If you're wondering why you should buy this new edition of *Government by the People*, here are 10 good reasons!

1. The first two years of the **Obama administration** are explored throughout the book, including analysis of important legislation such as health care reform and financial reform, foreign policy decisions and developments in Iraq and Afghanistan, and Supreme Court appointments. Coverage has also been updated to include discussion of the **2010 midterm campaigns and elections,** and figures and tables have been updated with the latest data.

2. We have integrated the **latest examples and scholarship** on American politics and government, including recent Supreme Court decisions, the economic conditions at the end of 2010, and comparisons with countries around the world.

3. A **new Introduction chapter** provides brief historical background of the founding of our country and explains the book's thematic approach of a government by the people. Vital for students with little background in the discipline, it will help them to hit the ground running with the course. Bookended with the Introduction, the **Conclusion** summarizes our history of government by the people and emphasizes the importance of active citizenship.

4. **Chapter Learning Objectives are more fully integrated** into the chapters, providing stronger pedagogical guidance for navigating the chapter content. Objectives are also used to structure end-of-chapter content, which includes a **Summary and Self-Test**, allowing students to assess their understanding of each objective.

5. **New Part Openers preview the broad themes** of each group of chapters and help students step back from the details to understand the bigger picture. Organized around Course Learning Objectives, they summarize the important overall concepts students should master by the end of the course. A comprehensive **Course Exam**, appearing at the end of the text, allows students to test their mastery of the course material as a whole.

6. **New features** are built around the framework of a government of, by, and for the people. **Of the People** boxes explore the diversity of Americans and assess how they compare to the global community; **By the People** boxes demonstrate nontraditional and accessible ways students can participate in government and public service; and **For the People** boxes remind students of the important accomplishments achieved by our government. These features help today's students see the relevance of government and the important role that they as citizens play in this country's present and future.

7. Being part of a government by the people requires consideration of differing points of view. **You Will Decide** boxes, updated with the latest in-the-news topics, explore questions that citizens and policy analysts alike wrestle with, like the advantages and disadvantages of a national presidential primary, or the need for restrictions on civil liberties during the war on terror, and then ask students to weigh options for resolving these issues.

8. The **visual program**, updated for currency and relevance, has also been developed to be more pedagogically effective in helping students build their study skills and get more out of the visuals. Photo captions include analysis questions designed to promote critical thinking and stimulate class discussion, and figures are accompanied by visual literacy questions that ensure students are accurately reading and assessing the data.

9. All chapters revised with an emphasis on anticipating areas of student confusion and revising explanations to address those areas of common difficulty. In particular, the discussion in Chapter 9 on bureaucratic agencies and in Chapter 13 on the public policy process have been revised and reorganized for greater clarity and comprehension.

10. **MyPoliSciLab** has been revised and integrated with this edition to make learning more effective. This best-selling online resource offers a wide array of multimedia activities, including videos, simulations, exercises, and online newsfeeds.

PEARSON

ELECTORAL COLLEGE VOTES IN THE 2008 ELECTION

THE UNITED STATES
A political map showing the number of electoral votes per state

Obama/Biden 365
McCain/Palin 173
Washington 11
Oregon 7
California 55
Nevada 5
Idaho 4
Montana 3
Wyoming 3
Utah 5
Arizona 10
Colorado 9
New Mexico 5
North Dakota 3
South Dakota 3
Nebraska 5
Kansas 6
Oklahoma 7
Texas 34
Minnesota 10
Iowa 7
Missouri 11
Arkansas 6
Louisiana 9
Wisconsin 10
Illinois 21
Michigan 17
Indiana 11
Ohio 20
Kentucky 8
Tennessee 11
Mississippi 6
Alabama 9
Georgia 15
Florida 27
South Carolina 8
North Carolina 15
Virginia 13
West Virginia 5
Pennsylvania 21
New York 31
Vermont 3
New Hampshire 4
Maine 4
Massachusetts 12
Rhode Island 4
Connecticut 7
New Jersey 15
Delaware 3
Maryland 10
Washington D.C. 3
Alaska 3
Hawaii 4

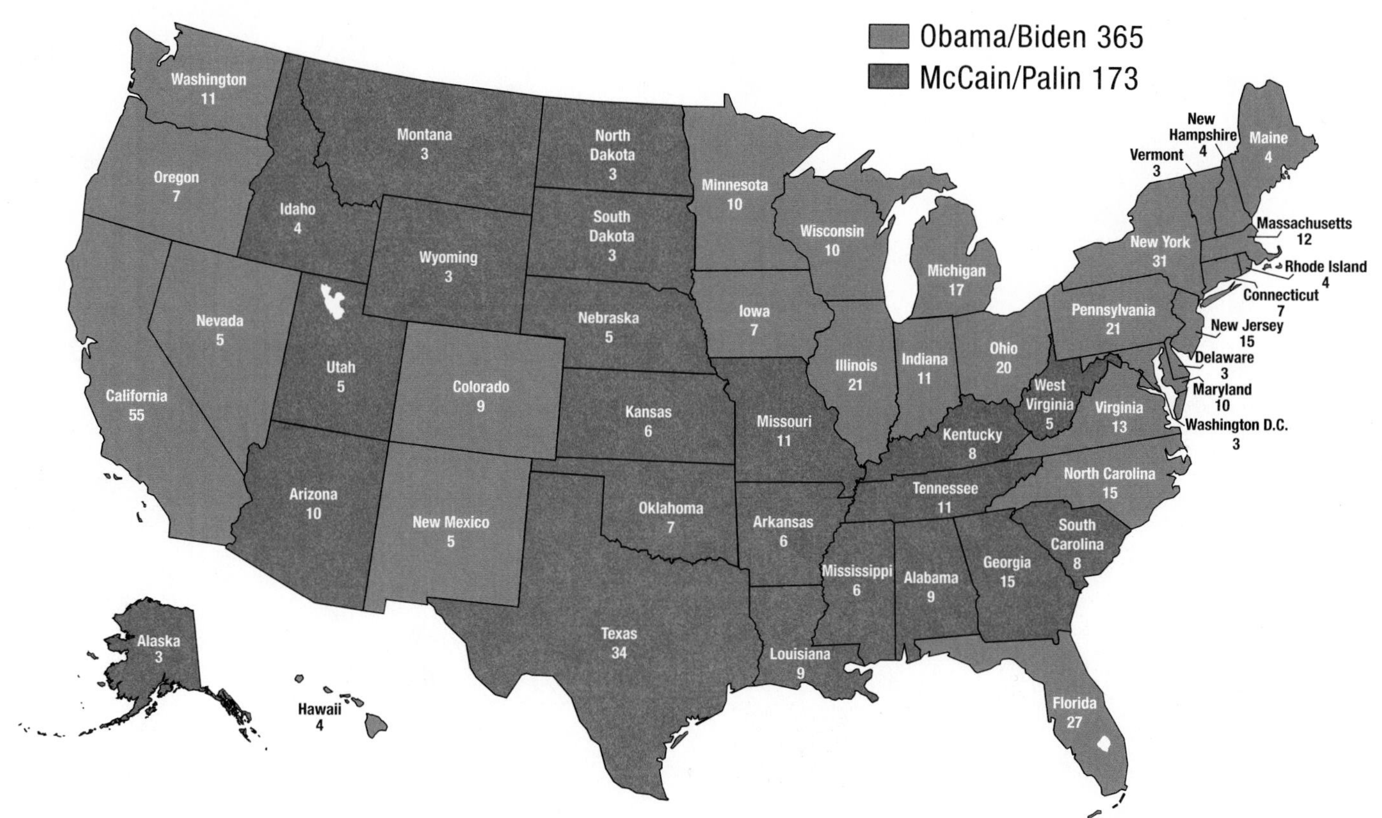

A political map with states drawn in proportion to the number of electoral votes

Maine 4
New Hampshire 4
Vermont 3
Massachusetts 12
Rhode Island 4
Connecticut 7
New York 31
Washington 11
Oregon 7
Montana 3
North Dakota 3
South Dakota 3
Minnesota 10
Wisconsin 10
Michigan 17
Idaho 4
Wyoming 3
Iowa 7
Nebraska 5
Nevada 5
Utah 5
California 55
Colorado 9
Kansas 6
Illinois 21
Indiana 11
Ohio 20
Pennsylvania 21
New Jersey 15
Delaware 3
Maryland 10
West Virginia 5
Virginia 13
Kentucky 8
Missouri 11
Tennessee 11
North Carolina 15
Arizona 10
New Mexico 5
Oklahoma 7
Arkansas 6
Mississippi 6
South Carolina 8
Alabama 9
Georgia 15
Texas 34
Louisiana 9
Washington D.C. 3
Alaska 3
Hawaii 4
Florida 27
Obama victory
McCain victory

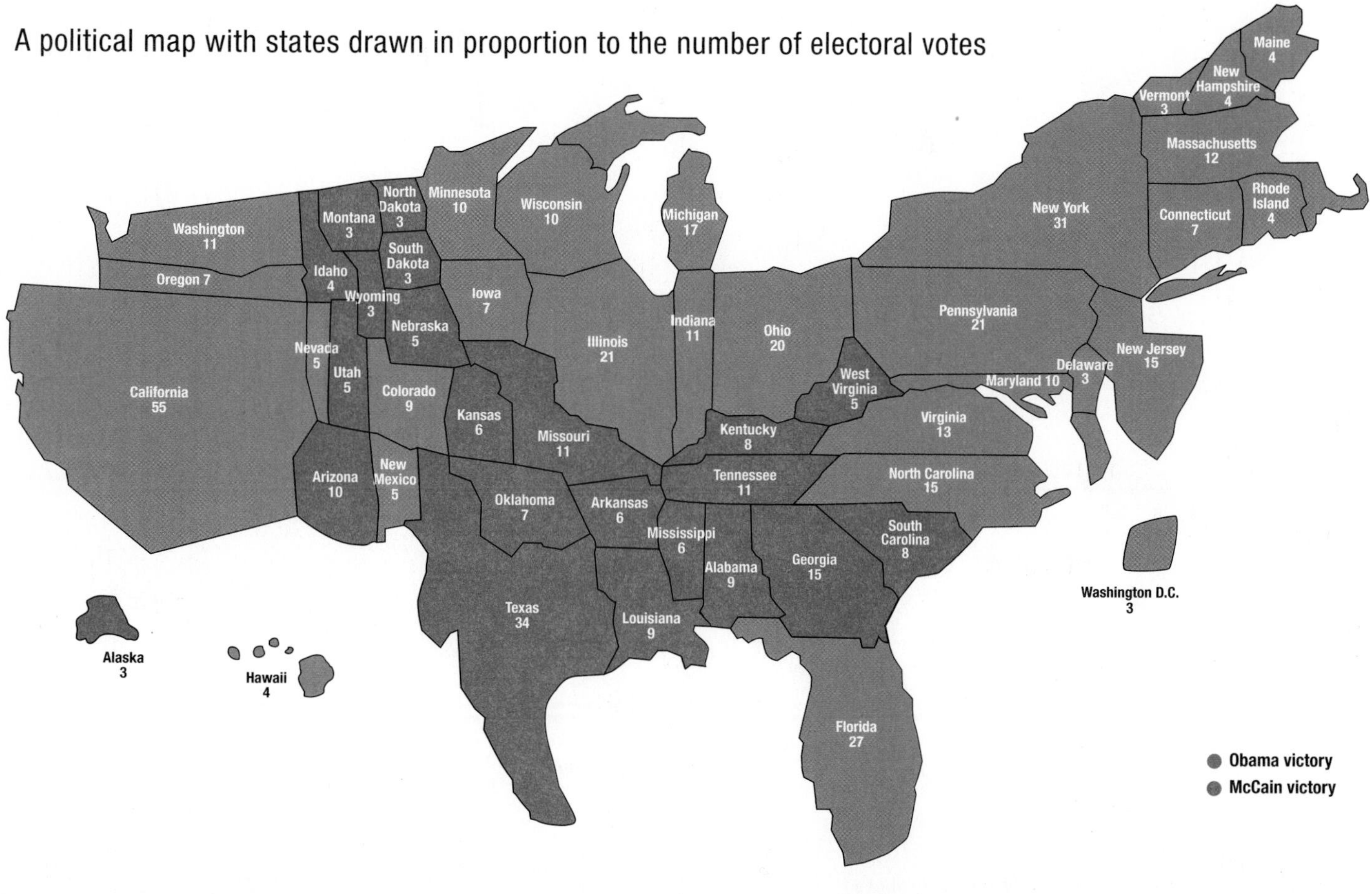

GOVERNMENT BY THE PEOPLE

GOVERNMENT BY THE PEOPLE

DAVID B. MAGLEBY
Brigham Young University

PAUL C. LIGHT
New York University

CHRISTINE L. NEMACHECK
The College of William and Mary

2011 Brief Edition

Longman
Boston Columbus Indianapolis New York San Francisco Upper Saddle River
Amsterdam Cape Town Dubai London Madrid Milan Munich Paris Montreal Toronto
Delhi Mexico City São Paulo Sydney Hong Kong Seoul Singapore Taipei Tokyo

Executive Editor: Reid Hester
Editorial Assistant: Elizabeth Alimena
Director of Development: Meg Botteon
Associate Development Editor: Donna Garnier
Supplements Editor: Corey Kahn
Senior Media Producer: Regina Vertiz
Senior Marketing Manager: Lindsey Prudhomme
Production Manager: Bob Ginsberg
Project Coordination, Text Design, and Electronic Page Makeup: Integra Software Services, Inc.
Cover Design Manager/Cover Designer: John Callahan
Cover Illustration/Photo: Michael Eudenbach/Aurora Photos
Photo Researcher: Teri Stratford
Senior Manufacturing Buyer: Dennis J. Para
Printer and Binder: RR Donnelley & Sons Company/Willard
Cover Printer: Lehigh Phoenix

For permission to use copyrighted material, grateful acknowledgment is made to the copyright holders on pp. 489–491, which are hereby made part of this copyright page.

Library of Congress Cataloging-in-Publication Data

Magleby, David B.
Government by the people: national, state, and local/David B. Magleby, Paul C. Light, Christine L. Nemacheck.—2011 ed.
p. cm.
Includes bibliographical references and index.
ISBN 978-0-205-80670-6
1. United States—Politics and government—Textbooks. I. Light, Paul Charles. II. Nemacheck, Christine L. III. Title.
JK276.G68 2011
320.473—dc22

2010045839

Longman
is an imprint of

PEARSON

www.pearsonhighered.com

1 2 3 4 5 6 7 8 9 10—DOW—13 12 11 10

ISBN-13: 978-0-205-80670-6
ISBN-10: 0-205-80670-8

BRIEF CONTENTS

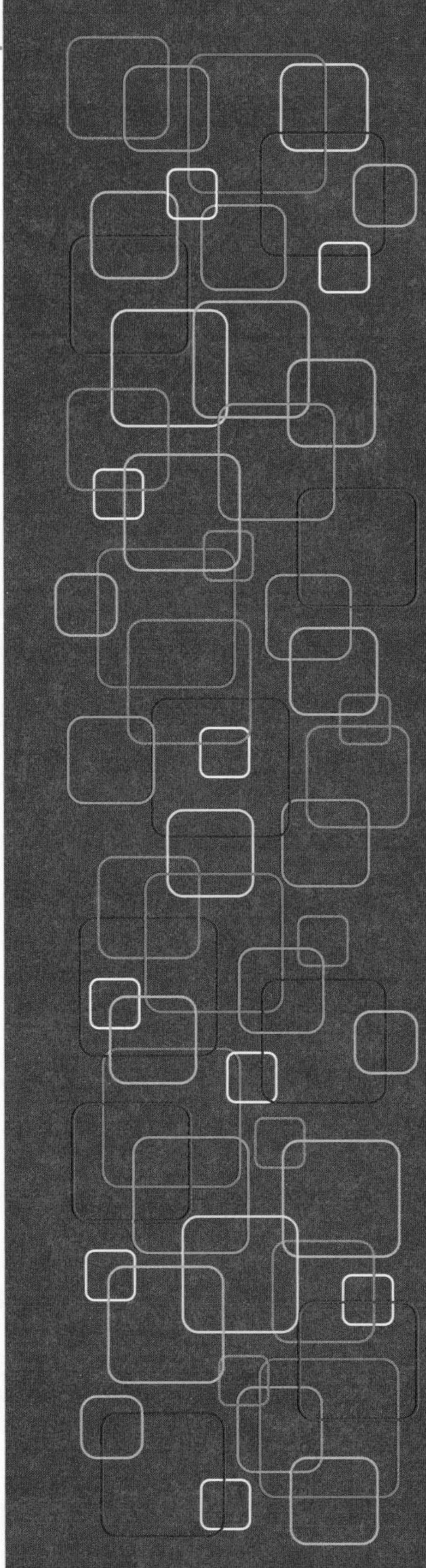

CONTENTS

COURSE **OBJECTIVES**

PART I Constitutional Principles

CHAPTER 1 Constitutional Democracy

Identify the philosophical principles on which our democratic republic is based, and describe the creation and adoption of the Constitution and the Bill of Rights

CHAPTER 2 American Federalism

Explain federalism in America, and analyze the relationship between the federal and state and local governments.

PART II The Political Process

CHAPTER 3 The American Political Landscape

Describe how geographic and demographic differences among Americans affect political beliefs and policy preferences.

CHAPTER 4 Political Parties and Interest Groups

Explain the role of political parties in American government, and evaluate the efforts of interest groups to influence elections and legislation.

CHAPTER 5 Public Opinion and Participation

Explain differences in opinions and rates of participation, and evaluate the importance of public opinion and participation in a democracy.

CHAPTER 6 Campaigns, Elections, and the Media

Describe the rules for elections in America, and assess the impact of the media on elections, public opinion, and governance.

PART III Policy Making Institutions

CHAPTER 7 Congress

Identify the legislative powers of Congress, and compare and contrast the House of Representatives and the Senate.

CHAPTER 8 The Presidency

Identify the powers of the president for leading the nation.

CHAPTER 9 The Federal Bureaucracy

Describe the role of the federal bureaucracy in implementing the laws.

CHAPTER 10 The Judiciary

Explain the role of the courts in the system of checks and balances, and evaluate the challenges for judicial independence.

PART IV Individual Rights and Liberties

CHAPTER 11 Civil Liberties

Describe the individual liberties protected in the Bill of Rights, and evaluate the limitations on these rights.

CHAPTER 12 Civil Rights

Explain how Congress and the Supreme Court have expanded and protected civil rights.

PART V The Politics of National Policy

CHAPTER 13 Making Economic and Social Welfare Policy

Identify the steps in the policy-making process and describe the government's role in economic and social policy making.

CHAPTER 14 Making Foreign and Defense Policy

Describe the tools of foreign policy making, and evaluate the status of America's current foreign policy interests.

PREFACE

We welcome you to the study of American government at the college level. The importance and relevance of the topics covered in our book have been reinforced by today's pressing economic, social, and foreign policy challenges. Governmental decisions made now will have lasting implications.

We title this book *Government by the People* because we want to emphasize the important role people play in our constitutional democracy. Understanding American politics and government must include an appreciation of the people, their similarities and differences, their beliefs and attitudes, and their behaviors.

The study of American government should be engaging, relevant, and rigorous. As authors of this book, we see politics and government as topics worthy of careful study. Constitutional democracy—the kind we have in the United States—is exceedingly hard to achieve, equally hard to sustain, and often hard to understand. Our political history has been an evolution toward an enlarged role for citizens and voters. Citizens have more rights and political opportunities in 2010 and 2011 than they had in 1800 or 1900. The framers of our Constitution warned that we must be vigilant in safeguarding our rights, liberties, and political institutions. But to do this, we must first understand these institutions and the forces that have shaped them.

We want you to come away from reading this book with a richer understanding of American politics, government, the job of politicians, and the important role you, as a citizen, play in this country's present and future. We hope you will participate actively in making this constitutional democracy more vital and responsive to the urgent problems of the twenty-first century.

What's New in This Edition

The new edition of *Government by the People* builds on the long-standing reputation of this book for strong coverage of the foundations of American government that is accurate, accessible, and current. We have integrated the latest in scholarship on American politics and government, the 2010 midterm elections, recent Supreme Court appointments and decisions, and comparisons with countries around the world into a book that introduces you to the subject and the discipline of political science.

Building on the theme of the people in government, we examine government through a new set of features that we have named *Of the People*, *By the People*, and *For the People*. These features explore who the American people are, how they compare to people and cultures around the world, the ways they are engaging in their government, and the important accomplishments that have resulted.

Growing from the success of the previous edition, this edition expands on the framework of learning pedagogy to help you navigate each chapter's discussion, focus on the most important concepts, and understand American politics and government. After surveying American government and politics courses taught around the country, we developed a list of Learning Objectives—the concepts professors teaching this course most often want their students to understand—to shape and guide the development of this edition. Each part opens with a list of Course Objectives, which provides students with a big picture overview of the broad concepts they will encounter, giving them a better understanding of how to focus their reading and studying for each section. At the end of the book, they will be able to test their mastery of the course material as a whole through the comprehensive Course Exam. Paralleling this structure, each chapter opens with a list of Chapter Objectives, highlighting the learning goals for that chapter. Chapter Objectives are called out in the text margins as the key concepts are discussed, and a summary and self-test at the end of each chapter provide students with a final check of their understanding of the chapter.

Chapter-by-Chapter Changes:

Introduction. New to this edition is an introductory chapter, which places in historical context the idea of self-government and introduces concepts that provide a foundation for understanding our distinctive constitutional democracy. Each of the features, designed to reinforce learning, are introduced in this chapter.

Chapter 1 begins to explore the context of our experiment in constitutional democracy. In this edition, we have an expanded section on the conditions that help democracy endure. We also examine the Constitutional Convention and subsequent ratification debates, which continue to be central to understanding American government. The judiciary's role in interpreting the Constitution is explained, and students are challenged to consider how the document should be understood in light of current constitutional debates. Methods for proposing amendments include examples to clarify the two methods. A new feature explores the process for becoming an American citizen, and immediately after this chapter, you will find a copy of the U.S. Constitution. We place it here rather than in an appendix at the back of the book because we think it is very important that you read and think about this remarkable document.

Chapter 2 uses the recent state regulations on texting while driving to introduce the chapter. The discussion of federalism has been expanded to compare the advantages and disadvantages of a federal system of government in the United States. Analysis of the centralist and decentralist arguments has been reorganized and clarified. A new feature shows students how to track and monitor distribution of funds from the national stimulus package.

Chapter 3 opens with a new introduction on the use of microtargeting to explore how and why people see politics and government differently. A more informed understanding of politics comes from an appreciation that social, economic, and other characteristics of people influence political behavior. Using the most current U.S. census and other data, we examine these relationships. Many people bring to their study of politics an assumption that other people see things the way they do, often not realizing the influences that have helped shape them. A new feature shows how students are spreading awareness of poverty in America. Equality, one of the core elements of the American political culture, is examined in the context of the effort to provide access and opportunity for the disabled.

Chapter 4 is about political parties and interest groups and the reality that as we become involved in politics, we generally do so as part of groups. The chapter begins with a discussion of the Tea Party Movement's involvement in recent campaigns and influence in framing issues. The chapter details the role of political parties in the American context. We explore the importance of parties generally and as part of the way elections are funded. The ways groups seek to influence public policy are also a central focus. In this new edition, we have expanded coverage of lobbying, including the diversity among lobbyists, recent efforts to regulate lobbying and common strategies used by lobbyists, and how students can get involved in lobbying for education policy.

Chapter 5 begins with a discussion of the recent surge in use of absentee ballots and early voting and examines the implications of this for 2010 and 2012, and more generally. We examine how Americans form political opinions and how public opinion is measured. The section on liberalism, conservatism, and criticisms of both has been updated to reflect recent issues, elections, and events. The chapter also explores the implications of many Americans being middle-of-the road or not having thought much about ideology. The discussion of participation and voting has been updated to reflect the events and outcomes of the 2008 and 2010 elections.

Chapter 6 opens by discussing the importance of money in elections, and particularly the substantial increase in individual contributions to candidates in 2008. The rules of elections matter in important ways that this chapter explores at the congressional and presidential levels. One important resource in elections is money. This area has seen significant changes in recent years, and this chapter has been revised accordingly and in light of the 2008 and 2010 elections. We also discuss the role of the media in elections and campaigns, and in particular the declining importance of newspapers and the growing role of the Internet. We explain the origins of the Internet in a new feature. Social networking is one place that young people in particular learn about news and discuss it with each other. Although where people go to get news is changing, the central importance of a free and attentive media has not changed.

Chapter 7 opens with Senator Evan Bayh's reflections on his time in Congress to introduce how the framers designed the legislative branch and how it actually works today. The chapter has been updated to reflect the 2010 congressional elections and recent congressional decisions on major legislation such as health care reform. The chapter also has new content on public approval of Congress, and new features discuss the agenda of Congress and how individuals can influence that agenda.

Chapter 8 begins by exploring presidential decision making through the example of President Obama's formulation of a strategy for the war in Afghanistan. The chapter includes updated information on Obama's use of the veto power and executive orders, use of executive privilege, and continued controversies over the war power and legislative signing statements. The chapter also addresses recent decisions involving the president's role during periods of economic and international crises.

Chapter 9 explains the factors that led to the British Petroleum (BP) oil spill in the Gulf to introduce the federal bureaucracy. It includes an updated section on defining bureaucracy, the organization of government, and the four types of bureaucratic organizations. The chapter also analyzes the types of federal government employees and the changing size of government. New features discuss how to bring transparency to the federal bureaucracy.

Chapter 10 uses the Supreme Court's decision in *Citizens United* v. *Federal Election Commission* and President Obama's critique of the decision at the 2010 State of the Union Address as a vehicle to consider the appropriate role of the courts in a separation-of-powers system. Appointments to the federal courts, and particularly the U.S. Supreme Court, increasingly focus attention on the judiciary and the important role judges play in American politics. The president's most recent Supreme Court appointments are discussed, as is diversity on the federal bench. The section on Supreme Court decision making has been revised to more clearly guide the students through the entire process.

Chapter 11 focuses on civil liberties, including an enhanced discussion on individual rights in an age of terrorism. The chapter includes a comprehensive overview of due process rights, property rights (as explored in *Kelo* v. *City of New London*) privacy rights, including abortion and sexual orientation, the rights of the accused, and the death penalty, with a focus on the Supreme Court's treatment of juvenile offenders, including the decision in *Graham* v. *Florida*. New features demonstrate how the federal government and students help guarantee Sixth Amendment rights.

Chapter 12 examines civil rights through a discussion of the Court's most recent decisions on the use of race in student assignment to public schools and through a historical overview of judicial and legislative action concerning discrimination based on race, sex, religion, ethnic origin, age, sexual orientation, and physical handicap. Barack Obama's victory in the 2008 presidential election is added to the discussion of racial equality, and Hillary Clinton's and Sarah Palin's campaigns are included in the discussion of women's rights. The chapter also includes an enhanced discussion of citizenship rights and the continuing debate over rights for same-sex couples.

Chapter 13 expands the last edition's brief introduction to public policy to provide a more thorough discussion of the process. It begins with a definition of public policy, including the various types of public policy, and then explores the eight steps in making public policy. The chapter discusses economic policy using updated budget and expenditure data throughout the narrative and in figures and tables. The discussion of the Federal Reserve System includes analysis of the prime interest rate and the Federal Reserve's recent activity to stimulate the economy. The chapter includes expanded discussion of help for the unemployed, details of the health care reform bill, and updated information on the impact of No Child Left Behind. A new feature shows students how to get involved in improving the health and education of children in their community.

Chapter 14 focuses on five key priorities in foreign policy today. The discussion of the war in Iraq has been updated to reflect events of the past two years and now incorporates coverage of the increased U.S. involvement in Afghanistan. A new feature shows students how to make a difference by ensuring their university is making ethical foreign investments.

Conclusion. We end the book with a concluding chapter returning to the broad themes of the book and calling on all citizens to take politics and government seriously.

A FOCUS ON FOUNDATIONS . . .

Read by over one million students, this new edition of the classic *Government by the People* has been substantially rewritten and redesigned to assist you in your study of American government and politics.

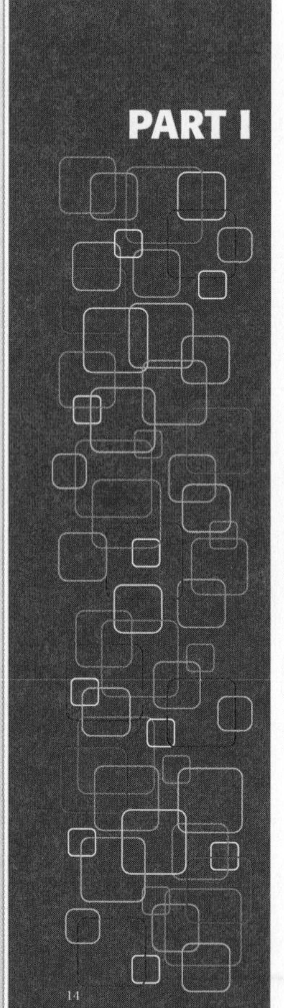

Constitutional Principles

THE BIG PICTURE

The U.S. Constitution provides our basic framework of government. It has resulted in great stability in governance for more than 220 years, but its success was in no way guaranteed. Indeed, its ratification came after significant debate and compromise and a previous governing document (The Articles of Confederation) that remained in effect for only eight years. Debates centered on such issues as the relative power of small and large states and the conflict between the ideal of individual freedom and the reality of slavery. In this section, we discuss the development of the U.S. Constitution, the debates and values that shaped the document and continue to shape our discussions about the appropriate role of government today, the genius of a separation-of-powers system, and the compromises that led to our unique balance of federal and state authority throughout the United States.

Throughout these first three chapters, we emphasize the importance of participation, politics, and compromise in developing and ratifying our founding document. We are a government by the people, but we are people with differing views and opinions on major issues of our day, just as the framers differed in their views of how our government should operate. Many of the issues about which we, as Americans, disagree today, such as health care reform, economic policy, and the United States' involvement in international affairs, mirror the kinds of debates that occurred in the founding era. They concern basic assumptions about the appropriate role of government, individual responsibility, and the degree to which the United States should be isolated from, or involved in, world affairs, including international conflict. As you read through this section, we challenge you to think about the ways you currently participate in our democratic system and perhaps consider a new way in which you might make your voice heard.

New! **Part Openers** identify the **Big Picture** themes and explain the overall **Course Learning Objectives** for each set of chapters. These will give you a better understanding of how to focus your reading and studying for the section, and will help you to integrate concepts across chapters.

COURSE EXAM

Introduction: Government by the People

1. Who is considered to be the architect of the Constitution?
   a. Thomas Jefferson
   b. George Washington
   c. John Adams
   d. James Madison

2. How did the Mayflower Compact become an important model for government in America?

3. Which philosopher wrote that people once lived in a state of nature but could enter into self-government through a social contract?
   a. David Hume
   b. John Locke
   c. Jean-Jacques Rousseau
   d. Thomas Hobbes

4. For which of the terms is the following definition most appropriate? "The belief that the authority and legitimacy of government is based in the consent and authority of the individuals living within its boundaries."
   a. Pure democracy
   b. Popular sovereignty
   c. Individualism
   d. Freedom of speech

Part I Constitutional Principles

Chapter 1: Constitutional Democracy
Identify the philosophical principles on which our democratic republic is based.

c. That Marbury was entitled to his commission and Madison should have delivered it to him
d. That the proper court could issue a writ of mandamus, even against so high an official as the secretary of state

New! At the end of the book you'll be able to test your mastery of the course material as a whole through the comprehensive **Course Exam.**

. . . A FOCUS ON GUIDED LEARNING

American Federalism

The relationship of the national government to the states has been the subject of intense debate since the founding.[1] In 1787, members of what would become the Federalist Party defended the creation of a strong national government, whereas the Antifederalists warned that a strong national government would overshadow the states. The great debate over which level of government best represents the people continues to rage.

State governments have often complained that the national government is either taking over their responsibilities or controlling too much of what they do. Yet, in policy areas such as civil rights, educational opportunities for people with disabilities, and handgun control, the states have been slow to respond to citizens, and the national government has taken steps to deal with these issues.

At the same time, states retain enormous authority under the Constitution to regulate life within their borders. Working with the local governments they create, states police the streets, fight fires, impose their own taxes, create most of the laws that govern their citizens, define the meaning of marriage, set the rules for elections and register voters, run the public schools, and administer most of the programs to help the poor, even when the money for those programs comes from the national government.

In recent years, for example, states have become increasingly involved in regulating cell phone use and texting while driving. As the number of text messages sent in the United States increased from 57.2 billion in 2005 to more than 600 billion in 2008, states became increasingly concerned that texting was an even greater threat to safety than talking on cell phones. According to recent studies, drivers who are texting while driving are significantly more likely to drift out of their lane and look away from the cars in front of them. As a result, they are much more likely to be in life-threatening accidents than drivers who talk on cell phones, who themselves are already more likely to be in life-threatening accidents than those who keep their eyes on the road and hands on the wheel.[2] As with talking on cell phones, younger drivers are much more likely to text than older drivers.

The pressure to pass new laws banning texting while driving increased in 2009, when British television began running a public service advertisement showing the grizzly results of a fictitious accident. The four-minute advertisement is graphic, bloody, and terrifying. It is so disturbing that viewers must be 18 to watch the film on YouTube, although anyone can watch a 2009 *Today Show* story about the film at http://www.youtube.com/watch?v=vOTbAbKoL28.

States are reacting to the threat by passing new laws to ban texting while driving. By the end of 2009, 18 states were already imposing stiff fines for texting while driving under a general ban on distracted driving, and some were stripping driver's licenses from first-time drivers caught texting on the road. Delaware, Indiana, Kansas, Maine, Mississippi, and West Virginia now prohibit texting while driving for drivers with learning permits or probationary licenses, while Missouri prohibits texting while driving for anyone under age 21.

Enforcement is the problem with such bans. Police cannot be everywhere watching every possible violation, and text messaging is particularly hard to spot. This is why state-sponsored education campaigns built around the kind of intense messages in the British television advertisement may be the only way to frighten drivers away from the practice. Under the Constitution, it is mostly up to the states to figure out both what to do about texting while driving and how to enforce the laws they make.

3

CHAPTER OUTLINE & CHAPTER LEARNING OBJECTIVES

Defining Federalism

3.1 Interpret the definitions of federalism, and assess the advantages and disadvantages of the American system of federalism.

The Constitutional Structure of American Federalism

3.2 Differentiate the powers the Constitution provides to national and state governments.

The National Courts and Federalism

3.3 Assess the role of the national courts in defining the relationship between the national and state governments, and evaluate the positions of decentralists and centralists.

The National Budget as a Tool of Federalism

3.4 Analyze the budget as a tool of federalism, and evaluate its impact on state and local governments.

The Politics of Federalism

3.5 Evaluate the current relationship between the national and state governments and the future challenges for federalism.

CHAPTER OUTLINE & CHAPTER LEARNING OBJECTIVES

Defining Federalism

3.1 Interpret the definitions of federalism, and assess the advantages and disadvantages of the American system of federalism.

CHAPTER SUMMARY

3.1 Interpret the definitions of federalism, and assess the advantages and disadvantages of the American system of federalism.

A federal system is one in which the constitution divides powers between the central government and lower-level governments such as states or provinces. But, over time, there has been support for different balances between state and government power such

Each chapter begins with a **Chapter Outline** that breaks down larger subjects into important subparts and previews the topics to come. **Chapter Learning Objectives** help you identify the kinds of learning you will be expected to do with each chapter. We also integrate the Chapter Learning Objectives throughout the chapter and return to them at the end of the chapter in a short **Chapter Summary**. This closely knit pedagogical system helps you navigate through chapter discussions and demonstrate that you have mastered the concepts.

CHAPTER SELF-TEST

3.1 Interpret the definitions of federalism, and assess the advantages and disadvantages of the American system of federalism.

1. Match each term with its appropriate definition:

a. Dual federalism	i. The power of the national government is limited in favor of the broad powers reserved to the states
b. Cooperative federalism	ii. All levels of government are engaged in a variety of policy areas, without rigid divisions between governmental jurisdictions
c. Marble cake federalism	iii. Local governments, state governments, and the national government offer various "packages" of taxes and services, and citizens can choose which package they like best

a. A unitary state
b. A federalist state
c. A confederation
d. A territorial union

3. Federalism affords five be
benefit along with a sente

3.2 Differentiate the power provides to national an

4. Determine whether the fo to the national governme shared by both:
a. Power to establish cour
b. Power to tax citizens an
c. Express powers stated i
d. Power to oversee prima education

To assist you in preparing for exams and make your learning experience more effective, we have prepared a **Chapter Self-Test** of multiple choice and essay questions. Before you take an exam, take this practice test to make sure you understand the chapter.

GOVERNMENT...

These features demonstrate how a government of, by, and for the people is put into practice, and highlight the important role of the people in our government.

OF THE PEOPLE
America's Changing Face

In important ways, the people of the United States today are much more diverse than at any previous time. This feature explores the impact of the ever-increasing level of diversity in the American political landscape, including how race and gender are changing the way the American government works. These unique boxes are designed to reflect the concerns and experiences of ethnic and minority groups in American politics.

Where Americans Come From and Where They Live

The United States is a nation of immigrants who have arrived from many parts of the world. Throughout the decades, the portrait of immigrants has been changing from mostly white to mostly minority. In 2008, for example, 38 million Americans, or 12.5 percent, were foreign born, consisting of 16 million naturalized citizens, 10 million long-term visitors, and 12 million undocumented immigrants. The number of unauthorized, or illegal, immigrants has fallen somewhat in recent years due to the economic recession, which has depressed employment opportunities.

Many foreign-born residents live in the nation's largest cities. The New York City-area population includes more than 5 million foreign-born residents, while Los Angeles includes another 4.5 million; Miami, slightly more than 2 million; Chicago, 1.6 million; and San Francisco, 1.3 million. Although the inner cities host a majority of foreign-born residents, there has been recent movement of immigrants to the suburbs and some movement toward certain areas of the country such as the southwest.

The changing face of America brings great diversity in all aspects of life, from schools to farm fields and small businesses. It enriches the quality of life through the mix of new cultures and old and can often be a source of innovation in how the economy operates. Diversity also brings complaints about the national government's effort to close its borders to illegal immigrants. Some groups complain that illegal immigrants take jobs that should go to U.S. citizens, whereas others worry about the costs associated with high-poverty rates. Governments at all levels must reconcile these complaints with our history of welcoming immigrants from all around the world.

QUESTIONS

1. How are foreign-born citizens from different regions of the world different from each other?
2. Why do you think foreign-born citizens tend to live in our nation's largest cities?
3. How do foreign-born citizens contribute to the nation's quality of life?

The Statue of Liberty symbolizes America's long tradition of welcoming immigrants to its shores. The inscription at the base of the statue reads: "Give me your tired, your poor, Your huddled masses yearning to breathe free, The wretched refuse of your teeming shore. Send these, the homeless, tempest-tost to me, I lift my lamp beside the golden door!"

Other areas 10%
Asia 9%
Other Latin America
Europe

Other areas 7%
Europe 13%
Asia 27%
Mexico 30%
Other Latin America 23%
2007

...ographic Trends in Metropolitan America," Washington, D.C.:

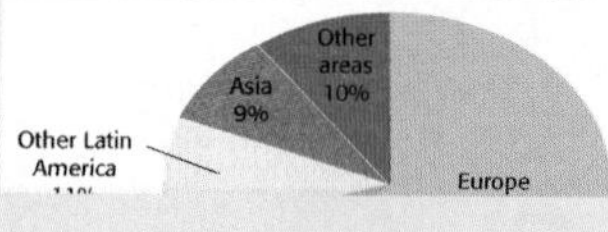

Global Opinion on the Role of Government

State and local governments are on the front lines of most programs for helping the needy. They provide much of the money and/or administration for unemployment insurance for the jobless, health care clinics and hospitals for the poor, school lunch programs for hungry children, and homeless shelters. Although many U.S. citizens see poverty firsthand as volunteers for local charities such as food pantries, some have doubts about how much government should do to help poor people who cannot take care of themselves. According to the Pew Global survey, citizens of other nations vary greatly on the question.

These opinions reflect very different social and economic conditions in each country. Japan has a culture of self-reliance that puts the burden on individuals to help themselves, while Nigeria continues to suffer from some of the highest poverty rates in the world. In this regard, U.S. citizens tend to mirror the Japanese—they want government to help the less fortunate but also want the less fortunate to help themselves. As a general conclusion, citizens of wealthier nations think poor people should take advantage of the opportunities that already exist in their economies, whereas citizens of poor nations believe that government should be more aggressive in providing support.

This does not mean wealthier nations are uncaring toward citizens in need, but it does suggest that they sometimes view of race, gender, or circumstance have the same opportunity to participate in politics, self-government, and the economy. Most Americans want to help the less fortunate, but only when they are truly needy, not when they fail because they will not help themselves.

QUESTIONS

1. What are the advantages of having the government provide services for the poor? What are the advantages of relying on individual citizens to seize opportunities for themselves?
2. Why might more wealthy nations be more likely to believe that individuals ought to take care of themselves and not rely on the state?
3. Which level of government might be most effective in providing services to the poor?

Agreement with the statement:
It is the responsibility of the (state or government) to take care of the very poor people who can't take care of themselves.

70, 60, 50, 40, 30, 20, 10, 0
Britain, China, India, Japan, Mexico, Nigeria, United

OF THE PEOPLE
The Global Community

speaks to the increasingly global context of American politics, examining public opinion from around the world on political issues and institutions. The experiences and opinions of people in other countries can both impact and provide insight into our own political system and culture.

...OF, BY, FOR THE PEOPLE

By the People

MAKING A DIFFERENCE

Improving Health One Playground at a Time

Citizens can make an immediate difference on public policy by simply changing the way they behave. They can stop smoking, change their diets, and get more exercise every day. They can also lobby their local governments to build more sidewalks and bike paths so that other citizens can exercise safely. They can push school boards to remove sugary drinks and junk food from school vending machines and cafeterias, support efforts to bring full-service grocery stores such as Whole Foods to low-income neighborhoods, and even plant community gardens.

Playgrounds are an easy place to start. According to KaBoom!, which is a charitable organization that built more playgrounds in 2010 than any state or city in America, 60 minutes of exercise a day can reduce health care costs dramatically in the future. Yet, there are thousands of "play deserts" across the country, often in dense urban areas, in which there is no space for children to play. You can see what is in your community by visiting maps.kaboom.org.

Students can easily find a "play-space" where a new playground would improve the opportunity for healthy exercise for low-income children. They can then join the KaBoom! building team as volunteers.

CRITICAL THINKING QUESTIONS

1. What can you do today to reduce health care costs in the future?
2. Why are playgrounds so important to communities? And why are there so few playgrounds in low-income communities?
3. What other resources do low-income communities need to be healthier places to live?

First Lady Michelle Obama brings D.C. school children to her organic garden to educate them about locally grown, healthful food.

BY THE PEOPLE
Making A Difference
Over the course of U.S. history, the people have become more and more involved in their own government. Active citizens have made real progress toward solving problems through involvement in government or public service. As you review this box, consider ways you can make a difference.

For the People

GOVERNMENT'S GREATEST ENDEAVORS

Clean Air and Water

One of the most visible forms of economic regulation involves nearly 60 years of effort to protect the nation's air and water from pollution. Although early laws such as the 1948 Water Pollution Act and the 1963 Clean Air Act established a federal role in protecting the environment, the 1970 Clean Air and 1972 Clean Water Acts provided much of the legal power to make progress in both areas.

During the past 30 years, the levels of most air pollution covered by the Clean Air Act have fallen dramatically as the U.S. Environmental Protection Agency has established ever-tighter rules promoting more efficient automobiles and cleaner-burning fuels. Although it is hard to find a single American city where the air quality has not improved, air pollution continues to spread to rural areas such as national parks where automobile pollution is concentrated as tourists arrive in record numbers.

Similarly, it is hard to find a single body of water or river that is not significantly cleaner because of the Clean Water Act. However, as the nation has learned more about pollutants such as arsenic, the pressure to improve water quality has increased. The Obama administration has been moving to expand both acts to cover new pollutants, while tightening limits on acceptable levels of exposure. It is also pushing for legislation to address the rising global temperature.

The federal government is becoming more concerned about the global environment, including the melting of the polar ice caps, which may raise sea levels dramatically throughout the next 100 years.

Despite these successes, there are many challenges ahead in keeping the air and water clean. The 2010 Gulf oil spill is a good example. As technology has become more sophisticated, the oil industry has been drilling at much greater depths below the water and in much more fragile environments. The Gulf oil spill shows how risky such drilling is, especially since the federal rules governing oil exploration were more than 30 years old when the spill occurred.

CRITICAL THINKING QUESTIONS

1. How clean should the air and water be in order to be declared "clean"?
2. How can the federal government protect the environment without hurting industry and creating unemployment when dirty factories must close?
3. What can citizens do to improve the environment through their own actions?

FOR THE PEOPLE
Government's Greatest Endeavors Throughout the country's history, the government has achieved remarkable goals in the service of the people. This feature explores these important accomplishments, such as building an interstate highway system, fighting discrimination, and eradicating diseases.

RESOURCES IN PRINT AND ONLINE

NAME OF SUPPLEMENT	PRINT	ONLINE	AVAILABLE	DESCRIPTION
MyClassPrep		✓	Instructor	This new resource provides a rich database of figures, photos, videos, simulations, activities, and much more that instructors can use to create their own lecture presentation. For more information visit *www.mypoliscilab.com*
Instructor's Manual 0205060439		✓	Instructor	Offers chapter overviews, lecture outlines, teaching ideas, discussion topics, and research activities. All resources hyperlinked for ease of navigation.
Test Bank 0205060420		✓	Instructor	Contains over 100 questions per chapter in multiple-choice, true-false, short answer, and essay format. Questions are tied to text Learning Objectives and have been reviewed for accuracy and effectiveness.
MyTest 0205075657		✓	Instructor	All questions from the Test Bank can be accessed in this flexible, online test generating software.
PowerPoint Presentation 0205060463		✓	Instructor	Slides include a lecture outline of the text, graphics from the book, and quick check questions for immediate feedback on student comprehension.
Transparencies 0205060471		✓	Instructor	These slides contain all maps, figures, and tables found in the text.
Pearson Political Science Video Program	✓		Instructor	Qualified adopters can peruse our list of videos for the American government classroom. Contact your local Pearson representative for more details.
Classroom Response System (CRS) 0205082289		✓	Instructor	A set of lecture questions, organized by American government topics, for use with "clickers" to garner student opinion and assess comprehension.
American Government Study Site		✓	Instructor/ Student	Online package of practice tests, flashcards and more organized by major course topics. Visit ***www.pearsonamericangovernment.com***
You Decide! Current Debates in American Politics, 2011 Edition 020511489X	✓		Student	This debate-style reader by John Rourke of the University of Connecticut examines provocative issues in American politics today by presenting contrasting views of key political topics.
Voices of Dissent: Critical Readings in American Politics, Eighth Edition 0205697976	✓		Student	This collection of criticale essays assembled by William Grover of St. Michael's College and Joseph Peschek of Hamline University goes beyond the debate between mainstream liberalism and conservatism to fundamentally challenge the status quo.
Diversity in Contemporary American Politics and Government 0205550363	✓		Student	Edited by David Dulio of Oakland University, Erin E. O'Brien of Kent State University, and John Klemanski of Oakland University, this reader examines the significant role that demographic diversity plays in our political outcomes and policy processes, using both academic and popular sources.
Writing in Political Science, Fourth Edition 0205617360	✓		Student	This guide, written by Diane Schmidt of California State University—Chico, takes students through all aspects of writing in political science step-by-step.
Choices: An American Government Database Reader		✓	Student	This customizable reader allows instructors to choose from a database of over 300 readings to create a reader that exactly matches their course needs. For more information go to ***www.pearsoncustom.com/database/choices.html.***
Ten Things That Every American Government Student Should Read 020528969X	✓		Student	Edited by Karen O'Connor of American University. We asked American government instructors across the country to vote for the ten things beyond the text that they believe every student should read and put them in this brief and useful reader. Available at no additional charge when packaged with the text.
American Government: Readings and Cases, Eighteenth Edition 0205697984	✓		Student	Edited by Peter Woll of Brandeis University, this longtime best-selling reader provides a strong, balanced blend of classic readings and cases that illustrate and amplify important concepts in American government, alongside extremely current selections drawn from today's issues and literature. Available at a discount when ordered packaged with this text.
Penguin-Longman Value Bundles	✓		Student	Longman offers 25 Penguin Putnam titles at more than a 60 percent discount when packaged with any Longman text. Go to ***www.pearsonhighered.com/penguin*** for more information.
Longman State Politics Series	✓		Student	These primers on state and local government and political issues are available at no extra cost when shrink-wrapped with the text. Available for Texas, California, and Georgia.

* Visit the Instructor Resource Center to download supplements at www.pearsonhighered.com/educator

Save Time and Improve Results with

PEARSON **mypoliscilab**™

The most popular online teaching/learning solution for American government, MyPoliSciLab moves students from studying and applying concepts to participating in politics. Completely redesigned and now organized by the book's chapters and learning objectives, the new MyPoliSciLab is easier to integrate into any course.

✔ STUDY A flexible learning path in every chapter.

Pre-Tests. See the relevance of politics with these diagnostic assessments and get personalized study plans driven by learning objectives.

Pearson eText. Navigate by learning objective, take notes, print key passages, and more. From page numbers to photos, the eText is identical to the print book.

Flashcards. Learn key terms by word, definition, or learning objective.

Post-Tests. Featuring over 50% new questions, the pre-tests produce updated study plans with follow-up reading, video, and multimedia

Chapter Exams. Also featuring over 50% new questions, test mastery of each chapter using the chapter exams.

✔ APPLY Over 150 videos and multimedia activities.

Video. Analyze current events by watching streaming video from the AP and ABC News.

Simulations. Engage the political process by experiencing how political actors make decisions.

Comparative Exercises. Think critically about how American politics compares with the politics of other countries.

Timelines. Get historical context by following issues that have influenced the evolution of American democracy.

Visual Literacy Exercises. Learn how to interpret political data in figures and tables.

MyPoliSciLibrary. Read full-text primary source documents from the nation's founding to the present.

✔ PARTICIPATE Join the political conversation.

PoliSci News Review. Read analysis of—and comment on—major new stories.

AP Newsfeeds. Follow political news in the United States and around the world.

Weekly Quiz. Master the headlines in this review of current events.

Weekly Poll. Take the poll and see how your politics compare.

Voter Registration. Voting is a right—and a responsibility.

Citizenship Test. See what it takes to become an American citizen.

✔ MANAGE Designed for online or traditional courses.

Grade Tracker. Assign and assess nearly everything in MyPoliSciLab.

Instructor Resources. Download supplements at the Instructor Resource Center.

Sample Syllabus. Get ideas for assigning the book and MyPoliSciLab.

MyClassPrep. Download many of the resources in MyPoliSciLab for lectures.

The icons in the book and eText point to resources in MyPoliSciLab.

With proven book-specific and course-specific content, MyPoliSciLab is part of a better teaching/learning system only available from Pearson Longman.

✔ To see demos, read case studies, and learn about training, visit **www.mypoliscilab.com.**

✔ To order this book with MyPoliSciLab at no extra charge, use **ISBN 0-205-07324-7.**

✔ Questions? Contact a local Pearson Longman representative: **www.pearsonhighered.com/replocator.**

 Follow MyPoliSciLab on Twitter.

ACKNOWLEDGMENTS

The writing of this book has profited from the informed, professional, and often critical suggestions of our colleagues around the country. This and previous editions have been considerably improved as a result of reviews by the following individuals, for which we thank them all:

Scott Adler, *University of Colorado*
Wayne Ault, *Southwestern Illinois College–Belleville*
Paul Babbitt, *Southern Arkansas University*
Thomas Baldino, *Wilkes University*
Barry Balleck, *Georgia Southern University*
Robert Ballinger, *South Texas College*
Jodi Balma, *Fullerton College*
Jeff Berry, *South Texas College*
Cynthia Carter, *Florida Community College–Jacksonville, North Campus*
Leonard Champney, *University of Scranton*
Mark Cichock, *University of Texas at Arlington*
Alison Dagnes, *Shippensburg University*
Paul Davis, *Truckee Meadows Community College*
Ron Deaton, *Prince George's Community College*
Robert DeLuna, *St. Philips College*
Anthony Di Giacomo, *Wilmington College*
Richardson Dilworth, *Drexel University*
Rick Donohoe, *Napa Valley College*
Art English, *University of Arkansas, Little Rock*
Alan Fisher, *CSU–Dominguez Hills*
Bruce Franklin, *Cossatot Community College of the University of Arkansas*
Eileen Gage, *Central Florida Community College*
Richard Glenn, *Millersville University*
David Goldberg, *College of DuPage*
Nicholas Gonzalez, *Yuen DeAnza College*
Charles Grapski, *University of Florida*
Billy Hathorn, *Laredo Community College*
Max Hilaire, *Morgan State University*
James Hoefler, *Dickinson College*
Justin Hoggard, *Three Rivers Community College*
Gilbert Kahn, *Kean University*
Rogan Kersh, *Syracuse University*
Todd Kunioka, *CSU–Los Angeles*
La Della Levy, *Foothill College*
Jim Lennertz, *Lafayette College*
John Liscano, *Napa Valley College*
Amy Lovecraft, *University of Alaska–Fairbanks*
Howard Lubert, *James Madison University*
Lowell Markey, *Allegany College of Maryland*
Larry Martinez, *CSU–Long Beach*
Toni Marzotto, *Towson University*
Michael McConachie, *Collin County Community College*
Brian Newman, *Pepperdine University*
Adam Newmark, *Appalachian State University*
Randall Newnham, *Penn State University–Berks*
Keith Nicholls, *University of South Alabama*
Sean Nicholson-Crotty, *University of Missouri–Columbia*
Richard Pacelle, *Georgia Southern University*
William Parente, *University of Scranton*
Ryan Peterson, *College of the Redwoods*
Robert Rigney, *Valencia Community College–Osceola Campus*
Bren Romney, *Vernon College*
Jack Ruebensaal, *West Los Angeles College*
Bhim Sandhu, *West Chester University*
Gib Sansing, *Drexel University*
Colleen Shogan, *George Mason University*
Tom Simpson, *Missouri Southern*
Linda Simmons, *Northern Virginia Community College–Manassas Campus*
Dan Smith, *Northwest Missouri State University*
Jay Stevens, *CSU–Long Beach*
Lawrence Sullivan, *Adelphi University*
Halper Thomas, *CUNY–Baruch*
Jose Vadi, *CSU–Pomona*
Avery Ward, *Harford Community College*
Shirley Warshaw, *Gettysburg University*
Ife Williams, *Delaware County Community College*
Margie Williams, *James Madison University*
Christy Woodward-Kaupert, *San Antonio College*
Chris Wright, *University of Arkansas–Monticello*
Martha Burns, *Tidewater Community College*
David Caffey, *Clovis Community College*
Ann Clemmer, *University of Arkansas at Little Rock*
Ellen Creagar, *Eastern Wyoming College*
Robert Locander, *Lone Star College North Harris*
Sean Mattie, *Clayton State University*
Jerry Murtagh, *Fort Valley State University*
Tally Payne, *Casper College*
Mark Peplowski, *College of Southern Nevada*
Geoff Peterson, *University of Wisconsin–Eau Claire*
Dennis Pope, *Kean University*
Jonathan Reisman, *University of Maine at Machias*
Sean Savage, *Saint Mary's College*
Carolyn Schmidt, *Florida Community College Jacksonville*
Kevin Sims, *Cedarville University*
Melanie Young, *University of Nevada Las Vegas*

Government by the People began in 1948 when two young assistant professors, James MacGregor Burns of Williams College and Jack W. Peltason of Smith College, decided to partner and write an American government text. Their first edition had a publication date of 1952. Their aim was to produce a well-written, accessible, and balanced look at government and politics in the United States. As authors have become a part of this book, they have embraced that objective. Tom Cronin of Colorado College and David O'Brien of the University of Virginia have been coauthors and made important contributions to the book. As the current authors of *Government by the People,* we are grateful for the legacy we have inherited.

Writing the book requires teamwork—first among the coauthors who converse often about the broad themes, features, and focus of the book and who read and rewrite each other's drafts; then with our research assistants, who track down loose ends and give us the perspective of current students; and finally with the editors and other professionals at Pearson Longman. Important to each revision are the detailed reviews by teachers and researchers, who provide concrete suggestions on how to improve the book. Our revision of the chapters on state and local government especially benefited from the tremendous input of Tom Carsey at the University of North Carolina. We are grateful to all who helped with this edition.

Research assistants for the current edition of *Government by the People* are Rebecca Eaton, Jeff Edwards, Bret Evans, Maren Gardiner, Eric Hoyt, David Lassen, Virginia Maynes, Haley McCormick, Kristen Orr, and Case Wade of Brigham Young University.

We also express appreciation to the superb team at Longman, especially Political Science Editor Eric Stano, who has been wonderfully supportive. Donna Garnier, our Development Editor, kept us on schedule and added helpful insights all along the way. We also appreciate the work Bob Ginsberg for production, Heather Johnson at Elm Street Publishing for page layout, Teri Stratford for photo research, and John Callahan for cover design.

We also want to thank you, the professors and students who use our book, and who send us letters and email messages with suggestions for improving *Government by the People.* Please write us in care of the Political Science Editor at Pearson Longman, 51 Madison Avenue, New York, NY 10010, or contact us directly:

David B. Magleby Distinguished Professor of Political Science and Dean of FHSS, Brigham Young University, Provo, UT 84602, david_magleby@byu.edu

Paul C. Light Paulette Goddard Professor of Public Service at New York University and Douglas Dillon Senior Fellow at the Brookings Institution, pcl226@nyu.edu

Christine L. Nemacheck Alumni Memorial Distinguished Associate Professor of Government at The College of William & Mary, Williamsburg, VA 23187, clnema@wm.edu

ABOUT THE AUTHORS

David B. Magleby is nationally recognized for his expertise on direct democracy, voting behavior, and campaign finance. He received his B.A. from the University of Utah and his Ph.D. from the University of California, Berkeley. Currently Distinguished Professor of Political Science, Senior Research Fellow at the Center for the Study of Elections and Democracy, and Dean of the College of Family, Home and Social Sciences at Brigham Young University (BYU), Professor Magleby has also taught at the University of California, Santa Cruz, and the University of Virginia. He and his students have conducted statewide polls in Virginia and Utah. For the 1998–2008 elections, he has directed national studies of campaign finance and campaign communications in competitive federal election environments involving a consortium of academics from nearly 80 universities and colleges in 38 states. This research is summarized in seven edited books. In addition, he is coeditor of a long-standing series of books on financing federal elections. In partnership with colleagues, he has been studying the implementation of new voting technology, work funded in part by the National Science Foundation. He has been a Fulbright Scholar at Oxford University and a past president of Pi Sigma Alpha, the national political science honor society. Magleby is the recipient of many teaching awards, including the 1990 Utah Professor of the Year Award from the Council for the Advancement and Support of Education and the Carnegie Foundation, the 2001 Rowman & Littlefield Award for Innovative Teaching in Political Science, and several department and university awards. At BYU, he served as chair of the Political Science Department before being named dean. He is married to Linda Waters Magleby. They are the parents of four and grandparents of one.

Paul C. Light is the Paulette Goddard Professor of Public Service at New York University's Wagner School of Public Service. He received his B.A. from Macalester College and his Ph.D. from the University of Michigan. Professor Light has a wide-ranging career in both academia and government. He has worked on Capitol Hill as a senior committee staffer in the U.S. Senate and as an American Political Science Association Congressional Fellow in the U.S. House of Representatives. He has taught at the University of Virginia, University of Pennsylvania, and Harvard University's John F. Kennedy School of Government. He has also served as a senior adviser to several national commissions on federal, state, and local public service. He is the author of 15 books on government, public service, and public policy. Light's current research focuses on government reform, Congress, the presidency, and social entrepreneurship. His latest books are *A Government Ill Executed* (Harvard University Press, 2008) and *The Search for Social Entrepreneurship* (Brookings Institution Press, 2008). He was the founding director of the Brookings Institution's Center for Public Service and continues his research on how to invite Americans to serve their communities through public service. His work has been funded by the Douglas Dillon Foundation, the Pew Charitable Trusts, and the David and Lucille Packard Foundation, among many others. He is also an expert on preparing government, charitable organizations, and private corporations for natural and human-made disasters, and he was a recognized leader in the response to Hurricane Katrina in 2005. He has testified before Congress more than a dozen times in the last five years.

Christine L. Nemacheck is the Alumni Memorial Distinguished Associate Professor of Government at The College of William & Mary. She received her B.A. from the University of Michigan and her Ph.D. from The George Washington University. Professor Nemacheck has previously taught at Iowa State University. Her research focuses on judicial selection and the role of the courts in a separation-of-powers system. Her book, *Strategic Selection: Presidential Selection of Supreme Court Justices from Herbert Hoover through George W. Bush* was published in 2007. Other work on judicial selection has appeared in political science and law review journals. Her research, which is primarily archival, has been funded by numerous grants and awards from presidential library foundations. Nemacheck has received a number of awards for her teaching and research activity, including the Alumni Fellowship Award for excellence in teaching at The College of William & Mary, a Coco Faculty Fellowship, and she was named a Dean's Distinguished Lecturer in 2010. She is the coeditor of the Pi Sigma Alpha Undergraduate Journal of Politics, which will be housed at The College of William & Mary through the spring 2013 semester.

GOVERNMENT BY THE PEOPLE

INTRODUCTION

Government by the People

CHAPTER **OUTLINE**

In 1620, the *Mayflower,* with 102 passengers, including 19 adult women and 33 children, set sail for America. Earlier settlements like Jamestown had not initially included women and children, but the Pilgrim's colony at Plymouth would. Before embarking, the Pilgrims sought approval from the Virginia Company to establish a new colony and were granted an area of land, or patent, located south of the 41st parallel, near the Hudson River. Because of poor winds and a near shipwreck on shoals near Cape Cod, they came ashore a good deal north of their planned landing place. There they found an abandoned Native American settlement named Patuxet, whose inhabitants had died in 1617 from illnesses like small pox and yellow fever, which were attributed to contact with earlier European fishermen, traders, and explorers.

Because the terms of their patent did not apply to the place they decided to establish their settlement, there were concerns that some of the group, not feeling bound by their prior agreement, would leave. A contemporary account of the Pilgrims recorded, "This day, before we came to harbour, it was thought good there should be an association and agreement, that we should combine together in one body, and to submit to such government and governors as we should by common consent agree to make and choose."[1] On November 11, 1620, 41 of the male passengers on the *Mayflower* signed a document pledging to create a system of self-governance.[2] They stated:

> Having undertaken, for the glory of God, and advancement of the Christian faith and honor of our King and country, a voyage to plant the first colony in the northern parts of Virginia, do by these presents, solemnly and mutually in the presence of God, and one of another, covenant and combine ourselves together into a civil body politic, for our better ordering and preservation and furtherance of the ends aforesaid; and by virtue hereof to enact, constitute and frame such just and equal laws, ordinances, acts, constitutions and offices, from time to time, as shall be thought most meet and convenient and for the general good of the colony; unto which we promise all due submission and obedience.

This document, called the **Mayflower Compact,** is an enduring example of self-government. The compact was intended to unify the group for the arduous tasks before them of building a settlement, planting and harvesting crops so that they could survive the next winter, and defending themselves against potentially hostile Native Americans.[3] Although some historians view the compact as more about surviving than about self-government,[4] this voluntary action by the Pilgrims became an important model. For example, John Quincy Adams (president from 1825–1829) reflected that the signing was "perhaps the only instance in human history, of that positive, original social compact, which speculative philosophers have imagined as the only legitimate source of government. Here was a unanimous and personal assent by all the individuals in a community, to the association by which they became a nation."[5]

Although the debate about what motivated the signers of the Mayflower Compact continues, what may be more important is the fact that it became an important example to later settlers and revolutionaries of self-government and provided what some have called the "seeds" of later American constitutional government.[6] Scholar Louis Hartz described "the concept of a written constitution" as "the end product of a chain of historical experiences that went back to the Mayflower Compact and the Plantation Covenants of the New England towns."[7] American colonists celebrated Forefathers' Day, commemorating the landing of the Pilgrims at Plymouth, which came to be seen, in the words of one scholar, as "part of the repudiation of English Domination and as the inauguration of indigenous American government."[8] In the 1830s and 1840s, the Whig Party praised the Mayflower Compact "as a milestone in the growth of social order and cohesion."[9]

Mayflower Compact
A governing document created by the members of the *Mayflower* to temporarily establish self-government in the Mayflower Colonies in America.

The Idea of America

This book is about the continuing great experiment in self-government launched more than two centuries ago. We will examine the historical context and current practices of the institutions and political processes of American government. As the title to our book signals, a focus of the book is the role played by the people in their government. The idea of government by the people predated the Revolutionary War. It was important to the Pilgrims aboard the *Mayflower* who wrote and signed the Mayflower Compact, committing to a system of democratic government to promote the "general good of the colony."[10] Those who later signed the Declaration of Independence perceived government to derive its powers from the people, and when government violated that public trust, it was a legitimate cause for revolution.

In many respects, the early experience of the Pilgrims mirrors a set of enduring elements that form what we might call the idea of America. These elements include individualism, a desire for self-government, the pursuit of opportunity and a commitment to equality of opportunity, a commitment to freedom of religion, and the importance of economic liberty. A list of concepts like this was identified by Alexis de Tocqueville, the French aristocrat who visited the United States in the 1820s and whose book *Democracy in America* (written for French readers and published in 1835) remains insightful. Other writers more recently have identified a similar set of ideas as the enduring elements of the American political tradition.[11] We will focus here on five core values: individualism, popular sovereignty, equality of opportunity, freedom of religion, and economic liberty. We discuss these briefly here and then return to them again in Chapter 4.

Individualism

Although the term **individualism** was first used by de Tocqueville to describe the American focus on the importance of the individual in comparison to a focus on a group, society, or nation, the concept of individualism is much older. Individualism emphasizes the importance of individual rights, worth, freedom, and well-being. The idea of individualism is central to democracy, with the idea that each person has one vote, and to economic liberty, in which individuals may own property. In the United States, individual economic freedoms are protected, as are political freedoms. Consider the rhetoric of contemporary political campaigns and the arguments politicians make, which often center on individualistic themes.

Popular Sovereignty

As illustrated by the examples of the Mayflower Compact, the Declaration of Independence, and the Constitution, central to the American view of politics is the idea that the ultimate political authority rests with the people and that the people can create, alter, or abolish government. This idea is sometimes called **popular sovereignty.** On some occasions, as with the Mayflower Compact and Declaration of Independence, popular sovereignty is exercised by the people directly. More often, it is exercised through representative institutions, such as Congress or local decision-making bodies whose members are elected by the people. But self-government is practiced whenever people write, amend, or revise local, state, or federal constitutions or laws. Popular sovereignty is a political extension of individualism. The notion that individuals have rights, including most fundamentally political and economic rights, undergirds popular sovereignty.

Implicit in the idea of popular sovereignty is the idea of individual responsibility for self-government. If individuals in a constitutional democracy will not exercise self-government through participation in the governing process, the system ceases to function. Also important to American political thought is the enduring suspicion of political power, especially concentrated political power—a suspicion that should motivate but sometimes hinders civic involvement. As we frequently explore in this book, government

individualism
The moral, political, and ethical philosophy of life that emphasizes individual rights, effort, and independence.

popular sovereignty
The belief that the authority and legitimacy of government is based in the consent and authority of the individuals living within its boundaries.

by the people is both a right and a responsibility. As we will also show, Americans value popular rule while being critical of government.

Equality of Opportunity

In the lexicon of core American values, equality is important, but its meaning has changed dramatically over time and means different things to different people. In the early twenty-first century, political scientist Jack Citrin wrote: "If liberty is the most basic American political value, equality is a close second."[12] Yet the signers of the Mayflower Compact, Declaration of Independence, and Constitution did not include any women or persons of color—a contradiction of modern ideas about equality. And in what aspects can all persons be considered "equal," when individuals differ widely in such things as aptitude, motivation, and inheritance? A more functional objective for American government is **equality of opportunity:** all individuals regardless of race, gender, or circumstance have the same opportunity to participate in politics, self-government, and the economy.

Freedom of Religion

The framers understood the importance of freedom of conscience and freedom of worship to a free society. **Freedom of religion** has always been important to a large proportion of Americans. Indeed, as one author has noted, "American political culture celebrates freedom of religion, not freedom from religion."[13] Of course, freedom of religion does not extend to religious practice that is contrary to public peace or morality, or that causes harm to others. Central to the view of the founders was the importance of a separation of church and state, which requires, in part, that there be no religious test for public office, meaning that an individual need not belong to a particular church in order to hold office and, at least since passage of the Constitution, that there be no national church. The example of the Mayflower Pilgrims is informative, as the Separatists had fled England rather than accept King James's official state church.

Economic Liberty

The economic application of the idea of individualism is **economic liberty.** A driving force for much of the immigration to the United States from the Mayflower Pilgrims to the present day has been the pursuit of economic opportunity and the idea that, in this new world, individuals can shape their own destinies. Given the remnants of feudalism still existing in sixteenth- and seventeenth-century Europe, the possibility of owning property in the new world meant freedom and wealth for individuals. Property rights were also important to America's founders, as was protecting the functioning of a free market. To them, economic liberty came as a reaction to tariffs as well as trade and production restrictions imposed by governments under a system called mercantilism. The American Revolution was a reaction against these practices in favor of economic liberty for individuals and a view that government should have limited involvement in regulating the economy.

Economic liberty has been possible in the United States in part because of our initiative but also because of our resource advantages. As Benjamin Freedman has written, "There are many countries with abundant natural resources, and other physical advantages, but among large nations, only in America have they been used to produce such a consistently high level of income, and with consistent economic growth over time."[14] Today, government plays a larger role in economic affairs, but the idea that individuals are free to pursue their own self-interest and be rewarded for their innovations remains central.

Although the ideals of individualism, self-government, equality of opportunity, freedom of religion, and economic liberty were articulated early in our nation's history and have endured, the extent to which they have been put into practice has varied over time. Take the concept of equality, for example, which was one of the "self-evident" truths listed by Thomas Jefferson in the Declaration of Independence. The actual

equality of opportunity
All individuals, regardless of race, gender, or circumstance have the opportunity to participate in politics, self-government, and the economy.

freedom of religion
The belief that individuals living in a society should be free to exercise their personal religious convictions without government restrictions.

economic liberty
The belief that individuals should be allowed to pursue their economic self-interest without government restrictions.

The pilgrims' experiment in self-government encompassed many of the same values of our government today. ■ *What can you infer from the painting and from your knowledge of the conditions when the Pilgrims arrived about the importance of individual participation in government and society in early America?*

practice of Jefferson and other founders in owning slaves was contrary to equality. Even after slavery was abolished, state-sanctioned discrimination against blacks continued and was clearly inegalitarian.[15] Although our constitutional democracy is imperfect in attaining the full measure of any of these values, Americans were path breakers in their effort to move toward them. As we examine American government in practice over time and especially today, these values remain important to contextualizing government and politics in the United States.

A Distinctive Constitutional Democracy

Before moving ahead, we need to define some of the basic terms we will be using throughout this book. **Government** refers to the procedures and institutions (such as elections, courts, and legislatures) by which a people govern and rule themselves. **Politics,** at least in our system of government, is the process by which people decide who shall govern and what policies shall be adopted. Such processes invariably require discussions, debates, and compromises about tactics and goals. **Politicians** are the people who fulfill the tasks of overseeing and directing a government. Some politicians—legislators, mayors, and presidents—come to office through election. Nonelected politicians may be political party officials or aides, advisers, or consultants to elected officials. **Political science** is the study of the principles, procedures, and structures of government and the analysis of political ideas, institutions, behaviors, and practices.

As we demonstrate throughout the book, an understanding of history is important to putting government and politics in context. That was also the case with the establishment of our Constitutional structure. Many of those who led the American Revolution and wrote the U.S. Constitution were familiar with the writings of thinkers like Locke, Hobbes, Hume, and Rousseau, who had written in the century or so before the 1770s, as well as with philosophers who wrote centuries earlier, like Aristotle.[16] These influential thinkers, like the founders themselves, relied on their understanding and reading of history, their observation of human behavior, and what they called "right reason," which essentially meant that an argument or idea seemed sensible.[17]

Out of this intellectual tradition had emerged a view that people have inherent rights. John Locke, the English philosopher, wrote that people were once free, living in what he called the "state of nature."[18] In this condition, according to Locke, they enjoyed rights to life, liberty, and property, and they could freely enter into what he called a "social contract" to govern themselves.[19] Louis Hartz explained, nearly a half-century ago, the appeal of Locke in the new world: "In America, one not only found a society sufficiently fluid to give a touch of meaning to the individualist norms of Locke, but one also found letter-perfect replicas of the very image he used. There was a frontier that was a veritable state of nature. There were agreements, such as the Mayflower Compact, that were veritable social contracts."[20] Indeed, Locke's ideas about inherent rights and the necessity of popular consent to government are echoed in Jefferson's words in the Declaration of Independence.[21]

The philosophical debate over human tendencies as either virtuous or evil was also important to the thinking of our republic's founders. Predisposition to do evil included such vices as pride, greed, superstition, injustice, bigotry, betrayal, and overweening self-interest. David Hume, the Scottish philosopher, warned that people following their self-interest could infringe on the rights and liberties of others. But Hume did not always see self-interest as a danger. Guided by law, self-interest could motivate work and innovation.[22] Designing a government that would not fall prey to humans' worst tendencies and might direct these tendencies to productive ends was thus a major aim of the Constitution. The founders were also influenced by philosophers like Jean-Jacques

government
The processes and institutions through which binding decisions are made for a society.

politics
The process by which decisions are made and carried out within and among nations, groups, and individuals.

politician
An individual who participates in politics and government, often in the service of a group or political community.

political science
An academic discipline that studies the theory and practice of politics and government. It is one of the social sciences that use data and methods that overlap with Anthropology, Economics, Geography, History, Psychology, and Sociology.

Rousseau, who saw people as not inherently inclined to evil and as possessing a drive for public service. For Rousseau, citizen involvement was essential. He wrote, "As soon as any man says of the affairs of the State, 'What does it matter to me?' the State may be given up for lost."[23]

Unlike the governing systems in Europe, which grew out of centuries of feudalism, government as it developed in America was based on the idea that individuals have rights distinct from those granted by any government. Following Locke, the Constitution's founders believed that government derived its powers from the consent of the governed; in other words, individuals can agree to form a government with powers specified by those individuals. This type of agreement, sometimes called a **social contract,** had appeared in informal contexts throughout the world for centuries, and it was especially attributed to ancient Rome. At the same time, the American Revolution, the Constitution, and early governing conditions were something new in world history. As Peter Shuck and James Wilson have noted, "nobody then knew what it meant to live in a country where equality of condition was so widespread and where the common people actually ruled themselves."[24] A central and recurrent element of the idea of America then is that government by the people is preferred to other forms of government.

Understanding and applying lessons from history were important to those who signed the Declaration of Independence in 1776 and designed our distinctive Constitution in 1787. They were aware of the Mayflower Compact. More broadly, they knew of the successes and failures of past experiments with self-government, and they were well versed in political ideas. In today's world, as our generation works to sustain constitutional democracy, an understanding of history and politics is also critical.

The founders also shared a common perspective on the rule of law through courts and an idea of representation based on their background as Englishmen. The lack of responsiveness of Parliament and the King to their frequent petitions reinforced their sense that they needed to "throw off such Government, and to provide new Guards for their future security."[25] What the founders prescribed as *the structure of government* was written into the Constitution, and the *protections from government* became the Bill of Rights. The need for both structure and protection was reinforced by their common experience with monarchy under King George III and with ineffective governments under the Articles of Confederation.

The designers of our constitution were at least as unified in what they did *not* want to include in their design of government as in what they did want to include. They did not want to have a monarchy, they did not want to create a government so strong that it could threaten rights, and they did not want to establish a state religion. Nor did they wish to foster mob rule by providing too great a provision for democracy.

social contract
An agreement whereby individuals voluntarily commit to establish a government that will protect the common interests of all.

For James Madison and others who participated in creating our constitutional democracy, there were predictable patterns to human history and human nature. Taking into account these regularities was something Madison described as political science. But shouldn't science apply to things like gravity, motion, and molecules, and not to something like politics? You may be asked this question if you decide to major in political science.

Educated men of the period considered science, as well as politics and economics, within their sphere of knowledge. Influenced by Isaac Newton's discoveries, they were fascinated by machinery that operated by balancing forces one against another. The founders thought the Constitution should embody the principles of such machines, with each part of government exerting force upon the others. Newton's success in describing physical laws reinforced the founders' belief that they could identify, understand, and harness forces in human nature.

James Madison can be thought of as the architect of the constitution. He was its principle author and one of its strongest supporters as a contributing author of the *Federalist Papers*.

In a famous essay now known as Federalist Paper #10, Madison claims it is possible and important to understand and predict human nature because out of that understanding came ways to limit the negative tendencies of people. Madison identified the following aspects of human nature that need to be considered in designing a government: "zeal for different opinions,... attachment to different leaders,... [and the] propensity of mankind to fall into mutual animosities most commonly concerning the unequal distribution of property."[26] Madison, borrowing from Locke, connected understanding of human nature to constitutional structure, as follows: "If men were angels, no government would be necessary. If angels were to govern men, neither external nor internal controls on government would be necessary."[27] In other words, human nature as Madison understood it required some type of government to regulate citizens' behavior and some type of control over that government to regulate citizen-politicians' behavior, as well.

Madison's idea of harnessing human capacity for evil found fullest expression in the provisions for dividing powers among the branches. The president cannot sit in the legislature; a senator cannot also be in the House. The president shares in legislation with the power to sign and veto bills. Congress shares in the executive power by providing all the money, but the spending is done by the executive branch. The president has the power to conduct foreign relations and wage war, but Congress must ratify treaties and provide declarations of war. Most appointments are made by the president, but Congress must concur. The judiciary can check both of the other branches by determining if executive or legislative actions are consistent with the Constitution. The executive has the power to appoint federal court judges and the Senate must consent to these appointments. Each branch thus is given ways to check the others. For Madison, there was a science of politics that included understanding human nature and designing constitutional mechanisms to channel power to good, and not bad, ends.

American Government Today

As important as the study of government and politics was to the founders, it is just as relevant today. Government and politics matter. Consider such areas as the economy, educational opportunity, and public health. One of the lessons from the government's poor response to Hurricane Katrina in 2005 is that in such times we all greatly depend on government to provide safety and security. Without that security, we face a world of anarchy. Even though government can fail, as it did in its response to Katrina, it can also succeed, as it did when the NASA space program placed astronauts on the moon, polio was largely eradicated, and the cold war was peacefully resolved. As referenced earlier, we title this book *Government by the People* because we want to emphasize the important role people play in our constitutional democracy. Understanding American politics and government must include an appreciation of the people, their similarities and differences, their beliefs and attitudes, and their behaviors. Examining such aspects of our population as race, ethnicity, gender, age, religion, income, and region helps us see how the diversity of our country is important politically.

Constitutional democracy—the kind we have in the United States—is exceedingly hard to achieve, equally hard to sustain, and often hard to understand. Our political history has been an evolution toward an enlarged role for citizens and voters. Citizens have more rights and political opportunities in 2011 and 2012 than they had in 1800 or 1900. The framers of our Constitution warned that we must be vigilant in safeguarding our rights, liberties, and political institutions. But to do this, we must understand these institutions and the forces that have shaped them.

Government Of, By, and For the People

Our emphasis on the important role people play in our constitutional democracy extends not only through the text but also through the features. The features—titled Of, By, and For the People—are intended to help you understand how the theory of self-government is put into practice and see the important role that you as a citizen play in this country's present and future.

This title of this book and these features are drawn from President Abraham Lincoln's famous Gettysburg Address in 1863. In his brief but powerful speech, Lincoln reminded Americans of their heritage of self-government. He began by referring to the Declaration of Independence and the enduring commitment to the principle of human equality, and he closed with the admonition that those who had died, giving "the last full measure of devotion" to preserve the United States, should lead the living to resolve "that government of the people, by the people, for the people, shall not perish from the earth." We use these

Of the People

AMERICA'S CHANGING FACE

From the Mayflower to Today

Understanding how the American population has changed is examined in boxes in each chapter, which we have labeled "Of the People: America's Changing Face." From the initial landing of the *Mayflower* to today, the people who make up America have changed, and these changes have affected government and society in the United States.

Of the 102 Pilgrims who started the Plymouth settlement, 52 were male, and in other early settlements like Jamestown the settlers were all male. Yet by the time the first census of the United States was conducted in 1790, the population was nearly equally divided between men and women, and has remained so since.

All of those on the Mayflower were European Caucasian, but the population of the area was largely native peoples. As many as 72,000 native people occupied New England in 1610, but by the time the Pilgrims arrived in 1621 that number had been reduced by epidemics.* The population of what became the United States grew more racially diverse with the arrival of African slaves in Jamestown in 1619. The number of slaves of African descent increased to more than 1.2 million in the 1810 census, two years after Congress banned the practice of importing slaves in 1808.†

The average age of the Mayflower settlers was 32. In the 1800 census of the United States, the median age was 16. Over time the median age rose to 22.9 in 1900 and 35.8 in 2000. The rise in median age over the course of U.S. history is due to advances in medical care, better hygiene, and nutrition.

Throughout the book we will examine how the changing population in the United States has affected our politics and government. It is important to understand the changing characteristics of the people in a government by the people.

CRITICAL THINKING QUESTIONS

1. Why might the age, race or gender of people be important to a study of government?
2. What are some of the implications of an increasingly older population?
3. What are the implications of America becoming more diverse?

* Sherburne F. Cook, "The Indian Population of New England in the Seventeenth Century," *Publications in Anthropology,* 12 (1976):84.

† James A. McMillon. *The Final Victims: Foreign Slave Trade to North America, 1783–1910.* University of South Carolina Press. (Columbia: South Carolina 2004), 56.

three important ways in which Lincoln defined American government as grounded in "the people" to drive our features.

Of the People

One interpretation of the phrase "of the people" is that our nation by design does not have a monarchy. The phrase answers the question "Who governs?" with the answer, "The people do." Political leaders in the United States are not born into positions of power, as political leaders have been for much of history. Moreover, as we explore in this book, "the people" have changed throughout the course of U.S. history and have come to be a more inclusive group. In each chapter, we explore the implications of the changing face of America for our experiment in self-government through the feature *Of the People: America's Changing Face* (see box above).

Although the subject of this book is government and politics in the United States of America, there are important lessons to be learned from how other societies are governed as well. Given our emphasis on the role of people in government, each chapter also includes a comparison of how people in different countries and cultures view the same question or challenge through the feature *Of the People: The Global Community* (see the box on the following page).

By the People

The phrase "government by the people" communicates that people are active or engaged in their self-government. Throughout the course of U.S. history, the people have become more and more involved in their own government. For example, U.S. senators, once elected by state legislatures, are now elected by the people. The right to vote has been dramatically expanded over time. The 2008 elections demonstrated the power of the Internet as a means to participate in politics. In addition to being active citizens, individuals can and do make a difference in their communities in

Of the People THE GLOBAL COMMUNITY

Opinion of the United States

As Americans, we assume the world has a high regard for our country and what it stands for. Our history of freedom and our sustained constitutional democracy stand out in world history. But how do the people in other countries actually view the United States? The Pew Global Attitudes survey included a question that asked respondents the following question: "Please tell me if you have a very favorable, somewhat favorable, somewhat unfavorable, or very unfavorable opinion of the United States."

In the year following the election of Barack Obama, people's views toward the United States became more favorable in all of the countries in our sample. The most dramatic change in views toward the United States occurred in Mexico, which had a 22 percentage point rise in the proportion seeing the United States very or somewhat favorably in 2009 as compared to 2008. In the United States, the increase was insignificant, indicating that who currently occupies the White House matters less to Americans' views of their own country than to those in other countries.

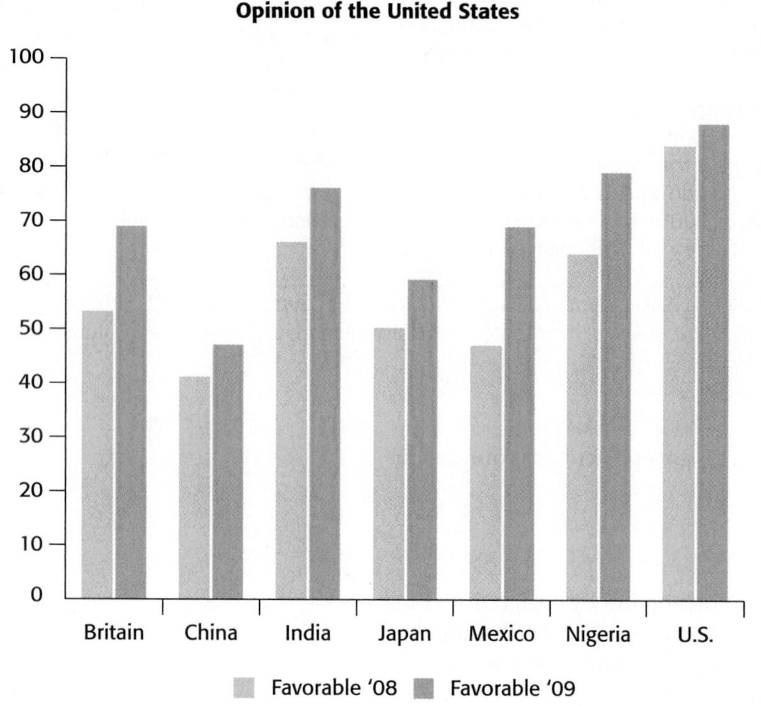

The people of the world had a great deal of interest in the 2008 U.S. presidential election. The initial impact of that election and President Obama's early speeches and actions appears to have had a positive impact on how the world sees the United States. Over time, especially as President Obama and his administration make unpopular decisions, these numbers will likely drop.

CRITICAL THINKING QUESTIONS

1. Why is it important how the people in other countries view the United States?
2. Why do you think residents of China have the least favorable views toward the United States of our sample countries?
3. What about the election of Barack Obama in 2008 may explain why people in the nations presented here now view the United States more favorably?

addressing important problems. Seemingly small acts by individuals, many of them young people, have the potential to make real progress toward solving problems. In each chapter of the book, we include an example of how people are making a difference through involvement in government or public service. As you review this *By the People: Making a Difference* feature (see the box on the following page) in each chapter, consider ways you can make a difference.

For the People

Abraham Lincoln's final way of linking the people to their government implies that government exists for the people—and that what is good for the people should guide the government's aims. In the case of the United States, the Constitution's preamble spells out the government's assignments: to achieve justice, domestic tranquility, security ("common defense"), and general welfare. Throughout the country's history, the government has achieved remarkable goals in the service of the people, such as building an interstate highway system, promoting space exploration, fighting discrimination in public spaces and the workplace, and reducing the crime rate. In each chapter, we explore the

By the People MAKING A DIFFERENCE

Greg Mortenson and Girls' Schools in Pakistan and Afghanistan

While recovering from an unsuccessful attempt to climb K2, the world's second-highest mountain, 36-year-old Greg Mortenson lived in Korphe, a small village in Pakistan. The people of the village could not afford to pay a school teacher's salary (valued at US $1 a day), so children met on their own and, lacking school supplies, wrote with sticks in the dirt. Mortenson resolved to build a school for the people in Korphe.

Mortenson began his fundraising for the school by writing nearly 600 letters to American celebrities and business leaders. Only NBC's Tom Brokaw responded, sending a check for $100. It was a group of elementary school children in River Falls, Wisconsin—donating $623.40 in pennies—who helped Mortenson find a way to raise the money needed. That early donation led to many others, and Mortenson later founded Pennies for Peace, a program that raises money from school children to build schools in remote areas of Afghanistan and Pakistan.* So far, Mortenson has established 78 schools, and all of his schools offer education to girls as well as boys.

A striking aspect of Greg Mortenson's story is the difference an individual can make in the lives of others and in influencing the conversation about public policy. The Pennies for Peace website (http://www.penniesforpeace.org/) provides resources for setting up programs at local schools that would not only raise money but would also help American students broaden their cultural horizons and learn about their capacities as philanthropists. Visit the Central Asia Institute (CAI) Web site for additional ideas on how to help fundraise in your own community: www.ikat.org.

CRITICAL THINKING QUESTIONS

1. How did Mortenson get the idea to raise money for girls' schools in Pakistan and Afghanistan?
2. Might the "Pennies for Peace" idea be a model to raise money for other important needs?
3. Why would educating girls and boys in villages in Pakistan and Afghanistan foster a more peaceful society?

* Pennies for Peace, http://www.penniesforpeace.org/ (accessed November 30, 2009).

important accomplishments of government in the service of its citizens through the feature *For the People: Government's Greatest Endeavors* (see the box on the following page).

Learning Objectives

While we hope the thematic "Of, By, and For the People" approach shows you the importance of our constitutional democracy, we also employ a Learning Objectives framework to help you use this book to succeed in the course. Using the Course and Chapter Objectives can help you to systematically build your understanding of the fundamentals and develop the skills necessary to analyze, evaluate, and engage in the study of political science.

What are Learning Objectives? Your professor, the department, and the college faculty will often have identified key learning objectives as the important concepts, skills, motivation, and knowledge you should have acquired through completion of the course, major, or in your undergraduate education. Some examples of Learning Objectives for the Introduction to American Government course include understanding the historical foundations and development of American government, being able to identify and discuss the governmental and political institutions, and being able to think critically and analytically about important issues.

In this textbook, we list and explain these most common **Course Learning Objectives** at the beginning of each part of the book (for example, the Political Process). There, you will find a brief part opener in which we identify the **Big Picture** themes and explain the Course Learning Objectives for this part (see sample). This will give you a better understanding of how to focus your reading and studying for that section and will help you integrate information across chapters. Keep these Course Learning Objectives in mind as you make your way through the chapters in a section, and revisit them at the end of a section to make sure you

For the People

GOVERNMENT'S GREATEST ENDEAVORS

Making Government by the People More of a Reality

Moving from the idea that the people could govern themselves—as expressed by the Mayflower Pilgrims and the early colonists in North America—to actually accomplishing that ambition in the form of a government is a theme we will return to again and again in this book. Take the simple act of voting, for example. Owning property was commonly required of those who voted in the early years of the United States. By the election of Andrew Jackson in 1828, the right to vote had been extended to white males, without regards to owning property, at least in federal elections.

Later, as a result of the Civil War and the Fifteenth Amendment (1870), the Constitution was amended to say states could not deny the right to vote "on account of race, color, or previous condition of servitude." A half-century later, the Nineteenth Amendment (1920) was adopted granting the right to vote to women. More recently, the Constitution has been amended to prohibit poll taxes (Twenty-Fourth Amendment in 1964) and lowering the voting age to 18 (Twenty-Sixth Amendment (1971). There was resistance to each of these changes, with none more intense than the Civil War. And yet, 200 years after the signing of the Declaration of Independence, our notions of who may and who may not participate in elections has changed dramatically.

However, barriers to full participation still remain. The United States, in most states, retains a system of voter registration that requires people to complete a process of registering with local or state officials well in advance of the election. As recent elections taught us, the ballots or voting machines we use to cast our ballots are far from perfect. An enduring debate centers on whether a goal of government should be to make voting easier. But when examined over the broad sweep of U.S. history, one of government's greatest successes is the expansion of voting to more and more people.

CRITICAL THINKING QUESTIONS

1. What have been the benefits to our democracy of extending the right to vote to more people?
2. Should the right to vote be extended to persons age 16 and older? Why or why not?
3. How does requiring people to register to vote before election day and register again each time they move discourage participation?

understand all of these big picture concepts. At the end of the book, you'll be able to test your mastery of the course material as a whole through the comprehensive **Course Exam**.

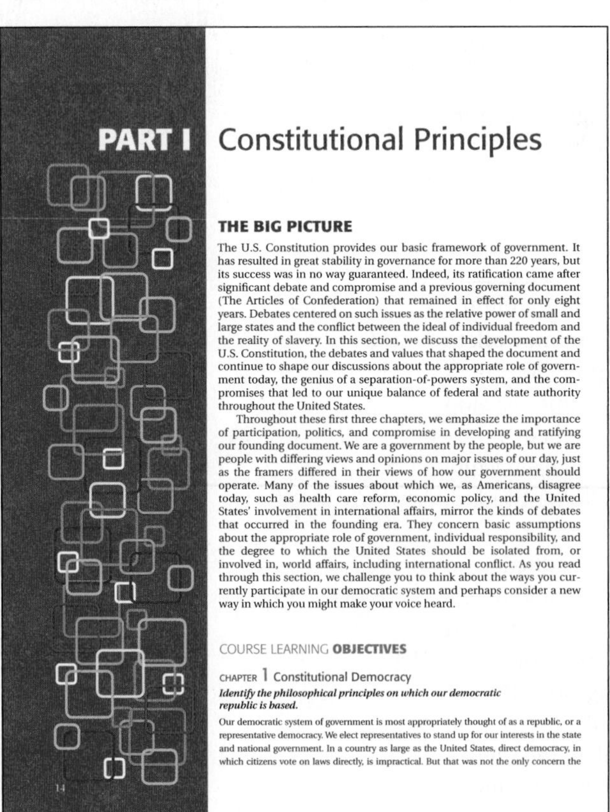

PART I Constitutional Principles

THE BIG PICTURE

The U.S. Constitution provides our basic framework of government. It has resulted in great stability in governance for more than 220 years, but its success was in no way guaranteed. Indeed, its ratification came after significant debate and compromise and a previous governing document (The Articles of Confederation) that remained in effect for only eight years. Debates centered on such issues as the relative power of small and large states and the conflict between the ideal of individual freedom and the reality of slavery. In this section, we discuss the development of the U.S. Constitution, the debates and values that shaped the document and continue to shape our discussions about the appropriate role of government today, the genius of a separation-of-powers system, and the compromises that led to our unique balance of federal and state authority throughout the United States.

Throughout these first three chapters, we emphasize the importance of participation, politics, and compromise in developing and ratifying our founding document. We are a government by the people, but we are people with differing views and opinions on major issues of our day, just as the framers differed in their views of how our government should operate. Many of the issues about which we, as Americans, disagree today, such as health care reform, economic policy, and the United States' involvement in international affairs, mirror the kinds of debates that occurred in the founding era. They concern basic assumptions about the appropriate role of government, individual responsibility, and the degree to which the United States should be isolated from, or involved in, world affairs, including international conflict. As you read through this section, we challenge you to think about the ways you currently participate in our democratic system and perhaps consider a new way in which you might make your voice heard.

COURSE LEARNING **OBJECTIVES**

CHAPTER 1 Constitutional Democracy

Identify the philosophical principles on which our democratic republic is based.

Our democratic system of government is most appropriately thought of as a republic, or a representative democracy. We elect representatives to stand up for our interests in the state and national government. In a country as large as the United States, direct democracy, in which citizens vote on laws directly, is impractical. But that was not the only concern the

14

Part openers identify the Big Picture themes and explain the Course Learning Objectives for the section.

To understand these big picture concepts, you'll first need to understand the basics, so at the chapter level, there are **Chapter Learning Objectives.** These are the specific concepts you should understand after studying each chapter. For example, in the chapter on the Constitution, you'll see the objectives include such goals as being able to describe the basic structure of the Constitution and the Bill of Rights, comparing and contrasting the branches of government, explaining how we make changes to the Constitution, etc. These Chapter Learning Objectives appear as a list at the beginning of each chapter but also appear in the chapter where the concept is discussed. Refer to these Chapter Learning Objectives as you read through the chapters to make sure you understand the key concepts. We recap the objectives in a **Summary** at the end of the chapter, and we provide a set of review questions in the **Self-Test** to help you assess your progress in meeting the Chapter Learning Objectives and so that you know where to focus your studying (see sample).

Both the Course Learning Objectives and Chapter Learning Objectives can help guide you in your reading and studying of the course material, but asking your own questions as you read will also help you understand and apply the material. One way to prepare for exams is to turn chapter titles or major headings into possible essay questions. The chapter title "Making Economic Policy," for example, can be turned into a question like, "Explain how economic policy is made in the United States, and assess the strengths and weaknesses of that process in light of the economic crisis of 2008–2009." If you approach the book with questions in mind, you will often have better recall of the content and you will develop a capacity in critical thinking, which is one of the intellectual skills that can come from a college education. You can use the Course Learning Objectives and Chapter Learning Objectives as a good jumping off point and a model for this method of organization and study.

Conclusion

A text like *Government by the People* is intended to assist you in your study of American government. As authors of the book, we find the subject fascinating. As teachers of this course, we realize there is a great deal of material to learn. Our aim is to organize the subject matter and current research in a thorough, balanced, and engaging way. *Government by the People* provides a foundation for your course but also for other courses that will follow.[28] As we introduce you to American government at a college level, we are also introducing you to political science as a discipline. An academic discipline is a way of thinking about the world in a systematic and rigorous way. Yale Law School Dean Robert Post defined a discipline as "not merely a body of knowledge but also a set of practices by which that knowledge is acquired, confirmed, implemented, preserved, and reproduced."[29]

CHAPTER **SUMMARY**

6.1 Explain the role of interest groups and social movements in American politics.

Interest groups form when a collection of people share similar political goals and organize to achieve them. Sometimes, these groups are based on a shared group identity, such as race, ethnicity, gender, or sexual orientation. Others are based on specific policy issues, such as reducing taxes or combating global warming. Still others claim to operate in the public interest on broad issues, such as educating voters or reducing the federal deficit. Interest groups sometimes begin as social movements, which consist of many people at the grassroots level who are interested in a significant issue, idea, or include people with many other cross-cutting inter- concern and take action to support or oppose it. ests, which both reduces and stabilizes their influence.

6.4 Describe lobbyists and the activities through which they seek to influence policy.

Lobbyists represent organized interests before government. Lobbying involves communicating with legislators and executive-branch officials, making campaign contributions, and assisting in election activity, especially through political action committees (PACs). Interest groups also communicate their message directly to the public through mass mailings, advertising, and online media.

CHAPTER **SELF-TEST**

6.1 Explain the role of interest groups and social movements in American politics.

1. Briefly explain the differences between *special interests* and *public interests.*
2. Describe what a social movement is and explain how it differs from an interest group or public interest.
3. In two or three sentences, analyze how the idea of pluralism explains the founders' method for protecting against overwhelming factions.

6.2 Categorize American interest groups into types.

4. Match each interest group with the category it most closely fits.

a. American Gaming Association	i. Public
b. National Right to Life	ii. Government
c. Project Vote Smart	iii. Economic
d. American-Israel Political Action Committee	iv. Ideological
e. The State Department	v. Foreign policy

End of chapter Summary and Self-Test can help you assess your progress in meeting the Chapter Learning Objectives.

We want you to come away from reading this book with a richer understanding of American politics, government, the job of politicians, and the important role you, as a citizen, play in this country's present and future. We hope you will participate actively in making this constitutional democracy more vital and responsive to the urgent problems of the twenty-first century.

Finally, as you begin your American government course, and perhaps your study of the political science discipline, keep in mind the wisdom of early education reformer Horace Mann. Regarding Americans' quest for equality, he said, "Education, then, beyond all other devices of human origin, is the great equalizer of the conditions of men—the balance-wheel of the social machinery."[30]

KEY TERMS

Mayflower Compact, p. 3
individualism, p. 4
popular sovereignty, p. 4
equality of opportunity, p. 5
freedom of religion, p. 5
economic liberty, p. 5
government, p. 6
politics, p. 6
politician, p. 6
political science, p. 6
social contract, p. 7

ADDITIONAL RESOURCES

FURTHER READING

ALEXIS DE TOCQUEVILLE, *Democracy in America,* 2 vols. (1835).

ROBERT A. DAHL, *On Democracy* (Yale University Press, 1998).

LOUIS HARTZ, *The Liberal Tradition in America* (Harcourt, 1955).

PAULINE MAIER, *American Scripture: Making the Declaration of Independence* (Vintage Books, 1997).

PIPPA NORRIS, ED., *Critical Citizens: Global Support for Democratic Institutions* (Oxford University Press, 1999).

ROBERT PUTNAM, *Making Democracy Work* (Princeton University Press, 1993).

MICHAEL J. SANDEL, *Democracy's Discontent: America in Search of a Public Philosophy* (Belknap Press, 1996).

CASS R. SUNSTEIN, *Designing Democracy: What Constitutions Do* (Oxford University Press, 2001).

GARRY WILLS, *A Necessary Evil: A History of American Distrust of Government* (Simon & Schuster, 1999).

PETER H. SCHUCK and JAMES Q. WILSON, *Understanding America: The Anatomy of an Exceptional Nation* (Public Affairs, 2008).

WEB SITES

loc.gov The Library of Congress's Web site contains historical information on America's founding documents as well as general history information.

tocqueville.org This site explains the life and works of Alexis de Tocqueville.

Liberty Fund (libertyfund.org) Publishes books and materials and sponsors conferences related to freedom and personal responsibility.

Mayflower Society (themayflowersociety.com) The Mayflower Society has as one of its primary purposes furthering the understanding of the Mayflower Compact.

Philosophy Pages (philosophypages.com/ph/index.htm) This site provides information on a wide range of political philosophers.

bc.edu/centers/cloughcenter/ Located at Boston College, the Clough Center for the Study of Constitutional Democracy seeks to foster self-government and reflection on constitutional government.

PART I Constitutional Principles

THE BIG PICTURE

The U.S. Constitution provides our basic framework of government. It has resulted in great stability in governance for more than 220 years, but its success was in no way guaranteed. Indeed, its ratification came after significant debate and compromise and a previous governing document (The Articles of Confederation) that remained in effect for only eight years. Debates centered on such issues as the relative power of small and large states and the conflict between the ideal of individual freedom and the reality of slavery. In this section, we discuss the development of the U.S. Constitution, the debates and values that shaped the document and continue to shape our discussions about the appropriate role of government today, the genius of a separation-of-powers system, and the compromises that led to our unique balance of federal and state authority throughout the United States.

Throughout these first chapters, we emphasize the importance of participation, politics, and compromise in developing and ratifying our founding document. We are a government by the people, but we are people with differing views and opinions on major issues of our day, just as the framers differed in their views of how our government should operate. Many of the issues about which we, as Americans, disagree today, such as health care reform, economic policy, and the United States' involvement in international affairs, mirror the kinds of debates that occurred in the founding era. They concern basic assumptions about the appropriate role of government, individual responsibility, and the degree to which the United States should be isolated from, or involved in, world affairs, including international conflict. As you read through this section, we challenge you to think about the ways you currently participate in our democratic system and perhaps consider a new way in which you might make your voice heard.

COURSE LEARNING **OBJECTIVES**

CHAPTER 1 Constitutional Democracy

Identify the philosophical principles on which our democratic republic is based, and describe the creation and adoption of the Constitution and the Bill of Rights.

Our democratic system of government is most appropriately thought of as a republic, or a representative democracy. We elect representatives to stand up for our interests in the state and national government. In a country as large as the United States, direct democracy, in which citizens vote on laws directly, is impractical. But that was not the only concern the framers had with direct democracy. They also feared that a direct democracy would fall prey to the tyranny of the majority and the changing whims of the people.

Strongly held principles such as the importance of personal liberty, individualism, equality of opportunity, and popular consent motivate our democratic structures and policies. An educated public who share basic democratic values and have the freedom to own property make democratic governance possible. To ensure its continuity, it is necessary to maintain free, fair, and frequent elections, which guarantees individual freedom to express ideas and assemble with others and a system of majority or plurality rule.

The framers' success in writing a new constitution and getting it ratified was in no way guaranteed. There was a great deal of debate at the Constitutional Convention and during the drive for ratification over the relative authority of a new national government and the states about the protection of minority rights and individual liberties and about the relative power of the three branches of government. Debates between the Federalists and the Antifederalists raged in newspaper editorials as states considered whether to ratify the new Constitution. Such debates led to the development of a bicameral legislature to balance power between small and large states and to the separation of powers between three branches of government, with a built-in system of checks and balances, to prevent the rise of a tyrannical government. Although the document that emerged reflected many of the Federalists' goals, it was not ratified until it also included the Bill of Rights, which detailed some of our most prized individual liberties, as called for by the Anti-Federalists.

The Constitution also includes a process for amendments as would be needed over time to meet changing needs and circumstances. As an instrument of government, it is important that the document is capable of change as the nation and its values evolve. However, to ensure the stability of our democratic system, it should not be so easy to change as to be rendered meaningless as a governing document. Thus, the framers struck a balance, as they did on so many issues. In order to amend the Constitution, supermajorities are required in both houses of Congress (or in state conventions) and among the states.

CHAPTER 2 American Federalism

Explain federalism in America, and analyze the relationship between the federal and state and local governments.

Federalism is a system of government in which power is divided between a central government and subdivisional governments; in the United States, those subdivisions are referred to as states. Under a system of federalism, neither the national government nor the states depend on the other for power, and neither government can usurp the other's authority. Instead, the power for each is derived from the people and, in our case, their views as represented in the Constitution.

Although the Constitution describes the authority that belongs to the national government and the states, not everyone agrees on what the document means and the appropriate balance of power. Some argue for a more limited national government in favor of greater power for the states, whereas others prefer a stronger central government. Supreme Court cases have defined many aspects of the relationship between the national and state governments, and amendments to the Constitution have also affected this relationship. Over time, depending on conditions in the country and the parties in government, national and state power has ebbed and flowed.

CHAPTER

1

Constitutional Democracy

U.S. Government and Politicians in Context

1.1 Use the concept of constitutional democracy to explain U.S. government and politics.

Defining Democracy

1.2 Differentiate democracy from other forms of government, and identify conditions, values, political processes, and political structures conducive to a successful democracy.

The Constitutional Convention of 1787

1.3 Assess the important compromises reached by the delegates to the Constitutional Convention of 1787.

To Adopt or Not to Adopt?

1.4 Evaluate the arguments for and against the ratification of the Constitution.

Constitutional Foundations

1.5 Describe the basic structure of the Constitution and its Bill of Rights.

Checking Power with Power

1.6 Analyze how the Constitution grants, limits, separates, and balances governmental power.

Judicial Review and the "Guardians of the Constitution"

1.7 Show how the use of judicial review strengthens the courts in a separation of powers system.

The peaceful transfer of power following elections is a process that U.S. citizens take for granted. Many people view elections with disdain, saying things like, "Voting does not matter," "Nothing ever changes," or "It's just all politics." But in fact, U.S. elections are remarkable and consequential. They conclude with a rare event in human history: the peaceful transfer of political power. What is unusual is what is *not* happening. Most of the time in most nations, those in power got there because either they were born to the right family or they killed or jailed their opponents. During most of history, no one, especially not an opposition political party, could openly criticize the government, and a political opponent was an enemy. England's King George III is reported to have said that George Washington would be "the greatest man alive in the world" if he were to voluntarily step down as president after two terms.[1]

After the 2008 election outcome appeared certain, John McCain graciously conceded defeat to Barack Obama and the process of organizing a new administration began. Obama's victory meant the eight-year Republican control of the presidency shifted to the Democrats. Even though the days before the election, John McCain, his running mate, Alaska Governor Sarah Palin, and their followers were insisting that if Barak Obama and his running mate, Delaware Senator Joe Biden, won the election, there would be dire economic and national security consequences, once the votes were counted, there was no serious consideration that anybody other than Barack Obama would become president. Outgoing president George Bush did not attempt to prolong his time in office by calling on the military to keep Obama from taking power. McCain's supporters did not take up arms or go underground to plan a revolution or leave the country. Instead, they almost immediately began planning how they could win the next election. Nor did Obama or his followers seriously think about punishing McCain and his supporters once they gained power. The Democrats wanted to throw the Republicans out of office, not in jail. In all these ways, the election of 2008 was a routine transfer—a constitutional democracy at work.

The peaceful transfer of power from one party and presidential administration to another is only one example of the successful functioning of our political system. In this chapter, we begin our exploration of the successful U.S. experiment with government by the people by taking a closer look at the meaning of democracy and the events that created the constitutional democracy of the United States.

U.S. Government and Politicians in Context

As the oldest constitutional democracy in the world, the United States of America has survived for more than two centuries, yet it is still a work in progress. We think of it as an enduring, strong government, but our constitutional political system is built on a fragile foundation. The U.S. Constitution and Bill of Rights survive not because we still have the parchment they were written on, but because each generation of U.S. citizens has respected, renewed, and worked to understand the principles and values found in these documents. Each generation has faced different challenges in preserving, protecting, and defending our way of government.

The U.S. constitutional democracy, founded on enduring values, has shown resilience and adaptability. We have held 112 presidential and midterm elections (including the 2010 election), and we have witnessed the peaceful transfer of power from one party to another

Constitutional Change

1.8 Outline how the Constitution is changed through informal and formal methods.

on dozens of occasions. The United States has succeeded largely because its citizens love their country, revere the Constitution, and respect the free enterprise system. We also believe that debate, compromise, and free elections are the best ways to reconcile our differences. From an early age, we practice democracy in elementary school elections, and even though we may be critical of elected leaders, we recognize the need for political leadership. We also know there are deep divisions and unsolved problems in the United States. Many people are concerned about the persistence of racism, about religious bigotry, and about the gap in economic opportunities between rich and poor. And we want our government, in addition to defending us against terrorism and foreign enemies, to address domestic problems like basic health care and education.

LEARNING **OBJECTIVE**

1.1 Use the concept of constitutional democracy to explain U.S. government and politics.

But what is this government of which we expect so much? The reality is that "government by the people" is built on the foundation of hundreds of thousands of our fellow citizens: the people we elect and the people they appoint to promote the general welfare, provide for domestic tranquility, and secure the blessings of liberty for us.

More than any other form of government, the kind of democracy that has emerged under the U.S. Constitution requires active participation and a balance between faith and skepticism. Government by the people does not, however, mean that *everyone* must be involved in politics and policy making or that those who are involved need to do so through traditional avenues such as campaigning for a political candidate or interning in a representative's office. Some individuals, however, run for office seeking to represent the voters, many of whom will always be too busy doing other things, and some of whom will always be apathetic about government and politics. Moreover, the public must be sufficiently attentive, interested, involved, informed, and willing, when necessary, to criticize and change the direction of government.

Thomas Jefferson, author of the Declaration of Independence and one of our best-known champions of constitutional democracy, believed in the common sense of the people and in the possibilities of the human spirit. Jefferson warned that every government degenerates when it is left solely in the hands of the rulers. The people themselves, Jefferson wrote, are the only safe repositories of government. He believed in popular control, representative processes, and accountable leadership. But he was no believer in the simple participatory democracy of ancient Greece or revolutionary France, where all eligible citizens were directly involved in decision making in the political process. Even the power of the people, Jefferson believed, must be restrained from time to time.

Government by the people requires faith in our common human enterprise, a belief that the people can be trusted with their own self-government, and an optimism that when things begin to go wrong, the people can be relied on to set them right. But we also need a healthy skepticism. Democracy requires us to question our leaders and never entrust a group or institution with too much power. And even though constitutional advocates prize majority rule, they must think critically about whether the majority is always right.

Constitutional democracy requires constant attention to protecting the rights and opinions of others, to ensure that our democratic processes serve the principles of liberty, equality, and justice. Thus, a peculiar blend of faith and caution is warranted when dealing with the will of the people.

Constitutional democracy means government by representative politicians. A central feature of democracy is that those who hold power do so only by winning a free and fair election. In our political system, the fragmentation of powers requires elected officials to mediate among factions, build coalitions, and work out compromises among and within the branches of our government to produce policy and action. We expect our politicians to operate within the rules of democracy and to be honest, humble, patriotic, compassionate, well informed, self-confident, and inspirational. We want politicians, in other words, to be perfect, to have all the answers, and to have all the "correct" values (as we perceive them). We want them to solve our problems, yet we also make them scapegoats for the things we dislike about government: taxes, regulations, hard times, and limits on our freedom. Many of these ideals are unrealistic, and no one could live up to all of them. Like all people, politicians live in a world in which perfection may be the goal, but compromise, ambition, fund raising, and self-promotion are necessary.

Thomas Jefferson, author of the Declaration of Independence, third president of the United States, and founder of the University of Virginia.

U.S. citizens will never be satisfied with their political candidates and politicians. The ideal politician is a myth. Politicians become "ideal" only when they are dead. Politicians and candidates, as well as the people they represent, all have different ideas about what is best for the nation. Indeed, liberty invites disagreements about ideology and values. That is why we have politics, candidates, opposition parties, heated political debates, and elections.

Defining Democracy

LEARNING **OBJECTIVE**

1.2 Differentiate democracy from other forms of government, and identify conditions, values, political processes, and political structures conducive to a successful democracy.

The distinguishing feature of democracy is that government derives its authority from its citizens. In fact, the word comes from two Greek words: *demos,* "the people," and *kratos,* "authority" or "power." Thus **democracy** means *government by the people,* not government by one person (a monarch, dictator, or priest) or government by the few (an oligarchy or aristocracy).

The word "democracy" is nowhere to be found in the Declaration of Independence or in the U.S. Constitution, nor was it a term the founders used. Ancient Athens, a few other Greek city-states, and the Roman Republic had a **direct democracy** in which citizens assembled to discuss and pass laws and select their officials. Most of these Greek city-states and the Roman Republic degenerated into mob rule and then resorted to dictators or rule by aristocrats. When this nation was founded, *democracy* was used to describe unruly groups or mobs, and a system that encouraged leaders to gain power by appealing to the emotions and prejudices of the people. In 1787, James Madison, in *The Federalist,* No. 10, reflected the view of many of the framers of the U.S. Constitution when he wrote, "Such democracies [as the Greek and Roman] . . . have ever been found incompatible with personal security, or the rights of property; and have in general been as short in their lives, as they have been violent in their deaths" (*The Federalist,* No. 10, is reprinted in the Appendix at the back of this book). Madison feared that empowering citizens to decide policy directly would be dangerous to freedom, minorities, and property and would result in violence by one group against another.

Over time, our democracy has increasingly combined representative and direct democracy. The most important examples of direct democracy were added roughly a century ago and include the **direct primary,** in which voters, rather than party leaders or other elected officials, select who may run for office; the **initiative** and **referendum,** which allow citizens to vote on state laws or constitutional amendments; and the **recall,** which lets voters remove state and local elected officials from office between elections. Initiatives and referendums are not permitted in all states, but where they are available, they have been used frequently. In 2008, California's Proposition 8 divided the state on the issue of gay marriage. Proposition 8 was an initiative stating that "only marriage between a man and a woman is valid or recognized in California." Overall, $73.4 million was spent by the two sides in an intensely fought campaign. The measure was passed with 52 percent of the vote and was deemed constitutional by the California Supreme Court in 2009.

Today, it is no longer possible, even if it were desirable, to assemble the citizens of any but the smallest towns to make their laws or select their officials directly. Rather, we have invented a system of representation. Democracy today means **representative democracy,** or a *republic,* in which those who have governmental authority get and retain that power directly or indirectly by winning free elections in which all adult citizens are allowed to participate. These elected officials are the people who determine budgets, pass laws, and are responsible for the performances of government. The framers used the term "republic" to avoid any confusion between direct democracy, which they disliked, and representative democracy, which they liked and thought secured all the advantages of a direct democracy while curing its weaknesses.

Many of the ideas that came to be part of the Constitution can be traced to philosophers' writings—in some cases, centuries before the American Revolution and the constitutional convention. Among those philosophers the framers would have read and been influenced by were Aristotle, Hobbes, Locke, and Montesquieu. Aristotle, a Greek philosopher writing in the fourth century BC, had provided important ideas on a political unit called a state but also on the idea of a constitution and on various forms of governing.[2] John Locke, an English philosopher, also profoundly influenced the authors of the Declaration of Independence and Constitution. Locke rejected the idea that kings had a

democracy
Government by the people, both directly or indirectly, with free and frequent elections.

direct democracy
Government in which citizens vote on laws and select officials directly.

direct primary
An election in which voters choose party nominees.

initiative
A procedure whereby a certain number of voters may, by petition, propose a law or constitutional amendment and have it submitted to the voters.

referendum
A procedure for submitting to popular vote measures passed by the legislature or proposed amendments to a state constitution.

recall
A procedure for submitting to popular vote the removal of officials from office before the end of their term.

representative democracy
Government in which the people elect those who govern and pass laws; also called a *republic.*

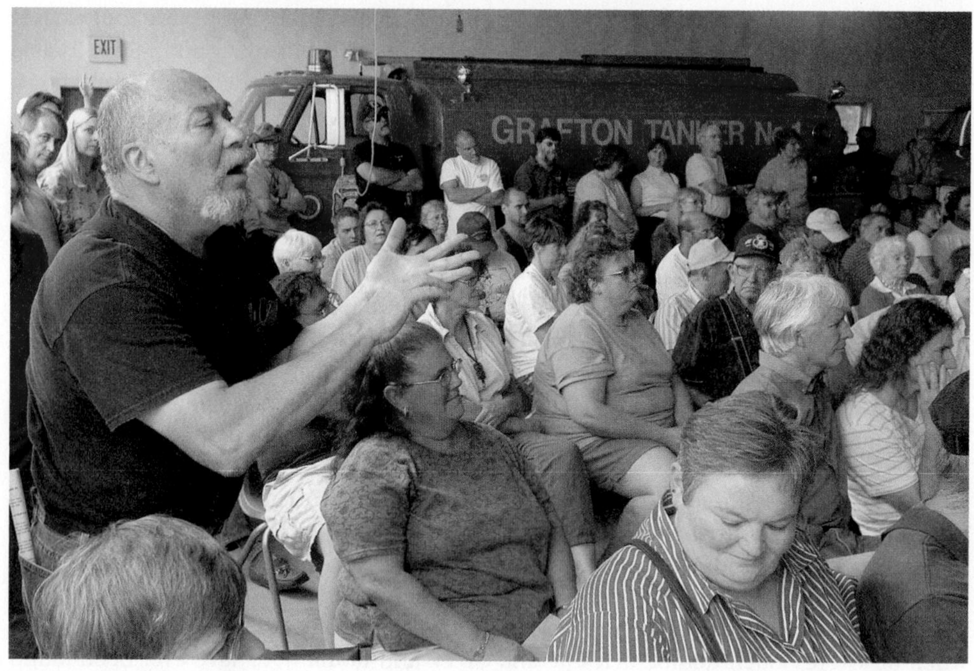

A New Hampshire man speaks at a local town meeting. Since Colonial times, many local governments in New England have held meetings in which all community members are invited to attend and discuss their opinions with public officials. ■ *Why is this form of direct democracy practiced primarily in small towns and communities?*

divine right to rule, advocated a constitutional democracy, and provided a philosophic justification for revolution.[3] Locke, like his fellow Englishman Thomas Hobbes, asserted that there was a social contract whereby people formed governments for security and to avoid what he called the state of nature, where chaos existed and where "everyone was against everyone."[4]

In defining democracy, we need to clarify other terms. **Constitutional democracy** refers to a government in which individuals exercise governmental power as the result of winning free and relatively frequent elections. It is a government in which there are recognized, enforced limits on the powers of all governmental officials. It also generally includes a written set of governmental rules and procedures—a constitution. The idea that constitutional provisions can limit power by having another part of the government balance or check it is one more good example of how the founders applied ideas from earlier thinkers—in this case, the French philosopher Charles de Montesquieu.[5]

Constitutionalism is a term we apply to arrangements—checks and balances, federalism, separation of powers, rule of law, due process, and a bill of rights—that require our leaders to listen, think, bargain, and explain before they make laws to prevent them from abusing power. We then hold them politically and legally accountable for the way they exercise their powers.

Like most political concepts, democracy encompasses many ideas and has many meanings. It is a way of life, a form of government, a way of governing, a type of nation, a state of mind, and a variety of processes. We can divide these many meanings of democracy into three broad categories: a system of interacting values, a system of interrelated political processes, and a system of interdependent political structures.

constitutional democracy
Government that enforces recognized limits on those who govern and allows the voice of the people to be heard through free, fair, and relatively frequent elections.

constitutionalism
The set of arrangements, including checks and balances, federalism, separation of powers, rule of law, due process, and a bill of rights, that requires our leaders to listen, think, bargain, and explain before they act or make laws. We then hold them politically and legally accountable for how they exercise their powers.

Democracy as a System of Interacting Values

A constitutional democracy is strengthened by an educated and prosperous public that has confidence in its ability to work out differences through the political process. A set of interacting values provides a foundation for that public confidence. As discussed in the Introduction, personal and economic liberty, individualism, equality of opportunity, and popular sovereignty are at the core of democratic values.

Personal Liberty The essence of liberty is *self-determination,* meaning that all individuals must have the opportunity to realize their own goals. Liberty is not simply the absence of external restraint on a person (freedom *from* something), it is also a person's freedom and capacity to reach his or her goals (freedom *to* do something). Moreover, both history and reason suggest that individual liberty is the key to social progress. The greater the people's freedom, the greater the chance of discovering better ways of life.

In Cuba government is based on centralized control and loyalty to the state. Here, students attend a state-sponsored ceremony to mark the start of the school year.

Individualism Popular rule in a democracy flows from a belief that every person has the potential for common sense, rationality, and fairness. Individuals have important rights; collectively, those rights are the source of all legitimate governmental authority and power. These concepts pervade democratic thought, and constitutional democracies make the *person*—rich or poor, black or white, male or female—the central measure of value.

Not all political systems put the individual first. Some promote **statism,** a form of government based on centralized authority and control, especially over the economy. China, Vietnam, and Cuba, for example, take this approach. In a modern democracy, the nation, or even the community, is less important than the individuals who compose it.

Equality of Opportunity The democratic value of *equality* enhances the importance of the individual: "All men are created equal and from that equal creation they derive rights inherent and unalienable, among which are the preservation of liberty and the pursuit of happiness." So reads Jefferson's first draft of the Declaration of Independence. But what does equality mean? And equality for whom? Does equality of opportunity mean that everyone should have the same place at the starting line? Or does it mean that society should try to equalize the factors that determine a person's economic or social well-being? These enduring issues often arise in American politics.

Popular Sovereignty The animating principle of the American Revolution, the Declaration of Independence, and the resulting new nation was popular sovereignty—the idea that ultimate political authority rests with the people. This means that a just government must derive its powers from the consent of the people it governs, or **popular consent.** A commitment to democracy thus means that a community must be willing to participate and make decisions in government. These principles sound unobjectionable, but in practice, they mean that people must be willing to lose when more people vote the other way.

Democratic Values in Conflict The basic values of democracy do not always coexist happily. Individualism may conflict with the collective welfare or the public good. Self-determination may conflict with equal opportunity. A media outlet's freedom to publish classified documents about foreign or defense policy may conflict with the government's constitutional requirement to "provide for the common defense."

Much of our political debate revolves around how to strike a balance among democratic values. How, for example, do we protect the Declaration of Independence's unalienable rights of life, liberty, and the pursuit of happiness, while trying to "promote the general Welfare" as the Constitution announces?

Democracy as a System of Interrelated Political Processes

In addition to meeting a few key conditions and having a consensus of core democratic values, a successful, democratic government requires a well-defined political process as well as a stable governmental structure. To make democratic values a reality, a nation must incorporate them into its political process, most importantly, in the form of free and fair elections, majority rule, freedom of expression, and the right of its citizens to peaceably assemble and protest.

statism
The idea that the rights of the nation are supreme over the rights of the individuals who make up the nation.

popular consent
The idea that a just government must derive its powers from the consent of the people it governs.

Of the People

THE GLOBAL COMMUNITY

Importance of Freedoms

As illustrated by the Pilgrims and those that followed, the United States has been known as a place where people value freedom. In today's world, what value do the people of the United States place on different freedoms, and how do they compare to the rest of the world? The respondents in the Pew Global survey were asked: "Thinking about your own personal life, which of these is MOST important to you: Being free to say whatever you want in public, Being free to practice your religion, Being free from hunger and poverty, Being free from crime and violence?"

To the worldwide population in the survey of 47 nations, the answer given most often to the question of what was most important was to be free from poverty (33 percent). This was also the most frequent response given in Britain (40 percent) and Nigeria (36 percent). In the United States, respondents are more evenly divided across the four competing values than in any other country.

In Japan, India, and Mexico, freedom to say whatever a person wanted to in public was the most frequently given response. Given the poverty in India and Mexico, this is a surprising answer. Both of these countries are relatively new democracies, so perhaps a political freedom like freedom of speech is more frequently cited there than in countries where it may be taken for granted. In Japan, this may be a reflection of the fact that the Japanese lost freedom of speech protections in the late nineteenth century and did not regain them until they were reinstated in the post–World War II constitution.

Being free to practice religion was most important to only 3 percent in Japan and 7 percent in Britain. In contrast, it was most important to 28 percent in the United States, where this value nearly tied for first place with being free from crime. The very clear differences in countries in what freedom they most valued is striking. Industrialized or wealthy countries do not always value the same things, nor do developing or less wealthy countries. When selecting from among these values, there is something distinctive about each country.

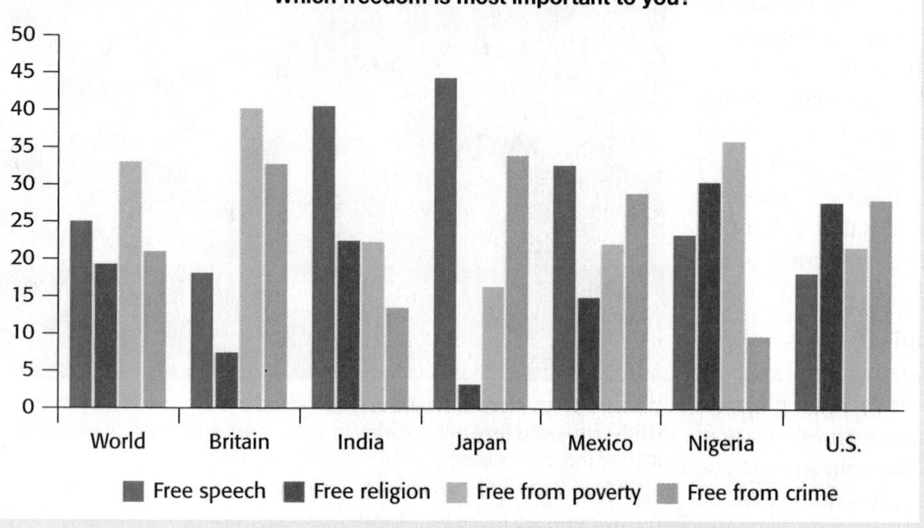

CRITICAL THINKING QUESTIONS

1. Why do many Americans say that they personally value freedom of religion as the most important value? What are the implications of this for American politics?
2. How can we account for the vast difference in what the people in these different countries most highly value?

Free and Fair Elections Democratic government is based on free and fair elections held at intervals frequent enough to make them relevant to policy choices. Elections are one of the most important devices for keeping officials and representatives accountable to the voters. The United States actively supports such elections throughout the world.

Crucial to modern-day definitions of democracy is the idea that opposition political parties can exist, can run candidates in elections, and have a chance to replace those who currently hold public office. Thus *political competition and choice* are crucial to the existence of democracy. Although free and fair elections do not imply that everyone will have equal political *influence*, they do have equal voting power, and each citizen—president or plumber, corporate CEO or college student—casts only one vote.

majority rule
Governance according to the expressed preferences of the majority.

majority
The candidate or party that wins more than half the votes cast in an election.

plurality
The candidate or party with the most votes cast in an election, not necessarily more than half.

Majority and Plurality Rule Governance according to the expressed preferences of the majority, or **majority rule,** is a basic rule of democracy. The **majority** candidate or party is the one that receives *more than half* the votes and so wins the election and takes charge of the government until the next election. In practice, however, democracies often function by **plurality** rule. Here, the candidate or party with the *most* votes wins the election, even though the candidate or party may not have received more than half the votes because votes were divided among three or more candidates or parties.

Should the side with the most votes always prevail? American citizens answer this question in various ways. Some insist that majority views should be enacted into laws and regulations. However, an effective representative democracy requires far more than simply counting individual preferences and implementing the will of most of the people. In a constitutional democracy, the will of a majority may run counter to the rights of individuals. For example, the Supreme Court struck down a 1964 California initiative where the majority voted to allow discrimination against minorities in the sale of residential housing.[6]

The framers of the U.S. Constitution wanted to guard society against oppression of any one faction of the people by any other faction. The Constitution reflects their fear of tyranny by majorities, especially momentary majorities that spring from temporary passions. They insulated certain rights (such as freedom of speech) and institutions (such as the Supreme Court and, until the Constitution was changed in 1913, even the Senate) from popular choice. Effective representation of the people, the framers insisted, should not be based solely on parochial interests or the shifting breezes of opinion.

Freedom of Expression Free and fair elections depend on voters having access to facts, competing ideas, and the views of candidates. This means that competing, nongovernment-owned newspapers, radio stations, and television stations must be allowed to flourish. If the government controls what is said and how it is said, elections cannot be free and fair, and there is no democracy. We examine free expression in greater detail in Chapter 11.

The Right to Assemble and Protest Citizens must be free to organize for political purposes. Obviously, individuals can be more effective if they join with others in a party, a pressure group, a protest movement, or a demonstration. The right to oppose the government, to form opposition parties, and to have a chance to defeat incumbents is a defining characteristic of a democracy.

Democracy as a System of Interdependent Political Structures

Democracy is, of course, more than the values and processes we have discussed so far. Its third characteristic is political structures that safeguard these values and processes. The Constitution and its first ten amendments—the Bill of Rights—set up an ingenious structure that both grants and checks government power. A system of political parties, interest groups, media, and other institutions that intercede between the electorate and those who govern reinforces this constitutional structure and thus helps maintain democratic stability.

The U.S. constitutional system has five distinctive elements: *federalism,* the division of powers between the national and state governments; *separation of powers* among the executive, judicial, and legislative branches; *bicameralism,* the division of legislative power between the House of Representatives and the Senate; *checks and balances* in which each branch is given the constitutional means, the political independence, and the motives to check the powers of the other branches so that a relative balance of power between the branches endures; and a judicially enforceable, written, explicit *Bill of Rights* that provides a guarantee of individual liberties and due process before the law. We will discuss all of these in more detail later in this chapter.

Conditions Favorable for Constitutional Democracy

Although it is hard to specify the precise conditions essential for establishing and preserving a democracy, and it does not always flourish, we can identify some patterns that foster its growth.

Educational Conditions The exercise of voting privileges requires an educated citizenry. But a high level of education (measured by the number of high school diplomas and university degrees granted) does not guarantee democratic government. Still, voting makes little sense unless many of the voters can read and write and express their interests and

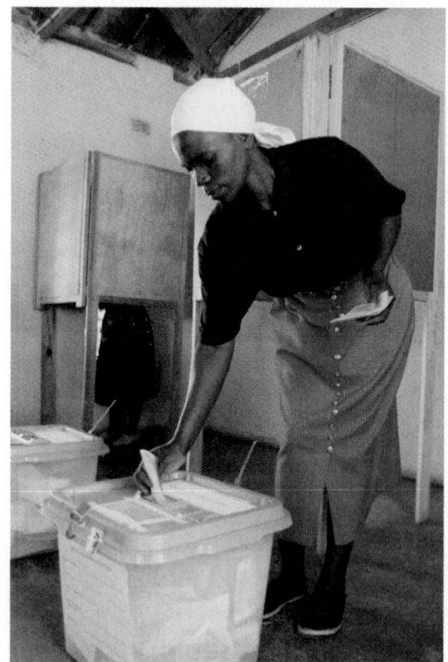

A woman casts her vote in Harare, Zimbabwe, where long lines formed at the polling stations hours before they opened. ■ *What factors make democratic government more difficult to maintain in countries such as Zimbabwe?*

opinions. The poorly educated and illiterate often get left out in a democracy. Direct democracy puts a further premium on education.[7]

Economic Conditions A relatively prosperous nation, with an equitable distribution of wealth, provides the best context for democracy. Starving people are more interested in food than in voting. Where economic power is concentrated, political power is also likely to be concentrated; thus, well-to-do nations have a better chance of sustaining democratic governments than do those with widespread poverty. As a result, the prospects for an enduring democracy are greater in Canada or France than in Zimbabwe or Egypt.

Private ownership of property and a market economy are also related to the creation and maintenance of democratic institutions. Freedom to make economic choices is linked to other freedoms like freedom of religion and the right to vote. Democracies can range from heavily regulated economies with public ownership of many enterprises, such as Sweden, to those in which there is little government regulation of the marketplace, such as the United States. But there are no democracies with a highly centralized, government-run economy and little private ownership of property. When we examine experiments with democracy in other countries, we can find examples of democracies that struggled in settings in which conditions were not favorable. Economic challenges during the Weimar Republic in Germany (1919–1933) undermined that short-lived experiment in self-rule.[8]

Social Conditions Economic development generally makes democracy possible, but proper social conditions are necessary to make it real.[9] In a society fragmented into warring groups that fiercely disagree on fundamental issues, government by discussion and compromise is difficult, as we have seen in Afghanistan and Iraq. When ideologically separated groups consider the issues at stake to be vital, they may prefer to fight rather than accept the verdict of the ballot box, as happened in the United States in 1861 with the outbreak of the Civil War.

In a society that consists of many overlapping associations and groupings, however, individuals are less likely to identify completely with a single group and give their allegiance to it. For example, Joe Smith is a Baptist, an African American, a southerner, a Democrat, an electrician, and a member of the National Rifle Association, and he makes $50,000 a year. On some issues, Joe thinks as a Baptist, on others as a member of the NRA, and on still others as an African American. Joe and his fellow Americans may differ on some issues and agree on others, but they share an overriding common interest in maintaining a democracy.[10]

Ideological Conditions American adults have basic beliefs about power, government, and political practices—beliefs that arise from the educational, economic, and social conditions of their individual experience. From these conditions must also develop a general acceptance of the ideals of democracy and a willingness of a substantial number of people to agree to proceed democratically. This acceptance is sometimes called the *democratic consensus.* Widely accepted ideals of democracy include one person, one vote; majority rule; freedom of speech; and freedom of assembly. Absent such a consensus, attempts at democracy will be ill-fated. For example, China has made major strides in improving its educational and economic circumstances in recent years, but it lacks a democratic consensus or the institutions and liberties vital to a democracy.

Political scientists have long tried to determine what factors contribute to stability in a democracy. Comparative studies have often linked factors such as national prosperity, education, and literacy to democratic success. Table 1–1 lists several different dimensions for the countries that we will be comparing to the United States throughout the book.

We have now discussed the values, political processes, and political structures that help foster viable constitutional democracy, as well as the conditions conducive to it. These provide a foundation on which we can assess governments throughout the world, as well as the extraordinary story of the founding and enlargement of constitutional democracy in the United States, to which we turn next.

TABLE 1–1 Conditions for Democratic Stability

	World	Britain	China	India	Japan	Mexico	Nigeria	United States
Population (millions; July 2007 est.)	6,790.06	61.11	1,338.61	1,156.90	127.08	111.21	149.23	307.21
Median Age	28.4	40.2	34.1	25.3	44.2	26.3	19	36.7
Life Expectancy	66.1	79.1	73.5	66.1	82.12	76.1	46.9	78.1
Literacy								
Male	87%	99	95.1	73.4	99	92.4	75.7	99
Female	77%	99	86.5	47.8	99	89.6	60.6	99
Government Type		Constitutional monarchy	Communist state	Federal republic	Constitutional monarchy	Federal republic	Federal republic	Federal republic
GDP[1]	$57.53	2.20	4.76	1.24	5.05	0.87	0.17	14.27
Freedom House[2]		Free	Not Free	Free	Free	Free	Partly free	Free

■ These countries vary dramatically in many aspects. For example, note the extremely young population of Nigeria compared to the generally older population of Japan. *What are the implications of this difference for both governments?* Notice that the U.S. population is less than one-fourth that of China. *How might population size affect some of these factors?* Compare the differences in literacy between men and women in India, Nigeria, and China. *What do you think accounts for these differences?*

NOTES: (1) Calculated based on the country's official exchange rate in trillions of USD; (2) For more on Freedom House's Freedom Index, see www.freedomhouse.org/template.cfm?page=351&ana_page=333&year=2007.

SOURCE: Central Intelligence Agency, *The World Factbook*, at https://www.cia.gov/library/publications/the-world-factbook/geos/us.html; and Freedom House, *Freedom in the World 2009: The Annual Survey of Political Rights and Civil Liberties*, at www.freedomhouse.org/template.cfm?page=363&year=2009.

The Constitutional Convention of 1787

LEARNING **OBJECTIVE**

1.3 Assess the important compromises reached by the delegates to the Constitutional Convention of 1787.

The delegates who assembled in Philadelphia in May 1787 had to establish a national government powerful enough to prevent the young nation from dissolving but not so powerful that it would crush individual liberty. This meeting became the **Constitutional Convention.** What these men did continues to have a major impact on how we are governed. It also provides an outstanding lesson in political science for the world.

The Delegates

The various states appointed 74 delegates, but only 55 arrived in Philadelphia. Of these, approximately 40 actually took part in the work of the convention. It was a distinguished gathering. Many of the most important men of the nation were there: successful merchants, planters, bankers, lawyers, and former and present governors and congressional representatives (39 of the delegates had served in Congress). Most had read the classics of political thought. Most had experience constructing local and state governments. Many had also worked hard to create and direct the national confederation of the states. And the Constitutional Convention also included eight of the 56 signers of the Declaration of Independence.

The convention was as representative as most political gatherings were at the time: the participants were all white male landowners. These well-read, well-fed, well-bred, and often well-wed delegates were mainly state or national leaders, for in the 1780s; ordinary people were not likely to participate in politics. (Even today, farm laborers, factory workers, and truck drivers are seldom found in Congress—although a haberdasher, a peanut farmer, and a movie actor have made their way to the White House.)

Although active in the movement to revise the Articles of Confederation, George Washington had been reluctant to attend the convention and accepted only when persuaded that his prestige was needed for its success. He was selected unanimously to preside over the meetings. According to the records, he spoke only twice during the deliberations, but his influence was felt in the informal gatherings as well as during the sessions. Everyone understood that Washington favored a more powerful central government led by a president. In fact, the general expectation that he would be the first president played

Constitutional Convention
The convention in Philadelphia, from May 25 to September 17, 1787, that debated and agreed on the Constitution of the United States.

Of the People

AMERICA'S CHANGING FACE

The Constitutional Convention

If the Constitutional Convention were convened today, how would the delegates compare to the all-white, all-male, property-owning delegates who drafted the Constitution in Philadelphia in 1787? One likely similarity is that they would be successful and generally well-educated individuals willing to engage in public service.

Many of those who drafted the Constitution had served in state legislatures. If the Constitutional Convention were held today and included state legislators, it would be much more diverse. Nearly 25 percent of most state legislators are now female, including at least a third in Maryland, Delaware, Arizona, Colorado, Kansas, Nevada, and Vermont. At the same time, state legislatures remain almost entirely white—only 9 percent were African American in 2009, and only 3 percent were Hispanic.*

Many of those who drafted the Constitution were also lawyers and successful business managers. If the Constitutional Convention were held today and included these professions, the proportion of women participating would be between 35 and 40 percent, and 15 percent of the delegates would not be white.† Although these proportions show a growing diversity among the delegates who might be called to Philadelphia today, they do not yet reflect the diversity of the population at large.

CRITICAL THINKING QUESTIONS

1. How would the recent changes in U.S. demographics translate into changes in the content of any constitution produced by a Constitutional Convention held today?
2. Why are lawyers disproportionately represented in politics, both today and at the Constitutional Convention? What difference does having so many lawyers as constitution makers have on the process and on the document they produce?

* Conference of State Legislators, "2009 African American Legislators," http://www.ncsl.org/Default.aspx?TabId=14767 (accessed February 16, 2010).

† U.S. Equal Employment Opportunity Commission, "Diversity in Law Firms," 2003, http://www.eeoc.gov/eeoc/statistics/reports/diversitylaw/lawfirms.pdf.

a crucial role in the creation of the presidency. "No one feared that he would misuse power. . . . His genuine hesitancy, his reluctance to assume the position, only served to reinforce the almost universal desire that he do so."[11]

To encourage everyone to speak freely and allow delegates to change their minds after debate and discussion, the proceedings of the convention were kept secret and delegates were forbidden to discuss them with outsiders. The delegates also knew that if word of the inevitable disagreements got out, it would provide ammunition for the enemies of the convention.

Consensus

Critical to the success of the Constitutional Convention were its three famous compromises: the compromise between large and small states over representation in Congress, the compromise between North and South over the regulation and taxation of foreign commerce, and the compromise between North and South over the counting of slaves for the purposes of taxation and representation. There were other important compromises. Yet, on many significant issues, most of the delegates were in agreement.

All the delegates publicly supported a republican form of government based on elected representatives of the people. This was the only form the convention seriously considered and the only form acceptable to the nation. Equally important, all the delegates opposed arbitrary and unrestrained government.

Most of the delegates were in favor of *balanced government* in which no single interest would dominate and in which the national government would be strong enough to protect property and business from outbreaks like the 1786 insurrection in western Massachusetts when Daniel Shays led farmers to revolt over foreclosures on their property. **Shays' Rebellion** reinforced the need for a stronger central government.

Shays' Rebellion
A rebellion led by Daniel Shays of farmers in western Massachusetts in 1786–1787 protesting mortgage foreclosures. It highlighted the need for a strong national government just as the call for the Constitutional Convention went out.

Benjamin Franklin, the 81-year-old delegate from Pennsylvania, favored extending the right to vote to all white males, but most of the delegates believed landowners were the best guardians of liberty. James Madison feared that those without property, if given the right to vote, might combine to deprive property owners of their rights. Delegates agreed in principle on limited voting rights but differed on the kind and

Representing different constituencies and different ideologies, the Constitutional Convention devised a totally new form of government that provided for a central government strong enough to rule but still responsible to its citizens and to the member states.

amount of property owned as a prerequisite to vote. The framers recognized that they would jeopardize approval of the Constitution if they made the qualifications to vote in federal elections more restrictive than those of the states. As a result, each state was left to determine its own qualifications for electing members of the House of Representatives, the only branch of the national government that was to be elected directly by the voters.

Within five days of its opening, the convention voted—with only the Connecticut delegates dissenting—that "a national government ought to be established consisting of a supreme legislative, executive, and judiciary." This decision profoundly changed the nature of the union, from a loose confederation of states to a true nation.

Few dissented from proposals to give the new Congress all the powers of the old Congress, plus all other powers necessary to ensure that state legislation would not challenge the integrity of the United States. After the delegates agreed on the extensive powers of the legislative branch and the close connection between its lower house and the people, they also agreed that a strong executive, which the Articles of Confederation had lacked, was necessary to provide energy, direction, and a check on the legislature. They also accepted an independent judiciary without much debate. Other issues, however, sparked conflict.

Conflict and Compromise

Serious differences among the various delegates, especially between those from the large and small states, predated the Constitutional Convention. With the success of the War of Independence, the United States gained the formerly British land west of the colonial borders. States with large western borders such as Virginia claimed that their borders should simply be extended. Colonies without open Western borders such as New Jersey and Connecticut took exception to these claims, reinforcing the tension between the colonies. The matter was resolved in the Land Ordinance of 1785 and the Northwest Ordinance of 1787, when all states agreed to cede the western lands to the national government and permit them to eventually become part of new states rather than expand the borders of existing states. But the rivalries between the former colonies remained sharp at the convention in Philadelphia in 1787. For example, the large states also favored a strong national government (which they expected to dominate), while delegates from small states were anxious to avoid being dominated.

This tension surfaced in the first discussions of representation in Congress. Franklin favored a single-house national legislature, but most states had had two-chamber legislatures since colonial times, and the delegates were used to this system. **Bicameralism**—the principle of the two-house legislature—reflected delegates' belief in the need for balanced government. The Senate, the smaller chamber, would represent the states and to some extent the wealthier classes, and it would offset the larger, more democratic House of Representatives.

The Virginia Plan The Virginia delegation took the initiative. They presented 15 resolutions known as the **Virginia Plan.** This called for a strong central government with a legislature composed of two chambers. The voters were to elect the members of the more representative chamber, which would choose the members of the smaller chamber from nominees submitted by the state legislatures. Representation in both houses would be based on either wealth or population. Wealth was based on a 1783 law where "general expenses were apportioned on the basis of land values with their improvements." The more wealthy states were also the more populous ones—Massachusetts, Pennsylvania, and Virginia—which gave them a majority in the national legislature.

The Congress that the Virginia Plan would have created was to have all the legislative power of its predecessor under the Articles of Confederation, as well as the power "to legislate in all cases in which the separate States are incompetent," to veto state legislation that conflicted with the proposed constitution, and to choose a national executive with extensive jurisdiction. A national Supreme Court, along with the executive, would have a qualified veto over acts of Congress. In sum, the Virginia Plan would have created a strong national government with disproportionate power to the more populous states.

The New Jersey Plan The Virginia Plan dominated the discussion for the first few weeks. That changed when delegates from the small states put forward their plan. William Paterson of New Jersey presented a series of resolutions known as the **New Jersey Plan.** Paterson did not question the need for a strengthened central government, but he was concerned about how this strength might be used. The New Jersey Plan would give Congress the right to tax and regulate commerce and to coerce states, and it would retain the single-house or unicameral legislature (as under the Articles of Confederation) in which each state, regardless of size, would have the same vote.

The New Jersey Plan contained the germ of what eventually came to be a key provision of our Constitution: the *supremacy clause.* The national Supreme Court was to hear appeals from state judges, and the supremacy clause would require all judges—state and national—to treat laws of the national government and the treaties of the United States as superior to the constitutions and laws of each of the states.

For a time, the convention was deadlocked. The small states believed that all states should be represented equally in Congress, especially in the smaller "upper house" if there were to be two chambers. The large states insisted that representation in both houses be based on population or wealth, and that voters, not state legislatures, should elect national legislators. Finally, the so-called Committee of Eleven, a committee of 11 men, one from each of the member states, was elected to devise a compromise.[12] On July 5, it presented its proposals, including what came to be known as the great or Connecticut Compromise.

The Connecticut Compromise The **Connecticut Compromise** (so labeled because of the prominent role the Connecticut delegation played in constructing it) called for one house in which each state would have an equal vote, and a second house in which representation would be based on population and in which all bills for raising or appropriating money—a key function of government—would originate. This proposal was a setback for the large states, which agreed to it only when the smaller states made it clear this was their price for union. After the delegates accepted equality of state representation in the Senate, most objections to a strong national government dissolved. (Table 1–2 outlines the key features of the Virginia Plan, the New Jersey Plan, and the Connecticut Compromise.)

bicameralism
The principle of a two-house legislature.

Virginia Plan
The initial proposal at the Constitutional Convention made by the Virginia delegation for a strong central government with a bicameral legislature dominated by the big states.

New Jersey Plan
The proposal at the Constitutional Convention made by William Paterson of New Jersey for a central government with a single-house legislature in which each state would be represented equally.

Connecticut Compromise
The compromise agreement by states at the Constitutional Convention for a bicameral legislature with a lower house in which representation would be based on population and an upper house in which each state would have two senators.

TABLE 1–2 The Constitutional Convention: Conflict and Compromise

Virginia Plan	New Jersey Plan	Connecticut Compromise
Legitimacy derived from citizens, based on popular representation	Derived from states, based on equal votes for each state	Derived from citizens and the states
Bicameral legislature, representation in both houses determined by population	Unicameral legislature, representation equal by state	Bicameral legislature with seats in the Senate apportioned by states and seats in the House apportioned by population
Executive size undetermined, elected and removable by Congress	More than one person, removable by state majority	Single executive elected by electoral college, not removable by state majority
Judicial life tenure, able to veto state legislation	No federal judicial power over states	Judicial life tenure, able to veto state legislation in violation of constitution
Legislature can override state laws	Government can compel obedience to national laws	
Ratification by citizens	Ratification by states	Ratification by states, with process open to citizen ratification

North–South Compromises Other issues split the delegates from the North and South. Southerners were afraid that a northern majority in Congress might discriminate against southern trade. They had some basis for this concern. John Jay, a New Yorker who was secretary of foreign affairs for the Confederation, had proposed a treaty with Great Britain that would have given advantages to northern merchants at the expense of southern exporters of agricultural products such as tobacco and cotton. To protect themselves, the southern delegates insisted that a two-thirds majority in the Senate be required to ratify a treaty.

One subject that appears not to have been open for resolution was slavery. The view widely shared among historians is that the states with a greater reliance on slaves would have left the convention if the document had reduced or eliminated the practice. The issue did arise on whether to count slaves for the purpose of apportioning seats in the House of Representatives. To gain more representatives, the South wanted to count slaves; the North resisted. After heated debate, the delegates agreed on the **three-fifths compromise.** Each slave would be counted as three-fifths of a free person for the purposes of apportionment in the House and of direct taxation. This fraction was chosen because it maintained a balance of power between the North and the

three-fifths compromise
The compromise between northern and southern states at the Constitutional Convention that three-fifths of the slave population would be counted for determining direct taxation and representation in the House of Representatives.

The Connecticut compromise created a bicameral legislature, with seats in the Senate apportioned by states and seats in the House apportioned by population. ■ *How did this decision affect the relative sizes of the House chambers (left) and those of the Senate (right)?*

South. The compromise also included a provision to eliminate the importation of slaves in 20 years, and Congress did so in 1808. The issue of balance between North and South would recur in the early history of our nation as territorial governments were established and territories that applied for statehood decided whether to permit or ban slavery.

Other Issues Delegates also argued about other issues. Should the national government have lower courts, or would one federal Supreme Court be enough? This issue was left to Congress to resolve. The Constitution states that there shall be one Supreme Court and that Congress may establish lower courts.

How should the president be selected? For a long time, the convention favored allowing Congress to pick the president, but some delegates feared that Congress would then dominate the president, or vice versa. The convention also rejected election by the state legislatures because the delegates distrusted the state legislatures. The delegates finally settled on election of the president by the **electoral college,** a group of individuals equal in number to the U.S. senators and representatives. Originally, it was thought electors would exercise their own judgment in selecting the president. But the college quickly came to reflect partisanship, and today, for most states, electors cast ballots for the candidate who wins the popular vote of that state. (We discuss the electoral college in greater detail in Chapter 6.) This was perhaps the delegates' most novel contribution as well as the most contrived, and it has long been one of the most criticized provisions in the Constitution.[13] (See Article II, Section 1 of the Constitution, which is reprinted following this chapter.)

After three months, the delegates stopped debating. On September 17, 1787, all but three of those still present signed the document they were recommending to the nation. Others who opposed the general drift of the convention had already left. Their work well done, the delegates adjourned to the nearby City Tavern to celebrate.

According to an old story, a woman confronted Benjamin Franklin as he left the last session of the convention.

"What kind of government have you given us, Dr. Franklin?" she asked. "A republic or a monarchy?"

"A republic, Madam," he answered, "if you can keep it."

To Adopt or Not to Adopt?

LEARNING **OBJECTIVE**

1.4 Evaluate the arguments for and against the ratification of the Constitution.

The delegates had gone far. Indeed, they had disregarded Congress's instruction to do no more than revise the Articles of Confederation. In particular, they had ignored Article XIII, which declared the Union to be perpetual and prohibited any alteration of the Articles unless Congress and *every one of the state legislatures* agreed—a provision that had made it impossible to amend the Articles. The convention delegates, however, boldly declared that their newly proposed Constitution should go into effect when ratified by popularly elected conventions in nine states.

They turned to this method of ratification for practical considerations as well as to secure legitimacy for their proposed government. Not only were the delegates aware that there was little chance of winning approval of the new Constitution in all state legislatures, but many also believed that a constitution approved *by the people* would have higher legal and moral status than one approved only by a legislature. The Articles of Confederation had been a compact of state governments, but the Constitution was based on the will of the people (recall its opening words: "We the People . . ."). Still, even this method of ratification would not be easy. The nation was not ready to adopt the Constitution without a thorough debate.

electoral college
The electoral system used in electing the president and vice president, in which voters vote for electors pledged to cast their ballots for a particular party's candidates.

Federalists
Supporters of ratification of the Constitution and of a strong central government.

Antifederalists
Opponents of ratification of the Constitution and of a strong central government generally.

Federalists Versus Antifederalists

Supporters of the new government, by cleverly appropriating the name **Federalists,** forced their opponents to be known as the **Antifederalists** and pointed out the negative character of the arguments opposing ratification. While advocating a strong national government but also retaining state prerogatives, the Federalists took some of the sting out of charges that they were trying to destroy the states and establish an all-powerful central government.

The split was in part geographic. Seaboard and city regions tended to be Federalist strongholds; backcountry regions from Maine (then part of Massachusetts) through Georgia, inhabited by farmers and other relatively poor people, were generally Antifederalist. The underlying regional and economic differences led to fears by those opposing the new form of government that it would not protect individual rights, and reinforced the "Antifederalist charge that the Constitution was an aristocratic document."[14] But as in most political contests, no single factor completely accounted for the division between Federalists and Antifederalists. Thus, in Virginia, the leaders of both sides came from the same general social and economic class. New York City and Philadelphia strongly supported the Constitution, yet so did predominantly rural New Jersey and Connecticut.

The great debate was conducted through pamphlets, newspapers, letters to editors, and speeches. It provides an outstanding example of a free people publicly discussing the nature of their fundamental laws. Out of the debate came a series of essays known as ***The Federalist,*** written under the pseudonym Publius by Alexander Hamilton, James Madison, and John Jay to persuade the voters of New York to ratify the Constitution. *The Federalist* is still "widely regarded as the most profound single treatise on the Constitution ever written and as among the few masterly works in political science produced in all the centuries of history."[15] (Three of the most important *Federalist* essays, Nos. 10, 51, and 78, are reprinted in the Appendix of this book.)

The Federalist
Essays promoting ratification of the Constitution, published anonymously by Alexander Hamilton, John Jay, and James Madison in 1787 and 1788.

Antifederalists opposed the creation of a strong central government. They worried that, under the Constitution, Congress would "impose barriers against commerce," and they were concerned that the Constitution did not do enough to ensure "frequent rotation of office," meaning elected officials could not be recalled through elections and over time would become less concerned with their constituents.[16]

The Antifederalists' most telling criticism of the proposed Constitution was its failure to include a bill of rights.[17] The Federalists believed a bill of rights was unnecessary because the proposed national government had *only* the specific powers that the states and the people delegated to it. Thus, there was no need to specify that Congress could not, for example, abridge freedom of the press because the states and the people had not given the national government power to regulate the press in the first place. Moreover, the Federalists argued, to guarantee some rights might be dangerous, because rights not listed could be assumed to be denied. The Constitution itself already protected some important rights—the requirement of trial by jury in federal criminal cases, provided for in Article III, for example. Hamilton and others also insisted that paper guarantees were feeble protection against governmental tyranny.

The Antifederalists were unconvinced. If some rights were protected, what could be the objection to providing constitutional protection for others? Without a bill of rights, what was to prevent Congress from using one of its delegated powers to abridge free speech? If bills of rights were needed in state constitutions to limit state governments, why did the national constitution not include a bill of rights to limit the national government? This was a government further from the people, they contended, with a greater tendency to subvert natural rights than was true of state governments.

Patrick Henry's famous cry of "Give me liberty or give me death!" helped rally support for the revolution against Britain. Later, he was an outspoken opponent of ratification of the Constitution and was instrumental in forcing adoption of the Bill of Rights.

TABLE 1–3 Ratification of the U.S. Constitution

State	Date
Delaware	December 7, 1787
Pennsylvania	December 12, 1787
New Jersey	December 18, 1787
Georgia	January 2, 1788
Connecticut	January 9, 1788
Massachusetts	February 6, 1788
Maryland	April 28, 1788
South Carolina	May 23, 1788
New Hampshire	June 21, 1788
Virginia	June 25, 1788
New York	July 26, 1788
North Carolina	November 21, 1789
Rhode Island	May 29, 1790

■ *By what date did the Constitution have enough state support to go into effect? Why was it still important for the remaining states to ratify the Constitution?*

The Politics of Ratification

The absence of a bill of rights in the proposed Constitution dominated the struggle over its adoption. In taverns, churches, and newspaper offices, people were muttering, "No bill of rights—no Constitution!" This feeling was so strong that some Antifederalists, though they were far more concerned with states' rights than individual rights, joined forces with those wanting a bill of rights in order to defeat the proposed Constitution.

The Federalists began the debate over the Constitution as soon as the delegates left Philadelphia in mid-September 1787. Their tactic was to secure ratification in as many states as possible before the opposition had time to organize. The Antifederalists were handicapped because most newspapers supported ratification. Moreover, Antifederalist strength was concentrated in rural areas, which were underrepresented in some state legislatures and in which it was more difficult to arouse the people to political action. The Antifederalists needed time to organize, while the Federalists moved in a hurry.

Most of the small states, now satisfied by getting equal Senate representation, ratified the Constitution without difficulty. Delaware was the first, and by early 1788, Pennsylvania, New Jersey, Georgia, and Connecticut had also ratified (see Table 1–3). In Massachusetts, however, opposition was growing. Key leaders, such as John Hancock and Samuel Adams, were doubtful or opposed. The debate in Boston raged for most of January 1788 and into February. But in the end, the Massachusetts Convention narrowly ratified the Constitution in that state, 187 to 168.

By June 21, 1788, Maryland, South Carolina, and New Hampshire had also ratified, giving the Constitution the nine states required for it to go into effect. But two big hurdles remained: Virginia and New York. It would be impossible to begin the new government without the consent of these two major states. Virginia was crucial. As the most populous state and the home of Washington, Jefferson, and Madison, Virginia was a link between North and South. The Virginia ratifying convention rivaled the Constitutional Convention in the caliber of its delegates. Madison, who had only recently switched to favoring a bill of rights after saying earlier that it was unnecessary, captained the Federalist forces. The fiery Patrick Henry led the opposition. In an epic debate, Henry cried that liberty was the issue: "Liberty, the greatest of earthly possessions ... that precious jewel!" But Madison promised that a bill of rights embracing the freedoms of religion, speech, and assembly would be added to the Constitution as soon as the new government was established. Washington tipped the balance with a letter urging ratification. News of the Virginia vote, 89 for the Constitution and 79 opposed, was rushed to New York.[18]

The great landowners along New York's Hudson River, unlike the southern planters, opposed the Constitution. They feared federal taxation of their holdings, and they did not want to abolish the profitable tax New York had been levying on trade and commerce with other states. When the convention assembled, the Federalists were greatly outnumbered, but they were aided by Alexander Hamilton's strategy and skill, and by word of Virginia's ratification. New York approved by a margin of three votes. Although North Carolina and Rhode Island still remained outside the Union (the former ratified in November 1789, the latter six months later), the new nation was created. In New York, a few members of the old Congress assembled to issue the call for elections under the new Constitution. Then they adjourned without setting a date for reconvening.

Constitutional Foundations

LEARNING **OBJECTIVE**

1.5 Describe the basic structure of the Constitution and its Bill of Rights.

The Constitution of the United States is the world's oldest written constitution. Some 224 other countries have written constitutions, but more than half (122) have been adopted or significantly revised since 1990, with 17 new ones ratified since 2000. Nine countries have no written constitution, including Oman, New Zealand, and the United Kingdom.[19]

By the People

MAKING A DIFFERENCE

Becoming an American Citizen

Many Americans take their government for granted and have not thought much about the importance of their citizenship in this country. That is not the case for those who have gone through the process of securing U.S. citizenship. The process involves a detailed application, a criminal records search, information about your family, and an interview that includes an assessment of proficiency in English and knowledge of the U.S. government and Constitution. You can view samples of these civics questions by clicking on the "Naturalization Test" at http://www.uscis.gov/files/nativedocuments/M-685.pdf. How would you do on the oral exam? One current sample question, for example, asks applicants: "The idea of self-government is in the first three words of the Constitution. What are these three words?" The correct answer is "We the people." To pass the test, an applicant must answer six of the ten questions correctly.*

For many people wanting to become U.S. citizens, the application process, interview, and examination are intimidating. The U.S. Committee for Refugees and Immigrants (USCRI) is a group that makes a difference in helping people attain U.S. Citizenship. USCRI is the nation's oldest (founded in 1911) and largest network of nonprofit organizations serving foreign-born people. USCRI has resettled a quarter million refugees in the past two decades. USCRI has a "Partnership for Citizenship Program" that helps individuals prepare to become citizens. Some of those seeking citizenship are refugees who also need assistance in such basics as writing resumes and preparing for job interviews, as well as information on where they can go for food, clothing, and housing.

You can make a difference by volunteering at an agency assisting refugees and others in your community. Some universities, like Harvard University, have programs where undergraduates tutor individuals to prepare them for the citizenship exam. If your institution does not have such a program, you might organize one. Given your study of American government, you will be especially prepared to assist in the English and Civics preparation for the citizenship screening interview.

CRITICAL THINKING QUESTIONS

1. Would all Americans take citizenship more seriously if they had to apply for citizenship and pass an oral exam on U.S. government?
2. How restrictive should the government be in extending citizenship?

* U.S. Citizenship and Immigration Services, "The Naturalization Test," http://www.uscis.gov/portal/site/uscis/menuitem (accessed April 27, 2010).

Understanding the Constitution and considering its strengths and weaknesses is a necessary step in studying and participating in U.S. government. After such a study, one student turned his college research paper at the University of Texas into a successful drive to ratify the Twenty-Seventh Amendment (concerning congressional salaries) in 1992. We may not all achieve such a result through our participation, but by being more knowledgeable about our system, we can better protect our own individual liberties, evaluate the appropriate authority of various elected and appointed governmental officials, and understand what it means to have a government with powers that are separated, shared, and checked.

In addition to being the oldest written Constitution in the world, the U.S. Constitution is also one of the shortest. The original Constitution, excluding the Bill of Rights, contains only 4,543 words. In comparison, India's constitution is 117,000 words, and the longest state constitution—that of Alabama—is over 350,000 words. Its basic structure is straightforward. Article I establishes a bicameral Congress, with a House of Representatives and a Senate, and empowers it to enact legislation, for example, governing foreign and interstate commerce (as discussed further in Chapter 7). Article II vests the executive power in the president (as discussed in Chapter 8), and Article III vests the judicial power in the Supreme Court and other federal courts that Congress may establish (as discussed in Chapter 10). Article IV guarantees the privileges and immunities of citizens and specifies the conditions for admitting new states. Article V provides for the methods of amending the Constitution, and Article VI specifies that the Constitution and all laws made under it are the supreme law of the land. Finally, Article VII provides that the Constitution had to be ratified by 9 of the original 13 states to go into effect. In 1791, the first 10 amendments, the Bill of Rights, were added, and another 17 amendments have been added since.

Despite its brevity, the Constitution firmly established the framers' experiment in free-government-in-the-making that each generation reinterprets and renews. That is why after more than 220 years we have not had another written Constitution—let alone two, three, or more, like other countries around the world. Part of the reason is the widespread acceptance

Citizens can view the original U.S. Constitution at the National Archives in Washington DC. ■ *What effects might displaying the Constitution as it is pictured here have on the way citizens think about the document?*

of the Constitution across our population. But the Constitution has also endured because it is a brilliant structure for limited government and one that the framers designed to be adaptable and flexible. The entire Constitution and its amendments appear at the end of this chapter.

As the Constitution won the support of citizens in the early years of the Republic, it took on the aura of **natural law**—law that defines right from wrong, which is higher than human law. Like the crown in Great Britain, the Constitution became a symbol of national unity and loyalty, evoking both emotional and intellectual support from Americans, regardless of their differences. The framers' work became part of the U.S. creed and culture.[20] The Constitution stands for liberty, equality before the law, limited or expanded government—indeed, it stands for just about anything anyone wants to read into it.

Even today, U.S. citizens generally revere the Constitution, although many do not know what is in it. A poll by the National Constitution Center found that nine of ten U.S. adults are proud of the Constitution and feel it is important to them. However, a third mistakenly believe the Constitution establishes English as the country's official language. One in six believes it establishes the United States as a Christian nation. Only one in four could name a single First Amendment right. Although two in three knew the Constitution created three branches of the national government, only one in three could name all three branches.[21]

The Constitution is more than a symbol, however. It is the supreme and binding law that both grants and limits powers. "In framing a government which is to be administered by men over men," wrote James Madison in *The Federalist*, No. 51, "the great difficulty lies in this: You must first enable the government to control the governed; and in the next place oblige it to control itself." (See *The Federalist*, No. 51, in the Appendix of this book.) The Constitution is both a positive instrument of government, which enables the governors to control the governed, and a restraint on government, which enables the ruled to check the rulers. How does the Constitution limit the power of the government? How does it create governmental power? How has it managed to serve as a great symbol of national unity and, at the same time, as an adaptable instrument of government? The secret is an ingenious separation of powers and a system of checks and balances that limits power with power.

Checking Power with Power

LEARNING **OBJECTIVE**

1.6 Analyze how the Constitution grants, limits, separates, and balances governmental power.

natural law
God's or nature's law that defines right from wrong and is higher than human law.

federalism
A constitutional arrangement in which power is distributed between a central government and subdivisional governments, called states in the United States. The national and the subdivisional governments both exercise direct authority over individuals.

"If men were angels," James Madison argued in *The Federalist,* No. 51, "no government would be necessary. If angels were to govern men, neither external nor internal controls on government would be necessary."[22] But the framers knew well that men were not angels, and thus, to create a successful government, they would need to create a government of *limited* authority. How? Within the government, competing interests would check each other, and, externally, the governed would check the government through elections, petitions, protests, and amendments. The framers wanted a stronger and more effective national government than they had under the Articles of Confederation. But they were keenly aware that the people would not accept too much central control. Efficiency and order were important concerns, but liberty was more important. The framers wanted to ensure domestic tranquility and prevent future rebellions, but they also wanted to forestall the emergence of a homegrown King George III. Accordingly, they allotted certain powers to the national government and reserved the rest for the states, thus establishing a system of **federalism** (whose nature and problems we discuss in Chapter 2). Even this was not enough. The framers believed additional restraints were needed to limit the national government.

The most important means they devised to make public officials observe the constitutional limits on their powers was *free and fair elections,* through which voters could throw out of office those who abuse power. Yet the framers were not willing to depend solely on political controls because they did not fully trust the people's judgment. "Free government is founded on jealousy, and not in confidence," said Thomas Jefferson. "In questions of power, then, let no more be heard of confidence in man, but bind him down from mischief by the chains of the Constitution."[23]

No less important, the framers feared a majority might deprive minorities of their rights. This risk was certainly real at the time of the framing, as it is today. "A dependence on the people is, no doubt, the primary control on the government," Madison contended in *The Federalist,* No. 51, "but experience has taught mankind the necessity of auxiliary precautions."[24] What were these "auxiliary precautions" against popular tyranny?

James Madison was the fourth president of the United States (1809–1817) and an author of *The Federalist Papers.* Madison's view on a separated system of government in which each branch checks the power of other branches shapes our governmental structure. ■ *How did Madison's beliefs about the nature of man affect his views on the best structure for our federal government?*

Separation of Powers

The first step against potential tyranny of the majority was the **separation of powers,** the distribution of constitutional authority among the three branches of the national government. In *The Federalist,* No. 47, Madison wrote, "No political truth is certainly of greater intrinsic value, or is stamped with the authority of more enlightened patrons of liberty, than that... the accumulation of all powers, legislative, executive, and judiciary, in the same hands... may justly be pronounced the very definition of tyranny."[25] Chief among the "enlightened patrons of liberty" to whose authority Madison was appealing were the eighteenth-century philosophers John Locke and Montesquieu, whose works most educated citizens knew well.

The intrinsic value of the dispersion of power, however, is not the only reason the framers included it in the Constitution. It had already been the general practice in the colonies for more than 100 years. Only during the Revolutionary period did some of the states concentrate authority in the hands of the legislature, and that unhappy experience as well as that under the Articles of Confederation confirmed the framers' belief in the merits of the separation of powers. Many attributed the evils of state government and the lack of energy in the central government under the Articles of Confederation to the lack of a strong executive to check legislative abuses and to give energy and direction to administration.

Still, separating power by itself was not enough. It might not prevent the branches of the government and officials from pooling their authority and acting together, or from responding alike to the same pressures—from the demand of a majority to restrict handgun ownership, for example, or to impose confiscatory taxes on the rich. If separating power was not enough, what else could be done?

Checks and Balances: Ambition to Counteract Ambition

The framers' answer was a system of **checks and balances** (see Table 1–4). "The great security against a gradual concentration of the several powers in the same department," wrote Madison in *The Federalist,* No. 51, "consists in giving to those who administer each department the necessary constitutional means and personal motives to resist encroachments of the others.... Ambition must be made to counteract ambition."[26] Each branch therefore has a role in the actions of the others (see Figure 1–1).

Congress enacts legislation, which the president must sign into law or veto. The Supreme Court can declare laws passed by Congress and signed by the president unconstitutional, but the president appoints the justices and all the other federal judges, with the Senate's approval. The president administers the laws, but Congress provides the money to run the government. Moreover, the Senate and the House of Representatives have absolute veto power over each other because both houses must approve bills before they can become law.

Not only does each branch have some authority over the others, but also each is politically independent of the others. Voters in each local district choose members of the House; voters in each state choose senators; the president is elected by the voters in all

separation of powers
Constitutional division of powers among the legislative, executive, and judicial branches, with the legislative branch making law, the executive applying and enforcing the law, and the judiciary interpreting the law.

checks and balances
A constitutional grant of powers that enables each of the three branches of government to check some acts of the others and therefore ensures that no branch can dominate.

TABLE

1–4 The Exercise of Checks and Balances, 1789–2010

Vetoes Presidents have vetoed more than 2,500 acts of Congress. Congress has overridden presidential vetoes more than 100 times.

Judicial Review The Supreme Court has ruled more than 175 congressional acts or parts thereof unconstitutional.

Impeachment The House of Representatives has impeached two presidents, one senator, one secretary of war, and 15 federal judges; the Senate has convicted seven of the judges but neither president.

Confirmation The Senate has refused to confirm nine cabinet nominations. Many other cabinet and subcabinet appointments were withdrawn because the Senate seemed likely to reject them.

SOURCE: The American Presidency Project, University of California, Santa Barbara, http://www.presidency.ucsb.edu/data/vetoes.php.
For additional resources on the Constitution, go to www.archives.gov/exhibits/charters/constitution.html.

■ *Does the relative infrequency of veto overrides surprise you? Why or why not? Are there other checks Congress can use against the president?*

the states through the electoral college. With the consent of the Senate, the president appoints federal judges, who remain in office until they retire or are impeached.

The framers also ensured that a majority of the voters could win control over only part of the government at one time. In an off-year (nonpresidential) election where a new majority might take control of the House of Representatives, the president still has at least two more years, and senators hold office for six years. Finally, there are independent federal courts, which exercise their own powerful checks.

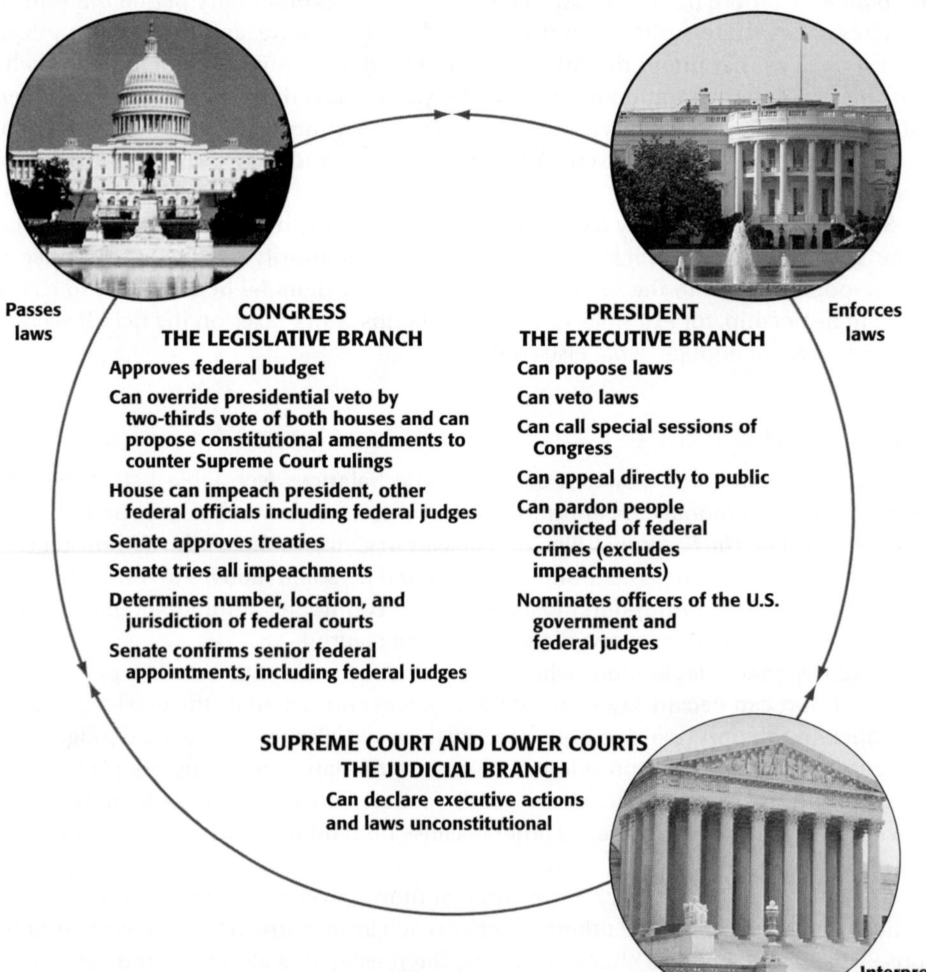

FIGURE 1–1 **The Separation of Powers and Checks and Balances.**
■ *Does the fact that the judiciary has the fewest number of checks make it the least powerful?*

Distrustful of both the elites and the masses, the framers deliberately built into our political system mechanisms to make changing the system difficult. They designed the decision-making process so that the national government can act decisively only when there is a consensus among most groups and after all sides have had their say. "The doctrine of the separation of powers was adopted by the convention of 1787," in the words of Justice Louis D. Brandeis, "not to promote efficiency but to preclude the exercise of arbitrary power. The purpose was not to avoid friction, but, by means of the inevitable friction incident to the distribution of the governmental powers among three departments, to save the people from **autocracy**"[27]—a system in which one person has control over the populace. Still, even though the fragmentation of political power written into the Constitution remains, constitutional silences, or topics the Constitution does not address, and subsequent developments have modified the way the system of checks and balances works.

autocracy
A type of government in which one person with unlimited power rules.

judicial review
The power of a court to refuse to enforce a law or a government regulation that in the opinion of the judges conflicts with the U.S. Constitution or, in a state court, the state constitution.

Judicial Review and the "Guardians of the Constitution"

LEARNING **OBJECTIVE**

1.7 Show how the use of judicial review strengthens the courts in a separation of powers system.

The judiciary has become so important in our system of checks and balances that it deserves special attention. Judges did not claim the power of **judicial review**—the power to strike down a law or a government regulation that judges believe conflicts with the Constitution—until some years after the Constitution had been adopted. From the beginning, however, judges were expected to check the legislature. "The independence of judges," wrote Alexander Hamilton in *The Federalist,* No. 78 (which appears in the Appendix), "may be an essential safeguard against the effects of occasional ill humors in the society."[28]

Judicial review is a major contribution of the United States to the art of government, one that many other nations have adopted. In Canada, Germany, France, Italy, and Spain, constitutional courts review laws referred to them to ensure that the laws comply with their constitutions, including with the charter of rights that is now part of those constitutions.[29]

Origins of Judicial Review

The Constitution says nothing about who should have the final word in disputes that may arise over its meaning. Scholars have long debated whether the delegates to the Constitutional Convention of 1787 intended to give the courts the power of judicial review. The framers clearly intended that the Supreme Court have the power to declare state legislation unconstitutional, but whether they meant to give it the same power over *congressional* legislation and the president is not clear. Why didn't the framers specifically provide for judicial review? Probably because they believed justices could infer they had the power, from certain general provisions and the necessity of interpreting and applying a written constitution.

The Federalists—who urged ratification of the Constitution and controlled the national government until 1801—generally supported a strong role for federal courts and thus favored judicial review. Their opponents, the Jeffersonian Republicans (called *Democrats* after 1832), were less enthusiastic. In the Kentucky and Virginia Resolutions of 1798 and 1799, respectively, Jefferson and Madison (who by this time had left the Federalist camp) came close to arguing that state legislatures—and not the Supreme Court—had the ultimate power to interpret the Constitution. These resolutions seemed to question whether the Supreme Court even had final authority to review *state* legislation, a point about which there had been little doubt.

When the Jeffersonians defeated the Federalists in the election of 1800, the question of whether the Supreme Court would actually exercise the power of judicial review was still undecided. Then in 1803 came *Marbury* v. *Madison,* the most path-breaking Supreme Court decision of all time.[30]

Chief Justice John Marshall (1755–1835) is our most influential Supreme Court justice. Appointed in 1801, Marshall served until 1835. Earlier he had been a staunch defender of the U.S. Constitution at the Virginia ratifying convention, a member of Congress, and a secretary of state. He was one of those rare people who served in all three branches of government. ■ *What might the federal courts look like today if the Marshall Court did not reach the outcome it did in Marbury* v. *Madison?*

Marbury v. *Madison*

President John Adams and fellow Federalists did not take their 1800 defeat by Thomas Jefferson easily. Not only did they lose control of the executive office, they also lost both houses of Congress. That left the judiciary as the last remaining Federalist stronghold.

To further shore up the federal judiciary, the outgoing Federalist Congress created dozens of new judgeships. By March 3, 1801, the day before Jefferson was due to become president, Adams had appointed, and the Senate had confirmed, loyal Federalists to all of these new positions. Although the commissions were signed and sealed, a few, for the newly appointed justices of the peace for the District of Columbia, were not delivered. John Marshall, the outgoing secretary of state and newly confirmed chief justice of the Supreme Court, left the delivery of these commissions for his successor as secretary of state, James Madison.

This "packing" of the judiciary angered Jefferson, now inaugurated as president. When he discovered that some of the commissions were still lying on a table in the Department of State, he instructed a clerk not to deliver them. Jefferson could see no reason why the District needed so many justices of the peace, especially Federalist justices.[31]

William Marbury never received his commission and decided to seek action from the courts. Section 13 of the Judiciary Act of 1789 authorized the Supreme Court "to issue **writs of mandamus,**" orders directing an official, such as the secretary of state, to perform a duty, such as delivering a commission. Marbury went directly to the Supreme Court and, citing Section 13, made his request.

Marbury's request presented Chief Justice John Marshall and the Supreme Court with a difficult dilemma. On the one hand, if the Court issued the writ, Jefferson and Madison would probably ignore it. The Court would be powerless, and its prestige, already low, might suffer a fatal blow. On the other hand, by refusing to issue the writ, the judges would appear to support the Jeffersonian Republicans' claim that the Court had no authority to interfere with the executive. Would Marshall issue the writ? Most people thought he would; angry Republicans even threatened impeachment if he did so.

On February 24, 1803, the Supreme Court delivered what is still considered a brilliantly written and politically savvy decision. First, Marshall, writing for a unanimous Court, took Jefferson and Madison to task. Marbury was entitled to his commission, and Madison should have delivered it to him. Moreover, the proper court could issue a writ of mandamus, even against so high an officer as the secretary of state.

However, Marshall concluded that Section 13 of the Judiciary Act, giving the Supreme Court original jurisdiction to issue writs of mandamus, was in error. It impermissibly expanded the Court's original jurisdiction, which is detailed in Article III of the Constitution. Marshall concluded that the grant of original jurisdiction in Article III was meant to be limited to those cases explicitly mentioned: when an ambassador, foreign minister, or a state is a party. Because none of these was at issue in Marbury's request for the writ of mandamus, the Court deemed Section 13 of the Judiciary Act contrary to the Constitution. Given that Article VI provided that the Constitution is the "supreme Law of the Land," and judges took an oath to uphold the Constitution, any law in conflict with it could not withstand the Court's review.

Although the Federalists suffered a political loss in not seating all their "midnight judges" on the bench, Marshall and the Court gained a much more important power to declare laws passed by Congress unconstitutional. Subsequent generations might have interpreted *Marbury* v. *Madison* in a limited way, such as that the Supreme Court had the right to determine the scope of its own powers under Article III, but Congress and the president had the authority to interpret their powers under Articles I and II. But throughout the decades, building on Marshall's precedent, the Court has taken the commanding position as the authoritative interpreter of the Constitution.

Once we accept Marshall's argument that judges are the official interpreters of the Constitution, several important consequences follow. The most important is that people can challenge laws enacted by Congress and approved by the president. Simply by bringing a lawsuit, those who lack the clout to get a bill through Congress can often secure a judicial hearing. And organized interest groups often find they can achieve

writ of mandamus
A court order directing an official to perform an official duty.

For the People
GOVERNMENT'S GREATEST ENDEAVORS

Increasing Access to Higher Education

The framers believed an educated public was essential to a strong government. As Thomas Jefferson wrote late in his life, "I know no safe depository of the ultimate powers of the society but the people themselves; and if we think them not enlightened enough to exercise their control with a wholesome discretion, the remedy is not to take it from them, but to inform their discretion by education. This is the true corrective of abuses of constitutional power."*

For most of American history, however, the federal government left college education to individuals and the states, and did not become involved in providing access to college until World War II. With more than 15 million soldiers about to return home in search of jobs and opportunity, Congress passed the Servicemen's Readjustment Act of 1944, popularly known as the GI Bill. It provided grants for college and other benefits to war veterans.

It was not until the late 1950s, though, that the federal government developed programs to help students from low-income families attend college. In 1958, Congress passed the National Defense Education Act in an effort to educate new scientists and engineers to fight the cold war with the Soviet Union. It provided money to fund students pursuing degrees in technical fields or modern languages, each considered essential for building weapons and collecting intelligence.

More recently, Congress has passed the Post 9/11 GI Bill to provide benefits to veterans who have been on active duty in the military for 90 or more days since September 10, 2001. As such, members of the National Guard and Reserve will qualify for benefits along with active duty service members. Through the new provisions, veterans can get up to 100 percent tuition reimbursement as well as funds for books and housing. Under this program and others, millions of college students have been able to finance their college education.

CRITICAL THINKING QUESTIONS

1. Why do you think it took so long for the federal government to become involved in education?
2. Are there public benefits to having federal tax dollars go toward such programs? Are there disadvantages?

* Thomas Jefferson, Letter to William Charles Jarvis, September 28, 1820.

goals through litigation that they could not attain through legislation. Litigation thus supplements, and at times even takes precedence over, legislation as a way to make public policy.[32]

Constitutional Change

LEARNING **OBJECTIVE**

1.8 Outline how the Constitution is changed through informal and formal methods.

As careful as the Constitution's framers were to limit the powers they gave the national government, the main reason they assembled in Philadelphia was to create a stronger national government. Having learned that a weak central government was a danger to liberty, they wished to establish a national government within the framework of a federal system with enough authority to meet the needs of all time. They made general grants of power, leaving it to succeeding generations to fill in the details and organize the structure of government in accordance with experience.

Informal Change

Our formal, written Constitution is only the skeleton of our system. It is filled out in numerous ways that we must consider part of our constitutional system in a larger sense. In fact, our system is kept up to date primarily through changes in the informal, unwritten Constitution. These changes exist in certain basic statutes and historical practices of Congress, presidential actions, and court decisions.

Congressional Elaboration Because the framers gave Congress authority to provide for the structural details of the national government, it is not necessary to amend the Constitution every time a change is needed. Rather, Congress can create legislation to meet the need, with what we refer to as **congressional elaboration.** The Judiciary Act of 1789, for example, laid the foundation for our national judicial system, just as other laws established the organization and functions of all federal executive officials subordinate to the president and enacted the rules of procedure, internal organization, and practices of Congress.

congressional elaboration
Congressional legislation that gives further meaning to the Constitution based on sometimes vague constitutional authority, such as the necessary and proper clause.

Another example of this congressional elaboration of our constitutional system is the use of the impeachment and removal power. An **impeachment** is a formal accusation against a public official and the first step in removing him or her from office. Constitutional language defining the grounds for impeachment is sparse. Look at the Constitution and note that Article II, the Executive Article, calls for removal of the president, vice president, and all civil officers of the United States on impeachment for, and conviction of, "Treason, Bribery, or other High Crimes and Misdemeanors." But, what does that mean? The question is not an easy one as there is a general lack of consensus on its meaning. In fact, the last time the House of Representatives formally accused a president of an impeachable offense, President Bill Clinton in 1998, House members had nearly 20 scholars testify before them as to the clause's meaning, and they still did not find consensus on it. Although the Constitution provides for the basic procedural structure of impeachments, it leaves up to Congress determining when a president's actions amount to an impeachable offense.

Presidential Practices Although the formal constitutional powers of the president have not changed, the office is dramatically more important and more central today than it was in 1789. Vigorous presidents—George Washington, Thomas Jefferson, Andrew Jackson, Abraham Lincoln, Theodore Roosevelt, Woodrow Wilson, Franklin Roosevelt, Harry Truman, Lyndon Johnson, Bill Clinton, and George W. Bush—have boldly exercised their political and constitutional powers, especially during times of national crisis such as the current war against international terrorism and the 2008 economic crisis. Their presidential practices have established important precedents, building the power and influence of the office.

impeachment
A formal accusation by the lower house of a legislature against a public official; the first step in removal from office.

executive order
A directive issued by a president or governor that has the force of law.

executive privilege
The power to keep executive communications confidential, especially if they relate to national security.

impoundment
Presidential refusal to allow an agency to spend funds that Congress authorized and appropriated.

A major practice is the use of **executive orders,** which carry the full force of law but do not require congressional approval. Executive orders direct the executive branch to take some action, such as President Franklin Roosevelt's 1942 order to intern Japanese-Americans during World War II or President Truman's order to integrate the armed forces in 1948. Presidents have long used these orders to achieve goals that may lack congressional support. Other practices include **executive privilege,** the right to confidentiality of executive communications, especially those that relate to national security; **impoundment** by a president of funds previously appropriated by Congress; the power to send armed forces into hostilities; and the authority to propose legislation and work actively to secure its passage by Congress.

Foreign and economic crises as well as nuclear-age realities and the war against international terrorism have expanded the president's role: "When it comes to action risking nuclear war, technology has modified the Constitution: the President, perforce, becomes the only such man in the system capable of exercising judgment under the extraordinary limits now imposed by secrecy, complexity, and time."[33] The presidency has also become the pivotal office for regulating the economy and promoting the general welfare through an expanded federal bureaucracy (as we discuss in Chapter 9). In addition, the president has become a leader in sponsoring legislation as well as the nation's chief executive.

President Bill Clinton was impeached by the House of Representatives in December 1998 for perjury and obstructing justice, but he was acquitted by the Senate. ■ *What kind of official wrongdoing should amount to an impeachable offense, and who should be responsible for determining this?*

Judicial Interpretation In its decision in *Marbury* v. *Madison* (1803),[34] the Supreme Court established that it was the judiciary's responsibility to interpret the Constitution. Through this practice, the courts have made far-reaching decisions that have settled, at least for a time, what some of the vague clauses of the document mean. For example, the Supreme Court ruled that segregation by race, even when equal facilities were provided, violated the requirements of the equal protection clause (*Brown* v. *Board of Education* [1954]),[35] and that Americans have a constitutionally protected right to privacy, even though the word "privacy" appears nowhere in the Constitution (*Griswold* v. *Connecticut* [1965]).[36] In both of

YOU WILL DECIDE Should We Interpret the Constitution According to Original Intent or Today's Needs?

Debate about how to interpret the Constitution began almost immediately, and, as we have seen, it continues to this day, with very important practical implications for citizens.

One kind of constitutional interpretation is the **originalist approach.** Originalists believe that the Constitution should be understood according to the framers' intent. If the exact wording of the document does not provide a conclusive answer, most originalists consider the context of the times in which it was written and interpret it in light of that history. Especially important are writings or speeches by the founders themselves or by proponents of subsequent amendments.

A second approach to interpreting the Constitution sees it as a changing and evolving document that provides a basic framework for government but that allows, and even encourages, new generations to interpret ideas such as "equal justice" and "due process" in light of the needs of their time. This **adaptive approach** may mean that subsequent generations will interpret the same document differently from prior generations.

The adaptive approach makes the court a more powerful institution in U.S. government. The originalist approach forces people and institutions to adopt amendments if they want constitutional change.

What do you think? Should we interpret the Constitution according to the framers' original intent, or should it be considered in light of the needs of today's society? What are some of the arguments for or against each approach?

THINKING IT THROUGH

Differences between the adaptive and the originalist views do not necessarily align with political labels such as *conservative* or *liberal*, although they may in particular cases. For example, Justice Antonin Scalia, who tends to be originalist in his approach, voted in *District of Columbia* v. *Heller* to strike down the District's prohibition on registering handguns through a close reading of the original, literal meaning of the Second Amendment. Because the Amendment indicates that "the right of the people to keep and bear Arms, shall not be infringed," Justice Scalia, writing for the majority of the Court, determined that individual citizens had a constitutionally protected right to own handguns.

Justice Stephen Breyer typically favors a more adaptive approach. In his dissent to the Court's majority opinion, Justice Breyer argues that the Court must consider the District of Columbia's restriction on handguns in light of present day conditions, such as the public safety concerns raised by gun violence. Justice Breyer weighs an individual's right to own a handgun and the District's responsibility to protect its citizenry, and sided with the District of Columbia.

If the Constitution is indeed open to changing interpretations, are any constitutional principles absolute and *not* open to new interpretation? This danger in the adaptive approach worries some because the selection of judges is only indirectly democratic, and, with lifetime appointments, judges could lose the people's confidence yet retain their power. There are problems with the originalist approach as well. A global economy, electronic and mass media, and the need to respond immediately to national security threats are only some examples of circumstances the founders could not consider or address in the Constitution. In other instances, such as with privacy, for example, the original wording of the Constitution implies an interpretation but does not explicitly say it.

Critical Thinking Questions

1. How do you think we should interpret the Constitution? What are the best arguments of both sides of this question?
2. Why does it matter whether we take an originalist or an adaptive approach to interpreting the Constitution?

these cases and a myriad of others, the Court's definition of what the Constitution meant led to changes in our political system without any amendment to the document itself. Although there is relatively little current debate over the judiciary's authority to interpret the Constitution, there is substantial disagreement over *how* it should be read. (See the You Will Decide box.)

originalist approach
An approach to constitutional interpretation that envisions the document as having a fixed meaning that might be determined by a strict reading of the text or the framers' intent.

adaptive approach
A method used to interpret the Constitution that understands the document to be flexible and responsive to the changing needs of the times.

Formal Change

The idea of a constantly changing system disturbs many people. How, they contend, can you have a constitutional government when the Constitution is constantly being twisted by interpretation and changed by informal methods? This view fails to distinguish between two aspects of the Constitution. As an expression of *basic and timeless personal liberties,* the Constitution does not, and should not, change. For example, a government cannot destroy free speech and still remain a constitutional government. In this sense, the Constitution is unchanging. But when we consider

Outside the 1984 Republican National Convention, Gregory Johnson burned an American flag to protest the Reagan administration's policies. The U.S. Supreme Court upheld his right to do so as a protected form of expression under the First Amendment. ■ *Why do you think that legislators have been so persistent in proposing amendments to bar flag burning?*

the Constitution as an *instrument of government* and a positive grant of power, we realize that if it did not grow with the nation it serves, it would soon be irrelevant and ignored.

The framers could never have conceived of the problems facing the government of a large, powerful, and wealthy nation of approximately 300 million people at the beginning of the twenty-first century. Although the general purposes of government remain the same—to establish liberty, promote justice, ensure domestic tranquility, and provide for the common defense—the powers of government that were adequate to accomplish these purposes in 1787 are simply insufficient more than 220 years later. The framers knew that future experiences would call for changes in the text of the Constitution and that it would need to be formally amended. In Article V, they gave responsibility for amending the Constitution to Congress and to the states. The president has no formal authority over constitutional amendments; presidential veto power does not extend to them, although presidential influence is often crucial in getting amendments proposed and ratified.

Proposing Amendments The first method for proposing amendments—and the only one used so far—is by *a two-thirds vote of both houses of Congress.* Dozens of resolutions proposing amendments are introduced in every session, but Congress has proposed only 31 amendments, of which 27 have been ratified (see Figure 1–2).

Why is introducing amendments to the Constitution so popular? In part because groups frustrated by their inability to get things done in Congress hope to bypass it. In part because Congress, the president, interest groups, or the public may want to overturn unpopular Supreme Court decisions. In part because the nation needs to make government more responsive to changing times. Although amendments are debated rather frequently, very few have made it through Congress to begin the ratification process.

Congress, the president, interest groups, and the public were all involved in an effort to overturn the Supreme Court's decision to strike down a Texas law barring flag burning (*Texas* v. *Johnson* [1989]).[37] Though Congress attempted to bypass the decision with the Federal Flag Protection Act of 1989, which prohibited intentionally burning or defiling the flag, the Court struck down that law as well (*United States* v. *Eichman* [1990]).[38] In doing so, the Court ruled that the First Amendment protects burning the flag as a form of political speech.

Following its failure to overturn the decision through new laws, Congress has made repeated efforts to send a constitutional amendment banning flag burning to the states.[39] The House of Representatives has voted seven times since the early 1990s on an amendment

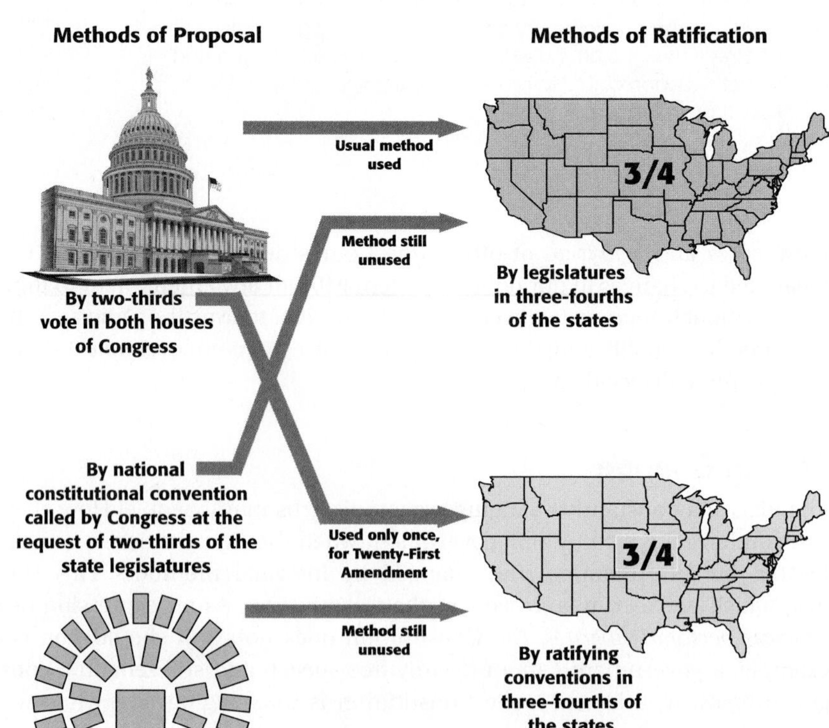

FIGURE 1–2 **Four Methods of Amending the Constitution.**
■ *Why do you think Congress has been reluctant to call for a national constitutional convention?*

prohibiting the "physical desecration of the flag of the United States," but the Senate has been unable to garner the necessary two-thirds vote. It came close to succeeding in June 2006, but the vote fell one short of the number required to send the amendment to the states for ratification.[40]

The second method for proposing amendments—*a convention called by Congress* at the request of the legislatures in two-thirds of the states—has never been used. Under Article V of the Constitution, Congress could call for such a convention without the concurrence of the president. This method presents difficult questions.[41] First, can state legislatures apply for a convention to propose specific amendments on one topic, or must they request a convention with full powers to revise the entire Constitution? How long do state petitions remain alive? How should delegates to a convention be chosen? How should such a convention be run? Congress has considered bills to answer some of these questions but has not passed any, in part because most members do not wish to encourage a constitutional convention for fear that once in session it might propose amendments on any and all topics.

Under most proposals, each state would have as many delegates to the convention as it has representatives and senators in Congress. Finally, and crucially, a constitutional convention would be limited to considering only the subject specified in the state legislative petitions and described in the congressional call for the convention. Scholars are divided, however, on whether Congress has the authority to limit what a constitutional convention might propose.[42]

Ratifying Amendments After Congress has proposed an amendment, the states must ratify it before it takes effect. Again, the Constitution provides two methods, and Congress may choose: approval by the legislatures in three-fourths of the states or approval by special ratifying conventions in three-fourths of the states. Congress has submitted all amendments except one—the Twenty-First (to repeal the Eighteenth, the Prohibition Amendment)—to the state legislatures for ratification.

Seven state constitutions specify that their state legislatures must ratify a proposed amendment to the U.S. Constitution by majorities of three-fifths or two-thirds of each chamber. Although a state legislature may change its mind and ratify an amendment after it has voted against ratification, the weight of opinion is that once a state has ratified an amendment, it cannot "unratify" it.[43]

The Supreme Court has said that ratification must take place within a "reasonable time" so that it is "sufficiently contemporaneous to reflect the will of the people."[44] However, when Congress approved ratification of the Twenty-Seventh Amendment, it had been before the nation for nearly 203 years, so there seems to be no limit on what it considers a "reasonable time." In fact, ratification ordinarily takes place rather quickly—one-third of all amendments were ratified within about one year, and 80 percent were ratified within about two years. Congress will probably continue to stipulate that ratification must occur within seven years of the date it submits an amendment to the states.

CHAPTER **SUMMARY**

1.1 Use the concept of constitutional democracy to explain U.S. government and politics.

The United States operates under a constitutional democracy. In our system, the Constitution lays out the basic rules of the game under which politicians act to accomplish their different agendas. "Politics" is a broad term that can be used to describe what happens between these politicians in pursuit of their goals. "Government" is another broad term that encompasses the many different institutions enumerated by the Constitution in which the politicians function. Political science studies the interaction among politics, politicians, the government, and, within the American context, our constitutional democracy.

1.2 Differentiate democracy from other forms of government, and identify conditions, values, political processes, and political structures conducive to a successful democracy.

The United States government is a representative democracy. The politicians in our system are elected representatives meant to stand up for the interests of their constituents. Representative democracy differs from direct democracy in the level of citizen participation.

Scholars have identified several conditions that may help democratic governments form and consolidate. Among these, educational, economic, social, and ideological conditions are the most important. These conditions further democratic values such as a belief in personal liberty, equality of opportunity, and popular consent. Our representative democracy functions through political structures including courts, legislatures, and the executive.

1.3 Assess the important compromises reached by the delegates to the Constitutional Convention of 1787.

The framers came up with some brilliant compromises to address these issues, such as the Connecticut Compromise that led to our current bicameral legislative branch. Other issues were put on hold. For example, the framers postponed dealing with slavery and compromised on counting slaves as three-fifths of a person for purposes of apportionment.

1.4 Evaluate the arguments for and against the ratification of the Constitution.

Some of the same themes that dominated the debate over ratification can still be heard today. Federalists argued for a central government that would be strong enough to make the newly united states capable of standing up to the great powers of the time. Antifederalists worried about what might come of a strong central government and were particularly concerned about the lack of any bill of rights in the document.

1.5 Describe the basic structure of the Constitution and its Bill of Rights.

The U.S. Constitution's first three articles establish the legislature, the executive, and the judiciary. The Bill of Rights, the first ten amendments to the Constitution, was added in 1791 and provides protections from federal government infringement on individual liberties.

1.6 Analyze how the Constitution grants, limits, separates, and balances governmental power.

The U.S. Constitution separates power vested in the legislature, which has the power to create law; the executive, with the power to enforce the law; and the judiciary, which interprets the law. None of the branches depends on the others for its authority, and each branch has the power to limit the others through the system of checks and balances. Competing interests within this structure check and balance one another.

1.7 Show how the use of judicial review strengthens the courts in a separation of powers system.

Judicial review is the power of the courts to strike down acts of Congress, the executive branch, and the states as unconstitutional. This authority provides the judiciary a powerful check on the other branches of government. The Supreme Court established its authority to rule an act of the federal legislature unconstitutional *in Marbury* v. *Madison*.

1.8 Outline how the Constitution is changed through informal and formal methods.

The constitutional system has been modified over time, adapting to new conditions through congressional elaboration, presidential practices, and judicial interpretation. Some jurists believe the Constitution is a static document with a set meaning, and they tend to interpret the Constitution according to a close reading of the text or according to what they think the framers' intended. Others consider the document's meaning to evolve with time and changing circumstances.

The framers also provided a formal procedure for amendment of the Constitution. An amendment must be both proposed and ratified: proposed by either a two-thirds vote in each chamber of Congress or by a national convention called by Congress on petition of the legislatures in two-thirds of the states; ratified either by the legislatures in three-fourths of the states or by special ratifying conventions in three-fourths of the states.

CHAPTER **SELF-TEST**

1.1 Use the concept of constitutional democracy to explain U.S. government and politics.

1. Write a short essay discussing the intersection between government and politics. In what ways are they similar? How are they different?
2. How would U.S. government be different if the Antifederalists had not been successful in pressing for a bill of rights?

1.2 Differentiate democracy from other forms of government, and identify conditions, values, political processes, and political structures conducive to a successful democracy.

3. Explain the differences between direct democracy and representative democracy. What concerns did the framers of the Constitution have about unlimited direct democracy?
4. Write a short essay explaining how specific values have contributed to the relative longevity of democracy in the United States. Which values seem most important to U.S. citizens?

1.3 Assess the important compromises reached by the delegates to the Constitutional Convention of 1787.

5. Which state was the compromise that led to a bicameral legislature named after?
   a. Rhode Island
   b. Connecticut
   c. New Hampshire
   d. Maine

6. Match the following articles with their appropriate subject (see the Appendix):

a. Art. I	i. Interstate Relations
b. Art. II	ii. Ratification
c. Art. III	iii. Congressional
d. Art. IV	iv. Amending Power
e. Art. V	v. Executive
f. Art. VI	vi. Supremacy Act
g. Art. VII	vii. Judiciary

1.4 Evaluate the arguments for and against the ratification of the Constitution.

7. Identify three or four historical tensions that impeded ratification of the Constitution and that have persisted into present-day politics.
8. Write a brief persuasive essay adopting the Antifederalist position against ratification of the Constitution. In your essay, list two or three arguments that you feel Federalists would put forward and then counter those with your persuasive arguments.

1.5 Describe the basic structure of the Constitution and its Bill of Rights.

9. The Constitution reflects the founders' respect for _______ law, which implies a universal sense of right and wrong.
   a. natural
   b. formal
   c. federal
   d. corporal

10. How does the U.S. Constitution compare to other constitutions around the world?

1.6 Analyze how the Constitution grants, limits, separates, and balances governmental power.

11. Write two or three paragraphs to explain the ways the writers of the constitution attempted to limit the power of the branches in the federal government.
12. Draw a diagram that shows how the different branches of government check one another. (Table 1–4 can provide useful examples.)

1.7 Show how the use of judicial review strengthens the courts in a separation of powers system.

13. Describe the details of *Marbury* v. *Madison* and who the major actors were. Explain why the case was heard in the first place. Describe the impact of the decision.
14. Many people are uncomfortable with what they term "activist judges." Explain the constitutional grounds for and against judicial activism in four sentences or less.

1.8 Outline how the Constitution is changed through informal and formal methods.

15. Write a two-paragraph essay in which you evaluate the arguments for a static or evolving interpretation of the Constitution.
16. The chapter lists two ways to propose amendments. Name these two ways, and describe how they are different. How is an amendment ratified?

mypoliscilab™ EXERCISES

Where participation leads to action!

Apply what you learned in this chapter on MyPoliSciLab.

Read on **mypoliscilab.com**

eText: Chapter 1

Study and **Review** on **mypoliscilab.com**

Practice Tests
Flashcards

Watch on **mypoliscilab.com**

Video: Mexico Border Security
Video: The Bailout Hearings
Video: Vaccines: Mandatory Protection

Explore on **mypoliscilab.com**

Simulation: You Are James Madison
Simulation: You Are Proposing a Constitutional Amendment
Comparative: Comparing Constitutions
Timeline: The History of Constitutional Amendments
Visual Literacy: The American System of Checks and Balances

Answers to selected questions: 5. b; 6. a. iii, b. v, c. vii, d. i, e. iv, f. vi, g. ii; 9. a

KEY TERMS

democracy, p. 19
direct democracy, p. 19
direct primary, p. 19
initiative, p. 19
referendum, p. 19
recall, p. 19
representative democracy, p. 19
constitutional democracy, p. 20
constitutionalism, p. 20
statism, p. 21
popular consent, p. 21
majority rule, p. 22
majority, p. 22
plurality, p. 22
Constitutional Convention, p. 25
Shays' Rebellion, p. 26
bicameralism, p. 28
Virginia Plan, p. 28
New Jersey Plan, p. 28
Connecticut Compromise, p. 28
three-fifths compromise, p. 29
electoral college, p. 30
Federalists, p. 30
Antifederalists, p. 30
The Federalist, p. 31
natural law, p. 34
federalism, p. 34
separation of powers, p. 35
checks and balances, p. 35
autocracy, p. 37
judicial review, p. 37
writ of mandamus, p. 38
congressional elaboration, p. 39
impeachment, p. 40
executive order, p. 40
executive privilege, p. 40
impoundment, p. 40
originalist approach, p. 41
adaptive approach, p. 41

ADDITIONAL RESOURCES

FURTHER READING

BERNARD BAILYN, ED., *The Debate on the Constitution: Federalist and Antifederalist Speeches, Articles, and Letters During the Struggle over Ratification,* 2 vols. (Library of America, 1993).

LANCE BANNING, *The Sacred Fire of Liberty: James Madison and the Founding of the Federal Republic* (Cornell University Press, 1995).

ROBERT A. DAHL, *How Democratic Is the American Constitution,* 2d ed. (Yale University Press, 2003).

ALAN GIBSON, *Understanding the Founding: Crucial Questions* (University Press of Kansas, 2007).

ALEXANDER HAMILTON, JAMES MADISON, AND **JOHN JAY,** *The Federalist Papers,* ed. Clinton Rossiter (New American Library, 1961). Also in several other editions.

PHILIP B. KURLAND AND **RALPH LERNER,** *The Founders' Constitution,* 5 vols. (University of Chicago Press, 1987).

SANFORD LEVINSON, *Our Undemocratic Constitution* (Oxford University Press, 2006).

JACK N. RAKOVE, *Original Meanings: Politics and Ideas in the Making of the Constitution* (Vintage Books, 1997).

MICHAEL SCHUDSON, *The Good Citizen: A History of American Civic Life* (Harvard University Press, 1998).

AKHIL REED AMAR, *America's Constitution: A Biography* (Random House, 2005).

CAROL BERKIN, *A Brilliant Solution: Inventing the American Constitution* (Harcourt, 2002).

STEPHEN BREYER, *Active Liberty: Interpreting Our Democratic Constitution* (Knopf, 2005).

MICHAEL KAMMEN, *A Machine That Would Go of Itself: The Constitution in American Culture* (Knopf, 1986).

LIBRARY OF CONGRESS, CONGRESSIONAL RESEARCH SERVICE, JONNY KILLIAN, ED., *The Constitution of the United States of America: Analysis and Interpretation* (U.S. Government Printing Office, 2006).

ANTONIN SCALIA, *A Matter of Interpretation: Federal Courts and the Law* (Princeton University Press, 1997).

CASS SUNSTEIN, *Designing Democracy: What Constitutions Do* (Oxford University Press, 2001).

JOHN R. VILE, ED., *Encyclopedia of Constitutional Amendments, Proposed Amendments, and Amending Issues, 1789–2002* (ABC-Clio, 2003).

WEB SITES

www.constitutionfacts.com/ This site provides quotes, facts, and quizzes about the Constitution.

www.people.brandeis.edu/~teuber/polphil.html This site provides resources for exploring the political philosophies important to the founders.

www.constitutioncenter.org/ The National Constitution Center's Web site includes information on the Constitution and its framers as well as an interactive constitution, online exhibits, and news updates.

www.memory.loc.gov/ammem/amlaw/lawhome.html This Library of Congress Web site is devoted to the Continental Congress and the Constitutional Convention. There are links to online documents contained in the Library's collection.

www.archives.gov/ The National Archives' Web site includes links to many online collections and historical documents.

On Reading the Constitution

More than 218 years after its ratification, our Constitution remains the operating charter of our republic. It is neither self-explanatory nor a comprehensive description of our constitiutional rules. Still, it remains the starting point. Many Americans who swear by the Constitution have never read it seriously, although copies can be found in most American government and American history textbooks.

Justice Hugo Black, who served on the Supreme Court for 34 years, kept a copy of the Constitution with him at all times. He read it often. Reading the Constitution would be a good way for you to begin (and then reread again to end) your study of the government of the United States. We have therefore included a copy of it at this point in the book. Please read it carefully.

The Constitution of the United States

The Preamble

We the People of the United States, in Order to form a more perfect Union, establish Justice, insure domestic Tranquility, provide for the common defence, promote the general Welfare, and secure the Blessings of Liberty to ourselves and our Posterity, do ordain and establish this Constitution for the United States of America.

Article I—The Legislative Article

Legislative Power

SECTION 1 All legislative Powers herein granted shall be vested in a Congress of the United States, which shall consist of a Senate and House of Representatives.

House of Representatives: Composition; Qualifications; Apportionment; Impeachment Power

SECTION 2

Clause 1 The House of Representatives shall be composed of Members chosen every second Year by the People of the several States, and the Electors in each State shall have the Qualifications requisite for Electors of the most numerous Branch of the State Legislature.

Clause 2 No Person shall be a Representative who shall not have attained to the Age of twenty five Years, and been seven Years a Citizen of the United States, and who shall not, when elected, be an inhabitant of that State in which he shall be chosen.

Clause 3 Representatives and direct Taxes[1] shall be apportioned among the several States which may be included within this Union, according to their respective Numbers, which shall be determined by adding to the whole Number of free Persons, including those bound to Service for a Term of Years, and excluding Indians not taxed, three fifths of all other Persons.[2] The actual Enumeration shall be made within three Years after the first Meeting of the Congress of the United States, and within every subsequent Term of ten Years, in such Manner as they shall by Law direct. The Number of Representatives shall not exceed one for every thirty Thousand, but each State shall have at Least one Representative; and until such enumeration shall be made, the State of New Hampshire shall be entitled to chuse three, Massachusetts eight, Rhode-Island and Providence Plantations one, Connecticut five, New-York six, New Jersey four, Pennsylvania eight, Delaware one, Maryland six, Virginia ten, North Carolina five, South Carolina five, and Georgia three.

Clause 4 When vacancies happen in the Representation from any State, the Executive Authority thereof shall issue Writs of Election to fill such Vacancies.

Clause 5 The House of Representatives shall chuse their Speaker and other Officers; and shall have the sole Power of Impeachment.

Senate Composition: Qualifications, Impeachment Trials

SECTION 3

Clause 1 The Senate of the United States shall be composed of two Senators from each State, chosen by the Legislature thereof,[3] for six Years; and each Senator shall have one Vote.

Clause 2 Immediately after they shall be assembled in Consequence of the first Election, they shall be divided as equally as may be into three Classes. The Seats of the Senators of the first Class shall be vacated at the Expiration of the second Year, of the second Class at the Expiration of the fourth Year, and of the third Class at the Expiration of the sixth Year, so that one third may be chosen every second Year; and if Vacancies happen by Resignation, or otherwise, during the Recess of the Legislature of any State, the Executive thereof may make temporary Appointments until the next Meeting of the Legislature, which shall then fill such Vacancies.[4]

Clause 3 No person shall be a Senator who shall not have attained to the Age of thirty Years, and been nine Years a Citizen of the United States, and who shall not, when elected, be an Inhabitant of that State for which he shall be chosen.

Clause 4 The Vice President of the United States shall be President of the Senate, but shall have no Vote, unless they be equally divided.

Clause 5 The Senate shall chuse their other Officers, and also a President pro tempore, in the Absence of the Vice President, or when he shall exercise the Office of President of the United States.

[1]Modified by the 16th Amendment
[2]Replaced by Section 2, 14th Amendment
[3]Repealed by the 17th Amendment
[4]Modified by the 17th Amendment

Clause 6 The Senate shall have the sole Power to try all Impeachments. When sitting for that Purpose, they shall be on Oath or Affirmation. When the President of the United States is tried, the Chief Justice shall preside: And no Person shall be convicted without the Concurrence of two thirds of the Members present.

Judgment in Cases of Impeachment shall not extend further than to removal from Office, and disqualification to hold and enjoy any Office of honor, Trust or Profit under the United States: but the Party convicted shall nevertheless be liable and subject to Indictment, Trial, Judgment and Punishment, according to Law.

Congressional Elections: Times, Places, Manner

SECTION 4 The Times, Places and Manner of holding Elections for Senators and Representatives, shall be prescribed in each State by the Legislature thereof; but the Congress may at any time by Law make or alter such Regulations, except as to the Places of chusing Senators.

The Congress shall assemble at least once in every Year, and such Meeting shall be on the first Monday in December, unless they shall by Law appoint a different Day.[5]

Powers and Duties of the Houses

SECTION 5

Clause 1 Each House shall be the Judge of the Elections, Returns and Qualifications of its own Members, and a Majority of each shall constitute a Quorum to do Business; but a smaller Number may adjourn from day to day, and may be authorized to compel the Attendance of absent Members, in such Manner, and under the Penalties as each House may provide.

Clause 2 Each House may determine the Rules of its Proceedings, punish its Members for disorderly Behaviour, and, with the Concurrence of two thirds, expel a Member.

Clause 3 Each House shall keep a Journal of its Proceedings, and from time to time publish the same, excepting such Parts as may in their Judgment require Secrecy; and the Yeas and Nays of the Members of either House on any question shall, at the Desire of one fifth of those Present, be entered on the Journal.

Clause 4 Neither House, during the Session of Congress, shall, without the Consent of the other, adjourn for more than three days, nor to any other place than that in which the two Houses shall be sitting.

Rights of Members

SECTION 6

Clause I The Senators and Representatives shall receive a Compensation for their Services, to be ascertained by Law, and paid out of the Treasury of the United States. They shall in all Cases, except Treason, Felony and Breach of the Peace, be privileged from Arrest during their Attendance at the Session of their respective Houses, and in going to and returning from the same; and for any Speech or Debate in either House, they shall not be questioned in any other Place.

Clause 2 No Senator or Representative, shall, during the Time for which he was elected, be appointed to any civil Office under the Authority of the United States, which shall have been created, or the Emoluments whereof shall have been encreased during such time; and no Person holding any Office under the United States, shall be a Member of either House during his Continuance in Office.

Legislative Powers: Bills and Resolutions

SECTION 7

Clause 1 All Bills for raising Revenue shall originate in the House of Representatives; but the Senate may propose or concur with Amendments as on other Bills.

Clause 2 Every Bill which shall have passed the House of Representatives and the Senate, shall, before it become a Law, be presented to the President of the United States; if he approve he shall sign it, but if not he shall return it, with his Objections to that House in which it shall have originated, who shall enter the Objections at large on their Journal, and proceed to reconsider it. If after such Reconsideration two thirds of that House shall agree to pass the Bill, it shall be sent, together with the Objections, to the other House, by which it shall likewise be reconsidered, and if approved by two thirds of that House, it shall become a Law. But in all such Cases the Votes of both Houses shall be determined by yeas and Nays, and the Names of the Persons voting for and against the Bill shall be entered on the Journal of each House respectively. If any Bill shall not be returned by the President within ten Days (Sundays excepted) after it shall have been presented to him, the Same shall be a Law, in like Manner as if he had signed it, unless the Congress by their Adjournment prevent its Return, in which Case it shall not be a Law.

Clause 3 Every Order, Resolution, or Vote to which the Concurrence of the Senate and House of Representatives may be necessary (except on a question of Adjournment) shall be presented to the President of the United States; and before the Same shall take Effect, shall be approved by him, or being disapproved by him, shall be repassed by two thirds of the Senate and House of Representatives, according to the Rules and Limitations prescribed in the Case of a Bill.

Powers of Congress

SECTION 8

Clause 1 The Congress shall have Power To lay and collect Taxes, Duties, Imposts and Excises, to pay the Debts and provide for the common Defence and general Welfare of the United

[5]Changed by the 20th Amendment

States; but all Duties, Imposts and Excises shall be uniform throughout the United States;

To borrow Money on the credit of the United States;

To regulate Commerce with foreign Nations, and among the several States, and with the Indian Tribes;

To establish an uniform Rule of Naturalization, and uniform Laws on the subject of Bankruptcies throughout the United States;

To coin Money, regulate the Value thereof, and of foreign Coin, and fix the Standard of Weights and Measures;

To provide for the Punishment of counterfeiting the Securities and current Coin of the United States;

To establish Post Offices and post Roads;

To promote the Progress of Science and useful Arts, by securing for limited Times to Authors and Inventors the exclusive Right to their respective Writings and Discoveries;

To constitute Tribunals inferior to the supreme Court;

To define and punish Piracies and Felonies committed on the high Seas, and Offences against the Law of Nations;

To declare War, grant Letters of Marque and Reprisal, and make Rules concerning Captures on Land and Water;

To raise and support Armies, but no Appropriation of Money to that Use shall be for a longer Term than two Years;

To provide and maintain a Navy;

To make Rules for the Government and Regulation of the land and naval Forces;

To provide for calling for the Militia to execute the Laws of the Union, suppress Insurrections and repel Invasions;

To provide for organizing, arming, and disciplining the Militia, and for governing such Part of them as may be employed in the Service of the United States, reserving to the States respectively, the Appointment of the Officers, and the Authority of training the Militia according to the discipline prescribed by Congress;

Clause 2 To exercise exclusive Legislation in all Cases whatsoever, over such District (not exceeding ten Miles square) as may, by Cession of particular States, and the Acceptance of Congress, become the Seat of the Government of the United States, and to exercise like Authority over all Places purchased by the Consent of the Legislature of the State in which the Same shall be, for the Erection of Forts, Magazines, Arsenals, dock-Yards; and other needful Buildings;—And

Clause 3 To make all Laws which shall be necessary and proper for carrying into Execution the foregoing Powers, and all other Powers vested by this Constitution in the Government of the United States, or in any Department or Officer thereof.

Powers Denied to Congress

SECTION 9

Clause 1 The Migration or Importation of such Persons as any of the States now existing shall think proper to admit, shall not be prohibited by the Congress prior to the Year one thousand eight hundred and eight, but a Tax or duty may be imposed on such Importation, not exceeding ten dollars for each Person.

Clause 2 The privilege of the Writ of Habeas Corpus shall not be suspended, unless when in Cases of Rebellion or Invasion the public Safety may require it.

Clause 3 No Bill of Attainder or ex post facto Law shall be passed.

Clause 4 No Capitation, or other direct, Tax shall be laid, unless in Proportion to the Census or Enumeration herein before directed to be taken.[6]

Clause 5 No Tax or Duty shall be laid on Articles exported from any State.

Clause 6 No Preference shall be given by any Regulation of Commerce or Revenue to the Ports of one State over those of another; nor shall Vessels bound to, or from, one State, be obliged to enter, clear, or pay Duties in another.

Clause 7 No Money shall be drawn from the Treasury, but in Consequence of Appropriations made by Law; and a regular Statement and Account of the Receipts and Expenditures of all public Money shall be published from time to time.

Clause 8 No Title of Nobility shall be granted by the United States: And no Person holding any Office of Profit or Trust under them, shall, without the Consent of Congress, accept of any present, Emolument, Office, or Title, of any kind whatever, from any King, Prince, or foreign State.

Powers Denied to the States

SECTION 10

Clause 1 No State shall enter into any Treaty, Alliance, or Confederation; grant Letters of Marque and Reprisal; coin Money; emit Bills of Credit; make any Thing but gold and silver Coin a Tender in Payment of Debts; pass any Bill of Attainder, ex post facto Law, or Law impairing the Obligation of Contracts, or grant any Title of Nobility.

Clause 2 No State shall, without the Consent of the Congress, lay any Imposts or Duties on Imports or Exports, except what may be absolutely necessary for executing its inspection Laws: and the net Produce of all Duties and Imposts, laid by any State on Imports or Exports, shall be for the Use of the Treasury of the United States; and all such Laws shall be subject to the Revision and Controul of the Congress.

Clause 3 No State shall, without the Consent of Congress, lay any Duty of Tonnage, keep Troops, or Ships of War in time of Peace, enter into any Agreement or Compact with another State, or with a foreign Power, or engage in War, unless actually invaded, or in such imminent Danger as will not admit of Delay.

[6]Modified by the 16th Amendment

Article II—The Executive Article

Nature and Scope of Presidential Power

SECTION 1

Clause 1 The executive Power shall be vested in a President of the United States of America. He shall hold his Office during the Term of four Years and, together with the Vice President, chosen for the same Term, be elected as follows:

Clause 2 Each State shall appoint, in such Manner as the Legislature thereof may direct, a Number of Electors, equal to the whole Number of Senators and Representatives to which the State may be entitled in the Congress: but no Senator or Representative, or Person holding an Office of Trust or Profit under the United States, shall be appointed an Elector.

Clause 3 The Electors shall meet in their respective States, and vote by Ballot for two Persons, of whom one at least shall not be an Inhabitant of the same State with themselves. And they shall make a List of all the Persons voted for, and of the Number of Votes for each; which List they shall sign and certify, and transmit sealed to the Seat of the Government of the United States, directed to the President of the Senate. The President of the Senate shall, in the Presence of the Senate and House of Representatives, open all the Certificates, and the Votes shall then be counted. The Person having the greatest Number of Votes shall be the President, if such Number be a Majority of the whole Number of Electors appointed; and if there be more than one who have such Majority and have an equal Number of Votes, then the House of Representatives shall immediately chuse by Ballot one of them for President; and if no Person have a Majority, then from the five highest on the List the said House shall in like Manner chuse the President. But in chusing the President, the Votes shall be taken by States, the Representation from each State having one Vote; A quorum for this Purpose shall consist of a Member or Members from two thirds of the States, and a Majority of all the States shall be necessary to a Choice. In every Case, after the Choice of the President, the Person having the greatest Number of Votes of the Electors shall be the Vice President. But if there should remain two or more who have equal Vote, the Senate shall chuse from them by Ballot the Vice President.[7]

Clause 4 The Congress may determine the Time of chusing the Electors, and the Day on which they shall give their Votes; which Day shall be the same throughout the United States.

Clause 5 No Person except a natural born Citizen, or a Citizen of the United States, at the time of the Adoption of this Constitution, shall be eligible to the Office of President; neither shall any Person be eligible to that Office who shall not have attained to the Age of thirty five Years, and been fourteen Years a Resident within the United States.

Clause 6 In Case of the Removal of the President from Office, or of his Death, Resignation, or Inability to discharge the Powers and Duties of the said Office, the Same shall devolve on the Vice President, and the Congress may by Law provide for the Case of Removal, Death, Resignation, or Inability, both of the President and Vice President, declaring what Officer shall then act as President, and such Officer shall act accordingly, until the Disability be removed, or a President shall be elected.[8]

Clause 7 The President shall, at stated Times, receive for his Services, a Compensation, which shall neither be increased nor diminished during the Period of which he shall have been elected, and he shall not receive within that Period any other Emolument from the United States, or any of them.

Clause 8 Before he enter on the Execution of his Office, he shall take the following Oath or Affirmation:—"I do solemnly swear (or affirm) that I will faithfully execute the Office of President of the United States, and will to the best of my Ability, preserve, protect and defend the Constitution of the United States."

Powers and Duties of the President

SECTION 2

Clause 1 The President shall be the Commander in Chief of the Army and Navy of the United States, and of the Militia of the several States, when called into the actual Service of the United States; he may require the Opinion, in writing, of the principal Officer in each of the executive Departments, upon any Subject relating to the Duties of their respective Offices, and he shall have the Power to grant Reprieves and Pardons for Offences against the United States, except in Cases of Impeachment.

Clause 2 He shall have Power, by and with the Advice and Consent of the Senate to make Treaties, provided two thirds of the Senators present concur; and he shall nominate, and by and with the Advice and Consent of the Senate, shall appoint Ambassadors, other public Ministers and Consuls, Judges of the supreme Court, and all other Officers of the United States, whose Appointments are not herein otherwise provided for, and which shall be established by Law: but the Congress may by Law vest the Appointment of such inferior Officers, as they think proper, in the President alone, in the Courts of Law, or in the Heads of Departments.

Clause 3 The President shall have Power to fill up all Vacancies that may happen during the Recess of the Senate, by granting Commissions which shall expire at the End of their next Session.

SECTION 3 He shall from time to time give to the Congress Information of the State of the Union, and recommend to their Consideration such Measures as he shall judge necessary and expedient; he may, on extraordinary Occasions, convene both Houses, or either of them and in Case of Disagreement between them, with Respect to the Time of Adjournment, he may adjourn them to such Time as he shall think proper; he shall receive Ambassadors and other public Ministers; he shall

[7]Changed by the 12th and 20th Amendments

[8]Modified by the 25th Amendment

take Care that the Laws be faithfully executed, and shall Commission all the Officers of the United States.

SECTION 4 The President, Vice President and all civil Officers of the United States, shall be removed from Office on Impeachment for, and Conviction of, Treason, Bribery, or other high Crimes and Misdemeanors.

Article III—The Judicial Article

Judicial Power, Courts, Judges

SECTION 1 The judicial Power of the United States shall be vested in one supreme Court, and in such inferior Courts as the Congress may from time to time ordain and establish. The Judges, both the supreme and inferior Courts, shall hold their Offices during good Behaviour, and shall, at stated Times, receive for their Services a Compensation, which shall not be diminished during their Continuance in Office.

Jurisdiction

SECTION 2 The judicial Power shall extend to all Cases, in Law and Equity, arising under this Constitution, the Laws of the United States, and Treaties made, or which shall be made, under their Authority;—to all Cases affecting Ambassadors, other public Ministers and Consuls;—to all Cases of admiralty and maritime Jurisdiction;—to Controversies to which the United States shall be a Party;—to Controversies between two or more States; between a State and Citizens of another State;[9]—between Citizens of different States;—between Citizens of the same State claiming Lands under Grants of different States, and between a State, or the Citizens thereof, and foreign States, Citizens, or Subjects.

In all Cases affecting Ambassadors, other public Ministers and Consuls, and those in which a State shall be Party, the supreme Court shall have original Jurisdiction. In all the other Cases before mentioned, the supreme Court shall have appellate Jurisdiction, both as to Law and Fact, with such Exceptions, and under such Regulations as Congress shall make.

The Trial of all Crimes, except in Cases of Impeachment, shall be by Jury; and such Trial shall be held in the State where the said Crimes shall have been committed; but when not committed within any State, the Trial shall be at such Place or Places as the Congress may by Law have directed.

Treason

SECTION 3 Treason against the United States, shall consist only in levying War against them, or in adhering to their Enemies, giving them Aid and Comfort. No Person shall be convicted of Treason unless on the Testimony of two Witnesses to the same overt Act, or on Confession in open Court.

The Congress shall have Power to declare the Punishment of Treason, but no Attainder of Treason shall work Corruption of Blood, or Forfeiture except during the Life of the Person attainted.

[9]Modified by the 11th Amendment

Article IV—Interstate Relations

Full Faith and Credit Clause

SECTION 1 Full Faith and Credit shall be given in each State to the public Acts, Records, and judicial Proceedings of every other State. And the Congress may by general Laws prescribe the Manner in which such Acts, Records and Proceedings shall be proved, and the Effect thereof.

Privileges and Immunities; Interstate Extradition

SECTION 2

Clause 1 The Citizens of each State shall be entitled to all Privileges and Immunities of Citizens in the several States.

Clause 2 A Person charged in any State with Treason, Felony or other Crime, who shall flee from Justice, and be found in another State, shall on Demand of the executive Authority of the State from which he fled, be delivered up, to be removed to the State having Jurisdiction of the Crime.

Clause 3 No person held to Service or Labour in one State, under the Laws thereof, escaping into another, shall, in Consequence of any Law or Regulation therein, be discharged from such Service or Labour, but shall be delivered up on Claim of the Party to whom such Service or Labour may be due.[10]

Admission of States

SECTION 3 New States may be admitted by the Congress into this Union; but no new State shall be formed or erected within the Jurisdiction of any other State; nor any State to be formed by the Junction of two or more States, or Parts of States, without the Consent of the Legislatures of the States concerned as well as of the Congress.

The Congress shall have Power to dispose of and make all needful Rules and Regulations respecting the Territory or other Property belonging to the United States; and nothing in this Constitution shall be so construed as to Prejudice any Claims of the United States, or of any particular State.

Republican Form of Government

SECTION 4 The United States shall guarantee to every State in this Union a Republican Form of Government, and shall protect each of them against Invasion; and on Application of the Legislature, or of the Executive (when the Legislature cannot be convened) against domestic Violence.

Article V—The Amending Power

The Congress, whenever two thirds of both Houses shall deem it necessary, shall propose Amendments to this Constitution, or, on the Application of the Legislatures of two thirds of several States, shall call a Convention for proposing Amendments,

[10]Repealed by the 13th Amendment

which, in either Case, shall be valid to all Intents and Purposes, as Part of this Constitution, when ratified by the Legislatures of three fourths of the several States, or by Conventions in three fourths thereof, as the one or the other Mode of Ratification may be proposed by the Congress; Provided that no Amendment which may be made prior to the Year One thousand eight hundred and eight shall in any Manner affect the first and fourth Clauses in the Ninth Section of the first Article; and that no State, without its Consent, shall be deprived of its equal Suffrage in the Senate.

Article VI—The Supremacy Act

Clause 1

All Debts contracted and Engagements entered into, before the Adoption of this Constitution, shall be as valid against the United States under the Constitution, as under the Confederation.

Clause 2

This Constitution, and the Laws of the United States which shall be made in Pursuance thereof; and all Treaties made, or which shall be made, under the Authority of the United States, shall be the supreme Law of the Land; and the Judges in every State shall be bound thereby, any Thing in the Constitution or Laws of any State to the Contrary notwithstanding.

Clause 3

The Senators and Representatives before mentioned, and the Members of the several State Legislatures, and all executive and judicial Officers, both of the United States and of the several States, shall be bound by Oath or Affirmation, to support this Constitution; but no religious Test shall ever be required as a Qualification to any Office or public Trust under the United States.

Article VII—Ratification

The Ratification of the Conventions of nine States, shall be sufficient for the Establishment of this Constitution between the States so ratifying the Same.

Done in Convention by the Unanimous Consent of the States present the Seventeenth Day of September in the Year of our Lord one thousand seven hundred and Eighty seven and of the Independence of the United States of America the Twelfth In Witness whereof We have hereunto subscribed our Names.

Amendments

The Bill of Rights

[The first ten amendments were ratified on December 15, 1791, and form what is known as the "Bill of Rights."]

Amendment 1—
Religion, Speech, Assembly, and Politics

Congress shall make no law respecting an establishment of religion, or prohibiting the free exercise thereof; or abridging the freedom of speech, or of the press; or the right of the people peaceably to assemble, and to petition the government for a redress of grievances.

Amendment 2—
Militia and the Right to Bear Arms

A well-regulated Militia, being necessary to the security of a free State, the right of the people to keep and bear Arms, shall not be infringed.

Amendment 3—Quartering of Soldiers

No Soldier shall, in time of peace be quartered in any house, without the consent of the Owner, nor in time of war, but in manner to be prescribed by law.

Amendment 4—Searches and Seizures

The right of the people to be secure in their persons, houses, papers, and effects, against unreasonable searches and seizures, shall not be violated, and no Warrants shall issue, but upon probable cause, supported by Oath or affirmation, and particularly describing the place to be searched, and the persons or things to be seized.

Amendment 5—Grand Juries,
Self-Incrimination, Double Jeopardy, Due Process,
and Eminent Domain

No person shall be held to answer for a capital, or otherwise infamous crime, unless on a presentment or indictment of a Grand jury, except in cases arising in the land or naval forces, or in the Militia, when in actual service in time of War or public danger; nor shall any person be subject for the same offence to be twice put in jeopardy of life or limb; nor shall be compelled in any criminal case to be a witness against himself, nor be deprived of life, liberty, or property, without due process of law; nor shall private property be taken for public use, without just compensation.

Amendment 6—
Criminal Court Procedures

In all criminal prosecutions, the accused shall enjoy the right to a speedy and public trial, by an impartial jury of the State and district wherein the crime shall have been committed, which district shall have been previously ascertained by law, and to be informed of the nature and cause of the accusation; to be confronted with the witnesses against him; to have compulsory process for obtaining Witnesses in his favor, and to have the Assistance of Counsel for his defence.

Amendment 7—Trial by Jury in Common Law Cases

In Suits at common law, where the value in controversy shall exceed twenty dollars, the right of trial by jury shall be preserved, and no fact tried by a jury shall be otherwise re-examined in any Court of the United States, than according to the rules of the common law.

Amendment 8—Bail, Cruel and Unusual Punishment

Excessive bail shall not be required, nor excessive fines imposed, nor cruel and unusual punishments inflicted.

Amendment 9—Rights Retained by the People

The enumeration in the Constitution, of certain rights, shall not be construed to deny or disparage others retained by the people.

Amendment 10—Reserved Powers of the States

The powers not delegated to the United States by the Constitution, nor prohibited by it to the States, are reserved to the States respectively, or to the people.

Amendment 11—Suits Against the States

[Ratified February 7, 1795]

The Judicial power of the United States shall not be construed to extend to any suit in law or equity, commenced or prosecuted against one of the United States by Citizens of another State, or by Citizens or Subjects of any Foreign State.

Amendment 12—Election of the President

[Ratified June 15, 1804]

The Electors shall meet in their respective states, and vote by ballot for President and Vice-President, one of whom, at least, shall not be an inhabitant of the same state with themselves; they shall name in their ballots the person voted for as President, and in distinct ballots the person voted for as Vice-President, and they shall make distinct lists of all persons voted for as President, and of all persons voted for as Vice-President, and of the number of votes for each, which lists they shall sign and certify, and transmit sealed to the seat of the government of the United States, directed to the President of the Senate;—The President of the Senate shall, in presence of the Senate and House of Representatives, open all the certificates and the votes shall then be counted;—The person having the greatest number of votes for President, shall be the President, if such number be a majority of the whole number of Electors appointed; and if no person have such majority, then from the persons having the highest numbers not exceeding three on the list of those voted for as President, the House of Representatives shall choose immediately, by ballot, the President. But in choosing the President, the votes shall be taken by states, the representation from each state having one vote; a quorum for this purpose shall consist of a member or members from two-thirds of the states, and a majority of all states shall be necessary to a choice. And if the House of Representatives shall not choose a President whenever the right of choice shall devolve upon them, before the fourth day of March next following, then the Vice-President shall act as President, as in the case of the death or other constitutional disability of the President.[11] The person having the greatest number of votes as Vice-President, shall be the Vice-President, if such a number be a majority of the whole numbers of Electors appointed, and if no person have a majority, then from the two highest numbers on the list, the Senate shall choose the Vice-President; a quorum for the purpose shall consist of two-thirds of the whole number of Senators, and a majority of the whole number shall be necessary to a choice. But no person constitutionally ineligible to the office of President shall be eligible to that of Vice-President of the United States.

Amendment 13—Prohibition of Slavery

[Ratified December 6, 1865]

Section 1 Neither slavery nor involuntary servitude, except as a punishment for crime whereof the party shall have been duly convicted, shall exist within the United States, or any place subject to their jurisdiction.

Section 2 Congress shall have power to enforce this article by appropriate legislation.

Amendment 14—Citizenship, Due Process, and Equal Protection of the Laws

[Ratified July 9, 1868]

Section 1 All persons born or naturalized in the United States, and subject to the jurisdiction thereof, are citizens of the United States and of the State wherein they reside. No State shall make or enforce any law which shall abridge the privileges or immunities of citizens of the United States; nor shall any State deprive any person of life, liberty, or property, without due process of law; nor deny to any person within its jurisdiction the equal protection of the laws.

Section 2 Representatives shall be apportioned among the several States according to their respective numbers, counting the whole number of persons in each State, excluding Indians not taxed. But when the right to vote at any election for the choice of electors for President and Vice President of the United States, Representatives in Congress, the Executive and Judicial officers of a State, or the members of the Legislature thereof, is denied to any of the male inhabitants of such State, being twenty-one[12] years of age, and citizens of the United States, or in any way abridged, except for participation in rebellion, or other crime, the basis of representation therein shall be reduced in the proportion which the number of such

[11] Changed by the 20th Amendment

[12] Changed by the 26th Amendment

male citizens shall bear to the whole number of male citizens twenty-one years of age in such State.

SECTION 3 No person shall be a Senator or Representative in Congress, or elector of President and Vice President, or hold any office, civil or military, under the United States, or under any State, who, having previously taken an oath, as a member of Congress, or as an officer of the United States, or as a member of any State legislature, or as an executive or judicial officer of any State, to support the Constitution of the United States, shall have engaged in insurrection or rebellion against the same, or given aid or comfort to the enemies thereof. But Congress may by a vote of two-thirds of each House, remove such disability.

SECTION 4 The validity of the public debt of the United States, authorized by law, including debts incurred for payment of pensions and bounties for services in suppressing insurrection or rebellion, shall not be questioned. But neither the United States nor any State shall assume or pay any debt or obligation incurred in aid of insurrection or rebellion against the United States, or any claim for the loss or emancipation of any slave; but all such debts, obligations and claims shall be held illegal and void.

SECTION 5 The Congress shall have power to enforce, by appropriate legislation, the provisions of this article.

Amendment 15—The Right to Vote

[Ratified February 3, 1870]

SECTION 1 The right of citizens of the United States to vote shall not be denied or abridged by the United States or by any State on account of race, color, or previous condition of servitude.

SECTION 2 The Congress shall have power to enforce this article by appropriate legislation.

Amendment 16—Income Taxes

[Ratified February 3, 1913]

The Congress shall have power to lay and collect taxes on incomes, from whatever source derived, without apportionment among the several States, and without regard to any census or enumeration.

Amendment 17—Direct Election of Senators

[Ratified April 8, 1913]

The Senate of the United States shall be composed of two Senators from each State, elected by the people thereof, for six years; and each Senator shall have one vote. The electors in each State shall have the qualifications requisite for electors of the most numerous branch of the State legislatures.

When vacancies happen in the representation of any State in the Senate, the executive authority of such State shall issue writs of election to fill such vacancies: Provided, That the legislature of any State may empower the executive thereof to make temporary appointment until the people fill the vacancies by election as the legislature may direct. This amendment shall not be so construed as to affect the election or term of any Senator chosen before it becomes valid as part of the Constitution.

Amendment 18—Prohibition

[Ratified January 16, 1919. Repealed December 5, 1933 by Amendment 21]

SECTION 1 After one year from the ratification of this article the manufacture, sale, or transportation of intoxicating liquors within, the importation thereof into, or the exportation thereof from the United States and all territory subject to the jurisdiction thereof for beverage purposes is hereby prohibited.

SECTION 2 The Congress and the several states shall have concurrent power to enforce this article by appropriate legislation.

SECTION 3 This article shall be inoperative unless it shall have been ratified as an amendment to the Constitution by the legislatures of the several states, as provided in the Constitution, within seven years from the date of the submission hereof to the States by the Congress.[13]

Amendment 19—For Women's Suffrage

[Ratified August 18, 1920]

The right of the citizens of the United States to vote shall not be denied or abridged by the United States or by any State on account of sex.

Congress shall have power, by appropriate legislation, to enforce the provision of this article.

Amendment 20—The Lame Duck Amendment

[Ratified January 23, 1933]

SECTION 1 The terms of the President and Vice President shall end at noon on the 20th day of January, and the terms of the Senators and Representatives at noon on the 3rd day of January, of the years in which such terms would have ended if this article had not been ratified, and the terms of their successors shall then begin.

SECTION 2 The Congress shall assemble at least once in every year, and such meeting shall begin at noon on the 3rd day of January, unless they shall by law appoint a different day.

SECTION 3 If, at the time fixed for the beginning of the term of the President, the President elect shall have died, the Vice President elect shall become President. If a President shall not have been chosen before the time fixed for the beginning of his term, or if the President elect shall have failed to qualify, then the Vice President elect shall act as President until a President shall have qualified; and the Congress may by law provide for the case wherein neither a President elect nor a Vice President elect shall have qualified, declaring who shall then act as President, or the manner in which one who is to act shall be selected, and such person shall act accordingly until a President or Vice President shall have qualified.

[13]Repealed by the 21st Amendment

SECTION 4 The Congress may by law provide for the case of the death of any of the persons from whom the House of Representatives may choose a President whenever the right of choice shall have devolved upon them, and for the case of the death of any of the persons from whom the Senate may choose a Vice President whenever the right of choice shall have devolved upon them.

SECTION 5 Sections 1 and 2 shall take effect on the 15th day of October following the ratification of this article.

SECTION 6 This article shall be inoperative unless it shall have been ratified as an amendment to the Constitution by the legislatures of three-fourths of the several States within seven years from the date of its submission.

Amendment 21—Repeal of Prohibition

[Ratified December 5, 1933]

SECTION 1 The eighteenth article of amendment to the Constitution of the United States is hereby repealed.

SECTION 2 The transportation or importation into any State, Territory, or Possession of the United States for delivery or use therein of intoxicating liquors, in violation of the laws thereof, is hereby prohibited.

SECTION 3 This article shall be inoperative unless it shall have been ratified as an amendment to the Constitution by conventions in the several States, as provided in the Constitution, within seven years from the date of the submission hereof to the States by the Congress.

Amendment 22—Number of Presidential Terms

[Ratified February 27, 1951]

SECTION 1 No person shall be elected to the office of the President more than twice, and no person who has held the office of President, or acted as President, for more than two years of a term to which some other person was elected President shall be elected to the office of the President more than once. But this Article shall not apply to any person holding the office of President when this article was proposed by the Congress, and shall not prevent any person who may be holding the office of President, or acting as President, during the term within which this Article becomes operative from holding the office of President or acting as President during the remainder of such term.

SECTION 2 This Article shall be inoperative unless it shall have been ratified as an amendment to the Constitution by the legislatures of three-fourths of the several states within seven years from the date of its submission to the States by the Congress.

Amendment 23—Presidential Electors for the District of Columbia

[Ratified March 29, 1961]

SECTION 1 The District constituting the seat of government of the United States shall appoint in such manner as the Congress may direct:

A number of electors of President and Vice President equal to the whole number of Senators and Representatives in Congress to which the District would be entitled if it were a State, but in no event more than the least populous State; they shall be in addition to those appointed by the States, but they shall be considered for the purposes of the election of President and Vice President, to be electors appointed by a State; and they shall meet in the District and perform such duties as provided by the twelfth article of amendment.

SECTION 2 The Congress shall have power to enforce this article by appropriate legislation

Amendment 24—The Anti-Poll Tax Amendment

[Ratified January 23, 1964]

SECTION 1 The right of citizens of the United States to vote in any primary or other election for President or Vice President, for electors for President or Vice President, or for Senator or Representative in Congress, shall not be denied or abridged by the United States or any state by reason of failure to pay any poll tax or other tax.

SECTION 2 The Congress shall have power to enforce this article by appropriate legislation.

Amendment 25—Presidential Disability, Vice Presidential Vacancies

[Ratified February 10, 1967]

SECTION 1 In case of the removal of the President from office or his death or resignation, the Vice President shall become President.

SECTION 2 Whenever there is a vacancy in the office of the Vice President, the President shall nominate a Vice President who shall take the office upon confirmation by a majority vote of both Houses of Congress.

SECTION 3 Whenever the President transmits to the President pro tempore of the Senate and the Speaker of the House of Representatives his written declaration that he is unable to discharge the powers and duties of his office, and until he transmits to them a written declaration to the contrary, such powers and duties shall be discharged by the Vice President as Acting President.

SECTION 4 Whenever the Vice President and a majority of either the principal officers of the executive departments, or of such other body as Congress may by law provide, transmit to the President pro tempore of the Senate and the Speaker of the House of Representatives their written declaration that the President is unable to discharge the powers and duties of his office, the Vice President shall immediately assume the powers and duties of the office as Acting President.

Thereafter, when the President transmits to the President pro tempore of the Senate and the Speaker of the House of Representatives his written declaration that no inability exists, he shall resume the powers and duties of his office unless the Vice President and a majority of either the principal officers of the executive departments, or of such other body as Congress may by law provide, transmit within four days to the President pro tempore of the Senate and the Speaker of the House of Representatives their written declaration that the President is unable to discharge the powers and duties of his office. Thereupon Congress shall decide the issue, assembling within forty-eight hours for that purpose if not in session. If the Congress, within twenty-one days after receipt of the latter written declaration, or, if Congress is not in session, within twenty-one days after Congress is required to assemble, determines by two-thirds vote of both houses that the President is unable to discharge the powers and duties of his office, the Vice President shall continue to discharge the same as Acting President; otherwise, the President shall resume the powers and duties of his office.

Amendment 26—Eighteen-Year-Old Vote

[Ratified July 1, 1971]

SECTION 1 The right of citizens of the United States, who are 18 years of age, or older, to vote shall not be denied or abridged by the United States or by any state on account of age.

SECTION 2 The Congress shall have power to enforce this article by appropriate legislation.

Amendment 27—Congressional Salaries

[Ratified May 7, 1992]

No law, varying the compensation for the services of the Senators and Representatives, shall take effect, until an election of Representatives shall be intervened.

CHAPTER 2

American Federalism

CHAPTER OUTLINE & CHAPTER LEARNING OBJECTIVES

Defining Federalism

2.1 Interpret the definitions of federalism, and assess the advantages and disadvantages of the American system of federalism.

The Constitutional Structure of American Federalism

2.2 Differentiate the powers the Constitution provides to national and state governments.

The National Courts and Federalism

2.3 Assess the role of the national courts in defining the relationship between the national and state governments, and evaluate the positions of decentralists and centralists.

The National Budget as a Tool of Federalism

2.4 Analyze the budget as a tool of federalism, and evaluate its impact on state and local governments.

The Politics of Federalism

2.5 Evaluate the current relationship between the national and state governments and the future challenges for federalism.

The relationship of the national government to the states has been the subject of intense debate since the founding.[1] In 1787, members of what would become the Federalist Party defended the creation of a strong national government, whereas the Antifederalists warned that a strong national government would overshadow the states. The great debate over which level of government best represents the people continues to rage.

State governments have often complained that the national government is either taking over their responsibilities or controlling too much of what they do. Yet, in policy areas such as civil rights, educational opportunities for people with disabilities, and handgun control, the states have been slow to respond to citizens, and the national government has taken steps to deal with these issues.

At the same time, states retain enormous authority under the Constitution to regulate life within their borders. Working with the local governments they create, states police the streets, fight fires, impose their own taxes, create most of the laws that govern their citizens, define the meaning of marriage, set the rules for elections and voter registration, run the public schools, and administer most of the programs to help the poor, even when the money for those programs comes from the national government.

In recent years, for example, states have become increasingly involved in regulating cell phone use and texting while driving. As the number of text messages sent in the United States increased from 57.2 billion in 2005 to more than 600 billion in 2008, states became increasingly concerned that texting was an even greater threat to safety than talking on cell phones. According to recent studies, drivers who are texting while driving are significantly more likely to drift out of their lane and look away from the cars in front of them. As a result, they are much more likely to be in life-threatening accidents than drivers who talk on cell phones, who themselves are already more likely to be in life-threatening accidents than those who keep their eyes on the road and hands on the wheel.[2] As with talking on cell phones, younger drivers are much more likely to text than older drivers.

The pressure to pass new laws banning texting while driving increased in 2009, when British television began running a public service advertisement showing the grizzly results of a fictitious accident. The four-minute advertisement is graphic, bloody, and terrifying. It is so disturbing that viewers must be 18 to watch the film on YouTube, although anyone can watch a 2009 *Today Show* story about the film, also available on YouTube.

States are reacting to the threat by passing new laws to ban texting while driving. By the end of 2009, 18 states were already imposing stiff fines for texting while driving under a general ban on distracted driving, and some were suspending the driver's license of anyone caught texting on the road. Delaware, Indiana, Kansas, Maine, Mississippi, and West Virginia now prohibit texting while driving for drivers with learning permits or probationary licenses, while Missouri prohibits texting while driving for anyone under age 21.

Enforcement is the problem with such bans. Police cannot be everywhere watching every possible violation, and text messaging is particularly hard to spot. This is why state-sponsored education campaigns built around the kind of intense messages in the British television advertisement may be the only way to frighten drivers away from the practice. Under the Constitution, it is mostly up to the states to figure out both what to do about texting while driving and how to enforce the laws they make.

In 2009, a small city in Britain began running a graphic four-minute television advertisement about the dangers of texting while driving. Many U.S. states have passed or are considering legislation banning the practice. ■ *What are some of the potential difficulties for drivers when the regulation of texting while driving is handled on a state-by-state basis?*

In this chapter, we first define federalism and its advantages and disadvantages. We then look at the constitutional basis for our federal system and how court decisions and political developments have shaped, and continue to shape, federalism in the United States. Throughout, you should think hard about how you influence the issues you care about, even in your local city council or mayor's office. The Constitution clearly encourages, and even depends on, you to express your view at all levels of government, which is why action in a single state can start a process of change that spreads to other states or the national government.

Defining Federalism

LEARNING **OBJECTIVE**

2.1 Interpret the definitions of federalism, and assess the advantages and disadvantages of the American system of federalism.

Scholars have argued and wars have been fought over what federalism means. One scholar recently counted 267 definitions of the term.[3]

Federalism, as we define it, is a form of government in which a constitution distributes authority and powers between a central government and smaller regional governments—usually called states, provinces, or republics—giving to both the national and the regional governments substantial responsibilities and powers, including the power to collect taxes and to pass and enforce laws regulating the conduct of individuals. When we use the term "federalism" or "federal system," we are referring to this system of national and state governments; when we use the term "federal government," here and in the other chapters of the book, we are referring to the national government headquartered in Washington, D.C.

The mere existence of both national and state governments does not make a system federal. What is important is that a *constitution divides governmental powers between the national government and smaller regional governments,* giving clearly defined functions to each. Neither the central nor the regional government receives its powers from the other; both derive them from a common source—the Constitution. No ordinary act of legislation at either the national or the state level can change this constitutional distribution of powers. Both levels of government operate through their own agents and exercise power directly over individuals.

federalism
A constitutional arrangement in which power is distributed between a central government and subdivisional governments, called states in the United States. The national and the subdivisional governments both exercise direct authority over individuals.

Constitutionally, the federal system of the United States consists of only the national government and the 50 states. "Cities are not," the Supreme Court reminded us, "sovereign entities." This does not make for a tidy, efficient, easy-to-understand system; yet, as we shall see, it has its virtues.

There are several different ways that power can be shared in a federal system, and political scientists have devised terms to explain these various kinds of federalism. At different times in the United States' history, our system of federalism has shared power based on each of the below interpretations.

- *Dual federalism* views the Constitution as giving a limited list of powers—primarily foreign policy and national defense—to the national government, leaving the rest to sovereign states. Each level of government is dominant within its own sphere.
- *Cooperative federalism* stresses federalism as a system of intergovernmental relationships in delivering governmental goods and services to the people and calls for cooperation among various levels of government.
- *Marble cake federalism* conceives of federalism as a mixed set of responsibilities in which all levels of government are engaged in a variety of issues and programs, rather than a layer cake, or dual federalism, with fixed divisions between layers or levels of government.[4]
- *Competitive federalism* views the national government, the 50 states, and the thousands of local governments as competing with each other over ways to put together packages of services and taxes.[5]
- *Permissive federalism* implies that, although federalism provides "a sharing of power and authority between the national and state government, the states' share rests on the permission and permissiveness of the national government."[6]
- *New federalism,* championed by former presidents Richard M. Nixon (1969–1974) and Ronald Reagan (1981–1989), presumes that the power of the federal government is limited in favor of the broad powers reserved to the states.

Alternatives to Federalism

Among the alternatives to federalism are **unitary systems** of government, in which a constitution vests all governmental power in the central government. The central government, if it so chooses, may delegate authority to constituent units, but what it delegates, it may take away. China, France, the Scandinavian countries, and Israel have unitary governments. In the United States, state constitutions usually create this kind of relationship between the state and its local governments.

At the other extreme from unitary governments are **confederations,** in which sovereign nations, through a constitutional compact, create a central government but carefully limit its authority and do not give it the power to regulate the conduct of individuals directly. The central government makes regulations for the constituent governments,

unitary system
A constitutional arrangement that concentrates power in a central government.

confederation
A constitutional arrangement in which sovereign nations or states, by compact, create a central government but carefully limit its power and do not give it direct authority over individuals.

State and local governments are responsible for policing the streets but not for enforcing federal laws. Nevertheless, they often work with national agencies such as the Federal Bureau of Investigation, Drug Enforcement Administration, or the Immigration and Customs Enforcement Bureau. ■ *What are some of the benefits of federal, state, and local law enforcement agencies working together against crime?*

Of the People

THE GLOBAL COMMUNITY

Global Opinion on the Role of Government

State and local governments are on the front lines of most programs for helping the needy. They provide much of the money and/or administration for unemployment insurance for the jobless, health care clinics and hospitals for the poor, school lunch programs for hungry children, and homeless shelters. Although many U.S. citizens see poverty firsthand as volunteers for local charities such as food pantries, some have doubts about how much government should do to help poor people who cannot take care of themselves. According to the Pew Global survey, citizens of other nations vary greatly on the question.

These opinions reflect very different social and economic conditions in each country. Japan has a culture of self-reliance that puts the burden on individuals to help themselves, while Nigeria continues to suffer from some of the highest poverty rates in the world. In this regard, U.S. citizens tend to mirror the Japanese—they want government to help the less fortunate but also want the less fortunate to help themselves. As a general conclusion, citizens of wealthier nations think poor people should take advantage of the opportunities that already exist in their economies, whereas citizens of poor nations believe that government should be more aggressive in providing support.

This does not mean wealthier nations are uncaring toward citizens in need, but it does suggest that they sometimes view poverty as the fault of the poor. In the United States, these opinions reflect the importance of equality of opportunity as a basic social value, meaning that all individuals regardless of race, gender, or circumstance have the same opportunity to participate in politics, self-government, and the economy. Most Americans want to help the less fortunate, but only when they are truly needy, not when they fail because they will not help themselves.

CRITICAL THINKING QUESTIONS

1. What are the advantages and disadvantages of having the government provide services for the poor?
2. Why might more wealthy nations be more likely to believe that individuals ought to take care of themselves and not rely on the state?
3. Which level of government might be most effective in providing services to the poor?

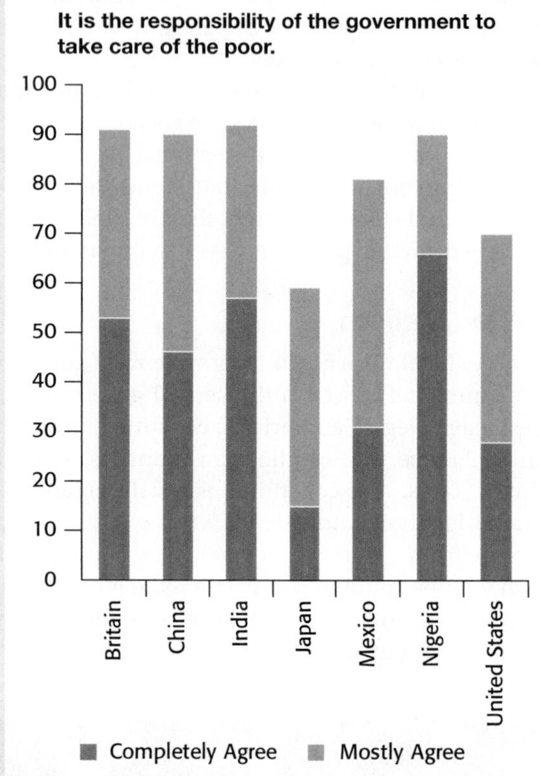

but it exists and operates only at their direction. The 13 states under the Articles of Confederation operated in this manner, as did the southern Confederacy during the Civil War.

There is no single model for dividing authority between the national and smaller regional governments of the other nations. Indeed, even in the United States, we have seen shifts in the balance of federal–state power throughout our history. Some countries have no federal system at all, whereas others have different variations of power sharing between the national and smaller regional governments.

For example, Britain's government is divided into three tiers: national, county, and district governments. County and district governments deliver roughly one-fifth of all government services, including education, housing, and police and fire protection. As a rule, most power is reserved for the central government on the theory that there should be "territorial justice," which means that all citizens should be governed by the same laws and standards. In recent years, however, Great Britain has devolved substantial authority to Scotland, Wales, and Northern Ireland.

Why Federalism?

In 1787, federalism was a compromise between centrists, who supported a strong national government, and those who favored decentralization. Confederation had proved unsuccessful. A unitary system was out of the question because most people were too deeply attached to their state governments to permit subordination to central rule. Many scholars think that federalism is ideally suited to the needs of a diverse people spread throughout a large continent, suspicious of concentrated power, and desiring unity but not uniformity. Yet, even though federalism offers a number of advantages over other forms of government, no system is perfect. Federalism offered, and still offers, both advantages and disadvantages for such a people.

Advantages of Federalism

Federalism Checks the Growth of Tyranny Although in the rest of the world federal forms have not always prevented tyranny (Germany's federal constitution did not, for example, prevent Hitler from seizing power in the 1930s), U.S. citizens tend to associate federalism with freedom.[7] When one political party loses control of the national government, it is still likely to hold office in a number of states and can continue to challenge the party in power at the national level. To the framers, who feared that a single interest group might capture the national government and suppress the interests of others, this diffusion of power was an advantage. There are now nearly 90,000 governments in the United States, including one national government, 50 state governments, and thousands of county, city, and town governments, as well as school boards and special districts that provide specific functions from managing hospitals or parks to mosquito control.[8] (See Figure 2–1 for the number of governments in the United States.)

Federalism Allows Unity Without Uniformity National politicians and parties do not have to iron out every difference on every issue that divides us, whether the issue is abortion, same-sex marriage, gun control, capital punishment, welfare financing, or assisted suicide. Instead, these issues are debated in state legislatures, county courthouses, and city halls. Information about state action spreads quickly from government to government, especially during periods when the national government is relatively slow to respond to pressing issues.

Federalism Encourages Experimentation As Justice Louis Brandeis once argued, states are "laboratories of democracy." If they adopt programs that fail, the negative effects are

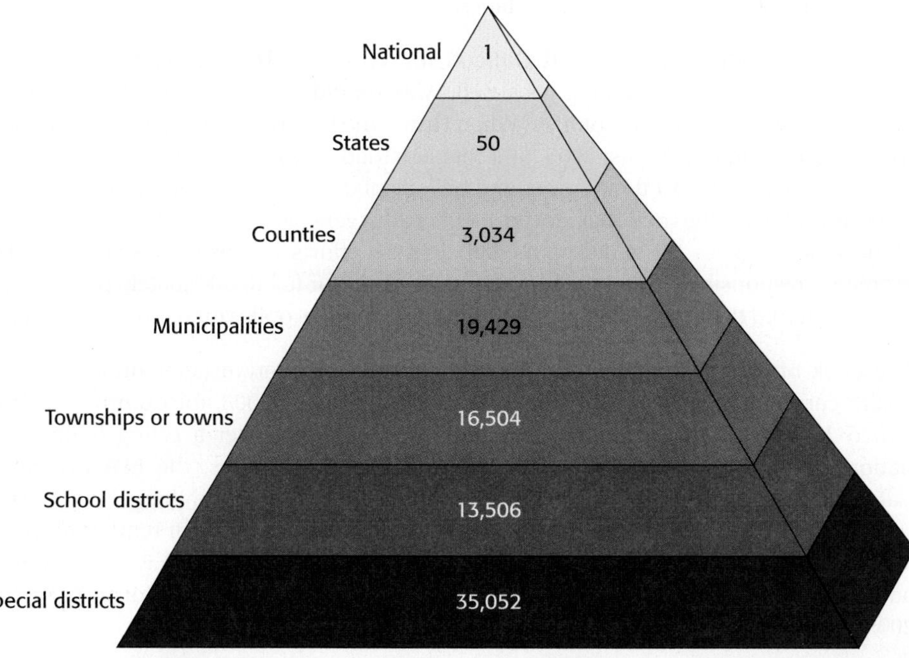

FIGURE 2–1 **Number of Governments in the United States, 2009.**
■ *How do the levels and numbers of governments in the United States help to prevent tyranny?*

SOURCE: U.S. Census Bureau, *Statistical Abstract of the United States*, www.census.gov/prod/2006pubs/07statab/stlocgov.pdf.

There are thousands of special districts in the United States that are responsible for providing specific services, such the Metropolitan Mosquito Control District in Minnesota. ■ *What are the advantages and disadvantages of dividing control of government services into local and special districts?*

limited; if programs succeed, they can be adopted by other states and by the national government. Georgia, for example, was the first state to permit 18-year-olds to vote; Wisconsin was a leader in requiring welfare recipients to work; California moved early on global warming; and Massachusetts created one of the first state programs to provide health insurance to all its citizens. Not all innovations, even those considered successful, become widely adopted.

Federalism Provides Training and Creates Opportunities for Future National Leaders Federalism provides a training ground for state and local politicians to gain experience before moving to the national stage. Presidents Jimmy Carter, Ronald Reagan, Bill Clinton, and George W. Bush previously served as governor of the respective states of Georgia, California, Arkansas, and Texas. In addition, three governors and one mayor ran for the Republican Party nomination for president in 2008, and another governor, Alaska's Sarah Palin, was selected as the Republican vice presidential candidate.

Federalism Keeps Government Closer to the People By providing numerous arenas for decision making, federalism provides many opportunities for Americans to participate in the process of government and helps keep government closer to the people. Every day, thousands of U.S. adults serve on city councils, school boards, neighborhood associations, and planning commissions. Federalism also builds on the public's greater trust in government at the state and local levels. The closer the specific level of government is to the people, the more citizens trust the government.

Disadvantages of Federalism

Dividing Power Makes It Much More Difficult for Government to Respond Quickly to National Problems There was a great demand for new efforts on homeland security after the September 11, 2001, terrorist attacks, and the national government created a new Department of Homeland Security in response. However, the department quickly discovered that there would be great difficulty coordinating its efforts with 50 state governments and thousands of local governments already providing fire, police, transportation, immigration control, and other governmental services.

The Division of Power Makes It Difficult for Voters to Hold Their Elected Officials Accountable When something goes well, who should voters reward? When something goes wrong, who should they punish? When Hurricane Katrina hit New Orleans and the surrounding areas in late August 2005 (and Rita less than a month later near Houston), many thousands of people lost their homes and billions of dollars in damage was done. Who was responsible? Did the national government and agencies like the Federal Emergency Management Agency (FEMA) drop the ball on relief efforts, or was it the state or local government's responsibility? Did the mayor and/or governor fail to adequately plan for such a crisis, or should the national government have had more supplies on hand in advance?

The Lack of Uniformity Can Lead to Conflict States often disagree on issues such as health care, school reform, and crime control. In January 2008, for example, California joined 15 other states in suing the national government over a ruling issued by the national Environmental Protection Agency (EPA). For decades, the EPA had allowed California to enact tougher air quality restrictions through higher mileage standards than required by the national Clean Air Act (first enacted in 1970). A similar request for permission to raise mileage standards was rejected in 2008, however, by the EPA under the Bush administration. The Obama Administration eventually approved California's request in 2009 and extended the higher mileage standards to all states.

Of the People

AMERICA'S CHANGING FACE

Where Americans Come From and Where They Live

The United States is a nation of immigrants who have arrived from many parts of the world. Throughout the decades, the portrait of immigrants has been changing from mostly white to mostly minority. In 2008, for example, 38 million Americans, or 12.5 percent, were foreign born, consisting of 16 million naturalized citizens, 10 million long-term visitors, and 12 million undocumented immigrants. The number of unauthorized, or illegal, immigrants has fallen somewhat in recent years due to the economic recession, which has depressed employment opportunities.

Many foreign-born residents live in the nation's largest cities. The New York City-area population includes more than 5 million foreign-born residents, while Los Angeles includes another 4.5 million; Miami, slightly more than 2 million; Chicago, 1.6 million; and San Francisco, 1.3 million. Although the inner cities host a majority of foreign-born residents, there has been recent movement of immigrants to the suburbs and some movement toward certain areas of the country such as the southwest.

The changing face of America brings great diversity in all aspects of life, from schools to farm fields and small businesses. It enriches the quality of life through the mix of old and new cultures, and can often be a source of innovation in how the economy operates. Diversity also brings complaints about the national government's effort to close its borders to illegal immigrants. Some groups complain that illegal immigrants take jobs that should go to U.S. citizens, whereas others worry about the costs associated with high-poverty rates. Governments at all levels must reconcile these complaints with our history of welcoming immigrants from all around the world.

The Statue of Liberty symbolizes America's long tradition of welcoming immigrants to its shores.

CRITICAL THINKING QUESTIONS

1. How are foreign-born citizens from different regions of the world different from each other?
2. Why do you think foreign-born citizens tend to live in our nation's largest cities?
3. How do foreign-born citizens contribute to the nation's quality of life?

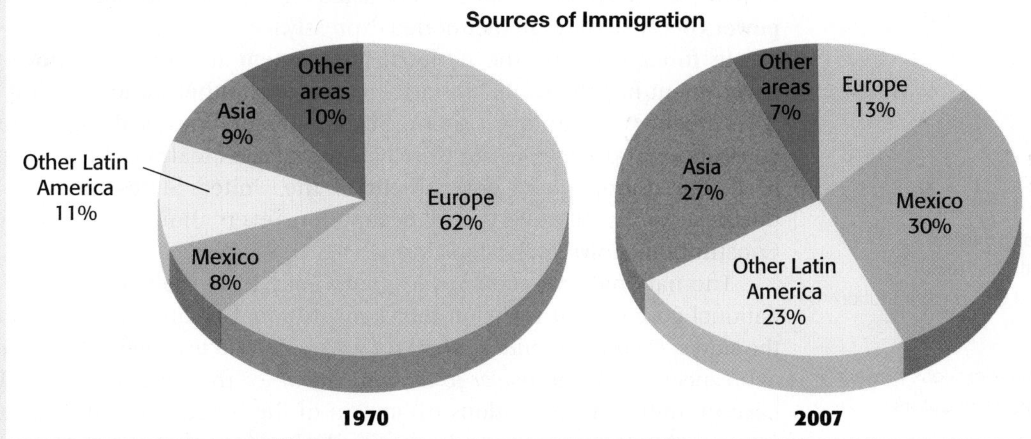

SOURCE: William H. Frey, Alan Berube, Audrey Singer, and Jill H. Wilson, "Getting Current: Recent Demographic Trends in Metropolitan America," Washington, D.C.: The Brookings Institution, 2009.

Variation in Policies Creates Redundancies and Inefficiencies The rules for environmental regulation, labor laws, teacher certification, gun ownership laws, and even the licensing requirements for optometrists vary throughout the 50 states, and this is on top of many federal regulations. Companies seeking to do business across state lines must learn and abide by many different sets of laws, while individuals in licensed professions must consider whether they face recertification if they choose to relocate to another state. One of the obstacles to health care reform debated throughout 2009 in Congress is the fact that each state has a different set of regulations for health insurance companies.

The Constitutional Structure of American Federalism

LEARNING **OBJECTIVE**

2.2 Differentiate the powers the Constitution provides to national and state governments.

The division of powers and responsibilities between the national and state governments has resulted in thousands of court decisions, as well as hundreds of books and endless speeches to explain them—and even then the division lacks precise definition. Nonetheless, it is helpful to have a basic understanding of how the Constitution divides these powers and responsibilities and what obligations it imposes on each level of government.

The constitutional framework of our federal system is relatively simple:

1. The national government has only those powers delegated to it by the Constitution (with the important exception of the inherent power over foreign affairs).
2. Within the scope of its operations, the national government is supreme.
3. The state governments have the powers not delegated to the central government except those denied to them by the Constitution and their state constitutions.
4. Some powers are specifically denied to both the national and state governments; others are specifically denied only to the states or to the national government.

Powers of the National Government

The Constitution explicitly gives legislative, executive, and judicial powers to the national government. In addition to these **delegated powers,** such as the power to regulate interstate commerce and to appropriate funds, the national government has assumed constitutionally **implied powers,** such as the power to create banks, which are inferred from delegated powers. The constitutional basis for the implied powers of Congress is the **necessary and proper clause** (Article I, Section 8, Clause 3). This clause gives Congress the right "to make all Laws which shall be necessary and proper for carrying into Execution the foregoing Powers, and all other Powers vested ... in the Government of the United States." (Powers specifically listed in the Constitution are also called **express powers** because they are mentioned expressly.)

In foreign affairs, the national government has **inherent powers.** The national government has the same authority to deal with other nations as if it were the central government in a unitary system. Such inherent powers do not depend on specific constitutional provisions but exist because of the creation of the national government itself. For example, the government of the United States may acquire territory by purchase or by discovery and occupation, even though no specific clause in the Constitution allows such acquisition.

The national and state governments may have their own lists of powers, but the national government relies on four constitutional pillars for its ultimate authority over the states: (1) the *national supremacy article,* (2) the *war power,* (3) the *commerce clause,* and especially (4) the *power to tax and spend* for the general welfare. These authorities have permitted a tremendous expansion of the functions of the national government. Despite the Supreme Court's recent declaration that some national laws exceed Congress's constitutional powers, the national government has, in effect, almost full power to enact any legislation that Congress deems necessary, so long as it does not conflict with the provisions of the Constitution designed to protect individual rights and the powers of the states. In addition, Section 5 of the Fourteenth Amendment, ratified in 1868, gives Congress the power to enact legislation to remedy constitutional violations and the denial of due process or equal protection of the laws.

delegated (express) powers
Powers given explicitly to the national government and listed in the Constitution.

implied powers
Powers inferred from the express powers that allow Congress to carry out its functions.

necessary and proper clause
The clause in the Constitution (Article I, Section 8, Clause 3) setting forth the implied powers of Congress. It states that Congress, in addition to its express powers, has the right to make all laws necessary and proper to carry out all powers the Constitution vests in the national government.

inherent powers
The powers of the national government in foreign affairs that the Supreme Court has declared do not depend on constitutional grants but rather grow out of the very existence of the national government.

The National Supremacy Article

One of the most important constitutional pillars is found in Article VI: "This Constitution, and the Laws of the United States which shall be made in Pursuance thereof; and all Treaties made...under the Authority of the United States, shall be the supreme Law of the Land; and the Judges in every State shall be bound thereby; any Thing in the Constitution or Laws of any State to the Contrary notwithstanding." All officials, state as well as national, swear an oath to support the Constitution of the United States. States may not override national policies; this restriction also applies to local units of government because they are agents of the states.

National laws and regulations of federal agencies *preempt* the field, so that conflicting state and local regulations are unenforceable. States must abide by the national government's minimum wage laws, for example, but are allowed to set the minimum wage higher if they wish.

The War Power The national government is responsible for protecting the nation from external aggression, whether from other nations or from international terrorism. The government's power to protect national security includes the power to wage war. In today's world, military strength depends not only on the presence of troops in the field but also on the ability to mobilize the nation's industrial might and apply scientific and technological knowledge to the tasks of defense. As Charles Evans Hughes, who became chief justice in 1930, observed: "The power to wage war is the power to wage war successfully."[9] The national government is free to create "no-fly" zones only for its military aircraft both within and across state borders, for example, and may use any airports it needs during times of war or peace.

The Power to Regulate Interstate and Foreign Commerce Congressional authority extends to all commerce that affects more than one state. Commerce includes the production, buying, selling, renting, and transporting of goods, services, and properties. The **commerce clause** (Article I, Section 8, Clause 1) packs a tremendous constitutional punch; it gives Congress the power "to regulate Commerce with foreign Nations, and among the several States, and with the Indian Tribes." In these few words, the national government has found constitutional justification for regulating a wide range of human activity because few aspects of our economy today affect commerce in only one state and are thus outside the scope of the national government's constitutional authority.

The landmark ruling of *Gibbons* v. *Ogden* in 1824 affirmed the broad authority of Congress over interstate commerce. The case involved a New York state license that gave Aaron Ogden the exclusive right to operate steamboats between New York and New Jersey. Using the license, Ogden asked the New York state courts to stop Thomas Gibbons from running a competing ferry. Although Gibbons countered that his boats were licensed under a 1793 act of Congress governing vessels "in the coasting trade and fisheries," the New York courts sided with Ogden. Just as the national government and states both have the power to tax, the New York courts said they both had the power to regulate commerce.

commerce clause
The clause in the Constitution (Article I, Section 8, Clause 1) that gives Congress the power to regulate all business activities that cross state lines or affect more than one state or other nations.

The national military has the power to set restrictions on airspace so that it can fly anywhere across the country without approval of state or local governments.
■ *Why does the national government have the final say on national security issues?*

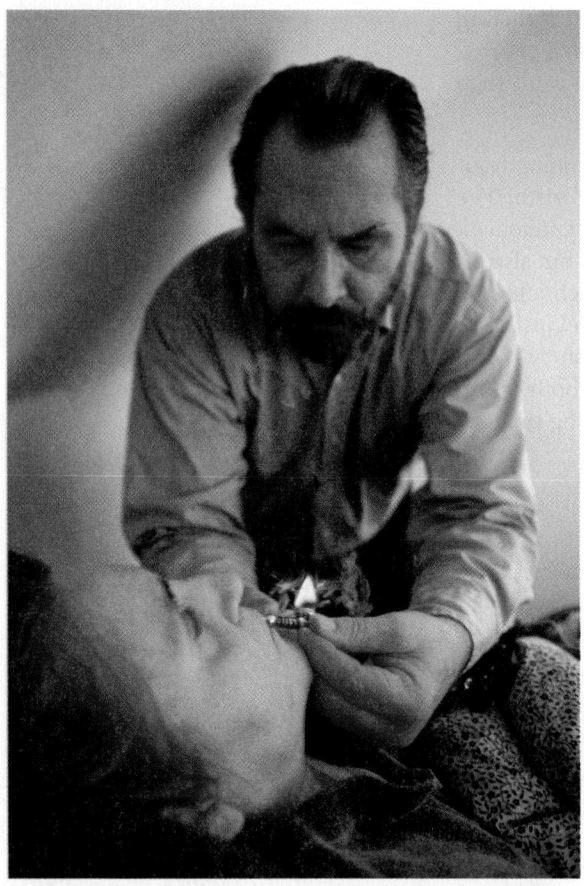

Though many states allow the use of medicinal marijuana, the Supreme Court decided that the national government could regulate its use in the states as a form of interstate commerce. ■ *Why did the Obama administration choose not to exercise this power to prohibit marijuana sales in states such as California that have legalized its use?*

Gibbons appealed to the Supreme Court and asked a simple question: Which government had the ultimate power to regulate interstate commerce? The Supreme Court gave an equally simple answer: The national government's laws were supreme.[10]

Gibbons v. *Ogden* was immediately heralded for promoting a national economic common market, in holding that states may not discriminate against interstate transportation and out-of-state commerce. The Supreme Court's brilliant definition of "commerce" as *intercourse among the states* provided the basis for national regulation of "things in commerce"[11] and an expanding range of economic activities, including the sale of lottery tickets,[12] prostitution,[13] radio and television broadcasts,[14] and telecommunications and the Internet.

The Power to Tax and Spend Congress lacks constitutional authority to pass laws solely on the grounds that they will promote the general welfare, but it may raise taxes and spend money for this purpose. For example, the national government lacks the power to regulate education or agriculture directly, but it does have the power to appropriate money to support education or to pay farm subsidies. By attaching conditions to its grants of money, the national government creates incentives that affect state action. If states want the money, they must accept the conditions.

When the national government provides the money, it determines how the money will be spent. By withholding or threatening to withhold funds, the national government can influence or control state operations and regulate individual conduct. For example, the national government has stipulated that federal funds should be withdrawn from any program in which any person is denied benefits because of race, color, national origin, sex, or physical handicap. The national government also used its "power of the purse" to force states to raise the drinking age to 21 by tying such a condition to federal dollars for building and maintaining highways.

Congress frequently requires states to provide specific programs—for example, provide services to indigent mothers and clean up the air and water. These requirements are called **federal mandates.** Often the national government does not supply the funds required to carry out "unfunded mandates" (discussed later in the chapter). Its failure to do so has become an important issue as states face growing expenditures with limited resources.

federal mandate
A requirement the national government imposes as a condition for receiving federal funds.

Powers of the States

The Constitution *reserves for the states all powers not granted to the national government,* subject only to the limitations of the Constitution. Only the states have the **reserve powers** to create schools and local governments, for example. Both are powers not given exclusively to the national government by the Constitution or judicial interpretation, so that states can exercise these powers as long as they do not conflict with national law.

The national and state governments also share powers. These **concurrent powers** with the national government include the power to levy taxes and regulate commerce internal to each state.

In general, states may levy taxes on the same items the national government taxes, such as incomes, alcohol, and gasoline, but a state cannot, by a tax, "unduly burden" commerce among the states, interfere with a function of the national government, complicate the operation of a national law, or abridge the terms of a treaty of the United States. Where the national government has not preempted the field,

Under national pressure, states have raised the drinking age to 21. States are also under pressure to monitor drunk driving more aggressively.

TABLE 2–1 The Constitutional Division of National and State Powers

Examples of Powers Delegated to the National Government	Examples of Powers Reserved for State Governments	Examples of Concurrent Powers Shared by the National and State Governments
Regulate trade and interstate commerce	Create local governments	Impose and collect taxes and fees
Declare war	Police citizens	Borrow and spend money
Create post offices	Oversee primary and elementary education	Establish courts
Coin money		Enact and enforce laws
		Protect civil rights
		Conduct elections
		Protect health and welfare

states may regulate interstate businesses, provided these regulations do not cover matters requiring uniform national treatment or unduly burden interstate commerce.

Who decides which matters require "uniform national treatment" or what actions might place an "undue burden" on interstate commerce? Congress does, subject to the president's signature and final review by the Supreme Court. When Congress is silent or does not clearly state its intent, the courts—ultimately, the Supreme Court—decide whether there is a conflict with the national Constitution or whether a state law or regulation has preempted the national government's authority.

Constitutional Limits and Obligations

To ensure that federalism works, the Constitution imposes restraints on both the national and the state governments. States are prohibited from doing the following:

1. Making treaties with foreign governments
2. Authorizing private persons to interfere with the shipping and commerce of other nations
3. Coining money, issuing bills of credit, or making anything but gold and silver coin legal tender in payment of debts
4. Taxing imports or exports
5. Taxing foreign ships
6. Keeping troops or ships of war in time of peace (except for the state militia, now called the National Guard)
7. Engaging in war

In turn, the Constitution requires the national government to refrain from exercising its powers, especially its powers to tax and to regulate interstate commerce, in such a way as to interfere substantially with the states' abilities to perform their responsibilities. But politicians, judges, and scholars disagree about whether the national political process—specifically the executive and the legislature—or the courts should ultimately define the boundaries between the powers of the national government and the states. Some argue that the states' protection from intrusions by the national government comes primarily from the political process because senators and representatives elected from the states participate in congressional decisions.[15] Others maintain that the Supreme Court should limit the national government's power and defend the states.[16]

On a case-by-case basis, the Court has held that the national government may not command states to enact laws to comply with or order state employees to enforce national laws. In *Printz* v. *United States,* the Court held that states were not required to conduct instant national background checks prior to selling a handgun.[17] Referring broadly to the concept of dual federalism discussed early in this chapter, the Supreme Court said that the national government could not "draft" local police to do its bidding. But as previously discussed, even if the national government cannot force states to enforce certain national laws, it can threaten to withhold its funding if states do not comply with national policies, such as lowering the minimum drinking age or speed limit.

reserve powers
All powers not specifically delegated to the national government by the Constitution. The reserve power can be found in the Tenth Amendment to the Constitution.

concurrent powers
Powers that the Constitution gives to both the national and state governments, such as the power to levy taxes.

The U.S. Supreme Court ruled that the national government cannot demand that states enforce the national law requiring handgun dealers to run background checks on potential buyers. States are free, however, to use a national registry of criminals in doing background checks, which almost all do. ■ *Should the national government extend gun control laws to flea markets, where guns are still sold without first checking the national registry? Under what authority could these laws be imposed?*

The Constitution also obliges the national government to protect states against *domestic insurrection*. Congress has delegated to the president the authority to dispatch troops to put down such insurrections when the proper state authorities request them.

Interstate Relationships

Three clauses in the Constitution, taken from the Articles of Confederation, require states to give full faith and credit to each other's public acts, records, and judicial proceedings; to extend to each other's citizens the privileges and immunities of their own citizens; and to return persons who are fleeing from justice.

Full Faith and Credit The **full faith and credit clause** (Article IV, Section 1), one of the more technical provisions of the Constitution, requires state courts to enforce the civil judgments of the courts of other states and accept their public records and acts as valid.[18] It does not require states to enforce the criminal laws or legislation and administrative acts of other states; in most cases, for one state to enforce the criminal laws of another would raise constitutional issues. The clause applies primarily to enforcing judicial settlements and court awards.

Interstate Privileges and Immunities Under Article IV, Section 2, individual states must give citizens of all other states the privileges and immunities they grant to their own citizens, including the protection of the laws, the right to engage in peaceful occupations, access to the courts, and freedom from discriminatory taxes. Because of this clause, states may not impose unreasonable residency requirements, that is, withhold rights to American citizens who have recently moved to the state and thereby have become citizens of that state.

full faith and credit clause
The clause in the Constitution (Article IV, Section 1) requiring each state to recognize the civil judgments rendered by the courts of the other states and to accept their public records and acts as valid.

extradition
The legal process whereby an alleged criminal offender is surrendered by the officials of one state to officials of the state in which the crime is alleged to have been committed.

interstate compact
An agreement among two or more states. Congress must approve most such agreements.

Extradition In Article IV, Section 2, the Constitution asserts that, when individuals charged with crimes have fled from one state to another, the state to which they have fled is to deliver them to the proper officials on demand of the executive authority of the state from which they fled. This process is called **extradition.** "The obvious objective of the Extradition Clause," the courts have claimed, "is that no State should become a safe haven for the fugitives from a sister State's criminal justice system."[19] Congress has supplemented this constitutional provision by making the governor of the state to which fugitives have fled responsible for returning them.

Interstate Compacts The Constitution also requires states to settle disputes with one another without the use of force. States may carry their legal disputes to the Supreme Court, or they may negotiate **interstate compacts.** Interstate compacts often establish interstate agencies to handle problems affecting an entire region. Before most interstate compacts become effective, Congress has to approve them. Then the compact becomes binding on all signatory states, and the federal judiciary can enforce its terms. A typical state may belong to 20 compacts dealing with such subjects as environmental protection, crime control, water rights, and higher education exchanges.[20]

The National Courts and Federalism

LEARNING **OBJECTIVE**

2.3 Assess the role of the national courts in defining the relationship between the national and state governments, and evaluate the positions of decentralists and centralists.

Although the political process ultimately decides how power will be divided between the national and the state governments, the national court system is often called on to umpire the ongoing debate about which level of government should do what, for whom, and to whom. The nation's highest court claimed this role in the celebrated case of *McCulloch* v. *Maryland.*

McCulloch v. *Maryland*

In *McCulloch* v. *Maryland* (1819), the Supreme Court had the first of many chances to define the division of power between the national and state governments.[21] Congress had established the Bank of the United States, but Maryland opposed any national bank and levied a $10,000 tax on any bank not incorporated in the state. James William McCulloch, the cashier of the bank, refused to pay on the grounds that a state could not tax an instrument of the national government.

Maryland was represented before the Court by some of the country's most distinguished lawyers, including Luther Martin, who had been a delegate to the Constitutional Convention. Martin said the Constitution did not expressly delegate to the national government the power to incorporate a bank. He maintained that the necessary and proper clause gives Congress only the power to choose those means and to pass those laws absolutely essential to the execution of its expressly granted powers. Because a bank is not absolutely necessary to the exercise of its delegated powers, he argued, Congress had no authority to establish it. As for Maryland's right to tax the bank, the power to tax is one of the powers reserved to the states; they may use it as they see fit.

Equally distinguished counsel, including Daniel Webster, represented the national government. Webster conceded that the power to create a bank is not one of the express powers of the national government. However, the power to pass laws necessary and proper to carry out Congress's express powers is specifically delegated to Congress. Although the power to tax is reserved to the states, Webster argued that states cannot interfere with the operations of the national government. The Constitution leaves no room for doubt; when the national and state governments have conflicts, the national government is supreme.

Speaking for a unanimous Court, Chief Justice John Marshall rejected every one of Maryland's contentions. He summarized his views on the powers of the national government in these now-famous words: "Let the end be legitimate, let it be within the scope of the Constitution, and all means which are appropriate, which are plainly adapted to that end, which are not prohibited, but consist with the letter and spirit of the constitution, are constitutional."

Having established the presence of *implied national powers,* Marshall then outlined the concept of **national supremacy.** No state, he said, can use its taxing powers to tax a national instrument. "The power to tax involves the power to destroy.... If the right of the States to tax the means employed by the general government be conceded, the declaration that the Constitution, and the laws made in pursuance thereof, shall be the supreme law of the land, is empty and unmeaning declamation."

It is difficult to overstate the long-range significance of *McCulloch* v. *Maryland* in providing support for the developing forces of nationalism and a unified economy. If the contrary arguments in favor of the states had been accepted, they would have strapped the national government in a constitutional straitjacket and denied it powers needed to deal with the problems of an expanding nation.

National Courts and the Relationship with the States

The authority of national judges to review the activities of state and local governments has expanded dramatically in recent decades because of modern judicial interpretations of the Fourteenth Amendment, which forbids states to deprive any person of life, liberty, or property without *due process of the law.* States may not deny any person the *equal protection of the laws,* including congressional legislation enacted to implement the Fourteenth Amendment. Almost every action by state and local officials is now subject to challenge before a federal judge as a violation of the Constitution or of national law.

Preemption occurs when a national law or regulation takes precedence over a state or local law or regulation. State and local laws are preempted not only when they conflict directly with national laws and regulations but also when they touch on a field in which the "federal interest is so dominant that the federal system will be assumed to preclude enforcement of state laws on the same subject."[22] Examples of federal preemption include laws regulating hazardous substances, water quality, clean air standards, and many civil rights acts, especially the Civil Rights Act of 1964 and the Voting Rights Act of 1965.

Throughout the years, federal judges, under the leadership of the Supreme Court, have generally favored the powers of the national government over those of the states. Despite the Supreme Court's recent bias in favor of state over national authority, few would deny the Supreme Court the power to review and set aside state actions. As Justice Oliver Wendell Holmes of the Supreme Court once remarked, "I do not think the United

national supremacy
A constitutional doctrine that whenever conflict occurs between the constitutionally authorized actions of the national government and those of a state or local government, the actions of the national government prevail.

preemption
The right of a national law or regulation to preclude enforcement of a state or local law or regulation.

States are responsible for registering voters, but the national government is responsible for assuring that state registration rules are Constitutional. ■ *How and why might state voter registration rules vary from state to state? Does this highlight a strength or weakness of federalism?*

States would come to an end if we lost our power to declare an Act of Congress void. I do think the Union would be imperiled if we could not make that declaration as to the laws of the several States."[23]

The Supreme Court and the Role of Congress

From 1937 until the 1990s, the Supreme Court essentially removed national courts from what had been their role of protecting states from acts of Congress. The Supreme Court broadly interpreted the commerce clause to allow Congress to do whatever Congress thought necessary and proper to promote the common good, even if national laws and regulations infringed on the activities of state and local governments.

In the past 15 years, however, the Supreme Court has signaled that national courts should be more active in resolving federalism issues.[24] The Court declared that a state could not impose term limits on its members of Congress, but it did so by only a 5-to-4 vote. Justice John Paul Stevens, writing for the majority, built his argument on the concept of the federal union as espoused by the great Chief Justice John Marshall, as a compact among the people, with the national government serving as the people's agent.

The Supreme Court also declared that the clause in the Constitution empowering Congress to regulate commerce with the Indian tribes did not give Congress the power to authorize national courts to hear suits against a state brought by Indian tribes.[25] Unless states consent to such suits, they enjoy "sovereign immunity" under the Eleventh Amendment. The effect of this decision goes beyond Indian tribes. As a result—except to enforce rights stemming from the Fourteenth Amendment, which the Court explicitly acknowledged to be within Congress's power—Congress may no longer authorize individuals to bring legal actions against states to force their compliance with national law in either national or state courts.[26]

Building on those rulings, the Court continues to press ahead with its "constitutional counterrevolution"[27] and return to an older vision of federalism from the 1930s. Among other recent rulings, in *United States* v. *Morrison,* the Court struck down the Violence Against Women Act, which had given women who are victims of violence the right to sue their attackers for damages.[28] Congress had found that violence against women annually costs the national economy $3 billion, but a bare majority of the Court held that gender-motivated crimes did not have a substantial impact on interstate commerce and that Congress had thus exceeded its powers in enacting the law and intruded on the powers of the states.

By the People

MAKING A DIFFERENCE

Monitoring the National Stimulus Package

In early 2009, Congress and President Barack Obama passed a nearly $800 billion spending package designed to stimulate the national economy. The number of unemployed Americans was rising fast, small businesses were closing, consumers were spending less, sales of new and old homes alike had fallen, and the economy was in the worst recession in decades. Under the stimulus, states were given nearly $260 billion to invest in projects that would put unemployed Americans back to work and restart the economy.

Much of this money was designed to support highway construction, new building projects, and scientific research but has been difficult to track. According to ongoing monitoring by the national government and outside groups, thousands of small companies are still receiving national dollars for a broad mix of projects.

Citizens can track the spending as a form of public service—the more they pay attention to the projects, the more the states pay attention to them. One way to monitor the spending is to pick a project and see what is actually happening. The first step in this monitoring is to find the project through Web sites such as recovery.gov or propublica.org. Citizens can click on a specific state at propublica.org, pick an individual county in that state, and see every project funded by the stimulus. Once citizens pick a project, they can visit the project and see what is actually happening. If the project is not even under way, citizens can report the inaction to the federal government through recovery.gov.

Colleges and universities have received a sizable amount of stimulus money. By early 2010, Florida's Alachua County had received more than $100 million. As home of the University of Florida, much of the money ended up in university research projects. According to the propublica.org list, the university received support for nearly 150 separate projects and student programs, while Santa Fe Community College received more than a dozen grants to support students with Pell Grants.

CRITICAL THINKING QUESTIONS

1. Why is monitoring the stimulus spending a form of public service?
2. What is the effect of visiting a project to see if it is working?
3. Does simply visiting the stimulus Web sites make any difference in telling Congress and the president that someone is watching?

University of Florida students conduct research with funds from the federal stimulus package.

These Supreme Court decisions—most of which split the Court 5 to 4 along ideological lines, with the conservative justices favoring states' rights—have signaled a shift in the Court's interpretation of the constitutional nature of our federal system. It is a shift that has been reinforced with the most recent Supreme Court appointments made by Presidents Bush and Obama. Chief Justice John Roberts and Justice Samuel Alito, each appointed by President George W. Bush, tend to favor the states, while justices Sonia Sotomayor and Elena Kagan, Obama appointees, tend to side with the national government.

The Great Debate Continues: Centralists Versus Decentralists

From the beginning of the Republic, there has been an ongoing debate about the "proper" distribution of powers, functions, and responsibilities between the national government and the states. Did the national government have the authority to outlaw slavery in the territories? Did the states have the authority to operate racially segregated schools? Could Congress regulate labor relations? Does Congress have the power to regulate the sale and use of firearms? Does Congress have the right to tell states how to clean up air and water pollution?

Today, the debate continues between **centralists,** who favor national action, and **decentralists,** who defend the powers of the states and favor action at the state and local levels on such issues as environmental and gun regulation.

centralists
People who favor national action over action at the state and local levels.

decentralists
People who favor state or local action rather than national action.

The Decentralist Position Among those favoring the decentralist or **states' rights** interpretation were the Antifederalists, Thomas Jefferson, the pre–Civil War statesman from South Carolina John C. Calhoun, the Supreme Court from the 1920s to 1937, and, more recently, Presidents Ronald Reagan and George H. W. Bush, the Republican leaders of Congress, former Chief Justice William H. Rehnquist, and current Justices Antonin Scalia and Clarence Thomas.

Most decentralists contend that the Constitution is basically a compact among sovereign states that created the central government and gave it limited authority. Thus the national government is little more than an agent of the states, and every one of its powers should be narrowly defined. Any question about whether the states have given a particular function to the central government or have reserved it for themselves should be resolved in favor of the states.

Decentralists believe that the national government should not interfere with activities reserved for the states. Their argument is based on the Tenth Amendment, which states: "The powers not delegated to the United States by the Constitution, nor prohibited by it to the States, are reserved to the States respectively, or to the people." Decentralists insist that state governments are closer to the people and reflect the people's wishes more accurately than the national government does.

Decentralists have been particularly supportive of the **devolution revolution,** which argues for returning responsibilities to the states.[29] In the 1990s, the Republican-controlled Congress gave states more authority over some programs such as welfare, and President Clinton also proclaimed, "The era of big government is over." However, he tempered his comments by adding, "But we cannot go back to the time when our citizens were left to fend for themselves," and despite its dramatic name, the revolution has fallen short of the hoped-for results.

Instead of a devolution revolution, the national government has actually grown stronger during the past decade. The national government has passed a number of laws that give states specific responsibilities in defending homeland security, including the implementation of national criteria for issuing driver's licenses. It has also ordered states not to sell any citizen's personal information to private companies, ended state regulation of mutual funds, nullified state laws that restrict telecommunication competition, and gave the national judiciary the power to prosecute a number of state and local crimes, including carjacking and acts of terrorism.

states' rights
Powers expressly or implicitly reserved to the states.

devolution revolution
The effort to slow the growth of the national government by returning many functions to the states.

Decentralists believe that education should be a state responsibility. However, because the national government provides money to the states, it has the power to impose strings on how the money is spent.
■ *What are some of the arguments for greater or less federal government involvement in public education?*

The Centralist Position The centralist position has been supported by presidents, Congress, and the Supreme Court. Presidents Abraham Lincoln, Theodore Roosevelt, Franklin Roosevelt, and Lyndon Johnson were particularly strong supporters, and the Supreme Court has generally ruled in favor of the centralist position.

Centralists reject the idea of the Constitution as an interstate compact. They view it as a supreme law established by the people. The national government is an agent of the people, not of the states, because it was the people who drew up the Constitution and created the national government. They intended that the national political process should define the central government's powers and that the national government be denied authority only when the Constitution clearly prohibits it from acting.

Centralists argue that the national government is a government of all the people, whereas each state speaks for only some of the people. Although the Tenth Amendment clearly reserves powers for the states, it does not deny the national government the authority to exercise all of its powers to the fullest extent. Moreover, the supremacy of the national government restricts the states because governments representing part of the people cannot be allowed to interfere with a government representing all of them.

The National Budget as a Tool of Federalism

LEARNING **OBJECTIVE**

2.4 Analyze the budget as a tool of federalism, and evaluate its impact on state and local governments.

Congress authorizes programs, establishes general rules for how the programs will operate, and decides whether room should be left for state or local discretion and how much. Most important, Congress appropriates the funds for these programs and generally has deeper pockets than even the richest states. Federal grants are one of Congress's most potent tools for influencing policy at the state and local levels.

Federal grants serve four purposes, the most important of which is the fourth:

1. To supply state and local governments with revenue
2. To establish minimum national standards for such things as highways and clean air
3. To equalize resources among the states by taking money from people with high incomes through federal taxes and spending it, through grants, in states where the poor live
4. To attack national problems but minimize the growth of federal agencies

Types of Federal Grants

The national government currently gives states three types of grants: *categorical-formula grants, project grants,* and *block grants* (sometimes called *flexible grants*). From 1972 to 1986, the national government also gave states a share of national tax revenues through *revenue sharing*. The program was terminated in an effort to reduce rising national budget deficits.

Categorical-Formula Grants The national government provides grants for specific purposes, such as promoting homeland security. By definition, these grants are distributed to the states based on population. Many categorical-formula grants require state governments to provide at least some of the total funding, often on a matching basis. Categorical-formula grants are tightly monitored to ensure that the money is spent exactly as directed. There are hundreds of grant programs, but two dozen, including Medicaid, account for more than half of total categorical-formula spending.

Project Grants The national government supports states through project grants for specific activities, such as scientific research, highway construction, and job training. Project grants are generally restricted to a fixed amount of time and can only be spent within tight guidelines. Many university-based medical schools rely on project grants to support their efforts to cure life-threatening diseases such as cancer and heart disease.

For the People
GOVERNMENT'S GREATEST ENDEAVORS

Supporting the States in Achieving National Goals

Throughout the decades, the national government has given state and local governments a long list of responsibilities for implementing national programs, such as health care for the poor, highway construction, and waste-water treatment. These programs involve important national goals for creating a healthy society and economy.

Most of these programs carry large amounts of national dollars, which allow the national government to set minimum standards for those who get unemployment insurance, public assistance, and medical care. National funds also offset state spending on both the administrative and program costs of achieving the national goals profiled throughout this book. But the national government relies on the states for the implementation of these programs.

Homeland security is a case in point. Following the 9/11 terrorist attacks on the World Trade Center and Washington, D.C. in 2001, the national government launched what President George W. Bush called the "war on terrorism." Local police departments are essential partners in the effort. They are linked to the national government through computer systems that contain the names of terrorist suspects and are often first at the scene of suspected terrorist acts such as the 2008 bombing of a Jewish center in New York City. The national government provides large amounts of funding to improve state and local defenses against terrorist attacks.

All totaled, the national government will spend nearly $600 billion in 2010 helping states achieve its broad goals for improving the quality of life in the United States, including $20 billion on transportation, $21 billion on education and job training, $43 billion on health care for the poor and substance abuse programs, and $36 billion on food and nutrition programs.* Although much of this money comes with tight restrictions on which citizens and projects qualify for funding, this spending indicates how much the national government is willing to invest in helping states help their citizens.

The national government works with state and local governments to ensure that airports are safe from terrorism. Baggage and passenger screeners are national government employees, but they work closely with local airports.

CRITICAL THINKING QUESTIONS

1. What are some of the advantages of national and local governments working collectively on problems like airport security? What are the disadvantages?
2. Why might the national government prefer working in cooperation with state governments?
3. How is airport security a form of marble cake federalism? How is it a form of cooperative federalism?

*SOURCE: U.S. Census Bureau, The 2010 Statistical Abstract: National Data Book, Table 419 (Washington, D.C.: U.S. Census Bureau, 2010).

Block Grants Block grants are broad grants to states for specific activities, such as public assistance, child care, education, social services, preventive health care, and health services. By definition, these blocks of funding are provided with very few requirements attached. States have great flexibility in deciding how to spend block grant dollars, but unlike programs such as national unemployment insurance that are guaranteed for everyone who qualifies for them, block grants are limited to specific amounts set by the national government.

The Politics of Federal Grants

Republicans "have consistently favored fewer strings, less federal supervision, and the delegation of spending discretion to the state and local governments."[30] Democrats have generally been less supportive of broad discretionary block grants, instead favoring more detailed, federally supervised spending. The Republican-controlled Congress in the 1990s gave high priority to creating block grants, but it ran into trouble when it tried to lump together welfare, school lunch and breakfast programs, prenatal nutrition programs, and child protection programs in one block grant.

The battle over national versus state control of spending tends to be cyclical. As one scholar of federalism explains, "Complaints about excessive federal control tend to be followed by proposals to shift more power to state and local governments. Then, when problems arise in state and local administration—and problems inevitably arise when any organization tries to administer anything—demands for closer federal supervision and tighter federal controls follow."[31]

The Americans with Disabilities Act of 1990 required state and local governments to improve access to buildings and public transportation for people with disabilities. The law covers all public colleges and universities. ■ *Why is enforcing the Americans with Disabilities Act so costly for state and local governments?*

Unfunded Mandates

Fewer federal dollars do not necessarily mean fewer federal controls. On the contrary, the national government has imposed mandates on states and local governments, often without providing federal funds. State and local officials complained about this, and their protests were effective. The Unfunded Mandates Reform Act of 1995 was championed by then-House Republican Speaker Newt Gingrich as part of the GOP's Contract with America. The act was considered part of what commentators called the "Newt Federalism."

The law requires Congress to evaluate the impact of unfunded mandates and imposes mild constraints on Congress itself. A congressional committee that approves any legislation containing a federal mandate must draw attention to the mandate in its report and describe its cost to state and local governments. If the committee intends any mandate to be partially unfunded, it must explain why it is appropriate for state and local governments to pay for it.

At least during its first 15 years, the Unfunded Mandates Reform Act has been mostly successful in restraining mandates.[32] According to the National Conference of State Legislatures, the national government has enacted only 11 laws that impose unfunded mandates. Three of these unfunded mandates involved increases in the minimum wage that apply to all state and local employees.

The Politics of Federalism

LEARNING **OBJECTIVE**

2.5 Evaluate the current relationship between the national and state governments and the future challenges for federalism.

The formal structures of our federal system have not changed much since 1787, but the political realities, especially during the past half-century, have greatly altered the way federalism works. To understand these changes, we need to look at some of the trends that continue to fuel the debate about the meaning of federalism.

The Growth of National Government

Throughout the past two centuries, power has accrued to the national government. As the Advisory Commission on Intergovernmental Relations observed in a 1981 report, "No one planned the growth, but everyone played a part in it."[33]

YOU WILL DECIDE Should the No Child Left Behind Act Be Renewed?

Early in 2002, President George W. Bush signed the No Child Left Behind Act into law, thereby creating one of the most significant mandates ever imposed on the states. Although primary and secondary education has long been considered an almost exclusive responsibility of state and local governments, the No Child Left Behind Act required states to create a new system of standardized testing for every public school. States could either implement the new mandate or lose their federal funding, which amounts to approximately 10 percent of all school budgets.

Under the No Child Left Behind Act, schools were required to adopt a number of separate reforms for improving student achievement. Students in grades three through eight were to be tested each year in reading and math, while students in high school were to be tested at least once in reading, math, and science. Based on the test results, schools were also required to show academic progress or risk the possibility of losing national funds.

Like many national laws, however, the No Child Left Behind Act is not permanent. It must be renewed every five years, which means that it can be changed. As they gain more experience with the act, parents and teachers will have more influence over the future of the tests and report cards that now govern their schools. Despite the five-year time limit, the law had not been formally reauthorized by September 2010, but continued to operate under a temporary extension.

What do you think? Should the No Child Left Behind Act be renewed? What arguments would you make for or against such an idea?

THINKING IT THROUGH

Parents and teachers already seem to agree that the No Child Left Behind Act created two problems that may need congressional attention.

First, some parents and teachers complain that instead of inspiring schools to focus on reading, math, and science, the act may encourage them to "teach to the test"—to prep students on how to take tests in reading, math, and science. There is no question, for example, that primary school students now spend enormous amounts of time practicing for the annual reading and math tests or that teachers are being encouraged to produce the highest scores possible, even if that occasionally means giving students extra practice on the test instead of instruction on basic skills. There have also been several highly publicized scandals in which schools cheated on the tests.

Second, parents and teachers worry that the national government has not provided enough funding to make the law work. Failing public schools cannot be improved simply by giving parents the right to remove their children, if only because they may not be able to find a better school. Moreover, new programs such as mentoring, afterschool tutoring, and summer school cost money that is often in short supply in large, urban school districts. These districts may also have much higher proportions of students who speak English as a second language, which can lead to lower test scores.

Despite these concerns, the act is almost certain to be renewed. Even though some say it focuses on testing, not learning, No Child Left Behind has created significant pressure for higher performance. The question is how its provisions might be changed to increase success.*

Actor Matthew McConaughey volunteers for Teach for America, a program that helps public schools by training young college graduates to spend two years teaching low-income students.

Critical Thinking Questions

1. What changes do you recommend when Congress and the president renew the No Child Left Behind Act?
2. Why does the support of teachers and parents matter to renewal of the No Child Left Behind Act?
3. Does the act ask too much of state and local governments given that the national government supplies only 10 percent of all school funding?
4. Should the national government be involved in issues like public education to make sure all states act the same way?

* Laura S. Hamilton et al., "Passing or Failing? A Midterm Report Card for 'No Child Left Behind,' " RAND Review, 31 (Fall 2007), pp. 16–25.

This shift occurred for a variety of reasons. One is that many of our problems have become national in scope. Much that was local in 1789, in 1860, or in 1930 is now national, even global. State governments could supervise the relationships between small merchants and their few employees, for instance, but only the national government can supervise relationships between multinational corporations and their thousands of worldwide employees, many of whom are organized in national unions.

As the economy grew rapidly during the early nineteenth century, powerful interests made demands on the national government. Business groups called on the government for aid in the form of tariffs, a national banking system, subsidies to railroads and the merchant marine, and uniform rules on the environment. Farmers learned that the national government could give more aid than the states, and they too began to demand help. By the beginning of the twentieth century, urban groups in general and organized labor in particular were pressing their claims. Big business, big agriculture, and big labor all added up to big government.

The growth of the national economy and the creation of national transportation and communications networks altered people's attitudes toward the national government. Before the Civil War, citizens saw the national government as a distant, even foreign, entity. Today, in part because of television and the Internet, most people know more about Washington than they know about their state capitals, and they know more about the president and their national legislators than about their governor, their state legislators, or even the local officials who run their cities and schools.

The Great Depression of the 1930s stimulated extensive national action on welfare, unemployment, and farm surpluses. World War II brought federal regulation of wages, prices, and employment, as well as national efforts to allocate resources, train personnel, and support engineering and inventions. After the war, the national government helped veterans obtain college degrees and inaugurated a vast system of support for university research. The United States became the most powerful leader of the free world, maintaining substantial military forces even in times of peace.

Although economic and social conditions created many of the pressures for expanding the national government, so did political claims. Once established, federal programs generate groups with vested interests in promoting, defending, and expanding them. Associations are formed and alliances are made. "In a word, the growth of government has created a constituency of, by, and for government."[34] The national budget can become a negative issue for Congress and the president if it grows too large, however. With the federal budget deficit rising rapidly in 2010, the Obama Administration was forced to back away from some of its largest spending programs and promise greater restraint.

The politics of federalism are changing, however, and Congress is being pressured to reduce the size and scope of national programs, while dealing with the demands for homeland security. Meanwhile, the cost of entitlement programs such as Social Security and Medicare are rising because there are more older people and they are living longer. These programs have widespread public support and to cut them is politically risky. "With all other options disappearing, it is politically tempting to finance tax cuts by turning over to the states many of the social programs . . . that have become the responsibility of the national government."[35]

The Future of Federalism

During recent decades, state governments have undergone a major transformation. Most have improved their governmental structures, taken on greater roles in funding education and welfare, launched programs to help distressed cities, expanded their tax bases by allowing citizens to deduct their state and local taxes from the national income tax, and assumed greater roles in maintaining homeland security and in fighting corporate corruption.

After the civil rights revolution of the 1960s, segregationists feared that national officials would work for racial integration. Thus, they praised local government, emphasized the dangers of centralization, and argued that the protection of civil rights was not a proper function of the national government. As one political scientist observed, "Federalism has a dark history to overcome. For nearly 200 years, states' rights have been asserted to protect slavery, segregation, and discrimination."[36]

Today, the politics of federalism, even with respect to civil rights, is more complicated than in the past. The national government is not necessarily more sympathetic to the claims of minorities than state or city governments are. Rulings on same-sex marriages and "civil unions" by state courts interpreting their state constitutions have extended more protection for these rights than has the Supreme Court's interpretation of the U.S. Constitution. Other states, however, are passing legislation that would eliminate such protections, and opponents are pressing for a constitutional amendment to bar same-sex marriages.

The national government is not likely to retreat to a more passive role. Indeed, international terrorism, the wars in Afghanistan and Iraq, and rising deficits have substantially altered the underlying economic and social conditions that generated the demand for federal action. In addition to such traditional challenges as helping people find jobs and preventing inflation and depressions—which still require national action—combating terrorism and surviving in a global economy based on the information explosion, e-commerce, and advancing technologies have added countless new issues to the national agenda.

Most American citizens have strong attachments to our federal system—in the abstract. They remain loyal to their states and show a growing skepticism about the national government. Yet, evidence suggests the anti-Washington sentiment "is 3,000 miles wide but only a few miles deep."[37] The fact is that we are pragmatists: We appear to prefer federal–state–local power sharing and are prepared to use whatever levels of government are necessary to meet our needs and new challenges.[38]

Federalism can be a source of great reward for the people, especially when it allows states to lead the nation in creating new programs to address problems such as global warming and health care access. If the people cannot move the national government toward action, they can always push their state and local governments. By giving them different leverage points to make a difference, the Constitution guarantees that government *is* by the people.

Federalism can also be a source of enormous frustration, especially when national and state governments disagree on basic issues such as civil rights and liberties. This is when the people need to step forward not as citizens of their states but as citizens of the nation as a whole. Even as they influence their state and local governments, the people must understand they have a national voice that often needs to be heard.

CHAPTER **SUMMARY**

2.1 Interpret the definitions of federalism, and assess the advantages and disadvantages of the American system of federalism.

A federal system is one in which the constitution divides powers between the central government and lower-level governments such as states or provinces. But, over time, there has been support for different balances between state and government power such as the shift from dual federalism to marble cake federalism. The federal system in the United States does protect us from tyranny, permit local variation in policy, and encourage experimentation, but it comes at the cost of greater complexity, conflict, and difficulty in determining exactly which level of government is responsible for providing which goods and services that citizens might demand.

2.2 Differentiate the powers the Constitution provides to national and state governments.

The Constitution provides three types of powers to the national and state governments: delegated powers to the national government, reserve powers for the states, and concurrent powers that the national and state governments share. Beyond delegated powers, the national government also has implied powers under the necessary and proper clause and inherent powers during periods of war and national crisis.

The national government's power over the states stems primarily from several constitutional pillars: the national supremacy clause, the war powers, its powers to regulate commerce among the states to tax and spend, and its power to do what Congress thinks is necessary and proper to promote the general welfare and to provide for the common defense. These constitutional pillars have permitted tremendous expansion of the functions of the national government.

2.3 Assess the role of the national courts in defining the relationship between the national and state governments, and evaluate the positions of decentralists and centralists.

The national courts umpire the division of power between the national and state governments. The Marshall Court, in decisions such as *Gibbons* v. *Ogden* and *McCulloch* v. *Maryland,* asserted the power of the national government over the states and promoted a national economic common market. These decisions also reinforced the supremacy of the national government over the states.

Today, debates about federalism are less often about its constitutional structure than about whether action should come from the national or the state and local levels. Recent Supreme Court decisions favor a decentralist position and signal shifts in the Court's interpretation of the constitutional nature of our federal system.

2.4 Analyze the budget as a tool of federalism, and evaluate its impact on state and local governments.

The major instruments of national intervention in state programs have been various kinds of financial grants-in-aid, of which the most prominent are categorical-formula grants, project grants, and block grants. The national government also imposes federal mandates and controls activities of state and local governments by other means.

2.5 Evaluate the current relationship between the national and state governments and the future challenges for federalism.

The national government has grown dramatically throughout the past 200 years. Its budget dwarfs many state budgets combined. As it has grown, the national government has asked states to do more on its behalf. States have pressed back against the national government, however, and continue to fight for their authority to use powers that are reserved for them under the Constitution.

CHAPTER **SELF-TEST**

2.1 Interpret the definitions of federalism, and assess the advantages and disadvantages of the American system of federalism.

1. Match each term with its appropriate definition:

a. Dual federalism	i. The power of the national government is limited in favor of the broad powers reserved to the states
b. Cooperative federalism	ii. All levels of government are engaged in a variety of policy areas, without rigid divisions between governmental jurisdictions
c. Marble cake federalism	iii. Local governments, state governments, and the national government offer various "packages" of taxes and services, and citizens can choose which package they like best
d. Competitive federalism	iv. A system that requires intergovernmental support to deliver goods and services to the people
e. Permissive federalism	v. Limited powers are given to the national government, while the rest are retained by the states; the Supreme Court resolves disputes between the two
f. New federalism	vi. Power is shared between the state and national governments, but the national government determines what powers are given to the states

2. Canada has a central government in Ottawa, the nation's capital, along with ten provinces and three territories, each of which has its own government. According to Canada's constitution, both the provinces and the central government have powers to tax and regulate individual citizens. Which type of government best describes Canada?
   a. A unitary state
   b. A cooperative federalist state
   c. A confederation
   d. A territorial union
3. Federalism affords five benefits to its citizens. List each benefit along with a sentence or two that describes it.

2.2 Differentiate the powers the Constitution provides to national and state governments.

4. Determine whether the following powers are delegated to the national government, reserved for the states, or shared by both:
   a. Power to establish courts
   b. Power to tax citizens and businesses
   c. Express powers stated in the Constitution
   d. Power to oversee primary and elementary education
   e. Inherent powers to present a united front to foreign powers
5. In one paragraph, explain the national supremacy article and discuss its consequences for state and local governments.
6. Create a diagram showing the relationships among *express, implied, inherent, reserved*, and *concurrent* powers.

2.3 Assess the role of the national courts in defining the relationship between the national and state governments, and evaluate the positions of decentralists and centralists.

7. In a few sentences, discuss the "constitutional counterrevolution" instigated by Chief Justice William Rehnquist and continued by Chief Justice John Roberts.
8. Discuss *McCulloch* v. *Maryland* and the reasons for its importance to federalism.
9. Write a persuasive essay appraising whether the balance of governmental power should lean more toward either

the national government or the states. Note the main arguments of both centralists and decentralists, and then refute the arguments of the side you disagree with.

2.4 Analyze the budget as a tool of federalism, and evaluate its impact on state and local governments.

10. Give an example of a program funded by (1) a *categorical-formula grant*, (2) a *project grant*, and (3) a *block grant*.
11. Identify which of the following is an example of a *federal mandate*:
    a. The New York state legislature passes a law requiring all New York school teachers to spend ten hours a year learning new teaching techniques.
    b. Congress passes a law requiring all coal plants in the United States to reduce their carbon emissions by 30 percent by 2015.
    c. The Supreme Court upholds a law requiring teenage women to get parental permission before having an abortion.
    d. The Federal Emergency Management Agency sends funds from the national government to help clean up after a tornado.
12. Explain why unfunded mandates can cause problems.

2.5 Evaluate the current relationship between the national and state governments and the future challenges for federalism.

13. Write an essay that explains the reasons for the growth of the national government since the founding and that outlines the pressures that exist today that encourage further expansion of the national government.
14. Analyze the arguments for and against turning over to the states many of the economic and social programs that have become the responsibility of the national government, and write a persuasive essay that advocates one of these positions.

Answers to selected questions: 1. a. i; b. iv; c. ii; d. iii; e. vi; f. v. 2. b 4. a. both; b. both; c. national; d. states; e. national 11. b

mypoliscilab™ EXERCISES

Where participation leads to action!

Apply what you learned in this chapter on MyPoliSciLab.

Read on **mypoliscilab.com**

eText: Chapter 2

Study and **Review** on **mypoliscilab.com**

Pre-Test
Post-Test
Chapter Exam
Flashcards

Watch on **mypoliscilab.com**

Video: The Real ID
Video: Water Wars
Video: Proposition 8

Explore on **mypoliscilab.com**

Simulation: You Are a Federal Judge
Simulation: You Are a Restaurant Owner
Comparative: Comparing Federal and Unitary Systems
Timeline: Federalism and the Supreme Court
Visual Literacy: Federalism and Regulations

KEY TERMS

federalism, p. 50
unitary system, p. 51
confederation, p. 51
delegated (express) powers, p. 56
implied powers, p. 56
necessary and proper clause, p. 56
inherent powers, p. 56
commerce clause, p. 57
federal mandate, p. 58
reserve powers, p. 59
concurrent powers, p. 59
full faith and credit clause, p. 60
extradition, p. 60
interstate compact, p. 60
national supremacy, p. 61
preemption, p. 61
centralists, p. 63
decentralists, p. 63
states' rights, p. 64
devolution revolution, p. 64

ADDITIONAL **RESOURCES**

FURTHER READING

SAMUEL H. BEER, *To Make a Nation: The Rediscovery of American Federalism* (Harvard University Press, 1993).

MICHAEL BURGESS, *Comparative Federalism Theory and Practice* (Routledge, 2006).

CENTER FOR THE STUDY OF FEDERALISM, *The Federalism Report* (published quarterly by Temple University; this publication notes research, books and articles, and scholarly conferences).

CENTER FOR THE STUDY OF FEDERALISM, *Publius: The Journal of Federalism* (published quarterly by Temple University; one issue each year is an "Annual Review of the State of American Federalism"; Web site is www.lafayette.edu/~publius).

TIMOTHY J. CONLAN, *From New Federalism to Devolution: Twenty-Five Years of Intergovernmental Reforms* (Brookings Institution Press, 1998).

DANIEL J. ELAZAR AND **JOHN KINCAID,** EDS., *The Covenant Connection: From Federal Theology to Modern Federalism* (Lexington Books, 2000).

NEIL C. MCCABE, ED., *Comparative Federalism in the Devolution Era* (Rowman & Littlefield, 2002).

PIETRO NIVOLA, *Tense Commandments: Federal Prescriptions and City Problems* (Brookings Institution Press, 2002).

JOHN T. NOONAN, *Narrowing the Nation's Power: The Supreme Court Sides with the States* (University of California Press, 2002).

WILLIAM H. RIKER, *The Development of American Federalism* (Academic Press, 1987).

DENISE SCHEBERLE, *Federalism and Environmental Policy: Trust and the Politics of Implementation* (Georgetown University Press, 2004).

KEVIN SMITH, ED., *State and Local Government, 2008–2009* (CQ Press, 2008).

CARL VAN HORN, ED., *The State of the States*, 4th ed. (CQ Press, 2008).

WEB SITES

www.OPM.gov The national government's Web site for all information on the civil service system. It contains the Factbook of basic demographic information on every federal employee.

www.USAjobs.gov The national government's Web site listing all available jobs. Also provides application information and online application forms.

www.USASpending.gov The national government's summary of all spending activity. Includes charts and graphs on overall spending trends and amounts of funding dedicated to specific programs.

www.ourpublicservice.org The Partnership for Public Service Web site. The Partnership is dedicated to improving the national government's workforce.

www.govexec.com The Web site for *Government Executive* magazine. The magazine provides a news stream on current news affecting the national bureaucracy.

PART II The Political Process

THE BIG PICTURE

Throughout the course of U.S. history, the role of the people in government has expanded significantly. In this section, we examine how people influence each other and impact their government. We begin by examining the U.S. political culture and the widely shared values people hold. Social and economic attributes of individuals like age, income, race, and education are often predictive of participation, vote choice, and attitudes. Although individual attributes and characteristics are important, much of politics is done through groups. How groups form and compete in our political system, their relative importance over time and across issues, and how government can harness the positive elements of groups without being captured by them are also main themes of this part of the book. Political parties are especially important to the functioning of democracy. How parties are formed and why they endure are important questions we explore.

The importance of measuring and understanding public opinion has grown as the role of people in our government has grown. How people see the political world is influenced by many factors, including their upbringing, peers, the media, and education. Americans vote more often and for more offices than do the citizens of any other democracy, and voting is only one of the modes of political participation people can engage in. Campaigns and elections seek to mobilize voters and persuade them to vote for one candidate or against the other, or to vote for or against a particular ballot measure. Understanding how elections are structured and conducted is important in assessing the strengths and weaknesses of our electoral democracy. One important source of information is the media. The media we turn to for news about the world has changed over time. An informed public is vital to meaningful participation.

COURSE LEARNING **OBJECTIVES**

CHAPTER 3 The American Political Landscape

Describe how geographic and demographic differences among Americans affect political beliefs and policy preferences.

The diversity of the U.S. population is important to American politics. Holding aside Native Americans and slaves who came here against their will, the remaining population descends from or are themselves immigrants. Such personal characteristics as ethnicity, gender, race, sexual orientation, income, education, occupation, and age are predictive of behaviors and attitudes that influence American politics. Where we live is also important because in our federal system people identify with their state. Differences also exist between those who live in rural, urban, or suburban areas. Yet all Americans are bound by a shared political culture consisting of common values about the worth and importance of individuals; a commitment to majority rule; free and fair elections; freedom of speech, press, and religion; limited government; and economic liberty. Political culture is learned in the family, reinforced in schools, and influenced by the media.

CHAPTER 4 Political Parties and Interest Groups

Explain the role of political parties in American government, and evaluate the efforts of interest groups to influence elections and legislation.

Political parties facilitate much of the workings of democratic government. Parties recruit and help elect candidates, simplify voting choices, and help organize government. Our electoral rules foster a two-party system, which has been competitive and stable over time. Parties are responsive to the views of party adherents and change positions over time. Occasionally new parties arise, and the public realigns with the parties. Most people have a party preference, although the strength of that affiliation varies. Parties raise money from individuals and interest groups and spend money in ways designed to foster electoral competition.

Interest groups arise when people with similar political interests organize to pursue those objectives. Interest groups vary in their size, resources, cohesiveness, leadership, and the techniques the group uses in attempting to influence government. Many groups are represented before government by lobbyists, individuals knowledgeable about the group and how the government works. Groups also attempt to build relationships with elected officials by funding their campaigns and by providing information to them. Government has attempted to check the power of any particular interest group through regulations and by encouraging interest group competition.

CHAPTER 5 Public Opinion and Participation

Explain differences in opinions and rates of participation, and evaluate the importance of public opinion and participation in a democracy.

Representative government is presumed to reflect the will of the people. Politicians, the media, and academics all want to measure public opinion. People have different levels of interest, awareness, and opinions on issues and adhere in varying degrees to political ideologies. To gauge public opinion accurately requires the application of scientific principles and care in asking questions. Opinions can change.

People in the United States have many ways they can participate in politics. Rates of participation are linked to education and age and vary by type of election or political activity. The most common form of participation is voting. Turnout varies by type of election and the interest of the voters. Better-educated and older persons vote more often. Party identification is an important predictor of how people vote, as are candidate appeal and issues.

CHAPTER 6 Campaigns, Elections, and the Media

Describe the rules for elections in America, and assess the impact of the media on elections, public opinion, and governance.

America's winner-takes-all rule in American elections encourages a two-party system. The electoral college system of choosing a president reinforces federalism but means the popular vote winner does not necessarily win the White House. Presidents are elected through state caucuses and primaries, a convention, and then the general election. Not all elections in the United States are competitive. Incumbents have important advantages and generally win in congressional contests. Successful candidates must be able to raise large amounts of money, much of it from individuals or groups with particular interests or agendas. Concerns over the influence of money on elections have led to reform efforts.

How people learn about politics and what events become news are influenced by the news media. Over time, the media has evolved and now includes newspapers, radio, television, the Internet, and even social media, like Facebook. People selectively attend to and interpret what news they see and hear. The media are important to election campaigns and debates over public policy and can provide an important check on the government.

CHAPTER 3

The American Political Landscape

A Land of Diversity

3.1 Relate differences in political culture to where people live and assess the importance of geography to the development of the U.S.

A Diverse People

3.2 Analyze how demographic factors—including race and ethnicity, religion, gender, family structures, education, income, class, and age—affect American politics.

The American Political Culture

3.3 Identify the most important elements of and sources for the American political culture.

Unity in a Land of Diversity

3.4 Evaluate the degree to which America has achieved a measure of unity in a land of diversity.

In recent elections, both parties have developed the ability to target their political communications to individual voters based on computer models they have developed from historic patterns and large sample-size polls that assess attitudes toward issues and candidates. This process is sometimes called data mining. Ohio Republican party chair Robert Bennett said, "We probably have more information about the average voter than they care for us to have."[1] The Republicans took the lead in this "microtargeting" activity in 2002 and 2004 with a massive voter file housed at the Republican National Committee named the "Voter Vault." Individuals who had been registered Republicans or who fit a certain profile in their age, gender, religion, and race were targeted for particular communications. New York U.S. Senator Charles Schumer, who headed the Democratic Senatorial Campaign Committee at the time, said of the GOP use of data in voter mobilization efforts: "In 2002 and 2004, the morning of Election Day, we thought we were going to win and we didn't. And the reason we didn't win the seats we thought we were going to win was because they had a much better get-out-the-vote operation."[2]

By 2008, the Democratic allies had heavily invested in their own voter files using a for-profit corporation called Catalist. Catalist lists among its clients Planned Parenthood, labor unions, Sierra Club, Rock the Vote, and other Democratic-leaning groups, and its files include more than 220 million names. Those doing the data mining and modeling can combine gender and age with consumer preferences—like the kind of cars a person owns or what types of magazines people read—to predict the message to which that voter will be most receptive. Among the variables in the Voter Vault and Catalist that are most important in predictive models are age, income, education, gender, religion, race, sexual orientation, partisanship, and ideology. In this chapter, we examine the political importance of several of these characteristics of individuals.

Do these social and economic differences still matter in American politics? The answer is clearly yes. In the United States, we celebrate our diversity and our immigrant past and proudly recite the words of Emma Lazarus, inscribed at the base of the Statue of Liberty: "Give me your tired, your poor, your huddled masses yearning to breathe free." Albert Einstein, who himself immigrated to the United States from Germany in the 1930s, once said that most people are incapable of expressing opinions that differ much from the prejudices of their social upbringing.[3] This **ethnocentrism**—selective perception based on our background, attitudes, and biases—is not uncommon. People often assume that others share their economic opportunities, social attitudes, sense of civic responsibility, and self-confidence, so in this chapter, we consider how our social environment explains, or at least shapes, our opinions and prejudices. In this chapter, we will also discuss why some individuals have more political self-confidence than others, a characteristic called **efficacy.**

Understanding the American political landscape requires us to consider the political culture of the Unites States. Widely shared values like individualism, liberty, freedom, equality, private property, limited government, and popular consent were once unrealized ideas of political philosophers, but became part of the foundation of the American political culture. The idea that each successive generation can make progress economically and socially is not only part of candidates' campaign rhetoric but remain widely shared values and aspirations.

This chapter explores the effects of regional or state identity on political perspectives; how differences in race, ethnicity, gender, family structure, religion, wealth and income, occupation, and social class influence opinions and voting choices; and the relationship

ethnocentrism
Belief in the superiority of one's nation or ethnic group.

efficacy
A sense of self-confidence in being able to produce a desired effect.

among age, education, and political participation. People's personal characteristics or attributes are important to political interest groups and political parties (Chapter 4); public opinion, participation, and voting (Chapter 5); and campaigns and elections (Chapter 6). This chapter lays the foundation of how different aspects of who we are as people influence how we behave politically.

A Land of Diversity

LEARNING **OBJECTIVE**

3.1 Relate differences in political culture to where people live and assess the importance of geography to the development of the U.S.

Most nations consist of groups of people who have lived together for centuries and who speak the same language, embrace the same religious beliefs, and share a common history. Most Japanese citizens are Japanese in the fullest sense of the word, and this sense of shared identity is generally as strong in Sweden, Saudi Arabia, and China. The United States is different. We have attracted the poor and oppressed, the adventurous, and the talented from all around the world, and we have been more open to accepting strangers than many other nations.

In the pages that follow, we examine a variety of factors that shape individuals' political orientation and views on such issues as health care and economic policy. What becomes clear through this discussion is that, in a nation as geographically large and ethnically diverse as the United States, many characteristics differentiate us from each other. They can also unite us.

Several elements of our diversity have political significance. Many retain an identity with the land of their ancestors, even after three or four generations. Families, churches, and other close-knit ethnic groups foster these ties. **Political socialization** is the process by which parents and others teach children about political values, beliefs, and attitudes. This teaching occurs in the home, in school, on the playground, and in the neighborhood. In addition to fostering group identities, political socialization also strongly influences how individuals see politics and which political party they prefer. Where we live and who we are in terms of age, education, religion, and occupation affect how we vote. Social scientists use the term **demography** to describe the study of such population characteristics. Persons in certain demographic categories tend to vote alike and to share certain **political predispositions** that can predict political behavior, despite individual differences within socioeconomic and demographic categories.

When social and economic differences reinforce each other, social scientists call them **reinforcing cleavages;** they can make political conflict more intense and society more polarized. In Italy, for example, the tendency of parts of the industrialized north to lean toward the Socialist or Communist Party, and of the poorer and more agrarian south to be politically conservative and Catholic, reinforces the divide between north and south that has existed for centuries.

Nations can also have **cross-cutting cleavages,** when, instead of reinforcing each other, differences pull people in different directions. To illustrate, if all the rich people in a nation belong to one religion and the poor to another, the nation would have reinforcing cleavages that would intensify political conflict between the groups. But if there are both rich and poor in all religions, and if people sometimes vote on the basis of their religion and sometimes on the basis of their wealth, the divisions would be cross-cutting. American diversity has generally been more of the cross-cutting than the reinforcing type. As a result, people have multiple allegiances that lessen political conflict. Winning in the American electoral system requires building a broad coalition that reinforces cross-cutting cleavages.

political socialization
The process by which we develop our political attitudes, values, and beliefs.

demography
The study of the characteristics of populations.

political predisposition
A characteristic of individuals that is predictive of political behavior.

reinforcing cleavages
Divisions within society that reinforce one another, making groups more homogeneous or similar.

cross-cutting cleavages
Divisions within society that cut across demographic categories to produce groups that are more heterogeneous or different.

Geography and National Identity

The United States is a geographically large and historically isolated country. In the 1830s, French commentator Alexis de Tocqueville studied its early development and observed that the country had no major political or economic powers on its borders "and consequently no great wars, financial crises, invasions, or conquests to fear."[4]

Of the People
THE GLOBAL COMMUNITY

Restricting Immigration

Immigration is an issue in many countries, not only in the United States. The Pew Global Attitudes Project asked individuals: "Please tell me whether you completely agree, mostly agree, mostly disagree, or completely disagree with this statement: We should restrict and control entry of people into our country more than we do now." In the figure below, we have combined those who completely and mostly agree into one category and those who mostly and completely disagree into another.

In the worldwide sample, more than two-thirds of the people agree that immigration should be more restricted than it is today. The country that departs the most from this view is Japan, where more people disagree (53 percent) than agree (44 percent) with making immigration more restrictive. One possible explanation for this is that, as a matter of policy, Japan has historically had low levels of immigration. In China, a country that has also had very little immigration, a greater percentage of respondents favor further restrictions than in Japan (58 percent), but that percentage is significantly lower than in other countries in our sample of nations.

Nearly three-quarters of Americans favor further restrictions on immigration. But people in Nigeria, Britain, and India are even more uniformly of this view. A striking 86 percent of people in India favor more restrictions on immigration. This attitude may be a result of the perceived problems in India arising from immigrants from Bangladesh. Most illegal immigrants in the United States today come from Mexico, and yet in Mexico, 69 percent favor further restrictions on immigration. This may be explained in part by the presence of illegal immigrants in Mexico from other Central and South American countries.

CRITICAL THINKING QUESTIONS

1. Why are people outside of Japan generally inclined to want to further restrict immigration?
2. Why would so many people in Mexico favor further restrictions on immigration in their country?
3. On many questions we examine, as many as 10 percent or more do not know their views. That is not the case with immigration, where no more than 4 percent report not knowing their views. Why is this the case?

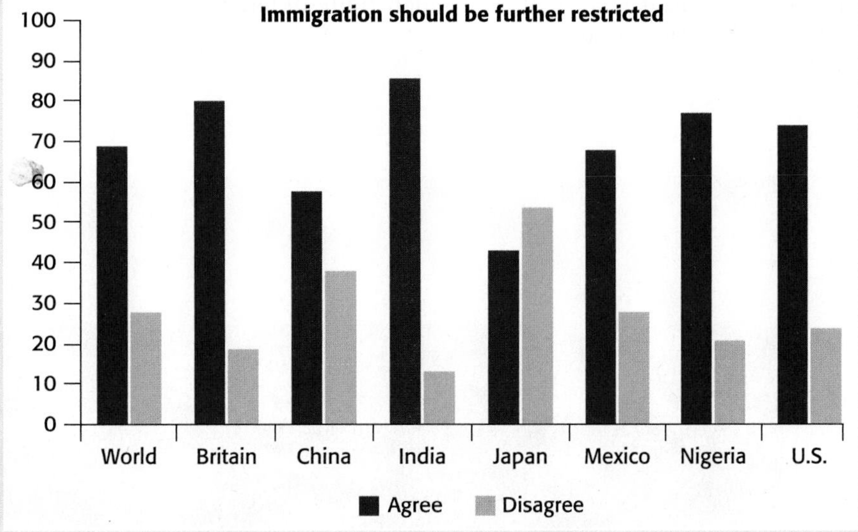

Geographic isolation from the major powers of the world during our government's formative period helps explain American politics.[5] The Atlantic Ocean served as a barrier to foreign meddling, giving us time to establish our political tradition and develop our economy.

Remarkably few foreign enemies have successfully struck within U.S. continental borders: most notably, England in the War of 1812, terrorists in the World Trade Center bombing in 1993, and the attacks of September 11, 2001.[6] Although geographic location may have previously provided a substantial buffer from foreign attack, technological advances make that less the case today. The ability of terrorists to harm the United States and other countries, especially if they are willing to die along with their victims, means that national defense and homeland security need to be rethought.

Size also confers an advantage. The Western frontier gave the expanding population of the United States room to spread out. This defused some of the political conflicts arising from religion, social class, and national origin because groups could isolate themselves from one another. Moreover, plentiful and accessible land helped foster the perspective that the United States had a **manifest destiny** to be a continental nation reaching from the Atlantic to the Pacific Ocean. Early settlers used this notion to justify taking land from Native Americans, Canadians, and Mexicans, especially the huge territory acquired after victory in the Mexican-American War.

The United States is also a land of abundant natural resources. We have rich farmland, which not only feeds our population but also makes us the largest exporter of food in the world.[7] We are rich in such natural resources as coal, iron, uranium, oil, and precious metals. All of these resources enhance economic growth, provide jobs, and stabilize government.

Our isolation, relative wealth, prosperity, and sense of destiny have fostered a view that the United States is different from the world. This *American exceptionalism*, a term first used by de Tocqueville in 1831, has historically been defined as "the perception that the United States differs qualitatively from other developed nations because of its unique origins, national credo, historical evolution, and distinctive political and religious institutions."[8] Exceptionalism can convey a sense of moral superiority or power that is not well received outside the United States, especially when the United States is seen to be acting in ways that other nations find objectionable or hypocritical.

Geography also helps explain our diversity. Parts of the United States are wonderfully suited to agriculture, others to mining or ranching, and still others to shipping and manufacturing. These differences produce diverse regional economic concerns, which in turn influence politics. For instance, a person from the agricultural heartland may see foreign trade differently from the way an automobile worker in Detroit sees it.

manifest destiny
A notion held by nineteenth-century Americans that the United States was destined to rule the continent, from the Atlantic to the Pacific.

The diversity of its natural resources, including farmland, forests, waterways, and coal mines, is one of the advantages of the United States' large landmass. ■ *To what specific aspects of America's national identity do these images speak?*

Regional Differences

Unlike the case in many other countries, geography in the United States does *not* define an ethnic or religious division. All the Serbians in the United States do not live in one place, nor do all French-speaking Catholics and Hispanic immigrants reside in others. Sectional, or regional, differences in the United States are primarily geographic, not ethnic or religious.

The most distinct section of the United States remains the South, although its differences from other parts of the country are diminishing. From the beginning of the Republic, the agricultural South differed from the North, where commerce and later manufacturing were more significant. But the most important difference between the regions was the institution of slavery. Northern opposition to slavery, which grew increasingly intense by the 1850s, reinforced sectional economic interests. The 11 Confederate states, by deciding to secede from the Union, reinforced a common political identity. After the Civil War, Reconstruction and the problems of race relations reinforced regional differences. The Civil War made the Democratic party the party of the South, and the Republican party (the party of Lincoln), the party of the North. The Democratic "solid South" remained a fixture of American politics for more than a century.

In addition to undergoing tremendous economic change, the large number of people moving to the South from other regions has diminished the sense of regional identity. The civil rights revolution of the 1960s eliminated legal and social barriers that prevented African Americans from voting, ended legal segregation, opened up new educational opportunities, and helped integrate the South into the national economy.

A Confederate flag flies outside South Carolina's memorial for Confederate soldiers ■ *Are there still significant regional differences that distinguish the U.S. South from other parts of the country?*

Starting in the mid 1960s, the South has become more reliably Republican. In 1992 and 1996, even with two southerners on the ticket—Bill Clinton and Al Gore—Democrats won only 4 of the 11 former Confederate states. In 2000 and 2004, Republican George W. Bush carried all 11 southern states, including Al Gore's home state of Tennessee in 2000 and vice presidential candidate John Edwards's home state of North Carolina in 2004. In 2008, Barack Obama made some inroads by winning in Florida, Virginia, and North Carolina, but in both North Carolina and Florida the margins were close.

The partisan shift in the South can also be seen in the rising percentage of state legislators who are Republicans, which grew from about 10 percent in the 1960s to nearly 50 percent in 2010. In 2010, Republicans controlled 8 of the 11 governorships in the former Confederate states. While remnants of the old Democratic "solid South" remain, politics in the region are becoming more predictably Republican.

Another sectional division is the **Sun Belt**—the 11 former Confederate states plus New Mexico, Arizona, Nevada, and the southern half of California. Sun Belt states are growing much more rapidly than the rest of the country (see Figure 3-1). Reapportionment has shifted seats in the House of Representatives to the Sun Belt, which has tended to help the Republican Party. Other sectional groupings of states include the "rust belt" of states in the Midwest where industrial production and jobs have left the region, leaving rusting factories vacant. States in the rust belt include Ohio, Pennsylvania, Michigan, and parts of Indiana and New York. The interior western states are another section with economic and political similarities. Much of the land in the West is owned by the federal government, which provides tension between state and local governments and the federal government.

Sun Belt
The region of the United States in the South and Southwest that has seen population growth relative to the rest of the country and which, because of its climate, has attracted retirees.

State and Local Identity

States have distinctive political cultures that affect public opinion and policies. Individuals often have a sense of identification with their state.[9] Part of the reason for

FIGURE 3–1 Percentage Change in Resident Population, 2000–2008.

■ *Which states saw the greatest shifts in population, and how might you account for some of those changes?*

SOURCE: U.S. Census Bureau, *Statistical Abstract of the United States: 2010* (U.S. Government Printing Office, 2009), p. 19.

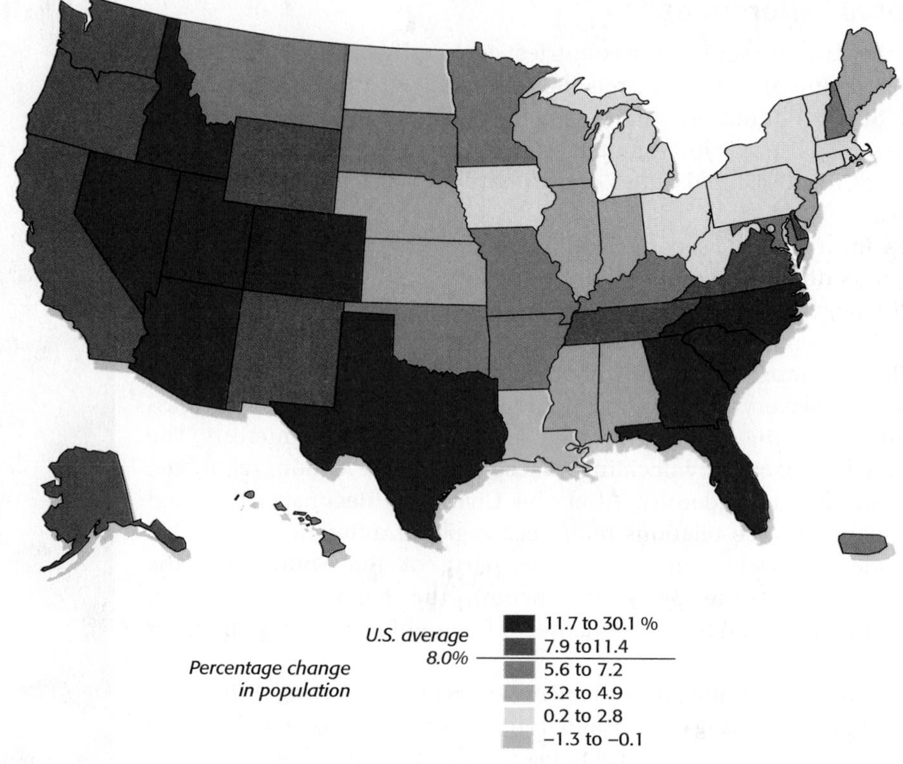

enduring state identities is that we elect members of Congress and the president at the state level. States such as Iowa and New Hampshire play important roles in narrowing the field of presidential candidates seeking their party's nomination. Differences in state laws relating to driving, drinking, gambling, and taxes reinforce the relevance of state identity. Colleges and universities may have the same effect while reinforcing competition between different states. California also stands out in American politics today, if only because nearly one of eight U.S. citizens lives in the state.[10] In economic and political importance, California is in a league by itself.

Urban and Rural Populations

Where we live can be categorized as one of three types of areas: **urban,** which is defined by the U.S. Census Bureau as "densely settled territory," also often the central part of a city; **suburban,** which is typically less densely settled and surrounds the central city; and **rural,** which is more sparsely populated areas and where farmers often reside. Four of five people in the United States now live in urban areas.[11] During the early twentieth century, the movement of population was from rural areas to central cities, which we call *urbanization,* but the movement since the 1950s has been from the central cities to their suburbs. Today, the most urban state is California (more than 94 percent of its population lives in cities or suburbs). Vermont is the least urban, with only 38 percent living in cities or suburbs.[12] Regionally, the West and Northeast are the most urban; the South and Midwest, the most rural.

urban
A densely settled territory that is often the central part of a city or metropolitan area.

suburban
An area that typically surrounds the central city, is often residential, and is not as densely populated.

rural
Sparsely populated territory and small towns, often associated with farming.

People move from cities to the suburbs for many reasons—better housing, new transportation systems that make it easier to get to work, a lower cost of living, the desire for cleaner air and safer streets. Another reason is "white flight," the movement of white people away from the central cities so that their children can avoid being bused for racial balance and attend generally better schools. White, middle-class migration to the suburbs has made American cities increasingly poor, African American, and Democratic.

Although four of five citizens live in urban areas, since approximately the 1950s, there has been a steady flow outward to the suburbs, particularly among the middle and upper classes.

A Diverse People

LEARNING **OBJECTIVE**

3.2 Analyze how demographic factors—including race and ethnicity, religion, gender, family structures, education, income, class, and age—affect American politics.

Sectional distinctions, which separate populations by geography and regions, less prominently distinguish us from one another in the United States today than they did a century or even a half-century ago. Today, we are more likely to define ourselves by a number of other characteristics, each of which may influence how we vote or think about candidates, issues, or policies.

Race and Ethnicity

Racial and ethnic differences have always had political significance. **Race** groups human beings with distinctive physical characteristics determined by genetic inheritance. Some scholars define it as more culturally determined than genetic.[13] **Ethnicity** is a social division based on national origin, religion, and language, often within the same race, and includes a sense of attachment to that group. Examples of ethnic groups with enduring relevance to American politics include Italian Americans, Irish Americans, Polish Americans, and Korean Americans, although most race and ethnicity issues in the United States today focus primarily on African Americans, Asian Americans, Native Americans, and Hispanics.

There are more than 39 million African Americans in the United States, nearly 13 percent of the population. Asian Americans constitute 4.4 percent of the population, and Native Americans, 1 percent.[14] Most American Hispanics classify themselves as white, although Hispanics can be of any race. At 46.9 million, Hispanics are the fastest-growing U.S. ethnic group, constituting nearly 15 percent of the population.[15] Because of differences in immigration and birthrates, non-Hispanic whites will decrease to approximately 50 percent of the population by 2050.[16]

Native Americans The original inhabitants of what became the United States have played an important role in its history and continue to be important to the politics of states like South Dakota, New Mexico, and Oklahoma. More than half the names of states and hundreds of the names of cities, rivers, and mountains in the United States are Native American. In recent U.S. Senate elections in South Dakota, the Native American vote has been important.[17] One-third of Native Americans and Alaskan Natives have incomes below the federal poverty level. This percentage is higher than those for African Americans and Hispanics.[18]

race
A grouping of human beings with distinctive characteristics determined by genetic inheritance.

ethnicity
A social division based on national origin, religion, language, and often race.

LeBron James, the two-time reigning NBA Most Valuable Player, earned nearly $15 million in salary last year and earns millions more through lucrative endorsements.

African Americans Most immigrants chose to come to this country in search of freedom and opportunity. In contrast, most African Americans came against their will, as slaves. Although the Emancipation Proclamation and Thirteenth Amendment ended slavery in the 1860s, racial divisions still affect American politics. Until 1900, more than 90 percent of all African Americans lived in the South; a century later, that figure was 55 percent.[19] Many African Americans left the South hoping to improve their lives by settling in the large cities of the Northeast, Midwest, and West. But what many of them found was urban poverty. More recently, African Americans have been returning to the South, especially its urban areas.

Most African Americans are more vulnerable economically than most whites. Income is correlated with education. Among recent high school graduates, 64 percent of white Americans go on to college, but only 58 percent of African Americans do.[20] Approximately 30 percent of whites graduate from college, whereas only about 20 percent of African Americans do.[21] African American median family income is close to $40,000, compared to about $64,000 for whites.[22] Approximately 22 percent of African American families live below the poverty level, compared to about 8 percent of white families.[23] However, African Americans have been doing better in recent years; 40 percent of African American households earned more than $50,000 in 2007 (compared to 62 percent of white households).[24] Some African Americans, like Miami Heat basketball player LeBron James and syndicated talk-show host and corporate chief executive Oprah Winfrey, have risen to the top of their professions in terms of earnings.

The African American population is much younger than the white population; the median age for whites in 2008 was 38.2 years, compared to 31.4 for African Americans.[25] The combination of a younger African American population, a lower level of education, and their concentration in economically depressed urban areas has resulted in a much higher unemployment rate for young African Americans. Unemployment can in turn contribute to social problems such as crime, drug and alcohol abuse, and family dissolution.

African Americans had little political power until after World War II. Owing their freedom from slavery to the "party of Lincoln," most African Americans initially identified with the Republicans, but this loyalty started to change in the 1930s and 1940s under President Franklin D. Roosevelt, who insisted on equal treatment for African Americans in his New Deal programs.[26] After World War II, African Americans came to see the Democrats as the party of civil rights. The 1964 Republican platform position on civil rights espoused *states' rights*—at the time, the creed of southern segregationists—in what appeared to be an effort to win the support of southern white voters. Virtually all African Americans voted for Lyndon Johnson in 1964, and in presidential elections between 1984 and 2008, their Democratic vote averaged more than 86 percent.[27]

In 2008, with an African American running for president, 95 percent of blacks voted for Obama and their share of total votes rose from 11 percent in 2004 to 13 percent in 2008.[28] Even though Obama and his campaign did not make race a major theme of their campaign, pollsters and pundits speculated about what effect his race would have on voters. Exit polls found Obama did better among white voters than John Kerry had done in 2004 and substantially better among Latinos and African Americans.

Further evidence of growing African American political power is the dramatic increase in the number of African American state legislators, which rose from 168 in 1970 to 623 in 2008.[29] Georgia has 55 African American state legislators, the most of any state. Alabama, Maryland, Mississippi, New York, and South Carolina all have more than 30.[30]

Ken Salazar, elected to the U.S. Senate from Colorado in 2004, is the fourth U.S. senator of Latino descent in American history. Salazar replaced Ben Nighthorse Campbell, a Native American and Republican, who did not seek reelection. Salazar previously served two terms as Colorado attorney general.

Hispanics Hispanic Americans are not a monolithic group, and although they share a common linguistic heritage in Spanish, they often differ from one another depending on which country they or their forebears emigrated from. Cuban Americans, for instance, tend to be Republicans, whereas Mexican Americans and Puerto Ricans living on the mainland are disproportionately Democrats.[31] Hispanics are politically important in a growing number of states. Nearly two-thirds of Cuban Americans live in Florida, especially in greater Miami. Mainland Puerto Ricans are concentrated in and around New York City; many Mexican Americans live in the Southwest and California. More than 13 million Hispanics live in California.[32]

Because Hispanics are not politically homogeneous, they are not as unified a voting bloc as African Americans. The many noncitizen Hispanics and the relative youth of the Hispanic population also diminish the group's political power. For example, 14.1 million foreign-born Hispanics are not citizens,[33] and of the estimated 11.6 million unauthorized immigrants, three-fifths are from Mexico.[34] This group cannot vote, nor can those under age 18, who make up a greater percentage of the Hispanic population than in other ethnic groups. The median age of Hispanics in 2008 was 27.7 years, more than ten years younger than whites (38.2 years), and younger than blacks (31.4 years).[35] Language problems also reduce Hispanic citizens' voter registration and turnout.

Both major parties are aggressively cultivating Hispanic candidates. Several Hispanics have been cabinet members. Ken Salazar, a Hispanic Democrat, was elected to the Senate in 2004 from Colorado, and he became secretary of the Interior in the Obama administration. Bob Menendez, a Democrat, was appointed to the Senate from New Jersey and then elected in a contested race in 2006. He served as head of the Democratic Senatorial Campaign Committee in the 2009–2010 election cycle.

Asian Americans The U.S. Census Bureau classifies Asian Americans together for statistical purposes, but like Hispanics, they show significant differences in culture, language, and political experience in the United States. Asian Americans include, among others, persons of Chinese, Japanese, Indian, Korean, Vietnamese, Filipino, and Thai origin, as well as persons from the Pacific Islands. As with Hispanics, there are differences among these subgroups.[36] For example, Japanese Americans were more likely to register as Democrats than were Korean Americans or other Asian Americans. Japanese Americans also were somewhat more likely to vote than other Asian-ethnic groups.[37]

Many Asian Americans have done well economically and educationally. Their income is well above the national median, and 52.6 percent have graduated from college, compared to 29.8 percent of whites and 19.6 percent of African Americans.[38]

The Ties of Ethnicity Except for Native Americans and the descendants of slaves, all U.S. citizens have immigrant ancestors who chose to come to the American continent. There have been two large waves of new immigrants to the United States. The first, 17.3 million people, came between 1900 and 1924, primarily from Southern and Eastern Europe. The second large wave is now under way. From 1991 to 2008, the United States has seen nearly 17.4 million immigrants, primarily from the Caribbean, Mexico, and Asian countries such as the Philippines, Vietnam, and China. Of this group, an estimated 11.6 million came into the country illegally.[39]

Large numbers of immigrants can pose challenges to any political and social system. Immigrants are often a source of social conflict as they compete with more established groups for jobs, rights, political power, and influence.

Religion

In many parts of the world, religious differences, especially when combined with disputes over territory or sovereignty, are a source of violence. The conflict between Israelis and Palestinians has motivated suicide bombers who kill Israeli civilians along with themselves, and Israelis who attack Palestinian settlements and leaders. The war between India and Pakistan over Kashmir is largely a religious battle between Muslims and Hindus, and the Shi'ite–Sunni conflict among different branches of Islam threatens the stability of the new government in Iraq.

Jews have often been the target of religious discrimination and persecution (anti-Semitism), which reached its greatest intensity in the Holocaust of the 1940s, during which the Nazis murdered an

Chinese American and Nobel Prize laureate Steven Chu is the Secretary of Energy in the Obama Administration. He is the second Chinese American to serve in a Presidential Cabinet.

YOU WILL

DECIDE Who Should the Census Count, and How Should They Be Counted?

As established in the Constitution, every ten years, the government conducts a count of all persons in the United States. For the 2000 census, the U.S. Census Bureau proposed using random sampling rather than attempting to count all households. The proposed sample approach would have contacted 90 percent of the households in a census tract consisting of roughly 1,700 individuals. The bureau would then check the accuracy of the sample by surveying 750,000 households throughout the nation and adjusting the final total accordingly. The sampling approach responded to complaints about the flawed 1990 census, which cost $2.6 billion (a 400 percent increase over the cost of the 1980 census) and failed to account for 10 million people while double-counting 6 million others, according to a study by the National Academy of Sciences.

In addition, although the census has always counted all individuals, citizens and noncitizens alike, it has not always asked about citizenship. Some members of Congress introduced legislation to require that citizenship be a question on the 2010 census and that illegal immigrants be excluded from the census count.

What do you think? As we assess the success of the 2010 census and look to future censuses, who should the census count, and how should they be counted? What arguments would you make for and against the use of sampling or questions about citizenship?

THINKING IT THROUGH

Both questions are really less about *how* to count as *whom* to count. The proposed sampling method would have produced a more accurate count of inner-city Hispanics and African Americans—the most difficult to count. Hispanics and African Americans are more likely to be homeless or living in poverty in urban areas. Using a sampling method would arrive at a more accurate count of these groups and would likely have resulted in a greater representation for Hispanics and African Americans in state legislatures and the U.S. House of Representatives. A more complete count of minorities could also mean that the Republican party would lose a few seats in the House to Democrats, which is one reason Republicans generally opposed the sampling approach while Democrats favored it.

The constitutionality of sampling is disputed, as the Constitution calls for an "actual enumeration" of the people. Democrats are quick to point out that under three presidents—Jimmy Carter, George H. W. Bush, and Bill Clinton—the Justice Department concluded that sampling is legal. Sampling as a method of determining population for congressional apportionment is not allowed under current law;* however, methods similar to sampling to fill in data missing from the "actual enumeration" has been upheld in the Supreme Court.†

Citizenship has been a question asked in the past in the census (1820–1960) but noncitizens have always been counted. Slaves counted as three-fifths of a person in the Constitution for apportionment purposes and the Fourteenth Amendment refers to the "whole number of persons" being counted without regard to citizenship. But counting illegal immigrants runs counter to our notions of political representation and is understandably unpopular. If illegal immigrants were excluded it could take away seats from states like California, Arizona, and Texas.

Critical Thinking Questions

1. Why do you think sampling may result in higher counts of minorities?
2. Do you think it is possible to decide questions about representation without considering partisan politics?
3. Should illegal immigrants and persons under age 18 be counted for purposes of apportioning seats in Congress or for counts of persons for distribution of federal monies to state and local governments?

* *Department of Commerce et al.* v. *U.S. House of Representatives et al.,* 119 S.Ct. 765 (1999).
† *Utah* v. *Evans,* 122 S.Ct. 2191 (2002).

estimated 6 million Jews.[40] The United States has not been immune from such hatred, despite its principle of religious freedom. In 1838, Governor Lilburn W. Boggs of Missouri issued an extermination order that made legal the killing of any Mormons in the state.[41]

Our government is founded on the premise that religious liberty flourishes when there is no predominant or official faith, which is why the framers of the Constitution did not sanction a national church. The absence of an official church does not mean that religion is unimportant in American politics; indeed, there were established churches in individual states in this country until the 1830s. At one time, people thought voters' religious preferences could prevent a Catholic from being elected president. John F. Kennedy's election in 1960 resolved that question. Nevertheless, a candidate's religion may still become an issue today if the candidate's religious convictions threaten to conflict with public obligations.

Religion has also been an important catalyst for political change. The Catholic Church helped overthrow communism in parts of Eastern Europe. Black churches provided many of the leaders in the American civil rights movement. More recently, political activity among fundamentalist Christians has increased. Led by ministers such as Pat Robertson and Focus on the Family leader James Dobson, evangelicals, sometimes called **fundamentalists,** are an important force in the Republican party and in some local governments.[42] Their agenda includes the return of school prayer, the outlawing of abortion, restrictions on homosexuals, opposition to gun control, and opposition to the teaching of evolution and sex education in public schools.

Many American adults take their religious beliefs seriously, more than do citizens of other democracies.[43] Thirty-seven percent attend houses of worship at least once a week; 16 percent, once or twice a month; and 18 percent more, at least several times a year.[44] Religion, like ethnicity, is a *shared identity.* People identify themselves as Baptist, Catholic, Jewish, Buddhist, or no religion at all. Sometimes religious attendance or nonattendance, rather than belonging to a particular religion or denomination, determines attitudes toward issues.

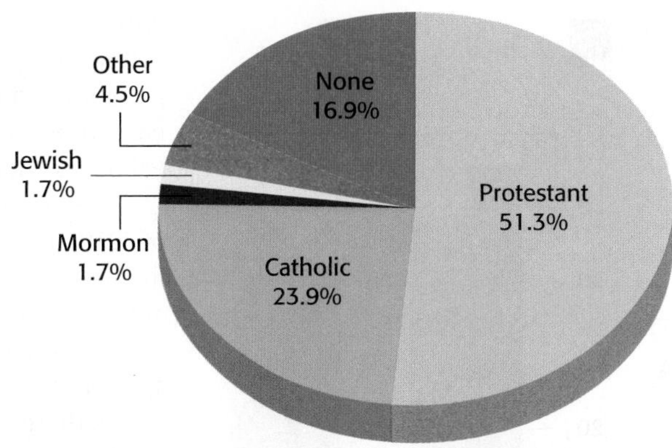

FIGURE 3–2 **Religious Groups in the United States.** Three-fourths of Americans describe themselves as Christian. ■ *In what areas of public policy do we see this playing a role? How important should religion be as a factor in making political decisions?*

SOURCE: U.S. Religious Landscape Survey, Pew Forum on Religion & Public Life, http://religions.pewforum.org. Copyright 2008 Pew Research Center.

The United States houses a tremendous variety of religious denominations. Approximately half the people in the United States describe themselves as Protestant, and the largest Protestant denomination is Baptist (see Figure 3-2). Because Protestants are divided among so many different churches, Catholics have the largest single membership in the United States, constituting slightly more than a quarter of the population.[45] Jews represent less than 2 percent of the population.[46] Muslims number more than 1.3 million, which is approximately one-half of 1 percent of the U.S. population.[47]

fundamentalists
Conservative Christians who as a group have become more active in politics in the last two decades and were especially influential in the 2000 and 2004 presidential elections.

Religion is important in American politics in part because people of particular religions are concentrated in a few states. Catholics number more than half the population of Rhode Island.[48] Baptists represent 16 percent of the American population; however, they account for roughly a third of the population of Mississippi and Alabama.[49] Mormons represent less than 2 percent of the American population but three-fifths of the population of Utah.[50] The state of New York has the highest percentage of Jews with 8.5 percent; the New York City metro area is 10.7 percent Jewish.[51]

Religious groups vary in their rates of political participation. In recent elections, Jews have the highest rate of reported voter turnout, more than 90 percent in 2000 and 2004, whereas those who claim no religious affiliation have the lowest, an average of roughly 60 percent in 2000, 2004, and 2008.[52] In recent presidential elections, most Protestants voted Republican, whereas most Catholics and Jews voted Democratic.[53] In 2008, McCain got 54 percent of the Protestant vote, but Obama did better among Protestants than either Gore in 2000 or Kerry in 2004. Obama received a majority of the Catholic vote.[54] The perception among many Catholics and Jews that the Democratic party is more open to them helps explain the strength of their Democratic identification.

Former governor of Arkansas Mike Huckabee appealed to conservative Christians by keeping religion central to his campaign for president in 2008. The Southern Baptist minister now hosts the Fox News talk show *Huckabee*, and there are speculations that he's gearing up for a 2012 presidential run.

Gender

For most of U.S. history, politics and government were men's business. Women first gained the right to vote primarily in the western territories, beginning with Wyoming in 1869 and Utah in 1870, and then in Colorado and Idaho before 1900.[55] The right was not extended nationally to women until 1920 with passage of the Nineteenth Amendment.

For a half-century after gaining the right to vote, American women voted at a lower rate than women in other Western democracies.[56] In 2008, as in the prior three presidential elections, slightly more women than men voted in the

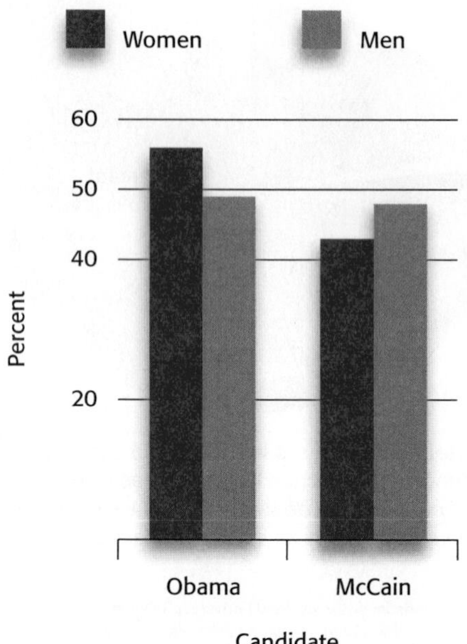

FIGURE 3–3 **Gender and the Vote for President.**

■ *What were some of the issues raised in the 2008 election that may have led women to vote disproportionately Democratic?*

SOURCE: 2008 CNN Exit Polls, http://www.cnn.com/ELECTION/2008/results/polls/ (accessed November 5, 2008).

presidential elections, and there is no significant difference between the genders in rates of voting in midterm elections.[57] Women have chosen to work within the existing political parties and do not overwhelmingly support female candidates, especially if they must cross party lines to do so.[58] For example, in 2008 polls found a majority of women saying Sarah Palin was not qualified to be president, and men more likely to support Palin.[59]

The number of women in Congress reached new highs in the 1990s. At the beginning of 2010, there were six female governors, 17 women serving in the Senate, and 76 women in the House. The proportion of women serving in the House of Representatives is approximately the same as in the Senate: about 17 percent. In contrast, some state legislative chambers like those in Colorado, Vermont, and New Hampshire are nearly 40 percent female.

Is there a **gender gap,** or a persistent difference between men and women in voting and in attitudes, on important issues? In recent elections, women have been more likely than men to vote for Democratic presidential candidates (see Figure 3–3). In 2000, Al Gore's share of the vote among women was 12 percent higher than among men.[60] In 2004, women preferred Kerry to Bush by 51 percent to 48 percent.[61] The gender gap was even wider in 2008, with women voting for Obama at 56 percent and McCain at 43 percent.[62] Men also gave Obama more votes than McCain, with 49 percent of men voting for Obama and 48 percent for McCain.

The women's movement in American politics seeks equal opportunity, education, jobs, skills, and respect in what has long been a male-dominated system.[63] Women are more likely than men to oppose violence in any form and are more likely to favor government-provided health insurance and family services. They also identify work and family issues such as day care, maternity leave, and equal treatment in the workplace as important.[64] Other gender issues, some of them focal points in recent elections, include reproductive rights and restrictions on pornography, gun control, and sexual harassment.[65]

There are serious income inequalities between men and women. Nearly twice as many women than men have an annual income of less than $15,000, and nearly three times as many men as women make more than $75,000 a year.[66] Because an increasing number of women today are the sole breadwinners for their families, the implications of this low income level are significant. Women earn on average less than men for the same work. After controlling for characteristics such as job experience, education, occupation, and other measures of productivity, a U.S. Census Bureau study shows that wage discrimination between the genders is 77 cents on every dollar.[67]

gender gap
The difference between the political opinions or political behavior of men and of women.

Unemployment in the economic recession of 2008–2010 affected more men than women. Four out of the five jobs lost in the recession were jobs held by men in such industries as manufacturing and construction.[68] The result of this unequal impact of the recession is that for the first time the number of women working could surpass men, though this may be a temporary change as the recession ends and men again find jobs.[69]

Annise Parker became the mayor of Houston, Texas, on January 2, 2010. She is the first openly gay mayor of a city with more than 1 million people, as well as Houston's second female mayor.

Sexual Orientation

The modern movement for expanded rights for gays and lesbians traces its roots to 1969, when New York City police raided the Stonewall Inn, a bar in Greenwich Village, and a riot ensued.[70] Since then, gays and lesbians have become more active and visible in pushing for legal rights and protections.

The precise number of homosexuals in the United States is unclear. Estimates range from 2 to 10 percent of the U.S. population.[71] Whatever its overall size, the gay and lesbian community has become important politically in several cities, notably San Francisco. Its lobbying power has increased noticeably in many states as well, and being gay or lesbian is no longer a barrier to election in many places.

The political agenda for gay and lesbian advocacy groups includes fighting discrimination, such as laws barring same-sex marriage and the military's "don't ask, don't tell" policy. On some fronts, the groups have been successful. Many local governments and private employers now grant health care and other benefits for same-sex domestic partners. Some states have legalized same-sex marriage, including Massachusetts, Connecticut, New Hampshire, Vermont, and Iowa, as well as the District of Columbia, and a number of others provide for some types of civil unions for same-sex couples.

The risk of having children later in life has recently been the subject of cover stories in newsmagazines. ■ *In what areas might the political views of individuals from traditional versus nontraditional family structures differ?*

Family Structure

Throughout the past half-century, the typical American family (mother and father married, with children in the home) has become anything but typical. The traditional family had several key characteristics: It married early, had children, and stayed together. Marriage itself used to be essential to be a family at all. However the number of American adults who live with someone of the opposite sex without being married increased to 5.5 percent of households in 2007.[72] Marriage also used to occur earlier in life, but people now marry later: The average age for first marriage for men is 28; for women it is 26.[73]

Children were also essential to traditional families, but birthrates have been falling for decades. Birthrates in the United States dropped in the late 1960s and 1970s. In the early 1960s, a woman statistically averaged approximately 3.5 children. By 2009, that number was at 2.1 children, barely meeting the 2.1 needed to replace the population. In other words, if the current trend continues, the native-born population will actually decrease over time.[74]

Finally, the traditional family stayed together, but the divorce rate has nearly doubled since 1950.[75] Today, it is estimated that about half of all marriages will end in divorce.[76] Divorce is one reason why the number of households headed by women has risen.

Education

Differences in education affect not only economic well-being but political participation and involvement as well. Thomas Jefferson wrote of education, "Enlighten the people generally, and tyranny and oppressions of body and mind will vanish like evil spirits at the dawn of day."[77] Most American students are educated in public schools. Nine of every ten students in kindergarten through high school attend public schools, and more than three of four college students are in public institutions.[78]

In 1992, for the first time, the number of American college graduates surpassed the number of persons who did not graduate from high school.[79] Slightly more than half of all U.S. adults have not gone to college, although many college students assume that nearly everyone goes to college. Approximately 30 percent of whites are college graduates, compared to 20 percent of African Americans and 13 percent of Hispanics; roughly 19 percent of African Americans and 41 percent of all Hispanics left school before completing high school (see Figure 3–4).[80]

Education is one of the most important variables in predicting political participation, confidence in dealing with government, and awareness of issues. Education is also related to the acquisition of democratic values. People who have failed to learn the prevailing norms of American society are far more likely to express opposition to democratic and capitalist ideals than those who are well educated and politically knowledgeable.[81]

Wealth and Income

The United States is a wealthy nation. Indeed, to some knowledgeable observers, "the most striking thing about the United States has been its phenomenal wealth."[82] Most American citizens lead comfortable lives. They eat and live well and have first-class medical care. But the unequal distribution of wealth and income results in political divisions and conflicts.

Wealth, the total value of someone's possessions, is more concentrated than income (annual earnings). The wealthiest families hold most of the property and other forms of wealth such as stocks and savings. Historically, concentrated wealth fosters an aristocracy.

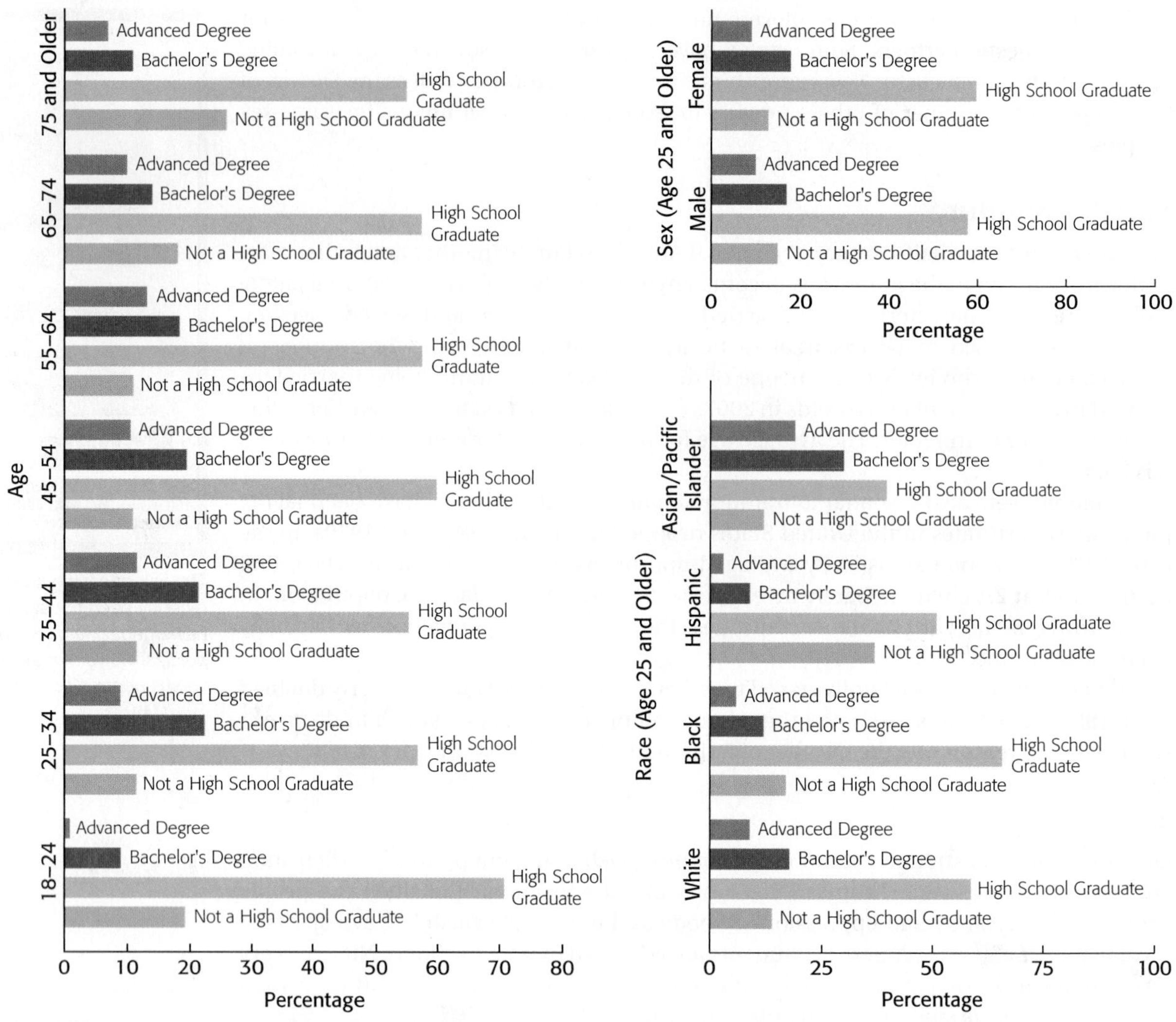

FIGURE 3–4 Educational Attainment in the United States.

■ *Based on the percentages of Americans who are high school graduates in each age bracket, what assumptions might you make about how the educational system and culture in America have changed?*

SOURCE: U.S. Census Bureau, *Educational Attainment in the United States: 2009*, www.census.gov/population/www/socdemo/education/cps2009.html.

The framers of the Constitution recognized the dangers of an unequal concentration of wealth. "The most common and durable source of factions has been the various and unequal distribution of property," wrote James Madison in *The Federalist*, No. 10 (reprinted in the Appendix). Economic differences often lead to conflict, and we remain divided politically along economic lines. Aside from race, income may be the single most important factor in explaining views on issues, partisanship, and ideology. Most rich people are Republicans, most poor people are Democrats, and this has been true since at least the Great Depression of the 1930s.

Between the 1950s and the 1970s, inflation-adjusted income doubled, but since then, it has fluctuated, with no substantial change over time.[83] As of 2007, 12.5 percent of the population fell below the poverty line and had the lowest per capita incomes, after factoring in family size.[84] In 2007, the official poverty level for a family of four with two children was an income below $21,027.[85] Families headed by a single female are more than two times as likely to fall below the poverty line than families headed by a single male, with 28.3 percent of all households headed by females falling below the poverty line.[86] Nearly 36 percent of the poor are children under age 18, and many appear to be trapped in a cycle of poverty where children raised in poverty are more likely to be poor as adults (see Figure 3–5).[87] African American and Hispanic children are more than twice as likely to be poor as white children.[88] The poor are a minority who lack political power.

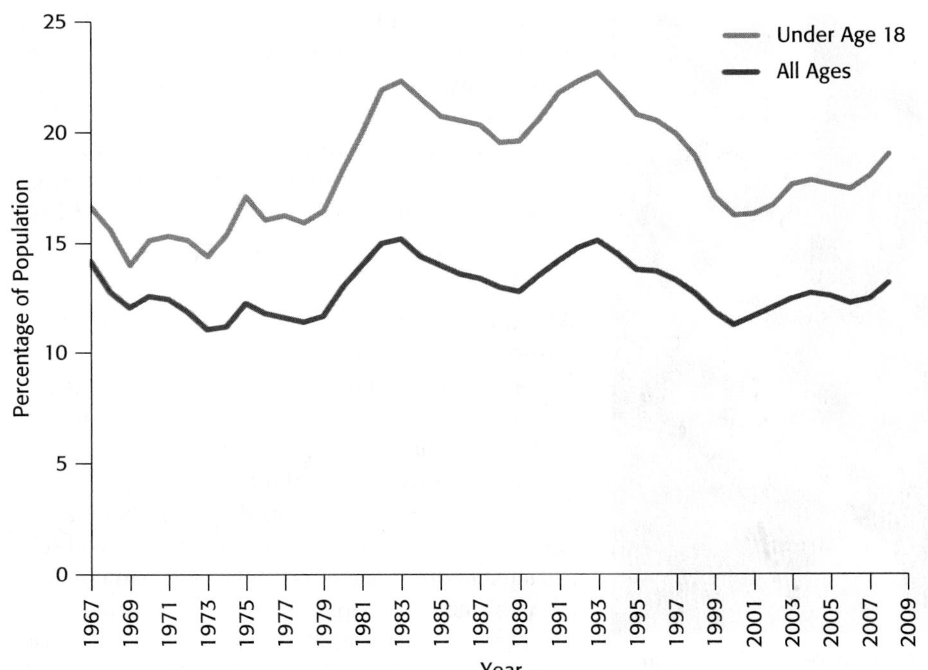

FIGURE 3–5 Percentage of Americans Living in Poverty, by Age, 1967–2009.
In 2008-2009, a poor economy and high unemployment contributed to a rise in the poverty rate. ■ *What other factors could influence the percentage of Americans classified as living in poverty at any given time?*

SOURCE: U.S. Census Bureau, "Table 3—Poverty Status, by Age, Race, and Hispanic Origin," http://www.census.gov/hhes/www/poverty/histpov/perindex.html (accessed September 29, 2009); and U.S. Census Bureau, "Table 2—Poverty Status by Family Relationships, Race, and Hispanic Origin," http://www.census.gov/hhes/www/poverty/histpov/perindex.html (accessed September 29, 2009).

They vote less than wealthier people and are less confident and organized in dealing with politics and government.

The distribution of income in a society can have important consequences for democratic stability. If enough people believe that only the few at the top of the economic ladder can hope to earn enough for an adequate standard of living, domestic unrest and even revolution may follow.

Occupation

In Jefferson's day and for several generations after, most people in the United States worked primarily on farms, but by 1900, the United States had become the world's leading industrial nation. As workers moved from farms to cities to find better-paying jobs, the cities rapidly grew. Labor conditions, including child labor, the length of the workweek, and safety conditions in mines and factories, became important political issues. New technology, combined with abundant natural and human resources, meant that the American **gross domestic product (GDP)** rose, after adjusting for inflation, by more than 460 percent from 1960 to 2007.[89] Gross domestic product is one measure of the size of a country's economy. It is the total market value of goods and services produced in that country in a specified period of time.

gross domestic product (GDP)
The total output of all economic activity in the nation, including goods and services.

The United States has entered what Daniel Bell, a noted sociologist, labeled the "postindustrial" phase of its development. "A postindustrial society, being primarily a technical society, awards less on the basis of inheritance or property...than on education and skill."[90] *Knowledge* is the organizing device of the postindustrial era. Postindustrial societies have greater affluence and a class structure less defined along traditional labor-versus-management lines. Figure 3–6, which shows the percentage of American workers in various occupations, demonstrates the changing dynamics of the country's labor force.

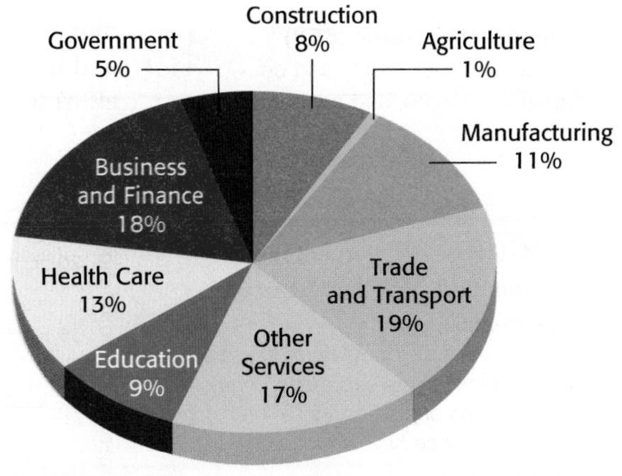

FIGURE 3–6 Employment by Occupational Groups, 2008.

SOURCE: U.S. Census Bureau, *Statistical Abstract of the United States: 2010* (U.S. Government Printing Office, 2010), p. 392.

The white-collar sector of our economy has grown tremendously throughout the past 50 years. This sector includes managers, accountants, and lawyers, as well as professionals and technicians in such rapid-growth areas as computers, communications, finance, insurance, and research. A dramatic decline in the number of people engaged in agriculture and a more modest decline in the

School teachers in the U.S. remain disproportionately female. ■ *Why do you think this has not changed, despite opportunities in other professions becoming more available to women?*

number of people in manufacturing (which together make up the blue-collar sector) has accompanied this shift. Today, agriculture employs 1 percent of working adults, and manufacturing employs 11 percent.[91] Federal, state, and local governments employ 5 percent of jobholders, while government expenditures account for 20 percent of our gross domestic product.[92]

Social Class

Why do U.S. citizens not divide themselves into social classes as Europeans do? American workers have not formed their own political party, nor does class seem to dominate our political life. Karl Marx's categories of *proletariat* (those who sell their labor) and *bourgeoisie* (those who own or control the means of production) are far less important here than they have been in Europe. Still, we do have social classes and what social scientists call **socioeconomic status (SES)**—a division of the population based on occupation, income, and education.

Most American adults say they are "middle class." Few admit to seeing themselves as lower class or upper class. In many other industrial democracies, large proportions of the population think of themselves as "working class" rather than middle class.[93]

What constitutes the "middle class" in the United States is highly subjective. For instance, some individuals perform working-class tasks (such as plumbing), but their income places them in the middle class or even the upper-middle class. A schoolteacher's income is below that of many working-class jobs, but in terms of status, teaching ranks among middle-class jobs.

Age

We are living longer, a phenomenon that has been dubbed the "graying of America" (Figure 3–7). This demographic change has increased the proportion of the population over the age of 65 and increased the demand for medical care, retirement benefits, and a host of other age-related services. Persons over the age of 65 constitute less than 13 percent of the population but account for more than 26 percent of the total medical expenditures.[94] With the decreasing birthrate discussed earlier, the graying of America has given rise to concern about maintaining an adequate workforce in the future.

Older adults are more politically aware and vote more often than younger ones, making them a potent political force. Their vote is especially important in western states and in Florida, the state with the largest proportion of people over the age of 65. In an effort to change this, several groups made registering younger voters and getting them to

socioeconomic status (SES)
A division of population based on occupation, income, and education.

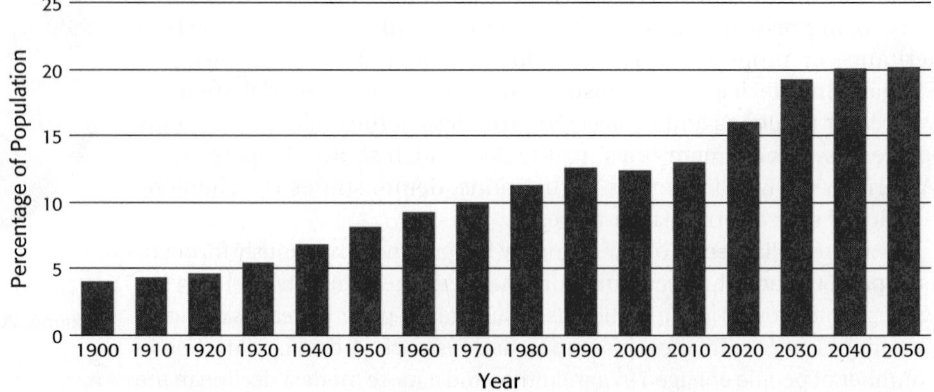

FIGURE 3–7 **Percentage of Population Over the Age of 65, 1900–2050.**
■ *How will the population 30 years from now compare to that of today? In what areas of politics and society might that difference have an impact?*

SOURCE: U.S. Census Bureau; U.S. Census Bureau, http://www.census.gov/compendia/statab/cats/population/estimates_and_projections_by_age_sex_raceethnicity.htm; and U.S. Census Bureau, *Statistical Abstract of the United States: 2010* (U.S. Government Printing Office, 2010), p. 12.

the polls a high priority in 2008. Exit polls from the 2008 election found that turnout among 18- to 29-year-olds rose from 48 percent in 2004 to 52 percent in 2008. An estimated 3.4 million more 18- to 29-year-olds voted in 2008.[95]

Age is important in terms of politics in two additional ways: lifecycle and generational effects. *Lifecycle effects* have shown that, as people become middle-aged, they become more politically conservative, less mobile, and more likely to participate in politics. As they age further and rely more on the government for services, they tend to grow more liberal.[96] Young people, in contrast, are more mobile and less concerned about the delivery of government services.

As was the case in 2004, the 2008 election cycle saw an increase in the number of young persons registering to vote. ■ *If young people were to turn out to vote at the same percentage as older people, in what areas of policy might the priorities of politicians change?*

Generational effects in politics arise when a particular generation has had experiences that make it politically distinct. For example, for those who lived through it, the Great Depression of the 1930s shaped their lifelong views of political parties, issues, and political leaders. Some members of this generation saw Franklin D. Roosevelt as the leader who saved the country by pulling it out of the Depression; others felt he sold the country down the river by launching too many government programs. More recently and to a lesser extent, the baby boomers shared a common and distinctive political experience. These Americans came of age politically in the 1960s and 1970s during the civil rights movement and the Vietnam War.

The American Political Culture

LEARNING **OBJECTIVE**

3.3 Identify the most important elements of and sources for the American political culture.

Many American citizens' first experience with democracy is a school election, sometimes as early as in elementary school. Other elements of our political culture are learned in the family or from peers. Many important elements of our political culture are widely shared by Americans, others are evolving, and some are no longer widely shared. American political culture centers on democratic values such as liberty, equality, individualism, justice, the rule of law, patriotism, optimism, and idealism.

Political scientists use the term **political culture** to refer to the widely shared beliefs, values, and norms citizens hold about their relationship to government and to one another. We can discover the specifics of a nation's political culture not only by studying what its people believe and say but also by observing how they behave. That behavior includes such fundamental decisions as who may participate in political decisions, what rights and liberties citizens have, how political decisions are made, and what people think about politicians and government generally.

political culture
The widely shared beliefs, values, and norms about how citizens relate to government and to one another.

Some elements of our political culture—such as our fear of concentrated power and our reverence for individual liberty—have remained constant over time. However, as discussed in the introduction, our ideas about **suffrage,** the right to vote, have changed from a belief that only property-owning white men should be allowed to vote to a conviction that all adults, excluding felons in some states, should have the right. Thus, citizens now vote in party primaries to select nominees for office, whereas for much of our history, party leaders determined who would run for office. The surge in political activity on the Internet in recent elections may be a harbinger of a new political culture in which citizens interact more with candidates, contribute money to campaigns, and mobilize each other.[97]

suffrage
The right to vote.

deliberation
The process whereby people or elected officials meet together to discuss and consider public matters.

The idea of people coming together, listening to each other, exchanging ideas, learning to appreciate each other's differences, and defending their opinions is sometimes called **deliberation** and builds what has been called **social capital.** Such interaction is thought to foster and strengthen community and relationships in ways that do not happen when citizens only cast ballots. Political scientist Robert Putnam has defined social capital as

social capital
Democratic and civic habits of discussion, compromise, and respect for differences, which grow out of participation in voluntary organizations.

"features of social organization such as networks, norms, and social trust that facilitate coordination and cooperation for mutual benefit."[98]

Shared Values

As discussed in the Introduction, the founders of our nation claimed that individuals have certain **natural rights**—the rights of all people to dignity and worth—and that government must be limited and controlled because it was a threat to those rights.

natural rights
The rights of all people to dignity and worth; also called *human rights.*

Liberty No value in the American political culture is more revered than liberty. "We have always been a nation obsessed with liberty. Liberty over authority, freedom over responsibility, rights over duties—these are our historic preferences," wrote the late Clinton Rossiter, a noted political scientist. "Not the good man but the free man has been the measure of all things in this sweet 'land of liberty'; not national glory but individual liberty has been the object of political authority and the test of its worth."[99] Not all students of U.S. political thought accept this emphasis on freedom and individualism over virtue and the public good and, in reality, both sets of values are important.[100]

Equality Thomas Jefferson's famous words in the Declaration of Independence express the strength of our views of equality: "We hold these truths to be self-evident, that all men are created equal, that they are endowed by their Creator with certain unalienable rights, that among these are life, liberty, and the pursuit of happiness." In contrast to Europeans, our nation shunned aristocracy, and our Constitution explicitly prohibits governments from granting titles of nobility. Although our rhetoric about equality was not always matched by our policy—slavery and racial segregation in schools—the value of social equality is now deeply rooted.

American citizens also believe in *political equality,* the idea that every individual has a right to equal protection under the law and equal voting power. Although political equality has always been a goal, it has not always been a reality. In the past, African Americans, Native Americans, Asian Americans, and women were denied the right to vote and otherwise participate in the nation's political life.

Equality encompasses the idea of *equal opportunity,* especially with regard to improving our economic status. American adults believe social background should not limit our opportunity to achieve to the best of our ability, nor should race, gender, or religion. The nation's commitment to public education programs such as Head Start for disadvantaged preschool children, state support for public colleges and universities, and federal financial aid for higher education reflects this belief in equal opportunity.

A teacher reads to her students as part of the Head Start program in Washington, D.C. ■ *How does the education system in the United States, including programs like Head Start and Race to the Top, reflect the principle of equal opportunity?*

For the People
GOVERNMENT'S GREATEST ENDEAVORS

Increasing Access for the Disabled

People today take for granted that Americans restricted to a wheelchair can have access to public transportation and buildings, that hearing-impaired persons can use telecommunications, and that persons with disabilities are not subject to discrimination. But this was not always the case.

Prior to 1990, when President George H. W. Bush signed into law the Americans with Disabilities Act (ADA), discrimination and other barriers existed that greatly restricted disabled persons. For example, one of those who fought hard for the Americans with Disabilities Act was Justin W. Dart Jr. Born into affluence, Dart contracted polio at age 18, shortly before entering the University of Houston. That institution denied him a teaching certificate because of his disability. After a career in business, Dart became an advocate for the rights of people with disabilities.

By establishing requirements for buildings and public transportation, persons with disabilities are now able to travel and enjoy going to a restaurant, hotel, or theater. Although many changes still need to be made, the improvements have made it much easier for persons with disabilities to participate in daily activities. Similarly, employment regulations have helped prevent discrimination and allowed these individuals to participate more fully in society. As you consider your college campus and community, imagine how different it would be if persons with disabilities were denied access to public transportation, buildings, and employment.

CRITICAL THINKING QUESTIONS

1. How does the Americans with Disabilities Act foster equality of opportunity?
2. What are the advantages to society of making public transportation, accommodations and buildings, and employment more accessible to persons with disabilities?
3. What are arguments you could make against legislation like the ADA?

Individualism The United States is characterized by a persistent commitment to the individual, who has both rights and responsibilities. As Peter Shuck and James Q. Wilson have recently written, "This belief in individualism causes Americans to place an unparalleled emphasis on the notion of individual rights in every area of social life and, correspondingly, to be suspicious of group rights."[101] Policies that limit individual choice generate intense political conflict. The debates over legalized abortion and universal health care are often framed in terms of our ability to exercise choices. Although American citizens support individual rights and freedoms, they also understand that their rights can conflict with another person's or with the government's need to maintain order or promote the general welfare.

democratic consensus
Widespread agreement on fundamental principles of democratic governance and the values that undergird them.

majority rule
Governance according to the expressed preferences of the majority.

Respect for the Common Person Most American adults prefer action to reflection. We are often anti-expert and sometimes anti-intellectual, and an emphasis on practicality and common sense has become part of our national image. Poets such as Walt Whitman and Carl Sandburg and storytellers such as Mark Twain, Will Rogers, Eudora Welty, and Garrison Keillor helped shape this tradition. Reverence for the common people helps explain our ambivalence toward power, politics, and government authority.

Joe the Plumber became a nationally recognized figure after Senator Obama and Senator McCain both referenced him repeatedly in the final presidential debate to demonstrate their understanding of the problems of the average American. ■ *Considering the social and economic conditions in the country, as well as the background of the presidential candidates, why might the image of Joe the Plumber have been so resonant for many Americans in 2008?*

Democratic Consensus As demonstrated in this chapter, we are a people from many different cultural and ethnic backgrounds, histories, and religions. Despite these differences, our political culture includes a **democratic consensus,** a set of widely shared attitudes and beliefs about government and its values, procedures, documents, and institutions. We have strong opinions about fundamental "rules of the game" such as who has power to do what, how people acquire power, and how they are removed from power. But this shared commitment does not necessarily mean that people vote, keep up with public affairs, or believe government is always fair or just.

We believe in **majority rule**—governance according to the preferences of the majority as expressed through regular elections. Yet we also believe that people in the minority should be free to try to win majority support for their opinions. Even though many lack strong party attachments, we favor a two-party system and the idea of competition between the parties. Our institutions are based on the principles of representation and consent of the governed. We believe in **popular sovereignty**—the idea that ultimate power resides in the people. Government exists to serve the people rather than the other way around. The government learns the will of the people through *elections,* the most important expression of popular consent and, to an extent, through public opinion polls (see Chapter 5). But sometimes other fundamental rights limit popular sovereignty and majority rule.[102]

The Constitution, especially the first ten amendments (the Bill of Rights) and the Thirteenth, Fourteenth, Fifteenth, and Nineteenth Amendments, spells out many of the limits on what governments can do. People, however, interpret what those rights actually mean in practice (see Table 3–1).

Justice and the Rule of Law Inscribed above the entrance to the U.S. Supreme Court are the words "Equal Justice Under Law." The *rule of law* means government is based on a body of law applied equally and by just procedures, as opposed to arbitrary rule by an elite whose whims decide policy or resolve disputes. In 1803, Chief Justice John Marshall summarized this principle: "The government of the United States has been emphatically termed a government of laws, not of men."[103] Americans strongly believe in fairness: Everyone is entitled to the same legal rights and protections.

To adhere to the rule of law, government should follow these five rules:

1. *Generality:* Laws should be stated generally and not single out any group or individual.
2. *Prospectivity:* Laws should apply to the present and the future, not punish something someone did in the past.
3. *Publicity:* Laws cannot be kept secret and then enforced.
4. *Authority:* Valid laws are made by those with legitimate power, and the people legitimate that power through some form of popular consent.
5. *Due process:* Laws must be enforced impartially with fair processes.

Nationalism, Optimism, and Patriotism The terrorist attacks of 2001 united the nation and reinforced American **nationalism.** As President George W. Bush said, "We are a different country than we were on September 10th: sadder and less innocent; stronger and more united; and in the face of ongoing threats, determined and courageous."[104] More than nine out of ten Americans are proud of their nationality.[105] More broadly, we believe in the freedom to improve ourselves and to achieve success with as little interference as possible from others or from government.

Despite dissatisfaction with the imperfections of government, we believe that America is better, stronger, and more virtuous than other nations. Americans are known for this strong sense of **patriotism.** Like every country, the United States has interests and motives that are selfish as well as generous, cynical as well as idealistic. Still, our support of human needs and rights throughout the world is evidence of an enduring idealism.

popular sovereignty
A belief that ultimate power resides in the people.

nationalism
An enduring sense of national identity or consciousness that derives from cultural, historic, linguistic, or political forces.

patriotism
Devotion to one's own country, often seeing it as better or stronger than other countries.

TABLE
3–1 What Do You Mean by Rights and Freedoms? It Depends

	Agree	Disagree	Don't Know
There has been real improvement in the position of African Americans.	61%	31%	8%
Freedom of speech should not extend to groups that are sympathetic with terrorists.	49	45	6
Books that contain dangerous ideas should be banned from public school libraries.	46	49	5
Abortions should be more difficult to obtain.	41	54	6
The police should be allowed to search the houses of known terrorist sympathizers without a court order.	33	64	3
School boards ought to have the right to fire teachers who are known homosexuals.	28	67	5

■ *If Americans generally express support for the concept of individual rights and freedom, what concerns might they be balancing those beliefs against in some of the issues for which they express low levels of support?*

SOURCE: Used by permission of The Pew Research Center for the People & the Press. *Trends in Political Values and Core Attitudes: 1987–2009; INDEPENDENTS TAKE CENTER STAGE IN OBAMA ERA,* May 21, 2009, http://people-press.org/report/517/political-values-and-core-attitudes (accessed December 4, 2009); and responses to abortion question obtained from Harris Poll, July 7–14, 2009, http://pollingreport.com/abortion.htm (accessed April 23, 2010).

Where We Learn the American Political Culture

One important source of political culture in the United States, as in other nations, is the family. Young children are taught what it means to be an American. They are curious about why people vote, what the president does, and whether Grandpa fought in Korea or Vietnam. Families are the most important reference group, with parents and siblings orienting each other to politics, the media, and the community more generally. Compared to families in other cultures, American families are much more egalitarian, with children having more input in family decisions than in other cultures.[106]

Public schools are another source of the American political culture. Children and teachers often begin the school day by saluting the flag, reciting the Pledge of Allegiance, or singing the national anthem. Political and economic values are part of the curriculum and are put into practice in school elections and other activities.[107] Colleges and universities also help foster the American political culture. Students who attend college are often more confident than others in dealing with bureaucracy and politics generally and are more likely to participate in politics, vote, and know more about government.[108]

American churches, synagogues, and mosques have long fostered a common understanding of right and wrong and of freedom—including freedom of religion, individualism, pluralism, and civic duty. Two scholars have recently written, "Surrounding and shaping American culture is a remarkably strong religious tradition and an inventive, though sometimes repellent, popular culture of religiosity."[109] Churches do not all take the same positions on political issues, but they have played important roles in such major social and political movements as the abolition of slavery, the expansion of civil rights, and opposition to war.

In modern times, the mass media have taken over some functions the family used to perform. By the time children leave high school, they will have spent more time watching television than talking to their parents. They may have learned more about politics from Comedy Central and Jon Stewart than from their parents, schools, or other media.[110] Finally, American adults educate each other about political values at work, at PTA meetings, and in more expressly political activities.

The American Dream

Many of our political values come together in the **American dream,** a complex set of ideas that holds that the United States is a land of opportunity where individual initiative and hard work can bring economic success. Whether fulfilled or not, this dream speaks to our most deeply held hopes and goals. Its essence is expressed in our enthusiasm for **capitalism,** an economic system based on private property, competitive markets, economic incentives, and limited government involvement in the production, pricing, and distribution of goods and services.[111]

The concept of *private property* enjoys extraordinary popularity in the United States. Most cherish the dream of acquiring property and believe that the owners of property have the right to decide how to use it. And yet the unequal distribution of property, observed by James Madison and still an issue today, is an enduring cause of faction or political division.* The conflict in values between a *competitive economy,* in which individuals reap large rewards for their initiative and hard work, and an *egalitarian society,* in which everyone earns a decent living, carries over into politics. How the public resolves this tension changes over time and from issue to issue.

As important as the American dream is as an aspiration, it remains unfulfilled. As discussed earlier in this chapter, the gap between rich and poor has grown in recent years, and a sharp income difference between whites and blacks remains tenacious.[112] For more people than we want to admit, chances for success still depend on the family they were born into, the neighborhood they grew up in, or the college they attended. An underclass persists in the form of impoverished families, malnourished and poorly educated children, and the homeless.[113] Many cities are actually two cities, where some residents live in luxury, others in squalor.

American dream
The widespread belief that the United States is a land of opportunity and that individual initiative and hard work can bring economic success.

capitalism
An economic system characterized by private property, competitive markets, economic incentives, and limited government involvement in the production, distribution, and pricing of goods and services.

*James Madison, "The Federalist #10" in The Federalist Papers (New York: Penguin Books, 1987) p.124.

Of the People

AMERICA'S CHANGING FACE

Immigrants and Assimilation into American Political Culture

As a nation of immigrants, the United States has assimilated individuals from many countries. This process takes time as new immigrants learn the language, pursue education, and begin to understand the institutions and process of government, including elections.

The scholar Samuel Huntington and others have argued that immigrants from Mexico are less likely to support core American values or learn English and have "a strong resistance to acculturation...[and] persistence of their communal bonds."* Huntington's findings have been challenged. One study found that "nearly all Hispanic adults born in the United States of immigrant parents report they are fluent in English," suggesting assimilation after the first generation.† The data presented in the figure are from a survey of Latinos in the United States. Latinos who are not American citizens are more likely to identify themselves with their country of birth and less likely to describe themselves as "American," but for both groups, the political focus is on the United States.

The immigration/assimilation debate inspires strong emotions on both sides. Some, like Huntington, fear that the influx of immigration will challenge "American" ideals. These groups and individuals are fearful that the immigration trends will mean the end of something—although they rarely specify what that will be. Fox News commentator John Gibson called on his presumably white viewers to "make more babies," otherwise, in "twenty-five years...the majority of the population [will be] Hispanic."‡ The United States has been down this road before. In the 1850s, following a devastating period of famine due to a potato mold, Irish émigrés began arriving in the Americas in droves. Today, more than 34 million Americans claim Irish ancestry—that number is more than nine times the population of Ireland today.§ However, in the 1850s, these immigrants were held in contempt. They were predominantly Catholic and generally poor. In short, they represented—at least in the minds of their contemporaries—a threat to American culture.

CRITICAL THINKING QUESTIONS

1. What factors may make it more or less difficult to assimilate new waves of immigrants into U.S. society today?
2. How does the racial composition of the United States affect the country's political culture?
3. Is the comparison between the Irish immigration of the 1850s and our current situation valid?

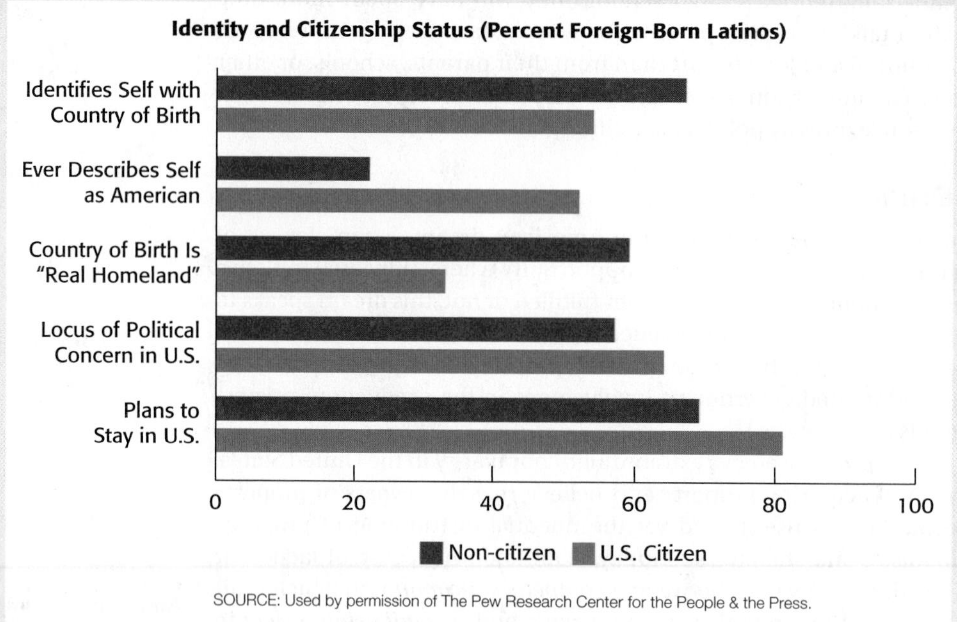

SOURCE: Used by permission of The Pew Research Center for the People & the Press.

* Samuel P. Huntington, *Who Are We? The Challenges to America's National Identity* (Simon & Schuster, 2004), pp. 189–190.

† Shirin Hakimzadeh and D'Vera Cohn, "English Usage Among Hispanics in the United States," *Pew Hispanic Center*, November 29, 2007; see also Mary C. Water and Tomas R. Jimenez, "Assessing Immigrant Assimilation: Empirical and Theoretical Challenges," *Annual Review of Sociology* (2005), pp. 105–125; and Jack Citrin, Amy Lerman, Michael Murakami, and Kathryn Pearson, "Testing Huntington: Is Hispanic Immigration a Threat to American Identity?" *Perspectives on Politics*, March 2007.

‡ John Gibson, "My Word," *Fox News*, May 11, 2006.

§ U.S. Census Bureau, "Facts for Features: Irish-American Heritage Month," March 10, 2006, www.census.gov/Press-Release/www/releases/archives/facts_for_features_special_editions/006328.html.

A contrast in housing can be seen in the two photos of New York City. On the left is the Plaza Hotel. On the right the Bronxdale houses, low-income public housing. ■ *Looking at the disparity of wealth that these images indicate, do you think they reaffirm that the American dream is still alive, or demonstrate that it's unattainable for most Americans?*

Most people today support a semi-regulated or mixed free enterprise system that checks the worst tendencies of capitalism, but they reject excessive government intervention. Much of American politics centers on how to achieve this balance. Currently, most people agree that some governmental intervention is necessary to assist those who fall short in the competition for education and economic prosperity and to encourage ventures that, though they have substantial public benefit, might not be undertaken without government assistance.

Unity in a Land of Diversity

LEARNING **OBJECTIVE**

3.4 Evaluate the degree to which America has achieved a measure of unity in a land of diversity.

As remarkable as American diversity is, the existence of a strong and widely shared sense of national unity and identity may be even more remarkable. Economic and social mobility have unified much of the U.S. population. Education has been an important part of this, as was the nationalizing influence of World War II. We are united by our shared commitment to democratic values, economic opportunity, work ethic, and the American dream. Social scientists used to speak of the "melting pot," meaning that, as various ethnic groups associate with other groups, they are assimilated into U.S. society and come to share democratic values such as majority rule, individualism, and the ideal of the United States as a land of opportunity. Critics have argued that the melting pot idea assumes there is something wrong with differences between groups, and that these distinctions should be discouraged. In its place, they propose the concept of the "salad bowl," in which "though the salad is an entity, the lettuce can still be distinguished from the chicory, the tomatoes from the cabbage."[114]

As this chapter has demonstrated, regional, social, and economic differences have important political consequences. They influence public opinion, participation, voting, interest groups, and political parties. At the same time, our country has a widely shared political culture and has achieved a sense of unity despite our remarkable diversity.

By the People

MAKING A DIFFERENCE

Experiencing Poverty

As we have seen in this chapter, poverty is still a problem in the United States, with direct political implications. The poor vote at lower rates and participate in other ways with less frequency than the wealthy. This reduces their political power and, among other things, threatens to weaken politicians' support of the social welfare programs on which the poor rely.

The enduring challenges of poverty have prompted some young people to take action to try and raise awareness of the enduring inequalities and difficulties of poverty.

Students at Ohio Wesleyan University, for example, hold a hunger banquet where participants are assigned to different socioeconomic classes, which determine their quality and quantity of food. The 15 percent of the students who are assigned to the upper class get a fully catered meal served at tables with linens. For the 30 percent of attendees who constitute the middle class, their meal consists of rice and beans served at tables without decoration or linens. The remaining 60 percent represent the world's poor and are fed a single scoop of rice and given water to drink. They sit on the floor to eat. A keynote speaker reinforces the contrast between different groups in society, and canned goods collected at the event are donated to the local shelter.

Students at Central Michigan University create a similar experiential learning opportunity in which they seek to raise public awareness about homelessness. To visually evoke the experience of Michigan's homeless residents, students create a makeshift "Shanty Town" out of cardboard in which they spend one night.* As people come to see the Shanty Town, they are encouraged to contribute to a homeless shelter in their area.†

For participants in these events, the contrast between the experiences of people at different socioeconomic levels is a powerful teaching moment. You might plan a hunger banquet at your campus if you do not already have one. Oxfam, a nonprofit organization dedicated to ending global poverty and injustice, provides a Hunger Banquet Toolkit with instructions and tips for how to host your own event: http://actfast.oxfamamerica.org/uploads/OA-HBToolkit.pdf.

CRITICAL THINKING QUESTIONS

1. What are some reasons why the poor participate less in politics?
2. Why is it hard for those who have not experienced hunger or poverty to relate to the difficulties faced by poor people?
3. Do events like "hunger banquets" help raise awareness of the issue being showcased?

* Michigan State Housing Development Authority, "The State of Homelessness in Michigan: 2008 Annual Summary," *Statistical Abstract: 2010,* p. 18, http://www.mpca.net/homeless.html.

† Maryellen Tighe, "Students Stay in Cardboard Boxes for 24 Hours for Homeless Awareness," *Central Michigan Life,* November 20, 2009, http://www.cm-life.com/2009/11/20/students-stay-in-cardboard-boxes-for-24-hours-for-homeless-awareness/.

CHAPTER **SUMMARY**

3.1 Relate differences in political culture to where people live and assess the importance of geography to the development of the U.S.

The character of a political society and its social environment are important to understanding its politics and government. Because the United States is a large continental nation with abundant natural resources, political freedom, and economic opportunity, immigrants from many nations have come here. These characteristics help explain American politics and traditions, including the notions of manifest destiny, ethnocentrism, and isolationism. Social and economic differences can foster conflict and violence. The continuing controversy over illegal immigration in the United States is an example of such a conflict. U.S. law has fostered religious diversity, and residential and settlement patterns have reinforced ethnic identify for some groups.

For much of U.S. history, the South has been a distinct region in the United States, in large part because of its agricultural base and its history of slavery and troubled race relations. Today, the region is Republican and conservative. Recently, the most significant migration in the United States has been from cities to suburbs. Today, many large U.S. cities are increasingly poor, African American, and Democratic, surrounded by suburbs that are primarily middle class, white, and Republican.

3.2 Analyze how demographic factors—including race and ethnicity, religion, gender, family structures, education, income, class, and age—affect American politics.

Race has been and remains among the most important of the differences in our political landscape. Although we fought a civil war over freedom for African Americans, racial equality was largely postponed until the latter half of the twentieth century. Ethnicity, including the rising numbers of Hispanics, continues to be a factor in politics. The United States has many religious denominations,
and these differences, including between those who are religious and those who are not, help explain public opinion and political behavior. Gender, sexual orientation, and family structures have become more important in politics. Although some achieve great

wealth and there is a large middle class, poverty has grown throughout the past two decades, especially among African Americans, Native Americans, Hispanics, and single-parent households. Women as a group continue to earn less than men, even in the same occupations. Age and education are important to understanding political participation.

3.3 Identify the most important elements of and sources for the American political culture.

The American political culture consists of a widely held set of fundamental political values and accepted processes and institutions that help us manage conflict and resolve problems. American adults share a widespread commitment to classical liberalism, which embraces the importance of individual liberty, equality, individualism, power to the people, private property, limited government, nationalism, optimism, idealism, the democratic consensus, and justice and the rule of law. People respect the Constitution, the Bill of Rights, the two-party system, and the right to elect officials on the basis of majority rule. We learn American political culture in the family, schools, religious and civic organizations, and through the mass media and political activities. The American dream persists as an ideal, as American residents perceive this to be a land of opportunity and upward mobility.

3.4 Evaluate the degree to which America has achieved a measure of unity in a land of diversity.

Even though social, economic, and other differences abound, there is also a shared commitment to the ideals of constitutional democracy in the United States. The American dream continues to exist and reinforces this unity. Some events serve to reinforce this sense of unity like the terrorist attacks of September 11, 2001.

CHAPTER **SELF-TEST**

3.1 Relate differences in political culture to where people live and assess the importance of geography to the development of the U.S..

1. In a short paragraph, define ethnocentrism. Is it different from racism? Why or why not?
2. In a short essay, explain how the concept of manifest destiny relates to the current political geography of the United States.
3. Compared to other countries in the world, the United States does not have many deep cleavages. Why do you think this is? (Hint: Think about the differences between *cross-cutting cleavages* and *reinforcing cleavages.*) Explain your opinion in a short paragraph.
4. Population growth patterns include all the following, *except:*
   a. In the West, population growth is occurring among younger persons.
   b. Growth in the South is occurring primarily in the population over the age of 65.
   c. There has been a resurgence of industrial growth in the New England states.
   d. Sun Belt states have experienced greater economic growth than most other areas.
5. In a short essay, describe two or three ways in which urbanization has affected American politics.

3.2 Analyze how demographic factors—including race and ethnicity, religion, gender, family structures, education, income, class, and age—affect American politics.

6. List and describe seven demographic categories.
7. Studies show that, after we control for socioeconomic status, many apparent racial divisions disappear. In a short essay, explain how race and socioeconomic status are related.

3.3 Identify the most important elements of and sources for the American politicalculture.

8. Identify and define four shared political values.
9. Which of the following "has taken over some functions the family used to perform" in terms of political socialization?
   a. Schools
   b. Churches
   c. The Internet
   d. The mass media
10. What role do educational opportunity, economic wealth, and religious freedom play in achieving the American Dream?

3.4 Evaluate the degree to which America has achieved a measure of unity in a land of diversity.

11. During the 2008 presidential election and nomination contest, much was made of "identity politics" in which individuals vote for the candidate most like them demographically. From what you know about the 2008 campaigns, how important was identity politics to the outcome?
12. Remembering that they are correlated, explain in a short essay whether you think regional or demographic distinctions are more important in how Americans see themselves.

Answers to selected questions: 4. c; 9.d;

mypoliscilab EXERCISES

Where participation leads to action!

Apply what you learned in this chapter on MyPoliSciLab.

Read on **mypoliscilab.com**

eText: Chapter 3

Study and **Review** on **mypoliscilab.com**

Pre-Test
Post-Test
Chapter Exam
Flashcards

Watch on **mypoliscilab.com**

Video: The President Addresses School Children
Video: America's Aging Population
Video: Who is in the Middle Class?

Explore on **mypoliscilab.com**

Simulation: What Are American Civic Values?
Comparative: Comparing Political Landscapes
Visual Literacy: Using the Census to Understand Who Americans Are

KEY TERMS

ethnocentrism, p. 87
efficacy, p. 87
political socialization, p. 88
demography, p. 88
political predisposition, p. 88
reinforcing cleavages, p. 88
cross-cutting cleavages, p. 88
manifest destiny, p. 90
Sun Belt, p.91
urban, p. 92
suburban, p. 92
rural, p. 92
race, p. 93
ethnicity, p. 93
fundamentalists, p. 97
gender gap, p. 98
gross domestic product (GDP), p. 101
socioeconomic status (SES), p. 102
political culture, p. 103
suffrage, p. 103
deliberation, p.103
social capital, p.103
natural rights, p. 104
democratic consensus, p. 105
majority rule, p. 105
popular sovereignty, p. 106
nationalism, p.106
patriotism, p.106
American dream, p.107
capitalism, p.107

ADDITIONAL RESOURCES

FURTHER READING

EARL BLACK AND **MERLE BLACK,** *The Rise of Southern Republicans* (Belknap Press, 2002).

DAVID T. CANON, *Race, Redistricting, and Representation: The Unintended Consequences of Black Majority Districts* (University of Chicago Press, 1999).

MAUREEN DEZELL, *Irish America: Coming into Clover* (Anchor Books, 2000).

JULIE ANNE DOLAN, MELISSA M. DECKMAN, AND **MICHELLE L. SWERS,** *Women and Politics: Paths to Power and Political Influence* (Prentice Hall, 2006).

LOIS DUKE WHITAKER, ED., *Women in Politics: Outsiders or Insiders?* 4th ed. (Prentice Hall, 2005).

RODOLFO O. DE LA GARZA, LOUIS DE SIPIO, F. CHRIS GARCIA, JOHN GARCIA, AND **ANGELO FALCON,** *Latino Voices: Mexican, Puerto Rican, and Cuban Perspectives on American Politics* (Westview Press, 1992).

DONALD R. KINDER AND **LYNN M. SANDERS,** *Divided by Color: Racial Politics and Democratic Ideals* (University of Chicago Press, 1996).

TAEKU LEE, S. KARTHICK RAMAKRISHNAN, AND **RICARDO RAMIREZ,** *Transforming Politics, Transforming America: The Political and Civic Incorporation of Immigrants in the United States (Race, Ethnicity, and Politics)* (University Press of Virginia, 2006).

JAN E. LEIGHLEY, *Strength in Numbers? The Political Mobilization of Racial and Ethnic Minorities* (Princeton University Press, 2001).

PEL-TE LIEN, M. MARGARET CONWAY, AND **JANELLE WONG,** *The Politics of Asian Americans* (Routledge, 2004).

JEREMY D. MAYER, *Running on Race: Racial Politics in Presidential Campaigns, 1960–2000* (Random House, 2002).

NANCY E. McGLEN, KAREN O'CONNOR, LAURA VAN ASSENDELFT, AND **WENDY GUNTHER-CANADA,** *Women, Politics, and American Society,* 4th ed. (Longman, 2004).

S. KARTHICK RAMAKRISHNAN, *Democracy in Immigrant America: Changing Demographics and Political Participation* (Stanford University Press, 2005).

MARK ROBERT RANK, *One Nation, Underprivileged: Why American Poverty Affects Us All* (Oxford University Press, 2004).

ARTHUR M. SCHLESINGER JR., *The Disuniting of America* (Norton, 1992).

MARCELO M. SUAREZ-OROZCO AND **MARIELA PAEZ,** *Latinos: Remaking America* (University of California Press, 2002).

ALEXIS DE TOCQUEVILLE, *Democracy in America*, edited by J. P. Mayer, translated by George Lawrence (Doubleday, 1969). Originally published 1835.

KENNETH D. WALD, *Religion and Politics in the United States*, 5th ed. (Rowman & Littlefield, 2006).

JANELLE WONG, *Democracy's Promise: Immigrants and American Civic Institutions (The Politics of Race and Ethnicity)* (University of Michigan Press, 2006).

JEAN BETHKE ELSHTAIN, *Democracy on Trial* (Basic Books, 1995).

HERBERT MCCLOSKY AND **JOHN ZALLER,** *The American Ethos: Public Attitudes Toward Capitalism and Democracy* (Harvard University Press, 1984).

JOHN RENSENBRINK, *Against All Odds: The Green Transformation of American Politics* (Leopold Press, 1999).

GARRY WILLS, *A Necessary Evil: A History of American Distrust of Government* (Simon & Schuster, 1999).

WEB SITES

www.census.gov The census provides demographic statistics for the country as a whole and for all 50 states.

www.usa.gov/Citizen/Topics/History_Culture.shtml USA.gov provides information on a variety of subjects, including detailed information on America's cultural history.

www.religions.pewforum.org/reports The Pew Forum provides detailed information on the religious makeup of America.

www.pbs.org/peoplelikeus/ This PBS site gives stats, stories, and other information about class in America.

www.conginst.org A Web site that provides up-to-date survey data on the American political culture.

www.loc.gov The Library of Congress Web site; provides access to more than 70 million historical and contemporary U.S. documents.

CHAPTER

4

Political Parties and Interest Groups

CHAPTER OUTLINE & CHAPTER LEARNING OBJECTIVES

What Parties Do for Democracy

4.1 Identify the primary functions of parties in democracies.

American Parties Today

4.2 Differentiate the functions of parties as institutions, parties in government, and parties in the electorate.

How Parties Raise and Spend Money

4.3 Assess the regulation of party fundraising and expenditures.

A Nation of Interests

4.4 Explain the role of interest groups in American politics, and categorize interest groups into types.

Characteristics and Power of Interest Groups

4.5 Analyze sources of interest group power.

Influencing Government: Lobbyists and Spending

4.6 Identify ways lobbyists seek to influence policy and interest group spending affects elections.

Parties and Interest Groups in a Democracy

4.7 Evaluate the influence of political parties and interest groups on government in America.

In early 2009, not long after Barack Obama took office, groups started forming to protest the $787 billion economic stimulus package, officially known as the American Recovery and Reinvestment Act of 2009. These groups adopted the name "tea party," a reference to the Boston Tea Party of 1773 when colonists rebelled against what they thought to be unfair British taxes on tea. The group's general concerns are about increasing government spending and growing government power. As Congress considered and the House of Representatives passed health care reform, that provided another issue for the tea party groups to protest. During the summer recess, many members of Congress faced heckling and protests in their home districts, in part the result of tea party organizing.[1] In the early 2010 special election to fill former Senator Ted Kennedy's Senate seat in Massachusetts, Republican Scott Brown staged an upset attributed by some, in part, to the Tea Party Movement. The British magazine, *The Economist*, said after Brown's victory, "America's most vibrant political force at the moment is the antitax tea-party movement."[2]

Tea party activists have held protests and rallies in cities throughout the country, where the number of participants ranges from a couple of dozen to thousands.[3] The movement has also organized national bus tours to call attention to their agenda.[4] This element of the Tea Party Movement was organized by the "Our Country Deserves Better PAC," founded by a political consulting firm in Sacramento.[5] In February 2010, a group called Tea Party Nation held a National Convention, which featured a speech by former Alaska Governor and Republican vice presidential nominee Sarah Palin.[6]

The Tea Party Movement has adopted many of the same tools used by the Obama campaign and Democratic leaning interest groups in 2008, such as using the Internet to coordinate, communicate, and recruit volunteers.[7] As this movement demonstrates, interest groups use a variety of strategies from local citizens spontaneously organizing for some political purpose, to more organized election-focused political action committees (PACs). But the Tea Party Movement in 2010 operated largely within the Republican Party. Candidates backed by the movement defeated established candidates in several states and generally expressed more conservative views than the GOP candidates they defeated. The long-term influence of the Tea Party on the Republican Party is unknown, but it is important that the movement chose to work within the Republican Party rather than form a third party.

Party labels typically help voters get a sense for the candidates; without knowing anything about the individual candidate, voters can make reliable assumptions about the candidate's stance on issues based on his or her political party. E. E. Schattschneider, a noted political scientist once said, "The political parties created democracy, and modern democracy is unthinkable save in terms of the parties."[8] Parties and interest groups are both a consequence of democracy and an instrument of it. They serve many functions, including narrowing the choices for voters,[9] providing information to officeholders, setting policy agendas, and making national and state elections work.

This chapter begins by examining why parties are so vital to the functioning of democracy. Although U.S. political parties have changed over time, they remain important in three different settings: as institutions, in government, and in the electorate. We will look at the way parties facilitate democracy in all three. We then examine the full range of interest group activities, as well as efforts to keep in check the potentially negative impacts of factions.

What Parties Do for Democracy

LEARNING **OBJECTIVE**

4.1 Identify the primary functions of parties in democracies.

American political parties serve a variety of political and social functions, some well and others not so well. The way they perform them differs from place to place and time to time.

Party Functions

Political parties are organizations that seek political power by electing people to office who will help party positions and philosophy become public policy.

Organize the Competition Parties exist primarily as an organizing mechanism to win elections and thus win control of government. For some races, parties recruit and nominate candidates for office; register and activate voters; and help candidates by training them, raising money for them, providing them with research and voter lists, and enlisting volunteers to work for them.[10]

Local and judicial elections in most states are **nonpartisan elections,** which means no party affiliation is indicated. Such systems make it more difficult for political parties to operate—precisely why many jurisdictions have adopted this reform, contending that party affiliation is not important to being a good judge or school board member. Lacking a party cue as a simplifying device, voters turn to name familiarity of candidates or other simplifying devices like incumbency. These local elections are also often held at times other than when state or federal elections are held. As a result, fewer voters tend to turn out for nonpartisan elections than for standard partisan elections.[11]

Unify the Electorate Parties are often accused of creating conflict, but they actually help unify the electorate and moderate conflict, at least within the party. Parties have a strong incentive to fight out their internal differences but come together to take on the opposition. Moreover, to win elections, parties need to reach out to voters outside their party and gain their support. This action also helps unify the electorate, at least into the two large national political parties in the American system.

Parties have great difficulty building coalitions on controversial issues such as abortion or gun control. Not surprisingly, candidates and parties generally try to avoid defining themselves or the election in single-issue terms. Rather, they hope that if voters disagree with the party's stand on one issue, they will still support it because they agree on other issues. Deemphasizing single issues in this way helps defuse conflict and unify the electorate.

Help Organize Government Although political parties in the United States are not as cohesive as in some other democracies, they are important when it comes to organizing our state and national governments. Congress is organized along party lines. The political party with the most votes in each chamber elects the officers of that chamber, selects the chair of each committee, and has a majority on all the committees. State legislatures, with the notable exception of Nebraska, are also organized along party lines. The 2006 election gave the Democrats winning majorities in both houses of Congress, and as a result, Democrats took over all the committee chairs.

The party that controls the White House, the governor's mansion, or city hall gets **patronage,** which means it can select party members as public officials or judges. Such appointments are limited only by civil service regulations that restrict patronage typically to the top posts, but these posts, which number approximately 3,000 in the federal government (not including ambassadors, U.S. Marshals, and U.S. Attorneys), are also numerous at the state and local levels. Patronage provides an incentive for people to become engaged in politics and gives party leaders and elected politicians loyal partisans in key positions to help them achieve their policy objectives. Patronage, sometimes called the *spoils system*, has declined dramatically in importance.

Translate Preferences into Policy One of the great strengths of our democracy is that even the party that wins an election usually has to moderate what it does to win reelection. Thus, public policy seldom changes dramatically after elections. Nonetheless, the party that wins the election has a chance to enact its policies and campaign promises.

political party
An organization that seeks political power by electing people to office so that its positions and philosophy become public policy.

nonpartisan election
An election in which candidates are not selected or endorsed by political parties and party affiliation is not listed on ballots.

patronage
The dispensing of government jobs to persons who belong to the winning political party.

American parties have had only limited success in setting the course of national policy, especially compared to countries with strong parties. The European model of party government, which has been called a *responsible party system*, assumes that parties discipline their members through their control over nominations and campaigns. Officeholders in such party-centered systems are expected to act according to party wishes and vote along party lines—or they will not be allowed to run again under the party label, generally preventing their reelection. Candidates also run on fairly specific party platforms and are expected to implement them if they win control in the election.

Because American parties do not control nominations, they are less able to discipline members who express views contrary to those of the party.[12] The American system is largely *candidate-centered*; politicians are nominated largely on the basis of their qualifications and personal appeal, not party loyalty. In fact, it is more correct to say that in most contests, we have *candidate* politics rather than *party* politics. As a consequence, party leaders cannot guarantee passage of their program, even if they are in the majority.

Political parties help inform and motivate voters. Here a senior and political science major at Western Kentucky University makes calls from the local Republican Party headquarters urging voters to support GOP candidates

Provide Loyal Opposition The party out of power closely monitors and comments on the actions of the party in power, providing accountability. When national security is at issue or the country is under attack, parties restrain their criticism, as the Democrats in Congress did for some time after September 11, 2001. There is usually a polite interval following an election—known as the **honeymoon**—after which the opposition party begins to criticize the party that controls the White House, especially when the opposition controls one or both houses of Congress.[13] The length of the honeymoon depends in part on how close the vote was in the election, on how contentious the agenda of the new administration is, and on the leadership skills of the new president. Early success in enacting policy can prolong the honeymoon; mistakes or controversies can shorten it.

The Nomination of Candidates

From the beginning, parties have been the mechanism by which candidates for public office are chosen. The **caucus** played an important part in pre-Revolutionary politics and continued to be important in our early history as elected officials organized themselves into groups or parties and together selected candidates to run for higher office, including the presidency. This method of nomination operated for several decades after the United States was established.

As early as the 1820s, however, critics were making charges of "secret deals." Moreover, the caucus was not representative of people from areas where a party was in a minority or nonexistent as only officeholders took part in it. Efforts were made to make the caucus more representative of rank-and-file party members. The *mixed caucus* brought in delegates from districts in which the party had no elected legislators.

Then, during the 1830s and 1840s, a system of **party conventions** was instituted. Delegates, usually chosen directly by party members in towns and cities, selected the party candidates, debated and adopted a platform, and built party spirit by celebrating noisily. But the convention method soon came under criticism that it was subject to control by the party bosses and their machines.

To draw more voters and reduce the power of the bosses to pick party nominees, states adopted the **direct primary,** in which people could vote for the party's nominees for office. Primaries spread rapidly after Wisconsin adopted them in 1905—in the North, as a Progressive Era reform, and in the South, as a way to bring democracy to a region that had seen no meaningful general elections since the end of Reconstruction in the 1870s because of one-party rule by the Democrats. By 1920, direct primaries were the norm for some offices in nearly all states.

Today, the direct primary is the typical method of picking party candidates. Primaries vary significantly from state to state. They differ in terms of (1) who may run in

honeymoon
The period at the beginning of a new president's term during which the president enjoys generally positive relations with the press and Congress, usually lasting about six months.

caucus
A meeting of local party members to choose party officials or candidates for public office and to decide the platform.

party convention
A meeting of party delegates to vote on matters of policy and, in some cases, to select party candidates for public office.

direct primary
An election in which voters choose party nominees.

Iowa's Democratic caucus is an unwieldy and complex process. Here, a precinct captain takes a head count to determine support for various candidates. ■ *What kinds of voters do you think the caucus process would tend to exclude?*

a primary and how he or she qualifies for the ballot; (2) whether the party organization can or does endorse candidates before the primary; (3) who may vote in a party's primary—that is, whether a voter must register with a party to vote; and (4) how many votes are needed for nomination—the most votes (a plurality), more than 50 percent (a majority), or some other number determined by party rule or state law. The differences among primaries are not trivial; they have an important impact on the role played by party organizations and on the strategy used by candidates.

In states with **open primaries,** any voter, regardless of party, can participate in the primary of whichever party he or she chooses. This kind of primary permits **crossover voting**—Republicans and Independents helping to determine who the Democratic nominee will be, and vice versa. Other states use **closed primaries,** in which only persons already registered in that party may participate. Some states, such as Washington and California, experimented with *blanket primaries,* in which all voters could vote for any candidate, regardless of party. Blanket primaries permitted voters to vote for a candidate of one party for one office and for a candidate from another party for another office, something that is not permitted under either closed or open primaries. In 2000, the Supreme Court held that California's blanket primary violated the free association rights of political parties, in part because blanket primaries permit people who have "expressly affiliated with a rival" party to have a vote in the selection of a nominee from a different party.[14] In a detailed study of California's blanket primary, political scientists found that fewer than 5 percent of voters associated with one party actually voted for nominees from another party. In 2010, California voters overwhelmingly passed an initiative to change the state's primary system to allow voters to cast their primary ballot for a candidate from any party, with the top two vote getters then running in the general election. Proponents of the "top two vote getter" primary see it as fostering more moderate politics.[15]

open primary
A primary election in which any voter, regardless of party, may vote.

crossover voting
Voting by a member of one party for a candidate of another party.

closed primary
A primary election in which only persons registered in the party holding the primary may vote.

minor party
A small political party that persists over time, is often composed of ideologies on the right or left, or is centered on a charismatic candidate. Such a party is also called a *third party*.

Along with modern communications and fund-raising techniques, direct primaries have diminished the influence of leaders of political parties. Many critics believe this change has had more undesirable than desirable consequences. Party leaders now have less influence over who gets to be the party's candidate, and candidates are less accountable to the party both during and after the election.

Party Systems

Ours is a two-party system; most other democracies have a multiparty system. Although the United States has many **minor parties,** only the two major parties have much of a chance to win elections. Multiparty systems are almost always found in countries that have a parliamentary government, in contrast to our presidential system.

Parliamentary systems usually have a *head of state*, often called the president, but they also have a *head of the government*, often called the prime minister or chancellor, who is the leader of one of the large parties in the legislature. In Germany, the chancellor, currently Angela Merkel, is elected by parliament and holds the greatest share of executive power. Typically, the chancellor comes from the largest party of a coalition of two or more parties and maintains power throughout a four-year term. In Germany, the president's responsibilities are mostly ceremonial, and he or she is expected to function in a politically neutral way. In democracies like Germany with multiparty systems, because no one party has a majority of the votes, *coalition* governments are necessary. Minor parties can gain concessions—positions in a cabinet or support of policies they want implemented—in return for joining a coalition. Major parties need the minor parties and are therefore willing to bargain.

Angela Merkel is the first female Chancellor of Germany. Because Germany has a multiparty system, she has presided over several coalition governments.

Thus, the multiparty system favors the existence of minor parties by giving them incentives to persevere and disproportionate power if they will help form a government. In some multiparty parliamentary systems, parties run slates of candidates for legislative positions, and winners are determined by **proportional representation,** in which the parties receive a proportion of the legislators corresponding to their proportion of the vote. In our single-member district, **winner-take-all system,** only the candidate with the most votes in a district or state takes office.[16] Because a party does not gain anything by finishing second, minor parties in a two-party system can rarely overcome the assumption that a vote for them is a wasted vote.[17] For this reason, an election system in which the winner is the candidate in a single-member district with the plurality deciding the winner, there is tendency to have two parties. This regularity is called *Duverger's law.*[18]

Minor Parties: Persistence and Frustration

Although we have a primarily two-party system in the United States, we also have minor parties, sometimes called *third parties.* Candidate-based parties that arise around a candidate usually disappear when the charismatic personality does. In most states, candidates can get their names on the ballot as an Independent or minor party candidate by securing the required number of signatures on a nomination petition. This is hard to do. In 1992, Ross Perot spent his own money to build an organization of volunteers who put his name on the ballot in all 50 states. Minor party candidates such as Ralph Nader in 2000 secured their nominations as candidates of existing minor parties.

Minor parties that are organized around an ideology usually persist over a longer time than those built around a particular leader. Communist, Prohibition, Libertarian, Right to Life, and Green Parties are of the ideological type. Minor parties of both types come and go, and several minor parties usually run in any given election. Some parties arise around a single issue, like the Right to Life Party active in states like New York. The Green Party is another example of an ideological third party. Although they are often visible, minor parties have never won the presidency (see Table 4–1) or more than a handful of congressional seats.[19] They have done only somewhat better in gubernatorial elections.[20] They have never shaped national policy from *inside* the government, and their influence on national policy and on the platforms of the two major parties has been limited.[21] Minor parties operating in recent elections include the Libertarian, Green, and Reform Parties.

proportional representation
An election system in which each party running receives the proportion of legislative seats corresponding to its proportion of the vote.

winner-take-all system
An election system in which the candidate with the most votes wins.

American Parties Today

LEARNING **OBJECTIVE**
4.2 Differentiate the functions of parties as institutions, parties in government, and parties in the electorate.

American adults typically take political parties for granted.[22] If anything, most people are critical or distrustful of them. Some see parties as corrupt institutions, interested only in the spoils of politics. Critics charge that parties evade the issues, fail to deliver on their promises, have no new ideas, follow public opinion rather than lead it, or are just one more special interest.

TABLE 4–1 Minor Parties in the United States

Year	Party	Presidential Candidate	Percentage of Popular Vote Received	Electoral Votes
1832	Anti-Masonic	William Wirt	8	7
1856	American (Know-Nothing)	Millard Fillmore	22	8
1860	Democratic (Secessionist)	John C. Breckinridge	18	72
1860	Constitutional Union	John Bell	13	39
1892	People's (Populist)	James B. Weaver	9	22
1912	Bull Moose	Theodore Roosevelt	27	88
1912	Socialist	Eugene V. Debs	6	0
1924	Progressive	Robert M. La Follette	17	13
1948	States' Rights (Dixiecrat)	Strom Thurmond	2	39
1948	Progressive	Henry A. Wallace	2	0
1968	American Independent	George C. Wallace	14	46
1980	National Unity	John Anderson	7	0
1992	Independent	Ross Perot	19	0
1996	Reform	Ross Perot	8	0
2000	Reform	Pat Buchanan	0	0
2000	Green	Ralph Nader	3	0
2004	Reform	Ralph Nader	0	0
2008	Independent	Ralph Nader	0	0

There are 538 electoral votes cast in a presidential election. ■ *How does the percentage of popular vote received compare to the electoral votes received? How can you explain the difference in these numbers?*

SOURCE: C.Q. Press Voting and Elections Collection, 2010, http://library.cqpress.com/elections/search.php.

Still, most people understand that parties are necessary. They want party labels kept on the ballot, at least for congressional, presidential, and statewide elections. Most voters think of themselves as Democrats or Republicans and typically vote for candidates from their party. They collectively contribute millions of dollars to the two major parties.[23] Thus, they appreciate, at least vaguely, that you cannot run a big democracy without parties.

Both the Democratic and Republican national parties and most state parties are moderate in their policies and leadership.[24] Successful party leaders must be diplomatic; to win presidential elections and congressional majorities, they must find a middle ground among competing and sometimes hostile groups. Members of the House of Representatives, to be elected and reelected, have to appeal to a majority of the voters from their own district. As more districts have become "safe" for incumbents, the House has had fewer moderates and is prone to more partisan ideological clashes than the Senate.

Parties as Institutions

Like other institutions of government—Congress, the presidency, and the courts—political parties have rules, procedures, and organizational structure. What are the institutional characteristics of political parties?

national party convention
A national meeting of delegates elected in primaries, caucuses, or state conventions who assemble once every four years to nominate candidates for president and vice president, ratify the party platform, elect officers, and adopt rules.

National Party Leadership The supreme authority in both major parties is the **national party convention,** which meets every four years for four days to nominate candidates for president and vice president, to ratify the party platform, and to adopt rules.

In charge of the national party, when it is not assembled in convention, is the *national committee.* In recent years, both parties have strengthened the role of the

Of the People
THE GLOBAL COMMUNITY

A Competitive Two-Party System

Having a competitive two-party system is something that citizens of the United States take for granted, but not all countries place the same level of importance on it. In the Pew Global opinion survey in 2003 and 2009*, respondents were asked, "How important is it to you to live in a country where honest elections are held regularly with a choice of at least two political parties?"

Respondents from the United States were most likley to say that being able to choose from at least two political parties was very important, with 84 percent giving this response. In contrast, only 43 percent of respondents from Korea gave this answer, and slightly more than half in India thought a choice of at least two politial parties is very important. Mexico, a country which for many years was governed by one party, had slightly more than half of respondents thinking a choice between two parties is very important.

Germany, like many countries in Europe, has a strong party system and more than two competitive parties and had a similar pattern of opinion to the United States on the importance of a two-party system. When looking at a worldwide sample, approximately 60 percent think having a choice between two or more parties is very important.

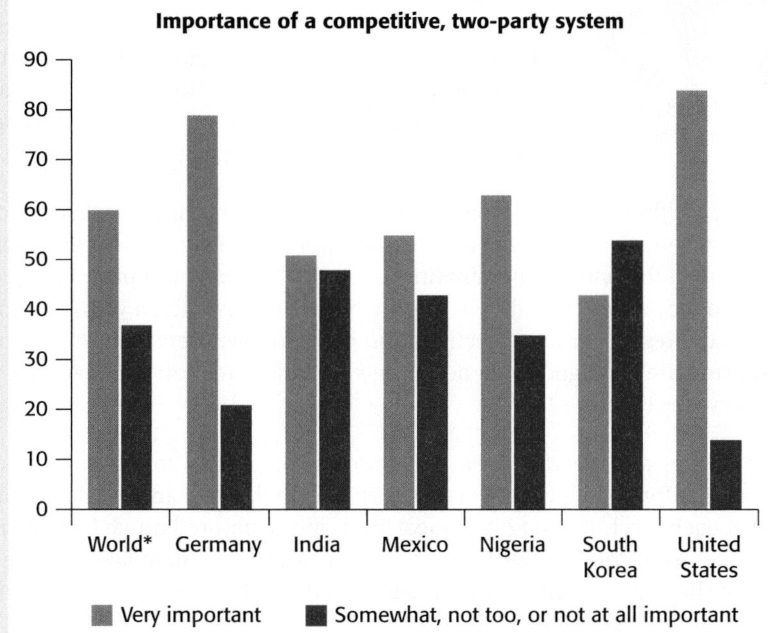

SOURCE: Data for Germany, South Korea, and the United States came from The Pew Global Attitudes Project, 2002. Data for the world average, India, Mexico, and Nigeria came from the Pew Global Attitudes Project, 2008. Note: Because not all countries were included in the 2009 Survey, we have included responses from the most recent survey for that country.

*The world average contains the average responses for the Pew sample for the question, which consists primarily of developing countries. It is not representative of the world as a whole.

CRITICAL THINKING QUESTIONS

1. What factors do you think explain people's belief that having a choice between at least two political parties is important?
2. Germany abandoned two parties with the rise to power of Hitler. To what extent do you think that experience influences the attitudes of Germans toward a competitive two-party system today?
3. South Korea is a neighbor to North Korea, one of the few remaining single-party states. Given this, why do you think South Koreans are not more inclined to see a competitive two-party system as very important?

*Some countries in our other *Global Community* boxes, such as China, were not included in the sample, in part because they do not have a competitive two or more party system.

national committee and enhanced the influence of individual committee members. The committees are now more representative of the party rank-and-file. But in neither party is the national committee the center of party leadership.

Each major party has a *national chair* as its top official. The national committee formally elects the chair, but in reality, this official is the choice of the presidential nominee. For the party that controls the White House, the chair actually serves at the pleasure of the president and does the president's bidding. Party chairs often change after elections. During the 2010 election cycle, the Republican National Committee (RNC) chair was Michael Steele, a former Maryland lieutenant governor who took the helm of the RNC after the 2008 election. Steele, an African American, became a visible spokesperson for the GOP and a critic of the Obama administration.

Michael Steele, Republican National Committee (RNC) Chairman, faced some opposition from within the party for his mismanagement of election spending and disappointing fundraising.

The Democratic National Committee (DNC) is led by former Virginia governor Tim Kaine. His term of service at the DNC started in 2009, overlapping with his last year as governor. Kane was considered as a possible running mate by Obama in 2008.

In addition to the national party committees, there are national congressional and senatorial campaign committees. These committees work to recruit candidates, train them, make limited contributions to them, and spend independently in some of the most competitive contests.[25] The National Republican Senatorial Committee (NRSC) and Democratic Senatorial Campaign Committee (DSCC) are led by senators elected to two-year terms by their fellow party members in the Senate. The National Republican Campaign Committee (NRCC) and Democratic Congressional Campaign Committee (DCCC) have leaders chosen in the same manner by fellow partisans in the House. Chairs of campaign committees are nominated by their party leadership and typically ratified by their party caucus.

Party Platforms Although national party committees exist primarily to win elections and gain control of government, policy goals are also important. Every four years, each party adopts a platform at the national nominating convention. The typical party *platform*—the official statement of party policy, that hardly anyone reads—is often a vague and ponderous document, the result of many meetings and compromises between groups and individuals. Platforms are ambiguous by design, giving voters few obvious reasons to vote against the party (see Figure 4–1).[26]

Parties at the State and Local Levels The two major parties are decentralized. They have organizations for each level of government: national, state, and local; and organize for elections at each level. The state and local levels are structured much like the national level. Each state has a *state committee* headed by a *state chair.* State law determines the composition of the state committees and regulates them. Members of state committees are usually elected from local areas.

Powerful state parties have developed in recent years. Despite much state-to-state variation, the trend is toward stronger state organizations, with Republicans typically being much better funded.[27] Some states have significant third and fourth parties. New York, for instance, has a Conservative Party in addition to the Democratic and Republican Parties. The role that minor parties play in statewide elections can be important, even though they rarely win office themselves.

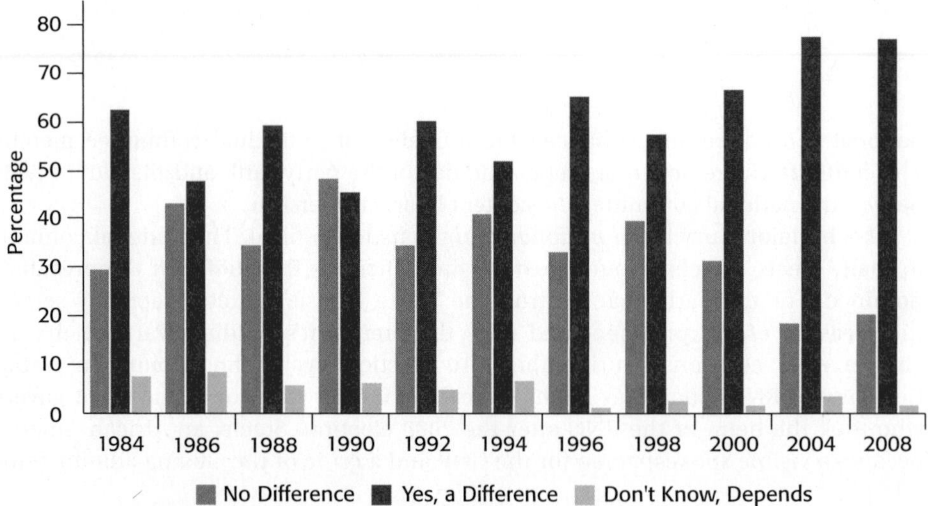

FIGURE 4–1 Difference in Perception of What the Parties Stand For, 1984–2008.
A National Election survey tracks responses to the question, "Do you think there are any important differences in what the Republicans and Democrats stand for?" ■ *Why would people be more likely to see differences between parties in presidential election years than in midterm election years?*

SOURCE: *2004 National Election Study,* "Important Difference in What Democratic and Republican Parties Stand For, 1952–2004" (Center for Political Studies, University of Michigan, 2004); and *2008 National Election Study* (Center for Political Studies, University of Michigan, 2008).

Below the state committees are county committees, which vary widely in function and power. These committees recruit candidates for such offices as county commissioner, sheriff, and treasurer. Often this means finding a candidate for the office, not deciding among competing contenders. For a party that rarely wins an election, the county committee has to struggle to find someone willing to run. When the chance of winning is greater, primaries, not the party leaders, usually decide the winner.[28] Many county organizations are active, distributing campaign literature, organizing telephone campaigns, putting up posters and lawn signs, and canvassing door-to-door. Other county committees do not function at all, and many party leaders are just figureheads.

Parties in Government

Political parties are central to the operation of our government. They help bridge the separation of powers and facilitate coordination between levels of government in a federal system.

In the Legislative Branch Members of Congress take their partisanship seriously, at least while in Washington. Their power and influence are determined by whether their party is in control of the House or Senate; they also have a stake in which party controls the White House. The chairs of all standing committees in Congress come from the majority party, as do the presiding officials of both chambers. Members of both houses sit together with fellow partisans on the floor and in committee. (We discuss the role of parties in Congress in greater detail in Chapter 7.) Political parties help bridge the separation of powers between the legislative and executive branches by creating partisan incentives to cooperate. Partisanship can also help unify the two houses of Congress.

Congressional staffs are also partisan. Members of Congress expect their staff—from the volunteer intern to the senior staffer—to be loyal, first to them and then to their party. Should you decide to go to work for a representative or senator, you would be expected to identify yourself with that person's party, and you would have difficulty finding a job with the other party later. Employees of the House and Senate—elevator operators, Capitol Hill police, and even the chaplain—hold patronage jobs. With few exceptions, such jobs go to persons from the party that has a majority in the House or the Senate.

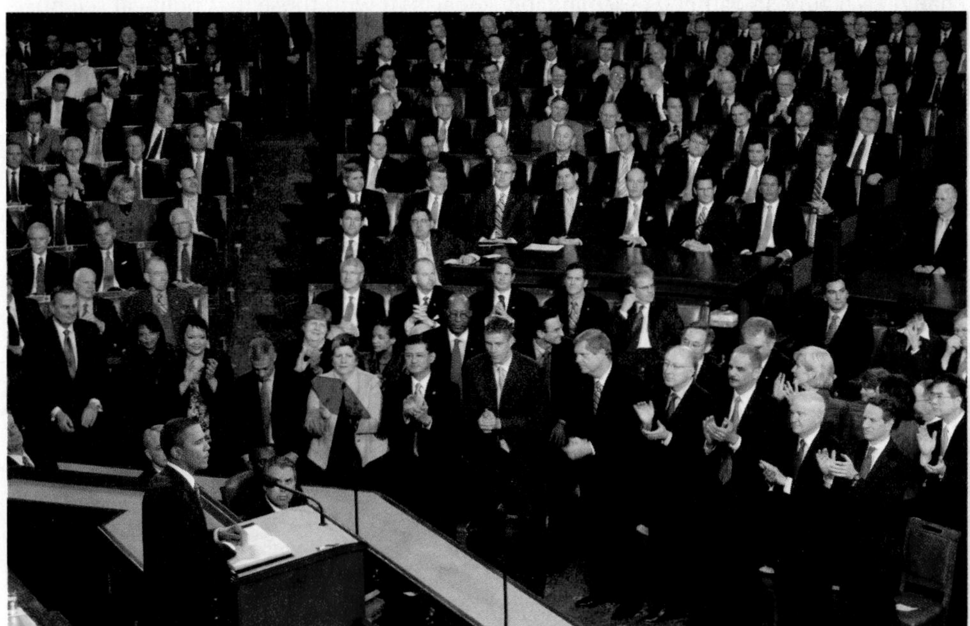

Members of Congress sit together by party during the annual State of the Union address and often respond to the speaker along partisan lines. As shown here during President Obama's 2010 address, they also tend to stand and applaud—or sit and not applaud—in unison as a party. ■ *Why do members of Congress choose to respond to an event like the State of the Union address as a party instead of as individuals?*

In the Executive Branch Presidents select nearly all senior White House staff and cabinet members from their own party. In addition, presidents typically surround themselves with advisers who have campaigned with them and proved their party loyalty. Partisanship is also important in presidential appointments to the highest levels of the federal workforce. Party commitment, including making campaign contributions, is expected of those who seek these positions.

In the Judicial Branch The judicial branch of the national government, with its lifetime tenure and political independence, is designed to operate in an expressly nonpartisan manner. Judges, unlike Congress, do not sit together by political party. But the appointment process for judges has been partisan from the beginning. The landmark case establishing the principle of judicial review, *Marbury* v. *Madison* (1803), concerned the efforts of one party to stack the judiciary with fellow partisans before leaving office.[29] (See Chapter 2.) Today, party identification remains an important consideration when nominating federal judges.

At the State and Local Levels The importance of party in the operation of local government varies among states and localities. In some states, such as New York and Illinois, local parties play an even stronger role than they do at the national level. In others, such as Nebraska, parties play almost no role. In Nebraska, the state legislature is expressly nonpartisan, although factions perform like parties and still play a role. Parties are likewise unimportant in the government of most city councils. But in most states and many cities, parties are important to the operation of the legislature, governorship, or mayoralty. Judicial selection in most states is also a partisan matter. Much was made by the 2000 Bush campaign of the fact that six of the seven Florida Supreme Court justices deciding the 2000 ballot-counting case in favor of Gore were Democrats. Democrats noted that the five U.S. Supreme Court justices who decided the election in favor of Bush were nominated by Republican presidents.

Parties in the Electorate

Political parties would be of little significance if they did not have meaning to the electorate. Adherents of the two parties are drawn to them by a combination of factors, including their stand on the issues; personal or party history; religious, racial, or social peer grouping; and the appeal of their candidates. The emphases among these factors change over time, but they are remarkably consistent with those that political scientists identified more than 40 years ago.[30]

Party Registration For citizens in most states, "party" has a particular legal meaning—**party registration.** When voters register to vote in these states, they are asked to state their party preference. They then become registered members of one of the two major parties or a third party, although they can change their party registration. The purpose of party registration is to limit the participants in primary elections to members of that party and to make it easier for parties to contact people who might vote for their party.

Party Activists Activists tend to fall into three broad categories: party regulars, candidate activists, and issue activists. *Party regulars* place the party first. They value winning elections and understand that compromise and moderation may be necessary to reach that objective. They also realize that it is important to keep the party together because a fractured party only helps the opposition.

Candidate activists are followers of a particular candidate who see the party as the means to elect their candidate. Candidate activists are often not concerned with the other operations of the party—with nominees for other offices or with raising money for the party. For example, people who supported Ron Paul in his unsuccessful run for the presidency as a Republican were candidate activists. Paul, a Libertarian Republican congressman from Texas, had previously run for the presidency as a Libertarian.

Issue activists wish to push the parties in a particular direction on a single issue or a narrow range of issues: the war in Iraq, abortion, taxes, school prayer, the environment, or civil rights, among others. To issue activists, the party platform is an important battleground because they want the party to endorse their position. Issue activists

party registration
The act of declaring party affiliation; required by some states when one registers to vote.

are also often candidate activists if they can find a candidate willing to embrace their position.

A member of the College Democrats at Ohio State University campaigns for Democratic candidates. While young people identify in greater numbers with the Democratic Party, exit polls suggest that many of the young Democratic voters newly registered in 2008 did not turn out for the 2010 election.

■ *Do you identify strongly with a political party?*

Party Identification

Party registration and party activists are important, but many voters are not registered with a political party. Most American adults are mere spectators of party activity. They lack the partisan commitment and interest needed for active involvement. This is not to say that they find parties irrelevant or unimportant. For them, partisanship is what political scientists call **party identification**—a psychological attachment to a political party that most people acquire in childhood from their parents.[31] This type of voter may sometimes vote for a candidate from the other party, but without a compelling reason to do otherwise, most will vote according to their party identification. Peers and early political experiences reinforce party identification as part of the political socialization process described in Chapter 3.

Political scientists and pollsters use the answers to the following questions to measure party identification: "Generally speaking, in politics, do you usually think of yourself as a Republican, a Democrat, an Independent, or what?" Persons who answer Republican or Democrat are then asked: "Would you call yourself a strong or a not very strong Republican/Democrat?" Persons who answer Independent are asked: "Do you think of yourself as closer to the Republican or the Democratic Party?" Persons who do not indicate Democrat, Republican, or Independent to the first question rarely exceed 2 percent of the electorate and include those who are apolitical or who identify with one of the minor political parties.

When these questions are combined in a single measure, there are seven categories of partisan identification: strong Democrats, weak Democrats, Independent-leaning Democrats, pure Independents, Independent-leaning Republicans, weak Republicans, and strong Republicans. During the more than 50-year period in which political scientists have been conducting such surveys, partisan preferences of the public as a whole have remained remarkably stable, even though new voters have been added to the electorate—minorities and 18- to 21-year-olds (see Table 4–2). For some sub-populations like Protestants and Catholics, partisan allegiances have changed over time (see *Of the People: America's Changing Face* box).

party identification
An affiliation with a political party that most people acquire in childhood.

TABLE 4–2 Party Identification, 1950s–2000s

Decade	Strong Democrat	Weak Democrat	Independent-Leaning Democrat	Independent	Independent-Leaning Republican	Weak Republican	Strong Republican	Other
1950*	23%	23%	8%	7%	7%	15%	13%	4%
1960	22	25	8	10	7	15	12	2
1970	17	24	12	14	10	14	9	2
1980	18	26	11	12	11	14	11	2
1990	18	19	13	10	12	15	13	1
2000†	18	16	16	10	12	13	14	2

* 1950s percentages based on years 1952, 1956, and 1958.
† 2000s percentages based on years 2000, 2002, 2004, and 2008.

NOTE: Data may not sum to 100 percent because of averaging.

■ *How has the strength of party identification changed over time?*

SOURCE: *National Election Study* (Center for Political Studies, University of Michigan, 2004).

Party identification is the single best predictor of how people will vote.[32] Unlike candidates and issues, which come and go, party identification is a long-term element in voting choice. The strength of party identification is also important in predicting participation and political interest. Strong Republicans and strong Democrats participate more actively in politics than any other groups and are generally better informed about political issues. Pure Independents are just the opposite; they vote at the lowest rates and have the lowest levels of interest and awareness of any of the categories of party identification. This evidence runs counter to the notions that persons who are strong partisans are unthinking party adherents and that Independents are informed and ideal citizens.[33]

Partisan Realignment

American political parties have evolved and changed over time, but some underlying characteristics have been constant. Historically, we have had a two-party system with minor parties. Our parties are moderate and accommodative, meaning they are open to people with diverse outlooks. Political scientist V. O. Key and others have argued that our party system has been shaped in large part by **realigning elections.** Also called *critical elections*, these are turning points that define the agenda of politics and the alignment of voters within parties during periods of historic change in the economy and society.

Realigning elections are characterized by intense voter involvement, disruptions of traditional voting patterns, changes in the relationships of power within the broader political community, and the formation of new and durable electoral groupings. They have occurred cyclically, about every 32 years, and tend to coincide with expansions of suffrage or changes in the rate of voting.[34] Political scientists generally agree that there have been four realigning elections in American party history: 1824, 1860, 1896, and 1932. Although some argued that the United States was due for another in the 1970s and 1980s, there is little evidence that such an election occurred or is likely in the immediate future.

In fact, as shown in Table 4–2, partisan identification has been stable for more than four decades, despite such changes to the electorate as adding minorities and 18- to 21-year-olds. In addition, as Figure 4–2 suggests, Americans have shown no consistent preference for one party over the other in their votes in presidential elections. In a time of electoral volatility, the basics of politics determine the winners and losers: who attracts positive voter attention, who strikes themes that motivate voters to participate, and who communicates better with voters.

realigning election
An election during periods of expanded suffrage and change in the economy and society that proves to be a turning point, redefining the agenda of politics and the alignment of voters within parties.

dealignment
Weakening of partisan preferences that point to a rejection of both major parties and a rise in the number of Independents.

However, some experts argue that Independents are increasing in number, suggesting that the party system may be in a period of **dealignment,** in which partisan preferences are weakening and there is a rise in the number of Independents. Indeed, the number of self-classified Independents has increased from 22 percent in the 1950s to 38 percent in 2009. However, two-thirds of all self-identified Independents are really partisans

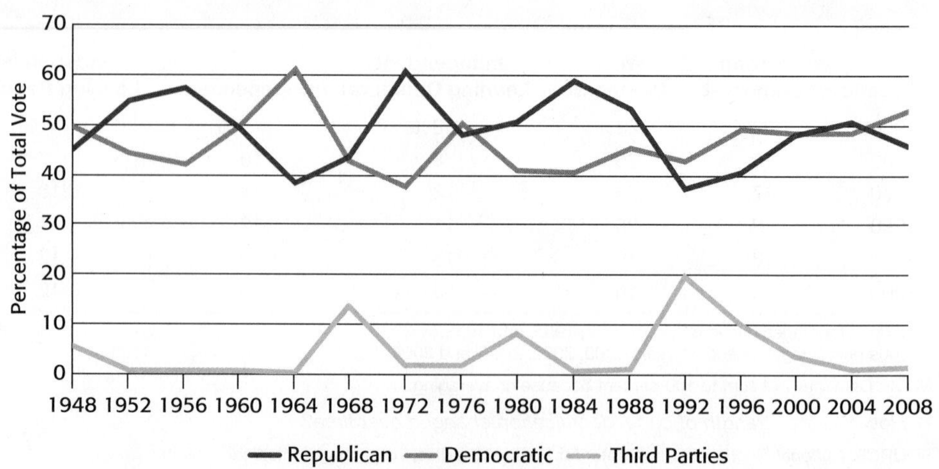

FIGURE 4–2 **Presidential Vote by Party.**
■ *Based on this graph, what share of the vote do third parties generally get? How many elections since 1952 have been exceptions to this?*

SOURCE: Stanley and Niemi, *Vital Statistics on American Politics 2009–2010*, pp. 20–21.

Of the People

AMERICA'S CHANGING FACE

Portrait of the Electorate

Throughout the 44-year period from 1964–2008, the demographic composition of the two major political parties has undergone some changes, while at the same time retaining some important similarities. Consistent with the Republican Party's having become stronger, we find slightly more Republicans than Democrats among men in 2008. In 1964, men were twice as likely to be Democrats as Republicans. Women are disproportionately Democratic in 2008, as they were in 1964. Lower-income voters have consistently been more Democratic, and higher-income voters more Republican. Younger voters in both 1964 and 2008 were more likely to be Democrats. In 1964, Democrats enjoyed strong support from Protestants, Catholics, and Jews. By 2008, Protestants were disproportionately Republican, and the Democratic margin among Catholics had dropped significantly. Jewish voters remained heavily Democratic. In 1964, 59 percent of whites were Democrats; by 2008, the white population was more Republican than Democratic. Blacks were heavily Democratic in both 1964 and 2008. The changing face of party composition has implications for electoral competition and campaign strategy.

CRITICAL THINKING QUESTIONS

1. Why have more white men become Republicans while white women have remained Democrats?
2. What might explain the shift to the GOP among Protestants and Catholics but not Jews?
3. How does the changing demographics of the two parties affect campaigns?

	1964			2008		
	Republican	**Democrat**	**Independent**	**Republican**	**Democrat**	**Independent**
Sex						
Male	30%	61%	8%	40%	46%	12%
Female	30	61	7	35	55	9
Race						
White	33	59	8	45	43	10
Black	8	82	6	6	85	8
Hispanic	—	—	—	22	63	14
Age						
18–34	26	64	9	30	56	12
35–45	32	59	8	41	47	10
46–55	26	65	8	41	49	9
56–64	28	66	6	35	54	11
65+	43	49	6	44	48	7
Religion						
Protestant	34	58	7	54	39	7
Catholic	22	70	9	39	51	10
Jewish	11	76	13	19	81	0
Other	28	55	16	28	58	13
Region						
Northeast	36	54	10	34	54	11
North-Central	36	55	8	36	51	11
South	20	71	7	42	46	11
West	30	63	7	32	60	7
Total	30	61	8	37	51	10

NOTE: Numbers may not add to 100 because of rounding. Independents that lean toward a party are classified with the party toward which they lean. Race is defined by the first race with which a respondent identifies. Income is classified as the respondent's household income.

SOURCE: *1964 National Election Study* (Center for Political Studies, University of Michigan, 1964); and *2008 National Election Study* (Center for Political Studies, University of Michigan, 2008).

TABLE
4–3 Voting Behavior of Partisans and Independents, 1992–2008

	Percent Voting for Democratic Presidential Candidate				
	1992	**1996**	**2000**	**2004**	**2008**
Strong Democrats	94%	96%	97%	98%	95%
Weak Democrats	69	84	85	85	86
Independent-Leaning Democrats	70	74	78	88	91
Pure Independents	41	39	45	58	55
Independent-Leaning Republicans	11	23	14	15	18
Weak Republicans	14	21	16	11	12
Strong Republicans	3	4	2	3	4

■ *How did the votes of Independents make a difference for President Obama in 2008?*

SOURCE: National Election Study Cumulative File (Center for Political Studies, University of Michigan, 2005); and 2008 National Election Study (Center for Political Studies, University of Michigan, 2008).

in their voting behavior and attitudes. Table 4–3 summarizes voting behavior in recent contests for president. One-third of those who claim to be Independents lean toward the Democratic Party and vote Democratic in election after election. Another third lean toward Republicans and just as predictably vote Republican. The remaining third, who appear to be genuine Independents, do not vote consistently and appear to have little interest in politics. Thus, despite the reported growth in numbers, there are proportionately approximately the same number of pure Independents now as in 1956.

How Parties Raise and Spend Money

LEARNING **OBJECTIVE**

4.3 Assess the regulation of party fundraising and expenditures.

Although parties cannot exert tight control over candidates, their ability to raise and spend money has had a significant influence. Political parties, like candidates, rely on contributions from individuals and interest groups to fund their activities. Because of the close connection political parties have with officeholders, the courts have long permitted regulation of the source and amount of money people and groups can contribute to parties, as well as the amount parties can spend with or contribute to candidates.

Under the post–Watergate reforms (Federal Election Campaign Act or FECA, as amended in 1974), contributions to the parties from individuals were limited to $20,000, whereas the limit for political action committees (PACs) was $15,000.[35] As we discuss in Chapter 6, PACs are more inclined to give to candidates than party committees.

After the 1976 election, both parties pressed for further amendments to FECA, claiming that campaign finance reforms resulted in insufficient money for generic party activities such as billboard advertising and get-out-the-vote drives. The 1979 amendments to FECA and the interpretations of this legislation by the Federal Election Commission (FEC) permitted unlimited **soft money** contributions to the parties by individuals and PACs for these party-building purposes. Unions and corporations were also allowed to give parties unlimited amounts of soft money. This unregulated money was thus easier to raise and could be spent in unlimited amounts as long as the parties could claim a party-building purpose.

In the 1996 election cycle, both parties found ways to spend this soft money to promote the election or defeat of specific candidates, effectively circumventing party spending limits.[36] In the 1998, 2000, and 2002 elections, congressional campaign committees, following the lead of the national party committees in the 1996 presidential election, raised unprecedented amounts of soft money. In 2000, all party committees combined raised $500 million in soft money. This money was spent in large amounts in the most competitive races. In many instances, this soft money paid for broadcast advertisements that did not even mention the party.[37]

soft money
Money raised in unlimited amounts by political parties for party-building purposes. Now largely illegal except for limited contributions to state or local parties for voter registration and get-out-the-vote efforts.

After repeated defeats in one or both houses of Congress for 15 years, Congress regulated this unrestricted soft money under the **Bipartisan Campaign Reform Act (BCRA)** in 2002. As we will see in Chapter 6, soft money was almost entirely banned under the Act, whereas the limits on individual contributions to candidates and party committees were roughly doubled and indexed to inflation, and a more realistic definition of what constituted election communications by groups was enacted.

The new laws raised serious questions about how the parties would cope without this once-unregulated money in 2004 and thereafter. In 2004, individual giving to both parties set new records, and the DNC and RNC raised as much in **hard money** from individuals and PACs as they had raised in both hard and soft money combined in 2000 or 2002. Much of this money is coming from individuals, including many small contributions.

Party Expenditures

Party committees are permitted to make contributions to candidates and can also spend a limited amount of money in what are called "coordinated expenditures." In the last several election cycles, the party committees have concentrated their contributions and coordinated expenditures in the most competitive contests.

Parties, like individuals and groups, can now also spend unlimited amounts for and against candidates as long as the expenditures are independent of the candidate or a party committee.[38] Unlike soft money, **party-independent expenditures** must use money raised with normal hard money contribution limits. As long as the party committees could use soft money, independent expenditures were of lesser importance, but with the BCRA ban on soft money, there has been a surge in party-independent expenditure activity (see Table 4–4).

Aside from the Democratic National Committee, all other party committees in Table 4–4 continued to spend heavily in independent expenditures in 2008. This money in 2008 was again spent in only a few competitive races. But where parties invest, they do so in substantial amounts.

During the debate over BCRA, and in the court case on its constitutionality, some, such as political scientist Sidney Milkes, speculated that BCRA's soft money ban would weaken political parties.[39] The surge in individual contributions has demonstrated the opposite; the DNC and RNC could and did find an alternative to unregulated money.

Bipartisan Campaign Reform Act (BCRA)
Largely banned party soft money, restored long-standing prohibition on corporations and labor unions use of general treasury funds for electoral purposes, and narrowed the definition of issue advocacy.

hard money
Political contributions given to a party, candidate, or interest group that are limited in amount and fully disclosed. Raising such limited funds was harder than raising unlimited soft money, hence the term "hard money."

party-independent expenditures
Spending by political party committees that is independent of the candidate. The spending occurs in relatively few competitive contests and is often substantial.

Former Alaska governor Sarah Palin speaks during the Republican 2010 Victory Fundraising Rally. Palin was instrumental in raising money for numerous winning Republican candidates. ■ *As Sarah Palin wasn't running in this election, why do you suppose she would campaign and raise money on behalf of Republican Party candidates?*

TABLE 4–4 Independent Expenditures by Party Committee, 1996–2008

	1996	1998	2000	2002	2004	2006	2008
DNC	$0	$0	$0	$0	$120,333,466	–$23,104	$1,104,113
DSCC	1,386,022	1,329,000	133,000	0	18,725,520	42,627,470	73,028,432
DCCC	0	0	1,933,246	1,187,649	36,923,726	64,141,248	81,641,424
RNC	0	0	0	500,000	18,268,870	14,022,675	53,459,386
NRSC	9,734,445	216,874	267,600	0	19,383,692	19,159,901	110,866,286
NRCC	0	0	548,800	1,321,880	47,254,064	82,059,161	30,971,545

NOTE: There was no independent spending by party committees before 1996. When party committees could spend soft money (1996–2002), they spent less in independent expenditures; when BCRA banned soft money in 2002, independent expenditures rose.

■ *Based on the data in this table, which election marked a substantial change in the amount of money spent independently by party committees? How did the spending between Democratic and Republican committees compare in 2008?*

SOURCE: Federal Election Commission, "Party Financial Activity Summarized for the 2004 Election Cycle," press release, March 2, 2005, www.fec.gov/press/press2005/20050302party/Party2004final.html; and David B. Magleby and Kelly D. Patterson, eds., *War Games: Issues and Resources in the Battle for Control of Congress*, monograph (Center for the Study of Elections and Democracy, 2007), p. 47.

It remains unclear whether the four congressional party committees can make up for the loss of soft money, but the surge in individual contributions to them is promising. The independent expenditure option allows parties to continue to direct money well in excess of the normal limits to races they thought were more competitive.

Compared to other countries, the United States has less public funding of political parties and candidates. Holding the United States aside, wealthier countries (by GDP per capita) have broader regulations than do less-wealthy countries. Britain and Japan, for example, both have limits on the sources of money allowed, disclosure, free television time to parties, and limits on paid television advertising.[40] In contrast, Nigeria only requires disclosure of donors, which could account for the overwhelming role that money plays in Nigerian elections.[41]

A Nation of Interests

LEARNING **OBJECTIVE**

4.4 Explain the role of interest groups in American politics, and categorize interest groups into types.

The founders of the Republic were very worried about groups with common interests, which they called **factions.** (They also thought of political parties as factions.) For the framers of the Constitution, the daunting problem was how to establish a stable and orderly constitutional system that would both respect the liberty of free citizens and prevent the tyranny of the majority or of a single dominant interest.

As a talented practical politician and a brilliant theorist, James Madison offered both a diagnosis and a solution in *The Federalist*, No. 10 (reprinted in the Appendix). He began with a basic proposition: "The latent causes of faction are... sown in the nature of man." All individuals pursue their self-interest, seeking advantage or power over others. Acknowledging that we live in a maze of group interests, Madison argued that the "most common and durable source of factions has been the various and unequal distribution of property." Madison called a faction "a number of citizens, whether amounting to a majority or minority of the whole, who are united and actuated by some common impulse of passion, or of interest, adverse to the rights of other citizens, or to the permanent and aggregate interests of the community." For Madison, "the *causes* of faction cannot be removed, and... relief is only to be sought in the means of controlling its *effects*."[42]

faction
A term the founders used to refer to political parties and special interests or interest groups.

pluralism
A theory of government that holds that open, multiple, and competing groups can check the asserted power by any one group.

James Madison played a critical role in drafting and enacting the Constitution, and many of its provisions are aimed at limiting the "mischiefs of faction." Separation of powers and checks and balances make it hard for a faction to dominate government. Staggered terms of office make it necessary for a faction to endure. But rather than trying to encourage one or another faction, the Constitution encourages competition between them. Indeed, checks and balances arguably function best when factions within the branches work to counter one another. The Constitution envisions a plurality of groups competing with each other, an idea that has been called **pluralism.**

How well pluralism has worked in practice is debated.[43] We will see that over time, government has sought to regulate factions as a response to the power some groups such as corporations, unions, and wealthy individuals have had in American government. The debate about how to check their power without damaging their liberty is an enduring one.

After the controversial election in Iran, protestors took to the streets to call for change, and the government responded with violence and repression. ■ *What aspects of the American democracy, which are not present in Iran, allow for groups to engage in peaceful protests?*

Some U.S. citizens identify with groups distinguished by race, gender, ethnic background, age, occupation, religion, or sexual orientation. Others form voluntary groups based on their opinions about issues such as gun control or tax reduction. When such associations seek to influence government, they are called **interest groups.**

Interest groups are also sometimes called "special interests." Politicians and the media often use this term in a pejorative way. What makes an interest group a "special" one? The answer is highly subjective. One person's *special* interest is another's *public* interest. However, so-called public interest groups such as Common Cause or the League of Women Voters support policies that not everyone agrees with. Politics is best seen as a clash among interests, with differing concepts of what is in the public interest, rather than as a battle between the special interests on one side and "the people" or the public interest on the other.

In fact, the term "special interest" conveys a selfish or narrow view, one that may lack credibility. For this reason, we use the neutral term "interest groups." An interest group simply speaks for some, but not all, of us. A democracy includes many interests and many organized interest groups. The democratic process exists to decide among them. Part of the politics of interest groups is thus to persuade the general public that their interest is more important.

Interest groups vary widely. Some are formal associations or organizations like the National Rifle Association (NRA); others have no formal organization. Some are organized primarily to persuade public officials on issues of concern to the group such as reducing greenhouse gases; others conduct research, or influence public opinion with published reports and mass mailings.

We can categorize interest groups into several broad types: (1) economic, including both business and labor; (2) ideological or single-issue; (3) public interest; (4) foreign policy; and (5) government itself. The varied and overlapping nature of interest groups in the United States has been described as *interest group pluralism*, meaning that competition among open, responsive, and diverse groups helps preserve democratic values and limits the concentration of power in any single group. We look at each category of interest group next.

Economic Interest Groups

There are thousands of economic interests: agriculture, consumers, plumbers, the airplane industry, landlords, truckers, bondholders, property owners, and more. Economic interests pursue what benefits them both financially and politically.

Business The most familiar business institution is the large corporation. Corporations range from one-person enterprises to vast multinational entities. General Motors, AT&T, Microsoft, Coca-Cola, McDonald's, Walmart, and other large companies exercise considerable political influence, as do hundreds of smaller corporations. For example, as Microsoft and Walmart came under heightened government and public scrutiny, their political contributions expanded.[44] Corporate power and a changing domestic and global economy make business practices important political issues.

interest group
A collection of people who share a common interest or attitude and seek to influence government for specific ends. Interest groups usually work within the framework of government and try to achieve their goals through tactics such as lobbying.

Cooperation between groups can increase their effectiveness, giving even small business an important voice in public policy. The Commerce Department includes a Small Business Administration. Small businesses are also organized into groups such as the

National Federation of Independent Business that help elect pro-business candidates and persuade the national government on behalf of its members.

Trade and Other Associations Businesses with similar interests join together as *trade associations*, as diverse as the products and services they provide. Businesses of all types are also organized into large nationwide associations such as the National Association of Realtors and smaller ones like the American Wind Energy Association.

The broadest business trade association is the Chamber of Commerce of the United States. Organized in 1912, the Chamber is a federation of thousands of local Chambers of Commerce representing millions of businesses. Loosely allied with the Chamber on most issues is the National Association of Manufacturers, which, since 1893, has tended to speak for the more conservative elements of American business.

Labor Workers' associations have a range of interests, including professional standards and wages and working conditions. Labor unions are one of the most important groups representing workers, yet the American workforce is the least unionized of almost any industrial democracy.[45] (See Figure 4–3.) The level of unionization has policy consequences. For example, a nation's minimum wage rates increase with unionization. The United States' minimum wage of $7.25 per hour is lower than in the more unionized United Kingdom, whose minimum wage is $8.83 per hour.[46]

Throughout the nineteenth century, workers organized political parties and local unions. Their most ambitious effort at national organization, the Knights of Labor, registered 700,000 members in the 1890s. But by approximately 1900, the American Federation of Labor (AFL), a confederation of strong and independent-minded national unions mainly representing craft workers, was the dominant organization. During the 1930s, unions more responsive to industrial workers broke away from the AFL and formed a rival national organization organized by industry, the Congress of Industrial Organizations (CIO). In 1955, the AFL and CIO reunited. Recently, more than a third of AFL-CIO members (4.5 of 13 million members), affiliated with the Service Employees International Union (SEIU), the International Brotherhood of Teamsters, and two other unions, split off from the AFL-CIO, forming a new group named the Change to Win Federation.[47] Unions today are thus less unified, but by 2007, dues paid to the AFL-CIO exceeded levels before the division.[48]

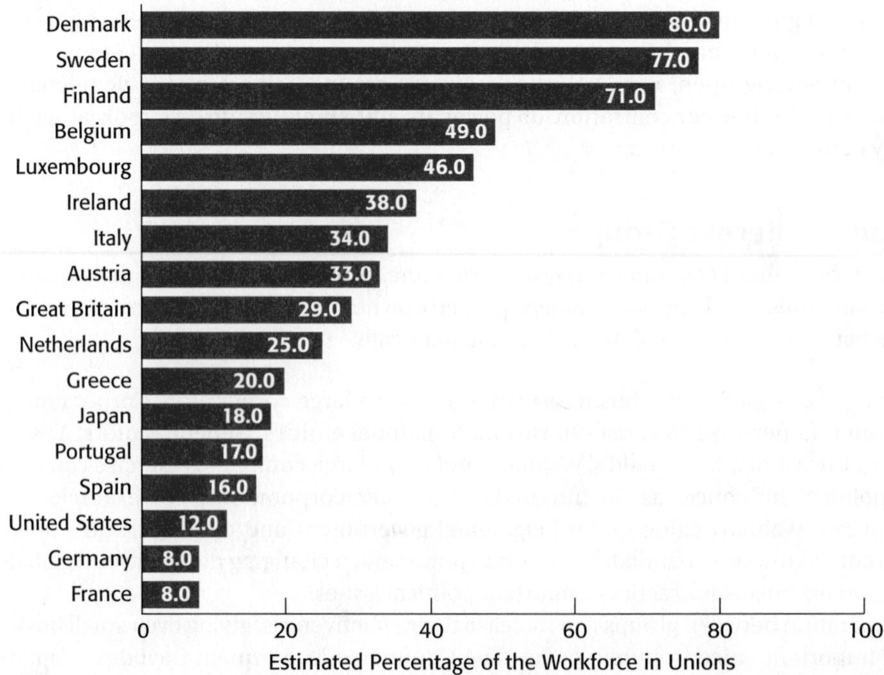

FIGURE 4–3 **Union Membership in the United States Compared to Other Countries.** ■ *How might aspects of American culture and ideology help explain the relatively low unionization of the American workforce?*

SOURCE: *European Foundation for the Improvement of Living and Working Conditions*, 2008 (Wyattville Road, Loughlinstown, Dublin 18, Ireland).

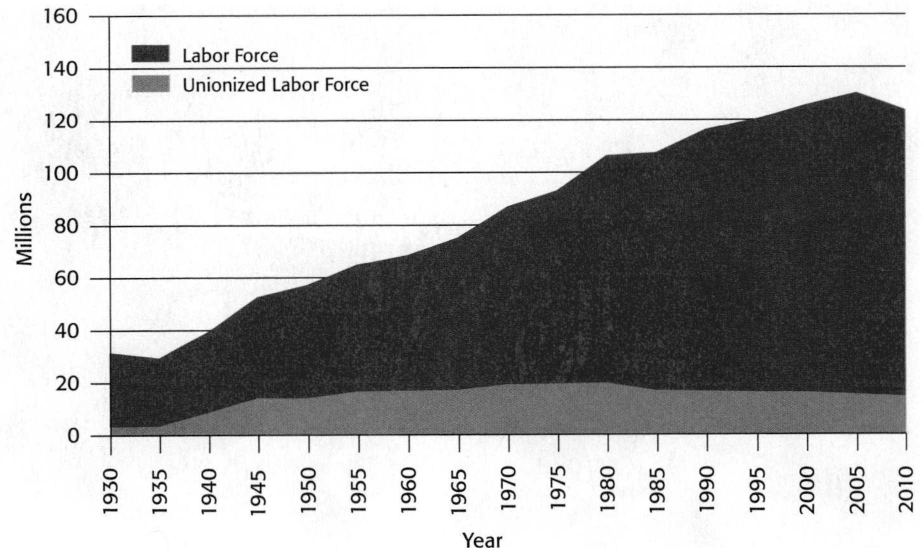

FIGURE 4–4 **Labor Force and Union Membership, 1930–2010.** ■ *How can you explain the steady upward growth of the labor force without a comparable growth in the unionized labor force?*

SOURCE: *The World Almanac and Book of Facts, 2000.* Copyright © 1999 Primedia Reference, Inc. Reprinted with permission, all rights reserved; and Barry Hirsch, Georgia State University, and David Macpherson, Florida State University, 1973–2007, "Union Membership, Coverage, Density, and Employment Among All Wage and Salary Workers, 1973–2007," http://www.unionstats.com.

The AFL-CIO speaks for approximately two-thirds of unionized labor,[49] but unions represent slightly more than 12 percent of the nation's workforce (see Figure 4–4).[50] The proportion of the U.S. workforce belonging to all unions has fallen, in part because of the shift from an industrial to a service and information economy. Dwindling membership limits organized labor's influence. Recently, however, some service and public sector unions have begun to expand, and even some doctors have unionized. Membership in SEIU rose from 1.58 million in 2006, a membership number little changed from 2003, to 2.2 million in 2009.[51]

Union membership is optional in states whose laws permit the **open shop,** in which workers cannot be required to join a union as a condition of employment. In states with the **closed shop,** workers may be required to join a union to be hired at a particular company if most employees at that company vote to unionize. In both cases, the unions negotiate with management, and all workers share the benefits the unions gain. In open-shop states, many workers may choose not to affiliate with a union because they can secure the same benefits that unionized workers enjoy without incurring the costs of joining the union. When a person benefits from the work or service of an organization like a union (or even a public TV or radio station) without joining or contributing to it, this condition is referred to as the **free rider** problem. We discuss how groups and government deal with the free rider challenge later in the chapter.

In the 2008 general election, unions were unified in backing Barack Obama for president and campaigned aggressively for pro-labor congressional, gubernatorial, and state legislative candidates. Traditionally identified with the Democratic Party, unions have not enjoyed a close relationship with Republican administrations. Given labor's limited resources, one option for unions is to form temporary coalitions with consumer, public interest, liberal, and sometimes even industry groups, especially on issues related to foreign imports. Labor has been unsuccessful in blocking free trade agreements like the North American Free Trade Agreement (NAFTA).[52]

Professional Associations Professional people join **professional associations** such as the American Medical Association (AMA) and the American Bar Association (ABA), which serve some of the same functions as unions. Other professions are divided into many subgroups. Teachers and professors, for example, belong to the National Education Association, the American Federation of Teachers, and the American Association of University Professors, and also to subgroups based on specialties, such as the Modern Language Association and the American Political Science Association.

open shop
A company with a labor agreement under which union membership cannot be required as a condition of employment.

closed shop
A company with a labor agreement under which union membership can be a condition of employment.

free rider
An individual who does not join a group representing his or her interests yet receives the benefit of the group's influence.

professional associations
Groups of individuals who share a common profession and are often organized for common political purposes related to that profession.

Barack Obama meets with labor union members over breakfast while campaigning for the Democratic nomination for the presidency. Labor unions have traditionally identified with the Democratic party. ■ *What can you learn from this photo about the demographics of a typical labor union and the issues with which members would be most concerned?*

Government, especially at the state level, regulates many professions. Lawyers are licensed by states, which, often as a result of pressure from lawyers themselves, set standards of admission to the state bar. Professional associations also use the courts to pursue their agendas. In the area of medical malpractice, for example, doctors lobby hard for limited-liability laws, while trial lawyers resist them. Teachers, hairstylists, and marriage therapists work for legislation that concerns them. It is not surprising, then, that groups representing professional associations such as the AMA and the National Association of Home Builders are among the largest donors to political campaigns.

Ideological or Single-Issue Interest Groups

Ideological groups focus on issues—often a single issue. Members generally share a common view and a desire for government to pursue policies consistent with it. Such *single-issue* groups are often unwilling to compromise. Right-to-life and pro-choice groups on abortion fit this description, as do the National Rifle Association and anti-immigration groups.

One of the most influential interest groups, the National Rifle Association promotes issues related to Second Amendment gun ownership rights. The NRA also sponsors firearm safety courses and shooting competitions across the United States. ■ *Why are single-issue groups like the NRA less willing to compromise on policy options than other kinds of interest groups?*

Public Interest Groups

Out of the political ferment of the 1960s came groups that claim to promote "the public interest." For example, Common Cause campaigns for electoral reform, for making the political process more open and participatory, and to stem media consolidation. Ralph Nader was instrumental in forming organizations to investigate and report on governmental and corporate action—or inaction—relating to consumer interests. Public interest research groups (PIRGs), as these groups are called, today seek to influence policy on Capitol Hill and in several state legislatures on environmental issues, safe energy, and consumer protection.

Foreign Policy Interest Groups

Interest groups also organize to promote or oppose foreign policies. Among the most prestigious is the Council on Foreign Relations in New York City. Other groups pressure Congress and the president to enact specific policies. For example, interest groups have been trying to influence American policy on China's refusal to grant independence for Tibet. Other groups support or oppose free trade. Foreign policy groups should not be confused with foreign governments and interest groups in other nations, which are banned from making campaign contributions but often seek to influence policy through lobbying firms.

Fears about a defect in Toyotas that led to an uncontrolled acceleration of the car resulted in a safety recall of 3.8 million vehicles. U.S. PIRG, the federation of state Public Interest Research Groups, was vocal about the need for the recall and played a role in the Senate hearings on product safety.

Public Sector Interest Groups

Governments are themselves important interest groups. Many cities and most states retain Washington lobbyists, and cities also attempt to influence Congress and the executive branch of the federal government. Governors are organized through the National Governors Association, cities through the National League of Cities, and counties through the National Association of Counties. Other officials—lieutenant governors, secretaries of state, mayors—have their own national associations.

Government employees form a large and well-organized group. The National Education Association (NEA), for example, has 3.2 million members.[53] The NEA endorses politicians from both parties but more typically supports Democrats. In 2008, the NEA endorsed Barack Obama for the presidency. The NEA fits the definition of a professional association, labor union, and public sector interest group. Public employees are increasingly important to organized labor because they constitute the fastest-growing unions.

Other Interest Groups

American adults are often emotionally and financially engaged by a wide variety of groups: veterans' groups, nationality groups, and religious organizations, among others. Individuals join groups because of a common interest or concern, because of a shared identification, or because of an issue or concern. Women's organizations have long been important in advocating for equal rights, most notably for the right to vote. An area of increasing activity is environmental groups.

Characteristics and Power of Interest Groups

LEARNING **OBJECTIVE**

4.5 Analyze sources of interest group power.

Groups vary in their goals, methods, and power. Among their most important characteristics are size, incentives to participate, resources, cohesiveness, leadership, and techniques. As we will demonstrate, these different resources and objectives help us understand the power and resources of interest groups.

Size and Resources

Obviously, size is important to political power; an organization representing 5 million voters has more influence than one speaking for 5,000. Perhaps even more important is the number of members who are active and willing to fight for policy objectives. Interest groups often provide tangible incentives to join, such as exclusive magazines, travel benefits, professional meetings and job opportunities, and discounts on insurance, merchandise, and admission to cultural institutions. Some are compelling enough to attract the potential free rider.[54]

Many government programs provide services that benefit everyone such as clean air, national defense, and public fireworks on July 4. One solution to the free rider problem is to pay for these widely shared benefits through taxes. Nongovernment service providers can require a number of people to pay for the service before providing it. It is then in everyone's interest to pay for the service or face the prospect that no

With a large membership and significant financial resources, the U.S. Chamber of Congress is active and influential in election campaigns. During the 2008 election the Chamber organized a "Vote for Business Bandwagon" to support candidates promoting economic policies beneficial to its members. Here, Chamber President and CEO Tom Donohue (left) meets with candidates in Denver.

one will have it. Groups rarely overcome the risk of free riders, but unless we offer some compensation for providing easily shared goods and services, they are not likely to be produced.

Although the size of an interest group is important to its success, so is its *spread*—the extent to which membership is concentrated or dispersed. Because automobile manufacturing is concentrated in Michigan and a few other states, the auto industry's influence does not have the same spread as the AMA, which has an active chapter in virtually every congressional district. Concentration of membership in a key battleground state, however, such as Cuban Americans in Florida or ethanol producers in Iowa, enhances that group's influence. Interest groups also differ in the extent to which they preempt or share a policy area.

Finally, groups differ in the extent of their *resources*—money, volunteers, expertise, and reputation. Some groups can influence many centers of power—both houses of Congress, the White House, federal agencies, the courts, and state and local governments—whereas others cannot.

Cohesiveness

Most mass-membership organizations include three types of members: (1) a relatively small number of formal leaders who may hold full-time, paid positions or devote much time, effort, and money to the group's activities; (2) a few hundred people intensely involved in the group who identify with its aims, attend meetings, pay dues, and do much of the legwork; and (3) thousands of people who are members in name only and cannot be depended on to vote in elections or act as the leadership wants.[55] When these groups share common views on the aims of the organization, the group is more cohesive.

Another factor in group cohesiveness is *organizational structure*. Some associations have a strong formal organization; others are local organizations joined into a loose state or national federation in which they retain a measure of separate power and independence.

Leadership

In a group that embraces many attitudes and interests, leaders may either weld the various elements together or sharpen their disunity. The leader of a national business association, for example, must tread cautiously between big business and small business, between exporters and importers, between chain stores and corner grocery stores, and between the producers and the sellers of competing products. The group leader is in the same position as a president or a member of Congress; he or she must know when to lead and when to follow.

Techniques for Exerting Influence

Our separation-of-powers system provides many access points for any group attempting to influence government. They can present their case to Congress, the White House staff, state and local governments, and federal agencies and departments. Efforts by individuals or groups to inform and influence public officials are called **lobbying.** Groups also become involved in litigation, protests, and election activities and even establish their own political parties. Groups vary in the extent to which they have widespread support that comes from the people (grassroots) vs. activity that is orchestrated or initiated centrally but looks to be grassroots (astroturf).[56]

lobbying
Engaging in activities aimed at influencing public officials, especially legislators, and the policies they enact.

Publicity, Mass Media, and the Internet One way to attempt to influence policy makers is through the public. Interest groups use the media—television, radio, the Internet including Web sites, newspapers, leaflets, signs, direct mail, and word of mouth—to influence voters during elections and motivate them to contact their representatives between elections. Businesses enjoy a special advantage because, as large-scale advertisers, they know how to deliver their message effectively or can find an advertising agency to do it for them. But organized labor is also effective in communicating with its membership through shop stewards, mail, phone calls, and personal contact.

Mobilization increasingly occurs through the Internet, especially through social media such as Facebook. Business organizations like the Business and Industrial Political Action Committee (BIPAC) have used the Internet to communicate with members and employees of affiliated businesses. BIPAC's Web site provides downloadable forms to request absentee ballots and the roll call votes of legislators on issues of interest to their businesses.[57] Some groups, such as MoveOn.org, operate almost exclusively online, while massive forums such as DailyKos.com and Townhall.com act as a clearinghouse for left- and right-wing causes. As one scholar noted, much of what modern interest groups do "could not work without the Internet."[58]

Energy Citizens, a interest group backed by the American Petroleum Institute, holds rallies against climate change legislation, which is under consideration by the Senate. ■ *Why might the oil and gas industry prefer using this technique of exerting influence?*

The Internet helps interest groups in two ways. First, it allows citizens to easily organize themselves for rallies, marches, letter-writing drives, and other kinds of civic participation. Second, the Internet opens new, exclusively online forms of political action, such as sending mass e-mails, posting videos, joining Facebook groups, donating money online, commenting on articles, and blogging. We discuss these developments in greater detail in Chapter 6.

Mass Mailing One means of communication that has increased the reach and effectiveness of interest groups is computerized and targeted mass mailing.[59] Before computers, interest groups could either cull lists of people to contact from telephone directories and other sources or send mailings indiscriminately. Today's computerized mailing-list technology can target personalized letters to specific groups. Environmental groups make extensive use of targeted mail and e-mail.[60]

Direct Contact with Government Organized groups have ready access to the executive and regulatory agencies that write the rules implementing laws passed by Congress. Government agencies publish proposed regulations in the ***Federal Register*** and invite responses from all interested persons before the rules are finalized—in the "notice and comments period."[61] Well-staffed associations and corporations use the *Register* to obtain the specific language and deadlines for pending regulations. Lobbyists prepare written responses to the proposed rules, draft alternative rules, and make their case at the hearings.

Litigation When groups find the political channels closed to them, they may turn to the courts.[62] The Legal Defense and Educational Fund of the National Association for the Advancement of Colored People (NAACP), for example, initiated and won numerous court cases in its efforts to end racial segregation and protect the right to vote for African Americans. Urban interests, feeling underrepresented in state and national legislatures, turned to the courts to press for one-person, one-vote rulings to overcome the disproportionate power rural interests had in legislatures and to otherwise influence the political process.[63]

In addition to initiating lawsuits, associations can gain a forum for their views in the courts by filing ***amicus curiae* briefs** (literally, "friend of the court" briefs), presenting arguments in cases in which they are not direct parties. It is not unusual for courts to cite such briefs in their opinions. Despite the general impression that associations achieve great success in the courts, groups are no more likely than individuals to win at the district court level.[64]

Federal Register
An official document, published every weekday, that lists the new and proposed regulations of executive departments and regulatory agencies.

amicus curiae brief
Literally, a "friend of the court" brief, filed by an individual or organization to present arguments in addition to those presented by the immediate parties to a case.

Protest To generate interest and broaden support for their cause, movements and groups often use protest demonstrations. For example, after the House of Representatives passed new laws on illegal immigration in 2006, pro-immigrant groups mounted protests in cities such as Phoenix and Washington, D.C., with more than 1 million participants.[65] Two months later, in a protest called "A Day Without Immigrants," more than 600,000 protesters gathered in Los Angeles to focus greater media attention on the important role immigrants play in the economy; similar rallies in Chicago drew more than 400,000 people.[66] (The legislation died when differences between the Senate and House versions of the bill could not be reconciled.) Other movements or groups that have used protest include the civil rights movement and antiwar, environmental, and antiglobalization groups.[67]

Candidate Support Most large organizations are politically engaged in some way, though they may be, or try to be, *nonpartisan.* Most organized interest groups try to work through *both* parties and want to be friendly with the winners, which often means they contribute to incumbents. But as competition for control of both houses of Congress has intensified and with presidential contests also up for grabs, many interest groups invest mostly in one party or the other.

Many interest groups publicly endorse candidates for office, either directly by issuing a statement or hosting an event, or indirectly by publishing scorecards of how candidates responded to roll call votes or questionnaires administered by the group. Some groups give candidates letter grades from A to F. The League of Conservation Voters names candidates it opposes to its "environmental dirty dozen," while praising others as "environmental champions."[68]

bundling
A tactic in which PACs collect contributions from like-minded individuals (each limited to $2,000) and present them to a candidate or political party as a "bundle," thus increasing the PAC's influence.

Ideological groups like Americans for Democratic Action and the American Conservative Union publish ratings of the voting records of members of Congress on liberal and conservative issues. Other interest groups, such as the U.S. Chamber of Commerce and the League of Conservation Voters, create scorecards of key legislative votes and report to their members how their representative voted on those issues.

Teachers in downtown Los Angeles protest proposed state budget cuts for education. Groups often use protest as a way of generating interest and increasing support for their causes. ■ *What are some of the factors that might make government officials more or less likely to respond to protests or demonstrations?*

Contributions to Campaigns Interest groups also form political action committees (PACs), which are the legal mechanism for them to contribute money to candidates, political party committees, and other political committees. One of the oldest PACs is the Committee on Political Education (COPE) of the AFL-CIO, but business groups and others have long existed to direct money to favored candidates. PACs also encourage other PACs to contribute to favored candidates, occasionally hosting joint fund-raisers for candidates. We discuss PACs in greater detail later in the chapter.

Individuals clearly associated with an interest group also contribute to campaigns as individuals in ways that make clear to the candidate the interest of the donor. Often one party gathers contributions from several individuals and then gives the checks made out to the candidate's campaign in a bundle, a process called **bundling.** This can also be done via the computer.

New Political Parties Another interest group strategy is to form a political party, not so much to win elections as to publicize a cause. Success in such cases may occur when a major party co-opts the interest group's issue. The Free Soil Party was formed in the mid-1840s to work against the spread of slavery into the territories, and the Prohibition Party was organized two decades later to ban the sale of liquor. Farmers have formed a variety of such parties. More often, however, interest groups prefer to work through existing parties.

Today, environmental groups and voters for whom the environment is a central issue must choose between supporting the Green Party, which has yet to elect a candidate to federal office, an Independent candidate such as Ralph Nader in 2008, or one of the two major parties. Sometimes minor-party candidates can spoil the chances of a major-party candidate. In a New Mexico congressional special election in 1997, the Green Party candidate won 17 percent of the vote, taking some votes from the Democrat and thereby helping to elect a Republican to what had been a Democratic seat. As discussed in the opener, the Tea Party Movement became a rallying cry for some candidates in 2010. However, although more closely identified with Republicans, the Tea Party Movement is not currently a party.

Influencing Government: Lobbyists and Spending

LEARNING **OBJECTIVE**

4.6 Identify ways lobbyists seek to influence policy and interest group spending affects elections.

Perhaps the most known—and vilified—technique for exerting influence is the use of professional **lobbyists,** or individuals employed by an interest group or corporation to try to influence policy decisions. The term "lobbying" was not generally used until around the mid-nineteenth century in the United States. These words refer to the lobby or hallway outside the House and Senate chambers in the U.S. Capitol and to those who hung around the lobby of the old Willard Hotel in Washington, D.C., when presidents dined there. The noun "lobby" is now used as a verb.

lobbyist
A person who is employed by and acts for an organized interest group or corporation to try to influence policy decisions and positions in the executive and legislative branches.

Despite their negative public image, lobbyists perform useful functions for government. They provide information for decision makers in all three branches of government, help educate and mobilize public opinion, help prepare legislation and testify before legislative hearings, and contribute a large share of the costs of campaigns. But many people fear that lobbyists have too much influence on government and add to legislative gridlock by stopping action on pressing problems.

revolving door
An employment cycle in which individuals who work for government agencies that regulate interests eventually end up working for interest groups or businesses with the same policy concern.

Who Are the Lobbyists?

The typical image of policy making is of powerful, hard-nosed lobbyists who use a combination of knowledge, persuasiveness, personal influence, charm, and money to influence legislators and bureaucrats. Often former public servants themselves, lobbyists are experienced in government and often go to work for one of the interests they dealt with while in government, or for a lobbying firm.

issue network
Relationships among interest groups, congressional committees and subcommittees, and the government agencies that share a common policy concern.

Moving from a government job to a job with an interest group—or vice versa—is so common that this career path is called the **revolving door.** Although it is illegal for former national government employees to directly lobby the agency from which they came, their contacts made during government service are helpful to interest groups. Many former members of Congress use their congressional experience as full-time lobbyists. In 2007, Congress passed the Honest Leadership and Open Government Act, which requires more disclosure of employment history of lobbyists, sets stricter limits on lobbyist activities, requires senators to wait two years before lobbying, and requires staff to wait one year before lobbying any Senate office. The Obama Administration used this lobbying list in prohibiting any registered lobbyists from serving in any White House or executive branch jobs.

Many lobbyists participate in **issue networks** or relationships among interest groups, congressional committees and subcommittees, and government agencies that share a common policy concern. Personal relationships among members of these groups can sometimes allow these networks to become so strong and mutually beneficial that they form a sort of subgovernment.

After leaving his position as White House Counsel, Greg Craig, shown here between former Chief of Staff Rahm Emmanuel and Press Secretary Robert Gibbs, became a partner in a Washington, D.C., law firm. While lawyers do not face the same "revolving door" restrictions as lobbyists, concerns were still raised regarding his recent insider status when it was announced that he would be advising Goldman Sachs, which was facing a lawsuit from the SEC.

For the People

GOVERNMENT'S GREATEST ENDEAVORS

Disclosure of Lobbyist Activity

Obtaining meaningful and timely disclosure of interest group and lobbyist activities is an important way to protect the political process from the undue influence of interest groups. During the last few decades, the government has been engaged in reform efforts seeking to achieve more meaningful disclosure.

One of the problems of prior efforts at disclosing lobbying activities was an imprecise definition of lobbying. The Lobbying Disclosure Act of 1995 (LDA) requires all lobbyists to register with the Clerk of the House of Representatives or the Secretary of the Senate and provides a more detailed definition of exactly what is considered lobbying and who is considered a lobbyist. Lobbyists must file quarterly reports about their lobbying activity, the compensation they received, the time they spent, and the expenses they incurred.

Congress and the president went a step further in 2007 with passage of amendments to the 1995 law known as the Honest Leadership and Open Government Act of 2007 (HLOGA). This law made the lobbyist registration and their reports publicly available online and permits the House clerk and Senate secretary to review the reports for accuracy. The HLOGA includes further restrictions on gifts, on privately funded travel for members of Congress, and requires lobbyists who bundle contributions from individual donors to disclose that activity.*

Although it appears some progress has been made in achieving greater disclosure of lobbying activity, some substantial gaps remain. A 2008 Government Accounting Office study of lobbyist filings found that approximately two-thirds of the details in the reports could not be verified and the level of detail in the reports was sometimes lacking.† In addition, disclosure laws do not apply to people who only indirectly try to influence policy or legislation through activities such as organizing *others* to write letters or call decision makers. These individuals have come to be known as "strategists" and currently fall outside of lobbyist regulations.

CRITICAL THINKING QUESTIONS

1. Why is disclosure assumed to limit abuses by lobbyists?
2. Why is there resistance to full and complete disclosure by lobbyists and legislators?

* Anthony Corrado, "The Regulatory Environment," in David B. Magleby and Anthony Corrado, eds., *Financing the 2008 Election* (Washington, D.C.: Brookings Institution Press, forthcoming).

† United States Government Accountability Office, "2008 Lobbying Disclosure: Observations on Lobbyists' Compliance with Disclosure Requirements," April 2009.

Legal and political skills, along with specialized knowledge, are so crucial in executive and legislative policy making that they have become a form of power in themselves. Elected representatives increasingly depend on their staffs for guidance, and these issue specialists know more about "Section 504" or "Title IX" or "the 2002 amendments"—and who wrote them and why—than most political and administrative leaders, who are usually generalists.[69] New laws often need specific rules and applications spelled out in detail by the agencies charged to administer them. In this rule-making activity, interest groups and issue networks assume even more significance.

Political Action Committees (PACs)

Interest groups also seek to influence politics and public policy by spending money on elections. A **political action committee (PAC)** is the political arm of an interest group legally entitled to raise limited and disclosed funds on a voluntary basis from members, stockholders, or employees in order to contribute funds to favored candidates or political parties. PACs link two vital techniques of influence—giving money and other political aid to politicians and persuading officeholders to act or vote "the right way" on issues. Thus, PACs are one important means by which interest groups seek to influence which legislators are elected and what they do once they take office.[70] We categorize PACs according to the type of interest they represent: corporations, trade and health organizations, labor unions, ideological organizations, and so on.

PACs grew in number and importance in the 1970s, in part because of campaign finance reform legislation enacted in that decade. The number of PACs registered rose from 608 in 1974 to 4,611 today.[71] Corporations and trade associations contributed most to this growth; today, their PACs constitute the majority of all PACs. Labor PACs, by contrast, represent less than 6 percent of all PACs.[72] But the increase in the number of PACs is less important than the intensity of PAC participation in elections and lobbying (see Figure 4–5).

Surprisingly, considering that the growth in numbers of PACs has occurred mainly in the business world, organized labor invented this device. In the 1930s, John L. Lewis, president of the United Mine Workers, set up the Non-Partisan Political League as the political

political action committee (PAC)
The political arm of an interest group that is legally entitled to raise funds on a voluntary basis from members, stockholders, or employees to contribute funds to candidates or political parties.

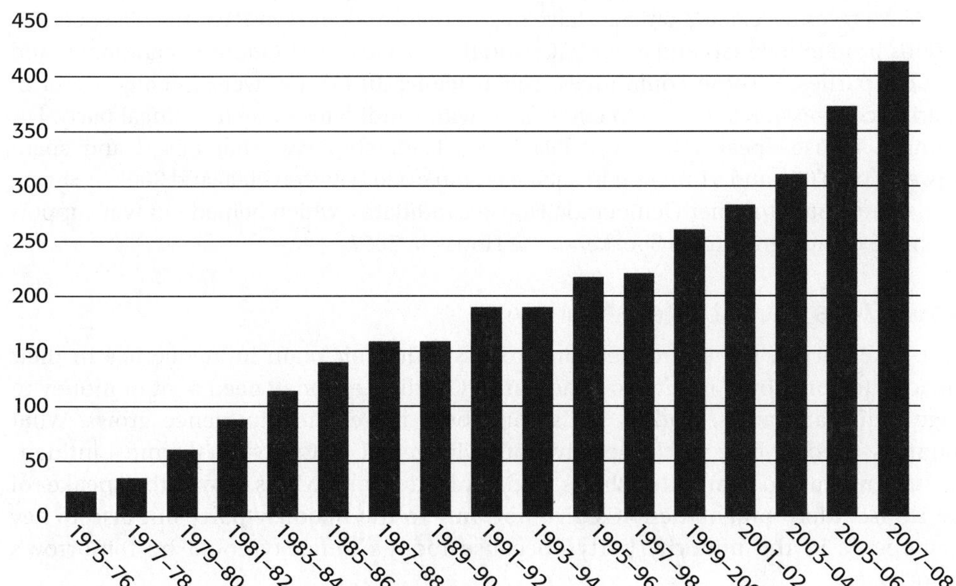

FIGURE 4–5 Total PAC Contributions to Candidates for U.S. Congress, 1975–2008 (in Millions).

SOURCE: Harold W. Stanley and Richard G. Niemi, *Vital Statistics on American Politics 2005–2006* (CQ Press), p. 103; and Federal Election Commission, "PAC Activity Continues to Climb in 2006," Press Release, October 5, 2007, www.fec.gov/press/press2007/20071009pac/20071009pac.shtml.

arm of the newly formed Congress of Industrial Organizations (CIO). When the CIO merged with the American Federation of Labor (AFL), the new labor group established the Committee on Political Education (COPE), a model for PACs generally whose activities we have already described. Some years later, manufacturers formed the Business and Industry Political Action Committee (BIPAC), but the most active business PAC today is the one affiliated with the National Federation of Independent Business.[73] Table 4–5 lists the most active PACs in elections since 2000.

TABLE 4–5 PACs That Gave the Most to Federal Candidates, Cumulatively, 2000–2008 (Millions of Dollars)

PAC	2000	2002	2004	2006	2008	Total
1. National Association of Realtors	$3.42	$3.65	$3.77	$3.75	$4.01	$18.61
2. National Auto Dealers Association	$2.50	$2.58	$2.58	$2.82	$2.86	$13.35
3. International Brotherhood of Electrical Workers	$2.46	$2.21	$2.30	$2.78	$3.33	$13.09
4. National Beer Wholesalers Association	$1.87	$2.07	$2.29	$2.95	$2.87	$12.04
5. National Association of Home Builders	$1.82	$1.92	$2.22	$2.90	$2.48	$11.35
6. International Brotherhood of Teamsters	$2.49	$2.33	$1.89	$2.07	$2.20	$10.99
7. American Federation of State, County, and Municipal Employees	$2.59	$2.42	$1.64	$2.05	$2.11	$10.81
8. United Auto Workers	$2.16	$2.34	$2.07	$2.22	$1.99	$10.77
9. Laborers Union	$1.79	$2.25	$2.25	$2.32	$2.05	$10.66
10. International Association of Machinists and Aerospace Workers	$2.18	$2.20	$1.91	$1.76	$2.33	$10.37

SOURCE: Federal Election Commission, "Growth in PAC Financial Activity Slows," Press Release, April 24, 2009, www.fec.gov/press/press2009/20090415PAC/20090424PAC.shtml (accessed March 15, 2010).

■ *What kinds of interests do the most active PACs support? What responsibility do candidates who receive funds have to those PACs?*

More recently, elected officials have begun to form their own PACs to collect contributions from individuals and other PACs and then make contributions to candidates and political parties.[74] These committees, called **leadership PACs,** were initially a tool of aspiring congressional leaders to curry favor with candidates in their political party. For example, House Speaker Nancy Pelosi has a leadership PAC that raised and spent between $900,000 and $1 million in each election cycle between 2000 and 2008.[75] She, in turn, contributed to other Democratic House candidates, which helped her win support when she campaigned to be Speaker of the House in 2007.

How PACs Invest Their Money

PACs take part in the entire election process, but their main influence lies in their capacity to contribute money to candidates. Candidates today need a lot of money to wage their campaigns. And as PACs contribute more, their influence grows. What counts is not only how much they give, but who gets it. PACs give to the most influential incumbents, to committee chairs, to party leaders and whips, and to the Speaker of the House. More pragmatic PACs give not only to the majority party but also to key incumbents in the minority party—because today's minority could be tomorrow's majority.

PACs are important not only because they contribute such a large share of the money congressional candidates raise for their campaigns but also because they contribute so disproportionately to incumbents. In the most recent election cycle, House incumbents seeking reelection raised 43 percent of the funds for their campaigns from PACs, compared to only 17 percent for the challengers opposing them. In total, House incumbents raised more than six PAC dollars for every one PAC dollar going to a challenger. Senate incumbents raise proportionately more from individuals but also enjoy a fundraising advantage among PACs compared to Senate challengers (see Figure 4–6). One reason members of Congress become entrenched in their seats is that PACs fund them. Many members of Congress thrive on the present arrangements, and the leaders and members of both parties actively compete for PAC dollars.

leadership PAC
A PAC formed by an officeholder that collects contributions from individuals and other PACs and then makes contributions to other candidates and political parties.

The law limits the amount of money that PACs, like individuals, can contribute to any single candidate in an election cycle. But raising money from PACs is more efficient for a candidate than raising it from individuals. Since the Democratic Party took control of Congress in 2007, some PACs have changed loyalties. In the House, approximately 60 percent of PAC money goes to Democrats and 40 percent to Republicans. Before Congress changed hands, just the opposite was true—approximately 60 percent of PAC

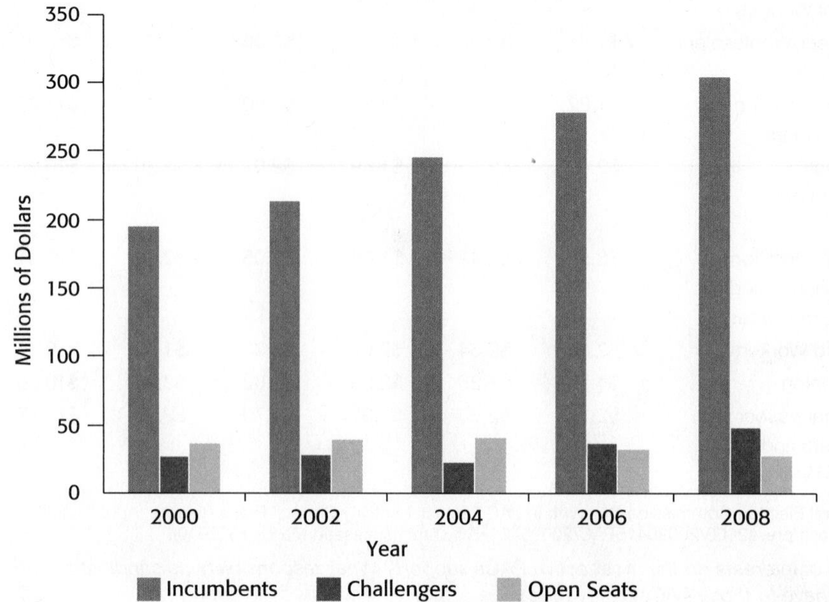

FIGURE 4–6 **PAC Contributions to Congressional Candidates, 2000–2008.**
■ *Over time, how has the distribution of PAC money changed? Why do PACs contribute so disproportionately to incumbents?*

SOURCE: Compiled from Federal Election Commission data, "Candidate Financial Summaries," www.fec.gov/finance/disclosure/ftpsum.shtml.

money went to Republicans. In the Senate, Republicans still receive more PAC money than Democrats, but the gap is decreasing.

Mobilizing Employees and Members

Another way interest groups can influence the outcome of elections is by persuading their employees, members, or stockholders to vote in a way consistent with the interests of the group. They accomplish this mobilization through targeted communications at the workplace, through the mail, on the telephone, or on the Internet. As we discuss elsewhere in this chapter, labor unions have been especially effective in member communications. Corporations and business associations have been following labor's lead. Membership organizations such as the NRA have also been able to mobilize their members and allied individuals and groups.[76]

Independent Expenditures

The Supreme Court in 1976 declared that limits on independent expenditures were unconstitutional when the contributions or expenditures were truly independent of a party or candidate. Hence, groups, like individuals, can campaign for or against a candidate, independent of a party or candidate committee and in addition to making contributions to candidates and party committees from their PAC. These **independent expenditures** are unlimited but must be disclosed to the Federal Election Commission (FEC). Interest-group independent expenditures fall well below PAC contributions to candidates and parties. Groups that have made heavy use of independent expenditures include MoveOn PAC, NRA, EMILY's List, several unions, National Right to Life PAC, the Club for Growth, and the National Association of Realtors. (See Table 4–6.) Independent expenditures enable groups to direct unlimited accounts of money to a particular race.

independent expenditures
The Supreme Court has ruled that individuals, groups, and parties can spend unlimited amounts in campaigns for or against candidates as long as they operate independently from the candidates. When an individual, group, or party does so, they are making an independent expenditure.

Campaigning Through Other Groups

For more than a century, reformers had sought disclosure of money in politics. In campaigns and elections, disclosure was often incomplete, and groups quickly found ways to avoid it. Then, the disclosure provisions of the Federal Election Campaign Act of 1971, amended in 1974, defined electioneering ads as communications that used words

TABLE 4–6 Independent Expenditures by Top Interest Groups, 2008

Interest Group	Expenditure
Service Employees International Union COPE	$39,556,155
National Rifle Association of America Political Victory Fund	18,047,203
National Republican Trust PAC	9,384,714
AFSCME	6,992,408
National Association of Realtors PAC	6,737,055
MoveOn.org PAC	6,649,335
United Auto Workers	4,874,803
American Federation of Teachers	3,867,811
Club for Growth	3,614,053
National Right to Life	3,584,697
League of Conservation Voters Action Fund	3,332,140
EMILY's List	3,202,778
Republican Majority Campaign	3,089,333

NOTE: Expenditures for all national affiliates of an organization are combined, but expenditures for state affiliates are excluded.

SOURCE: Federal Election Commission, ftp://ftp.fec.gov/FEC (accessed March 12, 2009).

In this image from one of Swift Boat Veterans for Truth's television advertisements, then-presidential nominee John Kerry's patriotism and Vietnam War record are called into question. ■ *What methods do issues groups have to influence elections that individual campaigns do not?*

such as "vote for" or "vote against" and made them subject to disclosure and spending limits.

For a time, citizens, journalists, and scholars had a complete picture of who was giving what to whom, and who was spending money and in what ways, to influence elections. That changed in 1996, when interest groups found a way to circumvent disclosure and contribution limits through **issue advocacy.** They simply made election ads without the words "vote for" or "vote against," and then they spent millions attacking or promoting particular candidates.

Labor unions were the first to exploit this tactic in a major way, spending an estimated $35 million in 1996, mostly against Republican candidates.[77] Corporations and ideological groups quickly followed labor's lead, spending millions on issue ads in 1996–2002.

In the post–campaign reform elections of 2004, 2006, and 2008, interest groups continued to mount their own campaigns against or for candidates in ways similar to the old issue advocacy. For example, a group of Vietnam War veterans formed a group they named Swift Boat Veterans for Truth and ran ads attacking Senator John Kerry's Vietnam War record.[78] Groups like Swift Boat Veterans for Truth are called **527 organizations** or groups because they are tax-exempt groups organized under section 527 of the Internal Revenue Service Code. They can run ads against or for candidates but under somewhat more restrictive conditions than existed before 2004.

During the 2004 election cycle, 527 groups were much more active on the liberal or Democratic side than on the conservative or Republican side. Democratic activists and allied interest groups understood that the Bipartisan Campaign Reform Act ban on soft money would leave the party and its presidential candidate at a disadvantage against the fund-raising prowess of President Bush and the Republicans. Interest groups allied to Democrats, including 527 groups, were again more active in 2006 than Republican-allied groups.

Interest groups also used other sections of the tax code to involve themselves in the election. Section 501(c) of the tax code permits some groups to organize, and for some purposes such as nonpartisan voter registration drives, donations to the group are tax deductible. Contributions to partisan groups such as the NRA and MoveOn are not tax deductible. Nor are contributions to labor unions and business groups such as the Chamber of Commerce.[79] In 2004, Republicans found more allies in 501(c) organizations.[80] In 2006 and 2008, 501(c) organizations were involved in activities that helped register and inform voters, often with an indirect benefit to one party. In 2008, groups on both sides of the partisan divide made use of 501(c) groups. Among those most active were Planned Parenthood, the League of Conservation Voters, and Defenders of Wildlife who mostly supported Democrats, and the Chamber of Commerce, which largely supported Republicans.[81]

Taken as a whole, interest groups spent more in 2007–2008 than they did in the prior presidential election cycle of 2003–2004. In 2007–2008, they spent an estimated $1.2 billion to influence federal elections.[82] Their level of 501(c) groups spending rose and PAC spending rose even more in 2007–2008, whereas their spending through Section 527 organizations declined.[83] Given the increase in PAC activity, Alan Cigler, an expert in interest groups, assesses the difference PACs made in 2008 and describes it as "robust" in contrast to spending activity by section 527 organizations. More broadly, 2008 saw a decline in Republican-ally involvement, especially at the end of the campaign, and a substantial effort by labor unions, especially the Service Employees International Union, in independent expenditure and 527 activities.[84]

issue advocacy
Unlimited and undisclosed spending by an individual or group on communications that do not use words like "vote for" or "vote against," although much of this activity is actually about electing or defeating candidates.

527 organization
A political group organized under section 527 of the IRS Code that may accept and spend unlimited amounts of money on election activities so long as they are not spent on broadcast ads run in the last 30 days before a primary or 60 days before a general election in which a clearly identified candidate is referred to and a relevant electorate is targeted.

YOU WILL DECIDE Should Corporations and Unions Be Unlimited in Funding Parties and in Running Issue Ads?

Does limiting the ability of corporations or unions to use their general or "treasury" funds for election-related expenditures violate the constitutional guarantee of freedom of speech? Corporations and unions, like other groups, are free to form political action committees to make contributions to candidates and parties. What has been at dispute is whether they could take their profits or general funds and spend those on electing or defeating candidates or in support of party efforts. For more than a century, federal law had banned unions and corporations from spending general or treasury funds on electoral politics.

These rules changed in 1979 when the Federal Election Commission allowed unions and corporations to give unlimited general treasury funds or profits to help political parties generally. This was called soft money. In 1996, unions and later corporations began spending unlimited and undisclosed amounts of money on "issue ads," which were really campaign commercials. The Bipartisan Campaign Reform Act banned soft money contributions to parties and more clearly defined election communications as to television or radio ads that refer to a specific candidate and that air within 30 days of the primary or 60 days of the general election. The Supreme Court initially upheld both bans but later reversed itself on election communications. Given this reversal, opponents of the soft money ban are likely to again challenge this provision in court.

What do you think? Should corporations and unions be unlimited in funding parties and in running issue ads? What are some arguments for or against this?

THINKING IT THROUGH

The Supreme Court in *McConnell* v. *FEC* cited a long list of precedents in upholding the limitation on unions and corporations using their general funds to influence elections.* The economic power of corporations such as Microsoft or major unions could, if unconstrained, drown out the voices of other participants and corrupt the electoral process.

But unions and corporations have a point in arguing that constraints on them are unfair when compared with the ability of wealthy individuals to spend unlimited amounts of their own money on politics via independent expenditures, which the Court allowed in its prior landmark decision, *Buckley* v. *Valeo*.† They would agree with Justice Scalia's dissent in *McConnell* v. *FEC* that restricting how much a group "can spend to broadcast [its] political views is a direct restriction on speech."‡

With respect to electioneering or issue ads, in 2007, the reconstituted Supreme Court in *FEC* v. *Wisconsin Right to Life, Inc.* said the BCRA language was too broad in defining electioneering and that unions and corporations had a right to communicate with voters about political topics in the days and weeks before primary and general elections.§ Chief Justice Roberts substituted a new, more loose definition of electioneering communication. In the past, language like that used by Chief Justice Roberts provided media consultants with enough latitude to craft election communications, arguing that they were about issues and not candidates. In 2010, the Supreme Court further broadened the opportunity for corporations and unions to engage in electioneering for or against candidates by reversing a long-standing ban on the use of corporate or union general funds, including profits.** This means that future elections could have substantial electioneering by unions and corporations on the eve of elections that is not subject to the other limitations of the law.

**McConnell* v. *FEC,* 124 S. Ct. 533 (2003).
†*Buckley* v. *Valeo,* 96 S. Ct. 760 (1976).
‡Justice Antonin Scalia, dissenting in *McConnell* v. *FEC,* 124 S. Ct. 618 (2003).
§*Federal Election Commission* v. *Wisconsin Right to Life Inc.,* 466 F. Supp. 2d 195 (2007).
***Citizens United* v. *Federal Election Commission,* 558 U.S. ___ (2010).

Parties and Interest Groups in a Democracy

LEARNING **OBJECTIVE**

4.7 Evaluate the influence of political parties and interest groups on government in America.

As we have demonstrated in this chapter, political parties are vital to the functioning of democracy. They organize electoral competition, unify large portions of the electorate, simplify democracy for voters, help transform individual preferences into policy, and provide a mechanism for opposition. Parties are just as important in organizing the government. They help straddle the separation of powers as fellow partisans cooperate between the executive and legislative branches or between the House and Senate. Senior government appointees get their jobs in part because of their party loyalty.

Interest groups also have an important impact on our politics and government, but whether their influence is a positive one is more debatable. Concern about the evils of interest groups has been a recurrent theme throughout U.S. history. James Madison, who wrote about the potential "mischiefs of faction," would likely be concerned to see how integrated

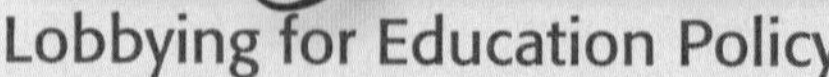

By the People

MAKING A DIFFERENCE

Lobbying for Education Policy

Lobbying on education policy has important implications for college students. Numerous policies and laws enacted by Congress directly affect students and universities, and so it is important for students and universities to try to influence these policies for their own best interests.

For example, approximately two-thirds of college students graduating in 2008 with a bachelor's degree had some debt, with the average amount more than $22,000.* Approximately 6 million students received a Federal Pell Grant in 2007–2008.† Congress recently enacted changes in student loans and Pell grants through two pieces of legislation—the College Cost Reduction and Access Act and the American Recovery and Reinvestment Act. Under these acts, the maximum Pell Grant scholarship for the 2009–2010 school year will be $5,350—more than $600 higher than in 2008–2009. Among the groups active in lobbying Congress on this matter were Sallie Mae, the nation's largest student lender, but also the Consumer Bankers Association and the National Direct Student Loan Coalition.

Most universities and colleges retain a lobbyist to help them secure the support of government, either at the state level, the federal level, or both. Public institutions rely more on the state legislature than do private institutions. You can search online to learn about whether your institution has a lobbyist and how much the institution spent lobbying last year. Find a site on lobbyists in your state—such as http://cal-access.sos.ca.gov/lobbying/ for California or http://www.ethics.state.tx.us/main/search.htm for Texas—to get information on how your school lobbies the state government.

CRITICAL THINKING QUESTIONS

1. Why do you think your university or college hires lobbyists?
2. On matters like changes in the laws relating to student loans, do you think students' perspectives are adequately represented before Congress and the bureaucracy?
3. Is the money your school spent on lobbyists well spent? Why or why not?

*FinAid Page, "Student Loans," FinAid Page, LLC, 2010, http://www.finaid.org/loans/ (accessed March 15, 2010).

†Betsy Miller Kittredge, "Managing Your Student Loans: July 1 College Affordability Benefits Every Borrower Should Know About," *Committee on Education and Labor*, May 14, 2009, http://edlabor.house.gov/blog/2009/05/managing-your-student-loans-up.shtml (accessed March 15, 2010).

into Washington interest groups are today. President Ronald Reagan in his Farewell Address warned of the power of "special interests,"[85] and President Dwight Eisenhower used his Farewell Address to warn against the "military-industrial complex," the alliance of defense industries and the U.S. military formed to pursue more spending on weapons.

One of the main arguments against interest groups is that they do not represent people equally. For example, fewer interest groups represent young or low-income people than represent senior citizens or corporations. Further, some groups are better organized and better financed, allowing them a decided advantage over more general groups. And the existence of a multiplicity of interests often leads to incoherent policies, inefficiency, and delay as lawmakers try to appease conflicting interests. In addition, the propensity of interest groups to support incumbents in elections increases the advantages of incumbency, which is often seen as undesirable.

Single-issue interest groups organized for or against particular policies—abortion, handgun control, tobacco subsidies, animal rights—have also aroused increasing concern in recent years. "It is said that citizen groups organizing in ever greater numbers to push single issues ruin the careers of otherwise fine politicians who disagree with them on one emotional issue, paralyze the traditional process of governmental compromise, and ignore the common good in their selfish insistence on getting their own way."[86]

Another area of concern related to both parties and interest groups is the raising and spending of vast amounts of money. Concern over the use of money—especially corporate funds – to influence politicians goes back more than a century. In 1921, President Warren G. Harding's administration allowed private companies to secretly lease public land in order to extract oil that had been reserved for the navy. In response to this "Teapot Dome scandal," Congress passed the Federal Corrupt Practices Act of 1925. It required disclosure reports, both before and after elections, of receipts and expenditures by Senate and House candidates and by political committees that sought to influence federal elections in more than one state.

But federal legislation was not very effective and was loosely enforced. The reform mood of the 1960s and the Watergate scandal of 1972 brought basic changes. The outcome was the Federal Election Campaign Act of 1971 (FECA), amended in 1974. We discuss FECA and the more recent Bipartisan Campaign Reform Act in greater detail in Chapter 6. The goals of these laws were to provide transparency regarding the sources and recipients of campaign funds and to regulate the use of money in elections in general.

Do campaign finance reforms and lobbying disclosure acts do enough to check the potential "mischiefs of faction"? What else—if anything—can be done? Most Americans agree with James Madison that the simple "remedy" of outlawing factions would be worse than the disease. It would be absurd to abolish liberty simply because it nourished faction. And the Constitution solidly protects the existence and activity of interest groups and lobbies. Moreover, interest groups provide important services, such as supplying needed and accurate information to government officials. The challenge, then, is how to regulate interest groups in a way that does not threaten our constitutional liberties.

An important part of campaigns is registering new voters and canvassing them about their views on issues. In this photo, a volunteer from an interest group focusing on get-out-the-vote efforts uses a palm pilot to record survey responses from a Minnesota family. ■ *In what ways can an interest group like this make America more democratic? Under what circumstances could they be accused of the "mischiefs of factions"?*

Interest groups and political parties also provide important ways for citizens to influence government. Because parties are the means by which politicians secure office, participation in the parties can help determine the course of American government. Parties also provide opportunities to learn about how other people see issues and to learn to compromise. Rather than being an impediment to democracy, they make government by the people possible. Interest groups provide important opportunities for individuals to work together to pursue common objectives. Sometimes, this means that individuals join existing groups; other times, they form new ones. Interest groups not only foster healthy competition in our politics, but they also teach important lessons about self-government.

CHAPTER **SUMMARY**

4.1 Identify the primary functions of parties in democracies.

Political parties are essential to democracy. They simplify voting choices, organize electoral competition, unify the electorate, help organize government by bridging the separation of powers and fostering cooperation among branches of government, translate public preferences into policy, and provide loyal opposition.

American elections are based on single-member-district, winner-take-all election rules. Compared to some European parties, American parties remain organizationally weak. Party nominees are determined through primaries, caucuses, or mixed systems under rules determined by each state.

4.2 Differentiate the functions of parties as institutions, parties in government, and parties in the electorate.

Parties play many different roles. As institutions, they are governed by their national and state committees, which are led by the party chairs, and they recruit and elect candidates, promote their party's principles, and keep the party organized. In government, Congress is organized around parties, and judicial and many executive branch appointments are based in large part on partisanship. In the electorate, parties actively seek to organize elections, simplify voting choices, and strengthen individuals' party identification. In recent years, there has been an increase in the number of persons who call themselves Independents. This trend is sometimes called dealignment, but most Independents are closet partisans who vote fairly consistently for the party toward which they lean.

4.3 Assess the regulation of party fundraising and expenditures.

With the rise of soft money in recent elections, parties had more resources to spend on politics. In 2002, Congress passed the Bipartisan Campaign Reform Act (BCRA), which banned soft money except for some narrowly defined and limited activities. The parties adapted to BCRA by building a larger individual donor base. Donors wanting to spend more than the BCRA limits did so in 2008 through a range of interest groups, many of which ran parallel campaigns with the candidates and parties.

4.4 Explain the role of interest groups in American politics, and categorize interest groups into types.

Interest groups form when a collection of people share similar political goals and organize to achieve them. Sometimes, these groups are based on a shared group identity, such as race, ethnicity, gender, or sexual orientation. Others are based on specific policy issues, such as reducing taxes or combating global warming. Still others claim to operate in the public interest on broad issues, such as educating voters or reducing the federal deficit.

Interest groups can be categorized as economic, ideological or single-issue, public interest, foreign policy, and government itself. Economic groups include corporations, labor unions, and professional and trade associations; they lobby officials and campaign for candidates whose trade, tax, and regulation policies favor their financial situation. Ideological groups typically pursue a single policy goal through many means. Public interest groups claim to work on behalf of all citizens and include watchdog groups and charities. Foreign policy groups work to influence some area of the United States' international affairs. Finally, government groups include public sector unions and other government entities.

4.5 Analyze sources of interest group power.

Size, resources, cohesiveness, leadership, and techniques, especially the ability to contribute to candidates and political parties and to fund lobbyists, affect interest group power. But the actual power of an interest group stems from how these elements relate to the political and governmental environment in which the interest group operates. Interest groups typically include people with many other cross-cutting interests, which both reduces and stabilizes their influence.

4.6 Identify ways lobbyists seek to influence policy and interest group spending affects elections.

Lobbyists represent organized interests before government. Lobbying involves communicating with legislators and executive-branch officials, making campaign contributions, and assisting in election activity.Interest groups spend money to lobby government officials and to involve themselves in elections, especially through the expanded use of PACs and 527 and 501(c) groups. Groups that lack money typically struggle to get their message out to the public and fail to influence public officials. Congress has enacted laws to regulate and reform excesses of interest groups in electoral democracy.

4.7 Evaluate the influence of political parties and interest groups on government in America.

Political parties are essential to the functioning of a democracy. While interest groups also perform important functions, James Madison's concerns about the "mischiefs of faction," especially in its tendency to foster instability and injustice, present a challenge today. The United States has generally responded by seeking to regulate lobbying and political money while preserving our constitutional liberty to create and join these groups. Both interest groups and political parties also provide important ways for citizens to influence government.

CHAPTER SELF-TEST

4.1 Identify the primary functions of parties in democracies.

1. Define the term *political party*, and explain the five major functions of political parties.
2. Keeping in mind the five functions of political parties, discuss in a few sentences why partisan fighting is an inevitable part of the party system.
3. In two or three sentences, explain why a vote for a third-party candidate in a U.S. election is typically considered a wasted vote.

4.2 Differentiate the functions of parties as institutions, parties in government, and parties in the electorate.

4. Match each of the following activities with the aspect of a political party it best represents—(a) parties as institutions, (b) in government, or (c) in the electorate.
   i. A student registers to vote, stating his party preference as Republican on the registration form before handing it to the county clerk
   ii. Howard Dean, chair of the Democratic National Committee, decides whether the votes of Democrats in Michigan and Florida should count during the 2008 presidential primaries
   iii. The Senate splits 55-to-45 on a bill authorizing funds for the Iraq War, with Republicans voting 44-to-5 in favor and Democrats voting 50-to-1 against
5. Many positions in the executive, legislative, and judicial branches of government are likely to be filled by loyal, active members of the political party in power. In one paragraph, discuss what problems may arise from this system.

4.3 Assess the regulation of party fundraising and expenditures.

6. Describe why soft money was banned by the Bipartisan Campaign Reform Act.
7. From where do the national party committees get most of their money today?
   a. Soft money
   b. Individual donors
   c. The general funds of unions and corporations
   d. Their parties' candidates

4.4 **Explain the role of interest groups in American politics, and categorize interest groups into types.**

8. Briefly explain the differences between *special interests* and *public interests*.
9. In two or three sentences, analyze how the idea of pluralism explains the founders' method for protecting against overwhelming factions.
10. Match each interest group with the category it most closely fits.

a. American Gaming Association	i. Public
b. National Right to Life	ii. Government
c. Project Vote Smart	iii. Economic
d. American-Israel Political Action Committee	iv. Ideological
e. The State Department	v. Foreign policy

4.5 **Analyze sources of interest group power.**

11. In a short essay, compare and contrast the three sources of interest group power: size, cohesiveness, and leadership. In your answer, provide an example of at least one group that exhibits each of the three sources and assess how it uses that power to influence national policy, and why.

12. Associations can gain a forum for their views by filing ________ briefs with courts.

4.6 **Identify ways lobbyists seek to influence policy and interest group spending affects elections.**

13. Explain and assess at least three ways in which lobbyists attempt to influence policy.
14. Describe what a PAC is and explain its characteristics.
15. List three or four arguments against allowing interest groups to donate money to political campaigns. Responding to those arguments, write a brief, persuasive essay explaining why interest groups should be allowed to donate money to political campaigns.

4.7 **Evaluate the influence of political parties and interest groups on government in America.**

16. Write a short, persuasive essay that explains why it is important to allow well-funded groups to function at the expense of less well-funded groups.
17. In a short essay, describe two or three benefits and two or three problems of parties, then argue for keeping or doing away with our current party system.

Answers to selected questions: 4. i. c, ii. a, iii. b; 7. b. 10. a. iii; b. iv; c. i; d. v; e. ii. 12. amicus

mypoliscilab EXERCISES

Where participation leads to action!

Apply what you learned in this chapter on MyPoliSciLab.

Read on **mypoliscilab.com**

eText: Chapter 4

Study and **Review** on **mypoliscilab.com**

Pre-Test
Post-Test
Chapter Exam
Flashcards

Watch on **mypoliscilab.com**

Video: Republicans and Democrats Divide on Tax Cut
Video: Senator Specter Switches Parties
Video: Tea Party Victories Concern for GOP
Video: American Cancer Society Recommendation
Video: Murtha and the PMA Lobbyists

Explore on **mypoliscilab.com**

Simulation: You Are a Campaign Manager: Help McCain Win Swing States and Swing Voters
Simulation: You Are an Environmental Activist
Comparative: Comparing Political Parties
Simulation: You Are a Lobbyist
Comparative: Comparing Interest Groups
Timelines: Interest Groups and Campaign Finance
Timeline: Third Parties in American History
Visual Literacy: State Control and National Platforms

KEY TERMS

political party, p. 116
nonpartisan election, p. 116
patronage, p. 116
honeymoon, p. 117
caucus, p. 117
party convention, p. 117
direct primary, p. 117
open primary, p. 118
crossover voting, p. 118
closed primary, p. 118
minor party, p. 118
proportional representation, p. 119
winner-take-all system, p. 119
national party convention, p. 120
party registration, p. 124
party identification, p. 125
realigning elections, p. 126
dealignment, p. 126
soft money, p. 128
Bipartisan Campaign Reform Act (BCRA), p. 129
hard money, p. 129
party-independent expenditures, p. 129
faction, p.130
pluralism, p. 130
interest group, p. 131
open shop, p.133
closed shop, p. 133
free rider, p. 133
professional associations, p. 133
lobbying, p.136
***Federal Register*,** p.137
***amicus curiae* brief,** p. 137
bundling, p.138
lobbyist, p. 139
revolving door, p.139
issue network, p.139
political action committee (PAC), p. 140
leadership PAC, p.142
independent expenditures, p.143
issue advocacy, p. 144
527 organization, p. 144

ADDITIONAL RESOURCES

FURTHER READING

JOHN H. ALDRICH, *Why Parties? The Origin and Transformation of Party Politics in America* (University of Chicago Press, 1995).

DAVID BOAZ, *Libertarianism: A Primer* (Free Press, 1998).

DONALD T. CRITCHLOW, *The Conservative Ascendancy: How the GOP Right Made Political History* (Harvard University Press, 2007).

LEON EPSTEIN, *Political Parties in the American Mold* (University of Wisconsin Press, 1986).

JOHN C. GREEN AND **DANIEL J. COFFEY,** EDS., *The State of the Parties: The Changing Role of Contemporary American Parties,* 6th ed. (Rowman & Littlefield, 2010).

MARJORIE RANDON HERSHEY, *Party Politics in America,* 14th ed. (Longman, 2010).

BRUCE E. KEITH, DAVID B. MAGLEBY, CANDICE J. NELSON, ELIZABETH ORR, MARK C. WESTLYE, AND **RAYMOND E. WOLFINGER,** *The Myth of the Independent Voter* (University of California Press, 1992).

MICHAEL S. LEWIS-BECK, HELMUT NORPOTH, WILLIAM G. JACOBY, AND **HERBERT F. WEISBERG,** *The American Voter Revisited* (University of Michigan Press, 2008).

DAVID B. MAGLEBY AND **ANTHONY D. CORRADO,** EDS., *Financing the 2008 Election* (Brookings Institution Press, 2011).

DAVID B. MAGLEBY, ED., *The Change Election: Money, Mobilization, and Persuasion in the 2008 Federal Elections* (Temple University Press, 2011).

L. SANDY MAISEL AND **KARA Z. BUCKLEY,** *Parties and Elections in America: The Electoral Process,* 5th ed. (Rowman & Littlefield, 2007).

STEVEN J. ROSENSTONE, ROY L. BEHR, AND **EDWARD H. LAZARUS,** *Third Parties in America: Citizen Response to Major Party Failure,* 2d ed. (Princeton University Press, 1996).

JAMES SUNDQUIST, *Dynamics of the Party System: Alignment and Realignment of Political Parties in the United States,* rev. ed. (Brookings Institution Press, 1983).

ALLAN J. CIGLER AND **BURDETT A. LOOMIS,** EDS., *Interest Group Politics,* 8th ed. (CQ Press, 2010).

MARTHA A. DERTHICK, *Up in Smoke,* 2d ed. (CQ Press, 2004).

KENNETH M. GOLDSTEIN, *Interest Groups, Lobbying, and Participation in America* (Cambridge University Press, 1999).

GENE GROSSMAN AND **ELHANAN HELPMAN,** *Special Interest Politics* (MIT Press, 2001).

KEVIN W. HULA, *Lobbying Together: Interest Group Coalitions in Legislative Politics* (Georgetown University Press, 1999).

MANCUR OLSON, *The Logic of Collective Action* (Harvard University Press, 1965).

JACK L. WALKER, JR., *Mobilizing Interest Groups in America: Patrons, Professions, and Social Movements* (University of Michigan Press, 1991).

WEB SITES

www.GOP.com; www.democrats.org These are the main Web sites of the Republican National Committee and Democratic National Committee, respectively. These sites have information about each party's national party convention and platform as well as party history and information about how to volunteer for party activities.

www.nrsc.org; www.dscc.org These are the Web sites for the National Republican Senatorial Committee and Democratic Senatorial Campaign Committee, respectively. These committees focus on helping their party's candidates win election to the United States Senate. Individuals can volunteer for and contribute to candidates on each site.

www.nrcc.org; www.dccc.org These are the Web sites for the National Republican Congressional Committee and Democratic Congressional Campaign Committee, respectively. These committees focus on helping their party's candidates win election to the United States House of Representatives. Individuals can volunteer for and contribute to candidates on each site.

www.gp.org The Web site for the Green Party of the United States. The site has information about the party's platform, party history, and how to volunteer for party activists and contribute financially.

www.opensecrets.org/parties/index.php The Center for Responsive Politics maintains this Web site with a large amount of information about how parties raise money.

www.fec.gov The Federal Election Commission site provides information on elections, campaign finance, parties, voting, and PACs.

www.pirg.org This is the Web site of the Public Interest Research Group (PIRG); this group has chapters on many college campuses. PIRG provides state-by-state policy and other information.

www.townhall.com This Web site of the American Conservative Union (ACU) provides policy and political information.

www.adaction.org The Web site of the American for Democratic Action provides information and ratings on members of Congress.

CHAPTER 5

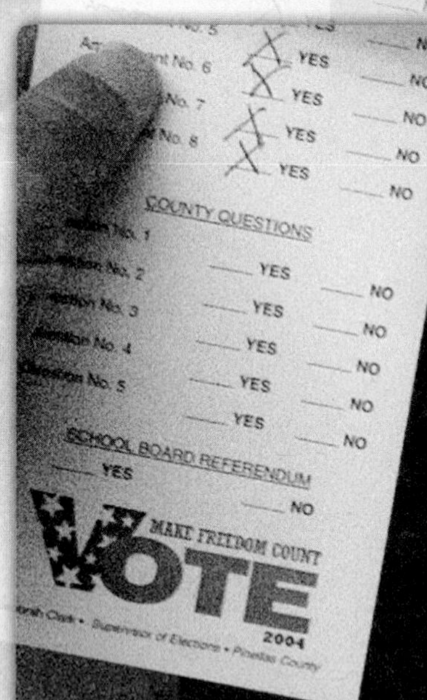
COUNTY QUESTIONS
SCHOOL BOARD REFERENDUM
MAKE FREEDOM COUNT
VOTE
2004

Public Opinion and Participation

CHAPTER **OUTLINE** & CHAPTER LEARNING **OBJECTIVES**

Forming Political Opinions and Values

5.1 Identify the forces that create and shape individuals' political attitudes.

Political Ideology and Attitudes Toward Government

5.2 Compare and contrast political ideologies and assess their importance in the contemporary American context.

Public Opinion: Taking the Pulse of the People

5.3 Outline the key dimensions of public opinion and how it is measured.

Participation: Translating Opinions into Action

5.4 Identify forms of political participation, and assess the effect on voter turnout of demographic, legal, and electioneering factors.

Voting Choices

5.5 Analyze the factors that influence voter choice.

For most of U.S. history, voting was something people did in person on a designated day during limited hours. Polling places included fire stations, schools, community centers, and a range of other locations. Under only very limited circumstances, like being out of town on election day, could a person request an *absentee ballot*, which allowed him or her to vote in advance of election day.

Beginning with some local elections in the 1970s, states like California and Oregon began to experiment with allowing voters to vote-by-mail in local elections.[1] In 1998, Oregon was the first state to switch to statewide elections done through the mail, an experiment that was widely seen as a success in that state. Voters who want to vote in person in Oregon can go to their county offices and vote in person, but relatively few do so. Election officials like vote-by-mail because it lowers cost and is easier to administer than an in-person voting process held on only one day. Vote-by-mail has been found to increase turnout, at least in the initial period after adoption,[2] and in Oregon, it continues to foster greater turnout in presidential general elections.[3] Opponents of vote-by-mail worry about potential abuses of the process where people might fraudulently cast the ballot of another person or bribe a person to vote a certain way and then mail in that person's ballot. Some see value in casting a ballot in public with other voters on a designated day. More fundamentally, some question the value of making it easier for people to vote, which voting by mail does. This viewpoint is based on the perceived importance of citizens being willing to invest time and effort, which in-person voting requires. To date, Oregon is the only state to have switched to vote-by-mail as its means to conduct elections.

Also during this same period, states liberalized their absentee voting rules to permit "no excuse" absentee voting, which meant people did not need to have a reason to request an absentee ballot. In the last few elections, states have also permitted voters to vote early at designated voting places. One advantage is voters do not have to request an absentee ballot—they can just show up to one of the early voting sites on an early voting day.

In 2008, 30 percent of all voters voted early or by absentee ballot, including virtually all of the votes cast in Oregon. This number is up from 22 percent in 2004 and 16 percent in 2000. In 2008, the percent of early or absentee votes was as high as 89 percent in Washington, 79 percent in Colorado, 67 percent in Nevada, and 62 percent in New Mexico.[4] With more and more voting happening before "election day," candidates have had to adapt their campaign strategies.

Making voting more accessible through vote-by-mail and "no-excuse" absentee voting is just the most recent reform intended to broaden electoral participation. In this chapter, we look at the nature and level of political participation in the United States and why people vote the way they do. We also explore public opinion, how to measure it, and what factors affect the formation of opinions. We begin by looking at how we get our political opinions, values, and ideology.

Forming Political Opinions and Values

LEARNING **OBJECTIVE**

5.1 Identify the forces that create and shape individuals' political attitudes.

No one is born with political views. Rather, they are learned and acquired through experience and association with other people. Socialization—the way in which we come to see society and ourselves and learn to interact with other individuals and groups—lays the foundation for political beliefs, values, ideology, and partisanship. It is a process that continues throughout our lives. How people come to see the political world can change, but our core values and beliefs are resistant to change. More transitory opinions, say, on banking regulation, tend to be volatile, whereas core values on such things as liberty or freedom tend to remain more stable. Discerning this difference is important for understanding the varied levels on which people think about politics.

Political Socialization

We develop our political attitudes from many mentors and teachers through a process called **political socialization.** This process starts in childhood, and families and schools are usually our two most important political teachers. We learn about our culture in childhood and adolescence, but we reshape our opinions as we mature.[5] Although the details of our political system may elude them, most young citizens acquire a respect for the Constitution and for the concept of participatory democracy, as well as an initially positive view of the most visible figure in our democracy, the president.[6]

The pluralistic political culture of the United States makes the sources of our views immensely varied. Political attitudes may stem from religious, racial, gender, or ethnic backgrounds or economic beliefs and values. But we can safely make at least one generalization: We form our attitudes through participation in *groups* (see Chapters 3 and 4). Close-knit groups such as the family are especially influential.

political socialization
The process—most notably in families and schools—by which we develop our political attitudes, values, and beliefs.

attitudes
An individual's propensity to perceive, interpret, or act toward a particular object in a particular way.

Family Most social psychologists agree that family is the most powerful socializing agent.[7] What we first learn in the family is not so much specific political opinions as basic **attitudes,** broad or general, that shape our opinions about our neighbors, political parties, other classes or types of people, particular leaders (especially presidents), and society in general. Attitudes are understood to be "a propensity in an individual to perceive, interpret, and act toward a particular object in particular ways."[8] Attitudes are often seen as positive or negative toward the object, person, or idea.

American children typically show political interest by age 10, and by the early teens, their awareness may be fairly high. People tend to belong to the same political party as their parents did. Does the direct influence of parents create the correspondence? Or does living in the same social environment—neighborhood, church, and socioeconomic group—influence parents and children? The answer is *both.* One influence often strengthens the other.

Presidents are important authority figures to children. Here a group of elementary school children watch a speech by President Obama on the importance of education. ■ *In what ways is this school functioning as an agent of political socialization?*

Schools Schools also mold young citizens' political attitudes. U.S. schools see part of their purpose as preparing students to be citizens and active participants in governing their communities and the nation. Especially important in fostering later political involvement are extracurricular activities such as student government and debate.[9]

From kindergarten through college, students generally develop political values consistent with the democratic process and supportive of the U.S. political system. In their study of U.S. history, they are introduced to our nation's heroes and heroines, important events, and the ideals of U.S. society. Other aspects of their experience, such as the daily Pledge of Allegiance and school programs or assemblies, reinforce respect for country. Children also gain practical experience in

By the People

MAKING A DIFFERENCE

Improving Literacy

In an extensive study released in 1993, between one-fifth and one-quarter of adult Americans were found to be illiterate, defined as being unable to "locate information in a text" or "make low-level inferences using printed material."* A follow-up study released in 2006 found no significant improvement in U.S. adult literacy.† Illiteracy, or the inability to use printed and written information effectively, is a significant problem for the illiterate individuals and for society as a whole. Most jobs require minimal literacy, as do daily activities like reading contracts or instructions on medications. Filling out governmental forms, including voter registration forms, and engaging in active citizenship in other ways is based on individuals being literate. Those not able to read often do not engage in active citizenship and exhibit a lack of confidence in dealing with other people and institutions.

You can make a difference in helping children and adults learn to read. Some college students have organized programs at their institutions to enhance literacy in their own communities. Baylor University, for example, has "Camp Success," which is a four-week language and literacy therapy camp for area children. Begun in 2003, the camp has had more than 500 children participate. Professor Michaela Ritter, who directs the camp, indicates that "most kids make from one to three years' progress" during the camp.‡

You do not have to find an organized program to make a difference in enhancing literacy. One-on-one reading with a child is something you can readily arrange in your local community. Most public schools are very eager for volunteers to read with struggling students, and local libraries often have such programs as well.

CRITICAL THINKING QUESTIONS

1. Does it surprise you that 20–25 percent of Americans are illiterate? Why or why not?
2. Why is literacy a condition of active citizenship?
3. Why do you think having a caring college student read with a younger person has such positive results?

* National Center for Education Statistics, *Adult Literacy in America* (April 2002), http://nces.ed.gov/pubs93/93275.pdf (accessed March 8, 2010).

† National Center for Education Statistics, *A First Look at the Literacy of America's Adults in the 21st Century* (2006), http://nces.ed.gov/NAAL/PDF/2006470.PDF (accessed March 8, 2010).

‡ http://www.wacotrib.com/news/content/news/stories/2009/07/03/07032009waccampsuccess.html

the way democracy works through elections for student government. In many states, high school and even college students are required by law to take courses in U.S. history or government to graduate.

Do school courses and activities give young people the skills needed to participate in elections and democratic institutions? A study of 18- to 24-year-olds commissioned by the National Association of Secretaries of State found that young people are lacking in "understanding about the democratic process . . . and information about candidates and political parties."[10] You and your classmates are not a representative sample, in part because you have more interest and knowledge than most people.

Peers and Friends People of all ages learn from peers and friends, but for younger people they are especially important. For example, friends help with adaptation to school, including college. The influence of friends and peers stems from the human desire to be like people around us.[11] Peer groups not only define fashion and social norms, they reinforce or may challenge what has been experienced in families. Technology has expanded the ways we interact with peers through Facebook or other social media.

The debate about whether there is peer pressure on college campuses to conform to certain acceptable ideas or to use particular language highlights how higher education can shape attitudes and values. One study suggests that college students are more likely than noncollege students of the same age to be knowledgeable about politics, more in favor of free speech, and more likely to talk and read about politics.[12]

Mass Media Like everyone else, young people are exposed to a wide range of media—school newspapers, national and local newspapers, the Internet, movies, radio, and television—all of which influence what they think, and like everyone else, they often pick and choose the media with which they agree, a process called **selective exposure.** The mass media also serve as agents of political socialization by exposing individuals to the values and behavior of others. Media influence is greater on attitudes about issues and individual politicians than on underlying values.[13]

selective exposure
Individuals choosing to access media with which they agree or avoiding media with which they disagree.

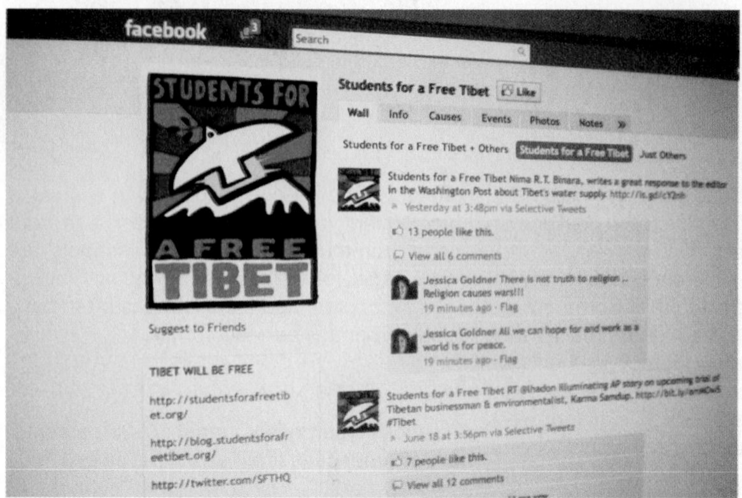

Facebook groups like Students for a Free Tibet allow peers to share their political interests and rally friends to their cause, all without leaving their dorm rooms. ■ *Has Facebook had an impact on your political opinions? How has it changed the way you interact with peers?*

Other Influences Religious, ethnic, and racial backgrounds as well as the workplace can also shape opinions, both within and outside the family. Some scholars have found, for example, that the religious composition of a community has a direct impact on knowledge, discussion, and self-confidence among students in dealing with politics.[14] But although generalizations about how people vote are useful, we have to be careful about stereotyping. For example, not all African Americans vote Democratic, and many Catholics disagree with their church's opposition to abortion. It is a mistake to assume that because we know a person's religious affiliation or racial background, we know his or her political opinions.

Stability and Change

Adults are not simply the sum of their early experiences, but adults' opinions do tend to remain stable. Even if the world around us changes rapidly, we are slow to shift our loyalties or to change our minds about things that matter to us. Political analysts are becoming more interested in how adults modify their views. A harsh experience—a war, an economic depression, or an event like the terrorist attacks of September 11, 2001—may be a catalyst that changes attitudes and opinions.

Because they are part of our core values, views on abortion, the death penalty, and doctor-assisted suicide, for example, tend to remain stable over time. On issues less central to our values, such as how a president is performing, opinions can change substantially. Figure 5–1 contrasts the public's opinion toward President George W. Bush with its views on abortion over time. Although the electorate's opinion of President Bush changed noticeably over time, opinions on abortion remained remarkably stable. On many issues, opinion can change once the public learns more about the issue or perceives another side to the question. These are the issues politicians can help shape by calling attention to them and leading the debate.

Awareness and Interest

Many people find politics complicated and difficult to understand. And they should because democracy is complicated and difficult to understand. The mechanics and structures of our government, such as how the government operates, how the electoral college works, how Congress is set up, and the length of terms for the president and for members of the Senate and House of Representatives are examples of such complexity that are important to our constitutional democracy.

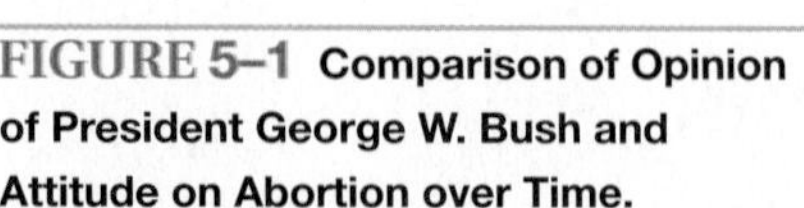

FIGURE 5–1 Comparison of Opinion of President George W. Bush and Attitude on Abortion over Time.
■ *Why is attitude on abortion so consistent in comparison to the fluctuation in opinion of President Bush over the same time period?*

SOURCE: Gallup and Gallup/USA Today polls, compiled by Polling Report, www.pollingreport.com/abortion and www.pollingreport.com/BushJob1.htm.

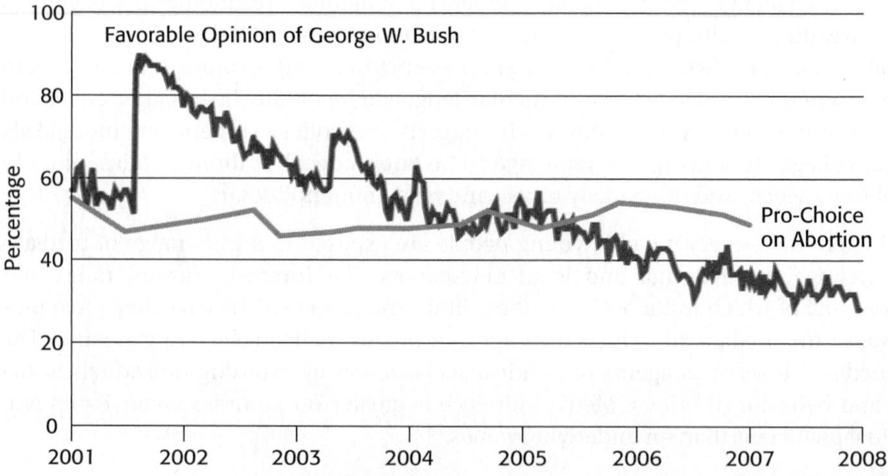

FIGURE 5–2 **Political Interest and Knowledge**

Do you know more than the average citizen? Test yourself! (Answers at right)

1. How many votes are needed in the Senate to break a filibuster?
   51, 60, 67, or 75
2. How many GOP senators voted for the health bill?
   0, 5, 10, or 20
3. Who is the chair of the GOP National Committee?
   Sarah Palin, Howard Dean, Michael Steele, or Newt Gingrich
4. What is the Dow Jones Industrial Average currently closest to?
   3,000; 5,000; 10,000; or 20,000
5. Who is the majority leader of the U.S. Senate?
   Harry Reid, Al Franken, Mitch McConnell, or Hillary Clinton
6. Stephen Colbert is which of the following:
   congressman, athlete, comedian and TV host, or hip-hop artist
7. In 2009, were there more U.S. deaths in Iraq or Afghanistan?
8. Where was the attempted "Christmas day" bomber trained?
   Israel, Syria, Afghanistan, or Yemen
9. Which of the following is the unemployment rate closest to?
   5%, 10%, 15%, or 20%
10. How many women are on the U.S. Supreme Court?:
    0, 1, 2, or 3
11. The U.S. imports what percentage of the oil it consumes?
    one-quarter, one-third, half, or two-thirds
12. Who holds the most U.S. debt?
    Japan, China, Saudi Arabia, or Canada

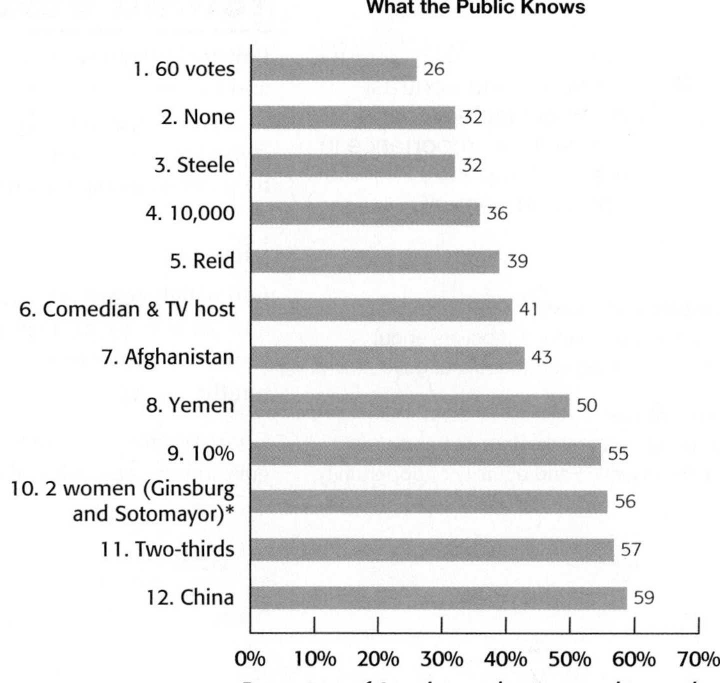

SOURCE: Pew Research Center, January 28, 2010, news release, http://people-press.org/reports/pdf/586.pdf.

Younger adults who remember learning the details in school typically know most about how the government works. In general, however, adults fare poorly when quizzed about their elected officials.[15] Slightly more than 15 percent know the names of the congressional candidates from their district.[16] With so few voters knowing the candidates, it is not surprising that "on even hotly debated issues before Congress, few people know where their Congress member stands."[17]

The public knows even less about important public policy issues (see Figure 5–2). In 2004, only 28 percent could identify William Rehnquist as the then chief justice of the U.S. Supreme Court. Fortunately, not everyone is uninformed or uninterested. Approximately 25 percent of the public is interested in politics most of the time. This is the **attentive public,** people who know and understand how the government works. They vote in most elections, read a daily newspaper, and talk politics with their families and friends. They tend to be better educated and more committed to democratic values than other adults.

At the opposite end of the spectrum are political know-nothings, people who are rarely interested in politics or public affairs and seldom vote. About one-third of American adults have indicated that they are interested in politics "only now and then" or "hardly at all."[18]

Between the attentive public and the political know-nothings are the *part-time citizens,* roughly 40 percent of the U.S. public. These individuals participate selectively in elections, voting in presidential elections but usually not in others. Politics and government do not greatly interest them, they pay only minimal attention to the news, and they rarely discuss candidates or elections with others.

Democracy can survive even when some citizens are passive and uninformed, as long as others serve as opinion leaders and are interested and informed about public affairs. Obviously, these activists will have much greater influence than their less-active fellow citizens.

attentive public
Citizens who follow public affairs carefully.

Political Ideology and Attitudes Toward Government

LEARNING **OBJECTIVE**

5.2 Compare and contrast political ideologies and assess their importance in the contemporary American context.

Political ideology refers to a consistent pattern of ideas or beliefs about political values and the role of government, including how it should work and how it actually does work.

Two major schools of political ideology dominate American politics: *liberalism* and *conservatism.* Two less popular schools of thought—*socialism* and *libertarianism*—also help define the spectrum of ideology. (See Table 5–1.)

Liberalism

political ideology
A consistent pattern of beliefs about political values and the role of government.

liberalism
A belief that government can and should achieve justice and equality of opportunity.

In the eighteenth and nineteenth centuries, classical liberals favored *limited government* and sought to protect people from governmental harassment in their political and economic lives. Over time, the liberal emphasis on individualism has remained constant, but the perception of the need for government changed.

Contemporary Liberals In its current U.S. usage, **liberalism** refers to a belief that government can bring about justice and equality of opportunity. Modern-day liberals wish

TABLE

5–1 Differences in Political Ideology

	Conservative	Moderate	Liberal	Don't Know/Haven't Thought About It
Sex				
Male	39%	23%	20%	18%
Female	31	24	22	23
Race				
White	39	24	21	17
Black	18	21	22	39
Asian	20	26	36	18
Hispanic	22	25	20	32
Age				
18–34	26	24	28	23
35–45	36	26	17	20
46–55	37	23	19	20
56–64	38	21	26	15
Religion				
Protestant	45	18	16	15
Catholic	31	28	18	23
Jewish	26	12	63	0
Education				
Less than high school	25	20	14	42
High school diploma	29	27	11	33
Some college	38	25	22	15
Bachelor's degree	42	21	32	5
Advanced degree	45	14	39	3
Party				
Democrat	13	27	37	23
Independent	14	35	11	40
Republican	70	15	5	11

This table displays how ideology is correlated to sex, race, age, religion, education, and political party. ■ *In which factors do you see the strongest and weakest correlations, and how might you account for that?*

SOURCE: Center for Political Studies, University of Michigan, *2008 American National Election Study Guide to Public Opinion and Electoral Behavior.*

to preserve the rights of the individual and the right to own private property, but they believe that some government intervention in the economy is necessary to remedy the shortcomings of capitalism. Liberals advocate equal access to health care, housing, and education for all citizens. They generally believe in affirmative action programs, protections for workers' health and safety, tax rates that rise with a person's income, and unions' rights to organize and strike. Liberals are generally more inclined to favor greater environmental protection and individual choice in such matters as same-sex marriage and abortion.

Liberals generally believe that the future will be better than the past or the present—that obstacles can be overcome and the government can be trusted to, and should, play a role in that progress. They contend that modern technology and industrialization cry out for government programs to offset the loss of liberties that the poor and the weak suffer.

Liberals led in expanding civil rights in the 1960s and 1970s and favor affirmative action today. Some liberals favor reducing the great inequalities of wealth that make equality of opportunity impossible. Most favor a certain minimum level of income for all. Rather than placing a cap on wealth, they want to build a floor beneath the poor. If necessary, they favor raising taxes to achieve these goals. In the recent health care reform debate, liberals favored a public option insurance plan providing something like Medicare for all citizens.

Patrick Leahy (D-Vermont) has promoted liberal programs and legislation for many years.

Criticisms of Liberalism Critics say liberals rely too much on government, higher taxes, and bureaucracy to solve the nation's problems. They argue that liberals have forgotten that government has to be limited if it is to serve our best interests. Too much dependence on government can corrupt the spirit, undermine self-reliance, and make people forget those cherished personal freedoms and property rights our Republic was founded to secure and protect. In short, critics of modern liberalism contend that the welfare and regulatory state liberals advocate will ultimately destroy individual initiative, the entrepreneurial spirit, and the very engine of economic growth that might lead to true equality of economic opportunity.

Since the late 1960s, Republicans have made liberalism a villain while claiming that their own presidential candidates represent the mainstream. Bill Clinton was careful not to label his programs liberal, focusing on the need for economic growth, jobs, and a balanced budget. He insisted he was a "New Democrat." Republicans, however, claim Democrats are liberals who favor "tax and spend" big government.

Conservatism

Belief in private property rights and free enterprise are cardinal attributes of contemporary **conservatism.** In contrast to liberals, conservatives want to keep government small, especially the national government, although they support a strong national defense. Conservatives take a more pessimistic view of human nature than liberals do. They maintain that people need strong leadership, firm laws, and strict moral codes. The primary task of government is to ensure order. Conservatives also believe that people are the architects of their own fortune and must solve their own problems and create their own successes.

Traditional Conservatives Conservatives are emphatically pro-business. They favor tax cuts and resist all but the minimum antitrust, trade, and environmental regulations on corporations. They believe that the sole functions of government should be to protect the nation from foreign enemies, preserve law and order, enforce private contracts, encourage economic growth by fostering competitive markets and free and fair trade, and promote family values. Conservatives believe that the market, not the government, should provide services. These views were tested by the Bush Administration's advocacy of a massive government bailout of financial institutions in 2008.

Conservatives opposed the New Deal programs of the 1930s, the War on Poverty in the 1960s, many civil rights and affirmative action programs, and the Obama Administration's push for a larger government role in health care in 2009 and 2010. Families and private charities, they say, can and should take care of human needs and social and economic problems. They believe government social activism has been expensive and counterproductive. State and local government should address those social problems that need a

conservatism
A belief that limited government ensures order, competitive markets, and personal opportunity.

Senator Jim DeMint (R-South Carolina) is both socially conservative—he is opposed to same-sex marriage—and fiscally conservative—he opposes increases in federal spending and speaks against the federal bailout of banks and other corporations.

government response. For example, conservatives have long held abortion to be a matter for state and local governments to decide, as well as education. President Bush's education reform created under the No Child Left Behind Act of 2002 encountered opposition from some of the most conservative and Republican states because they saw the policy as interfering with the ability of states and local school districts to manage education. Conservatives, especially those in office, do, however, selectively advocate government activism, often expressing a desire for a more effective and efficient government.

Social Conservatives Some conservatives focus less on economics and more on morality and lifestyle. Social conservatives favor strong governmental action to protect children from pornography and drugs. They want to overturn or repeal judicial rulings and laws that permit abortion, same-sex marriage, and affirmative action programs. This brand of conservatism—sometimes called the New Right—emerged in the 1980s. The New Right shares traditional conservatism's love of freedom and backs an aggressive effort to defend American interests abroad.

Accordingly, a defining characteristic of the New Right is a strong desire to impose *social controls*. Christian conservatives, who are disproportionately evangelical, want to preserve traditional values and protect the institution of the family. Groups promoting traditional marriage and committed parenting, like the Christian Coalition and Focus on the Family, wax and wane in importance. In 2008, the connection between Christian conservatives and the GOP was further reinforced by the candidacy of former Arkansas governor and ordained Baptist minister Mike Huckabee, who emphasized his Christianity in his 2008 campaign.[19]

Criticisms of Conservatism Not everyone agreed with Ronald Reagan's statement that "government is the problem." Indeed, critics point out that conservatives themselves urge more government when it serves their needs—to regulate pornography and abortion, for example—but are opposed to government when it serves somebody else's. Conservatives may also have fewer objections to big government when individuals have a choice in determining how government will affect them. Vouchers for schools, choices in prescription drug benefit plans, and options to manage Social Security savings are examples of such choices.[20]

Their great faith in the market economy often puts conservatives at odds with labor unions and consumer activists and in close alliance with businesspeople, particularly large corporations. Hostility to regulation and a belief in competition lead conservatives to push for deregulation. This approach has not always had positive results, as the collapse of many savings and loan companies in the 1980s[21] and the 2008 financial crisis, brought about by troubled subprime mortgages and other risky lending practices, illustrates.[22] Conservatives counter that, overall, it is still best to rely on the free market.

The policy of lowering taxes is consistent with the conservative hostility to big government. Many conservatives embrace the idea that, if the rich pay fewer taxes, they will spend and invest more, and the benefits of this increased economic activity will "trickle down" to the poor. But Democrats argue that most of the growth in income and wealth that followed the Bush tax cuts was largely concentrated among the well-to-do and that reduced taxes and increased government spending, especially for defense, tripled the deficit during the 1980s, when conservatives were in control.[23] Liberals charge that some conservatives repeatedly fail to acknowledge and endorse policies that deal with racism and sexism. They cite conservative opposition to civil rights laws in the 1960s and more recently to affirmative action.

Socialism and Communism

socialism
An economic and governmental system based on public ownership of the means of production and exchange.

Socialism is an economic and governmental system based on public ownership of the means of production and exchange. The nineteenth-century German philosopher Karl Marx once described socialism as a transitional stage of society between capitalism and communism. In a capitalist system, the means of production and most property are privately owned; under **communism,** the state owns property in common for all the people, and a single political party that represents the working classes controls the government.

In communist countries such as Cuba and China, the Communist Party allows no opposition. Some countries, such as Sweden, have combined limited government ownership and operation of business with democracy. Most western European countries and Canada have various forms of socialized or government-run medical systems and sometimes telecommunications networks, while keeping most economic sectors private.

Bernie Sanders, a self-described socialist, represents Vermont in the U.S. Senate as an Independent.

American socialists—of whom there are only a few prominent examples, including one United States senator, Vermont's Bernie Sanders—favor a greatly expanded role for the government but argue that such a system is compatible with democracy. They would nationalize certain industries, institute a public jobs program so that all who want to work could work, tax the wealthy much more heavily, and drastically cut defense spending.[24] Canada and most of the democracies of Western Europe are more influenced by socialist ideas than we are in the United States, but they remain, like the United States, largely market economies. Debate will continue about the proper role of government and what the market can do better than government can.[25]

Libertarianism

Libertarianism is a political ideology that cherishes individual liberty and insists on sharply limited government. It carries some overtones of anarchism, of the classical English liberalism of the nineteenth century (defined earlier in this chapter), and of a 1930s-style conservatism. The Libertarian Party has gained a small following among people who believe that both liberals and conservatives are inconsistent in their attitude toward the power of the national government.

Libertarians oppose nearly all government programs. They favor massive cuts in government spending and an end to the Federal Bureau of Investigation (FBI), the Central Intelligence Agency (CIA), the Internal Revenue Service (IRS), and most regulatory commissions. They oppose American participation in the United Nations and favor armed forces that would defend the United States only if directly attacked. They oppose *all* government regulation, including, for example, mandatory seat-belt and helmet laws, in part because they believe individuals will all benefit more from an undistorted free market, and more generally because they embrace the attitude "live and let live." Unlike conservatives, libertarians would repeal laws that regulate personal morality, including abortion, pornography, prostitution, and illicit drugs. A Libertarian Party candidate for president has been on the ballot in all 50 states in recent presidential elections, although the party has never obtained more than 1 percent of the vote, and in 2008, the party received less than one-half of 1 percent of the vote.

Political Ideology and the American People

For some people, ideological controversy today centers on the role of the government in improving schools, encouraging a stronger work ethic, and stopping the flow of drugs into the country. For others, ideology focuses on whether to permit openly gay people into the military or sanction same-sex marriages and on the best ways to instill moral values, build character, and encourage cohesive and lasting families. Ideology has economic, social/lifestyle, environmental, civil rights/civil liberties, and foreign/defense policy dimensions. It is not surprising that some individuals are liberal or conservative in one dimension but not another.

communism
A political, social, and economic system in which land and capital are collectively owned and political power is exercised by the masses.

libertarianism
An ideology that cherishes individual liberty and insists on minimal government, promoting a free market economy, a noninterventionist foreign policy, and an absence of regulation in moral, economic, and social life.

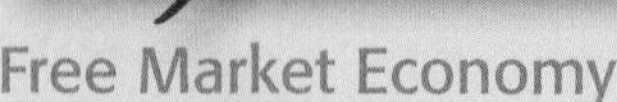

Of the People: THE GLOBAL COMMUNITY

Free Market Economy

The Pew Global data provide an interesting contrast among countries in how the people express agreement with the statement: "Most people are better off in a free market economy, even though some people are rich and some are poor." The figure below plots the percent that completely or mostly agree or disagree.

For most of the world, nearly two-thirds completely or mostly agree "that most people are better off in a free market economy." In Nigeria, nearly four out of five hold this view. In Japan, however, under half of the respondents felt that a free market economy was preferable.

If we look at people who agree more strongly to the question, 37 percent of people in Nigeria and 40 percent of people in India completely agree that most people are better off in a free market economy, even though some people are rich and some are poor. In contrast, only 7 percent of people in Japan and 17 percent of those in Britain held this view. The U.S and World samples are between these two extremes with approximately one in four completely agreeing.

CRITICAL THINKING QUESTIONS

1. What elements of a political culture might help explain positive feelings toward a free market economy?
2. Conversely, what elements of a political culture explain a more cautious view of a free market?
3. Why might people in Nigeria or India more strongly agree that a free market economy is preferable, even in the presence of economic imbalances?

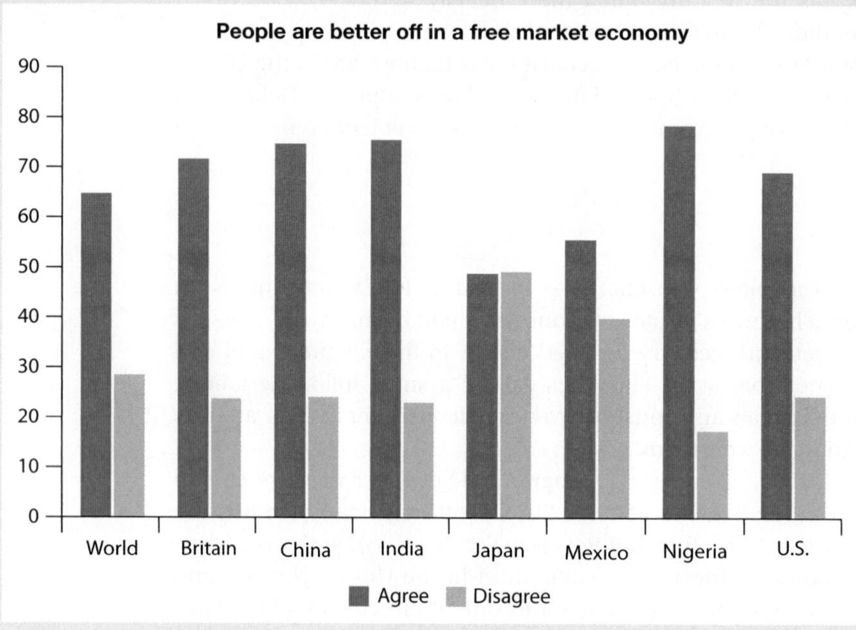

Despite the twists and turns of American politics, the distribution of ideology in the nation has been remarkably consistent (see Figure 5–3). Conservatives outnumber liberals, but the proportion of conservatives did not increase substantially with the decisive Republican presidential victories of the 1980s or the congressional victories of the 1990s.

Moreover, in the United States, most people are moderates or report not knowing whether they are liberal or conservative. In recent years, only 2–3 percent of the population saw themselves as extreme liberals, while extreme conservatives ranged from 2 to 4 percent (see Figure 5–4). These percentages have changed little over time. Despite claims by ideological extremes in both parties of a move to the right or to the left, there are simply more voters in the middle who are moderate or do not have a preferred ideology.[26] Both major parties target moderate or centrist voters, as reflected in the stands of the candidates on key issues.

For those with a liberal or conservative preference, ideology provides a lens through which to view candidates and public policies. It helps simplify the complexities of politics, policies, personalities, and programs. However, most voters are selective or even inconsistent in their political views. A voter may support increased spending for defense but vote for the party that is for reducing defense spending because he or she has always voted for that party or

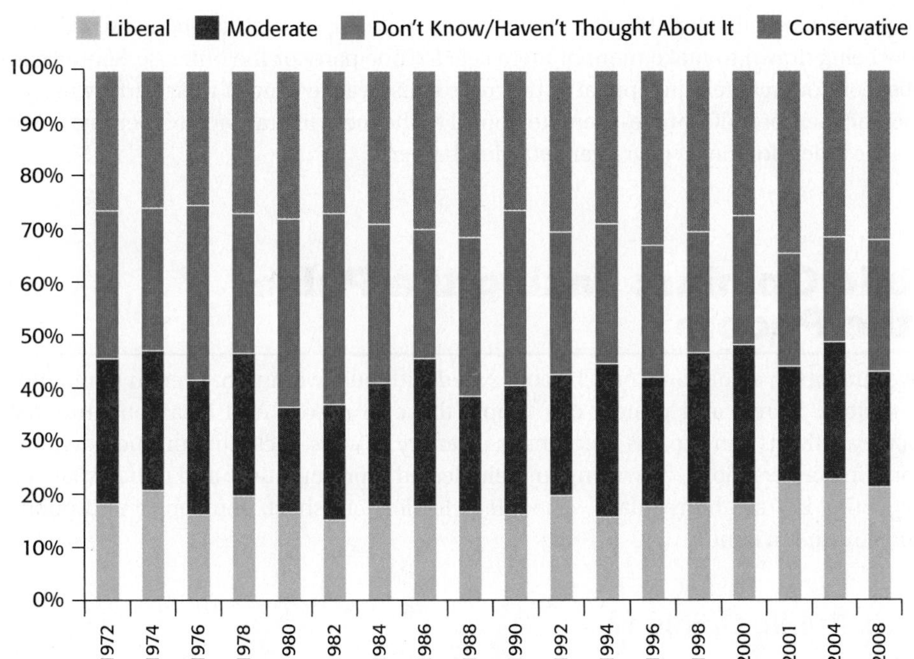

FIGURE 5–3 Ideology over Time.

■ *What factors might account for the stability in Americans' ideology over time?*

SOURCE: Center for Political Studies, University of Michigan, *2008 American National Election Study.*

prefers its stand on the environment. Or a person may favor tax cuts and a balanced budget while opposing substantial reductions in government programs. The degree to which people have ideologically consistent attitudes and opinions varies but is often relatively low.

The absence of widespread and solidified liberal and conservative positions in the United States makes for politics and policy-making processes that are markedly different from those in most nations. Policy making in this country is characterized more by ad hoc coalitions than by fixed alignments that pit one set of ideologies against another. Our politics are marked more by moderation, pragmatism, and accommodation than by a prolonged battle between competing philosophies of government. Elsewhere, especially in countries such as Sweden or Germany, where a strong Socialist, Green, or Christian Democratic party exists, things are different.

This does not mean that policies or ideas are not important in American politics. Since 1995, for instance, there has been a shift to more partisan and ideological voting in the House of Representatives. Part of the explanation is that Republicans have become more conservative and Democrats more liberal. Conservative Republicans have made large gains in the South, while the remaining Democrats in the South have become more liberal;[27] in other parts of the country, such as New England and parts of the Midwest, liberal Democrats

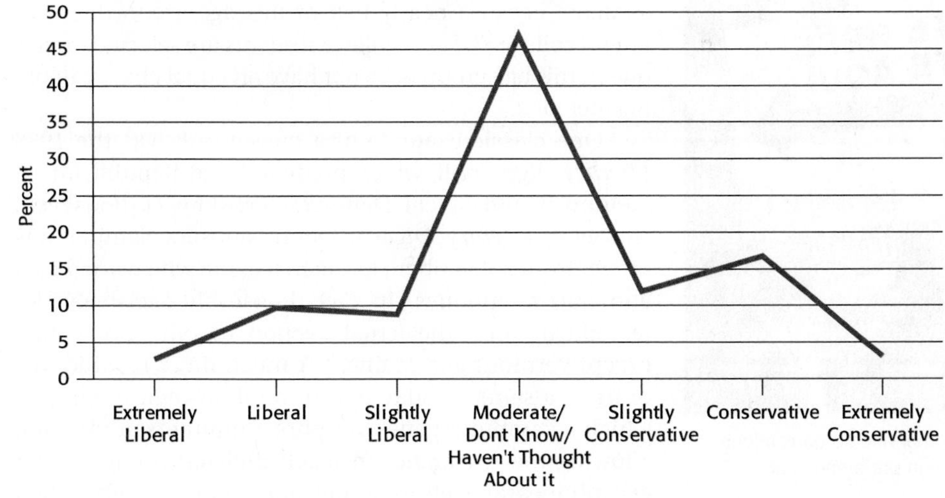

FIGURE 5–4 Distribution of Ideology in the United States.

■ *How does the ideology of the American people compare to that of American politicians and pundits? In what ways might this difference matter?*

SOURCE: Center for Political Studies, University of Michigan, *2008 American National Election Study.*

have replaced moderate Republicans. Perhaps even more important, congressional districts are now being drawn to make more of them safe for one party or the other, so Republican members of Congress tend to appeal to the more conservative wing of their party, whereas Democratic members of Congress tend to appeal to the more liberal wing of their party. We discuss these developments in greater detail in Chapter 7.

Public Opinion: Taking the Pulse of the People

LEARNING **OBJECTIVE**

5.3 Outline the key dimensions of public opinion and how it is measured.

All governments in all nations must be concerned with public opinion. Even in nondemocratic nations, unrest and protest can topple those in power. And in a constitutional democracy, citizens can express opinions in a variety of ways, including through demonstrations, in conversations, by writing to their elected representatives and to newspapers, and by voting in free and regularly scheduled elections. In short, democracy and public opinion go hand in hand.

What Is Public Opinion?

Politicians frequently talk about what "the people" think or want. But social scientists use the term "public opinion" more precisely: **Public opinion** is the distribution of individual preferences for or evaluations of a given issue, candidate, or institution within a specific population as measured by public opinion surveys. *Distribution* means the proportion of the population that holds a particular opinion, compared to people who have opposing opinions or no opinion at all. The most accurate way to study public opinion is through systematic measurement in polls or surveys. For instance, final preelection polls in 2008 by the Gallup Poll found that, among likely voters and removing those with no opinion, 54 percent said they were voting for Barack Obama, 44 percent said they were voting for John McCain, and 2 percent said they were voting for someone else.[28] The actual vote was Obama, 52 percent; McCain; 46 percent; and 1 percent voted for all others.

public opinion
The distribution of individual preferences for or evaluations of a given issue, candidate, or institution within a specific population.

random sample
In this type of sample, every individual has a known and equal chance of being selected.

In addition to polls conducted by Gallup, Pew, and other such organizations, newspapers and TV networks conduct polls on election preferences and numerous other subjects.

Measuring Public Opinion

In a public opinion poll, a relatively small number of people can accurately represent the opinions of a larger population if the researchers use *random sampling.* In a **random sample,** every individual in the group has a known and equal chance of being selected. For instance, a survey of 18- to 24-year-olds should not consist solely of college students because nearly half of this age group does not attend college.[29] If only college students are selected, everyone in this age group does not have an equal chance of being included.

One classic example of a flawed poll was the 1936 *Literary Digest* poll, which predicted that Republican Alf Landon would defeat Democrat Franklin D. Roosevelt. However, *Literary Digest*'s Depression-era sample was drawn from subscribers to the magazine who owned cars and had telephones. In fact, Roosevelt decisively defeated Landon in the actual election, carrying every state except Vermont and Maine.[30] A much more reliable way to draw a sample today is with random-digit dialing, in which a computer generates phone numbers at random, allowing the researcher to reach unlisted numbers and cell phones as well as home phones. Exit polls, when properly administered, interview voters at random as they leave the polls at a randomly selected set of precincts.

Even with proper sampling, surveys have a **margin of error,** meaning the sample accurately reflects the population within a certain range—usually plus or minus 3 percent for a sample of at least 1,000 individuals. If, for example, a preelection poll had one candidate getting 50 percent of the vote and another 48 percent, and the margin of error was plus or minus 3 percent, the first candidate's share could be as high as 53 percent or as low as 47 percent, and the second candidate's could be as high as 51 percent or as low as 45 percent. In such a race, the result would be within the margin of error and too close to say who was ahead. If the sample is sufficiently large and randomly selected, these margins of error would apply in about 95 of 100 cases. The final preelection survey results in 2008 were within this margin of error for the actual vote.

Chicago's *Daily Tribune* was so sure of its polling data in the 1948 election that it predicted a win for Republican Thomas Dewey before the results were final. A victorious Harry Truman displays the mistaken headline.

The *art of asking questions* is also important to scientific polling. Questions can measure respondents' factual knowledge, their opinions, the intensity of their opinions, or their views on hypothetical situations. The type of questions asked should be determined by the kind of information desired by the researcher. The way questions are worded and the order in which they are asked can influence respondents' answers. Researchers should pretest their questions to be sure they are as clear and as specific as possible. Professional interviewers, who read the questions exactly as written and without any bias in their voices, should ask them.

Open-ended questions permit respondents to answer in their own words rather than by choosing responses from set categories. These questions are harder to record and compare, but they allow respondents to express their views more clearly and may provide deeper insight into their thinking. (See Table 5–2.)

margin of error
The range of percentage points in which the sample accurately reflects the population.

TABLE 5–2 The Way You Ask the Question Matters

The way you ask a polling question can make a lot of difference in the way people answer it. Consider the following questions about the Holocaust, each of which was asked during early 1994. Read each question and consider how you would have responded if asked by an interviewer.

1. The term Holocaust usually refers to the killing of millions of Jews in Nazi death camps during World War II. Does it seem possible or does it seem impossible to you that the Nazi extermination of the Jews never happened?

   Possible—36.8% | Impossible—58.2% | Unsure, do not know, etc.—5.0%*

2. The term Holocaust usually refers to the killing of millions of Jews in Nazi death camps during World War II. Do you doubt that the Holocaust actually happened or not?

   Yes, doubt it happened—8.8% | No, do not doubt it happened—87.0% | Unsure, etc.—4.2%**

3. Just to clarify, in your opinion, did the Holocaust definitely happen, probably happen, probably not happen, or definitely not happen?

   Definitely happened—77.8% | Probably happened—17.2% | Probably did not happen—2.2% | Definitely did not happen—0.1% | Do not know, etc.—2.7%†

4. Does it seem possible to you that the Nazi extermination of the Jews never happened, or do you feel certain that it happened?

   Possible it never happened—1.1% | Feel certain it happened—91.2% | Do not know —7.7%‡

* Gallup (January 1994)
** Gallup (January 1994)
† Gallup (January 1994)
‡ Roper (April 1994)

■ *What about the question wording might explain the very different results in these polls? Which of the questions do you think led to the most accurate measure of opinion? Why?*

Scientific polls also require thorough *analysis and reporting of the results.* Scientific polls must specify the sample size, the margin of error, and when and where the poll was conducted. Moreover, because public opinion can change from day to day and even from hour to hour, polls are really only snapshots of opinion at a particular point in time.

Defining public opinion as the distribution of *individual preference* emphasizes that the unit of measurement is *individuals*—not groups. The **universe** or *population* is the group of people whose preferences the researcher wants to measure. The sample of whom we ask the questions in the survey should be representative of this universe. The universe of subscribers to *Literary Digest* was not representative of the universe of all voters in 1936, for instance, a major reason the poll incorrectly predicted the election.[31] When a substantial percentage of a sample agrees on an issue—say, that we should honor the U.S. flag—there is a *consensus.* But on most issues, opinions are divided. When two opposing sides feel intensely about an issue and the difference between the major alternatives is wide, the public is said to be *polarized.* On such issues, it can be difficult to compromise or find a middle ground. The Vietnam War in the 1960s and 1970s was a polarizing issue. A more recent example is gay marriage. Neither those who favor legalizing gay marriage nor those who unequivocally oppose it see much room for compromise. Somewhere in the middle are those who oppose gay marriage but favor giving gay couples legal rights through "civil unions."

Intensity The degree to which people feel strongly about their opinions, or **intensity,** produces the brightest and deepest hues in the fabric of public opinion. For example, some individuals mildly favor gun control legislation, others mildly oppose it; some people are emphatically for or against it; and some have no interest in gun control at all. Others may not have even heard of it. People who lost their jobs or retirement savings because of corporate scandals are likely to feel more intensely about enhanced regulation of corporations and accounting firms than those not directly affected. We typically measure intensity by asking people how strongly they feel about an issue or about a politician. Such a question is sometimes called a *scale.*

Latency When people hold political opinions but do not fully express them, they are described as **latent.** These opinions may not have crystallized, yet they are still important, because they can be aroused by leaders or events and thereby motivate people to support them. Latent opinions set rough boundaries for leaders who know that, if they take certain actions, they will trigger either opposition or support from millions of people. If leaders understand people's unexpressed wants, needs, and hopes, they will know how to mobilize people and draw them to the polls on election day. A recent example of a latent opinion is the concern for security from foreign enemies, which had not been an issue in the United States before the terrorist attacks of September 11, 2001. The need for homeland security has now become a **manifest opinion,** a widely shared and consciously held view.

Salience Issues that people believe are important to them are **salient.** Most people are more concerned about personal issues such as paying their bills and keeping their jobs than about national issues, but if national issues somehow threaten their security or safety, their salience rises sharply. Salience and intensity, though different, are often correlated on the same issue.

The salience of issues may change over time. During the Great Depression of the 1930s, people were concerned mainly about jobs, wages, and economic security. By the 1940s, with the onset of World War II, foreign affairs came to the forefront. In the 1960s, problems of race and poverty were important to many. In the 1970s, Vietnam and then the Watergate scandals became the focus of attention. The economy took center stage in 2008 with the country in a recession and banks struggling to stay afloat, and in response, Congress enacted a $700 billion infusion of federal dollars into the banking system. In 2009 and 2010, the focus turned more to job creation and reform of the financial system.

universe
The group of people whose preferences we try to measure by taking a sample; also called population.

intensity
A measure of how strongly an individual holds a particular opinion.

latency
Political opinions that are held but not yet expressed.

manifest opinion
A widely shared and consciously held view, such as support for abortion rights or for homeland security.

salience
An individual's belief that an issue is important or relevant to him or her.

Participation: Translating Opinions into Action

LEARNING **OBJECTIVE**

5.4 Identify forms of political participation, and assess the effect on voter turnout of demographic, legal, and electioneering factors.

U.S. citizens influence their government's actions in several ways, many of which the Constitution protects. In addition to voting in elections, they participate in Internet political blogs, join interest groups, go to political party meetings, ring doorbells, urge friends to vote for issues or candidates, sign petitions, write letters to newspapers, and call radio talk shows. This kind of "citizen-to-citizen" participation can be important and may become more so as more people use the Internet and its social capital-building applications, such as social networking sites.[32]

Protest is also a form of political participation. Our political system is remarkably tolerant of protest that is not destructive or violent. Boycotts, picketing, sit-ins, and marches are all legally protected. Rosa Parks and Martin Luther King Jr. used nonviolent protest to call attention to unfair laws (see Chapter 12). Relative to voting, few people participate in protests, but the actions of those who do can substantially shape public opinion as the Tea Party activities demonstrated in 2010.

Even in an established democracy, people may feel so strongly about an issue that they would rather fight than accept the verdict of an election. The classic example is the American Civil War. Following the election of 1860, in which Abraham Lincoln—an antislavery candidate who did not receive a single electoral vote from a slave state—won the presidency, most of the South tried to secede from the Union. The ensuing war marked the failure of democracy to resolve sectional conflict. Examples in our own time include antiabortion and animal rights groups that use violence to press their political agenda, and militia groups that arm themselves for battle against government regulations.

For most people, politics is a private activity. Some still consider it impolite to discuss politics at dinner parties. To say that politics is private does not mean that people do not have opinions or will not discuss them when asked by others, including pollsters. But many people avoid discussing politics with neighbors, coworkers, or even friends and family because it is too divisive or upsetting. Typically, less than one person in four attempts to influence how another person votes in an election,[33] and even fewer people contribute financially to a candidate.[34] Fewer still write letters to elected officials or to newspapers for publication or participate in protest groups or activities. Yet, despite the small number of people who engage in these activities, they can make a difference in politics and government. An individual or small group can generate media interest in an issue and thereby expand the issue's impact.

When the student pro-democracy protest was stopped by the Chinese government tanks in Tiananmen Square on June 5, 1989, one man stood up in defiance until he was pulled to safety by bystanders. ■ *In the United States, most protest is nonviolent, and dissidents work through the political system. Are there circumstances in which political violence is ever justified?*

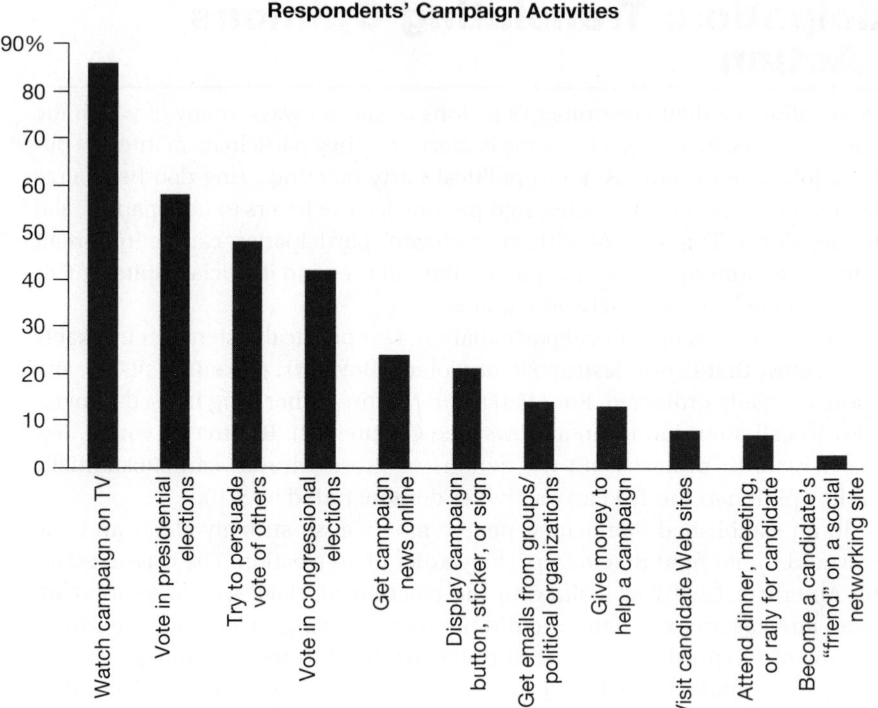

FIGURE 5–5 **Political Participation and Awareness in the United States.**

■ *Ten years from now, which of these activities would you expect to become more prevalent, and which less so?*

SOURCE: U.S. Census Bureau, *Statistical Abstract of the United States: 2006* (U.S. Government Printing Office, 2006), p. 263; *2008 National Election Study*, Center for Political Studies, University of Michigan; NES Guide to Public Opinion and Electoral Behavior, http://www.electionstudies.org/studypages/2008prepost/2008prepost.htm; and Pew Research Center, "Social Networking and Online Videos Take Off," January 11, 2008, www.pewinternet.org/pdfs/Pew_Media.

Levels of political participation rose during the 2008 presidential election, in part because of increased use of the Internet (see Figure 5–5). In 2008, the proportion reporting that they tried to influence another person's vote rose to nearly 50 percent. Candidates' Web sites allowed individuals to register with the campaign and be connected with other politically active individuals in their area. They also provided calling lists for volunteers to call from their own phones. Local campaign leaders in turn used the Internet to contact individuals in the area who had expressed an interest in working with the campaign. The Internet helped campaigns organize more effectively and made it easier for interested people to participate. Supporters of several candidates in 2008 went so far as to create their own music videos and political advertisements, which they uploaded to YouTube and other video-hosting Web sites. More candidates and interest groups also used the Internet for fund raising in the 2008 campaign. Candidates' Web sites made it easy for individuals to donate and to invite their friends to donate through e-mail, Facebook, MySpace, and other social-networking Web sites. In 2010, candidates and groups attempted to apply lessons learned in 2008 about internet communications, and both parties used the Internet more in fundraising.

Voting

Voting is our most typical political activity. The United States is a constitutional democracy with more than 200 years of free and frequent elections and a tradition of the peaceful transfer of power between competing groups and parties.

Originally, the Constitution left it to the individual states to determine who could vote, and qualifications for voting differed considerably from state to state. All states except New Jersey barred women from voting, most did not permit African Americans or Native Americans to vote, and until the 1830s, property ownership was often a requirement. By the time of the Civil War (1861–1865), however, every state had extended the franchise to all-white male citizens. Since that time, eligibility standards for voting have been expanded seven times by congressional legislation and constitutional amendments (see Table 5–3).

The civil rights movement in the 1960s made voting rights a central issue. In 1964, President Lyndon Johnson pushed for passage of the Twenty-Fourth Amendment, which banned poll taxes, and in 1965, for passage of the National Voting Rights Act, which outlawed the use of literacy tests as a requirement for voting. Anticipating that some state or local governments would change election rules to foster discrimination, the Act also required that any

TABLE 5–3 Changes in Voting Eligibility Standards Since 1870

Timeline	Change
1870	Fifteenth Amendment forbade states from denying the right to vote because of "race, color, or previous condition of servitude."
1920	Nineteenth Amendment gave women the right to vote.
1924	Congress granted Native Americans citizenship and voting rights.
1961	Twenty-Third Amendment permitted District of Columbia residents to vote in federal elections.
1964	Twenty-Fourth Amendment prohibited the use of poll taxes in federal elections.
1965	Voting Rights Act removed restrictions that kept African Americans from voting.
1971	Twenty-Sixth Amendment extended the vote to citizens age 18 and older.

■ *How have "the people" included in our government by the people changed since the founding of the country?*

changes to voting practices, requirements, or procedures must be cleared in advance with the Department of Justice or the U.S. District Court for the District of Columbia. The ban on the poll tax and the provisions of the Voting Rights Act resulted in a dramatic expansion of registration and voting by black Americans. Once African Americans were permitted to register to vote, "the focus of voting discrimination shifted...to preventing them from winning elections."[35] In southern legislative districts where black people are in the majority, however, there has been a "dramatic increase in the proportion of African American legislators elected."[36]

Registration One legal requirement—**voter registration**—arose as a response to concerns about voting abuses, but it also discourages voting. It requires voters to take an extra step—usually filling out a form at the county courthouse, when renewing a driver's license, or with a roving registrar—days or weeks before the election and every time they move to a new address. Most other democracies have automatic voter registration and some like Brazil, Greece, and the Philippines have mandatory voting. Average turnout in the United States, where voters must register before voting, is more than 30 percentage points lower than in countries such as Denmark, Germany, and Israel where voter registration is not required.[37] This was not always the case. In fact, in the 1800s, turnout in the United States was much like that of these countries today. It began to drop significantly around 1900, in part as a result of election reforms.

Laws vary by state, but every state except North Dakota requires registration, usually in advance. Idaho, Maine, Minnesota, New Hampshire, Wisconsin, and Wyoming permit election-day registration. The most important provision regarding voter registration may be the closing date. Until the early 1970s, closing dates in many states were six months before the election. Now, federal law prevents a state from closing registration more than 30 days before a federal election.[38] Other important provisions include places and hours of registration and, in some states, a requirement that voters show photo identification before voting.[39]

Motor Voter In 1993, the burdens of voter registration were eased a bit with the National Voter Registration Act—called the "Motor Voter" bill—which allows people to register to vote while applying for or renewing a driver's license. Offices that provide welfare and disability assistance can also facilitate voter registration. States may include public schools, libraries, and city and county clerks' offices as registration sites. The law requires states to allow registration by mail using a standardized form. To purge the voting rolls of voters who may have died or changed residence, states must mail a questionnaire to voters every four years. But Motor Voter forbids states from purging the rolls for any other reasons, such as because a person has not voted in multiple previous elections.

As a result of this law, more new voters have registered.[40] Data on the impact of Motor Voter suggest that neither Democrats nor Republicans are the primary beneficiaries because most new voters who have registered claim to be Independent.[41] Yet, Motor Voter does not appear to have increased turnout.

voter registration
A system designed to reduce voter fraud by limiting voting to those who have established eligibility to vote by submitting the proper documents, including proof of residency.

For the People

Helping America Vote

The exceedingly close Florida vote in the 2000 presidential election called attention to multiple problems with the voting process not only in that state but in many states. Among the problems were poorly maintained and outdated voting machines, confusing ballot designs, inconsistent rules for counting absentee ballots, and the need for more and better trained poll workers. In response to these and other problems, Congress enacted in 2002 the Help America Vote Act (HAVA).

HAVA for the first time established accessibility standards for voting systems in the United States. The Americans with Disabilities Act of 1990 required that voting places be accessible to persons with disabilities, but prior to HAVA, individuals with disabilities in some states could only vote with the assistance of a poll worker, which compromised the privacy of their vote. HAVA required that states provide voting machines for persons with disabilities, including the visually impaired, that allow these voters the same level of privacy as any other voter.

The system of voter registration in the United States is largely administered at the county level, and as such, there was widespread variability in the way counties maintained the list of registered voters. HAVA mandated the creation of statewide, computerized voter registration lists. The Act also mandated the creation of a toll-free phone number that individuals could use to learn about their registration status.

Poll workers are critical to the administration of elections. HAVA provides federal grants to help train poll workers and to involve college and high school students in assisting at the polls on election day. HAVA created the Election Assistance Commission to assist states with election administration and ensure that minimum federal standards in such areas as accessibility are met. Although problems remain in making elections work well, HAVA has helped state and local governments make substantial strides.

CRITICAL THINKING QUESTIONS

1. Why is the privacy of the voting act important to voters?
2. How would a common statewide list of registered voters enhance participation?
3. What are some other ways in which the voting process could be improved?

Absentee and Early Voting As discussed at the beginning of the chapter, many people choose not to vote in person at their local voting places on election day. Instead they use *absentee voting* to vote early by mail. Absentee voting has been used since the Civil War[42] and has recently become more popular. Three in ten voters in 2008 cast their vote away from a traditional, election-day polling location, the most in the history of the United States.[43] Another innovation designed to make voting easier is allowing people to vote early but at a polling location. This change was in part the result of concerns about having insufficient voting machines for election day. By 2008, 31 states allowed early voting without needing to claim travel, work, or other reasons to vote early.[44]

Turnout

The United States holds more elections for more offices than any other democracy. That may be why U.S. voters tend to be selective about which elections they vote in. We elect officeholders in **general elections,** determine party nominees in **primary elections,** and replace members of the House of Representatives who have died or left office in *special elections.*

Elections held in years when the president is on the ballot are called **presidential elections;** elections held midway between presidential elections are called **midterm elections,** and elections held in odd-numbered calendar years are called *off-year elections.* Midterm elections (such as the ones in 2006 and 2010) elect one-third of the U.S. Senate, all members of the House of Representatives, and many governors, other statewide officeholders, and state legislators. Many local elections for city council members and mayors are held in the spring of odd-numbered years.

Turnout—the proportion of the voting-age public that votes—is higher in general elections than in primary elections, and higher in primary elections than in special elections. It is also higher in presidential general elections than in midterm general elections, and higher in presidential primary elections than in midterm primary elections (see Figure 5–6).[45] Presidential elections attract greater interest and awareness. Turnout is also higher in elections in which candidates for federal office are on the ballot (U.S. senator, member of the House of Representatives, and

general election
Elections in which voters elect officeholders.

primary election
Elections in which voters determine party nominees.

presidential election
Elections held in years when the president is on the ballot.

midterm election
Elections held midway between presidential elections.

turnout
The proportion of the voting-age public that votes, sometimes defined as the number of registered voters that vote.

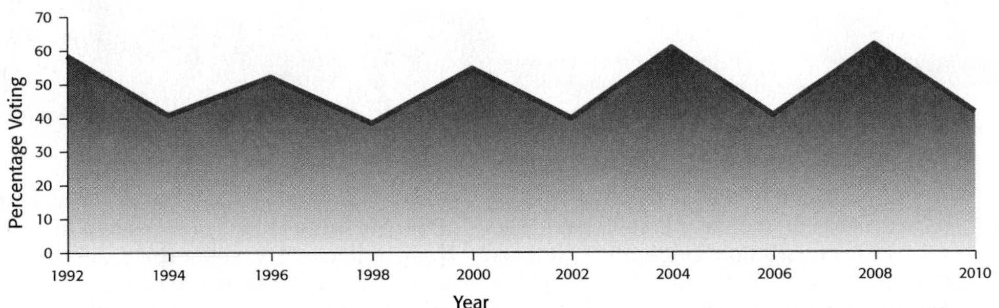

FIGURE 5–6 **Voter Turnout in Presidential and Midterm Elections, 1992–2010.**
■ *How can you explain the consistent pattern of voting demonstrated in the this graph?*

SOURCE: Curtis Gans, Howard W. Stanley, and Richard G. Niemi, *Vital Statistics on American Politics, 2009–2010* (CQ Press, 2010), pp. 4–5. U.S. Elections Project, George Mason University, http://elections.gmu.edu/Turnout_2010G.html.

president) than in state elections in years when there are no federal contests. Some states—for example, New Jersey, Virginia, and Kentucky—elect their governor and other state officials in odd-numbered years to separate state from national politics. The result is generally lower turnout. Finally, local or municipal elections have lower turnout than state elections, and municipal primaries generally have the lowest rates of participation.

Turnout reached more than 65 percent of those eligible to vote in the presidential election of 1960, but it declined to slightly more than 60 percent in 2004, and rose to 61.7 percent in 2008.[46] In midterm elections, turnout was 40 percent nationally in 2006, up about 1 percent from 2002 and up more than 2 percent since 1998. More competitive elections generate more interest among the public and more spending by the candidates, which in turn stimulate participation. However, more than 80 million eligible citizens failed to vote in the 2004 presidential election, and even more did not vote in midterm, state, and local elections.[47]

Who Votes?

The extent of voting varies widely among different groups. Level of education especially helps predict whether people will vote; as education increases, so does the propensity to vote. "Education increases one's capacity for understanding complex and intangible subjects such as politics," according to one study, "as well as encouraging the ethic of civic responsibility. Moreover, schools provide experience dealing with a variety of bureaucratic problems, such as coping with requirements, filling out forms, and meeting deadlines."[48]

Race and ethnic background are linked with different levels of voting, largely because they correlate with education. In other words, racial and ethnic minorities with college degrees vote at approximately the same rate as white people with college degrees. As a group, black people vote at lower rates than white people, although this is beginning to change.[49] In 2008, blacks were 13 percent of the vote, a 2 percent increase over 2004.[50] Despite efforts by both parties to mobilize Hispanics, the proportion of Hispanics voting in 2008 was only slightly over that in 2004, 49.9 percent as compared to 47.2 percent.[51]

Women, another historically underrepresented group, have voted in greater numbers than men since 1984.[52] That was true again in 2008.[53] Women's higher turnout is generally attributed to increasing levels of education and employment. Interest groups, including prominent pro-choice groups, have sought to mobilize female supporters of their agenda in recent elections.

Age is also highly correlated with the propensity to vote. As age increases, so does the proportion of persons voting. Older people, unless they are very old and infirm, are more likely to vote than younger people. The greater propensity of older persons to vote will amplify the importance of this group as baby boomers age and retire. In 2008, the number of young people voting was up substantially.[54] There were 3.4 million more voters

Voters wait to cast their ballots in a primary election. Voting reforms have led to more early voting, helping cut congestion on election day. ■ *What are the implications for political campaigns of greater levels of early voting?*

Of the People

AMERICA'S CHANGING FACE

Voter Turnout by Demographic Factors

Throughout the course of U.S. history, the right to vote has been extended and protected for women and racial minorities. Groups that did not have the franchise, or that had been effectively barred or discouraged from using it, have become as active in their rates of voting as white men.

In the following data, note that women have voted in higher percentages than men in each election since 1992. It took decades for women to reach this milestone and dismiss the old adage that "politics is men's business." The rate of voting among black persons was about 10 percentage points below white persons in 1992 and 1994, but more recently has lagged by only approximately 4 percentage points. Hispanics are not yet participating at rates similar to those of women and black persons. History suggests that over time this will change.

Percentage of People in Different Groups Who Voted

	1992	1994	1996	1998	2000	2002	2004	2006	2008
Sex									
Men	60%	44%	53%	41%	53%	41%	56%	42%	56%
Women	62	45	56	42	56	43	60	45	60
Race									
White	64	47	56	43	56	44	60	46	60
Black	54	37	51	40	54	40	56	39	61
Hispanic	29	19	27	20	28	19	28	19	32

SOURCE: U.S. Census Bureau, *Statistical Abstract of the United States: 2010* (U.S. Government Printing Office, 2009), p. 254.

CRITICAL THINKING QUESTIONS

1. Why might the rate of voting for women have increased over time?
2. How do presidential elections influence rates of voting? Why?
3. What factors might explain the change in the rate of voting among black persons?

under the age of 30 than had voted in 2004.[55] In 2010, President Obama held rallies on college campuses to encourage young people to vote. His party continued to do better among young voters than other voters, but turnout in this group was well below the 2008 level.

Mobilization

In a nation as evenly divided politically as the United States is now, candidates must also mobilize their most loyal supporters, or their "base." To do this, they reaffirm their support for issues or groups that matter to the base. In the 2008 "battleground" states where the vote seemed highly competitive, postcards urging residents to vote and phone calls reminding them it was election day bombarded voters who were already likely to vote and had already decided which candidate to support. In addition, the candidates and parties mobilized their supporters to vote early in states where it was possible. This effort, sometimes called "banking the vote," reduced the list of people the campaigns needed to mobilize on election day, when poll watchers would track those who had not yet voted and would urge those who had pledged support to vote.

Campaigners learn which issues matter to potential voters and which candidates these voters prefer by conducting interviews on the telephone or in person, a process called a *canvass.* Individuals who are undecided and probable voters in competitive races are likely to receive communications designed to persuade them to vote for a particular candidate. Interest groups and political parties may also conduct a canvass, followed by mail and phone calls that often reinforce the same themes the candidates themselves express.

Undecided or "swing voters" are a major focus of mobilization efforts, and they received a lot of attention in competitive states in recent elections. Both sides intensely courted these voters through numerous person-to-person contacts, mailings, telephone calls, and efforts to register new voters. Candidates, groups, and parties are all part of this "ground war." The volume of communication in competitive contests and battleground states in recent elections has been extraordinary. For example, there were 117 unique pieces of mail in New Mexico's 1st Congressional District race sent by candidates, parties, and groups, and there were at least 112 unique pieces of mail in the Colorado U.S. Senate race in that same year.[56]

Voting Choices

LEARNING **OBJECTIVE**

5.5 Analyze the factors that influence voter choice.

Why do people vote the way they do? Political scientists have identified three main elements of the voting choice: party identification, candidate appeal, and issues. These elements often overlap.

Voting on the Basis of Party

Party identification is our sense of identification or affiliation with a political party (see Chapter 4). It often predicts a person's stand on issues. It is part of our national mythology that we vote for the person and not the party. But, in fact, we vote most often for a person *from the party we prefer.* Although party identification has fluctuated in the past 40 years, it remains more stable than attitudes about issues or political ideology. Fluctuations in party identification appear to come in response to economic conditions and political performance, especially of the president. The more information voters have about their choices, the more likely they are to defect from their party and vote for a candidate from the other party.

The number of self-declared Independents since the mid-1970s has increased dramatically, and today, Independents outnumber Republicans and Democrats. But two-thirds of all Independents are, in fact, partisans in their voting behavior. There are three distinct types of Independents: Independent-leaning Democrats, Independent-leaning Republicans, and Pure Independents. Independent-leaning Democrats are predictably Democratic in their voting behavior, and Independent-leaning Republicans vote heavily Republican. Independent "leaners" are thus different from each other and from Pure Independents. Pure Independents have the lowest rate of turnout, but most of them generally side with the winner in presidential elections. Independent leaners vote at about the same rate as partisans and more than Pure Independents. Independent leaners vote for the party toward which they lean at approximately the same rate, or even more so, than weak partisans do. This data on Independents only reinforces the importance of partisanship in explaining voting choice. When we consider Independent-leaning Democrats and Independent-leaning Republicans as Democrats and Republicans respectively, only 10 percent of the population were Pure Independents in 2004.[57] In 2008, that number had risen slightly to 11 percent.[58] This proportion is consistent with earlier election years. In short, there are few genuinely Independent voters.

party identification
An informal and subjective affiliation with a political party that most people acquire in childhood.

candidate appeal
How voters feel about a candidate's background, personality, leadership ability, and other personal qualities.

Voting on the Basis of Candidates

Although long-term party identification is important, it is clearly not the only factor in voting choices. Otherwise, the Democrats would have won every presidential election since the last major realignment in partisanship, which occurred during the Great Depression in the election of Franklin Roosevelt in 1932. In fact, since 1952, there have been five Democratic presidents elected and the same number of Republicans.[59] The reason is largely found in a second major explanation of voting choice—**candidate appeal.**

Because they do not have the benefits of a well-known party, third-party candidates must rely on their personal appeal to voters. Independent Ross Perot's fiery style and sense of humor helped him garner 19.8 percent of the vote in 1992, the best showing for a third-party presidential candidate since 1912.

Candidate-centered politics means that rather than relying on parties or groups to build a coalition of supporters for a candidate, the candidates make their case directly to the voters. In many races, the parties and groups also make the candidate the major focus of attention, minimizing partisanship or group identification.[60] The fact that we vote for officials separately—president/vice president, senator, governor,

YOU WILL

DECIDE Should We Allow Voting by Mail and on the Internet?

During the past two centuries of constitutional government, this nation has gradually adopted a more expansive view of popular participation. It seems logical that the next step in our democratic progress is permitting voters to cast ballots through the mail or via the Internet. Not only would such a reform make voting easier, but it would permit us to have more elections. For example, when a city council wants voters to decide whether to build a new football stadium or when there is need for a special election to fill the term of a member of Congress who has died or resigned, election officials could mail out the ballots and then in two or three weeks count up those that have been returned. The state of Oregon has already conducted several general elections by mail, and other states have considered adopting the Oregon system.

What do you think? Should we move toward replacing the ballot box with the mailbox or the computer? What arguments would you make for and against such an idea?

THINKING IT THROUGH

One of the problems with making elections more frequent is that voters will tire. Americans already vote more frequently and for more offices than citizens of any other democracy. Asking them to make voting choices even more frequently could result in lower turnout and less rational consideration. Many voters may be unaware that an election is going on. Yet the advantage of the vote-by-mail system employed by Oregon and some cities and counties is that it increases turnout, at least initially. What political scientists dispute is whether such increases in participation will continue when the novelty wears off.

Some critics of voting by mail or electronic democracy worry about fraud. Even when voters are required to sign their mailed-in ballots, the possibility of forgery still exists. Also, voting by mail or computer has the possibility of allowing people to pressure or harass voters. Another concern is late returns. Concerns about electronic voting have been reinforced by claims that the computer software is not secure and that some electronic voting fails to count all the votes.*

Another criticism is that mail and electronic voting could be skewed toward participation by better-educated and higher-income voters, who routinely pay their bills by mail, make purchases on their computer, and own a personal computer with Internet access. Advocates of these new voting procedures contend that voters who do not own computers can drop off their ballots in some public building and that eventually computers will be available widely enough that access will not be a problem.†

If the integrity of the vote can be protected and the new ways of voting become widely accessible, such changes are probably inevitable. With more people having access to computers and confidence using them for important transactions, the Internet is likely to be used for voting in the future. Electronic voting has been tested for military personnel overseas,‡ and states like Michigan and Washington have experimented with new applications of computer voting.

Critical Thinking Questions

1. What advantages do you see in allowing people to vote via the Internet?
2. What would be the disadvantages of allowing Internet voting?
3. If we move to voting by Internet, how often do you think voters would be likely to participate in an election?

*E. J. Dionne, Jr., "Election Dangers to Be Avoided," *The Washington Post*, May 25, 2004.
†Adam J. Berinsky, Nancy Burns, and Michael W. Traugott, "Who Votes By Mail? A Dynamic Model of the Indiviual-Level Consequences of Voting-by-Mail Systems," *Public Opinion Quarterly* 65 (Summer 2001), pp. 178–197.
‡http://www.servesecurityreport.org/DoDMay2007.pdf.

state attorney general, and so on—means voters are asked repeatedly to choose from among competing candidates. Although the party of the candidates is an important clue to voters, in most contested races, voters also look to candidate-specific information.

Candidate appeal often includes an assessment of a candidate's character. Is the candidate honest? Consistent? Dedicated to "family values"? Does the candidate have religious or spiritual commitments? In recent elections, the press has sometimes played the role of "character cop," asking questions about candidates' private lives and lifestyles. The press asks these questions because voters are interested in a political leader's background—perhaps even more interested in personal character than in a candidate's political position on hard-to-understand health care or regulatory policy issues. Candidate appeal, or the lack of it—in terms of leadership, experience, good judgment, integrity, competence, strength, and energy—is sometimes more important than party or issues. In 2008, Republicans attempted to define Barack Obama as arrogant, aloof, and a celebrity. Democrats, while praising McCain as a war hero, tried to define him as out of touch and "more of the same [Bush]." Increasingly, campaigns today focus on the negative elements of candidates' history and personality. Opponents and the media are quick to point out a candidate's limitations or problems. This was the case again in 2010.

Voting on the Basis of Issues

Most political scientists agree that issues, though important, have less influence on how people vote than party identification and candidate appeal do.[61] This occurs partly because candidates often intentionally obscure their positions on issues—an understandable strategy.[62] When he was running for president in 1968, Richard Nixon said he had a plan to end the Vietnam War, which was clearly the most important issue that year, but he would not reveal the specifics. By not detailing his plan, he stood to gain votes both from those who wanted a more aggressive war effort and those who wanted a cease-fire. In 2008, Obama and the Democrats emphasized change from the Bush administration, a general theme that exploited public sentiment.

For issue voting to become important, a substantial number of voters must find the issue itself important, opposing candidates must take opposite stands on the issues, and voters must know these positions and vote accordingly. Rarely do candidates focus on only one issue. Voters often agree with one candidate on one issue and with the opposing candidate on another. In such cases, issues will probably not determine how people vote. But voters' lack of interest in issues does not mean candidates can take any position they please.[63]

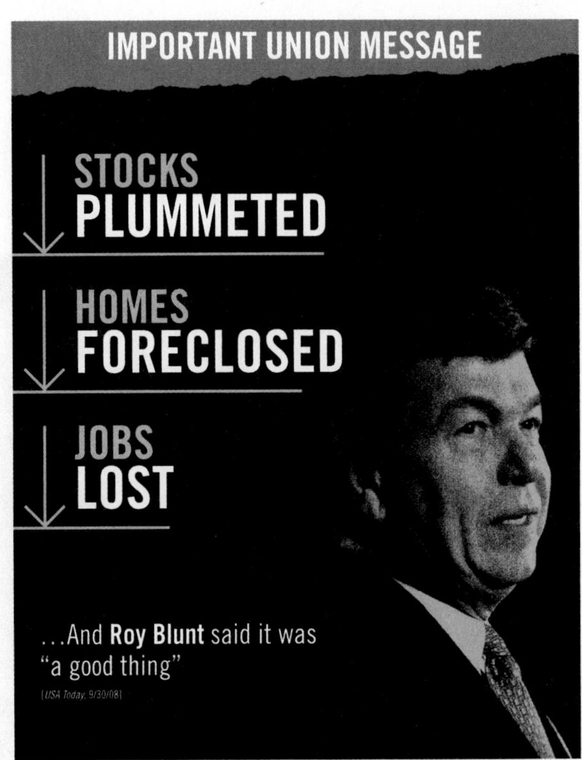

Exit polls indicated that the state of the economy was the most important issue to voters in 2010. In the Missouri Senate race, unions tried to portray House representative Roy Blunt as complicit in the failing economy, but the conservative Republican was nonetheless elected. ■ *What other issues in 2010 might have contributed to Blunt's win?*

Political parties and candidates often look for issues that motivate particular segments of the electorate to vote and on which the opposing candidate or party has a less popular position. These issues are sometimes called *wedge issues.* In recent elections, wedge issues have been gay marriage, the minimum wage, and abortion. One way to exploit a wedge issue is to place on the ballot an initiative to decide a proposed law or amendment on the issue. Both parties and allied groups are expanding their use of ballot initiatives in this way.

More likely than **prospective issue voting,** or voting based on what a candidate pledges to do about an issue if elected, is **retrospective issue voting,** or holding incumbents, usually the president's party, responsible for past performance on issues, such as the economy or foreign policy.[64] In times of peace and prosperity, voters will reward the incumbent. If the nation falls short on either, voters are more likely to elect the opposition.

But good economic times do not always guarantee that an incumbent party will be reelected, as Vice President Al Gore learned in 2000 when he was the Democratic candidate for president. Gore's inability to effectively claim credit for the good economic times hurt him, especially when Republicans contended that the American people, not the government under President Bill Clinton, had produced the strong economy.

The state of the economy is often the central issue in both midterm and presidential elections. Studies have found that the better the economy seems to be doing, the more congressional seats the "in" party retains or gains. The reverse is also true. The worse the economy seems to be doing, the more seats the "out" party gains.[65] Political scientists have been able to locate the sources of this effect in the way individual voters decide to vote. Voters tend to vote against the party in power if they perceive that their personal financial situations have declined or stagnated.[66] Anxiety over the economy and high unemployment were important to the vote in 2010, and the Democrats, as the party in power, were punished at the polls. Republicans also exploited fears about health care reform and growing federal budget deficits.

Unable to counter the Republican message on the economy, Democrats often resorted to attacking their opponent's record and policy positions. Harry Reid attacked his opponent Sharon Angle as a threat to Social Security, in Delaware Democratic allied

prospective issue voting
Voting based on what a candidate pledges to do in the future about an issue if elected.

retrospective issue voting
Holding incumbents, usually the president's party, responsible for their records on issues, such as the economy or foreign policy.

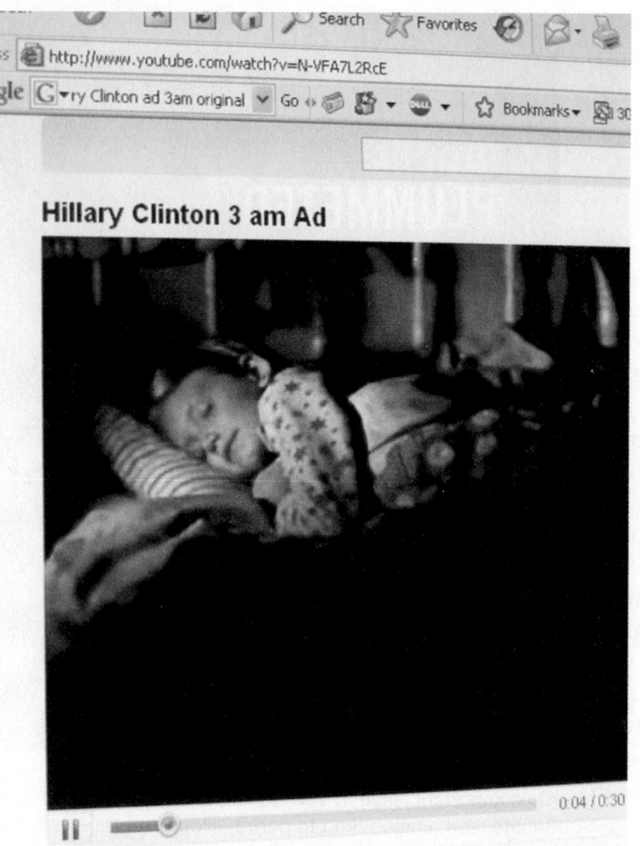

This advertisement from the Hillary Clinton campaign used a hypothetical national-emergency phone call at 3:00 AM to highlight her relative wealth of experience when compared to Barack Obama. ■ *What emotions does the imagery in this advertisement evoke?*

groups sent a mailer reminding voters that Republican Christine O'Donnell had reported dabbling "into witchcraft" in high school, and in California Barbara Boxer reminded voters that Carly Fiorina had been fired as CEO of Hewlett-Packard. These personal contrasts in some states worked to the Democrats' advantage. In contests for the House of Representatives and Governorships, these candidate and issue comparisons tended to work more to the Republicans' advantage.

The Impact of Campaigns

Candidates and campaigns are important to the voting choice. Given the frequency of elections in the United States and the number of offices people vote for, it is not surprising that voters look for simplifying devices such as partisanship to help them decide how to vote. Effective campaigns give them reasons to vote for their candidate and reasons to vote against the opposition.

Campaigns are a team sport, with the political parties and interest groups also important to the process of persuading and motivating voters.[67] Groups and parties are heavily engaged in all aspects of campaigns, and their efforts are often indistinguishable from the candidates' campaigns.

Although having enough money is needed for a competitive campaign, spending more money does not guarantee that a candidate will win. Effective campaigners find ways to communicate with voters that are memorable and persuasive.

CHAPTER **SUMMARY**

5.1 Identify the forces that create and shape individuals' political attitudes.

People's political attitudes form early in life, mainly through the influence of family. Schools, the media, social groups, and changing personal and national circumstances can cause attitudes to change, although most of our political opinions remain constant throughout life. Most people do not follow politics and government closely and have little knowledge of political issues.

5.2 Compare and contrast political ideologies and assess their importance in the contemporary American context.

The two most important ideologies in American politics are liberalism, a belief that government can and should help achieve justice and equality of opportunity, and conservatism, a belief in limited government to ensure order, competitive markets, and personal opportunity while relying on free markets and individual initiative to solve social and economic problems. Critics of liberalism contend that liberals, by favoring government solutions to problems, limit the capacity of markets to function well and create large and unmanageable bureaucracies. Critics of conservatism contend that some problems require government to become part of the solution and that too much faith in the market to solve the problem is misplaced. Socialism, which favors public ownership of the means of production, and libertarianism, which puts a premium on individual liberty and limited government, attract only modest followings in the United States.

Few in the United States are extremists. There are more conservatives than liberals, and ideology has come to be more important in the nomination battles in both parties and Congress. Because a large fraction of the public is moderate or has not thought much about ideology, politicians can expand their coalition of voters and supporters by being pragmatic. Because nonideological persons are less likely to vote, they are not as important in elections as the more committed ideologues. However, in close elections, these pragmatic centrist voters can be critical.

5.3 Outline the key dimensions of public opinion and how it is measured.

Public opinion is the distribution across the population of a complex combination of views and attitudes that individuals hold, and we measure it through careful, unbiased, random-selection surveys. Public opinion takes on qualities of intensity, latency, consensus, and polarization—each of which is affected by people's feelings about the salience of issues.

Sometimes, politicians follow prevailing public opinion on policy questions; in other cases, they attempt to lead public opinion toward a different policy option. Major events, such as economic crises and wars, affect both public opinion and government policy. Citizens who wish to affect opinion, policy, or both, can take action by voting or engaging in other forms of political participation.

5.4 Identify forms of political participation, and assess the effect on voter turnout of demographic, legal, and electioneering factors.

One of the hallmarks of democracy is that citizens can participate in politics in a variety of ways. Citizens who are dissatisfied with government can protest. Individual citizens participate by writing letters to elected officials, calling radio talk shows, serving as jurors, voting, or donating time and money to political campaigns. The Internet has allowed individuals to volunteer for campaigns in a wider variety of ways, to donate money more easily, and to produce content that can be uploaded onto the Internet and viewed by any interested people.

Better-educated, more affluent, and older people and those who are involved with parties and interest groups tend to vote more. The young vote the least. Voter turnout is usually higher in national elections than in state and local elections, higher in presidential elections than in midterm elections, and higher in general elections than in primary elections. Close elections generate interest and efforts to mobilize voters and thus have higher turnout than uncompetitive elections.

5.5 Analyze the factors that influence voter choice.

Party identification remains the most important element in determining how most people vote. It represents a long-term attachment and is a "lens" through which voters view candidates and issues as they make their voting choices. Candidate appeal, including character and record, is another key factor in voter choice. Less frequently, voters decide on the basis of issues.

CHAPTER **SELF-TEST**

5.1 Identify the forces that create and shape individuals' political attitudes.

1. Which of the following statements is true?
   a. Most people never change their political opinions.
   b. Most people change their political opinions quite often.
   c. Many people change their political opinions only when they meet new people.
   d. Many people change their political opinions after major experiences such as a war.
2. In a short essay, explain what the "attentive public" is. How are they different from part-time citizens and political know-nothings? Which group has greater influence on public policy?
3. In a short essay, identify and describe two major groups that influence the formation of individuals' political opinions and values. Which has had a greater influence in your life?

5.2 Compare and contrast political ideologies and assess their importance in the contemporary American context.

4. Identify each belief as either conservative or liberal:
   a. Belief that government can bring about equality of opportunity
   b. Belief that some government intervention in the economy is necessary to remedy the defects of capitalism
   c. Pessimistic view of human nature
   d. Preference for greater environmental protection
   e. Belief in keeping government small, especially the national government
   f. Preference for business
   g. Preference for individual choice in moral issues such as same-sex marriage and abortion
   h. Belief that the primary task of government is to ensure order
5. In a short essay, define three major criticisms of both conservatism and liberalism. Analyze these critiques and determine which criticism you find more persuasive.
6. In a short essay, compare and contrast the major beliefs of liberalism and conservatism. Consider each ideology's approach to moral, economic, and national defense issues. How are they alike? How are they different? Which do you think is more effective in today's world?

5.3 Outline the key dimensions of public opinion and how it is measured.

7. Which of the following was a major flaw in the 1936 *Literary Digest* poll?
   a. Biased questions
   b. A flawed sample
   c. Incorrectly counted results
   d. Poorly trained interviewers
8. What word describes opinions people may hold but have not fully expressed?
   a. Interest
   b. Salience
   c. Latency
   d. Intensity

5.4 Identify forms of political participation, and assess the effect on voter turnout of demographic, legal, and electioneering factors.

9. Which of the following is *not* a way individuals have used the Internet to participate in recent campaigns?
   a. Use candidate Web sites to participate in local caucuses
   b. Create campaign-centered music videos to upload to YouTube

c. Call other individuals using calling lists provided on a candidate's Web site
d. Invite other individuals to donate to campaigns through Facebook and MySpace

10. In a short essay, analyze the impact voter registration laws have on turnout. Consider state-specific laws, Motor Voter, and automatic registration. What changes, if any, do you think should be made to increase registration?

5.5 Analyze the factors that influence voter choice.

11. In a short essay, explain which is more common, prospective issue voting or retrospective issue voting, and why.
12. Think of the three main elements of vote choice—party identification, candidate appeal, and issues. In a short essay, evaluate which best explains the results of the 2008 presidential election.

Answers to selected Questions: 1. a; 4. a. liberal, b. liberal, c. conservative, d. liberal, e. conservative, f. conservative, g. liberal, h. conservative; 7. b; 8. c; 9. a;

mypoliscilab™ EXERCISES

Where participation leads to action!

Apply what you learned in this chapter on MyPoliSciLab.

Read on mypoliscilab.com

eText: Chapter 5

Study and **Review** on mypoliscilab.com

Pre-Test
Post-Test
Chapter Exam
Flashcards

Watch on mypoliscilab.com

Video: Obama Approval Rating
Video: Opinion Poll on the U.S. Economy
Video: Candidates Court College Students
Video: Chicago Worker Protest
Video: L.A. Riots: 15 Years Later
Video: Teen Sues for Equal Protection

Explore on mypoliscilab.com

Simulation: You Are a Polling Consultant
Simulation: You Are the Leader of Concerned Citizens for World Justice
Simulation: You Are an Informed Voter Helping Your Classmates
Comparative: Comparing Governments and Public Opinion
Timeline: War, Peace and Public Opinion
Visual Literacy: Voting Turnout: Who Votes in The United States?
Visual Literacy: Who Are Liberals and Conservatives? What's the Difference?

KEY TERMS

ADDITIONAL **RESOURCES**

FURTHER READING

R. MICHAEL ALVAREZ AND **JOHN BREHM,** *Hard Choices, Easy Answers: Values, Information, and American Public Opinion* (Princeton University Press, 2002).

R. MICHAEL ALVAREZ AND **THAD E. HALL,** *Electronic Elections: The Perils and Promises of Digital Democracy* (Princeton University Press, 2008).

HERBERT ASHER, *Polling and the Public: What Every Citizen Should Know,* 8th ed. (CQ Press, 2010).

BARBARA A. BARDES AND **ROBERT W. OLDENDICK,** *Public Opinion: Measuring the American Mind* (Wadsworth, 2006).

M. MARGARET CONWAY, *Political Participation in the United States,* 3d ed. (CQ Press, 2000).

ROBERT M. EISINGER, *The Evolution of Presidential Polling* (Cambridge University Press, 2002).

ROBERT S. ERIKSON AND **KENT L. TEDIN,** *American Public Opinion: Its Origins, Content, and Impact,* updated 8th ed. (Longman, 2010).

WILLIAM H. FLANIGAN AND **NANCY H. ZINGALE,** *Political Behavior of the American Electorate,* updated 12th ed. (CQ Press, 2009).

DONALD P. GREEN AND **ALAN S. GERBER,** *Get Out the Vote!: How to Increase Voter Turnout,* 2d ed. (Brookings Institution Press, 2008).

BRUCE E. KEITH, DAVID B. MAGLEBY, CANDICE J. NELSON, ELIZABETH ORR, MARK C. WESTLYE, AND **RAYMOND E. WOLFINGER,** *The Myth of the Independent Voter* (University of California Press, 1992).

V. O. KEY JR., *Public Opinion and American Democracy* (Knopf, 1961).

RICHARD G. NIEMI AND **HERBERT F. WEISBERG,** *Classics in Voting Behavior* (CQ Press, 1993).

RICHARD G. NIEMI AND **HERBERT F. WEISBERG,** *Controversies in Voting Behavior,* 4th ed. (CQ Press, 2001).

FRANK R. PARKER, *Black Votes Count: Political Empowerment in Mississippi After 1965* (University of North Carolina Press, 1990).

JAMES A. THURBER AND **CANDICE J. NELSON,** EDS., *Campaigns and Elections American Style,* 3d ed. (Westview Press, 2010).

MICHAEL W. TRAUGOTT AND **PAUL J. LAVRAKAS,** *The Voter's Guide to Election Polls,* 4th ed. (Rowman & Littlefield, 2008).

MARTIN P. WATTENBERG, *Is Voting for Young People?* (Longman, 2007).

JOHN ZALLER, *The Nature and Origins of Mass Opinion* (Cambridge University Press, 1992). See also *Public Opinion Quarterly, The American Journal of Political Science,* and *American Political Science Review.*

BRIAN DOHERTY, *Radicals for Capitalism: A Freewheeling History of the Modern American Libertarian Movement* (New York: Public Affairs, 2007).

E. H. H. GREEN, *Ideologies of Conservatism: Conservative Political Ideas in the Twentieth Century* (Oxford University Press, 2004).

CAROL A. HORTON, *Race and the Making of American Liberalism* (Oxford University Press, 2005).

IRVING KRISTOL, *Neoconservatism: The Autobiography of an Idea* (Free Press, 1995).

MICHAEL NEWMAN, *Socialism: A Very Short Introduction* (Oxford University Press, 2005).

MARCUS G. RASKIN, *Liberalism: The Genius of American Ideals* (Rowman & Littlefield, 2004).

WEB SITES

www.votesmart.org This is the Web site for Project Vote Smart. The site lists extensive nonpartisan information about candidates for both federal and state elections throughout the United States, including voting records and candidate positions.

www.govoteabsentee.org A collection of information and forms for individuals who would like to vote absentee in any state. This site is sponsored by an organization of current and recently graduated college students from around the country. You only need your home zip code in order to access the materials you will need to vote absentee in the next election.

www.rockthevote.org The home page for Rock the Vote, an organization that focuses on helping young people register to vote and participate in politics in general. The site includes voter registration materials, information on how to vote absentee, and information about other policy issues that young people may care about.

www.aapor.org As the home page of the American Association for Public Opinion Research, this site contains resources for both creators and users of polls and polling data. The site has information about how to accurately conduct a poll, how to understand polling data, and how to identify fake or poorly constructed polls.

www.stateline.org A University of Richmond/Pew Charitable Trust site dedicated to providing citizens with information on major policy issues.

CHAPTER

6

Campaigns, Elections, and the Media

Democracy in Action

The 2008 election set a new record for the most money raised and spent on federal elections. An estimated $6 billion was spent by candidates, political party committees, interest groups, and individuals on elections in 2007–2008.[1] This amounted to an increase of $1.4 billion over 2004 and more than $3 billion over 2000. Much of the increase came in spending by presidential candidates, who spent more than $1.8 billion, a nearly three-fold increase over what candidates spent in 2000.

Where does all this money come from? Under law, the nearly $6 billion spent on elections is reported to the Federal Election Commission (FEC) or Internal Revenue Service. In many cases, there are contributions limitations, or maximum amounts that individuals are allowed to donate, which means that candidates must find many donors. To maximize efficiency, candidates target individuals who could give the maximum allowable, which in 2007–2008 was $4,600. These donors provide an important jump-start to a campaign; their money helps fund the infrastructure of the campaign, such as the staff, early polling, and advertising, and helps the campaign raise more money. The media report the amount of money raised, which becomes a measure of how well or poorly a campaign is doing.

An unusual element of the 2008 election cycle was the success of the Obama campaign in raising money from individuals in relatively small amounts, under $200. Anthony Corrado, an expert on campaign finance, observed, "No previous presidential contender has ever raised as much money through small contributions as Obama did."[2] Roughly half of these small donors contributed for the first time during the last three months of the campaign, but many contributed several times during the election cycle.

Part of Obama's success in raising money was due to his innovative use of new media, especially the Internet. People were asked to volunteer, call or e-mail their friends, attend events, contribute money, and, most important, vote. It remains unclear whether the surge in numbers of individuals contributing money and the amount contributed in 2008 was a one-time event or if what happened can become part of American politics in the future. The Obama campaign combined a charismatic candidate with a compelling message who made skillful use of mass communications tools. Time will tell if others can learn from the way the 2008 campaign was financed in mounting future campaigns.

Money spent on elections is only one marker of their importance. Time devoted to campaigns by candidates, political parties, interest groups, and individuals is also substantial. Our system of federalism means we hold elections at the different levels of government. In the United States, citizens vote more often and for more offices than citizens of any other democracy. We hold thousands of elections for everything from community college directors to county sheriffs. Approximately half of a million persons hold elected state and local offices.[3] In 2010, we elected 37 U.S. senators,[4] all 435 members of the U.S. House of Representatives, 37 state governors, and, in many states, treasurers, secretaries of state, and judges.

In addition to electing people, voters in 27 states are allowed to vote on laws or constitutional amendments proposed by initiative petitions or on popular referendums put on the ballot by petition. In every state except Delaware, voters must approve all changes to the state constitution.

In this chapter, we explore our election rules and their impact on congressional and presidential campaigns. The media, as a source of political news, opinion, and advertisements, also plays a significant role in campaigns and elections. We assess the importance of the media in politics and government generally.

CHAPTER **OUTLINE** & CHAPTER LEARNING **OBJECTIVES**

Elections: The Rules of the Game

6.1 Assess the implications of election rules in the United States.

Congressional and Presidential Elections

6.2 Explain how congressional and presidential elections work.

Money in U.S. Elections

6.3 Evaluate the influence of money in American elections and the main approaches to campaign finance reform.

The Changing Landscape of the U.S. News Media

6.4 Outline changes in the nature and importance of the various news media.

Media Influence

6.5 Evaluate the media's influence on public opinion, elections, and governance.

Elections: The Rules of the Game

LEARNING **OBJECTIVE**

6.1 Assess the implications of election rules in the United States.

The rules of the game—the electoral game—make a difference. Although the Constitution sets certain conditions and requirements, state law determines most electoral rules. Our focus in this chapter is on presidential and congressional elections, although much of the discussion is also relevant to state and local elections.

Regularly Scheduled Elections

In our system, elections are held at fixed intervals that the party in power cannot change. It does not make any difference if the nation is at war, as we were during the Civil War, or in the midst of a crisis, as in the Great Depression; when the calendar calls for an election, the election is held. Elections for members of Congress occur on the first Tuesday after the first Monday in November of even-numbered years. Although there are exceptions (for special elections or peculiar state provisions), participants know *in advance* just when the next election will be. In most parliamentary democracies, such as Great Britain and Canada, the party in power can call elections at a time of its choosing. The predetermined timing of elections is one of the defining characteristics of democracy in the United States.

Fixed, Staggered, and Sometimes Limited Terms

Our electoral system is based on *fixed terms,* meaning the length of a term in office is specified, not indefinite. The Constitution sets the term of office for the U.S. House of Representatives at two years, the Senate at six years, and the presidency at four years.

Our system also has *staggered terms* for some offices; not all offices are up for election at the same time. All House members are up for election every two years, but only one-third of senators are up for election at the same time. Because presidential elections can occur two or four years into a senator's six-year term, senators can often run for the presidency without fear of losing their seat, as John Kerry did in 2004 and John McCain, Barack Obama, Hillary Clinton, and Joe Biden (for the vice presidency) did in 2008. But if their Senate term expires the same year as the presidential election, the laws of many states require them to give up their Senate seat to run for president, vice president, or any other position. An example of a state that permits a candidate to run for election to two offices is Connecticut, where Joseph Lieberman was reelected to the U.S. Senate in 2000 while being narrowly defeated in his race for vice president. Had he been victorious in both campaigns, he would have resigned his Senate seat.

The Twenty-Second Amendment to the Constitution, adopted in 1951, limits presidents to two terms. Knowing that a president cannot run again changes the way members of Congress, the voters, and the press regard the chief executive. A politician who cannot, or has announced he or she will not, run again is called a *lame duck.* Lame ducks are often seen as less influential because other politicians know that these officials' ability to bestow or withhold favors is coming to an end. Efforts to limit the terms of other offices have become a major issue in several states. The most frequent targets have been state legislators. One consequence of term limits is more lame ducks.

Term limits at the state level were largely adopted during the 1990s. Currently, 15 states have term limits for state legislatures. Six states have rescinded term limits. South Dakota voters were given the option of repealing term limits, and they overwhelmingly voted to keep them.[5] Despite their popularity at the state level, proposals for term limits on federal legislators have repeatedly been defeated when they have come to a vote in Congress. The Supreme Court, by a vote of 5-to-4, declared that a state does not have the constitutional power to impose limits on the number of terms for which its members of the U.S. Congress are eligible, either by amendment to its own constitution or by state law.[6] Congress has refused to propose a constitutional amendment to impose a limit on congressional terms.

Winner Take All

winner-take-all system
An election system in which the candidate with the most votes wins.

An important feature of our electoral system is the **winner-take-all system,** sometimes referred to as "first past the post" in other countries.[7] In most U.S. electoral settings, the

Of the People — THE GLOBAL COMMUNITY

Who Makes a Better Political Leader?

Voters in the United States have increasingly had the opportunity to vote for women for governor, president, vice president, senator, House representative, and other offices. How do people feel about women versus men serving in these offices? The Pew Global Attitudes survey asked respondents the following question: "Which of the following statements comes closest to your opinion about men and women as political leaders: Men generally make better political leaders than women, women generally make better political leaders than men, or, in general, women and men make equally good political leaders.

Holding aside Nigeria, the most common response in all countries in our sample is that men and women are equally qualified to be political leaders. In Britain, this response is given by 83 percent, perhaps a reflection of the fact that the position of prime minister in Britain has been held by a woman. Japan, Mexico, and the United States all have high proportions of respondents saying both genders make equally good leaders. However, in Nigeria, there is a preference for male leaders, with 48 percent saying they make better leaders. This likely stems from the political culture of Nigeria where women are often marginalized for social and religious reasons.*

Another way to look at these data is to compare the views of those who do not think men and women make equally good leaders. Of this group, people in India, Britain, Japan, and Mexico are about equally divided with some favoring men and others women. In the other countries and the world sample, men are preferred as leaders over women by about 3 to 1. Again, this is only among people who do not see the two genders as equally well-qualified.

CRITICAL THINKING QUESTIONS

1. What do you think the answer to this survey question would have been 100 years ago, 50 years ago, 20 years ago?
2. Why do we not see more women holding political office in the United States if 75 percent think men and women are equally well qualified?
3. If opinions have changed on this question over time, what factors might explain opinion change on this issue?

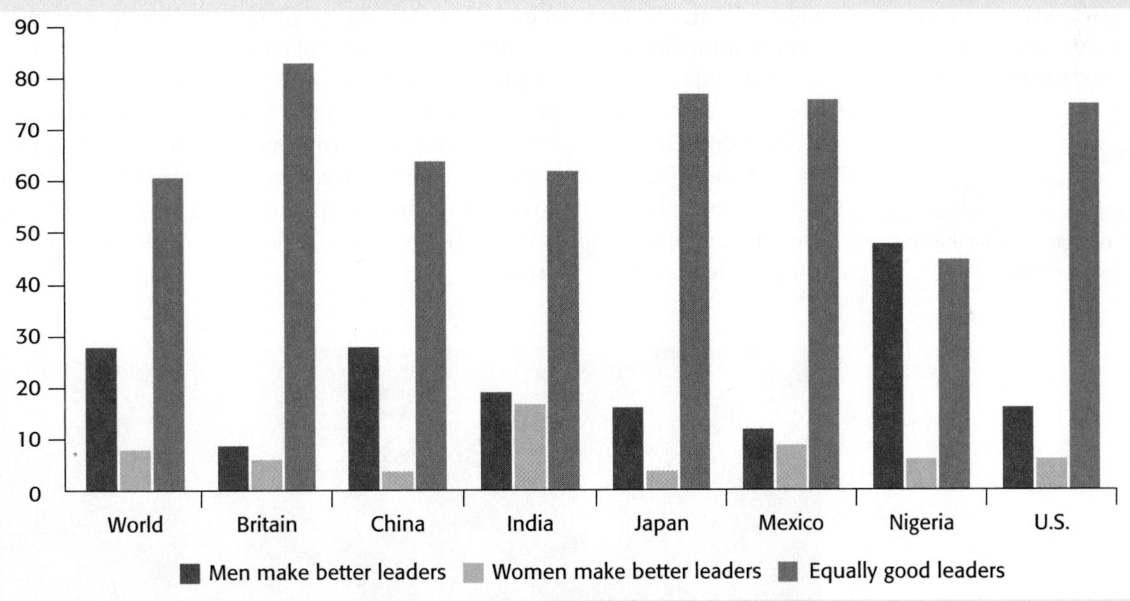

* Muhammad Mustapha, "In the Shadows of Men: Women's Political Marginalisation," *Inter Press Service,* March 12, 2010, http://ipsnews.net/news.asp?idnews=50648 (accessed May 6, 2010).

candidate with the most votes wins. The winner does not need to have a *majority* (more than half the votes cast); in a multicandidate race, the winner may have only a *plurality* (the largest number of votes). An example is the 2009 special election held in New York's 23rd Congressional District. In a three-candidate race, Democrat Bill Owens won with 48 percent of the vote, a plurality, not a majority. The Conservative party candidate Doug Hoffman received 46 percent of the vote, and the Republican Dierdre Scozzafava received less than 6 percent.[8] Winner-take-all electoral systems tend to reinforce moderate and centrist candidates because they are more likely to secure a plurality or a majority. Candidates in a winner-take-all system often stress that a vote for a minor party candidate is a "wasted vote" that may actually help elect the voter's least desired candidate.

Most U.S. electoral districts are **single-member districts,** meaning that in any district for any given election—senator, governor, U.S. House, and state legislative seat—the voters choose *one* representative or official.[9] When the single-member-district and winner-take-all systems are combined, minor parties find it especially hard to win. For example, even if a third party gets 25 percent of the vote in several districts, it still gets no seats. As discussed in Chapter 4, the single-member districts and winner-take-all system is different from a **proportional representation** system, in which political parties secure legislative seats and power in proportion to the number of votes they receive in the election. Countries that practice some form of proportional representation include Germany, Israel, Italy, and Japan.

The Electoral College

We elect our president and vice president not by a national vote but by an indirect device known as the **electoral college.** The framers of the U.S. Constitution devised this system because they did not trust the choice of president to a direct vote of the people. Under this system, each state has as many electors as it has representatives and senators. California therefore has 55 electoral votes (53 House seats and two Senate seats), whereas seven states and the District of Columbia have three electoral votes each.

Each state legislature is free to determine how it selects its electors. Each party nominates a slate of electors, usually longtime party workers. They are expected to cast their electoral votes for the party's candidates for president and vice president if their party's candidates get a plurality of the vote in their state. In our entire history, no "faithless elector"—an elector who does not vote for his or her state's popular vote winner—has ever cast the deciding vote, and the incidence of a faithless elector is rare.[10]

Candidates who win a plurality of the popular vote in a state secure all of that state's electoral votes, except in Nebraska and Maine, which allocate electoral votes to the winner in each congressional district plus two electoral votes for the winner of the state as a whole. Winning electors go to their state capital on the first Monday after the second Wednesday in December to cast their ballots. These ballots are then sent to Congress, and early in January, Congress formally counts the ballots and declares who won the election for president and vice president.

single-member district
An electoral district in which voters choose one representative or official.

proportional representation
An election system in which each party running receives the proportion of legislative seats corresponding to its proportion of the vote.

electoral college
The electoral system used in electing the president and vice president, in which voters vote for electors pledged to cast their ballots for a particular party's candidates.

In two of the four elections in which winners of the popular vote did not become president, the electoral college did not decide the winner. The 1824 election was decided by the U.S. House of Representatives. In the controversial 1876 presidential election between Rutherford B. Hayes and Samuel Tilden, the electoral vote in four states was disputed, resulting in the appointment of an electoral commission to decide how those votes should be counted. The Electoral Commission of 1877, depicted in the drawing, met in secret session, and after many contested votes, Hayes was elected.

It takes a majority of the electoral votes to win. If no candidate gets a majority of the electoral votes for president, the House chooses among the top three candidates, with each state delegation having one vote. If no candidate gets a majority of the electoral votes for vice president, the Senate chooses among the top two candidates, with each senator casting one vote.

When there are only two major candidates for the presidency, the chances of an election being thrown into the House are remote. But twice in our history, the House has had to act: in 1800, the House had to choose in a tie vote between Thomas Jefferson and Aaron Burr; and in 1824, the House picked John Quincy Adams over Andrew Jackson. The 1800 election prompted the Twelfth Amendment, ratified in 1804, requiring that electors in the electoral college vote for one person as president and for another as vice president.

As we were reminded in 2000, our electoral college system makes it possible for a presidential candidate to receive the most popular votes, as Al Gore did, and yet not get enough electoral votes to be elected president. Gore lost the electoral college vote 271 to 266, and George Bush became president.[11] This also happened in 1824, when Andrew Jackson won 12 percent more of the vote than John Quincy Adams; in 1876, when Samuel Tilden received more popular votes than Rutherford B. Hayes; and in 1888, when Grover Cleveland received more popular votes than Benjamin Harrison. It almost happened in 1916, 1960, and 1976, when the shift of a few votes in a few key states could have resulted in the election of a president without a popular majority.

The electoral college sharply influences presidential politics. To win a presidential election, a candidate must appeal successfully to voters in populous states such as California, Texas, Ohio, Illinois, Florida, and New York. California's electoral vote of 55 in 2008 exceeded the combined electoral votes of the 14 least populous states plus the District of Columbia. Sparsely populated states such as Wyoming and Vermont also have disproportionate representation in the electoral college because each has one representative, regardless of population. When the contest is close, as it was in recent elections, every state's electoral votes are crucial to the outcome, and so greater emphasis is given to states in which the contest is close[12] (see Table 6–1).

TABLE 6–1 2004 and 2008 Battleground States

As the table shows, many of the states that were battlegrounds in 2004, Obama took handily in 2008. In contrast, some states that voted strongly for Bush in 2004 became battlegrounds in 2008.

State	Electoral Votes in 2004 and 2008	Percent Difference in 2004 Popular Vote	Percent Difference in 2008 Popular Vote
Wisconsin	10	0.38 Kerry	13.91 Obama
New Mexico	5	0.79 Bush	15.13 Obama
Iowa	7	0.67 Bush	9.54 Obama
New Hampshire	4	1.37 Kerry	9.61 Obama
Pennsylvania	21	2.50 Kerry	10.32 Obama
Ohio	20	2.10 Bush	4.59 Obama
Nevada	5	2.59 Bush	12.50 Obama
Michigan	17	3.42 Kerry	16.47 Obama
Oregon	7	4.16 Kerry	16.35 Obama
Florida	27	5.01 Bush	2.81 Obama
Missouri	11	7.20 Bush	0.14 McCain
Virginia	13	8.20 Bush	6.30 Obama
North Carolina	15	12.44 Bush	0.32 Obama
Indiana	11	20.68 Bush	1.04 Obama

■ *Which states had the largest change in vote share to the two parties between 2004 and 2008? What do these states have in common?*

SOURCE: Federal Election Commission, "Election Results," http://www.fec.gov/pubrec/electionresults.shtml (accessed March 23, 2010).

Congressional and Presidential Elections

LEARNING **OBJECTIVE**

6.2 Explain how congressional and presidential elections work.

How candidates run for Congress differs depending on the nature of their district or state, on whether candidates are incumbents or challengers, on the strength of their personal organization, on how well known they are, and on how much money they have to spend on their campaign. There are both similarities and differences between House and Senate elections.

First, most congressional elections are not close. In districts where most people belong to one party or where incumbents are popular and enjoy fundraising and other campaign advantages, there is often little competition.[13] Districts are typically drawn in ways that enhance the reelection prospects of incumbents or one party, a process called *partisan gerrymandering.* We explore this process in greater detail in Chapter 7, which deals with Congress. Those who believe that competition is essential to constitutional democracy are concerned that so many officeholders have **safe seats.** When officeholders do not have to fight to retain their seats, elections are not performing their proper role.[14]

safe seat
An elected office that is predictably won by one party or the other, so the success of that party's candidate is almost taken for granted.

coattail effect
The boost that candidates may get in an election because of the popularity of candidates above them on the ballot, especially the president.

Competition is more likely when both candidates have adequate funding, which is not often the case in U.S. House elections. Elections for governor and for the U.S. Senate are more seriously contested and more adequately financed than those for the U.S. House.

Presidential popularity affects both House and Senate races during both presidential and midterm elections. The boost candidates get from running along with a popular presidential candidate from their party is known as the **coattail effect.** But winning presidential candidates do not always provide such a boost. The Republicans suffered a net loss of six House seats in 1988, even though George H. W. Bush won the presidency, and the Democrats suffered a net loss of ten House seats in 1992 when Bill Clinton won the presidential election. On the coattails of Barack Obama's convincing presidential win in 2008, the Democrats saw a net gain of 21 House seats and 8 Senate seats. Overall, "measurable coattail effects continue to appear," according to congressional elections scholar Gary Jacobson, but their impact is "erratic and usually modest."[15]

In midterm elections, presidential popularity and economic conditions have long been associated with the number of House seats a president's party loses.[16] These same factors are associated with how well the president's party does in Senate races, but the association is less strong.[17] Figure 6–1 shows the number of seats in the House of Representatives and U.S. Senate gained or lost by the party controlling the White House in midterm elections since 1954. In all of the midterm elections between 1934 and 1998, the party controlling the White House lost seats in the House. But in 1998 and 2002, the long-standing pattern of the president's party losing seats in a midterm election did not hold. In 2006, however, the long-standing pattern reemerged, with the Republicans losing 30 House seats and 6 Senate seats.[18] The net result of the Democrats success in 2006 and 2008 was that they had won many of the most competitive districts, making them vulnerable to the GOP in 2010.

In 2010, Republicans won a net gain of six U.S. Senate seats and more than sixty house seats. Putting this victory in historical perspective, this is the most house seats gained by a party since 1938 when the GOP had a net gain of 72 seats, and surpasses the 54 seats the Democrats lost in 1994 and 1946. Republicans did especially well in defeating centrist Democrats, sometimes called Blue Dog Democrats. More than half of this group in the House were defeated or retired in 2010.

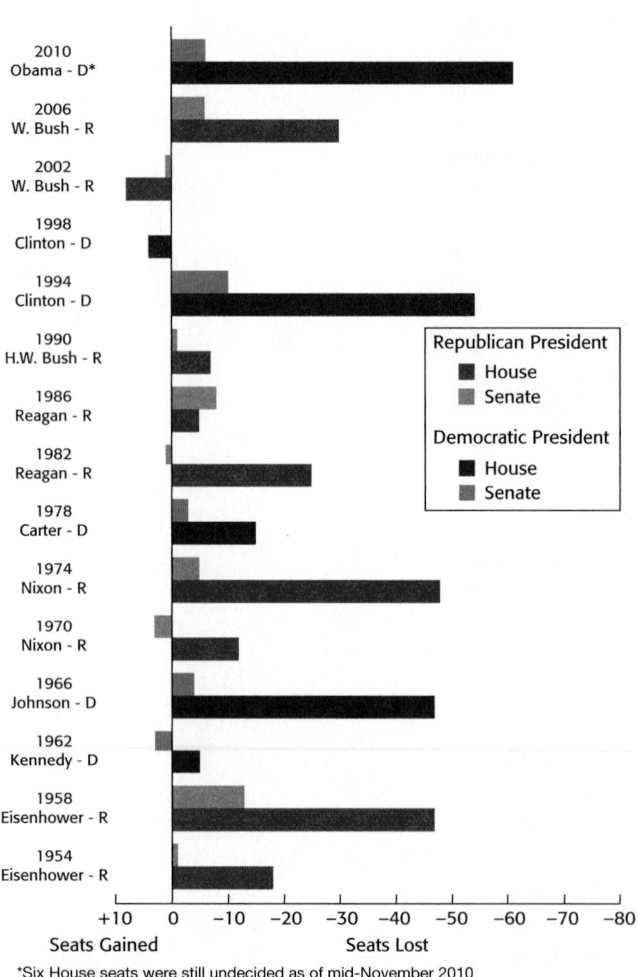

FIGURE 6–1 **Seats Gained or Lost by the President's Party in Midterm Elections, 1954–2010.**

■ *Based on past midterm elections, how does 2010 compare in terms of the seats lost by the President's party?*

SOURCE: Harold W. Stanley and Richard G. Niemi, *Vital Statistics on American Politics 2007–2008* (CQ Press, 2008), p. 54.

The House of Representatives

Every two years, as many as 1,000 candidates—including approximately 400 incumbents—campaign for Congress. Incumbents are rarely challenged for renomination from within their own party, and when they are, the challenges are seldom serious. In the 1990s, for example, on average only two House incumbents were denied renomination in each election. In 2010, four House incumbents were denied renomination, and 29 ran unopposed.[19] Challengers from other parties running against incumbents rarely encounter opposition in their own party.[20] In 2010, Tea Party-supported candidates denied renomination to two senators and defeated the party leader's preferred Senate candidates in Kentucky, Nevada and Delaware.

After losing in the Republican primary to Tea Party candidate Joe Miller, incumbent Senator Lisa Murkowski mounted a write-in campaign. While the results are still being tallied, Murkowski would be only the third Senator to be elected by write-in. ■ *Why is Murkowski's imcumbancy such an important factor in attempting a write-in campaign?*

Mounting a Primary Campaign The first step for would-be challengers is to raise hundreds of thousands of dollars (or even more) to mount a serious campaign. This requires asking friends and acquaintances as well as interest groups for money. Candidates need money to hire campaign managers and technicians, buy television and other advertising, conduct polls, and pay for a variety of activities. Another early step is to build a *personal organization.* A congressional candidate can build an organization while holding another office, such as a seat in the state legislature. A candidate's main hurdle is gaining visibility. Candidates work hard to be mentioned by the media. In large cities with many simultaneous campaigns, congressional candidates are frequently overlooked, and in all areas, television is devoting less time to political news.[21]

Campaigning for the General Election The electorate in a general election is different from that in a primary election. Many more voters turn out in general elections, especially the less-committed partisans and Independents. Partisanship is more important in a general election, as many voters use party as a simplifying device to select from among candidates in the many races they decide. Not surprisingly, candidates in districts where their party is strong make their partisanship clear, and candidates from a minority party deemphasize it. General elections also focus on the strengths and weaknesses of the candidates and their background, experience, and visibility. Political scientists describe this dimension as **candidate appeal.** Issues can also be important in general elections, but they are often more local than national issues. Occasionally, a major national issue arises that can help or hurt one party. Candidates who have differentiated themselves from their party or its leader can reduce the impact of such a **national tide** if it is negative. Some elections for Congress or the state legislature are in part referendums on the president or governor, but public opinion concerning the president or governor is rarely the only factor at play in these elections.

As we have mentioned, most incumbent members of Congress win reelection.[22] Since 1970, slightly more than 95 percent of incumbent House members seeking reelection have won, and since 2000, about 97 percent of incumbent House members running for reelection have been successful.[23] Incumbents have a host of advantages that help them win reelection. They are generally better known than challengers, something called **name recognition**. They are able to outspend challengers in campaigns by approximately 3 to 1 in the House and about 2.37 to 1 in the Senate.[24] In addition, incumbents generally win because their district boundaries have been drawn to be made up of voters who favor their party.

candidate appeal
The tendency in elections to focus on the personal attributes of a candidate, such as his or her strengths, weaknesses, background, experience, and visibility.

national tide
The inclination to focus on national issues, rather than local issues, in an election campaign. The impact of a national tide can be reduced by the nature of the candidates on the ballot who may have differentiated themselves from their party or its leader if the tide is negative, as well as competition in the election.

name recognition
Incumbents have an advantage over challengers in election campaigns because voters are more familiar with them, and incumbents are more recognizable.

The Senate

Running for the Senate is generally more high-profile than running for the House. The six-year term, the fact that there are only two senators per state, and the national exposure many senators enjoy make a Senate seat a glittering prize, leading to more intense competition. Individual Senate campaigns cost more than individual House races and are more likely to be seriously contested; though in the aggregate, because there are so many more House races, overall spending on House races surpasses overall spending on Senate races (see Figure 6–2).[25] The essential tactics are to raise large amounts of money, hire a professional and experienced campaign staff, make as many personal contacts as possible

FIGURE 6–2 Rising Campaign Costs in Congressional General Elections.

■ *What are some of the ways in which the rising cost of campaigns might impact who runs for office, how campaigns are funded, and the priorities of candidates?*

SOURCE: 1976–2004, Harold W. Stanley and Richard G. Niemi, *Vital Statistics on American Politics 2007–2008* (CQ Press, 2008), p. 101; 2006–2008, Center for Responsive Politics, "Price of Admission: Winners," www.opensecrets.org/bigpicture/stats.php?cycle=2008&display=T&Type=W. Amounts are in 2006 dollars.

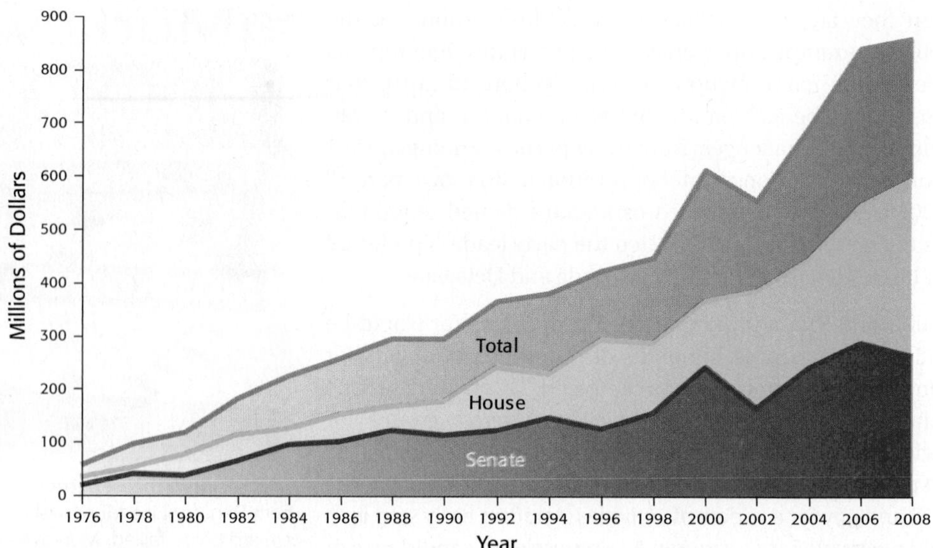

(especially in states with smaller populations), avoid giving the opposition any positive publicity, and have a clear and consistent campaign theme. Incumbency is an advantage for senators, although not as much as it is for representatives.[26] Incumbent senators are widely known but often so are their opponents, who generally raise and spend significant amounts of money.[27]

Running for President

Presidential elections are major media events, with candidates seeking as much positive television coverage as possible and trying to avoid negative coverage. The formal campaign has three stages: winning the nomination, campaigning at the convention, and mobilizing support in the general election.

Stage 1: The Nomination

Presidential hopefuls must make a series of critical tactical decisions. The first is when to start campaigning. For the presidential election of 2008, some candidates began soon after the 2004 presidential election.[28] Some candidates formally announced in December 2006, and most had announced by the end of February 2007. Republican Fred Thompson delayed his entry until September 6, 2007, a decision that meant he was less competitive in recruiting staff, fundraising, and visibility.[29] Early decisions are increasingly necessary for candidates to raise money and assemble an organization. Campaigning begins well before any actual declaration of candidacy, as candidates try to line up supporters to win caucuses or primaries in key states and to raise money for their nomination effort. This period in the campaign has been called the "invisible primary."[30]

One of the hardest jobs for candidates and their strategists is calculating how to deal with the complex maze of presidential primaries and caucuses that constitutes the delegate selection system. The system for electing delegates to the national party convention varies from state to state and often from one party to the other in the same state. In some parties in some states, for example, candidates must provide lists of delegates who support them months before the primary.

Another decision candidates must make is whether to participate in partial public financing of their campaigns. The presidential campaign finance system provides funds to match small individual contributions during the nomination phase of the campaign for candidates who agree to remain within spending limitations. George W. Bush declined federal funds in the 2000 and 2004 nomination phase, as did Democrats John Kerry and Howard Dean in 2004. In 2008, Barack Obama, Hillary Clinton, Mitt Romney, Rudy Giuliani, Ron Paul, Mike Huckabee, and Fred Thompson all turned down matching funds. Forgoing the public matching funds allows greater flexibility in spending campaign money and

By the People
MAKING A DIFFERENCE

Volunteering for a Campaign

You can make a difference in your community, state, or country by volunteering for a campaign. Campaigns are dependent on individuals like you to help make democracy happen. It is also a great way to learn about public opinion, representation, and the political process. If you decide to get involved, you may participate in a wide range of activities, including contacting voters in person, on the telephone, or through the Internet; helping with fundraising; or assisting in organizing events. Be sure to let the campaign know in what areas you have experience or expertise, such as database management or graphic design.

To have a good experience, it is important to understand that campaigns are hectic and intense. The election day cannot be postponed, and winning is the objective. But there is also an excitement and energy to campaigns that you will not forget. Because of the number and frequency of elections in the United States, there is likely a candidate or ballot measure campaign of some sort happening in your area that would welcome your assistance. Call, e-mail, or drop by the campaign office and inform the campaign manger of the kinds of things you would like to do and how you can assist.

You might also check on your campus to see if there is a possibility to do an internship with a campaign or if there is a clearing house for such opportunities. Occidental College, for example, had an internship program, "Campaign Semester," where a student could get a full semester's worth of college credit (16 credits) for volunteering full time with a presidential or U.S. Senate campaign.*

CRITICAL THINKING QUESTIONS

1. Why do many political leaders get their start in government or politics by volunteering in a campaign?
2. What aspect of campaigns most interests you?
3. If we judge a potential leader by the quality of his/her campaign, what are the markers of a good campaign?

* Peter Dreier and Caroline Heldman, "Campaign Semester Fall 2008," http://departments.oxy.edu/politics/campaignsemester.htm (accessed May 3, 2010).

removes the overall limit for this phase of the process. Most serious contenders for the White House are likely to decline federal matching funds in 2012 and beyond.

Presidential Primaries State presidential primaries, unknown before 1900, have become the main method of choosing delegates to the national convention. A delegate is a person chosen by local partisans to represent them in selecting nominees, party leaders, and party positions. Today, more than three-fourths of the states use presidential primaries. In 2008, 67 percent of the Democratic delegates and 77 percent of the Republican delegates were chosen in the primaries.[31] The rest of the delegates were chosen by state party caucuses or conventions or were party leaders who served as "superdelegates."

The states have different means of determining delegates, and state primaries allocate delegates using the following systems:[32]

- *Proportional representation:* Delegates to the national convention are allocated on the basis of the percentage of votes candidates win in the primary. This system has been used in most of the states, including several of the largest ones. The Democrats mandate proportional representation for all their primaries, with three-quarters of the states' delegates elected in primaries.[33]
- *Winner take all:* Whoever gets the most votes wins all that state's delegates or the share of delegates from each congressional district. Republicans use the winner-take-all system at the state level, and in 2008, most states used this rule at either the state or congressional district levels.[34] To win all the delegates of a big state such as California is an enormous bonus to a candidate, as it was to John McCain in 2008.
- *Superdelegates and delegate selection without a commitment to a candidate:* Following the 1972 election, there was an effort to give more influence in the selection of the presidential candidate to party leaders and elected officials. This led to the creation of superdelegates, which were delegates that were automatically selected due to their elected or party office or chosen by the state party committee. New York Republicans allow the state committee to select 12 at-large delegates who are officially unpledged, as are the party chair and national committee representatives.[35] In 2008, superdelegates cast the deciding vote for Obama because no candidate secured a majority of all delegates through the primary and caucus process.
- *Delegate selection and separate presidential poll:* In several states, voters decide twice: once to indicate their choice for president and again to choose delegates

pledged, or at least favorable, to a presidential candidate. In 2008, this was the process Democrats used in Texas, with a primary during the day to elect 126 delegates and a caucus that night electing 67 delegates. Republicans have long allowed a popularity vote or "beauty contest" in which votes indicate their preferred candidate but require a separate vote for delegates pledged to particular candidates.

Voters in states such as Iowa and New Hampshire, which are the first states to pick delegates, bask in media attention for weeks and even months before they cast the first ballots in the presidential sweepstakes. Because these early contests have had the effect of limiting the choices of voters in states that come later in the process, states have tended to move their primaries up in a process called "front loading." California, which traditionally held its primary in June, moved it to March in 2000 so that its voters would play a more important role in selecting the nominee. Other states did the same thing. Front loading was even more prominent in 2004 and 2008.[36] However, the parties have sought to prevent too much front loading. In 2008, when Florida and Michigan moved their primaries ahead of what party rules allowed, the Democratic National Committee (DNC) voted that delegates so selected would not be seated.[37] The controversy was resolved by giving each Florida and Michigan delegate a half vote, but at the convention, each delegate was given a full vote.

In 2008, the Republican nomination reached an early resolution, with John McCain effectively winning it after his victories in Ohio and Texas on March 4.[38] The Republican rules, which clearly advantage candidates who win states, even by narrow margins, helped McCain. The Democrats had a highly contested and protracted race that did not wrap up until June 2008, with voters in all states and territories voting in contested primaries and caucuses.

Caucuses and Conventions A meeting of party members and supporters of various candidates who may elect state or national convention delegates, who in turn vote for the presidential nominee, is called a **caucus.** In about a dozen states, one or both parties use a caucus or convention system (or both) to choose delegates.[39] Each state's parties and legislature regulate the methods used.[40] The caucus or convention is the oldest method of choosing delegates, and unlike the primary system, it centers on staffing local party positions such as voting district chair and often includes party discussions of issues and candidates in addition to a vote on candidates or policies. The best-known example of a caucus is in Iowa, because Iowa has held the earliest caucuses in the most recent presidential nominating contests.

In caucus or convention states, delegates who will attend the national party conventions are chosen by delegates to state or district conventions, who themselves are chosen earlier in county, precinct, or town caucuses. The process starts at local meetings open to all party members, who discuss and take positions on candidates and issues and elect delegates to represent their views at the next level. This process is repeated until conventions of delegates from a district or state choose delegates to the national nominating convention.

Strategies Presidential hopefuls face a dilemma: To get the Republican nomination, a candidate has to appeal to the more intensely conservative Republican partisans, those who vote in caucuses and primaries and actively support campaigns. Democratic hopefuls have to appeal to the liberal wing of their party as well as to minorities, union members, and environmental activists. But to win the general election, candidates have to win support from moderate and pragmatic voters, many of whom do not vote in the primaries. If candidates position themselves too far from the moderates in their nomination campaign, they risk being labeled extreme in the general election and losing these votes to their opponents.

Strategies for securing the nomination have changed throughout the years. Some candidates think it wise to skip some of the earlier contests and enter first in states where their strength lies. John McCain pursued such a strategy in 2000 and again in 2008, ignoring Iowa and concentrating on New Hampshire. In 2008, former New York City mayor Rudy Giuliani

caucus
A meeting of local party members to choose party officials or candidates for public office and to decide the platform.

YOU WILL DECIDE Should We Establish a National Presidential Primary?

States that have their caucuses or conventions early in the presidential selection process get more attention and have generally had a greater say in selecting the presidential candidates. For several election cycles prior to 2008, many states held presidential primaries after the nominee had effectively been selected. Continuing a trend from past election cycles, several states moved up their primary or caucus dates in 2008. The ordering of the states, with Iowa and New Hampshire first, has been disputed by other states that have proposed either a national primary or a set of regional primaries.

Another criticism of the current system is that the states asserting a claim to going first are not representative of their party or the country. Yet another problem is the threat of one party's voters participating in another's primary in hopes of nominating a weak candidate or prolonging the primary contest, such as when Rush Limbaugh urged Republicans, through his "Operation Chaos," to vote for Hillary Clinton to draw out the 2008 Democratic race for as long as possible. A national primary would give all U.S. voters an equal say as to whom their party nominee would be.

What do you think? Should we establish a national presidential primary? What are some of the arguments for or against it?

THINKING IT THROUGH

Our current system of state primaries or caucuses grows out of federalism and the rights of the states to govern elections. Mandating a national primary, though likely constitutional, would be a departure from federalism, and some may object to it as a step toward the federal government's controlling voter registration, voting technology, and other aspects of election administration that were long the province of the states. A national primary could force states that prefer the caucus system to adopt primaries. Because states sometimes combine the presidential primary with their primary for other offices, it may mean adding another election to the calendar.

A national primary would have the advantage of giving every voter an equal say in determining the nominee. It would also take away the kind of dispute that clouded the 2008 Democratic contest, in which Florida and Michigan voted earlier than the national party rules allowed, resulting in a disputed election.

A national primary would substantially change the nature of the campaign. Our current system means candidates with less money can spend more time meeting the voters of Iowa and New Hampshire and prove themselves in order to move on in the process. A national primary would help candidates with more money and greater name recognition because there would be little person-to-person campaigning.

Critical Thinking Questions

1. Do you think it is fair that Iowa and New Hampshire are always first in the nominating process?
2. What are the strengths and weaknesses of the current system?
3. When should a national primary be held, and why?

also bypassed Iowa, but unlike McCain, he did not win in New Hampshire and dropped out of the race after losing in Florida to McCain a few weeks later. Most candidates choose to run hard in Iowa and New Hampshire, hoping that early showings in these states, which receive a great deal of media attention, will move them into the spotlight for later efforts.

During this early phase, the ability of candidates to generate momentum by managing the media's expectations of their performance is especially important. Winning in the primaries thus centers on a game of expectations, and candidates may intentionally seek to lower expectations so that "doing better than expected" will generate momentum for their campaign. The media and pollsters generally set these expectations in their coverage of candidates. In 2008, polls consistently had Clinton in the lead in New Hampshire until the Iowa caucus the week before New Hampshire. With Obama's win in Iowa, however, Clinton's ability to win in New Hampshire was in doubt, and when she won, her victory was interpreted as a "stunner" by MSNBC.[41]

Stage 2: The National Party Convention

The delegates elected in primaries, caucuses, or state conventions assemble at their **national party convention** in the summer before the election to pick the party's presidential and vice presidential candidates. Conventions follow standard rules, routines, and rituals. Usually, the first day is devoted to a keynote address and other speeches touting the party and denouncing the opposition; the second day, to committee reports, including party and convention rules and the party platform; the third day, to presidential and vice presidential balloting; and the fourth day, to the presidential candidate's acceptance speech.

national party convention
A national meeting of delegates elected in primaries, caucuses, or state conventions who assemble once every four years to nominate candidates for president and vice president, ratify the party platform, elect officers, and adopt rules.

National party conventions used to be events of high excitement because there was no clear nominee before the convention. In the past, delegates also arrived at national nominating conventions with differing degrees of commitment to presidential candidates; some delegates were pledged to no candidate at all, others to a specific candidate for one or two ballots, and others firmly to one candidate only. Because of reforms encouraging delegates to stick with the person to whom they are pledged, there has been less room to maneuver at conventions. For a half century, conventions have ratified a candidate who has already been selected in the primaries and caucuses.

Despite the lack of suspense about who the nominee will be, conventions remain major media events. As recently as 1988, the major networks gave the Democratic and Republican national conventions gavel-to-gavel coverage, meaning that television covered the conventions from the beginning of the first night to the end of the fourth night. Now, the major networks leave comprehensive coverage to C-SPAN. The long-term decline in viewership and the reduced hours of coverage have altered the parties' strategies. The parties feature their most important speakers and highlight their most important messages in the limited time the networks give them. In 2008, coverage and viewership of the conventions increased; this was especially the case for the Obama, Palin, and McCain acceptance speeches. Acceptance speeches provide the nominess with an opportunity define themselves and their candidacy. An estimated 40 million people viewed the McCain speech, slightly higher than the number who saw Obama's acceptance speech.[42]

The Party Platform Delegates to the national party conventions decide on the *platform,* a statement of party perspectives on public policy. Why does anyone care what is in the party platform? Critics have long pointed out that the party platform is binding on no one and is more likely to hurt than to help a candidate by advocating positions unpopular to moderate or Independent voters, whose support the candidate may need to win in the general election. But presidential candidates, as well as delegates, take the platform seriously because it defines the direction a party wants to take. Also, despite the charge that the platform is ignored, most presidents try to implement much of it.[43]

The Vice Presidential Nominee The choice of the vice presidential nominee garners widespread attention. Rarely does a person actually "run" for the vice presidential nomination because only the presidential nominee's vote counts. But there is a good deal of maneuvering to capture that one vote. Sometimes, the choice of a running

The 2008 debate between the vice presidential candidates had a large audience. Prior to the debate, Republican nominee Sarah Palin had been criticized for her lack of knowledge in media interviews, which added to the voter interest. Both Democrat Joe Biden and Palin made no major mistakes in the debate. ■ *How important to an election are the debates? To what degree did the 2008 debates influence your opinion of the candidates?*

mate is made at the convention—not a time conducive to careful and deliberate thought. But usually, it is made before, and the announcement is timed to enhance media coverage and momentum going into the convention. The last time a presidential candidate left the choice of vice president to the delegates was the Democratic convention in 1956.

In 2008, Barack Obama selected Delaware Senator Joe Biden to be his running mate. Biden, who himself had twice been a candidate for the presidency including a bid in 2008, was seen as adding extensive foreign policy experience to the ticket because of his long service on the Senate Foreign Relations Committee. Biden was also expected to assist in winning working class and Catholic support in his native Pennsylvania and other battleground states. John McCain's selection of Alaska Governor Sarah Palin surprised many but quickly helped energize the Republican party base. Later in the campaign, Palin became a liability to the campaign as her media interviews were seen as showing a lack of knowledge and experience. Exit polls found that 60 percent of voters thought Palin was not qualified to be president, if necessary, compared with 31 percent having that view of Biden.[44]

The Value of Conventions Why do the parties continue to have conventions if the nominee is known in advance and the vice presidential nominee is the choice of one person? What role do conventions play in our system? For the parties, they are a time of "coming together" to endorse a party program and to build unity and enthusiasm for the fall campaign. For candidates, as well as other party leaders, conventions are a chance to capture the national spotlight and further their political ambitions. For nominees, they are an opportunity to define themselves in positive ways. The potential exists to heal wounds festering from the primary campaign and move into the general election united, but it is not always achieved. Conventions can be potentially divisive, as the Republicans learned in 1964 when conservative Goldwater delegates loudly booed New York governor Nelson Rockefeller, and as the Democrats learned in 1968 in Chicago when the convention spotlighted divisions within the party over Vietnam, as well as ugly battles between police and protesters near the convention hotels.

Nomination by Petition There is a way to run for president of the United States that avoids the grueling process of primary elections and conventions—if you are rich enough or well known enough to use it. Third-party and Independent candidates can qualify for the ballot by meeting each state's ballot access requirements. This takes time, organization, and money. In 2008, the petition process was as simple as submitting the signatures of 1,000 registered voters in Washington State[45] or by paying $500 in Colorado or Louisiana,[46] and as difficult as getting the signatures of currently registered voters equal to 2 percent of total votes cast in the last election in North Carolina (69,734 signatures).[47] Perennial third-party candidate Ralph Nader's name was on 45 state ballots plus the District of Columbia in 2008. He was not on the ballot in Georgia, Indiana, North Carolina, Oklahoma, and Texas.

Stage 3: The General Election

The national party convention adjourns immediately after the presidential and vice presidential candidates deliver their acceptance speeches to the delegates and the national television audience. Traditionally, the weeks between the conventions and Labor Day were a time for resting, for binding up wounds from the fight for the nomination, for gearing up for action, and for planning campaign strategy. In recent elections, however, the candidates have not paused after the convention but launched directly into all-out campaigning. In 2008, the Democratic race became a marathon with Senators Obama and Clinton campaigning in nearly every state and territory. This gave Obama some advantages in the general election as he was able to capitalize on late primaries and caucuses by easily carrying over his campaign organization into the general election. At the same time, the long nomination fight generated some hard feeling among Hillary Clinton supporters and gave Obama little time to refresh himself before the general election contest.

Democratic presidential nominee Barack Obama campaigned unceasingly throughout the summer and fall of 2008 in hopes of winning the election. ■ *Based on the setting of this photo, what kind of voters was Obama likely targeting on this campaign stop?*

Presidential Debates Televised presidential debates are a major feature of presidential elections. Presidential debates have come to be more of a joint appearance with opening and closing statements than a debate in which the candidates interact much with each other. Since 1988, the nonpartisan Commission on Presidential Debates has sponsored and produced the presidential and vice presidential debates. The commission includes representatives from such neutral groups as the League of Women Voters.

The 2008 presidential debates were widely watched and largely reinforced the candidate preferences of the viewers. Obama was seen as the "winner" by polls taken soon after all three debates. Obama in all three debates maintained a calm demeanor, even when it appeared McCain was trying to provoke him. McCain came out as more aggressive, especially in the third debate. But for voters who had not made up their minds, Obama made headway, denying McCain the chance to change the dynamic of the race. A recurrent theme in the debates was the economic crisis the country faced with home foreclosure, the collapse of large investment banks, and a looming recession. The economy became so central that in the last debate the war in Iraq was not mentioned by either candidate.

Minor party candidates often charge that those organizing debates are biased in favor of the two major parties. To be included in presidential debates, such candidates must have an average of 15 percent or higher in the five major polls the commission uses for this purpose. Candidates must also be legally eligible and on the ballot in enough states to be able to win at least 270 electoral votes.[48] In 2004 and 2008, Ralph Nader failed to meet these criteria for inclusion, as did both he and Patrick Buchanan in 2000.

Television and Radio Advertising Presidential candidates communicate with voters in a general election and in many primary elections through the media: broadcast television, radio, cable television, and satellite radio. Spending on television has risen from $623 million in 2000 to $1.2 billion in 2004 to $1.6 billion in 2008.[49] As with campaign activity generally—candidate visits and mail or phone calls about the candidates—the competitive or battleground states see much more activity. Candidates and their consultants believe that advertising on television and radio helps motivate people to vote and persuade voters to vote for them—or against their opponent. Political party committees and interest groups also run television and radio ads for and against candidates.

The Outcome Though each election is unique, politicians, pollsters, and political scientists have collected enough information to agree broadly on a number of basic factors they believe affect election outcomes. Whether the nation is prospering probably has the most

Republican presidential nominee John McCain worked seemingly endless hours to attract voters during the 2008 campaign season. ■ *What does the event poster tell you about the intended message of McCain's campaign tour?*

to do with who wins a presidential election, but as we have noted, most voters vote on the basis of party and candidate appeal.[50] Who wins thus also depends on voter turnout, and here the strength of party organization and allied groups is important. The Democrats' long-standing advantage in the sheer number of people who identify themselves as Democrats has declined in recent years and is mitigated by generally higher voter turnout among Republicans. Republican candidates also usually have better access to money, which means they can run more television ads in more places and more often.

After the votes are cast, they must be counted. And the way they are counted can be critical in close races. Even before the votes were counted in 2004 and 2008, both parties had deployed thousands of lawyers to observe the voting and ballot counting and to launch legal challenges if necessary. Although there were some problems with voting machines and long lines for people waiting to vote in 2008, there were not the kinds of legal challenges many had anticipated would arise over the use of provisional ballots or widespread challenges to voters because of home foreclosure or the voter not having a state-issued photo identification. The peaceful transfer of power from one individual or party to another, especially after such contested elections, is the culminating event in electoral democracy.

Money in U.S. Elections

LEARNING **OBJECTIVE**

6.3 Evaluate the influence of money in American elections and the main approaches to campaign finance reform.

Election campaigns cost money, and the methods of obtaining the money have long been controversial. Campaign money can come from a candidate's own wealth, political parties, interested individuals, or interest groups. Money is contributed to candidates for a variety of reasons, including ideology, group identification and support, and self-interest. Concern about campaign finance stems from the possibility that candidates or parties, in their pursuit of campaign funds, will decide it is more important to represent their contributors than their conscience or the voters. The potential corruption from politicians' dependence on interested money concerns many observers of U.S. politics.

The 1972 Watergate scandal—in which persons associated with the Nixon campaign broke into the Democratic Party headquarters to steal campaign documents and plant listening devices[51]—led to media scrutiny and congressional investigations that discovered that large amounts of money from corporations and individuals had been deposited in secret bank accounts outside the country for political and campaign purposes. The public outcry from these discoveries prompted Congress to enact the body of reforms that still largely regulate the financing of federal elections.

Efforts at Reform

Reformers have tried three basic strategies to prevent abuse in political contributions: (1) imposing limits on giving, receiving, and spending political money; (2) requiring public disclosure of the sources and uses of political money; and (3) giving governmental subsidies to presidential candidates, campaigns, and parties to reduce their reliance on campaign contributors. Recent campaign finance laws have tended to use all three strategies.

The Federal Election Campaign Act In 1971, Congress passed the Federal Election Campaign Act (FECA), which limited amounts that candidates for federal office could spend on advertising, required disclosure of the sources of campaign funds and how they are spent, and required political action committees to register with the government and report all major contributions and expenditures.

In 1974, the Watergate scandal helped push Congress to amend FECA in what was the most sweeping campaign reform measure in U.S. history. These amendments established more realistic limits on contributions and spending by candidates and party committees, strengthened disclosure laws, created the **Federal Election Commission (FEC)** to administer the new laws, and provided for partial public funding for presidential primaries and a grant to major party presidential candidates in the general election.

The Supreme Court in its 1976 *Buckley* v. *Valeo* decision overturned some provisions on grounds that they violated the First Amendment free speech protection.[52] The *Buckley* decision still allowed limitations on contributions and full and open disclosure of all fundraising activities by candidates for federal office, as well as the system of public financing for presidential elections.[53] However, the Supreme Court made a distinction between campaign spending and campaign contributions, holding that the First Amendment protects spending; therefore, although Congress may limit how much people contribute to somebody else's campaign, legislatures may not limit how much of their own money people spend on their own campaigns independent of a candidate or political party.

One of the success stories of FECA was that presidential candidates of both parties for 20 years chose to accept the limitations on fundraising and campaign spending that were part of the public financing provisions. During the nomination phase, candidates receive federal matching funds for campaign contributions up to $250. Accepting the federal matching funds means candidates accept state-by-state spending limits for the caucuses and the primaries. Major party candidates receive a grant for the general election but also stop their own fundraising. Until 2000, presidential candidates (except a few wealthy, self-financed candidates) accepted the voluntary limitations that come with partial public financing of presidential nomination campaigns.

In 2008, the number of candidates in both parties turning down the matching funds in the primaries increased, and included John McCain, Hillary Clinton, Mitt Romney, and Barack Obama. Obama, who originally indicated he would accept public funding in the general election, abandoned that position and ended up raising $639 million.[54] Obama was the first major party candidate since the system was created to reject taxpayers' money for the general election and ultimately had access to much higher funds for use in his campaign.

The Bipartisan Campaign Reform Act (BCRA) After years of legislative debate, Senate filibusters, and even a presidential veto, Congress passed and President Bush signed into law in 2002 the **Bipartisan Campaign Reform Act (BCRA).** This legislation, often known as the McCain–Feingold bill after its two chief sponsors in the Senate, was written with the understanding that it would immediately be challenged in court—and it was. The Supreme Court upheld most of the provisions of BCRA in *McConnell* v. *FEC.*[55] BCRA continued the public financing of presidential campaigns. It left unchanged the limits on spending by candidates for presidential nominations (on a state-by-state

Federal Election Commission (FEC)
A commission created by the 1974 amendments to the Federal Election Campaign Act to administer election reform laws. It consists of six commissioners appointed by the president and confirmed by the Senate. Its duties include overseeing disclosure of campaign finance information, public funding of presidential elections, and enforcing contribution limits.

Bipartisan Campaign Reform Act (BCRA)
Largely banned party soft money, restored a long-standing prohibition on corporations and labor unions for using general treasury funds for electoral purposes, and narrowed the definition of issue advocacy.

basis and in total) and in the presidential general elections for those candidates who accept public funding. Although recognizing that individuals are free to spend unlimited amounts on their own campaigns, BCRA provided increased contribution limits for candidates running against an opponent who was spending substantial amounts of his or her own money, a provision later declared unconstitutional in the Supreme Court.[56] Finally, it left unchanged the limits on the amounts the national parties can spend on presidential campaigns and on individual congressional and senatorial campaigns.

The limits under BCRA for individuals giving to candidates were increased and indexed to inflation, so that in 2010 individuals could give $4,800 to candidates running in a primary and general election. An individual can give up to $115,500 in the aggregate to federal candidates, national party committees, or PACs.

Soft Money The 1976 and 1978 elections, the first after FECA, saw less generic party activity and prompted parties to seek legislation and FEC rulings to allow for individuals or groups to avoid the contribution limits if the money they were giving was going to the political parties for "party-building purposes,"[57] such as voter registration drives or generic party advertising. This money came to be defined as **soft money,**[58] in contrast to the limited and more-difficult-to-raise **hard money** contributions to candidates and party committees that are committed to candidate-specific electoral activity. Over time, soft money became more important. The 1996 election saw aggressive soft money fundraising by the Clinton-Gore campaign, including opportunities for donors to have meetings with the president, to fly with him on Air Force One, and to spend the night in the Lincoln Bedroom at the White House. A congressional investigation into these and related concerns about campaign finance in the 1996 election cycle reinforced the case for reform.[59] From the perspective of the voter, the advertising purchased by soft money was indistinguishable from other campaign expenditures.[60]

Yet both parties continued to make raising and spending soft money a major priority, and soft money spending rose dramatically. All national party committees combined raised more than $509 million of soft money in the 1999-2000 election cycle, up from $110 million adjusted for inflation in 1991–1992.[61] And in 2002, the party committees raised more than $495 million combined in soft money.[62] Figure 6–3 plots the surge in soft money funds for the four congressional campaign committees.

Banning soft money became the primary objective of reformers and was one of the more important provisions in the BRCA. Soft money enabled large donors to be major players in campaign finance. It also strengthened the power of the national party committees, which allocated the money to state parties and indirectly to candidates. To the Supreme Court, which upheld the BCRA soft money ban, one of the major problems with soft money was that it purchased access to elected officials, and with that access came influence and the possibility or appearance of corruption.[63]

soft money
Money raised in unlimited amounts by political parties for party-building purposes. Now largely illegal except for limited contributions to state or local parties for voter registration and get-out-the-vote efforts.

hard money
Political contributions given to a party, candidate, or interest group that are limited in amount and fully disclosed. Raising such limited funds is harder than raising unlimited funds, hence the term "hard money."

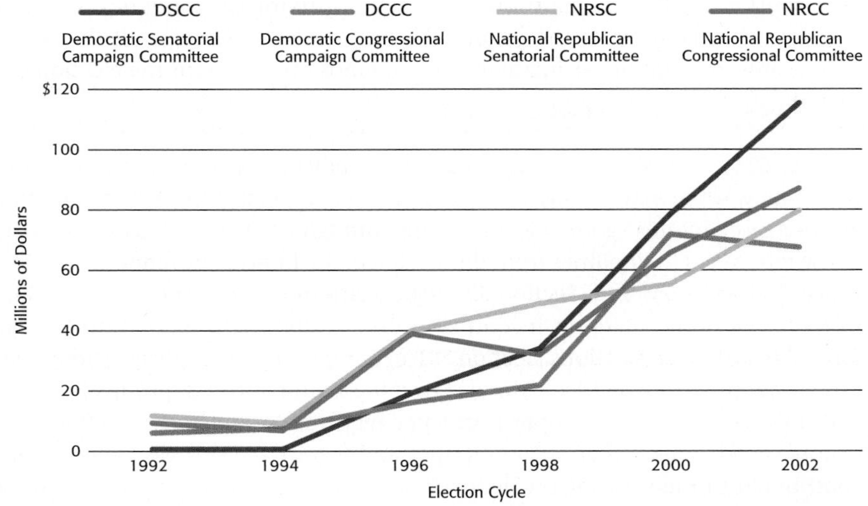

FIGURE 6–3 **Congressional Campaign Committee Soft Money Spending, 1994–2002.**

NOTE: The totals for each party do not equal the sum of the party committee receipts because the numbers provided by the FEC have been adjusted to account for transfers between party committees so as not to double-count money in the total receipts.

SOURCE: Federal Election Commission, "Party Committees Raise More Than $1 Billion in 2001–2002," press release, March 20, 2003, http://www.fec.gov/press/press2003/20030320party/20030103party.html. In constant, 2008 dollars.

Presidential elections have a well-earned reputation for brutality. This advertisement exploits the relationship between Barack Obama and his former pastor Jeremiah Wright in order to raise fears of Obama being too extreme for most voters.

Issue Advocacy Advertising Another way the post–Watergate election reforms were undermined was with the upsurge of interest groups running election ads with undisclosed and unlimited money. These ads typically attack a candidate, but the sponsor can avoid disclosure and contribution limitations because the ads do not use electioneering language, such as "vote for" or "vote against" a specific candidate. The Supreme Court in its 1976 *Buckley* v. *Valeo* decision on FECA defined election communication as "communications containing express words of advocacy of election or defeat, such as 'vote for,' 'elect,' 'support,' 'cast your ballot for,' 'Smith for Congress,' 'vote against,' 'defeat,' and 'reject.'"[64] Communications that did not use these "magic words" were defined as issue ads, not subject to disclosure required by FECA restrictions. Not surprisingly, interest groups and media consultants found a way to communicate an electioneering message without using the magic words. The 1996 election saw a surge in **issue advocacy.**

Campaign issue advertisements sponsored by interest groups are largely indistinguishable from candidate-run ads.[65] The same was also true for party ads paid for with soft money. In some competitive contests, interest groups and parties spent more money than the candidates did themselves. Typically, these party and group ads are even more negative than the ads run by candidates. Often the group identified as paying for the ad gave itself a nondescript name like "Citizens for..." or "Coalition Against..."

BCRA only partially addressed the issue ads loophole. It redefined "electioneering communications" to include much of what claimed to be issue ads. Under BCRA, an electioneering communication is "any broadcast, cable, or satellite communication which refers to a clearly identified candidate for Federal office [and in the case of House and Senate candidates is targeted to their state or district], is made within 60 days before a general, special, or runoff election for the office sought by the candidate; or 30 days before a primary or preference election."[66] In a 2007 decision, the Supreme Court in a 5-to-4 decision declared the BCRA "electioneering communication" definition too broad and substituted a new definition that an ad is considered "express advocacy" only if there is no reasonable way to interpret it except "as an appeal to vote for or against a certain candidate."[67] In 2008, unions made greater use of this new interpretation than did corporations. Unions like the Service Employees International Union (SEIU) were active in several battleground states. Corporations were less inclined than unions to exploit the 2007 court ruling but did contribute substantially to the Chamber of Commerce's large-scale effort to counteract the unions. The court also later rejected the BCRA ban on unions and corporations using their general funds on ads about the election or defeat of a candidate.[68]

issue advocacy
Promoting a particular position or an issue paid for by interest groups or individuals but not candidates. Much issue advocacy is often electioneering for or against a candidate, avoiding words like "vote for," and until 2004 had not been subject to any regulation.

527 organizations
Interest groups organized under Section 527 of the Internal Revenue Code may advertise for or against candidates. If their source of funding is corporations or unions, they have some restrictions on broadcast advertising.

Section 527 and 501(c) Organizations One predictable consequence of BCRA's ban on soft money, while leaving open the possibility of some electioneering communications, was increased interest-group electioneering through what are called 527 or 501(c) groups. These groups get their names from the section of the Internal Revenue Service code under which they are organized. Section **527 organizations** existed long before BCRA, but after BCRA, these groups had an incentive to expand their efforts. Section 527 groups are formed to influence elections. Section 501(c) groups include nonprofit groups whose purpose is not primarily political. Money given to Section 501(c)(3) groups is tax deductible, and they can engage in nonpartisan voter registration and turnout efforts but cannot endorse candidates. Other 501(c) groups can be and are expressly political, and money contributed to them is not tax deductible. Disclosure of contributions to these groups and spending by them are less frequent than for Section 527 groups, political parties, or PACs.[69]

In 2004, in the first post–BCRA election, the best-funded 527 organization was America Coming Together (ACT), which raised and spent an estimated $76 million in presidential battleground states to register and mobilize voters. However, the 527 group that may have had the greatest impact on the 2004 campaign was Swift Boat Veterans for Truth, which attacked Senator Kerry's war record. The modest initial budget for this group's ads generated widespread news coverage, especially on cable news stations. The message of the ads cut to the core of the persona that Kerry had presented at the Democratic National Convention. The attack by the Swift Boat Veterans was effective in part because of the lack of a strong response and rebuttal from Kerry, his campaign, or his party. These attacks led to a new term, being "swift-boated."[70]

Former White House advisor and Fox TV commentator Karl Rove, seen here on "Face the Nation" discussing the mid-term elections, helped organize the 527 group American Crossroads, which aimed to spend over $50 million to help elect Republicans. Most of the group's funding came from billionaires. ■ *Should there be stricter laws regulating 527 and other outside group spending, or is political spending an extension of free speech?*

Given the important role outside groups played in 2004 in attacking John Kerry and promoting George Bush as well in voter registration and mobilization, many anticipated they would play an even larger role in 2008. Although some groups ran ads for and against the presidential candidates, no group had the impact that Swift Boat Veterans for Truth had in 2004. In terms of voter mobilization, outside groups remained important in 2008. On the Democratic side, a group called America Votes coordinated the voter mobilization efforts. On the Republican side, business, pro-life, and gun rights groups were active. Some groups like the Chamber of Commerce invested heavily in supporting Senate candidates.

Unlike 2004 and 2006 when Democratic groups were more visible and spent more money, Republican allied groups played an important role in making more contests competitive in 2010 and in helping elect Republicans. Former Bush political strategist Karl Rove and others organized American Crossroads and Crossroads Grassroots Policy Strategies, while other prominent Republicans organized American Action Network and other groups. Moreover, these groups coordinated their spending with other GOP allied groups like the Chamber of Commerce, Club for Growth and the National Rifle Association. Some groups organized under sections of the law that allow them to not disclose their donors, and all groups could tap corporation and union general funds for the first time in decades. The threat of secret outside money was frequently cited by President Obama in his 2010 campaign appearances.

Independent Expenditures The Supreme Court made clear in its ruling on FECA in 1976 that individuals and groups have the right to spend as much money as they wish for or against candidates as long as they are truly independent of the candidate, they disclose their activity, and the money is not corporate or union treasury money. Some groups such as the American Medical Association, the National Education Association, and the National Rifle Association have long tried to influence elections independently rather than through a party committee or a candidate's campaign. As discussed in Chapter 4, the Supreme Court extended to political parties the same rights to make independent expenditures afforded to groups and individuals.[71]

BCRA does not constrain **independent expenditures** by groups, political parties, or individuals, as long as the expenditures by those individuals, parties, or groups are independent of the candidate and fully disclosed to the FEC. In 2008, independent expenditures by the party committee were important in some competitive contests. For example, in the North Carolina U.S. Senate race, the spending of $8.1 million by the Democratic

independent expenditures
Money spent by individuals or groups not associated with candidates to elect or defeat candidates for office.

Senatorial Campaign Committee helped Kay Hagan compete against Republican incumbent Elizabeth Dole, whose party spent $3.5 million independently.

Neither the DNC nor RNC made substantial independent expenditures in 2010 but the congressional campaign committees did. The Republicans and Democrats were at near parity in independent expenditures in U.S. House races, while the Democrats spent substantially more independently in U.S. Senate races than did the Republicans.

Continuing Problems with Campaign Finance

The continuing problems with federal election fundraising are easy to identify: dramatically escalating costs, a growing dependence on PAC money for congressional candidates, decreasing visibility and competitiveness of challengers (especially for the House), and the advantage wealthy individuals have in funding their own campaigns. BCRA reduced the danger of large contributions influencing lawmakers directly or indirectly through political parties. But large contributions can still influence the outcome of elections, as 527 and other groups have demonstrated. Supreme Court decisions have made campaign finance an increasingly deregulated activity. Interest groups like corporations and unions have been given much greater latitude to attempt to influence the outcome of elections.

The U.S. ideal that anyone—even a person of modest or little wealth—can run for public office and hope to win has become more of a myth than a reality.[72] Since FECA became law in 1972, total expenditures by candidates for the House of Representatives have more than doubled after controlling for inflation, and they have risen even more in Senate elections (see Table 6–2). One reason for escalating costs is the need for television advertising.

Unless something is done to help finance challengers, incumbents will continue to have the advantage in seeking reelection. Nothing in BCRA addresses this problem. Challengers in both parties are typically underfunded. The high cost of campaigns dampens competition by discouraging individuals from running for office. Moreover, unlike incumbents, whose salaries are being paid while they are campaigning and raising money, most challengers have to support themselves and their families throughout the campaign, which for a seat in Congress often lasts more than one year.

TABLE 6–2 Average Campaign Expenditures of Candidates for the House of Representatives, 1998–2008 General Election (in thousands of 2008 dollars)

	Incumbent	Challenger	Open Seat
Republican			
1998	725.4	270.7	843.4
2000	911.5	261.7	1289.9
2002	922.4	201.1	1234.9
2004	1129.5	259.3	1311.1
2006	1574.1	268.5	1422.4
2008	1456.2	375.8	1380.5
Democrat			
1998	584.8	253.3	778.2
2000	765.1	372.8	1090.4
2002	844.7	336.9	1079.6
2004	963.4	299.5	993.6
2006	1010.4	574.5	1465.6
2008	1252.4	612.9	1637.5

■ *What are the patterns of spending for incumbents, challengers, and open seat candidates, across both parties?*

SOURCE: Federal Election Commission, "FEC Reports on Congressional Financial Activity for 2000," press release, May 15, 2001; Federal Election Commission, "Congressional Candidates Spend $1.16 Billion During 2003–2004," press release, June 9, 2005; and Federal Election Commission, "Congressional Candidates Raised $1.42 Billion in 2007–2008," press release, December 29, 2009.

For most House incumbents, campaign money comes from political action committees (PACs), which we discussed in Chapter 4. In recent years, nearly two out of five incumbents seeking reelection raised more money from PACs than from individuals (see Figure 6–4).[73] Senators get a smaller percentage of their campaign funds from PACs, but because they spend so much more, they need to raise even more money from PACs than House incumbents do. Challengers receive little because PACs do not want to offend politicians in power. BCRA continued to cap PAC contributions at $10,000 for the primary and general election combined.

Campaign finance legislation cannot constitutionally restrict rich candidates—the Rockefellers, the Kennedys, the Perots, the Clintons, the Romneys—from spending heavily on their own campaigns. Big money can make a big difference, and wealthy candidates can afford to spend big money. In presidential politics, this advantage can be most meaningful before the primaries begin. The personal wealth advantage also applies to congressional and gubernatorial races. In the 2000 New Jersey U.S. Senate race, for example, Wall Street investment banker Jon Corzine spent a total of $60 million.[74] Corzine was elected to the U.S. Senate and later spent another $45 million of his own money on his successful 2005 gubernatorial election in New Jersey.[75] He spent another $28.5 million on his unsuccessful reelection bid in 2009. Overall then, Corzine spent $133.5 million in one decade on his own campaigns.[76] Meg Whitman, the unsuccessful Republican candidate for governor of California in 2010, spent over $140 million of her own money on her campaign, breaking the previous record held by New York Mayor Michael Bloomberg ($109 million).

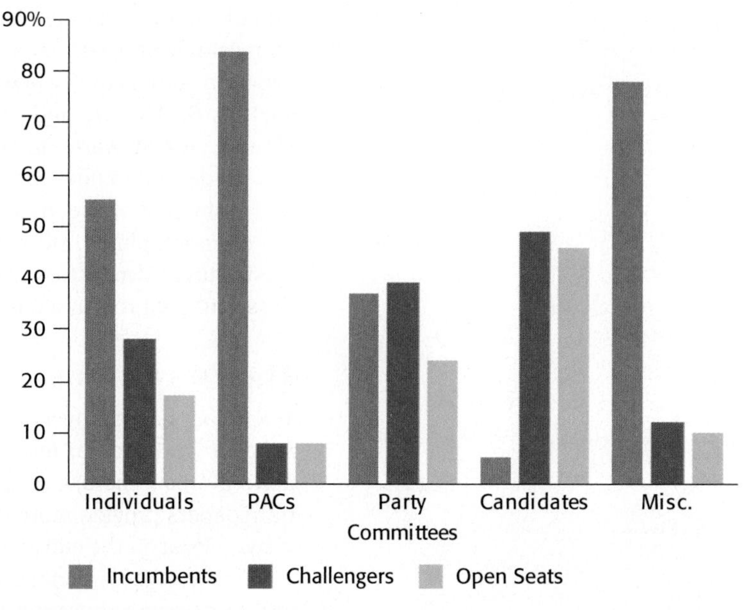

FIGURE 6–4 **How PACs and Others Allocated Campaign Contributions to House Candidates, 2007–2008.**

■ *Why might PACs be more apt than individuals or party committees to skew their funding so heavily to incumbents?*

SOURCE: Federal Election Commission, "PAC Activity Continues Climb in 2006," press release, October 5, 2007, http://www.fec.gov/press/press2007/20071009pac/20071009pac.shtml; and Federal Election Commission, "Growth in PAC Financial Activity Slows," press release, April 24, 2009, http://www.fec.gov/press/press2009/20090415PAC/20090424PAC.shtml.

BCRA made individuals more important as sources of money to candidates because it increased the amount they could give and indexed those limits to inflation. In the election cycles since BCRA took effect, there has been substantial growth in individual contributions, especially to the Democrats, who once were more reliant on soft money. As we have noted in the beginning of this chapter, the growth in individual contributions to both parties has been pronounced at the large and small donor levels.

Another development that has made individual donors more important is the Internet. Starting in 2000 with the McCain presidential campaign and then expanding with the Howard Dean candidacy for presidency in 2004, individuals started giving to candidates via the Internet. But it was the Obama campaign in 2008 that demonstrated the extraordinary power of the Internet as a means to reach donors and a way for people to contribute to a candidate. As former senator Tom Daschle said, the Internet "is an evolution away from Washington's control, away from the power that big money and big donors used to have a monopoly on."[77] It is clear that the Internet has the potential to change the way campaigns are funded.

After successfully running a self-financed campaign for the Senate, Jon Corzine spent millions of his own money on a successful bid for the governship of New Jersey, only to be defeated for reelection in 2009.

The Changing Landscape of the U.S. News Media

LEARNING **OBJECTIVE**

6.4 Outline changes in the nature and importance of the various news media.

The media, in particular the print media, have been called the "fourth estate" and the "fourth branch of government."[78] Evidence that the media influence our culture and politics is plentiful. In one form or another, the **mass media**—newspapers and magazines, radio, television (broadcast, cable, and satellite), the Internet, films, recordings, books, and electronic communication—reach nearly everyone in the United States.[79] The **news media** are the parts of the mass media that tell the public what is going on in the country and the world, although the distinctions between entertainment and news have become increasingly blurred. News programs often have entertainment value, and entertainment programs often convey news. Programs in this latter category include TV newsmagazines such as *60 Minutes* and *Dateline*; talk shows with hosts such as Larry King and Sean Hannity; Jon Stewart's parody of the news, *The Daily Show;* and *The Colbert Report.*

By definition, and to make money, the mass media disseminate messages to a large and often heterogeneous audience. Because they must have broad appeal, their messages are often simplified, stereotyped, and predictable. But how much political clout do the media have? Two factors are important in answering this question: the media's pervasiveness, and their role as a link between politicians and government officials and the public.

The Pervasiveness of Television

Television has changed U.S. politics more than any other invention. With its visual imagery and drama, television has an emotional impact that print media can rarely match.[80] It cuts across age groups, educational levels, social classes, and races. In contrast, newspapers provide more detail about the news and often contain contrasting points of view, at least on the editorial pages, that help inform the public.

The average American watches more than four and one-half hours of television a day, and most homes have more than two television sets.[81] Television provides instant access to news from around the country and the globe, permitting citizens and leaders alike to observe events firsthand. The growth of around-the-clock cable news and information shows is one of the most important developments in recent years.

mass media
Means of communication that reach the public, including newspapers and magazines, radio, television (broadcast, cable, and satellite), films, recordings, books, and electronic communication.

news media
Media that emphasize the news.

One of the biggest changes in U.S. electoral politics of the last half-century is that national news stations devote less time to coverage of politics, making television commercials even more important as a source of information about candidates and issues.[82] The amount of local television news devoted to politics has also been declining and now constitutes less than one minute per half-hour broadcast.[83] In large urban areas, viewers rarely see stories about their member of Congress, in part because those media markets usually contain several congressional districts. Newspapers do a better job of covering politics and devote more attention to it than television stations do.

For more than 40 years, Americans have been getting their news primarily from television. Whenever there is a crisis, most people turn first to television for information. No event in recent history has done more to underscore the importance of television as the primary source of news in contemporary U.S. society than the terrorist attacks that took place on September 11, 2001.

The Persistence of Radio

Television and the Internet have not displaced radio. On the contrary, radio continues to reach more U.S. households than television does. Only 1 household in 100 does not have a radio, compared with 2 in 100 without a television.[84] More than eight in ten people listen to the radio every week,[85] and nearly seven in ten do so every day.[86] Many consider the radio an essential companion when driving. Certainly American adults get more than "the facts" from radio; they also get analysis and opinion from commentators and talk show hosts.

Political campaigns continue to use radio to communicate with particular types of voters. Because radio audiences are distinctive, campaigns can target younger or older voters, women, Hispanics, and so on. Many candidates in 2008 used radio to "microtarget" particular audiences in this way.[87] One particularly important source of news on the radio is National Public Radio (NPR). An estimated audience of 14 million listens to programs such as *Morning Edition.*[88] NPR even rivals conservative radio commentator Rush Limbaugh for size of audience.[89]

The Declining Importance of Newspapers and Newsmagazines

Despite vigorous competition from radio and television, newspapers remain important. Daily newspaper circulation has been declining for the past 20 years from more than 62 million in 1990 to less than 49 million nationwide currently—or less than one copy for every six people.[90] The circulation figures for newspapers reflect a troubling decline in readership among younger persons: The percentage of young people who read newspapers on a regular basis declined by more than half between 1967 and 2008.[91]

Newspapers have become less profitable because of declining circulation, in part because the Internet provides instantly available information for free.[92] The Internet has also hurt newspapers' bottom line most by providing an alternative medium for retail advertisers, and particularly for classified ads via sites such as Craigslist. Newspapers once earned about 40 percent of their revenue from classifieds; today, they receive only 20 percent.[93]

In addition to metropolitan and local newspapers, Americans now have at least three national newspapers, *USA Today, The Wall Street Journal,* and *The New York Times.* With a circulation of nearly 2.1 million, *USA Today* has now replaced the *Wall Street Journal* as the top-circulating U.S. newspaper.[94] Newsmagazines, like newspapers, have also undergone major changes in recent years. Magazines such as *Time, Newsweek,* and *U.S. News and World Report* have experienced substantial declines in circulation and become less profitable. Declines in advertising revenue hurt the newsweeklies, as these magazines are called, just as it had hurt newspapers.[95]

Rush Limbaugh, seen here during his daily talk show, is an outspoken conservative and opinion leader with a substantial following.

The Growing Popularity of the Internet

From its humble beginnings as a Pentagon research project in the 1960s,[96] the Internet has blossomed into a global phenomenon. There are now more than 19 billion pages indexed by Yahoo on the Web,[97] and more than 117 million active domains have been registered worldwide.[98]

The Internet opens up resources in dramatic ways. One study found that nearly half of Internet users go online to search for news on a particular topic; somewhat smaller proportions go online for updates on stock quotes and sports scores. For approximately 37 percent of Internet users, the Internet is a primary source of news.[99] Internet users can also interact with politicians or other people about politics through e-mail, social networking sites, and blogs. Younger people, including teenagers, use the Internet extensively for schoolwork, and nearly three in four of them prefer it to the library.[100] A remarkable 63 percent of teenagers get news online, and the same proportion of teenagers use the Internet every day.[101]

The Internet provides an inexpensive way for candidates and campaigns to communicate with volunteers, contributors, and voters and promises to become an even larger component of future campaigns. Candidates' Web sites offer not only extensive information about the candidates themselves and their stands on issues but also tools for meeting fellow supporters, for receiving news and materials from the campaign, for volunteering, and for setting up personalized home pages.

During the past decade, there has been a dramatic increase in the use of social networking computer sites, and these have come to be important in American politics. Social networking sites allow individuals to create profiles and connect via the Web to other individuals via the site. Early sites had targeted populations like African Americans (BlackPlanet) or Asian Americans (AsianAvenue), but with the advent of Facebook, MySpace, and Twitter, social networking became a more generalized phenomenon. Since Facebook became available to more than only Harvard University students, the number of people with a Facebook profile has risen to an estimated 40 percent of all Americans over the age of 12,[102] and worldwide, there are nearly 500 million Facebook users.[103] Twitter has experienced similar growth.[104] Candidates like Barack Obama, political

People can now access news and other information through their cell phones. They are also frequently invited by news organizations to upload photos and video from their cell phones to help cover news events. ■ *Is this spread of citizen journalism a positive democratization of the news, or a negative removal of the standards and source-checking for publication?*

For the People
GOVERNMENT'S GREATEST ENDEAVORS

Creating the Internet

Presidential candidate Al Gore reaped some ridicule during the 2000 campaign when he claimed to have been instrumental in the "creation" of the Internet.* Gore had promoted the idea of a high-speed telecommunications network while in Congress and helped secure passage of legislation to expand the scope of the new technology in 1991, but the development of the Internet came from government agencies and government-funded researchers that predated Gore's activity. Private sector interests expanded and made the Internet more generally available, but the government was instrumental in its creation.

It began with the U.S. Air Force funding researchers at the RAND Corporation in the 1950s to develop technology to create a communications network that could survive nuclear attack. To avoid the problems that would result from an attack on what was a centralized communications system, researchers created a system that could function even if parts were destroyed, called distributed communications. Under the Defense Advanced Research Projects Agency (DARPA), government-funded researchers at the University of California, Los Angeles (UCLA), gave the concept its first large-scale test in 1969. The early system was intended for researchers and the military to be able to transmit information and share use of computers by granting remote access.

For decades, the government did not make access to the new technology generally available. Some entities like the National Science Foundation (NSF) developed NSFNET, linking much of the academic and research community. In 1993, Congress passed legislation allowing NSF to open NSFNET to commercial use, and by the mid-1990s, several commercial networks were in existence. Today, there are thousands of Internet service providers (ISPs) connecting an estimated 676 million computers worldwide to the Internet. More than half of these connected computers are in the United States, although China leads the world in estimated numbers of Internet users.† So the high-speed electronic communications network that you use for everything from e-mail to shopping to reading the latest news releases started as a government research endeavor.

CRITICAL THINKING QUESTIONS

1. How has the Internet changed your life?
2. What other inventions can be traced to government-funded research?
3. Does the Internet enhance national defense, the reason for its creation?

* CNN.com, "Transcript: Vice President Gore on CNN's 'Late Edition'," March 9, 1999 http://www.cnn.com/ALLPOLITICS/stories/1999/03/09/president.2000/transcript.gore/index.html (accessed June 8, 2010).

† CIA, "The World Factbook," https://www.cia.gov/library/publications/the-worldfactbook/rankorder/2184rank.html (accessed June 9, 2010).

863,956 WORLDS CIRCULATED YESTERDAY — The World. — 863,956 WORLDS CIRCULATED YESTERDAY

"Circulation Books Open to All."

MAINE EXPLOSION CAUSED BY BOMB OR TORPEDO?

Capt. Sigsbee and Consul-General Lee Are in Doubt---The World Has Sent a Special Tug, With Submarine Divers, to Havana to Find Out---Lee Asks for an Immediate Court of Inquiry---Capt. Sigsbee's Suspicions.

C[illegible] SIGSBEE, IN A SUPPRESSED DESPATCH TO THE STATE DEPARTMENT, SAYS THE ACCIDENT WAS MADE POSSIBLE BY AN ENEMY.

Dr. E. C. Pendleton, Just Arrived from Havana, Says He Overheard Talk There of a Plot to Blow Up the Ship---Capt Zalinski, the Dynamite Expert, and Other Experts Report to The World that the Wreck Was Not Accidental---Washington Officials Ready for Vigorous Action if Spanish Responsibility Can Be Shown---Divers to Be Sent Down to Make Careful Examinations.

The New York World a day after

As the nineteenth century progressed, literacy grew among the U.S. masses and more people began to get their news from newspapers. ■ *How did the popularization of the print media permanently change the way politicians and public officials relate with the press?*

movements like the Tea Party Movement, and even law enforcement have all used social networking in recent years.

The Press and Politics

The news media have changed dramatically throughout the course of U.S. history. When the Constitution was being ratified, newspapers consisted of a single sheet, often published irregularly by merchants to hawk their services or goods. But the framers understood the importance of the press as a watchdog of politicians and government, and the Bill of Rights guaranteed freedom of the press.

The new nation's political leaders, including Alexander Hamilton and Thomas Jefferson, recognized the need to keep voters informed. Political parties as we know them did not exist, but the support the press had given to the Revolution had fostered a growing awareness of the political potential of newspapers. Hamilton for the Federalists and Jefferson for the Republicans (later the Democrats) each recruited an editor to assist in the publication of a partisan newspaper. The two papers became the nucleus of a network of competing partisan newspapers throughout the nation. The early U.S. press served as a mouthpiece for political leaders and offered the opportunity for financial stability, but lacked journalistic independence.

During the Jacksonian era of the late 1820s and 1830s, the press began to shift its appeal away from elite readers and toward the mass of less-educated and less politically interested readers. Thus, increased political participation by the common people—along with the rise of literacy—began to alter the relationship between politicians and the press.

Some newspaper publishers began to experiment with a new way to finance their newspapers. They charged a penny a paper, paid on delivery, instead of the traditional annual subscription fee of $8 to $10, which most readers could not afford. The "penny press," as it was called, expanded circulation and increased advertising, enabling newspapers to become financially independent of the political parties. The penny press reshaped the definition of news as it sought to appeal to less politically aware readers with human interest stories and reports on sports, crime, trials, fashion, and social activities.

By the early twentieth century, many journalists began to argue that the press should be independent of the political parties. Objective journalism was also a reaction to exaggeration and sensationalism in the news media, something called *yellow journalism* at the time. Journalists began to view their work as a profession, and they established professional associations with journals and codes of ethics. Further strengthening the trend toward objectivity was the rise of the wire services, such as the Associated Press and Reuters, which remained politically neutral to attract more customers.

Franklin D. Roosevelt was the first president to recognize the effectiveness of radio to reach the public. His "fireside chats" were the model for later presidents.

Radio and television nationalized and personalized the news. People could now follow events as they were happening and not have to wait for the publication of a newspaper. From the 1920s, when radio networks were formed, radio carried political speeches, campaign advertising, and coverage of political events such as national party conventions.[105] Politicians could now speak directly to listeners, bypassing the screening of editors and reporters. Beginning in 1933, President Franklin Roosevelt used radio with remarkable effectiveness. Before then, most radio speeches were formal orations, but Roosevelt spoke to his audience on a personal level, seemingly in one-on-one conversations. These "fireside chats," as he called them, established a standard that politicians still follow today.

Television added a dramatic visual dimension, which increased audience interest in national events and allowed viewers to witness lunar landings and the aftermath of political assassinations, as well as more mundane events. By 1963, the two largest networks at the time, CBS and NBC, had expanded their evening news programs from 15 to 30 minutes. Today, news broadcasting has expanded to the point that many local stations provide 90 minutes of local news every evening as well as a half-hour in the morning and at noon. Programs such as *20/20* and other newsmagazine shows are among the most popular in the prime-time evening hours.

Cable television brought round-the-clock news coverage. During the Clinton impeachment hearings in 1998, the 2000 Florida ballot-counting controversy, and the "shock and awe" bombing of Iraq in March 2003, audiences around the world watched U.S. cable news for its instantaneous coverage.

News reporters today do more than convey the news; they investigate it, and their investigations often have political consequences. An investigative team at *60 Minutes* of CBS News broke the story of torture of Iraqi prisoners held by U.S. soldiers at Abu Ghraib in 2004,[106] and Dana Priest of *The Washington Post* revealed the existence of secret CIA prisons in 2005 that were being used to hold and interrogate suspected terrorists.[107] In many ways, the best example of the power of investigatory journalism is in the role the media played in the Watergate scandal.[108] Without persistent reporting by columnist Jack Anderson and two young *Washington Post* reporters, Robert Woodward and Carl Bernstein, the story would probably have been limited to a report of a failed burglary of the headquarters of the Democratic National Committee at the Watergate building.[109] The news reporting, coupled with congressional investigations, put a spotlight on the inner workings of the Nixon White House and the Nixon reelection committee, which had funded the attempted burglary and other political dirty tricks.

In 2004, an investigative team at CBS News uncovered and aired this and other photos of prisoner abuse in Abu Ghraib. Although the military had been privately investigating the situation for several months, the actions of the CBS reporters brought the tragedy into the national spotlight. ■ *Does the decline of the traditional news industry and increased media consolidation weaken the capabilities of investigatory journalism? Why or why not?*

The tradition of private ownership of the media continues, but has changed over time. Local firms used to own the regional newspapers, radio, and television stations. As in other sectors of the economy, media companies have merged and created large conglomerates of many newspapers and broadcasting stations. Some of these conglomerates are multinational. Rupert Murdoch, an Australian-born U.S. citizen and founder of the FOX Network, owns 35 television stations in the United States, DirecTV, 20th Century Fox, HarperCollins Publishers, MySpace.com, and *TV Guide*, which has

Of the People

AMERICA'S CHANGING FACE

Toward a More Representative Newsroom

The newspaper industry has worked hard to achieve greater diversity in the newsroom. The American Society of Newspaper Editors has stated that diverse newsrooms cover U.S. communities more effectively. Because many stories require contacts with a diverse public, the industry adopted a goal to make all newsrooms representative of the nation as a whole by 2025. Although the largest U.S. newspapers, such as *The New York Times* and *The Washington Post,* have made progress toward a more representative newsroom, smaller papers have had much more difficulty attracting and retaining minority reporters. Thus, less than 30 percent of smaller newspapers with circulations of less than 10,000 readers employ at least some minority reporters, compared with 100 percent of large newspapers with circulations of more than 500,000 readers. Moreover, the percentage of minority journalists varies greatly from one region of the country to another. Newspapers in the Midwest and New England have the smallest percentage of minority reporters, whereas newspapers in the western states have the highest percentage.

Diversity at U.S. Newspapers

	Women		**Minority***	
Position	**1999**	**2009**	**1999**	**2009**
Supervisors	34%	35%	9%	11%
Copy-Layout Editors	40	42	11	13
Reporters	40	39	13	14
Photographers	26	27	15	17

* African American, Asian American, Native American, and Hispanic.

SOURCE: American Society of Newspaper Editors, "Newsroom Employment Census," http://204.8.120.192/index.cfm?id=5650 (accessed April 22, 2010).

CRITICAL THINKING QUESTIONS

1. Why might more diverse newsrooms provide better news coverage?
2. Why are smaller newspapers less likely to have much diversity in their newsrooms?
3. What are some news topics where a more diverse newsroom might be important?

the largest magazine circulation in the United States. His most recent acquisition is *The Wall Street Journal,* giving him one of the few national newspapers in the United States.[110] Murdoch also owns nine newspapers abroad and two television networks—one in Asia and one in Europe.[111]

When television was in its infancy, radio networks and newspapers were among the first to purchase television stations. These mergers established cross-ownership patterns that persist today. The Gannett Company, for example, owns 100 daily newspapers in the United States and United Kingdom and 23 television stations and cable television systems—assets that provide news coverage to more than 21 million households in the United States.[112] At the same time, on the national level, the cable networks—CNN, Fox News, and others—have expanded the number of news sources available to the 90 percent of households receiving TV cable or satellite service.[113]

Glenn Beck, seen here on FoxNews, reaches substantial audiences through his cable news show, radio program, books, and recently launched Web site for political news and opinion. ■ *With which assessment of the nationalization of media do you agree more: that it allows for greater overall spread of information, or that it ensures only the loudest voices are heard?*

Will greater concentration of media ownership limit or restrict the free flow of information to the public? This concern is most evident in cities that once had two or more competing daily papers and now have only one newspaper. Although the number of local broadcast stations has not declined to the same extent, conglomerates without ties to the community now own more of these stations. The nationalization of media extends to some media personalities who have a large presence on television, radio, and through their books. Glenn Beck, for example, had two best-selling books in 2010, plus he hosted a talk radio program and a cable news show on Fox, enabling a wide public following.

Media Influence

LEARNING **OBJECTIVE**

6.5 Evaluate the media's influence on public opinion, elections, and governance.

When dramatic events such as the terrorist attacks on September 11, 2001, occur, we realize television's power to bring world events into our lives. Osama bin Laden, the purported mastermind behind those attacks, also understands the power of the media both inside and outside the United States, as evidenced by his release of videotapes of himself since the attacks.

Media and Public Opinion

Television's ability to present images and communicate events has influenced U.S. public opinion. Footage of the violence done to black and white protesters during the civil rights revolution of the 1950s and 1960s made the issue more real and immediate. News coverage of the war in Vietnam galvanized the antiwar movement in the United States because of the horrible images news shows brought into people's homes. The testimony of White House staff before the Senate about Watergate and later House Judiciary committees further weakened confidence in the Nixon administration. Television coverage of the terrorist attacks on the World Trade Center and the Pentagon and the devastation left by Hurricane Katrina and the earthquake in Haiti made indelible impressions on all who watched.

By calling public attention to certain issues, the media help determine what topics will become subjects of public debate and legislation.[114] However, the media do not have absolute power to set the public agenda. The audience and the nature of any particular issue limit it.[115] According to former Vice President Walter Mondale, "If I had to give up... the opportunity to get on the evening news or the veto power,... I'd throw the veto power away. [Television news] is the president's most indispensable power."[116]

Politicians, like everyone else, try to frame issues to win support, and they try to influence the "spin" the media will give to their actions or issues. The media provide the means. Objectors to normal trade relations with communist China frame that relationship as a human rights travesty. People who favor the right to have an abortion define the issue as one of freedom of choice; those who oppose it define it as murder. In referendum campaigns, the side that wins the battle of defining what the referendum is about, wins.[117]

We tend to blame the media for being either too conservative or too liberal. Conservatives often complain that the media are too liberal. For example, radio talk show host Rush Limbaugh even once said, "They all just happen to believe the same way.... They are part of the same culture as Bill Clinton."[118] Some liberal critics contend that the media reflect a conservative bias not only in what they report but also in what they choose to ignore. They point to Fox News as an example of conservative cable television. In fact, most U.S. news media are committed to being unbiased. Newspapers and television management go to some lengths to insulate reporters from their advertising and business operations, in part to reduce criticism about favorable editorial treatment of large advertisers or the corporate owners.

Some commentators have suggested that a possible bias flows from the fact that reporters and editors become too friendly with the people and organizations they write about. According to David Broder of *The Washington Post*, many members of the print and television media have crossed the line that should divide objective journalism from partisan politics. Broder opposes the idea of journalists becoming government officials and vice versa.[119] Others argue that journalists with previous government service have close working relationships with politicians and can give us a valuable perspective on government without losing their professional neutrality.

The media's alleged political bias is also a frequent target of criticism, in part because the journalists tend to be

Natural disasters in a distant part of the world become part of global news coverage, as with this earthquake in China in 2010. ■ *How might this image have affected the world's reaction to the crisis? Do the media have obligations in how they present these kinds of stories?*

TABLE 6–3 Partisanship and Ideology of Journalists, Policy Makers, and the Public

	Journalists	Policy Makers	Public
Party Identification			
Democrat	27%	43%	34%
Republican	4	24	28
Independent	55	26	21
Other	5	5	12
Do Not Know/Refused	9	2	4
Self-Described Ideology			
Liberal	25%	25%	21%
Moderate	59	52	37
Conservative	6	18	35
Do Not Know/Refused	11	5	7

■ *Why do you think journalists identify as Independent in a far greater percentage than policy makers or the public?*

SOURCE: The Kaiser Foundation, *The Role of Polls in Policy Making,* Combined Topline Results, June 2001, p. 27, www.kff.org/kaiserpolls/loader.cfm?url=/commonspot/security/getfile.cfm&PageID=13842.

more liberal than the rest of the public (see Table 6–3). Their worldview, some contend, may govern their choice of issues to cover and the way they cover them.[120] Critics counter that conservative forces in the media, such as corporate ownership, lead to disproportionate time and influence given to conservative pundits. The question of whether there is an ideological bias in the media has not been authoritatively answered. One bias that does not have a partisan or ideological slant is the bias toward sensationalism. Scandals happen to liberals and conservatives, Republicans and Democrats. Once the province of tabloids like the *National Enquirer,* stories about these scandals involving celebrities, sex, or both have become commonplace in the mainstream media.

political socialization
The process by which we develop our political attitudes, values, and beliefs.

selective exposure
The process by which individuals screen out messages that do not conform to their own biases.

Despite the varied means the media has for influencing public opinion, people are not just empty vessels into which politicians and journalists pour information and ideas. The way we interpret political messages depends on a variety of factors: political socialization, selectivity, needs, and our ability to recall and comprehend the message. We develop our political attitudes, values, and beliefs through an education process social scientists call **political socialization.**[121] (See Chapter 5 for more detail on this process.) The media are an important socializing force and help shape public perceptions and knowledge. Party identification is also a filter through which people view the media. Face-to-face contacts with friends and business associates (*peer pressure*) often have far more impact than the information or views we get from an impersonal television program or newspaper article. Strong identification with a party also acts as a powerful filter.[122] A conservative Republican from Arizona may watch the "liberal eastern networks" and complain about their biased news coverage while sticking to her own opinions. A liberal from New York will often complain about right-wing talk radio, even if he listens to it occasionally (see Figure 6–5).

Bill O'Reilly, conservative TV and radio pundit, appeared as a guest on Comedy Central's show *The Colbert Report,* which mocks conservative pundits. ■ *Do you think media bias is a significant impediment to obtaining nonpartisan news and information?*

We all practice **selective exposure**—screening out messages that do not conform to our own biases. We subscribe to newspapers or magazines or turn to television and cable news outlets that support our views.[123] We also

Party self-identification for regular viewers of:

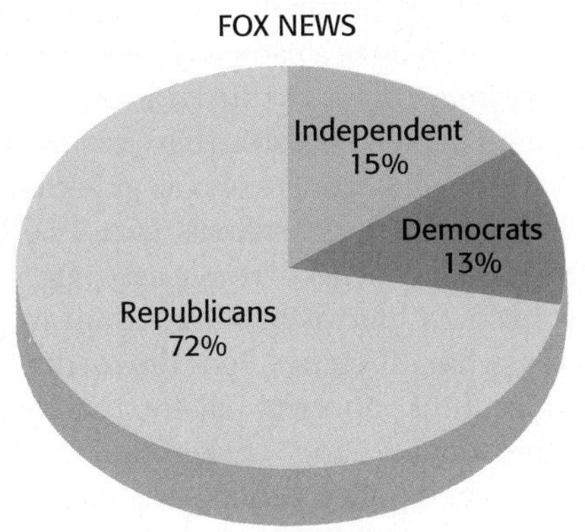

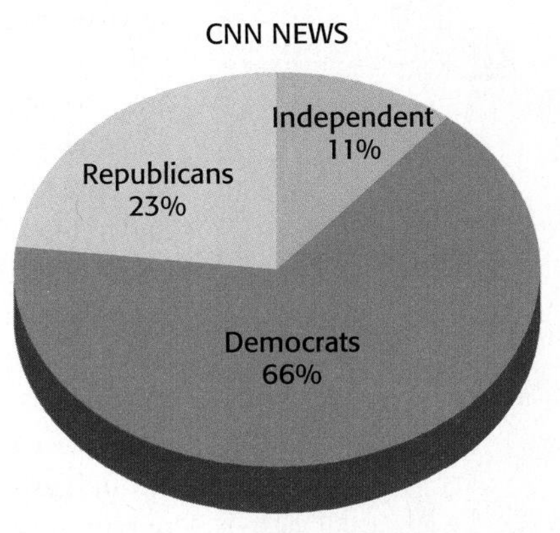

FIGURE 6–5 Partisanship and Preferred News Source.

■ *What do these figures imply about the practice of selective exposure?*

SOURCE: Pew Research Center for the People & the Press, "July 2009 Political-Media Survey" dataset, people-press.org/data archive.

practice **selective perception**—perceiving what we want to in media messages.[124] People read newspapers, listen to the radio, or watch television for different reasons.[125] Media affect people differently depending on whether they are seeking information about politics or want to be entertained. Members of the broader audience are also more likely to pay attention to news that directly affects their lives, such as interest rate changes or the price of gasoline.[126]

selective perception
The process by which individuals perceive what they want in media messages.

The Media and Elections

News coverage of campaigns and elections is greatest in presidential contests, less in statewide races for governor and U.S. senator, and least for other state and local races. Generally, the more news attention given the campaign, the less likely voters are to be swayed by any one source. Hence, news coverage is likely to be more influential in a city council contest than in an election for president or the Senate. For most city elections, there are only one or two sources of information about what candidates say and stand for; for statewide and national contests, there are multiple sources.

Diversification of the news media lessens the ability of any one medium to influence the outcome of elections. Campaigns have used the Internet and e-mail to reinforce voter preferences or help answer questions. Citizens can now interact with each other online on a wide range of political topics. In this sense, the Internet is like a town meeting, but one that people can attend without leaving their homes or offices. In recent elections, people have made greater use of blogs as sources of information, and campaigns have often created their own blogs. Of growing importance are political communications posted on YouTube or Facebook.

However, television is still the dominant media tool for candidates and campaigns. The extensive use of television has made looking and sounding good on television much more important. It has also led to the growth of the political consulting industry and made *visibility* the watchword in politics. Television strongly influences the public's idea of what traits are important in a candidate. Although the media insist that they pay attention to all candidates who have a chance to win, they also influence who gets such a chance. Consequently, candidates have to come up with creative ways to attract media attention. Candidates also schedule events—press conferences, interviews, and "photo ops"—in settings that reinforce their verbal messages and public image.

This ability of television to reach a mass audience and the power of the visual image on television has contributed to the rise of new

These photos from the Obama and Clinton election night speeches following the Iowa caucuses contrast two different ways to stage such a speech. The Clinton staging included former Secretary of State Madeleine Albright, union leaders, and other notables. Obama, on the other hand, is surrounded by a sea of ordinary people, many of them more diverse and younger than in the Clinton staging. As the campaign progressed, Clinton adopted what later became the Obama staging.

Scott Brown was elected to the U.S. Senate from Massachusetts in a special election in 2010. Part of his campaign persona was driving a pick-up truck, as seen in this photo. ■ *What other symbols do politicians use to convey desirable characteristics?*

players in campaign politics, most notably media consultants—campaign professionals who provide candidates with advice and services on media relations, advertising strategy, and opinion polling.[127] A primary responsibility of a campaign media consultant is to present a positive image of the candidate and to reinforce negative images of the opponent. Both parties have scores of media consultants who have handled congressional, gubernatorial, and referendum campaigns. These consultants have also been blamed for the negative tone and tactics of recent campaigns.

As television has become increasingly important to politics, the question arises, what difference does the media make in elections? Some critics think reporters pay too much attention to candidates' personality and background and not enough attention to issues and policy. Others say character and personality are among the most important characteristics for readers and viewers to know about. The public appetite for stories on candidates' personal strengths and weaknesses is not new and is likely to continue.

A common tendency in the media is to comment less on a candidate's position on issues than on a candidate's position in the polls compared with other candidates—what is sometimes called the **horse race.**[128] "Many stories focus on who is ahead, who is behind, who is going to win, and who is going to lose, rather than examining how and why the race is as it is."[129] Reporters focus on the tactics and strategy of campaigns because they think such coverage interests the public.[130] The media's propensity to focus on the "game" of campaigns displaces coverage of issues.

Paid political advertising, much of it negative in tone, is another source of information for voters. Political advertising has always attacked opponents, but recent campaigns have taken on an increasingly negative tone. A rule of thumb used to be to ignore the opposition's charges and thus avoid giving them, or the opposition, importance or standing. More recently, media advisers recommend responding quickly and aggressively to attacks.

Voters say the attack style of politics turns them off, but most campaign consultants believe that negative campaigning works. This seeming inconsistency may be explained by evidence suggesting that negative advertising may discourage some voters who would be inclined to support a candidate (a phenomenon known as *vote suppression*) while making supporters more likely to vote.[131] Other research suggests that negative advertising is more informative than positive advertising and does not discourage voter turnout, but it does alienate people from government.[132]

Newspapers and television seem to have more influence in determining the outcome of primaries than of general elections,[133] probably because voters in a primary are less likely to know about the candidates and have fewer clues about how they stand. By the time of the November general election, however, party affiliation, incumbency, and other factors diminish the impact of media messages. The mass media are more likely to influence undecided voters, who, in a close election, can determine who wins and who loses.

Does television coverage on election night affect the outcome of elections? Election returns from the East Coast come in three hours before the polls close on the West Coast. Because major networks often project the presidential winner well before polls close in western states, it can affect western voters. When one candidate appears to be winning by a large margin, it may make voters believe their vote is meaningless and dampen voter turnout. In a close presidential election, however, such early reporting may stimulate turnout because voters know their vote could determine the outcome. As the use of early voting and absentee ballots increases, the possible influence of exit polls has lessened.

horse race
A close contest; by extension, any contest in which the focus is on who is ahead and by how much rather than on substantive differences between the candidates.

The Media and Governance

When policies are being formulated and implemented, decision makers are at their most impressionable.[134] Yet by that time, the press has moved on to another issue. Lack of press attention to the way policies are implemented explains in part why we know less about how government officials go about their business than we do about heated legislative debates or presidential scandals. Only in the case of a policy scandal, such as the lax security surrounding nuclear secrets at Los Alamos National Laboratory, does the press take notice.

Some critics contend that the media's pressuring policy makers to provide immediate answers forces them to make hasty decisions, a particular danger in foreign policy: If an ominous foreign event is featured on television news, the president and his advisers feel bound to make a response in time for the next evening news broadcast. If he does not have a response ready by the late afternoon deadline, the evening news may report that the president's advisers are divided, that the president cannot make up his mind, or that while the president hesitates, his political opponents know exactly what to do.[135]

Presidents have become the stars of the media, particularly television, and have made the media their forum for setting the public agenda and achieving their legislative aims. Presidential news conferences command attention (see Table 6–4). Every public activity a president engages in, both professional and personal, is potentially newsworthy; a presidential illness can become front-page news, as can the president's vacations and pets.

Members of Congress have long sought to cultivate positive relationships with news reporters in their states and districts. They typically have a press relations staffer who informs local media of newsworthy events, produces press releases, and generally tries to promote the senator or representative.[136] Congress also provides recording studios for taping of news segments, and both parties have recording studios near the Capitol explicitly for electoral ads. Finally, politicians often appear on talk radio, which they can readily do from their offices in Washington. But the focus of this media cultivation is on the individual member and not on the institution of Congress as a whole.

TABLE 6–4 Presidential Press Conferences: Joint* and Solo Sessions, 1913–2010

President	Total	Solo	Joint	Joint as Percentage of Total	Months in Office
Wilson	159	159	0	0	96
Harding		No Transcripts Available			29
Coolidge	521	521	0	0	67
Hoover	268	267	1	0.4	48
Roosevelt	1020	984	33	3.2	145.5
Truman	324	311	13	4.0	94.5
Eisenhower	193	192	1	0.5	96
Kennedy	65	65	0	0	34
Johnson	135	118	16	11.9	62
Nixon	39	39	0	0	66
Ford	40	39	1	2.5	30
Carter	59	59	0	0	48
Reagan	46	46	0	0	96
G. H. W. Bush	143	84	59	41.3	48
Clinton	193	62	131	67.9	96
G. W. Bush	208	50	158	76	96
Obama†	39	17	22	56	21

* In a joint press conference, the president answers questions along with someone else, most often a foreign leader. In a solo session, only the president answers questions. There are three missing transcripts for Roosevelt and one for Johnson, which makes it impossible to determine whether those sessions were solo or joint ones.
† Obama through November 2010.

■ *How does President Obama's use of press conferences compare to his recent predecessors?*

SOURCE: Adapted from Martha Joynt Kumar, "Presidential Press Conferences: The Importance and Evolution of an Enduring Forum," *Presidential Studies Quarterly* 35, No. 1 (March 2005); and Kumar 2006, 2007, 2008, and 2010 updates.

U.S. President Barack Obama calls on reporters as he holds an impromptu news conference in the Brady Briefing Room of the White House in Washington on February 9, 2010. Obama urged compromise and bipartisanship with the Republican opposition on efforts such as health care and bringing down the deficit.

Congress is more likely to get negative coverage than either the White House or the Supreme Court. Unlike the executive branch, it lacks an ultimate spokesperson, a single person who can speak for the whole institution.[137] Congress does not make it easy for the press to cover it. Whereas the White House attentively cares for and feeds the press corps, Congress does not arrange its schedule to accommodate the media; floor debates, for example, often compete with committee hearings and press conferences.[138] Singularly dramatic actions rarely occur in Congress; the press therefore turns to the president to describe the activity of the federal government on a day-to-day basis and treats Congress largely as a foil to the president. Most coverage of Congress is about how it reacts to the president's initiatives.[139]

The federal judiciary is least dependent on the press. The Supreme Court does not rely on public communication for political support. Rather, it depends indirectly on public opinion for continued deference to or compliance with its decisions.[140] The Court does not allow television cameras to cover oral arguments, controls the release of audiotape, and bars reporters as well as anyone other than the justices when it meets to discuss cases.

Media, Elections, and Democracy

We have seen that elections matter in a constitutional democracy. They determine who holds office and what policies the government adopts. Elections are complex, and the rules of the game affect how it is played. Over time, the rules of the electoral game have changed, expanding the role of citizens and voters and making elections more fair and transparent. A system of fair elections must be well administered, so the outcome has legitimacy and voter confidence.

A free and thriving media is also central to the functioning of a constitutional democracy like that of the United States. The media perform a vital educational function, keeping the public informed of political events and issues of public interest. Nearly 70 percent of the public thinks the press is a watchdog that keeps government leaders from doing bad things.[141]

As the 2008 and 2010 elections demonstrated, people are increasingly using the Internet for the news. More broadly, campaigns and movements are exploiting the mobilization and fundraising potential of the Internet, as both the Obama campaign and Tea Party have shown.

Yet as important as these institutions and processes are, the participation of people in politics is essential. It is important for individuals to foster awareness of political issues, but also to critically analyze news and information. Individual citizens can make a difference in elections through voting, being active in selecting candidates, working for political parties, and organizing groups around common interests. Because candidates, parties, and groups need money and volunteers to operate, donating money and time are also important ways in which people invest in elections.

CHAPTER **SUMMARY**

6.1 Assess the implications of election rules in the United States.

The U.S. electoral system is based on winner-take-all rules, typically with single-member districts or single officeholders. These rules encourage a moderate, two-party system. Fixed and staggered terms of office add predictability to our electoral system. Although term limits have been popular with the public, Congress has not introduced any term limits to its members.

The electoral college is the means by which presidents are actually elected. To win a state's electoral votes, a candidate must have a plurality of votes in that state. Except in two states, the winner takes all. Thus, candidates cannot afford to lose the popular vote in the most populous states. The electoral college also gives disproportionate power to the largest and smallest states, especially if they are competitive. It has the potential to defeat the national popular vote winner.

6.2 Explain how congressional and presidential elections work.

Candidates for Congress must raise money, develop a personal organization, and increase visibility in order to be nominated for the election. Incumbents have significant advantages over their challengers, with House incumbents having stronger advantages than their Senate counterparts. The cost of elections and incumbency advantages make congressional elections widely noncompetitive.

The three stages in a presidential election are winning enough delegate support in presidential primaries and caucuses to secure the nomination, campaigning at the national party convention, and mobilizing voters in enough states to get the most votes in the electoral college. The nomination phase is dominated by more partisan and often more ideological voters. Early contests are often important, which means candidates start early. The connection phase is important in defining candidates for less engaged voters. The general election concentrates candidate time and money in a relatively few contested states.

6.3 Evaluate the influence of money in American elections and the main approaches to campaign finance reform.

The rising costs of campaigns have led to declining competition for congressional seats and increasing dependence on PACs and wealthy donors. Because large campaign contributors are suspected of improperly influencing public officials, Congress has long sought to regulate political contributions. The main approaches to reform have been (1) imposing limitations on giving, receiving, and spending political money; (2) requiring public disclosure of the sources and uses of political money; and (3) giving governmental subsidies to presidential candidates, campaigns, and parties, including incentive arrangements. Present regulation includes all three approaches.

6.4 Outline changes in the nature and importance of the various news media.

The news media include newspapers, magazines, radio, television, films, recordings, books, and electronic communications in all their forms. These means of communication have been called the "fourth branch of government," for they are a pervasive feature of U.S. politics. The media provide and carry information among political actors, the government, and the public.

Our modern news media emerged from a more partisan and less professional past. Journalists today strive for objectivity and also engage in investigatory journalism. Corporate ownership and consolidation of media outlets raise questions about media competition and orientation. Radio and television broadcasting have changed the news media, and these are the sources from which most people get their news. The Internet has recently emerged as a new source of both information and political participation.

6.5 Evaluate the media's influence on public opinion, elections, and governance.

The mass media's influence over public opinion is significant but not overwhelming. People may not pay much attention to the media or may not believe everything they read, see, or hear. People tend to filter the news through their political socialization, selectivity, needs, and ability to recall or comprehend the news. Little evidence exists of actual, deliberate bias in news reporting. The media's influence is most strongly felt in their ability to determine what problems and events will come to the public's attention and how those issues are framed.

Media coverage dominates presidential campaigns, and candidates depend on media exposure to build name recognition, a positive image, and thereby votes. Because of the way the media cover elections, most people seem more interested in the contest as a game or "horse race" than as a serious discussion of issues and candidates. Another effect of media influence has been the rise of image making and the media consultant.

The press serves as both observer and participant in politics and as a watchdog, agenda setter, and check on the abuse of power, but it rarely gives much attention to the implementation or administration phases of the policy process. Exceptions include major mistakes such as the government's response to Hurricane Katrina.

CHAPTER SELF-TEST

6.1 Assess the implications of election rules in the United States.

1. What aspects of the founders' design for our government does the electoral college reinforce? Why? Has the electoral college accomplished these objectives?
2. Write two to three paragraphs detailing what would likely happen to the major and minor parties in the United States if we adopted proportional representation.

6.2 Explain how congressional and presidential elections work.

3. The boost candidates from the president's party get from running along with a popular presidential candidate is known as the __________.
   a. safe effect
   b. wave effect
   c. coattail effect
   d. proportional effect

4. List four reasons why congressional elections are generally not very competitive.
5. Many think it would be better for the country if congressional elections were more competitive. Write a short persuasive essay defending the current system.
6. Choose from the following to complete the paragraph below: *strong partisans, moderates, win the nomination, win the election.*

   During the primary stage of the presidential campaign, candidates need to appeal to ________ in order to ________. During the general election, however, they need to appeal to ________ in order to ________.

6.3 Evaluate the influence of money in American elections and the main approaches to campaign finance reform.

7. Name and explain three ramifications of BCRA on political candidates and groups or individuals who contribute to their campaigns.
8. Describe how the FEC influences congressional and presidential fundraising.

6.4 Outline changes in the nature and importance of the various news media.

9. Briefly explain the distinction between the *mass media* and the *news media.*
10. Describe the major changes during the past century in how Americans get their news.

6.5 Evaluate the media's influence on public opinion, elections, and governance.

11. The process by which individuals perceive what they want to in media messages is ________.
    a. selective exposure
    b. political alienation
    c. selective perception
    d. political socialization
12. List four factors that limit the influence media have on public opinion, and explain each in a few sentences.
13. In a few sentences, explain how television and the media in general affect the choice of candidates for presidential elections.
14. Write a brief persuasive essay showing that the media's role in elections is a problem that calls for significant changes. Use the examples from the chapter as well as any personal experiences you have had.
15. In a short essay, discuss why the federal judiciary is the branch that is least dependent on the press.
16. In a short essay, describe how the president manipulates news coverage. In your opinion, is the president's ability to manipulate news coverage a positive or negative power?

Answers to selected questions: 3. c; 6. strong partisans, win the nomination; moderates, win the election; 11. c

mypoliscilab™ EXERCISES
Where participation leads to action!

Apply what you learned in this chapter with these resources on MyPoliSciLab.

Read on **mypoliscilab.com**

eText: Chapter 6

Study and **Review** on **mypoliscilab.com**

Pre-Test
Post-Test
Chapter Exam
Flashcards

Watch on **mypoliscilab.com**

Video: Dissecting Party Primaries
Video: Oprah Fires Up Obama Campaign
Video: Money in the 2008 Presidential Race
Video: State Primary Race
Video: YouTube Politics

Explore on **mypoliscilab.com**

Simulation: You Are a Media Consultant to a Political Candidate
Simulation: You Are the News Editor
Comparative: Comparing News Media
Timeline: Three Hundred Years of American Mass Media
Visual Literacy: Use of the Media by the American Public
Simulation: You Are a Campaign Manager: Lead Obama to Battleground State Victory
Simulation: You Are a Campaign Manager: McCain Navigates Campaign Financing
Comparative: Comparing Political Campaigns
Comparative: Comparing Voting and Elections
Timeline: Nominating Process
Timeline: Close Calls in Presidential Elections
Timeline: Television and Presidential Campaigns
Visual Literacy: Iowa Caucuses
Visual Literacy: The Electoral College: Campaign Consequences and Mapping the Results

KEY TERMS

ADDITIONAL RESOURCES

FURTHER READING

R. MICHAEL ALVAREZ, *Information and Elections* (University of Michigan Press, 1998).

LARRY M. BARTELS, *Presidential Primaries and the Dynamics of Public Choice* (Princeton University Press, 1988).

BRUCE BUCHANAN, *Presidential Campaign Quality: Incentives and Reform* (Pearson, 2004).

ANN N. CRIGLER, MARION R. JUST, AND **EDWARD J. MCCAFFERY,** EDS., *Rethinking the Vote: The Politics and Prospects of American Election Reform* (Oxford University Press, 2004).

RODERICK P. HART, *Campaign Talk* (Princeton University Press, 2000).

GARY C. JACOBSON, *The Politics of Congressional Elections,* 7th ed. (Longman, 2008).

KIM F. KAHN AND **PATRICK J. KENNEY,** *The Spectacle of U.S. Senate Campaigns* (Princeton University Press, 1999).

DAVID B. MAGLEBY AND **ANTHONY CORRADO,** EDS., *Financing the 2008 Election* (Brookings Institution Press, forthcoming).

DAVID B. MAGLEBY, ED., *The Change Election: Money, Mobilization, and Persuasion in the 2008 Federal Elections* (Temple University Press, 2011).

L. SANDY MAISEL AND **MARK D. BREWER,** *Parties and Elections in America: The Electoral Process,* updated 5th ed. (Rowman & Littlefield, 2009).

WILLIAM G. MAYER AND **ANDREW E. BUSCH,** *The Front-Loading Problem in Presidential Nominations* (Brookings Institution Press, 2004).

SAMUEL L. POPKIN, *The Reasoning Voter: Communication and Persuasion in Presidential Campaigns,* 2d ed. (University of Chicago Press, 1994).

STEPHEN J. WAYNE, *The Road to the White House 2008* (Wadsworth, 2008). See also *Public Opinion Quarterly, The American Journal of Politics,* and *American Political Science Review.*

STEPHEN ANSOLABEHERE AND **SHANTO IYENGAR,** *Going Negative: How Attack Ads Shrink and Polarize the Electorate* (Free Press, 1996).

MATTHEW BAUM AND **TIM J. GROELING,** *War Stories: The Causes and Consequences of Public Views of War* (Princeton University Press, 2010).

BRUCE BIMBER AND **RICHARD DAVIS,** *Campaigning Online: The Internet in U.S. Elections* (Oxford University Press, 2003).

KEITH BYBEE, *Bench Press: The Collision of Courts, Politics, and the Media* (Stanford Law and Politics Press, 2007).

JEFFREY E. COHEN, *The Presidency in the Era of 24-Hour News* (Princeton University Press, 2008).

JOHN G. GEER, *In Defense of Negativity: Attack Ads in Presidential Campaigns* (University of Chicago Press, 2006).

DORIS A. GRABER, *Mass Media and American Politics,* 8th ed. (CQ Press, 2009).

RODERICK P. HART, *Campaign Talk: Why Elections Are Good for Us* (Princeton University Press, 2002).

THOMAS A. HOLLIHAN, *Uncivil Wars: Political Campaigns in a Media Age* (Bedford/St. Martin's, 2009).

PHYLLIS KANISS, *Making Local News* (University of Chicago Press, 1997).

DARRELL M. WEST, *Air Wars: Television Advertising in Election Campaigns, 1952–2008,* 5th ed. (CQ Press, 2009).

WEB SITES

www.fec.gov The Web site of the Federal Election Commission. This site contains information on elections, voting, parties, PACs, and campaign finance.

www.politico.com This Web site focuses on political news and elections.

www.archives.gov/federal-register/electoral-college/calculator.html An electoral college calculator that lets you tally different predictions for the electoral vote; a fun way to get a good understanding of how the electoral college works.

www.sunshineingovernment.org/ The Web site for the Sunshine in Government Initiative, which is a coalition of media groups that focus on ensuring open and accountable government.

www.mrc.org/public/default.aspx The Web site for the Media Research Center, which calls itself "America's Media Watchdog." It is an attempt to try and balance news media, originally trying to correct a "liberal bias."

mediamatters.org/p/about_us/ The Web site for Media Matters for America, which tries to correct "conservative misinformation in the U.S. media."

www.prwatch.org/cmd/index.html The Center for Media and Democracy Web site, which tries to investigate issues and inform the public as well as promote transparency and promote "open content" media.

PART III Policy Making Institutions

THE BIG PICTURE

The U.S. Constitution established three branches of the federal government: Congress, the presidency, and the judiciary. The president also directs the federal bureaucracy, which implements the laws and enforces the court decisions that the three branches make. The three branches of government were designed to check and balance each other through a variety of mechanisms such as the presidential veto, judicial review, and congressional authority to pass, delay, or defeat legislation. Presidents are limited to two four-year terms; members of the Senate have six-year terms, but only a third of the Senate stands for election at a time; members of the House have two-year terms and all stand for election at the same time; and federal judges are appointed for life. Each branch also has different powers in the legislative process.

These checks and balances are part of a system of separate power, which is essential for controlling political ambition. James Madison believed that government must first control the people and then control itself. The Constitution was designed to pit each branch against the other in an effort to protect the nation from rapid swings in public policy. It allows Congress and the president to act only when there is great national consensus and then gives the judiciary the power to declare even popular laws unconstitutional.

The four chapters in this section describe each of the branches in detail and provide an introduction to the federal bureaucracy. Although the Constitution does not provide much detail on the bureaucracy, this "fourth branch" of government is responsible for converting laws into reality through a variety of techniques.

There are a number of ways that the public can influence decisions across these three branches, but citizens are up against a variety of forces, described in Part II of this book. Each of the three branches is built for stalemate unless citizens agree on the need for action.

COURSE LEARNING **OBJECTIVES**

CHAPTER 7 Congress

Identify the legislative powers of Congress, and compare and contrast the House of Representatives and the Senate.

Congress is the first branch of government mentioned in the Constitution. The founders believed that Congress would be the most active branch, except in times of great domestic and international threats to the survival of the nation. The Constitution gives Congress a long list of powers but divides authority in a bicameral, or two-house, system. Each house of Congress has its own responsibilities and operates under different calendars, leadership, and rules.

Because there are only 100 senators, the chamber is more flexible; because there are 435 representatives, the House has more rules for debate. Even as both chambers act together to check the president and the judiciary, each checks the other. The House of Representatives was given the power to initiate all revenue legislation, for example, whereas the Senate was given the power to confirm presidential appointees and approve treaties. Each also has the power to investigate the president and the federal bureaucracy, which puts pressure on executive decisions, and also to investigate violations of the law by citizens and private entities, such as businesses and charitable agencies.

As a general rule, members of Congress are usually reelected to their posts through the use of incumbency advantages such as name recognition. Nevertheless, there are times when the public turns strongly against incumbents, so members of Congress decide not to run for reelection or are defeated in primaries and the general election.

CHAPTER 8 The Presidency

Identify the powers of the president for leading the nation.

The U.S. president holds one of the most important jobs in the world. The Constitution gives the president a number of explicit and implied powers to protect the nation and provides the presidency with important checks on the legislature. The president also has a number of roles in drafting laws, negotiating international treaties, leading the federal bureaucracy, and building morale. Recent decades have produced a number of controversies surrounding the president's power, especially as commander in chief during wartime. These controversies often involve presidential assertions of significant implied powers to act in defense of the nation.

The president also has an important relationship with Congress. Although the two branches do pass important laws, they often disagree about the direction of the nation. The president has important tools for influencing Congress, but Congress has equally important tools for stopping the president. This is the essence of a separated powers system. Presidents often blame Congress for blocking key legislation, whereas Congress often argues that presidents claim powers that the Constitution gives to Congress.

CHAPTER 9 The Federal Bureaucracy

Describe the role of the federal bureaucracy in implementing the laws.

The Constitution left many of the key decisions about the future of the federal bureaucracy to the president and Congress. It instructs the president to appoint the senior political officers of government and gives Congress the power to create departments, independent stand-alone agencies, independent regulatory commissions, and quasi-government corporations. Several hundred presidential appointees lead the bureaucracy, but the civil service actually implements the laws, largely by making rules and regulations. The federal bureaucracy is also responsible for spending money on the programs that Congress and the president create.

Congress often delegates the implementation power to the bureaucracy by writing very general laws. This gives the bureaucracy great power to interpret congressional intent. The bureaucracy must translate general congressional intent into clear instructions that affect every American.

CHAPTER 10 The Judiciary

Explain the role of the courts in the system of checks and balances, and evaluate the challenges for judicial independence.

The Constitution created a single layer of the federal judiciary, the Supreme Court. It left the creation of "inferior courts" to Congress and the president through legislation. The Constitution gave the judiciary significant independence to make decisions on behalf of the nation. Over time, the Supreme Court expanded its role in checking the other branches by establishing its authority to decide whether even popularly enacted legislation was consistent with the Constitution. This role has evolved over time as the judiciary has taken a more active role in considering the constitutionality of the laws.

With life-terms, federal judges are theoretically insulated from political pressure. However, every federal judge must be nominated by the president and confirmed by the Senate, which creates political pressure on the appointments process. It is unusual that the Senate rejects the president's nominees, but the need for its approval influences the president's choices. Moreover, the president's choice of the Solicitor General, another appointment subject to Senate confirmation, affects the government's position on key cases. In addition, presidents appoint the U.S. Attorneys who initiate cases on behalf of the public and defend the government from citizens who challenge the laws.

CHAPTER 7

WIBC
INDY'S NEWS CENTER
93.1FM
NEWSTALK
1430 AM
WXNT
WTHR
FOX
59
NEWS
6 HD

Congress

The People's Branch

CHAPTER **OUTLINE** & CHAPTER LEARNING **OBJECTIVES**

Congressional Elections

7.1 Describe the congressional election process and the advantages it gives incumbents.

The Structure and Powers of Congress

7.2 Differentiate the powers of Congress, and compare and contrast the structure and powers of the House and Senate.

Congressional Leadership and Committees

7.3 Compare and contrast the leadership systems used in the House and Senate, and explain how work is done through congressional committees.

How a Bill Becomes a Law

7.4 Identify the steps by which a bill becomes a law and the ways a bill can be stopped at each step.

The Job of the Legislator

7.5 Characterize the two ways legislators represent their constituents, and identify the various influences on their votes.

An Assessment of Congress

7.6 Evaluate the influence of citizens on the legislative process.

Indiana Democratic Senator Evan Bayh dropped a bombshell on Washington on February 13, 2010. Elected to the Senate in 1998, Bayh would have been eligible for reelection in 2010, but he decided to retire early. He was an important swing vote for Senate Democrats in trying to pass legislation, but in retiring, Bayh joined a growing list of Democrats and Republicans who have given up on the bitter congressional infighting that had frozen action on critical legislation such as economic recovery, health care reform, global climate change, and efforts to trim the huge federal budget deficit.

Bayh was not particularly nervous about his reelection chances in Fall 2010. He has $13 million in the bank to defend his seat against challengers from his own party and his potential Republican opponent. Although some in Washington immediately concluded that he was going to take a year or two off to prepare for his own campaign against President Barack Obama in 2012, he made no mention of his plans in making his tough announcement. As the son of former Senator Birch Bayh, a leader in the old Senate of bipartisan compromise, Bayh, 54, was simply tired of the battles. Writing in the *New York Times* Sunday edition on February 23, he did not mince any words about his decision to leave. As a moderate Democrat, he felt increasingly isolated in his own party:

> When I was a boy, members of Congress from both parties, along with their families, would routinely visit our home for dinner or the holidays. This type of social interaction hardly ever happens today and we are the poorer for it. It is much harder to demonize someone when you know his family or have visited his home. Today, members routinely campaign against each other, raise donations against each other, and force votes on trivial amendments written solely to provide fodder for the next negative attack ad. It's difficult to work with members actively plotting your demise.[1]

Bayh called Congress a dysfunctional institution in which moderates were increasingly isolated from both parties. "It shouldn't take a constitutional crisis or an attack on the nation to create honest dialogue in the Senate." The frustrations he voiced were probably shared by many other senators, but he was still harsh toward his colleagues: "Milton Berle famously joked: 'You can lead a man to Congress, but you can't make him think.' "

Bayh was simply saying what most Americans think. They are disgusted by politics in Washington and disappointed that Obama had not been able to honor his campaign promise to change the tone in Washington. The Senate and House, too, have engaged in the familiar politics of partisanship and anger. Absent fundamental reform in campaign finance and electoral politics, and with party divisions ever more personal, Bayh said it was time to go.

In this chapter, we examine how the framers designed the legislative branch and how it actually works today. We will also explore the role of interest groups, colleagues, congressional staff, the two parties, and the president in shaping decisions; discuss how a bill becomes a law; and explore the ethics issue in more detail.

Before turning to these questions, however, we will look at how members of Congress reach office in the first place. The way we elect members of the House and Senate has a great deal to do with how they behave once in office, and it influences everything from committee assignments to legislative interests. We will also ask why individual members of Congress win reelection so easily.

Readers should also note that the word "Congress" is used several ways in government. The words "a congress" is a two-year body of elected officials and is numbered for the two-year period dating all the way back to the first congress convened after the Constitution was ratified. Thus, the 112th Congress convened exactly 224 years after the first one. The words "the Congress" refer to the institution itself as part of the three branches of government. A congress may stand for two years, but the Congress is a never-ending institution.

Congressional Elections

LEARNING **OBJECTIVE**

7.1 Describe the congressional election process and the advantages it gives incumbents.

There is only one Congress in the Constitution, but the 435 House members and 100 senators serve in bodies that are significantly different. One important distinction is the different election calendars. The framers believed these calendars would make the House and its members much more sensitive than senators to the opinions of their **constituents,** meaning residents of their districts or states.

House members and senators also run for their first elections under slightly different entry rules. House members must be 25 years old at the time they take office and must have been citizens for seven years, whereas senators must be 30 years old and have been citizens for nine years. House and Senate candidates must be residents of the states from which they are elected, but House members do not need to reside in their district. The framers hoped that by setting the Senate's requirements higher and giving its members a six-year term, they would shape the Senate as a check against what they saw as the less predictable House. Concerned about the "fickleness and passion" of the House of Representatives, James Madison in particular saw the Senate as "a necessary fence against this danger."[2] This is why the founders decided that senators would be selected by their state legislatures. Although the Constitution was amended in 1913 to require the direct election of all senators, the Constitution allows state governors to appoint senators to fill vacant posts until the next scheduled election for their seats.

Senators are not free to ignore their constituents, however. Because the framers did not limit the number of terms House members or senators can serve, they must defend their records at some point if they want to stay in office.

Drawing District Lines

constituents
The residents of a congressional district or state.

The framers of the Constitution set the Senate and the House apart in terms of the populations they serve. Every state has two senators, each of whom represents the entire state. Members of the House of Representatives, on the other hand, serve districts within

A campaign worker stays late after the Senator Arlen Specter's concession speech following his defeat in the Democratic Party's 2010 Pennsylvania Senate primary. Specter had often taken a moderate position on issues, and switched from the Republican to the Democratic party in 2009, citing that he was increasingly at odds with the Republican philosophy.

their states. A state's population determines the number of districts—hence, states with more citizens have more districts, and big states clearly have more influence in the House.

The exact number of districts in each state is determined by a national census of the population taken every ten years, which is also specified in the Constitution. The 2010 census is changing the distribution of congressional seats by giving growing states such as California and Texas more representatives. But the number of senators is fixed at two per state.

When the population changes, so does the potential number of districts, or seats in each state. This process of changing the number of seats allotted to each state is called **reapportionment.** Each seat in the House represents roughly 650,000 people. House members from small states often represent even fewer—Wyoming has only 580,000 people, for example, but each state is guaranteed one House member. Because the House limited the total number of districts to 435 after the 1910 census, the number of districts will not change after the 2010 census is completed, but the distribution of seats will.

The U.S. Congress has the power to change the number of seats per state, but the states have the power to determine the district lines. This process of converting the number of seats into districts is called **redistricting.**[3] Under the Constitution, states, not the federal government, are responsible for determining the time, place, and manner of elections, which includes district lines.

District lines can be drawn several ways to favor one party—a district can be "packed" with a large number of party voters, thereby diluting that party's strength in the districts next door, or a party stronghold can be dispersed into several districts, thereby possibly weakening that opposition party's strength in several districts. In extreme cases, this process is known as **gerrymandering,** a term dating to the early 1800s when Massachusetts governor Elbridge Gerry won passage of a redistricting plan that created a salamander-shaped district drawn to help his party win another seat.

Advantages of Incumbency

It only takes one defeat to end a House or Senate career, which is why so many House members and senators work so hard to create safe seats. A **safe seat** is almost certain to be won by the current officeholder, or **incumbent.** It usually occurs in a district where one party has a clear majority of voters, virtually ensuring the election of the candidate from the dominant party.

Although there are still competitive seats in the House, most are considered invulnerable to challenge. Of 435 seats up for election in 2010, roughly one quarter were considered truly competitive two-party seats. In some districts where one party dominates, there is occasional competition within the dominant party for the nomination, most often when an incumbent retires or runs for a different office. In contrast, Senate seats are considered more vulnerable. Opponents are often well financed, in part because Senate elections are so visible nationally. With only a third of the Senate up for reelection at any one time, the public can pay closer attention to campaign issues and advertisements, and the two parties can invest more money in their candidates.[4]

Incumbents benefit from several advantages:

- Under the franking privilege, incumbents do not have to pay postage on their mail to their district, except during the last 90 days before an election.
- Incumbents are allowed to send bulk e-mails any time.
- Incumbents have greater access to the media, especially on local or state issues, and have very high name recognition in their districts.
- Incumbents have a natural advantage in raising campaign contributions over their challengers, in part because they have such high odds of victory.
- Incumbents are usually better candidates than their challengers, in part because they have more experience.
- Incumbents have great influence in helping their constituents solve problems with government, and they often take credit for federal spending in their districts or state.

reapportionment
The assigning by Congress of congressional seats after each census. State legislatures reapportion state legislative districts.

redistricting
The redrawing of congressional and other legislative district lines following the census, to accommodate population shifts and keep districts as equal as possible in population.

gerrymandering
The drawing of legislative district boundaries to benefit a party, group, or incumbent.

safe seat
An elected office that is predictably won by one party or the other, so the success of that party's candidate is almost taken for granted.

incumbent
The current holder of elected office.

Members of Congress often appear at ribbon-cuttings for important public projects. Here, Senator Hutchinson helps open The Women's Museum in Dallas. ■ *How does this photo show several of the advantages an incumbent has?*

Incumbents also control federal spending for pet projects through **earmarks,** which are usually slipped into large legislative packages at the last minute. These earmarks instruct the executive branch to spend money on specific items such as new highways or research centers in individual congressional districts.[5]

earmarks
Special spending projects that are set aside on behalf of individual members of Congress for their constituents.

The 2010 Congressional Elections

The 2010 midterm elections produced dramatic gains for Republicans across the political landscape. They swept away dozens of incumbent Democrats in the House, made modest gains in the Senate, and emerged with much greater control of state governorships.

As the results rolled in on November 2, Democrats were not only shocked by the anger toward their candidates and president, but by the range of victories across the country. Republicans won more than sixty seats in the House, which was more than enough to recapture the majority they lost in 2006. Republicans also gained at least six seats in the Senate, which was still short of a majority, but enough to give them greater power in setting the agenda for the coming two years.

Republicans also gained at least eleven governorships, which gave them almost two-thirds of the key posts that will be so heavily involved in redistricting House seats in their states. Redistricting has already been scheduled in the wake of the 2010 census. Although state legislatures make the first decisions on where to draw the district lines, governors will have great influence in shaping the boundaries that will affect elections over the next decade.

The 2010 election involved record amounts of campaign spending, and the rise of a new corps of anti-government candidates who ran with the endorsement of the Tea Party, a highly conservative wing of the Republican Party. Although many Tea Party candidates were defeated in Republican primaries, their pressure for a radical turn toward more conservative policies resonated throughout the campaign. Many of the independents that had supported President Barack Obama in 2008 turned toward the Republicans in 2010.

The election was broadly interpreted as a rejection of the Obama administration's health bill, but also involved an angry reaction to the

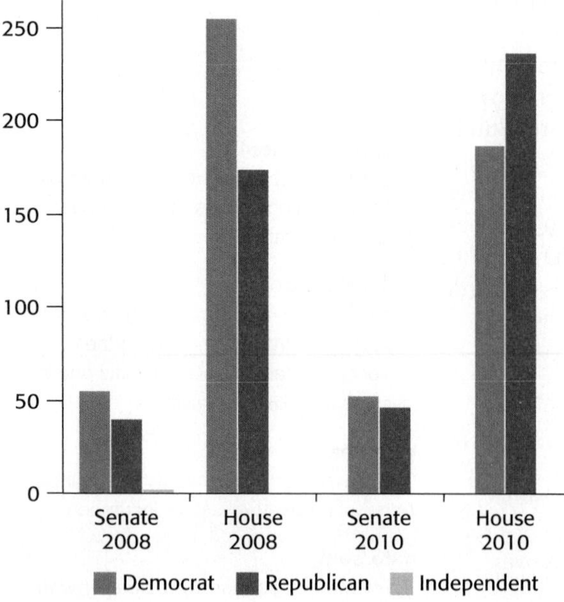

FIGURE 7–1 **Congressional Election Results, 2008 and 2010.**
■ *How did the party balance of Congress change after the 2010 elections, and what effect, if any, will that have on how Congress functions?*

NOTE: Some elections were still too close to call as of mid-November, 2010.

Members of Congress

Although the Constitution does not mention race, gender, or wealth among the qualifications for office, the framers expected members of Congress to be white male property owners. After all, women, slaves, and freed slaves could not vote, let alone hold office.

The framers would therefore be surprised at the face of Congress today. Recent Congresses have had record numbers of women and minorities. In 2008, New Hampshire's new Democratic senator Jeanne Shaheen became the 17th woman in the current Senate. All totaled, 95 women served in the 111th Congress, a record number.

[Hold for update]

These numbers would not have increased without the rise of a new generation of women and minority candidates. Although voting participation by women and minority groups has increased dramatically throughout the past half-century, it took time for women and minority candidates to gain the experience to increase the odds of their winning office.

Although Congress is becoming more diverse by race and gender, it still remains very different from the rest of the United States in income and occupation. Nearly one-third of the senators who served in the 111th Congress are millionaires, and more than half hold law degrees. At the current rate of change in the number of women, for example, it will take another 400 years before women constitute a majority in the House.

CRITICAL THINKING QUESTIONS

1. How does increasing diversity change the issues that Congress works on? Should Congress reflect the levels of diversity in the U.S. population in order to best represent our citizenry?
2. Does increasing diversity help strengthen public approval of Congress?
3. Did the election of Nancy Pelosi as Speaker of the House make any difference in the power of the office or the overall performance of Congress?

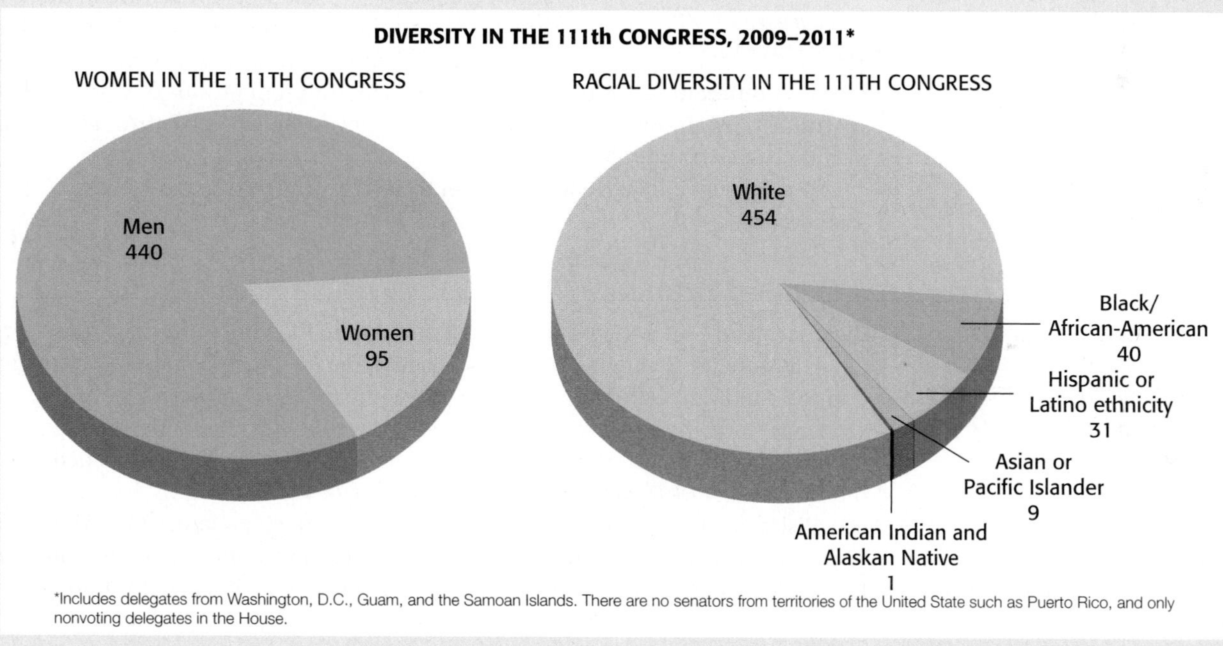

*Includes delegates from Washington, D.C., Guam, and the Samoan Islands. There are no senators from territories of the United State such as Puerto Rico, and only nonvoting delegates in the House.

SOURCE: Rutgers University, Eagleton Institute of Politics, Center for American Women and Politics, November 2008; updated by the authors.

continued economic woes following the 2008 banking failures, economic collapse, and rising unemployment. The economy was the number one issue listed by voters in explaining their vote. But they were also angry at "business-as-usual" in Washington. Many were disgusted by the polarization in Congress and the failure to push the economy forward.

The president's party almost always loses seats during midterm elections, but rarely loses its majority. The 2010 midterms was only the third time since the end of World War II that Republicans were able to take the House majority from a Democratic president—the first was in 1946 and the second in 1994. With government under divided control, both parties began preparing for a tough election battle in 2012.

With divided control in Congress, Washington girded for stalemate on a host of issues. Republicans promised to repeal the new health care bill, cut government spending by

Conservative Republican Marco Rubio won a three-way way race for the Senate in Florida, easily defeating once seemingly unbeatable Republican Governor Charlie Christ, who ran as an independent after Rubio defeated him in the Republican primary. Rubio is a national leader in the Tea Party movement. ■ *What does Rubio's election signal about where Florida's electoral votes might go in the 2012 presidential election?*

20 percent, and investigate waste in the economic stimulus package. There was little talk about working together across the party lines, suggesting that the 2012 election would involve more anger. However, Republicans were reminded that Democrats kept the presidency in both 1948 and 1996, suggesting that they need to do more than simply obstruct the president in order to win the presidency.

The Structure and Powers of Congress

The framers expected that Congress, not the president or the courts, would be the most important branch of government, which is why it is defined in Article I, Section 1 of the Constitution. Hence, they worried most about how to keep Congress from dominating the other branches.

In an effort to control Congress, they divided the legislative branch into two separate chambers, the House of Representatives and the Senate, which would "be as little connected with each other as the nature of their common functions and their common dependence on the society will admit."[6] Not only would House members and senators have different terms of office and represent different groups of voters (districts versus states), the framers originally wanted them to be selected through very different means (House by popular election and the Senate by state legislatures).

The framers allowed each chamber to set its own rules. Because it is so much larger than the Senate, the House has less time allowed for debate and more rules governing it.

LEARNING **OBJECTIVE**

7.2 Differentiate the powers of Congress, and compare and contrast the structure and powers of the House and Senate.

A Divided Branch

Bicameralism, or a two-house legislature, remains the most important organizational feature of the U.S. Congress. Each chamber meets in its own wing of the Capitol Building; each has offices for its members on separate sides of Capitol Street; each has its own committee structure, its own rules for considering legislation, and its own record of proceedings (even though the records are published together as the *Congressional Record*); and each sets the rules governing its own members (each establishes its own legislative committees, for example).[7] As James Madison explained in *The Federalist,* No. 51, "In order to control the legislative authority, you must divide it." (*The Federalist,* No. 51, is reprinted in the Appendix at the back of this book.)

bicameralism
The principle of a two-house legislature.

In the late 1970s, a handful of women members of the House created the Women's Caucus as a forum for discussing issues of concern to women. In the mid-1990s, the caucus was renamed the Caucus for Women's Issues and male members of the House were admitted. A history of women in Congress can be found at womenincongress.house.gov. ■ *Why do you think women still only make up about eighteen percent of Congress today?*

The Powers of Congress

The framers gave Congress a long list of express or **enumerated powers.** Because the Revolutionary War had been sparked by unfair taxation, the power "to lay and collect Taxes" was the very first of these powers. Another 17 express powers of Congress fall into five basic categories:

1. **The Power to Raise, Make, and Borrow Money.** Congress has the power to tax, borrow money, issue currency, and coin money.
2. **The Power to Regulate Commerce.** Congress has the power to regulate commerce between the United States and other nations, as well as between the states. It can also set standards for determining the value of products through weights and measures, establish uniform bankruptcy laws that govern private businesses, and promote the arts and sciences by granting copyright protection to authors and patents to inventors.
3. **The Power to Unify and Expand the Country.** Congress has the power to create post offices and postal roads, which link the states together; to determine the rules for becoming a citizen; and to acquire, manage, and dispose of federal land.
4. **The Power to Prepare and Declare War.** Alongside the power to declare war, Congress can raise, support, and regulate armies and a navy; provide for organizing, arming, disciplining, and calling on state militia (now called the National Guard); execute laws suppressing civil unrest; and repel foreign invasions.
5. **The Power to Create the Federal Judiciary.** Congress is responsible for creating all "inferior" courts below the Supreme Court and for determining their jurisdiction, as well as the appellate jurisdiction of the Supreme Court (discussed in Chapter 10).

Many of these powers are limited in some way, however. Congress has the power to collect taxes only for the common defense and general welfare of the nation, for example, and may not tax exports to other nations. Similarly, it may declare war, but only the president has the power to command the military.

The framers also gave Congress implied powers such as the power to "make all Laws which shall be necessary and proper for carrying into Execution the foregoing Powers, and all other Powers vested by this Constitution in the Government of the United States, or in any Department or Officer thereof."

Finally, the Constitution gave Congress important checks on government, including the power to remove the president and judges from office through the impeachment process. The House has the authority to charge, or impeach, a president or judge for committing "high crimes and misdemeanors," but the Senate has the responsibility to conduct the trial to determine guilt or innocence. Impeachment requires a majority vote in the House, but conviction requires a two-thirds vote of the Senate.

enumerated powers
The powers explicitly given to Congress in the Constitution.

The Constitution gives different duties to each chamber (see Table 7–1). The Senate has the power to give its advice and consent in confirming or rejecting the president's nominees for senior executive branch positions and for the federal courts. The Senate also has the power to give its advice and consent in approving or rejecting treaties made by the president. All treaties must be ratified by a two-thirds vote in the Senate before they can be enforced by the president.

The House has its own responsibilities, too, most notably the power to author "all bills for raising revenues." But these powers are less significant than those given to the Senate, in part because the framers worried that House members would be too close to the people and therefore more likely to act in haste. Although all revenue bills must originate in the House, for example, the Constitution invites the Senate to propose amendments to revenue bills, even to the point of changing everything except the title.

Alcee Hastings was one of only seven federal judges ever impeached and removed from office by Congress. He was impeached for corruption by the House in 1988 and removed by the Senate in 1989. Hastings was elected to the House in Florida's 23rd district in 1992, and continues to serve as a member of Congress today. ■ *Why is impeachment of judges and presidents so rare?*

Legislatures Around the World

Although the U.S. Congress is well known in other countries, Britain's parliament is the most visible legislature in the world. It is composed of two houses—the House of Commons, which is elected by the citizenry, and the House of Lords, which includes some individuals who have been given a lifelong title for achievement. Because the House of Lords has no durable legislative function beyond making small amendments in legislation, the British parliament is not considered a bicameral legislature.

TABLE 7–1 Differences Between the House of Representatives and the Senate

House	Senate
SIZE	SIZE
435 members	100 Members
ELECTIONS	ELECTIONS
Two-year term	Six-year term
All seats are open for election	One-third of seats are open for each election
Elected in districts	Elected in states
LEADERSHIP	LEADERSHIP
Strong leadership controls action by individual members	Weaker leadership provides more freedom to individual members
More powerful committee leaders	More equal distribution of power among committee members
LEGISLATION	LEGISLATION
Decision to consider legislation made by majority	Decision to consider legislation made by unanimous consent of all members; one senator can stop action
Responsible for moving first on raising revenues	Responsible for giving advice and consent on presidential appointees and treaties
All amendments to legislation must be approved for consideration in advance of legislative action	Amendments are generally allowed
DEBATE	DEBATE
Strict limits on debate	Flexible limits on debate approved by unanimous consent
Single member or group of members cannot stop debate once the bill is approved for action by the Rules Committee	Single member can stop action through the filibuster

■ *How are the rules for debate in the House and Senate related to their relative sizes and traditions?*

China has two legislatures, one controlled by the Communist Party and the other elected by the people for five-year terms. The People's Congress meets once a year and has up to 3,000 members. Although it has great formal powers, it yields to the party committees. Nevertheless, it has been asserting more power in recent years.

India has a parliamentary system, in no small measure because it was colonized by Britain. Its parliament has two chambers—the Lok Sabha (the House of the People) and Rajya Sabha (the Council of States). In recent years, the Council of States has become more influential to the point that the Indian system is bordering on a true bicameral legislature.

Mexico's legislature is one of the strongest in the world, at least in theory. Like the U.S. Congress, it is the first branch listed in the Mexican constitution. Like the U.S. Congress, too, it has two houses, both elected by the citizenry.

Congressional Leadership and Committees

LEARNING **OBJECTIVE**

7.3 Compare and contrast the leadership systems used in the House and Senate, and explain how work is done through congressional committees.

Given the differences between the chambers that are summarized in Table 7–1, we should not be surprised that the House and Senate have different kinds of leadership and rules. Whereas the House holds tight control over its large number of members, the Senate has much looser controls. This makes legislation easier to pass in the House and much more difficult in the Senate.

Leading the House of Representatives

The organization and procedures in the House are different from those in the Senate, largely because the House is more than four times as large as the Senate. A larger membership requires more rules, which means that *how* things are done affects *what* is done.

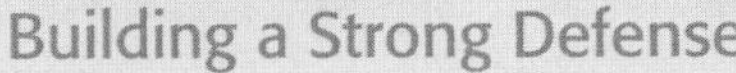

For the People

GOVERNMENT'S GREATEST ENDEAVORS

Building a Strong Defense

The United States spends more money on defense than any other nation in the world. In 2010 alone, the nation will spend more than $500 billion on defense. The Department of Defense, which houses all the military services, has invested heavily in sophisticated technologies that make the nation almost impossible to defeat in war. It is not clear, however, that these technologies ensure that the nation can win a war against the kind of deeply committed insurgents now fighting in Iraq and Afghanistan.

Presidents support a strong national defense, but Congress is responsible for authorizing the spending. Defense spending is spread across most of the states, and many congressional districts and congressional incumbents eagerly seek spending in their districts. The interests of the nation and individual members of Congress can align, as when Senator Bayh (D-Ind.), discussed in the opener, helped push an amendment through Congress to provide more armored Humvees for the soldiers in Iraq. The troops needed the equipment, and Bayh secured a lucrative manufacturing contract for a plant in Indiana.

The military continues to work on new technologies that may make soldiers safer on the battlefield. Troops can now use drones to launch long-range attacks against targets, and they have a variety of high-technology tools to survey the battlefield. Nevertheless, the military has been highly susceptible to the unsophisticated improvised explosive devices used in Iraq and Afghanistan, suggesting that strengthening our defense still needs to be a top priority.

Congress has invested heavily in advanced warfighting technology such as pilotless predator drones. These remotely controlled aircraft have been used frequently in the Afghanistan War.

CRITICAL THINKING QUESTIONS

1. Why do many members of Congress support high levels of defense spending?
2. Does the military buy the right equipment or the equipment that is right for political support?
3. How does U.S. defense spending affect global views of our nation?

The Speaker of the House Again because of its size, the House gives its leaders more power than the Senate, where individual senators have more power to refuse to act at all. The most powerful leader on Capitol Hill is the **Speaker** of the House.[8] Although the Speaker is formally elected by the entire House, the post is always filled by the majority party, which gives the party even more power. The Speaker has the power to recognize members who rise to speak, rule on questions of parliamentary procedure, and

Speaker
The presiding officer in the House of Representatives, formally elected by the House but actually selected by the majority party.

Because its membership is so much larger than the Senate, the House uses an electronic voting board above the balcony to keep track of member votes. The Senate still uses voice votes recorded by the clerk of the Senate. ■ *What are some of the challenges that the House faces more acutely than the Senate because of its size?*

Of the People — THE GLOBAL COMMUNITY

How the World Views the United Nations

The past half century has produced a long list of international organizations, such as the World Trade Organization, that are designed to encourage greater trade and economic coordination. In some ways, these organizations behave like a blend of legislatures and courts—they take votes on key issues and often impose penalties on nations that violate international rules.

The United Nations (U.N.) is the most visible of these international legislatures. With more than 190 member nations, the United Nations often makes decisions on war and peace, addresses international health, and draws on its members for its own peacekeeping forces that seek to maintain stability in war-torn countries. The United Nations has a general voting assembly of all members and a powerful Security Council that can veto action from the General Assembly. In a sense, the General Assembly is the legislature.

The world has different opinions on whether this "super-government" works. According to the Pew Global Survey, support for the United Nations has increased slightly throughout the past five years.

The Japanese remain skeptical of the United Nations, perhaps because their nation is not a permanent member of the Security Council. Moreover, Japan receives relatively little support from the United Nations' health programs and has been reluctant to contribute troops to U.N. peacekeeping forces.

CRITICAL THINKING QUESTIONS

1. In our sample of countries, people in Nigeria and Mexico have the most favorable opinions of the United Nations. Why might that be?
2. Why might Japan's not being a permanent member of the Security Council affect public opinion in Japan toward the United Nations?

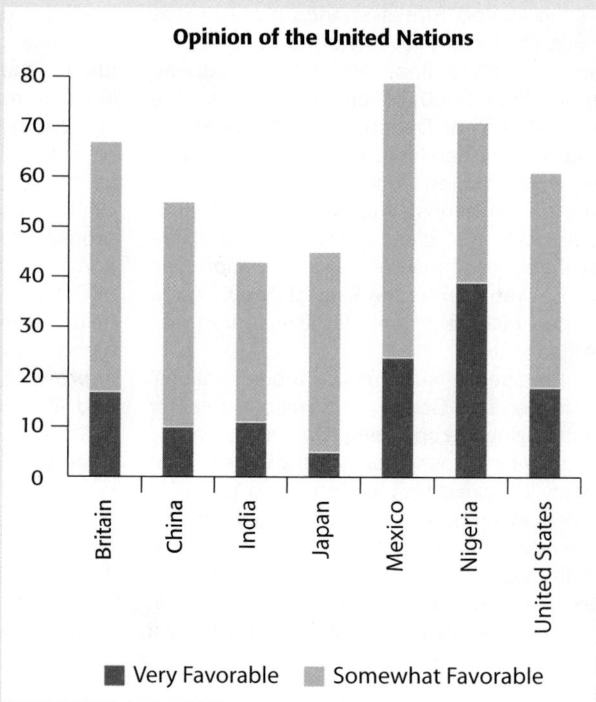

party caucus
A meeting of the members of a party in a legislative chamber to select party leaders and to develop party policy. Called a *conference* by the Republicans.

majority leader
The legislative leader selected by the majority party who helps plan party strategy, confers with other party leaders, and tries to keep members of the party in line.

minority leader
The legislative leader selected by the minority party as spokesperson for the opposition.

whip
The party leader who is the liaison between the leadership and the rank-and-file in the legislature.

closed rule
A procedural rule in the House of Representatives that prohibits any amendments to bills or provides that only members of the committee reporting the bill may offer amendments.

appoint members to temporary committees (but not to the major committees that help make the laws).

The Speaker is usually selected on a vote by the majority **party caucus,** called *the party conference* by Republicans, which is all of the members of a party in the legislative chamber. The caucus also elects party officers and committee chairs, approves committee assignments, and often helps the Speaker decide which issues will come first on the legislative calendar. However, because the Speaker is always selected first, he or she has the most important voice in determining all these choices.

Other House Officers The Speaker is assisted by the **majority leader,** who helps plan party strategy, confers with other party leaders, and tries to keep members of the party in line. The minority party elects the **minority leader,** who usually becomes Speaker when his or her party gains a majority in the House. (These positions are also sometimes called majority and minority *floor leaders.*) Assisting each floor leader are the party **whips.**

The House Rules Committee The House Rules Committee is almost certainly the most powerful committee in either chamber. Under the much tighter rules that govern the larger House, the Rules Committee decides the rules governing the length of the floor debate on any legislative issue and sets limits on the number and kinds of floor amendments that will be allowed. By refusing to grant a *rule,* which is a ticket to the floor, the Rules Committee can delay consideration of a bill. A **closed rule** prohibits amendments altogether or provides that only members of the committee reporting the bill may offer amendments; closed rules are usually reserved for tax and spending bills. An **open rule** permits debate within the overall time allocated to the bill.

Leading the Senate

The Senate has the same basic committee structure, elected party leadership, and decentralized power as the House, but because the Senate is a smaller body, its procedures are more informal, and it permits more time for debate. It is a more open, fluid, and decentralized body now than it was a generation or two ago. Indeed, it is often said that the Senate has 100 separate power centers and is so splintered that party leaders have difficulty arranging the day-to-day schedule.[9]

The Senate is led by the Senate majority leader, who is elected by the majority party. When the majority leader is from the president's party, the president becomes the party's most visible leader on Capitol Hill and in the nation as a whole. However, when the majority leader and the president are from different parties, the Senate majority leader is considered his or her party's national spokesperson. Senator Harry Reid (D-Nev.) was elected as the current Senate majority leader in 2007 after Democrats persuaded the two independents to help create a majority. Although that majority grew to 60 voters in 2009, it dropped to just a handful of seats after the 2010 midterm elections. Reid barely retained his seat after a tough reelection campaign against a well-financed opponent.

Although the majority leader has great authority, Senate floor debate is actually led by a **president pro tempore,** usually the most senior member of the majority party. Presiding over the Senate on most occasions is a thankless chore, so the president pro tempore regularly delegates this responsibility to junior members of the chamber's majority party. During controversial debates when there might be a tie vote, the vice president plays this role.

Party machinery in the Senate is similar to that in the House. There are party caucuses (conferences), majority and minority floor leaders, and party whips. Each party has a *policy committee,* composed of party leaders, which is theoretically responsible for the party's overall legislative program. In the Senate, the party policy committees help the leadership monitor legislation and provide policy expertise. Moreover, the Senate's rules allow individual senators to offer amendments on virtually any topic to a pending bill, occasionally allowing them to delay passage of a bill long enough to prevent passage.[10]

open rule
A procedural rule in the House of Representatives that permits floor amendments within the overall time allocated to the bill.

president pro tempore
An officer of the Senate selected by the majority party to act as chair in the absence of the vice president.

filibuster
A procedural practice in the Senate whereby a senator refuses to relinquish the floor and thereby delays proceedings and prevents a vote on a controversial issue.

cloture
A procedure for terminating debate, especially filibusters, in the Senate.

Individual senators also have the power to engage in unlimited debate, known as the **filibuster,** which was invented in the 1830s. A filibuster allows any individual senator to delay Senate proceedings by holding the floor continuously, thereby preventing action. Filibusters often begin with an individual senator issuing a legislative hold, putting a stop to all action. At one time, the filibuster was a favorite weapon of southern senators for blocking civil rights legislation.

A filibuster can be ended by invoking **cloture.** The rule specifies that the question of curtailing debate must be put to a vote two days after 16 senators sign a petition asking for cloture. If three-fifths of senators (60 of the 100 members) vote in favor of cloture, no senator may speak on the measure under consideration for more than one hour. Once invoked, cloture requires that the final vote on the measure be taken after no more than 30 hours of debate.[11]

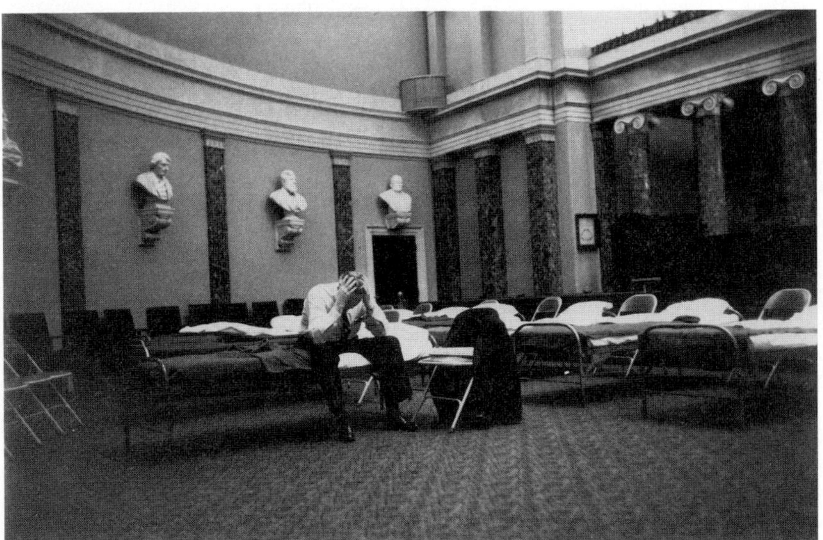

Old-fashioned filibusters went through the night. Here, a senator sits on his cot awaiting action to break a filibuster on the Civil Rights Act. Today, the threat alone of a filibuster can require that legislation has a supermajority in order to pass.

Congressional Committees

Committees are the workhorses of Congress. They draft legislation, review nominees, conduct investigations of executive branch departments and agencies, and are usually responsible for ironing out differences between House and Senate versions of the same legislation.

standing committee
A permanent committee established in a legislature, usually focusing on a policy area.

special or select committee
A congressional committee created for a specific purpose, sometimes to conduct an investigation.

joint committee
A committee composed of members of both the House of Representatives and the Senate; such committees oversee the Library of Congress and conduct investigations.

Types of Committees In theory, all congressional committees are created anew in each new Congress. But most continue with little change from Congress to Congress. **Standing committees** are the most durable and are the sources of most bills, whereas **special** or **select committees** come together to address both short-term and long-term issues such as investigating the September 11th terrorist attacks, but they rarely author legislation. **Joint committees** have members from both the House and the Senate and exist either to study an issue of interest to the entire Congress or to oversee congressional support agencies such as the Governmental Accountability Office (www.gao.gov).

Of the various types of committees, standing committees are the most important for making laws and representing constituents, and they fall into six types: (1) rules and administration, (2) budget, (3) authorizing, (4) appropriations, (5) revenue, and (6) oversight. (See Table 7–2.)

1. *Rules and Administration Committees* Rules committees in both chambers determine the basic operations of their chamber—for example, how many staffers individual members get and what the ratio of majority to minority members and staff will be. Again, because of the number of members it must control, the House Rules Committee is more powerful than its twin in the Senate. As noted earlier, the House Rules Committee has special responsibility

TABLE 7–2 Congressional Standing Committees, 2010–2011

House	Senate
RULES COMMITTEES	RULES COMMITTEE
House Administration	Rules and Administration
Rules	
Standards of Official Conduct	
BUDGET COMMITTEE	BUDGET COMMITTEE
Budget	Budget
AUTHORIZING COMMITTEES	AUTHORIZING COMMITTEES
Agriculture	Agriculture, Nutrition, and Forestry
Armed Services	Armed Services
Education and Labor	Banking, Housing, and Urban Affairs
Energy and Commerce	Commerce, Science, and Transportation
Financial Services	Energy and Natural Resources
Foreign Affairs	Environment and Public Works
Homeland Security	Foreign Affairs
Judiciary	Health, Education, Labor, and Pensions
Natural Resources	Judiciary
Science and Technology	Small Business and Entrepreneurship
Small Business	Veterans Affairs
Transportation and Infrastructure	
Veterans Affairs	
APPROPRIATIONS COMMITTEE	APPROPRIATIONS COMMITTEE
Appropriations	Appropriations
REVENUE COMMITTEES	REVENUE COMMITTEES
Budget	Budget
Ways and Means (Revenue and Budget)	Finance
OVERSIGHT COMMITTEES	OVERSIGHT COMMITTEES
Oversight and Government Reform	Homeland Security and Governmental Affairs

for giving each bill a rule, or ticket, to the floor of the House and determines what, if any, amendments to a bill will be permitted and how long the bill can be debated.

2. *Budget Committees* There is one budget committee for the House and Senate each. They were created as permanent standing committees in 1974 to give each chamber greater information and discipline on the overall federal budget. They set broad targets for spending and taxes at the start of each session of Congress and push authorizing and appropriations committees to follow those guidelines as they work on legislation. In theory, everything that the House and Senate do with the budget must be reconciled against the targets that the budget committees set.

3. *Authorizing Committees* Authorizing committees pass the laws that tell government what to do. The House and Senate education and labor committees, for example, are responsible for setting rules governing the federal government's student loan programs, including who can apply, how much they can get, where the loans come from, and how defaults are handled. Authorizing committees are also responsible for reviewing past programs that are about to expire. In the Senate, they also hold confirmation hearings for the president's political appointees.

4. *Appropriations Committees* Appropriations committees make decisions about how much money government will spend on authorized programs. Although there is only one appropriations committee in each chamber, each appropriations committee has one subcommittee for each of the 13 appropriations bills that must be enacted each year to keep government running.

5. *Revenue Committees* Revenue and budget committees deal with raising the money appropriating committees spend. Because it exists to raise revenues through taxes, the House Ways and Means Committee is one of the most powerful committees in Congress, for it both raises and authorizes spending. Although the appopriations committee determines how much is spent on specific programs, the Ways and Means Committee in the only committee in either chamber that can originate tax and revenue legislation. It is also responsible for making basic decisions on the huge Social Security and Medicare programs.

6. *General Oversight Committees* There are two major oversight committees in Congress: the House Oversight and Government Reform Committee and the Senate Homeland Security and Governmental Affairs Committee. Both committees have wide latitude to investigate the performance of government. They are also free to authorize programs for fixing government-wide programs. The oversight committees do not generally have authority to authorize such reforms for individual departments and agencies of government, however. This responsibility belongs to the specific authorizing committee responsible for the individual department or agency.

Choosing Committee Members Each political party controls the selection of standing committee members. Because some committees are more prestigious than others, the debate over committee assignments can be intense. These committees control more important programs or more money and give their members important advantages in helping their home districts.

Each chamber and party is responsible for choosing committee members. In the House, Republicans choose their committee members through their Committee on Committees, which is composed of one member from each state that has Republican representation in the House, whereas Democrats choose their committee members through their Steering and Policy Committee. In turn, Senate Republicans and Democrats both use their Steering Committees to make assignments. Both chambers make their selections based on an applicant's preferences, talent and party loyalty, and the needs of their district or state.

Most committee chairs are selected on the basis of the **seniority rule;** the member of the majority party with the longest continuous service on the committee becomes chair on the retirement of the current chair or a change in the party in control of Congress. The seniority rule lessens the influence of states or districts where the two parties are more evenly matched and where there is more turnover.[12]

Nancy Pelosi (above), Speaker of the House since 2007, lost her position as a result of the 2010 elections in which Republicans won more than enough seats to take over the majority. The new Speaker of the House is Ohio Republican John Boehner (below), a much more conservative member of his party

seniority rule
A legislative practice that assigns the chair of a committee or subcommittee to the member of the majority party with the longest continuous service on the committee.

Members of the Black Caucus often meet to decide what its members should do on particular issues. ■ *What are some of the advantages for members of Congress of organizing into caucuses based on shared interests?*

The choice of a committee chair in either chamber can make a very big difference on policy. Having decided not to run for reelection in 2010, Senate Banking Committee Chairman Chris Dodd (D-Conn.) turned over his chairmanship to Tim Johnson (D-S.D.). Dodd had been a passionate advocate of banking reform designed to protect consumers from credit card abuses. In contrast, Johnson was the only Democrat in the Senate to vote against Dodd's 2009 legislation to stop unreasonable credit card interest rates. South Dakota is home to many of the nation's largest credit card companies, most notably CitiBank, so Johnson will likely take the Banking Committee in a very different direction as long as Democrats control the Senate.

The Special Role of Conference Committees Given the differences between the House and the Senate, it is not surprising that the version of a bill passed by one chamber may differ substantially from the version passed by the other. Only if both houses pass an absolutely identical measure can it become law. Most of the time, one house accepts the language of the other, but approximately 10–12 percent of all bills passed, usually major ones, must be referred to a **conference committee**—a special committee of members from each chamber that settles the differences between versions.[13] Both parties are represented on conference committees, but the majority party has more members.

Caucuses Caucuses are best defined as informal committees that allow individual members to promote shared legislative interests. There are caucuses for House members only, for senators only, and for members of both chambers together.[14]

How a Bill Becomes a Law

LEARNING **OBJECTIVE**

7.4 Identify the steps by which a bill becomes a law and the ways a bill can be stopped at each step.

Congress operates under a system of multiple vetoes. The framers intentionally dispersed powers so that no would-be tyrant or majority could accumulate enough authority to oppress the nation. Follow a bill through the legislative process, and there are dozens of ways it can be killed. Only approximately one out of ten bills even receives minimal attention. In 2010, members of Congress introduced more than 1,500 bills but passed less than 300.[15]

How Ideas Become Bills

Most members come to Washington to make a difference for their party and country. Members of Congress clearly care about national issues such as education, energy, the economy, and foreign policy. In choosing ideas for legislation, they often secure their reputations as leading thinkers far into the future. Fifteen years after leaving the Senate, David L. Boren continues to provide national leadership as president of the University of Oklahoma and is often called upon for advice on difficult issues.

How Bills Become Laws

A bill must win many small contests on the way to final passage. There are four broad steps from beginning to end: (1) introduction, which means putting a formal proposal before the House or the Senate; (2) committee review, which includes holding a hearing and "marking up" the bill; (3) floor debate and passage, which means getting on the legislative calendar, passing once in each chamber, surviving a conference to iron out any differences between the House and Senate versions, and passing once again in each chamber; and (4) presidential approval. These steps are summarized in Figure 7–2: How a Bill Becomes a Law.

conference committee
A committee appointed by the presiding officers of each chamber to adjust differences on a particular bill passed by each in different form.

Introducing a Bill House members introduce a bill by placing it into a mahogany box (called the *hopper*) on a desk at the front of the House chamber; senators introduce a bill by

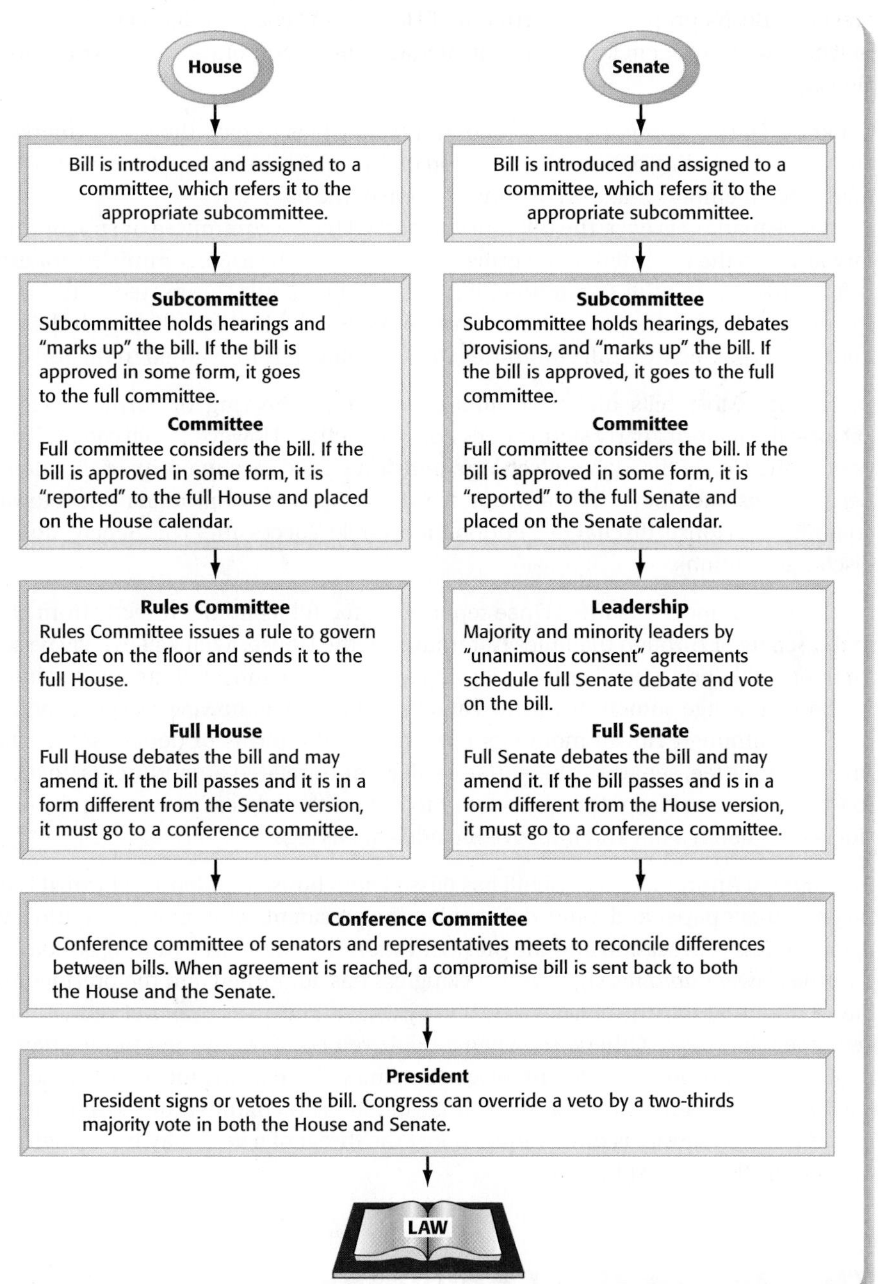

FIGURE 7–2 **How a Bill Becomes a Law.** ■ *Analyzing this legislative process, why is it so much easier for a bill to be killed than passed?*

either handing it to the clerk of the Senate or by presenting it to their colleagues in a floor speech. In the more informal Senate, members sometimes short-circuit the formalities by offering a bill as an amendment to pending legislation. A bill that comes from the House is always designated H.R. (House of Representatives) followed by its number, and a bill from the Senate is always designated S. (Senate) followed by its number. Presidents have no authority to introduce legislation, although they recommend many proposals.

Committee Review Once a bill has been introduced in either chamber, it is read into the record as a formal proposal and referred to the appropriate committee—tax bills to Ways and Means or Finance; farm bills to Agriculture; technology bills to Science, Space, and Technology; small business to Small Business; and so forth. The parliamentarian in each chamber decides where to send each bill.

The Referral Decision Although most bills are referred to a single committee, particularly complex bills may be referred simultaneously or sequentially to multiple committees.

President Bush's proposed Department of Homeland Security bill was so complicated and touched so many agencies that it was managed by a temporary special committee in the House.

Markup Once a committee or subcommittee decides to pass the bill, it "marks it up" to clean up the wording or amend its version of the bill. The term *markup* refers to the pencil marks that members make on the final version of the bill.

Once markup is over, the bill must be passed by the committee or subcommittee and forwarded to the next step in the process. If it is passed by a subcommittee, for example, it is forwarded to the full committee; if it is passed by a full committee in the House, it is then forwarded to the House Rules Committee for a rule that will govern debate on the floor; if it is passed by a full committee in the Senate, it is forwarded to the full chamber.

Discharge Most bills die in committee without a hearing or further review, largely because the majority party simply does not favor action. However, a bill can be forced to the floor of the House through a **discharge petition** signed by a majority of the membership. Because most members share a strong sense of reciprocity, or mutual respect toward other committees, House discharge petitions are rarely successful. The Senate does not use discharge petitions.

discharge petition
A petition that, if signed by a majority of the members of the House of Representatives, will pry a bill from committee and bring it to the floor for consideration.

rider
A provision attached to a bill—to which it may or may not be related—in order to secure its passage or defeat.

pocket veto
A veto exercised by the president after Congress has adjourned; if the president takes no action for ten days, the bill does not become law and is not returned to Congress for a possible override.

override
An action taken by Congress to reverse a presidential veto, requiring a two-thirds majority in each chamber.

Floor Debate and Passage Once reported to the full chamber directly from committee in the Senate or through the Rules Committee in the House, a bill will usually be scheduled for floor action or dropped entirely. Having come this far, most bills are passed into law.

Final passage sometimes comes at a very high price, however, especially for spending bills. Although House members must accept the terms of debate set by the House Rules Committee, senators often attach **riders,** or unrelated amendments, to a bill, either to win concessions from the sponsors or to reduce the odds of passage. Sponsors can use riders to sweeten a bill and improve the odds of passage.

Presidential Approval Once a bill has passed both houses in identical form, it is inscribed on parchment paper and hand-delivered to the president, who may *sign* it into law or *veto* it. If Congress is in session and the president waits ten days (not counting Sundays), the bill becomes law *without* his signature. If Congress has adjourned and the president waits ten days without signing the bill, it is defeated by what is known as a **pocket veto.** After a pocket veto, the bill is dead. Otherwise, when a bill is vetoed, it is returned to the chamber of its origin by the president with a message explaining the reasons for the veto. Congress can vote to **override** the veto by a two-thirds vote in each chamber, but assembling such an extraordinary majority is often difficult. Just the threat of a veto may be enough to derail a bill, but the threat must be real.

The Job of the Legislator

LEARNING **OBJECTIVE**

7.5 Characterize the two ways legislators represent their constituents, and identify the various influences on their votes.

Membership in Congress was once a part-time job. Legislators came to Washington for a few terms, averaged less than five years of continuous service, and returned to private life. Pay was low, and Washington was no farther than a carriage ride from home.[16]

Congress started to meet more frequently in the late 1800s, pay increased, and being a member became increasingly attractive.[17] In the 1850s, roughly half of all House members retired or were defeated at each election; by 1900, the number who left at the end of each term had fallen to roughly one-quarter; by the 1970s, it was barely a tenth. Even in the 1994 congressional elections, when Republicans won the House majority for the first time in 40 years, 90 percent of House incumbents who ran for reelection won.[18]

As members of Congress became attached to their careers, they began to abandon many of the norms, or informal rules, that once guided their behavior in office.[19] The old norms were simple. Members were supposed to specialize in a small number of issues (the norm of specialization), defer to members with longer tenure in office (the norm of seniority), never criticize anyone personally (the norm of courtesy), and wait their turn to speak and introduce legislation (the norm of apprenticeship). As longtime House Speaker

YOU WILL DECIDE Should Congress Create a College Football Playoff?

Congress had many issues on its agenda in 2010, including health care reform, unemployment, the wars in Iraq and Afghanistan, and global climate change. But as with other congresses in history, it also had time for less important bills. In December 2009, Representative Joe Barton (R-Tex.) introduced a bill to require the National Collegiate Athletic Conference to create a national football playoff.

Barton was incensed that the undefeated Texas Christian University football team, champion of the Mountain West Conference, had been excluded from the Bowl Championship Series (BCS) championship game in 2009. He was supported by members of the Western Athletic Conference, which was incensed that Boise State had been excluded in 2009, too.

Barton's bill was quite simple. It prohibited any person to promote, market, or advertise a post-season NCAA Division I football bowl game as a championship or national championship game unless it was the final game of a single elimination post-season playoff system for which *all* NCAA Division I schools are eligible. Using the Federal Trade Commission Act as the enforcement tool, the bill would subject the BCS to stiff penalties if it continued to advertise or otherwise promote its final game as a championship. In HR 390, "College Football Playoff Act," Congress found that college football games involve and affect interstate commerce, and therefore Congress had the constitutional power to act on the issue, and the economic reasons to protect non-BCS schools.

What do you think? Should Congress create a college football playoff? What are the arguments for and against this?

THINKING IT THROUGH

Barton was clearly serious about the legislation, as was a newly created political action committee called Playoff PAC, which funded an advertisement supporting a national playoff that aired during halftime of the TCU-Boise State game on Monday, January 4, 2010. (The commercial can be viewed at www.youtube.com/user/Playoff PAC.) Moreover, the public was sympathetic to the proposal. According to a December 2009 Quinnipiac University Poll, 63 percent of Americans approved of a new playoff system.

However, many members of Congress objected to using scarce legislative time for such a seemingly trivial issue. "With all due respect," Representative John Barrow (D-Ga.) told Barton, "I really think we have more important things to spend our time on." As for the public, despite support for a national playoff, nearly half also said that they did not think Congress should resolve the issue.

The case for reform was well made—most pundits and members of Congress appear to want a playoff system. So does President Obama. Just after winning the 2008 presidential election and right before the 2008 BCS that Florida won, Obama said he was in favor of a playoff.

Furthermore, Congress can handle multiple issues, big and small, at the same time, especially because most bills pass with minimal debate or controversy. As Representative Bobby Rush (D-Ill.) said, "We can walk and chew gum at the same time." (Updates on the bill can be found at www.GovTrac.us/Congress. Just enter the bill number in the search field.)

Critical Thinking Questions

1. Should Congress take on issues such a national college playoff game and steroid abuse by baseball players?
2. Does the playoff bill help or hurt Congress's reputation among the American public?
3. Should the president have made any comments on the bill? Does his support increase the chances of eventual passage?

SOURCE: ESPN.com, "Subcommittee OKs College Playoff Bill," December 9, 2009, accessible at http://sports.espn.go.com/espn/print?id=4727426&type=story.

Sam Rayburn once said, new members were to go along in order to get along, and to be seen and not heard.

Legislators as Representatives

Congress has a split personality. On the one hand, it is a *lawmaking institution* that writes laws and makes policy for the entire nation. In this capacity, all the members are expected to set aside their personal ambitions and perhaps even the concerns of their own constituencies.

Individual members of Congress perceive their roles differently. Some believe they should serve as **delegates** from their districts, finding out what "the folks back home" want and acting accordingly. The word "delegate" refers to a member who tries to do what constituents want. Other members see themselves as **trustees** to act and vote according to their own view of what is best for their district and state, and the nation. The word refers to a member who acts on what he or she thinks is best for the district and country.

delegate
An official who is expected to represent the views of his or her constituents even when personally holding different views; one interpretation of the role of the legislator.

trustee
An official who is expected to vote independently based on his or her judgment of the circumstances; one interpretation of the role of the legislator.

Former Oklahoma Senator David Boren (D) at work in the Senate. Future Secretary of Defense Robert Gates and Senator Robert Dole sit to his right. Boren retired in 1994 and currently serves as the co-chairman of the President's Intelligence Advisory Board under Barack Obama.

Most legislators shift back and forth between the delegate and trustee roles, depending on their perception of the public interest, their standing in the last and next elections, and the pressures of the moment. Most also view themselves more as free agents than as instructed delegates for their districts. And recent research suggests they often *are* free. Although approximately half of citizens do not know how their representatives voted on major legislation, most still believe their representative voted with the district or state. Moreover, members of Congress spend a great deal of time helping their constituency, reaching out to swing voters, and worrying about how a vote on a controversial issue will "play" back home.[20]

Members cannot represent their constituents through their experiences as ordinary Americans, however. They are certainly very different from the rest of the public. They are older on average, more educated, and less diverse by gender and race. They are also much more likely to be lawyers.

Making Legislative Choices

Approximately 8,000 bills are introduced in the House and Senate during a two-year Congress, but only a handful receive hearings, even fewer reach the floor, and one in eight become law. Although House members and senators cast 1,000 votes each year, most are voice votes on noncontroversial legislation and procedures.[21] Because members pay attention to different factors depending on the bill at hand, they vote on the basis of a long list of varying influences that are presented in alphabetical order below.

Colleagues Their busy schedules and the great number of votes force legislators to depend on the advice of like-minded colleagues and close friends in Congress. In particular, they look to respected members of the committee who worked on a bill.[22]

A member may also vote with a colleague in the expectation that the colleague will later vote for a measure about which the member is concerned—a practice called **logrolling,** meaning that members trade among themselves to get the legislation (log) moving. Some vote trading takes place to build coalitions so that members can "bring home the bacon" to their constituents. Other vote trading reflects reciprocity in congressional relations or deference to colleagues' superior information or expertise.

logrolling
Mutual aid and vote trading among legislators.

Congressional Staff The complexity of the issues and increasingly demanding schedules created a demand for additional congressional staff. Because both chambers have roughly equal amounts of money for staff, the 100 senators and their committees have much larger staffs than their 435 House counterparts. Many congressional staffers work in district and state offices back home to create great incumbency advantage.

Constituents Members of Congress rarely vote against the strong wishes of their constituents, but they often think their constituents are more interested in a particular issue than they really are.[23] Representatives mostly hear from the **attentive public**—meaning citizens who follow public affairs closely—rather than the general public. Members of Congress are generally concerned about how they will explain their votes, especially as election day approaches. Even if only a few voters are aware of their stand on a given issue, this group may make the difference between victory and defeat.

attentive public
Citizens who follow public affairs closely.

Ideology Members of Congress are influenced by their own experiences and attitudes about the role of government.[24] Ideology is closely related to a member's party as a predictor of congressional voting.

Party allegiance is not a perfect predictor of ideology. In 1994, for example, moderate and conservative Democrats created the "Blue Dog Coalition" to work for budget cuts and increased defense spending. Members called themselves "blue dogs" because they felt they had been "choked blue" by liberals in their party. By 2009, the coalition had 54 members, including some of the most senior members in the House. The coalition also had enough votes to force major compromises on a long list of legislative proposals, including the economic stimulus package and health care reform.

Interest Groups Interest groups influence the legislative process in many ways. They make contributions to congressional campaigns, testify before committees, provide information to legislative staff, and build public pressure for or against their cause. Congressional lobbying has existed since the early 1800s and is a perfectly legal exercise of the First Amendment right to petition government (see Chapter 4).

Interest groups often cancel each other out by taking opposing positions on issues, thereby killing a bill. Some of this maneuvering occurs at the subcommittee level and is almost invisible to the public. But it is always visible to the interest groups themselves and to Congress. "The result," says Senator Joe Lieberman (I-Conn.), "is that everyone on Capitol Hill is keeping a close eye on everyone else, creating a self-adjusting system of checks and balances."[25]

Constituents and interest groups often put pressure on Congress in person. Every January, opponents of abortion march on Washington. ■ *How does this march help citizens express their concerns? Do marches like this matter to congress?*

By the People

MAKING A DIFFERENCE

Staying in Touch with Congress

There are many ways that citizens can stay connected to Congress and their members, not the least of which are traditional means such as attending town hall meetings, sending letters, and voting.

More recently, however, members have started to use social networks such as Facebook to cultivate support and raise money. Some have even set up Twitter sites to keep their constituents informed on their work. As of January 2010, 19 members of the Senate and 51 members of the House were tweeting regularly with a mix of big and small news. They seem to accept TweetCongress.org's new version of the preamble to the Constitution: "We the Tweeple of the United States, in order to form a more perfect government, establish communication, and promote transparency do hereby tweet the Congress of the United States of America."

Their staffers keep track of the traffic, summarize the tweets, and provide advice on how to reach out more effectively to the kinds of people who tweet or use Facebook. Citizens can make a difference through these new media by commenting on blogs or setting up their own Twitter reviews.

QUESTIONS

1. Is social networking a new form of political participation? How did it affect President Obama's election chances?
2. Is tweeting an effective platform for sharing political ideas?
3. What other forms of social networking can be considered a form of public service? Do blogs qualify? What about Facebook?

Here is what Representative John Carter (R-Tex.) tweeted early in 2010:

R-TX John Carter: New year, same question: where are the jobs? http://ow.ly/Ud41 #jobs #tcot #tlot (via @replynnjenkins)

R-TX John Carter: If you're looking for work in the Austin area: Census Bureau plans to hire 4,000 in Central Texas for 2010 tally. http://shar.es/aQfEk

Party Members generally vote with their party. Whether as a result of party pressure or natural affinity, on major bills, most Democrats tend to be arrayed against most Republicans. Partisan voting increased in the House after the early 1970s and has intensified even more since the 1994 elections. Indeed, party-line voting has been greater in recent years than at any time in recent decades, in part because each party has become more liberal or more conservative. Since 2000, nearly 90 percent of congressional Democrats and Republicans have voted with their party on key votes, compared with less than 70 percent on average during the 1970s, and less than 80 percent in the 1980s.[26]

The President Presidents wield a variety of tools for influencing Congress, not least of which is the ability to distribute government resources to their friends. Presidents also help set the legislative agenda through their annual State of the Union Address, the budget, and assorted legislative messages, and they lobby Congress on particularly important issues.

When asked why they vote one way or the other, members of Congress tend to deny the president's influence. Presidents work hard to influence public opinion, and they have a long list of incentives to encourage congressional support, not the least of which are invitations to special White House dinners and federal grants to support key projects back home. Congress is also likely to rally around the president during times of national crisis, which is what helped Barack Obama win 97 percent of the congressional votes on which he took a clear position in 2009, easily besting every president since such scores were first collected more than 40 years ago.[27] (We will return to presidential influence in Congress in Chapter 8.)

Congressional Ethics

Members of Congress have never been under greater scrutiny regarding their conduct, in part because recent years have witnessed a parade of members accused and even convicted of trading their votes for cash and other gifts. "Super-lobbyist" Jack Abramoff admitted in 2006 that he had given several members of Congress free golfing trips, meals, and concert tickets in direct violation of congressional ethics rules.

Under the Constitution, Congress is responsible for punishing its own members. Although individual members are subject to federal prosecution for bribery and other criminal acts, the House and Senate set the more general rules for ethical conduct and investigate all complaints of misbehavior.

Under new rules enacted in September 2007, members of Congress may not accept any gifts or meals from any lobbyist. Although they can accept free admission at large meetings, conventions, discussions, and events where admission is free to other members, they may not accept free travel from any lobbyist.[28]

Finally, members may not accept any payment for making a speech, attending an event, or writing an article. Although they may accept free travel and expenses for making speeches and attending events, such travel must be related to their official duties as a member of Congress and publicly reported. These rules also apply to lobbyists, who may not offer gifts, free attendance, or travel.

The House and Senate enforce the rules through separate ethics committees (the House Committee on Standards of Official Conduct and the Senate Ethics Committee). Because the seats on both committees are equally divided between Democrats and Republicans (four on each side in the House, and three on each side in the Senate), and are filled through the normal committee selection process, members are under tremendous pressure not to hurt their own party.

Citizens can play an important role in monitoring congressional ethics, starting with careful monitoring of lobbying expenditures and campaign contributions. One of the best ways to get this information is from the Center for Responsive Politics, which operates a Web site called opensecrets.org. The Web site contains detailed information on what individual members of Congress spent on their campaigns, where the money came from, and how much they received from political action committees. The Web site also provides information on how much lobbyists spend each year trying to influence Congress. From 1989–2009, for example, AT&T spent more than $44 million lobbying Congress on cell phone issues, and state and local employee unions spent more than $41 million. By calling out their own reprsentatives on campaign spending and lobbying, citizens increase sensitivity to the issue that might lead to tighter regulations.

President Obama journeyed to Capitol Hill to address a joint session of Congress on the need for health care reform. Some Republicans booed the president during the speech, and one, Representative Joe Wilson (R-S.C.), was later reprimanded for shouting "you lie" in response to one of the president's explanations of the legislation. ■ *What are some of the reasons that the State of the Union address is such a good forum for the president to promote his legislative agenda?*

An Assessment of Congress

LEARNING **OBJECTIVE**

7.6 Evaluate the influence of citizens in the legislative process.

More than two centuries after its creation, Congress is a larger and very different kind of institution from the one the framers envisioned. It has become much more complex, more divided, and much more active. Although most incumbents are easily reelected, most campaign constantly to stay in office, creating what some observers have called the "permanent campaign." Members appear driven by their desire to win reelection, so that much of what takes place in Congress seems mainly designed to promote reelection. These efforts usually pay off: We have seen that those who seek reelection almost always win.

This *permanent campaign* also affects legislative progress. In an institution in which most members act as individual entrepreneurs, the task of providing institutional

House Republican majority leader Tom DeLay, otherwise known as "The Hammer," was driven out of office because of his connections to the Abramoff scandals. He later appeared on *Dancing with the Stars* in an effort to rehabilitate his reputation, but he lost in the early rounds.

leadership is increasingly difficult. With limited resources, and only sometimes aided by the president, congressional leaders are asked to bring together a diverse, fragmented, and independent institution. The congressional system acts only when majorities can be achieved. The framers clearly accomplished their original objective in creating a legislature that would rarely move quickly.

Citizens often complain about the lack of action, which is one reason why public approval of Congress is low. But citizens can play a role in speeding Congress up by demanding action from their own members. Even incumbents worry about losing elections. Indeed, as of late 2009, only 24 percent of Americans had a favorable view of Congress, compared with a 54 percent rating for President Obama. (See Figure 7–3 for the recent trend in public approval for Congress as measured by the NBC News/Wall Street Journal Poll.) By 2010, congressional approval remained at the all-time low.

Much of the public's recent discomfort with Congress involves the intense bargaining and conflict associated with passing major legislation such as health care reform. But in the longer term, it also reflects the performance of the economy. Americans are more favorable toward both Congress and the president when the economy is running smoothly, but they become understandably angry when the economy enters a downturn.

To the extent that citizens engage their members in tough conversations about the need to act on big issues such as health care, their members will listen. But individual citizens can be easily shouted down by organized interests and lobbyists. The question then is how to help citizens become more engaged in a constitutional system that sets checks and balances to stop action. Young Americans have a particular advantage in the effort—they understand the power of social networking.

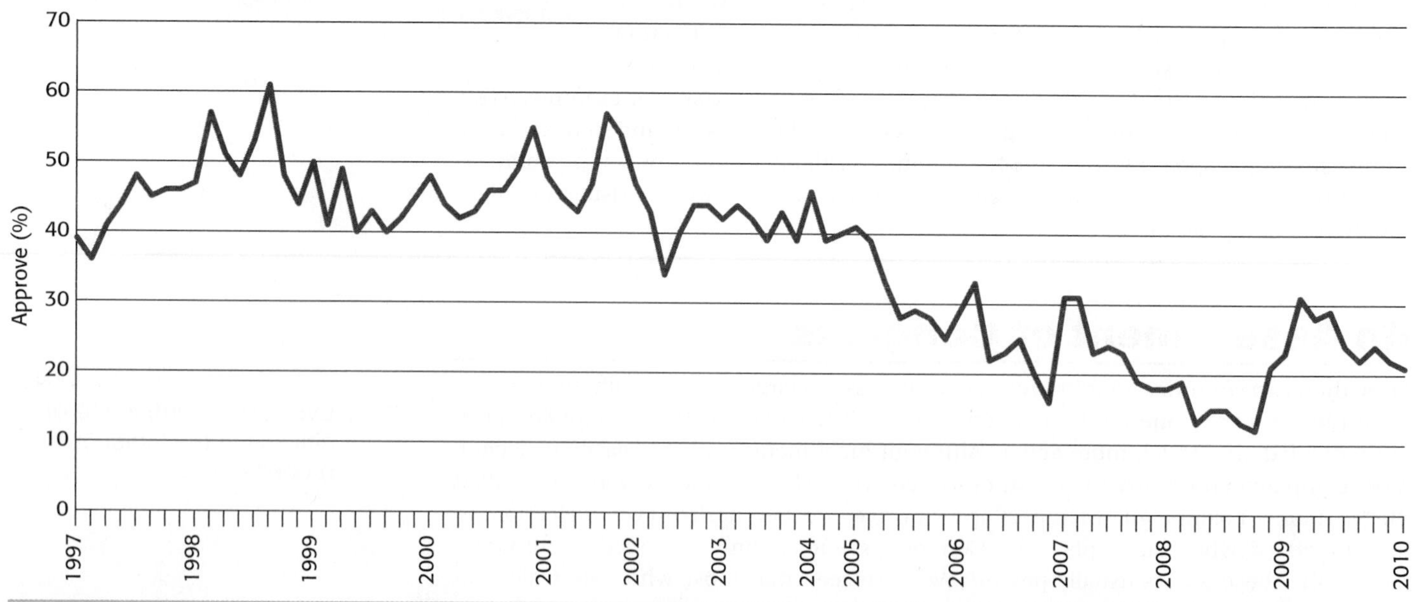

FIGURE 7–3 **Favorability Toward Congress, 1997–2010.** ■ *When were some of the highest and lowest points in Congressional approval? What reasons can you think of to explain these levels?*

SOURCE: http://pollingreport.com/congjob.htm, accessed May 16 2010.

CHAPTER SUMMARY

7.1 Describe the congressional election process and the advantages it gives incumbents.

The congressional election process requires decisions about who can run for office, when they run, and how long they serve. Most House elections concern local issues, whereas Senate elections are more likely to be about national concerns. Incumbents enjoy a variety of protections, including name visibility and the ability to send mail and other messages back home free of charge, to help constituents, and to raise money.

7.2 Differentiate the powers of Congress, and compare and contrast the structure and powers of the House and Senate.

Congress has express powers, implied powers, and checks and balances. The most important powers are the power to borrow and make money, regulate commerce, unify the country, declare and fund war, and create the inferior federal courts.

The most distinctive feature of Congress is its bicameralism, which the framers intended as a moderating influence on partisanship and possible error. The House has the power to propose legislation to raise revenue, whereas the Senate has the power to confirm presidential appointees (by a majority vote) and ratify treaties (by a two-thirds vote).

7.3 Compare and contrast the leadership systems used in the House and Senate, and explain how work is done through congressional committees.

The House is led by the Speaker, a majority and a minority leader, and whips in each party, whereas the Senate is led by a majority and a minority leader. The Senate is more difficult to lead because of its greater individualism, sometimes expressed through the use of holds and filibusters to control the legislative process.

Most of the work in Congress is done in committees and subcommittees, which are classified into six types: (1) rules and administration, (2) budget, (3) appropriations, (4) authorizing, (5) revenue, and (6) oversight. Authorizing committees author all legislation, whereas appropriations committees spend the money needed to implement the legislation.

7.4 Identify the steps by which a bill becomes a law and the ways a bill can be stopped at each step.

A bill moves through a tortuous process to become a law—an idea must first be converted into a proposal, then be introduced and referred to a committee, receive a hearing and markup, and move to the floor. Although all formal bills are referred to committees for consideration, very few receive a hearing, even fewer are marked up and sent to the floor, and fewer still are enacted by both chambers and signed into law by the president. In addition, the legislative obstacle course sometimes includes filibusters, riders, holds, and the occasional override of a presidential veto.

7.5 Characterize the two ways legislators represent their constituents, and identify the various influences on their votes.

Legislators must balance the needs of their constituents against the national good. In addressing constituent needs, they often act as representatives of public opinion in their home districts. In addressing national issues, they often act as trustees of the greater good. Members must balance these two roles.

Members of Congress vote on the basis of a long list of varying influences that include their colleagues, constituents, staff, ideology, their party, and the president. These influences vary in strength from issue to issue.

7.6 Evaluate the influence of citizens on the legislative process.

Citizens can influence Congress in many ways, not the least of which is voting in midterm elections, which have historically low turnout. They can also use a variety of methods to express their opinions, including Facebook and Twitter. And they register their concerns about the lack of progress on big issues such as health care through public opinion surveys and their level of congressional approval.

CHAPTER SELF-TEST

7.1 Describe the congressional election process and the advantages it gives incumbents.

1. How are congressional elections set, and where do they occur?
2. In a few sentences, outline the advantages an incumbent member of Congress has in elections.
3. HOLD FOR QUESTION ABOUT 2010 ELECTIONS

7.2 Differentiate the powers of Congress, and compare and contrast the structure and powers of the House and Senate.

4. List the five basic categories of congressional power.
5. Suggest three ways the two chambers of Congress check each others' power.
6. Write a brief essay explaining the major differences between the chambers of Congress and why the framers thought these differences were important.

7.3 Compare and contrast the leadership systems used in the House and Senate, and explain how work is done through congressional committees.

7. How is the leadership of the House different from the Senate?
8. How are members of Congress assigned to committees?

9. How do the differing committee structures in the House and Senate affect the way these bodies function?

7.4 Identify the steps by which a bill becomes a law and the ways a bill can be stopped at each step.

10. What are the steps in passing a law?
11. Why are conference committees so important to the legislative process?
12. Write a short essay on when and how to kill a bill.

7.5 Characterize the two ways legislators represent their constituents, and identify the various influences on their votes.

13. In a short essay, explain the major differences between a member of Congress acting as a trustee and acting as a delegate.
14. Imagine you are a member of Congress. In a paragraph, evaluate how you would determine your votes on bills. Would you vote the same way your constituency would, even if you disagreed? Would you vote against your party on a bad bill, even if it meant you would be barred from introducing legislation for your home state for the rest of the year?

7.6 Evaluate the influence of citizens on the legislative process.

15. Why are Americans often disappointed with the performance of Congress, and why do they give the president higher approval ratings than Congress? How might Congress improve its reputation?
16. Why would tweeting matter to a member of Congress?
17. Write a short essay on why voting is important. Are there times when voting is irrational?

mypoliscilab EXERCISES

Where participation leads to action!

Apply what you learned in this chapter on MyPoliSciLab.

Read on mypoliscilab.com

eText: Chapter 7

Study and Review on mypoliscilab.com

Pre-Test
Post-Test
Chapter Exam
Flashcards

Watch on mypoliscilab.com

Video: Unknown Wins South Carolina Senate Primary
Video: Kagan Hearing

Explore on mypoliscilab.com

Simulation: How a Bill Becomes a Law
Simulation: You Are a Member of Congress
Comparative: Comparing Legislatures
Timeline: The Power of the Speaker of the House
Visual Literacy: Congressional Redistricting
Visual Literacy: Why Is It So Hard to Defeat an Incumbent?

KEY TERMS

constituents, p. 220
reapportionment, p. 221
redistricting, p. 221
gerrymandering, p. 221
safe seat, p. 221
incumbent, p. 221
earmarks, p. 222
bicameralism, p. 224
enumerated powers, p. 225
Speaker, p. 227
party caucus, p. 228
majority leader, p. 228
minority leader, p. 228
whip, p. 228
closed rule, p. 228
open rule, p. 229
president pro tempore, p. 229
filibuster, p. 229
cloture, p. 229
standing committee, p. 230
special or select committee, p. 230
joint committee, p. 230
seniority rule, p. 231
conference committee, p. 232
discharge petition, p. 234
rider, p. 234
pocket veto, p. 234
override, p. 234
delegate, p. 235
trustee, p. 235
logrolling, p. 236
attentive public, p. 237

ADDITIONAL **RESOURCES**

FURTHER READING

E. SCOTT ADLER, *Why Congressional Reforms Fail: Reelection and the House Committee System* (University of Chicago Press, 2002).

SARAH A. BINDER, *Stalemate: Causes and Consequences of Legislative Gridlock* (Brookings Institution Press, 2003).

ROGER H. DAVIDSON, WALTER J. OLESZEK, AND **FRANCES E. LEE,** *Congress and Its Members,* 11th ed. (CQ Press, 2007).

CHRISTOPHER J. DEERING AND **STEVEN S. SMITH,** *Committees in Congress,* 3d ed. (CQ Press, 1997).

RICHARD F. FENNO, JR., *Home Style: House Members in Their Districts* (Little, Brown, 1978).

RICHARD F. FENNO JR., *Senators on the Campaign Trail: The Politics of Representation* (University of Oklahoma Press, 1996).

MORRIS P. FIORINA, *Congress: Keystone of the Washington Establishment,* 2d ed. (Yale University Press, 1989).

PAUL HERRNSON, *Congressional Elections,* 54th ed. (CQ Press, 2007).

GODFREY HODGSON, *The Gentleman from New York: Daniel Patrick Moynihan* (Houghton Mifflin, 2000).

GARY JACOBSON, *Politics of Congressional Elections,* 7th ed. (Longman, 2008).

LINDA KILLIAN, *The Freshmen: What Happened to the Republican Revolution?* (Westview Press, 1998).

THOMAS MANN AND **NORM ORNSTEIN,** *The Broken Branch: How Congress Is Failing America and How to Get It Back on Track* (Oxford University Press, 2006).

DAVID R. MAYHEW, *America's Congress: Actions in the Public Sphere, James Madison Through Newt Gingrich* (Yale University Press, 2002).

WALTER J. OLESZEK, *Congressional Procedures and the Policy Process,* 6th ed. (CQ Press, 2004).

RONALD M. PETERS JR., ED., *The Speaker: Leadership in the U.S. House of Representatives* (CQ Press, 1995).

BARBARA SINCLAIR, *Unorthodox Lawmaking: New Legislative Processes in the U.S. Congress,* 2d ed. (CQ Press, 2000).

WEB SITES

www.opencongress.org An easily accessible inventory of congressional activities and work, including lists of bills, members, committees, votes, issues, and campaign contributions.

www.GAO.gov The Web site for the Government Accountability Office, which provides studies on issues facing Congress.

www.CBO.gov The Web site for the Congressional Budget Office, which analyzes every bill for its costs and tracks key economic trends.

www.senate.gov The Senate's Web site. Pay particular notion to the historian's office and the oral histories section. Also click on "references," then "statistics and lists," "legislation and procedures," and "resume of congressional activity" to see how many bills have been introduced, have passed, how many days in sessions, and so forth.

www.house.gov The House's Web site. Links to all committees.

www.thomas.loc.gov The authoritative tracker of all legislation.

CHAPTER

8

The Presidency

The Personal Branch

President Barack Obama entered office with an extensive list of priorities for his first year. Name an international or domestic problem facing the nation, and Obama promised to address it. Within months of his inauguration on January 20, 2009, he had asked Congress for massive legislation to stimulate the sagging economy, health care for the nation's uninsured, action on global warming, new rules on credit card abuses, investments in the Interstate Highway System, action to curb tobacco use, expansion in volunteerism, greater openness in government, and improvements in education. It was the longest list of proposals since Lyndon Johnson pushed Congress to enact his "Great Society" reforms in the 1960s, and it reflected the president's extraordinary power to set the legislative agenda on Capitol Hill.

Obama's agenda included more than domestic proposals, however. His agenda also focused on the wars in Iraq and Afghanistan, both of which were central to his 2008 campaign for the presidency. He did not want the United States to withdraw its military forces immediately, but he clearly wanted to bring the wars to a successful end. Although military casualties were falling dramatically in Iraq, combat was increasing in Afghanistan. In 2009, 141 soldiers lost their lives in Iraq, compared with 491 deaths in Afghanistan. Half of the deaths in Iraq occurred in noncombat accidents, whereas nearly all of the deaths in Afghanistan came in firefights and bombings with insurgents.[1]

Obama came to his decision on Afghanistan after a long, often public process that involved a deep review of the situation. Unlike his predecessor, President George W. Bush, Obama rarely makes decisions on the spot. Rather, he tends to conduct what some critics call "seminars" on particular issues. He collects as much information as possible about a decision, seeks as many points of view as possible, and eventually reaches a decision based on his reading of the facts. His approach is admirable for its thoroughness but takes a great deal of time.

Obama used this long process in making his decision about Afghanistan. The process began with an initial request for 40,000 more troops from the U.S. military commander in Afghanistan. His hope was to bring enough troops to Afghanistan to pacify the entire country. Other advisors, including Vice President Joseph Biden, were skeptical about the effort. They proposed a much smaller increase in troops in the hope that the United States could help the Afghanistan government strengthen its military forces. As commander in chief under the Constitution, Obama had to make the final decision but was torn by the competing proposals.

The debate about the appropriate strategy dragged on for months as Obama worked through the issue. He finally decided to authorize 30,000 additional troops, but rather than focusing on defeating the Taliban, which had controlled Afghanistan when Osama bin Laden approved the terrorist attacks on New York City and Washington, D.C., in September 2001, Obama's objective was to "degrade" bin Laden's Al-Qaeda terrorist base. He also set a clear deadline for withdrawing the troops as quickly as possible. Obama wanted what he called a "faster surge" in U.S. troop strength and a much faster withdrawal.[2]

Obama's decision shows the extent of the president's authority to shape foreign policy through military action. Congress often complains about such decisions but is mostly unwilling to limit that action. As a result, citizens have few opportunities to influence foreign policy, and even less when the policies are secret. With so many other controversial issues confronting the country, the public did not react in any organized way to Obama's decision. There have been times in history, however, when citizen action has driven Congress and the president to alter foreign policy. Massive protests against the Vietnam War during the late 1960s clearly shaped the U.S. decision to end the conflict.

CHAPTER OUTLINE & CHAPTER LEARNING OBJECTIVES

The Structure and Powers of the Presidency

8.1 Describe the constitutional foundations of the presidency and of three presidential roles.

Controversies in Presidential Power

8.2 Evaluate the controversies surrounding presidents' assertion of additional executive powers.

Managing the Presidency

8.3 Outline the functions of the White House staff, Executive Office of the President, cabinet, and vice president.

The Job of the President

8.4 Characterize the various roles that presidents play.

Congress and the Presidency

8.5 Identify the sources of presidential–congressional conflict and the tools presidents use to influence Congress.

Judging Presidents

8.6 Identify factors that influence judgments about presidents.

Being president is one of the most difficult jobs in the world. Here, President Barack Obama meets with the four living ex-presidents to discuss general issues of governing the nation from the White House. ■ *What kind of knowledge can ex-presidents share with the current president, especially at the start of the new president's term in office?*

The framers of the Constitution both admired and feared the centralized leadership of a president. Although they knew a strong president was needed to protect the nation against foreign and domestic threats, they also worried about the potential abuse of power. This chapter will examine the framers' intent in designing the presidency, review the president's powers, and then turn to the continuing controversies surrounding the exercise of these powers. We will also explore the many jobs of the president and ask how Congress and the president work together and against each other in making the laws. We conclude with a discussion of how history judges presidents.

The Structure and Powers of the Presidency

LEARNING **OBJECTIVE**

8.1 Describe the constitutional foundations of the presidency and of three presidential roles.

The framers wanted the president to act with "dispatch" against threats, but they also worried that the president could become too powerful. Although they gave the president the power to run the executive branch, which now includes the White House and all departments and agencies, they limited the president's other powers to a relatively short list, including the power to wage wars declared by Congress, report to the nation from time to time on the State of the Union, nominate judges and executive appointees for Senate confirmation, and negotiate treaties. They wanted a presidential office that would steer clear of parties and factions, enforce the laws passed by Congress, handle communications with foreign governments, and help states put down disorders. They wanted a presidency strong enough to match Congress but not so strong that it would overpower Congress.

The framers believed the "jarrings of parties" in Congress were perfectly appropriate in making the laws but not in fighting wars and running the executive branch. They did not believe the president should have unlimited freedom to act, however. Having given a much longer list of powers to Congress, they saw the president as a powerful check on legislative action and essential to the administration of government. As Alexander Hamilton argued in *The Federalist,* No. 70, which explains the presidency in detail, "A feeble executive implies a feeble execution of the government. A feeble execution is but another phrase for a bad execution: And a government ill executed, whatever it may be in theory, must be in practice a bad government."[3]

Young citizens massed at the Lincoln Memorial on May Day, 1970, vowing to shut down the federal government to protest the Vietnam War. ■ *How might these protests have affected the president's abilities to make executive decisions about the war?*

parliamentary government
A form of government in which the legislature selects the prime minister or the president.

The Presidency and the Separation of Powers

Obama's power to act as commander in chief is part of the Constitution's separation of power. Even though Congress often gives the president the freedom to take action on foreign policy, it does retain the authority to cut off funding for foreign involvement, and the Senate is required to ratify all treaties with other nations.

Nevertheless, merely having three branches of a national government—legislative, executive, and judicial—does not by itself create a pure system of separated powers.

Unlike the United States, which has a separate path to the presidency through the electoral college, **parliamentary governments** elect their prime ministers from the parliament itself. In theory, this system makes the prime minister more influential—he or she controls both the executive and legislative branches. Great Britain is the oldest parliamentary government in the world, and its prime minister is possibly the most powerful. Becoming the prime minister is hardly easy—prime ministers must be members of Parliament, elected as their party's leader, and be able to lead their parties to a majority in a national election. Once in office, the prime minister has many of the same roles as the U.S. president.

India and Japan both follow this parliamentary system with several important differences. Like the British prime minister, the Indian prime minister can be removed from office through a vote of no confidence by the parliament. However, the Indian prime minister has the extraordinary power to suspend all political rights by declaring a national emergency. Even here, the parliament retains the power to overturn such declarations after two months. Also unlike the British system, the Indian system has often been governed by members of the same family. The Nehru family has ruled the country for nearly two-thirds of its 60 years of independence.

In the United States, however, the legislative, executive, and judicial branches are independent of one another. Although the legislative and executive branch are sometimes headed by the same political party, unified government can exist only if voters in enough states and districts vote for the same party over enough elections to control the House, Senate, presidency, and judiciary (whose members are nominated by the president and confirmed by the Senate).

The United States is one of the few world powers that is neither a parliamentary democracy nor a wholly executive-dominated government. Our Constitution plainly invites both Congress and the president to set policy and govern the nation.

David Cameron was selected as prime minister of the United Kingdom after a May 2010 election. He became the leader of government after collecting enough votes in parliament from a coalition of parties, none of which had won a clear majority in the election.

Leadership and policy change are likely only when Congress and the president, and sometimes the courts along with them, agree that new directions are desirable.

The Framers and the Presidency

The framers' most important decision about the presidency was also their first. Meeting on June 1, 1787, the Constitutional Convention decided there would be a single executive. Despite worries that a single president might lay the groundwork for a future monarchy, the framers also believed the new government needed energy in the executive. They were willing to increase the risk of tyranny in return for some efficiency.

Once past this first decision, the framers had to decide just how independent that executive would be from the rest of the national government. This meant finding an appropriate method of selection or election. Had they wanted Congress to select the president from among its members, the framers would have created a parliamentary system that would look more like the European governments we discussed previously. The delegates were initially divided on how the president would be selected. A small number favored direct election by the people, which Pennsylvania's James Wilson thought would ensure that the president was completely independent of Congress. The delegates rejected direct election in favor of the electoral college: Voters would cast their ballots for competing slates of electors, who would in turn cast their electoral votes for president.

The framers also gave the executive a four-year term of office, further balancing the House with its two-year terms and the Senate with its six-year terms. Although the framers were silent on the number of terms a president could serve, the Twenty-Second Amendment to the Constitution, ratified in 1951, limits presidents to two terms in office.

The framers created the position of vice president just in case the president left office before the end of the term. With little debate, they decided to give the vice president the power to break tie votes in the Senate. Otherwise, the vice president has no constitutional duties but to wait for the president to be incapacitated or otherwise unable to discharge the powers and duties of the presidency. In recent years, however, presidents have given their vice presidents greater responsibilities.[4]

The framers also established three simple qualifications for both offices. Under the Constitution, the president and vice president must be (1) at least 35 years old on inauguration day; (2) natural-born citizens of the United States, as opposed to immigrants who become citizens by applying to the U.S. government for naturalization; and (3) residents of the United States for the previous 14 years. The citizenship and residency requirements were designed to prevent a popular foreign-born citizen from capturing the office.

Presidents often make foreign policy and military decisions in the White House Situation Room. The room is in the basement of the White House and is completely secure. ■ *What might you expect in terms of the speed and cohesiveness of Situation Room decisions compared to legislative decisions?*

With this basic structure in place, the framers had to decide how the vice president would be selected. Once again, they created a remarkable electoral arrangement: The candidate who received the most electoral college votes would become president, and the candidate who came in second would become vice president. Any tie votes in the electoral college were to be broken by a majority vote in the House of Representatives.

It did not take long for the framers to discover the problem with this runner-up rule. The 1796 election produced Federalist President John Adams and Republican Vice President Thomas Jefferson. Because the two disagreed so sharply about the future of the country, Jefferson was rendered virtually irrelevant to government.

After a constitutional crisis in 1800, Congress decided to change the rule through a Constitution Amendment. Under the Twelfth Amendment, ratified in 1804, electors were allowed to cast separate votes for the president and vice president. This new practice encouraged candidates to run together as members of a **presidential ticket** that lists the presidential and vice presidential candidates first and second representatively.

Presidential Powers

Article II of the Constitution begins: "The executive Power shall be vested in a President of the United States of America." Presidents often use this **vesting clause** to argue that they control everything that happens in the executive branch after a bill becomes a law.[5] However, the Supreme Court has cast doubt on this breadth of the authority in a variety of past cases—presidents may control the executive branch, but they do not have unlimited command. The Supreme Court has also ruled that Congress cannot delegate powers to the president that the Constitution reserves for the legislative branch under Article I.

Although short, Article II does address foreign threats and the day-to-day operations of government, establishing the president's authority to play three central roles in the new government: (1) commander in chief, (2) diplomat in chief, and (3) administrator in chief.

It is important to note that the framers designed the presidency hoping George Washington would be the first to occupy the post. Washington commanded the public's trust and respect, and he was unanimously elected the first president of the new Republic. He understood that the people needed to have confidence in their fledgling government, a sense of continuity with the past, and a time of calm and stability free of emergencies and crises. He also knew that the new nation faced both domestic and foreign threats to its future.

As president, Washington set important precedents for the future. He not only established the legitimacy and basic authority of the office but negotiated the new government's first treaty, appointed its first judges and department heads, received its first foreign ambassadors, vetoed its first legislation, and signed its first laws, thereby demonstrating just how future presidents should execute and influence the laws.

Washington's most important precedent may have been his retirement after serving two terms. Although he would have been easily reelected to a third term, Washington believed two terms were enough and returned to his Mount Vernon estate in 1796. It was a precedent that held until Franklin Roosevelt's four terms and was finally enshrined in constitutional language under the Twenty-Second Amendment.

Commander in Chief

The Constitution explicitly states that the president is to be commander in chief of the army and navy, but the framers were divided over which branch would both declare and make war.[6]

The framers initially agreed that Congress would make war, raise armies, build and equip fleets, enforce treaties, and suppress and repel invasions, but they eventually changed the phrase "make war" to "declare war." At the same time, the framers limited the presidential war power by giving Congress the power to appropriate money for the purchase of arms and military pay and by giving the Senate the power to approve military promotions. Although Congress has the sole authority to declare war, presidents have used their power as commander in chief to order U.S. troops into battle without formal

presidential ticket
The joint listing of the presidential and vice presidential candidates on the same ballot, as required by the Twelfth Amendment.

vesting clause
The president's constitutional authority to control most executive functions.

Richard Nixon shocked the world when he traveled to the People's Republic of China in 1972. As a young Republican member of Congress, Nixon had built his early career as an anti-communist. As president, he decided that only a Republican like himself could open the door to a future relationship with the communist nation. ■ *What do people mean when they say that a presidential decision is "like Nixon going to China?"*

declarations dozens of times throughout the past century, including the recent wars in Afghanistan and Iraq. Presidents have often interpreted the war power even more broadly, as the Bush administration did in authorizing the domestic eavesdropping program.

Diplomat in Chief Article II also makes the president negotiator in chief of treaties with foreign nations, which must be approved by the Senate by a two-thirds vote. A **treaty** is a binding and public agreement between the United States and one or more nations that requires mutual action toward a common goal. The United States has signed hundreds of treaties throughout the past 200 years, including limits on the number of nuclear, biological, and chemical weapons. Although presidents cannot make treaties without Senate approval, past presidents have argued that they have the power to terminate treaties without Senate consent.

Presidents can also make **executive agreements** with the leaders of foreign nations. Unlike treaties, executive agreements are negotiated without Senate participation. In 2003, for example, the Bush administration negotiated a 22-item executive agreement with Mexico to create a "smart border" that would limit the movement of illegal aliens into the United States, while improving the flow of goods between the two nations. Although some executive orders are secret, most are made public.

Finally, presidents can make **congressional–executive agreements,** which are also negotiated between the president and leaders of other nations. Like treaties, congressional–executive agreements require mutual action toward a common goal. Unlike treaties, they require approval by both houses of Congress by a simple majority vote.

Administrator in Chief By giving the president the power to require the opinion of the principal officer in each of the executive departments "upon any subject relating to the duties of their respective offices," the Constitution puts the president in charge of the day-to-day operations of the federal departments and agencies.

Additional Executive Powers The Constitution also gives the president five additional powers to lead government: (1) the power to appoint judges and officers of government; (2) the power to veto legislation, thereby serving as a check on Congress; (3) the power to grant pardons to individuals convicted of federal, but not state, crimes, thereby providing a check against the judiciary; (4) the power to take care that the laws are faithfully executed, thereby giving the president sweeping authority to oversee the executive branch; and (5) the power to inform and convene Congress.

1. The Appointment Power The Constitution gives the president authority to appoint judges, ambassadors, and other officers of the executive branch subject to the advice and consent of the Senate, in the form of a simple majority of 51 votes.

This power gives presidents the ability to control what happens inside departments and agencies during their terms and to shape the federal judiciary far into the future. Presidents choose appointees on the basis of party loyalty, interest group pressure, and management ability. The Senate has failed to confirm only eight cabinet secretaries between 1789 and 2008, and only 36 of 159 nominations to the Supreme Court.

treaty
A formal, public agreement between the United States and one or more nations that must be approved by two-thirds of the Senate.

executive agreement
A formal agreement between the U.S. president and the leaders of other nations that does not require Senate approval.

congressional–executive agreement
A formal agreement between the U.S. president and the leaders of other nations that requires approval by both houses of Congress.

Of the People

THE GLOBAL COMMUNITY

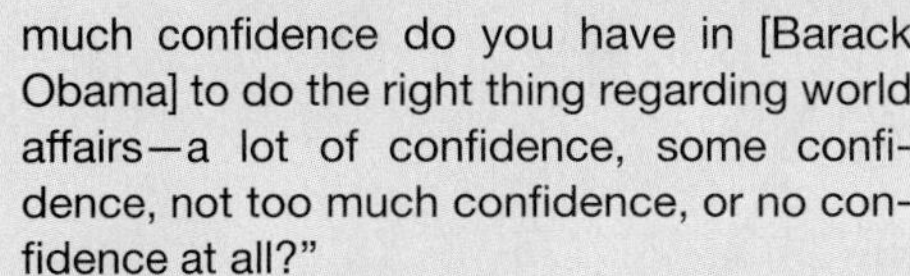

Opinions of Barack Obama

Presidents usually start their first terms in office with a burst of public support, both inside the United States and throughout the globe. Once they start making foreign policy decisions, their support tends to erode, especially if those decisions involve unpopular interventions such as the war in Iraq. Almost without exception, they end their terms in office less popular than they were at the beginning.

The pattern is clear in the Pew Global Survey, which took an early snapshot of Obama's popularity throughout the world in April 2009. Respondents were asked, "How much confidence do you have in [Barack Obama] to do the right thing regarding world affairs—a lot of confidence, some confidence, not too much confidence, or no confidence at all?"

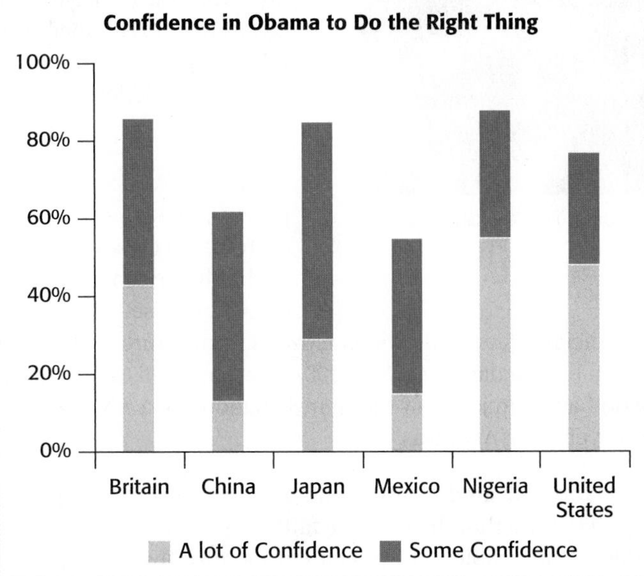

Obama's extraordinary popularity in Nigeria reflects both his personal ties to Africa as the son of a Kenyan citizen and his commitment to improved diplomatic ties with the region. Eighty-eight percent of Kenyans reported a lot or some confidence in Obama.

Obama's popularity at the start of his first year was in sharp contrast to George W. Bush's popularity in 2007. Only 16 percent of British citizens had a lot or some confidence in Bush in the middle of his sixth year, compared with 30 percent of the Chinese, 25 percent of Japanese, 16 percent of Mexicans, 55 percent of Nigerians, and only 37 percent of Americans.

CRITICAL THINKING QUESTIONS

1. Why was the world so enthusiastic about Barack Obama's presidency?
2. How does Obama's popularity translate into more effective foreign policy?
3. How will the increase in the U.S. troops in Afghanistan affect Obama's popularity both at home and abroad?

Presidents also have the power to make **recess appointments** when Congress takes a formal recess, or break, during the year. Although the power was originally intended to be used only when a vacancy occurs during the break, presidents now use recess appointments regularly to appoint particularly controversial nominees to office without Senate confirmation. These appointments end at the start of the Congress that is elected after the appointment is made.[7] Obama did not make any recess appointments in his first year in office.

2. The Veto Power The Constitution provides that bills passed by the U.S. House of Representatives and Senate "shall be presented to the President of the United States," and the president can then approve the measure or issue a **veto.** If a bill is vetoed by a president, it can be enacted only if the veto is overridden, which requires a two-thirds vote in each chamber of Congress.

A variation of the veto is the **pocket veto.** In the ordinary course of events, if a president does not sign or veto a bill within ten days after receiving it (not counting Sundays), the bill becomes law without the president's signature. But if Congress adjourns within the ten days, the president, by taking no action, can kill the bill with a pocket veto.

The power of a veto lies in the difficulty of overriding a president's decision. Recall that two-thirds of both houses must vote to overturn a veto. This requirement is a vital bargaining chip in the legislative process, in which the mere threat of a veto can

recess appointment
Presidential appointment made without Senate confirmation during Senate recess.

veto
A formal decision to reject a bill passed by Congress.

pocket veto
A formal decision to reject a bill passed by Congress after it adjourns—if Congress adjourns during the ten days that the president is allowed to sign or veto a law, the president can reject the law by taking no action at all.

President Obama nominated Judge Sonia Sotomayor to the Supreme Court in 2009. She was easily confirmed as the first Hispanic to join the court.

strengthen a president's hand. Historically, Congress has voted to override fewer than 10 percent of presidents' regular vetoes.

This veto threat is credible, however, only if the president is actually willing to use it. Whereas Ronald Reagan vetoed 78 bills in his two terms and Bill Clinton vetoed 37, George W. Bush issued only one veto during his first six years in office.

Once his Republican Party lost control of the House and Senate in 2007, however, Bush began using his veto power to stop Democratic legislation. In July 2007, for example, he vetoed legislation to allow federal funding of stem cell research.

3. The Pardon Power The pardon power can be traced directly to the royal authority of the king of England, and it is probably the most delicate power presidents exercise. It can shorten prison sentences, correct judicial errors, and protect citizens from future prosecution. It can also create controversy. On his last day in office in 2001, President Bill Clinton pardoned several of his associates who had been jailed in a long investigation of a real estate scandal dating back to his time as governor of Arkansas.

4. The Take Care Power Located near the end of Article II is the simple statement that the president "shall take Care that the Laws be faithfully executed." This **take care clause** makes the president responsible for implementing the laws Congress enacts, even through the override of a presidential veto.

Presidents sometimes use the take care clause to claim **inherent powers,** meaning powers they believe are essential to protecting the nation. Jefferson drew on this broad notion in making the Louisiana Purchase in 1803, for example. Abraham Lincoln extended the concept early in the Civil War to suspend the rights of prisoners to seek judicial review of their detention, to impose a blockade of Confederate shipping, and to expand the size of the army beyond authorized ceilings, all without prior congressional approval as required under the Constitution's lawmaking power.

5. The Power to Inform and Convene Congress. Under Article II, presidents are required "from time to time to give to the Congress Information of the State of the Union, and recommend to their Consideration such Measures as he shall judge necessary." Throughout the years, the phrase "from time to time" has evolved to mean a constant stream of presidential messages, as well as the annual **State of the Union Address** in late January or early February. This power gives presidents a significant platform for presenting their legislative agenda to both Congress and the people.

The president also has the power to convene Congress in extraordinary circumstances and recommend "such Measures as he shall judge necessary and expedient." In August 2010, for example, Obama convened Congress to push for health care reform.

Presidents also believe they have unilateral powers that are not subject to traditional checks and balances. The most important unilateral power involves decisions not to implement a law. These **signing statements** often make the case that a certain provision of a law is either unconstitutional or so vague it cannot be implemented. Between 2001 and early 2008, Bush issued more than 150 statements promising not to follow the laws he was signing.[8]

take care clause
The constitutional requirement (in Article II, Section 3) that presidents take care that the laws are faithfully executed, even if they disagree with the purpose of those laws.

inherent powers
Powers that grow out of the very existence of government.

State of the Union Address
The president's annual statement to Congress and the nation.

signing statements
A formal document that explains why a president is signing a particular bill into law. These statements may contain objections to the bill and promises not to implement key sections.

In his signing the Sudan Accountability and Divestment Act of 2007, President Bush noted that ordering states to jettison any investments made with companies doing business in Darfur conflicted with the president's authority to conduct foreign policy. His signing statement made clear Bush would implement the law selectively. ■ *Do signing statements such as this violate the constitution's requirement that the president faithfully execute the laws once they are signed?*

Presidential Removal and Succession

Having decided how a president would enter office and the length of the term of office, the framers also gave Congress the power to remove the president through **impeachment.** Under this constitutional check and balance, the House of Representatives is responsible for drafting the articles of impeachment that charge the president with treason, bribery, or other high crimes and misdemeanors. If the articles are approved by a majority vote in the House, the chief justice of the Supreme Court oversees a trial before the Senate. If two-thirds of the Senate vote to convict, the president is removed immediately from office.

impeachment
A formal accusation against the president or another public official; the first step in removal from office.

Impeachment charges have been filed against nine presidents in history, but the House has voted to impeach the president only twice: in 1868 against Andrew Johnson, and in 1998 against Bill Clinton. The Senate trials resulted in acquittals.

Although the framers did not limit the number of terms that a president could serve, the nation eventually ratified the Twenty-Second Amendment, which limits presidents to two terms in office. The ratification effort was led by Republicans who wanted to prevent a repeat of Franklin Roosevelt's four consecutive terms in office, which concentrated power in the White House and led to the great expansion of federal government power under the New Deal.

In 1967, the nation ratified the Twenty-Fifth Amendment, which allows for the temporary removal of the president due to illness or disability. The president can only be removed temporarily if (1) the vice president, and (2) a majority of either Congress or the president's own department secretaries declare the president to be unable to discharge the powers and duties of office. During the temporary removal of the president, the vice president becomes the acting president.

If the president dies or resigns from office, the vice president automatically becomes president and must nominate someone to be vice president. Under the Twenty-Fifth Amendment, the nominee for vice president must be confirmed by a majority vote in both houses of Congress.

Vice President Lyndon Baines Johnson takes the oath of office to become president on November 22, 1963, following the assassination of John F. Kennedy. In the wake of these events, the Twenty-Fifth Amendment was adopted to provide for replacing the vice president or removing a president from office for reasons of illness or disability.

Controversies in Presidential Power

LEARNING **OBJECTIVE**

8.2 Evaluate the controversies surrounding presidents' assertion of additional executive powers.

The president, today more visible than ever as a national and international leader, is still constrained by constitutional checks and balances. These do not stop presidents from asserting powers the framers intended for Congress or the judiciary, however.

The War Power

Article I of the Constitution gives Congress the power to declare war, but Article II gives the president the power to wage war as commander in chief. The framers recognized that declaring war was both one of the most important powers of government and one of the most easily abused. [9]

During the past half-century, U.S. presidents have ordered troops into battle in Korea, Vietnam, Grenada, Panama, Iraq (twice), Kosovo, and Afghanistan, all without asking Congress for a formal declaration of war. When they have asked for congressional approval, presidents have usually sought broad resolutions of support. In 2002, for example, Bush merely asked Congress to give him the authority to deploy U.S. forces as "he determines to be necessary and appropriate" to defend national security against the threat posed by Iraq. Although the request was eventually approved by wide margins in the House and Senate, White House lawyers also argued that the president already had the authority to act with or without congressional approval.[10]

Presidents and some scholars blame Congress for abdicating its constitutional authority to the presidency. Constitutional scholar Louis Fisher holds that Congress has repeatedly given up its fundamental war powers to the president. The framers knew what monarchy looked like and rejected it, writes Fisher. "Yet, especially in matters of the war power, the United States is recreating a system of monarchy while it professes to champion democracy and the rule of law abroad."[11]

Congress tried to reassert its role and authority in the use of military force at the end of the Vietnam War. In 1973, Congress enacted the War Powers Resolution over Nixon's veto. The law, still in place, declares that a president can commit the armed forces only (1) after a declaration of war by Congress, (2) by specific statutory authorization, or (3) in a national emergency created by an attack on the United States or its armed forces. After committing the armed forces under the third circumstance, the president is required to report to Congress within 48 hours. Unless Congress declares war, the troop commitment must be ended within 60 days.

executive privilege
The right to keep executive communications confidential, especially if they relate to national security.

This resolution signaled a new determination by Congress to take its prerogatives seriously, yet presidents have generally ignored it. And many leading scholars now believe that this earnest and well-intentioned effort by Congress to reclaim its proper role actually gave away more authority than previous practices had already done. Because presidents can declare a national emergency under almost any circumstances and often act under broad legislation that authorizes the use of force in ambiguous situations, the War Powers Resolution is almost always ignored.

Iranian president Mahmoud Ahmadinejad addresses the United Nations in 2007. Tensions began to rise dramatically between Iran and the United States late in the Bush administration. The Bush administration was particularly worried about the possibility that Iran was in the process of refining nuclear materials as part of a weapons program and threatened to use all powers in the U.S. arsenal to stop Iran's effort.

The Power to Invoke Executive Privilege

The courts have recognized that presidents have the power, or **executive privilege,** to keep secrets, especially if doing so is essential to protect national security or confidential White House conversations about public policy.

Some experts argue that executive privilege has no constitutional basis.[12] Yet presidents have withheld documents from Congress at least as far back as 1792, when President George Washington temporarily refused to share sensitive documents with a House committee studying an Indian massacre of federal troops. Thomas Jefferson and the primary author of the Constitution, James Madison, also withheld information during their presidencies.

Most scholars, the courts, and even members of Congress agree that a president does have the implicit, if not constitutionally explicit, right to withhold information that could harm national security. Presidents must keep secrets, and they often fight hard to do so. However, they cannot assert executive privilege in either congressional or judicial proceedings when it means refusing to cooperate in investigations of personal wrongdoing.

Nixon created enormous and continuing controversy over the term "executive privilege."[13] In an effort to hide his own role in the Watergate scandal, which involved a failed burglary of the Democratic National Committee offices during the 1972 election, Nixon refused to release the secret tapes of the White House meetings that led to a cover-up of the attempt. Nixon and his lawyers went so far as to claim that the decision to invoke executive privilege was not subject to review by Congress or the federal courts.

Ruling in an April 1974 unanimous decision, the Supreme Court acknowledged for the first time that presidents do indeed have the power to claim executive privilege if the release of certain information would be damaging to the nation's security interests. But the Court held that such claims are not exempt from review by the courts. More importantly for Nixon's future, the Court also held that national security was not threatened by the public release of the Watergate tapes. The Court ordered Nixon to yield his tapes, effectively dooming his presidency.[14]

The Bush administration formally invoked executive privilege four times between 2001 and 2007, and in late 2007, to prevent congressional testimony by two White House aides in a Justice Department scandal. As of early 2010, Obama has not invoked this power.

The Bush administration refused to release information on its use of "enhanced interrogation" techniques such as sleep deprivation at the Guantanamo interrogation facility. The decision was eventually reversed by the Obama administration, which released the Bush administration's "torture memos" in 2009.

The Power to Issue Executive Orders

Presidents execute the laws and direct the federal departments and agencies in part through **executive orders,** formal directives that are just as strong as laws and can be challenged in the courts. According to past Supreme Court decisions, executive orders are generally accepted as the law of the land unless they conflict with the Constitution or a federal law. Executive orders are numbered dating back to President George Washington's first order three months after his inauguration.

executive orders
Formal orders issued by the president to direct action by the federal bureaucracy.

Beginning with George Washington, presidents have issued nearly 14,000 executive orders. Presidents have used executive orders to implement a variety of decisions, including a declaration of U.S. neutrality in the war between France and England (1793). President George W. Bush issued 270 executive orders during his eight-year term, while Obama issued 37 in his first year. (See Figure 8–1 for a comparison of the number of executive orders issued, by president.) Obama's first executive order, issued the day after his inauguration, was an ethics pledge that all future executive appointees must sign. (An indexed list of all executive orders dating back to 1933 can be found at http://www.archives.gov/federal-register/executive-orders/disposition.html.)

The Budget and Spending Power

The Constitution explicitly gives Congress the power to appropriate money, but presidents are responsible for actually spending it. Congress dominated the budget-making process until 1921, when it approved the Budget and Accounting Act. That law required the president to submit annual budgets to Congress, and it established the Bureau of the Budget, which in 1970 became the Office of Management and Budget. Although the 1921 act also created the General Accounting Office as an auditing and oversight arm of Congress, presidents have played an increasingly powerful role in shaping the federal budget. (A detailed look at current federal spending can be found at www.USAspending.gov.)

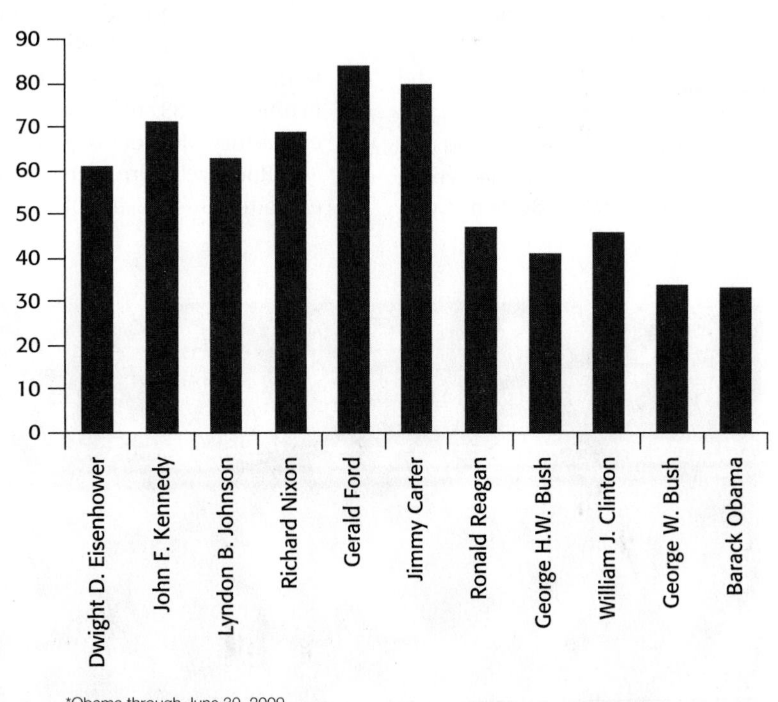

FIGURE 8–1 **Average Number of Executive Orders Issued Each Year, by President** ■ *Why has the average number of executive orders issued declined so much over the past six decades? What other tools might presidents now be using to influence policies and government?*

In 1974, Congress approved the Congressional Budget and Impoundment Control Act, which sharply curtailed the president's use of **impoundment,** or refusal to spend appropriations that had been passed into law. Enacted over Nixon's veto, the law gave Congress new powers to control its own budget process, created the Congressional Budget Office (CBO) to give the institution its own sources of economic and spending forecasts, and required the president to submit detailed requests to Congress for any proposed *rescission* (cancellation) of congressional appropriations.

In an effort to control its own tendency to overspend, Congress in 1996 voted to give the president greater budget power through the **line item veto,** which would have allowed presidents to strike out specific sections of an appropriations bill while signing the rest into law. In essence, the line item veto is a legal form of impoundment. Although many governors have the line item veto, the Supreme Court decided the law had disturbed the "finely wrought" procedure for making the laws and declared it unconstitutional in a 6-to-3 vote in 1998. If Congress wanted a new procedure for making the laws, Justice John Paul Stevens wrote for the majority, it would have to pursue a constitutional amendment.[15]

The Evolution of Presidential Power

The history of presidential power is one of steady, and uneven, growth. Of the individuals who have filled the office, approximately one-third have enlarged its powers. Andrew Jackson, Abraham Lincoln, Theodore Roosevelt, Franklin Delano Roosevelt, and Harry Truman all redefined the institution and many of its powers by the way they set priorities and responded to crises. Much of this expansion occurred during wartime or national crises such as the economic depression of the 1930s.

Nevertheless, today's presidency reflects precedents established by the nation's first chief executive, George Washington. The framers could not have anticipated the kinds of foreign and domestic threats that now preoccupy the office, but they did recognize the importance of the presidency in protecting the nation in times of trouble.

Today's presidency still bears the mark of George Washington, but also reflects the enormous expansion that occurred during the 1930s under Franklin Delano Roosevelt. During his 12 years in office, Roosevelt created an extraordinary record of achievement. He expanded the role of the president as commander, diplomat, and administrator in chief, while dominating Congress in both shaping and making the laws. Inaugurated for the first of his four terms in the midst of the Great Depression, Roosevelt took command, and his first 100 days in office in 1933 still stand as the most significant moment of presidential leadership in modern history. Most of his New Deal agenda for helping workers and the poor is still law today.

Roosevelt's impact extends well beyond the legislative agenda, however. He also exploited the powers of the presidency to build a highly personal relationship with the

impoundment
A decision by the president not to spend money appropriated by Congress, now prohibited under federal law.

line item veto
Presidential power to strike, or remove, specific items from a spending bill without vetoing the entire package; declared unconstitutional by the Supreme Court.

Franklin Roosevelt's Depression-era Works Progress Administration put millions of people to work on public projects, as depicted in this mural by Marvin Beerbohm, displayed at the Detroit Post Office. ■ *What does the mural tell you about the groups of people and industries that benefitted from the New Deal agenda?*

YOU WILL

DECIDE Should the Two-Term Limit Be Repealed?

The Twenty-Second Amendment was ratified in 1951 to limit the president's time in office to two terms whether served consecutively or not. If President Obama is defeated for reelection in 2012, for example, but ran again and won in 2016, he would still be limited to two terms total.

All of the presidents who have been elected since 1951 have supported repeal of the Twenty-Second Amendment. They argue that the amendment effectively renders them lame ducks in their second terms. Because they cannot stand for reelection, Congress and the public tend to ignore them as thoughts turn to who will be the president after them. Nor can they be held accountable in the voting booth for their second-term decisions.

What do you think? Should the two-term limit be repealed? What arguments would you make for or against such an idea?

THINKING IT THROUGH

The founders clearly believed that elections serve to discipline presidents for their actions, while the four-year term provides enough time to achieve policy results. They believed that steadiness in administration would help the country survive its early years, while giving the president a reason to create policies that would help the nation long into the future. Presidents are arguably more effective if their allies and opponents assume they may be running for another term. Otherwise, they become "lame ducks" early in their second terms, meaning that they have little influence.

Much as they may have applauded Washington's two-term precedent, the founders did not support the idea of a formal term limit—such a limit would have weakened the public's voice in keeping the president honest. Instead of starting a second term knowing they could not serve again, presidents would be able to keep Congress and the public guessing, thereby retaining influence until the last possible minute.

Critical Thinking Questions

1. Do presidents have so much power that they can almost guarantee reelection to more than two terms?
2. Does the two-term limit weaken the president's ability to influence the course of the nation in the second term?
3. What checks and balances ensure that presidents can be held accountable even if they are lame ducks?

U.S. public, using his "fireside chats" on radio to calm the public during the darkest days of the economic depression, while calling the nation to action during the early days of World War II. In doing so, he became the nation's communicator in chief, starting each broadcast with the simple phrase "My friends."

Managing the Presidency

LEARNING **OBJECTIVE**

8.3 Outline the functions of the White House staff, Executive Office of the President, cabinet, and vice president.

Presidents cannot do their jobs without help. Although some of that help comes from their *inner circle,* composed of their closest advisers, including the first lady, presidents rely on a vast array of support that extends well beyond 1600 Pennsylvania Avenue to include the executive branch as a whole.

The White House Staff

The president's most important advisers work inside the cramped confines of the West Wing of the White House.[16] Whereas presidents often view their cabinet secretaries as advocates of their departments, they view their White House staff as intensely loyal and responsive to the president, and the president alone.

Generally, the closer a staff member is to the president's Oval Office, the more power he or she has. However, power is also dependent on how the president organizes the staff for making decisions. Among modern presidents, Franklin Roosevelt and Lyndon Johnson both used the *competitive* approach for managing the White House staff, a "survival of the fittest" situation in which the president allows aides to fight each other for access to the Oval Office. Johnson sometimes gave different staffers the same assignment, hoping the competition would produce a better final decision.

In contrast, John Kennedy, Jimmy Carter, and Bill Clinton all used the *collegial* approach, encouraging aides to work together toward a common position. It is a

Rahm Emanuel resigned his seat in Congress to be Obama's chief of staff in 2009. Emmanuel left the White House late in 2010 to run for mayor of Chicago, a particularly powerful post in the Democratic Party given the city's strong Democratic base.

chief of staff
The head of the White House staff.

Executive Office of the President
The cluster of presidential staff agencies that help the president carry out his or her responsibilities. Currently, the office includes the Office of Management and Budget, the Council of Economic Advisers, and several other units.

friendlier way to work but may have the serious drawback of producing *groupthink*, the tendency of small groups to stifle dissent in the search for common ground.[17]

Finally, Dwight Eisenhower, Richard Nixon, Ronald Reagan, and George W. Bush all used the *hierarchical* approach, in which the president establishes tight control over who does what in making decisions. Presidents who use this approach usually rely on a "gatekeeper," or trusted adviser such as the chief of staff, to monitor the flow of information to and from the White House.

The White House Bureaucracy The White House staff grew steadily from the early 1900s through the early 1990s, then stabilized at roughly 400 today. The **chief of staff,** the president's most loyal assistant, heads the staff, which also includes the president's chief lawyer, speechwriters, legislative liaison staff, and press secretary.

There are at least two kinds of White House offices. *Political* offices are designed to help the president run for reelection, control the national party, and shape the president's image through press conferences, television and radio addresses, polling, and travel.

Policy offices are designed to shape the president's foreign and domestic program. Like congressional committees, these offices collect information and often write legislation. The list of policy offices includes the National Economic Council, which coordinates the president's economic agenda; the National Security Council, which helps set foreign policy; and the Office of Faith-Based and Community Initiatives, which encourages the use of religious institutions to help address community problems.[18]

The Executive Office of the President

The **Executive Office of the President (EOP)** was created in 1939 to give the president more help running the federal departments and agencies. The EOP consists of the Office of Management and Budget, the Council of Economic Advisers, and several other staff units. It also includes the White House staff, which is a distinct organization of staff who report solely to the president and are not ordinarily subject to Senate confirmation.

No one is quite sure how many people work in the EOP—although many staffers are on the White House budget, the EOP staff also includes between 2,000 and 6,000 staffers who are *detailed* to the White House by departments and agencies of government. Because they are paid by their departments and agencies, they do not show up on the traditional head-counts of EOP staff. (Biographies of all White House staff can be found at http://www.whorunsgov.com/Departments/White_House_Organizational_Chart, and is illustrated in Figure 8–2.)

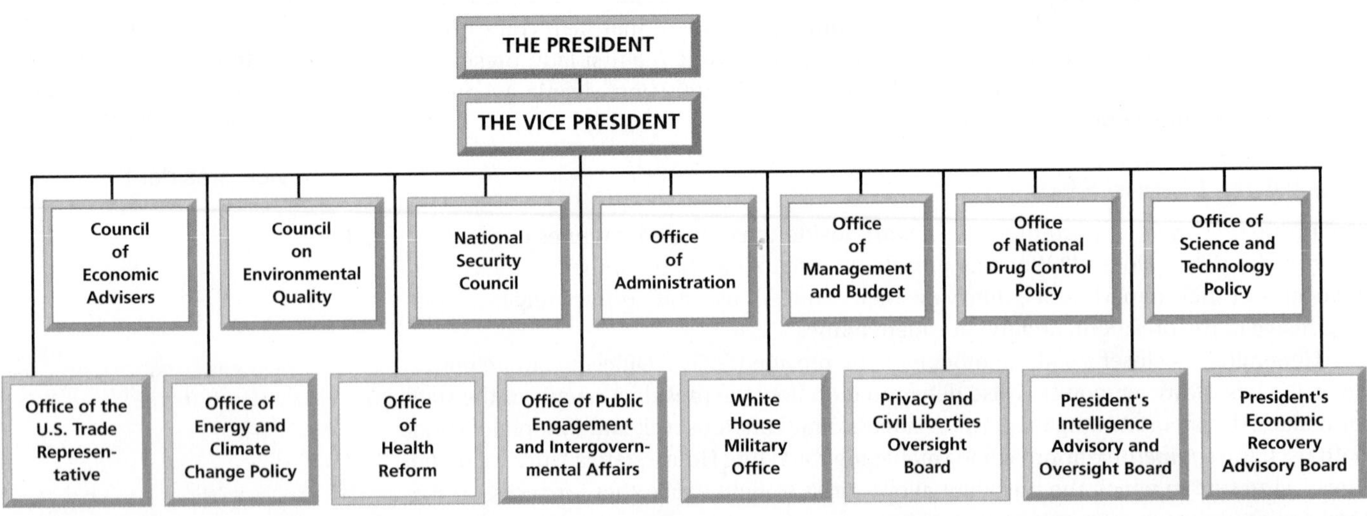

FIGURE 8–2 **Executive Office of the President.** ■ *Why are there so many separate offices under the president's direct command? And what do the kinds of offices President Obama includes in his Executive Office indicate about his policy priorities?*

SOURCE: Pollingreport.com

The President's Cabinet

As discussed above, the president's cabinet is composed of the Senate-confirmed secretaries and agency heads who are most important in giving the president advice. They meet regularly as a group with the president.

During the past 50 years, the president's cabinet has steadily become more diverse. Obama's first 20 cabinet appointees were the most diverse team in history but built on the gains made by women and minorities under Presidents Clinton and George W. Bush. The following chart shows the increasing diversity among the first round of cabinet appointments each president made.

This increasing diversity brings great assets to the White House. It provides greater creativity and life histories to the discussion of key issues such as economic growth, climate change, and health care reform. It also sends the message that a government of the people involves more than white males. With his appointments, Obama created the first cabinet with a majority of women and minorities.

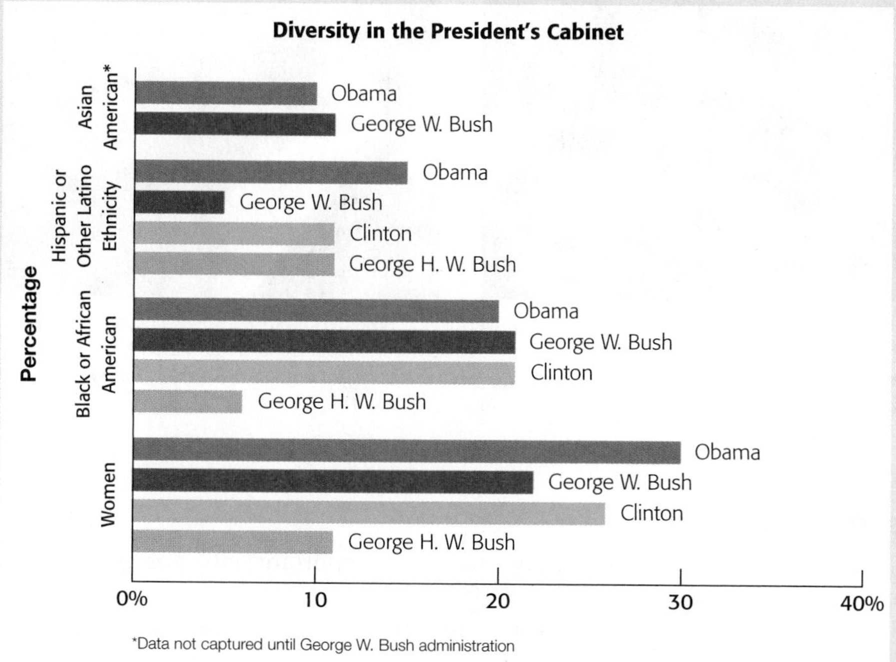

SOURCE: Author's analysis of appointment statistics.

CRITICAL THINKING QUESTIONS

1. Does partisanship predict the level of diversity in the cabinet? Why or why not?
2. Does diversity matter to presidential decisions? Should it?
3. The federal government's workforce is very diverse. How does diversity in the cabinet affect the performance of the federal bureaucracy?

The **Office of Management and Budget (OMB)** is the central EOP agency for making decisions about the budget. Its director advises the president in detail about the hundreds of government agencies—how much money they should be allotted in the budget and what kind of job they are doing. The OMB seeks to improve the planning, management, and statistical work of the agencies. It makes a special effort to see that each agency conforms to presidential policies in its dealings with Congress; each agency has to clear its policy recommendations to Congress through the OMB first.[19]

The Cabinet

It is hard to find a more unusual institution than the president's **cabinet.** The cabinet is not specifically mentioned in the Constitution, yet every president since 1789 has had one. Washington's consisted of his secretaries of state, treasury, and war, plus his attorney general.

Defining the Cabinet Defining the cabinet is the first major job for the president-elect. Today, the cabinet consists of the president, the vice president, the heads of the 15 executive departments, and several others a president considers essential officials.

The cabinet has always been a loosely designated body, and it is not always clear who belongs in it. In recent years, certain executive branch administrators and White House counselors have been accorded cabinet rank. Nineteen officials had cabinet status in the George W. Bush administration, including the 15 cabinet secretaries, the vice president, the chief of staff, and the director of national intelligence.

Office of Management and Budget (OMB)
A presidential staff agency that serves as a clearinghouse for budgetary requests and management improvements for government agencies.

cabinet
The advisory council for the president, consisting of the heads of the executive departments, the vice president, and a few other officials selected by the president.

Dick Cheney is widely regarded as the most powerful vice president in modern history. Although Joe Biden is well respected, he does not appear to have as much influence and has taken a less visible role as vice president. ■ *What are some of the factors that might impact how much influence a vice president has?*

The Vice Presidency

The vice presidency has not always been an important job. For most of U.S. history, the vice president was an insignificant officer at best and, at worst, a political rival who sometimes connived against the president. The office was often dismissed as a joke.

No matter how influential they become, vice presidents have only one major responsibility: to be ready to take the oath of office in case the president cannot discharge his duties. Nevertheless, vice presidents enter office with substantial access, including an office just down the hall from the president in the West Wing of the White House, a substantial staff of their own, and access to all of the information flowing into the Oval Office.

Vice President Dick Cheney is generally considered the most influential vice president in modern times. He had more than just access to President Bush, however. He was a trusted adviser to the Bush family and had served in Congress and as secretary of defense under the first president Bush.

Joe Biden has a very different, but still powerful, role in the Obama Administration. He was a strong voice in the president's Afghanistan decision, and he is in charge of the effort to stimulate the economy. He also meets regularly with the president and is often consulted by the White House before the president makes his decisions. He has a regular and private weekly lunch with Obama to discuss anything on their minds and also sits just down the hallway from the president's Oval Office.

The Job of the President

LEARNING **OBJECTIVE**

8.4 Characterize the various roles that presidents play.

U.S. citizens want the chief executive to be an international peacemaker as well as a national morale builder, a politician in chief as well as a commander in chief. They want the president to provide leadership on foreign, economic, and domestic policy. They also want presidents to be crisis managers and role models of a kind. They want them to be able to connect with ordinary people, yet be smarter, tougher, and more honest than the rest of us. (See Table 8–1 for what U.S. adults thought presidents could change about the world in 2008.)

TABLE 8–1 What Can Presidents Change?

Percentage of Americans Who Said the President Has a Great Deal of Influence Over Each of the Following Issues	
Housing prices	20%
Interest rates	23%
Inflation	30%
Gas prices	31%
Health care costs	38%
Federal budget deficit	48%
Taxes	48%
The way other countries view the United States	60%

SOURCE: Associated Press–Yahoo Poll, January 18, 2008.

Presidents as Morale Builders

As chief of state, the president must project a sense of national unity and authority as the country's chief ceremonial leader. The framers of the Constitution did not fully anticipate the symbolic and morale-building functions a president must perform. But over time, presidents have become national celebrities and command media attention merely by jogging, fishing, golfing, or going to church. By their actions, presidents can arouse a sense of hope or despair, honor or dishonor.

Morale building means much more than just ceremonies or prayers. At its finest, presidential leadership radiates national self-confidence and helps unlock the possibility for good that exists in the nation. That is certainly what George W. Bush intended in the days and weeks that followed September 11, 2001. By his words and deeds, he sought to simultaneously calm the nation and warn the rest of the world that the United States would not tolerate further terrorist attacks.

Presidents as Agenda Setters

By custom and circumstance, presidents are now responsible for proposing initiatives in foreign policy and economic growth and stability. Presidential candidates searching for campaign issues seize on new ideas, and these are later refined and implemented by the executive office staff, by special presidential task forces, and by Congress.[20]

Economic Policy Ever since the New Deal, presidents have been expected to promote policies to keep unemployment low, fight inflation, keep taxes down, and promote economic growth and prosperity. The Constitution does not specify these, but presidents know they will be held accountable for economic problems such as inflation and unemployment.

President Bush, flanked by firefighters and rescue workers, addresses a crowd at the scene of the terrorist attacks on the World Trade Center in New York on September 11, 2001. In times of crisis, the nation often rallies around the president despite political differences. ■ *What messages does Bush convey in this photo solely through visual cues?*

Presidents relax in many ways. President Ronald Reagan liked to chop wood at his California ranch, Bill Clinton liked to go jogging, George W. Bush went on frequent bike rides, and Obama likes to play pick-up games of basketball.
■ *How do images like this help presidents shape public perceptions of their human side?*

Social Policy Leadership is often defined as the art of knowing what followers want. John Kennedy and Lyndon Johnson did not launch the civil rights movement, for example. Nor did Bill Clinton or George W. Bush create public pressure for national health insurance or prescription drug coverage. But they all responded to the public demand by supporting legislation on each issue.

National Security Policy The framers foresaw a special need for speed and unity in dealing with other nations. The Supreme Court has upheld strong presidential authority in this area. In *United States* v. *Curtiss-Wright* (1936), the Court referred to the "exclusive power of the president as the sole organ of the federal government in the field of international relations—a power which does not require as a basis for its exercise an act of Congress, but which, of course, like every other governmental power, must be exercised in subordination to the applicable provisions of the Constitution."[21]

Presidents as Persuaders

Despite their formal powers, presidents spend most of their time *persuading* people. As Richard Neustadt argues, the power to persuade is the president's chief resource.[22] This power to persuade is based on the president's ability to communicate directly with members of Congress and the public through the skillful use of press conferences, speeches, and public events.

Presidents have reduced the number of their press conferences during the past five decades. Whereas Franklin Roosevelt averaged nearly seven press conferences a month during his dozen years in office, the past five presidents have averaged one. Although Barack Obama held three press conferences in his first six months, he did not hold another until 2010. "Going public" often means carefully staging events before friendly audiences that show strong support for the president.

Going public clearly fits with changes in the electoral process. Presidents now have the staff, the technology, and the public opinion research to tell them how to target their message, and they have nearly instant media access to speak to the public easily. And, as elections have become more image oriented and candidate centered, presidents have the incentive to use these tools to operate a permanent White House campaign.

Congress and the Presidency

LEARNING **OBJECTIVE**

8.5 Identify the sources of presidential–congressional conflict and the tools presidents use to influence Congress.

Congress and the presidency have a contentious relationship. They often work closely to address critically important problems but at other times are unable to reach agreement on equally difficult issues. They are most likely to agree in the first year of a president's first term and when one party controls both the White House and Congress, and they are more likely to fight late in the president's first term and off and on throughout the entire second term.

Given the separation of powers, it is a wonder that Congress and the president ever agree at all, which is exactly what the framers intended. The framers did not want the legislative process to work like an assembly line. Rather, they wanted ambition to counteract ambition as a way to prevent tyranny.

To the extent that they designed the legislative process to work inefficiently, the founders succeeded beyond their initial hopes. As hard as presidents work to win passage of their top priorities, they often complain that Congress is not listening. However, Congress listens more closely to its constituents, especially when the president's public approval is low. That is why so many of the Bush administration's second-term priorities never reached the floor of the House or Senate.

By the People
MAKING A DIFFERENCE

Public Service Through the White House Blog

Presidents pay attention to public opinion in many ways. Every president since the 1960s has appointed his own pollster to monitor public opinion. Presidents also travel frequently throughout the country lobbying for their programs, engaging citizens in town hall meetings, raising money for their political party, and campaigning for reelection.

Most of these activities are directed at relatively small numbers of citizens, which puts the burden on citizens to make contact with the president. Citizens are always welcome to send letters and e-mails to the president, but they rarely get a personal response. The White House receives 65,000 letters, 100,000 e-mails, 1,000 faxes, and between 2,500 and 3,500 phone calls per day, but only a handful of these messages end up on the president's desk.

At the start of his administration, however, Obama asked the White House mailroom to give him ten letters from ordinary Americans every day. Obama has been particularly interested in receiving real stories about the nation's current condition. "These letters, I think, do more than keep me in touch with what's happening around the country than anything else," Obama says in a White House video about the sorting process at http://www.whitehouse.gov/video/Inside-the-White-House-Letters-to-the-President. "Some of them are funny, some of them are angry, a lot of them are sad or frustrated about their current situation."

Under Obama, the White House established a series of forums for receiving public comments. On January 15, 2010, for example, the president's MySpace page had more than 160,000 friends, his Facebook page had nearly 500,000 friends, and his Twitter feed had more than 1.6 million followers. (All three destinations can be reached by entering MySpace.com, Facebook.com, or Twitter.com, followed by a backslash and the word "whitehouse.")

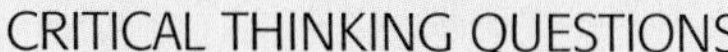

CRITICAL THINKING QUESTIONS

1. What kind of letter makes the most compelling reading in the White House and why?
2. Does a single hit on whitehouse.gov make any difference in the president's opinion?
3. What does the number of friends or followers actually tell the White House about public opinion? Are polls a better way for the president to understand what the country thinks?

Why Presidents and Congress Disagree

Congress and the president disagree for many reasons, not the least of which is the natural tendency of members of Congress to think about elections far into the future.

Competing Constituencies The framers guaranteed that members of Congress and the president would represent different constituencies, which often leads to conflict over major legislation. Members of Congress represent either states or local districts, whereas the president represents the nation as a whole. Although these constituencies often overlap, particularly in states that strongly support the president's election, members of Congress often worry most about how the laws and presidential actions will affect their home districts.

Competing Calendars The Constitution also ensures that Congress and the president will not share the same terms of office. Presidents can serve a maximum of eight years before leaving office, whereas senators and members of the House can serve for decades. Presidents enter office wanting everything passed at once, whereas members of Congress have plenty of time to wait.

President Jimmy Carter addresses the U.S. public in his first televised address to talk about energy policy. He made a deliberate choice to give the address sitting down near the fireplace dressed in a cardigan sweater as a way to calm the public's concern about increasing gasoline prices.

Competing Campaigns Finally, the Constitution ensures that Congress and the president will run different kinds of election campaigns. Most members of Congress finance their election campaigns with only minimal assistance from their national political party. They usually run independently of the president or national party platform. Even members of the president's own party have been known to ask the president not to visit their districts in particularly tight elections or when the president's public approval is falling. Whenever possible, members try to make elections about local, not national issues, which means the president is often completely ignored during the campaign.

Influencing Congress

Presidents have long had a substantial, if not always dominant, role in shaping what Congress does. Their primary vehicle for doing so is the president's agenda, an informal list of top legislative priorities. Whether through the State of the Union Address or through other messages and signals, presidents make clear what they think Congress should do.

It is one thing to proclaim a presidential priority, however, and quite another to actually influence congressional action. As Richard Neustadt argued in *Presidential Power,* a president's constitutional powers add up to little more than a job as the country's most distinguished office clerk. It is a president's ability to persuade others that spells the difference between being a clerk and being a national leader.[23]

The power to persuade on Capitol Hill is often measured through the **presidential support score,** calculated by counting the times the president wins key votes in Congress. Bush won more than 70 percent of his votes from 2001 to 2006, but only 38 percent in 2007.[24] Although his earlier high scores would seem to make him the most influential president in modern history, Bush earned the scores by taking relatively few positions on key votes that he knew he could win. Obama earned a record setting support score of almost 97 percent in 2009. Like Bush, Obama did so largely by limiting his positions to a handful of winnable votes.

Presidential Mandates Presidents who enter office with a large electoral margin, high public approval, and a party majority in Congress often claim a **mandate,** or public support, to govern. The winner-take-all nature of the electoral-college system tends to make the president's popular vote look larger than it truly is.

Obama decided to spend his 2008 presidential election mandate on just two priorities: an economic stimulus package and health care reform. His mandate was relatively modest, however. Although he did win an overwhelming share of the electoral vote, his popular vote total was only 53 percent, which limited his ability to claim a sweeping mandate for change. Moreover, the economic calamity that started in 2008 reduced public support for most new programs.

Public Approval The mandate to govern depends in part on public approval, which generally falls over time. (See Figure 8–3 for presidential approval trends throughout the past half-century.) Bush became the first incumbent president in modern history to win reelection despite starting his campaign with an approval rating below 50 percent. Although he regained ground after his second inauguration, his ratings continued to fall as his second term continued, which helps explain the declining number of congressional votes on which he took a position. He simply did not have enough *political capital* to take more positions.

Presidents also benefit from **rally points,** spikes in public approval following a domestic or international crisis. Rally points do not necessarily last long, however. George W. Bush's ratings jumped dramatically following the September 11, 2001, attacks when he called on the nation to support the war on terrorism but eventually fell back with the continued violence after the first months of the war in Iraq. His approval rating jumped 29 percent after the September 11 attacks and 12 percent after the start of the Iraq War in 2003.

Reputation The longer presidents stay in office, the better they get at being president. They learn how Washington works, what powers they can use to influence congressional

presidential support score
The percentage of times a president wins on key votes in Congress.

mandate
A president's claim of broad public support.

rally point
A rise in public approval of the president that follows a crisis as Americans "rally round the flag" and the chief executive.

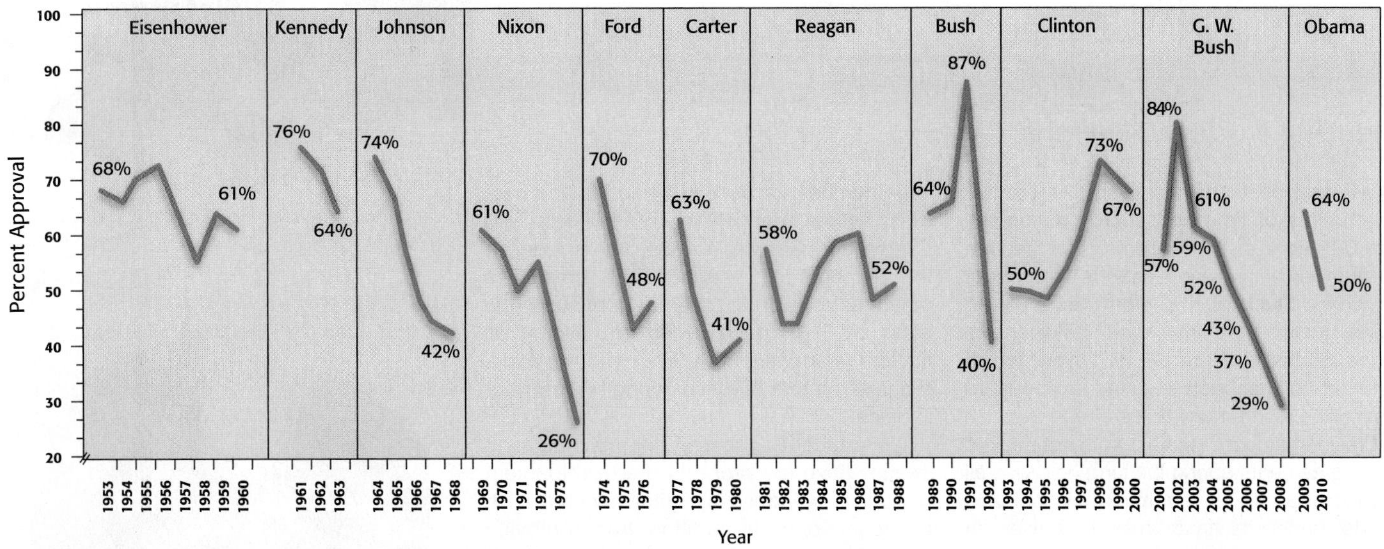

FIGURE 8–3 **Presidential Approval Ratings, 1953–2010.** ■ *How are all presidential approval ratings similar? Which president took office with the highest approval ratings, and which left with the lowest? What might explain the declines?*

NOTE: Percentage is from the first Gallup/*USA Today* poll taken each calendar year.

SOURCE: Gallup/*USA Today* poll, available at www.pollingreport.com.

action, and whom they need to convince to win passage of their top priorities. Presidents also learn how to use unilateral powers to accomplish some of their goals.

Nevertheless, presidents pay great attention to the steady erosion of public approval that occurs over time. As a result of this, they have the greatest potential influence at the very point when they know the least about being president, and they know the most about being president when they have the least influence.

Some experts believe the president's reputation has declined in recent years, in part due to political scandals. The controversy over the 2000 election raised questions about the legitimacy of the electoral process, and the war in Iraq led many to doubt President Bush's leadership in the war on terrorism. As a result, Congress may now be quicker to dismiss presidential positions.

Judging Presidents

LEARNING **OBJECTIVE**

8.6 Identify factors that influence judgments about presidents.

Presidents rise and fall in the historical rankings based on a number of factors. Some rise because they led the nation through periods of intense domestic or international crisis; others rise because they had a distinctive vision of where the nation should go on issues such as civil rights, social policy, or the economy. Rankings also include at least some assessment of how presidents fared as political and moral leaders of the nation.

History tends to judge wars and international crises as the most significant test of a president's leadership. Wars that end in stalemate tend to diminish a president's greatness, whereas wars that end in victory raise a president's ranking, especially when the nation's survival is threatened. Abraham Lincoln (the Civil War), Woodrow Wilson (World War I), and Franklin Delano Roosevelt (World War II) rank among the great presidents because of their leadership during just such wars, whereas Lyndon Johnson ranks much lower because of his role in the Vietnam stalemate.

Corruption and inability to deal with economic problems are sure paths to presidential failure. Warren Harding and Richard Nixon both rank as failures because of scandals that tarnished their presidencies, while Herbert Hoover is ranked a failure because of his lack of leadership at the start of the Great Depression. Although Lyndon Johnson launched a number of great domestic programs such as Medicare for older citizens and

For the People

GOVERNMENT'S GREATEST ENDEAVORS

Reducing Nuclear Weapons

Past presidents have invested enormous amounts of time and energy during the past 30 years to try to control and reduce the number of nuclear weapons throughout the world. Much of that work has involved efforts to stop the "arms race" between the United States and the Soviet Union, which together built enough nuclear weapons to destroy the world many times over.

Presidents negotiated a number of nuclear arms agreements during the long cold war, all of which had to be approved by the U.S. Senate under its treaty-making power. In 1972, for example, the Senate approved a freeze on the development of new weapons by the United States and Soviet Union that lasted through the 1970s. This Strategic Arms Limitation Treaty, negotiated by President Richard Nixon, froze the number of U.S. and Soviet missiles for five years.

In 1988, the Senate also approved a treaty banning the further development of shorter-range nuclear missiles that could be used in Europe and other "hot spots." This treaty, negotiated by President Ronald Reagan, marked the first time that the two nations also agreed to dismantle some of their existing weapons. Although both nations still have large numbers of nuclear weapons and missiles, further negotiations by Presidents Bill Clinton and George W. Bush have reduced the numbers of weapons and created a much safer world. Obama continued the effort by urging the world to destroy all nuclear weapons, but he was unable to make progress on that promise during his first year in office.

Unfortunately, these negotiations and treaties have not stopped the development of nuclear weapons by other nations, such as North Korea. In addition, Iran is moving forward with what it describes as a peaceful nuclear power program that foreign observers argue will produce the material for a nuclear weapon.

CRITICAL THINKING QUESTIONS

1. Why do nations seek nuclear weapons as part of their military strength?
2. What can the United States do to reduce the spread of nuclear weapons to other nations?
3. What can citizens do to put pressure on the United States and other nations to dismantle their nuclear weapons?

The United States and Russia negotiated a significant cut in nuclear weapons in May 2010 when they agreed to reduce the number of warheads to 1,500 in each country. However, the reduction still gives both nations the capacity to destroy each other many times over.

helped secure civil rights for African Americans, his role in the Vietnam War continues to cast a shadow on his presidential greatness.

It is too early to guess where George W. Bush will be ranked by history. His response to September 11, 2001, was steady and reassuring, and the nation rallied to his side in the first few weeks of the war in Iraq. At the same time, soaring budget deficits and questions about the war in Iraq undermined both his credibility and his public support. So did rising gasoline prices, the government's weak response to Hurricane Katrina in 2005, and the economic crisis that came at the end of his presidency in 2008.

At least for now, however, Bush seems destined for an average rating. According to public opinion polls taken in late 2006, only 19 percent of respondents rated Bush outstanding or above average, compared with 45 percent for Clinton, 32 percent for George H. W. Bush, 64 percent for Reagan, 38 percent for Jimmy Carter, and 23 percent for Gerald Ford. Of these presidents, only Reagan is likely to emerge as a great or near-great president in future polls.

Ultimately, a president's place in history is determined decades after he or she leaves office and varies over time. Reagan has moved up the charts with each passing survey, for example, as his role in ending the cold war takes on increasing visibility in an uncertain world. By remembering that there is a future accounting, presidents can find some inspiration for making the hard and sometimes unpopular choices that have led to greatness among their predecessors. Thus, the judgment of history may be one of the most important sources of accountability the nation has on its presidents.

CHAPTER SUMMARY

8.1 Describe the constitutional foundations of the presidency and of three presidential roles.

The framers wanted a presidency with enough authority to protect the nation from domestic and foreign threats but not so strong that it would become a threat to liberty. The framers gave the president three central roles in the new government: commander in chief, diplomat in chief, and administrator in chief. Presidents have expanded their powers in several ways throughout the decades. Crises, both foreign and economic, have enlarged these powers. When there is a need for decisive action, presidents are asked to supply it.

8.2 Evaluate the controversies surrounding presidents' assertion of additional executive powers.

The Constitution is not always clear on which branch has what powers, which creates controversies over the president's war power and authority to assert executive privilege, issue executive orders, and control the budget and spending process.

8.3 Outline the functions of the White House staff, Executive Office of the President, cabinet, and vice president.

Presidents manage the executive branch with the assistance of an intensely loyal White House staff, a much larger Executive Office of the President (EOP) that is anchored by the Office of Management and Budget (OMB), a cabinet of department secretaries that oversees the federal government's employees, and the vice president. The vice president's authority varies from president to president.

8.4 Characterize the various roles that presidents play.

We expect a great deal from our presidents. We want them to be crisis managers, morale builders, and agenda setters, but we also want them to be able to connect with average citizens. Presidents must also act as persuaders, using their staff, technology, and public opinion research to accomplish their agendas.

8.5 Identify the sources of presidential–congressional conflict and the tools presidents use to influence Congress.

The president and Congress often have a tense relationship because of different constitutional expectations and party divisions. Presidents have a variety of tools for influencing Congress, however, and use their political and personal resources to gain support for their policy proposals. Presidents have several powerful tools for influencing Congress. They can create mandates by helping members of Congress win elections, use their public approval to lobby Congress for action, and rely on the reputation of the presidency as a source of prestige.

8.6 Identify factors that influence judgments about presidents.

Presidential greatness is hard to define. Historians, political scientists, and the American public consider Washington, Jefferson, Lincoln, and Franklin Roosevelt as their greatest presidents. Greatness depends in part on how presidents deal with crisis and war.

CHAPTER SELF-TEST

8.1 Describe the constitutional foundations of the presidency and of three presidential roles.

1. Which of the following is NOT required for a person to be elected president of the United States?
   a. Be at least 35 years old
   b. Be a natural-born citizen of the United States
   c. Be affiliated with an officially organized political party
   d. Be a resident of the United States for the previous 14 years
2. What is the only constitutional duty of the vice president aside from waiting to take the place of the president if needed?
3. In one or two paragraphs explain the president's responsibility in each of the three roles discussed in the chapter.
4. In a short essay, discuss how the framers addressed their concerns about the presidency in the Constitution. In your opinion, have their protections worked?

8.2 Evaluate the controversies surrounding presidents' assertion of additional executive powers.

5. List and briefly explain the president's additional powers. Which of the president's additional executive powers are most important to the role as chief diplomat, chief lawmaker, manager in chief, and commander in chief?
6. Match each of the presidents listed below with the precedents they set while in office.

1. George W. Bush	a. Establishing a two-term precedent
2. George Washington	b. Creating a strong Executive Office of the President
3. Franklin D. Roosevelt	c. Expanding the president's war power

7. Which of these precedents is the most important to the president's success in Congress? Which is the most threatening to the separation of powers?

8.3 Outline the functions of the White House staff, Executive Office of the President, cabinet, and vice president.

8. Write a brief sentence defining the following parts of the president's staff:
   a. The White House staff
   b. The Cabinet
   c. The Executive Office of the President
   d. The Office of Management and Budget
9. List the three ways of organizing the White House staff and the benefits and weaknesses of each.
10. Table 8–1 lists a set of issues over which the President might be assumed to have some control. Chose three and write a brief essay explaining how the president could influence each.

8.4 Characterize the various roles that presidents play.

11. Briefly explain each of the president's roles listed below.
    a. Persuader
    b. Agenda setter
    c. Morale builder
12. Which role do you think is the most important at the start of a president's first term? Which is the most important during times of national crisis? How do the three roles work together, and when do they conflict?

8.5 Identify the sources of presidential–congressional conflict and the tools presidents use to influence Congress.

13. List the three main causes of conflict between the president and Congress.
14. Write a persuasive essay explaining how the current relationship between the president and Congress fulfills the framers' intentions for their roles and interactions.

8.6 Identify factors that influence judgments about presidents.

15. In a short essay, discuss factors other than winning wars that you think make a president "great." How would the most two recent presidents rank in your determination of presidential greatness?
16. How much should presidents worry about their standing in history when they are making decisions?

Answers for selected questions: 1. c; 6. Bush: c; Washington: a; Roosevelt: b

mypoliscilab™ EXERCISES

Where participation leads to action!

Apply what you learned in this chapter on MyPoliSciLab.

Read on **mypoliscilab.com**

eText: Chapter 8

Study and **Review** on **mypoliscilab.com**

Pre-Test
Post-Test
Chapter Exam
Flashcards

Watch on **mypoliscilab.com**

Video: Bush and Congress
Video: The Government Bails Out Automakers

Explore on **mypoliscilab.com**

Simulation: Presidential Leadership: Which Hat Do You Wear?
Simulation: You Are a President During a Nuclear Power Plant Meltdown
Comparative: Comparing Chief Executives
Timeline: The Executive Order Over Time
Visual Literacy: Presidential Success in Polls and Congress

KEY TERMS

parliamentary governments, p. 247
presidential ticket, p. 249
vesting clause, p. 249
treaty, p. 250
executive agreement, p. 250
congressional–executive agreement, p. 250
recess appointment, p. 251
veto, p. 251
pocket veto, p. 251
take care clause, p. 252
inherent powers, p. 252
State of the Union Address, p. 252
signing statements, p. 252
impeachment, p. 253
executive privilege, p. 254
executive orders, p. 255
impoundment, p. 256
line item veto, p. 256
chief of staff, p. 258
Executive Office of the President (EOP), p. 258
Office of Management and Budget (OMB), p. 259
cabinet, p. 259
presidential support score, p. 264
mandate, p. 264
rally point, p. 264

ADDITIONAL RESOURCES

FURTHER READING

THOMAS E. CRONIN AND **MICHAEL A. GENOVESE,** *The Paradoxes of the American Presidency,* 2d ed. (Oxford University Press, 2004).

TERRY EASTLAND, *Energy in the Executive* (Free Press, 1992).

FRED GREENSTEIN, *The Presidential Difference: Leadership Style from FDR to George W. Bush,* 2d ed. (Princeton University Press, 2004).

GENE HEALY, *The Cult of the Presidency: America's Dangerous Devotion to Presidential Power* (Cato Institute, 2008).

CHARLES O. JONES, *The Presidency in a Separated System,* 2d ed. (Brookings Institution Press, 2005).

SAMUEL KERNELL, *Going Public: New Strategies of Presidential Leadership,* 4th ed. (CQ Press, 2006).

GARY KING AND **LYN RAGSDALE,** *The Elusive Executive: Discovering Statistical Patterns in the Presidency,* 2d ed. (CQ Press, 2002).

SIDNEY M. MILKIS, *The President and the Parties: The Transformation of the American Party System Since the New Deal* (Oxford University Press, 1993).

MICHAEL NELSON, ED., *The Presidency and the Political System,* 9th ed. (CQ Press, 2009).

RICHARD E. NEUSTADT, *Presidential Power and the Modern Presidents* (Free Press, 1991).

BRADLEY H. PATTERSON JR., *The White House Staff: Inside the West Wing and Beyond* (Brookings Institution Press, 2002).

JAMES PFIFFNER, *The Modern Presidency,* 5th ed. (Wadsworth, 2008).

STEPHEN SKOWRONEK, *Presidential Leadership in Political Time: Reprise and Reappraisal* (University of Kansas Press, 2008).

WEB SITES

whitehouse.gov Every fact possible on the Obama presidency, including speeches, blogs, videos, and links to all major EOP.

loc.gov The Library of Congress Web site. Click on the presidential history link for portraits and details on each presidency.

millercenter.org/academic/americanpresident A huge inventory of resources on the American presidency, including research papers and oral histories from past administrations.

barackobama.com Information on Obama's call for citizen involvement.

presidency.org The Web site of the Center for the Presidency. Loaded with papers and facts.

presidency.ucsb.edu The largest inventory of information on what presidents do. Every State of the Union Address, executive orders, press conference transcripts, veto messages, and selected research papers. An invaluable resource for research papers.

CHAPTER 9

The Federal Bureaucracy

Executing the Laws

Understanding the Federal Bureaucracy

9.1 Outline the constitutional roots of the federal bureaucracy and pros and cons of bureaucratic administration.

The Four Types of Federal Organizations

9.2 Identify the four types of federal organizations.

Types of Federal Employees

9.3 Differentiate three types of federal employees, and explain how each is selected.

The Job of the Federal Bureaucracy

9.4 Analyze the bureaucracy's tools of implementation and their effectiveness.

Controlling the Federal Bureaucracy

9.5 Assess presidential and congressional efforts to control the federal bureaucracy.

Does the Federal Bureaucracy Work?

9.6 Evaluate the bureaucracy's effectiveness.

Early in the morning on April 20, 2010, British Petroleum was about to start producing oil from one of the deepest wells ever drilled in the Gulf of Mexico. Breaking through 5,000 feet below surface, the well was connected to a floating oil rig called the Deepwater Horizon. Hours before the Deepwater Horizon was to finish work, methane gas surged up the underwater pipe and exploded on the surface. Eleven oil workers were killed or lost at sea as the Deepwater Horizon was sinking. As it collapsed, the rig ripped free of the underwater oil pipe to the surface, which remained open because the underwater "blowout preventer" had failed. Within hours, the federal government discovered that the pipe was releasing thousands of gallons of oil per hour, creating the largest oil spill in U.S. history and threatening the entire Gulf coast.

The spill was caused by a number of failures, including British Petroleum's own haphazard safety precautions. However, the disaster was rooted in what President Barack Obama later called the "cozy relationship" between the federal government's Minerals Management Service (MMS) and the oil industry. Located within the Department of the Interior, the MMS was responsible for both regulating and promoting the industry. It set safety standards for offshore oil drilling even as it granted permits that allowed the industry to extract as much oil as possible. With the United States desperately trying to break its addiction to foreign oil, the MMS began to grant permits more freely and frequently waived safety requirements on deepwater drilling. For example, MMS decided that British Petroleum did not need an automatic cutoff valve on the Deepwater rig, waived the company's obligation to prove that its drilling would not cause environmental damage, and gave the company permission to test the Deepwater Horizon's blowout preventer at lower pressure standards than required under the MMS's own rules.

Confronted with these failures, Obama decided to overhaul MMS by breaking it into two new agencies, one for assuring safety and the other for granting permits. He also accepted the resignation of the political appointee heading the agency and gave the U.S. Coast Guard absolute authority to supervise British Petroleum's efforts to stop the spill. He also appointed a special commission to investigate the disaster, even as Congress launched its own investigations. Finally, Obama promised a new era of accountability at the MMS. However, MMS was the subject of numerous earlier investigations in previous decades, none of which had produced results. The fact that MMS continued to give the benefit of the doubt to the oil industry shows just how resistant some government agencies are to presidential and congressional control.

In this chapter, we examine the origins, functions, and realities of the federal bureaucracy as it works to faithfully execute the laws. We also explore how governmental departments, agencies, and employees are held accountable to the president, Congress, and the U.S. public.

This chapter uses the word "bureaucracy" to describe what political scientists call the federal administrative state. As we shall see, the word is sometimes used as a way to criticize government, while the word "bureaucrat" is often used to describe federal employees as poorly motivated and inefficient. Instead, we refer to federal employees as just that, federal employees. Some are very good at their work and are highly motivated to make a difference through their public service, but there are always a few employees in every organization, public or private, who do not work hard. The major difference is that private employees are relatively easy to fire, while poorly performing federal employees are protected against removal by a long list of laws.

Understanding the Federal Bureaucracy

LEARNING **OBJECTIVE**

9.1 Outline the constitutional roots of the federal bureaucracy and pros and cons of bureaucratic administration.

The framers clearly understood that the new national government would need an administrative system to protect the young Republic from foreign and domestic threats. They also understood that the new departments of government would need talented employees if they were to succeed. Although the framers hoped government employees would be motivated by the desire to serve their country, they knew government would have to pay those employees for their work.

Constitutional Controls

Under the Constitution, the federal bureaucracy is responsible for faithfully executing the laws on behalf of the president, Congress, and the judiciary. Although disagreements and factions were a normal and predictable part of making the laws, they were unacceptable when it came time for the laws to be executed. As Alexander Hamilton explained in *The Federalist,* No. 70, the new federal government would need a bureaucracy with the skill and motivation to convert laws into action, which he described as "the true test of a good government."[1]

The founders spent little time worrying about the administration of government, however. Instead, they left most of the details to future presidents. They believed that federal departments and agencies would be relatively small, and they expected Congress to establish the same departments that had existed under the Articles of Confederation, including the departments of war, state, and treasury, and the postal service.[2] Nevertheless, the framers made three key decisions about executing the laws that continue to shape federal administration to this day.

Alexander Hamilton helped set many of the precedents that govern the federal bureaucracy today. He was a strong advocate of what he called "execution in detail," which involved detailed rules that federal employees must follow, and he argued for an expansion in the number of federal employees as the federal government's mission expanded.

First, they prohibited members of the House and Senate from holding executive branch positions. They drew a sharp line on the issue in Article I, Section 6, of the Constitution: "No Senator or Representative shall, during the Time for which he was elected, be appointed to any civil Office under the Authority of the United States, which shall have been created, or the Emoluments whereof shall have been increased during such time, and no Person holding any Office under the United States, shall be a Member of either House during his Continuance in Office." Under this provision, Congress could not create executive jobs for its members, which was a common form of corruption in England before the Revolutionary War.[3]

Second, the framers decided to give the president complete authority to nominate the senior officers of government. Although they also gave the Senate authority to confirm or reject the president's appointees under the Constitution's "advice and consent" function, the framers made the president, not Congress, responsible for filling any vacancies in those jobs when the Senate is in recess. Although Article I does give Congress the power to create the departments of government and the Senate the power to confirm presidential appointees, both by a majority vote, the president emerged from the final days of the Constitutional Convention as the nation's *administrator in chief.* The framers saw direct presidential control of government as essential for faithfully executing the laws.

Third, the framers decided that the president, not Congress, is responsible for requiring the opinions of the "principal officer" of each executive department, which means the president is in charge of what presidential appointees do. The chief executive is not only responsible for hiring and supervising presidential appointees, however, but also has the power to fire appointees for any reason. Presidents routinely ask all their appointees to resign before the inauguration of a new president.

These decisions about presidential power did not give the president unlimited authority to execute the laws, however. Recall that Congress, not the president, has the power to create, reorganize, or abolish the departments and agencies of government in the first place and has the responsibility for appropriating the money to administer programs and hire government employees. They also gave the Senate the power to confirm certain presidential appointees, and they clearly expected both houses of Congress to monitor the workings of the executive branch.

Defining Bureaucracy

More than 200 years after the Constitution was written, the federal government is administered by one of the largest bureaucracies in the world. The federal bureaucracy is composed of 15 departments, 50 agencies, the U.S. Postal Service, and the armed services.

It also employs one of the largest workforces in the world. Nearly 4.5 million people worked for the federal government in 2010, including 700,000 postal workers, more than 2.2 million full-time federal employees, and 1.4 million military personnel. In addition, 7.6 million work for the federal government under contracts to private firms such as Lockheed Martin and Boeing, and 2.9 million work under federal grants to colleges, universities, and state and local governments. All told, the federal bureaucracy includes almost 15 million employees, only a handful of whom are visible to the public.[4] Figure 9–1 shows the numbers of full-time federal employees versus the number of contract employees. The former has been relatively stable throughout the last 20 years, whereas the latter has expanded rapidly.

At one time in history, **bureaucracy** actually meant fast, effective, and rational administration. In its ideal form, a bureaucracy made sure every job was carefully designed to ensure faithful performance by well-trained, highly motivated **bureaucrats,** or employees. According to German sociologist Max Weber, who wrote in defense of bureaucracy in the late 1800s, bureaucracies derive their strength from six characteristics:

1. *Specialization:* Bureaucracies break jobs into smaller and smaller parts so that every employee knows exactly what his or her job is. Because their jobs are so specialized, employees can be trained in enough detail to succeed.
2. *Centralization:* Bureaucracies concentrate authority at the top of the organization, where a single leader maintains control of all activity. This leader is in charge of every last person in the organization.
3. *Rules:* Bureaucracies implement policies through formal rules that govern everything that employees do.
4. *Standardization:* Bureaucracies make sure all decisions are the same—meaning every employee makes the same decisions in producing a product or making a ruling. Standardization assures customers and clients that they will be treated fairly whomever they talk to.
5. *Expertise:* Bureaucracies make sure all employees have the training and experience to do their jobs effectively and that they are given the tools such as information technology to succeed.
6. *Accountability:* Bureaucracies enforce these rules through a set of communication channels that allow the leaders of the organization to know exactly what is going on at all levels. The bureaucracy is structured so that employees follow orders or are fired.

bureaucracy
A form of organization that operates through impersonal, uniform rules and procedures.

bureaucrat
A career government employee.

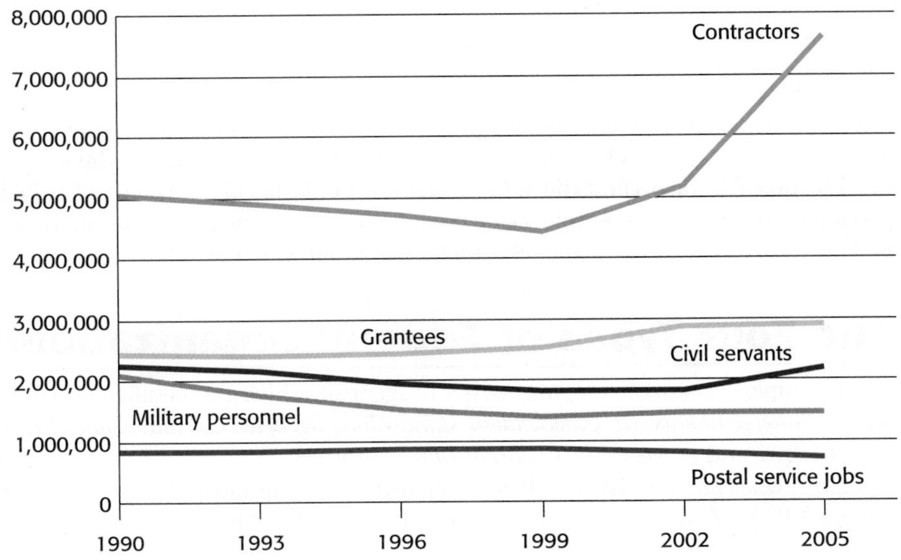

FIGURE 9–1 **Measuring the Estimated Total Number of Federal Employees.**

■ *Why has there been such a dramatic increase in the number of contracted employees?*

SOURCE: Paul C. Light, *A Government Ill Executed* (Harvard University Press, 2008).

Of the People — THE GLOBAL COMMUNITY

Global Views of Bribery

Bribery is not a significant problem in the U.S. federal bureaucracy, but it is a way of doing business in many countries. A bribe is merely a way for ordinary citizens to speed up the bureaucracy so that they can get building permits, resolve traffic fines without going to court, and receive basic benefits such as aid for the needy. Bribes are a sign that a government is unwilling to faithfully execute the laws for all of its citizens and show significant corruption within the system. As the Pew Global Survey shows, countries vary greatly in the degree of this kind of corruption. Respondents were asked, "In the past year, how often, if ever, have you had to do a favor, give a gift, or pay a bribe to a government official in order to get services or a document that the government is supposed to provide?"

The Pew survey shows great variation throughout the world in bribery and corruption. Some nations such as India tolerate very high levels of bribery, whereas other Asian nations have been more successful in limiting the practice.

One way to avoid corruption is to impose strong limits on employee conduct through tight monitoring by special units of government such as the U.S. government's offices of inspector general. These offices, which can be found through www.ignet.gov, are responsible for detecting and punishing fraud, waste, and abuse. They create deterrence by making sure federal employees understand that they might be caught and punished if they take bribes or other payments for favorable treatment. Higher-level federal employees are also required to file annual financial disclosure reports showing their financial transactions for the year. Citizens can also play a role in preventing fraud by reporting incidents of fraud, waste, and abuse through an inspector general's hotline.

CRITICAL THINKING QUESTIONS

1. What can international organizations such as the United Nations do to reduce government corruption throughout the world?
2. Do you have any theories about why the Pew Global Survey did not interview U.S., British, Chinese, and Japanese citizens about bribery?
3. Does financial exposure have any negative effects in discouraging people to take jobs in government?

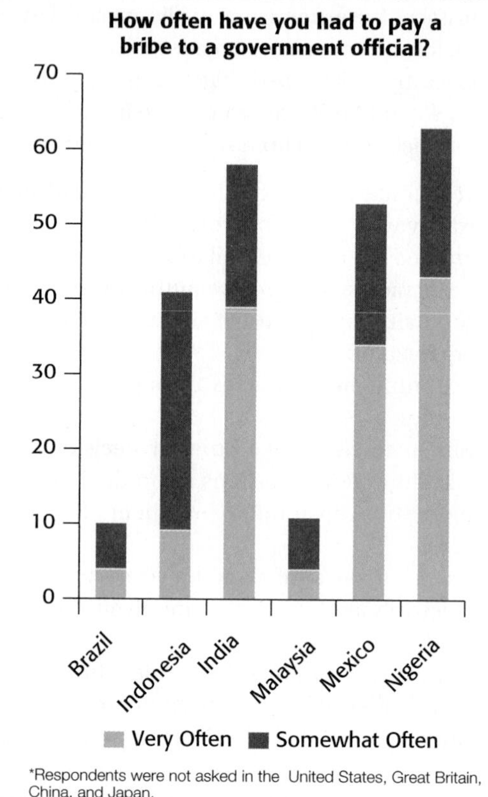

*Respondents were not asked in the United States, Great Britain, China, and Japan.

Over time, however, the bureaucracy has created dense layers of management—a problem because these layers keep information from moving up and down the organization quickly. Most federal organizations impose dozens of layers of management between the president and the federal employees who actually do the work. In addition, duplication and overlap between units can create confusion about who does what.

The Four Types of Federal Organizations

LEARNING **OBJECTIVE**

9.2 Identify the four types of federal organizations.

Federal employees work for departments and agencies, which are classified into four broad types: (1) *departments,* (2) *independent stand-alone agencies,* (3) *independent regulatory commissions,* and (4) *government corporations.* Although these terms are sometimes confusing, especially in the case of independent agencies versus independent regulatory commissions, they are the standard words used in the federal organization chart.

Duplication between agencies is evident in the procedures for protecting Americans from mad cow disease. The Department of Agriculture's Animal and Plant Health Inspection Service keeps diseased cattle out of the United States; the Department of Health and Human Services' Food and Drug Administration monitors cattle feed; and the Department of Agriculture's Food Safety and Inspection Service inspects cattle as they go to slaughter. ■ *Why is the federal bureaucracy, not the states, responsible for food safety?*

Departments tend to be the most common federal organizations, have the broadest missions, and usually have the largest number of federal employees. They are also the most visible organizations in government and are generally well known to the public.

Independent stand-alone agencies are also under the president's control but tend to have fewer federal employees and may have more focused missions than departments. In general, the word "independent" is used to distinguish agencies that exist outside a department from those that operate within a department such as the Department of Homeland Security. This chapter will generally use the term "independent stand-alone" agencies to describe what the federal government formally calls independent agencies.

Independent regulatory commissions are a special kind of independent agency. They are created to insulate the agency from congressional and presidential control through the appointment of a board of commissioners who serve for a fixed term of office and cannot be fired by the president.

Finally, **government corporations** are designed to operate much like private businesses and have special authorities to set the prices of their services. These corporations are quite rare and are often confused with departments and independent stand-alone agencies. The U.S. Postal Service is the biggest of the government corporations and is supposed to make money by delivering the mail. Amtrak is another example of a government corporation. It, too, is supposed to make money through ticket sales.

We will discuss each of the four types of federal organizations below.

department
Usually the largest organization in government with the largest mission; also the highest rank in the federal hierarchy.

independent stand-alone agency
A government agency that operates outside a traditional government department, but under the president's direct control.

independent regulatory commission
A government agency or commission with regulatory power whose independence is protected by Congress.

government corporation
A government agency that operates like a business corporation, created to secure greater freedom of action and flexibility for a particular program.

Departments Departments are the most visible organizations in the federal bureaucracy. Today's 15 departments of government employ more than 70 percent of all federal civil servants and spend 93 percent of all federal dollars. Fourteen of the departments are headed by secretaries; the 15th, the Justice Department, is headed by the attorney general. Many departments are collections of smaller agencies that are brought together under one organization chart. As Figure 9–2 shows, the Department of Health and Human Services contains more than a dozen smaller agencies as part of its overall structure.

Measured by the total number of employees, the five largest departments are the Defense Department; the Department of Veterans Affairs, which helps veterans return to

FIGURE 9–2 The Department of Health and Human Services.

■ *What are the benefits and drawbacks of having all of these organizations housed within the Department of Health and Human Services?*

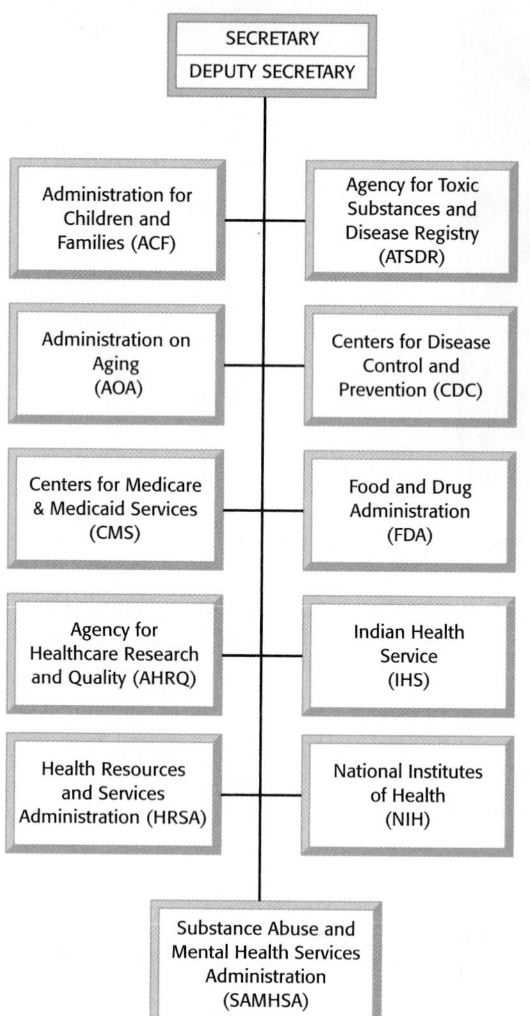

civilian life after military service; the Department of Homeland Security, created to protect the nation from terrorism; the Department of the Treasury, which manages the economy and raises revenues through the Internal Revenue Service; and the Department of Justice, which enforces the laws through the federal courts and investigates crime through the Federal Bureau of Investigation.

Measured by prestige, the Defense, Health and Human Services, Justice, State, and Treasury departments are considered part of the *inner cabinet* closest to the president, whereas the rest of the departments are considered part of the outer circle of departments that rarely receive the president's attention.

Measured by budget, the Department of Health and Human Services is the largest department of government and will become even larger as a result of health care legislation enacted in 2010. This department provides health insurance to the elderly through the huge Medicare program, helps states cover health care for the poor through the Medicaid programs, covers the cost of health insurance for children through the State Children's Health Insurance Program (SCHIP), and administers a variety of programs to help the poor. It also contains the Food and Drug Administration, the National Institutes of Health, and the Centers for Disease Control and Prevention, all of which protect the population from disease. The health care reforms signed into law in 2010 will be administered by the Centers for Medicare and Medicaid Services, which is also housed by this department.

The 15 federal departments were created using two very different models. The first approach to building a department focuses on creating an umbrella organization by combining a number of related independent agencies. The Department of Homeland Security, for example, was created by combining elements of 22 separate agencies, including the Immigration and Naturalization Service, the Customs Service, the Federal Emergency Management Agency, the Secret Service, portions of the Animal and Plant Health Inspection Service, and the Coast Guard, which is often viewed as a branch of the military.

The other approach to building a department is designed to create a single-purpose organization that owes its existence largely to the strength of an interest group. Congress created the Department of Veterans Affairs in 1989 under pressure from veterans' groups such as the American Legion and Veterans of Foreign Wars, who wanted their own advocate in the president's cabinet.

Independent Stand-Alone Agencies The word "independent" means at least two things in the federal bureaucracy. Applied to a regulatory commission, it means the agency is outside the president's control. Applied to an agency of government, it merely means separate from a traditional department. Whereas independent regulatory commissions do not report to the president, independent agencies do.

As a general rule, independent stand-alone agencies are smaller than federal departments and work on specific problems. Becoming an agency is often the first step toward becoming a department. The Veterans Administration was created in 1930 as an agency, for example, but it became a department only in 1989. Independent stand-alone agencies are usually headed by an administrator, the second most senior title in the federal bureaucracy behind secretary or attorney general. There are more than 50 such agencies today.

The spread of independent stand-alone agencies can add to confusion about who is responsible for what in the federal government. For example, the federal government has 15 different intelligence agencies, which include the CIA, the Defense Intelligence Agency, the FBI, and the NSA. These 15 agencies had a history of keeping secrets not only from the people but also from each other, which contributed to the intelligence failures leading up to the war in Iraq. In late 2004, Congress created a new national intelligence director to oversee all of these agencies and foster greater collaboration.

Politically, independent stand-alone agencies can sometimes be more important to the president than some cabinet departments. The director of the CIA or the administrator of the EPA may get a higher place on the president's agenda than the secretary of HUD (the Department of Housing and Urban Development) or agriculture, particularly when an issue such as international spying or global warming is in the headlines.

The following independent stand-alone agencies are considered among the most important in the bureaucracy:

- *Central Intelligence Agency* collects and interprets international intelligence.
- *Director of National Intelligence* coordinates intelligence collected by other government agencies.
- *Environmental Protection Agency* regulates and enforces laws to reduce pollution.
- *National Aeronautics and Space Administration* manages the U.S. civilian space program.
- *Small Business Administration* monitors the state of U.S. small businesses.
- *Social Security Administration* administers the Social Security program.

Independent Regulatory Commissions Although independent regulatory commissions are part of the federal bureaucracy, they have a measure of independence from both Congress and the president. By definition, these commissions are headed not by a single executive but by a small number of commissioners appointed by the president, with Senate confirmation, for fixed terms of office. Unlike other presidential appointees, commissioners cannot be removed from office without cause, which is defined by law to mean "inefficiency, neglect of duty, or malfeasance in office." As a result, independent regulatory commissions are less responsive to political pressure from either Congress or the president.

As Federal Reserve Board chair, Ben S. Bernanke is in charge of one of the most important independent regulatory commissions. Replacing Alan Greenspan, who had served for nearly 20 years, Bernanke has begun his second four-year term as chairman of the Federal Reserve Board. ■ *Why does the chairman of the Federal Reserve have a limited, four-year term when most presidential appointees do not?*

Throughout the decades, Congress has created dozens of independent regulatory commissions with the power to protect consumers (the Consumer Product Safety Commission), regulate stock markets (the Securities and Exchange Commission), oversee federal election laws (the Federal Election Commission), monitor television and radio (the Federal Communications Commission), regulate business (the Federal Trade Commission), control the supply of money (the Federal Reserve Board), and watch over nuclear power plants (the Nuclear Regulatory Commission). Many experts contend that the Federal Reserve Board chair is the second most influential person in making economic policy, and others would argue that the current chair, Ben S. Bernanke, is the most important leader in influencing public confidence about the economy.[5] Bernanke was appointed to a four-year term as a member of the Board in 2006, and he was reappointed in 2010.

Independent regulatory commissions are not completely independent, however. Their commissioners are appointed by the president and are subject to Senate confirmation, their annual budgets must be approved by Congress, and their decisions are subject to judicial review. Moreover, presidents make most appointments on the basis of party, which means that commissions are often highly political.

Independent regulatory commissions tend to be much less visible than departments until a crisis occurs. The Securities and Exchange Commission was on the front pages for three years, for example, as one corporation after another disclosed accounting fraud in their annual reports to investors. The SEC was created in the 1930s to restore investor confidence in the stock market after the Great Depression, but it was accused of being negligent in monitoring accounting practices at big companies such as Enron and WorldCom in the early 2000s. It also failed to detect Bernie Madoff's investment fraud, which cost investors more than $18 billion. In May 2010, however, a newly rebuilt SEC filed suit against the financial giant Goldman Sachs, alleging that the firm bet against the very mortgages it was selling on the open market.

The giant investment firm Goldman Sachs came under fire for its behavior in the 2008 economic collapse. It was accused of betting against investment packages that it sold to clients, which allowed the firm to make money even as its clients lost money. Congress began investigating the lack of federal oversight of the action in 2010.

The following independent regulatory commissions are considered among the most important in the federal bureaucracy:

- *Commodity Futures Trading Corporation* regulates the markets for commodities such as corn, wheat, precious metals, and other products used in manufacturing.

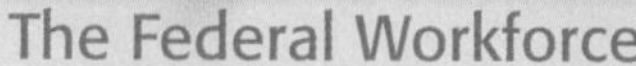

AMERICA'S CHANGING FACE

The Federal Workforce

The federal bureaucracy is more representative of the public now than it was in the 1950s, when most of its employees were white and most female employees were clerk-typists. Women held 44 percent of all federal jobs in 2007, whereas minorities held close to a third.

Even though the number of women and minorities in the federal workforce is at an all-time high, both groups still face barriers in rising to the top. First, women and minorities are not equally represented in all departments and agencies. They tend to be concentrated in departments with strong social service missions such as Education, Health and Human Services, Housing and Urban Development, and Veterans Affairs. Military and technical departments such as Defense, Energy, and Transportation have far fewer women employees.

Second, women and minorities are not represented at all levels of the federal bureaucracy. Women held 70 percent of lower-paying technical and clerical positions in 2007, and minorities were also heavily represented at the bottom of government. Together, women and minorities held barely 15 percent of the top jobs. Nevertheless, they are moving into the top jobs at a fast rate. Between 1994 and 2007, the number of women and minorities in professional and managerial jobs jumped from 44 percent to roughly 60 percent. (Further statistics on the federal workforce can be found by searching for "factbook" at http://www.opm.gov.)

CRITICAL THINKING QUESTIONS

1. Why should the federal bureaucracy try to recruit more women and minorities to its top jobs?
2. Does increasing diversity improve the bureaucracy's performance and accountability? Why or why not?
3. How can the bureaucracy enhance diversity in scientific and technical fields?

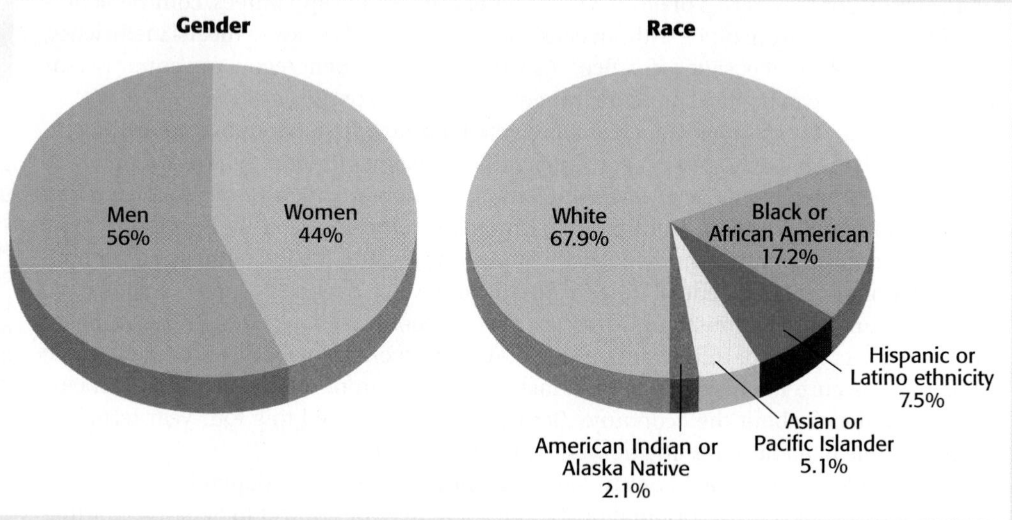

SOURCE: U.S. Office of Personnel Management, *Fact Book, 2007,* accessed at http://www.opm.gov/feddata/factbook/2007/2007FACTBOOK.pdf.

- *Consumer Product Safety Commission* monitors and regulates the safety of products released for public use, such as children's toys and cribs.
- *Equal Employment Opportunity Commission* regulates and enforces laws ensuring equality of access to jobs.
- *Federal Communications Commission* monitors and regulates use of the public airways for radio and television broadcasting, but its authority does not extend to cable television or satellite radio.
- *Federal Deposit Insurance Corporation* provides insurance for bank savings accounts up to $100,000.
- *Federal Election Commission* monitors and enforces federal campaign finance laws.
- *Federal Trade Commission* ensures that advertising for products is fair and truthful.
- *Federal Reserve Board* sets interest rates on borrowing.
- *Nuclear Regulatory Commission* regulates the nuclear power industry.
- *Securities Exchange Commission* regulates the stock markets that trade stocks in publicly held corporations.

Government Corporations Government corporations are perhaps the least understood organizations in the federal bureaucracy. Because they are intended to act more like businesses than like traditional government departments and agencies, they generally have more freedom from the internal rules that control traditional government agencies. They often have greater authority to hire and fire employees quickly and are allowed to make money through the sale of services such as train tickets, stamps, or home loans.[6]

Government corporations include organizations such as the Corporation for Public Broadcasting (which runs PBS television), the U.S. Postal Service, the National Railroad Passenger Corporation (better known as Amtrak), and AmeriCorps (which runs a national service program created by the Clinton administration), along with a host of financial enterprises that make loans of one kind or another.

Amtrak is a government corporation that is supposed to make money through its operations, but it lost more than $1 billion in 2009. Federal taxpayers must pick up the loss, which averaged $32 per Amtrak passenger. The U.S. Postal Service lost more than $3 billion in 2009, which was also covered by taxpayers. ■ *Do you think that the services these businesses provide justify allowing them to operate at a loss? Why might it be important that these services be provided by the government rather than a private business?*

Types of Federal Employees

The federal civilian workforce is composed of three different types of employees: (1) presidential appointees who run the bureaucracy; (2) members of the Senior Executive Service, which contains a mix of presidential appointees and civil servants; and (3) members of the civil service who execute the laws under the direction of presidential appointees and senior executives. (A full picture of the federal workforce would also include military personnel, but we will focus on civilian employees here.)

Presidential Appointees

LEARNING **OBJECTIVE**

9.3 Differentiate three types of federal employees, and explain how each is selected.

Roughly 3,000 presidential appointees head federal departments and agencies, including 600 administrative officers subject to Senate confirmation and another 2,400 who serve entirely "at the pleasure of the president." As political officers, presidential appointees generally leave their posts at the end of that president's term in office. The president also appoints another 1,000 U.S. marshals, U.S. attorneys, and ambassadors to foreign nations but usually makes these appointments on a nonpolitical basis.

Presidential appointees have some of the toughest jobs in the world. They work long hours, resolve complex disputes, and make important decisions about how the laws will be executed. Although many are selected on the basis of political connections, the top positions in the most important departments are generally reserved for individuals with significant leadership skills and experience.

Senior presidential appointees are selected through a four-step process. Except for individuals who are extraordinarily close to the president, the first step is to be selected by the White House Presidential Personnel Office. Most appointees are members of the president's party, and many contributed either time or money to the president's campaign.

The second step in becoming an appointee is to survive the White House clearance process, which is designed to ensure that candidates are legally qualified for office and pose no potential embarrassment to the president. All candidates receive a packet of forms that require detailed disclosure on every aspect of their personal and professional life, including job history, drug use, personal counseling, financial investments, and even traffic fines of more than $150.

The third step is the simplest: The president submits the name of the nominee on parchment paper to the clerk of the Senate. The document is placed in a special envelope, sealed with wax, and hand-delivered to the Senate when it is in session.

In the fourth step, the Senate refers each nomination to the appropriate confirmation committee, which conducts its own reviews. Depending on the position and the nominee, the Senate may ask to review the entire file developed by the White House, including the FBI's investigation. Once the review is complete, the committee holds a

Former Senate Majority Leader Tom Daschle was selected by President Obama as secretary of the Department of Health and Human Services. Daschle was forced to withdraw his name from consideration after reporting that he had underpaid his income taxes.

The Transportation Security Administration did not have an administrator in place when a terrorist attempted to blow up a Northwest Airlines flight on December 25, 2009. ■ *What other problems can arise when an agency doesn't have a senior official in place?*

hearing on the nomination and usually sends it to the floor of the Senate with a favorable recommendation. In turn, most nominations are approved by the Senate on voice votes.

Because the Senate acts through unanimous consent, individual senators can place *holds* on individual nominations to prevent confirmation. In 2009, for example, Senator Jim DeMint (R-S.C.) put a hold on Obama's choice for the top job at the Transportation Security Administration, which oversees airport security through its workforce of 45,000 baggage and passenger screeners. DeMint refused to release his hold unless the Obama administration promised not to allow the screeners to unionize. As a result, the Transportation Security Administration did not have an administrator in office when a terrorist attempted to explode a bomb on a flight from Amsterdam to Detroit on Christmas Day 2009.

The Senior Executive Service

Presidential appointees work closely with the 7,000 members of the **Senior Executive Service,** which includes roughly 6,400 career executives appointed through a rigorous review process and another 600 political executives appointed by the president without Senate confirmation. Career senior executives continue in their posts regardless of who happens to be president and are selected on the basis of merit. Except for a small number of political executives who are appointed for a limited time on the basis of political loyalty, members of the Senior Executive Service are selected through a highly competitive process that emphasizes their skills as managers.

When the number of presidential appointees and senior executives are added together, there are approximately 10,000 executives who run federal departments and agencies. The number has grown dramatically throughout the past three decades as the federal government has "thickened," with more layers of leadership and more leaders at each layer.[7] Some political scientists argue that Congress helped cause thickening by creating highly complex programs that demand close supervision, whereas others believe it is driven in part by a competition for power among competing organizations. According to this theory of public bureaucracy, bureaucratic organizations constantly seek to enhance their power, whether by creating new titles, adding more staff, or increasing their budgets.[8]

Senior Executive Service
Established by Congress in 1978 as a flexible, mobile corps of senior career executives who work closely with presidential appointees to manage government.

The Civil Service

The founders understood that the new federal government would need employees, and they would need to be paid. They also knew that most federal employees would not require Senate confirmation and that many of these employees would select government for their career. The founders believed that this **civil service** would outlast each administration, thereby providing steadiness for government.

For the first 100 years, however, members of the federal civil service were selected in part because of their political loyalty to the president's party. This **spoils system**—"to the

civil service
Federal employees who work for government through a competitive, not political, selection process.

spoils system
A system of public employment based on rewarding party loyalists and friends.

victor belong the spoils"—was substantially expanded by President Andrew Jackson after his election in 1829. Jackson believed that every job in government was a potential opportunity for employing his political allies. Thus, every job was subject to presidential control and filled on the basis of political connections and even bribes. Actual ability to do the work had almost nothing to do with obtaining an appointment, and few employees outlasted their president.

The spoils system gave the president's party complete control over almost every government job, from cabinet secretaries down to post office clerks. Under its method of *patronage,* presidents would patronize, or support, their allies by providing jobs and other benefits after an election.

The spoils system began to unravel when Congress created the modern civil service in 1883. Indeed, it was a job seeker who started the federal bureaucracy down the road toward today's civil service system. Unfortunately for President James Garfield, that job seeker happened to be both disappointed and a good shot. Garfield's assassination prompted Congress to pass the Pendleton Act of 1883, which created an independent Civil Service Commission to ensure that most federal jobs were awarded under a **merit system,** meaning on the basis of an individual's ability to do the work, not political connections.[9] See Figure 9–3 for the different types of federal employees.

FIGURE 9–3 **Types of Federal Employees.**
■ *What are the advantages and disadvantages of having so many more federal employees be civil service employees rather than presidential appointees?*

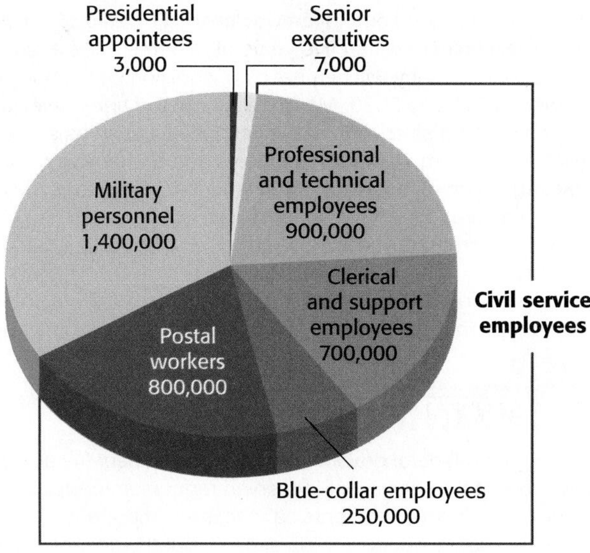

Ninety percent of federal employees are now selected on the basis of merit. Nearly all the rest are selected through hiring systems that emphasize a special skill such as medicine. The **Office of Personnel Management (OPM)** administers civil service laws and rules, whereas the independent **Merit Systems Protection Board** is charged with protecting the integrity of the federal merit system and the rights of federal employees. The Merit Systems Protection Board conducts studies of the merit system, investigates charges of favoritism, resolves employee complaints about unfair discipline, and orders corrective and disciplinary actions against an agency executive or employee when appropriate. (You can find a sampling of current federal job offerings at USAJobs in some chapter cites.

The Hiring Process

Unlike appointees selected by the president, most federal employees are recruited through the civil service. The civil service system was designed to reduce political corruption by promoting merit in the hiring process. But hiring on the basis of merit is not the only way government seeks to reduce corruption. As we shall see, it also regulates the political activities of civil servants.

Under Office of Personnel Management rules, most prospective government employees apply the way private employees do, by submitting an application. Federal organizations cannot select just anyone, however. They must keep careful records about each candidate and justify their decisions when challenged. Federal Organizations must also give veterans special consideration for most jobs and ensure that all jobs are filled through a truly competitive process. Each candidate must also provide certain information about his or her past, including education, work history, and criminal violations. Candidates must also declare any potential conflicts of interest that might affect their performance.

These procedures are intended to protect the merit principle and to meet the bureaucracy's need for qualified personnel. In practice, the two objectives sometimes conflict. In general, the federal hiring process takes six months on average, far longer than in most private businesses. Although the federal government offers a range of recruitment incentives such as partial loan forgiveness, many potential employees are unwilling to wait for a decision, especially in a highly competitive job market.

Regulating the Civil Service

In 1939, Congress passed the Act to Prevent Pernicious Political Activities, usually called the **Hatch Act** after its chief sponsor, Senator Carl Hatch of New Mexico. The act was designed to ensure that the federal civil service did not have disproportionate influence in the election of presidents and members of Congress. In essence, it permitted federal employees to vote in

merit system
A system of public employment in which selection and promotion depend on demonstrated performance rather than political patronage.

Office of Personnel Management (OPM)
An agency that administers civil service laws, rules, and regulations.

Merit Systems Protection Board
An independent agency that oversees and protects merit in the federal government personnel system.

Hatch Act
A federal statute barring federal employees from active participation in certain kinds of politics and protecting them from being fired on partisan grounds.

YOU WILL DECIDE Should You Apply for a Federal Job?

The average federal employee was nearly 50 years old in 2010, and nearly half are within five years of retirement. As a result, the federal bureaucracy will hire nearly one million new employees between 2011 and 2020. Many will be offered entry-level jobs that carry good salaries and special benefits such as student loan relief. Federal employees also receive comprehensive health care coverage, signing bonuses, a retirement plan, vacation days, and free child care. It is little wonder many college seniors say the federal government is the place to go for pay, benefits, and job security.

The federal government also offers some of the most interesting jobs in the world. Scientists and engineers can work on leading-edge space technologies at the National Aeronautics and Space Administration, biochemists and physicians can find great reward at the National Institutes of Health and the Centers for Disease Control, lawyers can help enforce important civil and criminal laws at the Department of Justice, and environmentalists can deal with global warming at the National Oceanographic and Atmospheric Administration or the Environmental Protection Agency.

What do you think? Would you consider working for the federal government? What are the pros and cons of these jobs?

THINKING IT THROUGH

Although the federal government offers good benefits and important work, it also has a well-deserved reputation for being a difficult place to work. Most students say the most important consideration in taking a job is not pay or job security but the chance to make a difference, the opportunity for promotions, and meaningful work. They also say they want a simple, easy hiring process that makes decisions quickly.

The federal government has many problems meeting these goals. Getting a federal job is a complicated, often confusing process that takes months to complete, and new recruits often leave because they feel trapped by a bureaucracy that allows little room for advancement. The government's biggest problem with retaining talented employees appears to be a lack of resources to actually do meaningful work. Young recruits complain they do not have enough access to training or new technology, and their organizations do not have enough people to execute the laws. (For a list of many, but not all, open federal jobs, visit www.USAJobs.gov.)

Many college seniors also say the federal government is a great place to work for anyone but them. They want the chance to make a difference *now,* not in 20 or 30 years. Although there are rewarding places to work in the federal bureaucracy, students rightly worry that they will land in a department or agency with little interest in giving them the tools to do their jobs well or the meaningful work they crave.

But public employment also provides opportunities to make a difference in a policy area of importance to the employee. Public employment may be open to people who lack the connections sometimes needed to secure jobs in the private sector. From auditing financial instutions for solvency to public health to the armed services, individuals can find job satisfaction in public employment.

Critical Thinking Questions

1. Why do college and university students put such a great emphasis on finding meaningful work?
2. Does the federal bureaucracy send the right message to students when it emphasizes the pay, benefits, and job security it can offer?
3. What can the federal bureaucracy do to make its jobs more attractive to this generation of employees?

government elections but not to take an active part in partisan politics. The Hatch Act also made it illegal to dismiss civilian employees for political reasons.[10]

In 1993, Congress, with the encouragement of the Clinton administration, overhauled the Hatch Act and made many forms of participation in partisan politics permissible. The revised act still bars federal officials from running as candidates in partisan elections, but it does permit most federal civil servants to hold party positions and involve themselves in party fund-raising and campaigning. This new law was welcomed by those who believed that the old act discouraged political participation by 3 million people who might otherwise be vigorous political activists.[11]

The new Hatch Act retains many restrictions on federal employees: They cannot raise campaign funds in their agencies, and those who work in such highly sensitive federal agencies as the CIA, the FBI, the Secret Service, and certain divisions of the IRS are specifically barred from nearly all partisan activity. Although public employees may in most cases express opinions about candidates and parties and contribute money to them, they *may not* be candidates for public office in partisan elections or use their jobs or authority for electoral purposes.

The vast majority of federal employees work outside of Washington, D.C., in regional federal offices, post offices, veterans medical centers, and a host of other big- and small-town federal service centers. In 1995, a homegrown antigovernment terrorist, Timothy McVeigh, bombed the federal building in Oklahoma City, killing 168 federal employees and some of their children who were in a federal day care center in the building.

The Role of Government Employee Unions

Since 1962, federal civilian employees have had the right to form unions or associations that represent them in seeking to improve government personnel policies, and approximately one-third of them have joined such unions. Some of the most important unions representing federal employees today are the American Federation of Government Employees, the National Treasury Employees Union, the National Association of Government Employees, and the National Federation of Federal Employees.

Unlike unions in the private sector, federal employee unions lack the right to strike and are not able to bargain over pay and benefits. But they can attempt to negotiate better personnel policies and practices for federal workers, they can represent federal employees at grievance and disciplinary proceedings, and they can lobby Congress on measures affecting personnel changes. They can also vote in elections. This is why members of Congress from districts with large numbers of federal workers often sit on the House and Senate civil service subcommittees.

The National Treasury Employees Union represents thousands of federal employees who work within government. Although it started out as a union for Treasury Department employees, it has expanded throughout the years. ■ *Should federal employees be allowed to strike? How would a strike affect public confidence in government?*

The Job of the Federal Bureaucracy

LEARNING **OBJECTIVE**

9.4 Analyze the bureaucracy's tools of implementation and their effectiveness.

Whatever their size or specialty, all federal organizations share one constitutional job: to faithfully execute, or implement, the laws.

Implementation covers a broad range of bureaucratic activities, such as writing checks at the Social Security Administration, inspecting job sites for the Occupational Safety and Health Administration, swearing in new citizens at the Immigration and Naturalization Service, or monitoring airline traffic for the Federal Aviation Administration. Some agencies implement the laws by spending money, others by raising revenues or issuing rules that govern what private citizens and businesses do, and still others by collecting information or conducting research. Whatever tool government uses, implementation is the act of converting a law into action.

Because Congress and the president could never pass laws detailed enough to deal with every aspect of their administration, they give federal departments and agencies **administrative discretion** to implement the laws in the most efficient and effective manner possible. This freedom varies from agency to agency, depending on both past performance and congressional politics. Political scientist Theodore Lowi believes that Congress often gives the federal bureaucracy vague directions because it is unable or unwilling to make the tough choices needed to resolve conflicts that arise in the legislative process. Congress gets the credit for passing a law, but the federal workforce gets the challenge of implementing an unclear law.[12]

implementation
The process of putting a law into practice through bureaucratic rules or spending.

administrative discretion
Authority given by Congress to the federal bureaucracy to use reasonable judgment in implementing the laws.

rule
A precise statement of how a law is implemented.

Federal Register
The official record of what the federal bureaucracy does.

Whether a law is clear or ambiguous, most agencies implement it through two means: administrative *regulations,* formal instructions for either running an agency or controlling the behavior of private citizens and organizations, and *spending,* the transfer of money to and from government. As noted earlier, the bureaucracy can only issue regulations that are authorized by Congress and the president through legislation, or ordered by the federal courts. In 2009, for example, Congress and the president gave the Food and Drug Administration formal authority to issue regulations governing the manufacturing of tobacco products such as cigarettes.

Making Regulations

As discussed in the chapter opener, **rules** are designed to convert laws into action. They tell people what they can and cannot do, as well as what they must or must not do. An Agriculture Department rule tells meat and poultry processors how to handle food; an Environmental Protection Agency rule tells automobile makers how much gasoline mileage their cars must get; a Social Security Administration rule tells workers how long they must work before they are eligible for a federal retirement check; an Immigration and Naturalization Service rule tells citizens of other nations how long they can stay on a student visa; and a Justice Department rule tells states what they must do to ensure that every eligible citizen can vote. All these rules can be traced back to legislation; they provide the details that laws leave out.

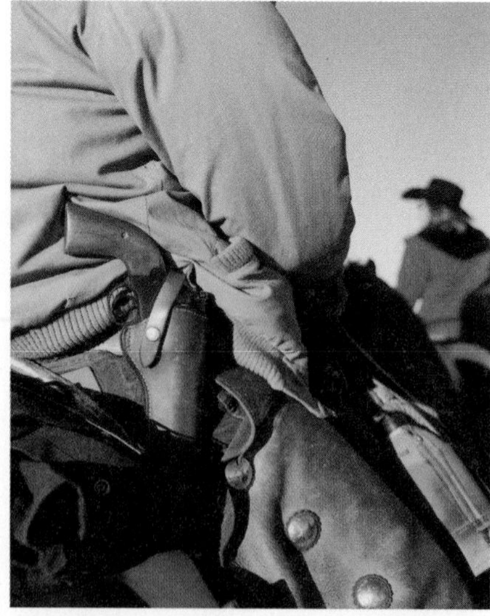

Just before he left office on January 20, 2009, President George W. Bush approved a new federal rule allowing national park visitors to carry concealed loaded weapons. The rule was endorsed by Congress and signed into law by President Obama in 2009. The Interior Department's National Park Service enforces the rule.

Rules are drafted and reviewed under the Administrative Procedure Act. Created in 1946 to make sure all rules are made visible to the public, the act requires that all proposed rules be published in the ***Federal Register.*** Publication in the federal government's newspaper marks the beginning of the "notice and comment" period, during which all parties affected by the proposed regulation are encouraged to make their opinions known to the agency. Because rules have the force of law and can become the basis for legal challenges, the process can take years from start to finish and consume thousands of pages of records. Some agencies even hold hearings and take testimony from witnesses in the effort to build a strong case for a particularly controversial rule.

The rule-making process does not end with final publication and enforcement. All rules are subject to the same judicial review that governs formal laws, thereby creating a check against potential abuse of power when agencies exceed their authority to faithfully execute the laws.

Spending Money

The federal bureaucracy also implements laws by spending money, whether by writing checks to more than 35 million Social Security recipients a year, buying billions of dollars'

For the People

GOVERNMENT'S GREATEST ENDEAVORS

Bringing Sunshine to Government

Congress, the president, and the federal judiciary have made many efforts to make government more open. Under the Administrative Procedure Act in 1946, for example, Congress required agencies to publish all proposed regulations in the *Federal Register* and give citizens a chance to make comments through direct access to government. Under the Sunshine Act in 1974, Congress required agencies to provide more access to records of key decisions and open their meetings to public participation. And under the Ethics in Government Act of 1978, Congress required presidential appointees to provide much more detailed information on their financial interests.

All of these laws promote the notion that sunshine is the best disinfectant for corruption, but none is more important than the Freedom of Information Act of 1966. Passed at the height of the Vietnam War, this law was designed to give citizens the power to demand the release of information from government through a Freedom of Information Act (FOIA) request. Such requests must be made through formal letters and notarized but force an agency such as the Federal Bureau of Investigation to make any information on any subject available. If the agency refuses to make the information available, it must provide a clear justification such as protecting national security.

Interest groups and the media often use FOIA requests to force the federal government to release particularly controversial documents. In October 2009, in response to a lawsuit brought by the American Civil Liberties Union, the federal courts ordered the Department of Justice to release hundreds of documents regarding the torture of suspected terrorists in U.S. custody overseas. The documents can be found at http://www.aclu.org/national-security/torture-documents-released-10302009.

The Obama Administration is trying to reenergize sunshine in government through a series of executive orders instructing the bureaucracy to provide more information to the public. Under a December 9, 2009, memorandum to the federal bureaucracy, the Obama administration ordered every department and agency to create separate Web sites for providing data to the public—the Web sites can be found at www.[agencyname].gov/open. The memorandum also ordered the bureaucracy to reduce the use of top-secret classifications to limit public access to information.

CRITICAL THINKING QUESTIONS

1. Would the framers support open government?
2. When should the bureaucracy refuse to release information? What rules should it use in making a decision to redact information?
3. Why do interest groups do much of the work on FOIA requests? Is their involvement good for citizen engagement?

~~TOP SECRET~~

217. (~~TS~~/ Detainees, both planners and operatives, have also made the Agency aware of several plots planned for the United States and around the world. The plots identify plans to attack the U.S. Consulate in Karachi, Pakistan; hijack aircraft to fly into Heathrow Airport loosen track spikes in an attempt to derail a train in the United States; blow up several U.S. gas stations to create panic and havoc; hijack and fly an airplane into the tallest building in California in a west coast version of the World Trade Center attack; cut the lines of suspension bridges in New York in an effort to make them collapse; This Review did not uncover any evidence that these plots were imminent. Agency senior managers believe that lives have been saved as a result of the capture and interrogation of terrorists who were planning attacks, in particular Khalid Shaykh Muhammad, Abu Zubaydah, Hambali, and Al-Nashiri.

218. (~~TS~~/ judge the reporting from detainees as one of the most important sources for finished intelligence. viewed analysts' knowledge of the terrorist target as having much more depth as a result of information from detainees and estimated that detainee reporting is used in all counterterrorism articles produced for the most senior policymakers. In an interview, the DCI

88

~~TOP SECRET~~

Even when information is released, it can be difficult to understand. The federal government can "redact" portions of particularly sensitive information to the point that documents are nearly impossible to read.

worth of military equipment, or making grants to state governments and research universities. Viewed in relative terms as a percentage of gross domestic product (GDP), federal spending more than doubled throughout the past half-century but began to shrink with the end of the cold war in 1989.

Most government spending is **uncontrollable,** or *nondiscretionary,* which means it is not subject to congressional or presidential control without substantial and often unpopular changes in the law. The bulk of uncontrollable, mandatory spending goes to **entitlement programs** such as Social Security and Medicare for older citizens, college loans, and help for the victims of natural disasters such as floods and hurricanes. Everyone eligible for these programs is *entitled* to benefits—hence, spending often rises automatically. (The amount of this *uncontrollable spending* in the 1962 and 2010 federal budget is shown in Figure 9–4.)

The largest share of uncontrollable spending goes to Social Security and Medicare, which are guaranteed to anyone who has paid taxes into the program for enough years.

uncontrollable spending
The portion of the federal budget that is spent on previously enacted programs, such as Social Security, that the president and Congress are unwilling to cut.

entitlement program
Programs such as unemployment insurance, disaster relief, or disability payments that provide benefits to all eligible citizens.

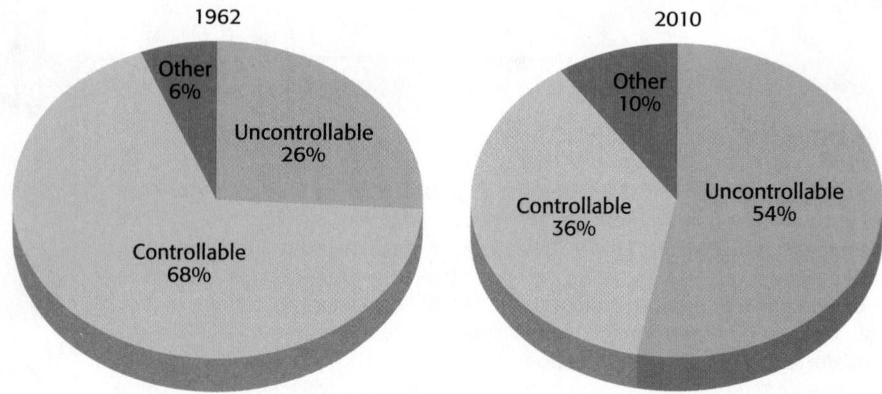

FIGURE 9–4 Uncontrollable Spending in 1962 and 2010.

■ *Why do you think there are so many federal programs today with uncontrollable spending?*

SOURCE: Office of Management and Budget, *Budget of the U.S. Government, Fiscal Year 2009, Historical Tables* (U.S. Government Printing Office, February 2008).

As a higher percentage of workers age throughout the next few decades, uncontrollable spending will almost certainly rise as Social Security and Medicare grow. The two programs are already the largest in the federal budget and will eventually account for more than half of all federal spending. In total, uncontrollable spending accounted for nearly $2 trillion in 2010, more than half of the federal government's spending.

A much smaller share of the uncontrollable budget goes to welfare for the poor and is linked to the performance of the economy. More unemployment, for example, means more federal unemployment insurance; more poverty means more food stamps, job training, temporary financial assistance, and other income support programs. On the other hand, spending for programs such as health research, highway construction, and defense weapons are discretionary.

Controlling the Federal Bureaucracy

LEARNING **OBJECTIVE**

9.5 Assess presidential and congressional efforts to control the federal bureaucracy.

Every president enters office promising to make federal agencies work better. Jimmy Carter, Ronald Reagan, Bill Clinton, George W. Bush, and Barack Obama all made bureaucratic reform a central part of their presidential campaigns. Carter promised to create a government as good as the U.S. people, Reagan promised to reduce waste in government, Clinton and Vice President Al Gore promised to reinvent government, Bush promised to make government friendlier to citizens, and Obama promised more government transparency.

Presidential Controls

Modern presidents invariably contend that they should be firmly in charge of federal employees because the chief executive is responsive to the broadest constituency. A president, they argue, must see that popular needs and expectations are converted into administrative action. The voters' wishes can be translated into action only if federal employees support presidential policies.

However, under the system of checks and balances, the party that wins the presidency does not acquire total control of the national government. The president is not even the undisputed master of the executive structure. Presidents come into an ongoing system over which they have little control and in which they have little leeway to make the bureaucracy responsive.

Still, the president has some control over federal departments and agencies through the powers of appointment, reorganization, and budgeting. A president can attempt to control the federal system by appointing or promoting sympathetic personnel, mobilizing public opinion and congressional pressure, changing the administrative apparatus, influencing budget decisions, using extensive personal persuasion, and if all else fails, shifting an agency's assignment to another department or agency (although such a shift requires tacit if not explicit congressional approval).[13]

Congressional Controls

Congress has a number of ways to control federal administration, whether by establishing agencies, formulating budgets, appropriating funds, confirming personnel, authorizing new programs or new shifts in direction, conducting investigations and hearings, or even terminating agencies.

Much of this authority is used to help constituents as they battle federal red tape. Members of Congress earn political credit by influencing federal agencies on behalf of their constituents. Still, Congress deserves at least some of the blame for having created the red tape in the first place, through such deeds as enacting pet programs, refusing to give federal agencies greater flexibility, delaying presidential appointments, and placing limits on bureaucratic discretion to protect some constituents but not others. Moreover, by demanding special attention for their constituents, members of Congress may undermine the fairness of the entire process. Like those who cut in line at a movie theater, they slow the progress for everyone but the special few who get their attention.

Individual committees generally specialize in the appropriations and oversight processes. They oversee policies of a particular cluster of agencies—often the agencies serving constituents in their own districts. Some legislators stake out a claim over specific areas. Members of Congress, who see presidents come and go, come to think they know more about particular agencies than the president does (and often they do). Some congressional leaders prefer to try to seal off "their" agencies from presidential direction and maintain their influence over public policy.

Former defense secretary Donald Rumsfeld resigned from office only days after the 2006 elections. His management of the war in Iraq had been widely criticized, and he was blamed for the deep Republican losses in the elections. In this way, citizens held government accountable through their votes against Republican candidates.

Shared Controls

Congress and the president spend a great deal of time and energy monitoring the federal bureaucracy through **oversight,** the technical term for their ongoing review.

oversight
Legislative or executive review of a particular government program or organization that can be in response to a crisis of some kind or part of routine review.

Presidents use a number of tools for keeping a watchful eye. They can put loyal appointees into the top jobs at key agencies; they can direct White House aides to oversee the work of certain agencies; and they can always call cabinet meetings to learn more about what is happening in the various departments. However, presidents tend to use the Office of Management and Budget (OMB) for most routine oversight. Departments and agencies must get the president's approval before testifying before Congress on pending legislation, making legislative proposals, or answering congressional inquiries about their activities. Under this **central clearance** system, OMB tells Congress whether the bureaucracy's requests for legislation are "in accordance" with the president's program (indicating the highest presidential support), "consistent with" the president's program (indicating at least moderate presidential support), or without objection (indicating little or no presidential interest).

Congress also has a number of tools for overseeing the federal bureaucracy, not least of which are the individual members of Congress themselves, who are free to ask agencies for detailed information on just about any issue. However, most members and committees tend to use the General Accounting Office or the Congressional Budget Office to conduct a study or investigation of a particular program.

Oversight is often conducted through external investigations launched by Congress or the president. In 2009, for example, the Obama Administration created a special commission to investigate the banking scandals that led to the financial collapse in 2008 and the $700 billion federal bailout called the Troubled Asset Relief Program (TARP). Investigations have covered a range of issues including Vietnam War, the Watergate scandal, the space shuttle *Challenger* disaster, and the September 11, 2001, terrorist attacks.

Congress often conducts oversight through very visible hearings with star witnesses. Congress did just that by bringing the chief executives of General Motors and Chrysler in 2009 to explain their use of federal bailout money to survive the economic downturn. ■ *Why do you suppose Congress brought the heads of the auto companies to the witness table in Capitol Hill, above, rather than conduct behind-the-scenes investigations?*

Together, Congress and the president conduct two basic types of oversight. One is "police patrol" oversight, in which the two branches watch the bureaucracy through a routine pattern. They read key reports, monitor the budget, and generally pay attention to

By the People

MAKING A DIFFERENCE

Joining the "Transparency Corps"

Under pressure from leading interest groups such as the Project on Government Oversight (www.pogo.org), OMB Watch (ombwatch.org), and the Sunlight Foundation (sunlightfoundation.com), the federal bureaucracy is releasing massive amounts of information to citizens. As the list of sources at www.data.gov shows, citizens can inspect virtually every corner of the bureaucracy except for national security and defense, which have tightly guarded Web sites.

There is also an enormous amount of information at private and interest group Web sites, including detailed information on congressional lobbying and fund raising at the Center for Responsive Politics (www.opensecrets.org), lists of wasteful government programs at Citizens Against Government Waste (www.cagw.org), and detailed biographies of every Obama administration appointee at *The Washington Post's* dot-com Web site (www.whorunsgovernment.com)

The problem with the bureaucracy is no longer too little public information, however, but perhaps too much. There is so much information that citizens simply cannot put it together. The Sunlight Foundation is trying to solve the problem by creating virtual teams of citizens, most of whom are students, to analyze government information and collect additional data. Its "Transparency Corps" is designed to give each member a specific assignment such as finding Twitter addresses for state legislators. "Use your Internet search 'kung fu' skills to track down whom among your state officials are on Twitter and what their usernames are," Sunlight tells its volunteers. "Don't know who your state officials are? No problem, you tell us your zip code, and we'll tell you who to look for."

The Transparency Corps is only one way citizens can monitor government. The more they do to make sense of government information, even by sorting information into graphs for data analysis at IBM's free Web site, http://manyeyes.alphaworks.ibm.com/manyeyes/, the more they can contribute to the information that experts read for input to major policy debates.

CRITICAL THINKING QUESTIONS

1. Is there too much information now flowing from Washington? Can the flood of information be used to suppress citizen engagement or discourage people from looking?
2. Why does the concept of the "Transparency Corps" lessen this information overload?
3. Should citizens trust the bureaucracy's information?

the way the departments and agencies are running. The goal is to deter problems before they arise.

The other form of oversight is "fire alarm" oversight, in which the two branches wait for citizens, interest groups, or the press to find a major problem and pull the alarm. The media play a particularly important role in such oversight, using the Freedom of Information Act to gain access to documents the federal bureaucracy keeps secret and often uncovering a scandal before a routine "police patrol" can discover the problem.

Can the Bureaucracy Regulate Itself?

central clearance
Review of all executive branch testimony, reports, and draft legislation by the Office of Management and Budget (OMB) to ensure that each communication to Congress is in accordance with the president's program.

Career administrators are in a good position to know when a program is not operating properly and what action is needed. But many people believe that federal employees care too much about their own pay, benefits, and job security to make things better. Some career employees act as if the expansion of their organization were vital to the public interest. They become more skillful at building political alliances to protect their organization than at building political alliances to ensure their programs' effectiveness.

Career administrators usually try hard to be objective, but they are inevitably political. Some have more bargaining and alliance-building skills than the elected and

Vice President Al Gore took the Clinton administration's campaign to cut government waste to the people when he appeared on *The David Letterman Show.* Gore and Letterman both wore goggles as Gore showed how to smash an ashtray under federal rules. ■ *What makes this demonstration so effective at showing the Clinton administration's commitment to better government?*

appointed officials to whom they report. In one sense, agency leaders are at the center of action in Washington. Over time, administrative agencies may become much closer to the interests they regulate than to the public they protect.

Interest groups work hard to cultivate the bureau chiefs and agency staffs who have jurisdiction over their programs. They also work closely with the committees and subcommittees of Congress that authorize, appropriate, and oversee programs run by these key bureaucracies. Recognizing the power of interest groups, bureau chiefs frequently recruit them as allies in pursuing common goals. These officials, interest groups, and congressional allies share a common view that more money should be spent on their federal programs.

Does the Federal Bureaucracy Work?

LEARNING **OBJECTIVE**

9.6 Evaluate the bureaucracy's effectiveness.

Despite their complaints about the federal bureaucracy, U.S. citizens are reluctant to support cutbacks in what government does. Most say the federal bureaucracy's biggest problem is not setting the wrong priorities but allowing inefficiency. We may complain about the red tape and waste in Washington, but the federal bureaucracy continues to make progress in solving some of the most difficult problems of modern society.

In today's climate of promises to cut big government, it is useful to recall Alexander Hamilton's warning about the dangers of a government ill executed. As he argued in *The Federalist,* No. 70: "A feeble execution is but another phrase for a bad execution; and a government ill executed, whatever it may be in theory must be in practice, a bad government."[14]

More than 200 years later, however, the federal government seems plagued by bad execution. The failures are all too familiar: taxpayer abuse by the Internal Revenue Service, security breaches at the nation's nuclear laboratories, missing laptops at the Federal Bureau of Investigation, the *Challenger* and *Columbia* space shuttle disasters, breakdowns in policing everything from toys to cattle, the sluggish response to Hurricane Katrina, miscalculations about the war in Iraq, a cascade of fraudulent defense contracts, continued struggles to unite the nation's intelligence services, backlogs at dozens of agencies, shortages of air traffic controllers and food inspectors, mistakes on the passenger screening lines, the Christmas Day bombing plot, the Gulf of Mexico oil spill, and negligent veteran's care.

As the federal government's agenda has expanded throughout the centuries, government has become increasingly difficult to manage. Its missions are critically important, but its organizations are dense with layer upon layer of management, rules, red tape, and old technologies; the presidential appointments process is needlessly complex and slow; many civil servants are motivated more by their job security than their mission; and the faithful execution of the laws now involves a large and mostly hidden workforce of contract employees that is hard to control.

This is not to suggest that the federal government is a wasteland of failure. To the contrary, the federal government accomplishes the impossible every day. And over time, as demonstrated in the *For the People: Government's Greatest Endeavors* boxes, the federal bureaucracy has accomplished much for betterment of society, including reducing diseases, building a strong national defense, and increasing access to education. But even federal employees have concerns about how the bureaucracy functions. Interviewed in mid-2008 by the U.S. Office of Personnel Management, less than half of a random sample of federal employees said their agencies were able to recruit employees with the right skills, slightly more than a third said promotions were based on merit, and even fewer said their agencies took steps to deal with poor performers.

It is not surprising that the public has serious doubts about the federal bureaucracy's performance, too. As Figure 9–5 shows, public confidence in the executive branch of government has been generally declining throughout the past ten years. The only major breaks in the decline came in 2002–2004 when the nation was pulled together by the response to the September 11, 2001, terrorist attacks and early success in Iraq, and in September 2009, as the economy showed early signs of recovery. Other surveys show similar patterns—trust in the bureaucracy rises with the economy and the popularity of the president and declines to traditionally low levels as enthusiasm wears off.

Improving public confidence in the bureaucracy depends in large part on the public itself. Citizens can make a great difference in shaping rules, monitoring bureaucratic performance, and prompting Congress and the president to adopt needed reforms to prevent government breakdowns. Citizens can also support the many interest groups that lobby for good government and can now keep their own watchful eye over government by visiting government Web sites and collecting information. There is an old saying in politics that Americans get the government they deserve. The more that citizens demand better government, the better government they get.

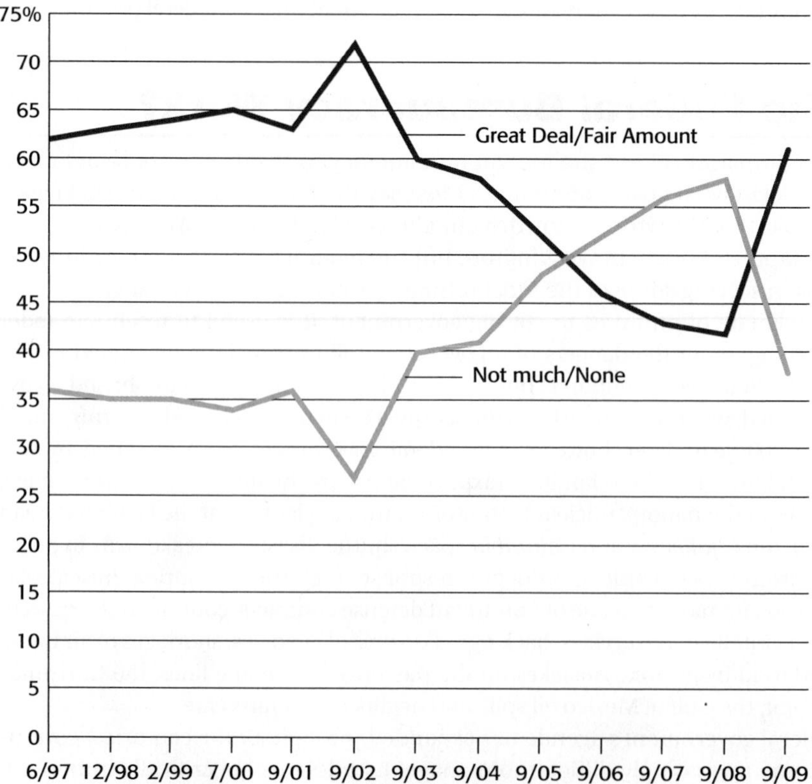

FIGURE 9–5 Trust in the Bureaucracy.

How much trust and confidence do you have at this time in the executive branch, headed by the president: a great deal, a fair amount, not very much, or none at all? ■ *What might explain the long-term decline in confidence in the federal bureaucracy? Why did confidence rise so dramatically in 2009?*

SOURCE: The Gallup Poll, available at http://pollingreport.com/institut.htm.

CHAPTER SUMMARY

9.1 Outline the constitutional roots of the federal bureaucracy and pros and cons of bureaucratic administration.

The founders assumed there would be a federal bureaucracy but that it would be small. Therefore, they left many of the details of the bureaucracy to the responsibility of future presidents. Although they did give the president the power to appoint the officers of government and require their opinions in writing, there are few constitutional rules for managing the bureaucracy. The chief benefits of bureaucracy are specialization, centralization, formal rules, standardization, expertise, and accountability. These factors create predictability by making sure all employees know their jobs. However, they can also create duplication and overlap, as well as needless levels of management.

9.2 Identify the four types of federal organizations.

There are four types of government organizations: (1) departments, (2) independent stand-alone agencies, (3) independent regulatory commissions, and (4) government corporations. Departments are generally the largest organizations in government and are often divided into members of the inner and outer cabinet; independent stand-alone agencies are generally smaller than departments but conduct important enforcement and policy work; independent regulatory commissions are insulated from political control through the appointment of commissioners with fixed terms of office who cannot be easily removed from office; and government corporations are designed to work more like a business and make a profit.

9.3 Differentiate three types of federal employees, and explain how each is selected.

Most presidential appointees are appointed by the president with Senate confirmation. Nearly all of these appointees are selected on the basis of political connections and ability to do the job. The president does not appoint members of the civil service. Civil servants are selected on the basis of merit. The federal government's Office of Personnel Management sets policy for recruiting and evaluating federal workers. Various restrictions prevent federal workers from running for political office or engaging in political fund-raising activities.

9.4 Analyze the bureaucracy's tools of implementation and their effectiveness.

The federal bureaucracy generally uses regulations or spending to implement the laws. The rule-making process is governed by the Administrative Procedure Act, whereas the spending process is governed by the federal budget. Most of the federal budget is uncontrollable, meaning that anyone who qualifies for programs such as Social Security, unemployment insurance, health care for the poor, and Medicare must be given benefits regardless of the impact on the federal budget.

9.5 Assess presidential and congressional efforts to control the federal bureaucracy.

The federal bureaucracy has at least two immediate supervisors: Congress and the president. It must pay considerable attention as well to the courts and their rulings and to well-organized interest groups and public opinion. Despite their efforts to ensure accountability, Congress and the president often give vague instructions to the administrative system, which gives the system significant discretion in implementing the laws.

9.6 Evaluate the bureaucracy's effectiveness.

Americans generally favor more government activism on virtually every program but have serious concerns about big government. They also express concerns about fraud, waste, and abuse in government.

CHAPTER SELF-TEST

9.1 Outline the constitutional roots of the federal bureaucracy and pros and cons of bureaucratic administration.

1. List key decisions the framers made about executing the laws that continue to shape federal administration to this day.
2. Which of the following is a weakness of the modern federal bureaucracy?
   a. Communication within a large organization is difficult.
   b. Few qualified individuals want to work in the bureaucracy.
   c. Today's jobs are overly simplistic and not attractive to young workers.
   d. Rules are almost impossible to enforce within a very large workforce.
3. In a short essay, identify and describe three strengths of bureaucracy. Focus on experiences you or someone you know has had with the federal bureaucracy. How could those experiences have been improved?

9.2 Identify the four types of federal organizations.

4. Which type of federal organization is the Federal Reserve Board?
   a. Department
   b. Independent agency
   c. Government corporation
   d. Independent regulatory commission
5. Which types of federal organizations report directly to the president? Which do not? Why are independent regulatory commissions structured to insulate their work from the president?

9.3 Differentiate three types of federal employees, and explain how each is selected.

6. What are the three types of government employees? To whom does each report? How are they selected?
7. Identify whether each of the following describes the spoils or the merit system:
   a. Andrew Jackson substantially expanded this system after his election in 1829.
   b. Federal jobs are filled on the basis of personal connections.
   c. Ninety percent of federal employees are selected through this system.
   d. This system gave the president's party nearly complete control over almost every government job.
   e. Federal jobs are filled on the basis of ability.
8. What is the main duty of the Office of Personnel Management?
   a. Protect the integrity of the federal merit system
   b. Administer civil service laws, rules, and regulations
   c. Research and interview each potential presidential appointee
   d. Provide information to the Senate about presidential appointees
9. How does the Hatch Act limit civil service political participation? Should civil servants have more rights to participate in politics and unions?

9.4 Analyze the bureaucracy's tools of implementation and their effectiveness.

10. What is the constitutional job shared by all federal organizations regardless of their size or specialty?
    a. To faithfully execute the laws
    b. To protect the president from harm
    c. To cooperate with Congress in all legal matters
    d. To aid the president in electing members of his or her party to political office
11. What is uncontrollable spending? What two programs receive the majority of these funds? Why? What implications could this reason have for the way your future tax dollars are spent?
12. Write a short essay on why regulations are such an important tool of government action.

9.5 Assess presidential and congressional efforts to control the federal bureaucracy.

13. Why do many members of Congress prefer the current, complicated federal bureaucracy to a more efficient alternative?
    a. It creates greater incumbency advantages in elections.
    b. A more complicated system creates more jobs for politicians' friends.
    c. The bureaucratic red tape allows for greater back-room deals.
    d. A more complicated system allows politicians greater freedom with less oversight from constituents.
14. Do the constitutional controls actually work to limit bureaucratic discretion? Is oversight an effective means for changing bureaucratic behavior?

9.6 Evaluate the bureaucracy's effectiveness.

15. Write a brief essay on different ways of measuring bureaucratic effectiveness.
16. Write a brief essay on why citizens have such low opinion of [?] the bureaucracy.

Answers to selected questions: 2. a; 4. d; 7. a: spoils, b: spoils, c: merit, d: spoils, e: merit; 8. b; 10. a; 13. a

mypoliscilab EXERCISES

Where participation leads to action!

Apply what you learned in this chapter on MyPoliSciLab.

Read on **mypoliscilab.com**

eText: Chapter 9

Study and **Review** on **mypoliscilab.com**

Pre-Test
Post-Test
Chapter Exam
Flashcards

Watch on **mypoliscilab.com**

Video: The CDC and the Swine Flu
Video: Internal Problems at the FDA

Explore on **mypoliscilab.com**

Simulation: You Are the President of MEDICORP
Simulation: You Are Deputy Director of the Census Bureau
Simulation: You Are a Federal Administrator
Simulation: You Are the Head of FEMA
Comparative: Comparing Bureaucracies
Timeline: The Evolution of the Federal Bureaucracy
Visual Literacy: The Changing Face of the Federal Bureaucracy

KEY **TERMS**

bureaucracy, p. 273
bureaucrat, p. 273
department, p. 275
independent stand-alone agency, p. 275
independent regulatory commission, p. 275
government corporation, p. 275
Senior Executive Service, p. 280
civil service, p. 280
spoils system, p. 280
merit system, p. 281
Office of Personnel Management (OPM), p. 281
Merit Systems Protection Board, p. 281
Hatch Act, p. 281
implementation, p. 284
administrative discretion, p. 284
rule, p. 284
***Federal Register*,** p. 284
uncontrollable spending, p. 285
entitlement program, p. 285
oversight, p. 287
central clearance, p. 288

ADDITIONAL **RESOURCES**

FURTHER READING

ROBERT D. BEHN, *Rethinking Democratic Accountability* (Brookings Institution Press, 2001).

BARRY BOZEMAN, *Bureaucracy and Red Tape* (Prentice Hall, 2000).

SHELLEY L. DAVIS, *Unbridled Power: Inside the Secret Culture of the IRS* (Harper Business, 1997).

JAMES W. FESLER AND **DONALD F. KETTL,** *The Politics of the Administrative Process,* 4th ed. (CQ Press, 2008).

JANE E. FOUNTAIN, *Building the Virtual State: Information Technology and Institutional Change* (Brookings Institution Press, 2001).

STEPHEN GOLDSMITH AND **WILLIAM EGGERS,** *Government by Network: The New Shape of the Public Sector* (Brookings Institution Press, 2005).

CHARLES T. GOODSELL, *The Case for Bureaucracy,* 4th ed. (CQ Press, 2003).

AL GORE, *Creating a Government That Works Better and Costs Less: The Report of the National Performance Review* (Plume-Penguin, 1993).

WILLIAM T. GORMLEY AND **STEVEN J. BALLA,** *Bureaucracy and Democracy: Accountability and Performance,* 2d ed. (CQ Press, 2007).

PHILIP K. HOWARD, *The Death of Common Sense: How Law Is Suffocating America* (Random House, 1994).

ANDREW KOHUT, ED., *Deconstructing Distrust: How Americans View Government* (Pew Research Center for the People and the Press, 1998).

PAUL C. LIGHT, *A Government Ill Executed: The Decline of the Federal Service and How to Reverse It* (Harvard University Press, 2008).

G. CALVIN MACKENZIE AND **MICHAEL HAFKEN,** *Scandal Proof: Do Ethics Laws Make Government Ethical?* (Brookings Institution Press, 2002).

KENNETH J. MEIER AND **LAURENCE J. O'TOOLE JR.,** *Bureaucracy in a Democratic State: A Governance Perspective* (Johns Hopkins University Press, 2006).

DAVID OSBORNE, *The Tools of Government: A Guide to the New Governance* (Oxford University Press, 2002).

JAMES Q. WILSON, *Bureaucracy: What Government Agencies Do and Why They Do It* (Basic Books, 1989). Four useful journals are the *Journal of Policy Analysis and Management, National Journal, Public Administration Review,* and *Government Executive.*

WEB SITES

www.omb.gov The source of information on the federal budget.

www.pogo.org The Project on Government Oversight, a source of investigations of the federal bureaucracy's performance.

www.washingpost.com Click on the "federal page" to find the latest news on what is happening in Washington.

www.ourpublicservice.org A source for information about the best places to work in the federal government.

www.USAJobs.gov Where federal agencies post federal jobs.

CHAPTER

10

The Judiciary

The Balancing Branch

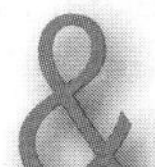

CHAPTER **OUTLINE** & CHAPTER LEARNING **OBJECTIVES**

Understanding the Federal Judiciary

10.1 Determine characteristics of the federal judiciary and implications of the adversarial process.

The Three Types of Federal Courts

10.2 Outline the structure of the federal court system.

The Politics of Appointing Federal Judges

10.3 Analyze the factors that play an important role in selecting judicial nominees.

How the Supreme Court Decides

10.4 Trace the process by which Supreme Court decisions are reached, and assess influences on this process.

Judicial Power and Its Limits

10.5 Assess the limits on judicial action and the role of the judiciary in a constitutional democracy.

On January 21, 2010, the U.S. Supreme Court announced its decision in a much-anticipated case dealing with federal campaign finance rules. The case, *Citizens United* v. *Federal Election Commission,*[1] dealt with the question of whether a documentary movie that was critical of Hillary Clinton, who was then running for the Democratic presidential nomination, violated the 2002 Bipartisan Campaign Reform Act's ban on corporation (and union) expenditures from their general funds—including profits—to advocate for the election or defeat of a candidate. In its 5-to-4 decision, the Court ruled that these expenditures cannot be limited under the First Amendment. This decision overturned long-standing restrictions on such spending and the Supreme Court's own precedent, which had allowed these restrictions due to the interest in preventing corruption, or the appearance of corruption, based on the potential for huge corporate general treasuries to disproportionately influence election outcomes.[2] As we discussed in Chapters 4 and 5, in *Citizens United,* the Supreme Court reaffirmed the free speech rights of corporations and ruled that the government had no right to limit that speech.

The Court's decision was met with a firestorm of criticism from commentators and politicians alike decrying the harm to the democratic process that would result from the Court's decision. Many members of Congress who had voted for the campaign reform legislation only eight years earlier disparaged the Court's opinion, arguing that the pro-business Roberts Court had struck yet another blow against the average citizen. The debate was amplified when, only six days later, President Obama openly criticized the Court's decision in his State of the Union Address. Six of the Court's nine justices attended the address and, as is their tradition, they sat mostly expressionless in the audience. That is, except for Justice Samuel Alito, who was caught on television cameras scowling and appearing to say "not true" in response to the president's remarks.

The unusual exchange between the president and justice provided extensive fodder for commentators and politicians and further criticism of both the president's comments in the State of the Union Address and Justice Alito's response. Debate over the exchange heated up again in early March when Chief Justice Roberts spoke about the event during a meeting with law students at the University of Alabama. Responding to a student's question, Roberts said he found the president's criticism of the Court at the State of the Union Address "very troubling" and suggested that event had turned into a "political pep rally" that perhaps the justices should not attend.[3]

The chief justice's remarks and the president's comments highlight a long-standing debate about the appropriate role of the Court in a separation-of-powers system. Is the Court part of the political process, or is it an apolitical institution operating outside the bounds of the political arena? In either case, it is clear that politics shape the courts, especially through the federal judicial appointment process, and the courts shape politics through the reach of their decisions.

In this chapter, we explore how the federal judiciary operates in a system of separated powers and examine the nomination process through which we staff the judiciary. The judicial branch is unlike the elected branches of government in several ways. We will first look at the way the framers envisioned the judiciary and discuss several of its important characteristics. After exploring the appointment process, we will discuss the Supreme Court in particular. Given that it is the court of last resort in the United States and has the final say on what the Constitution means, it is crucial to our understanding of the federal judiciary.

Understanding the Federal Judiciary

LEARNING **OBJECTIVE**

10.1 Determine characteristics of the federal judiciary and implications of the adversarial process.

The framers viewed the federal judiciary as an important check against both Congress and the president. But the judiciary lacked the institutional resources of the elected branches. As Alexander Hamilton wrote, "The Executive not only dispenses the honors, but holds the sword of the community. The legislature not only commands the purse, but prescribes the rules by which the duties and rights of every citizen are to be regulated. The judiciary, on the contrary, has no influence over either the sword or the purse."[4] So, in order to ensure the judicial check, the framers insulated the judiciary against both public opinion and the rest of government.

To protect the judiciary from shifts in public opinion, the framers rejected direct election. That was the method used to select many judges in the colonies, and it is still used today to choose some state and local judges. The framers also excluded the House, the more representative of the two bodies of Congress, from any role in either selecting or confirming federal judges. To protect the judiciary from Congress as a whole, no limits were allowed on judicial terms. Federal judges serve during good behavior, which typically means for life. And finally, to prevent Congress from assessing a financial penalty against the judiciary, judges' salaries cannot be reduced once confirmed.

These early decisions were essential to protect the judiciary's independence in resolving public disputes. Because it has no army or police force to enforce its will or make people obey its decisions, the judiciary must often rely on the public's respect to implement its decisions. This is sometimes a challenge, particularly when resolving controversial issues such as abortion rights or the rights of prisoners of war. Even in the face of these challenges, it is crucial that the judiciary maintain its independence.

However, in states where judges are chosen through popular elections, they are by definition accountable to the public. Although judicial elections arguably add accountability, some contend that it is accountability not to the average citizen but to the groups and corporations that contribute money to the judges' election campaigns. This is only one of the potential problems in systems that provide for greater accountability at the expense of judicial independence.

The appropriate balance between judicial independence and accountability is often at the forefront of debate about the best way to staff the judiciary. Some countries structure their appointment process so as to ensure independence. For example, in Japan, Great Britain, Germany, and France, individuals interested in the judiciary take a variety of competitive exams and go through specialized judicial training to become eligible for appointment to their country's courts. In other countries, like China, judicial independence has been difficult; many judges were simply transferred to the judiciary from military posts in the Communist Party. Since 1995, there have been efforts to improve the quality of the judiciary—judges must now have some basic legal education—but judicial independence is still not assured.

Characteristics of the Federal Judiciary

Civil and Criminal Law Federal judges play a central role in U.S. life. They rule on controversial issues such as partial-birth abortion and race-conscious school assignment, and they often decide whether laws are constitutional. Many of these decisions are based on Chief Justice John Marshall's successful claim of **judicial review**—the power to interpret the Constitution (see Chapter 1). Only a constitutional amendment or a later Supreme Court can modify the Court's decisions.

judicial review
The power of a court to refuse to enforce a law or government regulation that in the opinion of the judges conflicts with the U.S. Constitution or, in a state court, the state constitution.

Several important characteristics distinguish the judiciary from Congress, the presidency, and the administrative system. First, the federal judiciary is an **adversary system,** based on the theory that arguing over law and evidence guarantees fairness.[5] The courts provide a neutral arena in which two parties argue their differences and present evidence supporting those views before an impartial judge. Because the two parties in a case must bring their arguments before the judge, judges may not go looking for cases to decide; the adversary system thus imposes restraints on judicial power.

adversary system
A judicial system in which the court of law is a neutral arena where two parties argue their differences.

Texas uses a partisan election to determine its state supreme court justices. Here candidates Rick Green and Debra Lehman campaign for judicial office. ■ *What are the drawbacks to choosing judges through popular election? What are the advantages?*

The courts handle many kinds of legal disputes, but the most common are **criminal law,** which defines crimes against the public order and provides for punishment, and **civil law,** which governs relations between individuals and defines their legal rights. Here are several important distinctions between the criminal and civil law:

- In a criminal trial, a person's liberty is at stake (those judged guilty can be imprisoned); in a civil case, penalties are predominantly monetary.
- Criminal defendants who cannot afford attorneys are provided one by the government, but there is no right to a government-provided attorney in civil cases.
- Defendants generally have the right to a jury in criminal trials, but there is no constitutional right to a jury in state civil trials.

The federal government, not the judiciary, brings all federal criminal cases and can also be a party to a civil action. For example, when Martha Stewart was tried for securities fraud and obstruction of justice, the U.S. government brought the case. The federal judiciary decides the cases. Government **prosecutors,** acting on behalf of the public, choose whether and how to pursue a case against criminal **defendants** who may have violated the law. In some cases, they may decide to offer a **plea bargain,** an arrangement in which a defendant agrees to plead guilty to a lesser offense than he or she was charged with, to avoid having to face trial for a more serious offense and a lengthier sentence.

Cases and Controversies Unlike the legislature and the executive, the federal judiciary is a *passive* and *reactive* branch. It does not instigate cases, nor can it resolve every issue that comes before it. Federal judges decide only **justiciable disputes**—according to the Constitution, they are to decide *cases and controversies.* It is not enough that a judge believe a particular law to be unconstitutional; a real case must be litigated for a judge to reach that decision. In addition, the parties that raise a civil case must have *standing to sue.* That is, the **plaintiff,** the person who begins a civil suit, must have experienced or be in immediate danger of experiencing direct and personal injury. Hypothetical harm is not enough to warrant court review. In an adversary system like ours, it is essential that each side bring forth the best possible arguments before the judge or jury. Because the decision makers depend on the adversaries to bring all the relevant information before them, if one side does not truly have a stake in the outcome, the adversarial process breaks down.

criminal law
A law that defines crimes against the public order.

civil law
A law that governs relationships between individuals and defines their legal rights.

prosecutor
Government lawyer who tries criminal cases, often referred to as a district attorney or a U.S. Attorney.

defendant
In a criminal action, the person or party accused of an offense.

plea bargain
An agreement between a prosecutor and a defendant that the defendant will plead guilty to a lesser offense to avoid having to stand trial for a more serious offense.

justiciable dispute
A dispute growing out of an actual case or controversy that is capable of settlement by legal methods.

plaintiff
The party instigating a civil lawsuit.

By the People
MAKING A DIFFERENCE

Serving on a Jury: Your Civic Duty and an Interesting Experience

Any time you would like to observe what is going on in Congress, you can turn on your television and watch C-SPAN's coverage of the House and Senate. But if you want to observe the workings of the judicial branch, it is not as easy. Although some states allow cameras into their courtrooms, typically only high-profile cases get any media attention, and cameras are not allowed in most federal courts. One way you can both fulfill your responsibilities of citizenship and get a better understanding of how our judiciary functions is to serve on a jury. Most states and the federal government use driver registration records as well as local records for city or county utilities to call residents to serve on juries. So, as long as you have a driver's license and pay for local services, you are in the pool to be called as a juror.

Serving on a jury can be an enlightening experience and is a necessity for carrying out justice in the United States. The Sixth Amendment to the U.S. Constitution guarantees people the right to a jury trial when they are accused of violating a criminal law. Thus, your service on a jury is essential to protecting that constitutional right. Next time you are called to serve on a jury, do not try to avoid this service; seize it as an opportunity to see our justice system firsthand.

In addition to serving on a jury, you can also get an understanding of how our court system works by visiting your local court for a day. In general, trials are open to the public and you are welcome to observe the courtroom work. Find your local court and visit it for a day. Your court's public relations office typically provides information on current trials, and some courts even have formal tours that allow you to observe a trial and engage in a follow-up discussion afterward. See your local court's Web site for information.

CRITICAL THINKING QUESTIONS

1. Why do you think many judges are reluctant to allow cameras in their courtrooms?
2. Do you think driver's registration rolls and utility records are a good way to develop a jury pool? How else might a pool of eligible citizens be determined?
3. Why might some people be reluctant to serve on a jury? What could be done to relieve their concerns?

The federal judiciary has also been reluctant to hear disputes on powers the Constitution explicitly assigns to Congress or the president. It resists intervening in foreign policy questions respecting the power to declare war or economic questions such as the fairness of the federal tax system. The federal judiciary does decide questions about whether the federal government followed the laws, but it generally allows Congress and the president to resolve their differences through the normal legislative process.

Prosecuting Cases

The U.S. Department of Justice is responsible for prosecuting federal criminal and civil cases. The department is led by the United States **attorney general,** assisted by the **solicitor general,** 94 U.S. Attorneys, and approximately 1,200 assistant U.S. Attorneys. The solicitor general represents the federal government whenever a case appears before the Supreme Court, whereas U.S. Attorneys represent the government whenever a case appears before a lower federal court. U.S. Attorneys are appointed by the president with the advice and consent of the Senate, whereas the attorney general appoints each of the assistant U.S. Attorneys after consulting with the U.S. Attorneys in each district. Some districts have as few as 17 assistant U.S. Attorneys, as does the U.S. Attorney's Office for the district of North Dakota; the largest, the U.S. Attorney's Office for the District of Columbia, has more than 350.

United States attorney general
The chief law enforcement officer in the United States and the head of the Department of Justice.

solicitor general
The third-ranking official in the Department of Justice who is responsible for representing the United States in cases before the U.S. Supreme Court.

public defender system
An arrangement whereby public officials are hired to provide legal assistance to people accused of crimes who are unable to hire their own attorneys.

The federal judiciary also provides help to defendants who cannot afford their own attorneys in criminal trials. Traditionally, private attorneys have been appointed to provide assistance, but many state and federal courts employ a **public defender system.** This system provides lawyers to any defendant who needs one and is supervised by the federal judiciary to ensure that public defenders are qualified for their jobs.

The Three Types of Federal Courts

LEARNING **OBJECTIVE**

10.2 Outline the structure of the federal court system.

Article III of the Constitution is the shortest of the three articles establishing the institutions of government. Yet as brief as it is, it instructs the judiciary to resolve several kinds of cases, including those to which the United States is a party in enforcing the laws, for example, and disputes between citizens of two or more states.

Article III is not the only part of the Constitution dealing with the federal judiciary, however. The framers also gave Congress the power to establish "all tribunals inferior to the Supreme Court," which meant that Congress could establish the lower courts we discuss next.

The first Congress used this power to create a hierarchy of federal courts. Under the Judiciary Act of 1789, which was the very first law Congress passed, the federal judiciary was divided into a three-tiered system that exists to this day. The first tier consists of **district courts,** the middle tier of **circuit courts of appeals,** and the highest tier of only one court, the **Supreme Court.** The Supreme Court has **original jurisdiction,** the authority to hear a case essentially as a trial court would, only in cases involving ambassadors, other public ministers, and other diplomats, and cases in which a state or states are a party.

In all other cases, the Supreme Court has **appellate jurisdiction** and reviews decisions of other federal courts and agencies and appeals from state supreme court decisions that raise questions of federal law. In general, federal courts may decide only cases or controversies arising under the Constitution, a federal law, a treaty, or admiralty and maritime law; cases brought by a foreign nation against a state or the federal government; and diversity suits—lawsuits between citizens of different states—if the amount of the controversy exceeds $75,000.

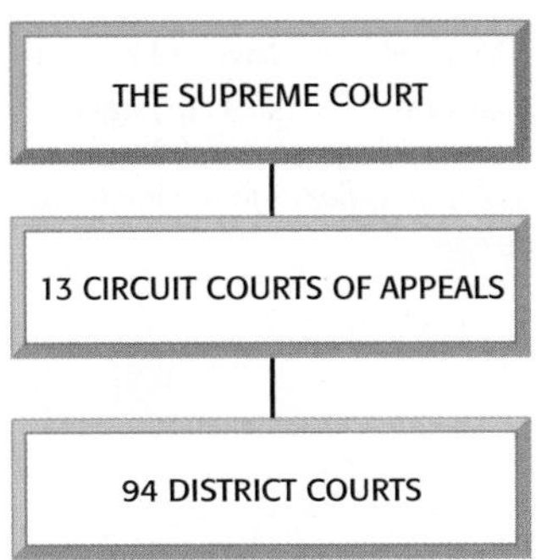

FIGURE 10–1 **The Structure of the U.S. Judiciary.**

■ *Why are there so many more district courts than there are circuit courts?*

Level One: District Courts

Although the Supreme Court and its justices receive most of the attention, the workhorses of the federal judiciary are the district courts in the states, the District of Columbia, and U.S. territories. In 2009, they heard more than 275,000 civil cases and more than 75,000 criminal cases.[6] There are 678 judgeships in the 94 district courts across the country, at least one in every state. (See Figure 10–1 for the three-tiered structure of the federal judiciary.)

District courts are the trial courts where nearly all federal cases begin. They make decisions on the death penalty, drug crimes, and other criminal violations. District judges normally hold trials and decide cases individually. However, because reapportionment of congressional districts and voting rights are so important to the nation, they hear cases concerned with these issues in three-judge panels.

Level Two: Circuit Courts of Appeals

All district court decisions can be *appealed,* or taken to a higher court for further review. Nearly all of these cases are reviewed by federal courts of appeals. Judges in these courts are bound by **precedent,** or decisions previously made by courts of appeals and the Supreme Court, but they have considerable discretion in applying these earlier decisions to specific new cases. Although most of their cases come upward from federal district courts, federal regulatory commissions bring their cases to the courts of appeals directly. For example, appeals of the Federal Energy Regulatory Commission's decisions may be heard by the U.S. Court of Appeals for the District of Columbia Circuit and by the U.S. Supreme Court.

Courts of appeals are located geographically in 11 *judicial circuits* that include all of the states and U.S. territories (see Figure 10–2 for a map of the states included in each of the 11 geographic circuits). A 12th is located in the District of Columbia and hears the largest number of cases challenging federal statutes, regulations, and administrative decisions. Circuit courts normally operate as panels of three judges; in 2009, they decided more than 57,000 cases.

Except in unusual circumstances, courts of appeals can resolve only cases that have been decided by district courts. Nevertheless, their decisions are usually final. Fewer than 1 percent of their decisions are appealed to the Supreme Court. (For more information about the federal judiciary, go to the Web site of the Administrative Office of the U.S. Courts at www.uscourts.gov.)

Level Three: The Supreme Court

The Constitution established only one court of appeals for the entire nation: the Supreme Court, or the "court of last resort." Once the Supreme Court decides, the dispute or case is over.

district courts
Courts in which criminal and civil cases are originally tried in the federal judicial system.

circuit courts of appeals
Courts with appellate jurisdiction that hear appeals from the decisions of lower courts.

Supreme Court
The court of last resort in the United States. It can hear appeals from federal circuit courts or state high courts.

original jurisdiction
The authority of a court to hear a case "in the first instance."

appellate jurisdiction
The authority of a court to review decisions made by lower courts.

precedent
A decision made by a higher court such as a circuit court of appeals or the Supreme Court that is binding on all other federal courts.

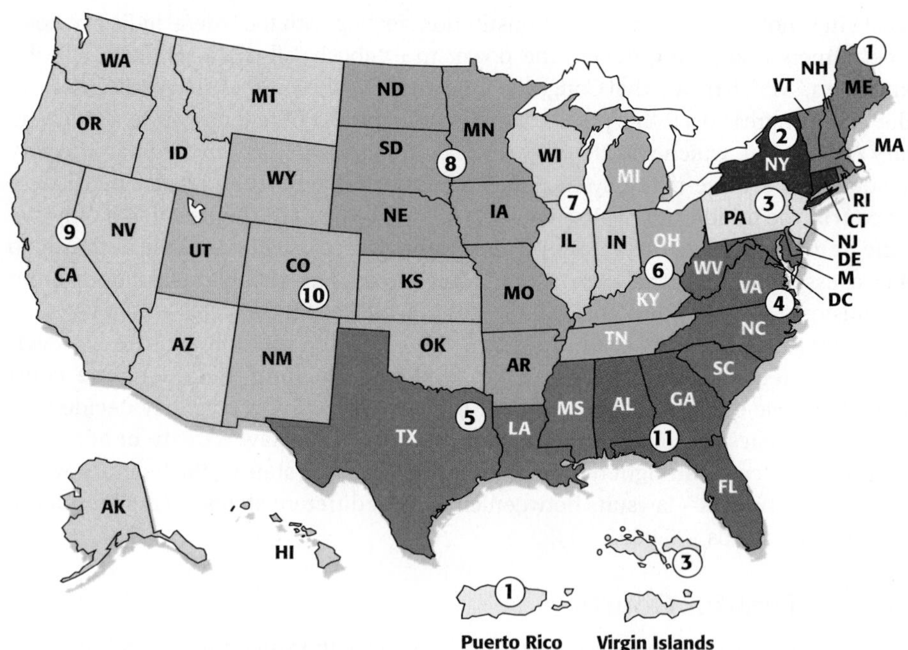

FIGURE 10–2 States Covered by the Eleven U.S. Circuit Courts of Appeals. ■ *Why are some circuits so much larger, geographically, than others? In what circuit do you reside?*

Compared with Congress and the presidency, the Supreme Court has changed the least since its creation. There are nine Supreme Court justices today, compared with six in 1789, and the Court moved into its own building only in 1935. Before then it had shared space with the House and Senate in the U.S. Capitol building. Unlike the current practice in both houses of Congress, oral arguments before the Court about individual cases are not televised, and the justices still appear in robes. Many of the Court's unique characteristics persist due to the constitutional protections the framers put in place. Given its importance, we will turn to a more in-depth discussion of the Supreme Court later in this chapter.

Judicial Federalism: State and Federal Courts

Unlike most countries, which have a single national judicial system that makes all decisions on criminal and civil laws, the United States has both federal and state courts. Each state maintains a judiciary of its own, and many large cities and counties have judicial systems as complex as those of the states. As in the federal system, state judicial power is divided between trial courts (and other special courts such as traffic courts) and one or more levels of appellate courts. State courts hear the overwhelming majority of cases in the U.S. legal system—approximately 90 million civil and criminal cases annually.

State courts primarily interpret and apply their state constitutions and law. When their decisions are based solely on state law, their rulings may not be appealed to or reviewed by federal courts. Only when decisions raise a federal question that requires the application of the Bill of Rights or other federal law are federal courts able to review them. Federal courts have **writ of *habeas corpus*** jurisdiction, or the power to release persons from custody if a judge determines they are not being detained constitutionally, and may review criminal convictions in state courts if they believe that an accused person's federal constitutional and legal rights have been violated (see Chapter 11). Except for habeas corpus jurisdiction, the Supreme Court is the only federal court that may review state court decisions, and only in cases presenting a conflict with federal law.

writ of *habeas corpus*
A court order requiring explanation to a judge why a prisoner is being held in custody.

Other than the original jurisdiction the Constitution grants to the Supreme Court, no federal court has any jurisdiction except that granted to it by an act of Congress. Congress controls the Supreme Court's appellate jurisdiction (as we will discuss later in the chapter) and also established the three-tiered structure of the federal court system through legislation, beginning with the Judiciary Act of 1789. Congress could technically eliminate the lower federal courts, but that is entirely unlikely given the heavy caseloads under consideration.

For the People

GOVERNMENT'S GREATEST ENDEAVORS

Reducing Crime

State and local governments are responsible for enforcing most laws against criminal activities such as murder, rape, and theft. However, the federal government provides money to help them do so, and it also enforces federal drug laws and gun controls. It has also helped fund larger police forces and imposed tougher sentences against federal crimes such as kidnapping and terrorism.

The federal government's biggest investment has been in providing money to help states control both street crimes and organized crime by the Mafia and other criminal organizations. In 1968, for example, Congress passed the Crime Control and Safe Streets Act, which gave millions of dollars to the states to increase their police forces and patrol the streets. The law also raised the minimum age for purchasing a handgun to 21 years of age.

The 1968 law set an important precedent for federal involvement in state and local crime control, which led to further controls on handguns and a new Crime Control and Safe Streets Act in 1994. Under the new law, the federal government gave states even more money to hire 100,000 new police officers and banned 19 types of assault weapons, such as the M-16 and AK-47, which are rapid-firing rifles often used by the military. The law also banned hate crimes such as painting Nazi slogans and swastikas on Jewish synagogues.

In part because of increased state and local action, national crime rates have fallen dramatically throughout the past quarter-century, particularly in large urban settings such as New York City. Crime fell through the 1990s and early 2000s, but there was an uptick in the number of violent crimes in 2005–2006. However, the rates in 2007–2008 have dropped back down below levels seen at the end of the 1990s but not yet to the lows of 2004. Preliminary rates for the first half of 2009 seem to indicate a further decline.*

CRITICAL THINKING QUESTIONS

1. Should the federal government be involved with state and local crime control?
2. What factors might drive the crime rate up or down?
3. How might criminal sentencing affect the crime rate?

* *Crime in the United States,* an annual publication of the Federal Bureau of Investigation, http://www.fbi.gov/ucr/ucr.htm#cius.

The Politics of Appointing Federal Judges

LEARNING **OBJECTIVE**

10.3 Analyze the factors that play an important role in selecting judicial nominees.

The Constitution sets absolutely no requirements for serving on the Supreme Court, nor did the first Congress create any requirements for the lower courts. Because judges were to be appointed by the president with the advice and consent of the Senate, the framers assumed that judges would be experienced in the law. As Alexander Hamilton explained, "there can be but few men in the society who will have sufficient skill in the laws to qualify them for the stations of judges. And making the proper deductions for the ordinary depravity of human nature, the number must be still smaller of those who unite the requisite integrity with the requisite knowledge."[7]

Much as the framers believed that the judiciary should be independent, the appointment process gives presidents and the Senate ample opportunity for influencing the direction of the courts. Indeed, George Washington established two precedents in judicial appointments. First, his appointees were his political and ideological allies—all of Washington's appointees belonged to his Federalist Party. Second, every state was represented on some court somewhere, thereby ensuring at least some representation across the nation.

Presidents have continued to follow Washington's lead on these two points. They nominate judges who are likely to agree with them on the key issues before the courts and tend to nominate judges from their own party. Presidents see these nominations as one of the most important legacies of their time in office. Indeed, if a president is able to appoint a 50-year-old justice, that person could continue to affect law in the United States for some 30 years beyond the president's time in office.

Presidents also routinely rely on the senators in a given state to make recommendations especially for district court appointments. Because judges serve for life, presidents see judicial appointments as an opportunity to shape the courts for decades to come. As Table 10–1 shows, federal court experience is the most common preparation for Supreme Court justices—in fact, 10 of the last 16 Supreme Court justices were federal lower-court judges at the time of their nomination. All of the current U.S. Supreme Court justices with the exception of the newest justice, Elena Kagan, have federal appeals court experience in particular.

TABLE 10–1 Moving Up to the Supreme Court

Job Experience	Number	Most Recent Example
Federal Judges	33	Sonia Sotomayor, 2009
Practicing Lawyers	22	Lewis F. Powell, 1971
State Court Judges	18	Sandra Day O'Connor, 1981
Cabinet Members	8	Labor Secretary Arthur Goldberg, 1962
Senators	7	Harold H. Burton (R-Ohio), 1945
Attorneys General	6	Tom C. Clark, 1949
Governors	3	Earl Warren (D-Calif.), 1953
Other	15	Solicitor General Elena Kagan, 2010

SOURCE: *CQ Weekly*, October 10, 2005, p. 2701, updated by authors.

■ *How might a justice's experience affect his or her[?] work on the Court? Why do you think so many federal judges have won appointment to the U.S. Supreme Court?*

Making the Initial Choices

Article II of the Constitution gives the president the power to appoint federal judges with the advice and consent of the Senate. Although that language may seem straightforward, it has caused great controversy over the Senate's appropriate role in federal judicial selection. The result is a judicial selection process in which presidents are likely to consult with members of Congress and particularly senators, especially if they want a smooth confirmation.

The process through which the president consults with members of Congress is complex and may differ from appointment to appointment, but one particularly important norm is **senatorial courtesy**—the custom of submitting the names of prospective judges for approval to the senators from the states in which the appointees are to work. The home-state senators, particularly if they are of the president's party, may also develop a list of candidates for the president's consideration. If the senators approve the nomination, all is well. But if negotiations are deadlocked between them, or between the senators and the Department of Justice, a seat may stay vacant for years.[8]

senatorial courtesy
The presidential custom of submitting the names of prospective appointees for approval to senators from the states in which the appointees are to work.

The custom of senatorial courtesy is not observed with Supreme Court appointments, but presidents do strategically consult with members of Congress, as President Clinton did on his 1993 and 1994 appointments of Justices Ruth Bader Ginsburg and Stephen Breyer. Clinton was especially willing to consult with Republican senator Orrin Hatch, then the Senate Judiciary Committee chair, because the Senate was controlled by Republicans and he needed their support. Before selecting Solicitor General Elena Kagan as his candidate to replace Justice Stevens on the Supreme Court, President Obama met with Senate leaders and consulted with every member of the Senate Judiciary Committee.

In preparation for her confirmation hearings, then Solicitor General Elena Kagan met with Senate Judiciary Committee members. Here Kagan meets with Senator Patrick Leahy (D-VT), the Chair of the Senate Judiciary Committee.
■ *Why do nominees take the time to meet with senators before the confirmation hearings?*

Presidents are also advised by their own White House staffs and the Justice Department in compiling a list of potential nominees. Especially in more recent administrations, the Justice Department's Office of Legal Policy and the White House Counsel's Office begin formulating lists of potential court appointees as soon as the president assumes office.

In addition to this process within the government, nongovernmental actors try to influence the selection process. The American Bar Association (ABA) has historically rated candidates being considered for appointment, but conservative groups' concern that the ABA rankings were biased in favor of more liberal judges led the Bush administration to end its preappointment involvement.

Liberal and conservative interest groups also provide their own views of nominees' qualifications for appointment. People for the American Way and the Alliance for Justice often support liberal nominees and oppose conservatives, whereas the Heritage Foundation and a coalition of 260 conservative organizations called the Judicial Selection Monitoring Project often support conservative judges and oppose liberals. These organizations once waited to express their opinions until after the president had sent the name of a nominee to the Senate, but now they are active before the choice is known, informing the media of their support or opposition to potential nominees.

After a contentious confirmation process in 1987, the Senate rejected Judge Robert Bork by a vote of 58 to 42. ■ *Why might senators vote against a judicial nominee? Are there valid reasons for opposing judicial nominees?*

Senate Advice and Consent

The normal presumption is that the president should be allowed considerable discretion in the selection of federal judges. Despite this presumption, the Senate takes seriously its responsibility in confirming judicial nominations, especially when the party controlling the Senate is different from that of the president. However, because individual senators can always threaten or actually mount a filibuster, even party control of the Senate is no guarantee that a nomination will succeed.

All judicial nominations are referred to the Senate Judiciary Committee for a hearing and a committee vote before consideration by the entire Senate. Like laws, judges are confirmed with a majority vote. Even before they receive a hearing, however, all district court nominees must survive a preliminary vote by the nominee's two home-state senators. Each senator receives a letter on blue paper, called a *blue slip,* from the committee asking for approval. If either senator declines to return the slip, the nomination is dead and no hearing will be held.

There are other ways to delay or defeat a judicial nominee, including the threat of a filibuster. Just as the Republican Senate majority had stalled Clinton nominations in the late 1990s, the Democratic majority stalled many of the Bush administration's nominees after it took control of the Senate in mid-2001. Democrats also stalled many of the Bush nominees even after Republicans regained control of the Senate following the 2002 midterm elections with both the threat and actual use of filibusters.[9] During his first 18 months in office, confirmation rates for President Obama's judicial nominees hit historic lows: only 37% of district court and 47% of appeals court nominees were confirmed. This compares to a confirmation rate of 85% for district court and 52% for appeals court nominees during President George W. Bush's first two years in office.[10] Even if the Senate delays or rejects a nomination, however, presidents always have the option of making *recess appointments* after the Senate adjourns at the end of a session. Presidents have made more than 300 recess appointments to the federal courts since 1789, including 15 Supreme Court justices who were initially seated as recess appointments.[11]

Before the mid-1950s, the Senate confirmation process was relatively simple and nonpartisan. Until then, the Senate Judiciary Committee did not even hold hearings to ask potential judges questions about their personal history and philosophy. However, as judges became more important in deciding civil rights and other controversial cases, the committee began interviewing candidates on various questions, sometimes imposing a *litmus test* by asking nominees about their positions on specific issues such as abortion. Nominees almost always refuse to answer such questions, to protect themselves from attack and reserve their judgment for actual future cases.

In 1987, however, Supreme Court nominee Robert Bork adopted a different and ultimately unsuccessful strategy. Because he had written so many law articles, made so many speeches, and decided so many cases as a circuit court judge, Bork sought to clarify his constitutional views in defending himself before the Judiciary Committee. His candor may well have contributed to the Senate's rejecting him, and that has made subsequent nominees even more reluctant to respond to similar questions.

For the first time in the Supreme Court's history, three of the court's nine justices are women: Justices Ginsburg, Sotomayor and Kagan. ■ *Is it important to have gender and racial diversity on the Supreme Court? Why or why not?*

Until recently, most judicial appointments, especially those for the district and circuit courts, were processed without much controversy. However, "now that lower-court judges are more commonly viewed as political actors, there is increasing Senate scrutiny of these nominees."[12] The battle over judicial confirmations ordinarily takes place in hearings before the Senate Judiciary Committee, although debates can also occur on the Senate floor after the committee has acted.[13] Supreme Court nominees have typically faced more scrutiny in the

Of the People

AMERICA'S CHANGING FACE

Diversity in the Federal Courts

The federal judiciary has long been dominated by white males. But diversity on the federal bench has been increasing during the last several decades, largely because of the judicial appointments of Presidents Jimmy Carter, George H. W. Bush, Bill Clinton, and George W. Bush. Although President Obama has only gotten 43% of his federal judges confirmed by the Senate through July 2010, he did appoint two women to the U.S. Supreme Court: Sonia Sotomayor, who is also the first Hispanic justice on the Court, and Elena Kagan, only the fourth woman ever to serve on the Court. He also appointed diverse candidates to the district and appellate courts. As of June 2010, President Obama had appointed 73 lower court judges. Twenty-five percent of those nominees are African-American, 10% are Hispanic, and 11% are Asian-American. Thirty-one of the nominees (42%) are women.

Although the number of women and minorities appointed to the federal courts has only recently increased significantly, the first female judge, Florence Allen, was appointed in 1934 by President Franklin D. Roosevelt. President Harry Truman named the first African American judge, William Henry Hastie, in 1950. President John F. Kennedy appointed the first Hispanic judge, Reynaldo G. Garza, in 1961, and President Richard M. Nixon in 1971 appointed the first Asian American judge, Herbert Choy. The first Native American judge, Billy Michael Burrage, was appointed in 1994 by President Clinton.

There are several arguments for diversifying the federal judiciary. First, some scholars have argued that a diverse federal judiciary may reach decisions that more accurately reflect the views of our diverse populations. But research has not provided much support for the contention that female or minority judges decide cases differently than do white male judges, with the exception of discrimination suits. Even if there are no differences in outcomes, others argue that simply having a federal judiciary that reflects the citizenry is important to maintaining the courts' legitimacy. In short, citizens place value in seeing someone like themselves on the federal judiciary.

CRITICAL THINKING QUESTIONS

1. How might a judge's race or gender affect decisions on the courts?
2. Should presidents consider judicial candidates' race or gender when making appointments to the federal courts?
3. What advantages or disadvantages might there be to having a diverse federal judiciary?

Justice Ruth Bader Ginsburg

Justice Sonia Sotomayor

Supreme Court Justices Clarence Thomas (left) and Anthony Kennedy.

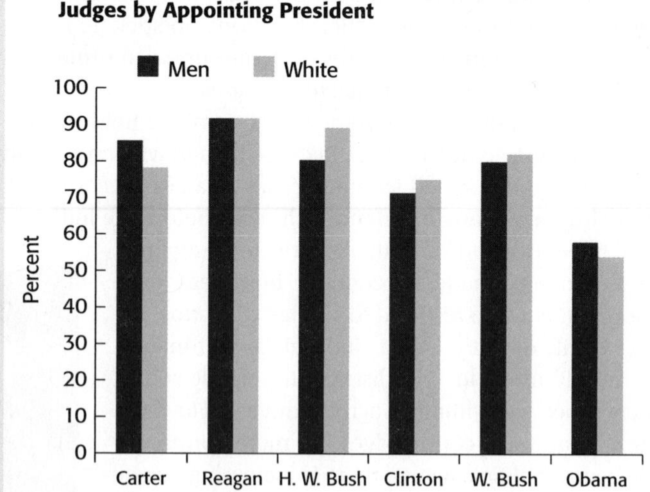

SOURCE: Sheldon Goldman, Elliot Slotnick, Genard Gryski, and Sara Schiavoni, "Picking Judges in Time of Turmoil: W. Bush's Judiciary During the 109th Congress," *Judicature* (May–June 2007). Data updated by authors.

confirmation process than have lower federal court judges. Indeed, the Senate has refused to confirm 31 of the 154 presidential nominations for Supreme Court justices since the first justice was nominated in 1789.

The Role of Ideology

Presidents so seldom nominate judges from the opposing party (only 10 percent of judicial appointments since the time of Franklin Roosevelt have gone to candidates from the opposition party) that partisan considerations are taken for granted. Today, more attention is paid to other characteristics, such as ideology, race, and gender.[14] (See *Of the People* box for more on the role of race and gender.)

Finding a party member is not enough; presidents want to pick the "right" kind of Republican or "our" kind of Democrat to serve as a judge. Thus judges picked by Republican presidents tend to be judicial conservatives, and judges picked by Democratic presidents are more likely to be liberals. Both these orientations are tempered by the need for judges to go through a senatorial confirmation process that must get bipartisan support.

As older, conservative judges appointed during the Reagan administration continued to retire, President George W. Bush worked hard to find younger conservative judges to fill the vacancies. Roberts and Alito were in their fifties when nominated for the Supreme Court and are likely to serve for decades. Many of the administration's lower-court appointees are also relatively young, which ensures their lasting impact. Like his recent predecessors, Bush had difficulty winning the support of opposition party senators for his judicial nominees. Democrats delayed Bush's most conservative nominees and held filibusters in order to prevent confirmation votes on ten circuit court nominees.

Alabama's Attorney General William Pryor was only 43 when he was confirmed for a life appointment as a federal judge on the 11th U.S. Circuit Court of Appeals. Here he testifies before the Senate Judiciary Committee. ■ *Are lifetime appointments to the federal courts problematic? Should there be term limits for these judges?*

The Role of Judicial Philosophy

A candidate's judicial philosophy also influences the selection process. Does a candidate believe that judges should interpret the Constitution to reflect what the framers intended and what its words literally say? Or does the candidate believe that the Constitution should be adapted to reflect current conditions and philosophies? Recall from our discussion in Chapter 1 that differences in constitutional interpretation can produce vastly different outcomes on the same legal question.

Presidents and senators also want to know how candidates see the appropriate role of the courts. Does the candidate believe that the courts should strike down acts of the elected branches if they violate broad norms and values that might not be explicitly stated in the Constitution? That is, does the candidate espouse the view of **judicial activism?** Or does the candidate believe in **judicial restraint,** which deems it appropriate for the courts to strike down popularly enacted legislation only when it clearly violates the letter of the Constitution? At the heart of this debate are competing conceptions of the proper balance between government authority and individual rights, and between the power of democratically accountable legislatures and that of courts and unelected judges.

Reforming the Selection Process

The televised confirmation hearings of Supreme Court nominees Robert Bork in 1987 and Clarence Thomas in 1991 provoked widespread complaints about the judicial selection process. Not only were the hearings lengthy and bitter, but they focused on personal issues that some critics believed were irrelevant to each nominee's qualification to serve. The hearings also included detailed questions about the nominees' positions on controversial issues, which neither was willing to answer.

The politics of judicial selection may shock those who like to think judges are picked strictly on the basis of legal merit and without regard for ideology, party, gender, or race. But as a former Justice Department official observed, "When courts cease being an instrument for political change, then maybe the judges will stop being politically selected."[15]

judicial activism
A philosophy proposing that judges should strike down laws that are inconsistent with norms and values stated or implied in the Constitution.

judicial restraint
A philosophy proposing that judges should strike down the actions of the elected branches only if they clearly violate the literal meaning of the Constitution.

YOU WILL

DECIDE Should the Federal Courts Be Active?

Given that a judicially active judge will be more willing to strike down the actions of the elected branches of government, it should not be surprising that legislators are interested to know how federal judicial candidates view judicial activism.

Throughout most of our history, federal courts have been more conservative than Congress, the White House, or state legislatures. Before 1937, judicial restraint was the battle cry of liberals who objected to judges' decisions to strike down many laws, such as state laws limiting the number of hours a person could work each week, that were passed to protect labor and women. These judges broadly construed the words of the Constitution to prevent what they thought were unreasonable regulations of property.

With Presidents Richard Nixon, Ronald Reagan, George H. W. Bush, and George W. Bush, however, these positions changed dramatically, and it was conservatives who advocated judicial restraint. What is needed, they argued, are judges who will step back and let Congress, the president, and the state legislatures regulate or forbid abortions, permit prayer in public schools, and not hinder law enforcement. Even though these presidents argued for restrained judges, many of the Supreme Court justices they appointed were quite active in overturning congressional legislation.

What do you think? Should the federal courts be judicially active? What arguments would you make for and against such a position?

THINKING IT THROUGH

Chief Justice John Marshall stated in 1803, "It is emphatically the province and duty of the judicial department to say what the law is."* The Court's decision in *Marbury* v. *Madison* established the use of judicial review to strike down congressional acts. Marshall saw this authority as essential to the Court's ability to check the other branches of government. Justices since Marshall have often been active in striking down legislation that infringes on the rights of minority groups. For example, the Supreme Court's decision in *Brown* v. *Board of Education of Topeka* (1954)† was an active one in that it struck down the state law requiring racial segregation in the public schools. The court's ability to take such action is often seen as an important check on the tyranny of the majority.

The courts have sometimes drawn criticism for too frequently striking down popularly supported legislation. The Roberts' Court decision to strike down restrictions on corporate and union spending from their general treasuries in *Citizens United* v. *Federal Election Commission*†† resulted in substantial criticism by those who supported such limitations. One school of thought holds that the federal judiciary, composed of unelected judges secure from public pressure, has a responsibility to use restraint in reaching its decisions.

Many critics of judicial activism argue that although the Supreme Court has the authority of judicial review, the Court must also respect the elected branches' interpretations of the constitutionality of their own actions. These critics assert that Congress is especially well situated to determine whether it is acting under the appropriate grant of authority in Article I, and the executive branch is in a similarly good position to evaluate its power under Article II. According to this perspective, the Court's view on the constitutionality of executive or legislative action is that of only one coequal branch of government.

Critical Thinking Questions

1. Under what circumstances do you think the Supreme Court should be active and strike down state or federal legislation?
2. Might it be preferable to have an unelected body decide whether legislation is constitutional? Why or why not?
3. Why do you think most people associate judicial activism with a liberal court?

* *Marbury* v. *Madison,* 5 U.S. 137 (1803).
† *Brown* v. *Board of Education of Topeka,* 347 U.S. 483 (1954).
†† *Citizens United* v. *Federal Election Commission,* 558 U.S. 50 (2010).

How the Supreme Court Decides

LEARNING **OBJECTIVE**

10.4 Trace the process by which Supreme Court decisions are reached, and assess influences on this process.

The Supreme Court is a unique institution. Its term runs from the first Monday in October through the end of June. The justices listen to oral arguments for two weeks each month from October to April and then adjourn for two weeks to consider the cases and to write opinions. By agreement, at least six justices must participate in each decision. Cases are decided by a majority vote. In the event of a tie, the decision of the lower court is sustained, although on rare occasions, the case may be reargued.

The Eight Steps to Judgment

When citizens vow to take their cases to the highest court of the land even if it costs their last penny, they underestimate the difficulty of securing Supreme Court review and misunderstand the Court's role. The rules for appealing a case are established by the Supreme Court and Congress. Since 1988, when Congress enacted the Act to Improve the Administration of Justice, the Supreme Court has not been obligated to grant review of most cases that come to it on appeal. Its *appellate jurisdiction* is almost entirely up to its discretion; the overwhelming majority of cases appealed to the Court will be denied review.

The process of deciding cases at the U.S. Supreme Court is substantially different than at other federal courts. The Court's first decision is to choose which of the thousands of appeals it will hear each year. Once it has decided to review a case, the Court must then decide the legal question at issue. Next, we discuss, step by step, the Court's process of accepting and deciding a case.

1. Reviewing Appeals Today, the decision to grant nearly all appeals is at the Court's discretion. Many appeals come to the Court by means of a petition for a **writ of certiorari,** a formal petition seeking the Court's review, or through an **in forma pauperis** ("as a pauper") petition, which avoids the payment of Court fees. The great majority of in forma pauperis petitions come from prisoners. In either case, the appeals may arise from any state supreme court or from the federal court system (see Figure 10–3 for a simplified description of the two paths to the Supreme Court).

The writs, which the Court can grant or deny, produce its agenda, or **docket.** The docket has grown significantly since the 1970s as citizens have brought more lawsuits, states have imposed more death sentences (which are often appealed), federal regulation has increased, and federal punishment for crimes has become more severe. However, as the number of appeals has grown, the Supreme Court's discretion to decide which cases it will review has allowed it to hear fewer and fewer cases (see Figure 10–4 representing the size of the Supreme Court's docket over time).[16]

2. Granting the Appeal The Supreme Court will review a case only if the claim raises a substantial question of federal or constitutional law with broad public significance—what kinds of affirmative action programs are permissible, whether individuals have a right to doctor-assisted suicide, or under what conditions women may have abortions. The Court also tends to review cases in which the courts of appeals disagree. Or a case may raise a constitutional issue on which a state supreme court has presented an interpretation with which the Court disagrees.

The Court decides whether to move forward based on the *rule of four.* If four justices are sufficiently interested in a petition, it will be granted and the case brought up for review. The justices' law clerks work as a group, in what is known as the *cert pool,* to read the petitions and write a memorandum on each, recommending whether a review should be granted. These memos circulate to all the justices except Justice Samuel Alito, who opted out of the cert pool in September 2008.

writ of certiorari
A formal writ used to bring a case before the Supreme Court.

in forma pauperis
A petition that allows a party to file "as a pauper" and avoid paying Court fees.

docket
The list of potential cases that reach the Supreme Court.

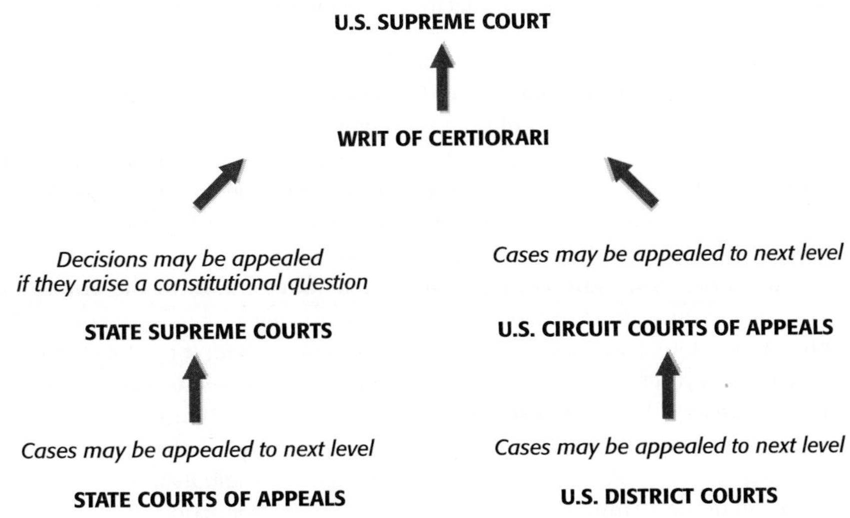

FIGURE 10–3 **How Most Cases Rise to the Supreme Court.**

■ *Under what conditions can a case that starts off in the state courts be appealed to the U.S. Supreme Court?*

FIGURE 10–4 The Supreme Court Caseload.

■ *Why do you think the Supreme Court's docket has gotten so much larger over time? Why has the number of cases decided declined at the same time?*

SOURCE: Lee Epstein, Jeffrey A. Segal, Harold J. Spaeth, and Thomas G. Walker, *The Supreme Court Compendium: Data, Decisions, and Developments* (CQ Press, 2007), figures updated by the authors.

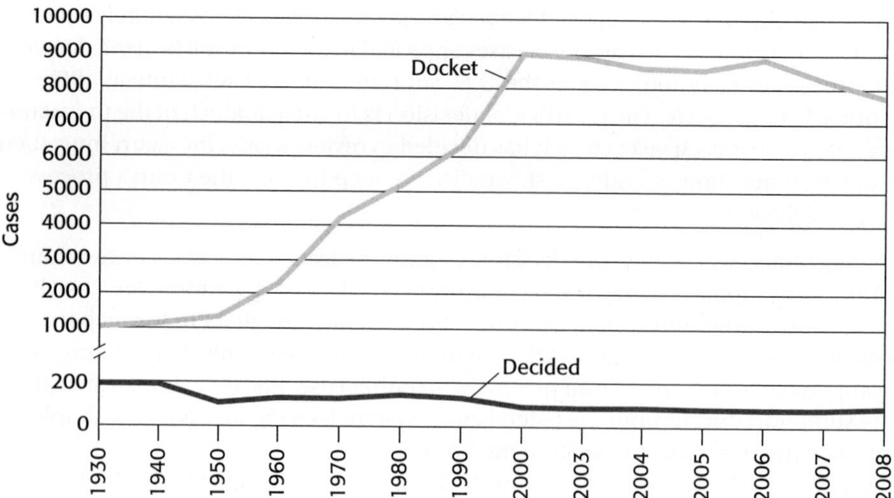

Denying a writ of certiorari does not mean the justices agree with the decision of the lower court, nor does it establish precedent. Refusal to grant a review can indicate all kinds of possibilities. The justices may wish to avoid a political "hot potato," or they may be so divided on an issue that they are not yet prepared to take a stand, or they may want to let an issue "percolate" in the federal courts so that the Court may benefit from their rulings before it decides.

3. Briefing the Case After a case is granted review, each side prepares written *briefs* presenting legal arguments, relevant precedents, and historical background for the justices and their law clerks to study and on which to base their decisions. Prior decisions by the U.S. Supreme Court itself are most highly desirable as precedent; however, the Court may also consider cases decided by the lower federal courts as well as state supreme courts in reaching its decision, depending on the issue presented.

In writing these briefs, the appellants are often aware of the justices' views or concerns about their case, and they attempt to address those concerns. Indeed, attorneys readily admit that they sometimes frame their briefs to appeal to a particular justice on the Court, one they suspect may be the swing, or deciding, vote in the case. Often, outside groups interested in the case file ***amicus curiae* briefs** (Latin for "friend of the court"), through which they can make arguments specific to their members and of interest to the justices.

***amicus curiae* brief**
Literally, a "friend of the court" brief, filed by an individual or organization to present arguments in addition to those presented by the immediate parties to a case.

4. Holding the Oral Argument After the Court grants review, a case is set for oral arguments—briefs must be filed according to a timely schedule and arguments are usually heard within three to four months. Lengthy oratory before the Supreme Court, once lasting for several days, is a thing of the past. As a rule, counsel for each side is now allowed only 30 minutes. In order to ensure compliance with this rule, lawyers use a lectern with two lights: A white light flashes five minutes before time is up. When the red light goes on, the lawyer must stop, even in the middle of a sentence.

The entire procedure is informally formal. Sometimes, to the annoyance of attorneys, justices talk among themselves or consult briefs or books during oral arguments. Other times, if justices find a presentation particularly bad, they will tell the attorneys so. Justices freely interrupt the lawyers to ask questions and request additional information. In recent years, "the justices seem barely able to contain themselves, often interrupting the answer to one question with another query."[17] Hence the 30-minute limit can be problematic, especially when the solicitor general participates, because his or her time comes out of the 30 minutes of the party he or she is supporting.

If a lawyer is having a difficult time, the justices may try to help out with a question. Occasionally, justices bounce arguments off an attorney and at one another. Justice Antonin Scalia is a harsh questioner. "When Scalia prepares to ask a question, he doesn't just adjust himself in his chair to get closer to the microphone like the others; he looks like a vulture, zooming in for the kill. He strains way forward, pinches his eyebrows, and poses the question, like '... do you want us to believe?' "[18] Justice Ruth Bader Ginsburg is a particularly persistent questioner, frequently rivaling Scalia, whereas Justice Clarence Thomas almost never asks a question at all. (You can hear oral arguments in landmark cases [www.oyez.org] and argument transcripts are now made available on the Court's Web site on the same day as the case is heard [www.supremecourt.gov]).

5. Meeting in Conference When in session, the justices meet on Friday mornings to discuss the cases they heard that week. These conference meetings are private; no one is allowed in the room except the justices themselves. As a result, much of what we know about the justices' conferences come from their own notes taken during the meetings.

The conferences are typically a collegial but vigorous give-and-take. The chief justice presides, usually opening the discussion by stating the facts, summarizing the questions of law, and suggesting how to dispose of each case. Each justice, in order of seniority, then gives his or her views and conclusions. The justices do not typically view this as a time to convince others of their views on the case; that will come later as drafts of the opinion are circulated between chambers. After each justice has given his or her view of the case, the writing of the majority opinion is assigned. By practice, if the chief justice is in the majority, he can either assign the opinion to a justice also in the majority or choose to write the opinion himself. If he is not in the majority, the most senior justice in the majority makes that determination.

6. Explaining the Decision The Supreme Court announces and explains its decisions in **opinions of the Court.** These opinions are the Court's principal method of expressing its views and reasoning to the world. Their primary function is to instruct judges of state and federal courts how to decide similar cases in the future.

Although the writing is assigned to one justice, the opinion must explain the reasoning of the majority. Consequently, opinions are negotiated documents that require the author to compromise and at times bargain with other justices to attain agreement.[19]

A justice is free to write a **dissenting opinion** if desired. Dissenting opinions are, in Chief Justice Charles Evans Hughes's words, "an appeal to the brooding spirit of the law, to the intelligence of a future day."[20] Dissenting opinions are quite common, as justices hope that someday they will command a majority of the Court. If a justice agrees with the majority on how the case should be decided but differs on the reasoning, that justice may write a **concurring opinion.**

Judicial opinions may also be directed at Congress or at the president. If the Court regrets that "in the absence of action by Congress, we have no choice but to . . . " or insists that "relief of the sort that petitioner demands can come only from the political branches of government," it is asking Congress to act.[21] Justices also use opinions to communicate with the public. A well-crafted opinion may increase support for a policy the Court favors.

7. Writing the Opinion Writing the opinion of the Court is an exacting task. The document must win the support of at least four—and more, if possible—intelligent, strong-willed persons. Assisted by the law clerks, the assigned justice writes a draft and sends it to colleagues for comments. If the justice is lucky, the majority will accept the draft, perhaps with only minor changes. If the draft is not satisfactory to the other justices, the author must rewrite and recirculate it until a majority reaches agreement.

The two weapons that justices can use against their colleagues are their votes and the threat of dissenting opinions attacking the majority's opinion. Especially if the Court is closely divided, one justice may be in a position to demand that a certain point or argument be included in, or removed from, the opinion of the Court as the price of his or her vote. Sometimes such bargaining occurs even though the Court is not closely divided. An opinion writer who anticipates that a decision will invite critical public reaction may want a unanimous Court and compromise to achieve unanimity. For this reason, the Court delayed declaring school segregation unconstitutional, in *Brown* v. *Board of Education* (1954), until unanimity was secured.[22] The justices understood that any sign of dissension on this major social issue would be an invitation to evade the Court's ruling.

8. Releasing the Opinion In the past, justices read their entire opinions from the bench on "opinion days." Now, they generally give only brief summaries of the decision and their opinions. Occasionally, when they are unusually unhappy with an opinion, justices read

opinion of the Court
An explanation of a decision of the Supreme Court or any other appellate court.

dissenting opinion
An opinion disagreeing with the majority in a Supreme Court ruling.

concurring opinion
An opinion that agrees with the majority in a Supreme Court ruling but differs on the reasoning.

Of the People

THE GLOBAL COMMUNITY

Importance of an Impartial Judiciary

In the United States, as in most Western democracies, an independent judiciary serves a crucial role in maintaining democracy and protecting individual rights. In a separation-of-powers system like the United States, the judiciary maintains checks on the other branches of government and has the power to invalidate their actions when they violate the Constitution. It also ensures that the government treats all citizens fairly and impartially; no person is above the law. A Pew Global Attitudes Project survey asked respondents from around the world how important it was to live in a country where the judicial system treats everyone the same.

Even if it is not a present reality, most countries see an impartial judiciary where the judicial system treats everyone the same as an important goal. Nearly 90 percent of respondents in the United States indicated that it is very important that the judicial system treat everyone equally, and support in Germany nearly mirrors that in the United States. However, in other countries such as India, Mexico, Nigeria, and South Korea, there are fewer respondents who agree that an impartial judiciary is very important. It is, perhaps, not surprising that in countries where impartial justice is less assured that respondents value it less than in countries such as the United States and Germany where impartiality is expected in the court systems.

CRITICAL THINKING QUESTIONS

1. In what ways could a judicial system show favoritism toward particular groups or individuals?
2. How do you think judicial elections might affect impartiality?
3. Would you expect greater or less impartiality of judges who gain their seats through popular elections?

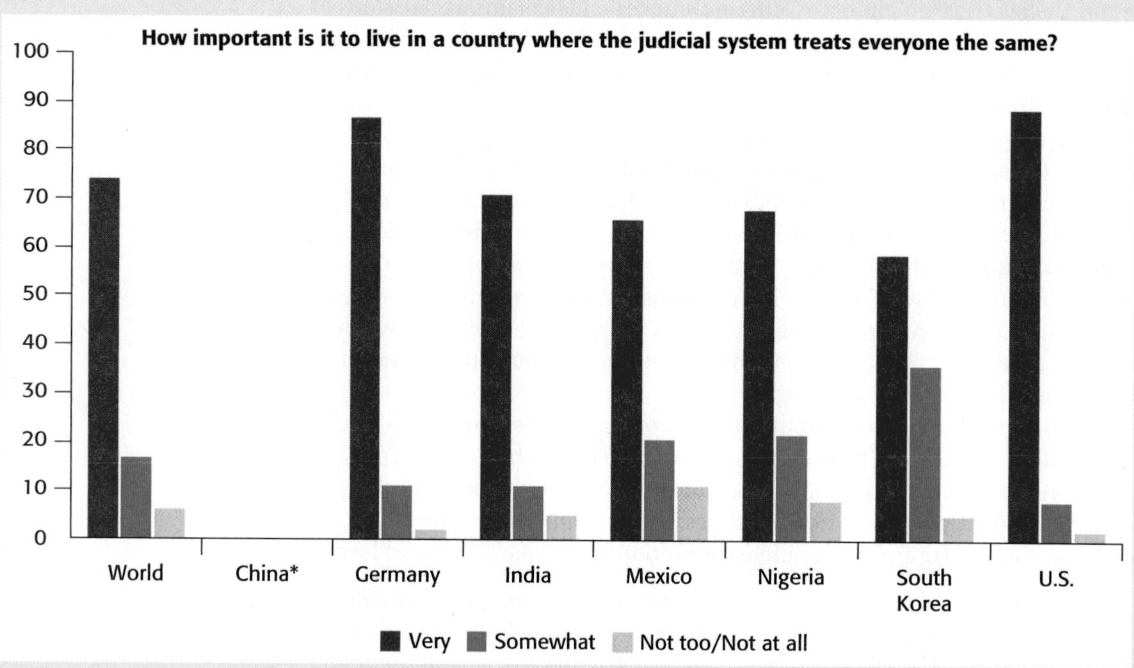

The Pew Global Attitudes Project, 2002. *Data was not collected in China, in part because they do not have an impartial judiciary.

portions of their dissenting opinions from the bench as Justice Stevens did in *Citizens United* v. *Federal Election Commission*.[23] Copies of the Court's opinions are immediately made available to reporters and the public and published in the official *United States Supreme Court Reports*. Since April 2000, the Court has made its opinions immediately available on its Web site (www.supremecourt.gov).

Influences on Supreme Court Decisions

Given the importance of cases that reach the U.S. Supreme Court, the complexity of the Court's decision-making process is not surprising. Supreme Court precedent is a primary influence, but if it were the only one, the lower courts could resolve the question themselves. Typically, there are conflicting precedents, and justices must decide which applies most closely to the legal question at hand.

Outside groups and other legal actors can also influence the Court's decisions. Interest groups' *amicus curiae* briefs may influence a justice's view of the case or the implications of a particular outcome. The chief justice can also affect decision making by the way he frames a case at the conference as well as by his choice of the justice to write the opinion based on the conference vote. Law clerks can affect the Court's decisions by the advice they give their justices, as well as by their role in reviewing the cases appealed to the Court.

The Chief Justice The chief justice of the United States is appointed by the president and confirmed by the Senate, like other federal judges. Yet the chief justice heads the entire federal judiciary; as a result, he (so far in our history, all have been men) has greater visibility than if selected by rotation of fellow justices, as in the state supreme courts, or by seniority, as in the federal courts of appeals. The chief justice has special administrative responsibilities in overseeing the operation of the judiciary, such as assigning judges to committees, responding to proposed legislation that affects the judiciary, and delivering the Annual Report on the State of the Judiciary.

But within the Supreme Court, the chief justice is only "first among equals," even though periods in Court history (such as the Warren Court) are often named after the chief justice. As Rehnquist said when he was still an associate justice, the chief deals not with "eight subordinates whom he may direct or instruct, but eight associates who, like him, have tenure during good behavior, and who are as independent as hogs on ice."[24] As political scientist David Danelski observes, "The Chief Justiceship does not guarantee leadership. It only offers its incumbent an opportunity to lead." Yet the chief justice "sets the tone, controls the conference, assigns the most opinions, and usually, takes the most important, nation-changing decisions for himself."[25]

Law Clerks Beginning in the 1920s and 1930s, federal judges began hiring the best recent graduates of law schools to serve as clerks for a year or two. As the judicial workload increased, more law clerks were appointed, and today, each Supreme Court justice is entitled to four. These are young people who have graduated from a leading law school and have previously clerked for a federal or state court.

Each justice picks his or her own clerks and works closely with them throughout the term. Clerks screen writs of certiorari and prepare draft opinions for the justices. As the number of law clerks and computers has increased, so has the number of concurring and dissenting opinions. Today's opinions are longer and have more footnotes and elaborate citations of cases and law review articles. This is the result of the greater number of law clerks and the operation of justices' chambers like "nine little law firms," often practicing against each other.[26]

Debate swirls about the degree to which law clerks influence the Court's decisions.[27] Some scholars contend that law clerks have had too much influence, especially as they help write early drafts of their justices' opinions. Others contend that justices select clerks with views very similar to their own, so to the extent law clerks are able to advance their views, they reflect those of the justice they serve. Regardless of this disagreement, however, there is widespread acceptance of law clerks' influence in the decision to grant certiorari. Law clerks' dominance at this stage of the decision-making process surely provides them with an opportunity at least to influence the Court's docket.

Chief Justice William Rehnquist (on the left) was very popular among his colleagues, both liberal and conservative. He was known for his general efficiency in running the Court and his fairness in assigning opinions. Here he meets with law clerks in his chambers. ■ *Should law clerks play such an important role in deciding which cases the Court will hear?*

The Solicitor General Attorneys in the Department of Justice and other federal agencies participate in more than

The U.S. Supreme Court is tradition bound. For example, when a male solicitor general appears before the Court, he wears a traditional vest, morning coat, and striped pants. The same applies on the rare occasion when the attorney general appears before the Court, as General Michael Mukasey did in 2008.

half of the cases the Supreme Court agrees to decide and therefore play a crucial role in setting its agenda. As we noted earlier in this chapter, the solicitor general is responsible for representing the federal government before the Supreme Court and is sometimes called the "tenth justice." Because the U.S. government may not appeal any case upward without the solicitor general's approval, the solicitor general has significant influence over the kinds of cases the Supreme Court eventually sees.[28]

The solicitor general also files *amicus curiae* briefs in cases in which the federal government is not a party. The practice of filing *amicus curiae* briefs guarantees that the Department of Justice is represented if a suit questions the constitutionality of an act of Congress or the executive branch. The solicitor general may also use these briefs to bring to the Court's attention the views of the current administration.

Citizens and Interested Parties Citizens, interest groups, and organizations may also file *amicus curiae* briefs if they claim to have an interest in the case and information of value to the Court.[29] An *amicus* brief may help the justices by presenting arguments or facts the parties to the case have not raised. In recent decades, interest groups have increasingly filed such briefs in an effort to influence the Court and to counter the positions of the solicitor general and the government. For example, in *Grutter* v. *Bolinger* (2003), a case concerning affirmative action in college admissions, a record 102 *amicus* briefs were filed.[30] Although *Grutter* is an outlier, *amicus* briefs are regularly filed in cases before the U.S. Supreme Court. Between 1990 and 2001, at least one *amicus* brief was filed in nearly 90 percent of the cases. Cases involving civil liberties, which we will discuss in Chapter 11, are particularly likely to result in *amicus* participation.[31] Interest groups may also file *amicus curiae* briefs to encourage the Supreme Court to review a case, although this strategy has almost no influence on how the case is decided.[32]

After the Court Decides

Victory in the Supreme Court does not necessarily mean that winning parties get what they want. Although the Court resolves many issues, it also sometimes *remands* the case, sending it back to the lower court with instructions to act in accordance with its opinion. The lower court often has considerable leeway in interpreting the Court's mandate as it disposes of the case.

The impact of a particular Supreme Court ruling on the behavior of individuals who are not immediate parties to a lawsuit is more uncertain. The most important rulings require a change in the behavior of thousands of administrative and elected officials. Sometimes, Supreme Court pronouncements are simply ignored. For example, despite the Court's holding that it is unconstitutional for school boards to require students to pray within a school, some schools continue this practice.[33] And for years after the Supreme Court held public school segregation unconstitutional, many school districts refused to integrate or even closed their public school system, as in Prince Edward County, Virginia, so as to avoid integration.[34]

LEARNING **OBJECTIVE**

10.5 Assess the limits on judicial action and the role of the judiciary in a constitutional democracy.

Judicial Power and Its Limits

Although the framers worked hard to create an independent federal judiciary, judges are limited in that they cannot ignore earlier decisions unless they have a clear reason to break with the past.

Adherence to Precedent

Just because judges make independent decisions does not mean they are free to do whatever they wish. They are subject to a variety of limits on what they decide—some imposed by the political system of which they are a part and some imposed by higher courts and the legal profession. Among these constraints is the policy of **stare decisis,** the rule of precedent.

Stare decisis pervades our judicial system and promotes certainty, uniformity, and stability in the law. Drawn from the Latin phrase "to stand by that which is decided," the term means that judges are expected to abide by previous decisions of their own courts and by rulings of superior courts. However, the doctrine is not very restrictive.[35] Indeed, lower-court judges sometimes apply precedents selectively, to raise additional questions about an earlier higher-court decision or to give the higher courts a chance to change a precedent entirely.

Stare decisis is even less controlling in the field of constitutional law. Because the Constitution itself, rather than any one interpretation of it, is binding, the Court can *reverse* a previous decision it no longer wishes to follow, as it has done hundreds of times. Supreme Court justices are therefore not seriously restricted by stare decisis. Liberal Justice William O. Douglas, for one, maintained that stare decisis "was really no sure guideline because what did the judges who sat there in 1875 know about, say, electronic surveillance? They didn't know anything about it."[36] Anticipating Justice Stevens' strong dissent in *Citizens United* v. *Federal Election Commission* in which the Court overturned two of its previously decided cases, Chief Justice Roberts wrote that if stare decisis were an "inexorable command" or "mechanical formula of adherence to the latest decision... segregation would still be legal, minimum wage laws would be unconstitutional, and the Government could wiretap ordinary suspects without first obtaining warrants."[37] Since 1789, the Supreme Court has reversed nearly 200 of its own decisions and overturned more than 170 acts of Congress, as well as nearly 1,300 state constitutional and legislative provisions and municipal ordinances.[38]

Chief Justice John Roberts was appointed by President George W. Bush in 2005. He addressed students at the University of Alabama School of Law in 2010. ■ *What power does the Chief Justice have over the associate justices of the U.S. Supreme Court?*

Many Court observers expect the more conservative justices appointed during both Bush administrations to continue to move the law away from the right to abortion established in *Roe* v. *Wade* in 1973. Although they do not expect the Court to overturn the decision in a single, sweeping case, they do expect it to chip away at the precedent as more limited opportunities come before it.[39] The Court did just that when it upheld the federal Partial-Birth Abortion Ban Act in 2007. Although the act affected only late-term abortion procedures, the Court for the first time upheld an abortion restriction that did not provide an exception for the woman's health.[40]

Congressional and Presidential Action

Individual judges are protected from Congress and the president by their life tenure, but the judiciary as a whole can be affected by legislative decisions that alter both the number and the composition of the courts. Because the district and circuit courts are both created through legislation, they can be expanded or altered through legislation.

"Packing" the Court When a political party takes control of both the White House and Congress, it may see an opportunity to increase the number of federal judgeships. With divided government, however, when one party controls Congress and the other holds the White House, a stalemate is likely to occur, and the possibility for new judicial positions is greatly decreased. During Andrew Johnson's administration, Congress went so far as to reduce the size of the Supreme Court to prevent the president from filling two vacancies. After Johnson left the White House, Congress returned the Court to its former size to permit Ulysses S. Grant to fill the vacancies.

stare decisis
The rule of precedent, whereby a rule or law contained in a judicial decision is commonly viewed as binding on judges whenever the same question is presented.

In 1937, President Franklin Roosevelt proposed an increase in the size of the Supreme Court by one additional justice for every member of the Court over the age of 70, up to a total of 15 members. Ostensibly, his proposal to "pack" the court with new supporters was aimed at making the Court more efficient. In fact, Roosevelt and his advisers were frustrated because the Court had declared much of the early New Deal legislation unconstitutional. Despite Roosevelt's popularity, his "court-packing scheme" aroused intense opposition and his proposal failed. Although he lost the battle, the Court began to sustain some important New Deal legislation, and subsequent retirements from the bench enabled him to make eight appointments to the Court.

Changing the Jurisdiction Congressional control over the structure and jurisdiction of federal courts has been used to influence the course of judicial policy making. Although unable to get rid of Federalist judges by impeachment, Jefferson's Republican party abolished the circuit courts created by the Federalist Congress just before it lost control of Congress. In 1869, radical Republicans in Congress altered the Supreme Court's appellate jurisdiction in order to remove a case it was about to review weighing the constitutionality of some Reconstruction legislation.[41]

Each year, a number of bills are introduced in Congress to eliminate the jurisdiction of federal courts over cases relating to abortion, school prayer, and school busing, or to eliminate the appellate jurisdiction of the Supreme Court over such matters. These attacks on federal court jurisdiction spark debate about whether the Constitution gives Congress authority to take such actions. Congress has not yet decided to do so because it would amount to a fundamental shift in the relationship between Congress and the Supreme Court.

Judicial Power in a Constitutional Democracy

An independent judiciary is one of the hallmarks of a constitutional democracy and a free society. As impartial dispensers of equal justice under the law, judges should not depend on the executive, the legislature, parties to a case, or the electorate. But judicial independence is often criticized when judges make unpopular decisions. Perhaps in no other society do the people resort to litigation as a means of making public policy as much as they do in the United States. For example, the National Association for the Advancement of Colored People (NAACP) turned to litigation to get relief from segregation practices in the 1930s, 1940s, and 1950s. More recently, an increasing number of women's organizations, environmental groups, and religious and conservative organizations have also turned to the courts.[42]

Whether judges are liberal or conservative, defer to legislatures or not, try to apply the Constitution as they think the framers intended or interpret it to conform to current values, there are links between what judges do and what the people want. The people never speak with one mind and the links are not direct, but they are the heart of the matter.[43] In the first place, the president and the Senate are likely to appoint justices whose decisions reflect their values. Therefore, elections matter because the views of the people who nominate and confirm the judges are reflected in the composition and decisions of the courts. For instance, in *Planned Parenthood* v. *Casey* in 1992, the Supreme Court refused 5 to 4 to overturn *Roe* v. *Wade* and upheld its core ruling—that the Constitution protects the right of a woman to an abortion—although it also upheld state regulations that do not "unduly burden" that right.[44] This close vote made it clear that presidential elections could determine whether the right to abortion would continue to be protected.

If we as citizens oppose the Court's decisions, we have several avenues through which we can make our opposition known. By communicating with members of Congress, we can pressure them to pass legislation that limits the Court's ruling, as President Obama encouraged Congress to act to pare back the effects of the Court's decision in *Citizens United* during his 2010 State of the Union Address. We can organize to oppose a particular nomination to the federal judiciary, as many citizens did in response to Judge Robert Bork's nomination to the Supreme Court in 1986. When making our voting decisions, we can also consider the kinds of judges a presidential candidate is likely to appoint to the federal judiciary. In these ways and others, we can affect our federal courts. The Court's power rests, as former Chief Justice Edward White observed, "solely upon the approval of a free people."[45] No better standard for determining the legitimacy of a governmental institution has been discovered.

CHAPTER **SUMMARY**

10.1 Determine characteristics of the federal judiciary and implications of the adversarial process.

The courts provide a neutral arena in which two parties argue their differences and present evidence supporting those views before an impartial judge. As a result, the courts are largely *reactive;* judges have to wait for parties to a case to bring issues before the courts.

10.2 Outline the structure of the federal court system.

There are three levels of federal courts: (1) district courts, which hear original trials, (2) circuit courts of appeals, which can only review the process by which district courts made their decisions, and (3) the Supreme Court, which makes the final decision.

10.3 Analyze the factors that play an important role in selecting judicial nominees.

Partisanship and ideology are important factors in the selection of all federal judges. In making appointments to the federal courts, presidents must also consider the confirmation environment. They act strategically in selecting a candidate and consulting with Congress. In recent decades, candidates for the presidency and the Senate have made judicial appointments an issue in their election campaigns.

10.4 Trace the process by which Supreme Court decisions are reached, and assess influences on this process.

The Supreme Court has almost complete control over the cases it chooses to review as they come up from the state courts, the courts of appeals, and district courts. Law clerks and the solicitor general play important roles in determining the kinds of cases the Supreme Court agrees to decide. Its nine justices dispose of thousands of cases, but most of their time is concentrated on the fewer than 90 cases per year they accept for review. The Court's decisions and opinions establish guidelines for lower courts and the country.

In addition to Supreme Court precedent and justices' own preferences, a number of actors may influence the decision-making process. Law clerks often write early drafts of justices' opinions. *Amicus curiae* participants and the solicitor general's office sometimes affect the opinion-writing process through the briefs they file, as well as through points made during oral argument before the Court.

10.5 Assess the limits on judicial action and the role of the judiciary in a constitutional democracy.

Although the federal judiciary is largely independent, factors such as stare decisis, the appointment process, congressional control over its structure and jurisdiction, and the need for the other branches of government to implement its decisions limit the degree to which the courts can or are likely to act without the support of the other branches. As impartial dispensers of equal justice under the law, judges should not depend on the executive, the legislature, the parties to a case, or the electorate. But judicial independence is often criticized when judges make unpopular decisions.

CHAPTER **SELF-TEST**

10.1 Determine characteristics of the federal judiciary and implications of the adversarial process.

1. List and explain three potentially negative consequences of the adversarial process.
2. In a criminal action, the ________ is the person or party accused of an offense.
   a. plaintiff
   b. defendant
   c. public defender
   d. judge magistrate
3. Match the following terms to their definitions:
   a. plea bargain
   b. adversary system
   c. standing
   i. The requirement that a person has experienced direct and personal injury in order to file a lawsuit.
   ii. System that holds arguing over law and evidence, which may or may not arrive at the truth, guarantees fairness in the judicial system.
   iii. System whereby defendants agree to plead guilty to a lesser crime to avoid having to stand trial and face a sentence for a more serious crime.

10.2 Outline the structure of the federal court system.

4. Draw a diagram of the federal court system.
5. Match the following terms to their definitions:
   a. precedent
   b. original jurisdiction
   c. appellate jurisdiction
   i. The authority of a court to hear a case "in the first instance."
   ii. The authority of a court to review appeals of decisions made by the lower courts.
   iii. A decision made by a higher court, such as the Supreme Court, that is binding on all other federal courts.

10.3 Analyze the factors that play an important role in selecting judicial nominees.

6. In a short essay, explain why the judicial nomination process can be so contentious.
7. In two paragraphs, describe the way interest groups get involved in the nomination process.

10.4 Trace the process by which Supreme Court decisions are reached, and assess influences on this process.

8. Discuss two ways Supreme Court clerks can influence the outcomes in cases.
9. In one paragraph, explain why a justice would spend the time to write a dissenting opinion in a case decided by the Court.
10. Define *amicus curiae,* and describe a situation in which an *amicus* brief might be influential.
11. Write a brief essay distinguishing judicial activism from judicial restraint. How are they similar? In what ways are they different?

10.5 Assess the limits on judicial action and the role of the judiciary in a constitutional democracy.

12. Define stare decisis. Give one real-life example that illustrates this principle.
13. When Congress does not like a decision made by the Supreme Court, what kind of action can it take? In one paragraph, explain how Congress can constrain the Court.
14. Write a short essay detailing the role of the judiciary in our constitutional system. Could the system function without the judiciary? What adjustments would have to be made?

Answers to selected questions: 2. b; 3. a: iii, b: ii, c: i; 5. a: iii, b: i, c: ii

mypoliscilab™ EXERCISES

Where participation leads to action!

Apply what you learned in this chapter on MyPoliSciLab.

Read on **mypoliscilab.com**

eText: Chapter 10

Study and **Review** on **mypoliscilab.com**

Pre-Test
Post-Test
Chapter Exam
Flashcards

Watch on **mypoliscilab.com**

Video: Court Rules on Hazelton's Immigration Laws
Video: Prosecuting Corruption
Video: Most Significant Abortion Ruling in 30 Years
Video: Prosecuting Cyber Crime

Explore on **mypoliscilab.com**

Simulation: You Are a Young Lawyer
Simulation: You Are the President and Need to Appoint a Supreme Court Justice
Simulation: You Are a Clerk to Supreme Court Justice Judith Gray
Comparative: Comparing Judiciaries
Timeline: Chief Justices of the Supreme Court
Visual Literacy: Case Overload

KEY TERMS

judicial review, p. 296
adversary system, p. 296
criminal law, p. 297
civil law, p. 297
prosecutor, p. 297
defendant, p. 297
plea bargain, p. 297
justiciable dispute, p. 297
plaintiff, p. 297
United States attorney general, p. 298
solicitor general, p. 298
public defender system, p. 298
district courts, p. 299
circuit courts of appeals, p. 299
Supreme Court, p. 299
original jurisdiction, p. 299
appellate jurisdiction, p. 299
precedent, p. 299
writ of *habeas corpus*, p. 300
senatorial courtesy, p. 302
judicial activism, p. 305
judicial restraint, p. 305
writ of certiorari, p. 307
in forma pauperis, p. 307
docket, p. 307
***amicus curiae* brief,** p. 308
opinion of the Court, p. 309
dissenting opinion, p. 309
concurring opinion, p. 309
stare decisis, p. 313

ADDITIONAL **RESOURCES**

FURTHER READING

HENRY J. ABRAHAM, *Justices, Presidents, and Senators: A History of U.S. Supreme Court Appointments from Washington to Bush II,* 5th ed. (Rowman & Littlefield, 2008).

ROBERT A. CARP AND **RONALD STIDHAM,** *The Federal Courts* (CQ Press, 2001).

CORNELL CLAYTON AND **HOWARD GILMAN,** EDS., *Supreme Court Decision Making: New Institutionalist Approaches* (University of Chicago Press, 1999).

LEE EPSTEIN AND **JEFFREY A. SEGAL,** *Advice and Consent: The Politics of Judicial Appointments* (Oxford University Press, 2005).

LEE EPSTEIN, JEFFREY A. SEGAL, HAROLD SPAETH, AND **THOMAS WALKER,** EDS., *The Supreme Court Compendium,* 4th ed. (CQ Press, 2007).

SHELDON GOLDMAN, *Picking Federal Judges: Lower Court Selection from Roosevelt Through Reagan* (Yale University Press, 1997).

KERMIT L. HALL AND **KEVIN T. MCGUIRE,** EDS., *Institutions of American Democracy: The Judicial Branch* (Oxford University Press, 2005).

PETER IRONS, *A People's History of the Supreme Court* (Viking Press, 1999).

RANDOLPH JONAKAIT, *The American Jury System* (Yale University Press, 2003).

DAVID KLEIN, *Making Law in the U.S. Courts of Appeals* (Cambridge University Press, 2002).

FOREST MALTZMAN, JAMES F. SPRIGGS II, AND **PAUL J. WAHLBECK,** *Crafting Law on the Supreme Court: The Collegial Game* (Cambridge University Press, 2000).

CHRISTINE NEMACHECK, *Strategic Selection: Presidential Nomination of Supreme Court Justices from Herbert Hoover Through George W. Bush* (University of Virginia Press, 2007).

DAVID M. O'BRIEN, *Storm Center: The Supreme Court in American Politics,* 7th ed. (Norton, 2005).

J. W. PELTASON, *Federal Courts in the Political Process* (Doubleday, 1955).

TODD C. PEPPERS, *Courtiers of the Marble Palace: The Rise and Influence of the Supreme Court Law Clerk* (Stanford University Press, 2006).

TERRI JENNINGS PERETTI, *In Defense of a Political Court* (Princeton University Press, 1999).

GERALD N. ROSENBERG, *The Hollow Hope: Can Courts Bring About Social Change?* (University of Chicago Press, 1991).

PETER RUSSELL AND **DAVID M. O'BRIEN,** EDS., *Judicial Independence in the Age of Democracy: Critical Perspectives from Around the World* (University Press of Virginia, 2001).

ELLIOT E. SLOTNICK, *Judicial Politics: Readings from Judicature,* 3d ed. (American Judicature Society, 2005).

DONALD R. SONGER, REGINALD S. SHEEHAN, AND **SUSAN B. HAIRE,** *Continuity and Change on the United States Courts of Appeals* (University of Michigan Press, 2000).

ARTEMUS WARD AND **DAVID L. WEIDEN,** *Sorcerers' Apprentices: 100 Years of Law Clerks at the United States Supreme Court* (New York University Press, 2006).

WEB SITES

www.oyez.org Oyez is a Web site that contains links to audio recordings of Supreme Court oral arguments. It also provides an overview of the Court's decisions in many cases and links to other interesting Web sites on the judiciary.

www.supremecourt.gov This is a new Web site released by the Court in 2010. You can obtain oral argument transcripts, read the justices' biographies, and keep up to date with the Court's docket.

www.ncsconline.org The National Center for State Courts is an independent, nonprofit organization aimed at gathering data on state courts and improving the states' judicial administration.

PART IV Individual Rights and Liberties

THE BIG PICTURE

The original U.S. Constitution did not provide protections for an individual's right to express his or her views on the government or to worship freely. Nor did it affirm that all persons would be treated equally under the law. Today, we view these freedoms and rights as essential to democratic government, but this was not always the case. In this section, we discuss our basic freedoms, known as civil liberties, protected from improper government restriction in the Bill of Rights, as well as our civil rights, or the right to be free from irrational discrimination based on such factors as race, gender, or ethnic origin.

The struggle to protect and secure these rights and liberties has often been difficult, and even when protected appropriately, none of our rights are absolute. One of the most important constitutional developments that has occurred since the Constitution was ratified is known as incorporation—the act of applying the protections provided for in the Bill of Rights to the states. When it was ratified, the Bill of Rights applied only to the national government. The Antifederalists were mainly concerned with the new, powerful national government restricting individual rights. But, as the nation developed, it became clear that it was not only the national government that might impermissibly restrict these rights but also the states. The U.S. Supreme Court's decisions applying the protections found in the first ten amendments to the states have greatly changed the balance of power between the federal and state governments. The Court's rulings in these incorporation cases, as we discuss in Chapter 11, has made the federal courts largely responsible for protecting individual liberties against impermissible restriction by both the state and national governments.

The judiciary is the branch of government generally thought to protect these rights, and indeed the federal and state courts, and especially the U.S. Supreme Court, devote a good deal of time to doing just that. However, Congress has been especially important in providing protections against discrimination through the many pieces of civil rights legislation we discuss in Chapter 12. Many of the Supreme Court's most important civil rights decisions depended on congressional legislation prohibiting discrimination in voting, employment, housing, education, and federal financial assistance based on such factors as race, gender, age, national origin, or physical handicap.

COURSE LEARNING **OBJECTIVES**

CHAPTER 11 Civil Liberties

Describe the individual liberties protected in the Bill of Rights, and evaluate the limitations on these rights.

One of the major Anti-Federalist concerns over the new Constitution was its lack of explicit protections for individual liberties. As mentioned above, they were particularly concerned that a distant and powerful central government could trounce on the rights of individual citizens. Thus, they demanded that the Constitution include a Bill of Rights. In need of their votes for ratification, Federalists conceded to these demands.

The Bill of Rights provides protections for individuals' right to free speech, to practice religious beliefs freely, to petition government and assemble with like-minded individuals, to be free from unreasonable searches and seizures, to have a fair and speedy criminal trial, and to be free from cruel and unusual punishment, among others. But, these rights are not absolute. In certain circumstances, such as a national security threat, it may be necessary for the government to restrict speech. If one person's religious ritual threatens the life of another person, it too may be restricted. If there is a concern for a law enforcement officer's safety, searches that might otherwise be unreasonable may be permissible. In short, although our liberties are protected, these protections are not without exception. And, through our system of separated powers, it is the judiciary that decides the bound of such government restrictions.

CHAPTER 12 Civil Rights

Explain how Congress and the Supreme Court have expanded and protected civil rights.

Prior to the ratification of the Fourteenth Amendment, there was nothing in the Constitution that required states to treat all citizens equally. Indeed, even after the Fourteenth Amendment was ratified in 1868, providing for equal protection under the law, discrimination based on race and gender continued in the United States. Voting rights of former slaves were secured through the Fifteenth Amendment, ratified in 1870, and women's suffrage was garnered with the ratification of the Nineteenth Amendment in 1920. However, laws segregating society based on race and regulations that disadvantaged women in the workplace and property ownership continued well into the twentieth century. Through demonstrations and protests by civil rights activists supporting the rights of both African Americans and women, members of Congress finally felt the pressure necessary to pass civil rights legislation in the late 1950s and 1960s.

The federal courts have been an important institution in the fight for civil rights in the United States. They have heard cases challenging state and federal laws under the Fifth and Fourteenth Amendments, as well as cases challenging discrimination by private business owners who violated congressional civil rights legislation. The U.S. Supreme Court's decisions concerning equality of educational opportunity have been especially important to the civil rights movement, particularly the Court's decision in *Brown* v. *Board of Education* (1954) declaring that segregating students based on race was inherently unequal and thus violated the Fourteenth Amendment. However, the debate over the role of race in education continues. Today, the Court is more likely to confront affirmative action cases where universities, as well as elementary and secondary schools systems, have used race as a factor in admissions decisions.

CHAPTER

11

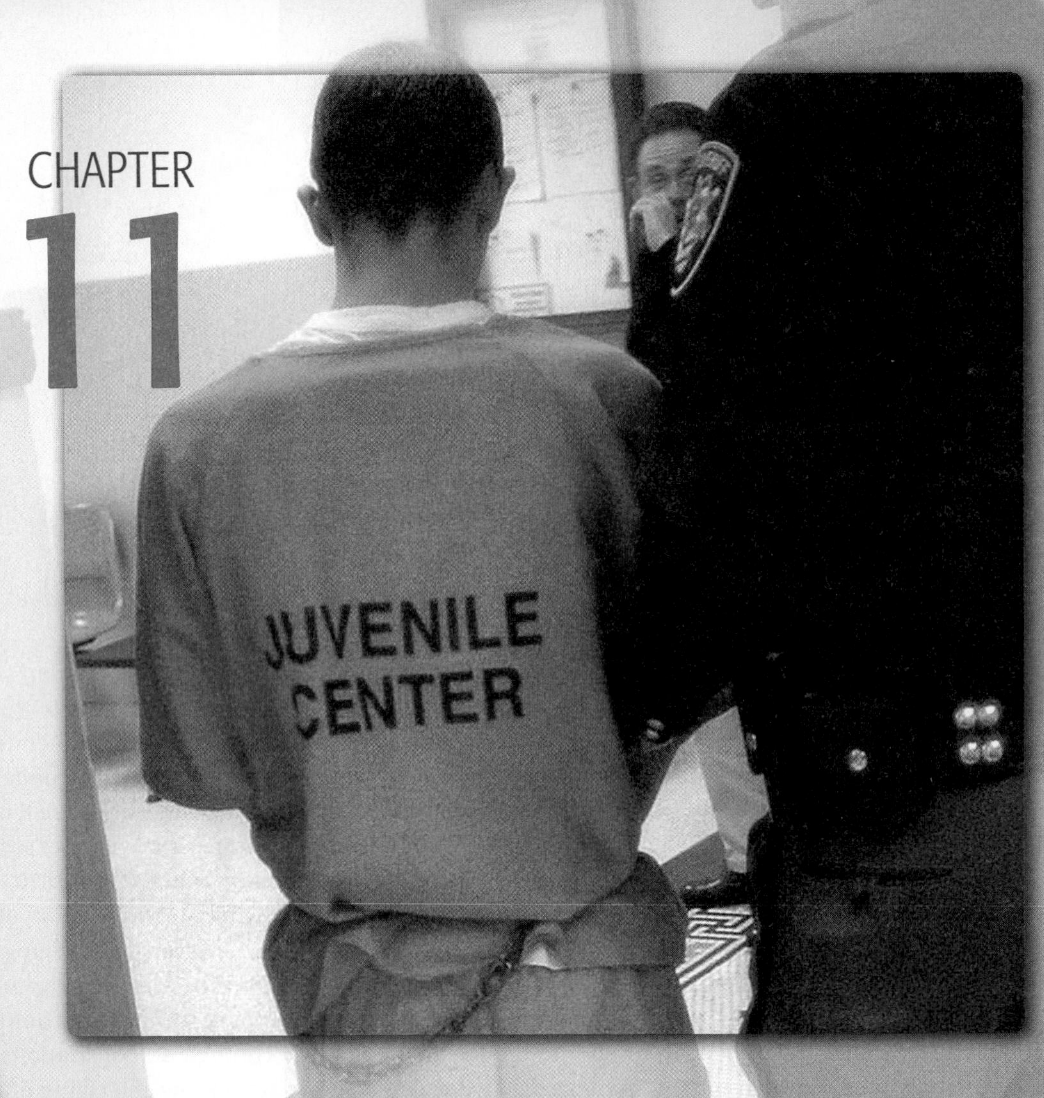

Civil Liberties

Protections Under the Bill of Rights

The Basis for Our Civil Liberties

11.1 Trace the roots of civil liberties in the original Constitution and their subsequent development in the Bill of Rights.

First Amendment Freedoms

11.2 Outline the First Amendment freedoms and the limitations on them.

Property Rights

11.3 Explain how the Constitution protects property rights.

Due Process Rights

11.4 Distinguish between procedural and substantive due process.

Privacy Rights

11.5 Assess the kinds of behavior that may be covered by a constitutional right to privacy.

Rights of Criminal Suspects

11.6 Characterize the constitutional rights of criminal suspects.

Protecting Our Civil Liberties in an Age of Terror: Whose Responsibility?

11.7 Evaluate the roles of institutions and the people in protecting civil liberties.

Sixteen-year-old Terrance Graham attempted to rob a restaurant in July 2003. When the manager would not give Graham and his accomplices money, one of them hit the manager with a steel bar. Graham fled the scene but was later arrested and charged as an adult of a first-degree felony (burglary with assault or battery) with a maximum sentence of life in prison. Graham pled guilty to the crime and was sentenced to serve nine months in county jail and three years of probation.

But, six months after he was released from jail, Graham, then 17, was arrested on new felony charges: home invasion, robbery, and eluding police. He was also charged with violating his probation for his first criminal conviction. This time, Graham was sentenced to life in state prison without the possibility of parole. Graham's sentence was upheld by the Florida Court of Appeal and his attorney thus appealed to the U.S. Supreme Court arguing that Graham's sentence violated the Eighth Amendment ban on cruel and unusual punishment.

The Supreme Court has become more engaged recently in the way juveniles are treated in the criminal justice system, and the degree to which they are culpable in the same way as adults. The Eighth Amendment protects criminal suspects against cruel and unusual punishment, but the question facing the Court is whether there should be different standards for juvenile offenders. In *Roper* v. *Simmons* (2005), the Court relied on the decisions of state legislatures, scientific research on juvenile brain development, and international opinion against the death penalty for juveniles in deciding that the death penalty for minors violates the Eighth Amendment.[1] Would they apply a similar line of reasoning to Terrance Graham's case and rule that sentencing a juvenile offender to a life sentence without the possibility of parole also fails to meet the standards of the Eighth Amendment?

On May 17, 2010, the Supreme Court, for many of the same reasons it invalidated the death penalty for juvenile offenders, ruled that it did. They decided that life sentences without the possibility of parole for juveniles convicted of nonhomicidal crimes violate the Eighth Amendment. Due to the potential for juveniles to mature and rehabilitate, the criminal justice system must provide juvenile offenders with some opportunity to show that they are "fit to rejoin society."[2] The Eighth Amendment is only one of several protecting the liberties of criminal suspects. Often these defendants are not the most sympathetic petitioners before the courts. But as Justice Felix Frankfurter observed, "The history of liberty has largely been the history of observance of procedural safeguards." Further, these safeguards have frequently "been forged in controversies involving not very nice people."[3] Our Constitution, and the Bill of Rights in particular, mandate that in order to deprive someone of their freedom, we must guarantee fairness and protect individual liberties.

In this chapter, we examine the fundamental liberties protected in a free society. These include freedom of speech and assembly, the right to practice one's religion without government interference, the right to bear arms, the right to be free from unreasonable searches and seizures, the right to be free from self-incrimination and double jeopardy, and the right to be represented by an attorney in a criminal proceeding. These freedoms are essential to self-determination and self-governance—government by the people. Yet they have also been vulnerable during times of war and, many would argue, are now threatened because of security measures put into place to combat international terrorism.[4] Regardless of the times, however, these liberties mean nothing if citizens do not challenge the government when they think it has impermissibly limited those freedoms. Unless we act as caretakers of our liberties, we lose them.

The Basis for Our Civil Liberties

LEARNING **OBJECTIVE**

11.1 Trace the roots of civil liberties in the original Constitution and their subsequent development in the Bill of Rights.

Before we delve into a discussion of freedoms, we will clarify several terms—*civil liberties, civil rights,* and *legal privileges*—often used interchangeably when discussing rights and freedoms.

Civil liberties are the constitutional protections of all persons against governmental restrictions on the freedoms of conscience, religion, and expression. Civil liberties are secured by the First Amendment and the due process clauses of the Fifth and Fourteenth Amendments, among others.

Civil rights are the constitutional rights of all persons to due process and the equal protection of the laws: the constitutional right not to be discriminated against by governments because of race, ethnic background, religion, or gender. These civil rights are protected by the due process and equal protection clauses of the Fifth and Fourteenth Amendments and by the civil rights laws of national and state governments. We discuss them further in Chapter 12.

Legal privileges, like the right to welfare benefits or to have a driver's license, are granted by governments and may be subject to conditions or restrictions.

Rights in the Original Constitution

Even though most of the framers did not think a bill of rights was necessary, they considered certain rights important enough to spell them out in the Constitution (see Table 11–1).

Foremost among constitutional rights, and deserving of particular mention here, is the **writ of *habeas corpus*.** Literally meaning "you have the body" in Latin, this writ is a court order directing any official holding a person in custody to produce the prisoner in court and explain why the prisoner is being held. Throughout the years, it developed into a remedy for any illegal confinement. People who are incarcerated have the right to appeal to a judge, usually through an attorney, stating why they believe they are being held unlawfully and should be released. The judge then orders the jailer or a lower court to justify why the writ should not be issued. If a judge finds that a petitioner is detained unlawfully, the judge may order the prisoner's immediate release.

writ of *habeas corpus*
A court order requiring explanation to a judge as to why a prisoner is being held in custody.

The Supreme Court has recently underscored the fundamental nature of the right to a writ of *habeas corpus* in several decisions. In them, the Court rejected the Bush administration's position that it could indefinitely hold foreign nationals and U.S. citizens deemed "enemy combatants" in its war against terrorism. In *Hamdan* v. *Rumsfeld* (2006),[5] the Court rebuffed the Bush administration's position that it had the authority to try enemy combatants by military commissions, rather than in civilian courts or in court martial. The Court also rejected the argument that the Bush administration could ignore the

TABLE 11–1 Rights in the Original Constitution

1. *Habeas corpus*
2. No bills of attainder (legislative act that sentences a person or group to punishment without a trial)
3. No *ex post facto* laws
4. No titles of nobility (aristocratic titles that had also been barred by the Articles of Confederation)
5. Trial by jury in national courts
6. Protection for citizens as they move from one state to another, including the right to travel
7. Protection against using the crime of treason to restrict other activities; limitation on punishment for treason
8. Guarantee that each state has a republican form of government
9. No religious test oaths as a condition for holding a federal office
10. Protection against the impairment of contracts (forbids states from passing laws that effectively invalidate contracts)

■ *Why might some rights be mentioned both in the original Constitution and the Bill of Rights?*

Geneva Conventions, which specify that the accused has a right to see and hear the evidence for alleged crimes. In the aftermath of the Court's decision in *Hamdan,* Congress passed the Military Commissions Act of 2006, providing for enemy combatants' trial before military commission. Hamdan was tried by a military commission and although he was found guilty of supporting terrorism, a jury gave him only a 66-month sentence with credit for 61 months he had already served in the U.S. military prison at Guantanamo Bay, Cuba. He was sent back to his home country of Yemen in November 2008.[6]

In its 2008 decision in *Boumediene* v. *Bush,* the Supreme Court stood firm in its holding that Guantanamo Bay detainees have the right to pursue *habeas* review in the federal courts. In doing so, the Court struck down as unconstitutional the section of the Military Commissions Act barring the federal courts from hearing enemy combatants' *habeas corpus* petitions.[7]

Although the Court has emphasized the importance of *habeas corpus* generally, it has restricted its use, particularly for *habeas* appeals made by prisoners in the state criminal justice system. In these cases, the number of appeals has been restricted and the federal courts must defer to state judges unless their decisions were clearly "unreasonable."[8]

The Constitution also bars ***ex post facto* laws,** retroactive criminal laws making an act a crime that was not a crime when it was committed, increasing the punishment for a crime after it was committed, or reducing the proof necessary to convict for a crime after it was committed. However, the prohibition does not restrict retroactive application of a law that benefits an accused person, such as decreasing the punishment for a particular crime; nor does it apply to civil laws.

The Bill of Rights and the States

Most of the liberties we address in this chapter did not appear in the original Constitution. The Constitution drawn up in Philadelphia included guarantees of a few basic rights discussed previously, but it lacked a specific bill of rights similar to those in most state constitutions (see Chapter 1). Our civil liberties are found in the Bill of Rights, which is the first ten amendments to the Constitution, added in 1791.

The Bill of Rights originally applied *only to the national government,* not to state governments.[9] Why not to the states? The framers were confident that citizens could control their own state officials, and most state constitutions already had bills of rights. Furthermore, it would not have been politically feasible for the new Constitution to restrict state governments in this way. It was the new and distant central government the people feared. As it turned out, those fears were largely misdirected.

It was not until the Fourteenth Amendment was adopted in 1868 that there became a way for the restrictions in the Bill of Rights to be applied to the states. Because the Fourteenth Amendment applies explicitly to the states, supporters contended that its **due process clause**—declaring that no person shall be deprived by a state of life, liberty, or property without due process of law—limits states in precisely the same way the Bill of Rights limits the national government. But for decades, the Supreme Court refused to interpret the Fourteenth Amendment in this way. Then, in *Gitlow* v. *New York* (1925), the Court reversed this trend and decided that when fundamental liberties, such as the "freedom of speech and of the press—which are protected by the First Amendment from abridgment by Congress"—are at stake, the due process clause of the Fourteenth Amendment prohibits the state from infringing on those liberties just as the First Amendment prohibits Congress.[10]

Gitlow v. *New York* was a revolutionary decision. For the first time, the U.S. Constitution was interpreted to protect freedom of speech from abridgment by state and local governments. This landmark decision changed the balance of federalism in the United States. State actions that deprived citizens of fundamental liberties could now be challenged as a constitutional violation. In the 1930s and continuing at an accelerated pace during the 1960s, through the **selective incorporation** of provision after provision of the Bill of Rights into the due process clause, the Supreme Court applied the most important of these rights to the states.[11]

Today, the Fourteenth Amendment imposes on the states all the provisions of the Bill of Rights the Court has deemed essential to ordered liberty (see Figure 11–1). Although

ex post facto law
A retroactive criminal law that works to the disadvantage of a person.

due process clause
A clause in the Fifth Amendment limiting the power of the national government; a similar clause in the Fourteenth Amendment prohibiting state governments from depriving any person of life, liberty, or property without due process of law.

selective incorporation
The process by which provisions of the Bill of Rights are brought within the scope of the Fourteenth Amendment and so applied to state and local governments.

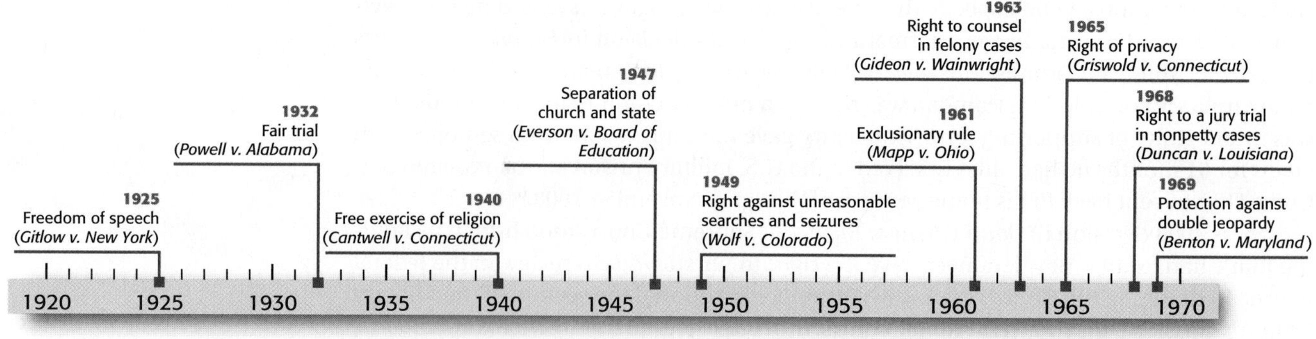

FIGURE 11–1 **Timeline of Selective Incorporation.**
■ *Examine the kinds of rights that the Court first began to incorporate. How are those different than the rights incorporated later, particularly in the 1960s?*

the Court had not incorporated a right since 1969, in 2010, it considered whether the Second Amendment ought to apply to the states as well as the federal government. In *McDonald* v. *Chicago,* the Court incorporated the Second Amendment protection of the right to bear arms to the states (*McDonald* v. *Chicago,* 561 U.S. ___ (2010)). As a result, state restrictions on handguns and other arms are now subject to strict constitutional review. Although the Supreme Court ruled that states have to abide by the Second Amendment, it left the decision as to whether Chicago's handgun restrictions violate the Second Amendment to the lower courts.

Selective incorporation of most provisions of the Bill of Rights into the Fourteenth Amendment is probably the most significant constitutional development that has occurred since the Constitution was written. It has profoundly altered the relationship between the national government and the states. It has made the federal courts, under the guidance of the Supreme Court, the most important protectors of our liberties—not the individual states. It has created a consistent national standard for interpreting the rights and liberties found in the Bill of Rights.

First Amendment Freedoms

LEARNING **OBJECTIVE**

11.2 Outline the First Amendment freedoms and the limitations on them.

Freedom of Religion

The first words of the First Amendment are emphatic and brief: "Congress shall make no law respecting an establishment of religion, or prohibiting the free exercise thereof." Though terse, it contains two important clauses: the *establishment* clause and the *free exercise* clause. Part of what makes religious liberties questions so interesting and difficult is that these clauses are often in tension with one another. Does a state scholarship for blind students given to a student who decides to attend a college to become a clergy member violate the establishment clause by indirectly aiding religion? Or would denying the scholarship violate the student's free exercise of religion? In dealing with the questions posed here, the Supreme Court ruled that providing such scholarship benefits does not go so far as to violate the establishment clause, but neither does the free exercise clause require that states provide the benefits.[12]

establishment clause
A clause in the First Amendment that states that Congress shall make no law respecting an establishment of religion. The Supreme Court has interpreted this to forbid governmental support to any or all religions.

The Establishment Clause In writing what has come to be called the **establishment clause,** the framers were reacting to the English system, wherein the crown was (and still is) the head not only of the government but also of the established church—the Church of England—and public officials were required to take an oath to support the established church as a condition of holding office. At least partly because of the brevity of the establishment clause, there is much debate as to its meaning. Some, such as the late Chief Justice William Rehnquist, contend it means *only* that the government cannot establish an official national religion nor prefer one sect or denomination to another.[13] Others argue that it requires the government to maintain neutrality, not only among religious denominations but also between religion and nonreligion.

Of the People: THE GLOBAL COMMUNITY

Separating Government from Religion

Throughout the world, there is substantial consensus that there ought to be some separation between religious beliefs and government policy. However, there are important differences between countries in which citizens believe more fully in such separation versus those in which citizens tend to agree with the idea. A Pew Global Attitudes Survey asked respondents for their level of agreement with the statement: "Religion is a matter of personal faith and should be kept separate from government policy." According to the survey, a majority of respondents in Great Britain, India, Nigeria, and the United States, completely agreed that government ought to be kept separate from religion.*

Although most countries' constitutions or laws provide for protections for religious liberties, enforcement of these rights vary, as does the degree to which government and religion are separate. For example, in Nigeria, in which tensions between Christians and Muslims have been on the rise, a separate court system exists for each group. Many Nigerian states use Shari'a courts in criminal and civil matters involving Muslims but common law courts for non-Muslims.† In other countries, such as India, there are differences between the national and state governments' involvement in religion. There, the national government has generally remained outside the religious sphere, but some state governments have enforced and enacted "anticonversion" laws.

The percentage of respondents completely agreeing that government policy and religion should be kept separate was significantly lower in China (21 percent), Japan (33 percent), and Mexico (38 percent). In China, the government sanctions only five religions known as "patriotic religious associations" (PRAs): Buddhist, Taoist, Muslim, Catholic, and Protestant. Only these PRAs can legally operate places of worship.

In Japan and Mexico, religious freedoms are constitutionally protected and the Mexican Constitution provides for a separation between church and state. However, particularly in Mexico, there is a great degree of religious homogeneity that might diminish the importance of separating government policy from religion in the eyes of many citizens. The great majority (approximately 88 percent) of Mexicans identify themselves, at least nominally, as Catholic.

CRITICAL THINKING QUESTIONS

1. Why might it be problematic to have the government involved in sanctioning religious groups as it does in China?
2. Do you think beliefs about separating government and religion depend on whether a person belongs to a religious minority? Should it?
3. How might religious homogeneity affect citizens' views of whether their government ought to be separate from the religion?

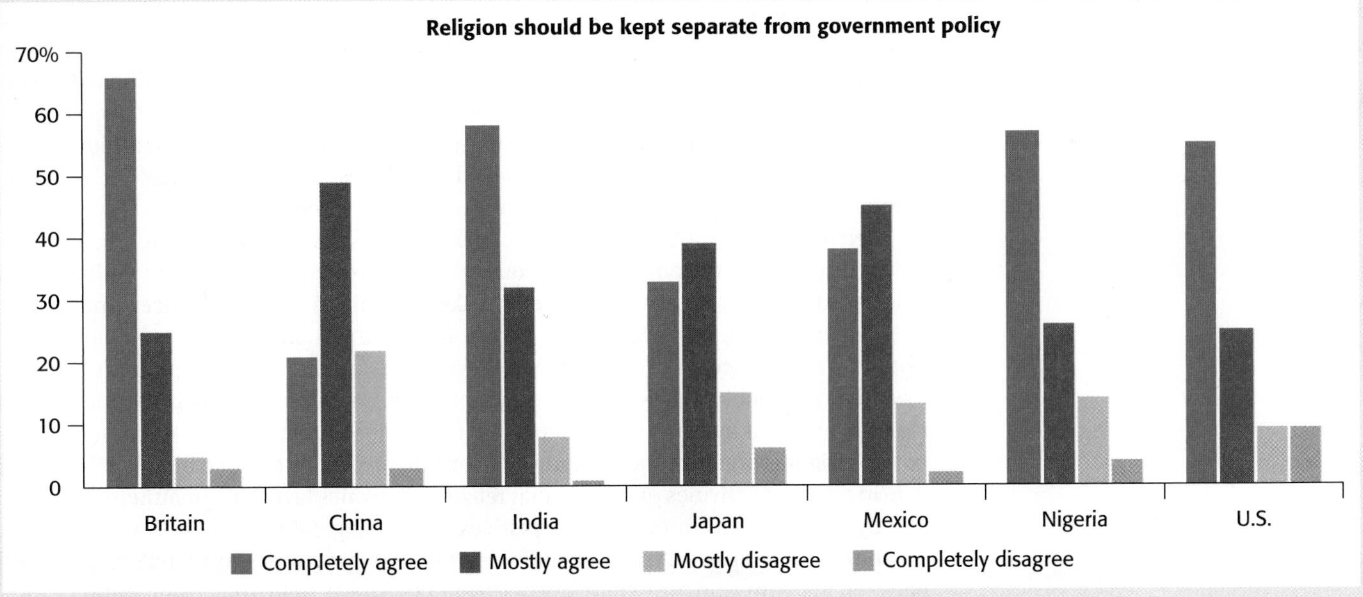

* Pew Research Center, "National Global Attitudes Survey," October 4, 2007.
† U.S. State Department, Bureau of Democracy, Human Rights, and Labor. "International Religious Freedom Report 2009," October 26, 2009, http://www.state.gov/g/drl/rls/irf/2009/index.htm.

Those who favor government neutrality regarding religion use the metaphor, coined by Thomas Jefferson, of a "wall of separation" to explain the strict separation between government and religion the clause requires. The metaphor was the basis for the Supreme Court's opinion in *Everson* v. *Board of Education of Ewing Township* (1947). The Court's 5-to-4 decision in the case, allowing government funds to reimburse parents for transporting children to private religious schools, is indicative of the confusion over

A singular religious display on government property, like this one of the nativity at City Hall in Dearborn, Michigan, might lead a reasonable observer to believe that the government was endorsing Christianity. Holiday displays with a variety of religious traditions represented along with some secular holiday symbols, such as a Christmas tree or Santa Claus, are considered acceptable. ■ *Why might displays that include references to several religious traditions pass constitutional scrutiny?*

the establishment clause. All nine justices agreed that the wall of separation was the appropriate interpretation of the clause, yet they were divided five to four on whether the township's action violated that test.[14]

The Court's use of the wall of separation was hardly its last attempt at resolving debate over the establishment clause's interpretation. In *Lemon* v. *Kurtzman* (1971), the Court laid down the three-part *Lemon* test. To pass constitutional muster, (1) a law must have a secular legislative purpose, (2) it must neither advance nor inhibit religion, and (3) it must avoid "excessive government entanglement with religion."[15] Because the *Lemon* test has not been consistently used, however, the justices remain divided over how much separation between government and religion the First Amendment requires.

In addition to the *Lemon* test, former Justice Sandra Day O'Connor championed what is known as the *endorsement* test. She believed that the establishment clause forbids governmental practices that a reasonable observer would view as endorsing religion, even if there is no coercion.[16] For example, if a reasonable person would understand a crèche (nativity scene) displayed at the entrance to a county courthouse to be government endorsement of religion, Justice O'Connor would vote to strike down the practice.[17] Justices Antonin Scalia and Clarence Thomas joined Chief Justice Rehnquist in supporting a *nonpreferentialist* test.[18] As mentioned previously, they believed that the Constitution prohibits favoritism toward any particular religion but does not prohibit government aid to *all* religions. In their view, government may accommodate religious activities and even give nonpreferential support to religious organizations so long as government does not coerce individuals to participate in religious activities or give certain religious activities favorable treatment.[19]

By contrast, the more liberal justices—including John Paul Stevens, Ruth Bader Ginsburg, and Stephen Breyer—usually maintained that there should be *strict separation* between religion and the state.[20] They generally have held that even indirect aid for religion, such as scholarships or teaching materials and aids for students attending private religious schools, crosses the line separating the government from religion. But today, this view is not able to command a majority on the Court.

free exercise clause
A clause in the First Amendment that states that Congress shall make no law prohibiting the free exercise of religion.

The Free Exercise Clause The right to hold any or no religious belief is one of our few absolute rights because it occurs solely within each person. The **free exercise clause** affirms that no government can compel us to accept any creed or to deny us any right because of what we do or do not believe. Requiring religious oaths as a condition of public employment or as a prerequisite for running for public office is unconstitutional. In fact, the original Constitution states, "No religious Test shall ever be required as a Qualification to any Office or public Trust under the United States" (Article VI).

Of the People

AMERICA'S CHANGING FACE

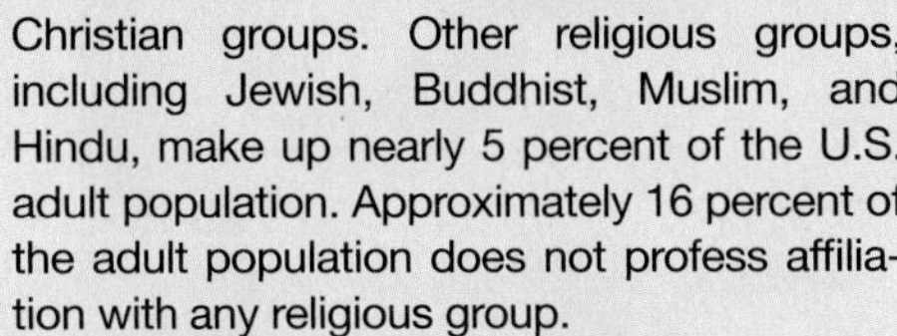

Religious Diversity in the United States

From the beginning, religious freedom has been an important tenet of government in the United States. This was largely due to the fact that many of those who settled in the American colonies had experienced religious persecution in their former countries. Even so, many of those early immigrants were not so tolerant of those whose beliefs differed from their own. Respecting religious differences was difficult, even though those differences were largely between sects of Christianity.

Differences among religious beliefs today are substantially greater than when the United States was founded, and it appears that the country is on a path to even greater religious diversity. A report by the Pew Forum on Religion & Public Life provides evidence on religious affiliation in the United States.* Today, approximately 79 percent of adults identify themselves as Christian. However, that label masks substantial differences in beliefs among Protestants, Catholic, and other Christian groups. Other religious groups, including Jewish, Buddhist, Muslim, and Hindu, make up nearly 5 percent of the U.S. adult population. Approximately 16 percent of the adult population does not profess affiliation with any religious group.

Indications are that the United States is likely to become more religiously diverse in the coming years. Protestants, who currently make up a bare majority of the population, are more prevalent among the older population than among younger Americans. And immigrants to the United States tend to bring religious diversity with them. Approximately two-thirds of Muslims and more than 80 percent of those identifying themselves as Hindu are immigrants to the United States. As the country becomes more religiously diverse, protecting Americans' right to exercise their religious beliefs takes on greater importance and, in some cases, greater controversy.

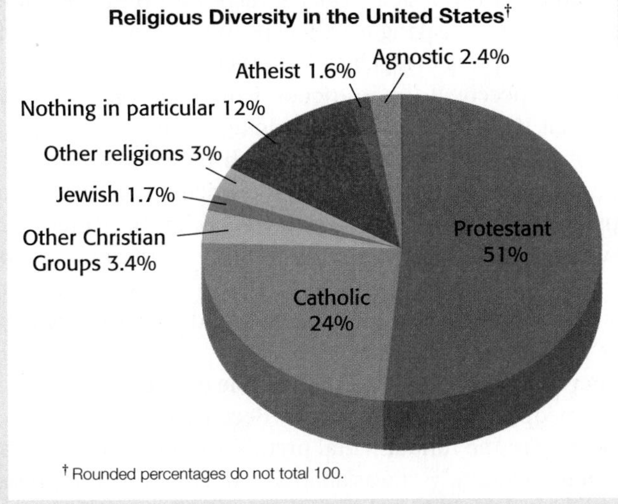

CRITICAL THINKING QUESTIONS

1. How might religious diversity in the United States affect the Supreme Court's decisions on religious liberties? Should it?
2. Do you think religious beliefs affect voting decisions? Why or why not?

* The Pew Forum on Religion & Public Life, *U.S. Religious Landscape Survey Religious Affiliation: Diverse and Dynamic*, February 2008, http://religions.pewforum.org/pdf/report-religious-landscape-study-full.pdf.

Although carefully protected, the right to practice a religion, which typically requires some action such as proselytizing or participating in a religious ritual, is more likely to be restricted than the right to hold particular beliefs. Before 1990, the Supreme Court carefully scrutinized laws allegedly infringing on religious practices and insisted that the government provide some compelling interest to justify actions that might infringe on someone's religion. Then, in *Employment Division* v. *Smith* (1990), the Court significantly altered the interpretation of the free exercise clause when it determined that the government does not always need to show a compelling interest if its laws infringe on religious exercise.[21] As long as a law is generally applicable and does not single out and ban religious practices, the law may be applied to conduct even if it burdens a particular religious practice.[22]

Free Speech and Free People

Government by the people is based on every person's right to speak freely, to organize in groups, to question the decisions of the government, and to campaign openly against them. Only through free and uncensored expression of opinion can government be kept responsive to the electorate and political power transferred peacefully. Elections, separation of powers, and constitutional guarantees are meaningless unless all persons have the right to speak frankly and to hear and judge for themselves the worth of what others have to say.

Even though the First Amendment explicitly denies Congress the power to pass any law abridging freedom of speech, the courts have never interpreted the amendment in

For many Native Americans, peyote is necessary to practice their religious beliefs. But the Supreme Court has ruled that states barring peyote do not need to create specific exceptions for its use in religious practices. ■ *Why do you think some states might not provide exemptions for the use of peyote in religious practices? Should they?*

Police arrested Scott Tyler of Chicago after he set fire to an American flag on the steps of the Capitol building in Washington, D.C. The Supreme Court afterward ruled that free speech covers even "symbolic speech" such as burning the U.S. flag. ■ *Would the Court's ruling on burning the flag differ if a riot were about to ensue as a result of that action?*

absolute terms. Like almost all rights, the freedoms of speech and of the press are limited. In discussing the constitutional power of government to regulate speech, we distinguish among *belief, speech,* and *action.*

At one extreme is the right to *believe* as we wish. Despite occasional deviations in practice, the traditional view is that government should not punish a person for beliefs or interfere in any way with freedom of conscience. At the other extreme is *action,* which the government may restrain. As the old saying goes, "Your right to swing your fist ends where my nose begins."

Speech stands somewhere between belief and action. It is not an absolute right, like belief, but neither is it as exposed to governmental restraint as is action. Some kinds of speech—libel, obscenity, fighting words, and commercial speech (discussed shortly)—are not entitled to constitutional protection. But many problems arise in distinguishing between what does and does not fit into the categories of unprotected speech. People disagree, and it usually falls to the courts to decide what free speech means and to defend the right of individual and minority dissenters to exercise it.

Plainly, questions of free speech require that judges weigh a variety of factors: What was said? In what context and how was it said? Which level of government is attempting to regulate the speech—a city council speaking for a few people, or Congress speaking for many? How is the government attempting to regulate the speech—by prior restraint (censorship) or by punishment after the speech? If the restriction is made to preempt publication (prior restraint), it is likely to fail. Why is the government doing so—to preserve the public peace or to prevent criticism of the people in power? Although the courts tend to be receptive to restrictions that are a genuine threat to public safety, restrictions on criticism are likely to fail.

Today, the Supreme Court generally holds that speech is protected unless it falls into one of four narrow categories—*libel, obscenity, fighting words,* and *commercial speech.* This is a change from its position at the beginning of the twentieth century, when the Court variously relied on one of three tests: the bad tendency test, the clear and present danger test, and the preferred position doctrine.

The **bad tendency test** presumed it was reasonable to forbid speech that tends to corrupt society or cause people to engage in crime. Because the test too broadly restricted speech and ran "contrary to the fundamental premises underlying the First Amendment as the guardian of our democracy,"[23] it was abandoned. The **clear and present danger test** provided that government could restrict speech *only* if it presented an immediate danger—for example, a false shout of "Fire!" in a crowded theater or speech leading to a riot, the destruction of property, or the corruption of an election. This clear and present danger test required the government to show the intended speech clearly resulting in imminent danger in order to restrict the important right of free speech.

The last of the three historic tests, the **preferred position doctrine,** was advanced in the 1940s when the Court applied all the guarantees of the First Amendment to the states (as discussed earlier). It comes close to the position that freedom of expression—the use of words and pictures—should rarely, if ever, be curtailed. This interpretation gives these freedoms, especially freedom of speech and of conscience, a preferred position in our constitutional hierarchy.

Although these tests are no longer applied, they provide a background for the current judicial approach to government regulation of speech, which represents an expansion of these more narrow constraints. Today, free speech and expression are constitutionally protected, and courts strictly scrutinize government regulation of such speech.

Protected Speech

Of all the forms of governmental interference with expression, judges are most suspicious of those that impose **prior restraint**—censorship before publication. Prior restraints include governmental review and approval before a speech can be made, before a motion picture can be shown, or before a newspaper can be published. Most prior restraints are unconstitutional, as the Court has said: "Any system of prior restraints of expression comes to this Court bearing a heavy presumption against its constitutional validity."[24] About the only prior restraints the Court has approved relate to military and national security matters—such as the disclosure of troop movements[25]—and to high school authorities' control over student newspapers.[26]

Even for an important purpose, a legislature may not pass a law that impinges on First Amendment freedoms if other, less drastic means are available. For example, a state may protect the public from unscrupulous lawyers but not by forbidding attorneys from advertising their fees for simple services. The state could adopt other ways to protect the public from such lawyers that do not impinge on their freedom of speech; it could, for example, disbar lawyers who mislead their clients.

Laws that regulate some kinds of speech but not others, or that regulate speech expressing some views but not others, are likely to be struck down. But those that are **content neutral or viewpoint neutral**—that is, laws that apply to *all* kinds of speech and to *all* views—are more likely to be safe. For example, the Constitution does not prohibit laws forbidding the posting of handbills on telephone poles. However, laws prohibiting only religious handbills or only handbills advocating racism or sexism would probably be declared unconstitutional because they would limit the content of handbills rather than restrict all handbills regardless of what they say.

Unprotected Speech

Unprotected speech lacks redeeming social value and is not essential to democratic deliberations and self-governance. The Supreme Court holds that all speech is protected unless it falls into one of four narrow categories: *libel, obscenity, fighting words,* or *commercial speech.* This does not mean that the constitutional issues relating to these kinds of speech are simple. How we prove *libel,* how we define *obscenity,* how we determine which words are *fighting words,* and how much *commercial speech* may be regulated remain hotly contested issues.

Libel

At one time, newspaper publishers and editors had to take considerable care about what they wrote to avoid prosecution by the government or lawsuits by individuals for **libel**—published defamation or false statements. Today, as a result of gradually rising constitutional standards, it has become more difficult to win a libel suit against a newspaper or magazine.

In *New York Times* v. *Sullivan* and subsequent cases, the Court established guidelines for libel cases and severely limited state power to award monetary damages in libel suits brought by public officials against critics of official conduct. Neither public officials nor public figures can collect damages for comments made about them unless they were made with *actual malice,* meaning that the "statements were made with a knowing or reckless disregard for the truth."[27] Nor can they collect damages even when subject to outrageous, clearly inaccurate parodies and cartoons. Such was the case when *Hustler* magazine printed a parody of the Reverend Jerry Falwell; the Court held that parodies and cartoons cannot reasonably be understood as describing actual facts or events.[28]

Obscenity and Pornography

Obscene publications are not entitled to constitutional protection, but members of the Supreme Court, like everyone else, have difficulty defining obscenity. As Justice Potter Stewart put it, "I know it when I see it."[29]

In *Miller* v. *California* (1973), the Court finally agreed on a constitutional definition of **obscenity.** A work may be considered legally obscene if (1) the average person, applying contemporary standards of the particular community, would find that the work, taken as a whole, appeals to a prurient interest in sex; (2) the work depicts or describes in a patently offensive way sexual conduct specifically defined by the applicable law or authoritatively construed (meaning that the legislature must define in law each obscene act); and (3) the work, taken as a whole, lacks serious literary, artistic, political, or scientific value.[30] As a result, cities such as New York City use zoning

bad tendency test
An interpretation of the First Amendment that would permit legislatures to forbid speech encouraging people to engage in illegal action.

clear and present danger test
An interpretation of the First Amendment that holds that the government cannot interfere with speech unless the speech presents a clear and present danger that it will lead to evil or illegal acts.

preferred position doctrine
An interpretation of the First Amendment that holds that freedom of expression is so essential to democracy that governments should not punish persons for what they say, only for what they do.

prior restraint
Censorship imposed before a speech is made or a newspaper is published; usually presumed to be unconstitutional.

content or viewpoint neutrality
Laws that apply to all kinds of speech and to all views, not only that which is unpopular or divisive.

unprotected speech
Libel, obscenity, fighting words, and commercial speech, which are not entitled to constitutional protection in all circumstances.

libel
Written defamation of another person. For public officials and public figures, the constitutional tests designed to restrict libel actions are especially rigid.

Internet bloggers pose an interesting twist on libel law. Bloggers can be sued for libel, just as print newspapers can, but bloggers' anonymity sometimes makes such suits more challenging. However, there are legal provisions to force Internet service providers to reveal the identity of a person who posts material online. ■ *Should the law treat bloggers differently than journalists? What other new media might pose difficult questions for the courts?*

New York City used zoning laws to eliminate adult entertainment and bookstores from Times Square. As a result, the area has once again become a vibrant center of the city and a prominent tourist attraction. ■ *Should states and cities be able to eliminate adult entertainment all together? Why or why not?*

laws to regulate where adult theaters and bookstores may be located,[31] and they may ban totally nude dancing in adult nightclubs.[32]

Fighting Words and Commercial Speech **Fighting words** were held to be constitutionally unprotected because "their very utterance may inflict injury or tend to incite an immediate breach of peace."[33] That the words are abusive, offensive, and insulting or that they create anger, alarm, or resentment is not sufficient. Thus, a four-letter word worn on a sweatshirt was not judged to be a fighting word in the constitutional sense, even though it was offensive and angered some people. The word was not aimed at any individual, and those who were offended could look away.[34] In recent years, the Court has overturned convictions for uttering fighting words and struck down laws that criminalized "hate speech." However, hate crime statutes, which do not limit a person's expression but instead allow courts to consider motive in criminal sentencing, have been broadly upheld.[35]

Commercial speech—such as advertisements and commercials—used to be unprotected because it was deemed to have lesser value than political speech. But the Court has reconsidered and extended more protection to commercial speech, as it has to fighting words. In *44 Liquormart, Inc.* v. *Rhode Island* (1996), for instance, the Court struck down a law forbidding advertising the price of alcoholic drinks.[36] It now appears that states may forbid and punish only false and misleading advertising, along with advertising promoting the sale of anything illegal—for example, narcotics. Although the Supreme Court has not specifically removed commercial speech from the nonprotected category, it has interpreted the First, Fifth, and Fourteenth Amendments to provide considerable constitutional protection for it.

Freedom of the Press

We have seen that courts are immediately skeptical of prior restraints and have carefully protected the right to publish information, no matter how journalists get it. However, they have not recognized additional protections to allow journalists to withhold information from grand juries or legislative investigating committees. Without this right to withhold information, reporters insist they cannot assure their sources of confidentiality, and they will not be able to get the information they need to keep the public informed.

The Supreme Court, however, has refused to acknowledge that reporters, and presumably scholars, have a constitutional right to ignore legal requests such as subpoenas and to withhold information from governmental bodies.[37] In 2005, *New York Times* reporter Judith Miller was jailed for two months for refusing to disclose her sources to a grand jury. Many states have passed *press shield laws* providing some protection for reporters from state court subpoenas, and Congress is currently deliberating on a federal shield law known as the Free Flow of Information Act.

When the First Amendment was written, freedom of the press referred to leaflets, newspapers, and books. Today, the amendment protects other media as well, and much debate centers on the degree of protection that should be afforded to broadcast media and the Internet.

Broadcast and Cable Communications Despite the rise of the Internet, television remains an important means of distributing news and appealing for votes. Yet of all the mass media, broadcasting receives the least First Amendment protection. Congress has established a system of commercial broadcasting, supplemented by the Corporation for Public Broadcasting, which provides funds for public radio and television. The Federal Communications Commission (FCC) regulates the entire system by granting licenses, regulating their use, and imposing fines for indecent broadcasts.

The First Amendment would prevent censorship if the FCC tried to impose it. The First Amendment does not, however, prevent the FCC from imposing sanctions on stations that broadcast indecent or filthy words, even if those words are not legally obscene.[38] Nor does the First Amendment prevent the FCC from refusing to renew a license if, in its opinion, a broadcaster does not serve the public interest. In the wake of Bono's 2003 Golden Globes acceptance speech including a certain indecent word and Janet Jackson's 2004

obscenity
The quality or state of a work that, taken as a whole, appeals to a prurient interest in sex by depicting sexual conduct in a patently offensive way and that lacks serious literary, artistic, political, or scientific value.

fighting words
Words that by their very nature inflict injury on those to whom they are addressed or incite them to acts of violence.

commercial speech
Advertisements and commercials for products and services; they receive less First Amendment protection, primarily to discourage false and misleading ads.

Although government may impose reasonable restrictions on the place and manner in which leaflets are posted, many college "hate speech" restrictions have been struck down because they unlawfully single out a certain kind of speech. ■ *Why is it constitutionally impermissible to single out a particular kind of speech?*

Super Bowl performance in which her breast was exposed, heightened attention was focused on the issue of FCC sanctions. At least partly in response, President Bush signed a law in 2006 authorizing the FCC to fine broadcasters up to $325,000 for each instance of indecent broadcasting. Although the Court has continued to uphold restrictions on the broadcast media, cable operators are given greater latitude in their programming.[39]

The Internet The Internet presents an interesting problem in determining the appropriate level of First Amendment protection. In many ways, it functions as a newspaper—providing news and information critical to an informed citizenry. But it is also a commercial marketplace where millions of U.S. consumers buy books, clothing, jewelry, airplane tickets, stocks, and bonds.

In general, attempts to regulate Internet content have been unsuccessful. In its major ruling on First Amendment protection for the Internet, *Reno* v. *American Civil Liberties Union* (1997), the Court struck down provisions of the Communications Decency Act of 1996 that had made it a crime to send obscene or indecent messages to anyone under the age of 18. In doing so, the Court emphasized the unique character of the Internet, holding that it is less intrusive than radio and broadcast television.[40] In response to *Reno* v. *ACLU,* Congress passed the Child Online Protection Act of 1998 (COPA), which made it a crime for a commercial Web site to knowingly make available to anyone under the age of 17 sexually explicit material considered "harmful to minors" based on "community standards." But the Supreme Court held that the law was unenforceable because imposing criminal penalties was not the least drastic means of achieving Congress's goals; Internet filters and adult checks could block minors' access to sites with sexually explicit material.[41]

When Cher used profanity in reference to her critics as she accepted a Billboard Music Award, the FCC ruled that the broadcast was indecent, a determination upheld by the U.S. Supreme Court in 2009 (*Fox* v. *FCC*, 556 U.S. _____ (2009)). However, litigation on the FCC's policy on profanity is ongoing and a court of appeals has determined that its current policy is unconstitutionally vague. ■ *Why does broadcast media receive comparatively little First Amendment protection?*

Freedom of Assembly

Khallid Abdul Muhammad, a known racist and anti-Semite, organized what he called a "Million Youth March" in New York City in 1998. Mayor Rudolph

People who want to express their views, like this person protesting the construction of a Islamic community center near Ground Zero in New York City, must obtain the proper permits or paperwork. But the government may not deny their permit requests because it disagrees with the group's message. ■ *Under what circumstances might a government constitutionally deny a permit to assemble and protest?*

Giuliani denied a permit for the march on the grounds that it would be a "hate march." A federal appeals court upheld a lower-court ruling that denial of the permit was unconstitutional. However, a three-judge panel placed restrictions on the event, limiting its duration to four hours and scaling it back to a six-block area. The march proceeded, surrounded by police in riot gear who broke up the demonstration after Muhammad delivered a vitriolic speech against the police, Jews, and city officials. This is a classic free speech problem: The First Amendment protects speech regardless of whether it is popular. It is almost always easier, and certainly politically more prudent, to maintain order by curbing unpopular groups' public demonstrations.

Time, Place, and Manner Regulations The Constitution protects the right to speak, but it does not give people the right to communicate their views to everyone, in every place, at every time they wish. No one has the right to block traffic or to hold parades or make speeches in public streets or on public sidewalks whenever he or she wishes. Governments may not censor what can be said, but they can make "reasonable" *time, place,* and *manner* regulations for protests or parades.

Depending on the place where the expressive activities are to occur, such as public parks, public school buildings, or government offices, the Court has been more or less willing to permit speech activities subject to reasonable time, place, and manner restrictions. It is essential, however, that any restriction be applied evenhandedly and that the government not act because of *what* is being said, rather than how, where, or by whom.

Does the right of peaceful assembly include the right to violate a law nonviolently but deliberately? We have no precise answer, but in general, **civil disobedience,** even if peaceful, is not a protected right. When Martin Luther King Jr. and his followers refused to comply with a state court's injunction forbidding them to parade in Birmingham, Alabama, without first securing a permit, the Supreme Court sustained their conviction, even though there was serious doubt about the constitutionality of the injunction and the ordinance on which it was based.[42]

More recently, the First Amendment right of antiabortion protesters to picket in front of abortion clinics has come into conflict with a woman's right to go to an abortion clinic. Protesters have often massed in front of clinics, shouting at employees and clients and blocking entrances to the clinic. The Supreme Court has struck down provisions that prohibit protesters from expressing their views. But it has upheld injunctions that keep antiabortion protesters outside a buffer zone around abortion clinics and also upheld injunctions that were issued because of the protesters' previous unlawful conduct.[43]

civil disobedience
Deliberate refusal to obey a law or comply with the orders of public officials as a means of expressing opposition.

property rights
The rights of an individual to own, use, rent, invest in, buy, and sell property.

First Amendment freedoms are crucial for the survival of our republican form of democracy. It is of utmost importance that individuals be able to make their voices heard regardless of the political views they wish to express. However, these freedoms alone do not provide full protection from arbitrary or impermissible government infringements on our liberties more generally. Historically, U.S. political thinking and political institutions have emphasized the close connection between liberty and owning property, and between property and power. One of the framers' central goals was to establish a government strong enough to protect people's rights to use and enjoy their property. Next, we turn our attention to amendments in the Bill of Rights protecting property, due process, privacy, and the rights of criminal suspects.

Property Rights

LEARNING **OBJECTIVE**
11.3 Explain how the Constitution protects property rights.

Property does not have rights; people do. People have the right to own, use, rent, invest in, buy, and sell property. The framers wanted to limit government so that it could not endanger that right. As a result, the Constitution has a variety of clauses protecting **property rights.**

Although the right of property ownership is highly regarded, both the national and state governments have the power of **eminent domain**—the power to take private property for public use—but the owner must be fairly compensated. What constitutes "taking" for purposes of eminent domain? Ordinarily, but not always, the taking must be direct, and a person must lose title and control over the property. Sometimes, especially in recent years, the courts have found that a governmental taking has gone "too far," and the government must compensate its owners even when title is left in the owner's name.[44] These are called **regulatory takings,** meaning the regulation has effectively taken the land by restricting its use. Thus, compensation is required when government creates landing and takeoff paths for airplanes over property adjacent to an airport, which makes the land unsuitable for its original use (say, raising chickens).[45] The government may, however, impose land use and environmental regulations, temporarily prohibiting the development of a property, without compensating the owners.[46]

In a controversial ruling with wide-ranging ramifications for urban planners and homeowners, a bare majority of the Court upheld the use of the government's power of eminent domain to condemn and take private property, with just compensation, for the purpose of advancing the economic development of a community. *Kelo* v. *City of New London* (2005) held that "public use" was not limited to eminent domain to build a road or a bridge but includes "promoting economic development," even if the property was taken and sold for development to private developers.[47] Public reaction to the Court's decision in *Kelo* was extremely negative. In a clear reminder that the Court is only one instrument of government, many states and localities acted swiftly to pass laws that barred authorities from taking private property for such purposes.

"Just compensation" is not always easy to define. When there is a dispute over compensation, the courts make the final resolution based on the rule that "the owner is entitled to receive what a willing buyer would pay in cash to a willing seller at the time of the taking."[48] An owner is not entitled to compensation for the personal value of an old, broken-down, dearly loved house—just the value of the old, broken-down house.

Major opposition to the Court's 2005 decision to allow New London, Connecticut, to take Susette Kelo's property led to many local ballot initiatives in the 2006 elections.
■ *How might ballot initiatives address citizens' concerns about the Court's decision in this case?*

Due Process Rights

LEARNING **OBJECTIVE**

11.4 Distinguish between procedural and substantive due process.

Perhaps the most difficult parts of the Constitution to understand are the clauses in the Fifth and Fourteenth Amendments forbidding the national and state governments to deny any person life, liberty, or property without "due process of law." Cases involving these guarantees have resulted in hundreds of Supreme Court decisions. Even so, it is impossible to explain *due process* precisely. In fact, the Supreme Court has refused to do so and has emphasized that "due process, unlike some legal rules, is not a technical conception with a fixed content unrelated to time, place, and circumstances."[49] We define **due process** as rules and regulations that restrain those in government who exercise power. There are, however, basically two kinds of due process: procedural and substantive.

Procedural Due Process

Traditionally, **procedural due process** refers not to the law itself but to *how a law is applied.* To paraphrase Daniel Webster's famous definition, the due process of law requires a procedure that hears before it condemns, proceeds upon inquiry, and renders judgment only after a trial or some kind of hearing. Originally, procedural due process was limited to criminal prosecutions, but it now applies to most kinds of governmental proceedings.

The liberties that due process protects include "the right of the individual to contract, to engage in any of the common occupations of life, to acquire useful knowledge, to marry, to establish a home and bring up children, to worship God according to the dictates of his own conscience, and generally to enjoy those common law privileges long recognized as essential to the orderly pursuit of happiness by free men."[50]

eminent domain
The power of a government to take private property for public use; the U.S. Constitution gives national and state governments this power and requires them to provide just compensation for property so taken.

regulatory taking
A government regulation that effectively takes land by restricting its use, even if it remains in the owner's name.

due process
Established rules and regulations that restrain government officials.

procedural due process
A constitutional requirement that governments proceed by proper methods; limits how government may exercise power.

Here a detainee is escorted by guards at the U.S. military prison at Guantanamo Bay, Cuba. Shortly after he took office, President Obama signed an executive order to close the facility in order to "restore the standards of due process and the core constitutional values that have made this country great even in the midst of war, even in dealing with terrorism."* ■ *Even with President Obama's executive order, why has it been so difficult to close the prison at Guantanamo Bay?*

*Susan Candiotti, Ed Hornick, and Jeanne Meserve, "What's Next for Guantanamo Bay Detainees?" CNN, *The First 100 Days*, January 26, 2009, http://www.cnn.com/2009/POLITICS/01/26/gitmo.next/index.html.

Substantive Due Process

Procedural due process limits *how* governmental power may be exercised; **substantive due process** limits *what* a government may do. Procedural due process mainly limits the executive and judicial branches because they apply the law and review its application; substantive due process mainly limits the legislative branch because it enacts laws. Substantive due process means that an "unreasonable" law, even if properly passed and properly applied, is unconstitutional. It means that governments *should not be allowed to do certain things.*

Substantive due process has deep roots in concepts of natural law and a long history in U.S. constitutional tradition. For most citizens most of the time, it is not enough merely to say that a law reflects the wishes of the popular or legislative majority. We also want our laws to be just, and we rely heavily on judges to decide what is just.

Privacy Rights

LEARNING **OBJECTIVE**

11.5 Assess the kinds of behavior that may be covered by a constitutional right to privacy.

The most important extension of substantive due process in recent decades has protected the right of privacy, especially marital privacy. Although the Constitution does not mention the right to privacy, in *Griswold* v. *Connecticut* (1965), the Supreme Court pulled together elements of the First, Third, Fourth, Fifth, Ninth, and Fourteenth Amendments to recognize that personal privacy is one of the rights the Constitution protects.[51] The decision remains highly controversial because the Bill of Rights does not specifically enumerate a right to privacy. Instead, the Court ruled that it was implied by the rights listed above.

This right has three aspects: (1) the right to be free from governmental surveillance and intrusion, especially with respect to intimate decisions on sexuality; (2) the right not to have the government make private affairs public; and (3) the right to be free in thought and belief from governmental regulations.[52] Thus, the right underlies our discussion later in this chapter of unreasonable searches and seizures, government surveillance, and self-incrimination. The right to privacy also encompasses two controversial issues: state regulation of abortion and private, adult consensual sexual conduct.

substantive due process
A constitutional requirement that governments act reasonably and that the substance of the laws themselves be fair and reasonable; limits what a government may do.

For the People

GOVERNMENT'S GREATEST ENDEAVORS

Protecting Sixth Amendment Rights of Indigent Defendants

Until 1963, defendants who could not afford an attorney to represent them in state criminal trials were left to defend themselves against charges brought by state prosecutors. Although the Sixth Amendment to the United States Constitution provided for an attorney in federal trials, it had not been incorporated against state infringement. However, all that changed when Clarence Earl Gideon appealed his conviction in the Florida state courts on the grounds that he was not provided with an attorney to fight charges that he had broken into a pool hall and stolen money from the cash register.

In *Gideon* v. *Wainwright,* the U.S. Supreme Court ruled that because of the complexities of the legal system and the potential for being deprived of one's basic liberty, the government must provide an attorney to a criminal defendant who cannot afford one. This is particularly important in an adversarial legal system such as we have in the United States, where the judge or jury, as a neutral decision maker, depends on the attorneys to bring forth all of the relevant evidence in a case. The Court's decision in *Gideon* v. *Wainwright* resulted in public defender services being provided throughout the United States. Each state has its own method to provide counsel to indigent defendants. For example, in some states, they have a statewide public defender service, and, in others, they use a combination of state-employed defense attorneys and private attorneys whom the state pays by the case to represent indigent defendants.

Providing a defense for indigent persons accused of a crime is essential to fulfilling the requirements of the Sixth Amendment. In 2007, more than 17,000 attorneys throughout some 964 public defender offices represented nearly 6 million cases involving indigent clients.* Although there are many concerns about the quality of representation provided to indigent defendants, including large caseloads and insufficient funding, indigent clients today are far better represented than they were some 40 years ago.

CRITICAL THINKING QUESTIONS

1. Why is it particularly important for indigent defendants to be represented by an attorney in an adversarial legal system?
2. Why might the Supreme Court have allowed the states to develop their own systems for providing indigent defendants with legal counsel?

* Public Defender Offices, 2007, Bureau of Justice Statistics, http://bjs.ojp.usdoj.gov/index.cfm?ty=pbdetail&iid=1758.

Abortion Rights

In *Roe* v. *Wade* (1973), the Supreme Court ruled that the right to privacy extended to a woman's decision, in consultation with her physician, to terminate her pregnancy. According to *Roe*'s "trimester framework," (1) during the first trimester of a woman's pregnancy, it is an unreasonable and therefore unconstitutional interference with her liberty and privacy rights for a state to set any limits on her choice to have an abortion or on her doctor's medical judgments about how to carry it out; (2) during the second trimester, the state's interest in protecting the health of women becomes compelling, and a state may make a reasonable regulation about how, where, and when abortions may be performed; and (3) during the third trimester, when the fetus becomes capable of surviving outside the womb, which the Court called "viability," the state's interest in protecting the unborn child is so important that the state can prohibit abortions altogether, except when necessary to preserve the life or health of the mother.[53]

The *Roe* decision led to decades of heated public debate and attempts by Presidents Ronald Reagan and George H. W. Bush to select Supreme Court justices who might reverse it. Nonetheless, *Roe* v. *Wade* was reaffirmed in *Planned Parenthood* v. *Casey* (1992). A bitterly divided Court upheld by a five-person majority (Justices O'Connor, Kennedy, Souter, Blackmun, and Stevens) the view that the due process clause of the Constitution protects a woman's liberty to choose an abortion prior to viability. The Court, however, held that the right to have an abortion prior to viability may be subject to state regulation that does not "unduly burden" it. In other words, the Court threw out the trimester framework and permitted states to make "reasonable regulations" on how a woman exercises her right to an abortion, so long as they do not prohibit any woman from making the ultimate decision on whether to terminate a pregnancy before viability.[54]

Applying the undue burden test, the Court has held, on the one hand, that states can prohibit the use of state funds and facilities for performing abortions; states may make a minor's right to an abortion conditional on her first notifying at least one parent

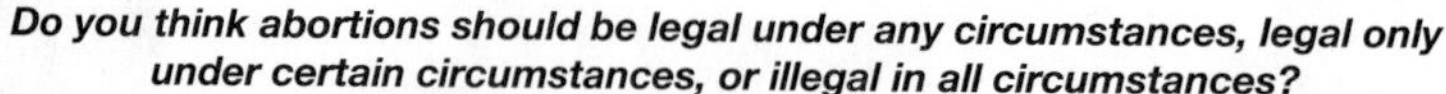

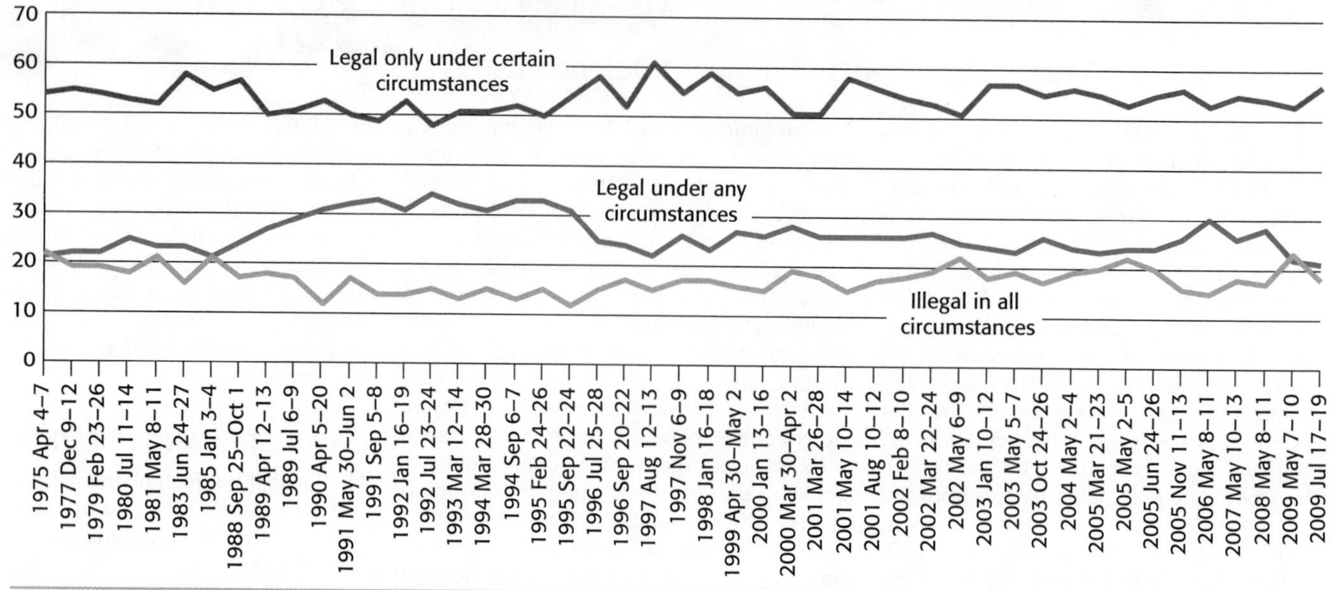

FIGURE 11–2 Public Opinion on Abortion Access.
Although there is great controversy over the issue of abortion, a majority of Americans has consistently agreed that abortion access should be "legal only under certain circumstances." ■ *Are the Supreme Court's rulings on abortion access generally in line with public opinion?*

or a judge; and states may require women to sign an informed-consent form and wait 24 hours before having an abortion. On the other hand, a state may not condition a woman's right to an abortion on her first notifying her husband. The Court also struck down Nebraska's ban on "partial birth" abortions in *Stenberg* v. *Carhart* (2000) because it completely forbade one kind of medical procedure and provided no exception for when a woman's health is at stake and thus imposed an "undue burden" on women.[55] But, more recently (in 2007), the Court ruled five to four to uphold a federal ban on abortion procedures that was nearly identical to the one struck down in *Stenberg* v. *Carhart*. It reasoned that because of "medical uncertainty" about the banned procedure's necessity, Congress was not required to include a health exception.[56]

Abortion continues to be a hotly contested issue before the courts. Here protesters on both sides of the abortion debate demonstrate in front of the Supreme Court building. ■ *What impact might such protestors hope to have by demonstrating in front of the Supreme Court? Should justices pay attention to these protests?*

Sexual Orientation Rights

Although there is general agreement on how much constitutional protection is provided for marital privacy, in *Bowers* v. *Hardwick* (1986), the Supreme Court refused to extend such protection to private relations between homosexuals.[57] By a 5-to-4 vote in *Bowers*, the Court refused to declare unconstitutional a Georgia law that made consensual sodomy a crime. But several state supreme courts, including Georgia's, upheld privacy rights for homosexual couples based on their own state constitutions rather than relying on the U.S. Constitution. Finally, in *Lawrence* v. *Texas* (2003),[58] the Court struck down Texas's law making homosexual sodomy a crime. Writing for the Court and noting the trend in state court decisions that did not follow *Bowers*, Justice Kennedy held the law to violate personal autonomy and the right of privacy. Dissenting, Justice Scalia, along with Chief Justice Rehnquist and Justice Thomas, warned that the decision might lead to overturning laws barring same-sex marriages, as some state courts and Canadian courts had already done. We will explore this further in Chapter 12 under discussions of equal protection under the law.

The right of privacy as an element of substantive due process is one of the developing edges of constitutional law, one about which people both on and off the Court have strong disagreements. How the Supreme Court handles privacy issues has become front-page news.

search warrant
A writ issued by a magistrate that authorizes the police to search a particular place or person, specifying the place to be searched and the objects to be seized.

Rights of Criminal Suspects

LEARNING **OBJECTIVE**
11.6 Characterize the constitutional rights of criminal suspects.

Despite what you see in police dramas on television and in the movies, law enforcement officers have no general right to break down doors and invade homes. They are not supposed to search people except under certain conditions, and they have no right to arrest them except under certain circumstances. They also may not compel confessions, and they must respect other procedural guarantees aimed at ensuring fairness and the rights of the accused. Persons accused of crimes are guaranteed these and other rights under the Fourth, Fifth, Sixth, Eighth, and Fourteenth Amendments.

Freedom from Unreasonable Searches and Seizures

According to the Fourth Amendment, "The right of the people to be secure in their persons, houses, papers, and effects, against unreasonable searches and seizures, shall not be violated, and no Warrants shall issue, but upon probable cause, supported by Oath or affirmation, and particularly describing the place to be searched, and the persons or things to be seized."

Protection from unreasonable searches and seizures requires police, if they have time, to obtain a valid **search warrant,** issued by a magistrate after the police indicate under oath that they have *probable cause* to justify it. Magistrates must perform this function in a neutral and detached manner and not serve merely as rubber stamps for the police. The warrant must specify the place to be searched and the things to be seized. *General search warrants*—warrants that authorize police to search a particular place or person without limitation—are unconstitutional. A search warrant is usually needed to search a person in any place he or she has an "expectation of privacy that society is prepared to recognize as reasonable," including, for example, in a hotel room, a rented home, or a friend's apartment.[59] In short, the Fourth Amendment protects people, not places, from unreasonable governmental intrusions.[60]

The Fourth Amendment presents a complex area of the law that includes many possible exceptions to the warrant requirement. Beyond obtaining a search warrant, there are several other conditions in which a search might be considered "reasonable" according to the language of the Fourth Amendment. Key to determining whether a *warrantless search* is permissible are factors such as whether a person's consent to a search is coerced or whether an officer's or the public's safety is at risk. The Fourth Amendment does not apply to every encounter between individuals and law enforcement officials, however.

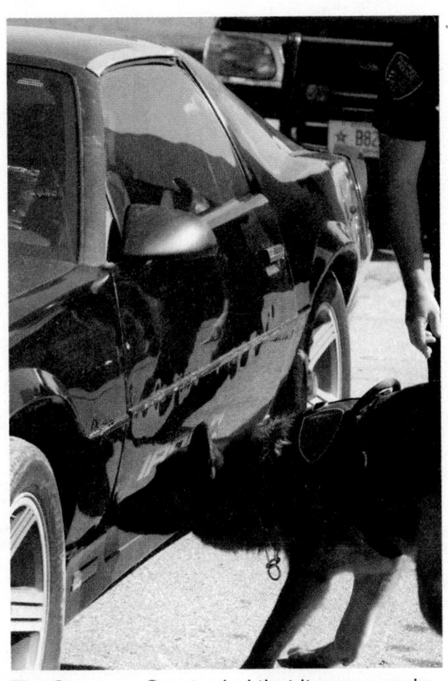

The Supreme Court ruled that it was permissible for police to use a drug-sniffing dog in a routine traffic stop without violating the Fourth Amendment protections against unreasonable search and seizure. (*Illinois* v. *Caballes*, 543 U.S. 405 (2005)). ■ *In what kinds of places might you have a reasonable expectation of privacy?*

Following September 11, 2001, airport security was tightened throughout the country. Such extensive searches are lawful because they are technically voluntary, meaning a person could choose not to fly. ■ *Should the same kind of searches be permissible before people board local public transportation such as buses or subways?*

If the police only ask questions or even seek consent to search an individual's person or possessions in a noncoercive atmosphere, and there is no detention, the person's physical liberty has not been limited. But if the person refuses to answer questions or consent to a search, and the police, by either physical force or a show of authority, restrain the movement of the person, even though there is no arrest, the Fourth Amendment comes into play.[61] For example, if police approach people in airports and request identification, this act by itself does not constitute a detention.[62]

The Supreme Court also upheld, in *Terry* v. *Ohio* (1968), a *stop and frisk* exception to the warrant requirement when officers have reason to believe someone is armed and dangerous or has committed or is about to commit a criminal offense. The *Terry* search is limited to a quick pat-down to check for weapons that may be used to assault the arresting officer, to check for contraband, to determine identity, or to maintain the status quo while obtaining more information.[63] If individuals who are stopped for questioning refuse to identify themselves, they may be arrested, although police must have a reasonable suspicion that they are engaged in criminal activities.[64] If an officer stops and frisks a suspect to look for weapons and finds criminal evidence that may justify an arrest, the officer can make a full search.[65]

Police and border guards may also conduct *border* searches—searches of persons and the goods they bring with them at border crossings.[66] The border search exception also permits officials to open mail entering the country if they have "reasonable cause" to suspect that it contains merchandise imported in violation of the law.[67]

The Exclusionary Rule

Before the development of the *exclusionary rule*, evidence obtained in violation of the Fourth Amendment might still be used at trial against a defendant. The remedy in such cases was the opportunity for the defendant to sue law enforcement. However, suing afterward did not resolve the denial of Fourth Amendment protection in the criminal action.

This changed in the federal courts in 1911 and was applied to the states in 1961. In *Mapp* v. *Ohio* (1961), the Supreme Court adopted a rule excluding from criminal trial evidence that the police obtained unconstitutionally or illegally.[68] This **exclusionary rule** was adopted to prevent police misconduct. Critics question why criminals should go free just because of police misconduct or ineptness,[69] but the Supreme Court has refused to abandon the rule. It has made some exceptions to it, however, such as cases in which police relied in "good faith" on a search warrant that subsequently turned out to be defective or granted improperly.[70]

exclusionary rule
A requirement that evidence unconstitutionally or illegally obtained be excluded from a criminal trial.

The Right to Remain Silent

During the seventeenth century, special courts in England forced confessions by torture and intimidation from religious dissenters. The British privilege against self-incrimination developed in response to these practices. Because they were familiar with this history, the framers of our Bill of Rights included in the Fifth Amendment the provision that persons shall not be compelled to testify against themselves in criminal prosecutions. This protection against self-incrimination is designed to strengthen the fundamental principle that no person has an obligation to prove innocence. Rather, the burden is on the government to prove guilt.

The Miranda Warning Police questioning of suspects is a key procedure in solving crimes. Approximately 90 percent of all criminal convictions result from guilty pleas and never reach a full trial. Police questioning, however, can easily be abused. Police officers sometimes forget or ignore the constitutional rights of suspects, especially those who are frightened and ignorant. Unauthorized detention and lengthy interrogation to wring confessions from suspects, common practice in police states, have also occurred in the United States.

To put an end to such practices, the Supreme Court, in *Miranda* v. *Arizona* (1966), announced that no conviction could stand if evidence introduced at the trial had been obtained by the police during "custodial interrogation" unless suspects were notified that they have a right to remain silent and that anything they say can and will be used against them; to terminate questioning at any point; to have an attorney present during questioning by police; and to have a lawyer appointed to represent them if they cannot afford to hire their own attorney.[71] If suspects answer questions in the absence of an attorney, the burden is on prosecutors to demonstrate that suspects knowingly and intelligently gave up their right to remain silent. Failure to comply with these requirements leads to reversal of a conviction, even if other evidence is sufficient to establish guilt.

Critics of the *Miranda* decision believe the Supreme Court severely limited the ability of the police to bring criminals to justice. Throughout the years, the Court has modified the original ruling by allowing evidence obtained contrary to the *Miranda* guidelines to be used to attack the credibility of defendants who offer testimony at trial that conflicts with their statements to the police. But the Court has reaffirmed *Miranda*'s constitutional necessity as recently as 2000 (*Dickerson* v. *United States*).[72]

Fair Trial Procedures

Many people consider the rights of persons accused of a crime to be less important than other rights. Nonetheless, they guarantee that all persons accused of crimes will have the right to representation by counsel and to a fair trial by an impartial jury. Procedural

The case of Ernesto Miranda (right) led to the Supreme Court decision in 1966 requiring suspects in police custody to be advised of their constitutional right to remain silent and to have an attorney present during questioning. ■ *Why is it important that criminal suspects know their rights?*

protections are guaranteed at each of the stages in the criminal process: (1) pretrial, (2) trial, (3) sentencing, and (4) appeal.

Before a person can be forced to stand trial for a criminal offense (except for members of the armed forces or foreign terrorists), they must be *indicted* by a grand jury, or before a judge in what is called an *information* proceeding. A **grand jury** is concerned not with a person's guilt or innocence, as a **petit jury** would be, but merely with whether there is enough evidence to warrant a trial. The grand jury has wide-ranging investigatory powers and "is to inquire into all information that might bear on its investigations until it is satisfied that it has identified an offense or satisfied itself that none has occurred."[73] The strict rules that govern jury proceedings, and the exclusionary rule to enforce the Fourth Amendment, do not apply, and the grand jury may admit hearsay evidence. If a majority of the grand jurors agree that a trial is justified, they return a *true bill,* or **indictment.** During this stage of the criminal process and throughout the remaining stages, suspects have the right to an attorney, even if they cannot afford one on their own. Communication between the accused and counsel is privileged and cannot be revealed to a jury.

The Constitution guarantees the accused the right to be informed of the nature and cause of the accusation so that he or she can prepare a defense. After indictment, prosecutors and the defense attorney usually discuss the possibility of a **plea bargain** whereby the defendant pleads guilty to a lesser offense that carries a lesser penalty. Prosecutors, facing more cases than they can handle, like plea bargains because they save the expense and time of going to trial and they result in a conviction. Likewise, defendants are often willing to "cop a plea" for a lesser offense to avoid the risk of more serious punishment for the original indictment.

After indictment and preliminary hearings that determine bail and what evidence will be used against the accused, the Constitution guarantees a *speedy and public trial.* Do not, however, take the word "speedy" too literally. Defendants are given time to prepare their defense and often ask for delays because time works to their advantage. In contrast, if the government denies the accused a speedy trial, not only is the conviction reversed, but the case must also be dismissed outright.

An *impartial jury,* one that meets the requirements of due process and equal protection, consists of persons who represent a fair cross section of the community. Although defendants are not entitled to juries that reflect their own race, sex, religion, or national origin, government prosecutors cannot strike people from juries because of race or gender, and neither can defense attorneys use what are called *peremptory challenges* to keep people off juries because of race, ethnic origin, or sex.[74]

During the trial, the defendant has a right to obtain witnesses in his or her favor and to have the judge subpoena, or order, witnesses to appear at the trial and testify. Both the accused and witnesses may refuse to testify on the grounds that their testimony would tend to incriminate themselves. If witnesses testify, both the prosecution and the defense have the right to confront and cross-examine them.

The sentencing phase begins with the conclusion of the trial. Here, the jury recommends a verdict of guilty or not guilty. If the accused is found guilty, the judge usually hands down the sentence, although in some cases, juries also impose the sentence according to the judge's instructions. The Eighth Amendment forbids the levying of excessive fines and the inflicting of cruel and unusual punishment.

Although the crime rate has generally declined in the past few years, public concern about crime remains high. At the national and state levels, presidents, governors, and legislators vie with one another to show their toughness on crime. California, Virginia, Washington, and other states have "three strikes and you're out" laws, requiring a lifetime sentence without the possibility of parole for anyone convicted of a third felony, even if it is a minor offense. In some states, the felonies must be for violent crimes; in others, any three felonies will do. For example, the Supreme Court in *Ewing* v. *California* (2003) upheld California's tough law for committing three felonies, ruling that a 25-years-to-life sentence for a nonviolent third felony conviction for stealing three golf clubs did not violate the prohibition against cruel and unusual punishment.[75]

grand jury
A jury of 12 to 23 persons, depending on state and local requirements, who privately hear evidence presented by the government to determine whether persons shall be required to stand trial. If the jury believes there is sufficient evidence that a crime was committed, it issues an indictment.

petit jury
A jury of 6 to 12 persons that determines guilt or innocence in a civil or criminal action.

indictment
A formal written statement from a grand jury charging an individual with an offense; also called a *true bill*.

plea bargain
An agreement between a prosecutor and a defendant that the defendant will plead guilty to a lesser offense to avoid having to stand trial for a more serious offense.

By the People

MAKING A DIFFERENCE

Providing Legal Aid: Not Only for Law Students

Many law students spend time working at a legal aid clinic or volunteering for a legal aid society. They might provide legal advice, draft briefs, and even represent clients who cannot afford their own attorney. As discussed in this chapter's "For the People" box, criminal defendants who cannot afford to pay for their own legal representation are entitled through the Sixth Amendment to government-provided representation, but there are no constitutional requirements for attorneys in civil litigation and most states do not provide them.

Although many legal aid programs are aimed at law students, undergraduates also have the opportunity to provide legal help for those who cannot afford an attorney. Some legal aid societies welcome students as individual volunteers, and some court systems even cooperate with universities to provide organized programs for students as part of their service-learning programs.

For example, several California universities work with the Los Angeles Superior Court through a program called Justice Corps.* Through the program, the court trains students to work with self-represented litigants in court-based self-help programs. Some students with language skills are able to assist non-English speakers in navigating through the court system. Others conduct legal research and provide other assistance to people who may be fighting eviction or trying to obtain a civil restraining order. Programs like Justice Corps provide incredible opportunities to learn about the legal system and provide services to those in need.

In addition to organized programs, most local legal aid societies are continually looking for volunteers to help staff their offices, work with clients, and even perform routine maintenance. Lacking specialized legal skills need not prevent you from volunteering to make justice available to all citizens. Check to see if your college or university has an organized program for students to volunteer in the legal system. Does your community have a legal aid society? Sign up to volunteer your time for an hour or two a week.

CRITICAL THINKING QUESTIONS

1. Why are attorneys provided for indigent defendants in criminal cases but not for indigent litigants in civil case? Should attorneys be provided for those who cannot afford representation in civil cases?
2. What barriers might non-native English speakers encounter in the U.S. court system?

* See http://www.lasuperiorcourt.org/outreach/ui/#JusticeCorps.

In the final stage of the criminal process, defendants may *appeal* their convictions if they claim they have been denied some constitutional right or the due process and equal protection of the law. The Fifth Amendment also provides that no person shall be "subject for the same offense to be twice put in jeopardy of life or limb." **Double jeopardy** does not prevent punishment by the national and the state governments for the same offense, or for successive prosecutions for the same crime by two states. Nor does the double jeopardy clause forbid civil prosecutions, even after a person has been acquitted in a criminal trial for the same charge.[76]

The Death Penalty

The United States is unusual among industrialized nations in its retention and use of the death penalty. In December 2007, the United Nations General Assembly adopted a resolution calling for a worldwide moratorium on the death penalty. More than half of the countries throughout the world, 135, have abolished capital punishment for all or most crimes, and the trend has been growing. The United States and Japan are the only two industrialized countries that retain the death penalty. Most of the 62 countries that still impose capital punishment are in Africa, the Middle East, the Caribbean, and Central America.

After a ten-year moratorium on executions in the late 1960s and early 1970s, the U.S. Supreme Court ruled that the death penalty is not necessarily cruel and unusual punishment if it is imposed for crimes that resulted in a victim's death, if the courts "ensure that death sentences are not meted out wantonly or freakishly," and if these processes "confer on the sentencer sufficient discretion to take account of the character and record of the individual offender and the circumstances of the particular offense to ensure that death is the appropriate punishment in a specific case."[77]

The Rehnquist Court made it easier to impose death sentences, cut back on appeals, and carry out executions. More states have added the death penalty (35 states now have it),

double jeopardy
Trial or punishment for the same crime by the same government; forbidden by the Constitution.

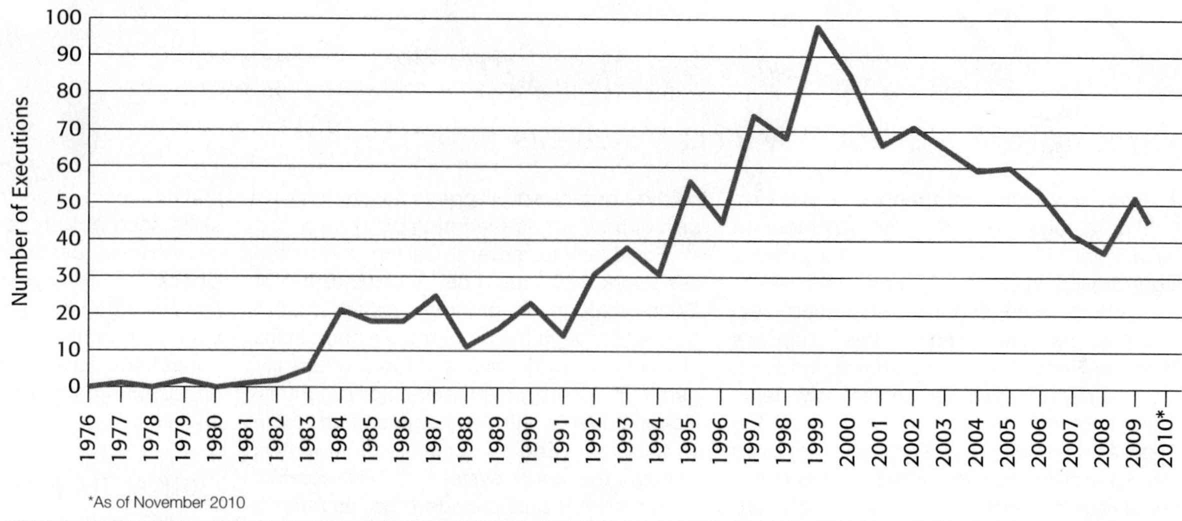

FIGURE 11–3 Number of Executions by Year, 1976–2010.

■ *What factors might explain the decline in the number of executions beginning in 2000?*

and the federal government has increased the number of crimes for which the death penalty may be imposed. As a result, the number of persons on death row has increased dramatically. Since capital punishment was reinstated in 1976, more than 1,000 people have been executed nationwide, and more than 3,300 are on death row.[78] (See Figure 11–3.) However, concerns have also grown about the fairness with which capital punishment is imposed. DNA tests that have established the innocence of a sizable number of those convicted of murder have increased these concerns.[79] Since 1973, more than 130 people who were convicted of murder and sentenced to death have been exonerated.[80] Much of this work has been done by the Innocence Project, which is a charitable organization that searches for wrongful convictions. (Visit the Innocence Project at innocenceproject.org.)

The prohibition against cruel and unusual punishment also forbids punishments grossly disproportionate to the severity of the crime. In 2002, the Supreme Court overruled an earlier decision and held that it is excessive and disproportionate to execute mentally retarded convicted murderers because they cannot understand the seriousness of their offense.[81] Using similar reasoning four years later, the Court ruled that executing minors also violated the Eighth Amendment.[82]

The Court continued its trend in limiting the use of the death penalty by deciding in *Kennedy* v. *Louisiana* (2008) that death could not be used when the defendant was convicted of child rape in which a death did not result, nor was it intended (the Court had previously ruled that the death penalty violated the Eighth Amendment in the case of adult rape).[83] In March 2008, however, the Court, in a 7-to-2 vote, upheld lethal injections as a constitutionally permissible means of carrying out executions.[84]

Protecting Our Civil Liberties in an Age of Terror: Whose Responsibility?

LEARNING **OBJECTIVE**

11.7 Evaluate the roles of institutions and the people in protecting civil liberties.

As the discussion regarding the appropriate venue for trying suspected terrorists illustrates (see "You Will Decide"), the debate over adequate protections of individual liberties is ongoing. Today, there is particular concern about how to protect those liberties in the face of terrorist threats. As Justice Oliver Wendell Holmes wrote in his famous decision in *Schenck* v. *United States* (1919), "when a nation is at war, many things that might be said in a time of peace" will not be permissible "so long as men fight."[85] How do we find the correct balance between security and protecting civil liberties?

Ensuring against another terrorist attack would be much easier if the government had open access to listen in on our conversations, search our possessions, and detain

YOU WILL

DECIDE Should Terrorism Suspects Be Tried in Civilian Courts?

As the United States fights the war on terror, complex issues of national security and individual liberties continue to arise. One pressing issue is whether those arrested for plotting terrorist activities should be tried in our civilian court system or by military tribunals. The debate has important implications as defendants in the criminal court system are afforded protections that are not available in the military system. In general, military commissions allow some evidence against a defendant that would not be admitted into a civilian court and thus, in theory, provide an advantage to the prosecution. For example, prosecutors cannot use testimony obtained through coercion in civilian courts. However, in military courts, even statements that are made under coercion can be used in some circumstances. And, unlike military court judges, federal court judges have life tenure and there are protections to ensure judicial independence. On the other hand, some argue that accused terrorists should be tried in civilian courts because that system has proven capable of administering justice for more than two centuries, in other cases involving terrorism, and shows the world we will not compromise our system of justice in the face of terrorist attacks.

What do you think? Should terrorism suspects be tried in military or civilian courts? What argument would you make for or against either proposition?

THINKING IT THROUGH

There are a number of competing arguments regarding the appropriate venue for trying terror suspects. Underlying many of these debates is the question of whether suspected terrorists should be treated as soldiers caught on a new kind of battlefield, or whether they are more appropriately thought of as criminals who have violated criminal laws.

Those who argue that suspected terrorists ought to be tried in military tribunals cite the additional protections afforded to defendants in the criminal court system. They argue that suspected terrorists should not be privy to such additional protections when a soldier fighting in a traditional war would not be afforded those benefits. Proponents of military trials also argue that trying terror suspects in civilian courts would give them an opportunity to advance their ideology, provide incentives to attack civilian rather than military targets, and result in increased security concerns for cities in which the trials are held.

Those who argue for trying suspected terrorists in the civilian courts cite the relative success of such trials since September 11 and the relative lack of similar success in the military system. Military trials have led to only three convictions of suspected terrorists in eight years, and two of those three defendants are now free—one sent back to his native country of Australia and the other is in Yemen. Furthermore, legal changes have led many to question the validity of military commissions; those convicted through the military system are likely to challenge those outcomes. Supporters of civilian trials also argue that such trials will result in greater respect for the U.S. legal system and provide a platform for showing the horrors of terrorism. They also point to the fact that the federal courts have procedures for dealing with classified information, and prosecutors would not pursue these cases unless there was sufficient unclassified evidence to obtain convictions.

Critical Thinking Questions

1. What are the most important differences between civilian and military courts?
2. How should concerns for citizens' safety be weighed against the need to provide for a fair trial?
3. Should the relative success of the two court systems be considered when determining the most appropriate venue in which to try suspected terrorists?

or question suspects without having to show cause for doing so. The need to protect national security and gather foreign intelligence presents a special problem for Fourth Amendment protections. Endorsing the president's claim that he can authorize warrantless wiretaps and physical searches of agents of foreign countries, Congress created the Foreign Intelligence Surveillance Court to review requests for warrantless wiretaps. The court consists of federal district judges and meets in secret. The USA PATRIOT Act, of 2001 (Uniting and Strengthening America by Providing Appropriate Tools Required to Intercept and Obstruct Terrorism) expanded the size of the court, lowered the requirement to approve warrants in cases involving terrorism, and permits searches for foreign intelligence and evidence of terrorist activities. Congress overwhelmingly voted to extend the PATRIOT Act, and in February 2010, President Obama signed a one-year extension of the Act into law without additional protections for civil liberties sought by many Democrats. The extension continued to authorize "roving wiretaps" to monitor one individual's use of multiple communication devices.[86]

Although the U.S. Supreme Court is often seen as the guardian of our civil liberties and minority rights in the United States, the actions of the legislature and executive in fighting the war on terror make clear that the judiciary is not the only branch of government concerned with protecting liberties and it cannot do this work alone. In fact, some scholars contend that through the legislation it passes, Congress is as important as the Court in protecting individual liberties.[87] And, as we discussed in Chapter 10, the judiciary relies on the legislative and executive branches to enforce and provide funding to carry out its decisions. What does that imply for the role you play in protecting our civil liberties?

It is essential for citizens to be active in protecting our civil liberties. If we do not elect representatives who will uphold our civil liberties, enforce the Court's decisions, and appoint judges who will respect the individual guarantees in the Constitution, we cannot expect that they will be protected. Furthermore, if we do not act when we know civil liberties are being violated, the courts cannot make rulings. The judiciary is a reactive institution. It depends on individual citizens, or individuals working in cooperation through interest groups, to challenge government restrictions on civil liberties.

CHAPTER **SUMMARY**

11.1 Trace the roots of civil liberties in the original Constitution and their subsequent development in the Bill of Rights.

Antifederalists were concerned that the new national government would infringe on individual rights. Although many state constitutions already protected civil liberties, the Bill of Rights was to prevent the national government from infringing on civil liberties.

11.2 Outline the First Amendment freedoms and the limitations on them.

The First Amendment forbids the establishment of religion and also guarantees its free exercise. These two freedoms, however, are often in conflict with each other and represent conflicting notions of what is in the public interest. The Amendment also includes protections for speech, the press, and the right of assembly. However, each of these are limited: not all speech is protected, members of the press have no greater rights than do ordinary citizens, and the right to peaceably assemble is subject to reasonable time, place, and manner restrictions.

11.3 Explain how the Constitution protects property rights.

The framers saw private property rights as essential for maintaining a republican system of government. Although the government may take private property for public use, it must provide adequate compensation. And, even when the Constitution might allow such a "taking," the political process may prevent it.

11.4 Distinguish between procedural and substantive due process.

The Constitution imposes limits not only on the procedures government must follow but also on the ends it may pursue. Some actions are out of bounds no matter what procedures are followed. Legislatures have the primary role in determining what is reasonable and what is unreasonable. However, the Supreme Court exercises its own independent and final review of legislative determinations of reasonableness, especially on matters affecting civil liberties and civil rights.

11.5 Assess the kinds of behavior that may be covered by a constitutional right to privacy.

The right to privacy is implied by a number of the protections in the Bill of Rights, including protections against unreasonable searches and seizures, the protection against self-incrimination, and the right to associate (and not associate) with those you choose. It also protects a woman's right to terminate pregnancy and intimate relationships between consenting adults, regardless of sexual orientation.

11.6 Characterize the constitutional rights of criminal suspects.

The framers knew from their own experiences that in their zeal to maintain power and to enforce the laws, especially in wartime, public officials are often tempted to infringe on the rights of persons accused of crimes. To prevent such abuse, the Bill of Rights requires federal officials to follow detailed procedures in making searches and arrests and in bringing people to trial.

11.7 Evaluate the roles of institutions and the people in protecting civil liberties.

Although the judiciary is often seen as the guardian of civil liberties, it cannot carry out this function alone. Congress and the president also play an important role in protecting civil liberties through the laws they make and enforce. In addition, the judiciary is a reactive institution; without citizens who are willing to challenge improper restrictions on liberties, the courts are unable to act.

CHAPTER SELF-TEST

11.1 Trace the roots of civil liberties in the original Constitution and their subsequent development in the Bill of Rights.

1. Explain the Federalists' concerns about adding a Bill of Rights to the Constitution. Were those concerns warranted?
2. In a few sentences, explain the significance of *Gitlow* v. *New York* and how it relates to the term *selective incorporation.*
3. List the four amendments in the Bill of Rights of which *no* part has been applied to states through the application of the Fourteenth Amendment. Why do you think these have not been incorporated?

11.2 Outline the First Amendment freedoms and the limitations on them.

4. In a paragraph, explain the tension that exists between the establishment and free exercise clauses of the First Amendment.
5. List the four categories of speech presently considered "unprotected," and give a brief definition of each.
6. Briefly define *prior restraint,* and explain the Supreme Court's position on it.
7. Imagine you are a newspaper editor who has just received a reliable tip that a prominent political leader fathered a child outside marriage. After checking the source, you run the story and are subsequently sued by the political leader. Write a short response defending your choice based on information in the chapter.

11.3 Explain how the Constitution protects property rights.

8. Your local city council has decided to develop a city park in your neighborhood. They offer you the fair market value for your home. If you prefer to stay in your house, can the city force you to move? In one paragraph, explain why or why not.

11.4 Distinguish between procedural and substantive due process.

9. Briefly define and contrast *procedural* and *substantive due process.*

11.5 Assess the kinds of behavior that may be covered by a constitutional right to privacy.

10. Which of the following is *not* an aspect of the right to privacy?
    a. The right to be free from government surveillance and intrusion
    b. The right not to have the government make private affairs public
    c. The right to be free in thought and belief from governmental regulations
    d. The right to perform religious acts as dictated by conscience on private property
11. Based on a credible tip, police officers obtain a search warrant to search your home. Can you deny them entry into your home based on your right to privacy? Explain your answer in one paragraph.
12. Match each of the following court cases with the significant precedent in the decision.

a. *Roe* v. *Wade*	i. Reaffirmed a woman's right to an abortion
b. *Romer* v. *Evans*	ii. Struck down a law criminalizing homosexual sodomy
c. *Lawrence* v. *Texas*	iii. Upheld Georgia law making consensual sodomy a crime
d. *Bowers* v. *Hardwick*	iv. Extended right to privacy to abortions
e. *Planned Parenthood* v. *Casey*	v. Struck down a constitutional amendment that banned state and local governments in Colorado from protecting homo-sexuals from discrimination

11.6 Characterize the constitutional rights of criminal suspects.

13. In a few sentences, describe the *exclusionary rule* and how it applies to the evolution of Fourth Amendment rights.
14. In a short essay, explain the procedures for a fair trial.

11.7 Evaluate the roles of institutions and the people in protecting civil liberties.

15. Write a paragraph discussing the limitations on the judiciary's ability to protect our civil liberties.

Answers to selected questions: 10. d; 12. a: iv, b: v, c: ii, d: iii, e: i

mypoliscilab EXERCISES

Where participation leads to action!

Apply what you learned in this chapter with these resources on MyPoliSciLab.

Read on **mypoliscilab.com**

eText: Chapter 11

Study and **Review** on **mypoliscilab.com**

Pre-Test
Post-Test
Chapter Exam
Flashcards

Watch on **mypoliscilab.com**

Video: Funeral Protestors Push the Limits of Free Speech
Video: D.C.'s Right to Bear Arms

Explore on **mypoliscilab.com**

Simulation: You Are a Police Officer.
Simulation: You Are a Supreme Court Judge Deciding a Free Speech Case
Simulation: Balancing Liberty and Security in a Time of War
Comparative: Comparing Civil Liberties
Timeline: Civil Liberties and National Security

KEY **TERMS**

ADDITIONAL **RESOURCES**

FURTHER READING

JEFFREY ABRAMSON, *We, the Jury: The Jury System and the Ideal of Democracy* (Harvard University Press, 2000).

STUART BIEGEL, *Beyond Our Control? Confronting the Limits of Our Legal System in the Age of Cyberspace* (MIT Press, 2001).

JAMES MACGREGOR BURNS AND **STEWART BURNS,** *A People's Charter: The Pursuit of Rights in America* (Knopf, 1991).

DAVID COLE AND **JAMES X. DEMPSEY,** *Terrorism and the Constitution,* 3d ed. (New Press, 2006).

LEE EPSTEIN and **THOMAS WALKER,** *Constitutional Law for a Changing America: Rights, Liberties, and Justice,* 7th ed. (CQ Press, 2009).

LOUIS FISHER, *The Constitution and 9/11: Recurring Threats to America's Freedoms* (University Press of Kansas, 2008).

LOUIS FISHER, *Religious Liberty in America: Political Safeguards* (University Press of Kansas, 2002).

ROBERT JUSTIN GOLDSTEIN, *Flag Burning and Free Speech: The Case of Texas v. Johnson* (University Press of Kansas, 2002).

ROGER HOOD, *The Death Penalty: A Worldwide Perspective,* 3d ed. (Oxford University Press, 2002).

LEONARD W. LEVY, *Emergence of a Free Press* (Oxford University Press, 1985).

ANTHONY LEWIS, *Gideon's Trumpet* (Random House, 1964).

CATHARINE A. MACKINNON, *Only Words* (Harvard University Press, 1993).

ALEXANDER MEIKLEJOHN, *Political Freedom: The Constitutional Powers of the People* (Harper & Row, 1965).

J. W. PELTASON AND **SUE DAVIS,** *Understanding the Constitution,* 16th ed. (Harcourt, 2004).

SHAWN FRANCIS PETERS, *Judging Jehovah's Witnesses: Religious Persecution and the Dawn of the Rights Revolution* (University Press of Kansas, 2002).

WILLIAM H. REHNQUIST, *All the Laws but One: Civil Liberties in Wartime* (Knopf, 1998).

BARRY SCHECK, PETER NEUFELD, AND **JIM DWYER,** *Actual Innocence: Five Days to Execution, and Other Dispatches from the Wrongly Convicted* (Doubleday, 2000).

NADINE STROSSEN, *Defending Pornography: Free Speech, Sex, and the Fight for Women's Rights* (Scribner, 1995).

MELVIN UROFSKY, ED., *100 Americans Making Constitutional History* (CQ Press, 2005).

MARY E. VOGEL, *Coercion to Compromise: Plea Bargaining, the Courts, and the Making of Political Authority* (Oxford University Press, 2001).

WELSH S. WHITE, *Miranda's Waning Protections: Police Interrogation Practices After Dickerson* (University of Michigan Press, 2001).

WEB SITES

www.law.cornell.edu/anncon/index.html Congressional Research Service's Annotated U.S. Constitution. For each of the constitutional clauses, it describes the convention and/or ratification debate as well as court decisions dealing with the clause.

www.oyez.org Web site containing MP3 files of oral arguments before the U.S. Supreme Court in both current and historical cases. There also are links to other great Supreme Court resources.

www.deathpenaltyinfo.org The Death Penalty Information Center Web site. Up-to-date information on death penalty statistics in the United States, changing state laws concerning the death penalty, and data on its use internationally.

www.firstamendmentcenter.org The First Amendment Center is affiliated with Vanderbilt University and the Freedom Forum, a nonpartisan foundation supporting the First Amendment. Its Web site contains research and analysis on a multitude of First Amendment questions and cases.

CHAPTER 12

Civil Rights

Equal Rights Under the Law

In 2000, Elizabeth Brose finished eighth grade in Seattle, Washington; the next fall, she would start high school. Under her school district's student assignment plan, Elizabeth, a white student, asked the district to assign her to Ballard High School, a newly remodeled school in her neighborhood with an excellent reputation. But race determined her assignment, and Brose was sent to Franklin High instead, a school eight miles away from her home where nonwhite students made up approximately 70 percent of the student body. When schools received too many applications, the Seattle School District used an "integration tiebreaker" to make schools more reflective of the district's racial composition as a whole.[1] Ballard would have had a heavily white student population without the tiebreaker, which meant Brose had to be assigned to Franklin.[2]

In 1978, Seattle became the first major U.S. city to use busing to integrate schools without a court order. Its plans had continued since, and although they clearly had popular support, it was not uniform. Some parents, especially those whose children were not placed in their chosen school, were strongly opposed to the program. Karen Brose, Elizabeth's mother, formed Parents Involved in Community Schools, a group opposed to Seattle's plan, and pursued the case in the courts.

Parents Involved in Community Schools was successful in its challenge. On June 28, 2007, the U.S. Supreme Court struck down Seattle's plan, as well as a similar plan used in Louisville, Kentucky. In its sharply divided (5-to-4) opinion, the Court ruled that Seattle had not shown that the goal of racial integration justified the method it used, which relied solely on race (and race broadly construed as white and nonwhite) as *the* factor in the admissions decision without other individualized assessment. In his opinion in the case, Chief Justice Roberts wrote, "The way to stop discrimination on the basis of race is to stop discriminating on the basis of race."[3]

The Seattle case highlights the United States' continuing dilemma concerning how to best ensure equality, and how to do so without violating the Constitution's protection from discrimination based on race. In this case, Elizabeth Brose's **civil rights** were at issue—her right not to be discriminated against because of race, religion, gender, or ethnic origin. The Constitution protects civil rights in two ways. First, it ensures that government officials do not impermissibly discriminate against us; second, it grants national and state governments the power to protect these civil rights against interference by private individuals.

Although the Constitution does not make any reference to "equality" (the Declaration of Independence proclaims "that all men are created equal," but equality is not mentioned in the Constitution or in the original Bill of Rights), we know that the framers believed all men—at least all white adult men—were equally entitled to life, liberty, and the pursuit of happiness. Although it took many years for the concept of equality to be extended to all people, the framers did create a system of government designed to protect what they called *natural rights.* (Today, we speak of *human rights,* but the idea is basically the same.) As we discussed in Chapter 1, by **natural rights,** the framers meant that every person, by virtue of being a human being, has an equal right to protection against arbitrary treatment and an equal right to the liberties the Bill of Rights guarantees.

These rights do not depend on citizenship; governments do not grant them. They are the rights of *all people.* In this chapter, we examine the protection of our rights from abuse *by government,* and the protection *through government* of our right to be free from abuse by our fellow citizens.

We will begin this chapter by discussing citizenship rights in general. Although natural rights do not depend on citizenship, the kinds of protections that can be denied based on citizenship have become increasingly important in recent years. We then discuss several groups'

CHAPTER OUTLINE & CHAPTER LEARNING OBJECTIVES

Equality and Equal Rights

12.1 Explain the concept of equality and assess the rights of citizens.

The Quest for Equal Justice

12.2 Compare and contrast the efforts of various groups to obtain equal protection of the law.

Equal Protection of the Laws: What Does It Mean?

12.3 Analyze the Supreme Court's three-tiered approach used to evaluate discriminatory laws.

Voting Rights

12.4 Trace the evolution of voting rights and analyze the protections provided by the 1965 Voting Rights Act.

Rights to Equal Access: Accommodations, Jobs, and Homes

12.5 Describe congressional legislation against discrimination in housing, employment, and accommodations.

Education Rights

12.6 Evaluate the historical process of school integration and the current state of affirmative action.

Equal Rights Today

12.7 Assess the status of civil rights in the United States today.

efforts to secure their civil rights and examine what we mean by "equal protection of the law." In doing so, we will pay particular attention to two laws essential to securing civil rights protections: the Civil Rights Act of 1964 and the Voting Rights Act of 1965. Finally, we examine the controversy over affirmative action. We will see that the debate over civil rights is not over and that the way we deal with it today will direct the path of civil rights in the future.

Equality and Equal Rights

LEARNING **OBJECTIVE**

12.1 Explain the concept of equality and assess the rights of citizens.

Citizens of the United States are committed to equality. "Equality," however, is an elusive term. The concept of equality on which we have the greatest consensus is that everyone should have *equality of opportunity* regardless of race, ethnic origin, religion, and, in recent years, gender and sexual orientation.

There is not much equal opportunity if one person is born into a well-to-do family, lives in a safe suburb, and receives a good education, while another is born into a poor, broken family, lives in a run-down inner-city neighborhood, and attends inferior schools. Some argue that providing equalizing opportunities for the disadvantaged through federal programs such as Head Start, which helps prepare preschool children from poor families for elementary school, are necessary to bridge this gap.

Traditionally, we have emphasized *individual* achievement, but in recent decades, some politicians and civil rights leaders have focused attention on the concept of *equality between groups*. When large disparities in wealth and advantage exist between groups—as between black and white people or between women and men—equality becomes a highly divisive political issue. Those who are disadvantaged emphasize economic and social factors that exclude them from the mainstream. They champion programs like **affirmative action** that are designed to provide opportunities for those who have been disadvantaged because they belong to a certain group. As we will discuss later in this chapter, such programs have been and continue to be controversial.

Finally, equality can also mean *equality of results*. A perennial debate is whether social justice and genuine equality can exist in a nation in which people of one class have so much and others have so little, and in which the gap between them is growing wider.[4] There is considerable support for guaranteeing a minimum floor below which no one should be allowed to fall, but American adults generally do not support an equality of results.

civil rights
The rights of all people to be free from irrational discrimination such as that based on race, religion, gender, or ethnic origin.

natural rights
The rights of all people to dignity and worth; also called *human rights*.

affirmative action
Remedial action designed to overcome the effects of discrimination against minorities and women.

naturalization
A legal action conferring citizenship on an alien.

Citizenship Rights

Although natural rights do not depend on citizenship, important legal rights come with citizenship. Citizenship determines nationality and defines who is a member of, owes allegiance to, and is a subject of the nation. But in a constitutional democracy, citizenship is an *office*, and like other offices, it carries with it certain powers and responsibilities. How citizenship is acquired and retained is therefore important.

Proud naturalized citizens are sworn in at a Constitution Day naturalization ceremony. Many similar ceremonies are held throughout the year.

How Citizenship Is Acquired and Lost

The basic right of citizenship was not given constitutional protection until 1868, when the Fourteenth Amendment was adopted; before that, each state determined citizenship. The Fourteenth Amendment states, "All persons born or naturalized in the United States, and subject to the jurisdiction thereof, are citizens of the United States and of the State wherein they reside." This means that all persons born in the United States, except children born to foreign ambassadors and ministers, are citizens of this country regardless of the citizenship of their parents.

Naturalization People can also acquire citizenship by **naturalization,** a legal act conferring citizenship on an alien—someone who is living in the United States but is not

TABLE 12–1 Requirements for Naturalization

An applicant for naturalization must:

1. Be over the age of 18.
2. Be lawfully admitted to the United States for permanent residence and have resided in the United States for at least five years and in the state for at least six months.
3. File a petition of naturalization with a clerk of a court of record (federal or state) verified by two witnesses.
4. Be able to read, write, and speak English.
5. Possess a good moral character.
6. Understand and demonstrate an attachment to the history, principles, and form of government of the United States.
7. Demonstrate that he or she is well-disposed toward the good order and happiness of the country.
8. Demonstrate that he or she does not now believe in, nor within the last ten years has ever believed in, advocated, or belonged to an organization that supports opposition to organized government, overthrow of government by violence, or the doctrines of world communism or any other form of totalitarianism.

For more information about immigration and naturalization, go to the Web site of the Federation for American Immigration Reform at www.fairus.org.

■ *How might the United States determine whether a potential citizen is of a "good moral character"?*

a citizen. Congress determines naturalization requirements (see Table 12–1 for the list of requirements). Today, with minor exceptions, nonenemy aliens over the age of 18 who have been lawfully admitted for permanent residence and who have resided in the United States for at least five years and in the state for at least six months are eligible for naturalization. Any state or federal court in the United States or the Immigration and Naturalization Service (INS) can grant citizenship. The INS, with the help of the FBI, makes the necessary investigations. Any person denied citizenship after a hearing before an immigration officer may appeal to a federal district judge.

Dual Citizenship Because each nation has complete authority to define nationality for itself, two or more nations may consider a person a citizen. **Dual citizenship** is not unusual, especially for people from nations that do not recognize the right of individuals to renounce their citizenship, called the **right of expatriation.** Children born abroad to U.S. citizens may also be citizens of the nation in which they were born. Children born in the United States of parents from a foreign nation may also be citizens of their parents' country.

Rights of U.S. Citizens

A person becomes a citizen of one of the 50 states merely by residing in that state. *Residence* as understood in the Fourteenth Amendment means the place a person calls home. The legal status of residence is not the same as physical presence. A person may be living in Washington, D.C., but be a citizen of California—that is, consider California home and vote in that state.

Most of our most important rights flow from *state* citizenship. In the *Slaughter-House Cases* (1873), the Supreme Court carefully distinguished between the privileges of U.S. citizens and those of state citizens.[5] It held that the only privileges of national citizenship are those that "owe their existence to the Federal Government, its National Character, its Constitution, or its laws." These privileges have never been completely specified, but they include the right to use the navigable waters of the United States and to protection on the high seas, to assemble peacefully and petition for redress of grievances, to vote if qualified to do so under state laws and have your vote counted properly, and to travel throughout the United States.

In times of war, the rights and liberties of citizenship are tested and have been curbed. The Supreme Court overruled President Abraham Lincoln's use of military courts to try civilians during the Civil War,[6] but it upheld the World War II internment of Japanese Americans in "relocation camps"[7] and has approved the use of military tribunals to try captured foreign saboteurs[8] who were held abroad, but it ruled that citizens may not be subject to courts-martial or denied the guarantees of the Bill of Rights.[9]

In the war against international terrorism, President George W. Bush issued orders declaring U.S. citizens "enemy combatants" for plotting with the Al-Qaeda network and

dual citizenship
Citizenship in more than one nation.

right of expatriation
The right to renounce one's citizenship.

Although the Court upheld the internment of Japanese American citizens during World War II, it was later determined that the government had misrepresented information to the Court about the potential threat they posed. It was not until 1988 that the U.S. government officially apologized for its actions, and Congress awarded reparations to those interned during the war. ■ *Under what, if any, circumstances should the government be able to intern American citizens?*

authorized their and other captured foreign nationals' detention in military compounds, without counsel or access to a court of law. However, even in these cases, prisoners have a right to have their detention reviewed, and the Court's decision in *Boumediene* v. *Bush* (2008) reinforced this right. Even detainees designated as enemy combatants have the right to appeal their detention in the federal courts.[10] The tension over protecting citizens' rights while fighting the war on terror continued in the Obama Administration. Faisal Shahzad, a naturalized U.S. citizen, was arrested for attempting to detonate a car bomb in Times Square in May 2010. Under the Court's ruling in *Boumediene*, Shahzad's case was heard in the federal court system. Shahzad was indicted by a federal grand jury on 10 terror-related charges, several of which carried life sentences in federal prison. Shahzad pleaded guilty to each of the charges in Manhattan's federal district court. On October 5, 2010, U.S. District Court Judge Miriam Goldman Cedarbaum sentenced Shahzad to life in prison without the possibility of parole.

Rights of Resident Aliens

During periods of suspicion and hostility toward aliens, the protections of citizenship are even more precious. Congress enacted the Enemy Alien Act of 1798, which remains in effect, authorizing the president during wartime to detain and expel citizens of a country with which we are at war. U.S. citizens may not be expelled from the country, but aliens may be expelled for even minor infractions.[11] The Supreme Court also upheld the 1996 amendments to the Immigration and Naturalization Act, which require mandatory detention during deportation hearings of aliens accused of certain crimes,[12] though they may not be held longer than six months.[13]

Still, the Constitution protects many rights of *all persons* not only of American citizens. Only citizens may run for elective office, and their right to vote may not be denied, but all other rights are not so literally restricted. Neither Congress nor the states can deny to aliens the rights of freedom of religion or freedom of speech. Nor can any government deprive any person of the due process of the law or equal protection under the laws.[14]

However, Congress and the states may deny or limit welfare and many other kinds of benefits to aliens. Congress has denied most federally assisted benefits to illegal immigrants and has permitted states to deny them many other benefits, making an exception only for emergency medical care, disaster relief, and some nutrition programs. The Court has also upheld laws barring the employment of aliens as police officers, schoolteachers, and probation officers.[15] Although states have considerable discretion over what benefits they give to aliens, the Supreme Court has held that states cannot constitutionally exclude children of illegal immigrants from the public schools or charge their parents tuition.[16]

The Quest for Equal Justice

LEARNING **OBJECTIVE**

12.2 Compare and contrast the efforts of various groups to obtain equal protection of the law.

The rights of citizenship have been prominent throughout our country's history, but not all people in the United States were originally granted full rights of citizenship. Here, we review the political history and social contexts in which constitutional challenges to laws and other government actions relating to civil rights for women and minorities arose. This history involves more than court decisions, laws, and constitutional amendments, however. It encompasses the entire social, economic, and political system. And although the struggles of all groups are interwoven, they are not identical, so we deal briefly and separately with each.

Racial Equality

U.S. citizens had a painful confrontation with the problem of race at the time of the Civil War (1861–1865). As a result of the northern victory, the Thirteenth, Fourteenth, and Fifteenth Amendments became part of the Constitution. The Thirteenth Amendment ended slavery, the Fourteenth ensures that all people are treated equally and establishes citizenship, and the Fifteenth Amendment protects citizens' voting rights. During Reconstruction in the late 1860s and 1870s, Congress passed civil rights laws to implement these amendments and established programs to provide educational and social services for the freed slaves. But the Supreme Court struck down many of these laws, and it was not until the 1960s that legal progress was again made toward ensuring African Americans their civil rights.

Segregation and White Supremacy Before Reconstruction programs could have any significant effect, the white southern political leadership regained power, and by 1877, Reconstruction was ended. Northern political leaders abandoned African Americans to their fate at the hands of their former white masters; presidents no longer concerned themselves with enforcing civil rights laws, and Congress enacted no new ones. The Supreme Court either declared old laws unconstitutional or interpreted them so narrowly that they were ineffective. The Court also gave such a limited construction to the Thirteenth, Fourteenth, and Fifteenth Amendments that they failed to accomplish their intended purpose of protecting the rights of African Americans.[17]

For nearly a century after the Civil War, white supremacy went unchallenged in the South, where most African Americans then lived. They were kept from voting; they were forced to accept menial jobs; they were denied educational opportunities; they were segregated in public and private facilities.[18] Lynchings of African Americans occurred on an average of once every four days, and few white people raised a voice in protest.

During World War I (1914–1918), African Americans began to migrate to northern cities to seek jobs in war factories. The Great Depression of the 1930s and World War II in the 1940s accelerated their relocation. Although discrimination continued, more jobs became available, and African Americans made social gains. As their migration from the rural South shifted the racial composition of cities across much of the United States, the African American vote became important in national elections. These changes created an African American middle class opposed to segregation as a symbol of servitude and a cause of inequality. There was a growing demand to abolish color barriers, and by the mid-twentieth century, urban African Americans were active and gaining political clout.

Slow Government Response By the 1930s, African Americans were challenging the doctrine of segregation in the courts, and after World War II, civil rights litigation began to have a major impact. Beginning with the landmark 1954 ruling in *Brown* v. *Board of Education of Topeka,* the Supreme Court prohibited racially segregated public schools[19] and subsequently struck down most of the devices that state and local authorities had used to keep African Americans from voting.[20] We discuss *Brown* and voting rights in detail later in the chapter. Although the Court reached rulings ending segregation, achieving a significant level of desegregation would require the other branches of government to act.

In the late 1940s and 1950s, Presidents Harry S. Truman and Dwight D. Eisenhower used their executive authority to fight segregation in the armed services and the federal bureaucracy. They directed the Department of Justice to enforce whatever civil rights

A significant sign of integration was Jackie Robinson's debut with the Brooklyn Dodgers in 1947, breaking Major League Baseball's "color line." Robinson was active in the civil rights movement with the National Association for the Advancement of Colored People (NAACP) and its Freedom Fund Campaign. In 2005, he was posthumously awarded a Congressional Gold Medal, the highest honor a civilian can receive. ■ *How might breaking the "color line" in Major League Baseball affect other efforts to integrate society?*

laws were on the books, but Congress still held back. In the late 1950s, an emerging national consensus in favor of governmental action to protect civil rights, plus the political clout of African Americans in the northern states, began to influence Congress. In 1957, northern and western members of Congress from both parties overrode a southern filibuster in the Senate and enacted the first federal civil rights laws since Reconstruction, the Federal Civil Rights Act of 1957, which made it a crime to intimidate or threaten African Americans exercising their right to vote.

A Turning Point Even after the Supreme Court declared racially segregated public schools unconstitutional, most African Americans still went to segregated schools, and there was widespread resistance to integration in the South. As we discuss in detail later in the chapter, many legal barriers to equal rights had fallen, yet most African Americans still could not buy houses where they wanted, compete fairly for the jobs they needed, send their children to well-equipped schools, eat in "white" restaurants, or walk freely on the streets of "white neighborhoods."

Still, change began to come by way of a massive social, economic, and political movement. It began in Montgomery, Alabama, on December 1, 1955, when Rosa Parks, an African American seamstress, refused to give up her seat to a white man on a bus as the law required her to do. She was removed from the bus, arrested, and fined. The black community responded by boycotting city buses.

The boycott worked and also produced a charismatic national civil rights leader, the Reverend Martin Luther King Jr. Through his doctrine of nonviolent resistance, King gave a new dimension to the struggle. Following a peaceful 1963 demonstration in Birmingham, Alabama, that was countered with fire hoses, police dogs, and mass arrests, more than a quarter of a million people converged on Washington, D.C., to hear King and other civil rights leaders speak. By the time the summer was over, hardly a city, North or South, had not had demonstrations, protests, or sit-ins; some cities erupted in violence.

This direct action had an effect. Many cities enacted civil rights ordinances, more schools were desegregated, and President John F. Kennedy urged Congress to enact a comprehensive civil rights bill. Late in 1963, the nation's grief over the assassination of President Kennedy, who had become identified with civil rights goals, added political fuel to the drive for decisive federal action to protect civil rights.[21] President Lyndon B. Johnson made civil rights legislation his highest priority. On July 2, 1964, after months of debate, he signed into law the Civil Rights Act of 1964, which forbids discrimination on the basis of race, color, religion, sex, or nationality.[22]

Rosa Parks's decision not to give up her seat on the bus in Montgomery, Alabama, sparked a boycott by African Americans who, for more than a year, refused to ride the segregated city buses. Rosa Parks died in 2006. ■ *How did the doctrine of nonviolent resistance affect the civil rights movement?*

Congressman John Lewis (D-Ga.), then the chair of the Student Nonviolent Coordinating Committee, led civil rights activists in a 1965 march across the Edmund Pettus Bridge in Selma, Alabama. ■ *What effect did the response of the Alabama state police and other law enforcement officials have on the civil rights movement?*

At the End of the Edmund Pettus Bridge On November 4, 2008, American voters elected Barack Obama president of the United States, the first time an African American candidate has been elected to the office. The historic election was one where the candidates, more so than at any time in the past, represented the diversity of the United States electorate. As President-Elect Obama discussed in his victory speech, this diversity was a direct result of the hard-won successes in our country's long battle over race and gender equality. Indeed, Congressman John Lewis, a long-time civil rights activist who was beaten by Alabama state police as he marched across Selma's Edmund Pettus Bridge in 1965, remarked that "Barack Obama is what comes at the end of that bridge in Selma."[23]

Women's Rights

The 2008 election broke other barriers besides race. The Democrats' other major contender for the presidential nomination was Hillary Clinton, who would have been the first woman nominated by a major party for the presidency. Because of the historic nature of the Obama candidacy, less attention was paid to the fact that Senator Clinton was herself breaking barriers in her string of primary election victories and near majority of elected delegates. In 2008, Alaska governor Sarah Palin ran as the vice presidential candidate on the Republican ticket, the first Republican and only the second time a woman has gained her party's nomination for that office.

The Seneca Falls Women's Rights Convention (1848), which launched the women's movement, attracted men and women who actively campaigned to abolish slavery and to secure the rights of African Americans and women. But as the Civil War approached, women were urged to abandon their own cause and devote their energies to ending slavery.[24] The Civil War brought the women's movement to a halt.

By the turn of the twentieth century, however, a vigorous campaign was under way for **women's suffrage**—the right of women to vote. The first victories came in western states, where Wyoming led the way. But many suffragists were dissatisfied with this state-by-state approach. They wanted a decisive victory—a constitutional amendment that would force all states to allow qualified women to vote. Finally, in 1919, Congress proposed the Nineteenth Amendment. Many southerners opposed the amendment because it gave Congress enforcement power, which might bring federal officials to investigate elections and ensure that it was being obeyed—an interference that could call attention to how blacks were being kept from voting.

women's suffrage
The right of women to vote.

Women won the right to vote with the ratification of the Nineteenth Amendment in 1920, but they were still denied equal pay and equal rights, and national and state laws imposed many legal disabilities on them, such as the lack of comparable pay and health benefits. In the 1970s and 1980s, the unsuccessful struggle to secure the adoption of the Equal Rights Amendment occupied much of the attention of the women's movement. But now there are other goals, and women have mobilized their political clout behind issues that range from equal pay to world peace, an end to sexual harassment, abortion rights, and the election of more women to office.[25]

Susan B. Anthony and Elizabeth Cady Stanton were the two most influential leaders of the women's suffrage movement in the nineteenth century. ■ *Why might the women's suffrage movement have had early success in western states?*

Since the late 1980s, the Supreme Court has been reluctant to expand the same level of Fourteenth Amendment protection against gender discrimination as it has against racial discrimination. But it did hold that Virginia could not create a separate military academy for women instead of admitting them into the all-male Virginia Military Institute, a 150-year-old state-run institution.[26]

And the courts have increasingly enforced the prohibition against sex discrimination in the 1964 Civil Rights Act and expanded it to forbid sexual harassment in the workplace. In 1986, the Court applied the Act to "quid pro quo" sexual harassment, in which an employer requires sexual favors from a person as a condition of employment (in hiring, promotions, and firing).[27] It has since ruled that the Act also forbids a "hostile environment," defined as a workplace "permeated" with intimidation, ridicule, and insult that is severe and pervasive, and this includes same-sex harassment.[28]

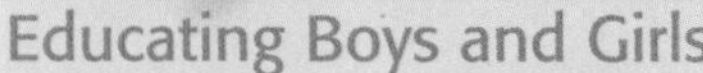

THE GLOBAL COMMUNITY

Educating Boys and Girls

Education is often seen as a necessary precondition to ensure equal opportunities for all members of society. A Pew Global survey asked respondents, "Which of the following statements comes closest to your opinion about educating children? It is more important for boys than girls, it is more important for girls than boys, or it is equally important for boys and girls."

Throughout the world, there is widespread consensus that it is important to provide educational opportunities for both boys and girls. In Western democracies such as Britain and the United States, this is particularly the case. In each country, 98 percent of respondents indicated that education was equally important for both boys and girls. Japanese respondents also indicated a very high level of support for equal educational opportunities; 95 percent of respondents thought education was equally important for both boys and girls.

Although there is general consensus on providing education to both boys and girls, there is some variation in the degree of that support. In China and India, 89 and 86 percent of respondents, respectively, indicated that education was important to both boys and girls. Even in regions of the world where there have not traditionally been educational opportunities for girls, such as in Nigeria, a full 84 percent of respondents indicated that it was equally important to provide these opportunities for both boys and girls, although there is still a fair number of respondents who indicate that it is more important to educate boys (14 percent).

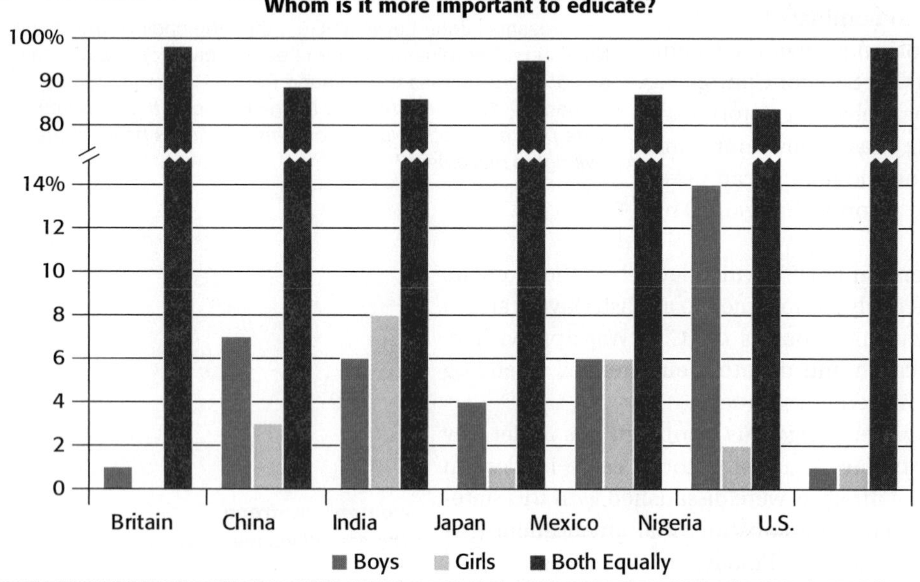

CRITICAL THINKING QUESTIONS

1. Why do you think some respondents indicated that it was more important to educate girls than boys?
2. Is it equally important that boys and girls should be educated together? Or, are separate educational facilities for boys and girls just as valuable as integrated facilities?
3. Is political equality possible without equal educational opportunities?

Many women still feel that a "glass ceiling" in large corporations prevents their advancement. But major progress has been made, with more and more women going to graduate and professional schools and into the media and business. Indeed, during the past three decades, more women have graduated from colleges and universities than men (see Figure 12–1).

Hispanics

The struggle for civil rights has not been limited to women and African Americans. Throughout U.S. history, many native-born citizens have considered new waves of immigrants suspect, especially if the newcomers were not white or English-speaking. Formal barriers of law and informal barriers of custom combined to deny equal rights to immigrants. But as groups established themselves—first economically and then politically—most barriers were swept away, and the newcomers or their children enjoyed the same constitutionally guaranteed rights as other citizens.

In many parts of the United States, Hispanics have not been able to translate their numbers into comparable political clout because of political differences among them and because many are not citizens or registered to vote. However, after California adopted Proposition 187 in 1994, which denied medical, educational, and social services to illegal immigrants, and Congress amended the federal welfare laws to curtail benefits to noncitizens, many immigrants rushed to become naturalized. Half of all Hispanic Americans live in

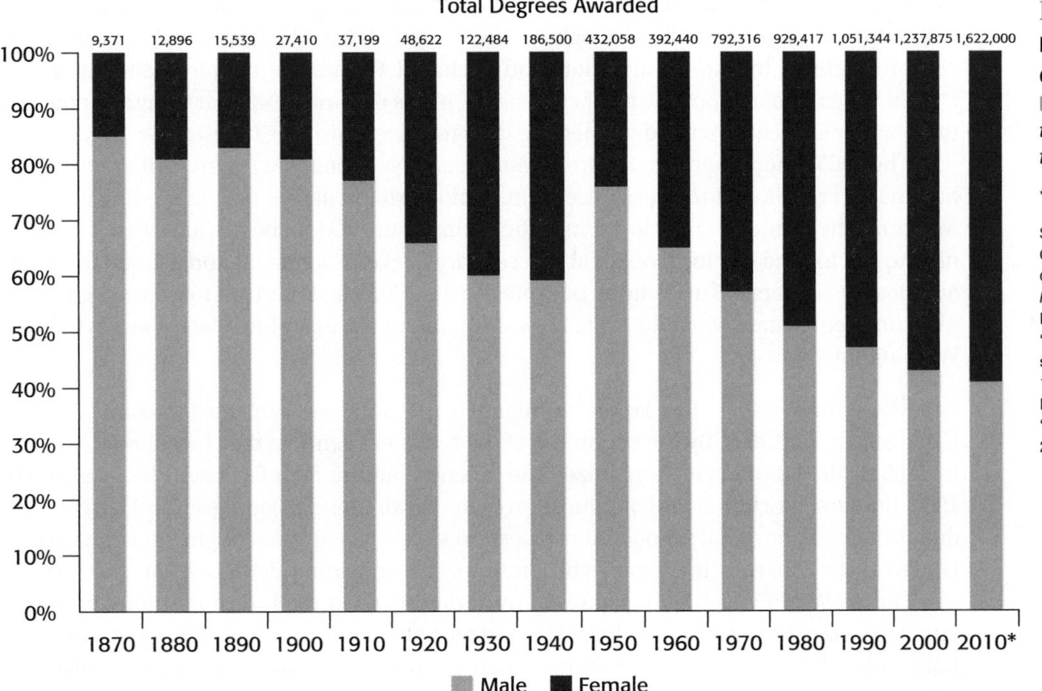

FIGURE 12–1 Percentage of Bachelor's Degrees Awarded, by Gender.

■ *What factors might affect the variation in men's college attendance from the 1920s through the 1950s?*

* Projected Data.

SOURCE: U.S. Department of Education, National Center for Education Statistics, *Earned Degrees Conferred*, 1869–1870 through 1964–1965; *Projections of Education Statistics to 2016;* Higher Education General Information Survey (HEGIS), "Degrees and Other Formal Awards Conferred" surveys, 1965–1966 through 1985–1986; and 1986–1987 through 2005–2006, Integrated Postsecondary Education Data System, "Completions Survey" (IPEDS-C:87–99), and Fall 2000 through Fall 2006.

two states: California and Texas. In 2001, California became the first big state in which white people are in the minority, and Texas followed in 2005; a majority of the population are racial minorities (majority-minority) in Hawaii, New Mexico, and the District of Columbia as well.[29]

The difficulty Hispanics have had in gaining political clout at the state level was highlighted in April 2010 as the Arizona legislature enacted immigration reform that was widely viewed as the broadest and strictest in generations. The law makes it a crime to fail to carry immigration documentation and authorizes law enforcement officials to detain anyone whom they suspect of being in the country illegally.[30] The law was immediately met with criticism, including remarks by President Obama, who called for federal immigration reform.

Arizona Governor Jan Brewer signs a controversial bill aimed at identifying, prosecuting, and deporting illegal immigrants. ■ *What factors might contribute to current concerns about illegal immigration?*

Asian Americans

The term "Asian American" describes approximately 10 million people from many different countries and ethnic backgrounds. Most do not think of themselves as Asians but as U.S. citizens of Chinese, Japanese, Indian, Vietnamese, Cambodian, Korean, or other specific ancestry. Although Asian Americans are often considered a "model minority" because of their successes in education and business, the U.S. Civil Rights Commission found in 1992 that "Asian Americans do face widespread prejudice, discrimination, and barriers to equal opportunity" and that racially motivated violence against them "occurs with disturbing frequency."[31] Discrimination against Asian Americans is, unfortunately, nothing new. The Naturalization Act of 1906, for example, made it impossible for any Asian American to become a U.S. citizen. Although the Act was challenged, the Supreme Court upheld its provision that only white persons and aliens of African nativity or descent were eligible for citizenship.[32]

Chinese Americans The Chinese were the first Asians to come to the United States. Beginning in 1847, when young male Chinese peasants came to the American West to escape poverty and to work in mines, on railroads, and on farms, the Chinese encountered economic and cultural fears by the white majority, who did not understand their language or their culture. Chinese Americans were recruited by the Central Pacific Railroad to work on the transcontinental railroad, but anti-Chinese sentiment grew. By the 1870s, attacks on "Chinatowns" began in cities throughout the United States. The Chinese Exclusion Act of 1882 restricted Chinese immigration and excluded Chinese immigrants already in the United States from the possibility of citizenship. It was not until 1943 that Congress repealed the Chinese Exclusion Act and opened the door to citizenship for Chinese Americans.

The 1965 amendments to the Immigration and Nationality Act went further to end the nationality criteria and thus equalize immigration criteria across race and ethnicity. Since that time, the Chinese have moved into the mainstream of U.S. society, and they are beginning to run for and win local political offices. Gary Locke, a Democrat and a graduate of Yale and Boston University Law School, became the first Chinese American to become governor of a continental state when, in 1996, he was elected to the first of two terms as governor of Washington.

Japanese Americans The Japanese migrated first to Hawaii in the 1860s and then to California in the 1880s. By the beginning of the twentieth century, they faced overt hostility. In 1905, white labor leaders organized the Japanese and Korean Exclusion League, and in 1906, the San Francisco Board of Education excluded all Chinese, Japanese, and Korean children from neighborhood schools. Some western states passed laws denying the right to own land to aliens who were ineligible to become citizens—meaning aliens of Asian ancestry.

During World War II, anti-Japanese hysteria provoked the internment of West Coast Japanese—most of whom were loyal U.S. citizens guilty of no crimes—in prison camps in California, Colorado, and other states. Their property was often sold at deep discount rates, and many of them lost their businesses, jobs, and incomes. Although Japanese Americans challenged the curfews and internment policies, the U.S. Supreme Court upheld the government's actions. In *Korematsu* v. *United States* (1944), the Court ruled that under the threat to national security, it could not reject congressional and military judgment that disloyalty existed and must be segregated.[33] Following the war, the exclusionary acts were repealed, though discrimination against Japanese Americans persisted, such as the limits placed on Japanese American student enrollment at many colleges and universities. In 1988, President Ronald Reagan signed a law providing $20,000 restitution to each of the approximately 60,000 surviving World War II internees.

Other Asian Americans Like other Asian Americans, Koreans faced overt discrimination in jobs and housing, but a Korean middle class has been growing, with many Korean Americans becoming teachers, doctors, and lawyers.[34]

When Filipinos first came to the United States in the early twentieth century, they were considered U.S. nationals because the Philippine Islands were a U.S. possession. Nonetheless, they were denied rights to full citizenship and faced discrimination and even violence, including anti-Filipino riots in the state of Washington in 1928 and later in California, where nearly one-third of the more than 1.5 million Filipinos in the United States live.[35] Their economic status has improved, but their influence in politics remains as small as their numbers.

The newest Asian arrivals consist of more than a million refugees from Vietnam, Laos, and Cambodia, who first came to the United States in the 1970s and settled mostly in California and Louisiana. Although this group included middle-class people who left Vietnam after the communist victory there in 1975, it also consisted of many "boat people," so called because they fled Vietnam in small boats, arriving in the United States without financial resources. In a relatively short time, most of these new Asian Americans established themselves economically. Although they are starting to have political influence, some remain socially and economically segregated.

Congressman Anh "Joseph" Cao (R-La.) escaped to the United States from Vietnam in 1975. He represents Louisiana's 2nd Congressional District. ■ *How might having greater representation of minority groups in Congress affect the kind of policy that is enacted?*

Native Americans

Nearly half of the more than 2 million Native Americans in the United States live on or near a *reservation*—a tract of land given to the tribal nations by treaties with the federal government—and are enrolled as members of one of the 550 federally recognized tribes, including 226 groups in Alaska.[36] Native Americans speak approximately 200 different languages, although most also speak English.

The history of discrimination against Native Americans in the United States is a great stain on our human rights record. Although discrimination against African Americans often gets more attention in civil rights discussions, legally sanctioned discrimination against Native Americans followed a similar path. Efforts to forcibly move Native American tribes off their land and farther west as more whites migrated to the Midwest and western states are well known. The Indian Removal Act, passed in 1830, required that all Native American tribes be moved from the East and Southeast. The Act also authorized the use of force to meet its goals. It is estimated that 4,000 of the 18,000 Cherokee Indians forced to move west into what became eastern Oklahoma in the late 1830s died on the "Trail of Tears."[37]

Native American rights organizations, including the American Indian Movement, protested discrimination against Native Americans in housing, employment, and health care. Over time, other civil rights groups, such as the American Civil Liberties Union (ACLU), have joined the fight to protect Native American civil rights. Currently pending suits allege discrimination against Native Americans in the public schools, as well as in the U.S. Department of Agriculture's farm-loan programs.

As a result of these efforts and of a greater national consciousness, most citizens are now aware that many Native Americans continue to face discrimination and live in poverty. Unemployment on many reservations continues to be 50 to 60 percent. Some reservations lack adequate health care facilities, schools, housing, and jobs. Congress has started to compensate Native Americans for past injustices and to provide more opportunities to develop tribal economic independence, and judges are showing greater vigilance in enforcing Indian treaty rights.

Equal Protection of the Laws: What Does It Mean?

LEARNING **OBJECTIVE**

12.3 Analyze the Supreme Court's three-tiered approach used to evaluate discriminatory laws.

The **equal protection clause** of the Fourteenth Amendment declares that no state (including any subdivision thereof) shall "deny to any person within its jurisdiction the equal protection of the laws." Although no parallel clause explicitly applies to the national government, courts have interpreted the Fifth Amendment's **due process clause,** which states that no person shall "be deprived of life, liberty, or property, without due process of law," to impose the same restraints on the national government as the equal protection clause imposes on the states.

Note that the clause applies only to the actions of *governments,* not to those of private individuals. If a private person performs a discriminatory action, that action does not violate the Constitution. Instead, it may violate federal and state laws passed to protect people from irrational discrimination by private parties.

The equal protection clause does not, however, prevent governments from discriminating in all cases. What the Constitution forbids is *unreasonable* classifications. In general, a classification is unreasonable when there is no relationship between the classes it creates and permissible governmental goals. A law prohibiting redheads from voting, for example, would be unreasonable. In contrast, laws denying persons under the age of 18 the right to vote, to marry without the permission of their parents, or to apply for a driver's license appear to be reasonable (at least to most persons over the age of 18).

equal protection clause
A clause in the Fourteenth Amendment that forbids any state to deny to any person within its jurisdiction the equal protection of the laws. By interpretation, the Fifth Amendment imposes the same limitation on the national government. This clause is the major constitutional restraint on the power of governments to discriminate against persons because of race, national origin, or sex.

due process clause
A clause in the Fifth Amendment limiting the power of the national government; a similar clause in the Fourteenth Amendment prohibits state governments from depriving any person of life, liberty, or property without due process of law.

Constitutional Classifications and Tests

One of the most troublesome constitutional questions is how to distinguish between constitutional and unconstitutional classifications. The Supreme Court uses three tests for this purpose: the *rational basis* test, the *strict scrutiny* test, and the *heightened scrutiny* test.

rational basis test
A standard developed by the courts to test the constitutionality of a law; when applied, a law is constitutional as long as it meets a reasonable government interest.

strict scrutiny test
A test applied by the court when a classification is based on race; the government must show that there is a compelling reason for the law and no other less restrictive way to meet the interest.

heightened scrutiny test
This test has been applied when a law classifies based on sex; to be upheld, the law must meet an important government interest.

The Rational Basis Test The traditional test to determine whether a law complies with the equal protection requirement—the **rational basis test**—places the burden of proof on the parties attacking the law. They must show that the law has no rational or legitimate governmental goals. Recall from Chapter 11 that when the court reviews the government's reason for legislating, it engages in substantive due process. Traditionally, the rational basis test applied only to legislation affecting economic interests and, with two exceptions in the last 70 years, the Court has upheld the legislation and deferred to legislative judgments.[38] But recently, the Court has applied the test when noneconomic interests are challenged.[39]

Suspect Classifications and Strict Scrutiny When a law is subject to the **strict scrutiny test,** the burden is on the government to show that there is both a "compelling governmental interest" to justify such a classification and no less restrictive way to accomplish this compelling purpose. The Court applies the strict scrutiny test to suspect classifications. A *suspect classification* is one through which people have been deliberately subjected to severely unequal treatment or that society has used to render people politically powerless.[40] When a law classifies based on race or national origin, the legislation immediately raises a red flag regardless of whether it is intended to aid or inhibit a particular race or nationality. For example, the Supreme Court has held that laws that give preference for public employment based on race are subject to strict scrutiny.

Quasi-Suspect Classifications and Heightened Scrutiny To sustain a law under the **heightened scrutiny test,** the government must show that its classification serves "important governmental objectives." Heightened scrutiny is a standard first used by the Court in 1971 to declare classifications based on gender unconstitutional. As Justice William J. Brennan Jr. wrote for the Court, "There can be no doubt that our nation has had a long and unfortunate history of sex discrimination. Traditionally, such discrimination was rationalized by an attitude of 'romantic paternalism,' which in practical effect put women, not on a pedestal, but in a cage."[41] In recent years, the Supreme Court has struck down most laws brought before it that were alleged to discriminate against women but has tended to do so on the basis of federal statutes like the 1964 Civil Rights Act (for other legislation, see Table 12–2).

TABLE 12–2 Major Civil Rights Laws

• Civil Rights Act, 1957	Makes it a federal crime to prevent persons from voting in federal elections.
• Civil Rights Act, 1964	Bars discrimination in employment or in public accommodations on the basis of race, color, religion, sex, or national origin; created the Equal Employment Opportunity Commission.
• Voting Rights Act, 1965	Authorizes the appointment of federal examiners to register voters in areas with a history of discrimination.
• Age Discrimination in Employment Act, 1967	Prohibits job discrimination against workers or job applicants aged 40 through 65 and prohibits mandatory retirement.
• Fair Housing Act, 1968	Prohibits discrimination on the basis of race, color, religion, or national origin in the sale or rental of most housing.
• Title IX, Education Amendment of 1972	Prohibits discrimination on the basis of sex in any education program receiving federal financial assistance.
• Rehabilitation Act, 1973	Requires that recipients of federal grants greater than $2,500 hire and promote qualified handicapped individuals.
• Fair Housing Act Amendments, 1988	Gave the Department of Housing and Urban Development authority to prohibit housing bias against the handicapped and families with children.
• Americans with Disabilities Act, 1990	Prohibits discrimination based on disability and requires that facilities be made accessible to those with disabilities.
• Civil Rights Act, 1991	Requires that employers justify practices that negatively affect the working conditions of women and minorities or show that no alternative practices would have a lesser impact. Also established a commission to examine the "glass ceiling" that keeps women from becoming executives and to recommend how to increase the number of women and minorities in management positions.

■ *Do you think the "glass ceiling" still exists? Why or why not?*

Poverty and Age Just as race and sex classifications receive elevated scrutiny, some argue that economic and age classification ought to be subject to some heightened review. The Supreme Court rejected the argument "that financial need alone identifies a suspect class for purposes of equal protection analysis."[42] However, some state supreme courts (Texas, Ohio, and Connecticut) have ruled that unequal funding for public schools, as a result of "rich" districts spending more per pupil than "poor" districts, violates their state constitutional provisions for free and equal education.[43]

Age is not a suspect classification. Many laws make distinctions based on age to obtain a driver's license, to marry without parental consent, to attend schools, to buy alcohol or tobacco, and so on. Many governmental institutions have age-specific programs: for senior citizens, for adult students, and for people in mid-career. As Justice Sandra Day O'Connor observed, "States may discriminate on the basis of age without offending the Fourteenth Amendment if the age classification in question is rationally related to a legitimate state interest."[44]

Nevertheless, Congress has attempted to extend the protections against age discrimination to cover state employees, but the Supreme Court ruled that Congress lacks the constitutional authority to open the federal courts to suits by state employees for alleged age discrimination. State employees are limited to recovering monetary damages under state laws in state courts.[45]

Sexual Orientation In 1996, the U.S. Supreme Court struck down an initiative amending the Colorado Constitution that prohibited state and local governments from protecting homosexuals from discrimination.[46] The Court ruled in *Romer* v. *Evans* that this provision violated the equal protection clause because it lacked any rational basis and simply represented prejudice toward a particular group. Although in cases like *Romer* (1996) and *Lawrence* v. *Texas* (2003), discussed in Chapter 11, the Court found that state laws based on sexual orientation violated the U.S. Constitution, it has not elevated the level of scrutiny with which it reviews such classifications. However, as we discuss in the "You Will Decide" box, several state courts have ruled that their own state constitutions require at least the right to legal recognition of same-sex civil unions. The supreme courts of Massachusetts, California, Connecticut, and Iowa have gone even further to determine that their state constitutions require that marriage be open to same-sex as well as different-sex couples. Although the California Supreme Court's decision was negated by California voters in the 2008 election, a case challenging the CA initiative (Proposition 8) as a violation of the U.S. Constitution's equal protection clause is currently making its way through the federal courts.

Other countries provide more extensive protections from discrimination based on sexual orientation. The United Kingdom's Civil Partnership Act, which went into effect in December 2005, provides same-sex couples with the same Social Security and pension benefits, parental responsibility for partners' children, and next of kin rights in hospitals as married heterosexuals.[47] Mexico also prohibits discrimination based on sexual orientation, and same-sex unions are now recognized in Mexico City.[48] However, in other countries, homosexual behavior is a crime punishable by long prison sentences (in India) or by death (in Nigeria).[49]

Fundamental Rights and Strict Scrutiny The Court also strictly scrutinizes laws impinging on *fundamental rights.* What makes a right fundamental in the constitutional sense? It is not the importance or the significance of the right but whether it is explicitly or implicitly *guaranteed by the Constitution.* Under this test, the rights to travel and to vote have been held to be fundamental. Rights to education, to housing, or to welfare benefits have not been deemed fundamental. Important as they may be, no constitutional provisions specifically protect them from governmental regulation.

As mentioned previously, the Constitution, particularly the Fourteenth Amendment's equal protection clause, is only one of the legal bases for civil rights protections in the United States. Although we often think of court decisions when we think of the civil rights movement, many of the courts' rulings that upheld the civil rights of racial minorities and women were based on congressional legislation. Two pieces of legislation were particularly important to the civil rights movement: the Voting Rights Act of 1965 and the Civil Rights Act of 1964. We turn to these next.

Shelly Bailes and Ellen Pontac, who have been together for 34 years, were the first same-sex couple to marry in Yolo County, California, on June 16, 2008, after the California Supreme Court overturned a state statute banning same-sex marriage. On November 4 of that year, California voters passed Proposition 8, which amended the state constitution to bar same-sex marriage. However, the constitutionality of Proposition 8 is being challenged in the federal courts. A federal district court ruled that the proposition violated the 14th Amendment to the U.S. Constitution. The ruling is under appeal (*Perry* v. *Schwarzenegger*).

Voting Rights

LEARNING **OBJECTIVE**

12.4 Trace the evolution of voting rights and analyze the protections provided by the 1965 Voting Rights Act.

Under our Constitution, the states, not the federal government, regulate elections and voting qualifications. However, Article I, Section 4, gives Congress the power to supersede state regulations as to the "Times, Places, and Manner" of elections for representatives and senators. Congress has used this authority, along with its authority under Article II, Section 2, to set the date for selecting electors, to set age qualifications and residency requirements to vote in national elections, to establish a uniform day for all states to hold elections for members of Congress and presidential electors, and to give citizens who live outside the United States the right to vote for members of Congress and presidential electors in the states in which they are legal residents.

In spite of these protections, officials seeking to deny African Americans the right to vote developed biased registration requirements and even turned to intimidation and violence. Reports of violence and intimidation against black voters were frighteningly prevalent. One representative from Alabama described the efforts to deprive blacks of the right to vote this way: "At first, we used to kill them to keep them from voting; when we got sick of doing that, we began to steal their ballots; and when stealing their ballots got to troubling our consciences, we decided to handle the matter legally, fixing it so they couldn't vote."[51]

In many southern areas, **literacy tests** were used to discriminate against African Americans. Although poor white people often avoided registering out of fear of embarrassment from failing a literacy test, the tests were more often used to discriminate against African Americans.[52] White people were often asked simple questions; black people were asked questions that would baffle a Supreme Court justice. "In the 1960s, southern registrars were observed testing black applicants on such matters as the number of bubbles in a soap bar, the news contained in a copy of the Peking Daily, the meaning of obscure passages in state constitutions, and the definition of terms such as habeas corpus."[53] In Louisiana, 49,603 illiterate white voters were able to persuade election officials that they could understand the Constitution, but only two illiterate black voters were able to do so.

literacy test
A literacy requirement some states imposed as a condition of voting, generally used to disqualify black voters in the South; now illegal.

Local officials were also able to keep black voters from participating through the use of the **white primary.** In the one-party South of the early twentieth century, the Democratic party would hold whites-only primaries, effectively disenfranchising black voters because, in the absence of viable Republican candidates, the winner of the Democratic primary was guaranteed to win the general election.

white primary
A Democratic party primary in the old "one-party South" that was limited to white people and essentially constituted an election; ruled unconstitutional in *Smith* v. *Allwright* (1944).

YOU WILL DECIDE Should Marriage Be Limited to Heterosexual Couples?

On May 15, 2008, the California Supreme Court ruled that denying same-sex couples the opportunity to marry violated the state's constitutional guarantee of equal protection. The state supreme court's decision was immediately challenged by opponents who placed a constitutional amendment banning same-sex marriage on the 2008 ballot. The measure was narrowly approved by voters. However, that has not ended the legal battle. Citizens challenged the amendment, and the Federal District Court in the Northern District of California has struck down the ballot measure, ruling that it violates the 14th amendment's guarantee of equal protection under the law. That ruling is being appealed.

Proponents of same-sex marriage cite Supreme Court rulings that have upheld marriage as a fundamental right under the U.S. Constitution.[50] Under these rulings, supporters contend, depriving same-sex couples of the right to marry violates the basic concept of liberty. Others argue that same-sex marriage will provide the same sort of benefits to the community—having stable, caring families and children with two parents—as does heterosexual marriage.

Opponents of same-sex marriage feel equally strongly that such unions should be prohibited by law. They argue that allowing same-sex marriage will lessen the value of marriage and result in fewer heterosexual marriages. Furthermore, they argue that while heterosexual marriage furthers the state's legitimate interest in procreation, same-sex marriage does not and thus need not be sanctioned by the state.

California was only the second state to allow same-sex marriage. In November 2003, the Massachusetts Supreme Court held that the state constitution's guarantees of equality and due process were violated by a ban on same-sex marriage. On October 10, 2008, Connecticut's Supreme Court invalidated the state's civil union law to become the third state to legalize same-sex marriage. Iowa followed suit in April 2009. In the same month, Vermont became the first state to legalize same-sex marriage through the legislative process. New Hampshire did the same in June 2009. In December 2009, the District of Columbia also legalized same-sex marriage. In other states and localities, propositions and constitutional amendments providing for same-sex civil unions or barring any legal recognition of same-sex unions have been strongly debated.

What do you think? Should marriage be limited to heterosexual couples? What are the arguments for or against it?

THINKING IT THROUGH

The rights of homosexuals in the United States have never received the heightened protection against discrimination applied to classifications made on the basis of race or sex. The Court has ruled that government needs only a reasonable basis for legislating in order to permissibly classify individuals based on sexual orientation. Traditionally, legislation meant to uphold basic values and morals would pass such a test, and those opposed to same-sex marriage contend that it endangers the traditional notion of marriage and the value of the family unit. However, the Court, in *Romer* v. *Evans* (1996), struck down a Colorado constitutional amendment that made a distinction based on sexual orientation by ruling that it did not pass the test of rationality or reasonableness.

Opponents of same-sex marriage also object to state supreme courts' rulings on the basis of judicial activism (discussed in Chapter 10). Many opponents of state court decisions argue that same-sex marriage is not an issue for the courts to decide; instead, they contend, it should be decided through the democratic process, as it was in Vermont and New Hampshire.

Echoing arguments heard in the civil rights era, many who favor the right of same-sex couples to marry say that just as laws barring interracial marriage were declared to violate the Constitution's Fourteenth Amendment equal protection clause (in *Loving* v. *Virginia*, 1967), so do laws barring same-sex marriage. Supporters argue that once states provide an opportunity for legal recognition of marriage, they must do so equally. Although civil unions, an option provided for in four states (New Jersey, Washington, Oregon, and Nevada), typically offer many of the benefits afforded to married couples, they do not provide the equal recognition and legal rights of marriage.

Critical Thinking Questions

1. Why are state courts such an important part of the debate on same-sex marriage?
2. Why is the issue of same-sex marriage so hotly debated? What makes this issue such a difficult one?
3. When voters and courts disagree over a topic such as same-sex marriage, who should prevail?

Protecting Voting Rights

After years of refusing to overturn racially discriminatory voting requirements, the Supreme Court in the 1940s began to strike down one after another of the devices that states and localities had used to keep African Americans from voting. In *Smith* v. *Allwright* (1944), the Court declared the white primary unconstitutional.[54] Later, it struck down other methods. In 1960, the Court held that **racial gerrymandering**—drawing election districts to ensure that African Americans would be a minority in all districts—was contrary to the Fifteenth Amendment.[55] We discuss legislative redistricting in greater detail in Chapter 7. In 1964, the Twenty-Fourth Amendment eliminated the **poll tax**—payment required as a condition for voting—in presidential and congressional elections. In 1966, the Court held that the Fourteenth Amendment forbade the poll tax as a condition in any election.[56]

racial gerrymandering
The drawing of election districts so as to ensure that members of a certain race are a minority in the district; ruled unconstitutional in *Gomillion* v. *Lightfoot* (1960).

poll tax
Tax required to vote; prohibited for national elections by the Twenty-Fourth Amendment (1964) and ruled unconstitutional for all elections in *Harper* v. *Board of Elections* (1966).

By the People
MAKING A DIFFERENCE

Protecting Student Voting Rights

Concern over student voting rights dates back to the 1940s and 1950s, when some states such as Kentucky and Georgia granted voting rights to 18-year-olds.* The Twenty-Sixth Amendment, which was ratified in 1971, grants all 18- to 21-year-old citizens the right to vote. There was substantial interest in increasing turnout among young voters in the 2008 presidential elections, and much of this effort was focused on college students. Throughout the United States, college students were urged to register to vote, and many sought to do so from their college campuses.

However, some states have strict residency and identification requirements that make it difficult for students to vote. Leading up to the 2008 election, congressional hearings were held to investigate reports that college students had been told they could not vote in the state in which they were attending college if their parents had claimed them as a dependent in another state.† Other reports included a local election official misleading students that registering to vote in their college town might result in losing their residency-based scholarships.‡

What efforts are made to encourage student voter registration on your college campus? In Ohio, Secretary of State Jennifer Bruner developed a Web site to assist students in the registration process whether they attend college in the place where they are a permanent resident or whether they are Ohio residents who attend college out of state and want to vote there.$ Do you have something similar in your state or through your college? Check your school's Web site and find out what you need to do to vote in the next election and help to protect students' voting rights. If you have more time, you might even become involved in a student voting registration campaign. Rock the Vote has volunteer Street Teams and Student Public Interest Research Groups (PIRGs) organize efforts to encourage student voting throughout the United States. You could get involved in PIRG's New Voters Project** or start up a group of your own.

CRITICAL THINKING QUESTIONS

1. Why might some local political leaders prefer it if college students did not vote in their local elections?
2. Why might you prefer to vote where you go to college instead of in your hometown?
3. Should voting rights be extended to 16-year-olds? Why or why not?

* Thomas H. Heale, "The Eighteen-Year-Old Vote: The Twenty-Sixth Amendment and Subsequent Voting Rates of Newly Enfranchised Age Groups" *Congressional Research Service,* May 20, 1983.

† "Members of Congress Worry That Students Are Being Misled About Voting Rights," *Chronicle of Higher Education,* September 24, 2008.

‡ Nikki Schwab, "Confusing Voter Registration Laws Could Affect Presidential Election," *US News and World Report,* September 24, 2008.

$ www.sos.state.oh.us/SOS/CollegeResources.aspx.

** www.studentpirgs.org/new-voters-project/#.

majority-minority district
A congressional district created to include a majority of minority voters; ruled constitutional so long as race is not the main factor in redistricting.

The Voting Rights Act of 1965

For two decades after World War II, under the leadership of the Supreme Court, many limitations on voting were declared unconstitutional, but as has often been the case, the Court acting alone was unable to open the voting booth to African Americans. Finally, Congress acted in passing the Voting Rights Act of 1965. It was renewed in 1982, and in 2006, it was extended for another 25 years.

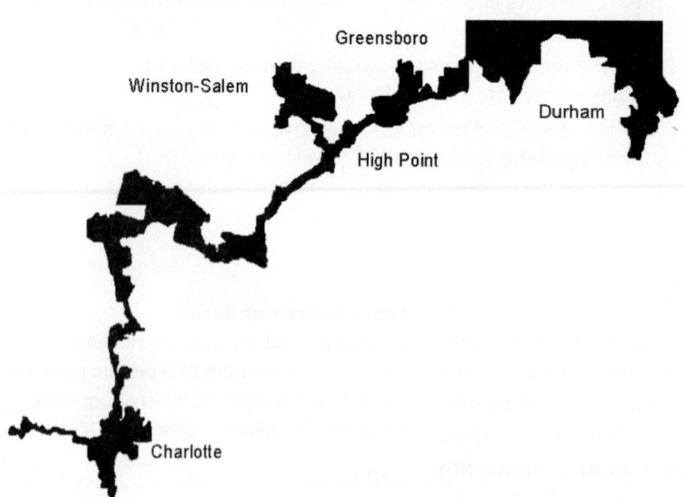

North Carolina's challenged "I-85 district" stretched more than 160 miles through the central region of the state. ■ *What changes did North Carolina have to make to comply with the Voting Rights Act?*

The Voting Rights Act prohibits voting qualifications or standards that result in a denial of the right of any citizen to vote on account of race and color. It also bars any form of threats or intimidation aimed at preventing citizens from voting. Under the Act, the Department of Justice must also review changes in voting practices or laws that may dilute the voting power of these groups,[57] such as changes in candidacy requirements and qualifications or boundary lines of voting districts.[58] The requirement that states obtain Justice Department clearance was recently challenged in the federal courts. But in June 2009, the U.S. Supreme Court upheld the requirement.[59]

In a series of cases beginning with *Shaw* v. *Reno* (1993), the Supreme Court announced that state legislatures could consider race when they drew electoral districts to increase the voting strength of minorities. However, the Court ruled that states could not make race the sole or predominant reason for drawing district lines. A test case examined the North Carolina legislature's creation of a **majority-minority district** that was 160 miles long and in some places only an interstate highway wide. The Supreme Court ruled that it was wrong to force states to create as many majority-minority districts as possible. To comply with the Voting Rights Act, the Court explained, states must provide for districts roughly proportional to the minority voters' respective shares in the voting-age population.[60]

Rights to Equal Access: Accommodations, Jobs, and Homes

LEARNING **OBJECTIVE**

12.5 Describe congressional legislation against discrimination in housing, employment, and accommodations.

In 1883, the Supreme Court had declared unconstitutional an act of Congress that made it a federal offense for any operator of a public conveyance (such as a train or bus), hotel, or theater to deny accommodations to any person because of race or color, on the grounds that the Fourteenth Amendment does not give Congress such authority.[61] Until the Supreme Court finally moved to strike down such laws in the 1950s, southern states had made it illegal for white and black people to ride in the same train cars, attend the same theaters, go to the same schools, be born in the same hospitals, drink from the same water fountains, or be buried in the same cemeteries. **Jim Crow laws,** as they came to be called, blanketed southern life.

The Court reinforced legalized segregation under the Fourteenth Amendment's equal protection clause in *Plessy* v. *Ferguson* (1896). In the *Plessy* decision, the Supreme Court endorsed the view that government-imposed racial segregation in public transportation, and presumably in public education, did not necessarily constitute discrimination if "equal" accommodations were provided for the members of both races.[62] But the "equal" part of the formula was meaningless. African Americans were segregated in unequal facilities and lacked the political power to protest effectively.

Beginning in the 1960s, however, Congress began to act to prevent such segregation. Its constitutional authority to legislate against discrimination by private individuals is no longer an issue because the Court has broadly construed the **commerce clause**—which gives Congress the power to regulate interstate and foreign commerce—to justify action against discriminatory conduct by individuals. Congress has also used its power to tax and spend to prevent not only racial discrimination but also discrimination based on ethnic origin, sex, disability, and age.

Civil Rights Act of 1964 and Places of Public Accommodation The key step in establishing rights of equal access was the Civil Rights Act of 1964. Title II of the Act makes it a federal offense to discriminate against any customer or patron in a place of public accommodation because of race, color, religion, or national origin. It applies to any inn, hotel, motel, or lodging establishment (except those with fewer than five rooms and where the proprietor also lives—in other words, small boardinghouses); to any restaurant or gasoline station that serves interstate travelers or sells food or products that are moved in interstate commerce; and to any movie house, theater, concert hall, sports arena, or other place of entertainment that customarily hosts films, performances, athletic teams, or other sources of entertainment that are moved in interstate commerce. Within a few months after its adoption, the Supreme Court sustained the constitutionality of Title II.[63] As a result, public establishments, including those in the South, opened their doors to all customers.

Civil Rights Act of 1964 and Employment In addition to dealing with equal access in public accommodations, the Civil Rights Act also barred discrimination in employment. Title VII of the 1964 Act made it illegal for any employer or trade union in any industry affecting interstate commerce and employing 15 or more people (and, since 1972, any state or local agency such as a school or university) to discriminate in employment practices against any person because of race, color, national origin, religion, or sex. Employers must create workplaces that avoid abusive environments. Related legislation made it illegal to discriminate against persons with physical handicaps, veterans, or persons over the age of 40.

Jim Crow laws
State laws formerly pervasive throughout the South requiring public facilities and accommodations to be segregated by race; ruled unconstitutional.

commerce clause
The clause of the Constitution (Article I, Section 8, Clause 3) that gives Congress the power to regulate all business activities that cross state lines or affect more than one state or other nations.

For the People

GOVERNMENT'S GREATEST ENDEAVORS

Reducing Workplace Discrimination

The United States has one of the most diverse workforces in the world. As diversity has grown, so have calls for protection against workplace discrimination. Many of these calls have been answered by the federal judiciary, where women, older Americans, and the disabled have won a series of victories ensuring their basic rights. But the courts did not act alone. These victories also involved congressional action through the 1964 Civil Rights Act, the 1967 Age Discrimination Act, and the 1990 Americans with Disabilities Act. Together, these three acts have created protections that have made reducing workplace discrimination one of the federal government's greatest achievements.

The 1964 Civil Rights Act was particularly important for guaranteeing equal rights for women. Under the original bill, women were not included in the law. Ironically, it was a conservative Democrat who added the word "sex" to the prohibition against discrimination on the basis of "race, color, religion, or national origin" in the Act. He did so in the belief that Congress would not pass a bill guaranteeing equality of the sexes. However, the bill did pass, and women had the legislation that would provide the opportunity to take employers to court for sex discrimination.

Disabled Americans won similar protection under the 1990 Americans with Disabilities Act. The fight for passage was led by Senator Bob Dole (R-Kans.), who had lost the use of his right arm in World War II. In addition to providing protection from discrimination, this Act also mandates that all public buildings and transportation be handicap accessible.

CRITICAL THINKING QUESTIONS

1. Are there other forms of workplace discrimination that should be protected but currently are not?
2. Might some victims of workplace discrimination be hesitant to bring a suit against their employers?
3. Sexual orientation is not listed in the Civil Rights Act. Should it be illegal to discriminate on the basis of sexual orientation?

A worker at Delaware's Industries for the Blind sews desert scarves for the U.S. military.

There are a few exceptions. Religious institutions such as parochial schools may use religious standards. Employers may take into account the age, sex, or handicap of prospective employees when occupational qualifications are absolutely necessary to the normal operation of a particular business or enterprise—for example, hiring only women to work in women's locker rooms.

The Equal Employment Opportunity Commission (EEOC) was created under the Act to enforce Title VII. The commission works together with state authorities to try to ensure compliance with the Act and may seek judicial enforcement of complaints against private employers. The attorney general prosecutes Title VII violations by public agencies. Not only can aggrieved persons sue for damages for themselves, but they can also sue for other persons similarly situated in a **class action suit.** For example, a pending class action lawsuit against Walmart alleges that the company discriminates against women in promotions and pay. The vigor with which the EEOC and the attorney general have acted has varied throughout the years, depending on the commitment of the president and the willingness of Congress to provide an adequate budget for the EEOC.[64]

class action suit
A lawsuit brought by an individual or a group of people on behalf of all those similarly situated.

restrictive covenant
A provision in a deed to real property prohibiting its sale to a person of a particular race or religion. Judicial enforcement of such deeds is unconstitutional.

The Fair Housing Act and Amendments Housing is the last frontier of the civil rights crusade, the area in which progress is slowest and genuine change most remote. Even after legal restrictions on segregated housing have been removed, housing patterns continue to be segregated. The degree to which housing also affects segregation in employment and the public schools makes it a particularly important issue. In 1948, the Supreme Court made racial or religious **restrictive covenants** (a provision in a deed to real property that restricts to whom it can be sold) legally unenforceable.[65] The 1968 Fair Housing Act forbids discrimination in housing, with a few exceptions similar to those mentioned in public accommodations. Owners may not refuse to sell or rent to any person because of race, color, religion, national origin, sex, or physical handicap or because a person has children. Discrimination in housing also covers efforts to deny mortgage loans to minorities.

The Department of Justice has filed hundreds of cases, especially against large apartment complexes, yet African Americans and Hispanics still face discrimination in housing. Some real estate agents steer African Americans and Hispanics toward neighborhoods that are not predominantly white and require minority renters to pay larger deposits than white renters. Yet victims complain about less than 1 percent of these actions because discrimination is so subtle that they are often unaware they are being discriminated against. However, more aggressive enforcement has increased the number of discrimination complaints the Department of Housing and Urban Development and local and state agencies receive.

Education Rights

LEARNING **OBJECTIVE**

12.6 Evaluate the historical process of school integration and the current state of affirmative action.

After the Court's decision in *Plessy*, segregated public as well as private facilities—such as schools, buses, and bathrooms—became the norm. However, in the late 1930s, African Americans started to file lawsuits challenging *Plessy*'s "separate but equal" doctrine. The National Association for the Advancement of Colored People's (NAACP) Legal Defense Fund (LDF) was active in challenging segregated educational facilities. The LDF cited facts to show that, in practice, separate was anything but equal and generally resulted in discrimination against African Americans.

Initially, the LDF showed that so-called equal facilities were in fact not equal, or simply not provided. Many of their early successes addressed inequality in higher education. States were forced to either provide separate graduate and law schools for African American students or integrate those they already had. A major success that laid the groundwork for the LDF's challenge in public secondary and elementary schools came when the Court ruled that not only did segregated facilities themselves have to be equal, but they also had to provide the same quality of benefits to black students as to their white counterparts.[66]

The End of "Separate but Equal": *Brown* v. *Board of Education*

Once the LDF had adequately established that segregated facilities were far from equal, it challenged the *Plessy* doctrine of "separate but equal" head on. And in *Brown* v. *Board of Education of Topeka* (1954), the Court finally agreed, ruling that "separate but equal" is a contradiction in terms. *Segregation is itself discrimination.*[67]

The question before the Court in *Brown* was whether separate public schools for black and white students violated the Fourteenth Amendment's equal protection clause. Relying heavily on arguments addressing the harm to all schoolchildren, black and white, caused by racial segregation, the Court struck down segregation in the public schools and, in so doing, overturned *Plessy* v. *Ferguson* (1896). A year later, the Court ordered school boards to proceed with "all deliberate speed to desegregate public schools at the earliest practical date."[68]

But many school districts moved slowly or not at all, and in the 1960s, Congress and the president joined even more directly to fight school segregation. Title VI of the Civil Rights Act of 1964, as subsequently amended, stipulated that federal dollars under any grant program or project must be withdrawn from an entire school or institution of higher education (including private schools) that discriminates "on the ground of race, color, or national origin," gender, age, or disability, in "any program or activity receiving federal financial assistance."

From Segregation to Desegregation—But Not Yet Integration

School districts that had operated separate schools for white children and black children now had to develop plans and programs to move from segregation to integration. Schools failing to do so were placed under court supervision to ensure that they were doing what was necessary and proper to overcome the evils of segregation. Simply doing away with laws mandating segregation would not be enough; school districts needed to actively integrate their schools.

Thurgood Marshall (center), George C. E. Hayes (left), and James Nabrit Jr. (right) argued and won *Brown* v. *Board of Education of Topeka* before the Supreme Court in 1954. ■ *Why do you think the NAACP Legal Defense Fund's strategy of using litigation to end segregation in education was successful?*

But because most white people and most African Americans continued to live in separate neighborhoods, merely removing legal barriers to school integration did not by itself integrate the schools. To overcome this residential clustering by race, some federal courts mandated busing across neighborhoods, moving white students to once predominantly black schools and vice versa. Busing students was unpopular and triggered protests in many cities.

The Supreme Court sustained busing only if it was undertaken to remedy the consequences of *officially* sanctioned segregation, **de jure segregation.** The Court refused to permit federal judges to order busing to overcome the effects of **de facto segregation,** segregation that arises as a result of social and economic conditions such as housing patterns.

After a period of vigorous federal court supervision of school desegregation programs, the Supreme Court in the 1990s restricted the role of federal judges.[69] It instructed some of them to restore control of a school system to the state and local authorities and to release districts from any busing obligations once a judge concludes that the authorities "have done everything practicable to overcome the past consequences of segregation."[70]

Political support for busing and for other efforts to integrate the schools also faded.[71] Many school districts eliminated mandatory busing, with the result that *Brown*'s era of court-ordered desegregation drew to a close. As a result, the percentage of southern black students attending white-majority schools fell from a high of 44 percent in 1988 to 30 percent in 2001, or approximately the same level it had been in 1969.[72] In the wake of such resegregation, some school districts have attempted to increase integration through race-conscious admission plans such as the Seattle plan discussed at the beginning of the chapter. Another method some schools have pursued, which has the benefit of presumptive constitutionality, is integration based on socioeconomic factors rather than race.[73]

de jure segregation
Segregation imposed by law.

de facto segregation
Segregation resulting from economic or social conditions or personal choice.

Of the People

AMERICA'S CHANGING FACE

Racial and Ethnic Diversity in U.S. Public Elementary and Secondary Schools

Since the 1970s, U.S. public schools as a whole have become more diverse. Over time, the percentage of white student enrollment in the public schools has dropped more than 20 percentage points, from 78 percent of schoolchildren between kindergarten and twelfth grade to slightly under 56 percent of the student population. The biggest increase for any minority group is certainly among Hispanic students, whose percentage of the student population has increased by more than 14 percentage points. One of many advantages of attending diverse schools is that students learn firsthand about different cultures. Furthermore, diverse education opportunities lead to increased interaction between racial groups as adults.*

However, as you can see by looking at the data by region, this diversity is not evenly distributed across all areas of the country. In the West, for example, white students do not even make up the majority of the student population, and the Hispanic student population is twice as large as it is in any other region. Because of these kinds of regional differences, as well as differences among school districts, often based on housing patterns, the increasing level of diversity across the student population is not necessarily reflected in individual schools or districts.

CRITICAL THINKING QUESTIONS

1. Why does diversity in the public school population vary by region?
2. Why have our public schools as a whole become more diverse over time?
3. Did the diversity in your school district reflect the overall diversity in your region of the country?

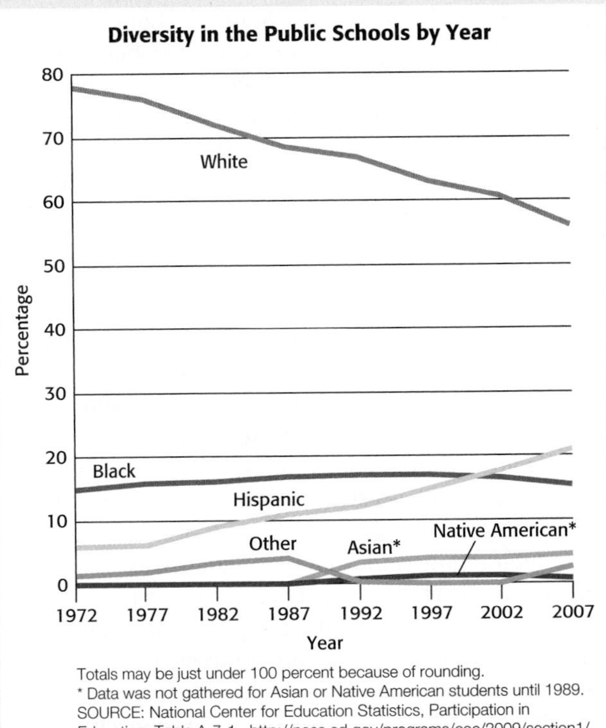

Totals may be just under 100 percent because of rounding.
* Data was not gathered for Asian or Native American students until 1989.
SOURCE: National Center for Education Statistics, Participation in Education, Table A-7-1, http://nces.ed.gov/programs/coe/2009/section1/table-1er-1.asp.

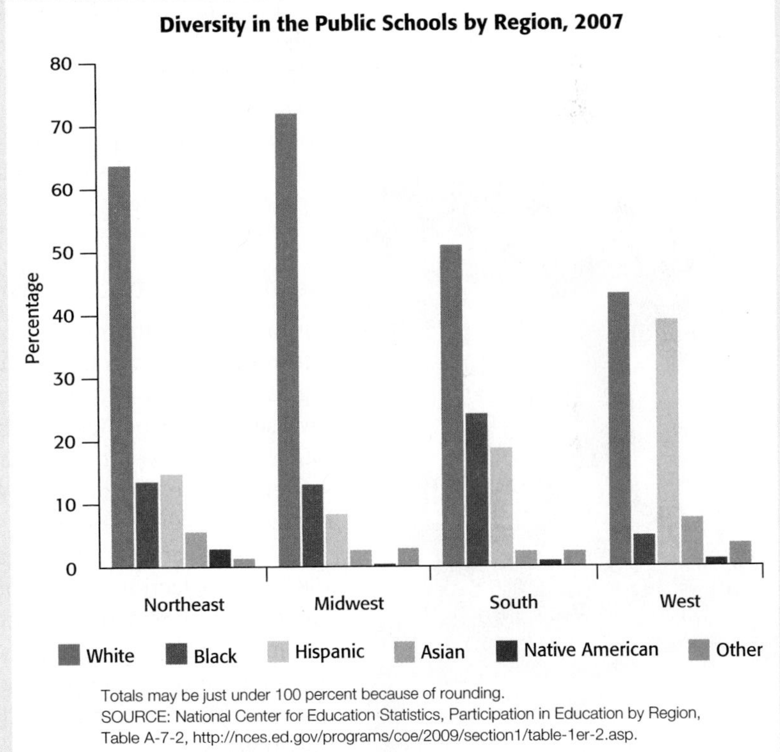

Totals may be just under 100 percent because of rounding.
SOURCE: National Center for Education Statistics, Participation in Education by Region, Table A-7-2, http://nces.ed.gov/programs/coe/2009/section1/table-1er-2.asp.

* U.S. Commission on Civil Rights, "The Benefits of Racial and Ethnic Diversity in Elementary and Secondary Education, November 2006, http://www.usccr.gov/pubs/112806diversity.pdf.

The Affirmative Action Controversy

When white majorities were using government power to discriminate against African Americans, civil rights advocates cited with approval the famous words of Justice John Marshall Harlan when he dissented from the *Plessy* decision: "Our Constitution is color-blind and neither knows nor tolerates class among citizens."[74] But by the 1960s, a new set of constitutional and national policy debates raged. Many people began to assert that government neutrality is not enough. If governments, universities, and employers simply stopped discriminating but nothing else changed, individuals previously discriminated against would still be kept from equal participation in U.S. life. Furthermore, when barriers to equality in education and employment advancement exist, we all suffer from a lack of diversity in society. Because discrimination had so disadvantaged some people and groups, they suffered disabilities that white males did not share in competing for openings in medical schools, for skilled jobs, or for their share of government grants and contracts.

Supporters call remedies to overcome the consequences of discrimination against African Americans, Hispanics, Native Americans, and women *affirmative action;* opponents call these efforts *reverse discrimination.* The Supreme Court's first major statement on the constitutionality of affirmative action programs came in a celebrated case relating to university admissions. Allan Bakke—a white male, a top student at the University of Minnesota and at Stanford, and a Vietnam War veteran—applied in 1973 and again in 1974 to the medical school of the University of California at Davis. In each of those years, the school admitted 100 new students, 84 in a general admissions program and 16 in a special admissions program created for minorities who had previously been underrepresented. Bakke was rejected in both years, while applicants with lower grade-point averages, test scores, and interview ratings were admitted through the special admissions program. Bakke brought suit in federal court, claiming he had been excluded because of his race, contrary to requirements of the Constitution and Title VI of the Civil Rights Act of 1964.

In *University of California Regents* v. *Bakke* (1978), the Supreme Court ruled the California plan unconstitutional[75] because it created a *quota*—a set number of admissions from which whites were excluded solely because of race. But the Court also declared that affirmative action programs are not necessarily unconstitutional. A state university may properly take race and ethnic background into account as "a plus," as one of several factors in choosing students because of its compelling interest in achieving a diverse student body.

Americans debate whether affirmative action is the best way to address the issue of past racial and ethnic quotas. ■ *Why has the Supreme Court upheld the use of race as part of and individualized assessment in university admissions?*

Reaffirming the Importance of Diversity

For many years following the *Bakke* decision, the Court refused to hear challenges to affirmative action in higher education, despite conflicting lower-court decisions leading to confusion and uncertainty about how colleges and universities could pursue diverse student bodies. The Supreme Court clarified the matter in 2003, reaffirming *Bakke* in two cases that challenged the admission policies for undergraduates and law students at the University of Michigan. Both policies sought to achieve diverse student bodies but in different ways.

The University of Michigan's undergraduate admissions program was based on a 150-point "selection index" that ranked applicants' test scores and grades for up to 100 points and allocated 40 points for other factors, including 4 points for children of alumni, 16 points for residents of rural areas, and 20 points for students from underrepresented minority groups or socially and economically disadvantaged families. Jennifer Gratz, a white high school student with a 3.8 GPA who was denied admission, challenged the program.

In *Gratz* v. *Bollinger* (2003), the Court struck down the policy as too mechanical and not narrowly tailored to giving applicants "individualized consideration" as *Bakke* required.[76] However, a bare majority of the Court upheld the University's law school admissions program that was also challenged. In *Grutter* v. *Bollinger* (2003), the Court ruled that the law school made "special efforts" to achieve racial and ethnic diversity, but unlike the undergraduate program, it did not use a point system based in part on race.[77] Writing for the Court, Justice O'Connor held that law school admissions were based on a "highly individualized, holistic review of each applicant's file" and did not use race as a factor in a "mechanical way." For that reason, it was consistent with *Bakke*'s holding that race may be used as a "plus factor" to achieve a diverse student body.

Although the Court further clarified the requirements to render an affirmative action program permissible, its ruling did not end the debate. We have seen that the Court does not always have the final word on such questions. Motivated groups have spurred consideration of affirmative action programs at the polls, and several states have abolished affirmative action. Michigan is one example. In the aftermath of the Court's ruling in *Gratz* and *Grutter*, Jennifer Gratz formed the Michigan Civil Rights Initiative to place on the state's 2006 election ballot an initiative banning affirmative action in public colleges and government contracting. The initiative won approval with 58 percent of the vote.[78] In addition to effectively nullifying the Supreme Court's decision as it applied to the University of Michigan, the initiative's success also highlights a motivated group of citizens' success in mobilizing the electorate.

California's Proposition 209 and Other Plans

Michigan is not alone in its efforts to end affirmative action through the democratic process. In 1995, the Regents of the University of California voted to eliminate race or gender as factors in employment, purchasing, contracting, or admissions. The following year, Californians voted overwhelmingly for Proposition 209 to amend the state constitution to forbid state agencies to discriminate against or grant preferential treatment to any individual or group on the basis of race, sex, color, ethnicity, or national origin in public employment, public education, or public contracting, except where necessary to comply with a federal requirement.

Seven other states (Texas, Louisiana, Mississippi, Georgia, Florida, Washington, and Nebraska) have also abandoned affirmative action programs—some like California, Michigan, and Washington because of voter opposition, and others like Texas and Georgia because federal courts held that such programs were unconstitutional.[79] Some have also opted for a strategy of automatic admissions for a certain percentage of all high school graduates to maintain diversity in colleges and expand educational opportunities for minorities. California offers admission to the top 4 percent of high school graduates, Texas to the top 10 percent, and Florida to the top 20 percent.

Jennifer Gratz (right) was the successful plaintiff in *Gratz* v. *Bollinger*; Barbara Grutter (left) was unsuccessful in challenging the University of Michigan law school's admission program, which the Supreme Court upheld due to its individualized approach. ■ *Why did the Court uphold the University of Michigan's law school program but strike down its undergraduate admission program?*

Equal Rights Today

LEARNING **OBJECTIVE**

12.7 Assess the status of civil rights in the United States today.

Today, civil rights legislation, executive orders, and judicial decisions have lowered, if not fully removed, legal barriers to full and equal participation in society. Important as these victories are, according to civil rights leader James Farmer, "They were victories largely for the middle class—those who could travel, entertain in restaurants, and stay in hotels. Those victories did not change life conditions for the mass of blacks who are still poor."[80]

As prosperous middle-class African Americans have moved out of inner cities, the remaining black *underclass*, as they have been called, has become even more isolated from the rest of the nation.[81] There are similar trends in Hispanic communities in Los Angeles, Dallas, and Houston.[82] Children are growing up on streets where drug abuse and crime are everyday events. They live in "separate and deteriorating societies, with separate economies, diverging family structures and basic institutions, and even growing linguistic separation within the core ghettos. The scale of their isolation by race, class, and economic situation is much greater than it was in the 1960s, with impoverishment, joblessness, educational inequality, and housing insufficiency even more severe."[83]

Some contend that we should pay attention to the plight of the underclass, and that instead of focusing on issues of race, we need to focus on class differences and support policies that provide jobs and improve education.[84] Others say there has to be a revival of the civil rights crusade, a restoration of vigorous civil rights enforcement, more job training, and, above all, an attack on residential segregation.[85] In any event, questions about how best to provide equal opportunities for all citizens remain high on the national agenda.

One of the many important lessons of the civil rights movement is that individuals can affect our government process. Without people like Rosa Parks, one woman sitting on a bus who refused to give up her seat, or Karen Brose, who fought for her daughter's right to attend her school of choice without regard to her race, we would not have experienced the monumental changes in our country's protection of all citizens' rights that we have seen during the last 100 years. By participating in our democratic system and challenging the status quo, we each play a part in promoting equal rights for all citizens.

CHAPTER **SUMMARY**

12.1 Explain the concept of equality and assess the rights of citizens.

Although there is no one agreed-upon definition of equality in the United States, there is general consensus that everyone should have an equal opportunity to succeed. The Constitution protects the acquisition and retention of citizenship. It protects the basic liberties of citizens as well as aliens, although in times of war, foreign terrorists may be detained and tried without the rights accorded to citizens and other aliens.

12.2 Compare and contrast the efforts of various groups to obtain equal protection of the law.

Although African Americans' rights were finally recognized under the Thirteenth, Fourteenth, and Fifteenth Amendments, the government failed to act to prevent racial discrimination for nearly a century thereafter. The women's rights movement was born partly out of the struggle to abolish slavery, and the women's movement learned and gained power from the civil rights movements of the 1950s and early 1960s. Concern for equal rights under the law continues today for African Americans and women as well as other groups, including Hispanics, Asian Americans, and Native Americans.

12.3 Analyze the Supreme Court's three-tiered approach used to evaluate discriminatory laws.

The Supreme Court uses a three-tiered approach to evaluate the constitutionality of laws that may violate the equal protection clause. The Court upholds most laws if they simply help accomplish a legitimate government goal. It sustains laws that classify people based on sex only if they serve important government objectives. It subjects laws that touch fundamental rights or classify people because of race or ethnic origin to strict scrutiny and sustains them only if the government can show that they serve a compelling public purpose.

12.4 Trace the evolution of voting rights and analyze the protections provided by the 1965 Voting Rights Act.

A series of constitutional amendments, Supreme Court decisions, and laws passed by Congress have now secured the right to vote to all citizens age 18 and older. Following the Voting Rights Act of 1965, the Justice Department can oversee practices in locales with a history of discrimination. Recent Supreme Court decisions have refined the lengths to which legislatures can go, or are obliged to go, in creating majority-minority districts.

12.5 Describe congressional legislation against discrimination in housing, employment, and accommodations.

By its authority under the interstate commerce clause (Article 1, Section 8), Congress has passed important legislation barring discrimination in housing and accommodations. The Civil Rights Act of 1964 outlawed discrimination in public accommodations. This Act also provided for equal employment opportunity. The Fair Housing Act of 1968 and its 1988 amendments prohibited discrimination in housing.

12.6 Evaluate the historical process of school integration and the current state of affirmative action.

Brown v. *Board of Education of Topeka* (1954) struck down the "separate but equal" doctrine that had justified segregated schools, but school districts responded slowly. Full integration has proved elusive, as many white citizens have left the inner cities, and their schools, predominantly black or Hispanic.

The desirability and constitutionality of affirmative action programs that benefit members of groups subjected to past discrimination divide the nation and the Supreme Court. Remedial programs tailored to overcome specific instances of past discrimination are likely to pass the Supreme Court's suspicion of classifications based on race, national origin, and sex. The Court has also reaffirmed the importance of diversity in education and employment.

12.7 Assess the status of civil rights in the United States today.

Legal barriers to full and equal participation in American society have been largely eliminated. However, the fight to protect civil rights of women and minority groups continues. Some argue that in continuing to meet the challenges of inequality, we should focus on economic integration, job training, and better education opportunities.

CHAPTER **SELF-TEST**

12.1 Explain the concept of equality and assess the rights of citizens.

1. Naturalization requires new citizens to do all the following *except:*
   a. be able to read, write, and speak English.
   b. agree never to renounce their new citizenship.
   c. understand and have an attachment to the history and principles of the government of the United States.
   d. demonstrate they do not believe in, advocate, or belong to an organization that advocates violent overthrow of the government.
2. Americans determined to be enemy combatants in the war on terror have _________.
   a. to be incarcerated indefinitely in a military detention facility.
   b. the right to have their detainment reviewed.
   c. the right to be immediately released and deported.
   d. no explicit rights because they do not fall under U.S. or international law.
3. Differences in the way people understand the term "equality" can have important implications for which policies get enacted to deal with the problem. In two paragraphs, compare and contrast equality of opportunity with equality of results.

12.2 Compare and contrast the efforts of various groups to obtain equal protection of the law.

4. Place the following events in correct chronological order.
   a. Violent riots erupt in many cities.
   b. Lyndon B. Johnson signs the Civil Rights Act.
   c. Barack Obama is elected president of the United States.
   d. Martin Luther King gives his "I Have a Dream" speech.
   e. African Americans migrate to northern and western cities.
   f. *Brown* v. *Board of Education* ends segregated public schools.
5. Different racial and ethnic groups in the United States have had different results in their struggles to achieve economic, political, and social equality and success. In a paragraph, explore possible reasons for these differences.
6. In a paragraph, list the historical events that impeded the progress of women's rights and discuss the gains made by women in the twentieth century, particularly in its last three decades.
7. Native Americans today suffer poor health and extremely high unemployment. Write a paragraph recommending what the Native American community can do to achieve equality.

12.3 Analyze the Supreme Court's three-tiered approach used to evaluate discriminatory laws.

8. In a paragraph, define *rational basis test, strict scrutiny,* and *heightened scrutiny,* and explain the relationships among them.
9. Imagine you are a judge. In a case before you, Isaac Johnson, a construction worker, age 60, has sued his company, United Builders, for discrimination because he was fired. United Builders explains it is company policy to cease employment of those over the age of 60 because they are usually unable to do the heavy work of construction. Write an essay determining whether this is a case of unfair discrimination.

10. The Supreme Court has placed sexual orientation as a classification for the rational basis test. In a paragraph, explain why the Court has ruled this way and evaluate whether the justification is correct, too lenient, or too severe.

12.4 Trace the evolution of voting rights and analyze the protections provided by the 1965 Voting Rights Act.

11. Which of the following is *not* a provision of the Voting Rights Act?
    a. Threats or intimidation in any form to prevent citizens from voting are barred.
    b. Voting criteria that result in a denial of the right to vote based on race or color are barred.
    c. Political parties must make a "reasonable effort" to nominate minority candidates for public office.
    d. The Justice Department must review changes in voting laws that may dilute the voting power of racial groups.
12. In a few sentences, discuss the rationale for creating majority-minority districts and judge whether they have been a wise public policy.

12.5 Describe congressional legislation against discrimination in housing, employment, and accommodations.

13. In one or two sentences, explain how Congress has used the commerce clause to fight discrimination in public accommodations.
14. Which of the following is *not* prohibited by the Fair Housing Act?
    a. A bank denies an African American man a mortgage because he has poor credit and no savings.
    b. A landlord denies a woman an apartment because he is concerned that her two young children will bother the other tenants.
    c. The owner of several apartment complexes charges handicapped tenants an extra $10 rent to help pay for the buildings' wheelchair lifts.
    d. A real estate agent shows a Hispanic family mostly Hispanic neighborhoods because, she assumes, they are most likely to feel comfortable with people of their own race.

12.6 Evaluate the historical process of school integration and the current state of affirmative action.

15. List and summarize the main points made by the Supreme Court in *University of California Regents* v. *Bakke, Gratz* v. *Bollinger,* and *Grutter* v. *Bollinger.*
16. In one paragraph, review the most recent court decisions and state laws on affirmative action and predict what will happen to the policy in the future.

12.7 Assess the status of civil rights in the United States today.

17. Consider civil rights leader James Farmer's statement that victories of the civil rights movement were "victories largely for the middle class. . . ." In one paragraph, critique Farmer's statement. Do you agree with his assessment? Why or why not?

Answers for selected questions: 1. b; 2. b; 4. e, f, d, a, b, c; 11. c; 14. a

mypoliscilab™ EXERCISES

Where participation leads to action!

Apply what you learned in this chapter on MyPoliSciLab.

Read on **mypoliscilab.com**

eText: Chapter 12

Study and **Review** on **mypoliscilab.com**

Pre-Test
Post-Test
Chapter Exam
Flashcards

Watch on **mypoliscilab.com**

Video: Should Don't Ask Don't Tell Go Away?
Video: Supreme Court: No Race-Based Admissions

Explore on **mypoliscilab.com**

Simulation: You Are the Mayor and Need to Make Civil Rights Decisions
Comparative: Comparing Civil Rights
Timeline: The Civil Rights Movement
Timeline: The Mexican-American Civil Rights Movement
Timeline: The Struggle for Equal Protection
Timeline: Women's Struggle for Equality
Visual Literacy: Race and the Death Penalty

KEY TERMS

civil rights, p. 349
natural rights, p. 349
affirmative action, p. 350
naturalization, p. 350
dual citizenship, p. 351
right of expatriation, p. 351
women's suffrage, p. 355
equal protection clause, p. 359
due process clause, p. 359
rational basis test, p. 360
strict scrutiny test, p. 360
heightened scrutiny test, p. 360
literacy test, p. 362
white primary, p. 362
racial gerrymandering, p. 363
poll tax, p. 363
majority-minority district, p. 364
Jim Crow laws, p. 365
commerce clause, p. 365
class action suit, p. 366
restrictive covenant, p. 366
de jure segregation, p. 368
de facto segregation, p. 368

ADDITIONAL RESOURCES

FURTHER READING

RAYMOND ARSENAULT, *Freedom Riders: 1961 and the Struggle for Racial Justice* (Oxford University Press, 2006).

TAYLOR BRANCH, *At Canaan's Edge: America in the King Years, 1965–1968* (Simon & Schuster, 2006).

TAYLOR BRANCH, *Parting the Waters: America in the King Years, 1954–1963* (Simon & Schuster, 1988).

TAYLOR BRANCH, *Pillar of Fire: America in the King Years, 1963–1965* (Simon & Schuster, 1998).

GORDON H. CHANG, ED., *Asian Americans and Politics* (Stanford University Press, 2001).

CHARLES CLOTFELTER, *After Brown: The Rise and Retreat of School Desegregation* (Princeton University Press, 2004).

CLARE CUSHMAN, ED., *Supreme Court Decisions and Women's Rights* (CQ Press, 2000).

ARLENE M. DAVILA, *Latinos, Inc.: The Marketing and Making of a People* (University of California Press, 2001).

WILLIAM N. ESKRIDGE JR., *Gaylaw: Challenging the Apartheid of the Closet* (Harvard University Press, 2000).

RICHARD KAHLENBERG, *All Together Now: Creating Middle-Class Schools Through Public School Choice* (Brookings Institution Press, 2003).

RANDALL KENNEDY, *Race, Crime, and the Law* (Pantheon, 1997).

MICHAEL J. KLARMAN, *From Jim Crow to Civil Rights: The Supreme Court and the Struggle for Racial Equality* (Oxford University Press, 2006).

PHILIP A. KLINKER AND **ROGER M. SMITH,** *The Unsteady March: The Rise and Decline of Racial Equality in America* (University of Chicago Press, 2000).

PETER KWONG AND **DUSANKA MISCEVIC,** *Chinese America: The Untold Story of America's Oldest New Community* (New Press, 2006).

NANCY MCGLEN, KAREN O'CONNOR, LAURA VAN ASSELDFT, AND **WENDY GUNTHER-CANADA,** *Women, Politics, and American Society,* 3d ed. (Pearson/Longman, 2005).

GARY ORFIELD AND **CHUNGMEI LEE,** *Brown at 50: King's Dream or Plessy's Nightmare* (Civil Rights Project, Harvard University, 2004).

J. W. PELTASON, *Fifty-Eight Lonely Men: Southern Federal Judges and School Desegregation* (University of Illinois Press, 1971).

DAN PINELLO, *America's Struggle for Same-Sex Marriage* (Cambridge University Press, 2006).

RUTH ROSEN, *The World Split Open: How the Modern Women's Movement Changed America* (Viking Press, 2000).

JOHN DAVID SKRENTNY, ED., *Color Lines: Affirmative Action, Immigration, and Civil Rights Options for America* (University of Chicago Press, 2001).

GIRARDEAU A. SPANN, *The Law of Affirmative Action: Twenty-Five Years of Supreme Court Decisions on Race and Remedies* (New York University Press, 1999).

SUSAN F. VAN BURKLEO, *"Belonging to the World": Women's Rights and Constitutional Culture* (Oxford University Press, 2001).

WEB SITES

www.brennancenter.org/studentvoting This Web site for the Brennan Center for Justice, Student Voting Rights, contains state-by-state information on registration and voting requirements for students.

www.justice.gov/crt/ The Web site for the U.S. Department of Justice, Civil Rights Division, provides information on a variety of civil rights issues such as fair housing, hate crimes, and protecting voting rights.

www.uscis.gov The U.S. Citizenship and Immigration Services Web site provides an opportunity to test yourself on questions that could appear on a citizenship test. Click on the link to the "Naturalization Test" and see how well you do.

PART V The Politics of National Policy

THE BIG PICTURE

The Constitution was created as an overall framework for making public policies about who gets what, when, where, and how from the federal government. A public policy is a specific course of action that government takes to manage the economy, social needs, or foreign issues. Defined this way, public policy is an important outcome of politics. Government makes public policy through laws, presidential orders, judicial opinions, and rules.

The Constitution assumes that government will intervene in these areas to protect the nation from domestic and foreign threats such as economic crises, internal unrest, and foreign attacks. In theory, federal policies are designed to assume that every American enjoys the promise of life, liberty, and the pursuit of happiness, which implies that the federal government will make and implement policies to assure opportunity for every citizen. However, there are strong disagreements about when and how the federal government should intervene. The Constitution clearly tells Congress, the president, and the judiciary to defend the nation from harm but does not tell these institutions what to do. Much of the contemporary conflict over issues such as health care and unemployment involve deep disagreements about what life, liberty, and the pursuit of happiness mean. Should government leave these pursuits to the individual citizen or try to set the rules that create equal opportunity for every American? As we will see in this section, the Constitution leaves the answer to the political process and the institutions of government.

Citizens play a prominent role in the great debates about what the government should do in response to perceived threats. They make their opinions known through elections, direct contact with their representatives, legal action, and more aggressive engagement in direct decisions by the federal bureaucracy. The nation's political leaders also pay great attention to what the public thinks through opinion surveys and the media.

COURSE LEARNING **OBJECTIVES**

CHAPTER 13 Making Economic and Social Welfare Policy

Identify the steps in the policy-making process and describe the government's role in economic and social policy making.

The policy process is designed to act in response to economic, social, and foreign threats. The policy process produces different kinds of policies, including distributive, redistributive, and reverse distributive policies, which give and/or take benefits and resources from certain segments of society.

The process for making these choices is complex. It involves eight steps: (1) making assumptions about the problem, (2) setting the agenda, (3) deciding to act, which can involve decisions not to act at all, (4) deciding how much to do, (5) choosing a solution to the problem, (6) deciding who will deliver the goods or services, (7) making rules for implementation, and (8) running the program itself.

Once government decides to act, it has a variety of choices about how to distribute or take away benefits. It can spend money collected through taxes or financed through borrowing. It can create taxes to reward or punish certain behaviors such as home ownership or smoking. It can also provide direct goods and services by building highways or hospitals, protecting its citizens from risks such as unemployment, and establishing rules for public conduct. These choices are often subject to intense debate among citizens and their representatives over the proper role of government in society.

The federal government has a significant role both in protecting the nation from economic crisis and promoting growth and stability. It can intervene in the economy through monetary policy, which affect the cost of borrowing. Increases in the cost of money tend to cool off the economy during times of high inflation in prices, whereas decreases tend to stimulate the economy during times of high unemployment. Monetary policy is made by the Federal Reserve Bank, which is insulated from politics.

The federal government intervenes in the economy through fiscal policy, which involves spending and taxing. Tax increases and budget cuts tend to cool off the economy, whereas tax cuts and budget increases tend to stimulate the economy. Fiscal policy is made by Congress and the president and involves intense political infighting as citizens, interest groups, and private businesses seek protection and benefits from the legislative process.

In addition to monetary and fiscal policy, the federal government plays a significant role in promoting and regulating business through rules.

Along with state and local governments, the federal government is also responsible for protecting Americans from hardship. This role involves great political conflict between citizens who believe that most Americans face hardship because they do not work hard enough and those who believe that Americans are often victims of forces beyond their control.

The greatest breakthroughs in protecting citizens from hardship came during Franklin Roosevelt's New Deal and Lyndon Johnson's Great Society. The economic collapse that began with the stock market crash in 1929 produced New Deal programs to insure Americans from economic hardship, including Social Security, unemployment and disability insurance, the first school lunch program, and other short-term public jobs programs. In turn, the Great Society produced health insurance for older Americans (Medicare), nutrition assistance, supplemental income for poor older Americans, and urban development programs. Most of these programs have expanded throughout the years and now cost more in total than the defense budget. Most are also entitlement programs that are available to citizens who meet a "means-test" of their need.

CHAPTER 14 Making Foreign and Defense Policy

Describe the tools of foreign policy making, and evaluate the status of America's current foreign policy interests.

Foreign policy is primarily concerned with protecting the United States from foreign threats. However, the term "threat" is broadly defined to include much more than potential attacks on the nation. It also includes concerns about environmental damage, humanitarian aid, peace in the Middle East, and the spread of nuclear weapons. Although the United States has been engaged in two wars during the past two decades, it has also been using a blend of "hard" (military) and "soft" (diplomatic) power to achieve its goals. These two forms of power involve a number of federal government agencies, including the State and Defense Departments, intelligence agencies such as the Central Intelligence Agency, and the president's National Security Council. The military plays a particularly powerful role in reinforcing U.S. foreign policy through its 1.5 million members of the Air Force, Army, Navy, and Marine Corps. Soft power is enhanced by a strong defense, just as hard power is held in reserve by soft power.

CHAPTER 13

powerSHARES
Rehire The Workers
Fire the bankers
Bail out the People Movement
StopForeclosuresandEvictions.org
212-633-6646
Bail Out Students & Youth
Bail out the People Movement
StopForeclosuresandEvictions.org
212-633-6646
No money for Wall St. & War
Bail out the workers and the poor
Bail Out the People Movement
StopForeclosuresandEvictions.org
212-633-6646

Making Economic and Social Welfare Policy

After two years of slow growth, the United States economy reached a crisis point in late September 2008. Consumers were increasingly anxious about making even small purchases, home prices and car sales were falling, and more than 750,000 Americans had lost their jobs in the first nine months of the year.

Most importantly, the credit market was beginning to freeze, sharply limiting the amount of money available for borrowing. Credit is the essential grease that keeps the economy moving—consumers borrow to buy homes and cars, students borrow to buy books and pay tuition, small businesses borrow to buy new goods to sell, banks borrow money from other banks to cover the ups and downs of borrowing itself, and Wall Street borrows money to buy businesses and finance big investments. But credit was quickly disappearing as nervous lenders decided to sit on their money rather than make what they thought were risky loans.

On Sunday, September 28, Treasury Secretary Henry M. Paulson Jr. went to Capitol Hill to ask lawmakers for unprecedented authority to ease the credit crisis, which had begun in 2007 with a surge in the number of homeowners who could no longer pay their debts. These loan defaults continued to grow through the year and eventually created billions of dollars of "toxic debt," meaning loans that banks could not cover.

Paulson's proposal to buy $700 billion of this bad debt and keep it in the federal government's hands for future action provoked intense anger. Many Americans saw his proposal as a bailout for Wall Street firms that had made so much money making the bad loans. Americans wondered how the bailout, or rescue, as Paulson called it, would help them pay for health insurance, college loans, gasoline, and groceries.

Paulson's proposal was not only unprecedented, it was complex. Members of Congress had difficulty explaining it back home and wondered how they could vote for such an expensive program when the federal government itself was already borrowing heavily to finance itself. With the economy teetering on what Paulson and other experts said was a complete breakdown, Congress only had days to make a decision on what to do. Moreover, the 2008 presidential election was in full swing with Democrat Barack Obama and Republican John McCain unwilling to take a position on the controversial idea. Under intense pressure as the stock markets fell dramatically, Congress passed the bill on October 3, only ten days after Paulson made his stunning proposal.

It will take several years to know whether Paulson's gamble will work. The U.S. economy no longer operates independently of other economies across the globe. If the U.S. economy failed, these other economies would fail, and vice versa. Much of the money that was loaned to banks by 2010 had been returned to the federal government, though the public remains intensely angry about the huge bonuses that bankers and Wall Street investors continue to receive.

Just as economic policy has become more complex as the world has changed, so have social, foreign, and defense policy. Promoting the general welfare, providing for the common defense, and securing the blessing of liberty for all Americans is no longer a matter of occasional tinkering when events go badly. It is a full-time job for a government by the people.

This chapter will explore the various ways in which citizens and government both work to create and implement public policy. We will start with some simple definitions of public policy. We will then examine the process for making public policy. Laws do not implement themselves. They must be converted into action. The public policy process is the method for making laws a reality in American life. Finally, the chapter will explore how the federal government promotes the general welfare through economic policy and social programs.

CHAPTER OUTLINE & CHAPTER LEARNING OBJECTIVES

The Expansion of Social Policy in the Twentieth Century

13.9 Outline the evolution of social policy throughout the twentieth century.

Social Policy Challenges for the Future: Health, Education, and Crime

13.10 Evaluate the current status of and challenges for federal government policy in the areas of health care, education, and crime.

Citizens and Public Policy

13.11 Assess ways in which citizens can influence the public policy process.

One of the most meaningful ways citizens can help influence and implement public policy is by volunteering. In 2009, President Obama signed the Serve America Act, which was designed to increase volunteering opportunities.

Defining Public Policy

LEARNING **OBJECTIVE**

13.1 Relate politics and public policy, and differentiate three types of public policy.

When government decides to solve a problem, it does so through a **public policy,** a specific course of action that government takes to address a challenge such as global warming, health care, or unemployment. Government can convey a public policy to the nation in laws passed by Congress and signed by the president, in opinions issued by the Supreme Court, and/or in rules written by administrators.

But whatever its form, a public policy tells the nation and the world who is about to get what, when, and how from the federal government. As Table 13–1 shows, we can define **politics** as the interaction of the people and their government, whereas *policy* is the product of that give and take. If politics is a question of who gets what, when, where, and how from government, then policy is a formal statement of who has the greater power and what compromises have been reached. We define **policy makers** as the individuals and groups that make the actual choices to create a public policy—some policy makers are elected officials or government employees, whereas others are lobbyists and interest groups. Citizens are rarely considered to be policy makers.

public policy
A specific course of action that government takes to address a problem.

politics
The interaction of the people and their government, including citizens, interest groups, political parties, and the institutions of government at all levels. Politics is concerned with who gets what, when, where, and how from government.

policy makers
Individuals and groups that make the actual choices to create a public policy.

Types of Public Policy

Public policies do not all have the same impact on society. Some benefit all groups of citizens, others benefit one group of citizens by taking something away from another, and still others take benefits from all groups in an effort to create a better society for everyone. These choices create three specific types of public policy.[1]

TABLE **13–1** Politics and Policy

The People ⟶	Politics ⟶	Policies ⟶	Outcomes
Older Americans	Voting, joining AARP	Creating prescription drug coverage	Lower prescription drug costs
College students	Writing e-mails	Reducing college loan costs	Lower debt
Businesses	Contributing money to campaigns	Lower taxes	Higher profits
Environmental groups	Filing lawsuits	Enforcing smokestack rules	Cleaner air
Community	Setting up Facebook sites	Increasing police patrols	Safer neighborhoods

Citizens receive significant government support when they purchase their homes. They are allowed to reduce their taxes by subtracting the interest payments on their loans from their annual taxes and receive indirect federal funds for buying energy-efficient appliances. ■ *How does home ownership relate to the American dream, discussed in Chapter 3? Why does the federal government promote home ownership?*

Federal policies that offer new benefits to all citizens are called **distributive policy.** National parks, air traffic control, the interstate highway system, education funding, national defense, and Social Security are all distributive. They help all groups at some level, whether rich or poor. Although some may get more benefit than others from a particular program such as Social Security, which reduces poverty among low-income beneficiaries, every group receives at least something through distributive policy.

distributive policy
A public policy such as Social Security that provides benefits to all groups in society.

In contrast, federal policies that take resources away from one or more groups in society (usually through taxes) so that another group can benefit (usually through an entitlement program) are **redistributive policy.** Such programs benefit the less fortunate. Welfare, poverty programs, Head Start for poor preschool children, and special programs to help minority groups are redistributive. Some political scientists call them **zero-sum games,** meaning one group's gain (the program's benefits) is another's loss (the program's cost in taxes).

redistributive policy
A policy that provides to one group of society while taking away benefits from another through policy solutions such as tax increases to pay for job training.

zero-sum games
A policy that takes away exactly as much in benefits as another group gains.

Finally, federal policies that take resources from every group to solve a common problem by reducing benefits such as Social Security or raising taxes on all income levels are a form of **reverse distributive policy.**[2] When Social Security benefits are increased through annual cost-of-living-adjustments, it is a form of distributive policy, but when benefits are cut and taxes increased to provide more money for benefits, it becomes a reverse distributive policy by taking away something from all citizens.

reverse distributive policy
A policy that reduces benefits for all groups such as a tax increase in society, often by imposing rules that govern everyone.

The Eight Steps in Making Public Policy

LEARNING **OBJECTIVE**
13.2 Outline eight steps in making public policy, and assess types of policy solutions.

Every public policy reflects a series of separate decisions leading to its creation. The process can be viewed as a staircase that moves upward toward final implementation. But like any very long staircase, there are times when policy makers simply run out of energy to keep going. The process can even go back down the staircase as new ideas are introduced and Congress and the president go back down to revisit their earlier decisions. When the Obama administration entered office in 2009, for example, it reversed directions on many of the Bush administration's policies on issues such as global warming.

Whereas the Bush administration had long argued that global warming was not a national threat, the Obama administration moved quickly to push for stricter limits on carbon emissions by automobiles and power plants.

The public policy staircase has eight steps: (1) making assumptions about the problem at the beginning, (2) setting the agenda of problems to be addressed, (3) deciding to act, (4) deciding how much to do, (5) choosing a solution to the problem, (6) deciding who will deliver the goods or services, (7) making rules for implementation, and (8) final implementation as an ongoing policy. Figure 13–1 presents the staircase.

We will discuss each step next, but note that by its very nature, the choice to move forward (in step 3) is the most difficult, largely because of the complexity of passing a bill, issuing an executive order, or making a Supreme Court decision. It is often far easier to make what political scientists call a **nondecision,** which means the policy process stops before final action. A nondecision can take place at any step on the staircase.

Making Assumptions About the Problem

Every government decision starts with assumptions about the future. Is the economy going to get stronger? If so, perhaps employment will go up and the costs of supporting the unemployed will go down. Is terrorism going to increase? If so, perhaps the federal government needs to inspect more cargo ships in search of bombs and other threats. Answers to questions about the future shape decisions about what the federal government might do.

Setting the Agenda

nondecision
A decision not to move ahead with the policy process. In short, it is a decision not to decide.

policy agenda
The list of issues that the federal government pays attention to.

Choosing the problem to be solved is the essential decision in setting the **policy agenda.** The policy agenda, as political scientist John Kingdon defines it, "is the list of subjects or problems to which governmental officials, and people outside of government closely associated with those officials, are paying some serious attention at any given time."[3]

Thus defined, the agenda is a direct product of politics and reflects broad social goals embraced by the people and their government, such as liberty, equality, individualism, and respect for the common person. These values are core to the ideology that shapes the

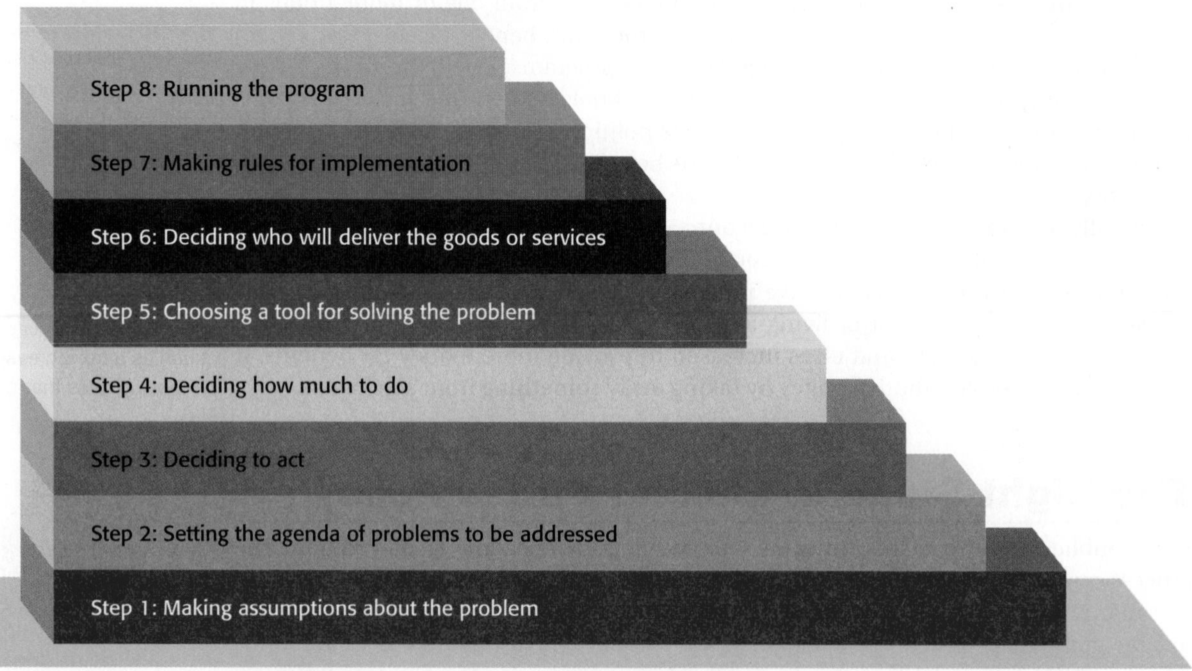

FIGURE 13–1 **The Eight Steps in Making Public Policy.**
■ *Why is step three the most difficult step?*

policy agenda, but they often conflict with each other as ideas move toward public policies. Everyone wants the American dream, for example, but we often disagree on how to get it. Politics affects the rise and fall of these ideologies through elections, party identification, interest group pressure, and a variety of other political expressions.

Nevertheless, the public's attention span can be very short. Problems identified through scientific research such as global warming may be the easiest to ignore, partly because there always seem to be numbers to refute a given analysis. Even as former Vice President Al Gore was accepting the Nobel Peace Prize for his work on global warming, a group of scientists challenged much of the evidence on which his work was based. The media can also play a role by magnifying or downplaying the impact of a particular story.

Policy makers set the agenda using many of the same criteria they apply to other political decisions—public opinion, interest group pressure, their own beliefs, ideology, party affiliation, and loyalty to their institution. In recent years, they have also come to rely on a small number of think tanks to help them sort through the stream of possible problems. A **think tank** is an organization composed of scholars who study public policy. Many are located in Washington, D.C., so that they can be closer to the national political process. Unlike a college or university, which also produces policy research, a think tank exists almost entirely to influence the immediate agenda. Thus, many are described as either liberal or conservative.

Former Vice President Al Gore clearly helped set the agenda for global warming with his Academy Award-winning documentary, *An Inconvenient Truth.* In the movie, Gore outlined what he believed were the negative impacts of global warming, and called citizens and policy makers to action. ■ *How else can citizens help set the policy making agenda?*

Deciding to Act

The fact that a problem exists does not automatically mean that Congress, the president, or the courts will try to solve it. Some problems help policy makers achieve their personal or political goals, such as reelection or a place in history, in which case they decide to act, whereas others do not, in which case they pick other problems to solve.

Policy makers also clearly understand that public pressure for action ebbs and flows over time. In fact, writes political scientist Anthony Downs, "American public attention rarely remains sharply focused upon any one domestic issue for very long—even if it involves a continuing problem of crucial importance to society." According to Downs, the public follows an **issue-attention cycle** in which each problem "suddenly leaps into prominence, remains there for a short time, and then—although still largely unresolved—gradually fades from the center of public attention."[4]

think tank
A nongovernmental organization that seeks to influence public policy through research and education.

issue-attention cycle
The movement of public opinion toward public policy from initial enthusiasm for action to realization of costs and a decline in interest.

Global warming is a recent example. Public concern about the issue has gone up and down throughout the years, reflecting competing concerns about the economy and doubt about specific solutions. Figure 13–2 shows the trends according to a variety of polls. As the polls show, the issue-attention cycle varies with a number of factors, most notably the economy. Citizens want government to act even when policy affects economic growth but not when the economy is in trouble. Although global warming is

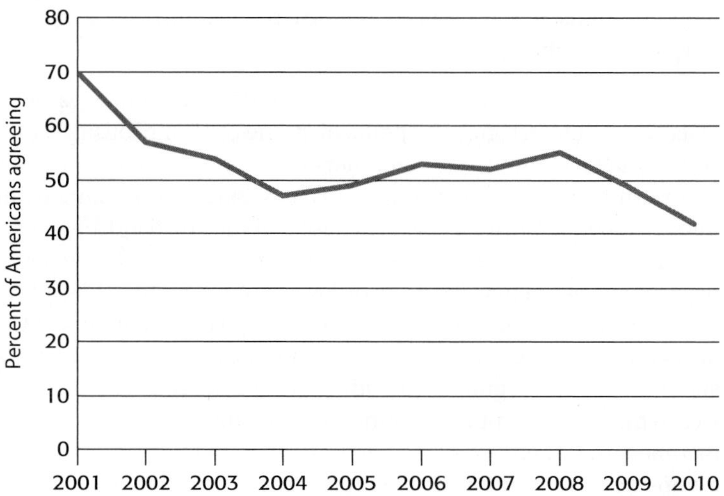

FIGURE 13–2 Concerns About the Environment, 2000–2010.

Agreement with the statement: "Protection of the environment should be given priority, even at the risk of curbing economic growth." ■ *What is one important reason why support for environmental action started to fall in 2008?*

SOURCE: Polls on global warming are available at http://www.polling-report.com.

still an issue for most Americans, it has been sliding somewhat throughout the past few years, suggesting that the issue-attention cycle is at work.

- This cycle starts with what Downs described as the "pre-problem stage," the rise of some "highly undesirable social condition" such as global warming that has yet to capture public attention.
- The issue-attention cycle continues with "alarmed discovery and euphoric enthusiasm," the sudden emergence of an issue as a topic for public debate. Books are written, documentaries made, speeches retooled, and campaigns rebuilt, all based on the sudden passion that generates public concern.
- The cycle moves onward with the realization that change will incur significant cost. It is one thing to worry about greenhouse gases and quite another to pay more for clean electricity or buy smaller, more efficient cars. The greater the cost of solving a problem, especially if it means tax increases or benefit cuts, the more strongly people pull back from their euphoric view of change.
- The cycle continues with the "gradual decline of intense public interest." Having pressed hard for action on an issue such as universal health insurance, the public may begin to realize that change is nearly impossible given the array of political forces fighting for a nondecision.
- The cycle ends with what Downs calls the "post-problem stage." The problem moves into "prolonged limbo—a twilight realm of lesser attention or spasmodic recurrences of interest."

The ultimate decline of public interest is not inevitable. But if we expect problems to be solved immediately, we will only be disappointed. Civil rights took 100 years to become a reality, for example. Although issues such as global warming seem to demand that we take immediate action before the damage is beyond repair, we must acquire enough understanding of the problem, and of the policy process, to stay actively engaged for the long term.

Deciding How Much to Do

Once the federal government decides it *wants* to do something about a problem, the next difficult decision is *how much* to do. Government can launch a comprehensive program such as Social Security or Medicare, or it can expand a smaller program bit by bit over time.

incremental policy
Small adjustments to existing public policies.

punctuating policy
Radical changes to public policy that occur only after the mobilization of large segments of society to demand action.

iron triangle
A policy-making instrument composed of a tightly related alliance of a congressional committee, interest groups, and federal department or agency.

issue network
A policy-making instrument composed of loosely related interest groups, congressional committee, presidential aides, and other parties.

Incremental or Comprehensive Policy

An **incremental policy** makes a small-scale adjustment in an existing program, whereas a *comprehensive* or **punctuating policy** creates a dramatic change in the government's role. Incremental policies are generally the easiest to create, if only because they build on past decisions in very small ways, such as increasing the amount of federal support for colleges by a few hundred dollars. Punctuating policies, such as providing national prescription drug coverage for older adults, often require citizens, interest groups, political parties, and policy makers to mobilize in a broad movement for change.

Iron Triangles and Issue Networks

Fundamental changes often depend on alliances of citizens, interest groups, political parties, private businesses, government agencies, congressional committees, and others who come together to place an issue on the agenda and push for or against change. Alliances called **iron triangles** exist for decades; **issue networks** cooperate for a specific cause and then disband.

An iron triangle has three sides that hold together for long periods of time: (1) a federal department or agency, (2) a set of loyal interest groups, and (3) a House and/or Senate committee. Each side supports the other two. Loyal members of Congress work to protect or increase the agency's budget, allowing the agency to flourish, and pass legislation to support the interest groups, providing benefits for its members. Agencies give special services to the interest groups, keeping their members happy, and ensure the constituencies of members of Congress are provided for, aiding in congressional approval ratings. Interest groups give contributions and endorsements to loyal members of Congress, aiding in their

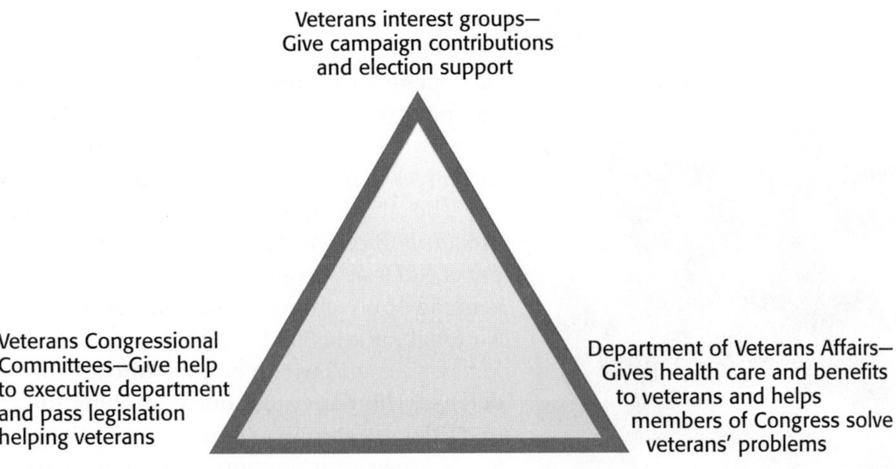

FIGURE 13–3 Iron Triangle.
■ *Why are iron triangles so hard to break?*

reelection, and support the activities and requests of the agency, enhancing their legitimacy. Policy making for veterans, for example, is achieved through an iron triangle composed of the Department of Veterans Affairs, the House and Senate Veterans Committees, and a long list of interest groups that represent veterans, such as the American Legion and Veterans of Foreign Wars. The basic structure of this iron triangle is presented in Figure 13–3.

Iron triangles have been largely replaced by much looser collections of participants in issue networks. As political scientist Hugh Heclo has argued, the notion that iron triangles make all policy was "not so much wrong as it was disastrously incomplete" in today's complicated policy environment.[5] The increasing number of small, highly specialized interest groups makes an iron triangle nearly impossible to create, if only because Congress and federal agencies can no longer identify a steady occupant for the third corner of the triangle. They have to find temporary allies, depending on the issue. There is nothing "iron" about such coalitions: They last only as long as an issue is hot.

Issue networks concentrate power in the relatively small number of individuals who organize and maintain them. These people make the key decisions about who participates and what they say. Some political scientists thus refer to the rise of well-financed issue networks—such as those that promote prescription drug coverage for older consumers or tax cuts for business—as a form of elitism, not pluralism, in which a very small number of actors accelerate or delay action. Medicare prescription drug coverage, for example, engaged an issue network of drug companies, the AARP, and hospitals.

Choosing a Solution

The federal government has five tools to solve most public problems: (1) spending money, (2) using taxes to regulate the economy and encourage certain behaviors, (3) providing goods and services directly, (4) providing protection against risk, and (5) creating standards, incentives, or penalties.[6]

The first option is *federal spending* for direct payments to individuals, hospitals, corporations, and other nations. Social Security is still the largest direct payment to individuals, whereas Medicare for older citizens' medical care is the largest direct payment to hospitals. The federal government also buys a huge amount of material to support the military, including fighter jets, body armor, gasoline, and food. In 2007, the Defense Department spent more than $200 billion on such purchases.

The second public policy option is the *use of taxes* to regulate the economy—lower taxes may stimulate a weak economy, whereas higher taxes may slow down a hot economy. The federal government can use the tax system to encourage certain behaviors such as buying a house, making contributions to charity, or even having children. Businesses receive tax credits and deductions for activities such as energy conservation and the

California and other states sued the national government to impose higher gas mileage standards on automobiles and light trucks. The Hummer is considered a light truck. ■ *Is regulation the best policy option for protecting the environment? What other kinds of policy solutions might the government attempt?*

purchase of some U.S.-made goods. Advocates of policies designed to curb global warming argue that the federal government should impose taxes on the amount of carbon gases that private companies produce. By creating such taxes, companies would have incentives to reduce their pollution or lose profits.

The third option for solving a problem is *providing goods and services* to the public. National parks such as Yosemite and the Grand Canyon generally only charge a modest admission fee, the National Air and Space Museum on the Washington Mall is free, and we do not pay directly for national defense. Ultimately, of course, nothing the government does is completely free—the National Air and Space Museum is supported by general taxes, as is the Defense Department.

The fourth option of public policy is to *guarantee protection* against risk, with a range of devices to encourage activities the private sector might not otherwise undertake. The most familiar protections are federal loan guarantees, under which the government promises to cover losses if a student, farmer, small business, or other borrower fails to repay a debt. Student loan programs have become more difficult to get in recent years because of the economic collapse and fears that students will not be able to repay their loans.

The final option to solve a problem is through **regulation** to encourage or discourage certain behaviors such as smoking, using illegal drugs, polluting, and driving safely. Regulation involves **rules,** which are precise legal statements implementing a public policy. They can impose penalties or rewards enforceable by, and open to challenge in, the courts.

Thus, regulation and rules are best viewed as tactics for achieving a particular result. In late 2009, for example, the Environmental Protection Agency was given the power to raise mileage standards as part of its general authority to protect the quality of the environment. These regulations are still being developed but are likely to affect everything from how much electricity kitchen appliances can use to curbs on pollution generated through power plants.

All five solutions are designed to produce *material* benefits for society. Some benefits are tangible, such as new roads, bridges, schools, and hospitals; others, such as higher pay, greater safety, better education, and cleaner air and water, can only be felt. In theory, action to reduce global warming will produce less violent hurricanes throughout the coming decades. Scientists tend to believe that hurricanes have become more dangerous because of the rise in sea temperatures, which fuel hurricanes.

Other solutions produce *symbolic* benefits, such as efforts to educate the public, study an issue, appoint a blue-ribbon commission, or highlight the need for future action. In theory, symbolic benefits highlight an emerging issue and create citizen action. In reality, they are sometimes a way to make a nondecision as policy makers merely express their concern and move to other tangible policies. It is not yet clear, for example, just how much global warming is caused by sources beyond government's control, but action to reduce global warming through international treaties can give the public a sense that the world is getting better.

regulation
A policy that encourages or discourages certain behavior by imposing a legally binding rule. Rules are made through a long process that begins with an act of Congress and ends with issuance of a final rule.

rule
A precise statement of how a law is implemented.

Deciding Who Will Deliver the Goods or Services

Part of selecting a solution to implement a policy is deciding who will actually implement the program. The answer is not always a federal employee.[7] Although federal employment has been steady at roughly 2 million workers since the early 1990s, the federal agenda has continued to grow. As a result, the government often depends on a largely hidden workforce of contractors, grantees, and state and local employees to achieve its policy goals.

There are four sources of what political scientists call *third-party government:* (1) private businesses, (2) colleges and universities, (3) state and local governments, and (4) charitable organizations.

Private firms provided most security services to protect U.S. diplomats during the Iraq War. In 2007, employees of Blackwater, Inc., were charged with the unprovoked killings of Iraqi citizens during one of its patrols. ■ *Why does the U.S. military continue to use private contractors to guard diplomats?*

Private Businesses Paid under contracts with federal departments and agencies, profit-making businesses do an increasing amount of federal work once done exclusively by federal employees.

Colleges and Universities Colleges and universities are a second option for implementing public policy, especially if it includes research.

State and Local Governments State and local employees do much of the real work of governing. They collect the trash; provide safe drinking water; vaccinate children; administer the airports; run the public schools, universities, and community colleges; oversee environmental laws; run almost all public hospitals; staff most of the nation's prisons; prosecute most of the crimes; and provide police and fire protection.

Charities Finally, the federal government often relies on charities such as the American Red Cross, the Salvation Army, the American Cancer Society, and religious institutions to maintain the social safety net through contracts and grants. It also relies on charities to help the nation respond to crises such as Hurricane Katrina.

The number of charities has more than tripled throughout the past half-century. Today's 1.5 million charities employ approximately 11 million people and spend nearly a trillion dollars per year. Most private colleges and universities are considered charities under federal law, for example, as are many hospitals.

Making Rules for Implementation

Rule making comes at the very end of the policy-making process and is virtually invisible to most citizens. Nevertheless, it is the essential step in converting the abstract ideas and language of laws, presidential orders, and court rulings into precise rules governing what individual members of the public, companies, government, states, and localities must do to achieve the goals of a specific policy.

Rules can be extraordinarily detailed and are sometimes difficult for even regulated parties to understand. Because they are so complicated, interest groups have much greater influence over their construction than citizens and even members of Congress.

Although the federal government has been issuing rules since 1789, the number of rules jumped dramatically during World War II and again in the 1970s.[8] The number of rules did not increase because rule making became easier, however. On the contrary, Congress made it more difficult to create a rule under the 1946 Administrative Procedure Act. We can see the growth of rules in the number of pages in the *Federal Register,* which provides a daily record of all new and proposed rules. Figure 13–4 shows the number of pages by decade.

The process starts when a bill is passed and signed into law, which is sent to the appropriate department or agency for "faithful execution," as the Constitution requires. With the legislative history as a guide to what Congress wanted, the department or agency then drafts a proposed rule. The rule itself generally consists of a statement of purpose, the actual rule, and a review of any research or legislative language that shaped it.

FIGURE 13–4 **Pages in the *Federal Register.***

■ *Why do the pages in the Federal Register continue to rise even though Congress is passing fewer pieces of legislation?*

SOURCE: U.S. Office of the Federal Register, "Annual Federal Register Pages Published."

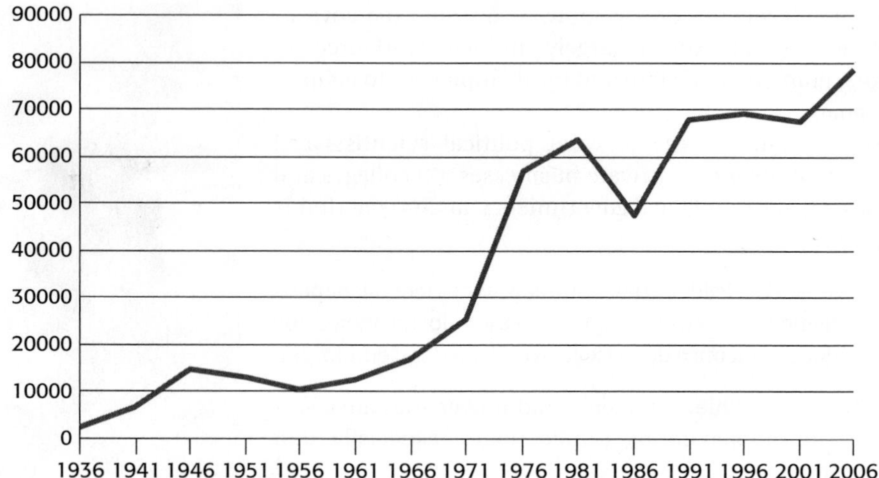

With the proposed rule in hand, the department or agency tells the public it is about to act. Under the Administrative Procedure Act, the department or agency must post a formal "Notice of Proposed Rulemaking" in the *Federal Register.*

Anyone affected by the rule has a short period of "notice and comment" to express concerns and suggest amendments through letters, e-mails, and personal testimony to government. After all the comments are reviewed, the department or agency publishes the final rule in the *Federal Register.* The rule goes into effect 30 days after it is published. Any citizen, including students, can provide comments regarding a proposed rule such as raising mileage standards, but they must first know when the proposed rule has been issued and when the notice-and-comment period starts and ends. The federal government publishes a list of all pending regulations and the timetable for action at http://www.regulations.gov/search/Regs/home.html#home. Under law, the federal government must review all comments and respond in a final summary of all comments.

Running the Program

Implementation does not end with release of a final rule. It continues with the day-to-day tasks of actually running a federal department or agency, making rules, supervising contractors, and evaluating impact. And as assumptions change and the issue-attention cycle takes hold, the policy-making process can begin again. As we shall see later in the chapter, the successful execution of the laws is hardly easy. It requires millions of federal employees; a long list of departments and agencies; intense oversight by Congress, the president, and the judiciary; and money—more than $3 trillion in 2008 alone.

The Order of Action

Making public policy is an often unpredictable process. It can start with any step and skip back and forth as politics shapes everything from the decision to act to running the program. The result is a policy-making process that is almost always in flux.

Some political scientists such as John Kingdon even think of this process as taking place in a "primordial swamp" of competing problems, solutions, political actors, citizens, pressure, and resources such as dollars, public support, and administrative energy.[9]

These policy "streams" are shaped by citizens, interest groups, presidents, and members of Congress and move through the institutions in search of each other. Thus, an idea for solving a problem such as a new weapons system or an increase in the minimum wage may linger in waiting for a specific problem such as terrorism or an increase in unemployment. Politics ties these various streams together into a public policy. According to this view, one reason immigration reform has not yet passed is that the streams of problems, solutions, and interests have yet to come together, in part because the political stream is so divided.

An Introduction to Economic Policy

LEARNING **OBJECTIVE**

13.3 Describe the federal government's economic policy making role and how economic performance is measured.

The federal government has been active in economic policy since the end of the Revolutionary War. The framers wanted a government strong enough to promote free trade, protect patents and trademarks, and enforce contracts between individuals and businesses. And they wanted a government with enough funding to build the postal roads, bridges, railroads, and canals that would allow the young economy to grow.

By creating a national government of limited powers and providing constitutional guarantees to protect property from excessive regulation, the framers succeeded in protecting capitalism. Part of the government's role is to stay out of the way as individuals and businesses create wealth through new ideas and hard work, but part is to promote the national welfare through **fiscal policy,** which uses federal spending and taxation to stimulate or slow the economy, and **monetary policy,** which manipulates the supply of money that individuals and businesses have in their hands to keep the economy from swinging wildly from boom to bust. In addition, the federal government promotes economic growth and trade and controls many economic decisions through regulations against certain kinds of business, labor, and environmental practices.

These tools are designed to smooth the ups and downs of the normal *business cycle.* Economists tend to focus on four discrete stages of the cycle: (1) *expansion,* in which the economy produces new jobs and growth; (2) *contraction,* as the economy starts to slow down; (3) *recession,* in which the economy reaches a trough of slow growth; and (4) *recovery,* in which the economy rebounds. A *depression* is an extremely deep form of recession that lasts much longer than the average recession. Depressions also produce extremely high unemployment. The Great Depression of the 1930s began with a stock market crash on October 29, 1929, which is still called *Black Friday,* and lasted until the early years of World War II more than ten years later. The goal of effective economic policy today is to make sure the peaks are not too high and the troughs are not too low.

We use two yardsticks to measure the performance of the economy. The first is **inflation,** which we track by comparing the price of goods and services such as gasoline, food, and housing over time. Inflation, a rising price level, is the primary risk during expansion and recovery. The second measure is **unemployment,** or the number of people looking for work at any given time. Unemployment among the employable is the greatest problem during contraction and recession.

In theory, inflation increases when unemployment drops (an increase in the workforce creates more demand for products, which raises prices), whereas inflation declines when unemployment increases (fewer workers creates less demand for products, which

fiscal policy
Government policy that attempts to manage the economy by controlling taxing and spending.

monetary policy
Government policy that attempts to manage the economy by controlling the money supply and thus interest rates.

inflation
A rise in the general price level (and decrease in dollar value) owing to an increase in the volume of money and credit in relation to available goods.

unemployment
The number of Americans who are out of work but actively looking for a job. The number does not usually include those who are not looking.

The economic cycle runs from expansion to recovery. Fiscal and monetary policies are designed to make sure the cycle is relatively stable. Here, unemployed workers during the Great Depression of the 1930s (left) and the recession of today (right) stand in line to apply for jobs and other assistance.
■ *How do the workers of the 1930s compare to those of today? And why is unemployment such an important measure of the health of the economy?*

lowers prices). This balance between the demand and supply of goods and services drives the business cycle: When supply is low and demand is high, prices rise; when supply is high and demand is low, prices fall. In reality, inflation and unemployment can rise or fall at the same time, as they did at the start of 2008. A simultaneous increase in inflation and unemployment is called **stagflation** (stagnation plus inflation). As of 2010, the economy was showing high levels of unemployment at approximately 10 percent but low levels of inflation.

We measure inflation with the *consumer price index (CPI),* which shows how much more or how much less consumers are paying for the same "basket of goods" over time. The major components of the CPI basket are food, shelter, fuel, clothing, transportation, and medical care. In turn, we measure unemployment simply by the percentage of able-bodied workers who are looking for jobs but cannot find them. This *unemployment rate* does not include able-bodied workers who have given up looking for work or taken jobs below their skill levels with lower pay.

Experts also use other measures to track the economy. These reveal whether the federal government is borrowing too much money (as measured by the budget deficit), whether it is selling too few goods and services to other nations (as measured by the balance of trade), and how much it is growing (as measured by year-to-year comparisons of the **gross domestic product [GDP]**). The gross domestic product, or GDP, shows the total value of all goods and services produced by the U.S. economy.

Fiscal Policy

LEARNING **OBJECTIVE**

13.4 Outline the way in which the federal government makes fiscal policy and the role of fiscal policy.

Congress and the president make fiscal policy by taxing, borrowing, and spending money. Nothing reflects the growth of federal programs and the rise of big government more clearly than increased spending by the national government. The 2008 rescue plan discussed at the start of this chapter is an example of a particularly aggressive fiscal policy. Under the plan, the federal government used its tax dollars to buy $700 billion of bad debt as a way to unclog the credit markets.

In general, increased government spending and lower taxes are ways to stimulate the economy, whereas decreased spending and higher taxes tend to slow the economy. Higher spending and tax cuts put more money in the pockets of consumers, which increases demand for goods and services, which in turn increases inflation and reduces unemployment. Conversely, lower spending and tax increases take money away from consumers, which reduces demand for goods and services, which in turn reduces inflation and increases unemployment.

The Federal Budget

Today, federal, state, and local governments spend an amount equal to approximately one-third of the nation's GDP. The national government is the biggest spender of all—it spends more than all state and local governments combined, or approximately 23 percent of GDP annually—nearly one dollar of every four spent in the U.S. economy.

Where the Money Comes From Although Benjamin Franklin once said nothing is more certain than death and taxes, he would be surprised at the range of taxes and other revenue sources used to fund federal spending today (see Figure 13–5 for the percentages from each source):

1. *Individual income taxes.* Taxes on individuals account for the largest share of the federal government's tax revenue. The income tax was prohibited under the Constitution until the Thirteenth Amendment was ratified in 1913.
2. *Payroll taxes.* Payroll taxes to pay for social insurance (Social Security and Medicare) are the second-largest and fastest-rising source of federal revenue. Most workers pay more in Social Security taxes than in federal income taxes.
3. *Corporate income taxes.* Corporate income taxes have fallen steadily from their historic high of two-fifths of federal revenues during World War II. Due to tax cuts and special

stagflation
A combination of an economic slowdown (stagnation) and a rise in prices (inflation).

gross domestic product (GDP)
The value of all goods and services produced by an economy during a specific period of time such as a year.

deductions, today they account for one-tenth of federal revenues, only one-fourth as much as the individual income tax.

4. *Excise taxes.* Federal **excise taxes** on the sale of liquor, tobacco, gasoline, telephones, air travel, and other so-called luxury items account for a very small percentage of the federal budget.
5. *Other sources.* Smaller taxes and fees include admission to national parks and camping fees in national forests, taxes on large estates left behind after death, and interest payments on government loans to college students.
6. *Borrowing.* When the federal government does not raise enough revenue to cover all its services, the only way to cover the resulting **budget deficit** is to borrow from citizens, banks, and even foreign governments, by selling Treasury notes and other investments such as saving bonds. As Figure 13–6 shows, borrowing to cover the deficit accounted for an estimated $1.3 trillion in federal revenues in 2008.[10,11]

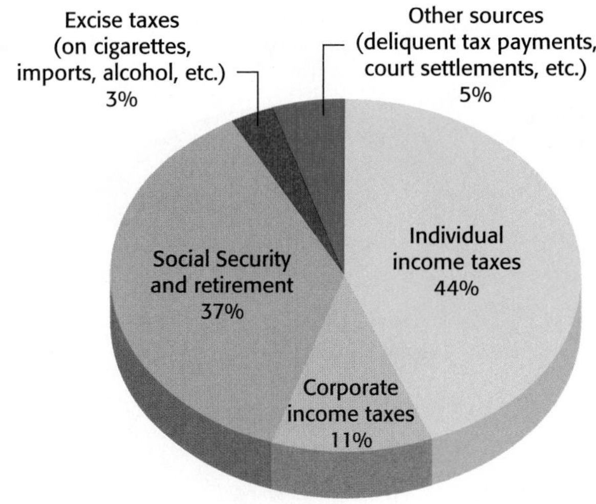

FIGURE 13–5 **Where the Money Comes From, 2010.**

■ *Are the majority of taxes collected by the government progressive or regressive?*

SOURCE: Summary Tables, *Budget of the United States, Fiscal Year 2011* (U.S. Government Printing Office, 2010).

Giving the people power over taxation was a major achievement in the development of self-government. "No taxation without representation" had been a battle cry in the Revolutionary War. The Constitution clearly provided that Congress "shall have Power to lay and collect Taxes, Duties, Imposts, and Excises" and that **tariffs,** or taxes on imports from other countries, and excise taxes have to be levied, or collected, uniformly throughout the United States.

Taxes are not only a means of raising money, however. In a broad sense, all taxation implies decisions about who gets what, when, where, and how. For example, a **progressive tax** that places higher taxes on individuals and families with higher incomes tends to help individuals and families with lower incomes. In contrast, a **regressive tax,** such as a sales tax collected on everyone's purchases of food and clothing, tends to hurt individuals and families with lower incomes.

Taxes also carry certain costs—it costs money to raise money. Like people who carry large balances on their credit cards, the United States must pay interest on its deficits. Government borrowing adds to the total **national debt,** which is the cumulative total of all deficits over time. In spring 2006, Congress raised the amount of money the federal government could borrow to $9 trillion, which would generate nearly $200 billion in interest payments during the year.

excise tax
A consumer tax on a specific kind of merchandise, such as tobacco.

budget deficit
The condition that exists when the federal government raises less revenue than it spends.

tariff
A tax levied on imports to help protect a nation's industries, labor, or farmers from foreign competition. It can also be used to raise additional revenue.

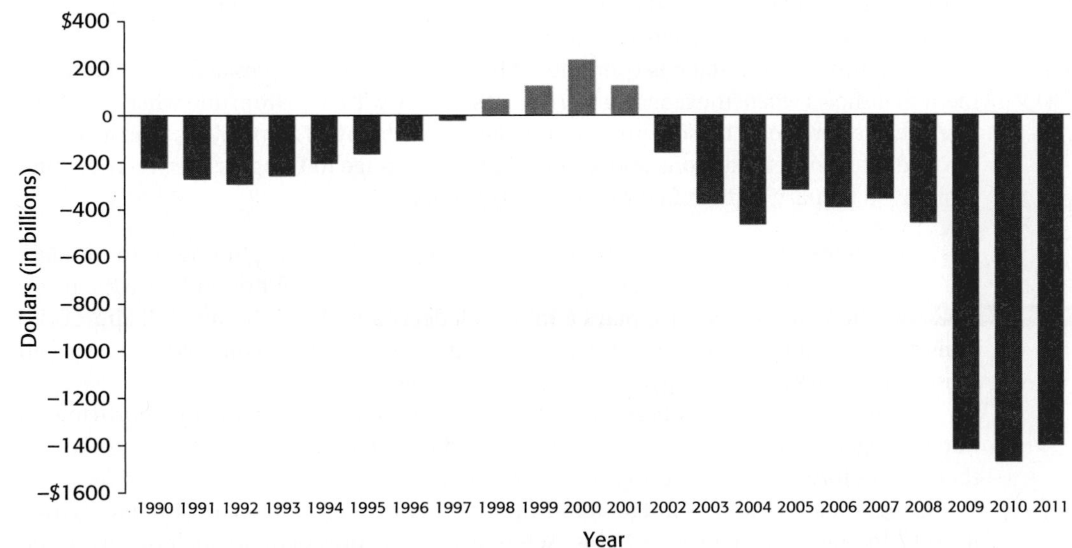

FIGURE 13–6 **The Federal Budget Deficit and Surplus.**

■ *Why has the budget deficit grown so rapidly in recent years?*

SOURCE: Summary Tables, *Budget of the United States, Fiscal Year 2011* (U.S. Government Printing Office, 2010).

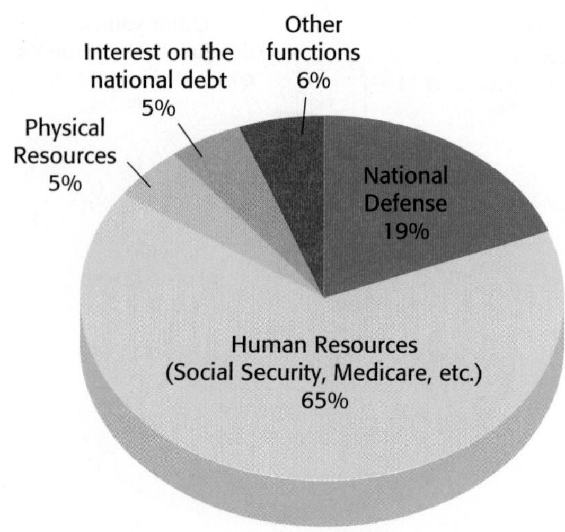

FIGURE 13–7 **Where the Money Goes, 2008.**

SOURCE: Summary Tables, *Budget of the United States, Fiscal Year 2009* (U.S. Government Printing Office, 2008).

Where the Money Goes Much of the money the federal government takes in is spent on benefit payments to individuals and on national defense. Measured in absolute dollars spent in 2006, nearly half of federal spending went to required benefit payments for individuals, such as Social Security, Medicare, Medicaid, and other major social programs. Most federal spending is **mandatory,** meaning that Congress and the president cannot use their discretion to change the spending rates. Mandatory programs include Social Security and Medicare for older people and other programs that pay any citizen who qualifies for support (see Figure 13–7). The rest of the spending is **discretionary,** meaning that Congress and the president can change the spending rates.

Two hundred years ago, revenues and spending were so small that neither had a significant impact on the overall economy. In the 2008 federal budget, even small changes in taxes and spending can alter the direction of the economy. However, because many federal programs are open to all eligible citizens, much of the federal budget is "uncontrollable" or nondiscretionary, meaning the bills must be paid regardless of the cost.

The Budget Process

Before Congress enacted the Budget and Accounting Act of 1921, each executive agency dealt with Congress on its own, requesting that the legislature appropriate funds for its activities with little or no presidential coordination. Today, the president is required by law to submit an annual budget proposal for all agencies together.

The Executive Branch The federal government's fiscal, or spending, year begins every October 1. But the budget process begins nearly two years in advance, when the various departments and agencies estimate their needs and propose their budgets to the president.[12] While Congress is debating the budget for the coming fiscal year, the agencies are making estimates for the year after that. Agency officials take into account not only their needs as they see them but also the overall presidential program and the probable reactions of Congress. Departmental budgets are detailed; they include estimates of expected needs for personnel, supplies, office space, and the like.

The **Office of Management and Budget (OMB)** is responsible for overseeing the budget process on behalf of the president. Once OMB receives each agency's budget request, its budget examiners review each agency's budget and reconcile it with the president's overall plans. OMB then holds informal hearings with every department and agency to give each one a chance to clarify and defend its estimates.

Once this give-and-take is over, the OMB director gives the president a single document that shows where the federal government's money will come from and where it will go. The president reviews these figures and makes adjustments. The president must submit the budget recommendations and accompanying message to Congress between the first Monday in January and the first Monday in February.

The Legislative Branch The president's proposal is only the beginning of the budget process. Under the Constitution, Congress must appropriate the funds and raise the taxes. However, the White House also plays a role in all decisions, if only because all appropriations and tax proposals are subject to a presidential veto. Presidents often threaten to veto these bills as a way of winning passage of their priorities.

Congress acts on the budget in several steps. It starts its process by approving an initial budget resolution that sets the broad spending and revenue goals for the process. It then moves forward with hearings on the budget proposal.

Congress adopted the Budget and Impoundment Control Act of 1974 to strengthen its role in the budget process. This Act requires the president to include proposed changes in tax laws, estimates of amounts of revenue lost through existing preferential tax treatments, and five-year estimates of the costs of new and continuing federal programs. The Act also calls on the president to seek authorizing legislation for a program a year before asking Congress to fund it.

progressive tax
A tax graduated so that people with higher incomes pay a larger fraction of their income than people with lower incomes.

regressive tax
A tax whereby people with lower incomes pay a higher fraction of their income than people with higher incomes.

national debt
The total amount of money the federal government has borrowed to finance deficit spending throughout the years.

mandatory spending
Required spending under the federal budget.

discretionary spending
Spending that can be altered by congressional and presidential action.

Office of Management and Budget (OMB)
The presidential staff agency that serves as a clearinghouse for budgetary requests and management improvements for government agencies.

The 1974 Budget Act also created the **Congressional Budget Office (CBO),** an independent agency that prepares budget data on behalf of Congress, and Congress only. By February 15 of each year, the CBO director presents an analysis of the president's budget proposal to the House and Senate budget committees. The CBO director also provides Congress with biannual forecasts of the economy, analyzes alternative fiscal policies, prepares five-year cost estimates for bills proposed by congressional committees, and undertakes studies requested by committees.

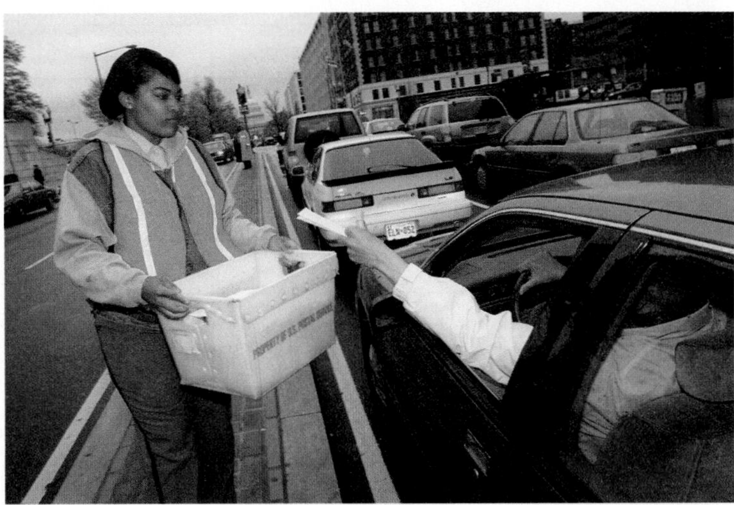

All individual income taxes are due on April 15 of each year. Here, cars line up as taxpayers drop their tax returns at the U.S. Postal Service to make sure they are postmarked on April 15. Failure to pay income taxes on time can result in a fine.

Tax Expenditures

Tax expenditures are a final type of fiscal policy that uses the tax code to provide special tax incentives or benefits to individuals and businesses for economic goals such as homeownership, retirement savings, and college education. The federal government spent more than $900 billion in tax expenditures in 2008. Put another way, the federal government lost more than $900 billion in revenue it would have collected without these tax breaks.

The Politics of Taxing and Spending

In addition to raising funds to run the government, taxes also promote economic growth and reward certain types of behavior, such as contributing to charities. Critics suggest that tax legislation helps individual members of Congress raise campaign funds—laws permitting several of the most popular corporate deductions must be renewed every year, for example, which gives Congress members a chance to show their support for corporations regularly, and corporations a chance to show their support for Congress, too.[13]

The **sales tax,** which is used only at the state and local levels in the United States, is widely used in Europe in a slightly different version. Called the **value-added tax (VAT),** it applies to the increased value of a product *at each stage of production and distribution* rather than just at the point where it is sold to a customer. A loaf of bread would thus have value added several times: The farmer would pay a value-added tax on the grain before selling to the miller, who would be taxed before selling to the baker, and so forth. Some see the value-added tax as a way to infuse a large amount of new revenue into the federal government.

Congressional Budget Office (CBO)
An agency of Congress that analyzes presidential budget recommendations and estimates the costs of proposed legislation.

tax expenditure
A loss of tax revenue due to federal laws that provide special tax incentives or benefits to individuals or businesses.

sales tax
A general tax on sales transactions, sometimes exempting such items as food and drugs.

value-added tax (VAT)
A tax on increased value of a product at each stage of production and distribution rather than just at the point of sale.

Monetary Policy

LEARNING **OBJECTIVE**

13.5 Outline the way in which the federal government makes monetary policy and the role of monetary policy.

Monetary policy is the second way the federal government manages the economy. The core element of monetary policy is the idea that prices, incomes, and economic stability reflect growth in the amount of money that circulates through the economy at any one time. Advocates of aggressive monetary policy contend that the money supply is the key factor affecting the economy's performance. Even as the federal government used fiscal policy to buy bad debt in 2008, it also used monetary policy to pump more money into the economy to provide greater access to credit.

The Federal Reserve System

Monetary policy is not made by Congress or the president but by the Board of Governors of the **Federal Reserve System** (often simply called "the Fed"). The chair and six members of the Fed's Board of Governors are appointed by the president with

Federal Reserve System
The system created by Congress in 1913 to establish banking practices and regulate currency in circulation and the amount of credit available. It consists of 12 regional banks supervised by the Board of Governors. Often simply called "the Fed."

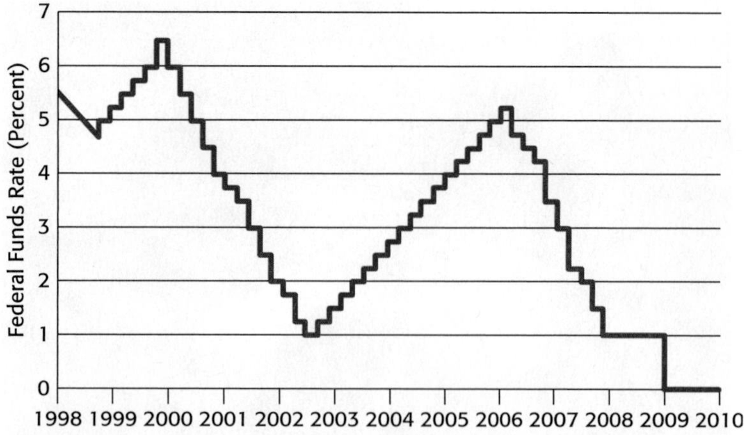

FIGURE 13–8 **Federal Funds Rate, 1998–2010.**

■ *Why did the Federal Reserve Board reduce interest rates so drastically in 2007?*

SOURCE: The Federal Reserve Board, Open Market Operations, federalreserve.gov/monetarypolicy/fomc.htm, September 1, 2010.

Senate consent to 14-year terms; a different member's term expires every two years. As an independent regulatory commission, the Fed is effectively insulated from politics. The governors supervise 12 regional Federal Reserve banks located across the country, each headed by a president and run by a nine-member board of directors chosen from the private financial institutions in each region. The current Fed chair is Ben S. Bernanke, who is thus one of the most powerful policy makers in the world and may have more say over economic performance than the president and Congress.

The Fed has several basic tools for influencing the economy, but its most important involves changing the interest rates banks must pay the Fed for borrowing money, which is called the **federal funds rate.** Increasing the rate slows down the economy by increasing costs for money and credit; lowering the interest rate stimulates the economy by making money more easily available for investment and growth.

The cost of borrowing money is linked to the interest rate a bank's best customers receive on their short-term loans. In turn, this *prime rate* is linked to the interest rates on student loans, home mortgages, car loans, and credit card debt. As Figure 13–8 shows, during the last several years, the Fed has swung between trying to stimulate the economy, slow the economy, and stimulate the economy again.

federal funds rate
The amount of interest banks charge for loans to each other.

laissez-faire economics
A theory that opposes governmental interference in economic affairs beyond what is necessary to protect life and property.

Keynesian economics
An economic theory based on the principles of John Maynard Keynes stating that government spending should increase during business slumps and be curbed during booms.

protectionism
A policy of erecting trade barriers to protect domestic industry.

trade deficit
An imbalance in international trade in which the value of imports exceeds the value of exports.

World Trade Organization (WTO)
An international organization derived from the General Agreement on Tariffs and Trade (GATT) that promotes free trade around the world.

General Agreement on Tariffs and Trade (GATT)
An international trade organization with more than 130 members that seeks to encourage free trade by lowering tariffs and other trade restrictions.

Government and Economic Policy

The Great Depression of the 1930s tested competing theories about helping the economy. Some economists urged the government to reduce spending, lower taxes, curb the power of labor, and generally leave business and the economy alone. This first theory is called **laissez-faire economics.**

Another group, deeply influenced by the work of the English economist John Maynard Keynes,[14] recommended that when consumer spending and investment decline, government spending and investing should increase. Government must do the spending and investing during a recession because private enterprise will not or cannot.

This second theory is called **Keynesian economics.** When the economy is in a recession, Keynesians press for more government spending on goods and services to inject money into the economy and stimulate growth. Keynesians believe this spending will "prime the pump" for increased economic activity and stimulate new jobs for the unemployed. When people have more money in their pockets, Keynesians believe at least some of it will be spent—in economic terms, consumer demand will increase.

Promoting the Economy

LEARNING **OBJECTIVE**

13.6 Identify ways in which the federal government seeks to promote economic growth.

Federal economic policy does more than try to smooth the ups and downs of the business cycle. It also tries to promote economic growth, often measured by the number of new jobs or businesses created. Growth creates jobs for individual workers, which in turn produces higher revenues, which in turn produces either greater savings or more federal spending. U.S. economic policy has two goals: (1) to promote economic growth so that the United States remains a world leader in terms of quality of life, and (2) to regulate business activity so that no single industry or company has an unfair edge in competing for success.

Promoting Economic Growth

The first goal of economic policy is promoting economic growth. The framers believed that developing a strong economy was part of securing the "blessings of liberty," and they encouraged U.S. exports by creating a navy to protect cargo ships. Throughout history, the federal government created a number of departments and agencies to protect that hoped-for growth, including the departments of Agriculture and Commerce and the Small Business Administration.

World War II stimulated a huge rise in the production of weapons, airplanes, and tanks, and many women entered the workforce in manufacturing jobs while the men were at war. ■ *What impact did World War II have on the industrial economy? What is the relationship between war and the economy today?*

Promoting International Trade

Worries about international competition often lead domestic producers to call for **protectionism,** which can take the form of special taxes, or tariffs, placed on imported goods to make them more expensive. Most economists oppose protectionism because it prevents efficient use of resources and because consumers pay much more for protected products than they otherwise would in the world economy. Tariffs merely divert attention from real solutions such as increased productivity and capital investments, and they inevitably invite retaliation from foreign countries.

Trade barriers are less severe today than they were in the 1930s. But restrictions still exist. Certain tariffs, limits on imported goods, and import regulations limit U.S. consumption of foreign products. Most exist to protect U.S. farmers, businesses, or workers in certain industries, but they often do more harm than good by leading other countries to put tariffs and other restrictions on U.S. goods. The result has been a persistent **trade deficit** in which the United States imports far more than it exports.

The World Trade Organization In 1947, a group of countries formed a trade organization to negotiate free trade by lowering tariffs, quotas (limits on the quantity of a particular product that may be imported), and other disadvantages countries face when trading. Today, the **World Trade Organization (WTO)** enforces trade agreements that include more than 130 countries, and its membership accounts for four-fifths of the world's trade.

North American Free Trade Agreement (NAFTA)
An agreement signed by the United States, Canada, and Mexico in 1992 to form the largest free trade zone in the world.

The WTO has conducted eight rounds of negotiations during the past six decades, all of which have amended the **General Agreement on Tariffs and Trade (GATT)** to encourage free trade. The WTO is responsible for overseeing GATT and resolving disputes; it can impose fines and penalties on nations that create protectionist policies.

Not everyone believes free trade should be unlimited, however. Labor unions, environmentalists, and human rights advocates argue that U.S. trade policies spur the creation of low-wage jobs abroad and encourage child labor, pollution, and worker abuse in countries such as China and India that export large quantities of goods to the United States.

The growth of the global economy has produced efforts to protect U.S. workers from unfair dumping of low-priced products in the United States. Here, cargo containers filled with goods await delivery within the United States. Some goods are priced unfairly because of lower wages in other less-developed countries. ■ *Do you think the U.S. trade deficit is a problem? If so, what should be done?*

The North American Free Trade Agreement In 1992, the United States, Canada, and Mexico signed the **North American Free Trade Agreement (NAFTA),** which formed the largest geographical free trade zone in the world. Although President George H. W. Bush signed NAFTA near the end of his presidency, the agreement could not become law until ratified by Congress. President Bill Clinton promoted NAFTA, even though many members of his own party were its most vigorous opponents. Congress passed it by a thin margin in a bipartisan vote with Democrats in the minority.

Regulating the Economy

LEARNING **OBJECTIVE**

13.7 Categorize ways in which the federal government seeks to regulate the economy, and explain the deregulation movement.

The second goal of U.S. economic policy is to regulate business activities that may create unfair advantages. U.S. workers believe in competition among businesses, but they also want a level playing field, meaning no industry or company cheats its way to the top or abuses its employees or the environment along the way.

The Constitution explicitly authorizes Congress to regulate commerce among the states and with foreign nations. In our earliest years, Congress used this regulatory power to impose or suspend tariffs on imports from other nations. In the nineteenth century, the federal government created a number of agencies to regulate the conduct of citizens and commercial enterprises with an eye toward promoting economic development. Among these were the Army Corps of Engineers (1824), the Patent and Trademark Office (1836), the Steamboat Inspection Service (1837), and the Copyright Office of the Library of Congress (1870). In 1887, Congress created the Interstate Commerce Commission to deal with widespread dissatisfaction over the practices of railroads.

Regulating Corporations

In a broad sense, regulation is any attempt by the government to control the behavior of corporations, other governments, or citizens. Regulation by government interjects political goals and values into the economy in the form of rules that direct behavior in the marketplace. These rules have the force of law and are backed by the government's police powers.

Congress has created two types of regulatory agencies: independent agencies under the president's control and independent regulatory commissions insulated from Congress and the president. The heads of independent agencies are nominated by the president and confirmed by the Senate, but they do not have terms of office and serve at the pleasure of the president. Independent regulatory commissioners are also appointed by the president and confirmed by the Senate, but they serve for specific terms of office and cannot be removed by a president except for cause.

Although the national government has been regulating interstate commerce since 1789, it was generally reluctant to regulate private businesses until after the Civil War. As the U.S. economy grew, so did the need for rules governing business and labor. Congress created the Interstate Commerce Commission (ICC) in 1887; the first of many independent regulatory commissions, the ICC regulated railroads and other transportation industries but was abolished in the late 1970s as part of the deregulation movement, which we discuss later in this chapter. Additional regulations were created to end monopolies, increase food safety, prevent environmental pollution, improve automobile safety, and prevent employment discrimination on the basis of race, color, national origin, religion, sex, and age.

monopoly
Domination of an industry by a single company; also the company that dominates the industry.

antitrust legislation
Federal laws (starting with the Sherman Antitrust Act of 1890) that try to prevent a monopoly from dominating an industry and restraining trade.

Both political parties say regulatory overkill threatens to overwhelm entrepreneurs and divert them from building vital, innovative companies. Nevertheless, even opponents of regulation recognize that the market does not always solve every problem. The question is not whether there are both costs and benefits from regulation, however, but whether the balance is right. Conservatives tend to overstate the costs of many regulations and understate the benefits, whereas liberals tend to overstate the benefits and understate the costs.

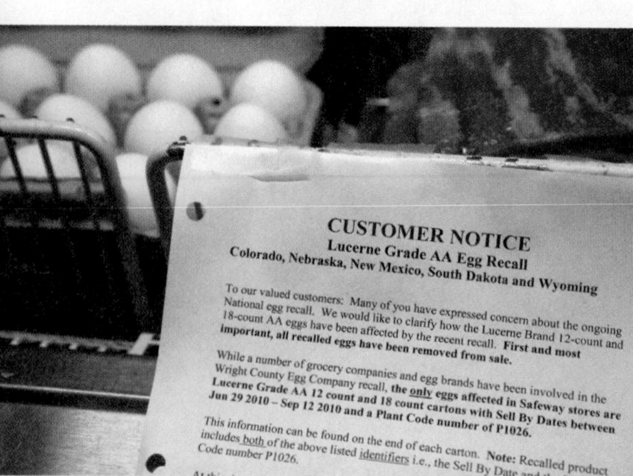

In August 2010, the Food and Drug Administration ordered grocery stores to remove almost 25 million eggs from their shelves due to an outbreak of salmonella, a deadly disease. ■ *Why does the federal bureaucracy, not state and local governments, regulate the food system?*

Regulating Competition

Business regulation increased in three major waves during the past century. The first came in the 1910s, the second in the 1930s, and the third in the late 1960s through 1980. In each case, changing circumstances gave rise to the legislation.

Perhaps the most important responsibility of government regulation in a free market system is to maintain competition. When one company gains a **monopoly,** or several create an *oligopoly,* the market system operates ineffectively. The aim of **antitrust legislation** is to prevent monopolies, break up those that exist, and ensure competition. In the past, so-called natural monopolies, such as electric utilities and telephone companies, were protected by the government because it was assumed that in these fields, competition would be grossly inefficient.

In the late nineteenth century, social critics and populist reformers believed that the oil, sugar, whiskey, and steel industries were deceiving consumers, in large part because of the rise of large monopolies called **trusts.** Once they became aware of abuses in these industries, citizens began to call for more government regulation. In 1890, Congress responded by passing the Sherman Antitrust Act, designed "to protect trade and commerce against unlawful restraints and monopolies." However, the Sherman Antitrust Act had little immediate impact; presidents made few attempts to enforce it, and the Supreme Court's early interpretation of the Act limited its scope.[15]

Congress added the Clayton Act to the antitrust arsenal in 1914. This Act outlawed such specific abuses as charging different prices to different buyers in order to destroy a weaker competitor, granting rebates, making false statements about competitors and their products, buying up supplies to suppress competition, and bribing competitors' employees. In addition, *interlocking directorates* (in which an officer or director in one corporation served on the board of a competitor) were banned, and corporations were prohibited from acquiring stock in competing companies if such acquisitions substantially lessened interstate competition. That same year, Congress established the Federal Trade Commission (FTC), run by a five-person board, to enforce the Clayton Act and prevent unfair competitive practices. The FTC was to be the "traffic cop" for competition.[16]

Regulating the Use of Labor

Most laws and rules curb business practices and steer private enterprise into socially useful channels. But regulation cuts two ways. In the case of U.S. workers, most laws in recent decades have tended not to restrict labor but to confer rights and opportunities on it. Actually, many labor laws do not touch labor directly; instead, they regulate labor's relationship with employers.

Federal regulations protect workers in the following important areas, among others:

1. *Public contracts.* The Walsh-Healey Act of 1936, as amended, requires that most workers employed under contracts with the federal government be paid at least the average or prevailing wage for that job, and that they be paid overtime for all work in excess of 8 hours per day or 40 hours per week.
2. *Wages and hours.* The Fair Labor Standards Act of 1938 set a maximum workweek of 40 hours for all employees engaged in interstate commerce or in the production of goods for interstate commerce (with certain exemptions). Work beyond that amount must be paid for at 1.5 times the regular rate.
3. *Child labor.* The Fair Labor Standards Act of 1938 prohibits children from working in any industry that engages in interstate commerce, which essentially means that all child labor is illegal.
4. *Industrial safety and occupational health.* The Occupational Safety and Health Act of 1970 created the first comprehensive federal industrial safety program. It gave the secretary of labor broad authority to set safety and health standards for companies engaged in interstate commerce.

Federal regulations also protect employees' right to organize unions. Under the 1935 National Labor Relations Act (usually called the Wagner Act), for example, the federal government gave workers significant new rights to organize unions, while prohibiting businesses from discriminating against union members or refusing to bargain in good faith with union representatives.

Congress passed a major modification of the labor laws in 1947, the Labor-Management Relations Act, commonly called the Taft-Hartley Act. The Act outlawed the **closed shop,** a company in which only union members in good standing may be hired; permitted the **union shop,** a company in which new employees are obligated to join the union within a stated period of time; prohibited employers from refusing to bargain with employees; allowed courts to issue **labor injunctions** forbidding specific individuals or groups from performing acts considered harmful to the rights or property of an employer or community; and structured the process of **collective bargaining** between unions and employers to set wages, benefits, and working conditions.

trust
A monopoly that controls goods and services, often in combinations that reduce competition.

closed shop
A company with a labor agreement under which union membership is a condition of employment.

union shop
A company in which new employees must join a union within a stated time period.

labor injunction
A court order forbidding specific individuals or groups from performing certain acts (such as striking) that the court considers harmful to the rights and property of an employer or a community.

collective bargaining
A method whereby representatives of the union and employer determine wages, hours, and other conditions of employment through direct negotiation.

For the People

GOVERNMENT'S GREATEST ENDEAVORS

Clean Air and Water

One of the most visible forms of economic regulation involves nearly 60 years of effort to protect the nation's air and water from pollution. Although early laws such as the 1948 Water Pollution Act and the 1963 Clean Air Act established a federal role in protecting the environment, the 1970 Clean Air and 1972 Clean Water Acts provided much of the legal power to make progress in both areas.

During the past 30 years, the levels of most air pollution covered by the Clean Air Act have fallen dramatically as the U.S. Environmental Protection Agency has established ever-tighter rules promoting more efficient automobiles and cleaner-burning fuels. Although it is hard to find a single American city where the air quality has not improved, air pollution continues to spread to rural areas such as national parks where automobile pollution is concentrated as tourists arrive in record numbers.

Similarly, it is hard to find a single body of water or river that is not significantly cleaner because of the Clean Water Act. However, as the nation has learned more about pollutants such as arsenic, the pressure to improve water quality has increased. The Obama administration has been moving to expand both acts to cover new pollutants, while tightening limits on acceptable levels of exposure. It is also pushing for legislation to address the rising global temperature.

The federal government is becoming more concerned about the global environment, including the melting of the polar ice caps, which may raise sea levels dramatically throughout the next 100 years.

Despite these successes, there are many challenges ahead in keeping the air and water clean. The 2010 Gulf oil spill is a good example. As technology has become more sophisticated, the oil industry has been drilling at much greater depths below the water and in much more fragile environments. The Gulf oil spill shows how risky such drilling is, especially since the federal rules governing oil exploration were more than 30 years old when the spill occurred.

CRITICAL THINKING QUESTIONS

1. How clean should the air and water be in order to be declared "clean"?
2. How can the federal government protect the environment without hurting industry and creating unemployment when dirty factories must close?
3. What can citizens do to improve the environment through their own actions?

Protecting the Environment

Until the 1960s, the United States did little to protect the environment, and the little that was done was by state and local governments. Recently, the federal government has taken on new responsibilities, starting with passage of the Clean Air and Water Acts in the early 1970s. These put new limits on the amount of pollution companies could release into the environment and launched a long list of laws regulating things, such as leaking underground storage tanks, garbage, and encouraging energy conservation and recycling. Congress also created the Environmental Protection Agency (EPA) to enforce the new laws.

Perhaps the most controversial environmental regulations are **environmental impact statements,** which assess the potential effects of new construction or development on the environment. Most projects using federal funds must prepare such statements, and since 1970, thousands have been filed. Supporters contend that the statements reveal major environmental risks in new construction projects and can lead to cost savings and greater environmental awareness. Critics claim that they represent more government interference, paperwork, and delays in the public and private sectors.

Environmental impact statements are only one form of environmental regulation, however. In 1990, Congress amended the Clean Air Act to tighten controls on automobiles and the fuel they use. Building on earlier mileage regulation, the 1990 amendments required automakers to install pollution controls to reduce emissions of hydrocarbons and nitrogen oxides and set stiff standards for the kinds of gasoline that can be sold. The 1990 Act also required power companies to cut pollution from coal-burning power plants, phased out the use of certain chemicals that harm the earth's protective ozone layer and may contribute to global warming, and set new limits on a long list of cancer-causing pollutants. In 2005, the Bush administration implemented a new set of relatively loose regulations supporting its Clear Skies initiative, but most of these regulations were repealed and replaced by more stringent limits by the Obama administration.

environmental impact statement
A statement required by federal law from all agencies for any project using federal funds to assess the potential effect of the new construction or development on the environment.

Corporate Responsibility

Many corporations have been dealing with the increased pressure to be more responsible by creating programs to give money and volunteer time to their communities. The Gap has pledged to provide a portion of every sale to charities through "Product Red," and other corporations have promised to be more environmentally conscious. These efforts at **corporate social responsibility** have increased public confidence in big business.

There are three forms of corporate social responsibility. The first is corporate giving to charities. Many corporations have foundations that give 1 or 2 percent of their annual profits to specific causes. The second is free consulting and advertising to help charities become more effective in making their voices heard. The third pairs corporations and charities in partnership activities such as annual walks for cancer. Many corporations also give their employees paid time off to volunteer.

The Deregulation Movement

One response to criticisms of government regulation of the economy is **deregulation,** the reduction or abolition of federal regulation in a particular sector of the economy. Deregulation began in 1977 with the airline, trucking, and railroad industries and has continued with banking and telecommunications.

At the same time that the federal government has been working to deregulate certain industries, it has also created new procedures to limit the amount of regulation it can impose. In 1993, for example, President Clinton issued an executive order prohibiting agencies from issuing regulations unless the benefits of the regulations (in lives saved, for example) outweighed the costs. In 2001, President Bush followed suit by imposing a 60-day hold on all regulations published by the Clinton administration until his administration could ensure that they passed the benefit/cost test.

No industry has undergone more extensive deregulation than the transportation industry. During the past generation, airlines, trucking, and railroads have been granted considerable freedom in conducting their operations. No deregulation effort has been more visible to consumers than airline deregulation.

The federal government began regulating aviation when it established the Civil Aeronautics Board (CAB) in 1938 to control rates and fares, protecting airlines from unreasonable competition. Critics charged that under regulation, airlines competed only in the frequency of flights and in the services they offered, forcing consumers to pay higher fares than needed.

After years of debate, Congress abolished the CAB in 1978, allowing the market to set fares through competition. The end of airline regulation has created problems but has resulted in generally lower fares, greater choice of routes and fares in most markets, and more efficient use of assets by the industry.[17] If an airline is overcharging passengers, a competitor will eventually steal those travelers away. Carriers have thus had to streamline their operations in order to survive in a competitive market. Southwest, AirTran, and JetBlue Airlines are examples of discount airlines that took advantage of deregulation to take on larger airlines.[18]

But recent mergers of major airlines have worsened the problems that deregulation and cancellation of service brought to small and medium-sized cities in many states and localities. The post–September 11 collapse in travel pushed several airlines toward bankruptcy, which in turn prompted Congress to provide loans to many airlines to help them through the crisis. Under economic pressure, many airlines stopped providing basic services such as meals, and some have demanded deep cutbacks in wages and benefits from their employees. However, some newer airlines such as Jet Blue and Southwest have been highly profitable offering low-cost services across the nation.

corporate social responsibility
Efforts by corporations to improve their reputations by paying attention to their contributions to the social good.

deregulation
A policy promoting cutbacks in the amount of federal regulation in specific areas of economic activity.

JetBlue offers its customers numerous amenities, including free snacks and personal televisions for in-flight entertainment. ■ *How did the deregulation movement allow for the rise of companies such as JetBlue? How has JetBlue been so successful as a start-up airline?*

The Role of the Federal Government in Social Policy

LEARNING **OBJECTIVE**

13.8 Outline the goals of the federal government's social policy and the forms of protection it provides.

Most Western governments expanded their social programs long before the United States did. American adults generally believed that people who could not succeed in a nation as big, rich, and open as the United States simply weren't working hard enough. This commitment to *rugged individualism* meant that government, whether local, state, or federal, played only a limited role in people's lives. Rather grudgingly, state governments in the early twentieth century extended relief to low-income groups, especially the old, the blind, and the orphaned. But government aid was limited, and most low-income people relied on charity for help, as many still do.[19]

This is not to suggest that the federal government ignored domestic policy, however. From its founding, the government took care of its military veterans. Indeed, with the Revolutionary War barely over, the Continental Congress established the nation's first programs to help soldiers disabled in battle and to provide retirement pensions for officers, well before the new government was even created.

These early programs set two important precedents for contemporary domestic policy. First, they established the notion that some people would be automatically entitled to certain government benefits on the basis of an eligibility requirement such as service in the nation's armed forces. Thus, veterans' relief was the nation's first **entitlement,** under which the government provides benefits to any citizen who is eligible regardless of need. Throughout the decades since, Congress and the president have created dozens of entitlement programs, including Social Security and Medicare. Both programs provide benefits to anyone who has paid taxes for them and are available once an individual reaches retirement age.

Second, these early programs also established government's right to restrict some benefits to only those citizens who could actually prove their need for help. In the original program, for instance, only poor veterans could go to old soldiers' homes. These were early examples of what we now call **means-tested entitlements,** under which citizens must prove they are poor enough to deserve the government's help. Throughout the decades since, Congress and the president have created dozens of means-tested entitlement programs, including Supplemental Security Income and food stamps. Both programs provide benefits only to those who can prove they are below a certain income level.

entitlements
Programs such as unemployment insurance, disaster relief, or disability payments that provide benefits to all eligible citizens.

means-tested entitlements
Programs such as Medicaid and welfare under which applicants must meet eligibility requirements based on need.

Having entered the twentieth century with only a handful of domestic programs, most of which were built around helping veterans, the federal government left the century with a deep inventory of such programs. According to the 2008 *Catalog of Federal Domestic Assistance,*

Although the federal government has become much more involved in helping the needy, private charities still provide nearly three-quarters of the free food for the hungry in the United States. ■ *Why are both private charities and government programs important for social welfare in America?*

which lists every one of the federal government's approximately 1,250 domestic funding programs in a searchable database (www.cfda.gov), there are at least 38 separate programs for farmers, another 35 for college and university students, 34 for women, and 44 for infants.

The Goals of Social Policy

Because most of these programs are restricted to one group of citizens only, they are often described as *categorical* aid. Simply typing a search term online such as "students," "elderly," "children," "disabled," "workers," "farmers," "women," or "veterans" reveals just how much help the federal government provides in each category. But regardless of category, federal domestic policy focuses on two broad goals.

The first goal is to protect citizens against social and economic problems by creating a **social safety net,** whether through relief for unemployed workers, health care for the elderly, emergency shelter for the homeless, or school lunches for poor children, most of which are available to citizens only on the basis of a means test that proves they need help. Although almost all citizens are covered by federal unemployment insurance through a payroll tax, only workers who have been laid off from their jobs through no fault of their own can qualify for benefits, and then only for a relatively brief period of time.

The second goal of federal social policy is to raise the quality of life for all, whether by improving air and water quality, building roads and bridges, regulating air traffic, fighting crime, or strengthening local schools through federal aid. Nearly all federal aid to the states for these purposes is distributed by formula on the basis of population, not need.

Types of Protection

Most scholars trace the federal government's effort to protect citizens against economic and personal hard times to the Great Depression and the Social Security Act of 1935. Although Franklin Roosevelt's New Deal agenda stimulated a remarkable expansion in the federal government's domestic policy role, federal, state, and local governments were helping citizens long before the Depression hit. However, as the nation sunk deeper into economic distress, Congress and the president soon invented two very different types of federal programs to protect citizens against hardship, both of which continue today.

social safety net
The many programs that the federal government provides to protect Americans against economic and social misfortune.

public assistance
Aid to the poor; "welfare."

social insurance
Programs in which eligibility is based on prior contributions to government, usually in the form of payroll taxes.

Public Assistance One type of help for the poor is called **public assistance,** or "welfare." The first public assistance programs were actually created in the late 1800s, when states established aid programs to help poor single mothers and their children. Although these programs were often described as "mothers' pensions" to create the impression that the beneficiaries had earned the benefits through some contribution, they created a precedent for many of the federal government's later antipoverty programs.

Most of these programs are means-tested entitlement programs. As noted earlier, such programs require applicants to disclose all financial assets and income to prove they fall below the poverty line, generally calculated as three times the amount of money an individual or family needs to purchase the food for a nutritious diet. This poverty level changes with the size of the family and the cost of living. For 2008, individuals who made slightly more than $10,000 and families of four who made slightly more than $21,000 were eligible for means-tested assistance.[20]

In absolute numbers, most poor people are white. As a percentage within their own population, however, a larger proportion of African Americans and Hispanics are poor. Moreover, in both absolute and proportional terms, more women than men are poor. Indeed, some scholars refer to the relatively recent rise in poverty among women as the "feminization of poverty."[21]

Food stamps, which today are often distributed as debit cards for food purchases, allow needy families to purchase nutritious food. In 2010, the food stamp program fed 1 in 8 Americans and 1 in 4 children in America. ■ *Why were food stamps created as an entitlement program?*

Social Insurance The second type of protection against hardship is **social insurance,** government programs that provide

Of the People

THE GLOBAL COMMUNITY

Experience with Poverty

The social safety net is a response to continuing problems such as hunger, disease, and poverty. Although countries vary greatly in the amount of need, the Pew Global Survey shows that significant percentages of citizens go without access to basic human needs every year.

The survey asked respondents, "Have there been times during the last year when you did not have enough money to (a) buy food your family needed, (b) pay for medical care your family needed, (c) and buy clothing your family needed?"

These answers provide a barometer of economic and social progress. All nations were hard hit by the 2008 recession, but the safety net appears to have been stronger in Britain, China, India, and Japan than it was in Mexico, Nigeria, and the United States.

China shows the greatest variation in the strength of its safety net—whereas its citizens report fewer problems buying food and clothing, a third said they had problems with access to health care in 2009. The problem lies in the rapid expansion of the Chinese population, which is putting pressure on the health system. Although the Chinese economy is growing rapidly too, the country has faced difficulty converting its growth into health care access.

CRITICAL THINKING QUESTIONS

1. Besides the economy, why might citizens in some countries have greater problems getting access to basic necessities such as food, health care, and clothing?
2. Does this lack of access have an impact on trust in government and other measures of citizen participation? What is the effect of hunger and poverty on how citizens think of other freedoms?
3. Why do so many Americans report lack of access to basic necessities? Are you surprised?

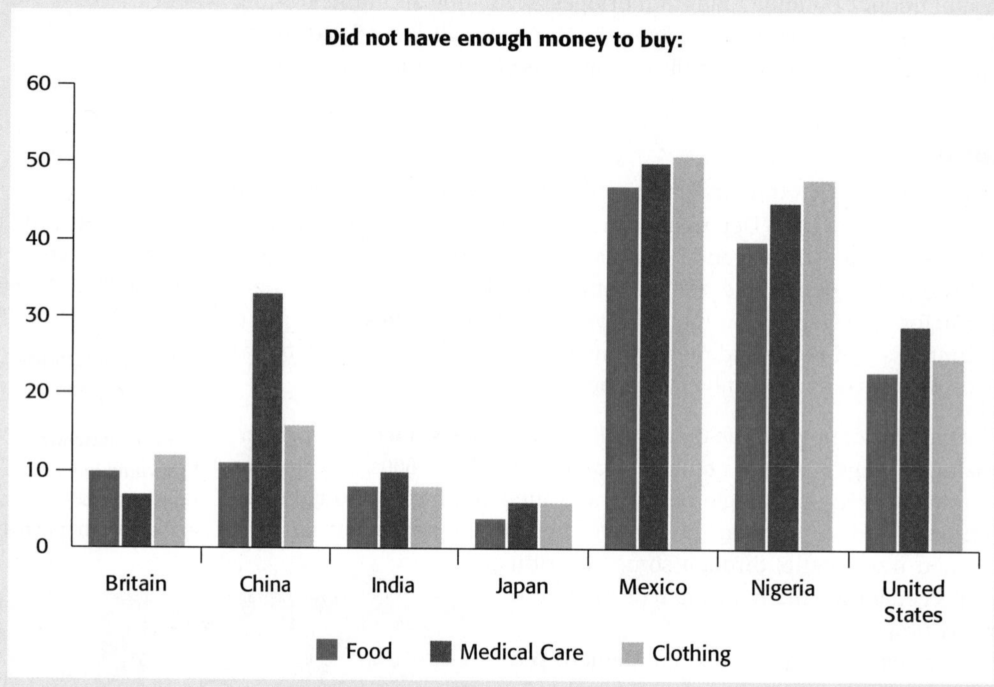

benefits to anyone who is eligible because of either past service (veterans, miners, merchant marines) or prepayments of some kind (payroll taxes for Social Security and Medicare or insurance premiums).

Many federal assistance programs are partnerships with state governments. There are two reasons for the connection. First, except for veterans' policy, states have been responsible for protecting their citizens against hardship since the United States was formed. Second, state and local governments have the administrative agencies to stay in touch with recipients of aid, whether to make sure they are actually eligible for support or to provide services such as job training or school lunches.

Because states vary greatly in their generosity, most federal assistance is designed to set a minimum floor of support that individual states can raise on their own. The most generous states in the country tend to be located in the Northeast and West, where living costs tend to be higher and legislatures more liberal, whereas the least generous tend to be found in the South. In this way, states act as a check on the federal government's ability to raise benefits too far, frustrating those who believe that the federal government should set a uniform level of benefits for all citizens.

The Expansion of Social Policy in the Twentieth Century

LEARNING **OBJECTIVE**

13.9 Outline the evolution of social policy throughout the twentieth century.

The federal government's commitment to helping the poor and improving the quality of life expanded rapidly during the Great Depression, which followed the stock market crash of 1929. The social safety net built by state and local governments and private charities at that time simply could not meet the needs of the huge increase in the homeless, unemployed, and poor.

The New Deal

Franklin Roosevelt was responsible for the expansion of social programs during the 1930s. As part of his New Deal agenda, the federal government began making loans to states and localities to help the poor, and soon it launched a long list of programs to help older workers (Social Security), the jobless (unemployment insurance), and the poor (Aid to Families with Dependent Children).

The First 100 Days Before creating these signature New Deal programs, however, the Roosevelt administration moved quickly to help low-income Americans. The first 100 days of 1933 produced the most significant list of legislation ever passed in U.S. history, including the Federal Emergency Relief Administration (FERA), which was established to give unemployed workers cash grants to get them through the summer.

The list of "alphabet agencies" grew longer as the administration created a host of new programs to help the poor, including the Works Progress Administration (WPA), which was created in 1935 to provide work for millions of unemployed, and the Civilian Conservation Corps (CCC), which put millions of young people to work clearing trails and building roads in the national forests and parks. Between 1933 and 1945, for example, the WPA put 8.5 million people to work at a cost of $10 billion. All told, the WPA built 650,000 miles of roads, 125,000 public buildings, 8,200 parks, and 850 airports. Though the wages were hardly generous, these and other New Deal programs created a national safety net to catch those in need. It is little wonder that scholars describe the New Deal as the "big bang" of social policy.[22] Although the distinction between the worthy and unworthy poor still remained, joblessness was no longer defined as merely a problem of individual idleness or the unwillingness to work.

Help for Older Citizens Once past the immediate crisis, the Roosevelt administration began designing the flagship programs of the New Deal. First on the list was **Social Security,** enacted in 1935 and still the federal government's most popular social program. Social Security was designed to meet two goals: (1) provide a minimum income for poor beneficiaries, and (2) ensure that benefits bear a relationship to the amount of payroll taxes a beneficiary actually paid. Supported by equal contributions from employers and employees, the program now covers more than 90 percent of the U.S. workforce.[23] Employees pay half of the annual Social Security tax, which applies to income up to $102,000 per year. The tax is identified on pay stubs as FICA, which stands for the Federal Insurance Contribution Act, and also covers disability insurance for injuries on the job.

Social Security was expanded in 1939 to include financial support for survivors of workers covered by Social Security when the retired worker died, and in 1954, it was expanded again to include support for disabled workers and the children of deceased or disabled workers. Benefit levels were raised repeatedly during the first 40 years of the program, often just before an election. The increases became so frequent and so costly that in 1975, Congress finally indexed benefits to rise only with inflation. Under legislation enacted in 1983, the Social Security retirement age started to rise in 2003 and will reach 67 by the year 2027.

Social Security
A combination of entitlement programs, paid for by employer and employee taxes, that includes retirement benefits, health insurance, and support for disabled workers and the children of deceased or disabled workers.

Many senior citizens rely on Social Security benefits to see them through their retirement years. This entitlement program covers more than 90 percent of the American workforce. ■ *What are the arguments for and against making Social Security a means-tested program?*

Until the 1970s, steady growth in Social Security benefits was relatively uncontroversial, largely because "the costs were initially deceptively low," making the system politically painless.[24] It is now the world's largest insurance program for retirees, survivors, and people with disabilities. In 2008, Social Security and Medicare expenditures totaled $966 billion.

Help for the Poor The federal government began protecting women and children against poverty when Congress passed the Infancy and Maternity Protection Act of 1921. Supported by many of the same women's groups that had just won ratification of the Nineteenth Amendment, which gave women the right to vote, the Act gave the newly created federal Children's Bureau funds to encourage states to create new maternal, infant, and early childhood health programs.

This precedent eventually produced the Aid to Families with Dependent Children (AFDC) program in 1935.[25] As its name suggests, AFDC tried to reduce public opposition to expanded benefits by shifting the focus away from what the mother had done or not done to deserve poverty, and onto the children, who suffered whatever the cause. Under the program, states were given federal money to establish cash grants for poor families under two conditions: states had to (1) match the federal funds with some contribution of their own and (2) establish a means-test for all families receiving benefits.

Congress also established the school lunch program during the New Deal as a way to both feed the hungry and strengthen the ailing farm economy. The Federal Surplus Relief Corporation began purchasing surplus agriculture products for low-income families in 1935 and launched the nation's first school lunch programs for poor children shortly thereafter. By 1941, more than 5 million children were receiving free school lunches, consuming more than 450 million pounds of surplus pork, dairy products, and bread. Although the program was disbanded during World War II because of food shortages, it was restored under the 1946 National School Lunch Act. As President Harry Truman said at the signing ceremony, "No nation is any healthier than its children." He could have added that many draftees had been rejected for service in World War II because of malnutrition.

Help for the Disabled and Unemployed The New Deal created two new federal programs to help disabled workers and the unemployed. Both were established under the Social Security Act in 1935.

Under the Disability Insurance program, workers can apply for government benefits if they have been injured on the job. They must have been disabled for at least five months and be unable to continue on the job. The process for earning a disability payment, which covers part of a worker's monthly salary, is very strict. Only 20 percent of applications are approved. The worker has to present detailed evidence that the disability

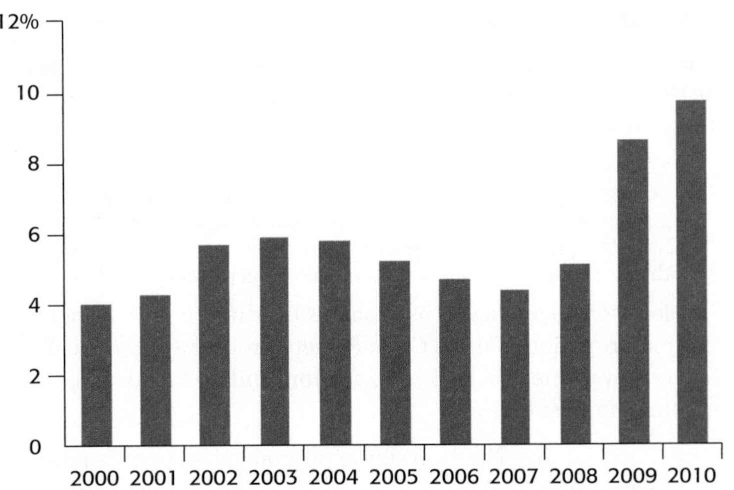

FIGURE 13–9 Unemployment in the United States.

■ *How does the unemployment rate today compare to the average rate over the last decade? What percentage unemployment is acceptable?*

SOURCE: U.S. Bureau of Labor Statistics.

was work, not age related, for example, and must prove that the disability is long term. Approximately 3 million Americans received disability support in 2009.

Unemployment insurance is available to workers who have lost their jobs because of economic conditions. Workers cannot receive benefits if they quit their jobs by their own choice—for example, if they have children, get married, move to another part of the country—or are fired for poor performance. Federal unemployment insurance is jointly administered by the federal government and the 50 states and is covered by monthly premiums that are automatically deducted from paychecks. Employers also pay monthly premiums for their employees. Unemployed workers cannot receive more than half their monthly pay, up to specific limits—in New York, for example, the maximum payment is approximately $500 a month, but it is less than half that amount in Arizona. During normal economic times, the benefit is paid for 26 weeks (see Figure 13–9 for the recent unemployment rate).

Although these programs sound generous, and are sometimes abused by employees who invent disabilities, they provide the bare minimum for survival. They are often the only sources of income that stand between a family and homelessness, hunger, and the loss of health care.

The federal government has several programs to make sure that women, children, and infants receive nutritious food. School lunch programs sometimes provide the only full meal of the day for the nation's poorest children. ■ *Why does federal spending on early childhood health save money in the longer term?*

The Great Society

The second major expansion of social policy came in the 1960s with what became known as the Great Society. At a commencement speech at the University of Michigan in May 1964, President Lyndon Johnson described his vision of the Great Society:

> The Great Society rests on abundance and liberty for all. It demands an end to poverty and racial injustice.... But that is just the beginning. The Great Society is a place where every child can find knowledge to enrich his mind and to enlarge his talents.... It is a challenge constantly renewed, beckoning us toward a destiny where the meaning of our lives matches the marvelous products of our labors.[26]

Johnson's agenda was as broad as his rhetoric, and Congress enacted much of it in a fairly short period of time. Great Society programs dramatically increased the role of the federal government in health, education, and welfare through a number of programs that continue to exist today:

- *Food Stamps.* The food stamp program gives poor families coupons to purchase the basics of a healthy, nutritious diet. The average benefit is approximately $90 per person per month. The program was renamed SNAP in 2009 (Supplemental Nutrition Assistance Program).
- *Head Start.* Head Start is a preschool program designed to help poor children get ready for kindergarten. The program serves more than 900,000 children each year at a cost of approximately $7,000 per child. Nearly 30 percent of Head Start teachers and staff are parents of Head Start children or were Head Start children themselves.
- *Medicare.* As noted earlier, **Medicare** was created in 1965 to provide health care to older citizens. It provides all reasonable hospital, medical, and prescription drug insurance. The hospital insurance is funded by a 1.42 percent tax on employees and employers. Medicare pays for inpatient hospital care, skilled nursing care, and other services. Individuals can purchase additional Medicare insurance to cover some expenses not traditionally covered by Medicare. With enactment in 2010 of Obama's health care plan, Medicare will become the largest federal spending program by 2015, if not sooner.
- *Medicaid.* **Medicaid** was created in 1965 to provide basic health services for poor families. The program is administered and partially funded by state governments and covers items such as hospital care and family planning. Obama's health care plan expanded Medicaid dramatically as a way to provide more coverage for the poor.
- *Supplemental Security Income.* The SSI program was created in 1972 to provide an extra measure of support for the elderly, the poor, and the blind or disabled. Levels of SSI support vary by state to reflect cost-of-living differences, so the program provides monthly benefit checks ranging from only $1 to approximately $800. SSI benefits are financed by general tax revenues and administered by the Social Security Administration.
- *Housing Assistance.* The Department of Housing and Urban Development, which was created in 1965, administers a number of programs designed to help low-income families find affordable, safe housing, in part by giving property owners subsidies to make up the difference between what tenants can pay and what the local housing market will bear.

Medicare
A national health insurance program for the elderly and disabled.

Medicaid
A federal program that provides medical benefits for low-income people.

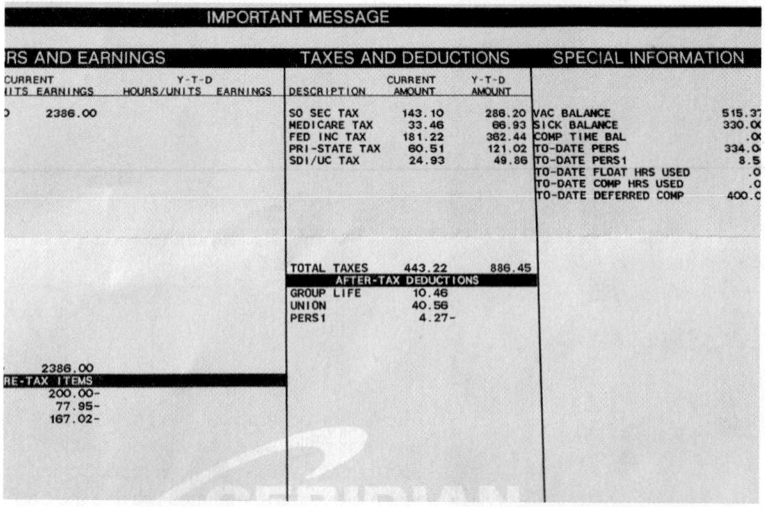

IMPORTANT MESSAGE

RS AND EARNINGS

CURRENT ITS EARNINGS	Y-T-D HOURS/UNITS	EARNINGS
2386.00		
2386.00		

RE-TAX ITEMS
200.00-
77.95-
167.02-

TAXES AND DEDUCTIONS

DESCRIPTION	CURRENT AMOUNT	Y-T-D AMOUNT
SO SEC TAX	143.10	286.20
MEDICARE TAX	33.46	66.93
FED INC TAX	181.22	362.44
PRI-STATE TAX	60.51	121.02
SDI/UC TAX	24.93	49.86
TOTAL TAXES	443.22	886.45

AFTER-TAX DEDUCTIONS

GROUP LIFE	10.46
UNION	40.56
PERS1	4.27-

SPECIAL INFORMATION

VAC BALANCE	515.37
SICK BALANCE	330.00
COMP TIME BAL	.00
TO-DATE PERS	334.0
TO-DATE PERS1	8.5
TO-DATE FLOAT HRS USED	.0
TO-DATE COMP HRS USED	.0
TO-DATE DEFERRED COMP	400.0

Social Security and Medicare taxes are withdrawn from regular paychecks and are called payroll taxes. The FICA (Federal Insurance Contribution Act) tax is collected on all payroll checks up to certain limits on income. ■ *How much do you pay in taxes in each of your paychecks?*

Reforming Welfare

Republicans have not been the only critics of the New Deal and Great Society welfare programs. President Bill Clinton made welfare reform a centerpiece of his reelection agenda in 1996, promising to "end welfare as we know it."[27]

Working with the new Republican congressional majority, Clinton won passage of the Personal Responsibility and Work Opportunity Reconciliation Act in 1996, which replaced the New Deal's AFDC with Temporary Assistance for Needy Families (TANF).

YOU WILL

DECIDE Should the Federal Government Promote Marriage?

Although the 1996 welfare reform legislation focused on replacing welfare with work, it also ordered the federal government to promote marriage. Advocates argue that marriage improves the lives of both children and parents. Married adults, whether women or men, are happier, healthier, and wealthier than their unmarried peers and are more likely to give their children a healthier start in life. Some advocates even argue that more marriages would reduce health costs by reducing depression and crime.*

The federal government can promote marriage in two ways. First, it can reduce the penalties it imposes on welfare recipients who get married. Under current law, for example, a single mother working full time at a minimum-wage job who marries stands to lose as much as $8,000 per year in cash and noncash benefits. Second, it can promote marriage through advertising, counseling, or even providing cash grants for getting married.

What do you think? Should the federal government enact policies that promote marriage? What are the arguments for both sides of the issue?

THINKING IT THROUGH

Although the federal government has long engaged in activities designed to promote vaccinating children, quitting smoking, wearing seat belts, and driving under 55 miles per hour, not everyone believes that promoting marriage is the answer to reducing the welfare rolls.

Critics note, for example, that domestic violence and child abuse occur almost as frequently in married as in unmarried households. They also worry that government grants for marriage would promote a rash of false marriages designed to get the cash. Most important, opponents believe that the best way to improve conditions for welfare recipients is to find them good-paying jobs. They look to states such as Minnesota that have created strong welfare-to-work programs that do not punish married women for getting a job.

Nevertheless, marriage appears to affect income. Two paychecks are better than one, and married couples may be more likely to save money for the future. Marital stability also positively influences child well-being on several measures, and marriage fosters healthier living habits as the marriage partners help monitor each other in such areas as smoking, weight gain, and drug use. These effects can be benefits to society in general.

The question, however, is whether they are a consequence of marriage or simply a product of adults living together. Absent a solid answer, support for marriage may be more an indicator of a person's ideology and religion than a position based on careful research.

Critical Thinking Questions

1. Should the federal government promote social values such as marriage?
2. How is promoting marriage similar to and different from other federal programs such as its campaign to stop smoking?
3. Why is marriage considered a way to reduce poverty? Are there other or better ways to achieve the same goal?

* See, for example, Ron Haskins and Isabel V. Sawhill, *Work and Marriage: The Way to End Poverty and Welfare*, Welfare Reform & Beyond Brief No. 28 (Brookings Institution, 2003).

Under the new rules, federally funded public assistance is limited to five years during a person's lifetime, and all recipients must enter some kind of work training program within two months of receiving initial benefits. Although states can exempt up to 20 percent of cases from the work requirements and time limits—an exemption intended for blind and disabled persons—the message to recipients is clear: Find work soon.

The law originally excluded legal immigrants from many welfare programs, but at the strong urging of the governors, most welfare benefits were later restored to legal immigrants. To discourage people on welfare from moving to states with more generous assistance payments, the law gave states the option of limiting welfare to newcomers from other states. This provision was declared unconstitutional by a federal district court judge, however, who said it "denies 'equal protection of the laws' to indigent families moving from one state to another."[28] The decision was not appealed.

Social Policy Challenges for the Future: Health, Education, and Crime

LEARNING **OBJECTIVE**

13.10 Evaluate the current status of and challenges for federal government policy in the areas of health care, education, and crime.

Even if states take on a greater social policy role, the federal government is sure to remain the greatest source of funding for the safety net. As Figure 13–10 shows, human resource spending for programs such as Social Security, Medicare, Medicaid, and child nutrition has doubled since 1950. The figure also shows a very slight increase in

FIGURE 13–10 Changing Priorities in the Federal Budget.

■ *What parts of the federal government have seen the greatest change over the last 50 years? What explains these changes in spending priorities?*

SOURCE: Historical Tables, *Budget of the United States, Fiscal Year 2011* (U.S. Government Printing Office, February 2011).

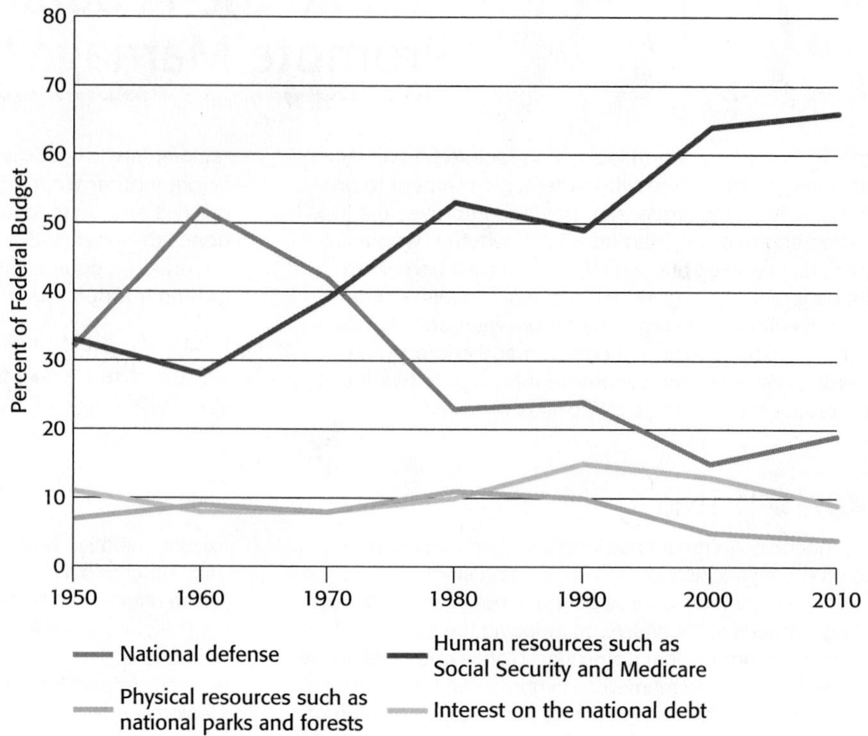

spending on physical resources, such as roads and bridges, due to the large, one-time infusion of money through the economic stimulus package. However, the figure does not show the projected interest on the national debt beyond 2010—according to the White House Office of Management and Budget, estimated interest payments will swell to $551 billion in 2015.

The Federal Role in Health Care

Medicare is only one of the federal government's many health programs. The federal government has been instrumental in reducing disease since 1887, when then it opened a one-room laboratory on Staten Island, New York, to study infectious diseases carried to the United States on passenger ships. In time, that one-room laboratory expanded into the National Institutes of Health (NIH), a conglomeration of 37 separate institutes on a 300-acre campus in Bethesda, Maryland.

The surgeon general of the United States is arguably the most visible health care official in government. As head of the Public Health Service (PHS), the surgeon general oversees a diverse array of health care researchers at NIH and elsewhere. Federally funded researchers study causes and seek cures for serious diseases. The PHS also grants fellowships for health research to scientists and physicians and administers grants to states and local communities to help improve public health. Another federal agency promoting health is the Food and Drug Administration (FDA), which oversees the development of new drugs and ensures food safety through inspections of the nation's food supply.

Dozens of other federal agencies work to improve public health. The Centers for Disease Control and Prevention (CDC) in Atlanta is also actively engaged in preventing disease. The CDC and its 7,800 "disease detectives" have been at the forefront of identifying a host of mystery illnesses, including the respiratory disease that attacked attendees at an American Legion convention in 1976 (Legionnaire's disease), toxic shock syndrome in 1980, and hepatitis C in 1989, as well as tracking down the causes of major health disasters, including the outbreak of swine flu in 2009. The swine flu outbreak produced a massive effort to vaccinate Americans against the virus, which was especially threatening to young adults.

Despite its success in improving the nation's health, the federal government faces two major health care challenges in the future: containing costs and expanding coverage.

Young adults proved particularly susceptible to the new swine flu virus that emerged in 2009. The federal government accelerated development of the vaccine to prevent the spread of the disease on college campuses.

The Rising Cost of Health Care Health care costs in the United States have nearly quadrupled, after controlling for inflation, since 1970.[29] Although costs slowed with the rest of the economy in 2001, they are expected to escalate rapidly as the nation ages throughout the next two decades. Health costs rose 4.4 percent in 2007 and another 6.0 percent in 2008.[30] It's too early to know if the Patient Protection and Affordable Health Care Act will reduce these increases.

As people live longer, of course, they place greater demands on the health care system, as well as on the Social Security program. New and advanced medical technology—life-support systems, ultrasound, sophisticated X-ray equipment, and genetic counseling—have all increased the costs of health care. Longer life expectancies also place greater demands on other social policies, subtracting from funding for public assistance and other forms of social insurance.

In addition, costs have risen because of new technologies that are now widely available. Nuclear magnetic imaging, or as it is more commonly known, magnetic resonance imaging (MRI), is now routinely used to diagnose a host of diseases easily detected through more traditional tests. Once a medical center purchases this kind of expensive technology, its physicians are given incentives to use it, which increases patients' health care costs.

At least part of the cost crisis is avoidable. Medicare alone spends billions of dollars each year treating smoking-related diseases, and throughout the next 20 years, the costs to treat such diseases will continue to rise. Other illnesses at least partly related to lifestyle choices include heart disease, liver disease, HIV/AIDS, and the epidemic of health disorders caused or made worse by obesity, such as diabetes.

Covering the Uninsured Despite passage of the Medicare program in 1965, the United States did not provide comprehensive insurance to the rest of the uninsured until 2010. Until then, most uninsured Americans either relied on public clinics, emergency room care, or simply lived without health or dental care.[31]

The Patient Protection and Affordable Health Care Act was designed to cover as many of these Americans as possible but was one of the most complicated laws passed in recent history. The bill was more than 1,200 pages long and contained a long list of changes in how health care is delivered and to whom. Its key provisions involved expansions of existing health care programs such as Medicaid for the poor and the creation of new health insurance "exchanges" in each state as a source of insurance for Americans who could not buy insurance from private companies. It also contained tax increases and benefit cuts for Medicare. The main provisions of the Act are:

- Most Americans will be required to buy health insurance starting in 2014 and will be fined by the federal government if they do not do so.
- Individuals who cannot buy affordable insurance will be able to purchase insurance from a state insurance exchange.
- Insurance companies will be prevented from denying coverage to people for any reason, including preexisting conditions, such as high blood pressure, cancer, or mental illness.
- Insurance companies will have to extend coverage for young Americans up to 26 years of age under their parents' insurance.
- The Medicaid program will be expanded to all poor Americans under the age of 65, including the unemployed and unmarried individuals.

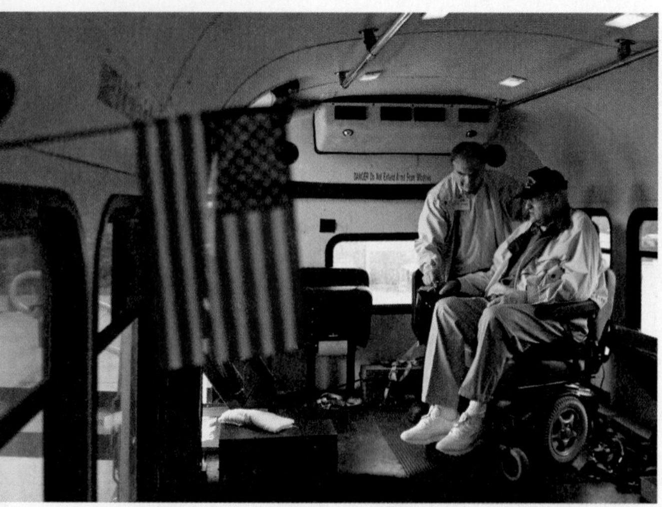

Medicare is not the only federal government health program. The federal government has dozens of health programs, including the Department of Veterans Affairs hospital system, which is open only to veterans.

- General Medicare benefits will not be cut, and all older Americans will qualify for free preventive care, but the special Medicare Advantage program for higher-income beneficiaries will be frozen, and some benefits will be abolished.
- Individual Americans will pay a tax on "Cadillac" insurance plans that offer broader coverage at a much higher cost.
- The Medicare payroll tax will rise 0.9 percent for Americans who make more than $200,000 per year.

Because these changes will be phased in throughout the next decade, it is not clear just how much the new reforms will cost on a yearly basis. Moreover, it is not clear that older Americans will accept the changes in Medicare. Some argue that the Medicare changes will be repealed as they approach full implementation in 2011. Moreover, the reforms are extremely difficult to implement, in part because they rely on the states to form the new insurance exchanges on their own. At least for now, the health care reform is a work in progress and will rely on faithful execution to have its full effects.

The Federal Role in Education

The federal government has been a partner in education at least since the Northwest Ordinance of 1785, in which Congress set aside land in every township for a public school. In 1862, the Morrill Land-Grant Colleges Act provided grants of land to states for universities specializing in the mechanical or agricultural arts. The U.S. Office of Education was established in 1867 to oversee these programs, but the scope of federal involvement was modest by today's standards. Even the G.I. Bill, which helped provide a college education for approximately 20 million World War II veterans, was seen more as an employment program than an educational one.

During the Cold War, however, education became one part of the national defense. When the Soviet Union launched *Sputnik*—the first human-made satellite to orbit the earth—in 1957, Congress responded in 1958 by passing the National Defense Education Act to upgrade science, language, and mathematics courses.

Elementary and Secondary Education Kindergarten through high school education is generally seen as a state and local responsibility. Most children go to public schools run by local school boards and funded, at least partly, by property taxes. Because school districts vary greatly in the wealth of their residents, children from poor districts are much more likely to have lower-quality public schools than those from wealthier districts. As a result, public schools vary in the quality of teacher preparation, student performance, dropout rates, and educational opportunities provided to minority students.

There have been many efforts to improve the performance of public schools, including the No Child Left Behind Act. Here, a teacher for the nongovernmental Knowledge Is Power Program (KIPP) works with poor children to improve their performance.

As concerns about the quality of public education increased during the 1990s, however, the federal government became more engaged in local education, first by setting national goals for student achievement, then by passing the No Child Left Behind Act in 2002. Under the Act, in return for federal funding, states were required to annually test at least 95 percent of all third and eighth graders in reading and mathematics. In addition, states were required to grade schools as passing or failing, to set higher standards for teachers, and to give students in failing schools the option to move to higher-performing schools. Schools must either improve test scores each year or risk being labeled "in need of improvement." Under the Act, all students are supposed to be proficient in reading and mathematics by 2014.

Although the No Child Left Behind Act set higher standards, it increased federal spending for education by only a tiny percentage.

By the People

MAKING A DIFFERENCE

Improving Health One Playground at a Time

Citizens can make an immediate difference on public policy by simply changing the way they behave. They can stop smoking, change their diets, and get more exercise every day. They can also lobby their local governments to build more sidewalks and bike paths so that other citizens can exercise safely. They can push school boards to remove sugary drinks and junk food from school vending machines and cafeterias, support efforts to bring full-service grocery stores such as Whole Foods to low-income neighborhoods, and even plant community gardens.

Playgrounds are an easy place to start. According to KaBoom!, which is a charitable organization that built more playgrounds in 2010 than any state or city in America, 60 minutes of exercise a day can reduce health care costs dramatically in the future. Yet, there are thousands of "play deserts" across the country, often in dense urban areas, in which there is no space for children to play. You can see what is in your community by visiting maps.kaboom.org.

Students can easily find a "play-space" where a new playground would improve the opportunity for healthy exercise for low-income children. They can then join the KaBoom! building team as volunteers.

CRITICAL THINKING QUESTIONS

1. What can you do today to reduce health care costs in the future?
2. Why are playgrounds so important to communities? And why are there so few playgrounds in low-income communities?
3. What other resources do low-income communities need to be healthier places to live?

First Lady Michelle Obama brings D.C. school children to her organic garden to educate them about locally grown, healthful food.

Under great pressure during the economic downturn, many states complained that they did not have enough funding to test every student every year or to meet the law's requirement for teacher training and certification. In addition, schools with many disabled or special-needs students were being unfairly categorized as "failing" because they could not meet the test-score requirement. As of late 2010, Congress was still working to change the Act to put a greater emphasis on teacher performance. At the same time, the Obama Administration launched an effort to reward states for increasing the number of charter schools.

Parents ask more of their schools than just to educate their children. Schools are now a major means of providing basic nutrition to millions of poor children. They screen at-risk children and attempt to get them medical and psychological assistance; they seek to socialize students into acceptable behaviors, often in the face of increasing violence in the surrounding neighborhoods; and they often reach out to families to provide basic help in parenting.

Higher Education The federal government also provides help to colleges and universities. In 2010, the federal government provided approximately $90 billion of the financial aid that college students receive. Pell grants for low-income students and low-interest guaranteed student loans continue to be the biggest source of college costs for low-income students.

In 1998, Congress added three new programs to improve the odds that low-income children will make it to college: (1) GEAR UP, which supports early interventions to help students complete high school; (2) the Learning Anytime Anywhere Partnerships (LAAP), which provide federal funding for distance learning through the Internet; and (3) a new initiative designed to improve teacher quality in primary and elementary schools. Although the three programs account for less than 1 percent of federal spending for education, they acknowledge the link between the quality of primary and elementary education and college success, as well as the need to act early to increase the odds of success for low-income students.

The September 11, 2001, terrorist attack on New York City and Washington, D.C., sparked a massive federal investment in homeland security.

The Federal Role in Crime Control

Like education, controlling crime is primarily a state and local matter. The federal government has passed sweeping legislation helping state and local governments pay for crime control. Often, the federal government acts more as a banker than a police officer, providing grants to states and local governments to hire their own police officers, build more prisons, improve drug enforcement, and prosecute organized crime. The federal government must also enforce its own laws against activities such as counterfeiting and pollution, while protecting the borders and preventing drugs from flowing into the country.

The federal government enforces its laws primarily through the Department of Justice, which contains the Federal Bureau of Investigation (FBI). The FBI was created in 1908 and charged with gathering and reporting evidence in matters relating to federal criminal laws. In addition, the FBI provides fingerprint identification and laboratory services to local law enforcement on a cooperative basis and has new responsibilities in the war on terrorism. Other law enforcement agencies of the federal government include the Drug Enforcement Agency (DEA), which is responsible for preventing the flow of illegal narcotics and other illegal drugs into the United States, patrolling U.S. borders, and conducting joint operations with countries where drugs are produced. The Bureau of Alcohol, Tobacco, Firearms, and Explosives monitors the sale of destructive weapons and guns inside the United States, regulates alcoholic beverage production, and oversees the collection of taxes on alcohol and tobacco.

Terrorism is clearly the federal government's top crime priority today. Only weeks after the September 11, 2001, terrorist attacks on New York City and Washington, D.C., Congress passed a massive antiterrorism law, and it created the new Department of Homeland Security the following summer. For his part, President Bush created the Office of Homeland Security within the White House in October 2001, merging 22 agencies and 180,000 federal employees, and ordered a complete reorganization of the Federal Bureau of Investigation in early 2002 to create a stronger focus on preventing terrorism.

Citizens and Public Policy

LEARNING **OBJECTIVE**

13.11 Assess ways in which citizens can influence the public policy process.

Despite calls for limiting the role of the federal government in public policy, most citizens and public officials understand that the federal government must be active in the economic life and social welfare of the nation. It should continue to collect taxes, regulate the money supply, prevent monopolies that would hurt consumers, protect workers and the environment, and promote free trade. The federal government should have a role in providing decent housing, adequate health care, and a solid education for all citizens. The question is not whether the nation will provide a safety net for its low-income citizens but how strong the net will be and who will be responsible for providing it.

Yet public policy is not made in a vacuum, and does not solely involve the federal government. Rather, it is a process that can involve citizens, interest groups, political parties, legislators, judges, and government institutions. Citizens have many levers that give them influence. They can certainly vote —the higher the participation, the more the process will heed their voice. But because voting is a blunt instrument of participation that does not convey precise information about what they want, citizens must also find other pathways to influence, including joining interest groups, writing letters, sending e-mails, confronting legislators at community meetings, and even running for office themselves. Citizens can exert influence on economic policy by purchasing (or boycotting) goods and services. They can write letters to their members

Of the People

AMERICA'S CHANGING FACE

Who Volunteers?

The United States is a nation of volunteers. In 2008, 61 million Americans volunteered in one way or another, giving an average of 52 hours during the year. Valuing each hour at $22, Americans give more than $200 billion worth of energy to charity, thereby allowing federal, state, and local governments to focus more of their resources on the needy. Many charities rely on volunteers as mentors for children, ushers at religious services, counselors at job training programs, and campaign workers.

Not every American volunteers at equal levels, however. According to the U.S. Bureau of Labor Statistics, middle-aged Americans are the most likely to volunteer, in part because many are at the stage of life when they are more likely to engage in their local schools and communities. They may not have more time to give but are somewhat more motivated. Those with college degrees are also more likely to volunteer, largely because they know how to volunteer and have more income to pay for child care and other support when they take time to give time to charities.

Given these income and educational differences, it is not surprising that different groups of Americans are more or less likely to volunteer. As the following table shows, education and the income that goes with it is the single best predictor of whether Americans volunteer.

All of these percentages have declined since 2004 and may reflect the effect of the deep recession that began in 2008. People gave less money to charities during the recession and had less time to give. Interestingly, however, people who were unemployed in 2008 were just as likely to volunteer as people who were fully employed. Overall, the number of volunteers declined from 65 million in 2004 to 61 million in 2008. Younger Americans showed the greatest increase in volunteering during that period, however, increasing from 41 hours per year to 48 hours on average.

Volunteering may have declined in part because some charities went out of business during the recession, whereas many others cut back on their ability to recruit and manage volunteers. Volunteers need fulfilling work to draw them into a charity. If their talents are not well used, many simply do not return. At least some volunteering among young Americans is for service-learning programs at their local schools and colleges.

CRITICAL THINKING QUESTIONS

1. Why do you volunteer? What was your experience?
2. Why do college graduates volunteer more than citizens with less education? Why are young Americans less active than middle-aged Americans?
3. What can charities do to improve the volunteer experience?

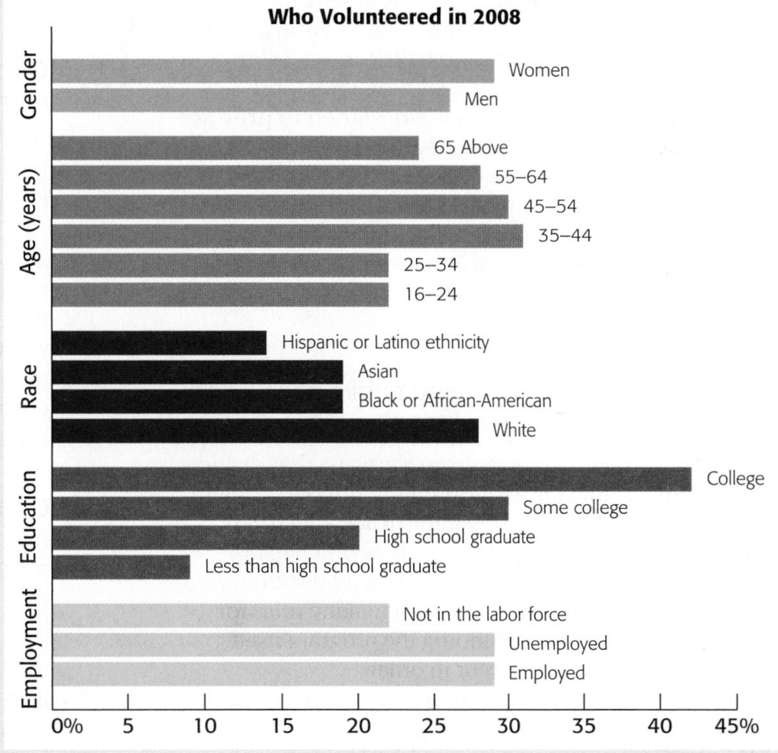

SOURCE: U.S. Bureau of Labor Statistics, "Volunteering in the United States," January 2009, press release. The information is updated each year and can be found at http://www.bls.gov/cps/.

of Congress when significant legislation, such as action to protect homeowners from unscrupulous lenders, comes to a vote. Citizens can influence social policy by joining interest groups that represent low-income Americans. They can also volunteer for specific programs that are designed to help the needy. Although the federal government has created dozens of programs to help the needy, the nation still relies heavily on charities to fill gaps in coverage, whether through food pantries and soup kitchens or early childhood programs. In turn, these programs rely on volunteers.

There is no question that citizens want action on the big problems highlighted in this chapter. They know that safeguarding Social Security, reducing global warming, and fixing the economy so that everyone rises on the basis of merit will not happen without pressure. Citizen action is more successful when it involves clear ideas for an alternative policy. It is rarely enough to merely demand that government act. It is also important to tell government what to do. This means thinking through the options and making a clear, well-developed argument for change and pursuing it aggressively through our complicated policy process.

CHAPTER **SUMMARY**

13.1 Relate politics and public policy, and differentiate three types of public policy.

Public policy is the product of politics, which resolves the question of who gets what, when, where, and how from government. Politics involves the interaction of the people and their government. It affects policy through activities such as voting, joining interest groups and political parties, congressional bargaining, ratifying treaties, signing laws, and administering laws. Policies are designed to produce certain outcomes, such as a healthier society.

There are three types of policy: distributive (which provides benefits to all groups in society), redistributive (which provides benefits to one group in society at the expense of another), and reverse distributive (which eliminates benefits to all groups in society).

13.2 Outline eight steps in making public policy, and assess types of policy solutions.

Every public policy emerges from a process that includes eight steps: (1) making assumptions about the problem, (2) setting the agenda, (3) deciding to act, which can involve nondecisions, (4) deciding how much to do, (5) choosing a solution to the problem, (6) deciding who will deliver the goods or services, (7) making rules for implementation, and (8) running the program itself. The steps do not always occur in order.

There are five solutions of policy: (1) spending, (2) taxing, (3) directly providing goods and services, (4) providing protection against risk, and (5) creating standards, incentives, or penalties. There are also different ways of delivering services through third-party government, which include private businesses, colleges and universities, state and local governments, and charities.

13.3 Describe the federal government's economic policy making role and how economic performance is measured.

Inflation and unemployment are considered the two most important measures of economic performance, although we also use the size of the federal budget deficit, the U.S. trade deficit or surplus with other nations, and gross domestic product (GDP). Inflation and unemployment tend to move together in opposite directions—inflation rises as unemployment drops, and it falls as unemployment rises. Other measures of economic performance include the amount of government spending and the balance of trade.

13.4 Outline the way in which the federal government makes fiscal policy and the role of fiscal policy.

Fiscal policy consists of economic policies made by Congress, the president, and the judiciary. There are two basic types—collecting revenues through taxes and fees and spending money through the federal budget. Increasing government spending stimulates the economy, thereby reducing unemployment, whereas increasing taxes generally slows economic growth, thereby curtailing inflation. The federal government also spends money through tax expenditures hidden from public view.

13.5 Outline the way in which the federal government makes monetary policy and the role of monetary policy.

Monetary policy, made by the Federal Reserve Board (the Fed), is designed to affect the flow of money through the economy. The Fed's most important tool is the federal funds rate, the amount of interest it allows banks to charge each other on short-term loans. Raising the cost of money is generally a way to slow down the economy and reduce inflation; lowering the cost of money ignites the economy and reduces unemployment.

13.6 Identify ways in which the federal government seeks to promote economic growth.

The federal government has long promoted the economy and specific industries. It also promotes trade and commerce with other nations, including efforts to reduce barriers to imports and exports, stabilize prices of certain goods and services, and encourage innovation through patents and other protections.

13.7 Categorize ways in which the federal government seeks to regulate the economy, and explain the deregulation movement.

Economic regulation is designed to control the behavior of the economy in a variety of ways such as preventing monopolies, reducing environmental pollution, and protecting workers. Many regulations were designed to curb specific abuses and promote competition.

The deregulation movement is driven by the belief that regulations are too costly and often fail to achieve their desired ends. Democrats and Republicans have both supported deregulation of key industries during the past four decades, but it sometimes produces new problems that create a backlash in favor of reregulation.

13.8 Outline the goals of the federal government's social policy and the forms of protection it provides.

The goals of social policy are to create a safety net to protect citizens against social and economic problems and to raise the quality of life for all. The two types of social policy are public assistance (usually means-tested) and social insurance. Public assistance takes many forms, including direct payments to the poor, the unemployed, and the disabled; food stamps; job training; housing subsidies; free school lunches; tax credits; and subsidized medical care. Social insurance (usually an entitlement), such as Social Security, is provided to anyone who has paid enough in contributions to receive support after meeting certain requirements, such as reaching retirement age.

13.9 Outline the evolution of social policy throughout the twentieth century.

The greatest expansion in the federal government's social programs occurred in two eras: (1) Franklin Roosevelt's New Deal from 1933 to 1945, and (2) Lyndon Johnson's Great Society from 1964 to 1969. The New Deal created a number of public assistance and social insurance programs such as job training for the unemployed, Social Security, and Aid to Families with Dependent Children; the Great Society produced help for the homeless, more job training, and Medicare.

13.10 Evaluate the current status of and challenges for federal government policy in the areas of health care, education, and crime.

Health care is well on track to becoming the federal government's largest social program, in part because health care costs are rising rapidly with the increasing lifespan and new technologies. In 2010, Congress passed a new health insurance program to provide greater access for millions of uninsured Americans. The federal government plays an important role in funding public schools and pushing national goals for better education and is also heavily engaged in helping finance college and university education. Crime control has also been part of the national agenda for decades, especially related to drugs, but has become much more visible as part of the war on terrorism.

13.11 Assess ways in which citizens can influence the public policy process.

Citizens can make their voices heard through both traditional and nontraditional means, including voting, joining interest groups, writing letters, sending e-mails, confronting legislators at community meetings, and even running for office themselves.

CHAPTER **SELF-TEST**

13.1 Relate politics and public policy, and differentiate three types of public policy.

1. Which is *not* a way government can convey public policy?
   a. A petition signed by voters
   b. Rules written by administrators
   c. Opinions issued by the Supreme Court
   d. A law passed by Congress and signed by the president
2. Which type of public policy includes programs like public assistance to poor people?
   a. Distributive policy
   b. Redistributive policy
   c. Semi-distributive policy
   d. Reverse distributive policy
3. What is reverse distributive policy, and why is it rare?

13.2 Outline eight steps in making public policy, and assess types of policy solutions.

4. Which of the steps in making public policy is the most difficult?
   a. Deciding to act
   b. Running the program
   c. Making rules for implementation
   d. Making assumptions about the problem
5. List three of the solutions the federal government uses to address public policy problems, and describe how they work in practice.
6. In a short essay, select three steps of the policy-making process and describe how a college student and a senior citizen can influence them. Consider each individual's desires and needs.

13.3 Describe the federal government's economic policy making role and how economic performance is measured.

7. Explain the interaction between *inflation* and *unemployment*. Define the terms, and draw a diagram to demonstrate their relationship.
8. Differentiate fiscal policy from monetary policy.

13.4 Outline the way in which the federal government makes fiscal policy and the role of fiscal policy.

9. What are the main sources of income and biggest expenditures of the federal government?

13.5 Outline the way in which the federal government makes monetary policy and the role of monetary policy.

10. When the Federal Reserve Board lowers the federal funds rate, what is the intended consequence?
11. Write a brief persuasive essay explaining what you believe the government's proper role in the economy should be.

13.6 Identify ways in which the federal government seeks to promote economic growth.

12. Define protectionism, and provide examples.
13. Why does the federal government promote industries such as agriculture but not industries such as computers? Is federal promotion of certain industries fair to American consumers and taxpayers?

13.7 Categorize ways in which the federal government seeks to regulate the economy, and explain the deregulation movement.

14. In two or three paragraphs, explain the relationship between the real economic situation and economic theory. For example, when are people more likely to argue for *more* or *less* regulation?
15. Why does the federal government encourage corporate social responsibility? Why would corporate social responsibility help reduce federal spending?

13.8 Outline the goals of the federal government's social policy and the forms of protection it provides.

16. Which of the following is *not* a social insurance program?
    a. Medicare
    b. Food stamps
    c. Social Security
    d. Disability Insurance
17. In a short essay, identify the two types of programs the federal government uses to protect citizens against hardship. What are the requirements to receive each type of protection? On which type did the government spend more money in 2008? Analyze the connection between eligibility requirements and levels of spending.

13.9 Outline the evolution of social policy throughout the twentieth century.

18. Identify each social program with the appropriate period—the New Deal or the Great Society.
    a. Food stamps
    b. Social Security
    c. Disability Insurance
    d. Medicare
    e. Head Start
    f. Unemployment Insurance
19. In a short essay, analyze the future of Social Security. Consider how it is funded and what steps Congress may have to take to ensure its continued existence.

13.10 Evaluate the current status of and challenges for federal government policy in the areas of health care, education, and crime.

20. What are the most important provisions of the new health care reform?
21. In a short essay, compare the circumstances that prompted the No Child Left Behind Act with those that gave rise to an earlier social program—food stamps or Social Security, for instance. Identify and analyze concerns with No Child Left Behind in light of U.S. experience with long-running social programs.

13.11 Assess ways in which citizens can influence the public policy process.

22. Why are volunteers so important to implementing policy decisions?
23. Select one of the major trends likely to influence public policy in the future. In a short essay, describe a possible way the government could address the problems associated with this trend. Use the eight steps and five solutions described in this chapter as a basis for your plan.

Answers for selected questions: 1. a; 2. b; 4. a; 16. b; 18.a: Great Society, 18b: New Deal, 18c: New Deal, 18d: Great Society, 18e: Great Society, 18f: New Deal.

mypoliscilab EXERCISES

Where participation leads to action!

Apply what you learned in this chapter on MyPoliSciLab.

Read on mypoliscilab.com

eText: Chapter 13

Study and Review on mypoliscilab.com

Pre-Test
Post-Test
Chapter Exam
Flashcards

Watch on mypoliscilab.com

Video: Making Environmental Policy
Video: Recession Hits Indiana
Video: The Stimulus Breakdown
Video: Economic Policy Debate at the G20
Video: Fed Approves Mortgage Crackdown
Video: Raising The Minimum Wage
Video: Health Care Plan

Explore on mypoliscilab.com

Simulation: You Are the President and Need to Get a Tax Cut Passed
Simulation: Making Economic Policy
Comparative: Comparing Economic Policy
Comparative: Comparing Social Welfare Systems
Comparative: Comparing Health Systems
Timeline: Growth of the Budget and Federal Spending
Timeline: The Evolution of Social Welfare Policy
Visual Literacy: Evaluating Federal Spending and Economic Policy
Visual Literacy: Where the Money Goes

KEY TERMS

public policy, p. 380
politics, p. 380
policy makers, p. 380
distributive policy, p. 381
redistributive policy, p. 381
zero-sum games, p. 381
reverse distributive policy, p. 381
nondecision, p. 382
policy agenda, p. 382
think tank, p. 383
issue-attention cycle, p. 383
incremental policy, p. 384
punctuating policy, p. 384
iron triangle, p. 384
issue network, p. 384
regulation, p. 386
rule, p. 386
fiscal policy, p. 389
monetary policy, p. 389
inflation, p. 389
unemployment, p. 389
stagflation, p. 390
gross domestic product (GDP), p. 390
excise tax, p. 391
budget deficit, p. 391
tariff, p. 391
progressive tax, p. 392
regressive tax, p. 392
national debt, p. 392
mandatory spending, p. 392
discretionary spending, p. 392
Office of Management and Budget (OMB), p. 392
Congressional Budget Office (CBO), p. 393
tax expenditure, p. 393
sales tax, p. 393
value-added tax (VAT), p. 393
Federal Reserve System, p. 393
federal funds rate, p. 394
laissez-faire economics, p. 394
Keynesian economics, p. 394
protectionism, p. 394
trade deficit, p. 394
World Trade Organization (WTO), p. 394
General Agreement on Tariffs and Trade (GATT), p. 394
North American Free Trade Agreement (NAFTA), p. 395
monopoly, p. 396
antitrust legislation, p. 396
trust, p. 397
closed shop, p. 397
union shop, p. 397
labor injunction, p. 397
collective bargaining, p. 397
environmental impact statement, p. 398
corporate social responsibility, p. 399
deregulation, p. 399
entitlements, p. 400
means-tested entitlements, p. 400
social safety net, p. 401
public assistance, p. 401
social insurance, p. 401
Social Security, p. 403
Medicare, p. 406
Medicaid, p. 406

ADDITIONAL **RESOURCES**

FURTHER READING

JAMES E. ANDERSON, *Public Policymaking: An Introduction* (Houghton Mifflin, 2005).

THOMAS A. BIRKLAND, *An Introduction to the Policy Process: Theories, Concepts, and Models of Public Policy Making* (Sharpe, 2005).

M. MARGARET CONWAY, DAVID W. AHERN, AND **GERTRUDE A. STEURNAGEL,** *Women and Public Policy: A Revolution in Progress* (CQ Press, 2004).

CORNELIUS KERWIN, *Rulemaking: How Government Agencies Write Law and Make Policy* (CQ Press, 2003).

JOHN W. KINGDON, *Agendas, Alternatives, and Public Policies* (Longman, 2002).

B. GUY PETERS, *American Public Policy: Promise and Performance* (CQ Press, 2006).

ANDREW RICH, *Think Tanks, Public Policy, and the Politics of Expertise* (Cambridge University Press, 2005).

MARK E. RUSHEFSKY, *Public Policy in the United States: At the Dawn of the Twenty-First Century* (Sharpe, 2007).

PAUL A. SABATIER, ED., *Theories of the Public Policy Process* (Westview Press, 2007).

JOE SOSS, JACOB S. HACKER, AND **SUZANNE METTLER,** EDS., *Remaking America: Democracy and Public Policy in an Age of Inequality* (Russell Sage Foundation, 2007).

DEBORAH STONE, *Policy Paradox: The Art of Political Decision Making* (Norton, 1997).

STEPHEN G. BREYER, *Breaking the Vicious Circle: Toward Effective Risk Regulation* (Harvard University Press, 1993).

GARY BRYNER, *Blue Skies, Green Politics: The Clean Air Act of 1990 and Its Interpretation,* 2d ed. (CQ Press, 1995).

GARY BURTLESS, ROBERT J. LAWRENCE, ROBERT E. LITAN, AND **ROBERT J. SHAPIRO,** *Globaphobia: Confronting Fears About Open Trade* (Brookings Institution Press, 1998).

THOMAS W. CHURCH AND **ROBERT T. NAKAMURA,** *Cleaning Up the Mess: Implementation Strategies in Superfund* (Brookings Institution Press, 1993).

ROBERT W. CRANDALL AND **HAROLD FURCHTGOTT-ROTH,** *Cable TV: Regulation or Competition?* (Brookings Institution Press, 1996).

ROBERT M. ENTMAN, *Competition, Innovation, and Investment in Telecommunications* (Aspen Institute, 1998).

THOMAS L. FRIEDMAN, *The World Is Flat: A Brief History of the Twenty-First Century* (Farrar, Straus, & Giroux, 2005).

PHILIP K. HOWARD, *The Death of Common Sense: How Law Is Suffocating America* (Random House, 1994).

CORNELIUS M. KERWIN, *Rulemaking: How Government Agencies Write Law and Make Policy,* 2d ed. (CQ Press, 1998).

PAUL KRUGMAN, *The Return of Depression Economics and the Crisis of 2008* (W.W. Norton, 2009).

ROBERT KUTTNER, *Everything for Sale: The Virtues and Limits of Markets* (Knopf, 1997).

MICHAEL LEWIS, *The Big Short: Inside the Doomsday Machine* (W.W. Norton, 2010).

PETER G. PETERSON, *Facing Up: Paying Our Nation's Debt and Saving Our Children's Future* (Simon & Schuster, 1994).

ANDREW ROSS SORKIN, *Too Big to Fail: The Inside Story of How Wall Street and Washington Fought to Save the Financial System and Themselves* (Viking, 2010).

ALLEN SCHICK, *The Federal Budget: Politics, Policy, Process,* rev. ed. (Brookings Institution Press, 2007).

JOSEPH E. STIGLITZ, *Globalization and Its Discontents* (Norton, 2002).

DANIEL YERGIN AND **JOSEPH STANISLAW,** *The Commanding Heights: The Battle Between Government and the Marketplace That Is Remaking the Modern World* (Simon & Schuster, 1998).

JOHN BALDOCK, NICHOLAS MANNING, AND **SARAH VICKERSTAFF,** EDS., *Social Policy* (Oxford University Press, 2007).

DONALD L. BARLETT AND **JAMES B. STEELE,** *Critical Condition: How Health Care in America Became Big Business—and Bad Medicine* (Broadway Books, 2005).

BARBARA EHRENREICH, *Nickel and Dimed: On (Not) Getting By in America* (Metropolitan Books, 2001).

MICHAEL HILL, *Social Policy in the Modern World: A Comparative Perspective* (Wiley, 2006).

CHRISTOPHER JENCKS, *The Homeless* (Harvard University Press, 1994).

PAUL C. LIGHT, *Still Artful Work: The Continuing Politics of Social Security Reform* (McGraw-Hill, 1995).

DANIEL PATRICK MOYNIHAN, *Miles to Go: A Personal History of Social Policy* (Harvard University Press, 1996).

CHARLES MURRAY, *Losing Ground: American Social Policy, 1950–1980* (Basic Books, 1984).

PAUL E. PETERSON AND **MARTIN R. WEST,** EDS., *No Child Left Behind: The Politics and Practice of School Accountability* (Brookings Institution Press, 2004).

MARK ROBERT RANK, *One Nation Underprivileged: Why American Poverty Affects Us All* (Oxford University Press, 2005).

DAVID K. SHIPLER, *The Working Poor: Invisible in America* (Vintage Books, 2005).

R. KENT WEAVER, *Ending Welfare as We Know It* (Brookings Institution Press, 2001).

MARGARET WEIR, ED., *The Social Divide: Political Parties and the Future of Activist Government* (Brookings Institution Press, 1998).

BOB WOODWARD, *Agenda: Inside the Clinton White House* (Simon & Schuster, 1994).

WEB SITES

www.volunteermatch.org A very large Web site for finding volunteer opportunities.

www.idealist.org The place to go for information on jobs in charities.

www.volunteer.gov The federal government's Web site on volunteering.

www.regulations.gov The place to go for basic information on the rule-making process.

www.POGO.org The Project on Government Oversight, which follows federal policy.

OMB.gov All the information on what the federal government has spent in the past and will spend in the future. Specific information on historical trends can be found in the historical tables section of the federal budget.

Federalreserve.gov The key Web site for information on monetary policy.

Spending.gov An easily accessible source of information on where the federal dollars go.

ConcordCoalition.org A nonpartisan interest group that promotes reductions in the federal deficit.

CTJ.org The Citizens for Tax Justice (CTJ) Web site. CTJ is a conservative interest group that promotes reductions in federal taxes.

CBPP.org The Web site for the Center on Budget and Policy Priorities.

CBBP is a liberal interest group that provides analysis of fiscal policy and programs.

npr.org National Public Radio offers a free series of podcasts on our rapidly changing global economy called Planet Money.

Healthiergeneration.org The Web site for the Alliance for a Healthier Generation, an organization founded to promote healthier lives and sponsored by First Lady Michelle Obama.

CMS.gov The Web site for the Centers for Medicare and Medicaid Services, which administer the largest health programs in the federal government.

Health.gov A portal to every federal program that deals with health care.

www2.ed.gov/about/offices/list/fsa/index.html The Web site for the federal government's student loan programs.

FBI.gov The destination for finding details on crime, including statistics on major crimes (http://www.fbi.gov/ucr/cius2008/index.html).

CHAPTER 14

Making Foreign and Defense Policy

CHAPTER **OUTLINE**
CHAPTER LEARNING **OBJECTIVES**

Understanding Foreign Policy and Defense

14.1 Analyze the questions and responses that shape approaches to U.S. foreign policy and defense.

The Foreign Policy and Defense Agenda

14.2 Assess the status of each of the issues that currently dominate the foreign policy and defense agenda.

The Foreign Policy and Defense Bureaucracy

14.3 Outline the structure of the foreign policy and defense bureaucracy.

Foreign Policy and Defense Options

14.4 Evaluate the options for achieving foreign policy and defense goals.

Prospects for the Future

The conflict in Darfur, Sudan, began in 2003 when a small rebel group attacked Sudanese government targets. Frustrated by drought and unrelenting poverty in a territory the size of Texas, the people of Darfur did not demand independence but clearly demanded aid. The Sudanese government, however, seemed more concerned with driving black Africans out of Darfur than with ending poverty. If they could not be driven out, the Sudanese government decided they would be killed.

The government sent troops into battle backed by its air force. At the same time, it began arming its own rebel army called the Janjaweed, who soon took up the fight against the people of Darfur. Riding into villages and towns on camels and horses, the Janjaweed ravaged the population, raping and killing men, women, and children.

By the beginning of 2008, international aid groups put the number of dead at 200,000 and the number in refugee camps along the border with Chad at 2 million. Although the warring groups had signed a peace agreement in 2006, that quickly collapsed. And although the United Nations sent a peacekeeping force to the area, its 26,000 members were unarmed and unable to protect refugees who strayed from the camps in search of food and firewood. So the killing went on. The anti-Darfur rebels soon took their violence to the southern Sudan, where they opened a new war on black Africans.

Because the attacks have concentrated on the systematic elimination of a specific population, the black Africans in Sudan, many activists have accused the Sudanese government of engaging in genocide. Human rights groups such as the International Crisis Group and SaveDarfur.org, college students throughout the United States, and entertainers such as Don Cheadle and George Clooney have been among the most vocal advocates of a much stronger international response that would include a well-armed U.N. force. They have also demanded a much stronger stand by the United States against the warfare. They often refer to the lack of U.S. response to the Rwanda genocide in April 1994 and the failure to stop the killing in Kosovo in 1998. If these kinds of international atrocities cannot provoke international outrage and action, they ask, what will?

The question for the United States' foreign policy and defense agenda is, what kind of power could be used to stop the genocide?[1] The United States tried creating international pressure on the Sudanese government to halt the arming of the Janjaweed and other anti-Darfur rebel groups, but those efforts mostly failed. As much as activists demand action, the U.S. public has been mostly unwilling to support the use of military force in distant lands.

Thus, despite continued pressure from students throughout the United States and the world, the suffering in Darfur continues today. The problem with preventing atrocities is that the international community may know where atrocity is most likely to occur, but it rarely knows when. And once genocide begins, it can move very quickly, forcing the community to choose between quick but unpopular military action and painfully slow diplomatic persuasion.

This chapter will ask how we make choices in planning and executing foreign and defense policy. We will first examine key debates in making foreign and defense policy, look at basic terms and concepts, and examine some of today's greatest foreign policy challenges, such as the increased U.S. presence in fighting the war in Afghanistan. Then, we will turn to a discussion of the key actors in making U.S. foreign policy and appraise the range of tools the United States uses to accomplish its international goals. The chapter concludes with a more detailed assessment of defense policy.

Citizens clearly play a role in foreign and defense policy, whether through their advocacy and pressure or through their own decisions to join the public service or armed forces. They can also create change through voting, especially if a foreign policy such as the war in Iraq becomes a national issue as it did in the 2006 congressional elections. Of course, citizens also can affect policy by their unwillingness to act, as has widely been the case regarding Darfur. That said, citizens often feel that the foreign policy and defense bureaucracy is immune to criticism and that Congress gives too much freedom to the president.

Understanding Foreign Policy and Defense

LEARNING **OBJECTIVE**

14.1 Analyze the questions and responses that shape approaches to U.S. foreign policy and defense.

In the broadest sense, the primary goal of U.S. foreign and defense policy is to protect the nation from harm. Doing so requires more than building strong borders, however. The United States does not have the luxury of avoiding the rest of the world. As one of the world's great superpowers, it has accepted a range of obligations, including promoting democracy abroad in nations such as Iraq, providing help to victims of disaster such as the 2010 earthquake in Haiti, promoting greater economic ties across all nations, and fighting terrorism.

Although the United States supports greater freedom in the world, it has long been divided about its own role in international affairs. Some believe that the United States should defend itself against its enemies but remain isolated from the rest of the world; others question whether it should assume that other nations will act in their own self-interest, or if it should maintain a more hopeful vision of a peaceful world; still others debate whether the United States should use its substantial military strength to force other nations to support its positions, versus using its own history of civil liberties and rights to lead the world through example.

In general, these debates start with five basic questions: (1) Should the United States view the world realistically or idealistically? (2) Should it isolate itself from the world or accept a role in the international community? (3) Should it act on its own or only with the help of other nations? (4) Should it act first against threats to its safety or wait until it is attacked? and (5) Should it use its military and economic hard power or its diplomatic soft power? We will discuss each of these issues next.

realism
A theory of international relations that focuses on the tendency of nations to operate from self-interest.

idealism
A theory of international relations that focuses on the hope that nations will act together to solve international problems and promote peace.

Realism Versus Idealism

Historically, U.S. foreign and defense policy has been built on two very different views of the world. The first relies on **realism,** a belief that other nations are interested first and foremost in their own advancement, whether economic, political, or social, and in strengthening their own power.

Critics of realism argue that nations seek cooperation and stability, not power. This view invokes **idealism,** a belief that nations can work together to solve common problems such as global hunger and poverty with peace, not war, as the ultimate aim. Idealists view national power as a tool for good and for promoting democracy in other nations, not merely as a way to amass more military and economic resources.

Although realism and idealism represent two competing views of the world, they can become part of a broader, more integrated foreign and defense policy. Thus, the United States could be realistic about the need to work with dictators (realism) yet still believe that democracy is the best form of government (idealism). As President Bush often argued in the months leading to the war in Iraq, the United States had to be realistic about Iraq's interest in building biological, chemical, and nuclear weapons, even as he also argued that democracy would lead nations such as Iran and North Korea toward international cooperation and peace. Thus far, the Obama administration has taken a more idealistic approach to nuclear weapons, arguing that it is in the world's best interests to limit access to nuclear materials.

Aung San Suu Kyi has been a tireless supporter of human rights in Myanmar, which was formerly known as Burma. She has been under house arrest by the Myanmar government for 14 of the last 20 years in an effort to silence her advocacy.

Isolationism Versus Internationalism

Whether it is based on realism or idealism, U.S. foreign policy has reflected very different views of how it should respond to the rest of the world. Some back an approach based on

By the People

MAKING A DIFFERENCE

Promoting Ethical Investments by Colleges and Universities

Students who care about the tragedy in Darfur have many options for making their voices heard. They can certainly join organizations that are campaigning against the human rights abuse and can contribute time and money to organizations such Save Darfur (savedarfur.org). Save Darfur is an alliance of more than 100 organizations that are working to stop the violence.

Students can also put pressure on their own colleges and universities to stop investing in businesses that operate in Sudan. Colleges and universities have endowment funds, which they invest to generate income for everything from faculty to financial aid. Some of these investments might be with businesses that have ties to or interests with the Sudanese government. Products bought by universities could be made by businesses that do business with Sudan. Because these purchases and investments are helping these businesses, even indirectly, opponents of the Sudanese government argue that colleges and universities should cut off their support so that they do not support the Darfur oppression in any way.

The University of California system prohibited all such investments in Sudan in 2006, and many colleges and universities have followed suit. Much of the effort has come from students who have worked hard to understand how their colleges and universities invest their endowment money.

The first step in stopping such investments is to know which companies actually operate in Sudan, which is sometimes very difficult. Multinational corporations often operate through subsidiaries that might do business with a specific country. The only way to know is to get a list of all companies in an endowment portfolio or sponsor a general resolution ordering the endowment's investment managers to sell all investments in Sudan.

This is what students have done at colleges such as Amherst, Hampshire, and Smith College. Students at all three colleges pushed for socially responsible investing, which is the term for removing all questionable investments in activities that might harm the environment, undermine human rights, or violate generally accepted codes of ethics.

CRITICAL THINKING QUESTIONS

1. Should colleges divest in unethical investments even if doing so costs money that could support students?
2. How can a college know when it is making an unethical investment? Are broad policies that prohibit such investments enforceable?
3. How can students make sure that their colleges take action on issues such as Darfur? What kinds of political participation might work on your campus?

isolationism, a belief that the United States should stay out of international affairs unless other nations constitute a direct threat to its existence. The term was first used during the years leading up to World War I, when many Americans believed that the United States should stay out of the global conflict.

But isolationism is alive and well in the debate about whether the United States should remain in Iraq and Afghanistan. Isolationists argue that the United States should follow George Washington's advice to avoid international "entanglements," lest those entanglements lead the United States into wars that either cannot be won or have a high cost in American lives. They also argue that the United States should always focus first on its own interests.

Other citizens, including most foreign and defense policy experts, believe in **internationalism,** which says the United States must be engaged in international affairs to protect its own interests. Realists and idealists can disagree on the goals of U.S. foreign and defense policy, but they can still agree that the United States should engage the world on economic, political, and social issues such as human rights for oppressed people, global hunger, and the war on terrorism. Internationalists tend to view themselves as citizens of the world, not only the United States. They feel there are times when the United States should intervene, even when not directly threatened by another nation.

isolationism
The desire to avoid international engagement altogether.

internationalism
The belief that nations must engage in international problem solving.

Unilateralism Versus Multilateralism

Although internationalists agree that the United States should participate in world affairs, they have two very different views about how. Supporters of **unilateralism** believe that the United States has the right to act alone in response to threats, even if other nations are unwilling to help. They argue that it should never give other nations (or the United

unilateralism
A philosophy that encourages individual nations to act on their own when facing threats from other nations.

In early 2009, the United States received satellite photos of Iran's nuclear development. The United States responded by demanding more international penalties against Iran in an effort to strangle the country's economy. Iran continues to develop nuclear weapons and shows no readiness to negotiate. ■ *Why is the United States so concerned about Iran's effort to acquire a nuclear weapon?*

Nations) a veto over its actions, even if that means it acts alone in using its great military power.

In fact, President Bush announced a new unilateral policy immediately after the September 11, 2001, terrorist attacks on New York City and Washington, D.C. Under the **Bush Doctrine,** any nation that threatened the United States was automatically a potential target for unilateral action. The Bush Doctrine was built on three basic concepts:

1. The United States reserves the right to attack any nation that either harbors terrorists or constitutes a serious threat to the United States.
2. The United States reserves the right to act unilaterally against other nations even if it does not have the support of its allies.
3. The United States reserves the right to use massive force against its enemies, including nuclear weapons if needed.

Opponents of the Bush Doctrine support **multilateralism,** a belief that the United States should act only with the active support of other nations. According to its advocates, multilateralism not only increases the odds that other nations will share the burdens of war with the United States, but it also increases the potential that other nations will support the U.S. position once a war is over. At least partly because of the advantages of multilateralism, the Bush administration began backing away from the Bush Doctrine only three years after announcing it. Faced with mounting costs of rebuilding Iraq and reducing international tension with other Middle Eastern nations, the administration began working to bring other nations such as Russia, France, and Germany into the debate.

The Obama administration immediately renounced the Bush Doctrine. For example, it decided early on that it would not use nuclear weapons against Iran's nuclear program, even though those weapons could be used against the United States. However, the administration continues the long-standing U.S. practice of promising retaliation for attacks on U.S. citizens in other countries. It is particularly concerned about terrorist attacks around the world and inside the United States and is ready to respond immediately with strong military force.

Preemption Versus Provocation

For most of its history, the United States has waited to be provoked before going to war. Although there is considerable debate about what constitutes a provocation to war, **preemption** assumes the United States can attack first when it believes another nation constitutes a very serious threat. This approach was a centerpiece of the Bush Doctrine discussed above, based on the notion that the proliferation of **weapons of mass destruction** such as chemical, biological, or nuclear arms makes waiting for provocation much more dangerous than it once was. However, Iraq's weapons of mass destruction were never found despite an intense search—U.S. intelligence agencies were widely blamed for providing misleading intelligence perhaps under pressure from the Bush administration and Vice President Dick Cheney.

The war in Iraq is an example of preemption, which some experts call the nation's first "war of choice." Prior to Iraq, the United States only engaged in war in direct response to a first attack by an adversary. Believing that Iraq continued to hold weapons of mass destruction, the Bush administration decided to force Saddam Hussein from his dictatorship before he could use those weapons against the United States. Then-national security adviser Condoleezza Rice argued that the United States had a moral obligation to remove Hussein from power, even if doing so meant war. "This is an evil man who, left to his own devices, will wreak havoc again on his own population, his neighbors, and, if he gets weapons of mass destruction and the means to deliver them, on all of us," Rice told the British Broadcasting Corporation in August 2002. "There is a very powerful moral case for regime change. We certainly do not have the luxury of doing nothing."[2]

Bush Doctrine
A policy adopted by the Bush administration in 2001 that asserts America's right to attack any nation that has weapons of mass destruction that may be used against U.S. interests at home or abroad.

multilateralism
A philosophy that encourages individual nations to act together to solve international problems.

preemption
A policy of taking action before the United States is attacked rather than waiting for provocation.

weapons of mass destruction
Biological, chemical, or nuclear weapons that can cause a massive number of deaths in a single use.

Hard Power Versus Soft Power

Internationalists have different views of just how the United States should influence other nations in protecting itself. Some favor the use of **hard power,** or military and economic strength, whereas others favor **soft power,** or negotiation and diplomacy.[3]

Hard power depends almost entirely on a nation's ability to threaten or force another nation to act a certain way to avoid an attack. It relies on military strength as measured by the number of soldiers in uniform, their preparation for war, the quality of their equipment, and their nation's willingness to put them in harm's way.

We often associate hard power with the **theory of deterrence,** under which a nation creates enough military strength to ensure a massive response to any attack. During the cold war, the United States maintained more than enough nuclear weapons to deter the Soviet Union from using its nuclear weapons first and argued that sufficient bombs would survive any Soviet attack to ensure the destruction of the Soviet Union. This notion of *mutual assured destruction,* sometimes called MAD, was enough to keep both nations from using their nuclear weapons, but it kept each on constant alert just in case the other dared to act first.

President Jimmy Carter, Egyptian President Anwar El Sadat, and Israeli Prime Minister Menachem Begin share a famous handshake in 1978 agreeing to negotiate for peace in the Middle East. The three met at the U.S. president's retreat at Camp David, Maryland.
■ *How is this meeting an example of soft power?*

Soft power is based on more traditional diplomacy and a nation's reputation for keeping its word in honoring treaties, its readiness to provide financial aid, and its ability to find consensus by bargaining with allies and adversaries alike. The Obama administration has been a strong supporter of more diplomacy in international affairs, although it has shown a willingness to use hard power in Afghanistan.

Nations can use hard and soft power at the same time to resolve disputes. In fact, the threat of military force is often enough to produce a negotiated settlement, as was the case throughout the cold war.

The Foreign Policy and Defense Agenda

LEARNING **OBJECTIVE**

14.2 Assess the status of each of the issues that currently dominate the foreign policy and defense agenda.

The United States does not always have a choice about whether to act in world affairs. Many issues reach its borders that the country cannot avoid. These constitute the foreign and defense policy agenda, which currently focuses on seven major issues, presented here in alphabetical order: (1) controlling weapons of mass destruction, (2) ending the wars in Iraq and Afghanistan, (3) fighting terrorism, (4) negotiating peace in the Middle East, (5) promoting free trade abroad, (6) reducing global warming, and (7) strengthening democracy and international understanding. Just because an issue such as global diseases like HIV/AIDS is not on the list does not mean it is off the agenda. Rather, we focus here on the issues that appear to be at the top of the agenda today.

Controlling Weapons of Mass Destruction

The international community has been working for decades to reduce the threat of weapons of mass destruction. Although the world is particularly concerned about the development of such weapons in North Korea and Iran, the effort to reduce the spread of nuclear weapons actually started with nuclear disarmament talks between the United States and the Soviet Union in the 1970s.

With the end of the cold war in 1989, the United States and Russia began to look for new ways of reducing their nuclear arsenals, and in 2010, they agreed to reduce the number of nuclear warheads dramatically. Meeting in Prague on April 8, Russia and the United States agreed that each would reduce the number of nuclear warheads to 1,500, down from 2,200–2,700, respectively.

The world is still threatened by biological, chemical, and nuclear weapons, however. Although chemical weapons were outlawed by international agreement after World War I, at least nine countries say they have developed chemical weapons, such

hard power
Reliance on economic and military strength to solve international problems.

soft power
Reliance on diplomacy and negotiation to solve international problems.

theory of deterrence
A theory that is based on creating enough military strength to persuade other nations not to attack first.

as nerve gases, that kill on contact. Others continue to develop biological weapons that spread disease or poisons, and still others already have or intend to develop nuclear weapons.

The United States has been particularly concerned in recent years about Iran and North Korea's recent efforts to develop nuclear weapons, which the United States and many other nations believe they may use against Israel. In April 2006, for example, Iran declared its intent to continue building its nuclear power program, which could generate uranium for nuclear weapons. There is also concern about the possibility that terrorists could build and explode some kind of nuclear weapon in the United States.

Fighting Terrorism

The war on terrorism is a broad term used to describe efforts to control terrorist acts sponsored by other nations, such as Afghanistan, or acts undertaken by independent groups that operate without any connection to a government.

Although the war is most often associated with Osama bin Laden and his Al-Qaeda terrorist organization, dozens of other terrorist organizations exist. These groups have executed bombings in London, Madrid, Moscow, the Middle East, and throughout Southeast Asia, including Thailand, Malaysia, the Philippines, and Indonesia, where terrorists have carried out several bombings at or near popular tourist hotels. For example, in November 2008, terrorists conducted a coordinated attack on major hotels in Mumbai, India, that killed 172 citizens. The attack was followed in December with the attempted Christmas Day bombing of a Northwest Airlines flight from Amsterdam to Detroit. These attacks showed the power of violence as a tool of terrorism, and the media's widespread coverage of terrorist incidents like these also (unwittingly or not) spreads this fear. Groups that were once small and unknown can achieve widespread notoriety, which helps with fund raising and recruiting.

Negotiating Peace in the Middle East

Long before the September 11, 2001, terrorist attacks, the United States was working to secure peace between Israel and its neighbors, in part because the Middle East is such an

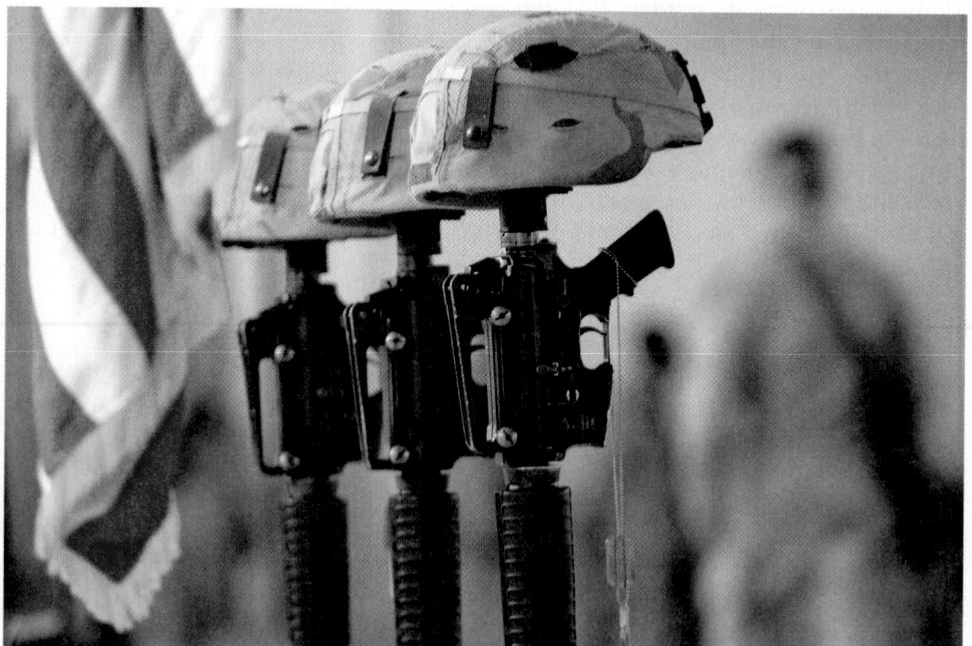

The war in Iraq, part of the ongoing war on terrorism, has cost the lives of more than 4,400 U.S. soldiers and more than 100,000 Iraqi civilians. ■ *Alongside the loss of life, what are the other costs of hard power?*

important source of the world's oil and in part because the United States has long considered Israel an ally. However, despite decades of U.S. efforts to promote peace in the region, the Middle East remains locked in a violent struggle over Israel's right to exist. Progress toward peace has been threatened by ongoing conflict with Arab nations and terrorist groups.

In 2002, however, the United States, Israel, and most Arab nations embraced "The Road Map to Peace." Under this agreement, signed in April 2003, Israel and its adversaries agreed to two broad steps toward peace. The Palestinian Authority, which represents citizens in territories captured by Israel in past wars, agreed to arrest, disrupt, and restrain individuals and groups that plan and conduct violent attacks on Israel. Israel in turn agreed to start dismantling settlements of Israeli citizens in the occupied territories to its south and east. Israel honored part of its end of the agreement starting in 2005 by beginning to dismantle settlements and turn over control of these territories to the Palestinian Authority. However, the dismantling of settlements happened in Gaza only; the settlements in East Jerusalem and the West Bank continue to expand. The dispute continues under the Obama administration, which is working toward a "soft power" resolution.

The Israeli-Palestinian conflict involves continued resistance to the creation of Israel, but it also involves ongoing international opposition to the construction of Israeli settlements in Palestinian territory.

Promoting Free Trade Abroad

As the world economy has grown, so has international competition with the United States. The United States has generally responded to this *globalization* with a basic policy of free trade, meaning a commitment to the free movement of goods across international borders. But it does not allow the unrestricted export of technologies that can be used to build nuclear weapons, and it has long protected certain defense industries that would be essential should it ever be forced into another world war. The United States has also used trade as a tool to promote human rights and democratic reform.

Conflicting goals have characterized the U.S. debate over free trade with China. On the one hand, China has a long history of violating basic human and democratic rights. But it also has one of the fastest-growing economies in the world. U.S. exports to China have tripled during the past decade, and imports from China have grown rapidly. The conflict between concern for human rights and a desire to benefit from China's growing economy became especially prominent when the Clinton administration asked Congress to grant **normal trade relations** status to China. Under normal trade relations, China would be given the same favorable trading terms, such as low tariffs on imports and exports, that other favored nations receive.

Typically, Congress grants normal trade relations under a "fast-track," or accelerated, basis by limiting its own debate to a simple yes-or-no, up-or-down vote with no amendments. Although Congress initially refused to use this process for China, it eventually approved the status and extended the president's authority to negotiate such trade agreements in the Trade Act of 2002.

Reducing Global Warming

The United States has a mixed record in efforts to control the global climate change often associated with greenhouse gases that trap heat in the environment and raise the world's temperature. Much of the recent increase in greenhouse gases is related to the release of carbon dioxide from the burning of fossil fuels such as gasoline and coal by automobiles and power plants.

Experts do not all agree that global warming is a problem. Nevertheless, rising temperatures appear to threaten the world's climate in two ways. First, as the average temperature rises, the polar ice caps and glaciers melt. As the water melts, the oceans rise, threatening low-lying areas across the world. By some estimates, New York City, the

normal trade relations
Trade status granted as part of an international trade policy that gives a nation the same favorable trade concessions and tariffs that the best trading partners receive.

Of the People

THE GLOBAL COMMUNITY

International Support for Ties with Business

Global citizens have very different views of ties between business and their countries. Some see the ties as essential for economic growth, whereas others worry that business is only interested in profits. In addition, some global citizens appear to worry about corruption in business dealings with their countries. They many even view business as too involved in local affairs.

Nevertheless, international trade is usually seen as a way to help nations reduce poverty. The Pew Global Survey shows that the world's citizens generally believe that global trade is very or somewhat good for their nation. Respondents were asked: What do you think about the growing trade and business ties between your country and other countries—do you think it is a very good thing, somewhat good, somewhat bad, or a very bad thing for your country?

Favorability toward global trade has fallen in most countries during the past three years, in part because of the economic recession. Although Indians have become more supportive of trade as their economy grows, Americans remain skeptical about business ties. Worries about the recession have driven these concerns higher within the nation as Americans blame business and trade for the high unemployment that has followed the economic collapse. However, most Americans understand that trade is one way to rebuild the economy as long as it flows both ways. They want more free trade between all nations.

In general, support for trade varies by the economic conditions of the world's nations. Poorer nations tend to see trade as a way out of poverty, but it is not always clear that trade has benefited them.

CRITICAL THINKING QUESTIONS

1. Why are less developed countries more supportive of international trade, and should they be so favorable?
2. What are the advantages of international trade in creating peaceful relations around the world?
3. How can trade damage a developing nation?

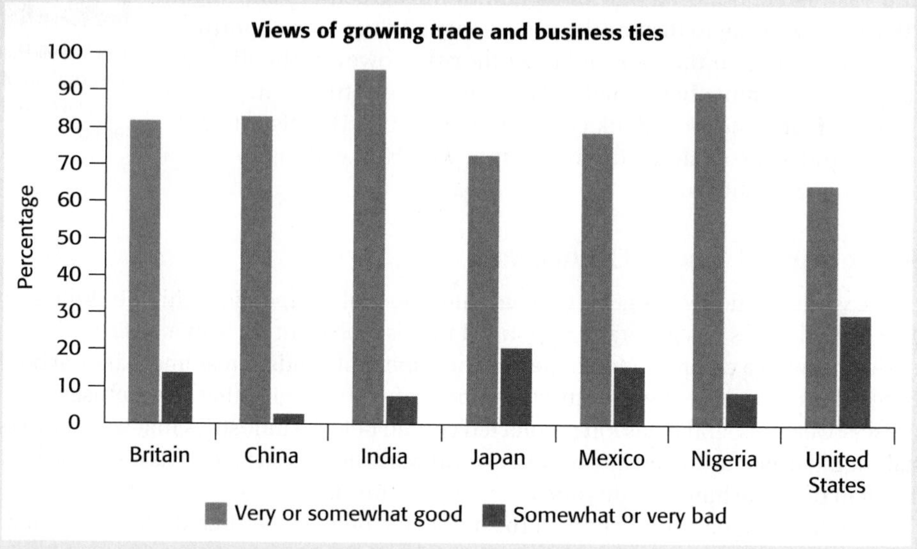

state of Washington, Florida, Louisiana, and other coastal areas could be completely under water within several hundred years. Second, as the average temperature rises, the weather becomes more unpredictable and potentially severe. Some experts attribute the recent increase in violent hurricanes such as Hurricane Katrina to global warming and predict more violent storms in the future.

The world acknowledged these problems when it adopted an international treaty called the Kyoto Protocol in 1997. Under the treaty, all participating nations agreed to reduce their emission of greenhouse gases by set amounts during the coming decades. Although 85 nations signed the agreement and 190 have ratified it, the United States has never ratified the treaty and has yet to embrace limits on burning fossil fuels, even though it produces a significant amount of the world's greenhouse gases. The United States has argued that the limits imposed by the Kyoto Protocol would weaken its economy. There is considerable debate today regarding the scientific evidence underpinning the call for action on global warming. Many of the world's largest carbon-producers met in Copenhagen in early 2010 but were unable to reach an agreement in setting targets.

In late 2009, the world's leaders met in Copenhagen to discuss targets for reducing global warming. The meeting failed to produce a formal agreement. ■ *Why is it so difficult to produce international agreements for reducing global warming?*

Ending the Wars in Iraq and Afghanistan

Iraq moved rapidly up the list of foreign-policy priorities in the days and weeks following the September 11, 2001, terrorist attacks. Convinced that Iraq possessed weapons of mass destruction that it was ready and willing to use against the United States, President Bush ordered the military to start planning for a preemptive war only six days after the attacks.[4] He also began building the case for action with the U.S. public and later made his argument before the United Nations.

> The United States has no quarrel with the Iraqi people; they've suffered too long in silent captivity. Liberty for the Iraqi people is a great moral cause, and a great strategic goal. The people of Iraq deserve it; the security of all nations requires it. Free societies do not intimidate through cruelty and conquest, and open societies do not threaten the world with mass murder. The United States supports political and economic liberty in a unified Iraq.[5]

President Bush, on the deck of the USS *Abraham Lincoln* on May 1, 2003, declares an end to major combat operations in Iraq. Since that time, thousands of injuries and deaths have occurred on both sides of the conflict. ■ *How is Bush's message reinforced visually by elements in this photograph?*

The Bush administration also argued that Iraq was manufacturing weapons of mass destruction such as nuclear missiles and poisons that it intended to use against the United States and its allies in the Middle East. In March 2003, the United States launched a massive attack on Iraq. U.S. troops quickly reached the outskirts of the nation's capital city and secured it during the next two days. On May 1, 2003, President Bush stood on the deck of the USS *Abraham Lincoln* underneath a banner that read "MISSION ACCOMPLISHED" and told the nation that "Major combat operations in Iraq have ended."

However, the United States never found any weapons of mass destruction in Iraq. More troubling, violence and political unrest increased following the early military victory. Under pressure from congressional Democrats and Republicans to do something to quell the violence, the president announced a "surge" of 28,000 troops in early 2007, raising the total U.S. presence to 160,000. The troops were deployed to Iraq's capital city, Baghdad, and other "hot spots" where terrorists were most active. The Obama administration continued the surge but promised to remove all U.S. combat troops as soon as possible. Nonetheless, the Obama administration also committed to leaving at least some troops in Iraq to train Iraqi soldiers.

However, the war in Iraq may have distracted the United States from maintaining pressure against Afghan terrorists, prompting calls for more troops.[6] The Obama administration answered these calls in 2009 by sending 40,000 more troops into battle. By March 2010, the number of U.S. troops killed in Afghanistan had crossed 1,000 and was larger than the troops killed in Iraq during the same period.

As discussed at the beginning of Chapter 8, the United States is currently committed to a "surge" strategy in which U.S. troops work with Afghan troops to stabilize key cities in the country. The U.S. and Afghan troops enter the city with massive force and move a civilian government into place as quickly as possible. The Obama administration hopes that this strategy will defeat terrorist forces that are seeking to recapture the country and has promised to end the surge in 2011.

Part of the peacemaking strategy in Afghanistan involves building a stronger Afghanistan government and military. The Obama administration's strategy is to train the Afghanistan military to take a greater role in fighting its adversaries. ■ *What are some of the difficulties in training and transferring authority to the Afghanistan military?*

Strengthening Democracy and International Understanding

The United States has long engaged in promoting democracy and its freedoms. It does so mostly through economic sanctions to increase the pain that might bring its adversaries to negotiations. However, some efforts conflict with other U.S. goals such as promoting international trade and fighting the war on terrorism. For example, the United States continues to promote international trade with China,

Celebrities work together on many humanitarian fund-raising efforts. In 2009, George Clooney organized a celebrity telethon to raise money for the victims of the Haitian earthquake. ■ *How can humanitarian aid help promote democracy abroad?*

one of the world's fastest-growing economies, even though China continues to deny its citizens basic rights such as a free press. In addition, the United States still provides aid to many Middle Eastern nations ruled by dictatorships in order to gain their help on the war on terrorism.

The United States also provides humanitarian aid to nations affected by natural disasters such as the 2010 earthquakes in Chile, Haiti, and China. Although dictators led many of the countries affected, the United States has long believed that citizens should not suffer during crises even though their governments are not free.

Finally, the United States uses programs such as the Peace Corps to promote international understanding. Peace Corps volunteers are expected to serve in another nation for two years and become part of the community they are serving. They work on a variety of projects, such as teaching mathematics and science, doing community development work, and improving water and sanitation systems. Most have a college degree, specific international experience, or both. Approximately 10 percent of the 7,300 current volunteers are over the age of 50. The Peace Corps covers travel and a minimum salary and typically trains volunteers in language and job skills for approximately three months before their service abroad.[7]

The Foreign Policy and Defense Bureaucracy

LEARNING **OBJECTIVE**

14.3 Outline the structure of the foreign policy and defense bureaucracy.

Even in troubled times, the president does not have absolute authority to act. Congress has the power to declare war, to appropriate funds for the armed forces, and to make rules that govern them. But the president is commander in chief and is authorized to negotiate treaties and receive and send ambassadors—that is, to recognize or refuse to recognize other governments. The Senate confirms U.S. ambassadorial appointments and gives consent (by a two-thirds vote) to treaty ratification.

Officially, the president's principal foreign policy adviser is the secretary of state, although others, such as the national security adviser or the vice president, are sometimes equally influential. In practice, the secretary of state delegates the day-to-day responsibilities for running the State Department and spends most of the time negotiating with the leaders of other countries.

However, foreign policy requires more than only one adviser. The application of hard and soft power is the responsibility of several major departments and agencies, including State, Defense, Treasury, Agriculture, Commerce, Labor, Energy, the Central Intelligence Agency (CIA), and the Department of Homeland Security.

The National Security Council

The key coordinating agency for the president is the National Security Council (NSC). Created by Congress in 1947, it serves directly under the president and is intended to help integrate foreign, military, and economic policies that affect national security. By law, it consists of the president, vice president, secretary of state, and secretary of defense. Recent presidents have sometimes also included the director of the CIA, the White House chief of staff, and the national security adviser as assistants to the NSC.

The national security adviser, appointed by the president, has emerged as one of the most influential foreign policy makers, sometimes rivaling the secretary of state in influence. Presidents come to rely on these White House aides both because of their proximity (down the hall in the West Wing of the White House) and because they owe their primary loyalties to the president, not to any department or program. Each president has shaped the NSC structure and adapted its staff procedures to suit his personal preferences. Throughout the years, however, the NSC, as both a committee and a staff, has taken on a major role in making and implementing foreign policy.

The State Department

The State Department is responsible for the diplomatic realm of foreign and defense policy. It is organized around a series of "desks" representing different parts of the world and foreign policy missions.

Duties The State Department is responsible for negotiating treaties with other nations and international organizations, protecting U.S. citizens abroad, promoting U.S. commercial interests in other nations, and granting visas to foreign visitors. The State Department also runs all U.S. embassies and consulates abroad. Embassies provide full diplomatic services on behalf of the United States and its citizens; consulates are smaller branch offices of embassies that help foreign citizens enter the United States through visas, or entry papers.

The State Department also plays a significant role in homeland security. Many of the September 11, 2001, attackers had entered the United States on student visas granted by the State Department's Bureau of Consular Affairs. Although their movements once in the United States were supposed to be monitored by the Justice Department's Immigration and Naturalization Service, the State Department was criticized for being too lax in granting visas to almost anyone with enough money to purchase an airline ticket.

The Foreign Service U.S. embassies are staffed largely by members of the U.S. Foreign Service. Although part of the State Department, the service represents the entire government and performs jobs for many other agencies. Its main duties are to carry out foreign policy as expressed in the directives of the secretary of state; gather political, economic, and intelligence data for U.S. policy makers; protect U.S. citizens and interests in foreign countries; and cultivate friendly relations with host governments and foreign peoples.

The Foreign Service is a select group of approximately 4,000 highly trained civil servants, comparable to army officers in the military and expected to take assignments anywhere in the world on short notice. Approximately two-thirds of U.S. ambassadors to approximately 160 nations come from the ranks of the Foreign Service. The others are usually presidential appointees confirmed by the senate.

The Foreign Service is one of the most prestigious, and most criticized, career services of the national government. Criticism sometimes comes as much from within as from outside. Critics claim that the organizational culture of the Foreign Service stifles creativity; attracts officers who are, or at least become, more concerned about their status than their responsibilities; and requires new recruits to wait 15 years or more before being considered for positions of responsibility. Like other federal agencies, most notably the CIA and the FBI, the Foreign Service has had great difficulty recruiting officers with Arabic-language skills, which clearly weakens each agency's ability to interpret, let alone collect, intelligence about the terrorist networks that have emerged in the Middle East and Asia.

Intelligence Agencies

Accurate, timely information about foreign nations is essential for making wise decisions. As the Senate Intelligence Committee and the national commission created to investigate the September 11, 2001, attacks both noted, the intelligence community failed to provide that information in time to prevent the attacks or change the course of the Iraq War.[8]

The Central Intelligence Agency The most important intelligence agency is the Central Intelligence Agency, created in 1947 to gather and analyze information that flows into various parts of the U.S. government from all around the world. In recent years, the CIA has had approximately 20,000 employees, who both collect information and shape the intelligence estimates that policy makers use to set priorities.

Although most of the information the CIA gathers comes from open sources such as the Internet, the CIA does use spies and undercover agents to monitor foreign threats. This secret intelligence occasionally supplies crucial data. But it is not all glamour; much is routine. Intelligence work consists of three basic operations: reporting, analysis, and dissemination. *Reporting* is based on close and rigorous observation of developments around the world; *analysis* is the attempt to detect meaningful patterns in what was observed in the past and to understand what appears to be going on now; *dissemination* means getting the right information to the right people at the right time.

The Broader Intelligence Community The CIA is only one of 15 intelligence agencies in the federal government, including the State Department's Bureau of Intelligence and Research; the Defense Department's Defense Intelligence Agency (which combines the intelligence operations of the Army, Navy, Air Force, and Marine Corps); the Federal Bureau of Investigation; the Treasury Department's Office of Terrorism and Finance Intelligence; the Energy Department's Office of Intelligence; the Homeland Security Department's Directorate of Information Analysis and Infrastructure Protection and Directorate of Coast Guard Intelligence; the National Security Agency (which specializes in electronic reconnaissance and code breaking); the National Reconnaissance Office (which runs the U.S. satellite surveillance programs); and the National Geospatial-Intelligence Agency (which collects and analyzes photographic imagery). Together, the 15 agencies constitute the *intelligence community.*

Because each was created to collect unique information (imagery, electronic intelligence, and so forth) for a unique client (the president, the secretary of defense, or others), historically, the agencies rarely shared information with each other. The lack of cooperation clearly affected the government's ability to prevent the September 11, 2001, attacks. "Many dedicated officers worked day and night for years to piece together the growing body of evidence on Al-Qaeda and to understand the threats," the 9/11 Commission concluded. "Yet, while there were many reports on bin Laden and his growing Al-Qaeda organization, there was no comprehensive review of what the intelligence community knew and what it did not know, and what that meant."[9]

Congress responded by creating a national intelligence director in 2004 to oversee all the intelligence offices. Under its legislation, the new director was responsible for providing the primary advice to the president on intelligence issues and was given the authority to increase or decrease the budgets of all other intelligence agencies. The director also oversees a new federal counterterrorism center, responsible for making sense of all national intelligence on potential terrorist threats to the United States. Despite the promise of more coordination, however, congressional critics in both parties complained that the new director merely added a layer of bureaucracy to an already cumbersome system.

The spirit of bipartisanship is reflected in the report of the 9/11 Commission, issued on July 22, 2004. The commission was made up of both Democrats and Republicans who managed to put their ideological differences aside and issue a report that is critical of both the Clinton and Bush administrations in their handling of terrorism. Shown here are 9/11 Commission co-chairs Thomas Kean and Lee Hamilton.

The Department of Defense

The president, Congress, the National Security Council, the State Department, and the Defense Department all make overall defense policy and attempt to integrate U.S. national security programs, but the day-to-day work of organizing for defense is the job of the Defense Department. Its headquarters, the Pentagon, houses within its 17.5 miles of corridors 23,000 top military and civilian personnel. The offices of several hundred generals and admirals are there, as is the office of the secretary of defense, currently Robert Gates, who provides civilian control of the armed services.

The Joint Chiefs of Staff The committee known as the Joint Chiefs of Staff serves as the principal military adviser to the president, the National Security Council, and the secretary of defense. It includes the heads of the Air Force, Army, Navy, and Marine Corps, and the chair and vice chair of the Joint Chiefs. The president, with the consent of the Senate, appoints all the service chiefs to four-year nonrenewable terms. Note that the twice-renewable two-year term of the chair of the Joint Chiefs is part of the process of ensuring civilian control over the military.

The Department of Defense Reorganization Act of 1986 shifted considerable power to the chair of the Joint Chiefs. Reporting through the secretary of defense, the chair now advises the president on military matters, exercises authority over the forces in the field, and is responsible for overall military planning. In theory, the chair of the Joint Chiefs can even make a military decision that the chiefs of the other services oppose.

Note, however, that the chair of the Joint Chiefs is *not* the head of the military. The chair and the Joint Chiefs are advisers to the secretary of defense and the president, but the president can disregard their advice and on occasion has done so. A president must weigh military action or inaction against the larger foreign and security interests of the nation.

As chair of the Joint Chiefs of Staff, Admiral Mike Mullen is the highest-ranking officer in the U.S. military. The chair and the Joint Chiefs are advisers to the secretary of defense and the president. ■ *Why does the military report to the president?*

The All-Volunteer Force The Constitution authorizes Congress to do what is "necessary and proper" in order to "raise and support Armies," "to provide and maintain a Navy," and "to provide for calling forth the Militia." The Joint Chiefs and the presidential appointees who serve as secretaries of the Air Force, Army, Navy, and Marine Corps oversee the 1.5 million soldiers who currently serve in what the founders might call the national militia.

During most of its history, the United States has used military conscription to raise and support its armed services. The draft, as it is called, was first used in 1862, during the Civil War, and again during World War I, World War II, and Vietnam. Shortly before the Vietnam War ended, Congress replaced the draft with an *all-volunteer force,* composed entirely of citizens who choose to serve.

Contractors The tools of war include contracts with private businesses. The U.S. defense budget reached $555 billion in 2008, not counting the costs of the wars in Afghanistan and Iraq. More than $400 billion of that total is for private business contracts, such as military equipment, computer programming, and housing for troops.

Defense spending fell dramatically at the end of the cold war as weapons systems were canceled or postponed, bases closed, ships retired, and large numbers of troops brought home from Germany, the Philippines, and elsewhere. The army was cut by more than 30 percent, and the National Guard and the military reserve were cut back by approximately 25 percent. As a result, defense spending also fell, dropping from 25 percent of total federal spending at the height of the cold war in the mid-1980s to 15 percent in 2000. It has been rising since, as has spending for the effort to curb terrorism.

Weapons are, in fact, a major U.S. industry, one that members of Congress work hard to promote and protect. As former World War II hero Dwight Eisenhower warned in his presidential Farewell Address in 1960, the United States must be wary of the *military-industrial complex* that supports increased defense spending as a way to protect jobs. Eisenhower's words are well worth rereading today:

> This conjunction of an immense military establishment and a large arms industry is new in the American experience. The total influence—economic, political, even spiritual—is felt in every city, every State house, and every office of the Federal government. We recognize the imperative need for this development. Yet we must not fail to comprehend its grave implications. Our toil, resources, and livelihood are all involved; so is the very structure of our society.
>
> In the councils of government, we must guard against the acquisition of unwarranted influence, whether sought or unsought, by the military industrial complex. The potential for the disastrous rise of misplaced power exists and will persist.[10]

Despite Eisenhower's warning, the military-industrial complex has grown dramatically since the 1950s.

Of the People

AMERICA'S CHANGING FACE

Diversity in the Military

The U.S. military has become much more diverse during the past three decades, in part because of much more aggressive recruiting of women and minorities. In 1990, for example, only 11 percent of all military personnel were women, and 28 percent were people of color. By 2006, which is the latest information available, 15 percent were women, and 39 percent were people of color.

The four armed services—the army, navy, Marine Corps, and air force—vary greatly in terms of diversity, however. Looking at new recruits in 2006, approximately 34 percent of the navy, 25 percent of the army, 23 percent of the air force, and 15 percent of the Marine Corps were African American, Hispanic, Asian American, or another minority group. At the same time, 24 percent of the air force, 19 percent of the navy, 17 percent of the army, and only 7 percent of the Marine Corps were women.

Several reasons explain why the armed forces have done better recruiting people of color than recruiting women. First, the military has worked hard to improve its reputation as an equal opportunity employer. Colin Powell's rise to the highest post in the armed services has often been used to show recruits of color that anything is possible in the military. Powell entered the military as a second lieutenant in 1958, served two tours of duty in Vietnam, and eventually became the first African American officer to chair the Joint Chiefs of Staff.

Second, the military has long focused on recruiting high school graduates who are not college-bound, which is a group that contains more people of color. The military has also developed several new programs that set aside substantial amounts of funding for future college tuition, which has also been effective in recruiting people of color.

CRITICAL THINKING QUESTIONS

1. What may explain the large percentages of minority soldiers in the military?
2. What may explain the much smaller percentages of women in the military?
3. Should the military represent all groups in society? Should combat soldiers be equally representative?

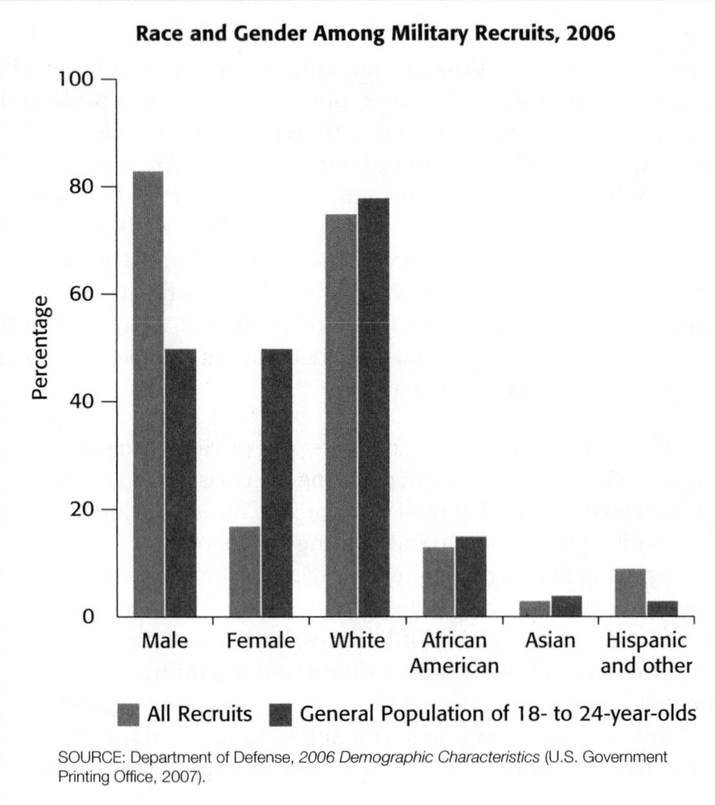

SOURCE: Department of Defense, *2006 Demographic Characteristics* (U.S. Government Printing Office, 2007).

Foreign Policy and Defense Options

LEARNING **OBJECTIVE**

14.4 Evaluate the options for achieving foreign policy and defense goals.

The United States has a number of tools for achieving foreign policy success, not the least of which is military might. But military might, or hard power as we discussed earlier, is no longer enough to ensure success, or even deter foreign threats. Without other forms of soft and hard power, such as conventional diplomacy to send its message clearly, foreign aid to help nations in need, economic sanctions to isolate its adversaries, and public diplomacy to help other nations understand its agenda, the nation will not succeed in reaching its foreign policy goals.

Conventional Diplomacy (Soft Power)

Much of U.S. foreign policy is conducted by the Foreign Service and ambassadors in face-to-face discussions across the world. International summit meetings, with their high-profile pomp and drama, are another form of conventional diplomacy. Even though traditional diplomacy appears more subdued and somewhat less vital in this era of personal leader-to-leader communication by telephone, fax, and teleconferencing, it is still an important, if slow, process by which nations can gain information, talk about mutual interests, and try to resolve disputes.

Conventional diplomacy can become hard power when the United States breaks diplomatic relations with another nation. Doing so greatly restricts tourist and business travel to a country and in effect curbs economic as well as political relations with the nation. Breaking diplomatic relations is a next-to-last resort (force is the last resort), for it undermines the ability to reason with a nation's leaders or use other diplomatic strategies to resolve conflicts. It also hampers our ability to get valuable information about what is going on in a nation and to have a presence there.

Secretary General Ban Ki-moon plays a central role in leading the United Nations. His job is to find common ground among nations of the world.

The United Nations is one of the most important arenas for traditional diplomacy. Established in 1945 by the victors of World War II, it now has 189 nation members. Despite its promise as a forum for world peace, the United Nations has been frustrated during its first 65 years. Critics contend that it has either ducked crucial global issues or was politically unable to tackle them. During much of that time, the U.N. General Assembly, dominated by a combination of Third World and communist nations, was hostile to many U.S. interests.

More recently, the five permanent members of the U.N. Security Council—the United States, China, Russia (which replaced the Soviet Union), Britain, and France—have usually worked in harmony. Moreover, the United Nations' assumption of responsibilities in the Persian Gulf War and its extensive peacekeeping missions in Cyprus and Lebanon have been notable examples of the effort to build the United Nations' respect. Several of the United Nations' specialized agencies—including the World Health Organization, the United Nations High Commission for Refugees, and the World Food Program—are considered major successes. But the review is much more mixed with respect to the United Nations' 63 peacekeeping efforts throughout its history. As of early 2010, the United Nations was engaged in at least 16 different peacekeeping missions, including the effort to protect civilians in the Darfur region of Sudan discussed at the beginning of this chapter.

Public Diplomacy (Soft Power)

In July 2002, President George W. Bush created the White House Office of Global Communications to address the question he asked before a joint session of Congress only a week after the terrorist attacks on New York City and Washington, D.C.: "Why do they hate us?" The Office of Global Communications is designed to enhance the United States' reputation abroad, countering its image as the "Great Satan," as some of its enemies describe it.[11]

Bush was not the first president to worry about the U.S. image abroad. President Franklin Roosevelt created the Office of War Information early in World War II, which in turn established the Voice of America program to broadcast pro-U.S. information into Nazi Germany. President Harry Truman followed suit early in the cold war with the Soviet Union by launching the Campaign of Truth, which eventually led to the creation of the U.S. Information Agency under President Dwight Eisenhower. Both agencies exist today and are being strengthened as part of the "new public diplomacy."

Public diplomacy is a blend of age-old propaganda techniques and modern information warfare. It has three basic goals: (1) to cast the enemy in a less favorable light among its supporters, (2) to mold the image of a conflict such as the war in Afghanistan, and (3) to clarify the ultimate goals of U.S. foreign policy. For example, the United States has tried to convince the people of Afghanistan that Osama bin Laden is the true enemy of the people, and that the war is not between Muslims and Western democracies but about preventing the deaths of innocent women and children in Afghanistan and the United States.

Foreign Aid (Soft Power)

The United States offers aid to more than 100 countries directly and to other nations through contributions to various U.N. development funds. Since 1945, the United States has provided approximately $400 billion in economic assistance to foreign countries. In recent years, however, its foreign aid spending has amounted to approximately $15 billion per year, or less than 50 percent of what it spent in inflation-adjusted dollars back in 1985.[12]

Most foreign aid goes to a few countries the United States deems to be of strategic importance to national security: Israel, Egypt, Ukraine, Jordan, India, Russia, South Africa, and Haiti. That list is sure to change in the future as the nation reallocates its budget to nations central to the war on terrorism. However, regardless of which nation receives the aid, most foreign aid is actually spent in the United States, where it pays for the purchase of U.S. services and products being sent to those countries. It thus amounts to a hefty subsidy for U.S. companies and their employees.

The American public thinks the United States spends much more on foreign aid than it actually does and therefore opposes increased spending. Although the United States is one of the largest foreign aid contributors in terms of total dollars, it ranks low among developed countries when aid is measured as a percentage of gross national income. A recent poll of U.S. citizens found that few supported increased foreign aid, and approximately half favored reducing it. The rest favor keeping foreign aid at the same level.[13] State Department officials are invariably the biggest advocates of foreign aid. Presidents also recognize the vital role foreign aid plays in advancing U.S. interests and have wanted to maintain the leverage with key countries that economic and military assistance provides. One major debate today is how much debt relief to provide for the world's poorest nations, especially ones that are hard hit by war and natural disasters such as Haiti.

Despite these arguments, Congress invariably trims the foreign aid budget, responding in part to polls that show most people erroneously believe that the United States spends more on foreign aid than it does on Medicare and other domestic priorities. Members of Congress often criticize foreign aid as a "Ghana versus Grandma" case. How, they say, can you give away taxpayers' money to some foreign country when we have poor older people who cannot afford their prescription drugs and decent medical help?[14]

Critics also note that U.S. foreign aid has subsidized the most autocratic and most corrupt of dictators. And there are plenty of instances in which foreign aid money has been stolen or misspent. Defenders counter that some corruption is inevitable.

Economic Sanctions (Hard Power)

The United States has frequently used economic pressure to punish other nations for opposing its interests. Indeed, it has employed economic sanctions more than any other nation—more than 100 times in the past 50 years. **Economic sanctions** deny export, import, or financial relations with a target country in an effort to change that country's policies. Those imposed on South Africa doubtless helped end apartheid and encourage democracy in that nation; sanctions on Libya helped end its nuclear weapons program. But sanctions imposed on Cuba have not had much effect in dislodging that nation's dictatorial regime.

The use of economic sanctions has varied throughout the years. They are especially unpopular among farmers and corporations that have to sacrifice part of their overseas markets to comply with government controls, and they rarely work as effectively as intended. They can also be costly to U.S. businesses and workers while intensifying anti-U.S. sentiment.

economic sanctions
Denial of export, import, or financial relations with a target country in an effort to change that nation's policies.

Military Intervention (Hard Power)

War is not merely an extension of diplomacy but rather the complete and total breakdown of diplomatic efforts. The United States has used military force in other

For the People

GOVERNMENT'S GREATEST ENDEAVORS

Rebuilding Europe After World War II

Approximately 50 years after the United States completed its most significant work rebuilding Europe after World War II, this endeavor still resonates as one of the its greatest achievements for the people. The roads, railroads, bridges, and factories that had been bombed into rubble were rebuilt; the economies that had been devastated by labor shortages were rekindled; and the hunger, homelessness, and unemployment that marked the end of war were dispatched as the war-torn continent healed.

A young West German boy clutches new shoes received from foreign aid after WWII.

By strengthening the economies of Western Europe, this endeavor simultaneously helped alleviate suffering abroad, contain communism, and create a vibrant market for American goods. It also created new economic competition that made the U.S. economy stronger, while forging a bond with future allies in the war against terrorism.

The centerpiece of rebuilding Europe was the 1948 Marshall Plan, named for its champion, General George C. Marshall, who had served as Army chief of staff during World War II and who had just joined the Truman administration as secretary of state. The essence of the Marshall Plan was simple: Inject billions in economic aid to get Europe moving again. The program, which was formally titled the European Recovery Plan, provided approximately $12 billion in aid to increase economic production, expand European trade, encourage new economic ties between former enemies, and put an end to the rampant economic chaos of the time.

The program was limited to four years and demanded cooperation from the nations it was designed to help. Nations could only receive help if they created a new organization to distribute the funding. Twenty-two European nations were invited to the first planning meeting in the summer of 1947, but only 16 showed up. The Soviet Union and its communist allies in Eastern Europe refused to attend, choosing instead to revive the Comintern, an international organization pledged to destroying world capitalism.

The Marshall Plan was a stunning foreign policy success, particularly in helping the United States contain communism. But it was also a great moral victory for America, prompting British Prime Minister Winston Churchill to call it "the most unsordid act in history."

CRITICAL THINKING QUESTIONS

1. Why was rebuilding Europe so important to the United States?
2. How is this kind of soft power being used today around the world?
3. Should the United States spend money helping future competitors such as Europe become self-sufficient?

nations on the average of almost once a year since 1789, although usually in short-term initiatives such as NATO's military activities in Bosnia and Kosovo. Although presidential candidate John Kerry argued that the Iraq War was the first time in history the United States had gone to war because it chose to, not because it had to, the country has actually sent forces into combat many times without a clear threat. It did not have to go to war against Spain in 1898 or send troops to Cuba, Haiti, the Dominican Republic, Lebanon, Mexico, Nicaragua, Somalia, South Vietnam, or even Europe in World War I.[15] (See Table 14–1 for the number of troops killed in the nation's major wars.)

Experts tend to agree that the use of force is most successful in small and even medium-sized countries for short engagements (Grenada, Panama, Kuwait, Kosovo, and Afghanistan). They also agree that it "often proves ineffective in the context of national civil wars (the United States in Vietnam; Israel in Lebanon)."[16]

Not all military action is visible to the public or even the intended target. Covert activities are planned and executed to conceal the identity of the sponsor. The United States repeatedly engaged in covert operations during the cold war, including early intervention in Vietnam and Central America, as well as in Afghanistan, where it supported rebels fighting the Soviet invasion. But covert activities in Cuba, Chile, and elsewhere have backfired, and support for this strategy has cooled in the post–cold war era.[17] Ironically, U.S. covert aid to the Afghan rebels eventually led to the Soviet withdrawal, which in turn led to the establishment of the Taliban, which allowed Osama bin Laden and his followers to establish training bases in its territory.

TABLE 14–1 The Costs of War

War	Number Killed
Revolutionary War	4,435
War of 1812	2,260
Civil War	214,939
Spanish-American War	385
World War I	53,402
World War II	291,557
Korean War	35,516
Vietnam War	58,516
Persian Gulf War	382
Iraq War	4,416*
Afghanistan War	1,233*

* Estimated figures as of August 2010.

SOURCE: *The Washington Post,* May 26, 2003; figures updated by authors.

YOU WILL

DECIDE Should Women Engage in Combat?

As the number of women in the armed forces has increased, so has the number of women who serve in combat zones. Whereas women constituted 6 percent of U.S. forces in the first war in Iraq in 1991, they made up 15 percent of forces in Iraq in 2008.

Although their jobs were in noncombat positions, Iraq and Afghanistan have been very dangerous places to serve—by July 2010, 113 female soldiers had been killed. Technically, the women killed in Iraq and Afghanistan did not die in combat operations. Under a 1994 order, women can fly combat aircraft to and from airfields, protect convoys, guard prisoners of war, and rescue wounded soldiers, but they may not participate in any "direct combat on the ground." Although the military is redesigning assignments to ensure that women have an equal opportunity to participate in noncombat operations, women are allowed to serve only in support units.

The military has changed dramatically in recent years—combat uses high-technology weapons and requires tight coordination of air, land, and sea operations, which can blur the lines between support and combat units. As war has become more complicated, experts are asking whether women should be given the order to engage in combat.

What do you think? Should women be engaged in direct ground combat? What are some of the arguments for or against this?

THINKING IT THROUGH

Opponents argue that men are physically superior to women—although there are many high-tech jobs in combat, there is nothing high-tech about a face-to-face encounter with a deadly enemy. These opponents believe that men are better suited to win these encounters. There is also concern that men and women would form personal relationships in combat units that might distract them as they enter battle, or that female soldiers might be in the early stages of pregnancy when called for combat.

Moreover, opponents feel women would be much more vulnerable to sexual harassment in combat units, which is obviously harder to police during battle.* There is already plenty of evidence that women in the military face discrimination and harassment. According to a recent investigation, approximately 3,000 women experienced some kind verbal and physical abuse in 2008 alone.†

Advocates of a combat role for women argue that physical differences are mostly irrelevant. All soldiers must meet certain physical qualifications such as height, weight, and conditioning. If women meet these criteria, they argue, they should be allowed to fight. After all, they go through the same boot camps as men and learn how to use the same weapons. With the armed services struggling to recruit new soldiers, advocates also argue, women constitute an important source of future volunteers.

Women now make up approximately 15 percent of the total enlistment in the U.S. armed forces.

Critical Thinking Questions

1. What are the political barriers against allowing women in combat?
2. Are women just as able to win the face-to-face battles that often arise in combat?
3. How can the military ensure that personal relationships do not affect combat decisions on the battlefield?

* Evan Thomas and Gregory L. Vistica, "Falling Out of the Sky," *Newsweek*, March 17, 1997, p. 26.
† http://www.time.com/time/magazine/article/0,9171,1968110,00.html.

Prospects for the Future

The world has become a much more uncertain place since the end of the cold war, if only because the United States now faces many potential "hot spots" where individual nations and groups can challenge its views. Moreover, the Internet has increased access to information around the world, the global economy has increased competition for jobs and markets, and the war on terrorism has increased anti-U.S. sentiment in many nations.

The United States is clearly struggling to address this uncertainty without frustrating the public or compromising basic democratic principles. On the one hand, for example, citizens favor open borders, easy movement of imports and exports, short lines at airports, quick access to information, and protection of their privacy. On the other hand, they want government to monitor terrorists, detect dangerous cargo, ensure airport security, keep secrets from the enemy, and make sure no one slips through the border to bring harm to the nation.

Osama bin Laden became America's number one public enemy after his Al-Qaeda organization took credit for destroying the World Trade Center on 9/11. ■ *What do Americans think when they see this image year after year? How important is it to capture bin Laden?*

Although these goals are not necessarily contradictory, they do require a careful balance of individual liberty and national interest. They also call for an effort to prevent the spread of terrorism by promoting global peace and understanding. The war on terrorism will not be won in a single battle with a single adversary, nor will weapons of mass destruction disappear without a broad international commitment to action. As the United States has learned during the hard months of combat in Iraq, coalition building may be difficult, frustrating, and most certainly time-consuming, but, ultimately, it may be the only option available. Having fought the Iraq War largely on its own, the United States has come to realize that it needs help to accomplish its goals.

Citizens can help the United States achieve its goals in many ways, whether by contributing or volunteering to provide humanitarian aid, serving in the military, or trying to improve the nation's reputation by addressing problems at home. At the same time, citizens can help change the foreign policy and defense agenda through active engagement in the political process. Their voices can be and have been heard on many issues, including Darfur. By putting pressure on the federal government, citizens can influence the priorities given to our foreign policy goals, while holding the nation's elected leaders accountable for what they do.

CHAPTER **SUMMARY**

14.1 Analyze the questions and responses that shape approaches to U.S. foreign policy and defense.

Views of foreign policy address five basic questions: Should the United States view the world realistically or idealistically? Should the United States isolate itself from the world or accept a role in the international community? Should the United States act on its own or only with the help of other nations? Should the United States act first against threats to its safety or wait until it is attacked? And should the United States use its military and economic hard power or its diplomatic soft power? Hard power relies on military and economic strength, whereas soft power uses diplomacy.

14.2 Assess the status of each of the issues that currently dominate the foreign policy and defense agenda.

The foreign policy and defense agenda contains a long list of issues, but seven are currently at the top of the list: controlling weapons of mass destruction such as nuclear missiles, fighting terrorism, negotiating peace in the Middle East, promoting free trade abroad, reducing global warming, ending the wars in Iraq and Afghanistan, and strengthening democracy and international understanding. Congress and the president do not always agree on the specific issues but tend to spend most of their time and the federal budget on them.

14.3 Outline the structure of the foreign policy and defense bureaucracy.

The defense bureaucracy involves a set of interlocking agencies that engage in many of the same issues. The National Security Council, State Department, intelligence agencies, and Defense Department all play a role in setting and administering foreign policy and defense. The Defense Department is designed to ensure civilian control of the U.S. military but seeks advice from the military through the Joint Chiefs of Staff, who oversee the all-volunteer force. Contractors deliver a large amount of goods and services to the department and are part of what President Eisenhower called the military-industrial complex.

14.4 Evaluate the options for achieving foreign policy and defense goals.

Foreign policy and defense options involve a mix of hard and soft power, including conventional diplomacy and foreign aid, economic sanctions, and military intervention.

CHAPTER SELF-TEST

14.1 Analyze the questions and responses that shape approaches to U.S. foreign policy and defense.

1. A policy of viewing the world idealistically requires accepting a role in the international community. In a few sentences, make two or three more connections between the five questions shaping U.S. foreign policy.
2. List and define the three components of the Bush Doctrine.
3. Decide whether the following are aspects of hard power or soft power.
   a. Negotiating with other nations
   b. Providing aid to developing countries
   c. Maintaining powerful military forces
   d. Using battlefield forces to defeat enemies
   e. Participating in international treaties and institutions

14.2 Assess the status of each of the issues that currently dominate the foreign policy and defense agenda.

4. List and describe five of the seven issues dominating the U.S. international agenda.
5. In a few sentences, explain two problems and two opportunities related to granting normal trade relations status to China.
6. In a few sentences, explain what the "surge" is, why it has been implemented, and its results so far.
7. Write a short essay discussing which of the seven issues on the U.S. agenda deserves the most attention. Explain how attention to it will most likely ensure peace and prosperity and why the other issues are less important.

14.3 Outline the structure of the foreign policy and defense bureaucracy.

8. Match each of the following government organizations with its appropriate description:

a. Contractor	i. The organization charged with gathering information from around the world
b. State Department	ii. A private business that develops and manufactures technology for the military
c. Joint Chiefs of Staff	iii. The organization responsible for negotiating treaties, protecting U.S. citizens abroad, and staffing embassies and consulates
d. National Security Council	iv. A council consisting of the heads of the army, navy, air force, and Marine Corps
e. Central Intelligence Agency	v. A committee of the president, vice president, secretaries of defense and state, and often others who make foreign policy

9. The foreign policy and defense bureaucracy is extremely complex and employs thousands of people. In a paragraph, suggest some of the problems that may arise from its size and complexity.
10. In two or three sentences, explain how the president is truly the commander in chief of the armed forces.

14.4 Evaluate the options for achieving foreign policy and defense goals.

11. Which of the following is an example of public diplomacy?
    a. Diplomats from Japan, China, and the United States negotiate with North Korea over ending its nuclear weapons program
    b. President Bush addresses the U.S. people about the Iraq War
    c. The State Department creates Web sites in Arabic showing that Al-Qaeda has killed thousands of fellow Muslims
    d. Executives from the United States' General Motors and Japan's Toyota discuss an auto industry trade agreement
12. In a few sentences, define conventional diplomacy and explain how it is related to hard power.
13. In an essay, discuss which foreign policy and defense tools, such as foreign aid or military force, would best keep the United States safe and improve its relationship with Iran. Also discuss which tools would likely *not* work or would make the situation worse.

Answers to selected questions: 3. a. soft, b. soft, c. hard, d. hard, e. soft; 8. a. ii, b. iii, c. iv, d. v, e. i; 11. c

mypoliscilab EXERCISES

Where participation leads to action!

Apply what you learned in this chapter on MyPoliSciLab.

Read on **mypoliscilab.com**

eText: Chapter 14

Study and **Review** on **mypoliscilab.com**

Pre-Test
Post-Test
Chapter Exam
Flashcards

Watch on **mypoliscilab.com**

Video: NYC's Subway Surveillance System
Video: Sanctions on Iran

Explore on **mypoliscilab.com**

Simulation: You Are President John F. Kennedy
Simulation: You Are the Newly Appointed Ambassador to the Country of Dalmatia
Simulation: You Are the President of the United States
Comparative: Comparing Foreign and Security Policy
Timeline: The Evolution of Foreign Policy
Visual Literacy: Evaluating Defense Spending

KEY TERMS

realism, p. 422
idealism, p. 422
isolationism, p. 423
internationalism, p. 423
unilateralism, p. 423
Bush Doctrine, p. 424
multilateralism, p. 424
preemption, p. 424
weapons of mass destruction, p. 424
hard power, p. 425
soft power, p. 425
theory of deterrence, p. 425
normal trade relations, p. 427
economic sanctions, p. 436

ADDITIONAL RESOURCES

FURTHER READING

KIMBERLY ANN ELLIOTT, GARY CLYDE HUFBAUER, AND **JEFFREY J. SCHOTT,** *Economic Sanctions Reconsidered,* 3d ed. (Peterson Institute, 2008).

LOUIS FISHER, *Presidential War Power,* 2d ed. (University Press of Kansas, 2004).

JOHN LEWIS GADDIS, *The Cold War: A New History* (Penguin, 2005).

OLE HOLSTI, *Public Opinion and American Foreign Policy,* rev. ed. (University of Michigan Press, 2004).

STEVEN W. HOOK AND **JOHN SPANNIER,** *U.S. Foreign Policy Since World War II, 18th ed.* (CQ Press, 2010).

LOCH K. JOHNSON, *Secret Agencies: U.S. Intelligence in a Hostile World* (Yale University Press, 1996).

JOYCE P. KAUFMAN, *A Concise History of U.S. Foreign Policy,* 2d ed (Rowman & Littlefield, 2010).

STEVEN KULL AND **I. M. DESTLER,** *Misreading the Public: The Myth of a New Isolationism* (Brookings Institution Press, 1999).

ROBERT S. LITWAK, *Rogue States and U.S. Foreign Policy: Containment After the Cold War* (Johns Hopkins University Press, 2000).

NATIONAL COMMISSION ON TERRORIST ATTACKS ON THE UNITED STATES, *The 9/11 Commission Report* (Norton, 2004).

JOSEPH NYE, *Soft Power: The Means to Success in World Politics* (Public Affairs, 2005).

MICHAEL E. O'HANLON, *How to Be a Cheap Defense Hawk* (Brookings Institution Press, 2002).

PAUL R. PILLAR, *Terrorism and U.S. Foreign Policy* (Brookings Institution Press, 2004).

ROSEMARY RIGHTER, *Utopia Lost: The United Nations and World Order* (Twentieth Century Fund, 1995).

STEPHEN R. WEISSMAN, *A Culture of Deference: Congress's Failure of Leadership in Foreign Policy* (Basic Books, 1995).

GEORGE C. WILSON, *This War Really Matters: Inside the Fight for Defense Dollars* (CQ Press, 2000).

WEB SITES

State.gov The State Department's Web site.

Defense.gov The Defense Department's Web site.

Foreignaffairs.com A leading magazine about foreign policy. Many articles are free.

Freedomhouse.org Freedom House is a charitable organization that follows threats to freedom around the world. It also provides news feeds on specific events.

Foreignpolicy.com Another leading magazine about foreign policy. Many articles are also free.

careers.state.gov/officer/index.html The place to go to apply to the foreign service.

CONCLUSION

Sustaining Constitutional Democracy

CHAPTER **OUTLINE**

The United States' founding generation fought an eight-year revolution to secure its rights and freedom. First at the Constitutional Convention in 1787 and later in the first Congress, they confronted the challenges of creating a government, writing a Constitution, and drafting a bill of rights that would protect rights to life, liberty, and self-government for themselves and subsequent generations. But they knew, as we also know, that passive allegiance to ideals and rights is never enough. Every generation must become responsible for nurturing these ideals by actively renewing the community and nation of which it is a part.

The framers knew about the rise and decline of ancient Athens. They were familiar with Pericles's funeral oration, which states that the person who takes no part in public affairs is a useless person, a good-for-nothing.[1] According to Pericles and many Athenians, the city's business was everyone's business. Athens had flourished as an example of what a civilized city might be, but it collapsed when greed, self-centeredness, and complacency set in. As time went on, the Athenians wanted security more than they wanted liberty, comfort more than freedom. In the end, they lost it all—security, comfort, and freedom. "Responsibility was the price every man must pay for freedom. It was to be had on no other terms."[2]

If we are to be responsible citizens, we must speak up for what we believe: support for or opposition to particular policies such as the war in Afghanistan, same-sex marriage, health care reform, and more or less regulation of the economy. The exchange of ideas helps produce more-representative policy and better-informed citizens. Our country needs citizens who understand that our well-being is tied to the well-being of our neighbors, community, and country.

More people today live under conditions of greater political freedom than at any previous time. The transition from living under authoritarian rule to shouldering political freedom is often difficult, as evidenced by the efforts to form democratic governments in Russia, Pakistan, and Honduras. Our experience in Iraq and Afghanistan also shows that imposing democracy on societies without the supporting values and institutions is problematic. Throughout history, most people have lived in societies in which a small group at the top imposed its will on others. Today, neither in Castro's Cuba nor in the military regime of North Korea, neither in the People's Republic of China nor in Saudi Arabia, do ordinary people have a voice in the type of decisions we routinely make in the United States: Should we attend college? What kind of employment should we seek? Who should be allowed to enter or leave the country? How much money should be spent for schools, economic development initiatives, health care, or environmental protection? We take for granted the freedom to make such decisions.

Elected leadership and constitutional structures and protections are important, but an active, committed citizenry is equally important. Freedom and obligation go together. Liberty and duty go together. The answer to a nation's problems lies not in producing a perfect constitution or a few larger-than-life leaders. The answer lies in encouraging a nation of attentive and active citizens who will, above and beyond their professional and private ambitions, care about the common concerns of the Republic and strive to make democracy work.

The Case for Government by the People

The essence of our Constitution is that it both grants power to government and withholds power from it. Fearing a weak national government and popular disorder, the framers wanted to strengthen the powers of the national government so that it could carry out its responsibilities, such as ensuring domestic order and maintaining national defense. They also wanted to limit state governments to keep them from interfering with interstate commerce and property rights. Valuing above all the principle of individual liberty, the framers wanted to protect the people from too much government. They wanted a limited government—yet one that could accomplish essential tasks. The solution was to divide up the power of the national government, to make it ultimately responsive, if only indirectly, to the voters.

Most citizens want an efficient and effective government that also promotes social justice. We want to maintain our commitment to liberty and freedom. We want a government that acts for the majority yet protects minorities. We want to safeguard our nation and our streets in a world full of change and violence. We want to protect the rights of the poor, the elderly, and minorities. Do we expect too much from our elected officials and public servants? Of course we do!

Constitutional democracy is a system of checks and balances. Government must balance individual liberties against the collective security needs of society. The questions always are: Which rights of which people are to be protected by what means and at what price to individuals and to the whole society? These questions have arisen again and again in the war on terrorism. The USA PATRIOT Act became law, allowing greater government surveillance and, arguably, security but at the expense of individual liberty. Criticized by both conservatives and liberals, the Act was renewed in 2006 but included some new limitations on government investigations.

Participation and Representation

No political problem is more complicated than working out the proper relationship between voters and elected officials. It is not only a simple matter of ensuring that elected officials do what the voters want them to do. Every individual has a host of conflicting desires, fears, hopes, and expectations, and no government can represent the conflicting desires and expectations of each individual.

Participation

Some propose to bypass this thorny problem of representation by vastly increasing the role of direct popular participation in decision making, through greater use of tools such as the initiative, referendum, or recall.[3] What some regard as the most perfect form of democracy would exist when every person has a full and equal opportunity to participate in all decisions and in all processes of influence, persuasion, and discussion that bear on those decisions. Direct participation in decision making, its advocates contend, will serve two major purposes. First, it will enhance the dignity, self-respect, and understanding of individuals by giving them responsibility for the decisions that shape their lives. Second, direct participation will act as a safeguard against undemocratic and antidemocratic forms of government and prevent the replacement of democracy by dictatorship or tyranny. Interests can be represented, furthered, and defended best by the people they directly concern.

New technologies and new uses of old technologies let governments appeal directly to voters and voters speak directly to public officials. We now have voting by mail in Oregon and other places, and some people advocate voting online. Digital town halls may be next. In the 2008 election, large numbers of voters, especially younger voters, communicated with each other and with the candidates via the Internet. The Internet was also an important fund-raising tool for Barack Obama and will likely grow in importance over time. The Internet is also now an important source of news and political advertising. All of these tools will become a bigger part of communications and interactions between citizens and their government.

Throughout the course of its history, the United States has shifted toward greater direct democracy, and this trend is likely to continue. Suffrage has expanded from only white male property owners being eligible to vote at the time of the founding to all

The United States holds more elections for more offices than any other democracy. ■ *Why is participation in the electoral process considered a key component of democracy in America?*

citizens 18 years of age or older being eligible to vote today. The founders designed a system that limited the use of direct representation to the House of Representatives. Today, both the House and Senate are directly elected. Moreover, with the advent of direct primaries, voters decide the nominees for federal office. The initiative and referendum process provides a direct way for citizens to enact or overturn laws and even recall those in government.

However, despite this trend toward increasing direct democracy, we still need elected officials to mediate among factions, build coalitions, and make the compromises necessary for producing policy and action. We also need institutions such as elected legislatures to digest complicated information and conduct impartial hearings to air competing points of view. As a practical matter, people simply cannot spend hours taking part in every decision that affects their lives. Thus, much of the work of government at all levels requires elected representatives.

Representation

Because we must have representatives, who shall represent whom? By electing representatives in a multitude of districts, we can build most minority interests and attitudes into our representative institutions. In the United States, we generally have election processes in which only the candidate receiving the greatest number of votes wins. But there are other ways. For example, Austria and Denmark use proportional representation—a system in which each party running receives the proportion of legislative seats corresponding to its proportion of votes.[4]

Representation can also be influenced by whether there is one party, two, or several. Ours is a strong two-party system that knits local constituencies into coalitions that can elect and sustain national majorities. A major factor in maintaining our two-party system is that single-member legislative districts, such as those for the U.S. Congress and state legislatures, tend to lead to two-party systems. This regularity, called *Duverger's law,* is generally seen as helping to moderate our politics.[5] In contrast, when countries adopt proportional representation, minor parties have greater influence.

Which is better, elected officials who represent coalitions of minorities or officials who represent a relatively clear-cut majority and have little or no obligation to the minority? The answer depends on what you expect from government. A system that represents coalitions of minorities usually reflects the trading, competition, and compromising that must take place in order to reach agreement among the various groups. Instead of acting for a united popular majority with a fairly definite program, either liberal or conservative, the government tries to satisfy all major interests by giving them a voice in decisions and sometimes a veto over actions.

Proponents of this form of representation argue that minority interests must be taken into consideration because the United States has not yet achieved equality in political access and representation. The U.S. Congress and many state legislatures, for example, still contain relatively few women and minorities. Critics also point to the extent of nonvoting and other forms of nonparticipation in politics. Low-income individuals are less well politically organized than upper-income individuals; strong organized groups are biased toward the status quo; a few corporations dominate television and the press; and the two major parties hold a virtual monopoly on party politics, which does not always offer the voters meaningful alternatives.

Critics of this philosophy of representation are concerned that our system of government is catering too much to minority interests with built-in procedures designed to curtail legislative majorities. For example, a Senate rule allows a minority to filibuster and block the will of the majority of senators. More broadly, rulings by the Supreme Court can overturn the will of the majority.[6]

These critics, who believe that governments should be more directly responsive to political majorities, can point to steady improvement in recent years in opening up access to the political system. Election laws have been changed to simplify voter registration, expand and improve voting procedures, and enforce one-person, one-vote standards. Efforts to limit the ability of rich people and well-financed interests to influence elections were cited by Congress as a motivation for passage of campaign finance reform in 2002, and by the Supreme Court in upholding most of that legislation in 2003.[7]

By this point, you undoubtedly appreciate that democracy has to mean much more than popular government and unchecked majority rule. A democracy needs competing politicians with differing views about the public interest. A vital democracy, living and growing, places its faith in the participation of citizens as voters, faith that they will elect not only people who mirror their views but leaders who will exercise their best judgment—"faith that the people will not condemn those whose devotion to principle leads them to unpopular courses, but will reward courage, respect honor, and ultimately recognize right."[8]

The Role of the Politician

Voters today have decidedly mixed views about elected officials. We realize that at their best, politicians are skillful at compromising, mediating, negotiating, and brokering—and that governing often requires these qualities. But we also suspect politicians of being ambitious, conniving, unprincipled, opportunistic, and corrupt.

Still, we often find that individual officeholders are bright, hardworking, and friendly (even though we may suspect they are trying to win our vote). And our liking sometimes turns into reverence after these same politicians die. George Washington, Abraham Lincoln, Dwight D. Eisenhower, and John F. Kennedy are acclaimed today. Harry Truman joked that "a statesman is a politician who has been dead for about ten or fifteen years."[9] Of course, we must put the problem in perspective. In all democracies, people probably expect too much from politicians and, at the same time, distrust those who wield power. Public officeholders tax us, regulate us, and conscript us, after all. We dislike political compromisers and ambitious opportunists—even though we may need such people to get things done.[10] At the same time, individuals can and do make a difference in shaping policy on the local, state, national, and international levels, whether the policy be about drunk driving, early childhood medical care, land mines, or using the courts to influence a policy agenda.

Politics and politicians, including those who work in Washington, are necessary and important to our freedom, security, and prosperity. Although people will disagree about

The U.S. Capitol in Washington, D.C., where both houses of Congress convene. Visitors are allowed to tour the Capitol and even watch Congress in session.

particular policies and processes, there is no disputing the need for government. Political leaders translate the fundamental needs of the people into practical demands on government.

We are fond of saying, "It's all politics." This greatly oversimplified observation implies that things would somehow be improved if we did not have politics and politicians. But politics is the lifeblood of democracy, and without politics, there is no freedom. A nation of subservient followers can never be a democratic one. A democratic nation requires educated, skeptical, caring, engaged, and conscientious citizens who will recognize when change is needed and have the courage to bring about necessary reforms and progress.[11] No matter how brilliant our Constitution or strong our economy, ultimately our system depends on individuals willing to study and speak out on issues, become involved in political parties, and run for and serve in office.

Experience teaches that power wielded justly today may be wielded corruptly tomorrow. It is right and necessary to protest when a policy is wrong or when the rights of other citizens are diminished. Democracy rests solidly on a realistic view of human nature. Criticism of official error is not unpatriotic. Our capacity for justice, as theologian and philosopher Reinhold Niebuhr observed, makes democracy possible. But our "inclination to injustice makes democracy necessary."[12] Democratic politics is the forum where, by acting together, citizens become and remain free.[13]

The ultimate test of a democratic system is the legal existence of an officially recognized opposition. A cardinal characteristic of a constitutional democracy is that it not only recognizes the need for the free organization of opposing views but also positively encourages this organization. Freedom for political expression and dissent is basic—even freedom to speak nonsense so that good sense not yet recognized gets a chance to be heard.[14]

The Importance of Active Citizenship

Crucial to democracy is belief in the free play of ideas. Only when the safety valve of public discussion is available, and when almost any policy is subject to perpetual questioning and challenge, can we be assured that both minority and majority rights will be served. To be afraid of public debate is to be afraid of self-government.

Thomas Jefferson once said, "Were it left to me to decide whether we should have a government without newspapers or newspapers without a government, I should

Education fosters self-confidence in dealing with bureaucracy, is a strong predictor of voting, and provides a knowledge base important to political influence. ■ *In what ways can educated participants have a real impact on our political system and public policies?*

not hesitate for a moment to prefer the latter."[15] Jefferson greatly valued an informed citizenry and had boundless faith in education. He believed that people are endowed with an innate sense of justice; the average person has only to be informed to act wisely. In the long run, said Jefferson, only an educated and enlightened democracy can hope to endure.

Education is one of the best predictors of voting, participation in politics, and knowledge of public affairs. People may not be equally invested or equally willing to invest in democracy, but those who are most attentive—frequently people like you who have gone to college—are more likely to have the willingness and self-confidence to see government and politics as necessary and important.

You now know how to influence public policy and the political process. You have gained an appreciation for the ways individuals and groups can both push and block an agenda. You know that many people choose not to participate in elections or politics, enhancing the power of those who do. Finally, you should also recognize that when individuals combine knowledge with political activity, they expand their influence.

Does political participation by committed individuals bring about constructive change? Remember that in the last half-century, restaurants, motels, and landlords once openly discriminated on the basis of race. Racial segregation in education existed in several states; segregated neighborhoods were a fact of life. Discriminatory practices denied blacks and poor whites access to voting. Women were discriminated against in the workplace and in government. Civil rights legislation and court cases have wrought remarkable changes. This is not to say that we have erased the legacies of racism and other kinds of discrimination from our national life. But as historian Arthur M. Schlesinger Jr. writes, "The genius of America lies in its capacity to forge a single nation from peoples of remarkably diverse racial, religious, and ethnic origins." Schlesinger acknowledges that our government and society have been more open to some than to others, "but it is more open to all today than it was yesterday and it is likely to be even more open tomorrow than today."[16]

Our political system is far from perfect, but it still is an open system and one that has become more and more democratic over time. People *can* fight city hall. People who disagree with policies in the nation can band together and be heard. We know only too well that the American dream is never fully attained. It must always be pursued.

Millions of citizens visit the great monuments in our nation's capital each year. They are always impressed by the memorials to Washington, Jefferson, Lincoln, Franklin D. Roosevelt, and the Vietnam, Korean, and World War II veterans. They are awed by the beauty of the Capitol, the Supreme Court, and the White House. The strength of the nation, however, resides not in these official buildings and monuments but in the hearts, minds, and behavior of citizens. If we lose faith, stop caring, stop participating, and stop believing in the possibilities of self-government, the monuments "will be meaningless piles of stone, and the venture that began with the Declaration of Independence, the venture familiarly known as America will be as lifeless as the stone."[17]

The future of our democracy will be shaped by citizens who care about preserving and extending our political rights and freedoms. Our individual liberties will never be assured unless we are willing to take responsibility for the progress of the whole community, to exercise our determination and belief in democracy. In the words of U.S. poet Archibald MacLeish: "How shall freedom be defended? By arms when it is attacked by arms, by truth when it is attacked by lies, by democratic faith when it is attacked by authoritarian dogma. Always, in the final act, by determination and faith."[18]

ADDITIONAL **RESOURCES**

FURTHER READING

DEREK BOK, *The Trouble with Government* (Harvard University Press, 2001).

RICHARD D. BROWN, *The Strength of a People: The Idea of an Informed Citizenry in America, 1650–1870* (University of North Carolina Press, 1996).

ROBERT A. DAHL, *On Democracy* (Yale University Press, 1998).

AMY GUTMANN AND **DENNIS THOMSON**, *Democracy and Discontent: Why Moral Conflict Cannot Be Avoided in Politics, and What Should Be Done About It* (Belknap Press, 1996).

WEB SITES

www.usa.gov/Contact/Elected.shtml This Web site provides links to contact information for the president and vice president, U.S. senators, U.S. representatives, state governors, and state legislators.

www.constitutionday.us/link_frameset.asp?url=http://www.constitutioncenter.org/constitution/ This is an "interactive Constitution" Web site, where you can search the Constitution by keywords or phrases, topics, or court cases.

www.dosomething.org/actnow/actionguide/how-get-involved-local-politics This Web site provides examples of how to get involved in community politics and includes a link to register to vote in your state.

www.rockthevote.com/ This Web site helps young people register to vote and get involved in politics.

APPENDIX

The Declaration of Independence

DRAFTED MAINLY BY THOMAS JEFFERSON, THIS DOCUMENT ADOPTED BY THE SECOND CONTINENTAL CONGRESS, AND SIGNED BY JOHN HANCOCK AND FIFTY-FIVE OTHERS, OUTLINED THE RIGHTS OF MAN AND THE RIGHTS TO REBELLION AND SELF-GOVERNMENT. IT DECLARED THE INDEPENDENCE OF THE COLONIES FROM GREAT BRITAIN, JUSTIFIED REBELLION, AND LISTED THE GRIEVANCES AGAINST GEORGE THE III AND HIS GOVERNMENT. WHAT IS MEMORABLE ABOUT THIS FAMOUS DOCUMENT IS NOT ONLY THAT IT DECLARED THE BIRTH OF A NEW NATION, BUT THAT IT SET FORTH, WITH ELOQUENCE, OUR BASIC PHILOSOPHY OF LIBERTY AND REPRESENTATIVE DEMOCRACY.

IN CONGRESS, JULY 4, 1776

(The unanimous Declaration of the Thirteen United States of America)

PREAMBLE

When, in the course of human events, it becomes necessary for one people to dissolve the political bands which have connected them with another, and to assume, among the powers of the earth, the separate and equal station to which the laws of nature and of nature's God entitle them, a decent respect to the opinions of mankind requires that they should declare the causes which impel them to the separation.

NEW PRINCIPLES OF GOVERNMENT

We hold these truths to be self-evident; that all men are created equal, that they are endowed by their Creator with certain unalienable rights, that among these are life, liberty, and the pursuit of happiness.

That, to secure these rights, governments are instituted among men, deriving their just powers from the consent of the governed.

That whenever any form of government becomes destructive of these ends, it is the right of the people to alter or to abolish it, and to institute new government, laying its foundation on such principles, and organizing its powers in such form, as to them shall seem most likely to effect their safety and happiness. Prudence, indeed will dictate that governments long established should not be changed for light and transient causes; and accordingly all experience hath shown that mankind are more disposed to suffer while evils are sufferable, than to right themselves by abolishing the forms to which they are accustomed. But when a long train of abuses and usurpations, pursuing invariably the same object, evinces a design to reduce them under absolute despotism, it is their right, it is their duty, to throw off such government, and to provide new guards for their future security.

REASONS FOR SEPARATION

Such has been the patient sufferance of these colonies; and such is now the necessity which constrains them to alter their former systems of government. The history of the present king of Great Britain is a history of repeated injuries and usurpations, all having in direct object the establishment of an absolute tyranny over these states. To prove this, let facts be submitted to a candid world.

He has refused his assent to laws, the most wholesome and necessary for the public good.

He has forbidden his governors to pass laws of immediate and pressing importance unless suspended in their operation till his assent should be obtained; and when so suspended, he has utterly neglected to attend to them.

He has refused to pass other laws for the accommodation of large districts of people, unless those people would relinquish the right of representation in the legislature, a right inestimable to them, and formidable to tyrants only.

He has called together legislative bodies at places unusual, uncomfortable, and distant for the depository of their public records, for the sole purpose of fatiguing them into compliance with his measures.

He has dissolved representative houses repeatedly, for opposing, with manly firmness, his invasions on the rights of people.

He has refused, for a long time after such dissolutions, to cause others to be elected; whereby the legislative powers incapable of annihilation, have returned to the people at large for their exercise; the state remaining, in the meantime, exposed to all the dangers of invasion from without and convulsions within.

He has endeavored to prevent the population of these states; for that purpose obstructing the laws of naturalization of foreigners, refusing to pass others to encourage their migration hither, and raising the conditions of new appropriations of lands.

He has obstructed the administration of justice, by refusing his assent to laws for establishing judiciary powers.

He has made judges dependent on his will alone for the tenure of their offices, and the amount and payment of their salaries.

He has erected a multitude of new offices, and sent hither swarms of officers to harass our people and eat out their substance.

He has kept among us, in times of peace, standing armies, without the consent of our legislature.

He has affected to render the military independent of, and superior to, the civil power.

He has combined with others to subject us to jurisdiction foreign to our constitution and unacknowledged by our laws, giving his assent to their acts of pretended legislation:

For quartering large bodies of armed troops among us;

For protecting them, by a mock trial, from punishment for any murders which they should commit on the inhabitants of these states;

For cutting off our trade with all parts of the world;

For imposing taxes on us without our consent;

For depriving us, in many cases, of the benefits of trial by jury;

For transporting us beyond seas, to be tried for pretended offenses;

For abolishing the free system of English laws in a neighboring province, establishing therein an arbitrary government, and enlarging its boundaries, so as to render it at once an example and fit instrument for introducing the same absolute rule into these colonies;

For taking away our charters, abolishing our most valuable laws, and altering, fundamentally, the forms of our governments;

For suspending our own legislatures, and declaring themselves invented with power to legislate for us in all cases whatsoever.

He has abdicated government here, by declaring us out of his protection and waging war against us.

He has plundered our seas, ravaged our coasts, burned our towns, and destroyed the lives of our people.

He is at this time transporting large armies of foreign mercenaries to complete the works of death, desolation, and tyranny already begun with circumstances of cruelty and perfidy scarcely paralleled in the most barbarous ages and totally unworthy of the head of a civilized nation.

He has constrained our fellow-citizens, taken captive on the high seas, to bear arms against their country, to become the executioners of their friends and brethren, or to fall themselves by their hands.

He has excited domestic insurrections among us, and has endeavored to bring on the inhabitants of our frontiers the merciless Indian savages, whose known rule of warfare is an undistinguished destruction of all ages, sexes, and conditions.

In every stage of these oppressions we have petitioned for redress in the most humble terms; our repeated petitions have been answered only by repeated injury. A prince whose character is thus marked by every act which may define a tyrant is unfit to be the ruler of a free people.

Nor have we been wanting in attention to our British brethren. We have warned them, from time to time, of attempts by their legislature to extend an unwarrantable jurisdiction over us. We have reminded them of the circumstances of our emigration and settlement here. We have appealed to their native justice and magnanimity; and we have conjured them, by the ties of our common kindred, to disavow these usurpations, which would inevitably interrupt our connections and correspondence. They, too, have been deaf to the voice of justice and of consanguinity. We must, therefore, acquiesce in the necessity which denounces our separation, and hold them, as we hold the rest of mankind, enemies in war, in peace, friends.

We, therefore, the representatives of the United States of America, in General Congress assembled, appealing to the Supreme Judge of the world for the rectitude of our intentions, do, in the name and by authority of the good people of these colonies, solemnly publish and declare, that these united colonies are, and of right ought to be, free and independent states; that they are absolved from all allegiance to the British crown, and that all political connection between them and the state of Great Britain is, and ought to be, totally dissolved; and that, as free and independent states, they have full power to levy war, conclude peace, contract alliances, establish commerce, and do all other acts and things which independent states may of a right do. And, for the support of this declaration, with a firm reliance on the protection of Divine Providence, we mutually pledge to each other our lives, our fortunes, and our sacred honor.

The Federalist, No. 10, James Madison

The Federalist, No. 10, written by James Madison soon after the Constitutional Convention, was prepared as one of several dozen newspaper essays aimed at persuading New Yorkers to ratify the proposed constitution. One of the most important basic documents in American political history, it outlines the need for and the general principles of a democratic republic. It also provides a political and economic analysis of the realities of interest group or faction politics.

To the People of the State of New York: Among the numerous advantages promised by a well-constructed union, none deserves to be more accurately developed than its tendency to break and control the violence of faction. The friend of popular governments, never finds himself so much alarmed for their character and fate, as when he contemplates their propensity of this dangerous vice. He will not fail, therefore, to set a due value on any plan which, without violating the principles to which he is attached, provides a proper cure for it. The instability, injustice, and confusion introduced into the public councils, have, in truth, been the mortal diseases under which popular governments have everywhere perished; as they continue to be the favorite and fruitful topics from which the adversaries to liberty derive their most specious declamations. The valuable improvements made by the American constitutions on the popular models, both ancient and modern, cannot certainly be too much admired; but it would be an unwarrantable partiality, to contend that they have as effectually obviated the danger on this side, as was wished and expected. Complaints are everywhere heard from our most considerate and virtuous citizens, equally the friends of public and private faith, and of public and personal liberty, that our governments are too unstable; that the public good is disregarded in the conflicts of rival parties; and that measures are too often decided, not according to the rules of justice, and the rights of the minor party, but by the superior force of an interested and overbearing majority. However anxiously we may wish that these complaints had no foundation, the evidence of known facts will not permit us to deny that they are in some degree true. It will be found, indeed, on a candid review of our situation, that some of the distresses under which we labor have been erroneously charged on the operations of our governments; but it will be found, at the same time, that other causes will not alone account for many of our heaviest misfortunes; and, particularly, for that prevailing and increasing distrust of public engagements, and alarm for private rights, which are echoed from one end of the continent to the other. These must be chiefly, if not wholly, effects of the unsteadiness and injustice, with which a factious spirit has tainted our public administrations.

By a faction, I understand a number of citizens, whether amounting to a majority of the whole, who are united and actuated by some common impulse of passion, or of interest, adverse to the rights of other citizens, or to the permanent and aggregate interests of the community.

There are two methods of curing the mischiefs of faction: the one, by removing its causes; the other, by controlling its effects.

There are again two methods of removing the causes of faction: the one, by destroying the liberty which is essential to its existence; the other, by giving to every citizen the same opinions, the same passions, and the same interests.

It could never be more truly said, than of the first remedy, that it was worse than the disease. Liberty is to faction what air is to fire, an aliment without which it instantly expires. But it could not be a less folly to abolish liberty, which is essential to political life, because it nourishes faction, than it would be to wish the annihilation of air, which is essential to animal life, because it imparts to fire its destructive agency.

The second expedient is as impracticable, as the first would be unwise. As long as the reason of man continues fallible, and he is at liberty to exercise it, different opinions will be formed. As long as the connection subsists between his reason and his self-love, his opinions and his passions will have a reciprocal influence on each other; and the former will be objects to which the latter will attach themselves. The diversity in the faculties of men, from which the rights of property originate, is not less an insuperable obstacle to an uniformity of interests. The protection of these faculties is the first object of government. From the protection of different and unequal faculties of acquiring property, the possession of different degrees and kinds of property immediately results; and from the influence of these on the sentiments and views of the respective proprietors, ensues a division of the society into different interests and parties.

The latent causes of faction are thus sown in the nature of man; and we see them everywhere brought into different degrees of activity, according to the different circumstances of civil society. A zeal for different opinions concerning religion, concerning government, and many other points, as well of speculation as of practice; an attachment to different leaders ambitiously contending for preeminence and power; or to persons of other descriptions whose fortunes have been interesting to the human passions, have, in turn, divided mankind into parties, inflamed them with mutual animosity, and rendered them much more disposed to vex and oppress each other, than to cooperate for their common good. So strong is this propensity of mankind, to fall into mutual animosities, that where no substantial occasion presents itself, the most frivolous and fanciful distinctions have been sufficient to kindle their unfriendly passions and excite their most violent conflicts. But the most common and durable source of factions, has been the various and unequal distribution of property. Those who hold, and those who are without property, have ever formed distinct interests in society. Those who are creditors, and those who are debtors, fall under a like discrimination. A landed interest, a manufacturing interest, a mercantile interest, a moneyed interest, with many lesser interests, grow up of necessity in civilized nations, and divide them into different classes, actuated by different sentiments and views. The regulation of these various and interfering interests forms the principal task of modern legislation, and involves the spirit of the party and faction in the necessary and ordinary operations of the government.

No man is allowed to be a judge in his own cause; because his interest will certainly bias his judgment, and, not improbably, corrupt his integrity. With equal, nay, with greater reason, a body of men are unfit to be both judges and parties at the same time; yet what are many of the most important acts of legislation, but so many judicial determinations, not indeed concerning the right of single persons, but concerning the rights of large bodies of citizens? And what are the different classes of legislators, but advocates and parties to the causes which they determine? Is a law proposed concerning private debts? It is a question to which the creditors are parties on one side, and the debtors on the other. Justice ought to hold the balance between them. Yet the parties are, and must be, themselves the judges; and the most numerous party, or, in other words, the most powerful faction, must be expected to prevail. Shall domestic manufacturers be encouraged, and in what degree, by restrictions on foreign manufacturers? Are questions which would be differently decided by the landed and the manufacturing classes; and probably by neither with a sole regard to justice and the public good. The apportionment of taxes, on the various descriptions of property, is an act which seems to require the most exact impartiality; yet there is, perhaps, no legislative act, in which greater opportunity and temptation are given to a predominant party to trample on the rules of justice. Every shilling, with which they overburden the inferior number, is a shilling saved to their own pockets.

It is in vain to say, that enlightened statesmen will be able to adjust these clashing interests, and render them all subservient to the public good. Enlightened statesmen will not always be at the helm, nor, in many cases, can such an adjustment be made at all, without taking into view indirect and remote considerations, which will rarely prevail over the immediate interest which one party may find in disregarding the rights of another, or the good of the whole.

The inference to which we are brought is, that the causes of faction cannot be removed; and that relief is only to be sought in the means of controlling its effects.

If a faction consists of less than a majority, relief is supplied by the republican principle, which enables the majority to defeat its sinister views, by regular vote. It may clog the administration, it may convulse the society; but it will be unable to execute and mask its violence under the forms of the Constitution. When a majority is included in a faction, the form of popular government, on the other hand, enables it to sacrifice to its ruling passion or interest, both the public good and the rights of other citizens. To secure the public good, and private rights, against the danger of such a faction, and at the same time to preserve the spirit and the form of popular government, is then the great object to which our inquiries are directed. Let me add, that it is the great desideratum, by which alone this form of government can be rescued from the opprobrium under which it has so long laboured, and be recommended to the esteem and adoption of mankind.

By what means is this object attainable? Evidently by one of two only. Either the existence of the same passion or interest in a majority, at the same time, must be prevented; or the majority, having such coexistent passion or interest, must be rendered, by their number and local situation, unable to concert and carry into effect schemes of oppression. If the impulse and the opportunity be suffered to coincide, we well know that neither moral nor religious motives can be relied on as an adequate control. They are not found to be such on the injustice and violence of individuals, and lose their efficacy in proportion to the number combined together; that is, in proportion as their efficacy becomes needful.

From this view of the subject, it may be concluded, that a pure democracy, by which I mean a society consisting of a small number of citizens, who assemble and administer the government in person, can admit of no cure for the mischiefs of faction. A common passion or interest will, in almost every case, be felt by a majority of the whole; a communication and concert, results from the form of government itself; and there is nothing to check the inducements to sacrifice the weaker party, or an obnoxious individual. Hence, it is, that such democracies have ever been spectacles of turbulence and contention; have ever been found incompatible with personal security, or the rights of property; and have in general been as short in their lives, as they have been violent in their deaths. Theoretic politicians, who have patronized this species of government, have erroneously supposed, that by reducing mankind to a perfect equality in their political rights, they would, at the same time be perfectly equalized and assimilated in their possessions, their opinions, and their passions.

A republic, by which I mean a government in which the scheme of representation takes place, opens a different prospect, and promises the cure for which we are seeking. Let us examine the points in which it varies from pure democracy, and we shall comprehend both the nature of the cure and the efficacy which it must derive from the union.

The two great points of difference, between a democracy and a republic, are, first, the delegation of the government, in the latter, to a small number of citizens, elected by the rest; secondly, the greater number of citizens, and greater sphere of country, over which the latter may be extended.

The effect of the first difference is, on the one hand, to refine and enlarge the public views, by passing them through the medium of a chosen body of citizens, whose wisdom may best discern the true interest of their country, and whose patriotism and love of justice, will be least likely to sacrifice it to temporary or partial considerations. Under such a regulation, it may well happen, that the public voice, pronounced by the representatives of the people, will be more consonant to the public good, than if pronounced by the people themselves, convened for the purpose. On the other hand the effect may be inverted. Men of factious tempers, of local prejudices, or of sinister designs, may by intrigue, by corruption, or by other means, first obtain the suffrages, and then betray the interest of the people. The question resulting is, whether small or extensive republics are most favourable to the election of proper guardians of the public weal; and it is clearly decided in favour of the latter by two obvious considerations.

In the first place, it is to be remarked that, however small the republic may be, the representatives must be raised to a certain number, in order to guard against the cabals of a few; and that however large it may be, they must be limited to a certain number, in order to guard against the confusion of a multitude. Hence, the number of representatives in the two cases not being in proportion to that of the constituents, and being proportionally greatest in the small republic, it follows, that if the proportion of fit characters be not less in the large than in the small republic, the former will present a greater option, and consequently a greater probability of a fit choice.

In the next place, as each representative will be chosen by a greater number of citizens in the large than in the small republic, it will be more difficult for unworthy candidates to practice with success the vicious arts, by which elections are too often carried; and the suffrages of the people being more free, will be more likely to centre in men who possess the most attractive merit, and the most diffusive and established characters.

It must be confessed, that in this, as in most other cases, there is a mean, on both sides of which inconveniences will be found to lie. By enlarging too much the number of electors, you render the representatives too little acquainted with all their local circumstances and lesser interests; as by reducing it too much, you render him unduly attached to these, and too little fit to comprehend and pursue great and national objects. The federal constitution forms a happy combination in this respect; the great and aggregate interests being referred to the national, the local and particular to the state legislatures.

The other point of difference is, the greater number of citizens, and extent of territory, which may be brought within the compass of republican, than of democratic government; and it is this circumstance principally which renders factious combinations less to be dreaded in the former, than in the latter. The smaller the society, the fewer probably will be the distinct parties and interests composing it; the fewer the distinct parties and interests, the more frequently will a majority be found of the same party; and the smaller the number of individuals composing a majority, and the smaller the compass within which they are placed, the more easily will they concert and execute their plans of oppression. Extend the sphere, and you take in a greater variety of parties and interests; you make it less probable that a majority of the whole will have a common motive to invade the rights of other citizens; or if such a common motive exists, it will be more difficult for all who feel it to discover their own strength, and to act in unison with each other. Besides other impediments, it may be remarked, that where there is a consciousness of unjust or dishonourable purposes, communication is always checked by distrust, in proportion to the number whose concurrence is necessary.

Hence, it clearly appears, that the same advantage, which a republic has over a democracy, in controlling the effects of faction, is enjoyed by a large over a small republic—is enjoyed by the union over the states composing it. Does this advantage consist in the substitution of representatives, whose enlightened views and virtuous sentiments render them superior to local prejudices, and to schemes of injustice? It will not be denied that the representation of the union will be most likely to possess these requisite endowments. Does it consist in the greater security afforded by a greater variety of parties, against the event of any one party being able to outnumber and oppress the rest? In an equal degree does the increased variety of parties, comprised within the union, increase the security? Does it, in fine, consist in the greater obstacles opposed to the concert and accomplishment of the secret wishes of an unjust and interested majority? Here, again, the extent of the union gives it the most palpable advantage.

The influence of factious leaders may kindle a flame within their particular states, but will be unable to spread a general conflagration through the other states; a religious sect may degenerate into a political faction in a part of the confederacy; but the variety of sects dispersed over the entire face of it, must secure the national councils against any danger from that source: a rage for paper money, for an abolition of debts, for an equal division of property, or for any other improper or wicked project, will be less apt to pervade the whole body of the union than a particular member of it; in the same proportion as such a malady is more likely to taint a particular county or district, than an entire state.

In the extent and proper structure of the union, therefore, we behold a republican remedy for the diseases most incident to republican government. And according to the degree of pleasure and pride we feel in being republicans, ought to be our zeal in cherishing the spirit, and supporting the character of federalists.

The Federalist, No. 51, James Madison

***The Federalist,* No. 51, also written by Madison, is a classic statement in defense of separation of powers and republican processes. Its fourth paragraph is especially famous and is frequently quoted by students of government.**

To what expedient, then, shall we finally resort, for maintaining in practice the necessary partition of power among the several departments as laid down in the Constitution? The only answer that can be given is that as all these exterior provisions are found to be inadequate the defect must be supplied, by so contriving the interior structure of the government as that its several constituent parts may, by their mutual relations, be the means of keeping each other in their proper places. Without presuming to undertake a full development of this important idea I will hazard a few general observations which may perhaps place it in a clearer light, and enable us to form a more correct judgment of the principles and structure of the government planned by the convention.

In order to lay a due foundation for that separate and distinct exercise of the different powers of government, which to a certain extent is admitted on all hands to be essential to the preservation of liberty, it is evident that each department should have a will of its own; and consequently should be so constituted that the members of each should have as little agency as possible in the appointment of the members of the others. Were this principle rigorously adhered to, it would require that all the appointments for the supreme executive, legislative, and judiciary magistracies should be drawn from the same fountain of authority, the people, through channels having no communication whatever with one another. Perhaps such a plan of constructing the several departments would be less difficult in practice than it may in contemplation appear. Some difficulties, however, and some additional expense would attend the execution of it. Some deviations, therefore, from the principle must be admitted. In the constitution of the judiciary department in particular, it might be inexpedient to insist rigorously on the principle: first, because peculiar qualifications being essential in the members, the primary consideration ought to be to select that mode of choice which best secures these qualifications; second, because the permanent tenure by which the appointments are held in that department must soon destroy all sense of dependence on the authority conferring them.

It is equally evident that the members of each department should be as little dependent as possible on those of the others for the emoluments annexed to their offices. Were the executive magistrate, or the judges, not independent of the legislature in this particular, their independence in every other would be merely nominal.

But the great security against a gradual concentration of the several powers in the same department consists in giving to those who administer each department the necessary constitutional means and personal motives to resist encroachments of the others. The provision for defense must in this, as in all other cases, be made commensurate to the danger of attack. Ambition must be made to counteract ambition. The interest of the man must be connected with the constitutional rights of the place. It may be a reflection on human nature that such devices should be necessary to control the abuses of government. But what is government itself but the greatest of all reflections on human nature? If men were angels, no government would be necessary. If angels were to govern men, neither external nor internal controls on government would be necessary. In framing a government which is to be administered by men over men, the great difficulty lies in this: you must first enable the government to control the governed; and in the next place oblige it to control itself. A dependence on the people is, no doubt, the primary control on the government; but experience has taught mankind the necessity of auxiliary precautions.

This policy of supplying, by opposite and rival interests, the defect of better motives, might be traced through the whole system of human affairs, private as well as public. We see it particularly displayed in all the subordinate distributions of power, where the constant aim is to divide and arrange the several offices in such a manner as that each may be a check on the other—that the private interest of every individual may be a sentinel over the public rights. These inventions of prudence cannot be less requisite in the distribution of the supreme powers of the State.

But it is not possible to give to each department an equal power of self-defense. In republican government, the legislative authority necessarily predominates. The remedy for this inconveniency is to divide the legislature into different branches; and to render them, by modes of election and different principles of action, as little connected with each other as the nature of their common functions and their common dependence on the society will admit. It may even be necessary to guard against dangerous encroachments by still further precautions. As the weight of the legislative authority requires that it should be thus divided, the weakness of the executive may require, on the other hand, that it should be fortified. An absolute negative on the legislature appears, at first view, to be the natural defense with which the executive magistrate should be armed. But perhaps it would be neither altogether safe nor alone sufficient. On ordinary occasions it might not be exerted with the requisite firmness, and on extraordinary occasions it might be perfidiously abused. May not this defect of an absolute negative be supplied by some qualified connection between this weaker department and the weaker branch of the stronger department, by which the latter may be led to support the constitutional rights of the former, without being too much detached from the rights of its own department?

If the principles on which these observations are founded be just, as I persuade myself they are, and they be applied as a criterion to the several State constitutions, and to the federal Constitution, it will be found that if the latter does not perfectly correspond with them, the former are infinitely less able to bear such a test.

There are, moreover, two considerations particularly applicable to the federal system of America, which place that system in a very interesting point of view.

First. In a single republic, all the power surrendered by the people is submitted to the administration of a single government; and the usurpations are guarded against by a division of the government into distinct and separate departments. In the compound republic of America, the power surrendered by the people is first divided between two distinct governments, and then the portion allotted to each subdivided among distinct and separate departments. Hence a double security arises to the rights of the people. The different governments will control each other, at the same time that each will be controlled by itself.

Second. It is of great importance in a republic not only to guard the society against the oppression of its rulers, but to guard one part of the society against the injustice of the other part. Different interests necessarily exist in different classes of citizens. If a majority be united by a common interest, the rights of the minority will be insecure. There are but two methods of providing against this evil: the one by creating a will in the community independent of the majority—that is, of the society itself; the other, by comprehending in the society so many separate descriptions of citizens as will render an unjust combination of a majority of the whole very improbable, if not impracticable. The first method prevails in all governments possessing an hereditary or self-appointed authority. This, at best, is but a precarious security; because a power independent of the society may as well espouse the unjust views of the major as the rightful interests of the minor party, and may possibly be turned against both parties. The second method will be exemplified in the federal republic of the United States. Whilst all authority in it will be derived from and dependent on the society, the society itself will be broken into so many parts, interests and classes of citizens, that the rights of individuals, or of the minority, will be in little danger from interested combinations of the majority. In a free government the security for civil rights must be the same as that for religious rights. It consists in the one case in the multiplicity of interests, and in the other in the multiplicity of sects. The degree of security in both cases will depend on the number of interests and sects; and this may be presumed to depend on the extent of country and number of people comprehended under the same government. This view of the subject must particularly recommend a proper federal system to all the sincere and considerate friends of republican government, since it shows that in exact proportion as the territory of the Union may be formed into more circumscribed Confederacies, or States, oppressive combinations of a majority will be facilitated; the best security, under the republican forms, for the rights of every class of citizen, will be diminished; and consequently the stability and independence of some member of the government, the only other security, must be proportionally increased. Justice is the end of government. It is the end of civil society. It ever has been and ever will be pursued until it be obtained, or until liberty be lost in the pursuit. In a society under the forms of which the stronger faction can readily unite and oppress the weaker, anarchy may as truly be said to reign as in a state of nature, where the weaker individual is not secured against the violence of the stronger; and as, in the latter state, even the stronger individuals are prompted, by the uncertainty of their condition, to submit to a government which may protect the weak as well as themselves; so, in the former state, will the more powerful factions or parties be gradually induced, by a like motive, to wish for a government which will protect all parties, the weaker as well as the more powerful. It can be little doubted that if the State of Rhode Island was separated from the Confederacy and left to itself, the insecurity of rights under the popular form of government within such narrow limits would be displayed by such reiterated oppressions of factious majorities that some power altogether independent of the people would soon be called for by the voice of the very factions whose misrule had proved the necessity to it. In the extended republic of the United States, and among the great variety of interests, parties, and sects which it embraces, a coalition of a majority of the whole society could seldom take place on any other principles than those of justice and the general good; whilst there being thus less danger to a minor from the will of a major party, there must be less pretext, also, to provide for the security of the former, by introducing into the government a will not dependent on the latter, or, in other words, a will independent of the society itself. It is no less certain that it is important, notwithstanding the contrary opinions which have been entertained that the larger the society, provided it lie within a practicable sphere, the more duly capable it will be of self-government. And happily for the *republican cause,* the practicable sphere may be carried to a very great extent by a judicious modification and mixture of the *federal principle.*

The Federalist, No. 78, Alexander Hamilton

THE FEDERALIST, NO. 78, WRITTEN BY ALEXANDER HAMILTON, EXPLAINS AND PRAISES THE PROVISIONS FOR THE JUDICIARY IN THE NEWLY DRAFTED CONSTITUTION. NOTICE ESPECIALLY HOW HAMILTON ASSERTS THAT THE COURTS HAVE A KEY RESPONSIBILITY IN DETERMINING THE MEANING OF THE CONSTITUTION AS FUNDAMENTAL LAW. HAMILTON IS OUTLINING HERE THE DOCTRINE OF JUDICIAL REVIEW AS WE NOW KNOW IT.

We proceed now to an examination of the judiciary department of the proposed government.

In unfolding the defects of the existing Confederation, the utility and necessity of a federal judicature have been clearly pointed out. It is the less necessary to recapitulate the considerations there urged as the propriety of the institution in the abstract is not disputed; the only questions which have been raised being relative to the manner of constituting it, and to its extent. To these points, therefore, our observations shall be confined.

The manner of constituting it seems to embrace these several objects: 1st. The mode of appointing the judges. 2nd. The tenure by which they are to hold their places. 3rd. The partition of the judiciary authority between different courts and their relations to each other.

First. As to the mode of appointing the judges: this is the same with that of appointing the officers of the Union in general and has been so fully discussed in the two last numbers that nothing can be said here which would not be useless repetition.

Second. As to the tenure by which the judges are to hold their places: this chiefly concerns their duration in office, the provisions for their support, the precautions for their responsibility.

According to the plan of the convention, all judges who may be appointed by the United States are to hold their offices *during good behavior;* which is conformable to the most approved of the State constitutions, and among the rest, to that of this State. Its propriety having been drawn into question by the adversaries of that plan is no light symptom of the rage for objection which disorders their imaginations and judgments. The standard of good behavior for the continuance in office of the judicial magistracy is certainly one of the most valuable of the modern improvements in the practice of government. In a monarchy it is an excellent barrier to the despotism of the prince; in a republic it is a no less excellent barrier to the encroachments and oppressions of the representative body. And it is the best expedient which can be devised in any government to secure a steady, upright, and impartial administration of the laws.

Whoever attentively considers the different departments of power must perceive that, in a government in which they are separated from each other, the judiciary, from the nature of its functions, will always be the least dangerous to the political rights of the Constitution; because it will be least in a capacity to annoy or injure them. The executive not only dispenses the honors but holds the sword of the community. The legislature not only commands the purse but prescribes the rules by which the duties and rights of every citizen are to be regulated. The judiciary, on the contrary, has no influence over either the sword or the purse; no direction either of the strength or of the wealth of the society, and can take no active resolution whatever. It may truly be said to have neither FORCE NOR WILL but merely judgment; and must ultimately depend upon the aid of the executive arm even for the efficacy of its judgments.

This simple view of the matter suggests several important consequences. It proves incontestably that the judiciary is beyond comparison the weakest of the three departments of power; that it can never attack with success either of the other two; and that all possible care is requisite to enable it to defend itself against their attacks. It equally proves that though individual oppression may now and then proceed from the courts of justice, the general liberty of the people can never be endangered from that quarter; I mean so long as the judiciary remains truly distinct from both the legislature and the executive. For I agree that "there is no liberty if the power of judging be not separated from the legislative and executive powers." And it proves, in the last place, that as liberty can have nothing to fear from the judiciary alone, but would have everything to fear from its union with either of the other departments, that as all the effects of such a union must ensue from a dependence of the former on the latter, notwithstanding a nominal and apparent separation; that as, from the natural feebleness of the judiciary, it is in continual jeopardy of being overpowered, awed, or influenced by its co-ordinate branches; and that as nothing can contribute so much to its firmness and independence as permanency in office, this quality may therefore be justly regarded as an indispensable ingredient in its constitution, and, in a great measure, as the citadel for the public justice and the public security.

The complete independence of the courts of justice is peculiarly essential in a limited Constitution. By a limited Constitution, I understand one which contains certain specified exceptions to the legislative authority; such, for instance, as that it shall pass no bills of attainder, no *ex post facto laws*, and the like. Limitations of this kind can be preserved in practice no other way than through the medium of courts of justice, whose duty it must be to declare all acts contrary to the manifest tenor of the Constitution void. Without this, all the reservations of particular rights or privileges would amount to nothing.

Some perplexity respecting the rights of the courts to pronounce legislative acts void, because contrary to the Constitution, has arisen from an imagination that the doctrine would imply a superiority to the judiciary to the legislative power. It is urged that the authority which can declare the acts of another void must necessarily be superior to the one whose acts may be declared void. As this doctrine is of great importance in all the American constitutions, a brief discussion of the grounds on which it rests cannot be unacceptable.

There is no position which depends on clearer principles than that every act of a delegated authority, contrary to the tenor of the commission under which it is exercised, is void. No legislative act, therefore, contrary to the Constitution, can be valid. To deny this would be to affirm that the deputy is greater than his principal; that the servant is above his master; that the representatives of the people are superior to the people themselves; that men acting by virtue of powers do not authorize, but what they forbid.

If it be said that the legislative body are themselves the constitutional judges of their own powers and that the construction they put upon them is conclusive upon the other departments it may be answered that this cannot be the natural presumption where it is not to be collected from any particular provisions in the Constitution. It is not otherwise to be supposed that the Constitution could intend to enable the representatives of the people to substitute their *will* to that of their constituents. It is far more rational to suppose that the courts were designed to be an intermediate body between the people and the legislature in order, among other things, to keep the latter within the limits assigned to their authority. The interpretation of the laws is the proper and peculiar province of the courts. A constitution is, in fact, and must be regarded by the judges as, a fundamental law. It therefore belongs to them to ascertain its meaning as well as the meaning of any particular act proceeding from the legislative body. If there should happen to be an irreconcilable variance between the two, that which has the superior obligation and validity ought, of course, to be preferred; or, in other words, the Constitution ought to be preferred to the statute, the intention of the people to the intention of their agents.

Nor does this conclusion by any means suppose a superiority of the judicial to the legislative power. It only supposes that the power of the people is superior to both, and that where the will of the legislature, declared in its statutes, stands in opposition to that of the people, declared in the Constitution, the judges ought to be governed by the latter rather than the former. They ought to regulate their decisions by the fundamental laws rather than by those which are not fundamental.

This exercise of judicial discretion in determining between two contradictory laws is exemplified in a familiar instance. It not uncommonly happens that there are two statutes existing at one time, clashing in whole or in part with each other and neither of them containing any repealing clause or expression. In such a case, it is the province of the courts to liquidate and fix their meaning and operation. So far as they can, by any fair construction, be reconciled to each other, reason and law conspire to dictate that this should be done; where this is impracticable, it becomes a matter of necessity to give effect to one in exclusion of the other. The rule which has obtained in the courts for determining their relative validity is that the last in order of time shall be preferred to the first. But this is a mere rule of construction, not derived from any positive law but from the nature and reason of the thing. It is a rule not enjoined upon the courts by legislative provision but adopted by themselves, as consonant to truth and propriety, for the direction of their conduct as interpreters of the law. They thought it reasonable that between the interfering acts of an equal authority that which was the last indication of its will should have the preference.

But in regard to the interfering acts of a superior and subordinate authority of an original and derivative power, the nature and reason of the thing indicates the converse of that rule as proper to be followed. They teach us that the prior act of a superior ought to be preferred to the subsequent act of an inferior and subordinate authority; and that accordingly, whenever a particular statute contravenes the Constitution, it will be the duty of the judicial tribunals to adhere to the latter and disregard the former.

It can be of no weight to say that the courts, on the pretense of a repugnancy, may substitute their own pleasure to the constitutional intentions of the legislature. This might as well happen in the case of two contradictory statutes; or it might as well happen in every adjudication upon any single statute. The courts must declare the sense of the law; and if they should be disposed to exercise WILL instead of JUDGMENT, the consequence would equally be the substitution of their pleasure to that of the legislative body. The observation, if it prove anything, would prove that there ought to be no judges distinct from that body.

If, then, the courts of justice are to be considered as the bulwarks of a limited Constitution against legislative encroachments, this consideration will afford a strong argument for the permanent tenure of judicial offices, since nothing will contribute so much as this to that independent spirit in the judges which must be essential to the faithful performance of so arduous a duty.

This independence of the judges is equally requisite to guard the Constitution and the rights of individuals from the effects of those ill humors which the arts of designing men, or the influence of particular conjunctures, sometimes disseminate among the people themselves, and which, though they speedily give place to better information, and more deliberate reflection, have a tendency, in the meantime, to occasion dangerous innovations in the government, and serious oppressions of the minor party in the community. Though I trust the friends of the proposed Constitution will never concur with its enemies in questioning that fundamental principal of Republican government which admits the right of the people to alter or abolish the established Constitution whenever they find it inconsistent with their happiness; yet it is not to be inferred from this principle that the representatives of the people, whenever a momentary inclination happens to lay hold of a majority of their constituents incompatible with the provisions in the existing Constitution would, on that account, be justifiable in a violation of those provisions; or that the courts would be under a greater obligation to connive at infractions in this shape than when they had proceeded wholly from the cabals of the representative body. Until the people have, by some solemn and authoritative act, annulled or changed the established form, it is binding upon themselves collectively, as well as individually; and no presumption, or even knowledge of their sentiments, can warrant their representatives in a departure from it prior to such an act. But it is easy to see that it would require an uncommon portion of fortitude in the judges to do their duty as faithful guardians of the Constitution, where legislative invasions of it had been instigated by the major voice of the community.

But it is not with a view to infractions of the Constitution only that the independence of the judges may be an essential safeguard against the effects of occasional ill humors in the society. These sometimes extend no farther than to the injury of the private rights of particular classes of citizens, by unjust and partial laws. Here also the firmness of the judicial magistracy is of vast importance in mitigating the severity and confining the operation of such laws. It not only serves to moderate the immediate mischiefs of those which may have been passed but it operates as a check upon the legislative body in passing them; who, perceiving that obstacles to the success of iniquitous intention are to be expected from the scruples of the courts, are in a manner compelled, by the very motives of the injustice they mediate, to qualify their attempts. This is a circumstance calculated to have more influence upon the character of our governments than but a few may be aware of. The benefits of the integrity and moderation of the judiciary have already been felt in more States than one; and though they may have displeased those whose sinister expectations they may have disappointed, they must have commanded the esteem and applause of all the virtuous and disinterested. Considerate men of every description ought to prize whatever will tend to beget or fortify that temper in the courts; as no man can be sure that he may not be tomorrow the victim of a spirit of injustice, by which he may be a gainer today. And every man must now feel that the inevitable tendency of such a spirit is to sap the foundations of public and private confidence and to introduce in its stead universal distrust and distress.

That inflexible and uniform adherence to the rights of the Constitution, and of individuals, which we perceive to be indispensable in the courts of justice, can certainly not be expected from judges who hold their offices by a temporary commission. Periodical appointments, however regulated, or by whomsoever made, would, in some way or other, be fatal to their necessary independence. If the power of making them was committed either to the executive or legislature there would be danger of an improper complaisance to the branch which possessed it; if to both, there would be an unwillingness to hazard the displeasure of either; if to the people, or to persons chosen by them for the special purpose, there would be too great a disposition to consult popularity to justify a reliance that nothing would be consulted by the Constitution and the laws.

There is yet a further and a weighty reason for the permanency of the judicial offices which is deducible from the nature of the qualifications they require. It has been frequently remarked with great propriety that a voluminous code of laws is one of the inconveniences necessarily connected with the advantages of a free government. To avoid an arbitrary discretion in the courts, it is indispensable that they should be bound down by strict rules and precedents which serve to define and point out their duty in every particular case that comes before them; and it will readily be conceived from the variety of controversies which grow out of the folly and wickedness of mankind that the records of those precedents must unavoidably swell to a very considerable bulk and must demand long and laborious study to acquire a competent knowledge of them. Hence it is that there can be but few men in the society who will have sufficient skill in the laws to qualify them for the stations of judges. And making the proper deductions for the ordinary depravity of human nature, the number must be still smaller of those who unite the requisite integrity with the requisite knowledge. These considerations apprise us that the government can have no great option between fit characters; and that a temporary duration in office which would naturally discourage such characters from quitting a lucrative line of practice to accept a seat on the bench would have a tendency to throw the administration of justice into hands less able and less well qualified to conduct it with utility and dignity. In the present circumstances of this country and in those in which it is likely to be for a long time to come, the disadvantages on this score would be greater than they may at first sight appear; but it must be confessed that they are far inferior to those which present themselves under the other aspects of the subject.

Upon the whole, there can be no room to doubt that the convention acted wisely in copying from the models of those constitutions which have established *good behavior* as the tenure of their judicial offices in point of duration, and that so far from being blamable on this account, their plan would have been inexcusably defective if it had wanted this important feature of good government. The experience of Great Britain affords an illustrious comment on the excellence of the institution.

Presidential Election Results, 1789–2008

Year	Candidates	Party	Popular Vote	Electoral Vote
1789	George Washington			69
	John Adams			34
	Others			35
1793	George Washington			132
	John Adams			77
	George Clinton			50
	Others			5
1796	John Adams	Federalist		71
	Thomas Jefferson	Democratic-Republican		68
	Thomas Pinckney	Federalist		59
	Aaron Burr	Democratic-Republican		30
	Others			48
1800	Thomas Jefferson	Democratic-Republican		73
	Aaron Burr	Democratic-Republican		73
	John Adams	Federalist		65
	Charles C. Pinckney	Federalist		64
1804	Thomas Jefferson	Democratic-Republican		162
	Charles C. Pinckney	Federalist		14
1808	James Madison	Democratic-Republican		122
	Charles C. Pinckney	Federalist		47
	George Clinton	Independent-Republican		6
1812	James Madison	Democratic-Republican		128
	DeWitt Clinton	Federalist		89
1816	James Monroe	Democratic-Republican		183
	Rufus King	Federalist		34
1820	James Monroe	Democratic-Republican		231
	John Quincy Adams	Independent-Republican		1
1824	John Quincy Adams	Democratic-Republican	108,740(30.5%)	84
	Andrew Jackson	Democratic-Republican	153,544(43.1%)	99
	Henry Clay	Democratic-Republican	47,136(13.2%)	37
	William H. Crawford	Democratic-Republican	46,618(13.1%)	41
1828	Andrew Jackson	Democratic	647,231(56.0%)	178
	John Quincy Adams	National Republican	509,097(44.0%)	83
1832	Andrew Jackson	Democratic	687,502(55.0%)	219
	Henry Clay	National Republican	530,189(42.4%)	49
	William Wirt	Anti-Masonic		7
	John Floyd	National Republican	33,108(2.6%)	11
1836	Martin Van Buren	Democratic	761,549(50.9%)	170
	William H. Harrison	Whig	549,567(36.7%)	73
	Hugh L. White	Whig	145,396(9.7%)	26
	Daniel Webster	Whig	41,287(2.7%)	14
1840	William H. Harrison	Whig	1,275,017(53.1%)	234
	Martin Van Buren	Democratic	1,128,702(46.9%)	60
1844	James K. Polk	Democratic	1,337,243(49.6%)	170
	Henry Clay	Whig	1,299,068(48.1%)	105
	James G. Birney	Liberty	63,300(2.3%)	
1848	Zachary Taylor	Whig	1,360,101(47.4%)	163
	Lewis Cass	Democratic	1,220,544(42.5%)	127
	Martin Van Buren	Free Soil	291,163(10.1%)	
1852	Franklin Pierce	Democratic	1,601,474(50.9%)	254
	Winfield Scott	Whig	1,386,578(44.1%)	42
1856	James Buchanan	Democratic	1,838,169(45.4%)	174
	John C. Fremont	Republican	1,335,264(33.0%)	114
	Millard Fillmore	American	874,534(21.6%)	8
1860	Abraham Lincoln	Republican	1,865,593(39.8%)	180
	Stephen A. Douglas	Democratic	1,381,713(29.5%)	12
	John C. Breckinridge	Democratic	848,356(18.1%)	72
	John Bell	Constitutional Union	592,906(12.6%)	79
1864	Abraham Lincoln	Republican	2,206,938(55.0%)	212
	George B. McClellan	Democratic	1,803,787(45.0%)	21
1868	Ulysses S. Grant	Republican	3,013,421(52.7%)	214
	Horatio Seymour	Democratic	2,706,829(47.3%)	80
1872	Ulysses S. Grant	Republican	3,596,745(55.6%)	286
	Horace Greeley	Democratic	2,843,446(43.9%)	66
1876	Rutherford B. Hayes	Republican	4,036,571(48.0%)	185
	Samuel J. Tilden	Democratic	4,284,020(51.0%)	184
1880	James A. Garfield	Republican	4,449,053(48.3%)	214
	Winfield S. Hancock	Democratic	4,442,035(48.2%)	155
	James B. Weaver	Greenback-Labor	308,578(3.4%)	
1884	Grover Cleveland	Democratic	4,874,986(48.5%)	219
	James G. Blaine	Republican	4,851,931(48.2%)	182
	Benjamin F. Butler	Greenback-Labor	175,370(1.8%)	
1888	Benjamin Harrison	Republican	5,444,337(47.8%)	233
	Grover Cleveland	Democratic	5,540,050(48.6%)	168

Presidential Election Results, 1789–2008 *(continued)*

Year	Candidates	Party	Popular Vote	Electoral Vote
1892	Grover Cleveland	Democratic	5,554,414(46.0%)	277
	Benjamin Harrison	Republican	5,190,802(43.0%)	145
	James B. Weaver	Peoples	1,027,329(8.5%)	22
1896	William McKinley	Republican	7,035,638(50.8%)	271
	William J. Bryan	Democratic; Populist	6,467,946(46.7%)	176
1900	William McKinley	Republican	7,219,530(51.7%)	292
	William J. Bryan	Democratic; Populist	6,356,734(45.5%)	155
1904	Theodore Roosevelt	Republican	7,628,834(56.4%)	336
	Alton B. Parker	Democratic	5,084,401(37.6%)	140
	Eugene V. Debs	Socialist	402,460(3.0%)	0
1908	William H. Taft	Republican	7,679,006(51.6%)	321
	William J. Bryan	Democratic	6,409,106(43.1%)	162
	Eugene V. Debs	Socialist	420,820(2.8%)	0
1912	Woodrow Wilson	Democratic	6,286,820(41.8%)	435
	Theodore Roosevelt	Progressive	4,126,020(27.4%)	88
	William H. Taft	Republican	3,483,922(23.2%)	8
	Eugene V. Debs	Socialist	897,011(6.0%)	0
1916	Woodrow Wilson	Democratic	9,129,606(49.3%)	277
	Charles E. Hughes	Republican	8,538,211(46.1%)	254
1920	Warren G. Harding	Republican	16,152,200(61.0%)	404
	James M. Cox	Democratic	9,147,353(34.6%)	127
	Eugene V. Debs	Socialist	919,799(3.5%)	0
1924	Calvin Coolidge	Republican	15,725,016(54.1%)	382
	John W. Davis	Democratic	8,385,586(28.8%)	136
	Robert M. La Follette	Progressive	4,822,856(16.6%)	13
1928	Herbert C. Hoover	Republican	21,392,190(58.2%)	444
	Alfred E. Smith	Democratic	15,016,443(40.8%)	87
1932	Franklin D. Roosevelt	Democratic	22,809,638(57.3%)	472
	Herbert C. Hoover	Republican	15,758,901(39.6%)	59
	Norman Thomas	Socialist	881,951(2.2%)	0
1936	Franklin D. Roosevelt	Democratic	27,751,612(60.7%)	523
	Alfred M. Landon	Republican	16,681,913(36.4%)	8
	William Lemke	Union	891,858(1.9%)	0
1940	Franklin D. Roosevelt	Democratic	27,243,466(54.7%)	449
	Wendell L. Willkie	Republican	22,304,755(44.8%)	82
1944	Franklin D. Roosevelt	Democratic	25,602,505(52.8%)	432
	Thomas E. Dewey	Republican	22,006,278(44.5%)	99
1948	Harry S Truman	Democratic	24,105,812(49.5%)	303
	Thomas E. Dewey	Republican	21,970,065(45.1%)	189
	J. Strom Thurmond	States' Rights	1,169,063(2.4%)	39
	Henry A. Wallace	Progressive	1,157,172(2.4%)	0
1952	Dwight D. Eisenhower	Republican	33,936,234(55.2%)	442
	Adlai E. Stevenson	Democratic	27,314,992(44.5%)	89
1956	Dwight D. Eisenhower	Republican	35,590,472(57.4%)	457
	Adlai E. Stevenson	Democratic	26,022,752(42.0%)	73
1960	John F. Kennedy	Democratic	34,227,096(49.9%)	303
	Richard M. Nixon	Republican	34,108,546(49.6%)	219
1964	Lyndon B. Johnson	Democratic	43,126,233(61.1%)	486
	Barry Goldwater	Republican	27,174,989(38.5%)	52
1968	Richard M. Nixon	Republican	31,783,783(43.4%)	301
	Hubert H. Humphrey	Democratic	31,271,839(42.7%)	191
	George C. Wallace	American Independent	9,899,557(13.5%)	46
1972	Richard M. Nixon	Republican	46,632,189(61.3%)	520
	George McGovern	Democratic	28,422,015(37.3%)	17
1976	Jimmy Carter	Democratic	40,828,587(50.1%)	297
	Gerald R. Ford	Republican	39,147,613(48.0%)	240
1980	Ronald Reagan	Republican	42,941,145(51.0%)	489
	Jimmy Carter	Democratic	34,663,037(41.0%)	49
	John B. Anderson	Independent	5,551,551(6.6%)	0
1984	Ronald Reagan	Republican	53,428,357(59%)	525
	Walter F. Mondale	Democratic	36,930,923(41%)	13
1988	George Bush	Republican	48,881,011(53%)	426
	Michael Dukakis	Democratic	41,828,350(46%)	111
1992	Bill Clinton	Democratic	38,394,210(43%)	370
	George Bush	Republican	33,974,386(38%)	168
	H. Ross Perot	Independent	16,573,465(19%)	0
1996	Bill Clinton	Democratic	45,628,667(49%)	379
	Bob Dole	Republican	37,869,435(41%)	159
	H. Ross Perot	Reform	7,874,283(8%)	0
2000	George W. Bush	Republican	50,456,169(48%)	271
	Al Gore	Democratic	50,996,116(48%)	266
	Ralph Nader	Green	2,767,176(3%)	0
2004	George W. Bush	Republican	60,608,582(51%)	286
	John Kerry	Democratic	57,288,974(48%)	252
	Ralph Nader	Independent	400,924(.35%)	0
2008	Barack Obama	Democratic	66,361,433(53%)	364
	John McCain	Republican	58,024,608(46%)	163

GLOSSARY

527 organization A political group organizes under section 527 of the IRS Code that may accept and spend unlimited amounts of money on election activities so long as they are not spent on broadcast ads run in the last 30 days before a primary or 60 days before a general election in which a clearly identified candidate is referred to and a relevant electorate is targeted.

adaptive approach A method used to interpret the Constitution that understands the document to be flexible and responsive to changing needs of the times.

administrative discretion Authority given by Congress to the federal bureaucracy to use reasonable judgment in implementing the laws.

adversary system A judicial system in which the court of law is a neutral arena where two parties argue their differences.

affirmative action Remedial action designed to overcome the effects of discrimination against minorities and women.

American dream The widespread belief that the United States is a land of opportunity and that individual initiative and hard work can bring economic success.

***amicus curiae* brief** Literally, a "friend of the court" brief, filed by an individual or organization to present arguments in addition to those presented by the immediate parties to a case.

Antifederalists Opponents of ratification of the Constitution and of a strong central government generally.

antitrust legislation Federal laws (starting with the Sherman Antitrust Act of 1890) that try to prevent a monopoly from dominating an industry and restraining trade.

appellate jurisdiction The authority of a court to review decisions made by lower courts.

attentive public Citizens who follow public affairs carefully.

attitudes An individual's propensity to perceive, interpret, or act toward a particular object in a particular way.

autocracy A type of government in which on person with unlimited power rules.

bad tendency test An interpretation of the First Amendment that would permit legislatures to forbid speech encouraging people to engage in illegal action.

bicameralism The principle of a two-house legislature.

Bipartisan Campaign Reform Act (BCRA) Largely banned party soft money, restored long-standing prohibition on corporation and labor unions use of general treasury funds for electoral purposes, and narrowed the definition of issue advocacy.

budget deficit The condition that exists when the federal government raises less revenue than it spends.

bundling A tactic in which PACs collect contributions form like-minded individuals (each limited to $2,000) and present them to a candidate or political party as a "bundle," thus increasing the PAC's influence.

bureaucracy A form of organization that operates through impersonal, uniform rules and procedures.

bureaucrat A career government employee.

Bush Doctrine A policy by the Bush administration in 2001 that asserts America's right to attack any nation that has weapons of mass destruction that may be used against U.S. interests at home or abroad.

cabinet The advisory council for the president, consisting of the heads of the executive departments, the vice president, and a few other officials selected by the president.

candidate appeal How voters feel about a candidate's background, personality, leadership, ability, and other personal qualities.

capitalism An economic system characterized by private property, competitive markets, economic incentives, and limited government involvement in the production, distribution, and pricing of goods and services.

caucus A meeting of local party members to choose party officials or candidates for public office and to decide the platform.

central clearance Review of all executive branch testimony, reports, and draft legislation by the Office of Management and Budget (OMB) to ensure that each communication to Congress is in accordance with the president's program.

centralists People who favor national action over action at the state and local levels.

checks and balances A constitutional grant of powers that enables each of the three branches of government to check some acts of the others and therefore ensure that no branch can dominate.

chief of staff The head of the White House staff.

circuit courts of appeal Courts with appellate jurisdiction that hear appeals from the decisions of lower courts.

civil disobedience Deliberate refusal to obey a law or comply with the order of public officials as a means of expressing opposition.

civil law A law that governs relationships between individuals and defines their legal rights.

civil rights The rights of all people to be free from irrational discrimination such as that based on race, religion, gender or ethnic origin.

civil service Federal employees who work for government through a competitive, not political selection process.

class action suit A lawsuit brought by an individual or a group of people on behalf of all those similarly situated.

clear and present danger test An interpretation of the First Amendment that holds that the government cannot interfere with speech unless the speech presents a clear and present danger that if will lead to evil or illegal acts.

closed primary A primary election in which only persons registered in the party holding the primary may vote.

closed rule A procedural rule in the House of Representatives that prohibits any amendments to bills or provides that only members of the committee reporting the bill may offer amendments.

closed shop A company with a labor agreement under which membership is a condition of employment.

cloture A procedure for terminating debate, especially filibusters, in the Senate.

coattail effect The boost that candidates may get in an election because of the popularity of candidates above them on the ballot.

collective bargaining A method whereby representatives of the union and employer determine wages, hours, and other conditions of employment through direct negotiation.

commerce clause The clause in the Constitution (Article 1, Section 8, Clause 1) that gives Congress the power to regulate all business activities that cross state lines or affect more than one state or other nations.

commercial speech Advertisements and commercials for products and services; they receive less First Amendment protection, primarily to discourage flase and misleading ads.

communism A political, social, and economic system based on public ownership of the means of production and exchange. (missing comma after social in text)

concurrent powers Powers that the Constitution gives to both the national and state governments, such as the power to levy taxes.

concurring opinion An opinion that agrees with the majority in a Supreme Court ruling but differs on the reasoning.

confederation A constitutional arrangement in which sovereign nations or states, by compact, create a central government but carefully limit its power and do not give it direct authority over individuals.

conference committee A committee appointed by the presiding officers of each chamber to adjust differences on a particular bill passed by each in different form.

Congressional Budget Office (CBO) An agency of Congress that analyzes presidential budget recommendations and estimates the costs of proposed legislation.

congressional elaboration Congressional legislation that gives further meaning to the Constitution based on sometimes vague constitutional authority, such as the necessary and proper clause.

congressional-executive agreement A formal agreement between the U.S. president and the leaders of other nations that requires approval by both houses of Congress.

Connecticut Compromise The compromise agreement by states at the Constitutional

Convention for a bicameral legislature with a lower house in which representation would be based on population and an upper house in which each state would have two senators.

conservatism A belief that limited government ensures order, competitive markets, and personal opportunity.

constituents The residents of a congressional district or state.

Constitutional Convention The convention in Philadelphia, from May 25 to September 17, 1787, that debated and agreed on the Constitution of the United States.

constitutional democracy Government that enforces recognizes limits on those who govern and allows the voice of the people to be heard through free, fair and relatively frequent elections.

Constitutional home rule State constitutional authorization for local governments to conduct their own affairs.

constitutionalism The set of arrangements, including checks and balances, federalism, separation of power, rule of law, due process, and a bill of rights, that requires our leaders to listen, think, bargain, and explain before they act or make laws. We then hold them politically and legally accountable for how they exercise their power.

content or viewpoint neutrality Laws that apply to all kinds of speech and to all views, not only that which is unpopular or divisive.

corporate social responsibility Efforts by corporations to improve their reputations by paying attention to their contributions to the social good.

criminal law A law that defines crimes against the public order.

cross-cutting cleavages Divisions within society that cut across demographic categories to produce groups that are more heterogeneous or different.

crossover voting Voting by a member of one party for a candidate of another party.

de facto segregation Segregation resulting from economic or social conditions or personal choice.

de jure segregation Segregation imposed by law.

dealignment Weakening of partisan preferences that point to a rejection of both major parties and a rise in the number of Independents.

decentralists People who favor state or local action rather than national action.

defendant In a criminal action, the person or party accused of an offense.

delegate An official who is expected to represent the views of his or her constituents even when personally holding different views; one interpretation of the role of the legislator.

delegated (express) powers Powers given explicitly to national government and listed in the Constitution.

deliberation The process where people or elected officials meet together to discuss and consider public matters.

democracy Government by the people, both directly or indirectly, with free and frequent elections.

democratic consensus Widespread agreement of fundamental principles of democratic governance and the values that undergird them.

demography The study of the characteristics of populations.

department Usually the largest organization in government with the largest mission; also the highest rank in the federal hierarchy.

deregulation A policy promoting cutbacks in the amount of federal regulation in specific areas of economic activity.

devolution revolution The effort to slow the growth of the national government by returning many functions to the states.

direct democracy Government in which citizens vote on laws and select officials directly.

direct primary An election in which voters choose party nominees.

discharge petition A petition that, if signed by a majority of the members of the House of Representatives, will pry a bill from committee and bring it to the floor for consideration.

discretionary spending Spending that can be altered by congressional and presidential action.

dissenting opinion An opinion disagreeing with the majority in a Supreme Court ruling.

distributive policy A public policy such as Social Security that provides benefits to all groups in society.

district courts Courts in which criminal and civil cases are originally tried in the federal judicial system.

docket The list of potential cases that reach the Supreme Court.

double jeopardy Trial or punishment for the same crime by the same government; forbidden by the Constitution.

dual citizenship Citizenship in more than one nation.

due process Established rules and regulations that restrain government officials.

due process clause A clause in the Fifth Amendment limiting the power of the national government; a similar clause in the Fourteenth Amendment prohibiting state governments from depriving any person of life, liberty, or property without due process of law.

earmarks Special spending projects that are set aside on behalf of individual members of Congress for their constiutuents.

economic sanctions Denial of export, import, or financial relations with a target country in an effort to change that nation's policies.

efficacy A sense of self-confidence in being able to produce a desired effect.

electoral college The electoral system used in electing the president and vice president, in which voters vote for electors pledged to cast their ballots for a particular party's candidates.

eminent domain The power of a government to take private property for public use; the U.S. Constitution gives national and state governments this power and requires them to provide just compensation for property so taken.

entitlement program Programs such as unemployment insurance, disaster relief, or disability payments that provide benefits to all eligible citizens.

entitlements Programs such as unemployment insurance, disaster relief, or disability payments that provide benefits to all eligible citizens.

enumerated powers The powers explicitly given to Congress in the Constitution.

environmental impact statement A statement required by federal law from all agencies for any project using federal funds to assess the potential effect of the new construction or development on the environment.

equal protection clause A clause in the Fourteenth Amendment that forbids any state to deny to any person within its jurisdiction the equal protection of the laws. By interpretation, the Fifth Amendment imposes the same limitation on the national government. This clause is the major constitutional restraint on the power of governments to discriminate against persons because of race, national origin, or sex.

established clause A clause in the First Amendment that states that Congress shall make no law respecting an establishment of religion. The Supreme Court has interpreted this to forbid government support to any or all religions.

ethnicity A social division based on national origin, religion, language, and often race.

ethnocentrism Belief in the superiority of one's nation or ethnic group.

ex post facto law A retroactive criminal law that works to the disadvantage of a person.

excise tax A consumer tax on a specific kind of merchandise, such as tobacco.

exclusionary rule A requirement that evidence unconstitutionally or illegally obtained be excluded from a criminal trial.

executive agreement A formal agreement between the U.S. president and the leaders of other nations that does not require Senate approval.

Executive Office of the President The cluster of presidential staff agencies that help the president carry out his or her responsibilities. Currently, the office includes the Office of Management and Budget, the Council of Economic Advisers, and several other units.

executive order A directive issued by a president or governor that has the force of law.

executive privilege The power to keep executive communications confidential, especially if they relate to national security.

extradition The legal process whereby an alleged criminal offender is surrendered by the officials of one state to officials of the state in which the crime is alleged to have been committed.

faction A term the founders used to refer to political parties and special interests or interest groups.

Federal Election Commission (FEC) A commission created by the 1974 amendments to the Federal Election Campaign Act to administer election reform laws. It consists of six commissioners appointed by the president and confirmed by the Senate. Its duties include overseeing disclosure of campaign finance information, public funding of presidential elections, and enforcing contribution limits.

federal funds rate The amount of interest banks charge for loans to each other.

federal mandate A requirement the national government imposes as a condition for receiving federal funds.

Federal Register An official document, published every weekday, that lists the new and proposed regulations of executive departments and regulatory agencies.

Federal Reserve System The system created by Congress in 1913 to establish banking practices and regulate currency in circulation and the amount of credit available. It consists of 12 regional banks supervised by the Board of Governors. Often simply called "the Fed."

federalism A constitutional arrangement in which power is distributed between a central government and subdivisional governments, called states in the United States. The national and the subdivisional governments both exercise direct authority over individuals.

Federalists Supporters of ratification of the Constitution and of a strong central government.

The Federalist Essays promoting ratification of the Constitution, published anonymously by Alexander Hamilton, John Jay, and James Madison in 1787 and 1788.

fighting words Words that by their very nature inflict injury on those to whom they are addressed or incite them to acts of violence.

filibuster A procedural practice in the Senate whereby a senator refuses to relinquish the floor and thereby delays proceedings and prevents a vote on a controversial issue.

fiscal policy Government policy that attempts to manage the economy by controlling taxing and spending.

free exercise clause A clause in the First Amendment that states that Congress shall make no law prohibiting the free exercise of religion.

free rider An individual who does not join a group representing his or her interests yet receives the benefit of the group's influence.

full faith and credit clause The clause in the Constitution (Article IV, Section 1) requiring each state to recognize the civil judgments rendered by the courts of the other states and to accept their public records and acts as valid.

fundamentalists Conservative Christians who as a group have become more active in politics in the last two decades and were especially influential in the 2000 and 2004 presidential election.

gender gap The difference between the political opinions or political behavior of men and of women.

General Agreement on Tariffs and Trade (GATT) An international trade organization with more than 130 members that seeks to encourage free trade by lowering tariffs and other trade restrictions.

general election Elections in which voters elect officeholders.

gerrymandering The drawing of legislative district boundaries to benefit a party, group, or incumbent.

government corporation A government agency that operates like a business corporation, created to secure greater freedom of action and flexibility for a particular program.

grand jury A jury of 12 to 23 persons, depending on state and local requirements, who privately hear evidence presented by the government to determine whether persons shall be required to stand trial. If the jury believes there is sufficient evidence that a crime was committed, it issues an indictment.

gross domestic product (GDP) The total output of all economic activity in the nation, including goods and services.

hard money Political contributions given to a party, candidate, or interest group that are limited in amount and fully disclosed. Raising such limited funds was harder than raising unlimited soft money, hence the term "hard money."

hard power Reliance on economic and military strength to solve international problems.

Hatch Act A federal statute barring federal employees from active participation in certain kinds of politics and protecting them from being fired on partisan grounds.

heightened scrutiny test This test has been applied when a law classifies based on sex; to be upheld; the law must meet an important government interest.

honeymoon The period at the beginning of a new president's term during which the president enjoys generally positive relations with press and Congress, usually lasting about six months.

horse race A close contest; by extension, any contest in which the focus is on who is ahead and by how much rather than on substantive differences between the candidates.

idealism A theory of international relations that focuses on the hope that nations will act together to solve international problems and promote peace.

impeachment A formal accusation by the lower house of a legislature against a public official; the first step in removal from office.

implementation The process of putting a law into practice through bureaucratic rules or spending.

implied powers Powers inferred from the express powers that allow Congress to carry out its functions.

impoundment Presidential refusal to allow an agency to spend funds that Congress authorized and appropriated.

incremental policy Small adjustments to existing public policies.

incumbent The current holder of elected office.

independent expenditures The Supreme Court has ruled that individuals, groups, and parties can spend unlimited amounts in campaigns for or against candidates as long as they operate independently from the candidate. When an individual, group, or party does so, they are making an independent expenditure.

independent regulatory commission A government agency or commission regulatory power whose independence is protected by Congress.

independent stand-alone agency A government agency that operates outside a traditional government department, but under the president's direct control.

indictment A formal written statement from a grand jury charging an individual with an offense; also called a *true bill.*

inflation A rise in the general price level (and decrease in dollar value) owing to an increase in the volume of money and credit in relation to available goods.

inherent powers The powers of the national government in foreign affairs that the Supreme Court has declared do not depend on constitutional grants but rather grow out of the very existence of the national government.

initiative A procedure whereby a certain number of voters may, by petition, propose a law or constitutional amendment and have it submitted to the voters.

intensity A measure of how strongly an individual holds a particular opinion.

interest group A collection of people who share a common interest or attitude and seek to influence government for specific ends. Interest groups usually work within the framework of government and try to achieve their goals through tactics such as lobbying.

internationalism The belief that nations must engage in international problem solving.

interstate compact An agreement among two or more states. Congress must approve most such agreements.

iron triangle A policy-making instrument composed of a tightly related alliance of a congressional committee, interest groups, and federal department or agency.

isolationism The desire to avoid international engagement altogether.

issue advocacy Promoting a particular position or an issue paid for by interest groups or individuals but no candidates. Much issue advocacy is often electioneering for or against a candidate, avoiding words like "vote for," and until 2004 had not been subject to any regulation.

issue network Relationships among interest groups, congressional committees and subcommittees, and the government agencies that share a common policy concern.

issue-attention cycle The movement of public opinion toward public policy from initial enthusiasm for action to realization of costs and a decline in interest.

Jim Crow laws State laws formerly pervasive throughout the South requiring public facilities and accommodations to be segregated by race; ruled unconstitutional.

joint committee A committee composed of members of both the House of Representatives and the Senate; such committees oversee the Library of Congress and conduct inves-tigations.

judicial activism A philosophy that judges should strike down laws that are inconsistent with norm and values state or implied in the Constitution.

judicial restraint A philosophy proposing that judges should strike down the actions of the elected branches only if they clearly violate the literal meaning of the Constitution.

judicial review The power of a court to refuse to enforce a law or a government regulation in the opinion of the judges conflicts with the U.S. Constitution or, in a state court, the state constitution.

justiciable dispute A dispute growing out of an actual case or controversy that is capable of settlement by legal methods.

Keynesian economics An economic theory based on the principles of John Maynard Keynes stating that government spending should increase during business slumps and be curbed during booms.

labor injunction A court order forbidding specific individuals or groups from performing certain acts (such as striking) that the court considers harmful to the rights and property of an employer or a community.

laissez-faire economics A theory that opposes governmental interference in economic affairs beyond what is necessary to protect life and property.

latency Political opinions that are held but not yet expressed.

leadership PAC A PAC formed by an office-holder that collects contributions form individuals other PACs and then makes contributions to other candidates and political parties.

libel Written defamation of another person. For public officials and public figures, the constitutional tests designed to restrict libel actions are especially rigid.

liberalism A belief that government can and should achieve justice and equality of opportunity.

libertarianism An ideology that cherishes individual liberty and insists on minimal government, promoting a free market economy, a non-interventionist foreign policy, and an absence of regulation in moral, economic, and social life.

line item veto Presidential power to strike, or remove, specific items from a spending bill without vetoing the entire package; declared unconstitutional by Supreme Court.

literacy test A literacy requirement some states imposed as a condition of voting, generally used to disqualify black voters in the South; now illegal.

lobbying Engaging in activities aimed at influencing public officials, especially legislators, and the policies they enact.

lobbyist A person who is employed by and acts for an organized interest group or corporation to try to influence policy decisions and positions in the executive and legislative branches.

logrolling Mutual aid and vote trading among legislators.

majority The candidate or party that wins more than half the votes cast in an election.

majority leader The legislative leader selected by the majority party who helps plan party strategy, confers with the other party leaders, and tries to keep members of the party in line.

majority rule Governance according to the expressed preferences of the majority.

majority-minority district A legislative district created to include a majority of minority voters; ruled constitutional as long as race is not the main factor in redistricting.

mandate A president's claim of broad public support.

mandatory spending Required spending under the federal budget.

manifest destiny A notion held by nineteenth-century Americans that the United States was destined to rule the continent, from the Atlantic to the Pacific.

manifest opinion A widely shared and consciously held view, such as support for abortion rights or for homeland security.

margin of error The range of percentage points in which the sample accurately reflects the population.

mass media Means of communication that reach the public, including newspapers and magazines, radio, television (broadcast, cable, and satellite), films, recordings, books, and electronic communication.

means-tested entitlements Programs such as Medicaid and welfare under which applicants must meet eligibility requirements based on need.

Medicaid A federal program that provides medical benefits for low-income people.

Medicare A national health insurance program for the elderly and disabled.

merit system A system of public employment in which selection and promotion depend on demonstrated performance rather than political patronage.

Merit Systems Protection Board An independent agency that oversees and protects merit in the federal government personnel system.

midterm election Elections held midway between presidential elections.

minority leader The legislative leader selected by the minority party as spokesperson for the opposition.

minor party A small political party that persists over time, is often composed of ideologies on the right or left, or is centered on a charismatic candidate. Such a part is also called a *third party*.

monetary policy Government policy that attempts to manage the economy by controlling the money supply and thus interest rates.

monopoly Domination of an industry by a single company; also the company that dominates the industry.

multilateralism A philosophy that encourages individual nations to act together to solve international problems.

name recognition Incumbents have an advantage over challengers in election campaigns because voters are more familiar with them, and incumbents are more recognizable.

national debt The total amount of money the federal government has borrowed to finance deficit spending throughout the year.

national party convention A national meeting of delegates elected in primaries, caucuses, or state conventions who assemble once every four years to nominate candidates for president and vice president, ratify the party platform, elect officers, and adopt rules.

national supremacy A constitutional doctrine that whenever conflict occurs between the constitutionally authorized actions of the national government and those of a state or local government, the actions of the national government prevail.

national tide The inclination to focus on national issues, rather than local issues, in an election campaign. The impact of a national tide can be reduced by the nature of the candidates on the ballot who may have differentiated themselves from their party or its leader if the tide is negative, as well as competition in the election.

nationalism An enduring sense of national identity or consciousness that derives from cultural, historic, linguistic, or political forces.

natural law God's or nature's law that defines right from wrong and is higher than human law.

natural rights The rights of all people to dignity and worth; also called *human rights*.

naturalization A legal action conferring citizenship on an alien.

necessary and proper clause The clause in the Constitution (Article 1, Section 8, Clause 3) setting forth the implied powers of Congress. It states that Congress, in addition to its express powers, has the right to make all laws necessary and proper to carry out all powers the Constitution vests in the national government.

New Jersey Plan The proposal at the Constitutional Convention made by William Paterson of New Jersey for a central government with a single-house legislature in which each state would be represented equally.

news media Media that emphasize the news

nondecision A decision not to move ahead with the policy process. In short, it is a decision not to decide.

nonpartisan election An election in which candidates are not selected or endorsed by political parties and party affiliation is not listed on ballots.

normal trade relations Trade status granted as part of an international trade policy that gives a nation the same favorable concessions and tariffs that the best trading partners receive.

North American Free Trade Agreement (NAFTA) An agreement signed by the United States, Canada, and Mexico in 1992 to form the largest free trade zone in the world.

obscenity The quality or state of a work that, taken as a whole, appeals to a prurient interest in sex by depicting sexual conduct in a patently offensive way and that lacks serious literary, artistic, political, or scientific value.

Office of Management and Budget (OMB) The presidential staff agency that serves as a clearinghouse for budgetary requests and management improvements for government agencies.

Office of Personnel Management (OPM) An agency that administers civil service laws, rules, and regulations.

open primary A primary election in which any voter, regardless of party, may vote.

open rule A procedural rule in the House of Representatives that permits floor amendments within the overall time allocated to the bill.

open shop A company with a labor agreement under which union membership cannot be required as a condition of employment.

opinion of the Court An explanation of a decision of the Supreme Court or any other appellate court.

originalist approach An approach to constitutional interpretation that envisions the document as having a fixed meaning that might be determined by a strict reading of the text of framers' intent.

original jurisdiction The authority of a court to hear a case "in the first instance."

override An action taken by Congress to reverse a presidential veto, requiring two-thirds majority in each chamber.

oversight Legislative or executive review of a particular government program or organization that can be in response to a crisis of some kind or part of routine review.

parliamentary government A form of government in which the legislature selects the prime minister or the president.

party caucus A meeting of the members of a party in a legislative chamber to select party leaders and to develop party policy. Called a *conference* by the Republicans.

party convention A meeting of party delegates to vote on matters of policy and, in some cases, to select part candidates for public office.

party identification An informal and subjective affiliation with a political party that most people acquire in childhood.

party-independent expenditures Spending by political party committees that is independent of the candidate. The spending occurs in relatively few competitive contests and is often substantial.

party registration The act of declaring party affiliation; required by some states when one registers to vote.

patriotism Devotion to one's own country, often seeing it as better or stronger than other countries.

patronage The dispensing of government jobs to persons who belong to the winning political party.

petit jury A jury of 6 to 12 persons that determines quilt or innocence in a civil or criminal action.

plaintiff The party instigating a civil lawsuit.

plea bargain An agreement between a prosecutor and a defendant that the defendant will plead guilty to a lesser offense to avoid having to stand trial for a more serious offense.

pluralism A theory of government holds that open, multiple, and competing groups can check the asserted power by any one group.

plurality The candidate or party with the most votes cast in an election, not necessarily more than half.

pocket veto A veto exercised by the president after Congress has adjourned; if the president takes no action for ten days, the bill does not become law and is not returned to Congress for a possible override.

policy agenda The list of issues that the federal government pays attention to.

policy makers Individuals and groups that make the actual choices to create a public policy.

political action committee (PAC) The political arm of an interest group that is legally entitled to raise funds on a voluntary basis from members, stockholders, or employees to contribute funds to candidates or political parties.

political culture The widely shared beliefs, values, and norms about how citizens relate to government and to one another.

political ideology A consistent pattern of beliefs about political values and the role of government.

political party An organization that seeks political power by electing people to office so that its positions and philosophy become public policy.

political predisposition A characteristic of individuals that is predictive of political behavior.

political socialization The process—most notably in families and schools—by which we develop our political attitudes, values, and beliefs.

politics The interaction of the people and their government, including citizens, interest groups, political parties, and the institutions of government at all levels. Politics is concerned with who gets what, when, where, and how from government.

poll tax Tax required to vote; prohibited for national elections by the Twenty-Fourth Amendment (1964) and ruled unconstitutional for all elections in *Harper* v. *Board of Elections* (1966).

popular consent The idea that a just government must derive its powers from the consent of the people it governs.

popular sovereignty A belief that ultimate power resides in the people.

precedent A decision made by a higher court such as a circuit court of appeals or the Supreme Court that is binding on all other federal courts.

preemption The right of a national law or regulation to preclude enforcement of a state or local law or regulation.

preferred position doctrine An interpretation of the First Amendment that holds that freedom of expressions is so essential to democracy that governments should not punish person for what they say, only what they do.

president pro tempore An officer of the Senate selected by the majority party to act as chair in the absence of the vice president.

presidential election Elections held in years when the president is on the ballot.

presidential support score The percentage of times a president wins on key votes in Congress.

presidential ticket The joint listing of the presidential and vice presidential candidates on the same ballot, as required by the Twelfth Amendment.

primary elections Elections in which voter choose party nominees.

prior restraint Censorship imposed before a speech is made or a newspaper is published; usually presumed to be unconstitutional.

procedural due process A constitutional requirement that governments proceed by proper methods; limits how government may exercise power.

professional associations Groups of individuals who share a common profession and are often organized for common political purposes related to the profession.

progressive tax A tax graduated so that people with higher incomes pay a larger fraction of their income than people with lower incomes.

property rights The rights of an individual to own, use, rent, invest, buy, and sell property.

proportional representation An election system in which each party running receives the proportion of legislative seats corresponding to its proportion of the vote.

prosecutor Government lawyer who tries criminal cases, often referred to as a district attorney or a U.S. Attorney.

prospective issue voting Voting based on what a candidate pledges to do in the future about an issue if elected.

protectionism A policy of erecting trade barriers to protect domestic industry.

public assistance Aid to the poor, "welfare."

public defender system An arrangement whereby public officials are hired to provide legal assistance to people accused of crimes who are unable to hire their own attorneys.

public opinion The distribution of individuals preferences for or evaluations of a given issue, candidate, or institution within a specific population.

public policy A specific course of action that government takes to address a problem.

punctuating policy Radical changes to public policy that occur only after the mobilization of large segments of society to demand action.

race A grouping of human beings with distinctive characteristics determined by genetic inheritance.

racial gerrymandering The drawing of election districts so as to ensure that members of certain race are a minority in the district; ruled unconstitutional in *Gomillion* v. *Lightfoot* (1960)

rally point A rise in public approval of the president that follows a crisis as Americans "rally round the flag" and the chief executive.

random sample In this type of sample, every individual has a known and equal chance of being selected.

rational basis test A standard developed by the courts to test the constitutionality of a law; when applied, a law is constitutional as long as it meets a reasonable government interest.

realigning election An election during periods of expanded suffrage and change in the economy and society that proves to be a turning point, redefining the agenda of politics and the alignment of voters within parties.

realism A theory of international relations that focuses on the tendency of nations to operate from self-interest.

reapportionment The assigning by Congress of congressional seats after each census. State legislatures reapportion state legislative districts.

recall A procedure for submitting to popular vote the removal of officials from office before the end of their term.

recess appointment Presidential appointment made without Senate confirmation during Senate recess.

redistributive policy A policy that provides to one group of society while taking away benefits from another through policy solution such as tax increases to pay for job training.

redistricting The redrawing of congressional and other legislative district lines following the census, to accommodate population shifts and keep districts as equal as possible in population.

referendum A procedure for submitting to popular vote measures passed by the legislature or proposed amendments to a state constitution.

regressive tax A tax whereby people with lower incomes pay a higher fraction of their income than people with higher incomes.

regulation A policy that encourages or discourages certain behavior by imposing a legally binding rule. Rules are made through a long process that begins with an act of Congress and ends with issuance of a final rule.

regulatory taking A government regulation that effectively takes land by restricting its use, even if its remains in the owner's name.

reinforcing cleavages Divisions within a society that cut across demographic categories to produce groups that are more heterogeneous or different.

representative democracy Government in which the people elect those who govern and pass laws; also called a *republic*.

reserve powers All powers not specifically delegated to the national government by the Constitution. The reserve power can be found in the Tenth Amendment to the Constitution.

restrictive covenant A provision in a deed to real property prohibiting its sale to a person of a particular race or religion. Judicial enforcement of such deeds is unconstitutional.

retrospective issue voting Holding incumbents, usually the president's party, responsible for their records on issues, such as the economy or foreign policy.

reverse distributive policy A policy that reduces benefits for all groups such as tax increases in society, often by imposing rules that govern everyone.

revolving door An employment cycle in which individuals who work for government agencies that regulate interests eventually end up working for interest groups or businesses with the same policy concern.

rider A provision attached to a bill—to which it may or may not be related—in order to secure its passage or defeat.

right of expatriation The right to renounce one's citizenship.

rule A precise statement of how a law is implemented.

rural Sparsely populated territory and small towns, often associated with farming.

safe seat An elected office that is predictably won by one party or the other, so the success of that party's candidate is almost taken for granted.

sales tax A general tax on sales transactions, sometimes exempting such items as food and drugs.

salience An individual's belief that an issue is important or relevant to him or her.

search warrant A write issued by a magistrate that authorizes the police to search a particular place or person, specifically the place to be searched and the objects to be seized.

selective exposure The process by which individuals screen out messages that do not conform to their own biases.

selective incorporation The process by which provisions of the Bill of Rights are brought within the scope of the Fourteenth Amendment and so applied to state and local governments.

selective perception The process by which individuals perceive what they want in media messages.

senatorial courtesy The presidential custom of submitting the names of prospective appointees for approval to senators from the states in which the appointees are to work.

Senior Executive Service Established by Congress in 1978 as a flexible, mobile corps of senior career executives who work closely with presidential appointees to manage government.

seniority rule A legislative practice that assigns the chair of a committee or subcommittee to the member of the majority party with the longest continuous service on the committee.

separation of powers Constitutional division of powers among the legislative, executive, and judicial branches, with the legislative branch making law, the executive applying and enforcing the law, and the judiciary interpreting the law.

Shays' Rebellion A rebellion led by Daniel Shays of farmers in western Massachusetts in 1786-1787 protesting mortgage foreclosures. It highlighted the need for a strong national government just as the call for a Constitutional Convention went out.

signing statements A formal document that explains why a president is signing a particular bill into law. These statements may contain objections to the bill and promises not to implement key sections.

single-member district An electoral district in which voters choose one representative or official.

Speaker The presiding officer in the House of Representatives, formally elected by the House but actually selected by the majority party.

special or select committee A congressional committee created for a specific purpose, sometimes to conduct an investigation.

social capital Democratic and civil habits discussion, compromise, and respect for differences, which grow out of participation in voluntary organizations.

social insurance Programs in which eligibility is based on prior contributions to government, usually in the form of payroll taxes.

social safety net The many programs that the federal government provides to protect Americans against economic and social misfortune.

Social Security A combination of entitlement programs, paid for by employer and employee taxes, that includes retirement benefits, health insurance, and support for disabled workers and the children of deceased or disabled workers.

socialism An economic and governmental system based on public ownership of the means of production and exchange.

socioeconomic status (SES) A division of population based on occupation, income, and education.

soft money Money raised in unlimited amounts by political parties for party-building purposes. Now largely illegal except for limited contributions to state and local parties for voter registration and get-out-the-vote efforts.

soft power Reliance on diplomacy and negotiation to solve international problems.

solicitor general The third-ranking official in the Department of Justice who is responsible for representing the United States in cases before the U.S. Supreme Court.

spoils system A system of public employment based on rewarding party loyalists and friends.

stagflation A combination of an economic slowdown (stagnation) and a rise in prices (inflation).

standing committee A permanent committee established in a legislature, usually focusing on a policy area.

State of the Union Address The president's annual statement to Congress and the nation.

states' rights Powers expressly or implicitly reserved to the states.

statism The idea that the rights of the nation are supreme over the rights of the individuals who make up the nation.

strict scrutiny test A test applied by the court when a classification is based on race; the government must show that there is a compelling reason for the law and no other less restrictive way to meet the interest.

strong mayor-council form A form of local government in which the voters directly elect the city council and the mayor, who enjoys nearly total administrative authority and appoints the department heads.

substantive due process A constitutional requirement that governments act reasonably and that the substance of the laws themselves be fair and reasonable; limits what a government may be.

suburban An area that typically surrounds the central city, is often residential, and is not as densely populated.

suffrage The right to vote.

Sun Belt The region of the United States in the South and Southwest that has seen population growth relative to the rest of the country and which, because of its climate has attracted retirees.

Supreme Court The court of last resort in the United States. It can hear appeals from federal circuit courts or state high courts.

take care clause The constitutional requirement (in Article II, Section 3) that presidents take care that the laws are faithfully executed, even if they disagree with the purpose of those laws.

tariff A tax levied on imports to help protect a nation's industries, labor, or farmers from foreign competition. It can also be used to raise additional revenue.

tax expenditure A loss of tax revenue due to federal laws that provide special tax incentives or benefits to individuals or businesses.

theory of deterrence A theory that is based on creating enough military strength to persuade other nations not to attack first.

think tank A nongovernmental organization that seeks to influence public policy through research and education.

three-fifths compromise The compromise between northern and southern states at the Constitutional Convention that three-fifths of the slave population would be counted for determining direct taxation and representation in the House of Representatives.

trade deficit An imbalance in international trade in which the value of imports exceeds the value of exports.

treaty A formal, public agreement between the United States and one or more nations that must be approved by two-thirds of the Senate.

trust A monopoly that controls good and services, often in combinations that reduce competition.

trustee An official who is expected to vote independently based on his or her judgment of the circumstances; one interpretation of the role of the legislator.

turnout The proportion of the voting-age public that votes, sometimes defined as the number of registered voters that vote.

uncontrollable spending The portion of the federal budget that is spent on previously enacted programs, such as Social Security, that the president and Congress are unwilling to cut.

unemployment The number of Americans who are out of work but actively looking for a job. The number does not usually include those who are not looking.

unilateralism A philosophy that encourages individual nations to act on their own when facing threats from other nations.

union shop A company in which new employees must join a union within a stated time period.

unitary system A constitutional arrangement that concentrates power in a central government.

universe The groups of people whose preferences we try to measure by taking a sample; also called population.

unprotected speech Libel, obscenity, fighting words, and commercial speech, which are not entitled to constitutional protection in all circumstances.

urban A densely settled territory that is often the central part of a city of metropolitan area.

U.S. attorney general The chief law enforcement officer in the United States and the head of the Department of Justice.

value-added tax (VAT) A tax on the increased value of a product at each stage of production and distribution rather than just at the point of sale.

vesting clause The president's constitutional authority to control most executive functions.

veto A formal decision to reject a bill passed by Congress.

Virginia Plan The initial proposal at the Constitutional Convention made by the Virginia delegation for a strong central government with a bicameral legislature dominated by the big states.

voter registration A system designed to reduce voter fraud by limiting voting to those who have established eligibility to vote by submitting the proper documents, including proof of residency.

weapons of mass destruction Biological, chemical, or nuclear weapons that can cause a massive number of deaths in a single use.

whip The party leader who is the liaison between the leadership and the rank-and-file in the legislature.

white primary A Democratic party primary in the old "one–party South" that was limited to white people and essentially constituted an election; ruled unconstitutional in *Smith* v. *Allwright* (1944).

winner-take-all system An election system in which the candidate with the most votes wins.

women's suffrage The right of women to vote.

World Trade Organization (WTO) An international organization derived from the General Agreement on Tariffs and Trade (GATT) that promotes free trade around the world.

write of certiorari A formal writ used to bring a case before the Supreme Court.

writ of *habeas corpus* A court order requiring explanation to a judge why a prisoner is being held custody.

writ of mandamus A court order directing an official to perform an official duty.

zero-sum games A policy that takes away exactly as much in benefits as another group gains.

NOTES

Introduction

1. Dwight B. Heath, ed., *Mourt's Relation: A Journal of the Pilgrims at Plymouth* (Bedford, MA: Applewood Books, 1963), p. 17.
2. November 11, 1620 on the Julian calendar would be on our present-day Gregorian calendar November 21, 1620.
3. Donald McQuade, Robert Atwan, Martha Banta, Justin Kaplan, David Minter, and Robert Stepto, *The Harper American Literature* (New York: Longman, 1998); John T. Wheelwright, *The Mayflower Pilgrims: Being a Condescension in the Original Wording and Spelling of the Story Written by Gov. William Bradford* (Boston: McGrath-Sherrill Press, 1930).
4. Nathaniel Philbrick, *Mayflower: A Story of Courage, Community, and War* (New York: Penguin Group, 2006), p. 42.
5. Ibid, p. 352.
6. Michael Kammen, *Mystic Chords of Memory: The Transformation of Tradition in American Culture* (New York: Vintage Books, 1993).
7. Louis Hartz, *The Liberal Tradition in America* (New York: Harcourt, Brace, and World, Inc., 1955), pp. 48–49.
8. Crispin Gill, *Mayflower Remembered: A History of the Plymouth Pilgrims* (New York: Taplinger Publishing, 1970), p. 155; Michael Kammen, *Mystic Chords of Memory: The Transformation of Tradition in American Culture* (New York: Vintage Books, 1993), p. 64.
9. Michael Kammen, *Mystic Chords of Memory: The Transformation of Tradition in American Culture* (New York: Vintage Books, 1993).
10. Mayflower Compact (1620), http://avalon.law.yale.edu/17th_century/mayflower.asp (accessed February 9, 2010).
11. Louis Hartz, *The Liberal Tradition in America* (New York: Harcourt, Brace, and World, Inc., 1955), p. 63; see also Jack Citrin, "Political Culture," in Peter H. Schuck and James Q. Wilson, eds., *Understanding America: The Anatomy of an Exceptional Nation* (New York City, NY: Public Affairs, 2008), pp. 147–148.
12. Jack Citrin, "Political Culture," p. 162.
13. Ibid, p. 170.
14. Benjamin M. Friedman, "The Economic System," in Peter H. Shuck and James Q. Wilson, eds., *Understanding America: The Anatomy of an Exceptional Nation* (New York: Public Affairs, 2008), p. x.
15. See Roger Smith, *Civic Ideals: Conflicting Visions of Citizenship in U.S. History* (Michigan: Book Crafters, 1997).
16. Carl J. Richard, *The Founders and the Classics: Greece, Rome, and the American Enlightenment* (Harvard University Press, 1995).
17. "Essex Result," *The Founders' Constitution*, April 29, 1778, http://press-pubs.uchicago.edu/founders/documents/v1ch4s8.html (accessed December 1, 2009).
18. John Locke, "The Second Treatise of Civil Government," http://www.constitution.org/jl/2ndtreat.htm (accessed May 20, 2010) (Chapter 7, Section 87, 2nd Treatise).
19. "Locke's Political Philosophy," *Stanford Encyclopedia of Philosophy*, November 9, 2005, http://plato.stanford.edu/entries/locke-political/ (accessed December 1, 2009).
20. Louis Hartz, *The Liberal Tradition in America*, pp. 60–61.
21. John Locke, "The Second Treatise of Civil Government," http://www.constitution.org/jl/2ndtreat.htm (accessed May 20, 2010) (Chapter 7, section 87, 2nd Treatise).
22. Frederick G. Whelan, *Hume and Machiavelli: Political Realism and Liberal Thought* (Lanham: Lexington Books, 2005), p. 43.
23. Jean-Jacques Rousseau, "The Social Contract," http://www.constitution.org/jjr/socon_03.htm (accessed May 20, 2010).
24. Peter H. Shuck and James Q. Wilson, eds., *Understanding America: The Anatomy of an Exceptional Nation* (New York, NY: Public Affairs, 2008), p. x.
25. The Declaration of Independence (1776).
26. James Madison, "The Federalist #10," in *The Federalist Papers* (New York: Penguin Books, 1987), p. 3.
27. James Madison, "The Federalist #51," in *The Federalist Papers* (New York: Penguin Books, 1987), p. 1.
28. We do not enter here into the famous debate in the philosophy of science about "normal science," "paradigm shifts," etc. Rather, we aspire to produce a text that details the foundation of what we do and do not know about the subject. See Thomas Kuhn, *The Structure of Scientific Revolutions*, 2d ed. (Chicago: University of Chicago Press, 1970), p. 1.
29. Robert Post, 2009, "Debating Disciplinarity," *Critical Inquiry*, 35 (Summer): 749–770.
30. Horace Mann, quoted in Gregory J. Fritzburg, "Schools Can't Do It Alone: A Broader Conception of Equality of Education," www.newhorizons.org/strategies/multicultural/fritzberg.htm (accessed October 30, 2009). This quote is from Mann's Twelfth Annual Report as Secretary of Massachusetts State Board of Education, http://www.tncrimlaw.com/civil_bible/horace_mann.htm (accessed May 20, 2010).

Chapter 1

1. David Boaz, "The Man Who Would Not Be King," *CATO Institute*, February 20, 2006, www.cato.org/pub_display.php?pub_id=5593 (accessed November 30, 2009).
2. Aristotle, *Politics* (Oxford University Press, 1998); and George Huxley, "On Aristotle's Best State," *History of Political Thought*, 6 (Summer 1985), pp. 139–149.
3. John Locke, *Two Treatises of Government and a Letter Concerning Toleration* (Yale University Press, 2003); and Virginia McDonald, "A Guide to the Interpretation of Locke the Political Theorist," *Canadian Journal of Political Science*, 6 (December 1973), pp. 602–623.
4. Thomas Hobbes, *Leviathan* (Oxford University Press, 1998); and Frank M. Coleman, "The Hobbesian Basis of American Constitutionalism," *Polity*, 7 (Autumn 1974), pp. 57–89.
5. Charles de Montesquieu, *The Spirit of the Laws* (Cambridge University Press, 1989); and E. P. Panagopoulos, *Essays on the History and Meaning of Checks and Balances* (University Press of America, 1986).
6. *Reitman* v. *Mulkey*, 387 U.S. 369 (1967).
7. David B. Magleby, *Direct Legislation: Voting on Ballot Propositions in the United States* (Johns Hopkins University Press, 1984), p. 119.
8. Sheri Berman, "Civil Society and the Collapse of the Weimar Republic," *World Politics*, 49, No. 3 (April 1997), pp. 410–429.
9. Seymour Martin Lipset, "The Social Requisites of Democracy Revisited," *American Sociological Review*, 59 (1994), pp. 1–22.
10. For a discussion of the importance for democracy of such overlapping group memberships, see David Truman's seminal work, *The Governmental Process*, 2d ed. (Knopf, 1971).
11. Seymour Martin Lipset, "George Washington and the Founding of Democracy," *Journal of Democracy*, 9 (October 1998), p. 31.
12. David O. Stewart, *The Men Who Invented the Constitution: The Summer of 1787* (Simon & Schuster: NY, 2007).
13. See the essays in Thomas E. Cronin, ed., *Inventing the American Presidency* (University Press of Kansas, 1989); see also Richard J. Ellis, ed., *Founding the American Presidency* (Rowman & Littlefield, 1999).

14. David McKay, *American Politics and Society* (Wiley-Blackwell: Malden, MA, 2009); see also Saul Cornell "Aristocracy Assailed: The Ideology of Backcountry Anti-Federalism," *Journal of American History*, 76 (March), p. 1156, www.jstor.org/stable/pdfplus/ 2936593.pdf.
15. Charles A. Beard and Mary R. Beard, *A Basic History of the United States* (New Home Library, 1944), p. 136.
16. W. B. Allen and Gordon Lloyd, eds., *The Essential Antifederalist* (University Press of America, 1985), pp. xi–xiii.
17. See Herbert J. Storing, ed., abridgment by Murray Dry, *The Anti-Federalist: Writings by the Opponents of the Constitution* (University of Chicago Press, 1985).
18. On the role of the promised Bill of Rights amendments in the ratification of the Constitution, see Leonard W. Levy, *Constitutional Opinions* (Oxford University Press, 1986), Chapter 6.
19. www.nationmaster.com.
20. Sanford Levinson, *Constitutional Faith* (Princeton University Press, 1988), pp. 9–52.
21. Richard Morin, "We Love It—What We Know of It," *The Washington Post National Weekly Edition* (September 22, 1997), p. 35.
22. Alexander Hamilton, James Madison, and John Jay, in Clinton Rossiter, ed., *The Federalist Papers* (New American Library, 1961).
23. Quoted in Alpheus T. Mason, *The Supreme Court: Palladium of Freedom* (University of Michigan Press, 1962), p. 10.
24. Hamilton, Madison, and Jay, *The Federalist Papers.*
25. Ibid.
26. Ibid.
27. Justice Brandeis dissenting in *Myers* v. *United States,* 272 U.S. 52 (1926).
28. Hamilton, Madison, and Jay, *The Federalist Papers.*
29. See Alec Stone Sweet, Wayne Sandholtz, and Neil Fligstein, *The Institutionalization of Europe* (Oxford University Press, 2001); Alec Stone Sweet, *Governing with Judges: Constitutional Politics in Europe* (Oxford University Press, 2000); and Anne-Marie Slaughter, Alec Stone Sweet, and J.H.H. Weiler, *The European Court and National Courts—Doctrine, Jurisprudence: Legal Change in Its Social Context* (Hart, 1998).
30. *Marbury* v. *Madison,* 5 U. S. 137 (1803).
31. Dumas Malone, *Jefferson the President: First Term, 1801–1805* (Little, Brown, 1970), p. 145.
32. J. W. Peltason, *Federal Courts in the Political Process* (Random House, 1955).
33. Richard E. Neustadt, *Presidential Power* (Free Press, 1990), pp. 180–181.
34. *Marabury* v. *Madison,* 5 U.S. 137 (1803).
35. *Brown* v. *Board of Education,* 347 U.S. 483 (1954).
36. *Griswold* v. *Connecticut,* 381 U.S. 479 (1965).
37. *Texas* v. *Johnson,* 491 U.S. 397 (1989).
38. *United States* v. *Eichman,* 496 U.S. 310 (1990).
39. John A. Clark and Kevin T. McGuire, "Congress, the Supreme Court, and the Flag," *Political Research Quarterly* 49 (1996), pp. 771–781.
40. Senate Joint Resolution 12, 109th Congress, 2d session.
41. Ann Stuart Diamond, "A Convention for Proposing Amendments: The Constitution's Other Method," *Publius* 11 (Summer 1981), pp. 113–146; and Wilbur Edel, "Amending the Constitution by Convention: Myths and Realities," *State Government* 55 (1982), pp. 51–56.
42. Russell L. Caplan, *Constitutional Brinksmanship: Amending the Constitution by National Convention* (Oxford University Press, 1988), p. x; see also David E. Kyvig, *Explicit and Authentic Acts: Amending the U.S. Constitution, 1776–1995* (University Press of Kansas, 1996), p. 440.
43. Samuel S. Freedman and Pamela J. Naughton, *ERA: May a State Change Its Vote?* (Wayne State University Press, 1979).
44. Kyvig, *Explicit and Authentic Acts,* p. 286; and *Dillon* v. *Gloss,* 256 U.S. 368 (1921).

Chapter 2

1. For further historical background, see Samuel J. Beer, *To Make a Nation: The Rediscovery of American Federalism* (Harvard University Press, 1993).
2. See "Eyes on the Road: States Crack Down on Texting While Driving," *State Health Notes,* 29, 523 (September 15, 2008), available at ncsl.org/default.aspx?tabid=14662.
3. William H. Stewart, *Concepts of Federalism* (Center for the Study of Federalism/University Press of America, 1984); see also Preston King, *Federalism and Federation,* 2d ed. (Cass, 2001).
4. Morton Grodzins, "The Federal System," in *Goals for Americans: The Report of the President's Commission on National Goals* (Columbia University Press, 1960).
5. Thomas R. Dye, *American Federalism: Competition Among Governments* (Lexington Books, 1990), pp. 13–17.
6. Michael D. Reagan and John G. Sanzone, *The New Federalism* (Oxford University Press, 1981), p. 175.
7. William H. Riker, *The Development of American Federalism* (Academic Press, 1987), pp. 14–15. Riker contends not only that federalism does not guarantee freedom but also that the framers of our federal system, as well as those of other nations, were animated not by considerations of safeguarding freedom but by practical considerations of preserving unity.
8. U.S. Census Bureau, *Statistical Abstract of the United States* (Government Printing Office, 2007), p. 487.
9. Charles Evans Hughes, "War Powers Under the Constitution," *ABA Reports,* 62 (1917), p. 238.
10. *Gibbons* v. *Ogden,* 22 U.S. 1 (1824).
11. *Reno* v. *Condon,* 528 U.S. 141 (2000).
12. *Champion* v. *Ames,* 188 U.S. 321 (1907).
13. *Caminetti* v. *United States,* 242 U.S. 470 (1917).
14. *Federal Radio Commission* v. *Nelson Brothers,* 289 U.S. 266 (1933).
15. See Jesse Choper, *Judicial Review and the National Political Process* (University of Chicago Press, 1980); and John T. Noonan Jr., *Narrowing the Nation's Power: The Supreme Court Sides with the States* (University of California Press, 2002).
16. See Michael S. Greve, *Real Federalism: Why It Matters, How It Could Happen* (American Enterprise Institute, 1999).
17. *Printz* v. *United States,* 521 U.S. 898 (1997); see also *New York* v. *United States,* 505 U.S. 144 (1992).
18. See *Franchise Tax Board of California* v. *Hyatt,* 538 U.S. 488 (2003).
19. *California* v. *Superior Courts of California,* 482 U.S. 400 (1987).
20. David C. Nice, "State Participation in Interstate Compacts," *Publius,* 17 (Spring 1987), p. 70; see also *Interstate Compacts and Agencies,* Council of State Governments (Author, 1995), for a list of compacts by subject and by state with brief descriptions.
21. *McCulloch* v. *Maryland,* 4 Wheaton 316 (1819).
22. Joseph F. Zimmerman, "Federal Preemption Under Reagan's New Federalism," *Publius,* 21 (Winter 1991), pp. 7–28.
23. Oliver Wendell Holmes Jr., *Collected Legal Papers* (Harcourt, 1920), pp. 295–296.
24. See, for example, *United States* v. *Lopez,* 514 U.S. 549 (1995).
25. *Seminole Tribe of Florida* v. *Florida,* 517 U.S. 44 (1996).
26. *Alden* v. *Maine,* 527 U.S. 706 (1999); *Kimel* v. *Florida Board of Regents,* 528 U.S. 62 (2000); *Vermont Agency of Natural Resources* v. *United States ex rel. Stevens,* 529 U.S. 765 (2000).
27. George Will, "A Revival of Federalism?" *Newsweek* (May 29, 2000), p. 78.
28. *United States* v. *Morrison,* 529 U.S. 598 (2000).
29. The term "devolution revolution" was coined by Richard P. Nathan in testimony before the Senate Finance Committee, quoted in Daniel Patrick Moynihan, "The Devolution Revolution," *New York Times* (August 6, 1995), p. B15.
30. John E. Chubb, "The Political Economy of Federalism," *American Political Science Review,* 79 (December 1985), p. 1005.
31. Donald F. Kettl, *The Regulation of American Federalism* (Johns Hopkins University Press, 1987), pp. 154–155.
32. See Paul J. Posner, *The Politics of Unfunded Mandates: Whither Federalism?* (Georgetown University Press, 1998).

33. *Restoring Confidence and Competence,* Advisory Commission on Intergovernmental Relations (Author, 1981), p. 30.
34. Aaron Wildavsky, "Bare Bones: Putting Flesh on the Skeleton of American Federalism," in *The Future of Federalism in the 1980s* (Advisory Commission on Intergovernmental Relations, 1981), p. 79.
35. Peterson, *Price of Federalism,* p. 182.
36. Dye, *American Federalism,* p. 199.
37. John J. DiLulio Jr. and Donald F. Kettl, *Fine Print: The Contract with America, Devolution, and the Administrative Realities of American Federalism* (Brookings Institution Press, 1995), p. 60.
38. John Kincaid, "Devolution in the United States," in Nicolaidis and Howse, eds., *The Federal Vision* (Oxford, 2002), p. 144.

Chapter 3

1. Lev Grossman, Viveca Novak, and Eric Roston, "Campaign '04: Technology: What Your Party Knows About You," *Time Magazine* (October 18, 2004), http://www.time.com/time/magazine/article/0,9171,995394-1,00.html (accessed March 8, 2010).
2. Senator Charles Schumer from an NPR story by Mara Liasson, "GOP Bets on Get-Out-Vote Campaign for Win," October 6, 2006, http:// www.npr.org/templates/story/story.php? storyId=6211237 (accessed March 8, 2010).
3. Albert Einstein, quoted in Laurence J. Peter, *Peter's Quotations* (Morrow, 1977), p. 358.
4. Alexis de Tocqueville, *Democracy in America,* edited by J. P. Mayer, translated by George Lawrence (Doubleday, 1969), p. 278. Originally published 1835 (Vol. 1) and 1840 (Vol. 2).
5. See John Lewis Gaddis, *Surprise, Security, and the American Experience* (Harvard University Press, 2005).
6. This excludes the Japanese attack on the U.S. territory of Hawaii in 1941 and other attacks on U.S. embassies or territories.
7. Food and Agriculture Organization of the United Nations, "Statistical Appendix," *Food Outlook,* 1 (June 2007), www.fao.org/docrep/010/ah864e/ah864e14.htm (accessed May 20, 2010).
8. Harold Hongju Koh, "On American Exceptionalism," *Stanford Law Review,* 55 (May 2003), p. 1481.
9. Robert S. Erikson, Gerald C. Wright, and John P. McIver, *Statehouse Democracy: Public Opinion and Policy in the American States* (Cambridge University Press, 1993).
10. *Statistical Abstract: 2010,* p. 18.
11. *Statistical Abstract: 2010,* p. 36.
12. Ibid.
13. David R. Harris and Jeremiah Joseph Sim, "Who is Multiracial? Assessing the Complexity of Lived Race," *American Sociological Review* (August 2002), p. 615.
14. *Statistical Abstract: 2010,* p. 25.
15. Ibid.
16. U.S. Census Bureau, "Projections of the Population and Components of Change for the United States: 2010 to 2050," *U.S. Department of Commerce,* http://www.census.gov/population/www/projections/summarytables.html (accessed May 20, 2010).
17. See James Meader and John Bart, "The More You Spend, the Less They Listen: The South Dakota U.S. Senate Race," in David B. Magleby and J. Quin Monson, eds., *The Last Hurrah? Soft Money and Issue Advocacy in the 2002 Congressional Elections* (Brookings Institution Press, 2004), p. 173; see also Elizabeth Theiss Smith and Richard Braunstein, "The Nationalization of Local Politics in South Dakota," in David B. Magleby and J. Quin Monson, eds., *Dancing Without Partners: How Candidates, Parties, and Interest Groups Interact in the New Campaign Finance Environment* (Center for the Study of Elections and Democracy, 2005), pp. 241–242.
18. Henry J. Kaiser Family Foundation, "Race, Ethnicity, and Healthcare Issue Brief," http://www.kff.org/minorityhealth/upload/7977.pdf (accessed March 1, 2010).
19. Robert D. Ballard, "Introduction: Lure of the New South," in Robert D. Ballard, ed., *In Search of the New South: The Black Urban Experience in the 1970s and 1980s* (University of Alabama Press, 1989), p. 5; and *Statistical Abstract: 2008,* p. 449.
20. *Statistical Abstract: 2010,* p. 447. Constant 2007 dollars.
21. Ibid., p. 458.
22. *Statistical Abstract: 2010,* p. 447.
23. *Statistical Abstract: 2010,* p. 13.
24. Jeremy D. Mayer, *Running on Race* (Random House, 2002), pp. 4, 297; see also Mark R. Levy and Michael S. Kramer, *The Ethnic Factor: How America's Minorities Decide Elections* (Simon & Schuster, 1973); and Mark Stern, "Democratic Presidency and Voting Rights," in Lawrence W. Mooreland, Robert P. Steed, and Todd A. Baker, eds., *Blacks in Southern Politics,* (Praeger, 1987), pp. 50–51.
25. For 1984–2000, see Harold W. Stanley and Richard G. Niemi, *Vital Statistics on American Politics, 2000–2001* (CQ Press, 2001), p. 122; for 2004, see Harold W. Stanley and Richard G. Niemi, *Vital Statistics on American Politics, 2005–2006* (CQ Press, 2006), p. 124.
26. BBC News, "The U.S. Election in Figures," http://news.bbc.co.uk/2/hi/americas/us_elections_2008/7715914.stm (accessed November 7, 2008).
27. Stanley and Niemi, *Vital Statistics on American Politics, 2009–2010,* pp. 53–54.
28. Ibid.
29. Matt Barreto, Rodolfo O. de la Garza, Jongho Lee, Jaesung Ryu, and Harry P. Pachon, "Latino Voter Mobilization in 2000," Tomás Rivera Policy Institute (2000), pp. 4–5, www.trpi.org/ PDFs/Voter_mobiliz_2.pdf; see also Richard E. Cohen, "Hispanic Hopes Fade," *National Journal* (February 2, 2002).
30. *Statistical Abstract: 2010,* p. 25.
31. *Statistical Abstract: 2010,* p. 46.
32. Michael Hoefer, Nancy Rytina, and Christopher Campbell, "Estimates of the Unauthorized Immigrant Population Residing in the United States: January 2008," Department of Homeland Security, http://www.dhs.gov/xlibrary/assets/statistics/publications/ois_ill_pe_2008.pdf (accessed February 2010).
33. *Statistical Abstract: 2008,* p. 13.
34. Andrew L. Aoki and Don T. Nakanishi, "Asian Pacific Americans and the New Minority Politics," *PS: Political Science and Politics* (September 2001), p. 605.
35. Ibid.
36. *Statistical Abstract: 2010,* p. 148.
37. Ibid., p. 47.
38. Leni Yahil, *The Holocaust: The Fate of European Jewry* (Oxford University Press, 1990).
39. Stephen C. LeSuer, *The 1838 Mormon War in Missouri* (University of Missouri Press, 1987), pp. 151–153.
40. Ronald Inglehart and Wayne E. Baker, "Looking Forward, Looking Back: Continuity and Change at the Turn of the Millennium," *American Sociological Review* (February 2000), pp. 29, 31.
41. Kenneth D. Wald and Allison Calhoun-Brown, *Religion and Politics in the United States,* 5th ed. (New York: Rowman and Littlefield, 2006), p. 9.
42. Pew Forum on Religious and Public Life, "Eastern, New Age Beliefs Widespread Many Americans Mix Multiple Faiths," December 2009, http://pewforum.org/newassets/images/reports/multiplefaiths/multiplefaiths.pdf (accessed February 18, 2010).
43. *Statistical Abstract: 2010,* p. 61.
44. Ibid.
45. Ibid.
46. *Statistical Abstract: 2010,* pp. 18, 59; see also www.thearda.com/mapsReports/reports/selectState.asp.
47. The Association of Religion Data Archives, "Southern Baptist Convention," 2000, http://www.thearda.com/Denoms/D_1087_d.asp (accessed February 22, 2010).
48. Ibid.
49. American Religion Data Archive, "Jewish Estimate—Number of Adherents," www.thearda.com/mapsReports/maps/map.asp?state=101&variable=20; ARDA; and "Metro Area Membership Report," www.thearda.com/mapsReports/reports/metro/5602_2000.asp.
50. CNN, "Exit Polls: Results," www.cnn.com/ELECTION/2000/results (accessed September 1, 2006).

51. Pew Forum on Religion and Public Life, "Voting Religiously" November 5, 2008, http://pewresearch.org/pubs/1022/exit-poll-analysis-religion (accessed February 19, 2010).
52. James West Davidson, William E. Gienapp, Christine Leigh Heyrman, Mark H. Lytle, and Michael B. Stoff, *Nation of Nations* (McGraw-Hill, 1990), pp. 833–834.
53. Margaret C. Trevor, "Political Socialization, Party Identification, and the Gender Gap," *Public Opinion Quarterly,* 63 (Spring 1999), p. 62.
54. *Statistical Abstract: 2006,* p. 263; Sue Tolleson-Rinehart and Jyl J. Josephson, eds., *Gender and American Politics* (Sharpe, 2000), pp. 77–78; and Center for American Women and Politics, "Gender Differences in Voter Turnout," 2009, http://www.cawp.rutgers.edu/fast_facts/voters/documents/genderdiff.pdf (accessed February 18, 2010).
55. Sue Tolleson-Rinehart and Jyl J. Josephson, *Gender and American Politics,* pp. 232–233; see also Cindy Simon Rosenthal, ed., *Women Transforming Congress* (University of Oklahoma Press, 2002), pp. 128–139.
56. Paul Steinhauser, "Men's Support Gives Palin Edge in Latest Poll," *CNN,* September 9, 2008, http://www.cnn.com/2008/POLITICS/09/09/palin.poll (accessed March 1, 2010).
57. Marjorie Connelly, "The Election; Who Voted: A Portrait of American Politics, 1976–2000," *New York Times* (November 12, 2000), p. D4.
58. *Statistical Abstract: 2006,* p. 247; and CNN, "U.S. President National Exit Poll," 2004, http://www.cnn.com/ELECTION/2004/pages/results/states/US/P/00/epolls.0.html (accessed February 18, 2010).
59. CNN, "Obama's Election Redraws America's Electoral Divide," November 5, 2008, http://www.cnn.com/2008/POLITICS/11/05/election.president/index.html (accessed February 18, 2010).
60. Diane L. Fowlkes, "Feminist Theory: Reconstructing Research and Teaching About American Politics and Government," *News for Teachers of Political Science* (Winter 1987), pp. 6–9; see also Sally Helgesen, *Everyday Revolutionaries: Working Women and the Transformation of American Life* (Doubleday, 1998); Karen Lehrman, *The Lipstick Proviso: Women, Sex, and Power in the Real World* (Anchor/Doubleday, 1997); Tanya Melich, *The Republican War Against Women: An Insider's Report from Behind the Lines* (Bantam Books, 1998); and Virginia Valian, *Why So Slow? The Advancement of Women* (MIT Press, 1998).
61. Arlie Russell Hochschild, "There's No Place Like Work," *New York Times* (April 20, 1997), p. 51.
62. The Pew Research Center, *Gay Marriage a Voting Issue, but Mostly for Opponents,* February 27, 2004, www.people-press.org/reports/display.php3?ReportID=204; and Alexis Simendinger, "Why Issues Matter," *National Journal* (April 1, 2000), based on data from a Pew Center Poll conducted March 15–19, 2000.
63. *Statistical Abstract: 2010,* p. 450.
64. U.S. Census Bureau, "Men's and Women's Earnings by State: 2008 American Community Survey," http://www.census.gov/prod/ 2009pubs/acsbr08-3.pdf (accessed February 22, 2010).
65. Catherine Rampell, "As Layoffs Surge, Women May Pass Men in Job Force," *New York Times* (February 5, 2009), http://www.nytimes.com/2009/02/06/business/06women.html.
66. Catherine Rampell, "Women Now a Majority in American Workplaces," *New York Times* (February 5, 2010),p. A10.
67. Anna Quindlen, "Some Struggles Never Seem to End," *New York Times* (November 14, 2001), p. H24.
68. "Gay and Lesbian Families in the U.S.," Urban Institute, http://www.urban.org/publications/ 1000491.html.
69. U.S. Census Bureau, "Unmarried-Partner Households by Region and Sex of Partners: 2007," *Statistical Abstract of the United States: 2010* (Washington, D.C.), p. 55.
70. U.S. Census Bureau, "Table MS-2. Estimated Median Age at First Marriage, by Sex: 1890 to the Present," January 2009, http://www.census.gov/population/socdemo/hh-fam/ ms2.csv (accessed February 23, 2010).
71. CIA World Factbook, "Country Comparison: Total Fertility Rate," 2009, https://www.cia .gov/library/publications/the-world-factbook/rankorder/2127rank.html (accessed February 23, 2010).
72. The census stopped releasing divorce data in 1998, possibly because several states stopped providing it.
73. *Statistical Abstract: 2010,* p. 94.
74. Thomas Jefferson to P. S. du Pont de Nemours, April 24, 1816, in Paul L. Ford, ed., *The Writings of Thomas Jefferson* (Putnam, 1899), Vol. 10, p. 25.
75. *Statistical Abstract: 2010,* p. 146.
76. *Statistical Abstract: 2008,* p. 146.
77. *Statistical Abstract: 2010,* p. 149.
78. Herbert McClosky and John Zaller, *The American Ethos: Public Attitudes Toward Capitalism and Democracy* (Harvard University Press, 1984), p. 261.
79. Raymond E. Wolfinger, Fred I. Greenstein, and Martin Shapiro, *Dynamics of American Politics,* 2d ed. (Prentice Hall, 1980), p. 19.
80. Harold W. Stanley and Richard G. Niemi, *Vital Statistics on American Politics, 2007–2008* (CQ Press, 2008), p. 374–375.
81. *Statistical Abstract: 2010,* p. 457.
82. U.S. Census Bureau, http://www.census.gov/hhes/www/poverty/threshld/thresh09.html.
83. *Statistical Abstract: 2010,* http://www.census .gov/prod/2008pubs/p60-235.pdf (accessed March 4, 2010), p. 13.
84. Ibid.
85. *Statistical Abstract: 2010,* p. 457.
86. U.S. Department of Commerce, Bureau of Economic Analysis, "Real Gross Domestic Product, 1 Decimal" (February 28, 2008), research.stlouisfed.org/fred2/data/GDPC1.txt.
87. Daniel Bell, *The Coming of Post-Industrial Society: A Venture in Social Forecasting* (Basic Books, 1973), p. xviii.
88. *Statistical Abstract: 2010,* p. 392.
89. *Statistical Abstract: 2010,* p. 427.
90. Gabriel A. Almond, G. Bingham Powell, Jr., Russell J. Dalton, and Kaare Strøm, eds., *Comparative Politics Today: A World View,* 9th ed. (Pearson Longman, 2008), p. 54.
91. Seymour Martin Lipset, *Continental Divide: The Values and Institutions of the United States and Canada* (Routledge, 1990), p. 170.
92. Nicholas L. Danigelis, Stephen J. Cutler, and Melissa Hardy, "Population Aging, Intracohort Aging, and Sociopolitical Attitudes," *American Sociological Review,* 72 (October 2007), p. 816.
93. David B. Magleby, J. Quin Monson, and Kelly D. Patterson, *Dancing Without Partners: How Candidates, Parties, and Interest Groups Interact in the Presidential Campaign* (Rowman & Littlefield, 2007); David B. Magleby, ed., *The Change Election: Money, Mobilization, and Persuasion in the 2008 Federal Elections* (Temple University Press, 2011).
94. Robert D. Putnam, "Bowling Alone: America's Declining Social Capital," *Journal of Democracy,* 6 (January 1995), pp. 65–78; see also Robert D. Putnam, *Bowling Alone: The Collapse and Revival of American Community* (Simon & Schuster, 2000); and Robert D. Putnam, "Bowling Together," *The American Prospect,* 13 (February 2002), p. 20.
95. Clinton Rossiter, *Conservatism in America* (Vintage Books, 1962), p. 72.
96. Bernard Bailyn, *The Ideological Origins of the American Revolution* (Belknap Press, 1967); Gordon S. Wood, *The Creation of the American Republic, 1776–1787* (University of North Carolina Press, 1969); and Jack Citrin, "Political Culture," in Peter H. Schuck and James Q. Wilson, eds., *Understanding America: The Anatomy of an Exceptional Nation* (New York: Public Affairs, 2008), pp. 160–161.
97. Peter H. Shuck and James Q. Wilson, eds., *Understanding America: The Anatomy of an Exceptional Nation* (New York: Public Affairs, 2008), p. 629.
98. See Ronald Dworkin, *Taking Rights Seriously* (Harvard University Press, 1977).
99. *Marbury* v. *Madison,* 5 U.S. 137 (1803).
100. "A Nation Challenged: Excerpts from President's Speech: 'We Will Prevail' in War on Terrorism," *New York Times* (November 9, 2001), p. B1.

101. Robert Coles, *The Political Life of Children* (Atlantic Monthly Press, 1986).
102. Fred I. Greenstein, *Children and Politics* (Yale University Press, 1965).
103. Raymond E. Wolfinger and Steven Rosenstone, *Who Votes?* (Yale University Press, 1980).
104. Peter H. Shuck and James Q. Wilson, "Looking Back" in Peter H. Schuck and James Q. Wilson, eds., *Understanding America: The Anatomy of an Exceptional Nation* (New York: Public Affairs, 2008), p. 630.
105. Rachel X. Weissman, "The Kids Are AllRight—They're Just a Little Converged," *American Demographics,* 20 (December 1998), pp. 30–32.
106. Jeremy Rifkin, *The European Dream* (Penguin, 2005).
107. When adjusted using the consumer price index (CPI1), the percentage of households earning more than $75,000 a year has risen from 10.1 percent in 1970 to 22.6 percent in 1999. U.S., Census Bureau, *Statistical Abstracts of the United States, 2001* (U.S. Government Printing Office, 2001), Table 661; see also Julia Isaac, "Economic Mobility of Black and White Families," *Economic Mobility Project,* Brookings Institution, November 2007.
108. See Michael B. Katz, *The "Underclass" Debate* (Princeton University Press, 1993); Theodore Dalrymple, *Life at the Bottom: The Worldview That Makes the Underclass* (Dee, 2001); and Charles A. Murray, *The Underclass Revisited* (AEI Press, 1999).
109. Carl N. Degler, *Out of Our Past: The Forces That Shaped Modern America,* 3d ed. (Harper & Row, 1984), p. 322.

Chapter 4

1. Peter Slevin, "Key Democrat Feels the Heat After Voting for House Plan," *Washington Post* (August 10, 2009), http://www.washingtonpost.com/wp-dyn/content/article/2009/08/09/AR2009080902428.html (accessed May 21, 2010).
2. "Stop! The Size and Power of the State Is Growing, and Discontent Is on the Rise," *The Economist* (2010), pp. 10–18.
3. Nate Silver, "Tea Party Nonpartisan Attendance Estimates: Now 300,000+ Tea Party Attendance Estimate," *FiveThirtyEight,* April 16, 2009, http://www.fivethirtyeight.com/2009/04/tea-party-nonpartisan-attendance.html, retrieved June 16, 2009 (accessed February 24, 2010).
4. Tea Party Express, "About," 2010, http://www.teapartyexpress.org/about/ (accessed February 22, 2010).
5. Our Country Deserves Better, "Campaigns," 2010, http://www.ourcountrydeservesbetter.com/campaigns (accessed February 22, 2010).
6. Kate Zernike, "Palin Assails Obama at Tea Party Meeting," *New York Times,* February 6, 2010, http://www.nytimes.com/2010/02/07/us/politics/08palin.html (accessed February 22, 2010).
7. Adam Nagourney, Jeff Zeleny, Kate Zernike, and Michael Cooper, "G.O.P. Used Energy and Stealth to Win Seat," *New York Times* (January 21, 2010).
8. E. E. Schattschneider, *Party Government* (Holt, Rinehart and Winston, 1942), p. 1.
9. See Scott Mainwaring, "Party Systems in the Third Wave," *Journal of Democracy* (July 1998), pp. 67-81.
10. Joseph A. Schlesinger, *Political Parties and the Winning of Office* (University of Michigan Press, 1994).
11. Robert R. Alford and Eugene C. Lee, "Voting Turnout in American Cities," *American Political Science Review* 62 (September), pp. 809–810.
12. Gary W. Cox and Mathew D. McCubbins, *Legislative Leviathan: Party Government in the House* (University of California Press, 1993).
13. David W. Brady and Craig Volden, *Revolving Gridlock: Politics and Policy from Carter to Clinton* (Westview Press, 1998); James A. Thurber, ed., *Divided Democracy: Cooperation and Conflict Between the President and Congress* (CQ Press, 1991); James A. Thurber, ed., *Rivals for Power: Presidential–Congressional Relations* (CQ Press, 1996); Charles O. Jones, *Separate but Equal Branches: Congress and the Presidency* (Chatham House, 1995), Chapters 5 and 6; and Jon R. Bond and Richard Fleisher, *The President in the Legislative Arena* (University of Chicago Press, 1990).
14. *California Democratic Party et al.* v. *Jones,* 120 S. Ct. 2402 (2000).
15. George Skelton, "California Open Primaries? Give Them a Chance," *Los Angeles Times,* February 11, 2010, http://articles.latimes.com/2010/feb/11/local/la-me-cap11-2010feb11 (accessed March 29, 2010).
16. For an analysis of the potential effects of different electoral rules in the United States, see Todd Donovan and Shawn Bowler, *Reforming the Republic: Democratic Institutions for the New America* (Prentice Hall, 2004).
17. William H. Riker, "The Two-Party System and Duverger's Law: An Essay on the History of Political Science," *American Political Science Review* 76 (December 1982), pp. 753–766. For a classic analysis, see E. E. Schattschneider, *Party Government* (Holt, Rinehart and Winston, 1942).
18. Maurice Duverger, *Party Politics and Pressure Groups* (Nelson, 1972), pp. 23–32.
19. Steven J. Rosenstone, Roy L. Behr, and Edward H. Lazarus, *Third Parties in America: Citizen Response to Major Party Failure,* 2d ed. (Princeton University Press, 1996); see also Xandra Kayden and Eddie Mahe, Jr., *The Party Goes On: The Persistence of the Two-Party System in the United States* (Basic Books, 1985), pp. 143–144. The Republican Party, which started as a third party, was one of the two major parties by 1860, the year Republican Abraham Lincoln won the Presidency; see Lewis L. Gould, *Grand Old Party: A History of the Republicans* (Random House, 2003), pp. 3–17.
20. Dean Lacy and Quin Monson, "The Origins and Impact of Voter Support for Third-Party Candidates: A Case Study of the 1998 Minnesota Gubernatorial Election," *Political Research Quarterly* 55(2), pp. 409–437.
21. On the impact of third parties, see Howard R. Penniman, "Presidential Third Parties and the Modern American Two-Party System," in William J. Crotty, ed., *The Party Symbol* (Freeman, 1980), pp. 101–117; see also Frank Smallwood, *The Other Candidates: Third Parties in Presidential Elections* (University Press of New England, 1983).
22. V. O. Key, Jr., *Political Parties and Pressure Groups,* 5th ed. (International, 1964); see also Marjorie Randon Hershey, *Party Politics in America,* 12th ed. (Longman, 2006).
23. Federal Election Commission, "National Party Activity Summarized," press release, October 30, 2006, www.fec.gov/press/press2006/20061030party/20061030party.html.
24. Hershey, *Party Politics in America.*
25. The early Republican efforts and advantages over the Democrats are well documented in Thomas B. Edsall, *The New Politics of Inequality* (Norton, 1984); and Gary C. Jacobson, "The Republican Advantage in Campaign Finances," in John E. Chubb and Paul E. Peterson, eds., *New Direction in American Politics* (Brookings Institution Press, 1985), p. 6; see also David B. Magleby and Kelly D. Patterson, "Rules of Engagement: BCRA and Unanswered Questions," in David B. Magleby and Kelly D. Patterson, eds., *The Battle for Congress: Iraq, Scandal, and Campaign Finance in the 2006 Election* (Paradigm, 2008), pp. 33–36.
26. David C. King, "The Polarization of American Political Parties and Mistrust of Government," in Joseph S. Nye, Philip Zelikow, and David C. King, eds., *Why People Don't Trust Government* (Harvard University Press, 1997); and National Election Study, "Important Difference in What Democratic and Republican Parties Stand For, 1952–2000," www.umich./nes/edu/nesguide/toptable/tab2b_4.htm.
27. See James L. Gibson, Cornelius P. Cotter, John F. Bibby, and Robert J. Huckshorn, "Assessing Party Organizational Strength," *American Journal of Political Science* 27 (May 1983), pp. 193–222; see also Cornelius P. Cotter, James L. Gibson, John F. Bibby, and Robert Huckshorn, *Party Organizations in American Politics* (University of Pittsburg Press, 1989).

28. Paul S. Herrnson, *Party Campaigning in the 1980s: Have the National Parties Made a Comeback as Key Players in Congressional Elections?* (Harvard University Press, 1988), p. 122.
29. *Marbury* v. *Madison,* 1 Cranch 137 (1803).
30. See Angus Campbell, Philip E. Converse, Warren E. Miller, and Donald E. Stokes, *The American Voter* (University of Chicago Press, 1960); Norman A. Nie, Sidney Verba, and John R. Petrocik, *The Changing American Voter,* enlarged ed. (Harvard University Press, 1979); and Warren E. Miller and J. Merrill Shanks, *The New American Voter* (Harvard University Press, 1996).
31. Campbell et al., *The American Voter,* pp. 121–128.
32. Ibid.
33. Bruce E. Keith et al., *The Myth of the Independent Voter* (University of California Press, 1992).
34. See V. O. Key, Jr., "A Theory of Critical Elections," *Journal of Politics* 17 (February 1955), pp. 3–18; Walter Dean Burnham, *Critical Elections and the Mainsprings of American Politics* (Norton, 1970), pp. 1–10; and E. E. Schattschneider, *The Semisovereign People: A Realist's View of Democracy in America* (Holt, Rinehart and Winston, 1975), pp. 78–80.
35. Nine percent of all voters were Pure Independents in 1956 and 1960; Keith et al., *The Myth of the Independent Voter,* p. 51. In 1992, the figure was also 9 percent; *1992 National Election Study* (Center for Political Studies, University of Michigan, 1992).
36. David B. Magleby and Candice J. Nelson, *The Money Chase: Congressional Campaign Finance Reform* (Brookings Institution Press, 1990), p. 16.
37. David B. Magleby, ed., *Outside Money: Soft Money and Issue Advocacy in the 1998 Congressional Elections* (Rowman & Littlefield, 2003); and David B. Magleby, ed., *The Other Campaign: Soft Money and Issue Advocacy in the 2000 Congressional Elections* (Rowman & Littlefield, 2003).
38. Jonathan S. Krasno and Daniel E. Seltz, *Buying Time: Television Advertising in the 1998 Congressional Elections,* report of a grant funded by the Pew Charitable Trusts (1998).
39. *Colorado Republican Federal Campaign Committee* v. *Federal Election Commission,* 518 U.S. 604 (1996).
40. Sidney M. Milkis, "Parties Versus Interest Groups," in Anthony Corrado, Thomas E. Mann, and Trevor Potter, eds., *Inside the Campaign Finance Battle: Court Testimony on the New Reforms* (Brookings Institution Press, 2003), p. 44.
41. "Comparative Data," in the Ace Electoral Knowledge Network Database, http://aceproject.org/epic-en (accessed March 30, 2010).
42. James Madison, *The Federalist,* No. 10, November 23, 1787, in Isaac Kramnick, ed., *The Federalist Papers* (Penguin, 1987), pp. 122–128.
43. See Robert Dahl, *Who Governs?* (Yale University Press, 1961).
44. Center for Responsive Politics, "Microsoft Corp: Donor Profile," http://www.opensecrets.org/orgs/summary.asp?ID=D000000115&Name=Microsoft+Corp (accessed May 21, 2010).
45. Gabriel A. Almond, G. Bingham Powell, Jr., Russell J. Dalton, and Kaare Strøm, *Comparative Politics Today,* 9th ed. (Pearson Longman, 2008), p. 70.
46. Minimum wage data compiled from International Labour Organization, Working Time Database, Minimum Wages Database, www.ilo.org/travaildatabase/servlet/minimumwages (accessed May 21, 2010); minimum wage rates converted to American dollars per hour based on a 40-hour workweek.
47. Change to Win, "About Us," 2010, http://www.changetowin.org/about-us.html (accessed March 15, 2010).
48. Office of Labor Management Standards, Union Reports, and Constitutions, http://www.dol .gov/olms/regs/compliance/rrlo/lmrda.htm (accessed May 21, 2010).
49. AFL-CIO, "About Us: Union Facts," www.aflcio .org/aboutus/faq/ (accessed May 21, 2010).
50. U.S. Bureau of Labor Statistics, www.bls.gov/cps/cpsaat40.pdf (accessed May 21, 2010).
51. Service Employees International Union, "Letters from President Andy Stern to SEIU Members: Where Do We Go from Here?," December 17, 2009, http://www.seiu.org/2009/12/letter-from-president-andy-stern-to-seiu-members-where-do-we-go-from-here.php (accessed February 24, 2010).
52. Alison Grant, "Labor Chief Sees Anti-Union Efforts Growing Bolder," (Cleveland) *Plain Dealer* (November 22, 2005), p. C1.
53. National Education Association, http://www.nea.org/home/1704.htm (accessed March 2, 2010).
54. Robert Salisbury, "Interest Representation: The Dominance of Institutions," *American Political Science Review,* 78 (March 1984), p. 66.
55. V. O. Key, Jr., *Public Opinion and American Democracy* (Knopf, 1961), pp. 504–507.
56. Daniel Stone, "The Browning of Grass Roots: How Astroturfing Is Taking Over Local Activism," *Newsweek,* August 20, 2009, http://www.newsweek.com/id/212934 (accessed April 29, 2010).
57. http://bipac.net/bipac_public/initial.asp (accessed May 21, 2010); see also David B. Magleby, Anthony Corrado, and Kelly D. Patterson, *Financing the 2004 Election* (Brookings Institute Press, 2006); and David B. Magleby, J. Quin Monson, and Kelly Patterson, *Electing Congress: New Rules for an Old Game* (Pearson Prentice Hall, 2007).
58. Andrew Chadwick, "Digital Network Repertoires and Organizational Hybridity," *Political Communication,* 24 (July–September 2007), p. 284.
59. R. Kenneth Godwin, *One Billion Dollars of Influence: The Direct Marketing of Politics* (Chatham House, 1988).
60. David B. Magleby, J. Quin Monson, and Kelly Patterson, *Electing Congress: New Rules for an Old Game* (Prentice Hall, 2006); see also David B. Magleby, J. Quin Monson, and Kelly D. Patterson, *Dancing Without Partners: How Candidates, Parties, and Interest Groups Interact in the Presidential Campaign* (Rowman & Littlefield, 2007); and David B. Magleby and Kelly D. Patterson, eds., *The Battle for Congress: Iraq, Scandal, and Campaign Finance in the 2006 Election* (Paradigm, 2008).
61. The *Federal Register* is published every weekday. You can find it at the library or on the Internet at www.gpoaccess.gov.
62. Lucius J. Barker, "Third Parties in Litigation: A Systemic View of the Judicial Function," *Journal of Politics,* 29 (February 1967), pp. 41–69; and Jethro K. Lieberman, *Litigious Society,* rev. ed. (Basic Books, 1983).
63. Gregory A. Caldeira and John R. Wright, "Organized Interests and Agenda Setting in the U.S. Supreme Court," *American Political Science Review,* 82 (December 1988), pp. 1109–1127; see also Gregory A. Caldeira and John R. Wright, "*Amici Curiae* Before the Supreme Court: Who Participates, When, and How Much?" *Journal of Politics,* 52 (August 1990), pp. 782–806.
64 Lee Epstein and C. K. Rowland, "Debunking the Myth of Interest Group Invincibility in the Courts," *American Political Science Review,* 85 (March 1991), pp. 205–217.
65. Robert D. McFadden, "Across the U.S., Protests for Immigrants Draw Thousands," *New York Times* (April 10, 2006), p. A14; and Anna Gorman and J. Michael Kennedy, "The Immigration Debate," *Los Angeles Times* (April 11, 2006), p. A11.
66. Judy Keen and Martin Kasindorf, "From Coast to Coast, 'We Need to Be Heard,' " *USA Today* (May 2, 2006), p. 3A.
67. See Kenneth Klee, "The Siege of Seattle," *Newsweek* (December 13, 1999), p. 30.
68. League of Conservation Voters, "Key Races of the 2004 Congressional Election Cycle," www.lcv.org/campaigns/2004-congressional/ (accessed May 21, 2010).
69. Hugh Heclo, "Issue Networks and the Executive Establishment," in Anthony King, ed., *The New American Political System* (American Enterprise Institute, 1978).
70. For evidence of the impact of PAC expenditures on legislative committee behavior and legislative involvement generally, see Richard L. Hall and Frank W. Wayman, "Buying Time: Moneyed Interests and the

Mobilization of Bias in Congressional Committees," *American Political Science Review,* 84 (September 1990), pp. 797–820.
71. Federal Election Commission, "Number of Federal PACs Increases," Press Release, March 9, 2009, http://www.fec.gov/press/press2009/20090309PACcount.shtml (accessed May 21, 2010).
72. Ibid.
73. Open Secrets, "Business Associations," July 13, 2009, http://www.opensecrets.org/pacs/industry.php?txt=N00&cycle=2008 (accessed March 17, 2010).
74. Amy Keller, "Leadership PACs 'Not Sinister,' FEC Told," *Roll Call* (February 27, 2003).
75. Open Secrets, opensecrets.org/pacs/lookup2 .asp?strid=C00344234&cycle=2008 (accessed May 21, 2010).
76. Paul Krugman, "Toward One-Party Rule," *New York Times* (June 27, 2003), p. A27.
77. For evidence of the impact of PAC expenditures on legislative committee behavior and legislative involvement generally, see Richard L. Hall and Frank W. Wayman, "Buying Time: Moneyed Interests and the Mobilization of Bias in Congressional Committees," *American Political Science Review,* 84 (September 1990), pp. 797–820.
78. Federal Election Commission, "Number of Federal PACs Increases," Press Release, March 9, 2009, http://www.fec.gov/press/press2009/ 20090309PACcount.shtml (accessed May 21, 2010).
79. Internal Revenue Code, Title 26, frwebgate.access.gpo.gov/cgi-bin/getdoc.cgi?dbname=browse_usc&docid=Cite:+26USC501 (accessed May 21, 2010).
80. Nicholas Confessore, "Bush's Secret Stash," *Washington Monthly,* 36 (May 2004), pp. 17–23.
81. Center for Responsive Politics, "527 Committees: Top 50 Federally Focused Organizations," http://www.opensecrets.org/527s/527cmtes.php:level=c&evele=1008 (accessed November 8, 2008).
82. David B. Magleby, "How the 2008 Elections Were Financed," in David B. Magleby, ed. *The Change Election: Money, Mobilization, and Persuasion in the 2008 Federal Elections,* pp. 41–45.
83. David B. Magleby, "How the 2008 Elections Were Financed," pp. 41–45.
84. David B. Magleby, "How the 2008 Elections Were Financed," p. 41.
85. E. J. Dionne, Jr., "Fear of McCain-Feingold," *Washington Post* (December 3, 2002), p. A25.
86. The Campaign Legal Center, "Interveners Urge Supreme Court to Sustain BCRA in Its Entirety," www.campaignlegalcenter.org/ press-814.html (accessed May 21, 2010).

Chapter 5

1. Priscilla L. Southwell and Justin Burchett, "Survey of Vote-by-Mail Senate Election in the State of Oregon," *PS: Political Science & Politics* 30 (1997), p. 53.
2. David B. Magleby, "Participation in Mail Ballot Elections," *Political Research Quarterly* 40 (1987), p. 81.
3. Paul Gronke, Eva Galanes-Rosenbaum, and Peter A. Miller, "Early Voting and Turnout," *PS: Political Science & Politics* 40 (2007), pp. 639–645.
4. http://elections.gmu.edu/Early_Voting_2008_Final.html.
5. Robert Coles, *The Political Life of Children* (Atlantic Monthly Press, 2000), pp. 24–25; see also Stephen M. Caliendo, *Teachers Matter: The Trouble with Leaving Political Education to the Coaches* (Greenwood Press, 2000).
6. James Garbarino, *Raising Children in a Socially Toxic Environment* (Jossey-Bass, 1995).
7. Gabriel A. Almond and Sidney Verba, eds. *The Civic Culture Revisited* (Little Brown, 1980), p. 13.
8. J. L. Glanville, "Political Socialization or Selection? Adolescent Extracurricular Participation and Political Activity in Early Adulthood," *Social Science Quarterly* 80 (1999), p. 279.
9. National Association of Secretaries of State, *New Millennium Project, Part I: American Youth Attitudes on Policies, Citizenship, Government, and Voting* (Author, 1999); and "Political Interest on the Rebound Among the Nation's Freshmen," Higher Education Research Institute, Fall 2003, www.gseis.ucla.edu/heri/03_press_release.pdf.
10. B. Bradford Brown, Sue Ann Eicher, and Sandra Petrie, "The Importance of Peer Group ("Crowd") Affiliation in Adolescence," *Journal of Adolescence* 9 (March 1986), pp. 73–96.
11. Kenneth Feldman and Theodore M. Newcomb, *The Impact of College on Students,* Vol. 2 (Jossey-Bass, 1969), pp. 16–24, 49–56; see also David O. Sears and Nicholas A. Valentino, "Politics Matters: Political Events as Catalysts for Preadult Socialization," *American Political Science Review* 91 (March 1997), pp. 45–65.
12. Daniel B. German, "The Role of the Media in Political Socialization and Attitude Formation Toward Racial/Ethnic Minorities in the U.S.," in Robert F. Farnen, ed., *Nationalism, Ethnicity, and Identity: Cross National and Comparative Perspective* (Transaction, 2004), p. 287.
13. James G. Gimpel, J. Celeste Lay, and Jason E. Schuknecht, *Cultivating Democracy: Civic Environments and Political Socialization in America* (Brookings Institution Press, 2003), p. 127 (see Chaper 5).
14. For a general discussion of political knowledge, see Michael Delli Carpini and Scott Keeter, *What Americans Know About Politics and Why It Matters* (Yale University Press, 1996).
15. *The 2000 National Election Study,* Center for Political Studies, University of Michigan; see also the NES Guide to Public Opinion and Electoral Behavior, www.umich.edu/nes/nesguide/nesguide.htm.
16. Erikson and Tedin, *American Public Opinion,* p. 304.
17. *The 2004 National Election Study* (Center for Political Studies, University of Michigan, 2004).
18. Michael Luo, "Huckabee Lays Out His Claim as an 'Authentic Conservative,'" *New York Times* (November 27, 2007), http:// www.nytimes.com/2007/11/27/us/politics/27adbox.html?_r=1&scp=1&sq=Huckabee%20Lays%20Out%20His%20Claim%20as%20&st=cse (accessed April 13, 2010).
19. Jonathan Rauch, "The Accidental Radical," *National Journal* (July 26, 2003), pp. 2404–2410.
20. Kathleen Day, *S&L Hell: The People and the Politics Behind the $1 Trillion Savings and Loan Scandal* (Norton, 1993).
21. Jon Hilsenrath, Serena Ng, and Damian Paletta, "Worst Crisis Since '30's, With No End Yet in Sight," http://online.wsj.com/article/SB122169431617549947.html (accessed May 20, 2010).
22. Sylvia Nasar, "Even Among the Well-Off, the Rich Get Richer," *New York Times* (March 5, 1992), p. A1.
23. Irving Howe, *Socialism and America* (Harcourt, 1985); and Michael Harrington, *Socialism: Past and Future* (Arcade, 1989).
24. Daniel Yergin and Joseph Stanislaw, *The Commanding Heights: The Battle Between Government and the Marketplace That Is Remaking the Modern World* (Simon & Schuster, 1998).
25. *American National Election Study: 1990,* Center for Political Studies, University of Michigan; and *Post-Election Survey,* April 1991.
26. Earl Black and Merle Black, *The Rise of Southern Republicans* (Belknap Press, 2002).
27. http://www.gallup.com/poll/111664/Gallup-Daily-Obama-Continues-Outpace-McCain.aspx (accessed November 7, 2008. Note: We removed the "no opinion" and percentaged the other categories to sum to 100 percent.
28. Thomas D. Snyder, Sally A. Dillow, and Charlene M. Hoffman, "Number of Persons Age 18 and Over, by Highest Level of Education Attained, Age, Sex, and Race/Ethnicity: 2005," *Digest of Education Statistics 2007* (U.S. Government Printing Office, 2008), p. 24.
29. Peverill Squire, "Why the 1936 *Literary Digest* Poll Failed," *Public Opinion Quarterly* 52 (Spring 1988), pp. 125–133.
30. Ibid., p. 128.
31. Nicole B. Ellison, Charles Steinfield, and Cliff Lampe, "The Benefits of Facebook 'Friends': Social Capital and College Students' Use of Online Social Network Sites," *Journal of Computer-Mediated Communication* 12 (2007), Art. 1.

32. Data from the American National Election Studies, Center for Political Studies, University of Michigan, 1948-2004, www.electionstudies.org/studypages/download/datacenter_all.htm.
33. *The 2008 National Election Study.*
34. Julie Bosman, "More Hiring and Advertising Ahead for Paul as the Donations Pour In," *New York Times,* December 18, 2007.
35. Frank R. Parker, *Black Votes Count: Political Empowerment in Mississippi After 1965* (University of North Carolina Press, 1990), p. 3.
36. Bernard Grofman and Lisa Handley, "The Impact of the Voting Rights Act on Black Representation in Southern State Legislatures," *Legislative Studies Quarterly* 16 (February 1991), pp. 111–128.
37. International Institute for Democracy and Electoral Assistance, "Voter Turnout from 1945 to Date: A Global Report on Political Participation," www.idea.int/voter_turnout/index.html.
38. Ibid., p. 24.
39. Raymond E. Wolfinger and Steven J. Rosenstone, *Who Votes?* (Yale University Press, 1980), pp. 78, 88.
40. Federal Election Commission, "The Impact of the National Voter Registration Act on Federal Elections 1999–2000," www.fec.gov.
41. See Raymond E. Wolfinger and Ben Highton, "Estimating the Effects of the National Voter Registration Act of 1993," *Political Behavior* (June 1998), pp. 79–104; and Raymond E. Wolfinger and Jonathan Hoffman, "Registering and Voting with Motor Voter," *PS: Political Science & Politics* (March 2001), pp. 85–92.
42. Quin Monson and Lindsay Nielson, "Mobilizing the Early Voter," paper presented at the annual meeting of the Midwest Political Science Association, Chicago, Ill., April 3–6, 2008; and Michael P. McDonald and Thomas Schaller, "Voter Mobilization in the 2008 Presidential Election," in David B. Magleby, ed., *The Change Election: Money, Mobilization, and Persuasion in the 2008 Federal Elections* (Temple University Press, 2011).
43. U.S. Census Bureau, "Voting and Registration in the Election of November 2004," www.census.gov/prod/2006pubs/p20–556.pdf.
44. The Early Voting Information Center, "Absence and Early Voting Laws," www.earlyvoting.net/states/abs/aws.php (accessed October 14, 2008).
45. For a discussion of the differences in the turnout between presidential and midterm elections, see James E. Campbell, "The Presidential Surge and Its Midterm Decline in Congressional Elections, 1868-1988," *Journal of Politics* 53 (May 1991), pp. 477–487.
46. David E. Rosenbaum, "Democrats Keep Solid Hold on Congress," *New York Times,* November 9, 1988, p. A24; Louis V. Gerstner, "Next Time, Let Us Boldly Vote as No Democracy Has Before," *USA Today,* November 16, 1998, p. A15; and Michael P. McDonald and Thomas Schaller, "Voter Mobilization in the 2008 Presidential Election," in David B. Magleby, ed., *The Change Election: Money, Mobilization, and Persuasion in the 2008 Federal Elections* (Temple University Press, 2011), p. 89.
47. North Carolina State Board of Elections, "Fact Sheet: Running for President of the United States of America," http://www.sboe.stak.nc.us/GetDocument.aspx?id=308.
48. Commission on Presidential Debates, www.debates.org/pages/news_040617_p.html.
47. Data from Curtis Gans, "President Bush, Mobilization Drives Propel Turnout to Post-1968 High; Kerry, Democratic Weakness Shown," *Center for Voting and Democracy,* November 4, 2004, www.fairvote.org/reports/csae2004electionreport.pdf.
48. Wolfinger and Rosenstone, *Who Votes?,* p. 102.
49. For a discussion of mobilization efforts and race, see Jan Leighley, *Strength in Numbers? The Political Mobilization of Racial and Ethnic Minorities* (Princeton University Press, 2001).
50. http://www.cnn.com/ELECTION/2008/results/ polls (accessed November 6, 2008).
51. David B. Magleby, "Elections as Team Sports: Spending by Candidates, Political Parties, and Interest Groups in the 2008 Election Cycle," in David B. Magleby, ed., The Change Election: Money, Mobilization, and Persuasion in the 2008 Federal Elections, p. 9.
51. U.S. Census Bureau, "Reported Voting and Registration by Race, Hispanic Origin, Sex, and Age Groups: November 1964 to 2008," *Voting and Registration,* July 2009, http://www.census.gov/hhes/www/socdemo/voting/publications/historical/index.html (accessed April 29, 2010).
52. Howard W. Stanley and Richard G. Niemi, *Vital Statistics on Politics, 1999–2000* (CQ Press, 2000), pp. 120–121; and Harold W. Stanley and Richard G. Niemi, *Vital Statistics on Politics, 2005–2006* (CQ Press, 2006), pp. 124–125.
53. http://www.cnn.com/ELECTIONS/2008/results/ polls (accessed November 6, 2008).
54. http://www.time.com/time/politics/article/ 0,8599,1708570,00.html (accessed April 16, 2010); and Heather Smith, Rock the Vote Executive Director, interview with David B. Magleby (March 25, 2009).
55. The Center for Information & Research on Civic Learning and Engagement, "Turnout by Education, Race, and Gender and Other 2008 Youth Voting Statistics," November 2008, http://www.civicyouth.org/?p=324 (accessed April 21, 2010).
56. David B. Magleby, ed., *The Change Election: Money, Mobilization, and Persuasion in the 2008 Federal Elections* (Temple University Press, 2011).
57. David B. Magleby, Candice J. Nelson, and Mark C. Westlye, "The Myth of the Independent Voter Revisited" Working Paper 10-01, Center for the Study of Elections and Democracy, Brigham Young University, January 2010. http://csed.byu.edu/Assets/Magleby%20Nelson%20Westlye%202010.pdf].
58. Ibid.
59. http://www.whitehouse.gov/history/presidents/ (accessed November 8, 2008).
60. David Menefee-Libey, *The Triumph of Campaign-Centered Politics* (Chatham House/Seven Bridges Press, 2000).
61. J. Merrill Shanks and Warren E. Miller, "Policy Direction and Performance Evaluation: Complementary Explanations of the Reagan Elections," *British Journal of Political Science* 20 (1990), pp. 143–235; and Warren E. Miller and J. Merrill Shanks, "Policy Direction and Performance Evaluation: Comparing George Bush's Victory with Those of Ronald Reagan in 1980–1984," paper presented at the annual meeting of the American Political Science Association, Atlanta, Ga., August 31–September 2, 1989.
62. Amihai Glazer, "The Strategy of Candidate Ambiguity," *American Political Science Review* 84 (March 1990), pp. 237–241.
63. Robert S. Erikson and David W. Romero, "Candidate Equilibrium and the Behavioral Model of the Vote," *American Political Science Review* 84 (December 1990), p. 1122.
64. Morris P. Fiorina, *Retrospective Voting in American National Elections* (Yale University Press, 1981).
65. Gerald H. Kramer, "Short-Term Fluctuations in U.S. Voting Behavior, 1896–1964," *American Political Science Review* 65 (March 1971), pp. 131–143; see also Edward R. Tufte, "Determinants of the Outcomes of Midterm Congressional Elections," *American Political Science Review* (September 1975), pp. 812–826; and Andrew E. Busch, *Horses in Midstream: U.S. Midterm Elections and Their Consequences* (University of Pittsburgh Press, 1999).
66. John R. Hibbing and John R. Alford, "The Educational Impact of Economic Conditions: Who Is Held Responsible?" *American Journal of Political Science* 25 (August 1981), pp. 423–439; and Morris P. Fiorina, "Who Is Held Responsible? Further Evidence on the Hibbing-Alford Thesis," *American Journal of Political Science* (February 1983), pp. 158-164.
67. David B. Magleby, "Electoral Politics as Team Sport: Advantage to the Democrats," in John C. Green and Daniel J. Coffey, eds., *The State of the Parties: The Changing Role of*

Contemporary American Parties (Rowman & Littlefield, 2011).

Chapter 6

1. David B. Magleby, "Adaptation and Innovation in the Financing of the 2008 Elections," in David B. Magleby and Anthony Corrado, eds., *Financing the 2008 Election* (Brookings Institution Press, 2010), Table 1–3.
2. Anthony Corrado, "Fund-raising Strategies in the 2008 Presidential Campaign," in James Thurber and Candice J. Nelson, eds., *Campaigns and Elections American Style* (Boulder, CO: Westview Press, 2009), p. 114.
3. U.S. Census Bureau, "Number of Elected Officials Exceeds Half Million—Almost All Are with Local Governments," press release, January 30, 1995.
4. U.S. Senate, www.senate.gov/general/contact_information/senators_cfm.cfm.
5. Associated Press, "Voters Retain State Term Limits," November 4, 2008, http://www.kxmb.com/News/293253.asp (accessed November 6, 2008).
6. *U.S. Term Limits Inc.* v. *Thornton*, 514 U.S. 799 (1995).
7. For an insightful examination of electoral rules, see Bernard Grofman and Arend Lijphart, eds., *Electoral Laws and Their Political Consequences* (Agathon Press, 1986).
8. New York State Board of Elections, "2009 Election Results: 23rd Congressional District," December 15, 2009, http://www.elections.state.ny.us/NYSBOE/Elections/2009/Special/23rdCDSpecial VoteResults.pdf (accessed May 19, 2010).
9. Arend Lijphart, "The Political Consequences of Electoral Laws, 1945–85," *American Political Science Review* 84 (June 1990), pp. 481–495; see also David M. Farrell, *Electoral Systems: A Comparative Introduction* (Macmillan, 2001).
10. There was one faithless elector in 2000 from the District of Columbia who abstained rather than cast her vote for Al Gore in order to protest the lack of congressional representation for Washington, D.C. See www.cnn.com/2001/ALLPOLITICS/stories/01/06/electoral.vote/index.html. The electoral college vote in 2004 had one faithless elector, an elector from Minnesota who voted for John Edwards instead of John Kerry.
11. As noted, one of Gore's electors abstained, reducing his vote from 267 to 266; www.cnn.com/2001/ALLPOLITICS/stories/01/06/electoral.vote/index.html.
12. Paul D. Schumaker and Burdett A. Loomis, *Choosing a President: The Electoral College and Beyond* (Seven Bridges Press, 2002), p. 60; see also George Rabinowitz and Stuart Elaine MacDonald, "The Power of the States in U.S. Presidential Elections," *American Political Science Review* 80 (March 1986), pp. 65–87; and Dany M. Adkison and Christopher Elliott, "The Electoral College: A Misunderstood Institution," *PS: Political Science and Politics* 30 (March 1997), pp. 77–80.
13. See, for example, David R. Mayhew, *Congress: The Electoral Connection* (Yale University Press, 1974); Richard F. Fenno, Jr., *Home Style: House Members in Their Districts* (Little, Brown, 1978); and James E. Campbell, "The Return of Incumbents: The Nature of Incumbency Advantage," *Western Political Quarterly* 36 (September 1983), pp. 434–444.
14. Gary King and Andrew Gelman, "Systemic Consequences of Incumbency Advantage in U.S. House Elections," *American Journal of Political Science* 35 (February 1991), pp. 110–137.
15. Alan I. Abramowitz, "Economic Conditions, Presidential Popularity, and Voting Behavior in Midterm Congressional Elections," *Journal of Politics* 47 (February 1985), pp. 31–43; see also Gary C. Jacobson, *The Politics of Congressional Elections*, 5th ed. (Addison-Wesley, 2001), pp. 146–153.
16. See Edward R. Tufte, *Political Control of the Economy* (Princeton University Press, 1978); see also his "Determinants of the Outcomes of Midterm Congressional Elections," *American Political Science Review* 69 (September 1975), pp. 812–826. For a more recent discussion of the same subject, see Jacobson, *Politics of Congressional Elections*, pp. 123–178.
17. Alan I. Abramowitz and Jeffrey A. Segal, "Determinants of the Outcomes of U.S. Senate Elections," *Journal of Politics* 48 (1986), pp. 433–439.
18. David B. Magleby and Kelly D. Patterson, eds., *The Battle for Congress: Iraq, Scandal, and Campaign Finance in the 2006 Election* (Paradigm, 2008).
19. Rhodes Cook, "Congress and Primaries: Looking for Clues to a Tidal Wave," *The Wall Street Journal*, July 24, 2008, http://blogs.wsj .com/political perceptions/2008/07/24/Congressional-Primaries-looking-for-clues-to-tidal-wave/.
20. Linda L. Fowler and Robert D. McClure, *Political Ambition: Who Decides to Run for Congress* (Yale University Press, 1989); and Paul S. Herrnson, *Congressional Elections: Campaigning at Home and in Washington*, 5th ed. (CQ Press, 2007), p. 45.
21. Kathleen Hall Jamieson, *Everything You Think You Know About Politics... and Why You're Wrong* (Basic Books, 2000), p. 38.
22. For a discussion of different explanations of the impact of incumbency, see Keith Krehbiel and John R. Wright, "The Incumbency Effect in Congressional Elections: A Test of Two Explanations," *American Journal of Political Science* 27 (February 1983), p. 140.
23. Harold W. Stanley and Richard G. Niemi, *Vital Statistics on American Politics 2009–2010* (CQ Press, 2010), pp. 45–47.
24. "Financial Activity of Senate and House General Election Campaigns," Federal Election Commission, http://www.fec.gov/press/press2009/2009Dec29Cong/4gen08.pdf.
25. Candice J. Nelson, "Spending in the 2000 Elections," in David B. Magleby, ed., *Financing the 2000 Election* (Brookings Institution Press, 2002), pp. 28–30.
26. Jonathan S. Krasno, *Challengers, Competition, and Reelection: Comparing Senate and House Elections* (Yale University Press, 1994), p. 2.
27. Alan I. Abramowitz, "Explaining Senate Election Outcomes," *American Political Science Review* 82 (June 1988), pp. 385–403.
28. Scott Shepard, "Politicians Already Looking to 2008 Election," *Austin (Texas) American-Statesman*, February 6, 2005; and Associated Press, "Former Bush Aide: 2008 Democratic Nomination Belongs to Hillary," April 30, 2005.
29. Susan Saulny, "Thompson Enters Race from 'Tonight Show' Couch," *New York Times*, September 6, 2007, p. A23.
30. Arthur Hadley, *Invisible Primary* (Prentice Hall, 1976).
31. "State by State Summary 2004 Presidential Primaries, Caucuses, and Conventions," www.thegreenpapers .com/P04/tally.phtml.
32. The descriptions of these types of primaries are drawn from James W. Davis, *Presidential Primaries*, rev. ed. (Greenwood Press, 1984), Chapter 3. See pp. 56–63 for specifics on each state (and Puerto Rico). This material is used with the permission of the publisher.
33. Paul T. David and James W. Caesar, *Proportional Representation in Presidential Nominating Politics* (University Press of Virginia, 1980), pp. 9–11.
34. Nelson W. Polsby and Aaron Wildavsky, *Presidential Elections: Strategies and Structures of American Politics*, 11th ed. (Rowman & Littlefield, 2004), p. 110.
35. The Green Papers, *The Green Papers, 2004 Presidential Primaries, Caucuses, and Conventions: New York Republican*, www.thegreenpapers.com/P04/NY-R.phtml.
36. Costas Panagopoulos, "Election Issues 2004 in Depth," *Campaigns & Elections* (May 2004), p. 48.
37. Lesley Clark, "DNC Votes to Strip Florida of Delegates: Florida's Status as a Key Presidential Prize Is in Doubt, with National Democratic Party Leaders Rejecting a State Plan to Hold an Early Primary," *Miami Herald*, August 26, 2007; see also "Campaign Briefing: On the Trail," *Newsday*, December 2, 2007, p. A3.
38. Jill Zuckman, "McCain Wins Nomination: Huckabee Steps Aside as Ex-Rival Targets Democrats," *Chicago Tribune*, March 5, 2008.
39. Federal Election Commission, "2004 Presidential Primary Dates and

Candidates Filing Deadlines for Ballot Access," May 26, 2004, www.fec.gov.

40. *California Democratic Party et al., Petitioners* v. *Bill Jones, Secretary of State of California et al.*, 530 U.S. 567 (2000).
41. "Stunner in N.H.: Clinton Defeats Obama," January 9, 2008, www.msnbc.msn.com/id/22551718/.
42. The viewership of conventions has declined as the amount of time devoted to conventions dropped. In 1988, Democrats averaged 27.1 million viewers and Republicans 24.5 million. By 1996, viewership for the Democrats was 18 million viewers on average; for the Republicans, it was 16.6 million. See John Carmody, "The TV Column," *The Washington Post*, September 2, 1996, p. D4. Viewership figures improved somewhat in 2000: Democrats averaged 20.6 million viewers and Republicans 19.2 million. See Don Aucoin, "Democrats Hold TV Ratings Edge," *The Boston Globe*, August 19, 2000, p. F3; and Jim Rutenberg and Brain Stelter, "Conventions, Anything but Dull, Are a TV Hit," *New York Times*, September 6, 2008.
43. Jeff Fishel, *Presidents and Promises* (CQ Press, 1984), pp. 26–28.
44. Joe Von Kanel and Hal Quinley, "Exit Polls: Obama Wins Big Among Young, Minority Voters," *CNN Politics.com*, November 4, 2008, http://www.cnn.com/2008/POLITICS/11/04/exit.polls/ (accessed April 28, 2010).
45. Sam Reed, "Washington State's February 19, 2008 Presidential Primary," www.secstate.wa.gov/elections/pdf/2008PP/PP%20MFQ%20Updated%20August%202007%20Final.pdf.
46. Richard Wagner, "Ballot Access News," www.ballot-access.org/2008/020108.html.
47. North Carolina State Board of Elections, "Fact Sheet: Running for President of the United States of America," http://www.sboe.stak.nc.us/GetDocument.aspx?id=308.
48. Commission on Presidential Debates, www.debates.org/pages/news_040617_p.html.
49. University of Wisconsin–Madison and the Brennan Center for Justice at NYU School of Law, "Political Advertising Nearly Tripled in 2000 with Half-a-Million More TV Ads," press release, March 14, 2001; David B. Magleby, "Elections as Team Sports: Spending by Candidates, Political Parties, and Interest Groups in the 2008 Election Cycle," in David B. Magleby, ed., *The Change Election: Money, Mobilization, and Persuasion in the 2008 Federal Elections* (Temple University Press, 2011).
50. Robert S. Erikson, "Economic Conditions and the Presidential Vote," *American Political Science Review* 83 (June 1989), pp. 567–575. Class-based voting has also become more important. See Robert S. Erikson, Thomas O. Lancaster, and David W. Romers, "Group Components of the Presidential Vote, 1952–1984," *Journal of Politics* 51 (May 1989), pp. 337–346.
51. David B. Magleby, "Elections as Team Sports: Spending by Candidates, Political Parties, and Interest Groups in the 2008 Election Cycle," in David B. Magleby, ed., *The Change Election: Money, Mobilization, and Persuasion in the 2008 Federal Elections*, p. 9.
52. Fortier and Ornstein, "The Absentee Ballot and the Secret Ballot."
53. Lewis L. Gould, *Grand Old Party: A History of the Republicans* (Random House, 2003), p. 236.
54. David B. Magleby and Candice J. Nelson, *The Money Chase: Congressional Campaign Finance Reform* (Brookings Institution Press, 1990), pp. 13–14.
55. http://www.opensecrets.org/pres08/summary.php?cycle=2008&cid=N00009638 (accessed November 6, 2008).
56. Anthony Corrado, Thomas E. Mann, Daniel R. Ortiz, and Trevor Potter, eds., *The New Campaign Finance Sourcebook* (Brookings Institution Press, 2005).
57. *Davis* v. *FEC*. 128 S.Ct. 2759. (2008).
58. Gould, *Grand Old Party*, pp. 389–391; and Jules Witcover, *Party of the People: A History of the Democrats* (Random House, 2003), pp. 589–590.
59. Anthony Corrado, "Money and Politics: A History of Campaign Finance Law," in *Campaign Finance Reform: A Sourcebook* (Brookings Institution Press, 1997), p. 32.
60. See Senate Committee on Governmental Affairs, "1997 Special Investigation in Connection with the 1996 Federal Election Campaigns," http://hsgac.senate.gov/sireport.htm.
61. *Buckley* v. *Valeo*, 424 U.S. 1 (1976).
62. David B. Magleby and Eric A. Smith, "Party Soft Money in the 2000 Congressional Elections," in David B. Magleby, ed., *The Other Campaign: Soft Money and Issue Advocacy in the 2000 Congressional Elections*, p. 29, 38; and David B. Magleby and Nicole Carlisle Squires, "Party Money in the 2002 Congressional Elections," in David B. Magleby and J. Quin Monson, eds., *The Last Hurrah? Soft Money and Issue Advocacy in the 2002 Congressional Elections* (Brookings Institution Press, 2004), pp. 44–5, Figure 2–2. http://hsgac.senate.gov/sireport.htm.
63. David B. Magleby and Nicole Carlisle Squires, "Party Money in the 2002 Congressional Elections," in *The Last Hurrah?* p. 45, Figure 2–2.
64. *McConnell* v. *Federal Election Commission*, 540 U.S. 93 (2003).
65. Corrado, Mann, Ortiz, and Potter, *The New Campaign Finance Sourcebook*, p. 79.
66. David B. Magleby, ed., *The Last Hurrah* (Brookings Institution Press, 2004), pp. 44–45.
67. *McConnell* v. *Federal Election Commission*.
68. *Federal Election Commission* v. *Wisconsin Right to Life, Inc.*, 551 U.S. 449 (2007).
69. See Joseph A. Pika, "Campaign Spending and Activity in the 2000 Delaware U.S. Senate Race," in David B. Magleby, ed., *Election Advocacy: Soft Money and Issue Advocacy in the 2000 Congressional Elections* (Center for the Study of Elections and Democracy, Brigham Young University, 2001), pp. 51–61.
70. Kate Snow, "Obama Could Get 'Swift Boated,'" *ABC News*, April 19, 2008, abcnews.go.com/Politics/story?id=4688386.
71. David B. Magleby, "Change and Continuity in the Financing of Federal Elections," in David B. Magleby, Anthony J. Corrado, and Kelly D. Patterson, eds., *Financing the 2004 Elections* (Brookings Institution Press, 2006), p. 15.
72 Corrado, Mann, Ortiz, and Potter, *The New Campaign Finance Sourcebook*, pp. 74–76.
73. *Colorado Republican Federal Campaign Committee* v. *Federal Election Commission*, 518 U.S. 604 (1996).
74. BCRA does allow candidates to pay themselves out of their campaign funds, something that helps less-affluent candidates run. But given the high cost of campaigns, such a strategy is often not going to be helpful to winning the election.
75. Federal Election Commission, "2000–2001 Financial Activity of Senate and House General Election Campaigns," www.fec.gov; and Federal Election Commission, "1999-2000 Financial Activity of Senate and House General Election Campaigns," www.fec.gov.
76. New Jersey Election Law Enforcement Commission, "Candidate Disclosure Report," http://www.elec.state.nj.us/ELECReport/StandardSearch.aspx.
77. Jose Antonia Vargas, "Campaign.USA: With the Internet Comes a New Political 'Clickocracy,'" *The Washington Post*, April 1, 2008, p. C01.
78. William Rivers, *The Other Government* (Universe Books, 1982); Douglas Cater, *The Fourth Branch of Government* (Houghton Mifflin, 1959); Dom Bonafede, "The Washington Press: An Interpreter or a Participant in Policy Making?" *National Journal*, April 24, 1982, pp. 716–721; and Michael Ledeen, "Learning to Say 'No' to the Press," *Public Interest* 73 (Fall 1983), p. 113.
79. Leslie G. Moeller, "The Big Four: Mass Media Actualities and Expectations," in Richard W. Budd and Brent D. Ruben, eds., *Beyond Media: New Approaches to Mass Communication* (Transaction Books, 1988), p. 15.
80. See Doris A. Graber, "Say It with Pictures: The Impact of Audiovisual News on Public Opinion Formation," paper presented at the annual meeting of the Midwest Political Science Association, April 1987, Chicago; and Benjamin I. Page, Robert Y. Shapiro, and Glenn R. Dempsey, "What Moves Public Opinion?" *American Political Science Review* 76 (March 1987), pp. 23–43.
81. U.S. Census Bureau, *Statistical Abstract of the United States: 2010* (U.S. Government Printing Office, 2010), pp. 693–694.
82. Jeffrey W. Koch, "Campaign Ads' Impact on Voter Certainty and Knowledge of Candidates' Ideological Positions," 2003,

American Political Science Association, http://www.allacademic.com// meta/p_mla_apa_research_citation/ 0/6/2/4/8/pages62486/p62486-1.php (accessed March 30, 2010).

83. Journalism.org, "Local TV," March 15, 2004, http://www.stateofthemedia.org/ 2004/narrative_localtv_contentanalysis.asp?cat=2&media=6 (accessed May 26, 2010); see also, Marc Fisher, "TV Stations Offer a Clear Picture of Indifference," *The Washington Post,* September 26, 2000, p. B1.
84. *Statistical Abstract of the United States: 2010,* p. 694.
85. *Statistical Abstract of the United States: 2010,* p. 694.
86. Mediamark Research Inc., "Mediamark Research Inc. Releases MediaDay Study," press release, June 25, 2007, http://www .mediamark .com/PDF/Mediamark %20Research%20Inc%20Releases %20MediaDay%20Study.pdf, (accessed April 2, 2008).
87. Robert J. Duffy, Kyle L. Saunders, and Joshua Dunn, "Colorado: Democrats Expand Their Base and Win Unaffiliated Voters," in David B. Magleby, ed., *The Change Election: Money, Mobilization, and Persuasion in the 2008 Federal Elections* (Temple University Press, 2011).
88. National Public Radio, "Morning Edition: About the Program," *NPR,* 2010, http:// www.npr.org/templates/story/story.php? storyId=5003 (accessed April 23, 2010).
89. Paul Farhi, "Limbaugh's Audience Size? It's Largely Up in the Air," *The Washington Post,* March 7, 2009, http://www. washingtonpost.com/wp-dyn/content/ article/2009/03/06/AR2009030603435.html (accessed April 30, 2010).
90. *Statistical Abstract of the United States: 2010,* p. 696.
91. Newspaper Association of America, "Readership," http://www.naa.org/ TrendsandNumbers/Readership.aspx (accessed March 30, 2010).
92. Nat Ives, "Publishers: Why Count Only People Who Pay?" *Advertising Age,* November 12, 2007, p. 8.
93. National Public Radio, "Extra! Extra! We Still Want News," *On the Media* (transcript), March 28, 2008, at http://www .onthemedia.org/transcripts/2008/ 03/28/05, accessed April 3, 2008; and Noam Cohen, "Craig (of the List) Looks Beyond the Web," *New York Times,* May 12, 2008, C1.
94. *The Washington Times,* "Circulation Declines Are Getting Steeper," http://www.washingtontimes.com/news/ 2009/apr/28/circulation-declines-are-getting-steeper/ (accessed May 26, 2010).
95. Stephanie Clifford, "Newsweek on Block as Era of the Newsweekly Fades" *New York Times,* May 5, 2010, http://www .nytimes.com/2010/05/06/business/ media/06newsweek.htm (accessed May 14, 2010).
96. Arthur L. Norberg and Judy E. O'Neill, *Transforming Computer Technology: Information Processing for the Pentagon, 1962–1986* (Johns Hopkins University Press, 1996).
97. Boutell.com, "WWW FAQS: How Many Web Sites Are There?," http://www.boutell. com/newfaq/misc/sizeofweb.html (accessed May 26, 2010).
98. Domain Tools, "Domain Counts & Internet Statistics," http://www .domaintools.com/internet-statistics/ (accessed May 26, 2010).
99. Alex Mindlin, "Web Passes Papers as a News Source," *New York Times,* January 4, 2009, http://www.nytimes.com/ 2009/01/05/business/media/05drill.html (accessed March 30, 2010).
100. Pew Internet & American Life Project, *Teens and Technology,* July 27, 2005, www .pewinternet.org/pdfs/PIP_Teens_Tech_ July2005web.pdf (accessed May 12, 2006).
101. Amanda Lenhart, Sousan Arafeh, Aaron Smith, and Alexandra McGill, "Writing, Technology, and Teens," *Pew Internet & American Life Project,* April 2008, http://www.pewinternet.org/ Reports/2008/Writing-Technology-and-Teens/04-The-Lives-of-Teens-and-Their-Technology/ 05-Many-teens-go-online-daily.aspx?r=1 (accessed May 26, 2010); and Amanda Lenhart, "Teens and Social Media: An Overview," *Pew Internet & American Life Project,* April 10, 2009, http://isites.harvard.edu/fs/docs/icb.topic 603902.files/Teens%20Social%20Media%20and%20Health%20-%20NYPH%20Dept %20Pew% 20Internet.pdf (accessed May 26, 2010).
102 http://www.edisonreserach.com/twiter_ usage_2010.php (accessed June 10, 2010)
103. Time.com, "How Facebook Is Redefining Privacy," (accessed June 10, 2010).
104. http://blog.nielsen.com/nielsenwire/ global/ facebook-and-twitter-post-large-year-over-year-gains-in-unique-users/ and http://blog.nielsen.com/ nielsenwire/global/led-by-facebook-twitter-global-time-spent-on-social-media-sites-up-82-year-over-year/ (accessed June 10, 2010).
105. During the 1930s, members of Congress on one network alone made more than 1,000 speeches. See Edward W. Chester, *Radio, Television, and American Politics* (Sheed & Ward, 1969), p. 62.
106. CBS News, "Abuse of Iraqi POWs by GIs Probed: 60 Minutes II Has Exclusive Report on Alleged Mistreatment," April 28, 2004, http://www.cbsnews.com/ stories/2004/04/27/60II/main614063 .shtml (accessed April 23, 2008).
107. Dana Priest, "CIA Holds Terror Suspects in Secret Prisons," *The Washington Post,* November 2, 2005, p. A01.
108. Fred Emery, *Watergate: The Corruption of American Politics and the Fall of Richard Nixon* (Touchstone, 1995).
109. Bob Woodward and Carl Bernstein, *All the President's Men* (Simon & Schuster, 1994).
110. Martin Peers, "Murdoch Wins His Bid for Dow Jones," *The Wall Street Journal,* August 1, 2007, p. A1.
111. News Corporation, home page, http:// www.newscorp.com/index.html (accessed April 3, 2008).
112. Gannett Company, "Company Profile," www.gannett.com/about/company_profile.htm (accessed April 22, 2010); and "Gannett Company, Inc: Company Information," *New York Times,* http:// topics.nytimes.com/topics/news/ business/companies/gannett_company/ index.html (accessed April 22, 2010).
113. Neilsen Company, "2010 Media Industry Facts," http://blog.nielsen.com/ nielsenwire/press/nielsen-fact-sheet-2010.pdf (accessed May 26, 2010); and "FCC Issues 12th Annual Report to Congress on Video Competition," press release, February 10, 2006, hraunfoss.fcc.gov/edocs_public/ attachmatch/DOC-263763A1.pdf (accessed May 11, 2006).
114. Shanto Iyengar, Mark D. Peters, and Donald R. Kinder, "Experimental Demonstrations of the 'Not-So-Minimal' Consequences of Television News Programs," *American Political Science Review* 76 (December 1982), pp. 848–858.
115. Ibid.; Maxwell E. McCombs and Donald L. Shaw, "The Agenda-Setting Function of the Mass Media," *Public Opinion Quarterly* 36 (1972), pp. 176–187; Maxwell E. McCombs and Sheldon Gilbert, "News Influence on Our Pictures of the World," in Jennings Bryant and Dolf Gillman, eds., *Perspectives on Media Effects* (Erlbaum, 1986), pp. 1–15; and Iyengar and Kinder, *News That Matters.*
116. Quoted in Michael J. Robinson and Margaret A. Sheehan, *Over the Wire and on TV: CBS and UPI in Campaign '80* (Russell Sage Foundation, 1983), p. xiii.
117. David B. Magleby, *Direct Legislation: Voting on Ballot Propositions in the United States* (Johns Hopkins University Press, 1984).
118. Rush Limbaugh, *See, I Told You So* (Pocket Books, 1993), p. 326.
119. David Broder, "Beware of the 'Insider' Syndrome: Why Newsmakers and News Reporters Shouldn't Get Too Cozy," *The Washington Post,* December 4, 1988, p. A21; see also Broder, "Thin-Skinned Journalists," *The Washington Post,* January 11, 1989, p. A21.
120. Daniel p. Moynihan, "The Presidency and the Press," *Commentary* 51 (March 1971), p. 43.
121. Kate Phillips, "Mistress of Edwards Ends Silence on Affair," *New York Times,* March 15, 2010, http://www.nytimes.com/ 2010/03/16/us/politics/16edwards.html (accessed May 26, 2010).
122. David M. Herszenhorn, "Senator Says He Had Affair with an Aide," *New York Times,* June 16, 2009, p. A17.
123. See, for example, Jack Dennis, "Preadult Learning of Political Independence: Media and Family Communications Effects," *Communication Research* 13 (July 1987), pp. 401–433; and Olive

Stevens, *Children Talking Politics* (Robertson, 1982).

124. Elihu Katz and Paul Lazarsfeld, *Personal Influence: The Part Played by People in the Flow of Mass Communications* (Free Press, 1955).
125. See Angus Campbell, Philip E. Converse, Warren E. Miller, and Donald E. Stokes, *The American Voter* (Wiley, 1960).
126. Pew Research Center for the People & the Press, Survey Reports, "News Audiences Increasingly Politicized," June 8, 2004, http://people-press.org/reports/display.php3?ReportID=215 (accessed May 26, 2010).
127. Larry J. Sabato, "Gerald Ford's 'Free Poland' Gaffe—1976," *The Washington Post*, www.washingtonpost.com/wp-srv/politics/special/clinton/frenzy/ford.htm (accessed May 9, 2006).
128. Quoted in Sabato, *Rise of Political Consultants*, p. 144.
129. John R. Zaller, *The Nature and Origins of Mass Opinion* (Cambridge University Press, 1992).
130. Shanto Iyengar and Donald R. Kinder, *News that Matters: Television and American Opinion* (University of Chicago Press, 1987), p. 2.
131. Thomas E. Patterson, *The Mass Media Election: How Americans Choose Their President* (Praeger, 1980), Chapter 12.
132. John H. Aldrich, *Before the Convention* (University of Chicago Press, 1980), p. 65; see also Patterson, *Mass Media Election.*
133. Stephen Ansolabehere and Shanto Iyengar, *Going Negative: How Political Advertisements Shrink and Polarize the Electorate* (Free Press, 1995).
134. William Glaberson, "A New Press Role: Solving Problems," *New York Times*, October 3, 1994, p. D6.
135. Patterson, *Mass Media Election*, pp. 115–117.
136. Lewis Wolfson, *The Untapped Power of the Press* (Praeger, 1985), p. 79.
137. Lloyd Cutler, "Foreign Policy on Deadline," *Foreign Policy* 56 (Fall 1984), p. 114.
138. Michael B. Grossman and Martha Joynt Kumar, *Portraying the President* (Johns Hopkins University Press, 1981), pp. 255–263; and Fredric T. Smoller, *The Six o'Clock Presidency: A Theory of Presidential Press Relations in the Age of Television* (Praeger, 1990), pp. 31–49.
139. Stephen Hess, *Live from Capitol Hill!* (Brookings Institution, 1991), pp. 62–76; and Timothy E. Cook, *Making Laws and Making News* (Brookings Institution, 1989), pp. 81–86.
140. Susan Heilmann Miller, "News Coverage of Congress: The Search for the Ultimate Spokesperson," *Journalism Quarterly* 54 (Autumn 1977), pp. 459–465.
141. Richard Davis, "Whither the Congress and the Supreme Court? The Television News Portrayal of American National Government," *Television Quarterly* 22 (1987), pp. 55–63.

Chapter 7

1. Evan Bayh, "Why I'm Leaving the Senate," *New York Times*, February 25, 2010, p. D8.
2. Charles Warren, *The Making of the Constitution* (Little, Brown, 1928), p. 195.
3. *Bush* v. *Vera*, 517 U.S. 952 (1996).
4. See David B. Magleby, *Last Hurrah? Soft Money and Issue Advocacy in the 2002 Elections* (Brookings Institution Press, 2004).
5. See Citizens Against Government Waste at www.cagw.org for the latest information on earmarks.
6. R. P. Fairfield, *The Federalist Papers* (Doubleday, 1961), p. 160.
7. See Roger H. Davidson and Walter J. Oleszek, *Congress and Its Members*, 10th ed. (CQ Press, 2005).
8. For discussion of the modern Speakership, see Barbara Sinclair, "House Majority Party Leadership in an Era of Legislative Constraint," in Roger H. Davidson, ed., *The Postreform Congress* (St. Martin's Press, 1992), pp. 91–111; and Ronald M. Peters, Jr., ed., *The Speaker: Leadership in the U.S. House of Representatives* (CQ Press, 1995).
9. For an insightful set of essays on Senate leadership, see Richard A. Baker and Roger H. Davidson, eds., *First Among Equals: Outstanding Senate Leaders of the Twentieth Century* (CQ Press, 1991).
10. Sarah A. Binder and Steven S. Smith, *Politics or Principles? Filibustering in the United States Senate* (Brookings Institution Press, 1997).
11. Helen Dewar, "Senate Filibuster Ends with Talk of Next Stage in Fight," *Washington Post*, November 15, 2003, p. A9.
12. Joel D. Aberbach, *Keeping a Watchful Eye: The Politics of Congressional Oversight* (Brookings, 1991).
13. "Résumé of Congressional Activity, 105th Congress," *Congressional Record*, Daily Digest, January 19, 1999, p. D29.
14. Davidson and Oleszek, *Congress and Its Members*, p. 307.
15. Sarah A. Binder, Thomas E. Mann, and Molly Reynolds, *One Year Later: Is Congress Still the Broken Branch?* (Brookings Institution Press, 2008).
16. For a history of the early Congresses, see James Sterling Young, *The Washington Community, 1800–1828* (Columbia University Press, 1966).
17. Davidson and Oleszek, *Congress and Its Members*, p. 30.
18. Nelson Polsby, "The Institutionalization of the U.S. House of Representatives," *American Political Science Association* (March 1968), pp. 144–168.
19. Herbert Asher, "The Learning of Legislative Norms," *American Political Science Review* 67 (June 1973), pp. 499–513.
20. See the case studies in Richard F. Fenno, Jr., *Senators on the Campaign Trail: The Politics of Representation* (University of Oklahoma Press, 1996), p. 331; see also Benjamin Bishin, "Constituency Influence in Congress: Does Subconstituency Matter?" *Legislative Studies Quarterly* (August 2000), pp. 389–415.
21. Statistics from congressional Web sites (www.senate.gov; www.house.gov); see also the Library of Congress Web site (thomas.loc.gov).
22. Bill Bradley, *Time Present, Time Past: A Memoir* (Knopf, 1996), Chapter 4.
23. From a 1999 CBS survey reported in "Poll Readings," *National Journal*, October 9, 1999, p. 2917.
24. Richard E. Cohen, "Vote Ratings," *National Journal*, February 21, 2005, p. 426.
25. Joseph I. Lieberman, *In Praise of Public Life* (Simon & Schuster, 2000), p. 109.
26. Catherine Richert, "Party Unity: United We Stand Opposed," *Congressional Quarterly Weekly*, January 14, 2008, p. 143.
27. *CQ Weekly*, January 11, 2010, p. 117.
28. Senate S. 1, *Honest Leadership and Open Government Act of 2007*, passed September 14, 2007.

Chapter 8

1. Adriana Lins de Albuquerque, Alicia Cheng, and Sarah Gephart, "A Year in Iraq and Afghanistan," *New York Times*, January 9, 2010, p. B10.
2. The story of Obama's decision was detailed by the *Washington Post* in an article by Anne E. Kornblatt, Scott Wilson, and Karen DeYoung, "Obama Pressed for a Faster Surge: Afghan Review a Marathon," December 6, 2009, p, A1.
3. Alexander Hamilton, James Madison, and John Jay, *The Federalist Papers* (Bantam Classic, 2003), pp. 426–427.
4. See Paul C. Light, *Vice Presidential Power* (Johns Hopkins University Press, 1984).
5. Richard Pious, *The American Presidency* (Basic Books, 1978).
6. This history of presidential powers draws heavily on Sidney M. Milkis and Michael Nelson, *The American Presidency: Origins and Development*, 1976–2000, 4th ed. (CQ Press, 2003).
7. See Al Kamen, "For Bush, the Fun Begins at Recess," *Washington Post*, June 29, 2007, p. A19; for a scholarly argument about this power, see the paper by Michael B. Rappaport, "The Original Meaning of the Recess Appointments Clause," October 6, 2004, at http://ssrn.com/abstract=601563.
8. See Phillip J. Cooper, "George W. Bush, Edgar Allan Poe, and the Use and Abuse of Presidential Signing Statements," *Presidential Studies Quarterly* 35 (September 2005), pp. 515–532.
9. Letter from Abraham Lincoln to his Illinois law partner W. H. Herndon, February 15, 1848, *in Abraham Lincoln,*

Speeches and Writings, 1832–1858 (Library of America, 1989), p. 175.
10. Miles A. Pomper, "Bush Hopes to Avoid Battle with Congress over Iraq," *Weekly*, August 31, 2002, p. 2251.
11. Louis Fisher, *Congressional Abdication on War and Spending* (Texas A&M University Press, 2000), p. 184.
12. Raoul Berger, Executive Privilege: *A Constitutional Myth* (Harvard University Press, 1974).
13. Mark J. Rozell, "The Law: Executive Privilege—Definition and Standards of Application," *Presidential Studies Quarterly* (December 1999), p. 924.
14. *United States v. Nixon*, 418 U.S. 683 (1974).
15. *Clinton et al. v. New York City et al.*, 524 U.S. 417 (1998).
16. See Bradley H. Patterson Jr., *The White House Staff: Inside the West Wing and Beyond* (Brookings Institution Press, 2000).
17. See Irving Janis, *Groupthink* (Houghton Mifflin, 1982).
18. For the views on presidents and the White House staff of a highly placed White House aide in several administrations, see David Gergen, *Eyewitness to Power: The Essence of Leadership,* Nixon to Clinton (Touchstone, 2000).
19. See Shelley Lynne Tomkins, *Inside OMB: Politics and Process in the President's Budget Office* (Sharpe, 1998).
20. See Paul C. Light, *The President's Agenda: Domestic Policy Choice from Kennedy Through Clinton* (Johns Hopkins University Press, 1999).
21. *United States v. Curtiss-Wright Export Corp.*, 299 U.S. 304 (1936).
22. Richard E. Neustadt, *Presidential Power and the Modern Presidents* (Free Press, 1991).
23. The phrase "power to persuade" is from Richard Neustadt, *Presidential Power and the Modern Presidents: The Politics of Leadership from Roosevelt to Reagan* (Free Press, 1990), p. 7.
24. Clea Benson, "Presidential Support: The Power of No," *CQ Weekly,* January 14, 2008, p. 132.

Chapter 9

1. Alexander Hamilton, James Madison, and John Jay, *The Federalist Papers* (Bantam Classic, 2003), p. 427.
2. See Stanley Elkins and Eric McKitrick, *The Age of Federalism* (Oxford University Press, 1993), pp. 50–51.
3. See John A. Rohr, *To Run a Constitution: The Legitimacy of the Administrative State* (University of Kansas Press, 1986).
4. Paul C. Light, *A Government Ill Executed: The Decline of the Federal Service and How to Reverse It* (Harvard University Press, 2008), Chapter 7.
5. Donald Kettl, *Leadership at the Fed* (Yale University Press, 1986).
6. James Fesler and Donald Kettl, *The Politics of the Administrative Process* (Chatham House, 1991).
7. See Paul C. Light, *Thickening Government* (Brookings Institution Press, 1995).
8. See Terry M. Moe, "The Politics of Structural Choice: Toward a Theory of Public Bureaucracy," in Oliver E. Williamson, ed., *Organization Theory: From Chester Barnard to the Present and Beyond* (Oxford University Press, 1990), pp. 140–162.
9. For an analysis of the use and abuse of the civil service system in the early twentieth century, see Stephen Skowronek, *Building a New American State* (Cambridge University Press, 1982).
10. See Jeanne Ponessa, "The Hatch Act Rewrite," *CQ Weekly,* November 13, 1993, pp. 3146–3147.
11. Theodore J. Lowi, Jr., *The End of Liberalism,* 2d ed. (Norton, 1979).
12. Eric Pianin, "EPA Aims to Change Pollution Rules," *The Washington Post,* December 5, 2003, p. A2.
13. Morris P. Fiorina, "Flagellating the Federal Bureaucracy," *Society* (March–April 1983), p. 73.
14. Alexander Hamilton, James Madison, and John Jay, *The Federalist,* ed. Benjamin Fletcher Wright (Cambridge, MA: Harvard University Press, 1961), p. 451.

Chapter 10

1. *Citizens United* v. *Federal Election Commission,* 558 U.S. ___ (2010).
2. *Austin* v. *Michigan Chamber of Commerce,* 494 U.S. 652 (1990).
3. Robert Barnes and Anne Kornblut, "It's Obama vs. the Supreme Court, Round 2, Over Campaign Finance Ruling," *The Washington Post,* March 11, 2010.
4. Roy P. Fairfield, ed., *The Federalist Papers* (Johns Hopkins University Press, 1981), p. 227.
5. Jerome Frank, *Courts on Trial: Myth and Reality in American Justice* (Princeton University Press, 1949), pp. 80–103; see also Martin Shapiro, *Courts* (University of Chicago Press, 1981); and Robert P. Burns, *A Theory of the Trial* (Princeton University Press, 1999).
6. Many of these workload statistics can be found in the Supreme Court's 2009, *Year-End Report on the Federal Judiciary* (U.S. Government Printing Office, December 31, 2009).
7. Fairfield, *The Federalist Papers,* p. 228.
8. Harold W. Chase, *Federal Judges: The Appointing Process* (University of Minnesota Press, 1972); and Sheldon Goldman, *Picking Federal Judges: Lower Court Selection from Roosevelt Through Reagan* (Yale University Press, 1997).
9. See David M. O'Brien, "Ironies and Disappointments: Bush and Federal Judgeships," in Colin Campbell and Bert A. Rockman, eds., *The George W. Bush Presidency* (CQ Press, 2004), pp. 133–157; and Brannon P. Denning, "The Judicial Confirmation Process and the Blue Slip," *Judicature* (March–April 2002), pp. 218–226.
10. Russell Wheeler, "Judicial Nominations in the First Fourteen Months of the Obama and Bush Administrations," *Governance Studies at Brookings* (April 7, 2010).
11. Scott E. Graves and Robert M. Howard, *Justice Takes a Recess: Judicial Appointments from George Washington to George W. Bush* (Lexington Books, 2009).
12. Lisa M. Holmes and Roger E. Hartley, "Increasing Senate Scrutiny of Lower Federal Court Nominees," *Judicature* (May–June 1997), p. 275.
13. George Watson and John Stookey, "Supreme Court Confirmation Hearings: A View from the Senate," *Judicature* (December 1987–January 1988), p. 193; see also John Massaro, *Supremely Political: The Role of Ideology and Presidential Management in Unsuccessful Supreme Court Nominations* (State University of New York Press, 1990).
14. Barbara A. Perry and Henry J. Abraham, "A 'Representative' Supreme Court? The Thomas, Ginsburg, and Breyer Appointments," *Judicature* (January–February 1998), pp. 158–165.
15. Donald Santarelli, quoted in Jerry Landauer, "Shaping the Bench," *The Wall Street Journal,* December 10, 1970, p. 1.
16. Lee Epstein, Jeffrey A. Segal, Harold J. Spaeth, and Thomas G. Walker. *The Supreme Court Compendium: Data, Decisions, and Developments* (CQ Press, 2007), figures updated by the authors.
17. Tony Mauro, "The Supreme Court as Quiz Show," *Recorder* (December 8, 1993), p. 10.
18. Joyce O'Connor, "Selections from Notes Kept on an Internship at the U.S. Supreme Court" (Fall 1988), *Law, Courts, and Judicial Process* 6 (Spring 1989), p. 44.
19. Forrest Maltzman, James F. Spriggs III, and Paul Wahlbeck, *Crafting Law on the Supreme Court: The Collegial Game* (Cambridge University Press, 2000).
20. Charles Evans Hughes, *The Supreme Court of the United States* (Columbia University Press, 1966), p. 68.
21. Daniel M. Berman, *It Is So Ordered: The Supreme Court Rules on School Segregation* (Norton, 1986), p. 114; and David M. O'Brien, *Storm Center: The Supreme Court in American Politics,* 7th ed. (Norton, 2005), pp. 262–272.
22. *Brown* v. *Board of Education of Topeka,* 347 U.S. 483 (1954).
23. *Citizens United* v. *Federal Election Commission,* 558 U.S. ___ (2010).
24. William H. Rehnquist, quoted in John R. Vile, "The Selection and Tenure of Chief Justices," *Judicature* (September–October 1994), p. 98.
25. David Danelski, "The Influence of the Chief Justice in the Decisional Process of the Supreme Court," in Thomas P. Jahnige and Sheldon Goldman, eds., *The Federal Judicial System: Readings in*

Process and Behavior (Holt, Rinehart and Winston, 1968), p. 148.
26. O'Brien, *Storm Center,* Chapter 3.
27. Artemus Ward and David L. Weiden, *Sorcerers' Apprentices: 100 Years of Law Clerks at the United States Supreme Court* (New York University Press, 2006); and Todd C. Peppers, *Courtiers of the Marble Palace: The Rise and Influence of the Supreme Court Law Clerk* (Stanford University Press, 2006).
28. Lincoln Caplan, *The Tenth Justice: The Solicitor General and the Rule of Law* (Knopf, 1987); and Rebecca Mae Salokar, *The Solicitor General: The Politics of Law* (Temple University Press, 1992).
29. Gregory A. Caldeira and John R. Wright, "Organized Interest and Agenda Setting in the U.S. Supreme Court," *American Political Science Review* 82 (December 1988), p. 1110; and Donald R. Songer and Reginald S. Sheehan, "Interest Group Success in the Courts: *Amicus* Participation in the Supreme Court," *Political Research Quarterly* 46 (June 1993), pp. 339–354.
30. *Grutter* v. *Bollinger,* 539 U.S. 306 (2003); Neal Devins, "Explaining Grutter v. Bollinger," *University of Pennsylvania Law Review,* 152, No. 1 (November 2003).
31. Paul M. Collins, Jr., *Friends of the Supreme Court: Interest Groups and Judicial Decision Making* (Oxford University Press, 2008).
32. Caldeira and Wright, "Organized Interest and Agenda Setting," *American Political Science Review* 82 (December 1988), p. 1118; and Songer and Sheehan, "Interest Group Success in the Courts," *Political Research Quarterly* 46 (June 1993).
33. Gerald N. Rosenberg, *Hollow Hope: Can Courts Bring About Sound Change?* (University of Chicago Press, 1991).
34. J. W. Peltason, *Fifty-Eight Lonely Men: Southern Federal Judges and School Desegregation* (University of Illinois Press, 1971); and Gary Orfield and Chungmei Lee, *Brown at 50: King's Dream or Plessy's Nightmare* (Civil Rights Project, Harvard University, 2004).
35. See Benjamin N. Cardozo, *The Nature of the Judicial Process* (Yale University Press, 1921)—a classic.
36. William O. Douglas, quoted in O'Brien, *Storm Center,* p. 184.
37. *Citizens United* v. *Federal Election Commission,* 558 U.S. _______ (2010), C. J. Roberts concurring.
38. Lee Epstein, Jeffrey A. Segal, Harold J. Spaeth, and Thomas G. Walker, *The Supreme Court Compendium: Data, Decisions, and Developments,* 4th ed. (CQ Press, 2007). Data through 2005–2006 Supreme Court term.
39. See Keith Perine, "Precedent Heeded, but Not Revered on High Court," *CQ Weekly,* November 28, 2005, pp. 3180–3184.
40. *Gonzales* v. *Carhart,* 550 U.S. 124 (2007).
41. Ex parte *McCardle,* 74 U.S. 506 (1869).
42. See Shawn Francis Peters, *Judging the Jehovah's Witnesses* (University of Kansas Press, 2002); Clyde Wilcox, *Onward, Christian Soldiers? The Religious Right in American Politics* (Westview Press, 1996); Mark Tushnet, *The NAACP's Legal Strategy Against Segregated Education, 1925–1950* (University of North Carolina Press, 1987); and Karen O'Connor, *Women's Organizations' Use of the Court* (Lexington Books, 1980).
43. J. W. Peltason, "The Supreme Court: Transactional or Transformational Leadership," in Michael R. Beschloss and Thomas E. Cronin, eds., *Essays in Honor of James MacGregor Burns* (Prentice Hall, 1988), pp. 165–180; and Valerie Hoekstra, *Public Reactions to Supreme Court Decisions* (Cambridge University Press, 2003).
44. *Planned Parenthood* v. *Casey,* 505 U.S. 833 (1992).
45. Edward White, "The Supreme Court of the United States," *American Bar Association Journal* 7 (1921), p. 341.

Chapter 11

1. *Roper* v. *Simmons,* 543 U.S. 551 (2005).
2. *Graham v. Florida,* ___U.S.____ (2010).
3. Justice Felix Frankfurther, dissenting in *United States* v. *Rabinowitz,* 339 U.S. 56 (1950).
4. Jeffrey Smith, *War and Press Freedom* (Oxford University Press, 1999); and David Cole, *Enemy Aliens: Double Standards and Constitutional Freedoms in the War on Terrorism* (New Press, 2003).
5. *Hamdan* v. *Rumsfeld,* 548 U.S. 557 (2006).
6. Josh White and William Branigin, "Hamdan to Be Sent to Yemen," *The Washington Post,* November 25, 2008.
7. *Boumediene* v. *Bush,* 553 U.S. _______ (2008).
8. *Felker* v. *Turpin,* 518 U.S. 651 (1996); *Winthrow* v. *Williams,* 507 U.S. 680 (1993); *McCleskey* v. *Zant,* 499 U.S. 467 (1991); and *Stone* v. *Powell,* 428 U.S. 465 (1976).
9. *Barron* v. *Baltimore,* 7 Peters 243 (1833).
10. *Gitlow* v. *New York,* 268 U.S. 652 (1925).
11. Richard C. Cortner, *The Supreme Court and the Second Bill of Rights: The Fourteenth Amendment and the Nationalization of Civil Liberties* (University of Wisconsin Press, 1981).
12. *Witters* v. *Washington Department of Services for the Blind,* 474 U.S. 481 (1986); and *Locke* v. *Davey,* 540 U.S. 712 (2004).
13. *Wallace* v. *Jaffree,* 472 U.S. 38 (1985).
14. *Everson* v. *Board of Education of Ewing Township,* 333 U.S. 203 (1947).
15. *Lemon* v. *Kurtzman,* 403 U.S. 602 (1971).
16. *Capital Square Review Board* v. *Pinette,* 515 U.S. 753 (1995).
17. *Allegheny* v. *ACLU,* 492 U.S. 573 (1989).
18. *Bowen* v. *Kendrick,* 487 U.S. 589 (1988); *Lee* v. *Weisman,* 505 U.S. 577 (1992); *Board of Education of Kiryas Joel Village School District* v. *Grumet,* 512 U.S. 687 (1994); and *Zelman* v. *Simmons-Harris,* 536 U.S. 629 (2002).
19. *Mitchell* v. *Helms,* 530 U.S. 793 (2000).
20. *Agostini* v. *Felton,* 521 U.S. 74 (1997).
21. *Employment Division of Human Resources of Oregon* v. *Smith,* 494 U.S. 872 (1990).
22. *Church of Lukumi Babalu Aye* v. *City of Hialeah,* 508 U.S. 520 (1993).
23. *Brown* v. *Hartlage,* 456 U.S. 45 (1982).
24. *New York Times Company* v. *United States,* 403 U.S. 670 (1971).
25. Ibid., *Near* v. *Minnesota,* 283 U.S. 697 (1930).
26. *Hazelwood School District* v. *Kuhlmeier,* 484 U.S. 260 (1988).
27. *New York Times* v. *Sullivan,* 376 U.S. 254 (1964).
28. *Hustler Magazine* v. *Falwell,* 485 U.S. 46 (1988).
29. Potter Stewart, concurring in *Jacobellis* v. *Ohio,* 378 U.S. 184 (1964).
30. *Miller* v. *California,* 413 U.S. 15 (1973).
31. *Young* v. *American Mini Theatres,* 427 U.S. 51 (1976); *Renton* v. *Playtime Theatres, Inc.,* 475 U.S. 41 (1986); and *City of Los Angeles* v. *Alameda Books, Inc.,* 535 U.S. 425 (2002).
32. *Barnes* v. *Glen Theatre, Inc.,* 501 U.S. 560 (1991); and *City of Erie* v. *Pap's A.M.,* 529 U.S. 277 (2000).
33. *Chaplinsky* v. *New Hampshire,* 315 U.S. 568 (1942).
34. *Cohen* v. *California,* 403 U.S. 115 (1971).
35. *Wisconsin* v. *Mitchell,* 508 U.S. 476 (1993).
36. *44 Liquormart, Inc.* v. *Rhode Island,* 517 U.S. 484 (1996); and *Thompson* v. *Western States Medical Center,* 535 U.S. 357 (2002).
37. *Branzburg* v. *Hayes,* 408 U.S. 665 (1972).
38. *Federal Communications Commission* v. *Pacifica Foundation,* 438 U.S. 726 (1978).
39. *United States* v. *Playboy Entertainment Group,* 529 U.S. 803 (2000); and *Denver Area Educational Television* v. *Federal Communications Commission,* 518 U.S. 727 (1996).
40. *Reno* v. *American Civil Liberties Union,* 521 U.S. 844 (1997).
41. *Ashcroft* v. *ACLU,* 542 U.S. 656 (2004).
42. *Walker* v. *Birmingham,* 388 U.S. 307 (1967).
43. *Madsen* v. *Women's Health Center,* 512 U.S. 753 (1994); *Schenck* v. *Pro-Choice Network,* 519 U.S. 357 (1997); and *Hill* v. *Colorado,* 530 U.S. 703 (2000).
44. *First English Evangelical* v. *Los Angeles County,* 482 U.S. 304 (1987); see Richard A. Epstein, *Taking: Private Property and the Power of Eminent Domain* (Harvard University Press, 1985).
45. *Lucas* v. *South Carolina Coastal Commission,* 505 U.S. 647 (1992).
46. *Tahoe-Sierra Council, Inc.* v. *Tahoe Regional Planning Agency,* 535 U.S. 302 (2002).
47. *Kelo* v. *City of New London,* 545 U.S. 469 (2005).
48. *United States* v. *554 Acres of Land,* 441 U.S. 506 (1979).
49. *Mathews* v. *Eldridge,* 424 U.S. 319 (1976), restated in *Connecticut* v. *Doeher,* 501 U.S. 1 (1991).
50. *Meyer* v. *Nebraska,* 262 U.S. 390 (1923).

51. *Griswold* v. *Connecticut,* 381 U.S. 479 (1965).
52. Philip B. Kurland, *Some Reflections on Privacy and the Constitution* (University of Chicago Center for Policy Study, 1976), p. 9. A classic and influential article about privacy is Samuel D. Warren and Louis D. Brandeis, "The Right to Privacy," *Harvard Law Review* (December 15, 1890), pp. 193–220.
53. *Roe* v. *Wade,* 410 U.S. 113 (1973).
54. *Planned Parenthood of Southeastern Pennsylvania* v. *Casey,* 505 U.S. 833 (1992).
55. *Stenberg* v. *Carhart,* 530 U.S. 914 (2000).
56. *Gonzales* v. *Carhart,* 550 U.S. 124 (2007).
57. *Bowers* v. *Hardwick,* 478 U.S. 186 (1986).
58. *Lawrence* v. *Texas,* 539 U.S. 558 (2003).
59. But see *Washington* v. *Chrisman,* 445 U.S. 1 (1982); and compare *Georgia* v. *Randolph,* 126 547 U.S. 103 (2006).
60. *Katz* v. *United States,* 389 U.S. 347 (1967).
61. *California* v. *Hodari D.,* 499 U.S. 621 (1991).
62. *Bond* v. *United States,* 529 U.S. 334 (2000).
63. *Terry* v. *Ohio,* 392 U.S. 1 (1968).
64. *Hiibel* v. *Sixth Judicial District of Nevada,* 542 U.S. 177 (2004).
65. *Minnesota* v. *Dickerson,* 508 U.S. 366 (1993).
66. *Almeida-Sanchez* v. *United States,* 413 U.S. 266 (1973); *United States* v. *Ortiz,* 422 U.S. 891 (1975); *United States* v. *Arvizu,* 534 U.S. 161 (2002); and *United States* v. *Flores-Montano,* 541 U.S. 149 (2004).
67. *United States* v. *Ramsey,* 431 U.S. 606 (1977).
68. *Mapp* v. *Ohio,* 367 U.S. 643 (1961).
69. Senate Committee on the Judiciary, the Jury, and the Search for Truth: The Case Against Excluding Relevant Evidence at Trial, Hearing Before the Committee, 104th Cong., 1st sess. (U.S. Government Printing Office, 1997).
70. *United States* v. *Leon,* 468 U.S. 897 (1984); and *Arizona* v. *Evans,* 514 U.S. 1 (1995).
71. *Miranda* v. *Arizona,* 384 U.S. 436 (1966); but see *Yarborough* v. *Alvarado,* 541 U.S. 652 (2004).
72. *Dickerson* v. *United States,* 530 U.S. 428 (2000).
73. *United States* v. *Enterprises, Inc.,* 498 U.S. 292 (1991).
74. *J. E. B.* v. *Alabama ex rel T. B.,* 511 U.S. 127 (1994); *Batson* v. *Kentucky,* 476 U.S. 79 (1986); *Powers* v. *Ohio,* 499 U.S. 400 (1991); *Hernandez* v. *New York,* 500 U.S. 352 (1991); and *Georgia* v. *McCollum,* 505 U.S. 42 (1990).
75. *Ewing* v. *California,* 538 U.S. 11 (2003).
76. *Benton* v. *Maryland,* 395 U.S. 784 (1969); see also *Kansas* v. *Hendricks,* 521 U.S. 346 (1997).
77. *Graham* v. *Collins,* 506 U.S. 461 (1993).
78. Death Penalty Information Center, "Facts About the Death Penalty," February 25, 2010, www.deathpenaltyinfo.org/documents/FactSheet.pdf.
79. Barry Scheck, Peter Neufeld, and Jim Dwyer, *Actual Innocence: Five Days to Execution and Other Dispatches from the Wrongly Convicted* (Doubleday, 2000); and Timothy Kaufman-Osborn, *From Noose to Needle: Capital Punishment and the Late Liberal State* (University of Michigan Press, 2002).
80. Death Penalty Information Center, "Innocence and the Death Penalty," May 2, 2008, www .deathpenaltyinfo.org/article.php?did=412#inn-yr-rc.
81. *Atkins* v. *Virginia,* 536 U.S. 304 (2002).
82. *Roper* v. *Simmons,* 543 U.S. 551 (2006).
83. *Kennedy* v. *Louisiana,* 554 U.S. _______ (2008).
84. *Baze* v. *Rees,* 553 U.S. _______ (2008).
85. *Schenck* v. *United States,* 249 U.S. 47 (1919).
86. "Congress Extends PATRIOT Act, No New Protections," *The Washington Post,* February 25, 2010.
87. Louis Fisher, *Religious Liberties in America: Political Safeguards* (University Press of Kansas, 2002).

Chapter 12

1. NewsHour Online, "Supreme Court Revisits Race in Public Schools," December 4, 2006, www.pbs.org/newshour/bb/law/july-dec06/scotus_12–04.html.
2. "How the Racial-Tiebreaker Case Began," *Seattle Times,* June 28, 2007.
3. *Parents Involved in Community Schools* v. *Seattle School District, No. 1,* 551 U.S. 701 (2007).
4. Andrew Hacker, *Two Nations: Black and White, Separate, Hostile, Unequal* (Scribner, 1992).
5. *Slaughter-House Cases,* 83 U.S. 36 (1873).
6. Ex Parte *Milligan,* 71 U.S. 2 (1866).
7. *Korematsu* v. *United States,* 323 U.S. 214 (1944).
8. Ex Parte *Quirin,* 317 U.S. 1 (1942).
9. *Reid* v. *Covert,* 354 U.S. 1 (1957).
10. *Boumediene* v. *Bush,* 553 U.S. _______ (2008)
11. *Matxhews* v. *Diaz,* 426 U.S. 67 (1976); and *Shaughnessy* v. *United States ex rel. Mezei,* 345 U.S. 206 (1953).
12. *Demore* v. *Kim,* 538 U.S. 510 (2003).
13. *Zadvydas* v. *Davis,* 533 U.S. 678 (2001).
14. *Yick Wo* v. *Hopkins,* 118 U.S. 356 (1886); *Kwong Hai Chew* v. *Colding,* 344 U.S. 590 (1953); *Zadvydas* v. *Davis,* 533 U.S. 678 (2001); *Rasul* v. *Bush,* 542 U.S. 466 (2004); and *Hamdi* v. *Rumsfeld,* 542 U.S. 507 (2004).
15. *Foley* v. *Connelie,* 435 U.S. 291 (1978); *Ambach* v. *Norwick,* 441 U.S. 68 (1979); *Cabell* v. *Chavez-Salido,* 454 U.S. 432 (1982).
16. *Plyler* v. *Doe,* 457 U.S. 202 (1982).
17. *Slaughter-House Cases,* 83 U.S. 36 (1873); and *Civil Rights Cases,* 109 U.S. 3 (1883).
18. *Plessy* v. *Ferguson,* 163 U.S. 537 (1896).
19. *Brown* v. *Board of Education of Topeka,* 347 U.S. 483 (1954); and *Brown* v. *Board of Education of Topeka,* 349 U.S. 294 (1955).
20. *Gomillion* v. *Lightfoot,* 364 U.S. 339 (1960).
21. Taylor Branch, *Parting the Waters: America in the King Years, 1954–1963* (Simon & Schuster, 1988); see also Harris Wofford, *Of Kennedys and Kings: Making Sense of the Sixties* (Farrar, Straus, & Giroux, 1980).
22. See Charles Whalen and Barbara Whalen, *The Longest Debate: A Legislative History of the 1964 Civil Rights Act* (Mentor, 1985); and Hugh Davis Graham, *The Civil Rights Era* (Oxford University Press, 1990).
23. David Remnick, *The Bridge: The Life and Rise of Barack Obama* (Knopf, 2010).
24. Ellen Carol Du Bois, *Feminism and Suffrage: The Emergence of an Independent Women's Movement in America, 1848–1869* (Cornell University Press, 1978); and Joan Hoff-Wilson, "Women and the Constitution," *News for Teachers of Political Science* (Summer 1985), pp. 10–15.
25. Susan M. Hartmann, *From Margin to Mainstream: American Women and Politics Since 1960* (Temple University Press, 1989); and Susan Gluck Mezey, *In Pursuit of Equality: Women, Public Policy, and the Federal Courts* (St. Martin's Press, 1992).
26. *United States* v. *Virginia,* 518 U.S. 515 (1996); see also Philippa Strum, *Women in the Barracks: The VMI Case and Equal Rights* (University Press of Kansas, 2002).
27. *Meritor Savings Bank, FBD* v. *Vinson,* 477 U.S. 57 (1986).
28. *Oncale* v. *Sundowner Offshore Services,* 523 U.S. 75 (1998); *Faragher* v. *City of Boca Raton,* 524 U.S. 775 (1998); and *Burlington Industries* v. *Ellerth,* 524 U.S. 742 (1998).
29. U.S. Census Bureau, "Texas Becomes Nation's Newest Majority-Minority State, Census Bureau Announces," August 11, 2005, www.census.gov/Press-Release/www/releases/archives/population/005514.html.
30. Randal C. Archibald, "Arizona Enacts Stringent Law on Immigration," *New York Times,* April 23, 2010.
31. Celia W. Dugger, "U.S. Study Says Asian Americans Face Widespread Discrimination," *New York Times,* February 29, 1992, p. 1, reporting on U.S. Civil Rights Commission, *Civil Rights Issues Facing Asian Americans in the 1990s* (U.S. Government Printing Office, 1992).
32. *Takao Ozawa* v. *United States,* 260 U.S. 178 (1922).
33. *Korematsu* v. *United States,* 323 U.S. 214 (1944).
34. Won Moo Hurh, *Korean Immigrants in America* (Fairleigh Dickinson University Press, 1984).
35. Antonio J. A. Pido, *The Filipinos in America: Macro/Micro Dimensions of Immigration and Integration* (Center for Migration Studies of New York, 1986).
36. Harold L. Hodgkinson, *The Demographics of American Indians: One Percent of the People, Fifty Percent of the Diversity* (Institute for Educational Leadership/Center for Demographic Policy, 1990), pp. 1–5.

37. "Assimilation, Relocation, Genocide: The Trail of Tears," *Indian Country Diaries*, PBS, November 2006, www.pbs.org/indiancountry/history/trail.html.
38. *Morey* v. *Doud*, 354 U.S. 459 (1957); and *Allegheny Pittsburgh Coal Co.* v. *County Commission*, 488 U.S. 336 (1989).
39. *City of Cleburne, Texas* v. *Cleburne Living Center*, 473 U.S. 432 (1985); *Heller* v. *Doe*, 509 U.S. 312 (1993); and *Romer* v. *Evans*, 517 U.S. 620 (1996).
40. *San Antonio School District* v. *Rodriguez*, 411 U.S. 1 (1973).
41. *Frontiero* v. *Richardson*, 411 U.S. 677 (1973).
42. *San Antonio School District* v. *Rodriguez*, 411 U.S. 1 (1973); and Douglas Reed, *On Equal Terms: The Constitutional Politics of Educational Opportunity* (Princeton University Press, 2001).
43. Matthew Bosworth, *Courts as Catalysts: State Supreme Courts and Public School Finance Equity* (State University of New York Press, 2001).
44. Sandra Day O'Connor, in *Kimel* v. *Florida Board of Regents*, 528 U.S. 62 (2000).
45. Ibid.
46. *Romer* v. *Evans*, 517 U.S. 620 (1996).
47. European Union and LGBT Rights, International Lesbian and Gay Association Europe, http:// www.ilga-europe.org/europe/guide/european_union/european_union_and_lgbt_rights.
48. Mexico City Passes Gay Union Law," BBC News, November 10, 2006, http://news.bbc.co.uk/2/hi/6134730.stm.
49. International Lesbian and Gay Association, www.ilga.org.
50. Leon F. Litwack, *Trouble in Mind: Black Southerners in the Age of Jim Crow* (1998), p. 227, as cited in James W. Fox, Jr., "Intimations of Citizenship: Repressions and Expressions of Equal Citizenship in the Era of Jim Crow," *Howard University Law Journal* (Fall 2006).
51. Harold W. Stanley, *Voter Mobilization and the Politics of Race: The South and Universal Suffrage*, 1952–1984 (Praeger, 1987).
52. Abigail M. Thernstrom, *Whose Votes Count? Affirmative Action and Minority Voting Rights* (Harvard University Press, 1987), p. 15.
53. *Smith* v. *Allwright*, 321 U.S. 64 9 (1944).
54. *Gomillion* v. *Lightfoot*, 364 U.S. 339 (1960).
55. *Harper* v. *Virginia Board of Elections*, 383 U.S. 663 (1966).
56. Thernstrom, *Whose Votes Count?* For a contrary view, see Bernard Grofman, Lisa Handley, and Richard G. Niemi, *Minority Representation and the Quest for Voting Equality* (Cambridge University Press, 1992).
57. *Morse* v. *Republican Party of Virginia*, 517 U.S. 116 (1996).
58. Northwest Austin Municipal Utility District Number One v. Holder, 557 U.S. _____ (2009)
59. *Shaw* v. *Reno*, 509 U.S. 630 (1993).
60. *Civil Rights Cases*, 109 U.S. 3 (1883).
61. *Plessy* v. *Ferguson*, 163 U.S. 537 (1896).
62. *Heart of Atlanta Motel* v. *United States*, 379 U.S. 421 (1964).
63. Darryl Van Duch, "Plagued by Politics, EEOC Backlog Grows," *Recorder* (August 18, 1998), p. 1; and David Rovella, "EEOC Chairman Casellas: 'We Are Being Selective,'" *National Law Journal* (November 20, 1995), p. 1.
64. *Shelley* v. *Kraemer*, 334 U.S. 1 (1948).
65. *Sweat* v. *Painter*, 339 U.S. 629 (1950).
66. *Brown* v. *Board of Education of Topeka*, 347 U.S. 483 (1954); see also J. W. Peltason, *Fifty-Eight Lonely Men: Southern Federal Judges and School Desegregation* (University of Illinois Press, 1971), p. 248.
67. *Brown* v. *Board of Education of Topeka*, 349 U.S. 294 (1955).
68. *Freeman* v. *Pitts*, 503 U.S. 467 (1992); and *Missouri* v. *Jenkins*, 515 U.S. 70 (1995).
69. See Gary Orfield, Susan E. Eaton, and the Harvard Project on School Desegregation, *Dismantling Desegregation: The Quiet Reversal of Brown* v. *Board of Education* (New Press, 1996).
70. Raymond Hernandez, "NAACP Suspends Yonkers Leader After Criticism of Usefulness of School Busing," *New York Times*, November 1, 1995, p. A13.
71. Gary Orfield and Chungmei Lee, *Brown at 50: King's Dream or Plessy's Nightmare?* (Civil Rights Project, Harvard University, 2004), http://www.civilrightsproject.ucla.edu/research/reseg04/brown50.pdf; see also Charles Clotfelter, *After Brown: The Rise and Retreat of School Desegregation* (Princeton University Press, 2004).
72. Richard Kahlenberg, *All Together Now: Creating Middle-Class Schools Through Public School Choice* (Brookings Institution Press, 2003).
73. John Marshall Harlan, dissenting in *Plessy* v. *Ferguson*, 163 U.S. 537 (1896).
74. *University of California Regents* v. *Bakke*, 438 U.S. 265 (1978); see also Howard Ball, *The Bakke Case* (University Press of Kansas, 2000).
75. *Gratz* v. *Bollinger*, 539 U.S. 244 (2003).
76. *Grutter* v. *Bollinger*, 539 U.S. 306 (2003).
77. Scott Jaschik, "Michigan Votes Down Affirmative Action," *Inside Higher Education* (November 8, 2006), www.insidehighered.com/news/2006/11/08/Michigan.
78. *Hopwood* v. *Texas*, 518 U.S. 1016 (1996).
79. James Farmer, quoted in Rochelle L. Stanfield, "Black Complaints Haven't Translated into Political Organization and Power," *National Journal* (June 14, 1980), p. 465.
80. Orfield and Lee, *Brown at 50;* and Clotfeler, *After Brown.*
81. D'Vera Cohn, "Hispanic Growth Surges Fueled by Births in U.S.," *The Washington Post*, June 9, 2005, p. A1.
82. Gary Orfield, "Separate Societies: Have the Kerner Warnings Come True?" in Fred R. Harris and Roger W. Wilkins, eds., *Quiet Riots: Race and Poverty in the United States—The Kerner Report Twenty Years Later* (Pantheon, 1988), p. 103; see also Nicholas Lehmann, *The Promised Land* (Knopf, 1991).
83. William J. Wilson, *The Truly Disadvantaged: The Inner City, the Underclass, and Public Policy* (University of Chicago Press, 1987), esp. Chapter 5; and Kevin Phillips, *The Politics of Rich and Poor* (Random House, 1995).
84. Gary Orfield and Carole Ashkinaze, *The Closing Door: Conservative Policy and Black Opportunity* (University of Chicago Press, 1991), pp. 221–234.

Chapter 13

1. See Paul C. Light, *Artful Work: The Politics of Social Security Reform* (Random House, 1985), for a discussion of rededistributive policy.
2. John Kingdon, *Agendas, Alternatives, and Public Policies* (Little, Brown, 1984), p. 3.
3. Anthony Downs, "The 'Issue-Attention Cycle,'" *Public Interest* 28 (Summer 1972), p. 38.
4. Hugh Heclo, "Issue Networks and the Executive Establishment," in A. King, ed., *The New American Political System* (American Enterprise Institute, 1978), pp. 87–124.
5. Lester Salamon and Michael Lund, "The Tools Approach: Basic Analytics," in L. Salamon, ed., *Beyond Privatization: The Tools of Government Action* (Urban Institute Press, 1989).
6. See Paul C. Light, *A Government Ill Executed: The Decline of the Federal Service and How to Reverse It* (Harvard University Press, 2008).
7. See Cornelius Kerwin, *Rulemaking: How Government Agencies Write Law and Make Policy* (CQ Press, 2003).
8. See Kingdon, *Agendas, Alternatives, and Public Policies*, for a description of the policy-making process.
9. Office of Management and Budget, *Budget of the U.S. Government, Fiscal Year 2009, Analytical Perspectives* (U.S. Government Printing Office, February 2008), p. 298.
10. Ibid., pp. 245, 332.
11. For a discussion of the budgetary cycle, see Allen Schick, *The Federal Budget: Politics, Policy, Process*, rev. ed. (Brookings Institution Press, 2000).
12. Efforts at past tax reform are described in Jeffrey H. Birnbaum and Alan S. Murray, *Showdown at Gucci Gulch: Lawmakers, Lobbyists, and the Unlikely Triumph of Tax Reform* (Vintage Books, 1988); see also Timothy J. Conlan, Margaret T. Wrightson, and David R. Beam, *Taxing Choices: The Politics of Tax Reform* (CQ Press, 1990).
13. The debate over Keynes and his economic theories is still alive in the United States. See Donald E. Moggridge, *Maynard Keynes: An Economist's Biography* (Routledge, 1992).

14. *United States* v. *E. C. Knight Co.*, 156 U.S. 1 (1895).
15. On the origins of the Federal Trade Commission and the role of Louis D. Brandeis, see Thomas K. McCraw, *Prophets of Regulation* (Belknap Press, 1984), Chapter 3.
16. For a useful history of airline deregulation, see Steven A. Morrison and Clifford Winston, *The Evolution of the Airline Industry* (Brookings Institution Press, 1995).
17. On Southwest Airlines and its longtime chief executive Herb Kelleher, see Kevin Freiberg and Jackie Freiberg, *Nuts!* (Bard Press, 1996).
18. Michael B. Katz, *In the Shadow of the Poorhouse: A Social History of Welfare in America* (Basic Books, 1986).
19. These numbers can be found at the Department of Health and Human Services Web site, aspe.hhs.gov/poverty/07poverty.shtml.
20. Gertrude Schaffner Goldberg and Eleanor Kremen, eds., *The Feminization of Poverty: Only in America?* (Greenwood Press, 1990).
21. See, for example, Margaret Weir, "Political Parties and Social Policymaking," in Margaret Weir, ed., *The Social Divide: Political Parties and the Future of Activist Government* (Brookings Institution Press, 1998).
22. Self-employed workers must cover both amounts, and many state and local government workers are not required to participate.
23. Martha Derthick, "No More Easy Votes for Social Security," *Brookings Review* 10 (Fall 1992), pp. 50–53.
24. See Theda Skocpol, *Protecting Soldiers and Mothers: The Political Origins of Social Policy in the United States* (Belknap Press, 1992), Chapter 9, for a history of the Act.
25. Lyndon Johnson, speech at the University of Michigan, May 1964, in *Congress and the Nation, 1965–1968: A Review of Government and Politics During the Johnson Years* (CQ Press, 1969), Vol. 2, p. 650.
26. William J. Clinton, acceptance speech, Democratic National Convention, Chicago, July 6, 1992.
27. Robert Pear, "Judge Rules States Can't Cut Welfare," *New York Times*, October 14, 1997, p. A1.
28. Centers for Medicare and Medicaid Services, "Health Accounts," www.cms.hhs.gov.
29. http://www.cms.hhs.gov/NationalHealthExpendData/downloads/highlights.pdf.
30. U.S. Census Bureau, www.census.gov.

Chapter 14

1. See Lee Feinstein, "Darfur and Beyond: What Is Needed to Prevent Mass Atrocities," *Council on Foreign Relations*, January 2007.
2. Condoleezza Rice, quoted in Glenn Kessler, "Rice Lays Out Case for War in Iraq," *The Washington Post*, August 16, 2002, p. A1.
3. See Joseph Nye, *Soft Power: The Means to Success in World Politics* (Public Affairs, 2005).
4. See Glenn Kessler, "U.S. Decision on Iraq Has Puzzling Past: Opponents of War Wonder When, How Policy Was Set," *The Washington Post*, January 12, 2003, p. A1, for a detailed history of the increasing interest in Iraq.
5. Remarks to the United Nations, September 12, 2003.
6. See Jason H. Campbell and Michael E. O'Hanlon, "The State of Iraq: An Update," *New York Times*, March 9, 2008, p. A28.
7. For more information, visit the Peace Corps Web site, www.peacecorps.gov. For a useful study of the Peace Corps, see Elizabeth Cobbs Hoffman, *All You Need Is Love: The Peace Corps and the Spirit of the 1960s* (Harvard University Press, 1998).
8. For a fascinating history of U.S. intelligence operations, see Christopher Andrew, *For the President's Eyes Only: Secret Intelligence and the American Presidency from Washington to Bush* (HarperCollins, 1995). See also Rhodri Jeffreys-Jones, *The CIA and American Democracy*, 2d ed. (Yale University Press, 1998).
9. National Commission on Terrorist Attacks on the United States, *The 9/11 Commission Report* (Norton, 2004), p. 12.
10. *Public Papers of the Presidents, Dwight D. Eisenhower* (U.S. Government Printing Office, 1960), pp. 1035–1040.
11. P. W. Singer, "Winning the War of Words: Information Warfare in Afghanistan," *Brookings Analysis Paper No. 5*, October 2001.
12. "U.S. Foreign Aid Spending Since World War II," *Public Perspective* 8 (August–September 1997), p. 11.
13. Gallup Poll, May 2000, www.gallup.com.
14. See Sebastian Mallaby, "Why So Stingy on Foreign Aid?" *The Washington Post National Weekly Edition*, July 3, 2000, p. 27.
15. See Robert Kagan, "The Kerry Doctrine," *The Washington Post*, August 1, 2004, p. B7, for this argument.
16. Gary Hufbauer and Jeffrey J. Schott, "Economic Sanctions and Foreign Policy," *PS: Political Science and Politics* 18 (Fall 1985), p. 278.
17. John Prados, *The President's Secret Wars: CIA and Pentagon Covert Operations Since World War II* (Morrow, 1986); and Daniel Patrick Moynihan, *Secrecy: The American Experience* (Yale University Press, 1998).

Conclusion

1. Thucydides, *History of the Peloponnesian War*, translated by Benjamin Jowett (Prometheus Books, 1998).
2. Edith Hamilton, *The Echo of Greece* (Norton, 1957), p. 47.
3. For a book advocating more direct democracy, see Ted Becker and Christa Daryl Slaton, *The Future of Teledemocracy* (Praeger, 2000); for a contrary view, see Richard J. Ellis, *Democratic Delusions: The Initiative Process in America* (University Press of Kansas, 2002).
4. For an extensive list of countries that use some form of proportional representation, see ACE The Electoral Knowledge Network, "Comparative Data: Electoral Systems," aceproject.org/epic-en/es.
5. For more on the relationship between electoral institutions and party systems, see Maurice Duverger, *Political Parties: Their Organization and Activity in the Modern State* (Wiley, 1954).
6. *Lawrence* v. *Texas*, 539 U.S. 558 (2003).
7. The Campaign Legal Center, www.campaignlegalcenter.org/BCRA.html; and *McConnell* v. *FEC*, 124 S. Ct. 619 (2003).
8. John F. Kennedy, *Profiles in Courage* (Pocket Books, 1956), p. 108.
9. Harry S. Truman, impromptu remarks before the Reciprocity Club, Washington, D.C., April 11, 1958, as reported by the *New York World-Telegram*, April 12, 1958, p. 4, www.bartleby .com/73/1405.html.
10. These books will give you insight into the life of public officeholders: Bill Clinton, *My Life* (Knopf, 2004); Harry Reid and Mark Warren, *The Good Fight* (Putnam Adult, 2008); George Tenet, *At the Center of the Storm: My Years at the CIA* (HarperCollins, 2007); and Alan Greenspan, *The Age of Turbulence* (Penguin, 2007).
11. See Kareem Abdul-Jabar and Alan Steinberg, *Black Profiles in Courage* (Morrow, 1996).
12. Reinhold Niebuhr, *The Children of Light and the Children of Darkness* (Scribner, 1944), p. xi.
13. See Bernard Crick, *In Defense of Politics*, rev. ed. (Pelican Books, 1983); and Stimson Bullitt, *To Be a Politician*, rev. ed. (Yale University Press, 1977).
14. See Nat Hentoff, *Free Speech for Me—but Not for Thee: How the American Left and Right Relentlessly Censor Each Other* (Harper Perennial, 1993).
15. Thomas Jefferson, letter to Edward Carrington, January 16, 1787, in Thomas Jefferson Randolph, ed., *Memoir, Correspondence, and Miscellanies, from the Papers of Thomas Jefferson*, 2d ed., Vol. 2 (Carvill, 1830), Letter 43. Available online from Project Gutenberg at www.gutenberg.org/files/16782/16782-h/16782-h.htm.
16. Arthur M. Schlesinger, Jr., *The Disuniting of America* (Norton, 1993), p. 134.
17. John W. Gardner, *Self-Renewal*, rev. ed. (Norton, 1981), p. xiv.
18. In George Field, ed., *Famous Words of Freedom*, (Freedom House, 1955).

CREDITS

Photo Credits

INTRODUCTION: 2: The Granger Collection, New York; **6:** The Granger Collection, New York; **7:** Bettmann/Corbis; **11:** Courtesy Central Asian Institute

CHAPTER 1: 16: Saul Loeb/AP Photo; **18:** Jim Young/Reuters/Corbis; **18:** Corbis Digital Stock; **20:** Lee Marriner/AP Photo; **21:** zumawire westphotos/Newscom; **21:** Cristobal Herrara/ AP Photo; **24:** Tsvangirayi Mukwazhi/AP Photo; **27:** Getty Images/Liaison; **29:** *(left)* Ian Wagreich/UPI; **29:** *(right)* Bettmann/Corbis; **31:** Bettmann/Corbis **34:** Massimo Borchi/ Corbis; **35:** Bettmann/Corbis; **37:** The Granger Collection, New York; **40:** U.S. Senate/ AP Photo; **42:** Image Works/Time & Life Pictures/Getty Images

CHAPTER 2: 48: Tony Avelar/The Christian Science Monitor/Getty Images; **51:** Damian Dovarganes/AP Photo; **54:** Johnny Crawford/ The Image Works; **55:** nagelstock/Alamy; **57:** Aaron D. Allmon II/U.S. Air Force via Getty Images; **58:** *(top)* Carl D. Walsh/Aurora; **58:** *(bottom)* Joe Raedle/Getty Images; **60:** Michael Smith/ News-com; **62:** Jonathan Nourok/Getty Images; **63:** Thomas Wright/ University of Florida/IFAS/AP Photo; **64:** Dream Pictures/Getty Images; **66:** Alex Wong/Getty Images; **67:** Ed Kashi/Corbis; **68:** Yael Swerdlow/AP Photo

CHAPTER 3: 86: David Grossman/Alamy; **90:** *(top)* Panoramic Images/Getty Images; **90:** *(bottom)* Corbis; **91:** Eric Draper/ AP Photo; **93:** *(left)* Patti McConville/Getty Images; **93:** *(right)* Mary Ann Chastain/AP Photo; **94:** *(top)* Doug Benc/Getty Images; **94:** *(bottom)* Mark Leffingwell/Getty Images; **95:** *(top)* Michael Reynolds/EPA/Corbis; **95:** *(bottom)* Carlos Barria/Reuters/Landov; **98:** David J. Phillip/AP Photo; **99:** Arthur Hochstein/Time Life Pictures/ Getty Images; **102:** Elizabeth Crews; **103:** William Thomas Cain/ Getty Images **104:** Paul Conklin/Photoedit; **106:** Madalyn Ruggiero/AP Photo; **109:** *(left)* Ellen McKnight/Alamy; **109:** *(right)* Bebeto Matthews/ AP Photo

CHAPTER 4: 114: Harrison McClary/Reuters/ Landov; **118:** Newscom; **189:** *(top)* Newscom; **119:** Reiner Jensen/Corbis; **122:** Sean Gardner/ Reuters/Landov; **124:** Pablo Martinez Monsivais/ AP Photo; **125:** Terry Gilliam/AP Photo; **129:** Scott Audette/ Reuters/ Landov; Billy Suratt/ Auma Press/Corbis; **131:** Morteza Nikoubazl/ Reuters/Landov; **134:** *(top)* Emmanuel Dunand/ Getty Images; **134:** *(bottom)* Teri Stratford/ Six-Cats Research Inc.; **135:** Matthew Staver/ Bloomberg via Getty Images; **136:** Photo by Ian Wagreich. Courtesy of U.S. Chamber of Congress; **137:** Al Grillo/AP Photo; **138:** Nick Ut/AP Photo; **139:** UPI/ Landov; **144:** Teri Stratford/Six-Cats Research Inc. **147:** Janet Hostetter/AP Photo

CHAPTER 5: 152: Tim Boyles/Getty Images; **154:** Mark Humphrey/AP Photo; **156:** Lynn Avedisian; **159:** Chris Kleponis/Newcom; **160:** Jacquelyn Martin/AP Photo; **161:** Tim Sloan/AFP/ Getty Images; **164:** Suzanne Dechillo/The New York Times/Redux; **165:** Bettmann/Corbis; **167:** Jeff Widener/AP Photo; **171:** Tom Olmscheid/AP Photo; **231:** Getty Images; **173:** AP Photo; **175:** AFL-CIO 2010; **175:** *(bottom)* Teri Stratford/ Six-Cats Research Inc.

CHAPTER 6: 180: Mark Weber/Landov; **184:** Marla Brose/Albuquerque Journal/AP Photo; **187:** Ben Margot/AP Photo; **194:** Mark Wilson/ Newscom; **195:** William Thomas Cain/Getty Images; **192:** Carlos Barria/Landov; **199:** Teri Stratford/Six-Cats Research Inc.; **201:** Getty Images; **202:** Shannon Stapleton/Corbis; **203:** *(top)* Jim Sulley/Wirepix/The Image Works; **204:** Bettmann/Corbis; **205:** *(top)* UPI/ Bettmann/Corbis; **205:** *(bottom)* Courtesy of Wikipedia .com/Zuma Press; **206:** Philadelphia Inquirer/ MCT/Landov; **207:** Liu Jin/AFP/ Getty Images; **208:** Adam Rountree/AP Photo; **209:** *(top)* Rick Bowmer/AP Photo; **209:** *(bottom)* JoeRaedle/Getty Images; **210:** Matthew Healey/ UPI/Landov; **212:** Mike Theiler/UPI/ Landov

CHAPTER 7: 218: AJ Mast/AP Photo; **220:** Jessica Kourkounis/The New York Times/Redux; **222:** Moses Olmos/Newscom; **224:** *(top)* Joe Burbank/MCT/Landov; **224:** *(bottom)* Win McNamee/Getty Images; **225:** Alexander Nemenov/AFP/Getty Images; **227:** *(top)* Sgt. James L. Haprer Jr./ USAF/AFP/Newscom; **227:** *(bottom)* Ron Sachs/ Newscom; **229:** *(top)* Paul Sakuma/AP Photo; **229:** *(bottom)* U.S. Senate Historical Office; **311:** Shawn Thew/EPA/Landov; **232:** Martin H. Simon/Corbis; **236:** Scott J. Ferrell/Getty Images; **237:** Mark Wilson/Getty Images; **239:** Tim Sloan/AFP/Getty Images; **240:** Adam Larkey/ABC via Getty Images

CHAPTER 8: 244: Tim Wimborne/Reuters/ Landov; **246:** J. Scott Applewhite/AP Photo; **247:** *(top)* Leif Skoogfors/Corbis; **247:** *(bottom)* EPA/ STR/Landov; **248:** ptsphotoshot/Newscom; **250:** AP Photo; **252:** UPI/Landov; **253:** *(top)* Ric Francis/AP Photo; **253:** *(bottom)* Cecil Stoughton/ Corbis; **254:** Behrouz Mehri/Getty Images; **255:** Kyodo via AP Photo; **256:** Smithsonian American Art Museum, Washington D.C./Art Resource; **258:** Greg Mathieson/Landov; **260:** *(left)* Karin Cooper/ CBS/AP Photo; **260:** *(right)* Alex Wong/ Getty Images; **261:** Win McNamee/Reuters/Getty Images; **262:** Newscom; **264:** Dirck Halstead/ Getty Images

CHAPTER 9: 270: Saul Loeb/AFP/Getty Images; **272:** The Granger Collection, New York; **275:** Sinclair Stammers/Photo Researchers; **277:** *(top)* Dennis Cook/AP Photo; **277:** *(bottom)* Evan Vucci/AP Photo; **279:** *(top)* Bizuayehu Tesfaye/AP Photo; **279:** *(bottom)* Manuel Balce Ceneta/AP Photo; **280:** Charles Rex Arbogast/AP Photo; **283:** *(top)* David Glass/AP Photo; **283:** *(bottom)* Gerald Herbert/AP Photo; **284:** JP Greenwood/Getty Images; **287:** *(top)* Mark Wilson/Getty Images; **287:** *(bottom)* Gerald Herbert/AP Photo; **289:** Alan Singer/CBS Television

CHAPTER 10: 294: Alex Wong/Getty Images; **297:** Morgan Smith, The Texas Tribune; **302:** Alex Wong/Getty Images; **303:** *(top)* Clary/UPI/ Corbis; **303:** *(bottom)* Chip Somodella/Getty Images; **304:** *(top left)* Brendan Smialowski/ Getty Images; **304:** *(top right)* Mark Wilson/ Getty Images; **304:** *(bottom)* Stephen Crowley/ The New York Times/Redux; **305:** Stephen Crowley/The New York Times/Redux; **311:** David Hume Kennerly/Getty Images; **312:** Bill O'Leary/The Washington Post; **313:** Jay Reeves/ AP Photo

CHAPTER 11: 320: Robert Caplin/AP Photo; **326:** Peter Yates/ Time Life Pictures/Getty Images; **328:** *(top)* Carl Iwasaki/Getty Images; **328:** *(bottom)* Charles Tasnadi/AP Photo; **329:** Chris Seward/The News & Observer/AP Photo; **330:** Michael Porro/Getty Images; **331:** *(top)* Nick Ut/AP Photo; **331:** *(bottom)* Michael Caulfield/Getty Images; **332:** Don Emmert/ AFP/Getty Images; **333:** Jessica Hill/AP Photo; **334:** Andres Leighton/AP Photo; **336:** Alex Wong/Getty Images; **337:** Nancy G. Fire Photography, Nancy Greifenhagen/Alamy; **338:** Mike Derer/AP Photo; **339:** Bettmann/ Corbis

CHAPTER 12: 348: Kevin P. Casey/The New York Times/Redux; **350:** Richard Ellis/Getty Images; **352:** Corbis; **354:** *(top)* Kidwiler Collection/Diamond Images/Getty Images; **354:** *(bottom)* Laurie P. Winfrey/Woodfin Camp; **355:** *(top)* Francis Miller/Time & Life Pictures/ Getty Images; **355:** *(bottom)* Bettmann/Corbis; **357:** Rick D'Elia/Corbis; **358:** Tim Sloan/AFP/ Getty Images; **362:** Rich Pedroncelli/AP Photo; **364:** National Conference of State Legislators; **366:** William Thomas Cain/Getty Images; **368:** Bettmann/ Corbis; **370:** Danny Moloshok/AP Photo; **371:** AP Photo

CHAPTER 13: 378: UPI/Landov; **381:** Rebecca Cook/ Reuters/Landov; **383:** Eric Lee/Lawrence Bender Prods./The Kobal Collection; **386:** AP Photo; **387:** Peter Andrews/Landov; **389:** *(left)* AP Photo; **389:** *(right)* Paul Sakuma/AP Photo; **393:** AFP/Getty Images; **395:** *(top)* Topham/The Image Works; **395:** *(bottom)* Nicki Nikoni/Getty Images; **396:** Rick Wilking/Reuters/Landov; **398:** Konrad teffen/University of Colorado/

Reuters/Landov; **399:** Landon Nordeman/Getty Images **400:** Alamy; **401:** Bob Daemmrich/The Image Works; **404:** Dennis MacDonald/ Photoedit; **405:** David Buffington/ Getty Images; **406:** Bonnie Kamin/Photoedit; **409:** Darron Cummings/AP Photo; **410:** *(top)* Brett Flashnick/ AP Photo; **411:** Larry owning/Reuters/Landov; **410:** *(bottom)* KIPP oundation/Ethan Pines Photography; **412:** Chao Soi Cheong/ AP Photo

CHAPTER 14: 420: Shezad Noorni/Majority World/The Image Works; **422:** Lee Jin Man/ AP Photo; **424:** Digital Globe/Reuters/ Landov; **425:** Karl Schumacher/AFP/Getty Images; **426:** Joe Raedle/Getty Images; **427:** Baz Ratner/Reuters/Landov; **428:** Bob Strong/ Reuters/Corbis; **429:** *(top)* AP Photo; **429:** *(bottom)* Chris Hondros/Getty Images; **430:** UPI; **432** Sean Heasley/Corbis; **433:** Patrick D. McDermott/ Landov; **435:** Geert Vanden Wijngaert/AP Photo; **437:** American Red Cross; **439:** Patrick Gelly/The Image Works; **438:** T. Campion/Corbis Sygma

CONCLUSION: 742: Kevin Fleming/Corbis; **745:** David R. Frazier/The Image Works; **747:** Tim Graham/Getty Images; **748:** Casey Cohen/ Photoedit

Text Credits

INTRODUCTION: 10: From "Obama More Popular Abroad Than at Home, Global Image of U.S. Continues to Benefit" July 2010, by Pew Global Attitudes Project. Copyright (c) 2010 by Pew Global Attitudes Project, a project of the Pew Research Center. Reprinted with permission.

CHAPTER 1: 22: From "Obama More Popular Abroad Than at Home, Global Image of U.S. Continues to Benefit" July 2010, by Pew Global Attitudes Project. Copyright (c) 2010 by Pew Global Attitudes Project, a project of the Pew Research Center. Reprinted with permission.

CHAPTER 2: 52: From "Obama More Popular Abroad Than at Home, Global Image of U.S. Continues to Benefit" July 2010, by Pew Global Attitudes Project. Copyright (c) 2010 by Pew Global Attitudes Project, a project of the Pew Research Center. Reprinted with permission. **55:** From GETTING CURRENT: RECENT DEMOGRAPHIC TRENDS IN METROPOLITAN AMERICA by William H. Frey, Alan Berube, Audrey Singer and Jill H. Wilson. Copyright (c) 2010 by William H. Frey, Alan Berube, Audrey Singer and Jill H. Wilson. Reprinted by permission of The Brookings Institution.

CHAPTER 3: 89: From "Obama More Popular Abroad Than at Home, Global Image of U.S. Continues to Benefit" July 2010, by Pew Global Attitudes Project. Copyright (c) 2010 by Pew Global Attitudes Project, a project of the Pew Research Center. Reprinted with permission. **98:** From "Data Points: Gender in the 2008 Election" by U.S. News Staff from U.S. NEWS AND WORLD REPORT, November 6, 2008. Copyright (c) 2008 by U.S. News and World Report Licensing. Reprinted by permission of Wright's Media.

CHAPTER 4: 120: From "Obama More Popular Abroad Than at Home, Global Image of U.S. Continues to Benefit" July 2010, by Pew Global Attitudes Project. Copyright (c) 2010 by Pew Global Attitudes Project, a project of the Pew Research Center. Reprinted with permission. **121:** From GUIDE TO U.S. ELECTIONS, 6e, Vol. 1. Copyright (c) 2010 by CQ Press. Reprinted with permission. **126:** From VITAL STATISTICS ON AMERICAN POLITICS, 2009-2010 by Harold W. Stanley and Richard G. Niemi. Copyright (c) 2010by Stanley and Niemi. Reprinted by permission of CQ Press.

CHAPTER 5: 157: From "Senate Legislative Process a Mystery to Many: Political Knowledge Update," January 28, 2010 by Pew Research Center for the People and Press, a Project of the Pew Research Center. Copyright (c) 2010 by Pew Research Center. Reprinted with permission. **162:** From "Obama More Popular Abroad Than at Home, Global Image of U.S. Continues to Benefit" July 2010, by Pew Global Attitudes Project. Copyright (c) 2010 by Pew Global Attitudes Project, a project of the Pew Research Center. Reprinted with permission.

CHAPTER 6: 183: From "Obama More Popular Abroad Than at Home, Global Image of U.S. Continues to Benefit" July 2010, by Pew Global Attitudes Project. Copyright (c) 2010 by Pew Global Attitudes Project, a project of the Pew Research Center. Reprinted with permission. **186:** From VITAL STATISTICS ON AMERICAN POLITICS, 2007-2008 by Harold W. Stanley and Richard G. Niemi. Copyright (c) 2008 by Stanley and Niemi. Reprinted by permission of CQ Press. **208:** From "National Survey of the Role of Polls in Policymaking—Combined Topline Results." Copyright (c) 2001 Henry J. Kaiser Family Foundation. Reprinted with permission. **211:** From "Presidential Press Conferences: The Importance and Evolution of an Enduring Forum" by Martha Joynt Kumar in PRESIDENTIAL STUDIES QUARTERLY, 35(1), March 2005. Copyright (c) 2005 by John Wiley and Sons. Reprinted with permission.

CHAPTER 7: 228: From "Obama More Popular Abroad Than at Home, Global Image of U.S. Continues to Benefit" July 2010, by Pew Global Attitudes Project. Copyright (c) 2010 by Pew Global Attitudes Project, a project of the Pew Research Center. Reprinted with permission. **240:** From The Wall Street Journal/NBC News Poll Approval Ratings from 1997-2010. Copyright (c) by Dow Jones and Company, Inc. Reprinted with permission.

CHAPTER 8: 251: From "Obama More Popular Abroad Than at Home, Global Image of U.S. Continues to Benefit" July 2010, by Pew Global Attitudes Project. Copyright (c) 2010 by Pew Global Attitudes Project, a project of the Pew Research Center. Reprinted with permission.

CHAPTER 9: 274: From GLOBAL OPINION TRENDS 2002-2007: A RISING TIDE LIFTS MOOD IN THE DEVELOPING WORLD by Pew Global Attitudes Project. Copyright (c) 2007 by Pew Global Attitudes Project, a project of the Pew Research Center. Reprinted with permission. **290:** From THE GALLUP POLL. Copyright (c) by Gallup. Reprinted with permission.

CHAPTER 10: 308: From THE SUPREME COURT COMPENDIUM: DATA, DECISIONS, AND DEVELOPMENTS by Epstein et al. Copyright (c) 2007 by Epstein et al. Reprinted by permission of CQ Press. **310:** From "Obama More Popular Abroad Than at Home, Global Image of U.S. Continues to Benefit" July 2010, by Pew Global Attitudes Project. Copyright (c) 2010 by Pew Global Attitudes Project, a project of the Pew Research Center. Reprinted with permission.

CHAPTER 11: 325: From "Obama More Popular Abroad Than at Home, Global Image of U.S. Continues to Benefit" July 2010, by Pew Global Attitudes Project. Copyright (c) 2010 by Pew Global Attitudes Project, a project of the Pew Research Center. Reprinted with permission. **327:** "U.S. Religious Landscape Survey," data from the GENERAL SOCIAL SURVEYS (1972–2006), by Pew Research Center's Forum on Religion & Public Life. Copyright (c) 2008 Pew Research Center. Reprinted with permission. **336:** From "U.S. Abortion Attitudes Closely Divided" by Lydia Saad from GALLUP, August 4, 2009. Copyright (c) 2009 by Gallup. Reprinted with permission.

CHAPTER 12: 357: From "Degrees of Separation" by Michael A. Fletcher from THE WASHINGTON POST, June 25, 2002. Copyright (c) 2002 by The Washington Post. Reprinted by permission of The Washington Post.

CHAPTER 13: 383: From The Polling Report, Inc. Copyright (c) 2010 by The Polling Report, Inc. Reprinted with permission. **402:** From "Obama More Popular Abroad Than at Home, Global Image of U.S. Continues to Benefit" July 2010, by Pew Global Attitudes Project. Copyright (c) 2010 by Pew Global Attitudes Project, a project of the Pew Research Center. Reprinted with permission.

CHAPTER 14: 428: From "Obama More Popular Abroad Than at Home, Global Image of U.S. Continues to Benefit" July 2010, by Pew Global Attitudes Project. Copyright (c) 2010 by Pew Global Attitudes Project, a project of the Pew Research Center. Reprinted with permission.

INDEX

D

E

F

G

O

P

Q

R

S

T

U

V

W

Z

COURSE EXAM

Introduction: Government by the People

1. Who is considered to be the architect of the Constitution?
   a. Thomas Jefferson
   b. George Washington
   c. John Adams
   d. James Madison

2. How did the Mayflower Compact become an important model for government in America?

3. Which philosopher wrote that people once lived in a state of nature but could enter into self-government through a social contract?
   a. David Hume
   b. John Locke
   c. Jean-Jacques Rousseau
   d. Thomas Hobbes

4. For which of the terms is the following definition most appropriate? "The belief that the authority and legitimacy of government is based in the consent and authority of the individuals living within its boundaries."
   a. Pure democracy
   b. Popular sovereignty
   c. Individualism
   d. Freedom of speech

Part I Constitutional Principles

Chapter 1: Constitutional Democracy
Identify the philosophical principles on which our democratic republic is based, and describe the creation and adoption of the Constitution and the Bill of Rights.

5. All of the following aspects of direct democracy were added *after* the constitution was signed EXCEPT:
   a. Direct primary elections of U.S. Senators
   b. Initiative process for enacting legislation
   c. Referendum on issues put forward by legislatures
   d. Recall of state government leaders
   e. Direct election of members of the House of Representatives

6. Some societies are better positioned to maintain a healthy democracy than are others. List and describe at least three of the conditions that lead to a strong democracy.

7. Which of the following is NOT a distinct element of the Constitution?
   a. Federalism
   b. Economic equality
   c. Bicameralism
   d. Bill of rights
   e. Separation of powers

8. In what ways did the Articles of Confederation differ from our current constitution?

9. What is the three-fifths compromise, and what social conditions led to the compromise? What parts of the country did the two different sides of the issue represent?

10. How has new technology and the media changed the system of checks and balances established by the Constitution?

11. The decision in the Supreme Court case *Marbury v. Madison* established which of the following?
    a. The Supreme Court's right to review acts of the national legislature
    b. The Supreme Court as the main interpreter of the Constitution
    c. That Marbury was entitled to his commission and Madison should have delivered it to him
    d. That the proper court could issue a writ of mandamus, even against so high an official as the secretary of state
    e. All of the above

12. Describe the two methods for proposing amendments to the U.S. Constitution and why you think that only one of these have been used thus far.

13. Which of the following applications of checks and balances has been used the most widely?
    a. Vetoes
    b. Judicial review
    c. Impeachment
    d. Confirmation

Chapter 2: American Federalism
Explain federalism in America, and analyze the relationship between the federal and state and local governments.

14. Define federalism and explain the ways governments at different levels can share power in different kinds of federalism.

15. Which one of the following is NOT an advantage of federalism?
    a. It checks the growth of tyranny.
    b. It encourages experimentation.
    c. It allows unity without uniformity.
    d. It encourages holding elected officials accountable through a division of power.
    e. It keeps government closer to the people.

16. What is the difference between delegated or express powers and implied powers? List some of both types.

17. A decentralist would agree with which one of the following statements?
    a. For the sake of national well-being, more power should be given to the federal government.
    b. Any question about whether the states have given a particular function to the central government or have reserved it for themselves should be resolved in favor of the states.
    c. The devolution revolution should be defeated.

d. Presidents Abraham Lincoln and Franklin Roosevelt had a correct understanding of the balance in power between the states and federal government.
e. The national government is an agent of the people, not the states.

18. Which of the following is one of the three types of federal grants currently given?
a. Welfare grant
b. Income equalization grant
c. Categorical-formula grant
d. Revenue sharing grant
e. Education grant

19. Historically, how had federalism been used to retain slavery, segregation, and discrimination? Provide arguments for and against retaining federalism given these patterns. Are there examples of states having laws today that treat people differently?

The Big Picture

20. Compare and contrast the originalist approach to interpreting the U.S. Constitution with the adaptive approach.

21. Explain how the system of federalism addressed the framers' concerns over the power of the new federal government.

Part II The Political Process

Chapter 3: The American Political Landscape
Describe how geographic and demographic differences among Americans affect political beliefs and policy preferences.

22. Name five of the shared values that contribute to American political culture.

23. Which of the following is NOT one of the characteristics of the rule of law?
    a. Laws should apply to the present and future, not punish something someone did in the past (Prospectivity).
    b. Laws should be specifically designed to promote different outcomes for particular groups or individuals in society (Specificity).
    c. Valid laws are made by those in legitimate power through popular consent (Authority).
    d. Valid laws cannot be kept secret and then enforced (Publicity).
    e. Laws must be enforced impartially and with fair processes (Due Process).

24. Explain the conflict in values between a *competitive economy* and an *egalitarian society.*

25. What is the difference between a reinforcing cleavage and a cross-cutting cleavage? Give some examples of each.

26. Define political socialization.

27. True or False: Religion has been an important catalyst for political change in the United States.

28. All of the following are true about women in the United States EXCEPT:
    a. Women are more likely to oppose violence in any form.
    b. There are serious income inequalities between men and women.
    c. The number of women in Congress reached new highs in the 1990s.
    d. Women are more likely to vote for female candidates.

Chapter 4: Political Parties and Interest Groups
Explain the role of political parties in American government, and evaluate the efforts of interest groups to influence elections and legislation.

29. Describe and give examples of four techniques interest groups use to exert influence.

30. The AFL-CIO is what type of interest group?
    a. Foreign Policy
    b. Public-Sector
    c. Ideological or Single-Issue
    d. Business
    e. Labor

31. Which piece of legislation doubled the allowed individual contribution limits and banned soft money?
    a. The Bipartisan Campaign Reform Act (BCRA)
    b. The Sherman Antitrust Act (SAT)
    c. The Elections and Campaigning Amendment (ECA)
    d. The Restoring Trust in Election Financing Act (RTEFA)
    e. The Federal Election Campaign Act of 1971 (FECA)

32. How do cross-cutting interests affect interest groups' influence?

33. Which of the following is NOT one of the functions of a lobbyist?
    a. Help members of Congress overcome party differences
    b. Help prepare legislation and testify before legislative hearings
    c. Provide information for decision makers in all branches of government
    d. Contribute a large share of the costs of campaigns
    e. Help educate and mobilize public opinion

34. Describe why third parties have difficulty obtaining support in the United States.

35. Which of the following is a feature of a parliamentary system rather than the U.S. party system?
    a. Winner-take-all
    b. Ideological parties
    c. Single-member districts
    d. Two dominant parties
    e. Candidate-centered campaigns

Chapter 5: Public Opinion and Participation
Explain differences in opinions and rates of participation, and evaluate the importance of public opinion and participation in a democracy.

36. Which of the following political ideologies is most likely to advocate affirmative action programs?
    a. Social conservative
    b. Contemporary liberal
    c. Libertarian
    d. Traditional conservative
    e. A and B

37. Which of the following political ideology(ies) is most likely to oppose government programs like those implemented in the New Deal of the 1930s?
    a. Contemporary liberal
    b. Libertarian
    c. Traditional conservative
    d. B and C
    e. All of the above

38. Which of the following is considered the most powerful agent of political socialization?
    a. Peers and friends
    b. Mass media
    c. Religious background
    d. Ethnic background
    e. Family

39. Define a random sample and explain what measures are taken when selecting a random sample to ensure it is representative of the population as a whole.

40. Generally, which of the following types of elections has the highest turnout?
    a. Primary election
    b. Midterm election
    c. Presidential election

d. Special election
e. Off-year election

41. Compare and contrast voting on the basis of party with voting on the basis of candidates.

42. Briefly describe some of the problems involved with counting Florida's ballots after the 2000 presidential election and what has been done to correct them.

Chapter 6: Campaigns, Elections, and the Media
Describe the rules for elections in America, and assess the impact of the media on elections, public opinion, and governance.

43. Compared with proportional representation, single-member districts typically:
a. Encourage more participation of minor parties.
b. Accurately reveal divisions in voter preferences.
c. Establish a clear winner.
d. Lead to greater ideological extremism.
e. None of the above

44. Partisan gerrymandering is:
a. The negative advertising between parties during elections.
b. The process of drawing district boundaries to benefit a certain party.
c. The support a congressional candidate receives from a popular president of the same party.
d. When members of Congress vote along strict party lines.

45. List and explain three key advantages incumbents enjoy in elections.

46. The Bipartisan Campaign Reform Act did all of the following EXCEPT:
a. Ban soft money.
b. Index contribution limits to inflation.
c. Restrict the way 527 groups communicate with voters.
d. Limit the amount candidates can spend on their own campaigns.
e. Provide a new definition for "electioneering communications."

47. Americans' number one news source is which of the following?
a. Television
b. Newspapers
c. Radio
d. Internet
e. Magazines

48. What is investigative journalism? Discuss the role it played in two events in U.S. history.

49. All of the following limit media influence EXCEPT:
a. Selective exposure
b. Needs of viewers and listeners
c. Audience fragmentation
d. Growth of the Internet
e. Selective perception

50. What has been the impact of television on candidates and elections?

51. How do presidents influence the media in order to push their agenda and reach their goals?

The Big Picture

52. How does America's two party system affect elections and the decisions of voters?

53. What are the primary arguments for and against strong campaign finance laws?

Part III Policy-Making Institutions

Chapter 7: Congress
Identify the legislative powers of Congress, and compare and contrast the House of Representatives and the Senate.

54. Which of the following is NOT an advantage incumbents enjoy?
    a. Franking privilege
    b. Greater access to the media
    c. Greater access to money
    d. More able to run as agent of change
    e. More visibility

55. Congressional regulation on semi trucks traveling across the country would be justified by which of the following enumerated powers?
    a. The power to raise, make, and borrow money
    b. The power to regulate interstate commerce
    c. The power to unify and expand the country
    d. The power to prepare and declare war
    e. The power to create monopolies

56. Compare and contrast the "delegate" and "trustee" approaches to representation.

57. Which of the following is NOT one of the types of congressional committees?
    a. Authorizing
    b. Oversight
    c. Budget
    d. Constitution
    e. Appropriations

58. Describe the roles of both the Speaker of the House and the Senate president.

Chapter 8: The Presidency
Identify the powers of the president for leading the nation.

59. Which of the following is NOT a presidential power given by the Constitution?
    a. The power to appoint judges
    b. The power to assume the role of commander in chief
    c. The power to declare war
    d. The power to be negotiate treaties
    e. The power to take care that the laws are faithfully executed

60. Discuss George Washington's and Franklin Delano Roosevelt's individual impacts on the Office of the Presidency.

61. Which power of the president did Congress curtail?
    a. The power to issue executive orders
    b. The executive privilege
    c. The use of signing statements
    d. The line item veto
    e. The use of impoundment

62. Which of the following has been said to most significantly enlarge presidential powers over time?
    a. Economic or foreign crises
    b. The power to appoint federal judges
    c. The line item veto
    d. Increasing use of signing statements

Chapter 9: The Federal Bureaucracy
Describe the role of the federal bureaucracy in implementing the laws.

63. With regard to the federal bureaucracy, all of the following are mandated in the Constitution EXCEPT:
    a. Current Representatives and Senators cannot hold executive branch positions.
    b. The president has complete authority to nominate senior government officers.
    c. The president has power to fill vacancies in the bureaucracy when the Senate is in recess.
    d. The president has power to create departments of government.
    e. The president is responsible to supervise the work of members of the bureaucracy.

64. Identify and explain key differences between independent regulatory commissions and independent stand-alone agencies.

65. Which of the following is NOT a part of the process for selecting presidential appointees?
    a. Selection of appointee by the White House Presidential Personnel Office
    b. The White House clearance process
    c. Review and hearing in a House committee
    d. Review and hearing in a Senate committee

66. The primary responsibility of all organizations in the federal bureaucracy is:
    a. Executing or implementing the laws
    b. Establishing entitlement programs and other services
    c. Responding to national disasters
    d. Overseeing the quality of goods produced within the United States
    e. Providing a check to the power of the president

67. In what ways can the president and Congress oversee and control the bureaucracy?

Chapter 10: The Judiciary
Explain the role of the courts in the system of checks and balances, and evaluate the challenges for judicial independence.

68. What does it mean that the federal judiciary is a passive and reactive branch?

69. In which of the following cases would the Supreme Court have original jurisdiction?
    a. A case involving a serial killer
    b. A case involving mass corporate fraud
    c. A case involving two states
    d. A case involving the governor of Texas
    e. A case involving a Tennessee church

70. Compare and contrast judicial activism and judicial restraint.

71. Which of the following is NOT one of the necessary steps the Supreme Court takes in making a judgment?
   a. Briefing the case
   b. Holding the oral argument
   c. Meeting in conference
   d. Reviewing public opinion
   e. Writing the opinion

The Big Picture

72. To what degree is the Supreme Court given policy-making power by the Constitution? What are the pros and cons of a Supreme Court that exerts strong influence over policy?

73. What are the strengths and weaknesses of a strong federal bureaucracy? What institutions are in place to control the federal bureaucracy, and do they do they do an adequate job?

Part IV Individual Rights and Liberties

Chapter 11: Civil Liberties
Describe the individual liberties protected in the Bill of Rights, and evaluate the limitations on these rights.

74. Which of the following is a correct definition of civil liberties?
    a. Constitutional protections of all persons against governmental restrictions on the freedoms of conscience, religion, and expression
    b. The constitutional rights of all persons to due process and the equal protection of the laws
    c. The constitutional right not to be discriminated against by governments because of race, ethnic background, religion, or gender
    d. Rights that are granted by governments and may be subject to conditions or restrictions
    e. All of the above

75. Which of the following kinds of speech is protected under the First Amendment?
    a. Libel
    b. Obscenity
    c. Fighting words
    d. Commercial speech
    e. Hate speech

76. What is the difference between procedural due process and substantive due process?

77. Which of the following court cases re-affirmed a woman's right to abort a pregnancy?
    a. *Roe* v. *Wade*
    b. *Planned Parenthood* v. *Casey*
    c. *Stenberg* v. *Carhart*
    d. *Bowers* v. *Hardwick*
    e. *Lawrence* v. *Texas*

Chapter 12: Civil Rights
Explain how Congress and the Supreme Court have expanded and protected civil rights.

78. Which one of the following is NOT a requirement for naturalization?
    a. Be over the age of 18
    b. Be able to read, write, and speak English
    c. Understand and demonstrate an attachment to the history, principles, and form of government of the United States
    d. Be lawfully admitted for permanent residence and have resided in the United States for at least 7 years
    e. Possess a good moral character

79. Name two specific rights that are derived from national citizenship in the United States.

80. Which amendment to the Constitution contains the equal protection clause?
    a. 5th
    b. 13th
    c. 14th
    d. 15th
    e. 19th

81. Explain the difference between *de jure* segregation and *de facto* segregation.

82. If the Supreme Court decides that a law is subject to strict scrutiny because it creates a suspect classification, which of the following must the government prove in order to justify that classification?
    a. That the classification serves a compelling government interest.
    b. That the classification rationally distinguishes between visible characteristics of people.
    c. That there is no less restrictive way to accomplish the government interest.
    d. A and C
    e. All of the above

The Big Picture

83. What are the primary arguments for and against affirmative action policies?

84. Why is free speech important to the survival of democracy? Are there situations where the right to free speech ought to be limited? Explain.

Part V The Politics of National Policy

Chapter 13: Making Economic and Social Welfare Policy
Identify the steps in the policy-making process and describe the government's role in economic and social policy making.

85. Which of the following is a redistributive policy?
 a. Social Security
 b. Education funding
 c. Interstate highway system
 d. Air traffic control
 e. Welfare

86. Which one of the following is NOT a necessary step in making public policy?
 a. Deciding to act
 b. Designing a political implementation strategy
 c. Setting the agenda of problems to be addressed
 d. Deciding how much to do
 e. Deciding who will deliver the goods or services

87. Compare and contrast incremental policy and punctuating policy. Give examples of each.

88. In recent years, the federal government has become more dependent on *third-party government*. Which one of the following is NOT a source of *third-party government*?
 a. State and local governments
 b. Colleges and universities
 c. Private businesses
 d. Charities
 e. The State Department

89. How can private citizens affect public policy?

90. Explain the difference between fiscal policy and monetary policy and how each can influence the nation's economy.

91. The acronym CPI means:
 a. Child Protection Initiative
 b. Consumer Price Index
 c. Contraction Predicted Inflation
 d. Commodity Price Index
 e. None of the above

92. The largest source of tax revenue for the federal government is:
 a. Payroll taxes
 b. Corporate income taxes
 c. Excise taxes
 d. Individual income taxes
 e. Estate taxes

93. Which organization oversees the budget process on behalf of the president?
 a. Office of Management and Budget
 b. Congressional Budget Office
 c. Internal Revenue Service
 d. Presidential Budget Office
 e. Federal Reserve

94. Explain how changes in the federal funds rate can affect the economy.

95. The Fair Labor Standards Act of 1938 regulated labor in which of the following areas?
 a. Wages and hours
 b. Child labor
 c. Industrial safety and occupational health
 d. Both A and B
 e. All of the above

96. What are entitlements? Name two examples of entitlement programs.

97. All of the following are programs instituted under President Lyndon Johnson's Great Society EXCEPT:
 a. Food Stamps
 b. Medicare
 c. Medicaid
 d. Social Security
 e. Housing Assistance

98. List five of the major provisions of the Patient Protection and Affordable Health Care Act.

99. How has the federal government attempted to set higher standards for public education, and what challenges has it faced?

Chapter 14: Making Foreign and Defense Policy
Describe the tools of foreign policymaking, and evaluate the status of America's current foreign policy interests.

100. Describe the contrasting theories of realism and idealism as they apply to foreign policy.

101. Which one of the following exemplify isolationism in foreign policy?
 a. The Iraq War
 b. Obama's decision to send more troops to Afghanistan
 c. Obama's vote against the Iraq War
 d. The War on Terror
 e. All of the above

102. Which one of the following is the most important intelligence unit?
 a. Federal Bureau of Investigation
 b. Bureau of Intelligence and Research
 c. Defense Intelligence Agency
 d. Central Intelligence Agency
 e. National Security Agency

103. What is the difference between soft power and hard power?

104. Which of the following is a type of hard power?
 a. Conventional diplomacy
 b. Foreign aid
 c. Economic sanctions
 d. Public diplomacy
 e. Image building

The Big Picture

105. What are the ways the federal government can influence the nation's economy? What are the pros and cons of governmental involvement in the economy?

106. Define redistributive social policy. What are the arguments for and against increasing wealth redistribution?

Conclusion: Sustaining Constitutional Democracy

107. Duverger's law is best described as:
    a. An observation that single-member legislative districts tend to lead to two-party systems
    b. A law proposed by Sen. Duverger (R-GA) prohibiting proportional representation in the U.S.
    c. A doctrine of political science equating democracy with economic prosperity
    d. A rule designating the procedure for the formation of House committees
    e. An observation that district lines tend to be drawn to maximize incumbent party strength

108. Why is active citizenship crucial for democracy?

ANSWERS

1. D
2. The Mayflower Compact became a model of how a group could unite under a unanimous agreement of self-government. The compact illustrated how the governed could be a legitimate source of government. Some say that it created the "seeds" of the American constitutional government and the written constitution.
3. B
4. B

PART I Constitutional Principles

5. Answer: E
6. High levels of education (an educated citizenry), a relatively prosperous and stable economy with a fairly equitable distribution of wealth, private ownership of property, a market economy, social stability (meaning peaceful relationships between different subgroups within a country), widely shared ideals of democracy (one person, one vote; freedom of speech; majority rule; and freedom of assembly) despite differing ideological views.
7. B
8. The Articles of Confederation lacked a strong executive and an independent judiciary. Under the Articles of Confederation, Congress had no direct authority over citizens. It could not levy taxes, regulate trade between states or with other nations, or prevent states from taxing each other's goods or issuing their own currencies. State governments could overturn national laws in practice. The Constitution reversed all of these characteristics.
9. The three-fifths compromise dealt with the method of counting slaves for the purpose of apportioning seats in the House of Representatives. Southern slave states wanted to count all slaves in their population, while northern free states did not want them to be included. With the three-fifths compromise, each slave would be counted as three-fifths of a person when determining apportionment of seats. This quelled the desires of both sides by maintaining a balance of power. The compromise also included a provision to eliminate the importation of slaves, which occurred in 1808.
10. Presidents have increased their power due to their ability to appeal directly to millions of people and to receive immediate access to public opinion. Interest groups are able to target thousands of letters and calls at members of Congress, to orchestrate campaigns to write letters to editors, and to organize and mobilize on the Internet. Nongovernmental institutions, such as special-interest groups and the press, have greater independence and influence. Wealthy individuals are able to bypass political parties and carry their message directly to the public.
11. E
12. Amendments can be proposed by a two-thirds vote of both houses of Congress or by a convention called by Congress at the request of the legislatures in two-thirds of the states. The latter method has never been used. Reasons for this may include that there are no specific directions in the Constitution for how delegates to such a convention would be selected or for the scope of amendments that may be considered by the convention once it is in session. Also, it may be more difficult to organize state legislatures in order to propose calling a convention.
13. A
14. Federalism is a constitutional arrangement in which power is distributed between a central government and subdivisional governments, called states in the United States. The national and subdivisional governments both exercise direct authority over individuals. The ways that governments at different levels can share power include:
    - Dual federalism: a limited list of powers are given to the national government, and the rest are reserved to the states.
    - Cooperative federalism: stresses intergovernmental relationships in delivering governmental goods and services.
    - Marble cake federalism: a mixed set of responsibilities where all levels of government engage in a variety of issues and programs (as opposed to dual federalism).
    - Competitive federalism: all levels of government compete with each other over ways to put together packages of services and taxes.
    - Permissive federalism: the states' share of power depends on the permission and permissiveness of the national government.
    - New federalism: the power of the federal government is limited in favor of the broad powers reserved to the states.
15. D
16. Delegated, or express, powers are powers explicitly given to the national government through statements in the Constitution. Implied powers are powers inferred from the express powers that are given to Congress in the Constitution. Express powers include the powers to declare war and to create post offices, while implied powers include the power to create banks.
17. B
18. C
19. State and national governments have disagreed often on civil rights and civil liberties issues. Thus, even when the national government outlawed slavery, segregation, and discrimination, states in which these new laws were not popular did not enforce these federal laws. Federalism also can create inconsistent laws among states that can create problems for people moving between states or for expanding businesses. Despite these potential problems, federalism has many advantages, including decentralization of power, and preventing the growth of tyranny. It also encourages experimentation in lower levels of government that might be adopted elsewhere. Finally, it keeps government closer to the people so that it can better engage more citizens in the governing process. There are laws today permitting same-sex marriage or civil unions in some states and not others.

20. Those who use an originalist approach to constitutional interpretation read the document literally and understand the words to mean what they meant at the time they were ratified. The adaptive approach is one through which the Constitution is seen as an evolving document that should be understood in light of society's norms and values.
21. The framers wanted a central government strong enough to address their concerns over the economy and international relations, but they also wanted government that was responsive to the diverse needs of state citizens. Federalism does both by providing the benefits of a strong central government balanced by smaller state governments that are closer to the people.

PART II The Political Process

22. Liberty, Equality, Individualism, Respect for the Common Person, Democratic Consensus—including majority rule and popular sovereignty, Justice and the Rule of Law, Patriotism, Optimism, Idealism.
23. B
24. A competitive economy allows individuals to reap large rewards for their initiative and hard work, while the goal of an egalitarian society is for everyone to earn a decent living. Conflicts between these value systems include whether or not people should be allowed to fail, or whether the success of some should be allowed to come at the expense of others.
25. Reinforcing cleavages are differences that reinforce each other and serve to polarize society. Cross-cutting cleavages pull the same people in different directions, thereby offsetting the polarizing effect of social and economic differences between people. An example of reinforcing cleavages includes the division between Northern and Southern Italy. American diversity has typically been considered more cross-cutting because most people fit it into several different social groups.
26. The process by which we develop our political attitudes, values, and beliefs.
27. True
28. D
29. Interest groups exert influence on policy by mobilizing the public, by executing mass mailings, and by contacting government directly about proposed rules and regulations. They may also influence rulemaking by making it difficult to enforce regulations and rules. Interest groups also exert influence by initiating lawsuits and by filing amicus curiae briefs for cases in which they are not directly involved.
30. E
31. A
32. Cross-cutting interests reduce and stabilize the influence of interest groups, which typically prevents any one group from assuming a commanding role in politics.
33. A
34. Third parties have difficulty obtaining support in the U.S. because our system of elections involves single-member districts and a winner-take-all system. These methods do not offer any incentive for a smaller third party to form, as it is unlikely that they would be able to obtain a plurality of votes. Also, our presidential system, where the head of government is not part of the legislative branch, makes development of a third party less likely.
35. B
36. B
37. D
38. E
39. A random sample is a sample in which each person in the population or group has an equal and known chance of being selected into the sample. Random-digit dialing, in which a computer generates phone numbers to include in a sample, can gather random samples. Similarly, exit polls target randomly selected voters leaving the polls to predict election results.
40. C
41. Citizens vote most often for a candidate from their preferred party. Voters use party identification as a way to more easily make decisions when they do not have detailed information on individual candidates. Alternatively, citizens may vote on the basis of a candidate when that candidate has made an appeal directly to voters.
42. Punch-card ballots had "hanging chads" or punches that did not completely perforate the card. Also, some counties in Florida used "butterfly ballots" on which the candidates' names were staggered on opposite sides of the ballot with the punch holes in a straight line in the middle of the ballot. Some voters complained these made it difficult to tell which candidate went with which punch. In order to fix these problems, Florida enacted legislation to modernize the voting process, to purchase more than $30 million worth of touchscreen machines, and to establish minimum standards for polling places and voting machines. On a federal level, the Congress passed the Help America Vote Act (HAVA) in 2002. This provided $3.9 billion of federal funds to modernize voting processes and to mandate that states keep accurate voter registration lists. Also under HAVA, if there is uncertainty surrounding a person's voter registration, he or she can cast a provisional ballot.
43. C
44. B
45. Incumbents typically enjoy better name recognition and greater visibility than challengers. Also, incumbents can reference their efforts on behalf of their constituents during their recent time in office, and they typically have access to greater funds than challengers. Finally, incumbents' district boundaries have usually been drawn in a way that benefits them.
46. D
47. A

48. In addition to reporting the news, journalists sometimes actually investigate emerging stories. Investigative reporters will reveal their findings to the public, which often has political consequences. For example, the reports on the torture of Iraqi prisoners at Abu Ghraib by U.S. soldiers in 2004, as well as the reports on Dana Priest's 2005 investigation of secret CIA prisons where suspected terrorists were held and interrogated, held enormous political and legal consequences. Reporters Jack Anderson, Robert Woodward, and Carl Bernstein's investigation of the attempted burglary at the Democratic National Committee headquarters in the Watergate building revealed the political corruption of the Nixon White House and reelection committee, ultimately leading to the former president's resignation.
49. D
50. Since the increased use of television during campaigns, candidates have become more focused on image and visibility. Mistakes made by candidates are more likely to be problematic for candidates with increased visibility and media coverage. Television has also made election issues more accessible to the public, but it has also contributed to the increased costs of campaigning. Furthermore, election night reporting has dampened voter turnout in western states because results from eastern states have already been counted and announced on television before some western voters get to the polls.
51. Presidents use the media to set the agenda and to push certain legislation. Presidents hold news conferences or may leak certain information and news to reporters. Any event that the president attends or activity he engages in is newsworthy.
52. The U.S. two-party system presents voters with candidates that are typically more centrist than might be the case with a multi-party system. In a winner-take-all system as we have in the U.S., voters who favor third party candidates might be less likely to vote, given that they know their favored candidate has little chance of winning the election.
53. One of the arguments against strong campaign finance laws is a concern with constitutionally protected free speech. Since candidates for office must spend money to convey their message, restricting the amount of money they can spend restricts their speech. Alternatively, proponents of strong campaign finance laws argue that they help to reign in well-financed special interests and allow individual citizens to affect campaigns through their contributions.

PART III Policy-Making Institutions

54. D
55. B
56. Delegates determine what their constituency wants and then acts accordingly. Trustees act and vote according to their own opinions of what is best for their constituency, state, and nation.
57. D
58. The Speaker of the House is the most powerful leader on Capitol Hill. This position is always filled by a member of the majority party. The Speaker has the power to rule on questions of parliamentary procedure, to recognize members who rise to speak, to appoint members to temporary committees, to reorganize House committees, to name committee chairs, to appoint allies to leadership posts, and to reduce the size of committee staffs. The president of the Senate is also the vice president of the United States but has little actual influence over Senate proceedings, only voting when there is a tie. The President pro tempore is generally the most senior member of the majority party in the Senate and acts as chair in the absence of the vice president. Often his or her senatorial responsibilities are delegated to junior members of the majority party.
59. C
60. George Washington established the legitimacy and authority of the presidency. He provided an example of how the president could carry out the duties assigned to him in the Constitution. His most important contribution was likely his resignation from office after serving for two terms. Franklin Roosevelt was most likely the first president to fully use the powers of the presidency as well as to dominate Congress. He also set a precedent of personal communication with American citizens.
61. E
62. A
63. D
64. Independent regulatory commissions are independent in the sense that they do not report to the president. Thus, these commissions are more insulated from politics, though the commissioners are appointed by the president and approved by Congress. Independent stand-alone agencies are independent from any department, but they report directly to the president.
65. C
66. A
67. Presidents control federal bureaucracy through the powers of appointment, reorganization, and budgeting. They can also influence the bureaucracy by mobilizing public opinion and support from Congress. The main ways Congress can control the bureaucracy is through formulating budgets, appropriating funds, confirming personnel, authorizing new programs, conducting investigations and hearings, and terminating agencies.
68. The Supreme Court cannot choose what issues will be brought to it. It can only address issues outside parties choose to litigate.
69. C
70. Judicial activism is the philosophy that judges should strike down laws that are inconsistent with norms and values stated or implied in Constitution. Judicial restraint is the philosophy that judges should strike down the actions of the elected branches only if they clearly violate the literal meaning of the Constitution.
71. D

72. The Constitution gives the Supreme Court the power to hear cases and controversies. It cannot take up issues that are not brought to it. It also cannot enforce its decisions. It must rely on the executive to do that. This keeps the Court, whose members are unelected, from having too much latitude to change policy, but it can also make it possible for the elected branches and the public to ignore unpopular rulings, even those that may protect minority rights.
73. A strong federal bureaucracy can provide expertise in implementing policy. But if the bureaucracy is too strong, it might frustrate the will of the elected branches. The president maintains a check on the bureaucracy through the power to appoint senior officials, and Congress maintains the power to appropriate funds as well as to create and eliminate bureaucratic agencies, with the president's cooperation.

PART IV Individual Rights and Liberties

74. A
75. E
76. Procedural due process mainly limits the executive and judicial branches because they apply the law and review its application. Substantive due process mainly limits the legislative branch because it actually creates and enacts laws.
77. B
78. D
79. The rights to use the navigable waters of the United States and protection on the high seas, to assemble peacefully and petition for redress of grievances, to vote if qualified to do so under state laws and have your vote counted properly, and to travel throughout the United States.
80. C
81. Officially sanctioned segregation is *de jure* segregation. Segregation that arises as a result of social and economic conditions such as housing patterns is *de facto* segregation.
82. D
83. One of the primary arguments in favor of affirmative action, particularly in education, is the need to promote diversity. One of the arguments against it is that the Fourteenth Amendment prohibits racial discrimination and while affirmative action programs may seek to promote diversity, they do so by discriminating based on race.
84. Democracy requires that citizens have the right to convey their ideas to each other, to their representatives, and to the country as a whole. Thus, free speech is essential for a healthy democracy. There are some instances in which free speech might not be protected, such as when it poses an immediate danger to national security or is judged to be obscene.

PART V The Politics of National Policy

85. E. Of the programs mentioned, only welfare takes money from one group and gives it exclusively to another group.
86. B. While B might be part of a president, party, or group's calculation when attempting to influence policy, it is not necessary in making public policy.
87. Incremental policy consists of small changes to existing policy, such as increasing funding to colleges by a few hundred dollars, whereas punctuating policy is more radical and can only occur after mobilization of large segments of society. An example of punctuating policy would be a health care bill that makes purchasing health insurance mandatory.
88. E
89. There are many possible ways for citizens to affect public policy, including joining interest groups, writing letters, sending e-mails, confronting legislators at community meetings, and even running for office.
90. Fiscal policy means using federal spending and taxation to stimulate or slow the economy. Monetary policy means manipulating the supply of money in the economy to smooth periods of growth and recession.
91. B
92. D
93. A
94. Increasing the federal funds rate increases the costs for money and credit, thus slowing the economy. Lowering the federal funds rate makes money more accessible for investment and growth, thus stimulating the economy.
95. D
96. Entitlements are programs under which the government provides benefits to all eligible citizens, regardless of need such as disaster relief or disability payments.
97. D
98. Provisions of the Patient Protection and Affordable Health Care Act include: most Americans will be required to purchase health insurance starting in 2014; insurance companies will be prevented from denying coverage for any reason; insurance companies will extend coverage under parents' plans for young Americans up through the age of 26; the Medicaid program will be extended to all poor Americans under 65; and individual Americans will pay a tax on "Cadillac" insurance plans.
99. Congress has enacted legislation concerning public education, including the Elementary and Secondary Education Act (1965) and the No Child Left Behind Act (2002). However, states have not always been favorable to such efforts, particularly when the federal laws require them to meet higher standards without sufficient resources.

100. Realism assumes that nations will act out of self-interest, while idealism is open to the idea that nations will work together to solve international problems.
101. C
102. D
103. Soft power relies on diplomacy to solve international problems, while hard power relies on economic and military strength.
104. C
105. There are a variety of ways in which the government can influence the nation's economy, including increasing or decreasing government spending, raising or lowering taxes, changing the federal funds rate, and increasing or lowering trade barriers. Some argue that government involvement improves economic growth and promotes a strong economy. Others argue that government regulation stifles competition and the potential for private industry to succeed.
106. Redistributive policies take benefits away from one group in society and provide benefits to another group in society. One argument in favor of such programs is that they provide benefits to those who truly need them. Opponents might argue that such programs penalize those who succeed by taxing them to redistribute benefits.
107. A
108. Active citizenship is crucial because democracy derives its power from the governed. Thus, in order to ensure that majority and minority rights are protected, the public must take an active role in governing whether through voting, voter mobilization and lobbying, and/or running for office. Active citizenship also ensures that policies are adequately discussed and debated before they are implemented.